P9-CPX-716

Contemporary Literary Criticism

Guide to Gale Literary Criticism Series

For criticism on	Consult these Gale series
Authors now living or who died after December 31, 1959	**CONTEMPORARY LITERARY CRITICISM (CLC)**
Authors who died between 1900 and 1959	**TWENTIETH-CENTURY LITERARY CRITICISM (TCLC)**
Authors who died between 1800 and 1899	**NINETEENTH-CENTURY LITERATURE CRITICISM (NCLC)**
Authors who died between 1400 and 1799	**LITERATURE CRITICISM FROM 1400 TO 1800 (LC)** **SHAKESPEAREAN CRITICISM (SC)**
Authors who died before 1400	**CLASSICAL AND MEDIEVAL LITERATURE CRITICISM (CMLC)**
Black writers of the past two hundred years	**BLACK LITERATURE CRITICISM (BLC)**
Authors of books for children and young adults	**CHILDREN'S LITERATURE REVIEW (CLR)**
Dramatists	**DRAMA CRITICISM (DC)**
Hispanic writers of the late nineteenth and twentieth centuries	**HISPANIC LITERATURE CRITICISM (HLC)**
Native North American writers and orators of the eighteenth, nineteenth, and twentieth centuries	**NATIVE NORTH AMERICAN LITERATURE (NNAL)**
Poets	**POETRY CRITICISM (PC)**
Short story writers	**SHORT STORY CRITICISM (SSC)**
Major authors from the Renaissance to the present	**WORLD LITERATURE CRITICISM, 1500 TO THE PRESENT (WLC)**
Major authors and works from the Bible to the present	**WORLD LITERATURE CRITICISM SUPPLEMENT (WLCS)**

ISSN 0091-3421

Volume 108

Contemporary Literary Criticism

Excerpts from Criticism of the Works
of Today's Novelists, Poets, Playwrights,
Short Story Writers, Scriptwriters, and
Other Creative Writers

Deborah A. Schmitt
EDITOR

Jeffrey W. Hunter
Tim White
CLC COORDINATORS

Tim Akers
Pamela S. Dear
Daniel Jones
John D. Jorgenson
Jerry Moore
Polly Vedder
Thomas Wiloch
Kathleen Wilson
ASSOCIATE EDITORS

WITHDRAWN FROM
J. EUGENE SMITH LIBRARY
EASTERN CONN. STATE UNIVERSITY
WILLIMANTIC, CT 06226-2295

GALE

DETROIT · LONDON

STAFF

Deborah A. Schmitt, *Editor*

Jeffrey W. Hunter, Timothy J. White, *Coordinators*

Tim Akers, Pamela S. Dear, Daniel Jones, John D. Jorgenson, Jerry Moore,
Polly Vedder, Thomas Wiloch, and Kathleen Wilson, *Associate Editors*

Tracy Arnold-Chapman, Jay Daniel, Linda Quigley,
Paul Serralheiro, and Fred Wheeler, *Contributing Editors*

Susan Trosky, *Permissions Manager*
Kimberly F. Smilay, *Permissions Specialist*
Steve Cusack and Kelly Quin, *Permissions Associates*
Sandy Gore, *Permissions Assistant*

Victoria B. Cariappa, *Research Manager*
Julia C. Daniel, Tamara C. Nott, Michele P. Pica, Tracie A. Richardson,
Norma Sawaya, and Cheryl L. Warnock, *Research Associates*
Laura C. Bissey, Alfred A. Gardner I, and Sean R. Smith, *Research Assistants*

Mary Beth Trimper, *Production Director*
Deborah L. Milliken, *Production Assistant*

Barbara J. Yarrow, *Graphic Services Manager*
Sherrell Hobbs, *Macintosh Artist*
Randy Bassett, *Image Database Supervisor*
Robert Duncan and Mikal Ansari, *Scanner Operators*
Pamela Reed, *Imaging Coordinator*

Since this page cannot legibly accommodate all copyright notices, the acknowledgments constitute an extension of the copyright notice.

While every effort has been made to ensure the reliability of the information presented in this publication, Gale Research neither guarantees the accuracy of the data contained herein nor assumes any responsibility for errors, omissions or discrepancies. Gale accepts no payment for listing, and inclusion in the publication of any organization, agency, institution, publication, service, or individual does not imply endorsement of the editors or publisher. Errors brought to the attention of the publisher and verified to the satisfaction of the publisher will be corrected in future editions.

The paper used in this publication meets the minimum requirements of American National Standard for Information Sciences—Permanence Paper for Printed Library Materials, ANSI Z39.48-1984. ⊚™

This publication is a creative work fully protected by all applicable copyright laws, as well as by misappropriation, trade secret, unfair competition, and other applicable laws. The authors and editors of this work have added value to the underlying factual material herein through one or more of the following: unique and original selection, coordination, expression, arrangement, and classification of the information.

All rights to this publication will be vigorously defended.

Copyright © 1998
Gale Research

Address until September 15, 1998:

835 Penobscot Building
Detroit, MI 48226-4094

Address after September 15, 1998:

27500 Drake Rd.
Farmington Hills, MI 48331-3535

All rights reserved including the right of reproduction in whole or in part in any form.

Library of Congress Catalog Card Number 76-46132
ISBN 0-7876-2031-9
ISSN 0091-3421

Printed in the United States of America
10 9 8 7 6 5 4 3 2 1

Contents

Preface vii

Acknowledgments xi

A. R. Ammons 1926- 1
American poet

Charles Bukowski 1920-1994 63
German-born American poet, novelist, and short story writer

Joel and Ethan Coen 1955- and 1958- 118
American screenwriters and filmmakers

Robert Coles 1929- 177
American psychiatrist, biographer, social commentator, and nonfiction writer

Chester Himes 1909-1984 218
American novelist, short story writer, autobiographer, and essayist

Langston Hughes 1902-1967 280
American poet, dramatist, novelist, nonfiction and short story writer

Joyce Carol Oates 1938- 338
American novelist, short story writer, poet, literary critic, essayist, nonfiction writer, and dramatist

Julia O'Faolain 1932- 398
English-born Irish short novelist, short story writer, editor, and translator

Literary Criticism Series Cumulative Author Index 431

Literary Criticism Series Cumulative Topic Index 499

CLC Cumulative Nationality Index 509

CLC-108 Title Index 525

Preface

A Comprehensive Information Source
on Contemporary Literature

Named "one of the twenty-five most distinguished reference titles published during the past twenty-five years" by *Reference Quarterly,* the *Contemporary Literary Criticism (CLC)* series provides readers with critical commentary and general information on more than 2,000 authors now living or who died after December 31, 1959. Previous to the publication of the first volume of *CLC* in 1973, there was no ongoing digest monitoring scholarly and popular sources of critical opinion and explication of modern literature. *CLC,* therefore, has fulfilled an essential need, particularly since the complexity and variety of contemporary literature makes the function of criticism especially important to today's reader.

Scope of the Series

CLC presents significant passages from published criticism of works by creative writers. Since many of the authors covered by *CLC* inspire continual critical commentary, writers are often represented in more than one volume. There is, of course, no duplication of reprinted criticism.

Authors are selected for inclusion for a variety of reasons, among them the publication or dramatic production of a critically acclaimed new work, the reception of a major literary award, revival of interest in past writings, or the adaptation of a literary work to film or television.

Attention is also given to several other groups of writers-authors of considerable public interest—about whose work criticism is often difficult to locate. These include mystery and science fiction writers, literary and social critics, foreign writers, and authors who represent particular ethnic groups within the United States.

Format of the Book

Each *CLC* volume contains about 500 individual excerpts taken from hundreds of book review periodicals, general magazines, scholarly journals, monographs, and books. Entries include critical evaluations spanning from the beginning of an author's career to the most current commentary. Interviews, feature articles, and other published writings that offer insight into the author's works are also presented. Students, teachers, librarians, and researchers will find that the generous excerpts and supplementary material in *CLC* provide them with vital information required to write a term paper, analyze a poem, or lead a book discussion group. In addition, complete bibliographical citations note the original source and all of the information necessary for a term paper footnote or bibliography.

Features

A *CLC* author entry consists of the following elements:

- The **Author Heading** cites the author's name in the form under which the author has most commonly published, followed by birth date, and death date when applicable. Uncertainty as to a birth or death date is indicated by a question mark.

- A **Portrait** of the author is included when available.

- A brief **Biographical and Critical Introduction** to the author and his or her work precedes the excerpted criticism. The first line of the introduction provides the author's full name, pseudonyms (if applicable), nationality, and a listing of genres in which the author has written. To provide users with easier access to information, the biographical and critical essay included in each author entry is divided into four categories: "Introduction," "Biographical Information," "Major Works," and "Critical Reception." The introductions to single-work entries—entries that focus on well known and frequently studied books, short stories, and poems—are similarly organized to quickly provide readers with information on the plot and major characters of the work being discussed, its major themes, and its critical reception. Previous volumes of *CLC* in which the author has been featured are also listed in the introduction.

- A list of **Principal Works** notes the most important writings by the author. When foreign-language works have been translated into English, the English-language version of the title follows in brackets.

- The **Excerpted Criticism** represents various kinds of critical writing, ranging in form from the brief review to the scholarly exegesis. Essays are selected by the editors to reflect the spectrum of opinion about a specific work or about an author's literary career in general. The excerpts are presented chronologically, adding a useful perspective to the entry. All titles by the author featured in the entry are printed in boldface type, which enables the reader to easily identify the works being discussed. Publication information (such as publisher names and book prices) and parenthetical numerical references (such as footnotes or page and line references to specific editions of a work) have been deleted at the editor's discretion to provide smoother reading of the text.

- Critical essays are prefaced by **Explanatory Notes** as an additional aid to readers. These notes may provide several types of valuable information, including: the reputation of the critic, the importance of the work of criticism, the commentator's approach to the author's work, the purpose of the criticism, and changes in critical trends regarding the author.

- A complete **Bibliographical Citation** designed to help the user find the original essay or book precedes each excerpt.

- Whenever possible, a recent, previously unpublished **Author Interview** accompanies each entry.

- A concise **Further Reading** section appears at the end of entries on authors for whom a significant amount of criticism exists in addition to the pieces reprinted in *CLC*. Each citation in this section is accompanied by a descriptive annotation describing the content of that article. Materials included in this section are grouped under various headings (e.g., Biography, Bibliography, Criticism, and Interviews) to aid users in their search for additional information. Cross-references to other useful sources published by Gale Research in which the author has appeared are also included: *Authors in the News, Black Writers, Children's Literature Review, Contemporary Authors, Dictionary of Literary Biography, DISCovering Authors, Drama Criticism, Hispanic Literature Criticism, Hispanic Writers, Native North American Literature, Poetry Criticism, Something about the Author, Short Story Criticism, Contemporary Authors Autobiography Series,* and *Something about the Author Autobiography Series.*

Other Features

CLC also includes the following features:

- An **Acknowledgments** section lists the copyright holders who have granted permission to reprint material in this volume of *CLC*. It does not, however, list every book or periodical reprinted or consulted during the preparation of the volume.

- Each new volume of *CLC* includes a **Cumulative Topic Index,** which lists all literary topics treated in *CLC, NCLC, TCLC,* and *LC 1400-1800.*

- A **Cumulative Author Index** lists all the authors who have appeared in the various literary criticism series published by Gale Research, with cross-references to Gale's biographical and autobiographical series. A full listing of the series referenced there appears on the first page of the indexes of this volume. Readers will welcome this cumulated author index as a useful tool for locating an author within the various series. The index, which lists birth and death dates when available, will be particularly valuable for those authors who are identified with a certain period but whose death dates cause them to be placed in another, or for those authors whose careers span two periods. For example, Ernest Hemingway is found in *CLC,* yet F. Scott Fitzgerald, a writer often associated with him, is found in *Twentieth-Century Literary Criticism.*

- A **Cumulative Nationality Index** alphabetically lists all authors featured in *CLC* by nationality, followed by numbers corresponding to the volumes in which the authors appear.

- An alphabetical **Title Index** accompanies each volume of *CLC.* Listings are followed by the author's name and the corresponding page numbers where the titles are discussed. English translations of foreign titles and variations of titles are cross-referenced to the title under which a work was originally published. Titles of novels, novellas, dramas, films, record albums, and poetry, short story, and essay collections are printed in italics, while all individual poems, short stories, essays, and songs are printed in roman type within quotation marks; when published separately (e.g., T. S. Eliot's poem *The Waste Land),* the titles of long poems are printed in italics.

- In response to numerous suggestions from librarians, Gale has also produced a **Special Paperbound Edition** of the *CLC* title index. This annual cumulation, which alphabetically lists all titles reviewed in the series, is available to all customers and is typically published with every fifth volume of *CLC.* Additional copies of the index are available upon request. Librarians and patrons will welcome this separate index: it saves shelf space, is easy to use, and is recyclable upon receipt of the next edition.

Citing *Contemporary Literary Criticism*

When writing papers, students who quote directly from any volume in the Literary Criticism Series may use the following general forms to footnote reprinted criticism. The first example pertains to material drawn from periodicals, the second to material reprinted in books:

[1]Alfred Cismaru, "Making the Best of It," *The New Republic,* 207, No. 24, (December 7, 1992), 30, 32; excerpted and reprinted in *Contemporary Literary Criticism,* Vol. 85, ed. Christopher Giroux (Detroit: Gale Research, 1995), pp. 73-4.

[2]Yvor Winters, *The Post-Symbolist Methods* (Allen Swallow, 1967); excerpted and reprinted in *Contemporary Literary Criticism,* Vol. 85, ed. Christopher Giroux (Detroit: Gale Research, 1995), pp. 223-26.

Suggestions Are Welcome

The editors hope that readers will find *CLC* a useful reference tool and welcome comments about the work. Send comments and suggestions to: Editors, *Contemporary Literary Criticism,* Gale Research, Penobscot Building, Detroit, MI 48226-4094.

Acknowledgments

The editors wish to thank the copyright holders of the excerpted criticism included in this volume and the permissions managers of many book and magazine publishing companies for assisting us in securing reproduction rights. We are also grateful to the staffs of the Detroit Public Library, the Library of Congress, the University of Detroit Mercy Library, Wayne State University Purdy/Kresge Library Complex, and the University of Michigan Libraries for making their resources available to us. Following is a list of the copyright holders who have granted us permission to reproduce material in this volume of *CLC*. Every effort has been made to trace copyright, but if omissions have been made, please let us know.

COPYRIGHTED EXCERPTS IN *CLC*, VOLUME 108, WERE REPRODUCED FROM THE FOLLOWING PERIODICALS:

African American Review, v. 26, Fall, 1992 for "The Chester Himes Mystique" by Gwnedoline L. Roget; v. 28, Winter, 1994 for "Limited Options: Strategic Maneuverings in Himes's Harlem" by Wendy W. Walters; v. 28, Fall, 1994 for "Heroic 'Hussies' and 'Brilliant Queers': Genderracial Resistance in the Works of Langston Hughes" by Anne Borden. Copyright © 1992, 1994 by the respective authors. All reproduced by permission of the respective authors.—*America,* v. 133, August 30, 1975 for "Women in the Wall" by Margaret Ferrari; v. 156, May 2, 1987 for a review of "The Irish Signorina" by T. Patrick Hill. © 1975, 1987. All rights reserved. Both reproduced by permission of the publisher and the respective authors.—*American Book Review,* March-May, 1995. © 1995 by *The American Book Review.* Reproduced by permission.—*American Film,* v. 16, August, 1991 for "What's The Goopus" by William Preston Robertson. Copyright 1991 by *American Film.* Reproduced by permission of the author./ v. 12, April, 1987. Copyright © 1987 by *American Film.*—*American Imago,* v. 45, Summer, 1988. © 1988 by Johns Hopkins University Press. Reproduced by permission of The Johns Hopkins University Press.—*The American Spectator,* v. 22, March, 1989. Copyright © *The American Spectator* 1989. Reproduced by permission.—*Arizona Quarterly,* v. 41, Spring, 1985. Copyright © 1985 by the Regents of the University of Arizona. Reproduced by permission of the publisher./ v. 49, Winter, 1993 for "Ammons Beside Himself: Poetics of The Bleak Periphery" by David R. Jarraway. Copyright © 1993 by the Regents of the University of Arizona. Reproduced by permission of the publisher and the author.—*Belles Lettres: A Review of Books by Women,* v. 9, Winter, 1993/94. Reproduced by permission.—*Book Week--The Sunday Herald Tribune,* October 25, 1964. © 1964, Washington Post Book World Service/Washington Post Writers Group. Reproduced by permission.—*Book World--The Washington Post,* February 2, 1986; May 8, 1988; December 23, 1990. © 1986, 1988, 1990, Washington Post Book World Service/Washington Post Writers Group. All reproduced by permission./ November 3, 1968 for "Journey to the End of Suburban Night" by R. V. Cassill; June 13, 1971 for "Judas-Hole Vision of Hell" by J. R. Frakes; August 23, 1991 for "Crass Consciousness" by Jonathan Rosenbaum. © 1968, 1971, 1991 Postrib Corp. All reproduced by permission of *The Washington Post* and the respective authors.—*Chicago Reader,* August 23, 1991 for "Crass Consciousness" by Jonathan Rosenbaum. Reproduced by permission.—*Chicago Tribune--Books,* January 30, 1994. © copyrighted 1994, Chicago Tribune Company. All rights reserved. Used by permission.—*The Christian Century,* v. 109, August 26-September 2, 1992. Copyright 1992 Christian Century Foundation. Reproduced by permission from *The Christian Century.*—*The Christian Science Monitor,* December 9, 1993. © 1993 The Christian Science Publishing Society. All rights reserved. Reproduced by permission from *The Christian Science Monitor.*—*The Chronicle of Higher Education,* v. XL, December 1, 1993. Copyright © 1993 *The Chronicle of Higher Education.* Reproduced with permission.—*CLA Journal,* v. 18, December, 1974; v. XX, June, 1977; v. XXI, December, 1977; v. 32, September, 1988. Copyright © 1974, 1977, 1988 by The College Language Association. All used by permission of The College Language Association .—*CM: Canadian Materials for Schools and Libraries,* November, 1984. Copyright 1984 The Canadian Library Association. Reproduced by permission of the Manitoba Library Association.—*Colby Quarterly,* v. XXVII, March, 1991; v. XXX, December, 1994. Both reproduced by permission.—*College Literature,* v. 22, October, 1995. Copyright © 1995 by West Chester University. Reproduced by permission of the publisher.—*Commentary,* v. 92, November, 1991 for "Hollywood's Holy Grail" by Richard Grenier. Copyright © 1991 by the American Jewish Committee. All rights reserved. Reproduced by permission of the publisher and the author.—*Contemporary Literature,* v. 30, 1989. © 1989 by the Board of Regents of the University of Wisconsin. Reproduced by permission of The University of Wisconsin Press.—*Contemporary Psychology,* v. 39, October, 1994 for "A Child Analyst for All Seasons: Anna Freud" by Paulina F. Kernberg. Copyright © 1994 by the American Psychological Association, Inc. Reproduced by permission of the publisher and the author.—*Critique: Studies in Contemporary Fiction,* v. XXXIII, Summer, 1992. Copyright 1992 by Helen Dwight Reid Educational Foundation. Reproduced with permission of the Helen Dwight Reid Educational Foundation, published by Heldref Publications, 1319 18th Street, NW, Washington, DC 20036-1802.—*Diacritics,* v. III, Winter, 1973. Copyright © Diacritics, Inc., 1973. Reproduced by permission.—*The Economist,* v. 246, February 17, 1973. Reproduced by permission. © 1973 The Economist Newspaper Group, Inc. Reproduced by permission.—*Éire-Ireland,* v. 21, Spring, 1986. Copyright © 1986 by the Irish American Cultural Institute. Reproduced by permission of the publisher.—*ENclitic,* v. 11, Summer, 1989 for "Bukowski's Hollywood" by Stan Theis (John O'Kane). Reproduced by permission of John O'Kane.—*Epoch,* v. XXVI, Spring, 1977. Copyright 1977 by Cornell University. Reproduced by permission.—*The Explicator,* v. 47, Fall, 1988; v. 49, Spring, 1991. Copyright © 1988, 1991 Helen Dwight Reid Educational Foundation. Both reproduced with permission of the Helen Dwight Reid Educational Foundation, published by Heldref Publications, 1319 18th Street, NW, Washington, DC 20036-1802.—*Film Comment,* v. 21, March/April, 1985 for "Bloodlines" by Hal Hinson; v. 26, September/October, 1990 for "Chasing the Hat" by Richard T. Jameson; v. 27, September-October, 1991 for "What's in the Box: Wrestling with 'Barton Fink'" by Richard T. Jameson. Copyright © 1985, 1990, 1991 by Film Comment Publishing Corporation. All reproduced by permission of the respective authors.—*Film Quarterly,* v. 50, Fall, 1996 for a review of 'Fargo' by Devin McKinney. Copyright © 1996 by the Regents of the University of California. Reproduced by permission of the publisher and the author.—*The Georgia Review,* v. LXIII, Summer, 1989. Copyright, 1989, by the University of Georgia. Reproduced by permission.—*The Gettysburg Review,* v. 6, Spring, 1993 for an Interview with Joyce Carol Oates by David Y. Todd. Reproduced by permission of David Y. Todd.—*Harvard Educational Review,* v. 63, 1993. Copyright © by the President and Fellows of Harvard College. Reproduced by permission.—*The Humanist,* v. 45, July/August, 1985 for "Reflections on My First Century" by Harry M. Geduld. Copyright © 1985 by the American Humanist Association. Reproduced by permission of the author.—*International Journal of Women's Studies,* v. 6, May/June, 1983 for "Catatonia and Feminity in Oates's `Do With Me What You Will'" by Janis P. Stout. Reproduced by permission of the author.—*The Iowa Review,* v. 18, Fall, 1988 for "The Grace of Slaughter: A Review-Essay of Joyce Carol Oates's `On Boxing'" by Gerald Early. Copyright © 1988 by The University of Iowa. Reproduced by permission of the author.—*The Langston Hughes Review,* v. 5, Fall, 1986; v. XI, Spring, 1992; v. XII, Spring, 1993. Copyright © 1986, 1992, 1993 by The Langston Hughes Society. All reproduced by permission.—*London Magazine,* v. 10, November, 1970; v. 14, January, 1975. © London Magazine, 1970, 1975. Both reproduced by permission.—*London Review of Books,* v. 18, March 7, 1995. Appears here by permission of the *London Review of Books./* v. 18, June 20, 1996 for "The Life of the Mind" by Michael Wood. Appears here by permission of the *London Review of Books* and the author.—*Los Angeles Times Book Review,* February 9, 1986; September 13, 1987; October 3, 1993; October 30, 1994. Copyright, 1986, 1987, 1993, 1994 *Los Angeles Times.* All reproduced by permission.—*Melus,* v. 20, Summer, 1995. Copyright, MELUS, The Society for the Study of Multi-Ethnic Literature of the United States, 1995. Reproduced by permission.—*Michigan Quarterly Review,* v, XXVIII, Winter, 1989 for an interview with A. R. Ammons by William Walsh. Copyright © The University of Michigan, 1989. All rights reserved. Reproduced by permission of A. R. Ammons and the Literary Estate of William Walsh./ v. XXXI, Summer, 1992 for "Heat and Cold: Recent Fiction by Joyce Carol Oates" by Sally Robinson. Copyright © The University of Michigan, 1992. Reproduced by permission of the author.—*The Midwest Quarterly,* v. XXVIII, Summer, 1987; v. XXXVIII, Autumn, 1996. Copyright, 1987, 1997 by *The Midwest Quarterly,* Pittsburg State University. Both reproduced by permission.—*Midwestern Miscellany,* v. XVIII, 1990 for "Threatening Places, Hiding Places: The Midwest in Selected Stories by Joyce Carol Oates" by Margaret Rozga. Copyright 1990 by The Society for the Study of Midwestern Literature. All rights reserved. Reproduced by permission of the publisher and the author.—*The Nation,* New York, v. 198, March 23, 1964. © 1964 *The Nation* magazine/ The Nation Company, Inc. Reproduced by permission.—*New York,* Magazine, v. 20, March 23, 1987. Copyright © 1987 K-III Magazine Corporation. All rights reserved. Reproduced with the permission of *New York* Magazine.—*The New York Review of Books,* v. XXXIX, January 16, 1992. Copyright © 1992 Nyrev, Inc. Reproduced with permission from *The New York Review of Books.—The New York Times Book Review,* September 10, 1967; January 19, 1986; September 6, 1987; February 26, 1989; v. 98, December 12, 1993; October 16, 1994;

v. XCIX, December 25, 1994; February 12, 1995; June 5, 1995; October 8, 1995; January 27, 1997. Copyright ©
1967, 1986, 1987, 1989, 1993, 1994, 1995, 1997 by The New York Times Company. All reproduced by
permission.—*The New York Times,* November 21, 1990. Copyright © 1990 by The New York Times Company.
Reproduced by permission.—*The New Yorker,* February 10, 1986; v. LXVI, January 7, 1991. © 1986, 1991 by *The
New Yorker* Magazine, Inc. All rights reserved. Both reproduced by permission.—*New Statesman & Society,* June
17, 1994. © 1994 Statesman & Nation Publishing Company Limited. Reproduced by permission.—*Pembroke
Magazine,* 1986 for "Poetic Metaphysic in A. R. Ammons" by D. R. Fosso; 1986 for "Scholar of Wind and Tree:
The Early Lyrics of A. R. Ammons" by Sister Bernetta Quinn. Copyright © Pembroke Magazine. Both reproduced
by permission of the respective authors.—*PHYLON: The Atlanta University of Race and Culture,* v. 48, Fall, 1987.
Copyright, 1987 by Atlanta University. Reproduced by permission of *PHYLON.*—*Poetry,* v. CLXIV, May, 1994
for "From a Toy" by Robert B. Shaw. © 1994 by the Modern Poetry Association. Reproduced by permission of the
Editor of *Poetry* and the author.—*Post Script: Essays in Film and The Humanities,* v. 8, Summer, 1989.
Reproduced by permission.—*Review: Latin American Literature and Arts,* v. 47, Fall, 1993. Copyright © 1993 by
the Americas Society, Inc. Reproduced by permission of the Americas Society, Inc.—*Review of Contemporary
Fiction,* v. 5, Fall, 1985. Copyright, 1985, by John O'Brien. Reproduced by permission.—*Rolling Stone,* June 17,
1976; May 21, 1987. © 1976, 1987 by Straight Arrow Publishers, Inc. All rights reserved. Both reproduced by
permission.—*Sight and Sound,* v. 56, Summer, 1987; v. 60, Winter, 1990/91; v. 1, September, 1991; v. 4, August,
1994; v. 6, June, 1996. Copyright © 1987, 1990, 1991. 1994, 1996 by The British Film Institute. All Reproduced
by permission.—*Small Press: The Magazine of Independent Publishing,* v. 8, February, 1990. Reproduced by
permission.—*The Southern Literary Journal,* v. XV, Fall, 1982. Copyright 1982 by the Department of English,
University of North Carolina at Chapel Hill. Reproduced by permission.—*Southwest Review,* Vol. 48, Autumn,
1963. Copyright © 1963 Southern Methodist University. Reproduced by permission.—*Stand Magazine,* v. 36,
Autumn, 1995 for "Recent Poetry" by Lawrence Sail. Copyright © 1995 by the author. Reproduced by
permission.—*Studies in American Humor,* v. 4, 1996. Copyright © 1996 by Southwest Texas State University.
Reproduced by permission.—*Studies in Short Fiction,* v. 27, Winter, 1990. Copyright 1990 by Newberry College.
Reproduced by permission.—*Tennessee Folklore Society Bulletin,* v. LVI, 1994. Copyright by The Tennessee
Folklore Society, 1994. All rights reserved. Reproduced by permission.—*Time,* New York, v. 127, March 17, 1986.
Copyright 1986 Time Warner Inc. All rights reserved. Reproduced by permission from *Time.*—*The Times Literary
Supplement,* n. 3813, April 4, 1975; September 25, 1992; December 24, 1993. © The Times Supplements Limited
1975, 1992, 1993. All reproduced from *The Times Literary Supplement* by permission.—*Twentieth Century
Literature,* v. 40, Winter, 1994. Copyright 1994, Hofstra University Press. Reproduced by permission.—*VLS,* June,
1991 for "The Collected Stories of Chester Himes" by James A. Miller. Copyright © V. V. Publishing Corporation.
Reproduced by permission of the author.—*Vogue,* April, 1994 for "Inside the Coen Heads" by Tad Friend.
Reproduced by permission of the author.—*The Wall Street Journal,* November 15, 1993. Reproduced with
permission of *The Wall Street Journal.* Copyright 1993 Dow Jone & Company, Inc. All rights reserved.—*World
Literature Today,* v. 66, Autumn, 1992; Autumn, 1995. Copyright © 1992, 1995 by the University of Oklahoma
Press. Both reproduced by permission.

**COPYRIGHTED EXCERPTS IN *CLC*, VOLUME 108, WERE REPRODUCED FROM THE FOLLOWING
BOOKS:**

Harrison, Russell. From *Against the Dream: Essays on Charles Bukowski.* Black Sparrow Press, 1994. Copyright
© 1994 by Russell Harrison. All rights reserved. Reproduced by permission.—Manske, Eva. From Neo-Realism in
Contemporary American Fiction. Edited by Kristiaan Versluys. Rodopi, 1992. © Editions Rodopi B. V. 1992.
Reproduced by permission.—Peters, Robert. From *Where the Bee Sucks: Workers, Drones and Queens of
Contemporary American Poetry.* Asylum Arts, 1994. Copyright © 1994 by Robert Peters. Reproduced by
permission.—Rampersad, Arnold. From *The Harlem Renaissance: Revaluations.* Edited by Amritjit Singh, William
S. Shriver and Stanley Brodwin. Garland Publishing, 1989. Copyright © 1989 Amritjit Singh, William S. Shriver
and Stanley Brodwin. Reproduced by permission.—Weeks, Ann Owens. From *Irish Women Writers: An Uncharted
Tradition.* University Press of Kentucky, 1990. Reproduced by permission of The University Press of Kentucky.

PHOTOGRAPHS AND ILLUSTRATIONS APPEARING IN *CLC,* VOLUME 108, WERE RECEIVED FROM THE FOLLOWING SOURCES:

Ammons, A.R., photograph. AP/Wide World Photos. Reproduced by permission.—Bukowski, Charles, photograph by Freddie Patterson. Archive Photos. Reproduced by permission.—Coen, Ethan and Joel Coen, photograph. AP/Wide World Photos, Inc. Reproduced by permission.—Coles, Robert, photograph. AP/Wide World Photos, Inc. Reproduced by permission.—Himes, Chester, photograph. AP/Wide World Photos. Reproduced by permission. —Hughes, Langston, photograph. The Bettmann Archive/Newsphotos, Inc./Corbis-Bettmann. Reproduced by permission.—Oates, Joyce Carol, photograph. AP/Wide World Photos. Reproduced by permission.

A. R. Ammons

1926-

(Full name Archie Randolph Ammons) American poet.

The following entry presents an overview of Ammons's career. For further information on his life and works, see *CLC*, Volumes 2, 3, 5, 8, 9, 25, and 57.

INTRODUCTION

A prolific writer, Ammons is widely considered among the most significant contemporary American poets. Often referred to as an Emersonian Transcendentalist, Ammons is praised for his sensitive meditations on the human capacity to comprehend the flux of the natural world. Initially characterized as a nature poet in the tradition of Walt Whitman and Robert Frost, Ammons frequently writes in a conversational tone and endows his verse with resonant images of detailed landscapes. While often linked with traditional literary movements, Ammons's poetry contains a modern skepticism which stems from his refusal to attach universal significance to religious or artistic doctrines. Abstaining from offering any facile resolutions to the tensions in his works, Ammons is concerned with broadening his readers' perceptions of their relationship to the world.

Biographical Information

Ammons was born in 1926 in Whiteville, North Carolina, where his father ran a small farm. He spent his first 17 years on the farm, and his poetry later exhibited a preoccupation with and an appreciation for natural processes. In 1943 he graduated from high school and got a job with a ship-building company in Wilmington. Ammons joined the U.S. Naval Reserve when he was 18 and served in the South Pacific for 19 months during World War II. After returning home in 1946, he entered Wake Forest College on the G.I. Bill. Ammons had begun writing poetry while in the South Pacific, and he continued throughout college. He graduated with a bachelor of science degree in 1949. After working briefly as the principal of the elementary school in Cape Hatteras, Ammons left North Carolina to pursue a Master's degree in English at the University of California at Berkeley. In 1952 he moved to New Jersey, where he worked for several years as an executive for a biological-glassware factory. Ammons showed his poetry to the poet and critic Josephine Miles, who encouraged him to publish his work. His first collection, *Ommateum with Doxology,* appeared in 1955. The book sold only 16 copies in five years and did not garner much critical attention. Ammons continued to write and struggled to find a publisher for the next nine years.

In 1963 he served as editor of *Nation,* and did a poetry reading at Cornell University. Ammons was offered a teaching position and eventually received an endowed chair as the Goldwin Smith Professor of Poetry. Ammons has since received increasing critical attention and acclaim, and has received numerous literary awards, including the National Book Award for Poetry for *Collected Poems* (1972), the Bollingen Prize in Poetry for *Sphere: The Form of a Motion* (1973), the National Book Critics Circle Award for Poetry for *A Coast of Trees* (1982), and the National Book Award for Poetry for *Garbage* (1993).

Major Works

Ammons's work, occupied with speculations about natural processes, shows an appreciation of nature, but it is not an idealized vision as in pastoral poetry. Although the poetic landscape of Ammons's earlier work is dominated by images from the natural world, he is not a nature poet per se. His poetry is concerned with humankind's relationship to nature. The major themes of his poetry include the dialectic between the one and the many, the relationships between species, and the ever-changing nature of experience. His first collection, *Ommateum with Doxology,* studies different ways of looking at the world. The word *ommateum* means "compound eye," and exhibits Ammons's use of scientific language and his multiple perspectives. One of Ammons's main concerns is apparent in his next collection, *Expressions of Sea Level* (1964), in which he expresses the desire for unity between the flesh and the spirit — the form and the formless. He uses images of the sea and wind to represent nature's perpetual motion, and suggests that man is only partially aware of external forces. Ammons's *Tape for the Turn of the Year* (1965) is a book-length poem that takes the form of a daily poetic journal and chronicles the poet's thoughts on the mundanity of everyday life. The poem was composed on adding machine tape, as was his later *Garbage. Sphere: The Form of a Motion* concerns humanity's struggle to impose order on a world which defies structure and to suspend the motion of natural forces. Ammons believes that anything is a suitable subject for poetry. His collection *Garbage* was inspired by a landfill he passed on the highway during a trip through Florida.

Critical Reception

Critics often refer to Ammons's work as Emersonian, asserting that his poetry shows the influence of the American Romantic tradition. Some critics assert that Ammons's work is more complicated than that, however, citing the lack of resolution and optimism in his poetry. Critics also point out the lack of an overriding doctrine in Ammon's work. Josephine Jacobsen states: "Though Ammons now and then reminds his reader of Emerson, there is an unbridgeable gap between the basically firm optimism of the transcendentalist, and the painful, theory-free search of the poet of 'Extremes and Moderations.'" In discussing Ammons's style, reviewers often note his natural and appropriate use of scientific language. As Ammon's career progressed, critics recognized a greater scope to his work and praised his ability to turn anything into poetry. Critics assert a continuity of theme and purpose in Ammons's work, and praise his ability to bring new life to his recurring concerns. Josephine Jacobsen says, "To be able to control so much renewal, to strengthen and deepen new insights and hints, upon so permanent a project, to maintain so much *oneness* and flexibility in such an unrelentingly coherent poetic purpose, is perhaps the most solid of Ammons's achievements."

PRINCIPAL WORKS

Ommateum with Doxology (poetry) 1955
Expressions of Sea Level (poetry) 1964
Corsons Inlet: A Book of Poems (poetry) 1965
Tape for the Turn of the Year (poem) 1965

Northfield Poems (poetry) 1966
Selected Poems (poetry) 1968
Uplands (poetry) 1970
Briefings: Poems Small and Easy (poetry) 1971
Collected Poems, 1951-1971 (poetry) 1972
Sphere: The Form of a Motion (poetry) 1973
Diversifications: Poems (poetry) 1975
For Doyle Fosso (poetry) 1977
Highgate Road (poetry) 1977
The Snow Poems (poetry) 1977
The Selected Poems: 1951-1977 (poetry) 1977; expanded
  edition, 1987
Breaking Out (poetry) 1978
Six-Piece Suite (poetry) 1978
Selected Longer Poems (poetry) 1980
Changing Things (poetry) 1981
A Coast of Trees: Poems (poetry) 1982
Worldly Hopes: Poems (poetry) 1982
Lake Effect Country: Poems (poetry) 1982
Sumerian Vistas: Poems, 1987 (poetry) 1987
The Really Short Poems of A. R. Ammons (poetry) 1991
Garbage (poem) 1993
The Best American Poetry 1994 [editor] (poetry) 1995

CRITICISM

Wendell Berry (review date 23 March 1964)

SOURCE: "Antennae to Knowledge," in *The Nation,* Vol. 198, No. 13, March 23, 1964, pp. 304-6.

[*In the following review, Berry discusses Ammons's focus on knowledge in his* Expressions of Sea Level, *and analyzes the poet's use of form and scientific language.*]

In this admirable book, [*Expressions of Sea Level*], Mr. Ammons' aim isn't beauty, though there are poems here that I think are beautiful, and it's not the suggestiveness which is sometimes meant by the word "poetic." His aim is knowledge, the getting of it and the use of it; the art of poetry is held out to the world like an antenna. A man who is concerned with knowing must necessarily be concerned with what he does not know; and one of the principles here is an honesty which insists on clarifying the difference and will then consider what is unknown or unaccountable: "I admit to mystery / in the obvious. . . ." The suggestive is confined to what is authentically mysterious. These poems take place on the frontier between what the poet knows and what he doesn't; perhaps that explains their peculiar life and sensitivity. They open to accommodate surprises and accidents. The poet's interest is extended generously toward what he didn't expect, and his poems move by their nature in that direction.

The poems are worked out, not by the application of set forms to their materials, but in an effort to achieve form—in accordance with a constant attentiveness to, a hope for, the possibility of form—the need of anything, once begun, to complete itself, meaningfully. Mr. Ammons' way in this can be seen in the poem called **"Mechanism."** The movement begins with a goldfinch lighting in a bush:

> the yellow
> bird flashes black wing bars
> in the new-leaving wild cherry
>   bushes by the bay. . . .
>
> flitting to a branch where
>   flash vanishes into stillness. . . .

And then there's a consideration of the multitudinous biological dependencies of the goldfinch—all the minute causes and effects of digestion, sex, instinct, habitat, etc., almost inscrutably complex, and involving a kind of miracle: "mind rising / from the physical chemistries. . . ." The poem then returns to the bird itself, a model of the world, both containing and caught up in the natural workings, ignorant of all of them, singing on its perch: the

> goldfinch, unconscious of the billion
>   operations
>   that stay its form, flashes,
>   chirping (not a
> great songster) in the bay cherry
>   bushes wild of leaf.

The form here is circular; we wind up where we started. But by the time we've come all the way around though the bird hasn't changed, we have. We've learned something. We see differently, and better. We've seen the world working, which is not only informative but dramatic. This gives a fair idea of how Mr. Ammons goes about his task. He attempts to mediate, make or discover an intelligible continuity between the complex and the simple, the vast and the small, the over-ruling laws of creation and the creatures.

In several of the poems there's a large proportion of scientific language. In the following you can see how the scientific talk is broken into, made flexible, by the commoner language of everyday:

> Honor a going thing, goldfinch,
>   corporation, tree,
>   morality: any working order
> animate or inanimate: it
>
> has managed directed balance,
> the incoming and outgoing energies
>   are working right. . . .

However, in lines where the language is predominantly or purely scientific the effect the poet's ear can have on it is extremely limited:

> honor the chemistries, platelets,
>   hemoglobin kinetics,
> the light-sensitive iris, the
>   enzymic intricacies
> of control. . . .

That language is by nature stiff, like a wooden shoe. No conceivable amount of use would limber it up. Except for the word "honor," the poet is taking the scientific vocabulary pretty much as it comes. About all he can hope to do with it, as a poet, is to place it exactly within the large rhythm of his poem—everything seems to depend on that.

"Mechanism," I believe, makes more use of this kind of language than any of the others. But so many of the poems include lines or passages that have the cadences of prose that I assume it must be deliberate, part of Mr. Ammons' usual method. The only near-equivalent or precedent for this, so far as I know, is the gathering in of prose quotations, statistics etc., in such modern poems as *Paterson* and *The Cantos*. And it works, I think, the same way: the prose detail is admitted raw into the poem not to be transformed into poetry by it but to be illuminated or newly clarified by the energy with which the poem surrounds it—and to serve the poem in some way in which only prose can serve it. This use of prose in poems may be justified by the poet's conviction that poetry might legitimately deal with subject matter which is customarily the subject matter of prose—his realization that some of the things he knows and is concerned about are new, and haven't been prepared for poetry by any considerable period of association or usage. What I'm indicating here is that Mr. Ammons aims to bring science into his poems as *subject matter*, not just to borrow words or images from it.

The poet attempting to lay hold of such materials is up against the possibility of enlarging the powers and working spaces of his art at the risk of weakening it. The effort is experimental in the purest sense of the word, and involves the risk of experiment. The only measure for it is: Does it work? Can the reader take it in?

I think that Mr. Ammons makes it work often and well. The poetry doesn't inhere consistently in the verbal texture of the poems, but in the forms, the arrangements of the contents. Sometimes the reader is unsure that what he's reading is poetry until he has read all the way through. But when he comes to the end of a poem like **"Mechanism"**—which attempts to bring to bear on the image of the singing bird, and to bring under the control of that poetic image, all that the poet *knows* about it—he's conscious that a unifying exciting energy has been released among the subject matters; and he knows that it's the energy of poetry, which takes over the language of science only as a resource, and causes it to belong to a larger, more exuberant statement than the specialized vocabulary alone could make. **"Mechanism"** isn't a biologist's poem; it's the poem of a poet who knows biology.

There's a nearly opposite kind of Ammons poem, represented here by **"Nelly Myers," "Hardweed Path Going"** and **"Silver."** These poems recollect the poet's country boyhood. Again the use of prose, this time a kind of narrative prose, is characteristic. And again the necessity for prose seems one of the conditions imposed by the materials. Here the subject matter is not difficult because, like the scientific, it has been kept pure of emotional or literary associations; it's difficult because it has been too much and too poorly written about—too much condescended to, you could say, by the conventions that claim to have been invented for it. I'm talking about all the oversweetening, distortion, falsification that have been left sticking to rural things by the pastoralizers, sentimentalizers and folksifiers since God knows when. Such things are usually both written and read about in a kind of institutional blindness to the sweat, crap, blood, and biting insects which are as much a part of the real experience as white lambs and new-mown hay. Mr. Ammons' poems of this life manage an honesty about it which is an achievement. He proceeds in these as he does in the poems of scientific lore, keeping a respectful loyalty to what he knows, refusing to think of it or write about it in any falsifying rhetoric. It must be given to the reader in the most direct way, otherwise there can be no meeting of minds.

The poem **"Nelly Myers"** is about a simple-minded woman of that name, a maker of brooms, who lived with the poet's family during his boyhood. The difficulty of writing this poem must have been Mr. Ammons' sense both of the uniqueness and the meaningfulness of her life, the presence of her life in his life. The two would, I imagine, have tended to cancel each other out: her uniqueness would have threatened to overpower her meaningfulness, make it incommunicable; or to emphasize the meaningfulness might have reduced her to a stereotype. Mr. Ammons' solution is to be openly personal. Some of the details of the poem are given with the directness, not even of prose fiction, but of biography:

> my grandmother, they say, took her
>   in
> when she was a stripling run away
>   from home
> (her mind was not perfect
>   which is no bar to this love song
>   for her smile was sweet,
>   her outrage honest and violent)
> and they say that after she worked

> all day her relatives
> would throw a handful of dried peas
>   into her lap
>   for her supper
> and she came to live in the house
>   I was born in the
> northwest room of. . . .

The poem is an elegy, and the relaxed passages of description or narrative support and give their specificness of feeling to an elegiac lyricism which is authentic and powerful, and which charges not just the passages in which it occurs purely, but the whole poem:

> oh I will not end my grief
> that she is gone, I will not end
>   my singing;
> my songs like blueberries
> felt-out and black to her searching
>   fingers before light
> welcome her
> wherever her thoughts ride with
>   mine, now or in any time
>   that may come
> when I am gone; I will not end
>   visions of her naked feet
> in the sandpaths: I will hear her
>   words

We're moved by Wordsworth's solitary highland lass because she's seen at a distance, and the poet is left free to suppose and suggest. We're moved by Nelly Myers because we're brought very close to her. She's not idealized, nor idealizable—she's too much present, we know too much about her. The power of the poem is that we're made to know her as she was, and to care for her as she was. Only the sympathy approaches some kind of ideal.

There is a wonderful eagerness in this book, a whetted appetite for the phenomena of seashores and farms and landscapes and factories. And the interest is not directed at things as objects or appearances, but at their ways—how they act, how they mix. The excitement of anything is that it moves, changes, influences other things—"boundless in its effect, / eternal in the working out / of its effect. . . ." Each poem is, in a way, an ecology—the revelation of a harmony which is both found and made.

Josephine Jacobsen (essay date Winter 1973)

SOURCE: "The Talk of Giants," in *Diacritics,* Winter, 1973, pp. 34-8.

[In the following essay, Jacobsen discusses the major sources of tension in Ammons's poetry, including limitation, utility and waste, and compensation, as well as the features which make Ammons's work so strong.]

The publication of A. R. Ammons' ***Collected Poems, 1951-1971,*** has focused attention on a poet who has quietly risen to the top rank of American poets. Actually, it was obvious in his first book (***Ommateum***), that his work was strong and original, and formidable in its promise. Belonging to no clique, identifiable by no gimmicks, he continued to publish increasingly commanding books, while still having a relatively narrow contact with the poetry-reading public. In the past ten years his poetry began to come into its own, with the publication of ***Expressions of Sea Level*** in 1964, and the rapid appearance of three other books, ***Corsons Inlet*** and ***Tape for the Turn of the Year*** in 1965, and ***Northfield Poems*** in 1966. By the time ***Selected Poems*** arrived in 1968, his stature had been fully recognized by a number of critics. From that period to the recent publication of his collected poems, his reputation has widened and deepened, and he is now being recognized for what he is—one of the finest American poets of his generation.

Ammons' poetry is a poetry which is profoundly American, without being in any way limited by this characteristic. His use of language, his vocabulary and phrasing are utterly and flexibly American. The universal terms of science emerge accurately and naturally from the poems' roots.

The poetry can now be read in its bulk and ripeness. It is science-minded, passionately absorbed with the processes around the poet, the constant, complex, fascinating processes of water, wind, season and genus. But if Ammons' poetry is in the tradition of "nature poets," its essence is far different from the lyric, limpid joy of John Clare, or the *pay-sage moralisé* of Wordsworth, or the somber farmer-wisdom of Robert Frost, or the myth-ridden marvels of D. H. Lawrence's tortoises, serpents and gentians. Ammons sees the datum of nature as *evidence;* intricate, interlocking fragments of a whole which cannot be totally understood, but which draws him deeper and deeper into its identity. No poet now writing in English has so thoroughly created on the page the huge suggestion of the whole through its most minute components.

One major aspect of the work is its concern with choices: limitation. There are choices for the root, the bird, the insect, the poet: and there are the limitations within which these choices operate. There are alternatives, but these are affected constantly by all the other alternatives chosen by contingent forms of life. The poet chooses between silence and words, and the proportion of each. Silence takes the forms of deliberate omission, understatement, statement in a lower or off-beat tone, abbreviation, refusal to be governed by the reader's satisfaction. **"Coon Song"** (***Collected Poems***), is a perfect example of the last. The coon, in actuality, has no alternatives, but the poet arbitrarily creates an alternative for him, without affirming it:

> You want to know what happened,
> you want to hear me describe it,
>   to placate the hound's mouth
>   slobbering in your own heart:
>
>   I am no slave that I
> should entertain you, say what you want
>   to hear, let you wallow in
>   your silt: one two three four five:
> one two three four five six seven eight nine ten:

The poem is moving underground, in silence, as the count goes on. In ***Tape for the Turn of the Year*** the process shows itself clearly: the thread of the poem, the authentic connection with the invoked Muse, is followed through the diversions of eating, getting the mail, shovelling snow, carting groceries, as the poem shows itself, dives into the ordinary detail which is part of its crucial silence, surfaces again.

Choices are limited, but vital. Does one love enough, and rightly? At what point does compassion rot into sentimentality, pessimism become ingratitude? At what point does optimism corrupt the attention to truth?

The choices: limitation duality becomes more important as the work progresses. Often the choice is more illusory than actual; usually something, somewhere else, is invisibly interacting to limit that choice. Nevertheless, the element of choice exists. In the case of the poet, it is brilliantly evident and utilized. He chooses the large, or the small, though inevitably, at their extremes and beyond his control, they will merge into the indefinable. He chooses speech, or that defining shadow of speech which is silence, attempting to employ just so much of silence as communication will allow. He chooses irregularities, within the limiting tone of the poem; the respites of colloquialisms, abbreviations, clowning, which are the poem's own kinds of varied silences. He chooses above all, not to make a choice final:

> my other word is
>   *provisional:*
> we'll talk about that
>   someday,
>   tho you may guess
> the meanings from *ecology:*
> don't establish the
>   boundaries
>   first,
>   the squares, triangles,
>   boxes

> of preconceived
> possibility,
> and then
>   pour
> life into them, trimming
> off left-over edges,
> ending potential:
>   let centers
>   proliferate
>   from
> self-justifying motions!

Over and over we are warned that the closed conclusion, like the attempt to distort evidence for the salvation of our hopes, is death. We are allowed only the constant tension between the defined and the indefinable, between the need to be identified and the need to be lost, between hope and reality:

> have I prettified the
> tragedies,
>   the irrecoverable
>   losses: have I
> glossed over the
> unmistakable evils:
> has panic
>   tried to make a flower:
>
>   then, hope distorts
>   me:
>   turns wishes into lies:
>
> I care about the statement
> of fact:
>   the true picture
>   has a beauty higher
>   than Beauty:

A second vital aspect of the poems is the concern with utility: waste. When Ammons writes in **"Catalyst"** (*Collected Poems*),

> Honor the maggot,
>   supreme catalyst
> he spurs the rate of change:
> tall scavengers are honorable: I love them
> all,
> will scribble as hard as I can for them)

his is not a merely ecological admiration for maximum efficiency. It is the admiration of the poet, this particular poet: the belief that the Muse is as formidably economical as the natural system of waste and replenishment. Poetry has no accidental lapses: instead, it continues to define, by its underground presence, by its silences and invisibilities, by

those surrounding silences which define its metaphors, as a plain sets forth a solitary tree.

> but betimes & at times
> let me out of here:
> I will penetrate into the
> void
> & bring back
> nothingness
> to surround all these
>   shapes with!

In Ammons' poetry there are differing silences—all useful, all used. There is the silence which ensues when the thing contemplated becomes too large or too small for speech, when the particular disappears into sizelessness, the sizelessness of the unimaginably small, the unimaginably great. In neither direction does the imagination cease to function, but silence takes over as its expression. Often one has very clearly this sense of a speech just beyond the imagination's speech: a minute, insect-like voice drilling at an unimaginable height: a subterranean, immense rumble at a depth too deep for the imagination to fathom. They meet. And this is the ultimate economy of Ammons' poetry. This *is* the talk of giants, illustrating the illusion of size: the atom which can destroy a mountain, the drop of water complex as a galaxy.

Sometimes this economy has a terrifying quality, and there is often the sense of the poet moving, carefully, through a world in which a more acute consciousness has been substituted for the "normal" illusory proportions. This is one reason why the earlier poems tend to confine overtly defined emotions to isolated poems, individual incidents. The vast process observed and reported on is so intricate, so incredibly able in its motions, so frighteningly economical, that all poetic energy is absorbed into that observing, that reporting. Conclusions, other than tentative conclusions on immediate evidence, are postponed, are presently inappropriate.

A pig, the comfortable familiar of a hundred mornings, will be slaughtered when the inescapable calendar says so: the individual and precious mule will be carted off when the inescapable financial calendar says so: a marvelous and battered human figure will shine out of the inescapable processes of pain and death. But what, if anything, this *means* cannot yet assert itself: there is still too much evidence to be accumulated. The pig will feed other bodies, the mule will balance a debt: the servant-friend's gnarled body responds to the demand of toil.

The parallels are too numerous and beautifully varied to belabor. Among these, the bones of the poet on which the wind will perform the song the poet did not manage: the glossy flies winging up from the dead cat's putrifaction; the poet's use of his tape, which permits and limits.

A third important tension of Ammons' poetry is that of levels: compensation, and this is perhaps most powerfully represented in the title poem of *Expressions of Sea Level,* one of the most remarkable poems of its time. It is as though this poetry, for an instant laid a finger on a pulsating heart exposed to touch. *Expressions of Sea Level* is a poem so close to non-verbal reality that the reader feels he is in the presence of some miraculously sensitive instrument. That instrument fixes the position of the poet, the spot from which he works. It establishes that fractional instant of balance, that living center of a shift so secret and so momentary as to be almost a metaphor in itself—a point from which all the infinite interplay, fluctuation, compensation, choices, are redistributed, redefined, again set in motion.

In a body of poetry which must reject, by its very nature, the appearance of a highly-organized overplan, it is no small triumph that the poems—the very long as well as the very short—show at almost unbroken parallel in their structure to their conception of the natural and poetic worlds. The ebb and flow, the periods of dryness, with catalogued details, provide a duplication of the poem's intent, a sort of root-tree, shaped like the tree in air.

The form of the lines upon the page turns out to be a physical expression of the poetry's basic element: a dominant sense of form, evidenced in flexibility and a variety of modes and tones. The lines in the long poems—and these are by far the greater number—assert a fundamental character: a breath-oriented, serious but not solemn, *discussion,* varying according to season, mood, the advent and termination of incidents; however indented, stretched, abbreviated, the discussion always maintains the balance between the poetry's intention and the levity of failures, disappointments, the ridiculous and necessary frustrations of actuality. The very real lyric quality in the poems is so conditioned by the other ingredients, humor, information, discoveries, that it can be easily missed.

Humor in Ammons' poems, being the manipulation of proportion, weaves in and out of even much of the serious poetry. It is overt in regard to the poet himself: he sees himself at once as a weed, a fool, and Ezra, the speech of the wind: above all, as a servant to the Muse:

> help me:
> I have this &
> > no other comfort:
> > > the song,
> the slight, inner
> unmistakable song you
> give me

> and nothing else! what
> > are you,
> some kind of strumpet?
> will you pull out on me?
> look: I have faith: I
> have faith: come or go:
> I'll always love you:
> I have nothing else:
> I have
> nothing else beside you:
> will you tear me
> > to pieces? I'll go
> on without you, until
> you come again:

The poet shoots himself down at the first hint of the portentous.

One major fact has contributed greatly to the strength and toughness of Ammons' writing: the matter of reinforcement. Most of those poets who signally avoid stasis, and the slow process of petrifaction within their own accomplishment, move sequentially, developing forward from past accomplishment by way of experiment, and advance upon new territory. Ammons has moved circularly, in the manner of seasons and tides, reinforcing the nature, the manner, the approaches of his poetry. New growth constantly appears, compelling changes by development, variation, richness, penetration. But what is happening is unmistakably, organically, what was happening in his very first poems. It is not just that one can identify an Ammons poem by its essential tone and flavor: it is that the concerns, the self-admonitions, the scrupulous search, the vast undertaking, are exactly that to which his first poems were addressed. To be able to control so much renewal, to strengthen and deepen new insights and hints, upon so permanent a project, to maintain so much *oneness* and flexibility in such an unrelentingly coherent poetic purpose, is perhaps the most solid of Ammons' achievements.

One of Ammons' preoccupations is the poet's relation to his reader. Ammons works within the tension between the wish and need to communicate, and a vigilant sense of the poet's need for freedom—freedom from the dictation of the reader's taste and approbation. (As for the more sordid dictates of poetic fashion, it would be hard to find any poet now writing more totally free from the taint of other-directed concessions to any sort of bandwagonism.) Dickinson and Hopkins come to mind, but each was sealed into (or freed by) certain rigid habits of life, while Ammons' work is freely exposed to an almost unnerving range of interests. His poetry, owing nothing to any school, group, clique, critical pressure, has developed its unique tone in a sort of solitary soliloquy which is simultaneously an open response to life, and a dialogue with the self. Its originality, so unostentatious as to make only a gradual impression, is amazing—far less an easily-identifiable matter of technique, vocabulary, subject matter, than of breath, tone and texture. It is this sort of originality which argues best for the permanent value of his poetry.

Ammons' sense of the necessity to communicate accounts in part for the organic quality of his poetry. Solipsism would be ludicrous: poetry must be a part of a speak-hear process of shared discovery. But a refusal of the hearer's influence comes at the point where any concession would distract the poet from the quest for his quarry, from the balanced point of a position which must be constantly realigned. The **"Coon Song,"** having addressed life, death, survival, defeat, at their deepest level, starts back abruptly from the reader's "Well, what happened?" pressure. Within the poem, nothing is inevitable: so the thread is roughly snapped. The near-solemn vocabulary is abruptly subverted. The coon, having a secret knowledge, will cause the hounds to disappear, but will end in disorder in the teeth of hounds:

> now there
> one two three four five
>   are two philosophies:
> here we go round the mouth-wet of hounds:
>
>   what I choose
>   is youse:
>   baby.

There is a very strong pressure on the poet to "reflect his own time." What is his identity—personal, political, social, national—within the parentheses of his dates of birth and death—specifically, the birth and death dates of his life as poet? If any demonstration were needed (which seems unlikely) that poetry of major caliber relates to, and indeed affects, every aspect of its own time, regardless of subject matter or specific reference, Ammons' poetry would afford it. American it is, as earlier noted, by its accent and tone. Its personal and social relevance to its own time comes through the compliment it pays to continuity: it examines doggedly those interactions of environment, characteristics, chance, and law, which shape human history. There is no section in his entire work which is not applicable to our immediate predicament. Unquestionably, a reader's taste for more explicitly considered human problems may be thwarted: Ammons' poetry supplies the key and the energy; it is up to the reader to open any door he wishes.

There is in the work, however, a growing sense of the personal emerging from the poetry, and this must be a consideration in any attempt to understand its present direction. Eighty lives are lost when a plane crashes over Delaware:

> grieved, we

> rejoice
> as a man rejoices saved
>   from death: we beg
> that men be spared
> calamity & the hard turn:
> we make an offering of our
> praise: we reaccept:
>
> our choice is
>   gladness:

Gladness is chosen; but it is a hard and constantly eroded choice. It is mostly in the recent work that human sorrow, of which the early deprivations were foretokens, has become more explicit. It is as though the poet's universe had to be formerly so passionately and protractedly examined that there was no room in the resulting poem for explicit expression of the havoc wrought on human affections and attachments. Eight years ago, a short poem gave full scope at last to sorrow. **"Dark Song"** (*Collected Poems*) says it all in twelve lines:

> Sorrow how high it is
> that no wall holds it
> back: deep
>
> it is that no dam undermines
> it: wide that it
> comes on as up a strand
>
> multiple and relentless:
> the young that are
> beautiful must die; the
>
> old, departing,
> can confer
> nothing.

The refusal of the work as a whole to tie itself to the occasional or topical, the stubbornness of its roots in the specific as part of the universal, are what makes the poetry relevant to contemporary problems. The poems are never as discrete as they seem. Just as every choice, every fragment of motion, affects multiple beings in unexpected ways, so the slightest ethical shift affects all human relations. In the poem **"Expressions of Sea Level,"** the secret moment of balance—leagues out, at an undefinable ocean-point—affects the tiny pools of minnows inland. The faintest suggestion of a shift sets in motion life and death forces. It would be nonsense to argue that this sort of poetry has little to do with the terrors and pressures of our daily life.

Although the poems use scientific terms freely, Ammons is sharply conscious of what must be the incorruptibility of the vocabulary in relation to its subject:

high-falutin
language does not
rest on the
cold water
all night
by
the luminous
birches:

    is too vivid
    for the eyes
    of pigeons,
    heads tucked
    under wings in
    first
patches of sunlight:

    is too noisy to
    endure
    the sleep of buds,
    the holding in
    of the huckleberry
blossom:

too voracious
    to spin,
    rest
    & change:

    is too clever
    for the frank
    honey-drop
    of the lily-pistil:

Ammons' poetry as a whole can be considered religious in character. It possesses the senses of humility and awe, and a kind of unconquerable expectation.
—*Josephine Jacobsen*

Ammons' poetry as a whole can be considered religious in character. It possesses the senses of humility and awe, and a kind of unconquerable expectation. This was foreshadowed in the earliest of books. But it was a preoccupation often submerged for long periods in simply paying attention, that special genius of Ammons. This attention often brought on dismaying results, results never distorted in the service of optimism. Though Ammons now and then reminds his reader of Emerson, there is an unbridgeable gap between the basically firm optimism of the transcendentalist, and the painful, theory-free search of the poet of **"Extremes and Moderations"** (*Collected Poems*). In "Unsaid," Ammons asked, earlier,

Have you listened for the things I have left out?
I am nowhere near the end yet and already
    hear
        the hum of omissions.
    the chant of vacancies, din of
silences:

Toward whichever side the balance tilts, there is a silence affirming the counterweight:

    I know
    the standing on loose
                            ground:
                        I know the
    violence, grief, guilt,
    despair, absurdity:
            the sky's raw:
            the star
    refuses our wish,
    obliterates us with
                permanence,
                scope of its
                coming and going:

    I know what it is
            to feel around in
            the dark
            for a hold
            & to touch
        nothing:
            we must bear
            the dark edges of
            our awareness:

Here, hope is silent.

    and when
    the Florentines painted
    radiant populations in
        the heavens, they were
                        not wrong:
                        each of

        us.
    says modern science, is
    radiant.
            tho
            below the
            visible spectrum:
    paradise will
    refine our radiance
    or give us better sight:
        we're fallen
        now:

we may be raised into
   knowledge & light:
   lower would be
longer & longer wavelengths
to dark's undisturbed constant:
may we
not go there
but ever and ever up
   singing into shining
light:

Here, it is sorrow which is silent.

More and more, in the recent poems, the personal emerges from the universal. But the foundation has been so strongly laid, the range of the search has been so wide, that this increasingly personal element, far from narrowing or weakening the poetry, is itself infused with an extraordinary strength, as though a quintessence of all the natural world had been concentrated in a human emotion.

It is obviously pointless to speculate about the future direction of the poetry, especially in view of Ammons' repeated refusal to impose a pattern, to provide that definition which is the final box:

   when we solve, we're
   saved by deeper problems:
      definition is death:
         the final box:
      hermetic seal:

But the pressure of a greater freedom to express the personal (always within the wider context), and the sense that for some time now he has been ready to draw conclusions, if always the most tentative, make Ammons' current poetry interesting in a way that little contemporary poetry attempts to be. It is interesting, also, that the culture which has produced this particular body of work has been, in general, the most antithetical to its elements. It is nature poetry from a nation hastily burying itself in concrete and plastic: a poetry conscious of immense reaches of time, in a period of changes so frenetic that a cardiogram of its heart would cause despair: a poetry of humility and patience in a setting of shrillness: a poetry of immense scope in a rabble of specialists. Perhaps such a period is best suited to produce just such poetry.

The one thing which can be predicted is that that scope will not shrink:

   is there a point of rest where
   the tide turns: is there one
   infinitely tiny higher touch
   on the legs of egrets, the

skin of back, bay-eddy reeds:
   is there an instant when fullness is,
   without loss, complete: is there a
   statement perfect in its speech:

   how do you know the moon
   is moving: see the dry
   casting of the beach worm
      dissolve at the
   delicate rising touch:

   that is the
   expression of sea level,
      the talk of giants,
   of ocean, moon, sun, of everything,
   spoken in a dampened grain of sand.

Jerald Bullis (review date Spring 1977)

SOURCE: A review of *The Snow Poems,* in *Epoch,* Vol. XXVI, No. 3, Spring, 1977, pp. 304-11.

[*In the following review, Bullis discusses the form and themes of Ammons's* The Snow Poems.]

The Snow Poems are actually one poem. It is a diary of the 1975-76 year: a record of Ammons's own experiences, observations, attitudes that begins in the fall with the bird migrations heading south and ends in the spring, with welcoming (the last word of the poem is "we(l)come") "a young / birch frilly in early-girlish / leaf." *The Snow Poems* is at the same time an almanac—a compendium of useful and interesting facts, proverbs, weather news. It is also an adventure story in which Ammons, in Ithaca, wanders far and the extravagance of the wandering becomes a reaffirmation of the poet's role as adventurer, as Odysseus (Odysseus's name, in Greek at least, meant trouble—it was his fate to odysseus himself and others heroically). Ammons's own wandersong precisely distinguishes the heroic potentiality of now from the models of unreclaimable times: without coming on in a high-hatted, grandeurish way. *The Snow Poems* radiates nobility, that quality Wallace Stevens remarked as being most conspicuously absent from modern literature. *One* of the values of this poem is its bulk, the overweeningness of its cry: it approximates the plenitude of the novel without falling into the worn-out procedures of the novel. It is Ammons's richest exemplification to date of the resolution made in the concluding lines of **"Corsons Inlet"** to "try / to fasten into order enlarging grasps of disorder, widening / scope." The extempore explorations of this long poem affirm Emerson's assertion that "the vision of genius comes by renouncing the too officious activity of the understanding, and giving leave and amplest privilege to the spontaneous sentiment."

This book could have been done as four or five books, but done in that way it would have been a piecemeal offering of several kinds of more-or-less acceptable poetic styles. In his earlier work Ammons has already experimented with lyric and meditative modes, testing the limits of free verse, incorporating levels of diction—such as the scientific—that have enlarged the scope of poetry; he has made the fable appear like a new genre, as if Emerson's mountain and squirrel had never had a quarrel (in which Bun replies—Bun being the squirrel—that "all sorts of things and weather / Must be taken in together, / To make up a year / And a sphere"— a wisdom about spheres that applies as well to *The Snow Poems* as it does to *Sphere: The Form of A Motion*). Ammons's successes with the medium-length conversational poem (after Coleridge's "Frost at Midnight"), the hymn, the metaphysical lyric, the "song," the pastoral-walk poem (after Frost's "The Wood Pile") are exemplary: in such poems as **"The City Limits," "Saliences,"** and **"Configurations,"** Ammons has extended the range of the short poem.

If Ammons were a *moderate poet* (a designation oxymoronic if not entirely moronic) then I suppose he would have kept plunking-out the kind of performance for which he has already received acclaim. But *The Snow Poems* is a more extravagant poem than any of the earlier poems, including the resuscitations of the *essai* in its original aleatory form: **"An Essay in Poetics," "Hiburnaculum," "Extremes and Moderations,"** and **"Summer Place"**; it is more openly autobiographical than any earlier poem: and it challenges our assumptions about what makes a statement "poetic" to an extent that even *Tape for the Turn of the Year* did not. Most of the "poems" of this poem have an entropic "organization"—the conclusions irrelevancies, seemingly—a kind of dribbling-off format, even to the shapes on the page. The sections are believably extra-vasational or, more like snow, precisely improvisational. Some of the sections seem to derive their forms from the spatial limitations and freedoms of the 9" x 11" page, written upon by a typewriter. In some of the sections one "poem" will proceed down the left side of the page, going right about half-way, and another— contrapuntal, complementary, dialectically?—will begin somewhere right-of-center. This technique seems a further development of Ammons's statement concerning nonlinear prosody published in *Poetry:* "What I think is illustrated by [the versification of a poem like Ammons's **'Close-Up'**] is that both ends are being played against a middle. The center of gravity is an imaginary point existing between the two points of beginning and end, so that a downward pull is created that gives a certain downward rush to the movement, something like a waterfall glancing in turn off opposite sides of the canyon, something like the right and left turns of a river."

Such typographical pyrotechnics aren't new. They get their freshness in *The Snow Poems* from Ammons's ability to amalgamate ranges of discourse—heretofore largely excluded from poetry—with such techniques. Though these poems may superficially resemble work by Charles Olson, look like some of Pound's *Cantos,* or portions of Williams's *Paterson,* Ammons's work actually exhibits a far different rhetorical stance. The discursive tendency of much of Carl Sandburg's and Robinson Jeffers's poetry—two unfashionable precursors with whom Ammons has not been allied— anticipates the openness of *The Snow Poems* more directly than the work of the above-mentioned poets. Not even Wallace Stevens, whose improvisatory and essayistic ensembles are more apparent prior attempts at making non-narrative long poems, could manage more than uneasy fusings of imagistic-symbolic and discursive writing, a problem Ben Belitt pointed out in a review of Stevens: "moved to formal discourse in the quest for order and certitude, [Stevens's] art has not up to the present permitted him to pursue such discourse or his temperament to accept it." To which Stevens replied in a letter to Belitt: "While you pointed out my difficulty in the second sentence of your review, it is a difficulty that I have long been conscious of and with which I am constantly struggling." Stevens struggled with this problem to the end, though late poems exhibit an Ammons-like acceptance of the antipoetic, as in "Reality Is an Activity of the Most August Imagination": "Last Friday, in the big light of last Friday night, / We drove home from Cornwall to Hartford, late." Ammons is the only modern poet I've encountered who seems to have gotten beyond the bugbears of imagism and symbolic systematizing: who doesn't seem to feel that the propositional, the baldly discursive, is innately antipoetic: who doesn't write as if abstractions were the Death of Poetry, as if proverbial announcement were something old-timey sayers could get to the sooth of, but that we cannot. At random:

>   so much works flawed
>   it makes you think
>   perfection not one of
>   nature's hangups
>
>   how could you, walking in the mts,
>   be big as the mts: only by
>   wandering: aimlessness
>   is as big as mts
>   it is not for the poet to
>   speak the speakable
>   that which long known & said
>   requires no energy
>   of finding or forming but to
>   murmur, stammer, swear, and
>   sing on the edges of or around
>   or deep into the unspeakable—

the reason it makes
no difference what people
think
is that they don't think
enough to make any
difference

you can't imitate
anybody really
and the extent
to which
you can't is
enough originality

poets add
obscurity
to the
inexplicable
for critics
who can't
get their
tools sharp on
the obvious

The intelligence and smiling acerbity of this aspect of *The Snow Poems* reminds me of the poetry of the T'ang poet Han-Shan:

A certain scholar named Mr. Wang
Was laughing at my poems for being so clumsy.
"Don't you know you can't have two accents here?
And this line has too many beats.
You don't seem to understand meter at all
But toss in any word that comes to mind."
I laugh too, Mr. Wang, when *you* make a poem,
Like a blind man trying to sing of the sun.

But the strength of *The Snow Poems* can't be demonstrated by snippets of quotation. And, though the problem of judgment with respect to this long poem may seem difficult, I think it is actually not. For those who have read Ammons's work from *Ommateum* through *Diversifications,* including this poem's important prelude, *Tape for the Turn of the Year, The Snow Poems* will seem the necessary unfolding of Ammons's venture. As Warner Berthoff has remarked of Emerson, "Once we begin to get the sense of how [Ammons] operates as a writer, our experience of reading him is likely to be full of double takes, and our admiration, sluggish and reluctant at first, so little taste remains with us for the mode of pastoral exhortation he seems to employ, springs forward by a geometric progression." Ammons's mode of pastoral exhortation is to try to hold in interpenetrant relation the dualistic categories with which, in order to communicate easily though imprecisely, we have oversimplified our language: I mean such categories as imagination/reality, inner/outer,

self/other, man/nature. This interpenetration of word and world, whereby abstract "themes" are divulged or adumbrated through hollyhocks, blue spruce, jays, brooks, mudpuddles, mountains and so on, is summarized ideogrammatically in **"The Word Crys Out"**: "wor(l)d." Ammons's insistence on seeing books in the running brooks, poetic theory in the ministrations of snow, enables a ghostly demarcating of rigid, highfalutin categories *within* a discursive context. For instance, in **"It's Half an Hour Later Before,"** the self is presented as a winter tree, probably about fifty years old, whose fine branches, as of imagination, snatch lyric flakes before they reach the ground they'll end up groundwater of, and whose big branches take on ridges-worth of saying, holding the evanescent in beads that light up nature, and man, for a spell:

winter trees aren't good
winnowers

nevertheless,
fine branches snatch flakes
and big branches take
single ridges: the chaff
  hits the ground
  but the caught
  turns to lit melt beads
  that light up
  trees in a different light:

If this poem is directed in any particular way, it is directed against destructive clarification. Ammons balks at harping on small ideas, neat schema, paradigmatic bliss. So the big idea that drifts through and settles on everything here like snow is that all is in all—the idea enunciated as fable in **"Ballad"** (*Diversifications*), in which the water oak and willow defend their respective territorial rights, with the poet as mediator. In this poem Ammons repeatedly asserts, exhorting by example, that

I do not, can not, will not
care for plain simple things
with straightforward fences round them:
I prefer lean, true
integrations of ongoing
with recurrences,
resemblances, half-adventitious or fortuitous
or as some would say accidental,
half-accidental,
not under a third

—the hedging on how much accidence is necessary typifies the complexity of statement in this poem, the major subject of which is poetry. Poems, like crows in the initial segment (**"Words of Comfort"**), "emphatically find dead / trees to sit in, / skinned branches, line up / into the wind / a black countercurrent / drippy but cool." This venturing begins "in a fallish time, / the birds' gatherings and flights / skim tree-tops, not / much entering in now, no nests, pausing to consider / or dwell, the wide / storm winter coming." And while *The Snow Poems* is a venturing away from "the wide / storm winter coming"—the winter of frozen possibility, personal extinction (always coming, but inevitably closer when one is "pushing fifty")—the book is at the same time a venturing into what can be found possible, established as abundance, *in* the venture of "pushing fifty" and heading into winter, unlike the birds.

One of the central ways in which this poem projects itself is to identify the poetic self with snow, an identification that is sometimes accentuated by the resemblance of snow to age, the winter of life, and discontent, a sense of lessening power, ("the sexual basis of all things rare is really apparent": *Sphere*); and so this poem prays for a snowing "of the / right consistency, / temperature, and / velocity" that will enable the cold-bright diffuse but still consistent lee-self to fall in a "building out over / space a / promontory of / considerable / reach in / downward curvature." The poem wondrously demonstrates that "snow / will do this / not once / but wherever possible, / a similarity of effect / extended / to diversity's / exact numeration."

I find this aspect of the generalized snow-metaphor beautiful as poetic defense—an offense not at all offensive. But I don't think Ammons is falling in downward curvature: the promontory of this poem speaks against that drift.

Actually, most of this poem, so far as I can tell, was written in that time when winter begins to fade into spring's necessary muckiness: from **"The Prescriptive Stalls As"** on, we're going from February toward and into April-May. The major gesture of the poem is away from, contrary to stasis, delimitation, ice—the easy victory of the professionally-wrought lyric—and toward enlarging possibility, spanglings of snowlight-meltings-and-meldings from the reservoirs of evergreens: "I stand for / whatever will not come round / or be whole / or made out or reduced."

The Snow Poems is a great poem. It tries to make the mind—rather, *let* the mind—accord with "necessity's inner accuracy": necessity's inner accuracy is nature's accuracy. The poem is a habitat, ecosystem, world, galaxy, universe—in which there are events and creatures of little note and others on up (or down) the scale to events and creatures of great note, magnificent with their breakings-out of the brush of silence, in order to leave a greater silence after their going again. It shows how the great poem of earth, if this isn't it, may be written: it reveals how what has been taken for the great poetry of earth is only "the smooth walks, trimmed hedges, posys and nightingales" of insular tradition. *The Snow Poems* calls for a view of nature (to continue to quote

Whitman) "in the prophetic literature of these States," that would place man in the light and dark of "the whole orb, with its geologic history, the cosmos, carrying fire and snow, that rolls through the illimitable areas, light as a feather, though weighing billions of tons"; it supports W. C. Williams's indictment of us by saying in its own way how the first settlers "saw birds with rusty breasts and called them robins," thought what they saw were not "robins" but thrushes "larger, stronger, and in the evening of a wilder, lovelier song."

This poem raises more questions about our aesthetic assumptions than a review can honestly deal with. If the segments of *The Snow Poems* were normal (Academico-American?) Western Adult Lyrics, then clearly some of the stuff would have to be left out. But to make that assertion seems more a criticism of our lyric-based poetics than a criticism of this particular poem, or any similar to it. The problem with aesthetic dicta is that they are of no use when one is confronted with work of major importance. Ammons's intention is obviously *not* to make a great pile of well-wrought urns. As Whitman asserted in the 1855 preface to *Leaves of Grass*, prophesying Ammons but speaking primarily of his own audacity, "Here is action untied from strings necessarily blind to particulars and details magnificently moving in vast masses. Here is the hospitality which forever indicates heroes." He was speaking of These States too: and said they await the gigantic and generous treatment worthy of them. And of the American poet: "he is greatest forever and forever who contributes the greatest original practical example. The cleanest expression is that which finds no sphere worthy of itself and makes one." And: "Great genius and the people of these states must never be demeaned to romances. As soon as histories are properly told there is no more need of romances." And: "The great poets are also to be known by the absence in them of tricks and by the justification of perfect personal candor." Here is one of my favorite properly told moments of history in *The Snow Poems:*

> what my father enjoyed
> most—in terms of pure,
> high pleasure—was
> scaring things: I remember
> one day he and
> I were coming up in Aunt
> Lottie's yard
> when there were these
> ducks ambling
> along in the morning sun,
> a few drakes, hens, and a string of
> ducklings,
> and my father took off his
> strawhat and
> shot it spinning out sailing in
> a fast curving glide over the

ducks so they
thought they were being
swooped by a hawk.
and they just, it looked
like, hunkered down on their
rearends and slid all the
way like they were
greased right under the house
  (in those days houses
    were built up off the ground)
my father laughed the purest,
highest laughter
till he bent over
thinking about those
ducks sliding under
there over nothing

D. R. Fosso (essay date 1986)

SOURCE: "Poetic Metaphysic in A. R. Ammons," in *Pembroke Magazine,* No. 18, 1986, pp. 158-63.

[*In the following essay, Fosso analyzes the ontological and cosmological concerns in Ammons's poetry.*]

His poems witness that A. R. Ammons knows what he is about and we who relish reading him are finding him out. Take a small poem of 1975, scarcely even one of his "rondures":

Metaphysic

Because I am
here I am
(nowhere)
else

A "metaphysic," of course, is one whose epistemological concerns are especially with ontology and cosmology. If one reads "Because I am / here I am," the statement is reflexive and ontological, doubly recalling the familiar causality of "I think; therefore I am." On the other hand, if one reads "Because I am here / I am (nowhere) else," the statement is relational and squints toward the enlargingly cosmologic. Since "(nowhere)" isn't anywhere, it gets shunted into parentheses and the word quickens in the eye with an assertion of immediacy, "(now/here)," while, if read that way, its homonymic pun on "hear" demands attention. Finally, the syllabic diminuendo of the lines, 4-3-2-1, makes the form an exercise in getting down to "one," the self ontologically understood and that ever-present "One/many" problem cosmologically understood. The problem is how to put the two together and the poem does just that when it reads two ways at the same time.

Ommateum, the first book, opens with **"So I Said I Am Ezra"** and rightfully so, for everything that Ammons has published originates from and returns to that poem. Its 27 lines are five sentences without punctuation as though the statements "said" dissolve uncertainly. Something happens to the personal pronouns as well. The first sentence, lines 1-3, has four of them while the last, lines 21-27, has only one stated and one understood. Increasingly, the speaker's attempt to find a relation "here" is thwarted by a hostile setting where "the wind whipped my throat / gaming for the sounds of my voice," that "gaming" making even more edgily unsettling the cruel "whipped." When in lines 4-5 the speaker "listened to the wind / go over my head and up into the night," we sense he means not just spatially, but also cognitively as when we say of something we don't understand, "that's over my head."

To assert so simply that "I am Ezra" and then to find no response, "he echoes from the waves," is a frightening condition of reflexiveness, so frightening indeed that it is "as if the wind were taking me away," that "me" not only in the sense of carrying me off but also in the full sense of "me-ness," being itself. And that is what is happening when, after three assertions of "I am Ezra," two of them isolated lines without relation, we come to line 23, "so I Ezra went out into the night." The verb of being has disappeared, an articulation without attribution, and "went out" is resonant with familiar idiom as in our saying "the light just went out," here "into the night." Ending with "the windy oats / that clutch the dunes of unremembered seas," the speaker's desperate clutching at a relation that is denied him, at an identity, at a being that "falls out of being," makes the poem a poignant ontological crisis in a cosmology wherein there are no bearings from which one can take assurance about the nature of self and other.

How different and how similar is the voice in **"Corsons Inlet,"** that utterance, so familiar, to which one returns with renewing wonder. It begins:

I went for a walk over the dunes again this morning to the sea,

not the night of Ezra with his "dunes / of unremembered seas," for here the "I" is conscious, in "again," of his return to these dunes that modify but stay as well. He continues:

then turned right along
    the surf
   rounded a naked headland
   and returned
  along the inlet shore:

Note an altered tonality here, the playfulness of not only turning to the "right" but also of moving "right along" and then doubleness of "returned" turning into "returned." The pattern of the speaker's movement is important ("turned" "rounded" "returned"), for his circulation through the inlet's seascape is a circle. This perceiving eye/I makes a circumference in his passages, and to know a circumference enables a center to be known. Hence, the "Inlet" stroll is an avenue into ontological understanding.

Refusing "forms," "perpendiculars," "straight lines, blocks, boxes, binds / of thought," refusing definitions ("shutting out and shutting in, separating inside / from outside"), this speaker is "willing to go along" (both in the sense of moving and of accepting), "To accept / the becoming thought" (both in the sense of handsomely attractive and of what is as a state of continuing), willing "to stake off no beginnings or ends," this last an assertion that experience is not a narrative with its linear assumptions of causality and its endorsement of purposiveness, of the existence of a *telos* ("ends"). Earlier, in lines 30-32, the speaker declared:

> but Overall is beyond me: is the sum of these events
> I cannot draw, the ledger I cannot keep, the accounting
> beyond the account.

"Overall" being that cosmologic transcendent *telos* that would make of experience a boxed in narrative, something "beyond me" (not only spatially too high but also cognitively out of one's reach as when we say, "that's beyond me"). The accounting ledger he "cannot keep" (both hold on to and keep in order); it will not be neatly quantified, tallied up, for it is "the accounting / beyond the account," what he cannot give an account of, though, of course, the poem does do just that, superbly.

Line 64 of this 128 line poem, a center around which the circling field of the speaker's perceptions make their arc, stations central concerns:

> caught always in the event of change:

"Caught" is the boxing in of linear cause and effect narrative that defines and thereby limits; "change" is the circling "field of action" animating ontologic and cosmologic possibilities. "Always" means "forever" but then slips freeingly into the simultaneous possibility of "all ways" just as "in the event of" signals the important occurrence of "the event" while also working as a phrase meaning "in the case of." This poem, so richly textured in word and phrase, destabilizes secure meanings into resonating possibilities. In such a world, in such a self, we, like Ammons, could well assert, "there is serenity," because, while "terror pervades," it "is not arranged, all possibilities / of escape open."

At the end, content to "see narrow orders, limited tightness," understanding his place in the proximate "now/here," the speaker refuses "that easy victory" wherein we would humble "reality to precept" by positing a linear narrative both ontologic and cosmologic, fraught with the purposive clarity of a telelogic Oneness. Rather, he will "try / to fasten into order," that is, into the order of this and his other poems, "enlarging grasps of disorder," thereby "widening / scope, but enjoying the freedom that / Scope eludes my grasp." The first "scope" is like the scope of a book, how much it covers, as well as that liberating domain when we say, "you have free scope." But that second "Scope" (like "Overall is beyond me" earlier) refers to what one can know or encompass or understand as when we say, "that's beyond my scope."

Finally, consider the last two lines:

> that I have perceived nothing completely,
> that tomorrow a new walk is a new walk.

What astonishes here is "nothing" which we receive two ways, both as "nothing at all" and as the state of "nothingness" absolutely conceived, that unutterable, unspeakable, unknowable, that One known so "completely" out of the many perceivings at **"Corsons Inlet"** where again the speaker will endlessly circle assured in his serenity "that tomorrow a new walk is a new walk."

In the dedicatory poem to *Sphere: the Form of a Motion,* "for Harold Bloom," "nothing" uneasily rings evasive astonishments while forming the backbone for the four-part development. Unlike Ezra at the shore of the Outer Banks of North Carolina, the speaker here stands at a high "Summit" of perception, but like Ezra's "whipped" and "ripped" surroundings, the wind here "tore about this / way and that in confusion." Ezra found no voice to echo his own, nothing relational, and the speaker here finds that the wind's "speech could not / get through to me nor could I address it." Ezra's yearning for relatedness is set forth even more poignantly here, and just as "nothing" appears four times, so, too, does the speaker's italicized *"Longing"* well up four times.

Seeking a distanced relation beyond the proximate, the speaker stands at a mastering summit of lengthened, spacious perspectives, a center surveying peripheries. Without, however, that cosmologic relationship, he feels ontologically as if he were "the alien in myself" and later "as foreign here as I had landed, a visitor." The cause of his disjunction is that "having been brought this far by nature I have been / brought out of nature" where "nature" means by his own inclination as well as by nature's evolutionary development to the point where he has a consciousness and a *"longing"* separate and apart from nature and which nature cannot respond to. The words of his conscious mind, *"tree" "rock" "stream" "cloud" "star,"* signify only positivist realities drained of any transcendental import. That "nature so grand" of the nineteenth century Emersonian sublime here is "reticent," uncommunicatively withholding.

In the third movement beginning in line 24 (each section introduced by "so I" phrasing), the speaker, like God in Eden, "gathered mud / and with my hands made an image for *longing.*" Failing to find its place in relation to that summit where "it completed / nothing," he returns to the city, builds "a house to set / the image in," and, for the first time, hears voices other than just his own, voices which, in concord with him, agree "that is an image for *longing,*" an image not of "nature so grand," that cosmologic and distanced image of "nothing" viewed from the summit. The ontologic ground for being, enclosed in the house of the proximate and the "now/here," is defined in respect to a *"longing"* for what cannot be but can be recognized in the relational longings of other men who know it when they feel it.

The poem ends in line 34 with the fourth use of the word "nothing" which by this time, through iteration and development, has hauntingly gathered complex meaning:

> and nothing will ever be the same again

On the one hand, everything is changed from what it was. On the other hand, "nothingness" absolutely conceived will be itself eternally. Just as in **"Corsons Inlet,"** we have mysteriously entered into the absent presence of the unspeakable whose hushed reticence enlarges the human sense of longing for what is not.

An exemplary composing of Ammons' cognitive quest is the 1971 poem, **"The Arc Inside and Out,"** its title playing with our familiar sense of knowing something "inside out," the "inside" being in this case the ontologic, the "outside" being the cosmologic. Fifteen stanzas organize three movements of approximately five stanzas each. In the first, lines 1-16, the speaker's epistemological method is that of "whittler and dumper," a method that is subtractive and reductive, seeking an ontologic essentiality, "the face-brilliant core / stone." In the second movement, lines 16-31, the method is opposite, that of an "amasser, heap shoveler," additive and comprehensive, to arrive at a cosmologic "plenitude / brought to center and extent." But in the third movement, both "ways to dream" are cognitive fictions rejected as "bumfuzzlement," the second to "the heterogeneous abundance / starved into oneness." Hence, at the end, there is the communing sustenance of what simply "is," "The apple an apple" and "the drink of water, the drink" as well as the restorative and easing "falling into sleep, dream, dream" ever renewing with possibilities beyond what simply "is." Serene assurance ends the poem:

> every morning the sun comes, the sun

comes in its apparent transcribing of an arc of circulation, "inside which is nothing, / outside which is nothing," that "nothing" which is again so hauntingly the known unknowable that is everything.

"Singling and Doubling Together," from his most recent book, **_Lake Effect Country,_** is a remarkable work that in epitome focuses and resolves for a moment central concerns of this poetic metaphysic, A. R. Ammons. Given the title and the first line,

> My nature singing in me is your nature singing,

we expect the possibility of "my" and "your" doubling in their song. The speaker's "nature" is to be a poetic singer of "your nature" voiced expressively in nature:

> you have means to veer down, filter through,
> and, coming in,
> harden into vines that break back with leaves,
> so that when the wind stirs
> I know you are there and I hear you in leafspeech,

In a book whose title is playfully drawn from the nature poets of the "lake country" as well as from the "lake effect" of dumping heavy snow on New York state when winter weather systems pass over the Great Lakes, one might recognize in the lines just cited the presence of precise meteorologic diction. "Veer down" is what the wind does when it shifts to a clockwise direction, in this case, when the "you" enters our finite world of time. "Filter through" is, in reference to physics, what permits certain electric frequencies to pass while preventing others. "Coming in" reminds of radio waves as when we say that "transmission is coming in good." In line 4, the "vines that break back with leaves," in respect to wind direction, suggest a shift to counter-clockwise. Hence, the high and unheard wind comes clockwise into leaves that turn it to a backwind, thereby, like a radio transmitter, making the unheard heard, the "leafspeech" of "your nature singing."

In stanza two, the "you" who sings arrives from "there beyond / tracings flesh can take" and cosmologically, like a great circle of transcendent immanence, from where it is "surrounding and informing the systems." This distanced unknowable is "as if nothing, and / where you are least knowable I celebrate you most," celebrate joyously as in this poem, a privately public testimonial singing.

While in stanza two the speaker could not follow "back into your heightenings" (both into your risings and your intensifyings and "back" in the sense of counter-clockwise, into your timelessness beyond our time and finiteness), follow to where "you" are "beyond / tracings" (tracings meaning to track as well as to find the source or origin), in stanzas three and four the direction of cognitive awareness is toward the "now/here." "Your nature" is manifest in the "heightening" angle of exactitude of a pheasant's ascent "to the roost cedar," a beautifully balancing movement of contrast to the "veer down" of line 2. Likewise, "when dusk settles," sounds of creaking and snapping in bushes turn the speaker into a transmitter of "your creaking / and snapping nature": "I catch the impact and turn / it back" (balancingly as the leaves that "break back" had done in line 2).

This "you" who is "least knowable" and is a "great high otherness" has "risked all the way into the taking on of shape / and time" to "fail and fail with me, as me," the transmitter whose frequencies are unsteady. When "you are incarnated into finite and temporal transmitters, then there is a "doubling together" in the last two stanzas as

> in the cries of that pain it is you crying and
> you know of it and it is my pain, my tears, my
> loss—

In this and because of this "doubling together," there is bestowed a "grace" "to bear in every motion." Against the shifting relativisms of the speaker's "embracing or turning away, staggering or standing still," there is firmly poised "your settled kingdom" that "sways in the distillations of light," a settledness in the closing lines that

> plunders down into the darkness with me
> and comes up nowhere again but changed into
> your
> singing nature when I need sing my nature
> nevermore.

The "doubling together" has become "nowhere" and "now/here," a wondrous alchemy of transformation wherein a union of doubling oneness, fulfilled and fulfilling, celebrates, in a change from the beginning, not "your nature singing" but "your / singing nature," yet another doubling together into oneness.

That double concern of the metaphysic, ontologic and cosmologic, has singled out here into the cognitive testimonial of a poetic *episteme*. What Ezra "said" and, finding no responding, reflexively experienced as an ontological crisis "taking me away," becomes here an ontologic assurance firmly knit to a cosmologic relatedness. In **"Corsons Inlet,"** the speaker, travelling a circumference, finds access to a center where "there is serenity," but here there is more, there is personal and public ritual of celebratory song. In **"for Harold Bloom,"** the quadruple "nothing" and *"longing"* arrive here at a filling up of both in a concordant "together." "Metaphysic" with its doubleness of reading posing the ques-

tion of the nature of self and other turns here to an answering and melodious "doubling together." And, finally, **"The Arc Inside and Out"** is heard here in a composure of song that is no "bumfuzzlement," as if the "dream" of discovered essentiality and plenitude has become a cognitive perception of the conscious self, this poetic metaphysic that is A. R. Ammons.

Sister Bernetta Quinn, OSF (essay date 1986)

SOURCE: "Scholar of Wind and Tree: The Early Lyrics of A. R. Ammons," in *Pembroke Magazine*, No. 18, 1986, pp. 236-47.

[*In the following essay, Quinn discusses the place of the physical world and the figure of Ezra in Ammons's poetry.*]

Beginning his 1968 *Selected Poems* "in the middle of the thing," A. R. Ammons as Ezra stands up against the physical universe simply by introducing himself to it: "So I said I am Ezra." The wind whipping his throat captures the words as a hunter might game, then whistles off into the dark night, a temperamental companion, or guide, as he is throughout the book. Rejected by the wind in his attempt to start a conversation, Ezra turns to the ocean but it too will have none of him, crashing surf blotting out his words. Pushed into unsteadiness by the returning wind, he faces the shore and says for the third time, "I am Ezra," then blown inward like a cloud of sand leaves the arrogant sea to splash through clumps of sea-oats frantically digging their fists of roots into dunes built up by forgotten waves. To trace the roles of wind and tree through this Old Testament prophet as "voice," not always Hebraic but often as American as its creator, is a useful way of charting some of the most fascinating poetic landscapes in contemporary letters.

The Biblical *persona* Ezra the scribe, of interest also to his namesake Pound, comes out of the time of the Babylonian captivity; it contributes the validity of "a local habitation and a name" to the work of Ammons, often disturbing in its formlessness and abstraction. Richard Howard in the essay which begins his *Alone in America*, finds reason for misgivings about as well as praise of this writer: after praising the fine passages in the first book he quotes eight lines which he calls wordy and shrill and wonders "whose voice it is that utters these hymns to—and against—Earth." Then he goes on to his own view about the choice of the sixth-century B.C. scholar in the Mosaic Law:

> In a later book too, 'I Ezra' returns, 'the dying portage of these deathless thoughts,' and we recall that this prophet is generally regarded as responsible for the revision and editing of the earliest books of

Scripture and the determination of the canon. The persona appears in Ammons' poems, I think, when he is desperate for an authoritative voice; the nature of his enterprise is so extreme, and the risks he is willing to take with hysterical form and unguarded statement . . . so parlous, that the need for such authority must be pretty constant.

Here, the word Ezra is not restricted to the Old Testament scribe favored by the Persian king to direct the return to Jerusalem; it includes as well A. R. Ammons speaking in his own voice, an analogous one.

Parallel to the Book of Ezra are the two Books of Esdras (an interchangeable name), classified in the Good News Bible as apocryphal. In the first chapter of the second of these the formula "I, Ezra" appears: "When I, Ezra, was a captive in Media during the reign of Artaxerxes," then after pages of the Lord's instructions to the chosen Israelite recurs as "I, Ezra, was on Mount Sinai," and again "I, Ezra, saw an enormous crowd on Mount Sion." According to an angel in the account of the seven visions with which Ezra is favored, these are persons who have put off their mortal robes and put on immortal ones to be crowned by the Son of God. The next chapter starts: "Thirty years after the fall of Jerusalem, I, Shealtiel (also known as Ezra) was in Babylon." In the initial revelation Ezra is asked by the angel Uriel: "How do you weigh out a pound of fire? How do you measure a bushel of wind? How do you bring back a day that is passed?" and though earlier Ezra has asserted that he can understand the ways of God Most High, he now admits that no human being can answer such questions.

It is easy to see why this part of Scripture would appeal to Ammons: Uriel uses the same conversational technique that the poet periodically adopts throughout *Selected Poems,* and later, as in *Northfield Poems.* The angel reports on how he has "heard the trees plotting together. They were saying, 'Let's go to war against the sea and push it back, so that we may have more room.' But the waves of the sea also plotted together and said, 'Let's conquer the woods and extend our territory,'" a passage which reads as if it were an invention of Ammons'. The rest of the visions brim with lively imagery and mystical insights into the same problems the lyrics confront: life/death, finitude/infinity, God/man.

In the second selection the wind takes notice of the scribe, contemptuously, true, but better such notice than nothing:

> The wind whipped at my carcass saying
> How shall I
>   coming from these fields
> water the fields of earth

The place is North Carolina, a rural district, the state in which Ammons was born in 1926. The trees there are dying, their branches drooping; in the fields the rye, oats, wheat are suffering the assault of combines, saying "Oh!" and "Oh!" and "Oh!" Wrapped in his own woe, the prophet (undesignated as such by name, but all genuine poets are prophets in the meaning of deeply understanding a present reality) is kin to them; as the wind scolds him he too cries "Oh!" and falls down in the dust. Eloi Leclerc in *The Canticle of Creatures Symbols of Union* writes appositely: "Francis speaks the language of a man who lives close to material things; who feels things co-existing at his side, mysteriously connected with his own destiny; and in whom these things elicit a genuine feeling of brotherhood."

So interrelated are the elements of landscape in Ammons that dialogue seems as natural as the speeches of the Poverello Francis Bernadone to his brothers and sisters sun, moon, fire, water, stars, wind in those conversations whereby he delivered his thoughts to God: "Creatures are a language expressive of the sacred because they put the soul in touch with itself and its primordial powers. Creatures are the outward form of a discourse that goes on deep within man." Not always, however, does Ammons' "voice" experience the rapport known to the Italian saint. In **"I went Out in the Sun,"** after failing to engage the wind or ocean in talk, tries the sun, as its flames burn above a desert willow under the shade of which the scholar is resting: "It's very hot in this country." But the sun ignores him.

In an attempt to get a rise out of the haughty planet, he continues: "The moon has been talking about you." The ruse works: "Well, what is it this time?" Like a true gossip, the man replies that the moon is denying she owes her light to solar energy. The only fitting answer the sun can think of is a burst of fire, almost scorching the willow. Troublemaker that he is, Ezra mutters: "Well, of course I don't know," at which the sun concludes their discussion by moving away, to the willow's relief. The scribe, having dug for water, hangs his shirt on the willow to dry, indulging in his memorable personification:

> This land where whirlwinds
>   walking at noon in tall columns of dust
>   take stately turns about the desert
>   in a very dry land

He sleeps until, awakened by the cold, he reaches for his shirt and says to the moon, "You make it the desert a pretty sigh," rewarded by her smile (Ammons usually employs the standard gender in relation to landscape figures). But the seeds of ill humor that he has planted have sprouted: the lunar planet sees the sun sulking behind the mountain over the ungrateful comment re her light. In defense of the culprit Ezra calls out, "Why are you angry with the moon?" reminding him that soon they shall all be lost in the emptiness.

In the early lyrics Ammons presents man and Nature as equals, companions even if not particularly congenial ones, "I" being closer to some than to others, closer for instance to the tree since both are organic and earthbound, unlike the heavenly bodies or the ocean. In **"The Whaleboat Struck"** after being shot in the throat by savages he leaves his body on the shore and walks away; a heavy wind catches his spirit but lets him go at hearing how vultures and flies are even at that moment feasting on his flesh. Days pass, until another wind blows by singing this melodious song:

> Bones
> lovely and white
> lie on the southern sand
> the ocean has washed bright

Ezra hurries to see his own beautiful bones in the sun; finding them picked clean, he chooses a rib and draws pictures in the sand until the ocean, all its green gone, is silent, and the wind too. Happy to be disembodied, he runs in and out of the waves to the tunes of Devonshire airs. It is in this poem that the participial phrase "Leaving myself on the shore" occurs, a line Howard calls "the first enunciation of the theme, in the crude form of a romantic pantheism" which the critic summarizes as the putting off of flesh and putting on of the universe. Indeed, the following selection, a farewell of the protagonist to the seen and spoken, seems evidence for such an opinion ("Turning a Moment to Say So Long").

> **In the early lyrics Ammons presents man and Nature as equals, companions even if not particularly congenial ones . . .**
> *—Sister Bernetta Quinn*

Although discrete from wind or tree Ezra finds himself identifying with the later in **"With Hopes of Hemp,"** wherein he binds himself to an oak tree, singing odes to its roots, heart, bark-fiber until he is empowered to sing "oak-songs" in response to "the raucous words of the night-clouds." But he knows that not all his being is earthbound: in the three-part **"Doxology,"** possessed of the wisdom the silent owl acquires near death according to legend, he transplants his soul to the wind, a way of attaining the fluidity he longs for (though concomitantly he desires the kind of survival an ancient amphora's designs afford). In the middle section he is enmeshed in the sleeping landscape, a part not only of wind and tree but of rock, moss, gooseberry hill, swamp, raccoon, crawfish, sun, sea, dawn, plain, seeking together with all of these to "learn the vowels of silence."

Ezra in his Hebrew identity speaks in **"Coming to Sumer,"** where irreverently he rifles the "Innisfree" huts along the river bank for their burial trappings: gold leaves, lapis lazuli beads ornamenting bones. Set in autumn, **"When I Set Fire to the Reed Patch"** returns the "voice" to interact with the wind as it scatters the burning thorny stems. As wisdom, sweeping a desertscape clean of the "lust prints of the sun," the wind takes the stage as actor again in **"A Treeful of Cleavage Flared Branching,"** the title with more than a hint of a metamorphosis comparable to that in Ezra Pound's "A Tree." It will not leave him alone, where he sits on the sand cradling a gold altarcone:

> The wind
> chantless of rain in the open place
> spun a sifting hum
> in slow circles round my sphere of grief

It will not agree to his staying rooted, the very next piece substantiating Richard Howard's statement in *Alone in America:* "Here is a man obsessed by Pure Being who must put up with a human incarnation when he would prefer to embody only the wind, the anima of existence itself." In **"I Set It My Task"** it picks him up bodily after sowing loose dreams in his eyes:

> and telling unknown tongues
> drawn me out beyond the land's end
> and rising in long
> parabolas of bliss
> borne me safety   perhaps a misprint
> from all those ungathered stones

Here the natural force has succeeded in making the poet his lyre, even as Shelley begged the West Wind to do. But its sway over him is intermittent. The seventeenth lyric in the 1968 volume goes back to the second Book of Esdras as it opens: "I Ezra the dying / portage of these deathless thoughts,"; the hero stands on a hill beneath a mountain and disclaims the importance of wisdom, represented by wind, to man—it belongs only to the gods, who don't need it (**"Whose Timeless Reach"**).

A description of the selection might well be a travelogue of the mind penetrating the "jungles" of matter. **"Driving Through"** discloses the veteran traveler crossing a twentieth-century desert at midnight; he takes out a notebook, an appropriate gesture for a poet as also the sharpening of a pencil, and evokes an apocalyptic vision of running mountains that skid over "the icy mirages of the moon," a vision also highlighting "stone mosaics of the flattest / places" and "a brimming smoketree," "a green / tiger with orange eyes." Daylight motorists later will never guess the wonders glorifying the night (who could imagine mountains tumbling down "laughing for breath?"), any more than they will be able to see his lonely house, destined finally to hold "laurel and a friend," one of those succinct Ammons endings which completely satisfy. This poet knows as he travels that he is more than a wayfarer (the wind has told him so) and continues to long for a place of abiding such as the tree-transformation in **"Song"** provides. Here he merges into a wooded slope, extending his arms to take up "the silence and spare leafage," exposing himself to wind and ice, which work fast at their task of disintegration, a task destined to turn him into a hump beneath the leaves "where chipmunks dig."

The three Hymns which follow addressed to the deity are among A. R. Ammons' triumphs. If Ezra ever finds God, he will have to go out over the sea marshes, the hills of tall hickory, crater lakes, canyons, upward through the diminishing air, past nocturnal clouds into the "empty stark," the missing noun intensifying the loneliness. At the same time, he knows that if he finds God he will have to stay with the earth, down to the least cell: "You are everywhere partial and entire / You are on the inside of everything and on the outside." He is the ant-soul (the name of the first book means "insect eye") running up and down the chasms of the sweetgum bark. The first Hymn ends in an oxymoron, wherein he says to God that if he finds him he will have to "go out deep into your far resolutions" but at the same time "stay here with the separate leaves" of the sweetgum tree in his *persona* as poet.

In the second Hymn, Ezra tells the Lord about going out to "the naked mountain" to see a single peachflower pushing its way through the ribs of a skeleton, as if in a Georgia O'Keeffe painting, praying with its petals and sepals in the spirit of Francis' Canticle. Startled by "a lost circling bee," he goes at sunset on that late December day "down to the stream / and wading in / lets the Lord's cold water run over his feet. The third Hymn is a prayer for a good death, when he, the "shriven celebrant," chilling, pulse slowing, will reach "home / dead on arrival."

"March Song" is Ezra's address at the approach of spring to the willows and cattails, praising the first as they return gold to their naked limbs and the second, fluffy again, leaving winter in their pale stems. But he does not want to be buried even under the beautiful willow (**"Ritual for Eating the World"**); coming upon a rope hanging in the bend of the rock he sings three verses of a cowboy song beginning "When I die don't bury me / under no weeping willer tree." With suicidal intent he seizes the rope, which breaks and forces him to re-accept his sordid world.

The wind, which has raced by like a ranch hand in the rope lyric set on the mesa top, becomes quite friendly in **"The Wide Land,"** eager to get Ezra's approval. They have the conversation denied the poet in the opening of the book. The wind apologizes for breaking up the desert chaparral ("you know I'm / the result of forces beyond my control," to which the poet says yes, he understands; but the wind continues to

explain, persisting in self-justification despite the other's "I know I know," a reassurance concluding with "No, I said you don't have / to explain / It's just the way things are."

Drawn back to a tree-disguise, Ezra in **"Mountain Liar"** (the title a pun on the lyre he lacks even though he tries to imitate Orpheus) deceives the mountains into thinking they can achieve their wish to fly to interstellar regions for a skating party. When they see him below them, or believe they do since actually they have not moved, only imagined they were gliding about amidst the stars shrieking for joy, they cry out at his deception "You wood." They are no more satisfied with "the way things are" than the wind, or that he is with his own nature. **"Gravelly Run,"** used later to name a collection, raises the supposition that perhaps man's blending in with the cosmos might not be enough; after all the main thing is to know self as "galaxy and cedar cone" know it, cedar cone serving for human person in his tree-role and galaxy for the nonconscious, a great abyss separating these: "the sunlight has never heard of tree," **"Gravelly Run"** says as it ends in what Howard calls a farewell to the spirit of place.

Reading Ammons correctly is not easy, because of his experimental punctuation, any more than it is clear at first what sense is intended by Williams in "Landscape with the Fall of Icarus," five sentences though without periods leading up to "This was / Icarus drowning." The colon is his most used mark, and not always conventionally so. In **"Gravelly Run"** it appears at the end of the first stanza, consisting of six uneven lines, implying that what precedes is in apposition to stanza two, the same procedure occurring throughout the next four stanzas. The eleventh line according to syntax would seem suitably ended with a period, the first three words of the lyric, "I don't know" forming a meditative comment sufficient unto itself. The third stanza is also a complete sentence, colon-concluded. The most beautiful passage is the next:

> holly grows on the banks in the woods there,
> and the cedars' gothic-clustered
>   spires could make
> green religion in winter bones:

The word *green* is especially effective, slanting both backwards and forwards, as sometimes happens in Robert Creeley ("Kore, Kore"). Five sentences and a fragment complete the piece, the colon last used taking the place of what convention would say called for a comma. Isn't it the sunlight that has never surrendered self among unwelcoming forms?

Ammons' poetry ought to have a marked appeal for children, for instance such a rich fabric of incidents and images as **"Prospecting,"** where the traveler comes to cottonwoods and willows at evening, makes camp, turns his mule loose, and then drowsing over the leaves sends out his loneliness to shake hands with the trees. This *poltergeist* runs up the black cliff to pull the moon over, howls with the coyotes, tells a night-circle of lizards ghost-stories while the Big Dipper pours out the night. With dawn his *alter ego* returns to wake him up, and they fit themselves together again for breakfast and the day, nocturnal adventures as forgotten as David's in Randall Jarrell's children's story *Fly by Night.*

Descendant of Joshua, the revered scribe Ezra, master of the Sacred Word, seems summoned back in **"Joshua Tree"** (a metamorphically significant title), with its very short lines, the first merely "The wind," which surprises the "I" weeping under this Biblical tree. Ezra gives the reason for his tears thus:

> and Oh I said
> I am mortal all right
> and cannot live,
> by roads
> stopping to wait
> for no one coming,
> moving on
> to dust
> and burned weeds,
> having no liturgy,
> no pilgrim,
> from my throat
> singing news of joy,
> no dome, alabaster wall,
> no eternal city

The wind points out that man is not meant to be a wayfarer, that the prophet should settle right there and make a well. But "I'm not like wind," remonstrates the weeper, "that dies and / never dies." He is destined to go on until some syllable of rain anoints his tongue, like the coal that cleansed the tongue of Isaiah. But in the event that no rain should ever fall he bids the wind "enter angling through / my cage / and let my ribs / sing me out."

Up to this point in *Selected Poems,* if Ezra is present he and "I" are fused, but in **"The Wind Coming Down From"** such is not the case: they are separate individuals, the Hebrew scholar taking the third person singular. The first four words of the poem, "summit and blue air," complete the prepositional phrase in the title, the only time in the book Ammons uses this device. The wind feels compassion for *le moi* of Ammons, only dust and completely at his mercy though an "instrument of miracle," and regrets his own volitionless role: "not air or motion / but the motion of air." He praises Ezra at the expense of the poet for his immortality and goes off to engage in erosion, the carving of monuments, "while Ezra / listens from terraces of mind" unreachable because

immaterial, safe from being cracked or shivered, the word used here, by the roots among which the poet feeds.

Sometimes the landscape elements speak only in indirect discourse, as in **"Close-up"** and **"Bourn,"** the latter title apparently taken from Hamlet's "undiscovered country from whose bourn / No traveler returns." It is instructive, if one wishes a familiarity with Ammons' art, to meditate on his craft in the second, where sea shores and willows sing and weep their unheeded warnings, he begins with the customary trait (in him) of surprising with an abstraction in the Auden manner instead of using the expected concrete word: "When I got past relevance." A study of the whole lyric reveals that his position in regard to the sea is with his back towards it and its willowedges, moving towards an "outward gray" he mistakes for a "foreign light," just the right adjective here. The shores sing to him to turn back from eternity, towards which like Emily in the chariot accompanied by Death he did not realize he was heading. Looking over his shoulder, he sees the "dancing" emblems of grief between him and the waves. Why *shores* is in the plural is not evident.

So he comes to "the decimal of being," the darkness of Dylan Thomas's waterbead in **"Refusal to Mourn the Death by Fire of a Child in London."** The reason for the title becomes clearer: "What light there / no tongue turns to tell / to willow and calling shore," the shore now singular, though the final stanza, one line only, pluralizes it again: "though willows sweep and shores sing always." Nature is volitionless, bound in this case to weep, and to sing always, whereas Ezra must bear the dreadful responsibility of choice.

"Mansion" puts him back into commerce once more with the wind, to whom he has decided to will his body. Grateful, eager to show appreciation, the wind asks how he can say thanks, and the "I" replies he desires nothing other than for the wind to swirl his dust around so that he can see what after the bequest is happening with the ocotillo, saguaro-wren, sky at sunset or dawn. More than once the sorrow of wind at its invisibility comes through in the poetry ("The wind was glad / and said it needed all / the body / it could get / to show its motions with"). (Later in the book **"Interference"** will show the sand materializing wind). The wind-resurrected skeleton of the poet's body as it will be offers a variation of the transformation to tree used earlier: "the tree of my bones."

Critic Richard Howard considers **"Guide"** one of the saddest of A. R. Ammons' lyrics, "an astonishing meditation." Since the noun reflects the mentor-relationship of wind and poet, there is an irony about the former's lament re "having / given up everything to eternal being but direction." East, West, North, South are all that is left of wind, as could be concluded from the nomenclature of the mythological figures in Botticelli's *The Birth of Venus.* The most central of the wind's "words to live by" is the sentence "You cannot come to unity and remain material," another way of putting Wallace Stevens' "Death is the mother of beauty." When Ezra tries to understand opposites within him or the uniqueness of a peachblossom, "the wind was gone and there was no more knowledge then."

The whole book might be called Ammons' *Consolations of Philosophy,* one chapter being **"The Golden Mean,"** advice by the wind, if it stands for wisdom concerning sexual love, care not to go too far: "withhold / enough to weather loss." Interestingly enough, the piece occupies the center of *Selected Poems.* Ammons takes three of the gifts of the Holy Spirit (wisdom, understanding, knowledge) and discusses them at some length. In the entire lyric, the only word which suggests an image is *dime,* not a total abstraction characteristic of Ammons' approach to poetry; apart from its line-divisions and lack of rhyme, also its cadences, **"The Golden Mean"** could conceivably be likened to **"The Vanity of Human Wishes." "Risks and Possibilities,"** which directly follows, redeems this "bodiless" effect by beginning with four pretty things which the poet has selected for a specific if unspecified addressee.

The examples are put in the form of numbered propositions, each heightening the attractiveness of the objects that the speaker has picked for the pleasure of his friend by a comparison: thunder like water "down the sky's eaves" to locusts in dogfennel; the yellow daisy to dawn; the constellations as somehow mirrored in a willow-slip, frog "language" as equated with daisy silences. This method is a good entrance into the theme of the poem: the sacramental unity of the universe. Each thing influences every other, not only on earth ("Never send to know . . .") but throughout creation: "the crawl of a slug / on the sea's floor / quivers the moon to a new dimension." One part of Nature echoes another: the leaves of a tree, the gills of a fish, a variant of Stevens' theory of "resemblances."

Like William Carlos Williams (Garrett Mountain as woman, the city of Paterson as man) Ammons likes to conceive of the human being anthropomorphically. In **"Terrain":**

> The soul is a region without definite boundaries
> 　it is not certain a prairie
> can exhaust it
> 　or a range enclose it
> it floats (self-adjusting) like the continental mass

Besides the above features, the soul has its hills, river-systems (complete with runs, such as Gravelly, and branches, lakes, marshes) for visualizing which the poet imagines winter tree-shadows, has deserts ('barren spots') and peat-bogs; and also its own weather, irrefutably, as the sciences of psy-

chology and psychiatry will testify to. Like any continent, the soul is subject to natural disasters: floods, whirlwinds. It even has its own moon, perhaps here a conventional emblem for the imagination.

"Raft" summons back the wind, so that he and Ezra can go off like two boys who want to play near the sea on a nice day: ". . . we stayed around for a while / trying to think / what to do." Just before dark, the wind stops, "breathless (a clever adjective) from playing." While the wind sleeps, the poet makes a round raft of rushes, then slips away from his companion ("I did not wake it to say goodbye"). At that hour the night is moonless. He waits for the sun to rise to ascertain direction, though when day comes he passes it without progress, not really sure which way he wants to go. As the sun goes down, along comes the wind "rushing before dark to catch (him)," truly his guide as in the lyric so named.

It would be a mistake in a discussion of landscape elements in Ammons to omit the marvelous configuration of sight and sound images in **"River,"** silver willows, forsythia, moonwaters, hidden bird. Its repetitions add a melancholy music. "I shall / go down" becomes "shall I / go down" in the third stanza, followed by the same nine lines as at the opening:

> 　　to the deep river, to the moonwaters,
> 　　　where the silver
> 　　willows are and the bay blossoms,
>
> 　　to the songs
> 　　　of dark birds
> 　　　　to the great wooded silence
> 　　of flowing
> 　　forever down the dark river
>
> 　　silvered at the moon-singing of hidden birds.

Because of this identity, the lyric is little more than a sigh of ecstasy at the beauty of a particular twenty-seventh of March, when spring blossoms trailed their yellow fragrance through the air, "alive" as amoebae in clear water.

"Expressions of Sea Level" calls for a Francis of Assisi, whom legend credits with an ability to read in the Book of the Creatures, in fact to speak its language. Changeless itself though capable of eroding and building, the ocean speaks without words, renders itself in silence, speaks at its edges instead of from its core through "wind and water, spray / swells, whitecaps, moans" as if in a dream. After two pages in the indicative mood comes a series of unanswered questions, ending:

> 　　that is the
> 　　　expression of sea level,

the talk of giants,
of ocean, moon, sun, of everything,
spoken in a dampened grain of sand.

The passage, reminiscent of Blake, prepares well for **"Still,"** the next lyric, where Ammons can find nothing lowly in the universe, not even the grain of sand, with which to identify himself. Like Whitman, he can only step back and marvel at "moss, beggar, weed, tick, pine, self, magnificent / with being!"

"Motion" combines what A. R. Ammons means by his manipulation of wind and tree images. In very short lines, three consisting of only two letters (*is, to*), he meditates on what semanticists call "the triangle of reference," the relation between a verbal symbol and what it points to, or, as the poet here adds, captures as in a net. The only likeness between a word and the thing it distinguishes occurs if onomatopoeia is present (whir). As Robert Penn Warren has remarked, however, sound-structures in the artifact itself go beyond this:

> but the music
> in poems
> is different,
> points to nothing,
> traps no
> realities, takes
> no game, but
> by the motion of
> its motion
> resembles
> what, moving, is—
> the wind
> underleaf white against
> the tree.

The long **"Saliences"** develops this thought.

In Ammons' rarified language, **"Saliences"** is a philosopher's hymn to the wind, its key word *variable,* applied first to geography, then (with the prefix *multi-*) to scope, next, elevated to noun, associated directly with the wind:

> a variable of wind
> among the dunes,
> making variables
> of position and direction and sound
> of every reed leaf
> and bloom

This variable also dominates sand, shells as they undergo weathering, grass, bayberry bushes, spiders knocked about on the bench "from footing to footing / hard across the dry

even crust / toward the surf." It changes from soft breeze to hard, steady gale; takes form from trees that harbor it briefly, or sandcrab trails, or reeds blown seaward. Overhead, it forces the gull to fly according to its formula, which determines the dropping of clam as well as the direction of flight. As Ezra the prophet traces its moods, paraphrase seems a legitimate means of keeping up with their rapid shifts.

More powerful in some ways than the ocean, the wind controls both surf and the coastal temperature: "wind, from the sea, high surf / and cool weather." It is "a factor in millions of events / leaves no two moments / on the dunes the same," those shapes (omnipresent in this poet) so convenient for use as transient outlines, a sign of metamorphosis as limestone is in Auden. **"Saliences"** affirms the existence of dunes of mind as well as of sand. How dull for the physical dunes without wind, for interior dunes without the wind of poetic imagination! In **"Dunes,"** Ammons the poet as tree confesses that "Taking root in windy sand / is not an easy / way / to go about / finding a place to stay," but this life requires the attempt, since as the last line says: "Firm ground is not available ground."

At this point in **"Saliences"** Ammons addresses the reader through the imperative mode: "keep / free to these events." As he has innumerable times before, he demands resistance to imprisonment, even what the world in general takes for granted: boundaries, fixed identities, any kind of stability. What wind is on a given day is no prediction. As the poem reaches its last section, Ammons mercifully deviates from abstraction to bring in details congruent to memories but not replicas: the way the waves look from a dune-rise, pink periwinkles edging a tidal pool, a bunch of deep-blue weeds, minnows and fiddler crabs filtering through thin water. Here he begins to lament rather than praise change, mourning the fled swallows of yesterday. By means of end-rhyme he emphasizes the thought: "where not a single single thing endures / the overall reassures": though the earth brings to grief "much in an hour that sang, leaped, swirled" (verbs descriptive of wind), it keeps on quietly turning, "beyond loss or gain"—not really beyond, but seeming so.

In the series of dizzy changes that comprise **"Configurations,"** the poet in five grammatically correct sentences proclaims that he is a bush, next, bird, wind, egg, then switches into an "I is" construction to repeat these, adding "I is a leaf." These disguises lose their grip on location: leaves fall, birds fly, nests tumble down spilling out eggs. The only hope for survival is to put down roots, like a shrub: "there is some relationship between proximity / to the earth and permanence." Yet wind and ice will break down even the shrub— but then, after all, the only existence any of these had was in his song. This lyric, like "prospecting," has the charm of children's literature, a charm which shines through in the chain of cockbird longing for henbird, it for nest, nest for earth, earth for sun, sun for—here, Ammons snaps off the list to conclude with his tree-metaphor, this time a talking tree: "please please / let me put on my leaves / let me let the sap go," to which the prudent bark answers "hush, hush / the time is not right." **"Halfway"** brights into focus in a minimum of words the autobiographical relationship between artist and art, its setting October:

>   . . . the
> birches
> in
>
> pools of them-
> selves, the yellow
> fallen
>
> leaves reflecting
> those on
> the tree that
> mirror the ground.

The subject of **"Portrait"** is the poet's life depicted as a leaf, tossed about by the autumn wind, facing destinies as different as being blown up a rise gay as a "spring catkin" or being flattened into the darkness of a stream-bottom. Like Randall Jarrell, who so feared loss of the ability to write, Ammons pleads: "come, / / wind, away from / water and let / song spring & / / leap with this / paper-life's / lively show."

Seldom does Ammons depart completely from realism, as he does in **"Winter Scene,"** the fantasy of which corresponds to James Wright's translation of Vallejo in "The Jewel": "If I stood upright in the wind / My bones would turn to dark emerald." In it a cherry tree, stripped by the season, holds up naked boughs except for those intervals when a jay swoops down into it: "then every branch / / quivers and / breaks out in blue leaves," probably just an impressionistic passage but able also to represent the poetic process, the imagined foliage like gold spun from straw.

Selected Poems, which started in dialogues between the poet and one or another elements in landscape, closes the same way. In the penultimate lyric, **"Kind,"** the giant redwood, miffed because passed over for the so-temporary weeds, half-hidden among stones, complains and is answered thus:

>   O redwood I said in this matter
> I may not be able to argue from reason
> but preference sends me stopping
> seeking
>   the least,
>   as finished as you
>   and with a flower

Here, again, is Tennyson's enigmatic blossom growing obscurely in its wall. The Book of the Creatures has a great deal to teach that apt scholar, A. R. Ammons, and he in turn is well-qualified to instruct with delight an evergrowing body of readers.

A. R. Ammons with William Walsh (interview date 6 March 1988)

SOURCE: "An Interview with A. R. Ammons," in *Michigan Quarterly Review,* Vol. XXVIII, No. 1, Winter, 1989, pp. 105-17.

[*In the following interview, conducted March 6, 1988 in Winston-Salem, North Carolina, Ammons discusses his life, work, and view of poetry.*]

When A. R. Ammons's ***Collected Poems 1951-1971*** appeared in 1972, Geoffrey H. Hartman wrote in *The New York Times Book Review* that it was "a remarkable book . . . his distinction as a major American poet will now be evident." A critical consensus has formed since then that Ammons is indeed one of the most important poets in our contemporary literature. He has published some seventeen volumes, including the ***Collected Poems*** (winner of the National Book Award for Poetry), ***Sphere: The Form of a Motion*** (winner of the 1973-1974 Bollingen Prize in Poetry), ***A Coast of Trees*** (winner of the National Book Critics Circle Award for Poetry, 1981), ***The Snow Poems, Corsons Inlet, Diversifications,*** and most recently ***The Selected Poems: Expanded Edition*** and ***Sumerian Vistas.*** Ammons was born in Whiteville, North Carolina. He is Goldwin Smith Professor of Poetry at Cornell University.

This interview was conducted on March 6, 1988, in Winston-Salem, North Carolina, at the house where Ammons and his wife were staying while on sabbatical.

[*WALSH:*] *I read an interview the other day where the guest was asked if there was a question he had always wanted to answer, but had never been asked.*

[AMMONS:] Most of the questions I have been asked have had to do with literary reputations rather than what I considered the nature of poetry, that is, what is poetry and how does it work? In what way is it an action or a symbolic action? In what way does poetry recommend certain kinds of behavior? Questions like that are of absorbing interest to me. What Robert Bly or somebody else is doing is of no interest to me whatsoever. I've written my poetry more or less in isolation without any day-to-day contact with other writers. Though I have read tidbits in anthologies of other people, I've made no study of anybody else's work, except in school where I read Shelley, Keats, Chaucer, and so on. I like questions that address, if they can, the central dynamics of this medium we work with, not that any answer is possible, but that we meditate the many ways in which it represents not only our verbal behavior but other representative forms of behavior—how poetry resembles other actions such as ice skating or football. That is to say, I think poetry is extremely important because it's central to other actions, and it should not be pushed far to the side as a strictly academic study or a technical investigation.

Do you think poetry is threatened by becoming an academic subject?

To the extent that it is a mere object of study, yes. I worry about that, because it means that the action of the poem and the mind, the action of the body of the poem itself, is going to be paraphrased into discursiveness—something is going to be said about it which will be different from the original action. And while I don't know how classes can be conducted any other way, that's not why poems are written. They are not written in order to be studied or discussed, but to be encountered, and to become standing points that we can come to and try to feel out, impressionistically, what this poem is recommending. Is it recommending in a loud voice, extreme action, or is its action small, does it think we should look closely at things, should we forget the little things and look at some big inner problem, should we understate our stances toward the world, or does hyperbole work better, is this a shallow poem, or is there some profound way that it achieves something it didn't even mean to achieve? In other words, we're trying to live our lives and we go to these representative, symbolic actions to test out what values seem to have precedence over others. If human beings in this country or wherever could approach poetry more in that way rather than as an historical or strictly theoretical form of study, then they might feel the ball of strength in poetry and come to it because it would inform and excite them the way Madonna does or punk rock does. Of course, I'm not insisting that poetry become a popular medium. It requires the attention that few people are willing to give it. I kind of wish that weren't so.

Many of the people I've come in contact with who don't read poetry say it's because they don't understand it.

"Understanding something" has been defined for them as a certain system of statements made about something. If they don't get a very good statement about the poems, it means they haven't opened themselves to the rhythm, pacing, sound of words, colors, and images that they are supposed to move into. Who understands his own body? I mean the gorillas have been walking around for two hundred and fifty thousand years with extremely complicated enzymic and other operations going on in their blood streams that they know nothing about, which prevented them not at all from being gorillas. We're the same case. What are we supposed to understand about poetry? I've studied and worked with poetry since I was eighteen. Poetry astonishes me day after day. I see something else that is somehow implicated in that. I never expect to understand it. You see, there's where the problem is. The kind of understanding that was defined for these people, most people, has been trivial and largely misses the poem.

You spent the first seventeen years of your life in the South, in Whiteville, North Carolina. Could you discuss your background leading up to your first interest in writing?

It covers the period people like to cover in ten years of psychotherapy and don't give up and walk away until they have an answer. [*Laughing*] I was born in 1926, just toward the end of the good times—the Twenties into the Depression. Our family had a pretty rough time on the farm. We had a small subsistence farm of fifty acres on which my grandfather had raised thirteen children, and which in my father's hands became a cash crop farm that was not large enough to raise enough cash. Yet, we didn't do the dozens of things that would have continued it as a subsistence farm. Apparently, my grandfather had done very well. So we were caught in that kind of bind, aggravated by the Depression, about which you've heard endless rumors—all true. [*Laughing*] It was a rather desperate time until the beginning of the war provided jobs for people, and changes—radical changes. Do you realize that when I was born in 1926 something like 85 percent of the people in the country were rural, lived on a farm, and now it's about 3 percent? So the most incredible silent revolution has taken place just in my lifetime.

After I graduated from high school in 1943 I worked for a ship-building company in Wilmington, then entered the Navy when I was eighteen. I was in the South Pacific for nineteen months, came back and entered Wake Forest College in the summer of 1946 on the G.I. Bill. Nobody in my family had gone to college before. It was a truly daunting experience for me. My major was premed and I minored in English, and then everything collapsed into a kind of general science degree.

You started in a premed program with hopes of becoming a doctor?

Yes, I did. I think it came out of a general interest in things and people and feelings. To be a doctor would have been to get completely out of the mess I was in as a farmer. It was a different social and economic level. I didn't pursue it beyond my undergraduate degree. I had wanted to stay a farmer, but my father sold the farm. So, that option was eliminated. I love the land and the terrible dependency on the weather and the rain and the wind. It betrays many a farmer, but makes the interests of the farmer's life tie in very immediately with everything that's going wrong meteorologically. I miss that. That's where I got my closeness and attention to the soil, weeds, plants, insects, and trees.

Prior to studying English in college had you written very much?

The first poem I wrote was in the tenth grade, where you have to write a poem in class. It was on Pocahontas. Then I didn't write anymore until I was in the South Pacific and discovered a poetry anthology when I was on the ship. Then I began to write experimentally and imitatively. There was a man on ship who had a Master's degree in languages and I began to study Spanish with him. We didn't have a text; he just made it up as he went along. It somehow gave me a smattering of grammar—you know how helpful it is with your own grammar to study another language. Pretty soon I was writing regularly. Then I came to Wake Forest where there were no creative writing classes, but I continued to write for four years. About a month before I left Wake Forest I finally got up the nerve to show some of my poems to the professors and they were very encouraging. From then on, my mind, my energies, were focused on poetry even though I had to do what everyone else does—try to figure out some way to make a living.

You didn't begin by sending your poems to small magazines, did you?

I didn't even know they existed. I was just totally ignorant of the literary scene. What a load that is on the mind not to know what the configuration, the landscape of the literary world is. I got married the year I was the principal of the elementary school in Cape Hatteras. From there we went to Berkeley, where I did further study in English, working toward a Master's degree. I took my poems to Josephine Miles, a fine poet and critic who died a couple of years ago. She consented to read my poems and said I should send them out. That's where I first heard about literary magazines.

Your first book of poetry, **Ommateum,** *failed terribly.*

I believe the publisher knew it wouldn't sell and so they only bound one hundred copies of the three hundred sheets pressed. It sold sixteen copies the first five years. Five libraries bought it—Princeton, Harvard, Yale, Berkeley, and Chapel Hill, only because they bought everything. My father-in-law sent forty copies to people he knew in South America. I bought back thirty copies for thirty cents each. So I guess you could say it failed miserably. One review in *Poetry* magazine, my first review, was favorable. But now **Ommateum** goes for about thirteen hundred dollars a copy.

The reason I brought this up is because you did not publish another collection of poetry for nine years. What transpired

in those nine years, between the time you wrote **Ommateum** *and* **Expressions of Sea Level,** *that produced a resounding critical change in your work?*

We cannot imagine, sitting here, how long nine years is. I just kept writing, resubmitting manuscripts, tearing them apart, putting them back together, getting rejected, trying again, and so on until I was finally rejected by everybody. I took my work to a vanity publisher in New York City and I was turned down by them, too. I went to Bread Loaf in 1961 and met Milton Kessler, who at that time was teaching at Ohio State University. He said their press was starting a poetry series and I should send my poems early on before the hundreds of manuscripts began to arrive. I did and they took it. It was favorably reviewed, but it took ten years for them to sell eight hundred copies. I used to get monthly statements from them saying this month we've sold three copies, this month we sold four. For ten years this happened, and I'm not sure they ever sold all one thousand copies. It is amazing how favorably it was reviewed. I just saw *The Oxford Companion to American Literature* which has an article on me saying from the day **Expressions of Sea Level** was published, A. R. Ammons was a major poet. . . . Nobody told me then that I was a major poet.

Now, as to what happened to the poetry itself, that's a story so long I wouldn't know how to tell you. I'd have to go back over the stages, the failures, the rebeginnings, and so on. It isn't easy to be a poet. I think if the young poets could realize *that* they would be off doing something else. It takes a long time. It took me a long time. I do believe there are poets who begin right at the top of their form, and usually are exhausted in five years. In a way I wasn't bad either early on. **Ommateum** remains a very powerful influence with me.

Who do you see as starting at the top of their form?

I just happen to think of James Tate, who won a national prize when he was twenty-two. I don't mean to say he burned out. There are poets who seem to be at their best right away. I'm a slow person to develop and change. The good side of that is that it leaves me so much more to do.

When you look back at the poems in **Ommateum** *as a whole what is your reaction? Do you still feel the same way?*

It's a very strong book. It may be my best book. **Expressions of Sea Level,** though more widely welcomed, more obviously ingratiates itself to an easier kind of excellence. The **Ommateum** poems are sometimes very rigid and ritualistic, formal and off-putting, but very strong. The review I got said, these poems don't care whether they are listened to or not. Which is exactly true. I had no idea there was such a thing as an audience; didn't care if there was. I was involved in the poem that was taking place in my head and on the page and that was all I cared about. If I had known there were millions of people out there wanting to buy my book, which of course is not the case, it would have been nice. But an audience meant nothing to me. Someone else said that I was a poet who had not yet renounced his early poems. I never intend to renounce those poems. [*Laughing*] I have published some inferior poems in each volume—that's inevitable. But as Jarrell said, if you are lucky enough to write a half a dozen good poems in your life, you would be lucky indeed.

Critics have traced your creative genealogy to several influences: Whitman, Thoreau, Emerson, Pound, Stevens, Frost. One critic stated, "Ammons's poetry is founded on the implied Emersonian division of experience into Nature and the Soul." Would you agree with their findings?

First of all, one has been influenced by everything in one's life, poetic and otherwise. There have been predominant influences, such as Robert Browning, whom I imitated at great length as an undergraduate, writing soliloquies and dramatic monologues, trying to get anywhere near the marvelous poems he wrote. I failed miserably. Whitman was a tremendous liberation for me. Emerson was there in the background; though I am said to be strongly Emersonian I sort of learned that myself. I haven't read him that much. When I read Emerson I see a man far wiser and more intelligent, and a better writer than myself, saying exactly what I would say if I could. That's scary in a way. We're still different in so many ways. But then I do believe I hear, at times, in my poems, distant echoes from every poet, not in terms of his own words, but as a presence. Frost is there, also Stevens. I have read very little Stevens, and basically he's not one of my favorite poets, though I think he's a good poet. They do say of me, even though the influences are there, that my voice remains my own, which is a mystery to me, but apparently it's true. I believe I assimilate from any number of others and other areas. I'm that kind of person—one who is looking for the integrated narrative. That's where my voice finds its capability of movement. It is my voice, but it is an integrated one. Does that sound right?

Oh, yes.

I just made it up. [*Laughing*]

How, then, would you describe your poetry?

It's a variable poetry that tries to test out to the limit the situation of unity and diversity—how variable and diverse a landscape of poetry can be and at the same time hold a growing center. I have written some very skinny poems you might call minimalist and I've written some very long-lined poems, such as **"Sphere."** In my early poems I was contemplating the philosophical issue of the One and the Many.

Your poetry deals principally with man in nature, the phenomena of the landscape—earth's nature. I've wondered, because of your scientific background, if you have ever thought about taking man off the earth into space? I don't mean to say science fiction poetry, but into the nature of space.

I don't believe I have, though I've thought a great deal about it—billions and billions of galaxies and billions and billions of stars in each one. Who was it said that if you stick out your arm at the end of space what does it stick into? If space is limited, what happens?

In about 90 percent of your poetry the reader is brought into the poem to witness the solitude of the speaker. Is this solitude your poetic vision of loneliness?

Yes.

Is it your loneliness you're writing about?

Yes it is. I really don't write to an audience. I never imagined an audience. I imagine other lonely people, such as myself. I don't know who they are or where they are, and I don't care, but they're the people whom I want to reach. It seems to me that the people who are capable of forming themselves into groups and audiences have something else to go on besides poetry. So let them go ahead. It could be political, sociological, mystical, or whatever. They're welcome to it and I hope they do a good job, but I am not part of that. I'm really an isolationist. And I know there are others like me. There is some element of ultimate loneliness in each person. In some people it's a crisis. Those are the pieces of loneliness I would like to share at this distance.

You published three major collections in a row: **Collected Poems 1951-71, Sphere: The Form of a Motion,** *and* **The Snow Poems.** *How does this affect a writer's sense that since what you're doing is working, you might as well keep doing the same thing?*

> **I can't get stuck in a pattern, because I don't believe in patterns. I believe in process and progression. I believe in centralizing, integration, that kind of ongoing narrative, more than I believe in the boxes of identification and completion.**
> **—A. R. Ammons**

I can't get stuck in a pattern, because I don't believe in patterns. I believe in process and progression. I believe in centralizing, integration, that kind of ongoing narrative, more than I believe in the boxes of identification and completion.

That's just the way I am structured as a human being. *The Collected Poems* contains two or three other previously unpublished books. I just dumped them in there. I had them, but didn't want to bother sending them out to magazines.

But *Sphere,* finally, was the place where I was able to deal with the problem of the One and the Many to my own satisfaction. It was a time when we were first beginning to see an image of the earth from outer space on the television screen, at a time when it was inevitable to think about that as the central image of our lives—that sphere. With *Sphere,* I had particularized and unified what I knew about things as well as I could. It didn't take long for me to fall apart or for that to fall apart, too. Thinking of the anger and disappointment that comes from such things . . . I wrote *The Snow Poems,* where I had meant to write a book of a thousand pages. I don't know why I didn't go ahead and do it, because I wanted to say here is a thousand pages of trash that nevertheless indicates that every image and every event on the planet and everywhere else is significant and could be great poetry, sometimes is in passages and lines. But I stopped at three hundred pages. I had worn myself and everybody else out. But I went on long enough to give the idea that we really are in a poetically inexhaustible world, inside and out.

Your work has been anthologized in many publications over the years. They usually publish "Corsons Inlet," "This Is," "Bridge," and "Visit." Of all your poems which do you think is your best work and will most likely survive?

I have always liked two poems of mine that are twins, **"Conserving the Magnitude of Uselessness"** and **"If Anything Will Level with You Water Will"** from the *Collected Poems.* I think those are fine poems, but other people don't reprint them. I think anthologists tend to imitate each other. If they find a poem anthologized, they put it in their anthology. I have a great many poems, to tell you the truth, that could just as well have been chosen for an anthology as the others.

Donald Justice said at one time that the United States has not produced a major poet in the last thirty years. Do you agree with this?

I agree with that. The possibility is that Ashbery is a major writer, but other than that I don't know any major writers, except possibly myself. The great poets of the first half of the century are not as great as we thought they were, but they are greater than anything since. I think Eliot was a great poet. I like Ransom a lot. I don't believe Lowell and Berryman are going to prove to be as strong as was thought. I hope I'm wrong about that. It seems to me that there are a million poets that write interesting verse, but I can't think of a single one that I would think of getting up in the morning

and going to find my life profoundly changed and enlightened and deepened by. Not a single one. Isn't that amazing? Or do I just not know about them? I don't mean an answer to life, I mean an encounter of intelligence, sensibility, feeling, vision. Where do I go for a verbal encounter that will be sufficient to cause me to feel that I should come back the next day and the next day to drink from that fountain again?

Do you think we will see a major poet evolve out of the last eleven or twelve years of the century or has the well dried up?

I think not. This century has had it. Like others, I believe that we've been replaying the seventeenth century in which a great deal of poetic energy in the first part of the century dried up into Dryden and Pope. Dryden at the end of the seventeenth and Pope at the beginning of the eighteenth. And we have started to take on a formalist cast now. Maybe we're going to need a century or two before we get back on line.

You've taught at Cornell since 1964.

Yes, that's right. Denise Levertov was poetry editor of *The Nation* and she wanted to take off for six months and she asked me to fill in for her. During that period I accepted a poem by David Ray. I didn't know who he was, but I published his poem. Some months later I was asked to read at Cornell, and it turned out that David Ray was a teacher there. I guess he was glad I published his poem and wanted to meet me. I went to read and they asked me why I wasn't teaching and I said because no one had ever asked me. They proceeded to ask me. I became a full professor in seven years. Some years later Yale made me an offer, so Cornell countered their offer and gave me an endowed chair. They have just honored me beyond all dreams. I teach part-time . . . one course that meets once a week. It's like having your life free. I go over every day and talk to students and go to meetings, but I don't have to.

Is it stimulating for your work to meet with the students everyday?

Not much any more. I need human contact, but it needn't be profound. To see someone and have a cup of coffee really restores me. See, I don't like to live alone. I don't think that I'm much of a teacher, but that's not what the students tell me. I never feel very competent. I don't think anyone who teaches poetry can feel very competent, because the subject is so overwhelming and it's easy to miss the center of it. Can you imagine in a creative writing class the interplay between the teacher and the student—how complex that is on both sides? Superficial, no matter how profound. It's so superficial and so mixed, "Help me, don't help me. Criticize this poem but only say good things. Don't tell me what my next move is. Tell me, but don't let me know that you told me what my next move is, so it will seem that I discovered it for myself. When I owe you something please be the first one to say I owe nothing." That is to say, the relationship is extremely complex and draining on that account. You would have to be superhuman to know what to do in that situation. I am, as it turns out, not superhuman. But they say I'm a good teacher, nevertheless. I do the best I can. I must say that I have a pretty quick eye on a poem. I can tell what it is likely to amount to or not amount to rather quickly. It's just a wonderful job, but I'm tired of it, only because of something they call "burnout." After having done something for twenty-five years I don't know what happens. I guess you begin hearing yourself say the same thing, repeating yourself.

When I first began to teach, I would go into the classroom and see eighteen or twenty individuals and I believed they were individuals. After about five years of teaching six courses per year, I would come into a writing class knowing full well that there were three or four basic problems. Diction—there is always too much poetic diction. There's the problem of shape, or the lack of it—some contact with an ideal form. There's the problem of consistency. It's not sufficient to have a good line and a good image, you need to write a whole poem. Then, as a teacher, you have to begin to nudge yourself and say, "This person sitting in front of you is not an example of one of these problems, he's a person. After awhile, if you have to nudge yourself too much, then it's time to quit.

If the burnout begins to weigh too heavily upon you, is there something that you would prefer doing instead of teaching?

I would like to, now, be designated, as anything in this world, POET. Not teacher, not professor, not farmer, but one who writes poems. What I would like to do now, since I have not allowed myself to do it in twenty years is to go out and meet the people who read my poems. I have been giving poetry readings lately which I did not do for a long, long time. I would like to stay home when I go back to Ithaca and write my poems, send them to magazines, go see people, because I don't know how to tell somebody else how to write.

You don't categorize yourself as particularly Southern, a Southern writer.

I feel my verbal and spiritual home is still the South. When I sit down and play hymns on the piano my belly tells me I'm home no matter where I am. So, yes, I am Southern, but I have been away from the immediate concerns of the South a long time. I guess we should define Southerner. Who are Southerners? Are they white, black? Does a black Southerner want to be separated from a Northerner? Does he feel the same boundary in the North as the Southerner often does? Also, the South has changed so much demographically that

it's difficult to know. I was just in the bank the day before yesterday and I told a young lady I was going back home to Ithaca. She had just moved down from Kingston, New York. She said she liked it, but missed the snow. At the next teller's window was a woman who said she was from New York. So there we were, the three of us, adjacent to each other from New York. The very same thing happened in the post office one morning.

How does a poet deal with this change?

I wonder. I don't think it has very much effect on me. The sources of poetry, by the time you are as old as I am, sixty-two, have taken all kinds of perspectives, and while the work may be changed in tone and mood by recent events, it's changed only slightly. Curvature of the narrative, by that time, becomes fairly well established, and while it can change, it won't change much.

You never dreamed of becoming a poet in the sense of receiving recognition for your work. You thought of yourself as being an amateur poet and not a "Poet." Once you began publishing, when did you begin to think of yourself as a "Poet?"

When I said amateur poet, I meant that I didn't want to professionalize it. It seems to have more spontaneity, immediacy and meaning to me when I think of it as just something I do. I worry when poetry is professionalized. I think maybe I am a poet. I keep getting letters from all over the world from people who say they are moved by this and that. Whatever it was that they were moved by is in the past for me. I just wrote a poem this morning. That's where I'm at. I try to live each day as I can. If I write a poem, fine. If I don't, that's fine. I think life ought to come first. Don't you? One is alive in the world with other people. I write poetry. Other people collect insects or rocks. I don't think I have answered this question very well, but you know how at some point in your life you have meditated deeply on a subject—you remember that you have meditated on it, you file it, and the next time you try to remember it you can't access it. You have to take thirty minutes to work your way there, then you might have something to say, or you might not. That's what just happened. [*Laughing*]

Do you think there are writers, poets, who take poetry too seriously, that they feel poetry is almost more important than life?

The solemn, the pompous, the terribly earnest are all boring.

We touched upon your childhood earlier and I'd like to ask if you have a favorite childhood memory?

I remember one Christmas when I got a little tin wagon with milk cans drawn by a mule or a horse. I must have been five or six. I remember getting back into bed and playing with that on top of the quilt, thinking it was absolutely marvelous.

Turning this around, do you have a least favorite childhood memory?

The most powerful image of my emotional life is something I had repressed and one of my sisters lately reminded me of. It was when my little brother, who was two and a half years younger than I, died at eighteen months. My mother some days later found his footprint in the yard and tried to build something over it to keep the wind from blowing it away. That's the most powerful image I've ever known.

Throughout your career you've professed formlessness and boundlessness. Have you found either?

I guess the other side of that question is, is there anything, in fact, in our world and perception that isn't formal in one way or the other? I guess not. The air between me and that oak tree is invisible and formless. I can't see the air. So I see nothing but form out the window. I know the air is there because I see it work on the trees, and so I begin to think there is an invisible behind the visible, and a formlessness, an ongoing energy that moves in and out of a discrete formation. It remains constant and comes and goes and operates from a world of residual formlessness. That space, at some point, develops what we perceive. In a way I have experienced the idea of formlessness and boundlessness, but these are imperceptible thanks to our senses.

For the last three or four months I have been profoundly occupied with the conceptual aspect of poetry—poetry that has some thought behind it. But also, the poem is a verbal construct that we encounter, learn from, make value judgements with, and go to to sort out possibilities in relation to our own lives in order to try to learn how to live. I'm sick and tired of reading poets who have beautiful images that don't have a damn thing to say. I want somebody who can think and tell me something. You reintegrate that into a larger thing where you realize that thought and loss are certainly not the beginning and end to things, but are just one element in the larger effort we are making, which is to try to learn how to live our lives.

Thomas Dilworth (essay date Fall 1988)

SOURCE: "Ammons's 'Coon Song,'" in *The Explicator,* Vol. 47, No. 1, Fall, 1988, pp. 40-3.

[*In the following essay, Dilworth interprets Ammons's "Coon Song."*]

"Coon Song" by A. R. Ammons is a remarkably metamorphic literary experience. It seems to deconstruct itself by denying its opening narrative description—about a raccoon surrounded by hunting dogs—in order to express something beyond the range of narration and description. The narrative is broken off by the poet's direct address to the reader, which initiates a dramatic monologue. Within this monologue, kinds of relationship between the poem (or poet) and the reader are in conflict. Because the dramatic monologue retains its reference to the initial narrative and because the dominant images of that narrative become metaphors in the monologue, the poem retains its unity. This achievement is especially impressive since the work tends to fly apart because of multiple generic metamorphoses. At eighty-eight lines, it is too long to reprint here in its entirety, so I will quote liberally as I interpret.

The initial narrative captures the moment before action, the imminent attack on the raccoon by the dogs:

> I got one good look
>   in the raccoon's eyes
>   when he fell from the tree
> came to his feet
>   and perfectly still
>   seized the baying hounds
> in his dull fierce stare,
>   in that recognition
>   all decision lost,
> choice irrelevant, before the
>   battle fell
>   and the unwinding
> of his little knot of time began. . . .

The narrative is followed by an editorial intrusion expanding on the notion of freedom and its limits: "Dostoevsky would think it important if the coon / could choose to / be back up the tree: / or if he could chose to be / wagging by a swamp pond, / dabbling at scuttling / crawdads." In one sense, the coon, like any victim, has no choice. He may fantasize himself into a safe, womb-like, leaf-lined hole "of a fallen oak." This is not, of course, a practical option, though it may constitute the sort of choice the poet reads in the coon's eyes: "reality can go to hell"—a metaphysical choice of sorts. Realistically, the only decision the coon can make is between "exposed tenders, / the wet teeth." Tenders, the ligaments at the back of the hounds' jaws, pun on the commercial term for "formal offers." Which mouth to choose is, for the coon, the only "problem to be / solved." Because the editorial intrusion is the sort that narrative can accommodate, no generic change has so far occurred.

But then the poet turns on the reader: "you want to know what happened, / you want to hear me describe it, / to placate the hound's-mouth / slobbering in your own heart." The poet catches us in voyeuristic expectation, wanting to witness the consummation of violence; as readers we become analogous to the blood-thirsty hounds. And a corresponding metaphor is implied: the poem—and then, as he speaks for himself, the poet—becomes the coon. (As hounds will consume the coon, readers consume the poem.) The imminent "unwinding" of the coon, we now realize, has affinity for the unwinding that takes place during literary analysis and may recall Wordsworth's dictum, "we murder to dissect." As if to avoid such analysis, the poem itself begins to unwind as the poet says about the fate of the coon: "I will not tell you."

But then, apparently contradicting himself, he relates that "the coon / possessing secret knowledge / pawed dust at the dogs / and they disappeared." The fantasy breaks the realism that has dominated the narrative and that will go on to characterize most of this dramatic monologue of direct address. As a consequence, the initial narrative is seen as fictitious and therefore, in its conclusion, as potentially a romance, in which the coon can make the dogs disappear. But then the poet undermines this possibility: "maybe he didn't: I am no slave that I / should entertain you, say what you want / to hear, let you wallow in / your silt."

Why silt? The only possible explanation is implied by references to the pond where crawdads scuttle. If the poet is now the coon, we readers have become crawdads scuttling in silt, which is the comfortable habitat of wish-fulfillment. The hunters (the hounds/readers) have become the hunted, and the coon/ poet has caught us, though almost immediately he allows us our freedom, in fact, insists on it.

At first this freedom seems contingent on the generosity of the poet, for he remains in control in so far as he generates what we consume and directs our mental and emotional response. But it is precisely to diminish this control and to increase our freedom that he institutes a new generic shift—to nonsense, which is, as Lewis Carroll realized, closely related to romance though it effects the collapse of all other generic modes: "one two three four five six seven eight nine ten: / (all this time I've been / counting spaces / while you were thinking of something else." We are forced to realize that the entire poem has been a counting of spaces, an artifice or conventional fiction and not only as narrative but as monologue. What we have accepted as imaginatively "real" in deference to primary literary convention is actually built on airy nothing. Literary "reality can go to hell."

This the poet further emphasizes as he returns us to romance: "mess in your own sloppy silt: / the hounds disappeared . . . into—the order / breaks up here—immortality: I know that's

where you think the brave / little victims should go." The effect of this is to make the reader realize that the element of direct address in the monologue is also a fiction since you, surely, are not the fictional reader. That reader is a projection of the poet, someone who was hound-like in wanting the coon killed but able to identify with the coon enough to want (or accept) its magically making away with the hounds. To that point you may well coincide with the projected reader. But now that the poet continues associating the reader with the hounds, he supposes that you identify emotionally with them. Behind the comedy of this final supposition is implied an immense passivity and egoism on the part of the reader that force you to disidentify with the fictional reader. The "silt," which that reader wallows in, is now not the fantastic escape of the coon from death but the escape of the hounds from death into "immortality," which the poet suggests is equally unreal.

He continues to free the reader from authorial control by generating more nonsense, which is now circular in its unwinding of the poem:

> I do not care what
> you think: I do not care what you think:
> I do not care what you
> think: one two three four five
> six seven eight nine ten: here we go
> round the here-we-go-round, the
> here-we-go-round, the here-we-
> go-round: coon will end in disorder at the
> teeth of hounds: the situation
> will get him. . . .

Twice we have been offered the contrasting outcomes of brutal realism and escapist romance or fantasy. Now the speaker presents "two philosophies" condensed into images: "spheres roll, cubes stay." If we read these as aesthetic philosophies and as reflecting the choices we have so far been given, the rolling spheres suggest romance, which has up to now been a wallowing in accommodating silt, and the static cubes suggest realism. As larger, ontological philosophies, the spheres suggest Platonic idealism; the cubes, Aristotelian realism.

In any case, the poet finally, enigmatically announces, "what I choose / is youse: / baby. With that decision, he transfers choice, placing responsibility squarely on the reader. How will you, whose "exposed tenders" have been chosen, consume this coon/poem? Will you choose escapist romance? Probably not, since the poet has biased you against romance as a mere wallowing in silt. Will you choose brutal realism? Although it seems more probable, he has also biased you against voyeuristic self-indulgence. Maybe you can refuse the choice.

But what you must accept is the freedom of the poet, who

is "no slave that" he "should entertain you." He has liberated himself. Moreover, because he has become analogous to the coon and because of the colloquial racist connotations of the word "coon," his self-liberation resonates with the civil rights movement already under way when this poem was first published.

Analogically, the meaning of the work is partly sociopolitical, but the experience that gives substance to the analogy is literary-analytical and consists of the liberation of the poet (and also the reader) from literary bondage through radical shifts in generic modality: from realistic narrative to dramatic monologue and, within monologue, between realism, romance, and nonsense. In the process, the reader's point of view is repeatedly altered and finally brought to the awareness that he or she is not the reader whom the poet addresses, is in no way accommodated by the poem, and is therefore as free as the poet.

Cary Wolfe (essay date Spring 1989)

SOURCE: "Symbol Plural: The Later Long Poems of A. R. Ammons," in *Contemporary Literature,* Vol. 30, No. 1, Spring, 1989, pp. 78-94.

[*In the following essay, Wolfe asserts that from "Essay on Poetics" on, "Ammons emphasizes the becoming, rather than the Being, of nature—the processes rather than the fixity of a* logos *which drives them." He notes a connection between Ammons's portrayal of nature and the English romantics.*]

For years now, Ammons criticism has in general followed Harold Bloom's reading of the poet out of the American transcendental—Bloom's "Emersonian"—tradition. Bloom's readings have been instructive, often exciting (and make for a compelling version of literary history); his work on Ammons and on other contemporary poets (Strand and Merwin come to mind) constitutes a fascinating thematics of what it is to be an American poet. In terms of poetics, however—and here I mean how a given poet *constitutes* his subject—Ammons needs to be examined in light of his highly ambivalent relationship with those writers who provided the poetic machinery for the transcendentalists in the first place—I refer, of course, to the English romantics. Here, I will replace Bloom's "Emerson" with the Coleridgean "symbol" and the romantic notion of the organic—though I hope to avoid what Frank Lentricchia has called the Bloomian "spirit of revenge." Rather, I want to argue that the romantic symbol must, for a poet like Ammons, be dealt with in the realm of poetics in much the same way that Emersonianism must be confronted as a kind of thematic bedrock for later American poets. The fact that Ammons's

later poetry is highly discursive—I mean this in relative terms, as compared with, say, the work of James Wright—makes this sort of approach all the more imperative for Ammons criticism. Furthermore, I want to argue that Ammons's significant modification of romantic poetics constitutes a resituating of the ideological role of poetic writing and of the "aesthetic" as traditionally conceived.

Bloom has dubbed Ammons "a poet of the Romantic Sublime," yet in a fundamental sense Ammons's sublime is both postromantic and post-Emersonian; for this one-time biologist, oneness with nature is a brute (and brutal) fact, a "one-sided extension"—as much a curse as a blessing—which is (in Emersonian terms) finally not a fullness but an emptiness, a lack of common ontological ground that makes knowledge possible.

Part of the reason Ammons is able to embrace nature (sometimes in terror) while at the same time avoiding the appropriations of the romantics is that from the **"Essay on Poetics"** on he adopts a different model of nature, one fundamentally different from the talking wind and mountains of the early poems. Drawing his new model from cybernetics, Ammons emphasizes the becoming, rather than the Being, of nature—the processes rather than the fixity of a *logos* which drives them. It is important to note just how strong the connection is between the nature of the **"Essay"** and that of cybernetic theory. In its very first line we find the melding of literary and cybernetic diction ("lyric information") that runs throughout the poem. Ammons is attempting here to deal with the questions of how nature can in some sense be known and how poetry can have anything to do with that knowledge. By adopting the cybernetic model, Ammons achieves a distinctive modification of the romantic idea of organic form, largely because in the new context the idea of the organic is itself redefined. We might say, following Lentricchia's assessment of Northrop Frye in *After the New Criticism,* that Ammons's new organic opens outward, is centrifugal rather than the centripetal "innate" form of Coleridge.

It may be helpful at this point to offer a few key concepts of the cybernetic model drawn from Gregory Bateson's landmark essay "Cybernetic Explanation." The cybernetic universe is above all relational and formal; communication is a product of redundancy and repetition of pattern (the usual figure for this concept is the signal-to-noise ratio—the signal is recognizable pattern, the noise, the unidentifiable random). Pattern, in turn, is closely wedded to predictability: "To guess, in essence, is to face a cut or slash in the sequence of items and to predict across that slash what items might be on the other side. . . . A pattern, in fact, is definable as an aggregate of events or objects which will permit in some degree such guesses when the entire aggregate is not available for inspection." In cybernetic explanation, "information and form are not items which can be localized" because they are relational correspondences (between message and referent, item and context) which resemble the ideas of contrast, frequency, symmetry, congruence, conformity, and so on—they are "of zero dimensions." The difference between a piece of paper and a cup of coffee, for example, is not in the paper, nor is it in the coffee—the contrast (and subsequent information) cannot be localized. Cybernetic epistemology posits a concept of mind which is organic but not organicist: "The individual mind is immanent, but not only in the body. It is immanent also in pathways and messages outside the body; and there is a larger Mind of which the individual mind is only a subsystem. This larger Mind . . . is . . . immanent in the total interconnected social system and planetary ecology." A final and important point from cybernetics is this: "All that is not information, not redundancy, not form and not restraints—is noise, the only possible source of *new* patterns."

The cybernetic model goes a long way, I think, in helping to explain the similarities and differences between the nature of the **"Essay"**—and to a large extent of all the later long poems—and that of the romantics. The opening of the **"Essay,"** in both diction and conception, shows clearly the shaping presence of a cybernetic kind of thinking; the poem aspires to express something like immanent mind through "information actual / at every point / / but taking on itself at every point / the emanation of curvature, of meaning." The nature of the **"Essay"** is a "bit-nature" where each instance of wholeness and form is "internally irrelevant to scope, / but from the outside circumscribed into scope." Eighteen lines into the poem we come upon the crucial passage, the critical "but," which clearly distinguishes the cybernetic character of Ammons's view of nature from that of the romantics:

> but then find the wholeness
>
> unbelievable because it permits
> another wholeness,
> another lyric, the same in structure,
>
> in mechanism of existence

"Wholeness" is presented in the **"Essay"** not as the purified essence of existence but as a *condition* of existence, not as *either* one or many but as "a one:many mechanism."

Frederick Buell calls Ammons's new model a "partial humanization of nature"; I believe what Ammons recognizes and what Buell is trying to get at is that nature is for us always already conceptualized, symbolized, abstract:

> I wonder if I'm really talking about
> the economy of the self. . . .

. . . .
> we never talk about anything but ourselves,
> objectivity the objective way of talking about
> ourselves

Ammons's shift to a "bit-nature," a nature not of Being but of evidence becoming information, "saliences," is not so much a willful move to humanize nature as it is a recognition of the abstract as a precondition of existence and of knowledge ("the manageable rafters of salience"); the attempt to deal only in the concrete results in the sort of dilemma discussed midway through **"Hibernaculum"**:

> nature seems firm with casual
>
> certainties (one could say a steel spike is a foot
> long) but pressed for certainty breaks out
> in bafflings of variability, a thousand close
>
> measuring of the spike averaged out and a
> thousand
> efforts to average out the variables in the instru-
> ments
> of measure or in the measuring environment
>
> (room temperature, humidity, the probable
> frequency
> the door to the room is opened): recalcitrance is
> built
> in perfectly, variations thereon perceived as
> possibility

This passage clearly echoes the cybernetic idea that conceptual "noise" (the recalcitrant, the as yet unpatterned or unassimilated) is the source of new patterns—variations on recalcitrance perceived as possibility. At the same time, the other end of the problem, so to speak—that of extreme abstraction—is constantly threatened with gaseous evaporation:

> the swarm at the
> subatomic level may be so complex and surprising
> that it puts
> quasars, pulsars and other matters to shame: I
> don't know:
>
> and "living world" on the other hand may be so
> scanty in its
> information as to be virtually of no account

We can see, then, that Ammons is being playful but also exercising a very concentrated economy of expression (underscored by the echo of "tree" in "true") when he writes, "true, I really ought to know where the tree is: but I know / it's in my backward." The organic becomes for Ammons a question of limits and perimeters. In contrast to *a* center, the location of "the primordial egg of truth," Ammons offers a mobile universe of which wholeness is an abstract condition, a beginning rather than a closure:

> a center's absolute, if relative: but every point in
> spacetimematter's
>
> a center: reality is abob with centers: indeed, there
> is
> nothing but centers

A center is, of course, an abstract matter; like form and information, it cannot be located but is rather the product of relational processes, as Ammons indicates in his grappling with the concrete particulars of trying to locate the tree in the back yard:

> I assume the fixed point would have to be
>   the core center of the planet, though I'm perfectly
> prepared to admit the core's involved
>   in a slow—perhaps universal—slosh that would
> alter the
>   center's position

Ammons's argument with the traditional idea of organic form is that it isn't organic enough; its organicism is based on an idea of closure and completion rather than on an ability to maintain an open, functioning relationship with the accidental and haphazard—an ability to translate "noise" into "signal":

>   I am not so much
> arguing with the organic school as shifting true
> organismus from
> the already organized to the bleak periphery of
> possibility,
> an area transcendental only by its bottomless
> entropy

Coincidental with Ammons's criticism of the closure of organic form as traditionally conceived is a similar attitude toward its analogues of symbol and lyric; the "already organized" is a condition for knowing which provides a "disposition" toward the unassimilated but can be changed by new data. The ontological point is of course that the "disposition" depends on the mechanism, and the sort of knowledge one derives depends upon both. The problem with the lyric is precisely its inflexibility as a mechanism for knowing; not open to the possibilities and potential waiting in the coincidental and the unassimilated, its intolerance gives the lyric its expressive power—its small explosion—but renders it, like some sort of exotic poodle, unfit for survival. The lyric is a "slight completion" (in both senses): "to be small and assembled! how comforting: but how perishable!" A similar distrust marks Ammons's attitude toward the idea of

symbol. If anything, the symbol isn't abstract *enough*: "and the symbol won't do, either: it differentiates flat / into muffling fact it tried to stabilize beyond." The point Ammons is making is de Man's in "The Rhetoric of Temporality": by holding that some things are concrete and others abstract, and by then privileging a kind of concrete abstraction, the traditional idea of symbol draws us into a pseudo-dialectic of subject and object. For Ammons, the concrete as such is a myth but is valuable as a function, a nexus of localization in the "one:many mechanism":

> it's impossible anyone should know anything
> about the concrete
> who's never risen above it, above the myth of
> concretion
>
> in the first place

For Ammons, the particulars of nature are not of value primarily because they are concrete but because they are *evidence*— and evidence only makes sense, has meaning, within a larger framework of abstraction kept honest, so to speak, by new evidence.
                               —*Cary Wolfe*

For Ammons, the particulars of nature are not of value primarily because they are concrete but because they are *evidence*—and evidence only makes sense, has meaning, within a larger framework of abstraction kept honest, so to speak, by new evidence. Ammons's empirical observation (as in, for example, sections 75-76 of *Sphere*), and his knowledge and use of the language of science, is unsurpassed in American poetry, yet almost always these empirical forays end in a questioning, a dizzying explosion into a new realm of complexities. Empirical observation pushed far enough dissolves, in one sense, into a question of the one and the many—finally, he writes, "a problem in rhetoric" which cannot be reconciled in language. (His discussion of "division" versus "differentiation" in **"Hibernaculum"** is helpful here.) Ammons's playful and prismatic variation upon Williams's "No ideas but in things" clarifies the point that the relationship between one and many, subject and object, symbol and symbolized is multivalent, always leaving an opening because always leaving something out:

>   the symbol apple and the
> real apple are different apples, though resembled:
> "no ideas but in
>
> things" can then be read into alternatives—"no
> things but in ideas,"

"no ideas but in ideas," and "no things but in
things": one thing
always to keep in mind is that there are a number
of possibilities

(Ammons characteristically underscores the point by the casual statement "one thing to keep in mind"—rather than "one *idea* to keep in mind.")

Ammons brings this sort of attitude to his discussion of the tree as paradigm of organic form, begun in the **"Essay"** and returned to regularly and finally as the oblique subject of *The Snow Poems*. What he refers to sarcastically as "the transcendental / vegetative analogy" is too tidy as an "analogy" and too simplistic as "vegetative." The "point of change" makes him realize that "actually, a tree / is a print-out: the tree becomes exactly what the locked genetic // code has preordained—allowing, of course, for variables." But Ammons goes on to consider the fact that the "locked" code is "apparently based on accidence, chance, unforeseeable distortion"—like his center, it is absolute, but relative. The problem of identity as a paradigm of organic form persists:

> if I back off to take the shape of a tree
> I gather blurs: when does water seeping into the
> roothairs
> pass the boundary after which it is tree

Ammons's symbolism is of a very different order; the tree becomes as much a symbol of difference and otherness—of all that it cannot contain—as it is a paradigm of identity and order.

The shift from tree as organic paradigm to tree as print-out is telling in a number of ways. The "point of change" can be expressed by the tree but cannot be located there, is not *in* the tree. If I examine the tree at different points over time, it will be each time, considered as a concrete thing, a different tree. I can induce change—its motion and perhaps its "drift"—from the variations, but the change is not in the tree, nor is it "between" one examined tree and another. The tree, in this sense, is like a frame of film; it has meaning only insofar as it is traced or inscribed with aspects of the frames which precede it and insofar as it serves to intimate some sense of predictability about the frames to follow.

The elm tree of *The Snow Poems* functions as a locus "to show change by reflecting light differently in a series of exposures." (It is worth noting here that Saussure used in his notes and lectures the terms "historical," "diachronic," and "cinematic" interchangeably to suggest that change or evolution is always an operation of abstracting change and continuity out of discontinuous items.) Ammons's shift to the print-out is, I believe, a movement away from the closed space of self-contained organic form which "partakes" (as

Coleridge put it) of transcendent substance, and toward an emphasis upon the metonymic nature of the tree as a product of the "contiguous" conditions of its environment and of our perception of it. The form is thus not finished but open to the accidental and haphazard (and thus to new information and patterning). The crucial difference is that Ammons goes out of his way to present his metonymies *as* metonymies, to remind us that, in his readings of parts of a world for the whole, it is the *mechanism* and not the substance that informs the meaning of the organic. I emphasize the metonymic nature of Ammons's symbol to point out how it is resolutely untranscendental, "local and mortal." As Kenneth Burke has written, "Viewed as a sheerly terministic, or symbolic function, that's what transcendence is: the building of a *terministic bridge* whereby one realm is *transcended* by being viewed *in terms of* a realm 'beyond' it." And, Burke adds, "*beyond* the here and now." It is Ammons's openness and inclusiveness which gives his symbol—in contrast to Coleridge's—a kind of centrifugal character (this is, I think, in part what is suggested by "the emanation of curvature" of "one curve, the whole curve" at the beginning of the **"Essay"**). Ammons's symbol is "translucent," but to its own provisionality. Poetry achieves the greatest scope of meaning not by exclusion of all that is not organic form but by inclusion of all that might be. Ammons's unique brand of symbolism is in part his strategy for dealing with the dilemma described by Geoffrey Hartman (and we should think here of Stevens's variation upon Williams's "El Hombre"):

> The aura of the symbol is reduced even as its autonomy is strengthened. It is ironic that, by the time of Stevens, "the philosophy of symbols" (as Yeats called it) confronts the poet with a new discontinuity: the symbols, or romantic relics, are so attenuated by common use that their ground (sky?) is lost. They become starry junk, and the poem is a device to dump them, to let the moon rise as moon.

Hartman's "starry junk" is in Ammons countered by the material of the moment—the "worn-outs, stiff-and-thins, the used-up literary." The "growing edge to change and surprise" of the poem can turn anything—trash included—into art with its "one:many mechanism" (while, Ammons would hope, retaining the essential "trash nature" of the bits). Unlike the early Ammons, the poet of wind and mountain, the last two long poems care less about the particular material of the poetry—rely less on wind or mountain—and more about making poetry out of whatever is at hand. Indeed, in both poems Ammons seems to gravitate toward the peripheries, away from the tidiness and centeredness of literary diction and lyric organization. We already see the desire for scope, whatever the risks, emerging in *Sphere*:

> I'm sick of good poems, all those little rondures

splendidly brought off, painted gourds on a shelf:
give me

the dumb, debilitated, nasty, and massive, if that's
the
alternative: touch the universe anywhere you touch
it
everywhere

The key word in all of this is *discontinuity*. Ammons, confronted with the question of how to make poetry possible in a postsymbolist (and in some senses postliterary) context, begins with the **"Essay"** a new type of writing which emphasizes the discontinuity between word and world, writing and speech, but at the same time has a profoundly orphic dimension.

Ammons began, with the Ezra persona of the early poems, in a mode that presented itself as already an analogue of expression: "*so* I said I am Ezra" has no antecedent in the poem. It can only be interpreted as the result of something occurring before the Ezra persona "speaks"—something "outside" the poem or just before it begins. The poem begs to be read as an analogue of speech, the speech an analogue of the Ezra persona, and the persona, finally, an analogue of a human speaker. Implicit in the idea of poem-as-analogue representation is a continuity across ontological levels: the graphic array of language is an analogue for the acoustic, which in turn is analogous to the verbal, the verbal to the intellectual. A paradigm of analogue representation would be the clock: the movement of the hand is an analogue for the movement of the earth. Analogue representation is based on a real correspondence between real magnitudes—representation is motivated by the nature of its object. It is highly conventionalized and metaphoric in the sense that the nature of the representation is motivated by the nature of its object—the circular movement of the hands by the circular movement of the earth, for instance.

Digital representation, on the other hand, makes a point of its discontinuity with real magnitudes and asserts its abstract and arbitrary conventional nature. It can, unlike analogue, represent, and indeed must make use of, negatives. Rather than a fixed analogous whole, the disruption of whose syntax would destroy the entire representation, the digital representation is discrete and infinitely divisible. The continuity between 11:57 and 11:58 is so because in the conventions of the system 8 follows 7, not because of its correspondence to the actual magnitude of that which it represents (as in the case of, say, a thermometer). Analogue representation will emphasize accuracy; digital will emphasize *specificity* (the ontological ground for accuracy having been removed). As Anthony Wilden points out, "The digital mode of language is denotative: it may talk about anything and does so in the language of objects, facts, events and the like. Its linguistic function is primarily the sharing of nameable information . . . its overall function is the transmission or sharing or reproduction of pattern and structures."

We see Ammons, from the **"Essay"** forward, develop a style and form which makes a point of disrupting the idea or impression that his poems are analogue representations. The form makes a point of its own arbitrariness, its discontinuity: the three-line or four-line "stanza" of the later long poems (excepting *The Snow Poems*) runs from margin to margin, the writing structured simply by arbitrary imposition (line breaks do not coincide with acoustic or syntactic breaks or with a sonnetlike "shift of mind" of the speaker). In **"Hibernaculum"** and in *Sphere,* the arbitrariness is further emphasized by the grouping of stanzas into numbered sections—the more apparent the graphic structure, the less it matters at any other level. The "structure" is there to present a visual array pleasing in itself and not as an analogue of the acoustic or intellectual dimensions. When we move inside the stanza, we find a similar discontinuity emphasized again by Ammons's punctuation; there are no periods ("a complete sentence is a complete thought") but only colons, creating a "closeless" structure. As Robert Pinsky has written, "In movement from part to part, the strings of repeated colons suggest a conflict between the stationary or simultaneous and the developing or sequential; each part explains every other part, with a minimum of the consecutive structuring in which part rests on part as in a building or a tree."

The most apparent structuring device is the "friction" between the "regular" stanzas and the staccato movement of the lines produced by the colon, but it cannot be located in either one. Ammons gives us not a consecutive structuring which builds an analogical whole, but a series of read-outs—meaning kept up in the air by its use in circulation. Again, the movement is not inward toward closure—a zeroing in on meaning—but is centrifugal, providing a "growing edge to change," "increasing the means and / assuring the probability of survival." Even though the later long poems are linear, they are at the same time primarily nonnarrative, relying not on a principle of consecutive structuring so much as on a kind of accretive activity which oscillates back and forth from center to periphery, from specific to general, and so on. We could say that, although the form on the page is (of necessity) linear, the governing and informing principle is radial, "circling about, repeating, and elaborating the central theme. It is all 'middle,' . . . with apparently interchangeable structural units." This is, I think, the logic implicit in Ammons's playful assertion in **"Summer Place":** "circle around the truth without telling / it and you tell it." The attempt to make the governing principle of form radial is already present in the title and impulse of *Sphere: The Form of a Motion:*

the essential without specification is boring
and specification without the essential is: both
ways out
leaves us divided but so does neither way:
unless—and here

is the whole possibility—both essential and
fashionable can
be surrounded in a specified radial essential

Ammons's salient interest in arcs and curves gives rise to a desire for "a form to complete everything with! orb," a form whose center ("disposition") remains intact (because mobile) even as the periphery expands. As Ammons has said in a recent interview, "a poem doesn't exist only in motion, in time. It seems to me that when you know the poem intimately you know it radially and complete. You have a non-linear perception of the whole thing."

Still, the poem must, to open outward to such knowledge, insist on its own discontinuity, must be "chocked full of resistance." Writing of *Sphere* in **"Summer Place,"** Ammons echoes the "recalcitrance built into nature" that resists "casual certainties," and he seems to want a similar resistance in his own work: "I wanted something / standing recalcitrant in its own nasty massiveness," "a big gritty poem that would just stand / there and spit." Underneath the complaining is, I think, a weariness of having the work taken as an analogue, a "fallacy of imitative form" too easily appropriated: "pretty soon you're a nature poet, everybody / saying, lands, something nice to go with dinner."

The Ammons of **"Summer Place"** and even more so of *The Snow Poems,* having generated a kind of radiant wholeness in the previous long poems, now emphasizes that his universe—as he had been saying all along—is a *discrete* whole (as in this example from the *OED:* "The parts of an animal form a concrete whole; but the parts of a society form a whole that is discrete"). This is, I think, the implicit logic behind much of Ammons's seemingly unpoetic diction of the "economy of the self"; Ammons resorts to terms like "currency," "interest," "account," "expenditure," "overinvestment" (a symbol is "the overinvested concrete"), "balance" ("all identities are imbalances") to speak of a wholeness while at the same time avoiding the ontological pitfalls of the language of organicism.

The discrete whole of society as theme is most explicit in **"Summer Place."** Concomitant with its patriotic ending and the inscription of *The Snow Poems* as a work "for my country" comes a shift inward toward the poet's own world, toward a poetry more explicitly discrete, separate, and discontinuous. The broad sweep of the earlier long poems is replaced by a more fragmented universe and the more intense internalization of voice of the highly "digital" *Snow*

Poems: the work is (based on internal evidence and chronology) a long poem, but broken up into pieces; the titles are not analogues of the "content" of the pieces, but simply read-outs taken from the first lines (which, in a long poem, are not first lines). The voice is a bit more irascible and the verse more recalcitrant toward wholeness, including in its conglomeration "outriders," marginal glosses and counters, and games both typographical and lexical. The material at hand of **"Summer Place"** becomes here the material conditions of the poet's environment—elm tree, typewriter, dictionary, paper.

At the end of *Sphere* and in **"Summer Place"** Ammons becomes more overtly concerned with the social and the political; but the essentially liberal polemics here are not, I would argue, the source of Ammons's true political force. Part of Ammons's project has been to dislodge poetry from its closed and rarefied space, to situate it in what he would call a larger "network" of relations, most of them not particularly "aesthetic." If we look at Ammons's writing as a cultural and therefore social act— as his extraliterary and political content begs us to—then what we see is a rewriting of the idea of poetry and of the role of literary culture. To emphasize the making and not the made, the mechanism and not the substance, is to engage a poetics of the centrifugal, to consciously resituate poetry—and, by extension, culture—in a network of relations both biological and social. If, as Lentricchia has suggested in his reading of Burke, "To make metaphor is to violate in one act the status quo of discourse and of society," then we can see how Ammons is attempting to restore and reassert the power of poetry to be something more than "superior amusement," more than the various but marginal repetition of the Beautiful in all its highly allusive forms. I say "restore" because in the above sense poetry is always radical, always a subversion of the language of the marketplace—even, as Burke has argued, antinomian: "Art's very accumulation (its discordant voices arising out of many systems) serves to undermine any one rigid scheme of living—and herein lies 'wickedness' enough."

Ammons would seek to undermine those habits and institutions that compromise our lived awareness of the "saliences," of "massive suasions." Here again we need Burke to complicate what might seem like an easy holism, a "natural fact": "Any reduction of *social* motives to terms of sheer 'nature' would now seem to me a major error. Naturalism has served as deceptively in the modern world as supernaturalism ever did in the past, to misrepresent motives that are intrinsic to the social order." What Burke is getting at but does not say is that "nature" masks ideology; indeed, if (as Ammons realizes) we encounter a nature that is always already abstract, how could it be otherwise? Ammons often says, with little or no ironic cover (but with perhaps more than a dash of sentimentality), that his later long poems are "ideal organizations":

> not homogeneous pudding but
>
> united differences, surface differences expressing
> the common,
> underlying hope and fate of each person and
> people, a gathering
> into one place of multiple dissimilarity

More important than the vision of genuine community here is the *writing* of it—through a poetics that goes beyond the romantics and thus speaks with special timeliness—into a radically decentered poetics not of Being but of beings, of a heterocosm "local and mortal." Truth then becomes not a metaphysical but a pragmatic matter: what, in the manner of the late William James, it is better for us to believe.

We could do worse than to read Ammons as something of a contemporary pragmatist, and in doing so helping to sharpen the contrast between the ideology of Ammons's work and the Emersonianism that Carlyle so much admired. We are, as Ammons reminds us in his earthbound variation of Emerson, "unmendably integral," and implied here is an imperative for conduct, but not only for the poem (as ideal organization) or the poet (as Emersonian representative man). Ammons's work is often the poetry of constraints and balances, of the local and mortal context; he rails against wastefulness in **"Extremes and Moderations,"** and in *Sphere* would ground the work of mind in the specificity of its objects:

> one terror mind brings on
> itself is that anything can be made of anything
> . . . .
>
> . . . scary to those who need prisons,
> liberating to those already in

Ammons reminds us again and again (and often in oblique reference to the romantic symbol) that "all identities and effects are / imbalances." Keeping in mind Ammons's linkage of poetics and ideology, then, we can read in the following passage on the symbolic a dark parable indeed:

> when an image or
> item is raised into class representative of cluster,
> clump,
>
> or set, its boundaries are overinvested, the
> supercharge is
> explosive, so that the burden of energy over-
> whelms the matter,

> and aura, glow, or spirituality results, a kind of
> pitchblende,
>
> radium, sun-like: and when the item is moved
> beyond class
> into symbol or paradigmatic item, matter is a mere
> seed
> afloat in radiance

The source of the sublime in Ammons is the confrontation between the knowledge that "the mind will forever work in this way" and the understanding that the larger network of which it is a part cannot, finally, be subjected to such "overinvestment." The effect of what I have called Ammons's metonymic symbolism is to go beyond representation, beyond the romantic symbolic; as Ammons puts it: "When we have made the sufficient mirror will / / it have been only to show how things will break." Ammons's ideal *organization* seeks to unseat the idea of poetry as the polishing of such a mirror, to show us how we might go about things with a full awareness of the local and mortal context, how we might socially be otherwise by coming to terms with the physical, biological network of necessity that can't be otherwise. This is the social message of Ammons, of the poetics not of partaking but of making: "when may it not be our / task so to come into the knowledge of the reality as to / participate therein."

Elizabeth McGeachy Mills (essay date Spring 1991)

SOURCE: "Ammons's 'Singing & Doubling Together,'" in *The Explicator*, Vol. 49, No. 3, Spring, 1991, pp. 187-90.

[*In the following essay, McGeachy Mills asserts that "In its every complexity" Ammons's 'Singing & Doubling Together,' "signals the mysterious, paradoxical, somehow linearly unknowable experience of doubling with the divine."*]

A. R. Ammons's poem **"Singing & Doubling Together"** demonstrates the power of carefully chosen signs to create and to recreate, while exposing through the medium of the poem a complex, nonrational experience of union.

Speaking in the first person, in the present tense, from within the event itself, the speaker describes a real experience—not hearsay, but sound personally heard. That sound joins the *I* to a *you* who is an equal subject in the poem and in the experience, but a superior power. Nowhere in the poem does the identity of either the speaker or the one addressed become more specific than the personal pronouns, which themselves stress the intimate contact between the two. Activities such as cutting the grass and picking up branches depict the *I* as human (line 20). The *you* is not doctrinally distinct—bearing no identity as specific as God the Father or the Taoist Way—but it is clearly divine, a mysterious spiritual power (perhaps the energizing life force) that is "as if nothing," or no thing. Although shapeless, it can take "on . . . shape"; though timeless, it can take on time. Initially, because the sound crosses a barrier from "there" to "here," the *you* controls it, sending it "in" the speaker from some "great high otherness," so that the speaker says, "you have means . . . I / can never follow." Through the "event" of the poem itself, however, the speaker utters his own sound, duplicating the power of the divine in his own song. From the simple interweaving ampersand in the poem's title through the intricately bound seven claims of the poem's one long sentence, the poet artfully employs specific devices as means to break out of his inarticulate human bondage into his own "leafspeech."

The argument of the poem emerges from one sentence with seven claims. Distinct punctuation (five colons and one dash) signals each part. As is true at every level of the poem, what appears simple becomes increasingly complex. The first line of the poem makes a straightforward declaration, which the rest of the poem expands through transformations of the basic assertion. The balanced parallelism of "My nature singing in me is your nature singing," the *I* linked to, and defined by, the *you* through the copula, gains complexity in the second claim, which explains the separating distance and dominance of the *you*. The *you*'s active force is reiterated and praised further in the third claim, but here the speaker joins in the communion. Claim four boldly presents the speaker as active: "I catch the impact and turn / it back," although the activity comes in response to the *you*'s motion. Moving from further description of the speaker's action, claim five, however, explores the shocking possibility that the *you* can "fail," not through motion but through nonmotion: "The still / of your great high otherness." Then the failures of claim five become the risky, incarnational pains of claim six, resulting in the explosive exclamation and question of grace in claim seven. That Ammons's song praising this complex, transforming unity develops from seven claims is surely no accident, for seven remains the traditional numerical symbol for the unity of heaven and earth.

The visual structure of the poem presents six stanzas of six lines each, giving the physical appearance of perfect balance. Just as the seven claims lie embedded in the one large assertion, suggesting the complexity of the whole, so the balance of the six stanzas contains variation in line length clearly representing each and "every motion" that the poem describes. A small graphic clue, the double space after the colon preceding "you are there beyond," emphasizes the gulf between the *you* and the *I*. A more obvious sign is the shortest line in the poem, the three-syllable "what but grace," a visually distinct line that depicts the breathtaking, yet ambivalent, question/exclamation of the poet's experience of

union. Although coming at the end of stanza five, it syntactically belongs to stanza six, thus linking the "pain," "tears," "loss" to the consolation of complete union.

Diction also signals the poem's complex experience. In the opening line, "nature" conjures multiple concepts: of essence, of reality, of character, of elemental and primitive forces and processes, of the physical world, and of the human personality, to name a few. The single word carries multiple meanings, which can combine in different ways. For instance, the paraphrase "My human personality singing in me is your physical universe singing" forms an insufficient gloss of the line, for it reduces the line's semantic power. A more complete rendering of the poet's meaning seems to be: "My essential/real/defining/uncivilized/physical/ spiritual nature singing in me is your essential/real/defining/uncivilized/physical/ spiritual nature singing"; the indeterminancy characteristic of homonymy allows the noun to shimmer with semantic options. Only as the poem develops does the essential difference in natures, one finite and human, the other infinite and divine, become clear. And that difference is itself called into question by the existence of the poem. Other words, such as "tracings" (meaning both "paths" and "outlines of shapes") and "still" (the adjective, meaning "the absence of sound or motion," and the adverb suggesting duration of time), provide further semantic doubleness.

Indexical signs such as the deictic words of relationship, "I" and "you," also signal doubleness; even as the pronouns suggest intimacy, they also stress difference since *I* is other than *you*. The deictic words of space—"in," "into," "back," "there," "away," "where," "here," "near," "up," "under," "somewhere," "hence," "nowhere"—reinforce the contrast of place between the speaker and the one addressed. Yet the multiplicity of that swooping motion or threatening stasis suggests that the *you* is both "everywhere" and, as the poet says, "in me."

Word repetition—sometimes exact, sometimes with slight variation—likewise signals the complex, often paradoxical, tension that the event arouses. "Nature," whose multiple meanings are evident, occurs in the poem six times in the singular and once in the plural. Such duplication, as well as the "I catch" repeated in stanzas three and four, the "creak" that becomes "creaking," the "snap," "snapping," and the "settles," "settled," intertwine the poem's separate parts. Repetition of identical words also stresses the speaker's difficulty in articulating the event. The abstraction "things" is repeated three times within two lines, emphasizing the helplessness of "things" (the material) in the face of the power of the "nothing" (no thing, not thing, the immaterial or spiritual). "Fail" appears four times in stanzas four and five, where repetition becomes most intense as the speaker confronts the mystifying paradox of incarnation, victorious life emerging from death's defeat. The most amazing repetition, however, is of *my/me/I* and *your/you/you* words. Eighteen of each group occur in this poem—a definite paralleling of words relating to the theme of the poem.

Although the most frequently used verb form in the poem is the present participle, appearing eighteen times and stressing continuing action, the poem ends with a projection from present time and present union toward a promise of future union. Death will not be the end of the speaker, who will be transformed, losing individual identity and gaining cosmic power at the same time, "changed into your singing nature when I need sing my nature nevermore." The progression is mysterious, from sound to divine silence, followed by human cries, then divine cries ending in transformation, the final syntax forming a chiasmus with the original assertion—my nature/your nature now becomes your nature/ my nature.

But what is the final nature of the union? Is the "nature" described here physical nature, from dust to dust? Will the poet only become part of the earth and so devolve into personal silence? Or is that "singing nature" spiritual? Will the poet finally become literally one with the word? The answer, enforced by the devices of the poem, remains ambiguous. In its every complexity the poem signals the mysterious, paradoxical, somehow linearly unknowable experience of doubling with the divine. It stands as evidence of the precarious moment the poet praises.

David R. Jarraway (essay date Winter 1993)

SOURCE: "Ammons Beside Himself: Poetics of 'The Bleak Periphery,'" in *Arizona Quarterly,* Vol. 49, No. 4, Winter, 1993, pp. 99-116.

[*In the following essay, Jarraway discusses Ammons's "Essay on Poetics" in relation to American literature.*]

In the context of American literature, the presentiment of the writer-as-critic or the critic-as-writer is likely to be inherently a more available one than in other literatures. This is due in no small part to the fact that American literature, as Kenneth Dauber pointed out several years ago, "is a literature whose primary concern has always been its own nature," and whose object, even in the classic period of American letters, "[is] its own process," the "act of writing" in other words, "into which all forms of the written are returned." American literature, therefore, will repeatedly sensitize us to a historical moment in the writing of its poetry in which the traditional "apology" conventionally located *outside* the artifact—one thinks, for instance, of the classic statements of poets such as Sidney, Shelley, and Wilde—will be gathered up *inside* the American poem, allowing the text itself

to become its own medium of authorization and legitimation. From the auto-affection of "Song of Myself," through to "Self-Portrait in a Convex Mirror," the romance in American poetry for self-reflexivity is given without apology—at least, without any kind of formal apology. Writing continually turning back upon itself in such a manner thus elides any clear separation between introspection and retrospection in the poet's art. "The Philosophy of Composition" then, as "Composition as Explanation" now, both seem somewhat beside the point when it is actually the practice that constitutes the theory (and the theory constituting the practice) that forms the basis of America's long-standing romance with text. In this regard, Gerald Graff has therefore been quite correct to surmise that "It has taken little time for earlier theories of Americanness of American literature to be written in the deconstructionist register . . . [since] Americanness lay not in the romance of the symbol or the frontier but in reflexive awareness of the problematic of writing itself, which is to say, in the romance of self-deconstruction and of heterogeneity." In keeping with "the 'secret' autobiographical agenda of [American] writing," A. R. Ammons thus contends that a poem, once it is thoroughly known, "contains / its [own] motion," and that this *modus operandi* can be reproduced completely whole to the mind—"all its shapeliness intact"—as the mind travels in and around it. He says this in a longer poem called, characteristically, **"Essay on Poetics,"** the significance of whose title I must return to later. Using this poem primarily, I would here like to explore Ammons' own re-versal of the classic defense in the self-reflexive scene of modern American poetry, and specifically, to investigate further both the possible and what I consider to be the *impossible* wager his textuality dares to encumber in so dividing, on both theoretical and/or practical levels, the discourse against itself.

The self-defensiveness of American letters as a whole, in view both of the absence of a historically stabilizing tradition within and the presence of a politically intimidating authority without, is by now a commonplace among the master-narratives attending to the sanctioning of American literature's own Declaration of Independence (for example, Weisbuch, Fredman). In the literature's repudiation of *arché* and deregulation of *telos,* one becomes rather easily persuaded to the view that writing is grounded in no metaphysical principle outside writing itself, indeed, that "we descend into the void that the loss of metaphysical grounds for words has opened up." At an early point in his **"Essay on Poetics,"** this appears to be a view to which Ammons is somewhat partial, a view of writing he labels "enterprise":

> enterprise is our American motif, riding horseback
>> between
> the obscure beginning and the unformulated
> conclusion,
>> thinking

grace that show of riding, the expertise, performance,
   the intricacy
of dealing: to be about something . . .

enterprise then's the American salience, rainbow
arch
colossus: but the aristoi are beauty, wealth, birth,
   genius &
virtue who should be governors: enterprise
somewhat,
   though
not necessarily, inconsistent with those, we lack
   governors:

With the disavowal of beginnings and endings, the emphasis of these lines lands firmly on the movement of the writing itself: riding, thinking, dealing, etc. Moreover, this is a
movement that, on the most basic level of the text, converges
into that "main confluence" of what Ammons calls his
"one:many" mechanism, and as an earnest of self-reflexion,
demonstrates what "all this essay is *about*" (emphasis
added). And just as many lines turn back on one movement
and many motions turn back on or are *contained* by one
mechanism—"whatever turns turns—in [on?] itself"—so, on
another level, many poems turn back onto one grand poem.
In the punning "lyric in[-]formation" that begins the essay,
therefore, the curvature of each turns back on the curvature
of all:

   . . . everything beefing up
   and verging out

   for that point in the periphery where
   salience bends into curve
   and all saliences bend to the same angle of

   curve and curve becomes curve, one curve, the
   whole
      curve:
   that is information actual
   at every point

   but taking on itself at every point
   the emanation of curvature, of meaning, all
   the way into the high
   recognition of wholeness, that synthesis,
   feeling, aroused, controlled, and released:

If the "high / recognition of wholeness" in this passage
clinches a gradually accretive and autotelic structuralism that
we tend to associate with High Modernism, it's surely no
accident. For in such a structure, where all objects turn back
upon and in a sense re-present their subjects, we are given
a system of signification which, in Mark Taylor's words,

"perfectly mirrors the structure of the modern subject that
begins with Descartes and comes to completion in Hegel's
speculative or specular System." Ending the recognition of
wholeness in the above passage by remarking upon "that synthesis" as it does, Ammons' modernist narrative here merely
serves to underscore how both "sign and subject are thoroughly reflexive," and so resemble the self-coinciding
artefact that produces nothing other than itself." "I've often
said," Ammons states in another place, "that a poem in becoming generates the laws of its / own becoming." With this
assertion, we finally begin to see how the aesthetic trajectory of the American poem is made even more intensely to
coincide with the historical and political trajectory that I alluded to previously in remarking upon a certain self-defensiveness in American poetry with respect to the whole notion
of authority—a defensiveness that can appear iconoclastic
equally from a Puritan as from a Modern (or Postmodern)
point of view. For in generating the laws of its own becoming, Ammons' discourse generates for itself as well an image of self-referentiality "without practical rhyme or reason
. . . [and] is at once eloquent testimony to the obscure origins and enigmatic nature of value in a society which would
seem everywhere to deny it, and an alternative to this sorry
condition." In the sheer pointlessness of its "enterprise,"
then, Ammons can joke that his American text "must be ever
in search of the rapier that / holds the world on guard!" In
the same gesture, however, it's impossible for Ammons to
escape sounding somewhat reactionary, if not paranoid—
"schizophrenic," as Deleuze and Guattari would perhaps say,
and as my title in part suggests. For, as Deleuze and Guattari
ask, "Isn't the destiny of American literature that of crossing limits and frontiers, causing deterritorialized flows of
desire to circulate, but also always making these flows trans-
port fascisizing, moralizing, Puritan, and familialist territo-
rialities?"

If whatever circulates, turns in (or on) itself in American
poetry's most self-reflective moments, Ammons' poetics
would argue that there ought really to be "no reason for confusion: that is / what this [essay] is about," after all. Yet a
discourse layering practice over theory and theory over practice in precisely the etymological sense suggested by the
word con-fusion is, in fact, the very thing this essay *is* about,
and this "thing" perhaps cannot slip by without the need for
some further questioning. Confusion, then, like the very self-
reflexivity it betokens, is simple and impossibly difficult, by
turns: "simple by grandeur, impossible by what all must answer there." And so we are given a quite intractable sense
in which Ammons, somewhat more hesitantly now, admits
his text may be far more profoundly divided against itself
than we might at first have thought. For what the text at the
level of a high recognition of wholeness finds impossible to
answer there is *how* all that simplicity and all that grandeur
of curvature comes into being in the first place. Wholly outside the plane of recognitive wholeness and synthesis, there-

fore, lies Ammons' quite different conception of reality. This is a reality that we're likely to find unbelievable (to recur to the poem's opening once again), "because it permits / another wholeness, / another lyric, the same in structure, / in mechanism of existence, but bearing a *different weight*" (emphasis added). What could this reality be?

For one thing, it appears to mark a level of discourse entirely resistant to any kind of unitive synthesis, the kind that eventuates, for example, when language is made to take hold of reality in an empirical, objective, or eidetic sense, as a parley to reflexive order. Reality "captured" in such a restrictively correspondent sense is entirely analogous to the educations of "arborescent" discourse described by Deleuze and Guattari, a hierarchical system of communication whose "corresponding models" (the imprint, engram, tracing, photograph, etc.) "still cling to the oldest modes of thought in that they grant all power to a memory or central organ." By contrast, as "an acentered nonhierarchical, nonsignifying system without a General and without an organizing memory or central automation" (the fascicle, map, *intermezzo,* etc.), "rhizomatic" discourse seeks to establish an *experimental* contact "with the real." Rather than an invocation of language, then, Reality, in this quite improvisational mode of discourse, is more like its provocation, and in Ammons' text, seems somewhat akin to Nietzsche's Chaos, Heidegger's Being, or Althusser's History—a radical multiplicity or Otherness that (simply) cannot be rationalized:

> . . . all I mean to suggest is that the reality under
>
> words (and images) is too multiple for rational
> assessment and
> that language moves by sailing over: the
> other way definition has is to accept the multiplic-
> ity
>
> of synthesis: of course, synthesis is at work in
> certain levels of
> analysis, but I mean by synthesis the primary
> intent: look
> at it this way: I am experiencing at the moment
> several
> clusters of entanglement:

In an even more revealing passage, we find the former rapier-like wit of the well-wrought poem's conception in the image of unenlightened "blades of reason" sinking and melting through the quite *other* motion of "reality's cold murky waters." Here, the verbal symbol operating on behalf of reason tries to control reality's "level of abstraction" by suppressing it, imagining that a symbolical salience of meaning—a "sheet of ice" in Ammons' very telling image—can perhaps be the last (and lasting) word on the matter. In thus heightening language "by dismissing reality" in this way,

the symbol only serves to violate reality, reducing it to what Ammons calls an "artificial clarity." The point is made even more emphatically in Ammons' **"Hibernaculum"**:

> . . . the poet, baited by illusion, figures
>
> that massive tangling will give locus to core-
> tangles
> and core-tangles to *the* core-tangle that will
> fix reality in staid complication, at that central
>
> core's center the primordial egg of truth: ah, what
> an
> illusion . . .

The fact of the matter, however, is that reality cannot be fixed, a point which Wallace Stevens only came to discover quite late in his own Modernist project. In more rigorously postmodern terms, Deleuze and Guattari view reality's construction through metaphor—the radical of all symbolization—as equally problematic: "There is no 'like' here. . . . The plane of consistency is the abolition of all metaphor; all that consists is Real . . . veritable black holes, actual organites, authentic sign sequences. It's just that they have been uprooted from their strata, destratified, decoded, deterritorialized, and that is what makes their proximity and interpenetration in the plane of consistency possible." Consequently, though language may be formed and sustained by reality, the symbol can only operate at an "impositional remove" from reality—a "nothing," as Ammons goes on to expand the notion in **"Hibernaculum,"** "an infinitesimal dot of void at the center of / the primordial egg" just described, a veritable black hole if you like. Like Paul de Man on the subject of "The Task of the Translator," then, Ammons fully owns up here to "the inadequacy of any symbol in relation to what it means." Paul de Man, of course, arrives at this conclusion after working many years on the symbol in the context of Romanticism. Using the word "image" rather than "symbol" (or "metaphor"), Rodolphe Gasché makes a similar point in this context, but he also hooks it up with the conventional reflexivity of language developed previously: "if [a word like 'hymen'] re-marks its textuality, it is not because it would be a totalizing emblem which, like the romantic image, would assume the eschatological function of subduing a text to having its meaning in reflecting itself." Once below this textual repression, however, it is precisely Ammons' point that "the symbol carries exactly the syrup of many distillations"—"hard endurance," it is true, but also "soft inquiry and turning."

The other thing about Reality that intensifies the division of Ammons' text at a deeper—perhaps more distilled—level than transparent self-coincidence is a certain opacity which the text sets up to frustrate every avenue to univocal meaning or singular truth. This is particularly evident when the

"Essay on Poetics" endeavors "to turn the essential image of a tree into the truest / rational wordage," "tree" into its etymology, in ME. *treue* and AS. *trewe* and G. *treu,* hoping at some point to end with Truth, and at last, "'conformity / with the facts.'" But like the highly perspectival character of Nietzsche's Fact or the inexhaustible nature of Heidegger's Thing, Ammons' Tree proves to be equally multiple and incorrigibly dense. Constantly influenced and influencing, it hardens and enters the ground at some "fairly reliable point" that does promise a degree of "general unalterability," but only to veer off at some other point, in "an outward, expanding / reticulation / too much to deal precisely with." The point of rupture here that makes all the difference, in Deleuze and Guattari's surprisingly similar terms, between a tree in its reductively transcendent or "arborescent" aspect, and its productively immanent or "rhizomatic" aspect is, in the more historically resonant terms alluded to earlier, a point of demarcation that separates American literature from all others:

> . . . [America] is not immune from domination by trees or the search for roots. This is evident [ ] in the literature, in the quest for a national identity and even for a European ancestry or genealogy (Kerouac going off in search of his ancestors). Nevertheless, everything important that has happened or is happening takes the route of the American rhizome: the beatniks, the underground, bands and gangs, successive lateral offshoots in immediate connection with an outside. American books are different from European books, even when the American sets off in pursuit of trees. The conception of the book is different. *Leaves of Grass* . . . there is the rhizomatic West, with its Indians without ancestry, its ever-receding limit, its shifting and displaced frontiers. There is a whole American "map" in the West, where even the trees form rhizomes.

What complicates this whole matter of mapping, of course, is language itself, and according to Ammons, its withholding of any "core center of the planet" from which to gauge the tree's true material being. And even if such a core could be settled upon, it would very soon betray the kind of "slow—perhaps universal—slosh" that before long gives every fixed point and every core position over to an entirely new set of references. This is rather like the hapless position of Borges' "Funes, the Memorius," in his confrontation with every last detail of a similar tree, and a thousand others besides. But if Funes is unaware that to think—to abstract and generalize—is to forget a difference, at least *that* lesson has not been lost on the writer of the present essay, whose own "wide application of averaging" seems the only way round a "massive pile-up of information" otherwise "recalcitrant to higher assimilations." I don't think Ammons means to imply here that the opacity of experience that greets us on this second level of his text necessarily strengthens and thereby privileges all that we secure for ourselves in the way of unity and wholeness found on the first. If the poem is making sense at all, there is a certain application of averaging operative at *both* levels. But what I do think we sense when the essay becomes more deeply divided on this second level is how it is enabled more completely to account for itself when the discourse seeks to become open to that which is other than itself. "Read a few lines along the periphery of any of the truly / great," Ammons instructs us, "and the knowledge delineates an open shore," and the experience of a "landless, orientationless" beyond. But to obtain experience in such a prospect—reductions, identities, suasions—is perhaps to know it for the first time in all of its "difficult absoluteness." "Philosophy," it has been said, "has its reasons for wanting to know beyond, across, and between what it itself is and what it is not . . . for being itself as well as being *other* than what it is." Yet can anything *less* be said about a literary text that problematizes its own identity to an equal degree?

From all of this, I think it might now be possible for us to see that the point in the self-reflexive scene of American poetry at which the same is divided against (or by) its other, that one is divided by many, and identity by difference is precisely the point at which Modernism gives place to Postmodernism, the point, that is to say, at which writing exceeds the symmetrical bifurcation between theory and practice and discovers in theory itself—Against Theory, if you will—a genuine source for its own production and power. In saying this, I entirely concur with Gerald Graff's recent suggestion that theory "is what is generated when some aspect of literature"—its conditions of production, in this case—"ceases to be given and becomes a question to be argued in a generalized way." In this way, the concern for the "poetics" of a text will yield a "description of the way in which a work means" that a concern for "hermeneutics" or the meaning itself of a work never can. In electing, therefore, to title his own work, **"Essay in Poetics,"** Ammons in the same way aims to foreground the productive syntactics of textuality rather than a reductive semantics—the how rather than the what—underscoring, in an important place near the end of the poem, that he is "more certain that [he is] about than what [he is] about." As with the co-dependent relation between Modernism and Postmodernism, of course, neither syntax nor meaning is completely separable from the other, the very "meaning-producing function" of all discourse residing in "the fundamental oneness of language." And it is this oneness, too, which is fundamental to Ammons' own "one: many" mechanism, no longer a shorthand for pluralism in the restricted and equilibrated economy of reflexion. "Bearing a different weight" now, to repeat the earlier citation, this one: many mechanism becomes something very much akin to "the primordial structure of repetition" in the more general economy of his text, manifest both from within *and* from the outside:

> that is, a different, perhaps contradicting,
> bit-nature and assimilation:
>
> wholeness then is a condition of existence,
> a one: many mechanism, internally irrelevant to
> scope,
> but from the outside circumscribed into scope:

As a gloss on the one: many mechanism here, particularly in relation to "the outside" in the final line, it may be instructive to recall the discursive "war machine's relation to an outside" in Deleuze and Guattari once again, a relation which is "not another 'model'" by which to represent or reproduce or replicate the world. As in the case with reality previously, "we think that one cannot write sufficiently in the name of an outside [for] the outside has no image, no signification, no subjectivity . . . with which to assemble in heterogeneity." In terms of this formulation for Ammons' one: many machine, then, we're now invited to view "the high levels of oneness" as relays of force, "examples of integration" that set limits against which a text's "energy flows with maximum / effect and economy," generating "numerous subordinations and divisions of diversity" for itself. The control of the flow and organization of the energy is signal here; Ammons says he cannot stress that enough. "If I am to celebrate multiplicity / unity, and such," he declares, "I'll be obliged to free myself by accepting certain limitations . . . [for] it seems to me / a possibility of unceasing magnitude that [only] these structures / permit these eventualities." Seen from the other side, as in **"Extremes and Moderations,"** limitation forms an extreme the "strictures and disciplines of which prevent loose-flowing phantasmagoria," and when broadly and densely exploited, empowers "the outbreak of dialectical alternatives." Derrida stresses the same point, time after time, in his own work:

> The adventurous excess of a writing that is no longer directed by any knowledge does not abandon itself to improvisation. The accident or throw of dice that "opens" such a text does not contradict the rigorous necessity of its formal assemblage. The game here is the unity of chance and rule, of the program and its leftovers or extras.

The "unity of chance and rule" states precisely the "oneness" that divides both Ammons and his text, and indeed Postmodernism more generally, against themselves, for it is "out / of that bind"—perhaps we should say, double-bind— as he says, "I proceed a little way into similarity and / withdraw a bit into differentiae." "In short," Deleuze and Guattari affirm, "there is no deterritorialization of the flows of schizophrenic desire that is not accompanied by global or local reterritorializations, reterritorializations that always reconstitute shores of representation." Hence, in Ammons, "one recognizes an ocean even from a dune." But Ammons' one: many mechanism can take off in the completely opposite direction, and through the deterritorialization of the previous "shores of representation," discover a repetitive means—"say ocean over / and over"—by which, in a passage already cited, to "delineate[ ] an open shore."

The most surprising thing about Ammons' essay, the thing that perhaps puts it most beside itself, comes with the revelation that, by the end, its theory really cannot be saying anything radically mind-altering or subversively earth-shattering at all. Those who detect in certain lines of Ammons' thought as I have outlined them yet another weary diatribe in the deconstructive mode, rife, once again, for institutional appropriation—or "routinization" or "domestication" or "neutralization"—at least have one thing right. There can be no mistaking the very conservative direction from which Ammons' theory comes. His is not a brief against lyricism or confessionalism or formalism or traditionalism or anything else. A delimitation of the self-reflexive gestures in American poetry is not an attack on those limits, but if anything, an *intensification* of them. To decipher, we proceed by way of the cipher, and to deconstruct, we honor not the destructiveness of human endeavor, but rather its opposite. "I am not so much / arguing with the organic school," he tells us at the conclusion, "as shifting true organismus from / the already organized to the bleak periphery of possibility." Along that "periphery of integrations"—the integration of chance and rule, again—there may be what he describes as "an exposure / to demons, thralls, witcheries, [a] maelstrom black / of possibility . . . an area transcendental only by its bottomless entropy." But that is a blackness, a bottomlessness, a bleakness seen only from "that point in the periphery where / salience bends [back] into curve" once again, the curve of sameness from which we began. It rings a kind of *cordon sanitaire* around all those who will not know, nor indeed would ever care to know, the possibility of something other. Yet what if what happens at the periphery presents us with the possibility of adding to our store of knowledge rather than merely recycling or recircling what we may already possess? In other words, "you start by delimiting a first line consisting of circles of convergence around successive singularities." But then, picking up on the gesture of intensification just noted, "you see whether inside that line new circles of convergence establish themselves, with new points located *outside* the limits and in other directions." As Ammons envisions the process, the curvature of sameness suddenly begins to take on the appearance of an effect constituted from a point at the furthest remove from sameness, that is to say, from a point of unlikeness or difference as *the* centrifugally fecundating category. And the burgeoning "strings of nucleations" engendered from this newly focused sense of otherness that eventually opens us up to greater knowledge and to greater insight—do these new lines of flight not please us so much more than merely "representative details" only because, at that same point on the periphery, but from where, this time, "the mind is brought to silence, the / non-verbal, and the still" from an *other* or *outside*—do these nucleations of mind not please us more because for the first time we are actually able "to see how [the mind's] motion goes?"

> . . . split its green periphery and divide: John's
> old tractor on the lawn only shows its steering
> wheel:
>   the
> snowplow's been by and blocked the driveway:
> it's
>   December 26:
> yesterday was Christmas: I got a pair of wat-
>   er-resistant gloves
> with a removable woolen lining: I got Phyllis three
>   charms for
>
> the bracelet I bought her in Rome: John got a
> snowsled,
>   a beautiful
> wooden train set, Lincoln logs, toggles, and
> several
>   things
> operated by non-included batteries: this morning
> he has
>   no fever:

In the "irreducible errancy of [the] parapraxis" here, in Mark Taylor's phrase—which can risk moving beyond the periphery only by moving through it—we approach generative and accumulative reaches of the expanding mind so insubstantial and inscrutable, so filled with the pure heat of "potentiality" and "undisclosed possibility," that we're given to stand in terror and amazement. And undoubtedly it's at that moment that we fall back into our more established and secure patterns of disciplinary discourse, rather pendantically attempting to talk a poem down through a study of its sources, its history, its influences, and other less "peripheral," though perhaps more widely footnoted and more amply rewarded ways.

This is not to imply, in a final word, that a Postmodern poetics of the "bleak periphery" is to be located at a diametrical remove from the study of history and culture and society, as some are likely to charge. If in bearing down on the force of articulation, "procedure's the only procedure," as we are given in conclusion to **"Hibernaculum,"** then one wants to have at one's disposal as many procedures as one can in order to circumscribe its motion and contextualize its operation, a kind of "pragrammatology," as Derrida would say, that would aim to take the whole sociohistorical situation of

the marking (and re-marking) into account. This also means, of course, that the "poetics" of force is not restricted merely to literary discourse, although to many, that would seem a fairly likely place within which to begin charting its motions. Once underway, however, the opportunities for expanding and exceeding the periphery, like the expanding energies of discursive expression itself, seem boundless:

> . . . I am seeking the
> mechanisms physical, physiological, epistemologi-
> cal,
>   electrical
>
> chemical, esthetic, social, religious by which
> many,
>   kept
> discrete as many, expresses itself into the
> manageable rafters of salience, lofts to compre-
> hension,
> breaks
>
> out in hard, highly informed suasions, the "gather-
> ing
> in the sky" so to speak

Once Ammons' poetics takes this final turn against its own containment within a purely Modernist literary self-reflexion, the only absolute limit it dares impose upon itself is "patience": the patience to understand how oneness cannot be useful "when easily derived," and to understand how manyness cannot be truthful when "thinly selective." Hence, Ammons' well-known ending to **"Corsons Inlet":**

> I see narrow orders, limited tightness, but will
> not run to that easy victory:
>   still around the looser, wider forces work:
>   I will try
> to fasten into order enlarging grasps of disorder,
> widening
> scope, but enjoying the freedom that
> Scope eludes my grasp, that there is no finality of
>   vision,
> that I have perceived nothing completely,
>   that tomorrow a new walk is a new walk.

If Ammons' bleak poetics risks leaving us with a theory of American literature that can't add up to some kind of high (re)cognition anymore, the ultimate reflection of some kind of metaphysical Being or Presence, perhaps it's because, like Neitzsche's well-known Becoming that can only be explained without recourse to final intentions, Ammons finds so much more to interest him at every moment. That is to say, his is a model of textuality "that is perpetually prolonging itself, breaking off and starting up again" simply because it is in the very character of American literature to "do away with foundations, nullify endings and beginnings . . . [in] a transversal movement that sweeps one *and* the other away . . . and picks up speed in the middle." The image of the periphery, in sum, seems an appropriate one with which to foreground this sense of a poetics processually "in the middle," that is to say, perpetually machining its way as a movement *in-between.* As readers and writers of contemporary American discourse, in a final citation from the *Anti-Oedipus,* "We no longer believe in a primordial totality that once existed, or in a final totality that awaits us at some future date. . . . We believe only in totalities that are *peripheral.* And if we discover such a totality alongside various separate parts, it is a whole *of* these particular parts but does not totalize them; it is a unity *of* all these particular parts but does not unify them; rather, it is added to them as a new part fabricated separately" (initial emphasis added). "Scope eludes my grasp," as Ammons has stated: "tomorrow a new walk is a new walk." And if *that* means nothing—"the greatest hazard of all is alien water," we learn in a final anecdote from **"Essay on Poetics"**—it could very well be that to risk meaning nothing, at last, is to begin to play. When one gets lost for fun, as Ammons' **"Essay"** wryly claims, "there's no chance of getting lost."

Pedro E. Ponce (review date 1 December 1993)

SOURCE: "A Poet's Long Path to Literary Honors," in *The Chronicle of Higher Education,* Vol. XL, No. 15, December 1, 1993, p. A6.

[*In the following review, Ponce discusses* Garbage, *stating that "As in his earlier poems, he uses an object as a springboard into thoughts of a universal significance."*]

Writers usually prefer not to have their work labeled as garbage, but the poet and Cornell professor A. R. Ammons has found phenomenal success with the label.

Garbage, his latest book, won Mr. Ammons his second National Book Award for Poetry two weeks ago. It is a single, 121-page poem inspired by a heap of garbage that Mr. Ammons saw in Florida.

For the author of 21 books, Mr. Ammons is reticent about his work. "It's just what I do," he says.

His colleagues are more forthright. David Bonanno, an editor at *The American Poetry Review,* says *Garbage* is "a major poem by a major poet."

Roald Hoffman, a Cornell chemistry professor who has published two books of poetry, calls Mr. Ammons "an inspiration." Over the last 10 years, Mr. Hoffmann has participated in an informal poetry-reading group with Mr. Ammons. "He's more than a fellow poet," says Mr. Hoffman, a winner of the 1981 Nobel Prize in chemistry. "He's sort of my guru."

Although Mr. Ammons says that poetry was his "governing energy from the age of 18," his path to publication was a long one. Born in Whiteville, N.C., in 1926, he attended Wake Forest University on the GI Bill after serving in the Navy during World War II.

He spent his first year out of college as the principal of an elementary school in Cape Hatteras, N.C. He moved to New Jersey and worked for 12 years as an executive for a biological-glassware factory.

In 1955 Mr. Ammons published his first book of poetry, **Ommateum, with Doxology.** Printed at his expense, the book, he says, sold 16 copies in five years.

In 1963, Mr. Ammons was asked to do a reading at Cornell University. He has been teaching poetry there ever since.

Nine years separated the publication of **Ommateum** and the appearance of his next book, **Expressions of Sea Level.** This was followed by **Corsons Inlet** in 1965.

In his early poems, the author wrestles with the conflict between the artist, who tries to structure the world, and the world itself, which defies structure. As expressed in the title piece of **Corsons Inlet,** "in nature there are few sharp lines." Mr. Ammons observes:

> I will try
> to fasten into order enlarging
> grasps of disorder, widening
> scope, but enjoying the freedom
>   that
> Scope eludes my grasp, that
>   there is no finality of vision,
> that I have perceived nothing
>   completely,
> that tomorrow a new walk
>   *is a new walk.*

Of Mr. Ammons's technique, Mr. Hoffmann says: "He makes us walk the hard edge of syntax. He uses language to make us read slower, to feel something in a way that no other poet does."

Since he began to publish steadily, Mr. Ammons has been no stranger to literary success. His work won the National Book Award for Poetry in 1973, the Bollingen Prize in Poetry in 1973-74, and the National Book Critics Circle Award for Poetry in 1981.

Garbage was conceived during a trip Mr. Ammons made to visit his mother-in-law in 1987. While driving on I-95, he saw a mountain of garbage at a landfill. He didn't stop, but the image stayed with him.

After an unsatisfactory first draft, he returned to the poem in earnest in 1989. He used a roll of adding machine tape to compose "because you don't have to stop to change the sheets of paper."

A heart attack later in the year and triple bypass surgery in 1990 forced him to set the poem aside again. The first five sections of the completed poem did not appear in print until 1992 in *The American Poetry Review,* but the positive response encouraged Mr. Ammons to submit it to his publisher.

Garbage comprises 18 sections that follow the poet's thoughts, both sacred and scatological, as he contemplates a pile of trash. As in his earlier poems, he uses an object as a springboard into thoughts of a universal significance:

> garbage has to be the poem of
> our time because
> garbage is spiritual, believable
> enough
>
> to get our attention, getting in
> the way, piling
> up, stinking, turning brooks
> brownish and
>
> creamy white: what else deflects
> us from the
> errors of our illusionary ways
> . . .

Of *Garbage,* Mr. Bonanno of *The American Poetry Review* says: "Part of what makes it a successful poem is that once he gets going, he can move so quickly from subject matter to subject matter and it's all of one piece." Mr. Bonanno likens the tone to the improvisational style of a jazz musician.

Mr. Ammons declines to discuss his future plans, except to say that he wants to retire from teaching after this academic year.

Despite his success, Mr. Ammons keeps a perspective on his work that is as uncompromising as his compressed and complicated use of language in poetry.

"The most important thing to me about poetry is writing the poem," he says. Reflecting on his long apprenticeship before publishing his poetry, he remarks, "Do you think the audience sustains you during that period? They're not even

there. I write poems whether anybody reads them or not. *I* read them."

Edward Hirsch (review date 12 December 1993)

SOURCE: "Trash and Other Wonders of Nature," in *The New York Times Book Review,* Vol. 98, December 12, 1993, p. 30.

[*In the following excerpt, Hirsch praises Ammons's* Garbage.]

Archie Randolph Ammons's book-length poem, **Garbage,** the winner of this year's National Book Award, has a rueful grandeur and characteristically splendid oddity. Following the abbreviated lyricism of the retrospective volume ***The Really Short Poems, Garbage*** is a single extended performance, a meditation, as the poet says, "assimilated into motion." Over the last 40 years Mr. Ammons has consistently demonstrated the democratic precept that "anything is poetry" and here he playfully takes up—takes on—the subject of trash. Thus a mountain of junk near the I-95 in Florida becomes the site of his moving and often comic speculations about natural processes:

> garbage has to be the poem of our time because
> garbage is spiritual, believable enough
>
> to get our attention, getting in the way, piling
> up, stinking, turning brooks brownish and
>
> creamy white: what else deflects us from the
> errors of our illusionary ways.

Like Wallace Stevens in "The Man on the Dump," Mr. Ammons is a philosophical poet whose abstruse flights—on the correspondences between the species, the commerce between the One and the Many, the mutability of experience—are brought back to earth by the bluntness of matter.

Garbage might well have been subtitled "Self-Portrait at 67" since it presents the poet in late middle age tallying things up, leaning forward or looking back even as he tries to dwell in the present, to stay available to the moment and make a clean sweep of the past.

"I can't believe / I'm merely an old person," he says near the beginning of the poem, "whose mother is dead, / whose father is gone and many of whose / friends and associates have wended away to the / ground." Yet he refuses to be encumbered by losses or memories, asserting "life is not first / for being remembered but for being lived!" The key to Mr.

Ammons's poetics, and possibly to his philosophy of life, is his scientific pragmatism, his determination to "study the motions" and then "take action," to "keep the mind / allied with the figurations of ongoing." His highest praise is reserved for the spiritual and material transformation of energy, an Emersonian commitment to "renewing change."

Garbage is written in a loose pentameter approximating speech. (Like his *Tape for the Turn of the Year,* it was composed on adding-machine tape.) In the past, many of Mr. Ammons's poems have felt like solitary neighborhood walks, but this is more like a long, companionable drive through the country. The poem moves freely, insistently, on a ribbon of two-line stanzas punctuated by the poet's quirky use of colons, what has been called his "colonization" of English. Its 2,200 odd lines are divided into 18 sections or chapters, each a momentary resting place before the speaker sets forth again for new territory. He never stays put for long, though he also moves generally in the direction of his main subject:

> no use to linger over beauty or simple effect:
> this is just a poem with a job to do: and that
>
> is to declare, however roundabout, sideways,
> or meanderingly (or in those ways) the perfect
>
> scientific and materialistic notion of the
> spindle of energy.

The engine of this poet's astonishing fluency is his resolve to stave off death by praising transfiguration and keeping on the move.

Garbage is a poem that enacts what it is about: "action and / action's pleasure." The poet avows no purpose and endorses a certain poetic aimlessness ("the right / time to write is when you have nothing to say"), yet the work repeatedly returns to, indeed is deeply informed by, a series of ethical propositions: "nature models values" and "likes a broad spectrum approaching disorder"; "right regard / for human life" must respect "all other forms of life"; we, too, are a form of trash, "plenty wondrous." In this major new installment to his life work, A. R. Ammons has given us an American testament that arcs toward praise, a poem of amplitude that confronts our hazardous ends and circles around to saying. "I'm glad I was here, / even if I must go."

Robert B. Shaw (review date May 1994)

SOURCE: "From A to Y," in *Poetry,* Vol. CLXIV, No. 2, May, 1994, pp. 97-107.

[*In the following excerpt, Shaw offers a mixed review of* Garbage.]

We have landfill to thank for A. R. Ammons's latest book-length poem. The sight of a huge mound of refuse beside I-95 in Florida was the epiphany that spurred him to this effort; like the garbage heap that fostered it, the resulting poem is imposing, at once anarchic and subject to a degree of formal design. It is also, fortunately, a lot more appealing. There is no question that you would rather read about the place as described by Ammons than be there. More than most poets, he knows what can be made of what others discard or overlook, reminding us how "anything / thrown out to the chickens will be ground fine / / in gizzards or taken underground by beetles and / ants: this will be transmuted into the filigree / / of ant feelers' energy vaporizations. . . ." Although his stance and central metaphor recall those of Wallace Stevens's "The Man on the Dump," Ammons's poem is broader in reference as it is longer in pages. Certainly, like Stevens, he is concerned with the processes of imagination and treats the theme memorably. One passage, on pages 42-43, is one of the most remarkable descriptions of what it is like to write a poem, from initial gropings to final formal embodiment, that I have ever seen in verse or prose. But *Garbage* isn't only an *ars poetica.* It explores a less allegorical dump than Stevens's, and reaches into cosmology, enriched with the lore of physics and biology, as well as personal speculations touching on mortality and the possibility of states which may transcend it.

Like his earlier *Tape for the Turn of the Year,* this poem was written on adding machine tape, this time, as Ammons mentions, "a little wider, just about / pentameter." While pairs of lines are spaced apart from one another on the page, this seems to be more in the interest of legibility than anything else. The work is divided, in a somewhat rough and ready way, into numbered sections. Since it is meditative, not narrative, and since Ammons is as fond of digression as he is brilliant at it, the evolution of the poem's themes is free-form, arbitrary, dependent on the poet's roving voice. Ammons himself, in one of a number of self-conscious passages, worries about how all this will hold together: "I'm running too many / threads and dropping too many stitches in this / / weaving which is about, what, *life* and, mais oui, / *death*." It is not a criticism but simply a description to say that the work struggles toward unity rather than achieving it. Like other modern long poems—*The Cantos, Paterson,* etc.—this is a congeries, not a single entity. I don't think this need be a problem for the reader who is enjoying what he reads, except perhaps toward the end. The poem doesn't work toward a single climax but offers a series of high points along the way; consequently the last lines seem more like a random cessation than a satisfying conclusion.

On the way, however, are numerous splendors and diversions. Ammons is intent to avoid the kind of long-poem solemnity that turns so easily into somnolence. He seasons his scoutings of the sublime with jokes, slang, ironies, Li'l

Abnerisms. To some (and I admit, to me) the folksiness seems disingenuous at times in a work which after all is eminently sophisticated in its aim and design. Whatever its excesses, this is an approach to style compatible with Ammons's profound engagement of the old passionately yoked dichotomy, flesh and spirit. As he puts it in Part 2:

> there is a mound,
>
> too, in the poet's mind dead language is hauled
> off to and burned down on, the energy held and
>
> shaped into new turns and clusters, the mind
> strengthened by what it strengthens: for
>
> where but in the very asshole of comedown is
> redemption: as where but brought low, where
>
> but in the grief of failure, loss, error do we
> discern the savage afflictions that turn us around:

One notices how effortlessly considerations of life and letters interpenetrate, and how the metaphor of the dump invigorates both. Later he will tell us, "life, life is like a poem: the moment it / begins, it begins to end: the tension this / / establishes makes every move and moment, every / gap and stumble, every glide and rise significant"—and as we approach the end of this wide-ranging poem we may find Ammons persuasive in his conviction that "anything, anything is poetry: effortlessness / / keys the motion; it is a plentiful waste and / waste of plenty."

In the conscious jumble of *Garbage* certain passages stand out as matching anything Ammons has written. I think especially of the wonderful colloquy with nature in Part 13, of which I can quote only a portion:

> I
> looked into the pit of death and it was there,
>
> the pit was, and the death: I circled it saying
> this looks like safety's surcease next to which
>
> risks' splits and roars, the sparrow's lone note
> in the gray tree, are radiances: the rocks
>
> came up to me in a wall saying they would say
> nothing, and the trees bent away as in wind
>
> their tops hanging on to silence, and I could
> make nothing out in the brook's fuzzy bustle:
>
> the bushes huddled down by the pinewoods as if
> looking for a path leading in, with no saying

> and no listening either, so I derived the nature
> of each thing from itself and made each derivation
>
> speak, the mountains quietly resounding and very
> authoritative, their exalted air perfect grain
>
> of the spiritual, the sense of looking down so
> scary half-love for height held. . . .

Garbage doesn't appear to have been printed on recycled paper: a missed opportunity. Looking ahead, though, the issue is irrelevant, since this is one poem readers are unlikely to be throwing out any time soon. . . .

Frank J. Lepowski (essay date Winter 1994)

SOURCE: "'How are we to find holiness?': The Religious Vision of A. R. Ammons," in *Twentieth Century Literature,* Vol. 40, No. 4, Winter, 1994, pp. 477-98.

[*In the following essay, Lepowski analyzes the religious element in Ammons's poetry and the poet's changing portrayal of God.*]

Critical attention to the religious element in the poetry of A. R. Ammons has generally subsumed it in an overall argument placing him as a modern Romantic visionary poet. Locating Ammons in this way has obscured somewhat the extent of his spirituality and its unique emotional tonality. A reading of Ammons sensitive to these may find in his development a spiritual pilgrimage with distinct phases. His idea of God, clearly present in the early poetry, undergoes a period of doubt, reconstruction, and denial in the middle of his career, and after a strong negation becomes a renewed theme in his later poetry. Meditation on the nature of God and interrogation of the visible world for revelation of the Divine occasion some of his most powerful writing.

Marius Bewley in an early review first pointed out that "Ammons *is* a mystical poet in the same sense that Whitman was." Somewhat later, Hyatt Waggoner discerned that "a sense of God's reality, whether as immanent or as *deus absconditus,* is everywhere present in the poems and should be recognized. . . . Ammons is a poet of religious vision," a view to which he has held true in subsequent assessments of Ammons's career, although he stresses a skeptical Ammons as well for whom religious beliefs "are like mirages, existing somewhere between fact and delusion." Helen Vendler has identified one of his greatest poems as a "a colloquy with God," yet elsewhere she qualifies Ammons as manifesting no more than a belief in a Quakerish "inner light," and certifies his work as being happily free of "disabling religious or ideological nostalgia." Vendler's uneasiness with Ammons's religiosity, even as her critical acuity registers its existence, indicates the difficulty others have had acknowledging it. The age wants to celebrate the poet, but is uncomfortable with the spiritual commitments that animate his work.

Ammons's belief in God's presence in the universe does not arise from allegiance to a particular institutional mode of revelation; in fact, while his early work can be quite overtly Christian, his later work includes elements of eastern religion. Furthermore, as both mystic and inheritor of the Williams branch of modernist tradition, he operates under Pound's injunction to "make it new," to perceive God and to articulate that knowledge without reference to institutions and sacred texts. Yet however syncretic or idiosyncratic his synthesis, there seems little doubt that Ammons, rather than showing "characteristic concepts and patterns of Romantic philosophy and literature" of "displaced and reconstituted theology or . . . a secularized form of devotional experience," instead shows a return to mystical devotional and meditation on the works and mind of God.

In the criticism of Ammons's work the religious has often been elided into the philosophical or psychological. Favoring the latter was Harold Bloom, who during the period of his own greatest influence was one of the first to champion Ammons. He applied a reading which relentlessly psychologizes the poet's work. Ammons is a Romantic seer whose achievement is the result of a creative will to power, continuously threatened by the universe's recalcitrance, and by the poet's awareness of the limits of his own mind. Bloom, like Waggoner, places Ammons in a visionary company of Strong Romantic Sensibilities, an avatar of his American predecessor Emerson. While philosophical similarities between Ammons and Emerson have been often noted, Bloom makes it an issue of filiation and treats the tensions in that relationship as the actual matter of the poetry.

Bloom invites us to admire the heroic struggle of a doomed subjectivity to establish its vision for a time, a struggle with the very fact of vision itself, a project in which "a poem is . . . as much an act of breaking as of making, as much a blinding as a seeing." When he traces the development of a poem he does so in primarily psychological terms, as when he sees the language of Ammons's **"Guide"** enacting "the psychic defenses of undoing and isolation, but only in order to recoil from this limitation so as to mount up into a daemonic Sublime, itself based upon a repression of this poet's deepest longings." To see Ammons's concern as the Sublime in isolation from what he tells us about the Divine is the "strong misreading" which has skewed the critical debate over Ammons. The primary question of interest for such critics becomes that of how successful a belated Romantic can be when transcendence has been rendered by the Zeitgeist an untenable alternative.

Portraying Ammons as a Romantic obscures the way his poetry reenacts spiritual inquiry and devotion, with a piety quite unlike anyone else in the American tradition, linking him more to the humility of George Herbert than to the vatic optimism of Ralph Waldo Emerson. In the present reading our goal is to show through a thorough examination of his *ouevre* the importance of the Divine in Ammons, who in his poetry offers a vision in which science tells of the works of God, whose presence is revealed to the patient and faithful inquirer.

Ammons's earliest strong expression of the Divine we find in the much-commented upon **"Hymn,"** in which the poet addresses God directly, uniting the question of His nature with Ammons's abiding philosophical preoccupation with the one:many problem. The first stanza begins with the line "I know if I find you I will have to leave the earth," and the second with the line "And I know if I find you I will have to stay with the earth," and between the poles of transcendence and immanence we may track Ammons's project.

To know God at His most universal, the poet will have to ascend past sea marshes, hills, crater lakes, and canyons, through the atmosphere and out into space: "way past all the light diffusions and bombardments / up further than the loss of sight / into the unseasonal undifferentiated empty stark." The poet's unpurgeable humanity and affiance to the things of this world make him pause when going out "past the blackset noctilucent clouds / where one wants to stop and look." God at His most absolute is infinite and eternal, hence "undifferentiated" and "unseasonal," and radically unembellished with anthropomorphic presence beyond the intimacy of address implied in the second person pronoun. To cross over into a transcendence so radical is incomprehensible and involves leaving the human completely behind.

Instead of pursuing God beyond this world, then, the poet seeks to find how God's presence may be revealed in the world of nature as perceived by the poet, moving from the macrocosm to the microcosm, "inspecting with thin tools and ground eyes" of science. In this direction faith ("trust") reposes in minute details of cell structure visible only through electron microscopy ("microvilli") or the tiny spore sacs of fungi ("sporangia") or animals so basic and rudimentary that they lack vascular systems ("coelenterates"). The Naturalist ultimately finds himself reduced to another point of human reluctance in this direction as he finds himself praying "for a nerve cell / with all the soul of my chemical reactions," which is to say that the scientific mode of perception, which helps the poet to understand creation at one level, when carried too far begins to radically diminish his humanity. Threatened in transcendence by expansion to a universal starkness, in the microcosm he is threatened by diminution through subdivision into the tiniest part of the whole.

These two motions are unified by the statement, "You are everywhere partial and entire / You are on the inside of everything and on the outside." The presence of the Godhead is everywhere in the universe; there is no place into which it does not reach, yet the poet's recognition of this still leaves him with an unavoidable human predicament. He is drawn both ways himself, for "if I find you I must go out into your far resolutions / and if I find you I must stay here with the separate leaves." He reiterates the two poles of spirit, essence and articulation, transcendence and immanence, one and many, with the final sense obtaining of the poet's remaining caught between them.

That the universal spirit we commonly call God is the object of address in this poem seems a not illogical supposition. The title of the poem, after all, is **"Hymn,"** referring to a genre in which "you" almost always means "God." All the aspects of the presence Ammons attributes to what he is addressing are easily comprehended within what has commonly been thought of as the Deity. Of the poem's many commentators, however, only Bewley unambiguously observes that Ammons is "addressing a cosmic God who is diffused throughout nature, yet presumably transcends it." Waggoner refers to the object of "you" as "One" (as in One:many) and circumspectly notes that "In traditional religious terms, which he normally avoids, these lines would imply the simultaneous Immanence and Transcendence of deity." Alan Holder states that "The *you* appears to be a principle of absolute being, existing outside the realm of seeing"; Nathan Scott holds that "it is Being itself, the aboriginal reality from which everything else springs. . . . Ammons choice of an anthropomorphic idiom for his salute to this aboriginal reality is merely a conceit"; Bloom sees "you" as "Emerson's 'Nature,' all that is separate from 'the Soul' . . . the found 'you' is: 'the NOT ME, that is, both nature and art, all other men and my own body.'" These last are strategies for eliding the religious into the philosophical or psychological, as the Divine is replaced with a principle or abstraction embodying some aspect of it. We can see in this one example the critical resistance that Ammons's religious sensibility faces.

Early in his career Ammons explicitly embraces Christianity. One poignant expression of it may be found in **"The Foot-Washing"** as the poet, summoning man and woman alike, enacts the same service that Christ performed for the Apostles (John 13:5-14). The ablution he has to offer is a healing one, which will cleanse the dust-humbled feet of his "brother," will heal with "serenity" the woman's "flat feet / yellow, gray with dust, / [her] orphaned udders flat." Of both brother and sister he asks forgiveness for himself, as if in apology to the broken and human for his visionary ambitions: "if I have failed to know / the grief in your gone time, / forgive me wakened now." The Christian pilgrimage here stands in rebuke, in its reminder of earthly suffering and require-

ment of charity, to the temptations of the egotistical sublime.

Another striking example of the Christian theme is **"Christmas Eve,"** in which he juxtaposes an account of the nativity with that of a contemporary American husband, trying to sneak a nap and decorate the tree before his wife comes home. The poem begins, however, with an evangelical excursus, seeming to preach the totalizing gospel of science:

> When cold, I huddle up, foetal, cross
> arms:
> but in summer, sprawl:
>
>   secret is plain old
> surface area,
> decreased in winter, retaining: in summer no
>   limbs touching—
> radiating:
> everything is physical:
>
>   chemistry is physical:
>   electrical noumenal mind
> is:
> (I declare!)

But the sleepy poet finds his "electrical noumenal mind" picturing Mary's experience by his own lights, the muse for the moment more morphic than orphic:

> Christmas Eve tonight: Joseph
> is looking for a place:
> Mary smiles but
>   her blood is singing:
>
>   she will have to lie down:
>   hay is warm:
> some inns keep only
> the public room warm: Mary
>
> is thinking, Nice time
>   to lie down,
> good time to be brought down by this necessity:

His reverie is repeatedly interrupted by such travelers from Porlock as a telephone call and the need to find an extension cord for the lights, so that the poem plays back and forth between the mundane and the spiritual. This oscillation, with its gently comic tone, reaches a sudden, wrenchingly personal fusion of the two realms:

> I better get busy
> and put the lights on—can't find
>   extension cord:
> Phyllis will be home, will say, The

tree doesn't have any lights!
I have tiny winking lights, too:
  she will like
them: she went to see her mother:

my mother is dead: she is
deep in the ground, changed: if she
rises, dust will blow all over the place and
  she will stand there shining,
smiling: she will feel good:
she will want
to go home and fix supper: first she
  will hug me:

an actual womb bore Christ,
divinity into the world:
  I hope there are births to lie down to
back
to divinity,
since we all must die away from here:

I better look for the cord:

The figure of Ammons's dead mother being resurrected, embracing him, all told in a guilelessly childlike tone, quite movingly bridges the personal and religious levels of the poem. That divinity ultimately receives the poem's assent over physics we see in the conclusion's treatment of Christ's mission:

  Christ was born
  in a hay barn among the warm cows and the
  donkeys kneeling down: with Him divinity
  swept into the flesh
    and made it real.

This final affirmation that the ultimate meaning of human life is a spiritual reality clarifies the irony involved in Ammons's initial invocation of physics to explain "everything." Scientific knowledge, while having its profound uses, does not begin to address human reality at the level Christ does.

We find a Christmas scene as well in Ammons's first long poem, the book-length poetic journal *Tape for the Turn of the Year,* which contains the following description of a church service, notable for his sincere, unironic, unalienated participation in it:

  I held a lighted candle
  in my hand—as all the
    others did—and helped
  sing "Silent Night": the
  church lights were doused:
    the preacher lit his

candle & from his the
  deacons lit theirs &
then the deacons went down
the aisles & gave light to
each row
& the light poured
down the rows &
the singing started:

The song and light create a setting for Ammons to testify to the nature of his religious faith. The communal celebration of the very origin of Christian belief contextualizes his more individualist credo regarding fundamental spiritual realities, given the scientific, objectifying name of "forces":

  though the forces
    have different names
  in different places &
  times, they are
  real forces which we
  don't understand:
    I can either believe
      in them or doubt them &
    I believe:
  I believe that man is
  small
  & of short duration in the
  great, incomprehensible,
  & eternal: I believe
  it's necessary to do
  good
  as we can best define it:
  I believe we must
  discover & accept the
    terms
    that best testify:
  I'm on the side of
  whatever the reasons are
    we are here:

  we do the best we can
  & it's not enough:

What is most interesting about this passage is the humility with which Ammons treats the divine mysteries; in fact, as Frederick Buell has observed, "his acceptance of uncertainty is Judeo-Christian in overtone." He accepts the limits of his knowledge yet accepts the knowledge as well. The relentless clarifications and revisions of the reasoning, scientific mind in Ammons pause at the threshold of revealed belief. Such intellectual humility and acceptance of the insufficiency of the human will is not what we think of as a trait of the dauntless Romantic seer.

This poem not only includes a credo specifying the articles

of faith, but also manifests faith's action in the form of a prayer for strength and guidance:

> God, help us: help us:
>
> we praise Your light:
> give us light to do what
> we can with darkness:
>
> > courage
> > to celebrate Your
> > light
> > even while the
> > bitterdrink
> > is being drunk:
>
> > give us the will
> > to love
> > those
> > who cannot love:
>
> > a touch of the dark
> > so we can know how one,
> > hungry for the light,
> > can
> > turn away:

Ammons concludes with a plea for "a song / sanctified / by Your divinity / to make us new / & certain of the right," lines which, in their naming the Lord as his muse emphasize what Vendler observes elsewhere in his work as the "utter congruence between Christian grace and *poiesis*." What is more audacious tonally than this public testimony of faith and prayer is the way he goes on to tell us that he "had / lunch after / 'who cannot love'— / soup, sandwich, milk," much as he used the mundane details of **"Christmas Eve"** to contextualize that poem's vision of divinity. The diary-like accumulation of the quotidian in this lengthy work makes the outbursts of religious vision all the more remarkable.

None more extraordinary, perhaps, than this act of surrendering himself to God's purposes, and in effect dedicating his poetic work to be part of His work:

> Lord, I'm in your
> hands: I surrender:
> > it's your will
> > & not mine:
> > you give me
> > singing shape
> & you turn me into dust:
>
> undefined &
> undefinable, you're
> > beyond reach:

> what form should my
> praise take?

The fruit of submission to God's will is poetic inspiration. Its result, seen in this key word of "praise," will appear often in Ammons, including poems during his middle period most commonly seen as purely Romantic. Clearly its object is divine, the Creator of all and His creation; the praise is the poet's just prayer. In *Tape* we encounter both spiritual longing and deep faith expressed so unaffectedly as to seem as natural as the meals, weather patterns, and other incidents that make up this extraordinary poetic journal. The absolute dependency of the human upon God for solace, for meaning, and for healing has not been more convincingly portrayed since Eliot. Ammons at this point in his career seems to view his own poetic vocation as a ministry in Christian terms, that of spreading testimony to God's grace and works.

The Divine continues as an abiding concern of Ammons in the work from the late 1960s through the early 1970s, but the perspective he takes on it changes. The poet comes to view God as a construct of the human imagination rather than as an independent, noumenal entity, the creator of the universe; he seems to agree with Blake that "all Deities reside in the human breast," and to begin to embrace a Religion of Man more Emersonian in tone. The reading of Ammons as latter-day Romantic may most convincingly be applied to works from this period.

In **"Hibernaculum,"** when Ammons addresses God there is uneasy qualification alien to the earlier poems: "dear God (or whatever, if anything, is / merciful) give us our lives, then, the full possession, / before we give them back." Diffidence about knowing *what* God is is a sign of piety; diffidence about knowing *whether* God is at all is a sign of profound religious doubt. A tone of resentment has entered into the prayer as well, understandable since God seems to exist only as an endlessly fillable blank, a sort of floating signifier, rather than a powerful being who would care to hear and answer prayers:

> I address the empty place where the god
> that has been deposed lived: it is the godhead: the
> yearnings that have been addressed to it bear
> > antiquity's
>
> 18
>
> sanction: for the god is ever re-created as
> emptiness, till force and ritual fill up and strangle
> his life, and then he must be born empty again: I
> accost the emptiness saying let all men turn their
> eyes to the emptiness that allows adoration's life:

The focus has changed from the originary, constitutive presence of God in creation, which animates the spiritual seeking of the early poems from **"Hymn"** through *Tape,* to the promptings of the human imagination that needs to create an object of veneration. Rather than witness to God's presence in creation, Ammons offers only "antiquity's sanction" to validate faith. Making the Divine the creation of the human, though much more easily assimilable to the rationalist and secularizing thrust of intellectual history since the eighteenth century, is a significant reversal of the stance we have seen in his earlier work.

The long poem *Sphere: The Form of a Motion* marks a certain climax of this humanistic version of the Divine. Here the will to believe poses grave dangers, because people invest the objects of their belief with considerable power over themselves, conceptions to which they become captive:

>   make a mighty
> force, that of a god: endow it with will, personal-
> ity,
>   whim:
> then, please it, it can lend power to you: but then
> you
> have created the possibility of its displeasure: what
>   you
> made to be greater than you is and enslaves you

From being the transcendent and immanent creator of all toward whom the spirit yearns, the Divine here has become a treacherous projection of the mind which usurps our freedom.

In keeping with the circularity of *Sphere's* motion, Ammons returns to this theme in a tone more seemingly reverential, referring to God in the second person rather than the third:

> spirit-being, great one in the world
> beyond sense, how do you fare and how may we
> fare to Thee:

>   69

>   . . .

> what is to be done, what is saving: is it so to come
> to know
> the works of the Most High as to assent to them
> and be
>   reconciled
> by them, so to hold those works in our imagina-
> tions as to
>   think

> them our correspondent invention, our best design
> within the

governing possibilities: so to take on the Reason
of the
  Most
High as to in some part celebrate Him and offer
Him not our

flight but our cordiality and gratitude: so to look to
the
moment of consciousness as to find there, beyond
all the
individual costs and horrors, perplexing pains and
seizures,
joy's surviving radiance:

The initial voice of prayer recalls *Tape,* but the view Ammons takes toward the Most High here is considerably more qualified. He seems to be uneasily fusing two contradictory propositions, that God is a creation of the human imagination, and that God has the omnipotent existence of the creator of all. He argues that the same power of mind by which we repeatedly imagine and destroy our gods is itself the acting power of God's imagination remaking itself. By looking inside ourselves to our own consciousness, we find the Most High's way at work, and in so doing our imagination serves as an essential vehicle of God's self-creation. This is Ammons's closest approach to the Emerson who declared "that man has access to the entire mind of the Creator, is himself the creator in the finite."

The overall movement of *Sphere* is toward affirming the world the way it is, in secular terms, as the place in which we have our happiness or not at all. In it alone may we find sufficient beauty to sustain us. We find "joy's surviving radiance" in the "moment of consciousness," that is through enjoying the motion of our minds in the here and now rather than in anticipation of a future transcendent state beyond our mortal life. This argument animates some of the great poems of his middle period, as for example **"The Arc Inside and Out,"** which, after luxuriating in both poles of thought, ends with an injunction to inhabit a state between both of these motions of the mind, to accept this life as it is as a resting point and enjoy it as such:

>   stay
> here, the apple an apple with its own hue
> or streak, the drink of water, the drink,

> the falling into sleep, restfully ever the
> falling into sleep, dream, dream, and
> every morning the sun comes, the sun.

The poet articulates so remarkably an edenic equipoise of mind and feeling that it seems churlish to question its durability as a position for living, or its suitability as an answer to the spiritual searching that drives so much of Ammons's earlier (and, as we shall see, later) verse. But it is hard, after reviewing the whole corpus of his poetry to date, not to assent to Waggoner's criticism of the poems of this middle period as being "not entirely consistent, in tone or statement, with the best of the earlier lyrics or even with the prayer . . . and the several credos . . . in *Tape.* A little more defensive, more guarded, more 'intellectually prudent.'" The poems of the period, roughly speaking, from *Uplands* through *Diversifications,* "have pulled back a little from the letting-go and letting-out of the earlier work. There is less abandon, more control. . . . Their style might be described as more 'mature,' but maturity brings losses as well as gains." Ultimately this position would not satisfy the poet, and in fact it inspired a thorough demolition of the optimistic humanism on which it is based.

After the climax of critical reception attendant upon the publication of **Collected Poems** and **Sphere,** which received the National Book Award and Bollingen Award respectively, Ammons shocked many of his readers with **The Snow Poems,** a book Waggoner found "trivial and dull," which moved him to wonder aloud, "Does Ammons write too much?" In context of our argument here, **The Snow Poems** is a descent to the underworld, an exploration of the abyss of mind and will wrestling with the most intractable material of the human condition in isolation from God and His grace. In this book (at almost three hundred pages his longest single work) the poet seems awash in ennui and depression alternating with terror, confined by quotidian life, taking tranquilizers to get by, haunted by memories of his dead father. Precious little of the buoyancy of his previous work is to be found, and even the qualified, constructed God of **Sphere** has vanished. Earlier in his career he pictures God's universal, beneficent consciousness as

> someone [who] has a clear vision of it all,
> exact to complete existence;
> loves me when I swear and praise
> and smiles, probably, to see me
> wrestle with sight

In **The Snow Poems** comes the bleak negation:

> is no one watching, of
> course not,
>   not even a gentle, universal
> principle with a calming circularity

The poet has a sense of utter cosmic abandonment so intense it pushes aside the effect of the tranquilizer he uses to blunt it:

> one is helpless: one weeps: e
> terror raves beyond the tear: q
> one is without help: u

> and then one sees or recalls   a
> that on the balance line between   n
> purchases and payoffs   i
> indifference looks neither this   l
> way nor that:
> our help is the call of
> indifference that says
> come where there is no
> need of help
> and have all the help you need.

Over the course of this book the poet enacts the drama of a resourceful mind isolated and unable to find a way to live with his human brokenness, most tellingly in the way in which he is haunted by the memory of his father, but really including all the other people and things in his life. In this record of spiritual isolation and alienation the vehicle of his "redemption" proves to be, oddly enough, a spring encounter with a neighbor's dog, whose kindly recognition endorses his existence from outside:

> . . . old fellow,
> friend, frizzled schnauzer
> runs out of the driveway
> and whines grievous
> pleasure
> stretching up toward my face:
> he knows me: we were
> friends last fall:
> I am myself:
> I am so scared and sad I can
> hardly bear to speak
> and yet delight breaks
> falls through me
> and drives me off laughing
> down a dozen brooks:

From this point the book's mood begins to rise from the Slough of Despond in which the poet has been caught, and move toward an acceptance of the world and his life in it, seen in essentially natural, secular terms.

In tracing the spiritual theme in Ammons's work, **The Snow Poems** stands as an oddly compelling record of a long, dark night of the soul, when the seeker feels himself abandoned by God, by the grace he had previously been able to find in the world of things, by what his understanding of the universe and his life has been. It is Ammons at his most reduced, least transcendental, least religious, least visionary; it is his fullest exploration of the estranged self in an abandoned universe. Its example points out as by relief the importance of the Divine in his work overall.

The Snow Poems contrasts dramatically with the book that follows it, *A Coast of Trees,* as Ammons takes up again his spiritual searching. The first poem, **"Coast of Trees,"** invokes the Taoist Way to describe the origin of observed creation and its ongoing course for the pilgrim, one who is asking a question absent throughout the preceding book, "How are we to find holiness?" Only by accepting our fallenness, our "helplessness" of which we make "first offer and sacrifice," by accepting "a shambles of / non-enterprise" which represents our conscious, calculating, making-sense-of-the-world's failure to control reality the way we want it to, may we come to "know a unity approach divided, a composure past / approach." It is after thus emptying ourselves of the pretensions and intrusions of willful consciousness that "with nothing, we turn / to the cleared particular, not more / nor less than itself," seeing things for what they are and neither exaggerating nor deprecating their significance, their proper place in creation. Which is to say that we see things in their place in the Divine Nature and the Divine Nature's place in them: "and we realize / that whatever it is it is in the Way and / the Way in it, as in us, emptied full."

Seeing things in themselves and in their place in the Way reminds us of our nature, and of our place in the Way. The poet's acceptance of the "shambles" in this poem denotes a chastened return to the spiritual humility seen in his earlier work; a taste of earth now leavens his religious sensibility, and the optimistic humanism of his middle period has been replaced by an acknowledgment that this life is a Vale of Sorrow to be endured before our emergence after death into a better life.

In the elegy **"In Memoriam Mae Noblitt"** this world, instead of being our sufficiency, is rather a temporary abode before the eternal one: "this is just a place," whereas

> our home which defines
> us is elsewhere but not
> so far away we have
> forgotten it:

Rejecting with Flannery O'Connor the notion that we are our own light, he questions:

> is love a reality we
> made here ourselves—
> and grief—did we design
>
> that—or do these,
> like currents, whine
> in and out among us merely
> as we arrive and go:

Our ultimate consolation turns out to be our destination after death, a return to our true home:

the reality we agree with,

> that agrees with us,
> outbounding this, arrives
> to touch, joining with
>
> us from far away:

The consolation of this eternal frame of reference in no way eliminates the death and suffering that blight our earthly life. Looking forward to the next hundred million years in **"Rapids,"** Ammons predicts that "the universe will probably not find / a way to vanish nor I / in all that time reappear." **"Sweetened Change," "Parting," "Givings,"** and **"An Improvisation for the Stately Dwelling"** are all in some sense meditations on death, the last marked particularly by spiritual compensation for earthly travail:

> I know a man whose cancer has
> got him just to the point
> he looks changed by a flight of stairs
> people pass him and speak
> extra-brightly
> he asks nothing else
> he is like a rock
> reversed, that is, the rock has a solid
> body and shakes only
> reflected in the water but he shakes
> in body only,
> his spirit a boulder of light

The problem of mortal suffering constitutes a constant counterpoint to spiritual reward which checks whatever temptation to the egotistical sublime the poet may still feel. In **"Swells,"** a symbolic meditation on the magnitude and amplitude of the waves of the ocean, the climax comes not in lofty cresting but rather in a shattering collapse back into the rag-and-bone-shop base of human life from which this meditation has sought to ascend but will not be permitted to escape: "the immediate threat / shot up in a disintegrating spray, the many thoughts and / sights unmanageable, the deaths of so many, hungry or mad." Ammons recognizes, in **"Breaking Out,"** that he has been "an earth thing all along," whose "feet are catching in the brush" now that the "balloons" of a self-deceiving afflatus have been released.

This dialectic of human sorrow and divine grace which consoles may be seen no more clearly than in the much-commented-on **"Easter Morning."** In fact, the poem could have been titled "Good Friday and Easter Morning" for it is a two-stage construction in which suffering and death in the first meets its complement of saving grace and resurrected spirit in the second. The *via dolorosa* is represented in a child's desperation, loneliness, and abandonment by his elders in which the poet sees that

the child in me that could not become
was not ready for others to go,
to go on into change, blessings and
horrors, but stands there by the road
where the mishap occurred, crying out for
help.

The aborted life of this child within him the mature poet
holds onto, suffers with over the course of his life. Ammons
speaks from the center of his brokenness and sorrow:

I stand on the stump
of a child, whether myself
or my little brother who died, and
yell as far as I can, I cannot leave this place, for
for me it is the dearest and the worst,
it is life nearest to life which is
life lost:

He finally embraces this locale, and the suffering it represents, as his own:

it is my place where
I must stand and fail,
calling attention with tears
to the branches not lofting
boughs into space.

Finally he clings to that failure and the pain it holds with a
certain tenacity, almost pride, since it defines him more truly
than any exultation in his power as a seer.

The reclamation of the poet's spirit arises in the final section from finding holiness in the purpose and beauty of the
natural world, or, as Vendler puts it, "grace—not offered by
Ammons as an 'equivalent' to Bunyan's grace, but as *the
same thing,* a saving gift from an external source," an observation as true of **"Easter Morning"** as it is of **"Grace
Abounding,"** the poem she has in mind. The contemplation
of the flight of a pair of eagles allows Ammons his "assuag-
ing human clarification":

it was a sight of bountiful
majesty and integrity: the having
patterns and routes, breaking
from them to explore other patterns or
better ways to routes, and then the
return: a dance sacred as the sap in
the trees, permanent in its descriptions
as the ripples round the brook's
ripplestone: fresh as this particular
flood of burn breaking across us now
from the sun.

The divinity revealed by nature, as announced by the poem's

title, makes **"Easter Morning"** a capstone of the rest of the
book's preoccupation with the human and the Divine.

The poem in which Ammons addresses God at the highest
and most reverent level of expression of which he is capable
comes from a later collection, *Lake Effect Country.* **"Singling & Doubling Together"** is like **"Hymn"** in that the
poet refers to God in the second person, achieving here
something of the tender familiarity we see in the poetry of
George Herbert. Unlike **"Hymn,"** in which God is sought
by moving outward into an unimaginable transcendence, or
downward into the minute particulars of the physical universe, the later poem finds Ammons recognizing God's grace
as a personal gift in his own human identity: "My nature
singing in me is your nature singing." The poem elaborates
the felt intimate presence of the Lord from His articulation
as well in the world of appearances:

you have means to veer down, filter through,
and, coming in,
harden into vines that break back with leaves,
so that when the wind stirs
I know you are there and I hear you in leafspeech

The poem does replicate the motion of the earlier **"Hymn"**
in tracing out a polar relationship between the most remote
and unknowable manifestation of the Godhead and its particular expressions in local nature, both the "far resolutions"
and the "separate leaves":

though of course back into your heightenings I
can never follow: you are there beyond
tracings flesh can take,
and farther away surrounding and informing the
systems,
you are as if nothing, and
where you are least knowable I celebrate you most

or here most when near dusk the pheasant squawks
and
lofts at a sharp angle to the roost cedar,
I catch in the angle of that ascent,
in the justness of that event your pheasant nature

God at His most infinite and eternal is remote and incon-
ceivable to the poet's mind, but in the natural world of creation reveals Himself in a variety of forms and ways of
being, including a "creaking / and snapping nature" in the
motion of bushes. In human form God shows a failing nature. Here as in **"Easter Morning"** failure summarizes what
it is to be human, a state of brokenness and pain, in which
God participates completely and sacrificially:

and you will fail me only as from the still
of your great high otherness you fail all things,

somewhere to lift things up, if not those things
again:

even you risked all the way into the taking on of
shape
and time fail and fail with me, as me,
and going hence with me know the going hence
and in the cries of that pain it is you crying and
you know of it and it is my pain, my tears, my loss

The final motion is that of testifying to God's forgiving grace, as the poet rededicates his art to His service, as he had done in *Tape for the Turn of the Year.* Ammons can see the desired end of his life's pilgrimage, the annihilation of his self in death, to be reunited with his Creator. Finally the poet looks forward to being liberated from his own particular voice to be blended with God's pure expression:

                              what but grace

have I to bear in every motion,
embracing or turning away, staggering or standing
  still,
while your settled kingdom sways in the distillations
  of light
and plunders down into the darkness with me
and comes nowhere up again but changed into
your singing
nature when I need sing my nature nevermore.

At this point in his poetic career Ammons is, like the George Herbert of "Love (III)," in communion with his creator. We sense a familiarity with God wrought of concentration, persistence, suffering, prayer, the reward of which is a trust foretelling eternal salvation.

Among Ammons's critics it has been easier to speak of the Sublime rather than the Divine, perhaps because the former is an ultimately subjective mode of expression, and can be tailored to the needs of the occasion as a one-size-fits-all spirituality replacement. Harold Bloom makes of it the centerpiece of an elaborate psychodrama in the poet's mind, the various discharges from which are the heart of his reading of Ammons. A critic like Nathan Scott can make it just consoling enough so that it becomes almost divine, without setting off the reflex of disbelief endemic to the modern mind. Given the ardor of Ammons's spiritual expression in these late poems, the lengths to which an otherwise sympathetic and acute commentator like Scott will go to elide the presence of God in **"Singling & Doubling Together"** indicates the operation of a powerful taboo:

In short, the "you" being addressed in **"Singling & Doubling Together"** is simply the Wholly Other,

the Incomparable, the "dearest freshness deep down things": it is none other than Being itself. . . . And this aboriginal reality is addressed as "you," not because Ammons conceives it to be *a* being with personal attributes but rather, presumably, because he feels it to present itself with the same sort of graciousness that one encounters in the love of another person. He chooses not, in other words, to talk about "God" but, rather, to speak of that which approximates what Teilhard de Chardin called *le milieu divin.* Or, we might say that Ammons is a poet of what Stevens in a late poem, "Of Mere Being," in *Opus Posthumous,* called "mere Being": we might say that he is a poet of that which, though not coextensive with all things, yet interpenetrates all things with the radiance of its diaphanous presence.

This fails to be a satisfying account of the poem because as we have just seen, Ammons addresses an omniscient creator who feels his pain, who participates in his fallen human life even though having high and eternal origin, which is to say it is exactly "a being with personal attributes" and not merely some abstraction of "Being itself," which would indeed be "mere Being." The poem is addressed to a sympathetic consciousness who shares the poet's sufferings and who, moreover, will ultimately save the poet from them. In short, the address is not to some abstraction of Being but rather to the God in whom "we live and move and have our being," not the milieu but the Presence itself, such convincing witness to which is quite rare in contemporary poetry.

The later poems in their working toward a state of communion represent a culmination of Ammons's engagement with the Divine as a poetic subject, which has taken several phases. In the earliest, he combines an examination of nature for signs of the Creator with a faith basically Christian in origin as seen in **"Hymn," "Christmas Eve,"** and *Tape for the Turn of the Year.* In his middle period, seduced by the egotistical sublime, he revises God into being a necessary construct of the human imagination, which needs to create a space to venerate. With the scorched-earth demolition in *The Snow Poems* of Romantic optimism Ammons shows the extremity of life without God in his most willful, isolated, and harrowing work, which clears the field for renewed spiritual pilgrimage in the later books. In these Ammons is strengthened to endure the trials of earthly life which threatened to undo him in *The Snow Poems,* and fixes his hope on eternal reward after death, nourished in his faith by signs of grace that he encounters in the natural world, and by God's speaking directly to his heart.

In its most affective lineaments, the idea of God that Ammons articulates is not dogmatic but partakes, rather, of the emotional context of personal spiritual encounter, and is revealed in an examination of nature as probing and scientific as one can imagine any poet performing. In the rigors of this unsparing intimacy we may see Ammons more fruitfully not as our Emerson, but rather our Herbert, not Romantic so much as truly Metaphysical. Such attention to nuance of thought and depth of feeling in spiritual experience grounds the rest of his concerns and makes Ammons's enterprise a singular achievement in modern American poetry.

Lawrence Sail (review date Autumn 1995)

SOURCE: "Recent Poetry," in *Stand Magazine,* Vol. 36, No. 4, Autumn, 1995, pp. 77-8.

[*In the following excerpt, Sail discusses the virtues and flaws of Ammons's* Tape for the Turn of the Year *and* Garbage.]

. . . Should a poem be, formally or thematically, open or closed? What is the poet's responsibility to himself or herself, to the poem, to the tradition, to the events of the twentieth century? Can the modesty that history may seem to demand also mislead into political oversimplification? Where does an awareness of complexity become clutter or prolixity? When does spacious equal specious? At what point might self-consciousness become self-defeat?

A. R. Ammons, now nearing his 70th year, would appear to have found a novel answer to such challenges in his long poem ***Tape for the Turn of the Year,*** dating from 1965 and now reissued. What he calls 'this foolish / long / thin / poem' aims to benefit from a mechanical imperative, as the blurb explains: 'In the form of a journal covering the period December 6, 1963, through January 10, 1964 . . . [it] . . . was written on a roll of adding-machine tape, then transferred foot by foot to manuscript. He chose this method as a serious experiment in making a poem adapt to something outside itself.' There follow 210 pages of vertical notebook, in a confident mode which has affinities with both Whitman and Ashbery. As far as I could see, the only full stops are those after the poet's initials: breaks are provided by vertical spacing, by question and exclamation marks and brackets, with the colon easily the most frequent irrigation in Ammons's sweeping landscapes. From ebullient listings to somewhat indulgent monologues, he develops a speculative vein which mostly gets away with stating what is mostly obvious. Less successful are the bathetic jokes, such as 'the snails are sluggish' or the spelling of Sisyphus as 'Sissy Fuss', though the poem ends with rather a neat joke as farewell—'so long'. The key Ammons word is 'exchanges'—he sees everything as transactional: the moment and eternity, loss and (re)gain, fragmentation and unity. He commutes between the language of philosophy, lyricism and a clipped-demotic register, conducts a running dialogue with the Muse, and frequently asks questions of himself, such as 'Why do I need to throw / this structure / against the flow / which I cannot stop?'—to which he provides an answer 55 pages on, suggesting that the thing is to 'leave structure / to the maker / & praise / by functioning'. If all this sounds too naked, it is fair to say that much of the poem is anchored in a good sense of the local: the winter landscape and weather, birds, the daily round, shopping, cooking, all play their part. One or two of the later entries (I'm thinking of 2 and 8 January in particular) sag a bit, partly because Ammons himself draws attention to the way in which he is waiting for the tape to run out and so for the poem to end.

Appearing in tandem with the ***Tape*** is another long Ammons poem, ***Garbage,*** written fully 30 years on and winner of the 1993 National Book Award for poetry. In 18 sections, mostly of five or so pages, it is written in unrhymed couplets, mostly with four or five stresses, and runs to 121 pages with seven full stops, and colon still king. Like ***Tape,*** it relies on the anchorage of vivid details—but here the debate is about meaning and the possibility of it, and much of Ammons's speculation centres round what kind of poem he should be writing. It can get pretty convoluted at times: '. . . I'm trying to mean what I / / mean to mean something: best for that is a kind / of matter-of-fact explicitness about the facts'. As before, the virtues and vices are closely entwined: Ammons can be self-critical and self-forgiving, sententious and acute, modest and smug. There are elements of greater strain in this poem than the earlier one and it is a bit relentless, like being constantly beaten over the head with good news. But it has really memorable things, too, such as this vivid picture of his father in hospital, 'gussied up with straps, in a wheelchair, a catheter leading / to the little fuel tank hung underneath, urine / the color of gasoline, my father like the / others drawn down half-asleep mulling over his / / wheels'. From his worst, it would be tempting to conclude that a long Ammons goes a little way: but the sheer energy and zest of the man are winning qualities—you imagine him sitting there, synapses sparking away as he leaps from the local to the cosmic and back again. And his poetry's real virtue is that; like Whitman's earth in 'To the sayers of words', it 'closes nothing, refuses nothing, shuts none out.'

Ian Sansom (excerpt date 7 March 1996)

SOURCE: "Cheesespreadology," in *London Review of Books,* Vol. 18, No. 5, March 7, 1996, pp. 26-7.

[*In the following excerpt, Sansom discusses Ammons's critical reception in England.*]

In a power-rhyming slap-happy parody of Thirties doom-mongering published in 1938 William Empson famously had 'Just a Smack at Auden':

> What was said by Marx, boys, what did he
> > perpend?
> No good being sparks, boys, waiting for the end.
> Treason of the clerks, boys, curtains that descend,
> Lights becoming darks, boys, waiting for the end.

By contrast, in a lecture on 'Rhythm and Imagery in English Poetry' to the British Society of Aesthetics in 1961, Empson gave William Carlos Williams and his reviewers an exasperated wallop:

> The most unexpected American critics will be found speaking of him with tender reverence; they feel he is a kind of saint. He has renounced all the pleasures of the English language, so that he is completely American; and he only says the dullest things, so he has won the terrible fight to become completely democratic as well. I think that, if they are such gluttons for punishment as all that, they are past help.

It may in fact have been Empson who by 1961 was past help—at only 55 he was already describing himself as an 'old buffer'—for he was clearly unable to pick up the subtleties of intonation in Williams's drawl in the way that he had instinctively been able to tune in to the rhythms of Auden's Oxford patter. Empson's is a classic English misreading and misunderstanding of American poetry, caused largely by lack of proximity but also by a wilful refusal to hear. 'I suspect,' Emerson wrote, 'that there is in an Englishman's brain a valve that can be closed at pleasure, as an engineer shuts off steam.'

The closing of the valve, the deliberate shutting off of steam, is one of the things that helps regulate English poetry, producing its iambic highs and lows, its mood-swings and its syncopations. In American poetry there is often no such clear cut-off, no shut-up or shut-down; the language seems to be on automatic, which can be disconcerting: 'the English often feel,' as Empson put it, 'that some Americans quack on with a terrible monotony and no pause for the opposite number to get in a word.' A. R. Ammons's poetry is a case in point: his massive oeuvre amounts to a kind of giant bulk bin fed by his extraordinary brush-equipped pick-up belt of a brain, which has managed to load and deliver material at a speed of about one collection every two years for forty years, yet it is an achievement which remains either politely ignored or quietly sniggered at in England. His titling his latest book *Garbage* probably won't help, but then his verse has always been something of a dumping ground for Platonic, Romantic and Emersonian notions of effluence,

confluence and the common harmony of the created order. As he put it in *Sphere: The Form of a Motion,*

> under all life, fly and
>
> dandelion, protozoan, bushamster, and ladybird,
> > tendon
> and tendrel (excluding protocelluar organelles) is
> > the same
>
> cell . . .

Indeed, Ammons's theory of poetic form, as set out in *Hibernaculum,* amounts to a kind of trashcan theory:

> much have I studied, trashcanology,
> > cheesespreadology,
> laboratorydoorology, and become much
> > enlightened and
> dismayed: have, sad to some, come to care as
> > much
> > > for
> a fluted trashcan as a fluted Roman column: flutes
> > > are
> flutes and the matter is a mere substance design
> > > takes
> its shape in . . .

According to William Rathje and Cullen Murphy, garbage archaeologists with the University of Arizona's Garbage Project, *garbage* 'refers technically to "wet" discards—food remains, yard waste, and offal', while *trash* refers to the 'dry' stuff—'newspapers, boxes, cans, and so on'. *Refuse,* however, covers both, and *rubbish* 'refers to all refuse plus construction and demolition debris'. It is worth bearing such distinctions in mind, for Ammons's *Garbage* is most certainly not *rubbish;* it is something far more wet and slippery. Ammons states that

> garbage has to be the poem of our time because
> garbage is spiritual, believable enough
> to get our attention, getting in the way, piling
> up, stinking . . .

Garbage for Ammons, in other words, is nothing so simple as evidence of mere over-consumption: it is a kind of sacrament, an outward and visible sign of certain inward and spiritual truths—in fact, another illustration of the truths and graces of the Emersonian version of Neoplatonism that he has been espousing since his first collection *Ommateum* and which found its most profound expression in *Corsons Inlet.* Ammons's is a philosophy in which, as he puts it in *Garbage,* 'all is one, one all'; it finds a natural expression in paradox—'we're trash, plenty wondrous'—and often comes close to sliding into determinism:

oh well: argument is like dining:
mess with a nice dinner long enough, it's garbage.

This kind of Transcendental shruggery gives his poetry its very un-English tone of patient endurance and content—'don't worry, be happy,' he counsels at one point in ***Garbage***—and in this latest collection results in a reconsideration of waste products and wasted moments:

Marine Shale are said to be 'able to turn

wastes into safe products': but some say these
'products are themselves hazardous wastes':

well, what does anybody want: is there a world
with no bitter aftertaste or post coital triste:

what's a petit mort against a high moment:
I mean, have you ever heard of such a thing . . .

The restless and continuous movement of Ammons's poetry is undoubtedly impressive but it is nonetheless semi-automatic: although he can and often does adjust the size of his nozzle to alter the pressure of mood, mode or tone in a poem, it's basically always the same stuff coming out. For example, ***Tape for the Turn of the Year,*** first published in 1965 and recently reissued, is pretty bog-standard Ammons, with its reflections on 'motions / and intermotions', and surely was and now most certainly is remarkable only for having been written on a roll of adding-machine tape. With the tape's length and breadth determining its shape and size, ***Tape for the Turn of the Year*** quite literally invites readers to never mind the quality but feel the width; when Ammons ends the poem with the throwaway phrase 'so long' some readers might welcome the words not only as a farewell but also as a statement of unfortunate fact.

The restless and continuous movement of Ammons's poetry is undoubtedly impressive but it is nonetheless semi-automatic: although he can and often does adjust the size of his nozzle to alter the pressure of mood, mode or tone in a poem, it's basically always the same stuff coming out.
—*Ian Sansom*

Ammons's extraordinary overflow also raises questions about quality control, a problem that he states as fact in **'Cold Rheum'**, from ***The Really Short Poems of A. R. Ammons:***

You can't

tell what's

snot from
what's not . . .

Of course, snot is not always to be sniffed at. There is a children's riddle:

Q: What is it that the rich man puts in his pocket
that the poor man throws away?
A: Snot.

Substitute 'American' for the riddle's 'rich man' and 'English' for 'poor' and you have a workable definition of the differences between American and English poetry. In a gloss on the snot riddle in his book *Rubbish Theory: The Creation and Destruction of Value,* Michael Thompson explains that the riddle

succeeds by playing upon that which is residual to our system of cultural categories. When, in the context of wealth and poverty, we talk of possessable objects we unquestioningly assume that we are talking about valuable objects. The category 'objects of no-value' is invisible and we only notice its existence when it is pointed out to us by the riddle. But the riddle contains much more than this. If the answer is simply 'an object of no-value' (say, pebbles or sweet papers) it is not very funny. What makes it funny is that the answer 'snot' is an object, as it were, of negative value; something that should be thrown away.

One might describe ***Garbage*** as the logical extension of Ammons's sustained attempt to dignify objects and experiences of no apparent value, a project in which silt, sludge and slurry are not so much by-products as the stuff of life.

FURTHER READING

Criticism

Baker, David. "The Push of Reading." *Kenyon Review* 16, No. 4 (Fall 1994): 161-76.
    Praises Ammons's *Garbage* as a "brilliant book."

Cushman, Stephen. "A. R. Ammons, or the Rigid Lines of the Free and Easy." In his *Fictions of Form in American Poetry,* pp. 149-86. Princeton, NJ: Princeton University Press, 1991.
    Analyzes the place of form in Ammons's poetry.

Deane, Patrick. "Justified Radicalism: A. R. Ammons with

a Glance at John Cage." *Papers on Language and Literature* 28, No. 2 (Spring 1992): 206-22.

> Discusses the implications of Ammons's use of adding machine tape to compose his *Tape for the Turn of the Year.*

Doreski, William. "Sublimity and Order in the *Snow Poems.*" *Pembroke Magazine,* No. 21 (1989): 68-76.

> Analyzes how Ammons's *The Snow Poems* "demonstrates the aesthetic possibilities and limitations of sequence."

Kirby, David. "Is There a Southern Poetry?" *The Southern Review* 30, No. 4 (Autumn 1994): 869-80.

> Discusses what is unique about southern poets, including A. R. Ammons.

Oates, Joyce Carol. "Books of Change: Recent Collections of Poems." *The Southern Review* 9 (1973): 1014-29.

> Praises Ammons's *Collected Poems 1951-1971,* and calls Ammons "timeless."

Spiegelman, Willard. "Myths of Concretion, Myths of Abstraction: The Case of A. R. Ammons." In his *The Didactic Muse,* pp. 110-46. Princeton, NJ: Princeton University Press, 1989.

> Analyzes the major themes found in Ammons's poetry throughout his career and how the poet deals with them.

Wolf, Thomas J. "A. R. Ammons and William Carlos Williams: A Study in Style and Meaning." *Contemporary Poetry* II, No. 3 (Winter 1977): 1-16.

> Analyzes William Carlos Williams's influence on Ammons's poetry.

Additional coverage of Ammons's life and career is contained in the following sources published by Gale Research: *Authors in the News,* **Vol. 1;** *Contemporary Authors,* **Vols. 9-12R;** *Contemporary Authors New Revision Series,* **Vols. 6, 36, 51;** *Dictionary of Literary Biography,* **Vols. 5, 165;** *DISCovering Authors Modules: Poets; Major Twentieth-Century Writers;* **and** *Poetry Criticism, Vol. 16.*

Charles Bukowski
1920-1994

(Henry Charles Bukowski, Jr.) German-born American poet, novelist, and short story writer.

The following entry provides an overview of Bukowski's career. For additional information on his life and works, see *CLC,* Volumes 2, 5, 9, 41, and 82.

INTRODUCTION

Charles Bukowski appears in many of his own works, in the quasi-anagrammaticalalter ego of Henry Chinaski, who takes on many varied personas. Some of these personas have been labeled by the critic Glenn Esterly in describing Bukowski: ". . . poet, novelist, short story writer, megalomaniac, lush, philanderer, living legend recluse, classical music aficionado, scatologist, loving father, sexist, physical wreck, jailbird, pain in the ass, genius, finagling horse player, outcast, antitraditionalist, brawler and ex-civil servant . . . ." Others would add a description of a caring, sensitive man with a finely-honed, self-deprecating sense of humor. Chinaski, like Bukowski, is able to step back and poke fun at his drunken, womanizing, excessively macho character. Avoiding maudlin sentimentality, Bukowski nevertheless brings a caring humanity to his characters who are typically outcasts living on the fringes of society. His sympathy comes from a perspective that success and failure are more a result of luck and social injustice than reflections of a person's worth. Bukowski's feelings for these characters is visible in the words of the lead character Belane from his last novel, *Pulp* (1994): "Of course, there were a lot of good people sleeping in the streets. They weren't fools, they just didn't fit into the needed machinery of the moment."

Biographical Information

Born August 16, 1920, in Andernach, Germany, Bukowski was brought to the United States by his family at the age of two. He grew up in the Los Angeles area, experiencing a brutal, unhappy childhood. His father, Henry Charles Bukowski, Sr., was a strict authoritarian who "disciplined" the young Bukowski regularly with a razor strop. A slight child, scarred by acne and boils, he was also victimized by schoolyard bullies. Bukowski often underplayed the cruelty of his father, suggesting that Charles Sr. helped harden him for survival in a cruel, brutal world. Bukowski began attending Los Angeles City College in 1939, but dropped out at the beginning of World War II and moved to New York with the aspiration of becoming a writer. He spent the next few years working a variety of menial jobs and writing, without

publishing success. Some critics have suggested his failure was a result of sending his work to inappropriate markets such as *Harper's Magazine.* Disgusted, he gave up writing entirely in 1946 and began a ten-year period of heavy drinking. The result, described in the short story collection *Life and Death in the Charity Ward* (1974), was a bleeding ulcer that nearly killed him. Bukowski took his survival as a sign of purpose and began writing again. Bukowski also credits his drinking with helping provide part of his artistic perspective. He said, "Drinking is an emotional thing. It joggles you out of the standardism of everyday life, out of everything being the same. It yanks you out of your body and your mind and throws you up against the wall. I have the feeling that drinking is a form of suicide where you're allowed to return to life and begin all over the next day. It's like killing yourself, and then you're reborn. I guess I've lived about ten or fifteen thousand lives now." The critic Loss Glazier alludes to this when he says, "He was able to turn his hand to fiction with a perspective unequaled in contemporary American letters. He had been through a stripping-down that would've killed any ordinary person. And yet Bukowski, rather than being weakened by each successive defoliation, seemed to get stronger with the knowledge of what was necessary."

Major Works

Bukowski was first published in the underground magazines and small presses, gaining a reputation largely by word of mouth. His first book of poetry, *Flower, Fist, and Bestial Wail* (1959), deals with common Bukowski themes of abandonment, desolation, and the absurdities of life and death. The subject matter of drinking, gambling, music, and sex was considered offensive by many critics, but others hailed his crisp, authentic voice. The collection *It Catches My Heart in its Hands* (1963), a selection of poems written between 1955 and 1963, deals with topics such as rerolled cigarette butts, winning at the races, and high-priced call girls. In a review of the work, the poet Kenneth Rexroth said that Bukowski "belongs in that small company of poets of real, not literary, alienation." Bukowski wrote over forty other books of poetry. In addition to poetry, he wrote several novels, drawing on experiences in his own life for subject matter. *Post Office* (1971) dealt with his years as a letter carrier and mail sorter, and explored the oppression of petty bureaucracy and the numbing effect of mindless, hard work. The character Chinaski's refusal to go along with the program, to play the game, made the novel an anthem for the oppressed underdog. In *Ham on Rye* (1982), a younger Chinaski is the protagonist. Bukowski's semi-autobiography deals with Chinaski's early years under the thumb of a brutal, oppressive father, and a painful adolescence, lonely and isolated. It moves on to his brief college experience, then the life of hard jobs and heavy drinking. Although his writing was not well known in the United States, he enjoyed considerable popularity in Europe, and publication of his work there began to give him a measure of financial success. This success was enhanced when he was asked to write a screenplay. The result was the movie *Barfly* (1987), starring Mickey Rourke as Chinaski at the age of twenty-four. Bukowski's experience with the making of the movie is documented in the novel *Hollywood* (1989). His last novel, *Pulp* (1994), was published a few months after his death from leukemia at age 73. On the surface, it is a spoof of the hard-boiled detective genre. But the humorous novel explores questions of identity, the meaning of life, and the interaction of literature and life.

Critical Reception

Throughout his career, Bukowski's reception by the critics was mixed. Many regarded his work as merely a re-hash of the sexual escapade literature of Henry Miller, covering ground that had already been explored, and adding nothing new. He is dismissed by some as a misogynist and sexist. But many critics perceive a tongue-in-cheek aspect behind the macho posturing. Russell Harrison observes, "The effect

of Bukowski's depiction of women, chauvinist though it can be, is quite different from what his predecessors and contemporaries produced. Although depicting Chinaski as sexist, Bukowski at the same time, and more tellingly, goes to great pains to undermine this position." Indeed, it would be more accurate to characterize Chinaski as "pseudo-macho." Harrison points out numerous examples in Bukowski's novels where traditional macho roles are reversed, where the woman is the sexual aggressor who wants a man for only one thing and dumps him if he cannot perform to her satisfaction. He says, ". . . we have an absolute reversal of the scene where the woman (traditionally viewed as the romantic in such situations) falls in love and it is the man who makes (or thinks) the distinction between love and sex." There is also an insight into human weakness that raises Bukowski's work above the gutter it describes. Elizabeth Young observes, "In addition to its acerbic edge, Bukowski's writing always possessed a sense of the frailty of human endeavor . . . Bukowski's was a lifelong struggle to express himself clearly, honestly and concisely. He has similarities with Henry Miller and, like Miller, has had trouble over his alleged 'sexism.' . . ." Several other critics also comment on the influences of Hemingway and Miller. Julian Smith says, "Ernest Hemingway, the most accessible modernist, provided Bukowski with a macho role model, an existential material, and an experimental style already pushed in the direction of American 'speech.'" Several critics have commented on the presence of Bukowski's voice in his work. As Smith notes, "The intrusions of the author/narrator into the text are integral to many Bukowski stories, not merely winking to the reader but pointing up the text's artificial, fictive status. A playfulness clearly places Bukowski in the same camp as the postmoderns. . . ." Throughout most of his poetry and fiction, Bukowski's real life is the subject matter. This became more evident as Bukowski began to achieve success and recognition. His persona of a hard-drinking, hard-living, tough guy began to become a burden. In the *Barfly* screenplay and the novel *Hollywood,* Bukowski probes the influence of money and fame on his alter-egos. Elizabeth Young, speaking of this transition, says that "Despite his decades of devoted reading and writing, his straightforward, largely autobiographical work received little attention until his middle years, when he was discovered by a disaffected post-Beat audience of younger readers. . . . His persona became increasingly fixed and near-parodic but he did attempt to write about the cryptic, complex ways of fame with honesty and intelligence." Bukowski dealt with the success of being offered a contract for a screenplay by doing one about his youth when he was an impoverished drunk. The theme of fame and money occurring by chance, and that the successful writer is the same person who was the hopeless drunk became central to much of Bukowski's work. Speaking of *Hollywood,* Stan Thies says, "Bukowski's foray through tinsel town doesn't produce the easy results we might expect. In a certain sense he sets a trap for the reader. Early on we are on the lookout for some scapegoat, someone who can be blamed for sustaining a world which so magically trades off quality and dealing. We never really find one, and perhaps we never really find the hero-god either." An actor thrives by losing the self while a writer such as Bukowski needs the self in order to record it. And it is this willingness to lay bare his exploration of his private self that many critics find as Bukowski's most valuable contribution to literature. The less autobiographical novel, *Pulp*, also deals with issues that are impending in Bukowski's life. As Dick Lochte observes, "*Pulp* was printed only months after his death . . . Though a few decades younger, [the novel's hero] Belane's sense of his own mortality is acute. Everywhere he looks he sees people and places he knew leaving the scene." The novel is described by some as a parody of the work of Chandler and Hammett, and credited with varying degrees of success on that level. But its exploration of the questions of mortality are more widely praised. George Stade says, "As parody, **Pulp** does not cut very deep. As a farewell to readers, as a gesture of rapprochement with death, as Bukowski's sendup and send-off of himself, this bio-parable cuts as deep as you would want."

PRINCIPAL WORKS

Flower, Fist, and Bestial Wail (poetry) 1959

Run with the Hunted (poetry) 1962

Poems and Drawings (poetry) 1962

It Catches My Heart in Its Hands: New and Selected Poems, 1955-1963 (poetry) 1963

Grasp the Walls (poetry) 1964

Cold Dogs in the Courtyard (poetry) 1965

Crucifix in a Deathhand: New Poems, 1963-1965 (poetry) 1965

The Genius of the Crowd (poetry) 1966

True Story (poetry) 1966

On Going Out to Get the Mail (poetry) 1966

To Kiss the Worms Goodnight (poetry) 1966

The Girls (poetry) 1966

The Flower Lover (poetry) 1966

Night's Work (poetry) 1966

2 by Bukowski (poetry) 1967

The Curtains Are Waving (poetry) 1967

At Terror Street and Agony Way (poetry) 1968

Poems Written before Jumping out of an 8-Story Window (poetry) 1968

If We Take. . . (poetry) 1969

The Days Run Away Like Wild Horses over the Hills (poetry) 1969

Another Academy (poetry) 1970

Fire Station (poetry) 1970

Post Office (novel) 1971

Erections, Ejaculations, Exhibitions, and General Tales of Ordinary Madness (short stories) 1972, abridged edition published as *Life and Death in the Charity Ward*, 1974

Mockingbird, Wish Me Luck (poetry) 1972

Me and Your Sometimes Love Poems (poetry) 1972

Notes of a Dirty Old Man (short stories) 1973

South of No North (short stories) 1973

While the Music Played (poetry) 1973

Love Poems to Marina (poetry) 1973

Burning in Water, Drowning in Flame: Selected Poems, 1955-1973 (poetry) 1974

Chilled Green (poetry) 1975

Africa, Paris, Greece (poetry) 1975.

Factotum (novel) 1975

Weather Report (poetry) 1975

Winter, No Mountain (poetry) 1975

Tough Company, [bound with *The Last Poem* by Diane Wakoski] (poetry) 1975

Scarlet (poetry) 1976

Maybe Tomorrow (poetry) 1977

Love Is a Dog from Hell: Poems, 1974-1977 (poetry) 1977

Women (novel) 1978

Legs, Hips, and Behind (poetry) 1979

Play the Piano Drunk Like a Percussion Instrument until the Fingers Begin to Bleed a Bit (poetry) 1979

A Love Poem (poetry) 1979

Dangling in the Tournefortia (poetry) 1981

Ham on Rye (novel) 1982

Horsemeat (novel) 1982

The Last Generation (poetry) 1982

Hot Water Music (short stories) 1983

Sparks (poetry) 1983

The Bukowski/Purdy Letters: A Decade of Dialogue, 1964-1974 [with Al Purdy] (letters) 1983

Barfly (novel) 1984

There's No Business (short stories) 1984

War All the Time: Poems, 1981-1984 (poetry) 1984

The Movie: Barfly (screenplay) 1987

The Roominghouse Madrigals: Early Selected Poems, 1946-1966 (poetry) 1988

Hollywood (novel) 1989

The Last Night of the Earth Poems (poetry) 1992

Pulp (novel) 1994

CRITICISM

Robert Wennersten (interview date December 1974/January 1975)

SOURCE: "Paying for Horses," in *London Magazine*, Vol. 1, No. 15, December 1974/January 1975, pp. 35-54.

[*In the following interview, Bukowski discusses his writing and life.*]

Charles Bukowski was born in Andernach, Germany. When he was two years old, his parents brought him to the United States; and he was raised in Los Angeles, where, after a long period of bumming around the country, he still lives.

Bukowski, mostly self-educated, began writing in his early twenties. Ignored, he stopped. Ten years later he started again and since then has published about twenty books of poetry, hundreds of short stories and one novel, **Post Office.** *Bukowski's writing is about an existence he once sought out for himself, so knows firsthand: he writes about the lower classes paddling as fast as they can to avoid drowning in the shit life pours on them. His characters, if they are employed at all, hold down dull, starvation-wage jobs. Off work they drink too much and live chaotically. Their attempts to make it—with women, at the race track or simply from day to day—are sometimes pathetic, sometimes nasty, often hilarious.*

On the day of this interview, Bukowski was living, temporarily, in a typical Los Angeles apartment building: low and square with a paved courtyard in the center. He was standing at the top of the stairs that led to his second-floor rooms. Broad, but not a tall man, he was dressed in a print shirt and blue jeans pulled tight under a beer belly. His long, dark hair was combed straight back. He had a wiry beard and moustache, both flecked with grey. "You didn't bring a bottle," he said slowly, chuckling and walking inside. "My girl was afraid you'd bring a fifth and get me so drunk that I wouldn't be able to take care of business when I see her tonight."

In the living room, he sat down on a bed which also served as a couch. He lit a cigarette, put it in an ashtray and clasped his hands between his knees. Aside from reaching for that cigarette or lighting another one, he seldom made a gesture. To the first questions, his answers were taciturn, just one or two sentences; yet he frequently accused himself of being long-winded. Reassured that he was not, he gradually became more and more talkative.

When the interview ended, Bukowski rose and walked to a table on the opposite side of the room. He picked up a pamphlet, flipped it open and said, "Look at this. Something's going on." The pamphlet turned out to be an autograph dealer's catalogue, and it listed about a dozen Bukowski letters for sale. He stared at the list a moment, tossed the catalogue back on the table and mumbled, "I'll make it, man. I'll make it."

[*Wennersten:*] *What were your parents and your childhood like?*

[*Bukowski:*] Oh, God. Well, my parents were of German ex-traction. My mother was born there; and my father's people were German, although he came out of Pasadena.

My father liked to whip me with a razor strop. My mother backed him. A sad story. Very good discipline all the way through, but very little love going either direction. Good training for the world, though, they made me ready. Today, watching other children, I'd say one thing they taught me was not to weep too much when something goes wrong. In other words, they hardened me to what I was going to go through: the bum, the road, all the bad jobs and the adversity. Since my early life hadn't been soft, the rest didn't come as such a shock.

We lived at 2122 Longwood Avenue. That's a little bit west and a little bit south of here. When I first started shacking with women, I lived near downtown; and it seems like through the years each move I make is further west and further north. I felt myself going towards Beverly Hills at one time. I'm in this place now, because I got booted out of the house where I lived with this lady. We had a minor split, so all of a sudden I came back south a bit. I got thrown off course. I guess I'm not going to make Beverly Hills.

What changes have you seen in Los Angeles during the years you've lived here?

Nothing astounding. It's gotten bigger, dumber, more violent and greedier. It's developed along the same lines as the rest of civilization.

But there's a part of LA—you take it away from Hollywood, Disneyland and the ocean, which are places I stay away from, except the beaches in wintertime when there's no one around—where there's a good, easy feeling. People here have a way of minding their own damned business. You can get isolation here, or you can have a party. I can get on that phone and in an hour have a dozen people over drinking and laughing. And that's not because I'm a writer who's getting known a little. This has always been, even before I had any luck. But they won't come unless I phone them, unless I want them. You can have isolation, or you can have the crowd. I tend to mix the two, with a preference for isolation.

One of your short stories has this line in it: "LA is the cruelest city in the world." Do you believe it is?

I don't think LA is the cruelest city. It's one of the least cruel. If you're on the bum and know a few people, you can get a buck here and there, float around and always find a place to lay up overnight. People will tolerate you for a night. Then you go to the next pad. I put people up overnight. I say, "Look, I can only stand you for one night. You've got to go." But I put them up. It's a thing people in LA do. Maybe they do it elsewhere, and I just haven't seen it.

I don't get the feeling of cruelty here that I get from New York City. Philadelphia has nice rays, too; it has a good feeling. So does New Orleans. San Francisco isn't all they say it is. If I had to rate cities, I'd put LA right up on top: LA, Philadelphia, New Orleans. Those are places where somebody can *live.*

I've left LA many times, but I always come back. You live in a town all of your life, and you get to know every street corner. You've got the layout of the whole land. You have this picture of where you are. When I hit a strange town, I seldom got out of the neighborhood. I'd settle within an area of two or three blocks: the bar, the room I lived in and the streets around them. That's all I knew about a town, so I always felt lost; I was never located, never quite knew where I was. Since I was raised in LA, I've always had the geographical and spiritual feeling of being here. I've had time to learn this city. I can't see any other place than LA.

Do you still travel a lot?

I've done my traveling. I've traveled so damn much, mostly via buses or some other cheap mode, that I've gotten tired of it. At one time I had this idea that one could live on a bus forever: traveling, eating, getting off, shitting, getting back on that bus. (I don't know where the income was supposed to come from.) I had the strange idea that one could stay in motion forever. There was something fascinating about constant motion, because you're not tied down. Well, it was fascinating for a while; and then I got un-fascinated, or non-fascinated. Now I hardly travel; I hate going to the drugstore.

What turned you off about New York?

I didn't like it. I didn't have a taste for it. I don't think I could ever like New York, and there's no need to go there. I guess New York was almost the beginning of American civilization. Now it's the top of our civilization. It represents what we mean. I don't like what we mean, what New Yorkers mean.

I landed there with $7 and no job. I walked out of the bus station into Times Square. It was when all the people were getting off their jobs. They came roaring out of these holes in the ground, these subways. They knocked me about, spun me about. The people were more brutal than any I'd ever seen anywhere else. It was dark and dank, and the buildings were so damned tall. When you only have $7 in your pocket and look up at those huge buildings . . . .

Of course, I deliberately went to New York broke. I went to every town broke in order to learn that town from the bottom. You come into a town from the top—you know, fancy hotel, fancy dinners, fancy drinks, money in your pocket—

and you're not seeing that town at all. True, I denied myself a full view. I got a bottom view, which I didn't like; but I was more interested in what was going on at the bottom. I thought that was the place. I found out it wasn't. I used to think the real men (people you can put up with for over ten minutes) were at the bottom, instead of at the top. The real men aren't at the top, middle or bottom. There's no location. They're just very scarce; there aren't many of them.

Why was San Francisco a disappointment?

You get the big build-up, you know, in literature and movies and God knows where else. I got up there and looked around, and it didn't seem to live up to it. The build-up was too big; so when I finally got there, there was a natural let-down. And when I hit San Francisco, I knew I had to hustle a job. I knew some guy would hire me, pay me a bit of money, and I'd have to bust my ass and be grateful that I had a job. It was the same as every place else.

Most cities are alike: you've got people, a business district, whore-houses, police who hassle you and a bunch of bad poets walking around. Maybe the weather is different, and the people have slightly different accents; that's about it. But, like I said, LA has a spiritual and geographical difference which, because I've been hanging around it, I've picked up on. I have an acquaintanceship with LA, you might say.

Now, women are a lot different than cities. If you're lucky, you do all right. You've got to be lucky with women, because the way you meet them is mostly through accident. If you turn right at a corner, you meet this one; if you turn left, you meet the other one. Love is a form of accident. The population bounces together, and two people meet somehow. You can say that you love a certain woman, but there's a woman you never met you might have loved a hell of a lot more. That's why I say you have to be lucky. If you meet someone up near that possible top, you're lucky. If you don't, well, you turned right instead of left, or you didn't search long enough, or you're plain, damned unlucky.

Did you do much writing while you were on the road?

I got some writing done in New York. In Philadelphia, St. Louis and New Orleans, too, in my early days. St. Louis was very lucky for me. I was there when I got rid of my first short story—to *Story* mag, which was quite a mag in its day. (They discovered William Saroyan and reprinted top-class writers.) I don't remember if I wrote the story in St. Louis, because I was moving pretty fast then; but I was there when it got accepted.

You've got to have a good city to write in, and you've got to have a certain place to live in to write. This apartment is not right for me; but I had to move right away, and I got tired of looking around. This place isn't rugged enough. The neighbors don't like any noise at all. It's very constrictive, but I'm not here most of the time. I'm usually over at Linda's big house. I write there and lay around. This place is for when things go wrong with her. Then I come running back here. I call it my office. You see, my typewriter isn't even here; it's over there. I used to pay rent over there. Then we had a split. Now I still live there, but I don't pay rent. That was a smart move.

How did you end up, at one point in your life, on the bum?

It just occurred. Probably through the drinking and disgust and having to hold a mundane job. I couldn't face working for somebody, that eight-to-five thing. So I got hold of a bottle and drank and tried to make it without working. Working was frankly distasteful to me. Starving and being on the bum seemed to have more glory.

There was this bar I went to in Philly. I had the same barstool—I forget where it was now; I think it was on the end—reserved for me. I'd open the bar early in the morning and close it at night. I was a fixture. I ran errands for sandwiches, hustled a little. I picked up a dime, a dollar here and there. Nothing crooked, but it wasn't eight to five; it was 5 a.m. to 2 a.m. I guess there were good moments, but I was pretty much out of it. It was kind of a dream state.

What poets do you like reading at the moment?

Auden was pretty good. When I was young and I read, I liked a lot of Auden. I was in a liking mood. I liked that whole gang: Auden, MacLeish, Eliot. I liked them at the time; but when I come back on them now, they don't strike me the same way. Not loose enough. They don't gamble. Too careful. They say good things, and they write it well; but they're too careful for me now.

And there's Stephen Spender. Once I was lying in bed, and I opened this book up. You know what happens when a poem hits you. I was thinking of that one with the touch of corn about the poets who have "left the air signed with their honor". That was pretty good. Spender got them off. I can't remember them all, but I know that he set me off three, four, five, six times. The more modern poets don't seem to do this to me.

It could be that I was more spiritually available to be turned on at that time and that I wasn't as much into the game. To be sitting in the stands as a spectator and see a guy hit a home run: Holy God, that ball goes flying over the fence, and it's a miracle. When you get down there and play with them and hit a few over yourself, you say, "That wasn't so hard. I just seemed to tap that ball, and it went over the wall." When you finally get into the game, miracles aren't as big as when

you're looking on from the sidelines. That has something to do with my lack of appreciation now.

Then you meet the writers finally, and that's not a very good experience. Usually, when they're not on the poem, they're rather bitchy, frightened, antagonistic little chipmunks. When they get turned on, art is their field; but when they get out of their field, they're despicable creatures. I'd much rather talk to a plumber over a bottle of beer than a poet. You can say something to a plumber, and he can talk back. The conversation can go both ways. A poet, though, or a creative person, is generally pushing. There's something I don't like about them. Hell, I'm probably the same way, but I'm not as aware of it as when it comes from another person.

Do the classical poets—say, Shakespeare—do anything for you?

Hardly. No, Shakespeare didn't work at all for me, except given lines. There was a lot of good advice in there, but he didn't pick me up. These kings running around, these ghosts, that upper-crust shit bored me. I couldn't relate to it. It had nothing to do with me. Here I am lying in a room starving to death—I've got a candy bar and half a bottle of wine—and this guy is talking about the agony of a king. It didn't help.

I think of Conrad Aiken as classical. He's hardly Shakespeare's time, but his style is classical. I feel it was influenced by the older poets way back. He is one of the few poets who turns me on with classical lines. I admire Conrad Aiken very much. But most of the—what shall I call them, purists?—don't pick me up.

There was one at the reading the other night. William Stafford. When he started turning on those lines, I couldn't listen. I have an instinctive radar, and it shut me off. I saw the mouth move, I heard sounds; but I couldn't listen. I don't want to take castor oil.

What do you look for in a good poem?

The hard, clean line that says it. And it's got to have some blood; it's got to have some humor; it's got to have that unnameable thing which you know is there the minute you start reading.

As I said, modern poets don't have it for some reason. Like Ginsberg. He writes a lot of good lines. You take the lines separately, read one and say, "Hey, that's a good line." Then you read the next one and say, "Well, that's a fair line"; but you're still thinking of the first line. You get down to the third, and there's a different twist. Pretty soon you're lost in this flotsam and jetsam of words that are words themselves, bouncing around. The totality, the total feel, is gone.

That's what happens a lot. They throw in a good line—maybe at the end, maybe in the middle or a third of the way down—but the totality and the simplicity are not there. Not for me, anyway. They may be there, but I can't find them. I wish they were there; I'd have better reading material. That's why I'm not doing all the reading I should, or like people say you should.

How much reading should you do? I've always thought that writers who don't read are like people who always talk and never listen.

I don't listen very well, either. I think it's a protective mechanism. In other words, I fear the grind-down of doing something that's supposed to have an effect on me. Instinctively, I know ahead of time that the effect won't be there. That's my radar again. I don't have to arrive there myself to know that there's not going to be anything there.

I hit the library pretty hard in my early days. I did try the reading. Suddenly I glanced around, and I was out of material. I'd been through all the standard literature, philosophy, the whole lot. So I branched out; I wandered around. I went into geology. I even made a study of the operation on the mesacolon. That operation was damned interesting. You know, the type of knives, what you do: shut this off, cut this vein. I said, "This isn't bad. Much more interesting than Chekhov." When you get into other areas, out of pure literature, you sometimes really get picked up. It's not the same old shit.

Anymore, I don't like to read. It bores me. I read four or five pages, and I feel like closing my eyes and going to sleep. That's the way it is. There are exceptions: J.D. Salinger; early Hemingway; Sherwood Anderson, when he was good, like, *Winesburg, Ohio* and a couple of other things. But they all got bad. We all do. I'm bad most of the time; but when I'm good, I'm damned good.

At one point in your life, you stopped writing for ten years. Why was that?

It started around 1945. I simply gave up. It wasn't because I thought I was a bad writer. I just thought there was no way of crashing through. I put writing down with a sense of disgust. Drinking and shacking with women became my art form. I didn't crash through there with any feeling of glory, but I got a lot of experience which later I could use—especially in short stories. But I wasn't gathering that experience to write it, because I had put the typewriter down.

I don't know. You start drinking; you meet a woman; she wants another bottle; you get into the drinking thing. Everything else vanishes.

What brought it to an end?

Nearly dying. I ended up in County General Hospital with blood roaring out of my mouth and my ass. I was supposed to die, and I didn't. Took lots of glucose and ten or twelve pints of blood. They pumped it straight into me without stop.

When I walked out of that place, I felt very strange. I felt much calmer than before. I felt—to use a trite term—easygoing. I walked along the sidewalk, and I looked at the sunshine and said, "Hey, something has happened." You know, I'd lost a lot of blood. Maybe there was some brain damage. That was my thought, because I had a really different feeling. I had this calm feeling. I talk so slowly now. I wasn't always this way. I was kind of hectic before; I was more going, doing, shooting my mouth off. When I came out of that hospital, I was strangely relaxed.

So I got hold of a typewriter, and I got a job driving a truck. I started drinking huge quantities of beer each night after work and typing out all these poems. (I told you that I didn't know what a poem is, but I was writing *something* in a poem form.) I hadn't written many before, two or three, but I sat down and was writing poems all of a sudden. So I was writing again and had all these poems on my hands. I started mailing them out, and it began all over. I was luckier this time, and I think my work had improved. Maybe the editors were readier, had moved into a different area of thinking. Probably all three things helped make it click. I went on writing.

That's how I met the millionairess. I didn't know what to do with these poems, so I went down a list of magazines and put my finger on one. I said, "All right. Might as well insult this one. She's probably an old woman in this little Texas town. I'll make her unhappy." She wasn't an old woman. She was a young one with lots of money. A beautiful one. We ended up married. I was married to a millionairess for two and a half years. I blew it, but I kept writing.

What happened to the marriage?

I didn't love her. A woman can only tolerate that so long unless she's getting some other type of benefit out of it, either fame or money from you. She got nothing out of our marriage, neither fame nor money. I offered her nothing. Well, we went to bed together. I offered her that, but that's hardly enough to hold a marriage together unless you're a real expert. I wasn't at the time. I was just some guy dressed in clothes who was walking across the room, eating an egg and reading a paper. I was tied up with myself, with my writing. I didn't give her anything at all, so I had it coming. I don't blame her, but she didn't give me much either.

She was arty and turned on to artistic types. She painted

badly and liked to go to art classes. She had a vocabulary and was always reading fancy books. Being rich, she was spoiled in that special way rich people are spoiled without knowing it. She had this air that the rich have. They have a superior air that they never quite let go of. I don't think that money makes much difference between people. It might in what they wear, where they live, what they eat, what they drive; but I don't think it makes *that* much difference between people. Yet, somehow, the rich have this separation value. When they have money and you don't, something unexplainable rises up between you. Now, if she'd given me half of her money so that I could have had half of her feeling, we might have made it. She didn't. She gave me a new car, and that was it; and she gave that to me *after* we split, not before.

In a short story you made a sort of self-pitying remark that went something like this: "Here I am, a poet known to Genet and Henry Miller, washing dishes."

Yes, that's self-pity. That's straight self-pity, but sometimes self-pity feels good. A little howl, when it has some humor mixed with it, is almost forgivable. Self-pity alone. . . . We all fail at times. I didn't do so well there.

I didn't do so well as a dish washer, either. I got fired. They said, "This man doesn't know how to wash dishes." I was drunk. I didn't know how to wash dishes, and I ate all their roast beef. They had a big leg of roast beef back there. I'd been on a drunk, and I hadn't eaten for a week. I kept slicing this goddamned leg. I ate about half of it. I failed as a dish washer, but I got a good feed.

Another time, though, you said you enjoyed anonymity, that you liked the idea of people not knowing who you are. That seems like a contradiction.

There's a difference between being known by another writer and being known by the crowd. A good workman—if we can call it that—like, a carpenter—wants to be known as a good carpenter by other carpenters. The crowd is something else; but to be known by another good writer . . . I don't find that detestable.

Do the critics' opinions of your work ever bother you?

When they say I'm very, very good, it doesn't affect me anymore than when they say I'm very, very bad. I feel good when they say nice things; I feel good when they say unnice things, especially when they say them with great vehemence. Critics usually go overboard one way or the other, and one excites me as much as the other.

I want reactions to my work, whether they be good or bad; but I like an ad-mixture. I don't want to be totally revered

or looked upon as a holy man or a miracle worker. I want a certain amount of attack, because it makes it more human, more like where I've been living all my life. I've always been attacked in one fashion or another, and it's grown on me. A little rejection is good for the soul; but total attack, total rejection is utterly destructive. So I want a good balance: praise, attack, the whole stewpot full of everything.

Critics amuse me. I like them. They're nice to have around, but I don't know what their proper function is. Maybe to beat their wives.

In **Post Office** *there's an episode about the flack you got from the government because of your writing. Did they actually give you a lot of trouble?*

My God, yes. The whole scene underground: one dim light, the handshake, sitting down at the end of a long table, two guys asking me little trap questions. I just told them the truth. Everything they asked, I told the truth. (It's only when you lie that you get your ass in the wringer. I guess the big boys have found that out now.) I thought, Is this America? Sure, I'll back it all the way as really happening. I wrote a short story about it, too.

You've been published a lot in the underground press. Those newspapers, now, seem to have lost their original vigor. What happened to them?

They've turned into a business, and the real revolutionaries were never there. The underground press was just lonely people who wanted to get around and talk to each other while putting out a newspaper. They went left wing and liberal, because it was the young and proper thing to do; but they weren't really interested in it. Those newspapers were kind of a lark. They were a sign to carry around, like wearing a certain type of clothing. I can't think of one underground newspaper that meant anything, shook anybody.

You mentioned your problems with women. Didn't one of your girl friends recently try to kill you?

She found me on my way to another lady's house. I had already been there and gone and was coming back with two six-packs and a pint of whiskey. I was quite high at the time. Her car was parked out in front, so I said, "Oh, jolly. I'll take her up and introduce her to the other one, and we'll all be friends and have drinks." No chance. She rushed me. She got those bottles out and started smashing them all up and down the boulevard—including the pint of whiskey. She disappeared. I'm out sweeping the glass up, and I hear this sound. I looked up just in time. She's got her car up on the sidewalk, rushing it towards me. I leaped aside, and she was gone. She missed.

Many of your stories read as if they're written off the top of your head. Do you write that way, or do you rewrite a great deal?

I seldom revise or correct a story. In the old days, I used to just sit down and write it and leave it. I don't quite do that anymore. Lately I've started dripping out what I think are bad or unnecessary lines that take away from a story. I'll subtract maybe four or five lines, but I hardly ever add anything.

And I can't write except off a typewriter. The typewriter keeps it strict and confined. It keeps it right there. I've tried to write longhand; it doesn't work. A pencil or a pen . . . it's too intellectual, too soft, too dull. No machine-gun sounds, you know. No action.

Can you write and drink at the same time?

It's hard to write prose when you're drinking, because prose is too much work. It doesn't work for me. It's too unromantic to write prose when you're drinking.

Poetry is something else. You have this feeling in mind that you want to lay down the line that startles. You get a bit dramatic when you're drunk, a bit corny. It feels good. The symphony music is on, and you're smoking a cigar. You lift the beer, and you're going to tap out these five or six or fifteen or thirty great lines. You start drinking and write poems all night. You find them on the floor in the morning. You take out all the bad lines, and you have poems. About sixty per cent of the lines are bad; but it seems like the remaining lines, when you drop them together, make a poem.

I don't always write drunk. I write sober, drunk, feeling good, feeling bad. There's no special way for me to be.

Gore Vidal said once that, with only one or two exceptions, all American writers were drunkards. Was he right?

Several people have said that. James Dickie said that the two things that go along with poetry are alcoholism and suicide. I know a lot of writers, and as far as I know they all drink but one. Most of them with any bit of talent are drunkards, now that I think about it. It's true.

Drinking is an emotional thing. It joggles you out of the standardism of everyday life, out of everything being the same. It yanks you out of your body and your mind and throws you up against the wall. I have the feeling that drinking is a form of suicide where you're allowed to return to life and begin all over the next day. It's like killing yourself, and then you're reborn. I guess I've lived about ten or fifteen thousand lives now.

Just a minute ago you mentioned classical music, and you

make remarks about it in lots of your stories. Are you seriously interested in it?

Not as a conscious thing. In other words, I have a radio—no records—and I turn that classical music station on and hope it brings me something that I can align with while I'm writing. I don't listen deliberately. Some people object to this in me. A couple of girl friends I've had have objected that I don't sit down and *listen*. I don't. I use it like the modern person uses a television set: they turn it on and walk around and kind of ignore it, but it's there. It's a fireplace full of coals that does something for them. Let's say it's something in the room with you that helps you, especially when you're living alone.

Say you work in a factory all day. When you come home, somehow that factory is still hanging to your bones: all the conversation, all the wasted hours. You try to recover from those eight, ten hours they've taken from you and use what juice you have left to do what you really want to do. First, I used to take a good, hot bath. Then I turned on the radio, got some classical music, lit a big cigar, opened a bottle of beer and sat down at the typewriter. All these became habitual, and often I couldn't write unless they were happening. I'm not so much that way now, but at the time I did need those props to escape the factory syndrome.

I like a certain amount of interruption when I'm writing. I do a lot of writing over at Linda's. She has two kids, and once in a while I like to have them run in. I like interruptions, as long as they're natural and aren't total and continuous. When I lived in a court, I put my typewriter right by the window. I'd be writing, and I'd see people walking by. Somehow that always worked into what I was doing at the moment. Children, people walking by and classical music are all the same that way. Instead of a hindrance, they're an aid. That's why I like classical music. It's there, but it's not there. It doesn't engulf the work, but it's there.

There's a certain Bukowski image that's been created: drunkard, lecher, bum. Do you ever catch yourself deliberately trying to live up to that image?

Sometimes, especially, say, at poetry readings where I have a bottle of beer by my hand. Well, I don't need that beer, but I can feel the audience relating when I lift that beer and drink it. I laugh and make remarks. I don't know if I'm playing the game or they're playing the game. Anyway, I'm conscious of some image that I've built up or that they've built, and it's dangerous. You notice that I'm not drinking today. I fooled you. Blew the image.

If I drink two or three days in a row, I get pretty bad. Like I said, I've been in the hospital. My liver is not in great shape, and probably neither are several other organs. I heat up very much; my skin gets red-hot. There are a lot of danger signs. I like drinking, but it should be alternated; so I take a few days off now and then, instead of running a string of drinking days and nights together like I used to. I'm fifty-three now; I want to stay in the game a while longer, so I can piss a lot of people off. If I live to be eighty, I'll really piss them off.

Are poetry readings as bad an experience as you make them out to be in a couple of your short stories?

They are torture, but I've got to pay for the horses. I guess I read for horses instead of people.

How much time do you spend at the track?

Too much, too much, and now I've got my girl friend hooked. I never mention the track to her, you know. We'll be lying down, and morning will come around. Or we'll be writing. (She writes in one corner of the room, and I write in another. We do pretty well that way.) We've been at the track all week, and I'll say, "We'll get some goddamned writing done today at last." All of a sudden, she says something about the race track. It could be just a word or two. I'll say, "All right, let's go. You said it." That always happens. If she'd keep her mouth shut, we'd never go. Between the two of us, we've got to solve that problem of one wanting to go and the other not.

Races are a drag-down. There are thirty minutes between races, which is a real murder of time; and if you lose your money on top of it, it's no good. But what happens is that you come home and think, "I've got it now. I know what they are doing out there." You get up a whole new system. When you go back, either they changed it a little or you don't follow your nose: you get off the system, and the horse comes in. Horses teach you whether you have character or not.

Sometimes we go to the thoroughbreds in the daytime, then we jump over and play the harness at night. That's eighteen races. When you do that, you've had it. You're so tired. It's no good. Between her and me, we've had a rough week; but track season closes in a few days, so my worries will be over. Race tracks are horrible places. If I had my way, I'd have them all burned down, destroyed. Don't ask me why I go, because I don't know; but I have gotten some material out of all that torture.

Horse racing does something to you. It's like drinking: it joggles you out of the ordinary concept of things. Like Hemingway used the bullfights, I use the race track. Of course, when you go to the track every day, that's no damned joggle: it's a definite bring-down.

What do you think about the Supreme Court's recent decision on pornography?

I agree with almost everybody else. It was silly to relegate it to the local area, the town or the city. I mean, a man makes a movie; he spends millions of dollars on it, and he doesn't know where to send it. They're going to love it in Hollywood and hate it in Pasadena. He'll have to sense out how each city is going to react. My idea on obscenity is to let everything go. Let everybody be as obscene as they wish, and it will dissipate. Those who want it will use it. It's hiding things, holding back that makes something so-called evil.

Obscenity is generally very boring. It's badly done. Look at the theaters that show porno films: they're all going broke now. That happened very quickly, didn't it? They lowered the price from $5 to 49 cents, and nobody wants to see them even for that. I've never seen a good porno film. They're all so dull. These vast mounds of flesh moving around: here's the cock; the guy has three women. Ho-hum. God, all that *flesh.* You know, what's exciting is a woman in clothes, and the guy rips her skirt off. These people have no imagination. They don't know how to excite. Of course, if they did, they'd be artists instead of pornographers.

I understand that **Post Office** *might be sold to the movies. If it is, will you write the screenplay?*

I would tend to back away from it. I'd rather put any energy I have (I almost said "left") into a piece of paper: beginning a new novel or finishing the one I'm at or starting a poem. I'm like any other guy who's doing what he wants to do in his own way.

It's such a whole new field that, unless I have total control, I don't want to enter it; and I'm not well enough known to get total control. Unless they gave me my own head, I wouldn't want to do it; and if they gave me my own head, *they* wouldn't want to do it. I don't want to fight all those people to get my thing across. Once again, the radar tells me there'd be too much trouble.

What are you working on now?

I'm putting a novel together. A book of short stories is coming out, and some of those are similar to chapters in the novel. So I'm pulling all these chapters out, patching it up and putting it back together. It's a good exercise. The novel is called **Factotum.** Factotum means a man of all trades, many jobs. It's about many of the jobs I've had. I took the glamorous chapters out, which is just as well. Now I can have the everyday humdrum thing of the alcoholic, low-class, as they call them, workers trying to make it. I got the idea, kind of, from *Down and Out in Paris and London.* I read that book and said, "This guy thinks something has happened to him? Compared to me, he just got scratched." Not that it wasn't a good book, but it made me think that I might have something interesting to say along those same lines.

One last question: Why do you put yourself down so much in your stories?

It's partly a kind of joke. The rest is because I feel that I'm an ass a lot of the time. If I'm an ass, I should say so. If I don't, somebody else will. If I say it first, that disarms them.

You know, I'm *really* an ass when I'm about half smashed. Then I look for trouble. I've never grown up. I'm a cheap drunk. Get a few drinks in me, and I can whip the world . . . and I want to.

Glenn Esterly (interview date 17 June 1976)

SOURCE: "The Pock-marked Poetry of Charles Bukowski: Notes of a Dirty Old Mankind," in *Rolling Stone,* June 17, 1976, pp. 28-34.

[*In the following interview, Esterly and Bukowski discuss topics such as the author's writing, his life, his relationships with women, and other issues.*]

In preparation for tonight's poetry reading, Charles Bukowski is out in the parking lot, vomiting. He always vomits before readings; crowds give him the jitters. And tonight there's a big crowd. Some 400 noisy students—many of whom have come directly from nearby 49rs tavern—are packed into an antiseptic auditorium at California State University at Long Beach on this fourth night of something called Poetry Week. Not exactly the kind of event calculated to set the campus astir, as evidenced by the sparse audiences for readings by other poets on the first three nights. But Bukowski always attracts a good crowd. He has a reputation here—for his performances as well as his poetry. Last time he was here, he had both an afternoon and an evening reading. In between, he got hold of a bottle and slipped over the edge. Too drunk to read at the evening performance, he decided to entertain the students by exchanging insults with them. It developed into quite a show.

Backstage, Leo Mailman, publisher of a small literary magazine and coordinator of tonight's reading, peeks between the stage curtains for a look at the audience and says: "A lot of these people are repeaters from his last reading. Some of them were disappointed by his drunkenness: they thought they got ripped off. But a lot of others were perfectly satisfied because they felt they got a look at the real Bukowski—you know, the legendary gruff, dirty old man, the drunk who

doesn't give a damn and goes around looking for fights. They saw Bukowski in the raw.

"At the other extreme, when I called him to make arrangements for this reading, he was completely sober and fell all over himself apologizing for the way he acted last time. He was very soft-spoken, telling me how sorry he was he got drunk and how he hoped to make it up to us this time. I was amazed. So who's to say which one is the real Bukowski—the hostile drunk who makes a spectacle of himself, or the humble, diffident guy who's worried that he might have let somebody down?"

A few minutes later, Bukowski, clad in an open-necked shirt, tattered charcoal *American Graffiti* era sport coat and baggy gray pants, shows up backstage, having finished his warm-up activities in the parking lot. Pale and nervous, he tells Mailman: "Okay, let's get this travesty over so I can collect my check and get the hell outta here." Then he lumbers out, unannounced, onto the stage. Mailman turns to Bukowski's companion, Linda King, a spirited, full-figured 34-year-old poet and sculptor who has survived a stormy relationship with the poet for five years. "Is he all right?" Mailman asks. "Sure," she says. "He's only had a few beers and he's feeling pretty good. He wants to do well tonight." As the audience begins applauding, Bukowski takes a chair behind a small table on the stage. Hunched over close to the microphone, he announces. "I'm Charles Bukowski," then takes a long hit from a thermos bottle filled with vodka and orange juice prompting cheers from several students. He grins a half-shy, half-sly grin. "I just brought a little vitamin *C* along for my health . . . . Well, here we are, on the poetry hustle again. Listen, I've decided to read all the serious poems first and get 'em outta the goddamn way so we can enjoy ourselves, okay?"

> **The crude, antisocial alcoholic is earning his living with his typewriter now, nailing the words to the page in intensely personal, rawly sensitive poems and wild, raunchy, anecdotal short stories that have earned him an international reputation with translations into other languages.**
> **—*Glenn Esterly***

As he begins reading, a coed in the third row who's seeing the poet for the first time turns to a friend and asks. "Do you think he's as ugly as they say?" Her friend puts her finger tips to her lips in contemplation as she sizes him up. "Yeah, but he's impressive-looking somehow. That face . . . he looks like he's lived a hundred years. It's kind of tragic and dignified at the same time."

That face. By any conventional standards it *is* ugly, and for most of Bukowski's 55 years that's exactly what people called it. That's what they called it during all those years when he was working at bone-crushing, mind-stultifying jobs in slaughterhouses and factories, living on the underside of the American Dream. But things have changed. The crude, antisocial alcoholic is earning his living with his typewriter now, nailing the words to the page in intensely personal, rawly sensitive poems and wild, raunchy, anecdotal short stories that have earned him an international reputation with translations into other languages. He writes about what he has experienced: poverty, menial jobs, chronic hangovers, hard women, jails, fighting the system, failing, feeling bad. The impression created is of someone with his foot in a trap who's trying to gnaw himself free at the ankle. Which could make for a lot of drab reading if it weren't for the fact that there's frequent relief in a sardonic humor that sometimes gives one the feeling that W.C. Fields has been reincarnated as a writer.

Bukowski's appeal was summed up before the reading by Gerald Locklin, a burly, bearded poet who teaches literature at Cal State. Locklin, who has been following Bukowski's progress for many years and has known him four years, was drinking beer with a couple students at the 49rs and observing: "I think of him as a survival study. This guy has not only survived problems that would kill most men, he's survived with enough voice and talent left to write about it. You know, you're always running into people in bars who say that if they could only write about their lives, it would make such great reading. Well, they never do, of course. But Bukowski has."

Locklin also believes Bukowski "deserves credit for leading us in a new direction in American poetry with his direct, spontaneous, conversational free-form style. Many poets had been talking for a long time about getting more of a narrative quality into their work, but until Bukowski no one really succeeded. He just did it naturally, without really thinking very much about it. The more traditional poets hate him for it, but I think the trend he started was long overdue. His kind of style has its dangers: it can result in a lot of very ordinary poetry, and Bukowski has written his share. But at his best he's hard to beat, believe me."

Another view has been provided by poet Hal Norse, who had a falling out with Bukowski after being close to him for several years. Writing about their relationship in the *Small Press Review,* Norse said: "Hateful as he can be—and, God, he can be so detestable you want to shove him up a camel's ass—somehow the warmth and snotty charm of the bastard come through so powerfully that he remains an attractive personality, ugliness and all."

So here the man is, making it at last. Sartre and Genet have

volunteered compliments about his poetry. His position as an underground folk hero is secure. Colleges fly him around the country for readings. Some critics have gone so far as to compare his prose stories to those of Miller, Hemingway. The National Endowment for the Arts has blessed him with a grant. A university has established a literary archive in his name. His early out-of-print books are valuable collectors' items. The *New York Review of Books,* for crying out loud, has reviewed him. Desirable young women keep knocking at his door. And now they call the face things like tragic . . . dignified . . . even beautiful. Bukowski appreciates the ironies of it.

The face, no bargain to begin with, has been abused terribly over the years. There was a blood disease that hospitalized him for months as a teenager with boils the size of small apples on his face and back ("It was my hatred for my father coming out through my skin—an emotional thing"), leaving a lifelong imprint of pockmarks. Later, there were the cruel whores who gouged out pieces of flesh with their fingernails when he was too drunk to fight back, leaving more scars. In the middle of these facial road maps of past troubles is a bulbous nose, swollen and lumpy and red in futile protest against the exorbitant amounts of alcohol, and above the nose two small gray eyes set deep into the huge skull stare out warily at the world. An unexpected feature of the Bukowski body are the hands: two quite delicate lands at the ends of muscular arms, the hands of an artist or musician. Beautiful hands, really. ("I tell the women that the face is my experience and the hands are my soul—anything to get those panties down.")

Those beautiful hands reach for his thermos bottle after each poem as he gathers momentum, reading about his women:

> this woman thinks she's a panther
> and sometimes when we are making
>   love
> she'll snarl and spit
> and her hair comes down
> and she looks out from the strands
> and shows me her fangs
> but I kiss her anyhow and
>   continue to love . . .

> **—"have you ever kissed a panther?"**

hard times:

> . . . the best one can settle for
> is an afternoon
> with the rent paid, some food in the
>   refrigerator,
> and death something like
> a bad painting by a bad painter

(that you finally buy because there's
 not
anything else
around).

—**"left with the day"**

the race track:

> . . . There are thoroughbred horses
> and thoroughbred bettors. What
>   you do is
> stay with your plays and let them
>   come to you.
>   Loving
> a woman is the same way, or loving
>   life. You've
> got to work a bit for it . . .

—**"a day at the oak tree meet"**

one of his favorite poets:

> . . . I find a black book by the typer:
> Jeffers' Be Angry at the Sun.
> I think of Jeffers often,
> of his rocks and his hawks and his
> isolation.
> Jeffers was a real loner.
> yes, he had to write.
> I try to think of loners who don't
>   break out
> at all
> in any fashion,
> and I think, no, that's not strong,
> somehow, that's dead.
> Jeffers was alive and a loner and
> he made his statements.
> his rocks and his hawks and his
>   isolation
> counted.
> he wrote in lonely blood
> a man trapped in a corner
> but what a corner
> fighting down to the last mark . . .

—**"he wrote in lovely blood"**

and life in general:

> . . . it's not the large things that
> send a man to the
> madhouse, death he's ready for, or
> murder, incest, robbery, fire, flood . . .
> no, it's the continuing series of

small *tragedies*
that send a man to the madhouse . . .
not the death of his love
but a shoelace that snaps
with no time left . . .

—**"the shoelace"**

The vodka is working; the old man is rolling. Bukowski is in good form, just full enough of booze to bring out the showman in him, and the audience responds enthusiastically. On the humorous lines he reads drolly, stretching out certain syllables for emphasis in his mortician's voice and managing to get the same inflections into the spoken word as he has on paper. Despite his often professed dislike for readings, he seems to be enjoying himself now, and to cap off the performance he surprises his listeners by reading a section from a novel in progress. An uninhibited account of an encounter with a fat, sex-starved middle-aged woman ("I'm sorry to say this actually happened to me"), it keeps the audience roaring with its outrageous exaggeration: "She flung herself upon me, and I was crushed under 220 pounds of something less than an angel. Her mouth was upon mine and it dripped spittle and tasted of onions and stale wine and the sperm of 400 men. Suddenly it emitted saliva, and I gagged and pushed her off . . . . Before I could move again she was upon me. She gripped my balls in both of her hands. Her mouth opened, her head lowered, she had me; her head bobbed, sucked, whirled. Although I was on the verge of vomiting, my penis kept growing. Then, giving my balls a tremendous yank while almost biting my pecker in half, she forced me to fall upon the floor. Huge sucking sounds fell upon the walls as my radio played Mahler. My pecker became larger, purple, covered with spittle. If I come, I thought, I'll never forgive myself . . . ."

As he ends, most of the students rise to give him an ovation. He takes off his glasses and gives the crowd a little wave. "Now let's all go out and get smashed." He gathers his papers and gets up to leave. The applause continues as he walks away and, obviously pleased, he suddenly turns back and leans over the microphone. For just a moment, his guard comes down. "You're full of love," he says "—ya mothers."

> with one punch at the age of 16 and ½,
> I knocked out my father,
> a cruel shiny bastard with bad
> breath . . .

—**"the rat"**

Henry Charles Bukowski, Jr., poet, novelist, short story writer, megalomaniac, lush, philanderer, living legend recluse, classical music aficionado, scatologist, loving father, sexist, physical wreck, jailbird, pain in the ass, genius, finagling horse player, outcast, antitraditionalist, brawler and ex-civil servant, is sitting in the small living room of his three-room furnished bungalow, a tacky $105-a-month apartment with worn carpeting, scruffy furniture and frazzled curtains. It's his kind of place, one of eight bungalows in a small court just off Western Avenue in a section of Hollywood heavily populated with massage parlors, pornographic movie theaters and takeout joints. The lady in the bungalow next to his is a stripper and another tenant manages the massage parlor across the street. Bukowski feels at home here. For eight years he had lived in a similar cottage where his writing flourished, despite the fact that the place was, according to all who had been there, the filthiest dwelling they had ever seen (Bukowski personally, however, was, and is, immaculate; he's in the habit of taking four or five baths a day). Then he moved into a much more expensive apartment in a modern complex but he felt out of place and his typewriter fell increasingly silent. So he moved into this bungalow in the hope it would restore the right creative feelings, and so far it has. He hasn't been here long enough for the dust and beer bottles to collect in any appreciable quantities, but he's working on it. The only notable features of the place are two paintings that hang on the walls. They're by Bukowski and they're not bad.

He is guzzling from a 16-ounce can of beer, part of two six-packs I've brought along to help smooth the interview. He doesn't bother to put the six-packs in the refrigerator; it's apparent he figures we'll drink them before the evening is over. Barefooted and dressed in blue jeans and a faded yellow short-sleeved shirt with a button missing at the navel, he looks loose and relaxed. More relaxed, in fact, than I am—that Bukowski countenance is, after all, a little overwhelming in a face-to-face confrontation. Then, too, I've learned enough about the man in talks with people who know him well to know that nothing with Bukowski is predictable. His acquaintances have told me that he'll tolerate me and my questions, but won't go so far as to be cordial. So I'm surprised when he goes out of his way to put me at ease, shoving a beer in my hand and announcing: "I've been drinking beer most of the day, but don't worry, kid—I'm not gonna stick my first through the window or bust up any furniture. I'm a pretty benign beer drinker . . . most of the time. It's the whiskey that gets me in trouble. When I'm drinking it around people, I tend to get silly or pugnacious or wild, which can cause problems. So when I drink it these days, I try to drink it alone. That's the sign of a good whiskey drinker anyway—drinking it by yourself shows a proper reverence for it. The stuff even makes the lampshades look different. Norman Mailer has uttered a lotta shit, but he said one thing I though was great. He said, 'Most Americans get their spiritual inspiration when they're intoxicated, and I'm one of those Americans.' A statement I'll back up 100%, *The Naked and the Dead* be damned. Only thing is a man

has to be careful how he mixes his alcohol and his sex. The best thing for a wise man is to have his sex before he gets drunk 'cause alcohol takes away from that old stem down there. I've been fairly successful at that so far." Grinning, he also informs me that a female friend had departed shortly before my arrival. "Yeah, I had her on that couch you're sitting on. She was pretty young, maybe 23 or 24. She was all right except she didn't know how to kiss. How come kissing the young ones is like kissing a garden hose? Christ, their mouths won't give, they don't know what to do. Ah, well, I shouldn't complain. That makes three different ladies in the last 36 hours. Man, I'll tell ya, women would rather screw poets than just about anything, even German shepherds. If I had only known about all this earlier, I wouldn't have waited till, was 35 to start writing poetry."

We start talking about his childhood going over the details, most of which are still painful for him: his upbringing in Los Angeles after being born in Andernach, Germany; the terrible plague of boils over his face and back, the constant beatings by his father, a milkman who carried Prussian discipline to extremes, whipping his son almost daily with a razor strop for all sorts of imagined offenses; the feeling, even as a young child, of alienation and isolation, of not belonging, of being somehow inferior and superior to his peers at the same time. "The school idiot always gravitated to me he recalls. "Ya know, the fucked up guy who was cross-eyed and wore the wrong kind of clothes and was always going around stepping in dog shit. If there was a pile of dog shit within ten miles, this guy would manage to step in it. So I sort of disdained him but somehow he'd wind up being my buddy. We'd sit around eating our pitiful peanut-butter sandwiches and watching the other kids play their games." Several other boys at school made a habit of beating up his hapless friend. For some reason, though, they left Bukowski alone. "They understood I was almost like him, almost as fucked up, but they were just a little wary of me," he says. "I seemed to have something extra, something in my demeanor that kept 'em from picking on me Maybe it was a wild look in my eyes, I don't know, but they seemed to sense that if they tried it with me they might be in for some trouble. And I guess they would have been too." His tone is casual, unemotional, but traces of bitterness sneak through. "I got pretty hard from all those beating from my father, ya know. The old man toughened me up got me ready for the world."

When he was 16, he came home drunk one night, got sick and vomited on the living room rug. His father grabbed him by the neck and began pushing his nose, like a dog's into the vomit. The son exploded, swinging from the heels and catching his father squarely on the jaw. Henry Charles Bukowski Sr. went down and stayed down a long time. He never tried to beat his son again.

At about the same time, young Charles started to frequent

public libraries. He had decided that being a writer made good sense for a loner; the solitude of it appealed to him. At the libraries he was looking for literary heroes. Browsing through the aisles, he would flip through the books and when he found a page that interested him, he took the book home to read. "I'd find one writer and another," he says, "and after a while I found that I'd discovered the same ones who had pretty much stood up over the years. I liked the Russians, Chekhov and the boys. There were some others, most of 'em going a long way back. One day I noticed a book in the stacks called *Bow Down to Wood and Stone* by Josephine Lawrence. The title caught my eye, so I paged through it, but just the title was good. Then I picked up a book right next to it and when I looked through it I said, 'Hey, this bastard can write.' It was by D.H. Lawrence. There's a bit of color for ya."

He was badly disappointed in the contemporary American writers of the day. "I kept thinking, 'They're playing it too safe; they're holding back, not dealing with reality.' At least reality as I knew it. Hell, I'd see these people in the libraries with their heads down on the tables, asleep, with the books open in front of 'em and flies buzzing around their heads. That's a pretty good comment on the books, huh? Yeah, I guess that about summed up what I thought of most of the writing. And the poetry—Jesus! When I was growing up, poets were thought of as sissies. It's easy to see why. I mean, ya couldn't figure out what the hell they were up to. The poem could be about somebody getting punched in the mouth, but the poet never would come out and *say* that somebody got punched in the mouth. The reader was supposed to plod through the fucking thing 18 times to somehow puzzle this out. So when it came to both fiction and poetry, I thought I had a chance to make it 'cause what was being written was so pale and lifeless. It wasn't that I was so good, it was just that they were so goddamn bad."

> . . . I can't help thinking of the years
> in lonely rooms when the only
> people who knocked were the land-
> ladies asking for the back rent . . .
> I lived with rats and mice and wine
> and my blood crawled the walls in a
> world I couldn't understand and still
> can't. Rather than live their life,
> I starved: I ran inside my own mind
> and hid. I pulled down all the shades
> and stared at the ceiling . . .
> I wanted to write but the typer was
> always in hock. I gave it up and
> drank . . .
>
> —*South of No North*

As a young man, Bukowski wrote hundreds of short stories,

sending them off to the wrong markets, magazines like *Harper's* and *Atlantic Monthly* where his style and subjects didn't have a chance. When the manuscripts kept coming back, he figured they weren't any good and threw them away. By the time he was 25 his efforts seemed so futile that he decided to abandon his writing ambitions completely. That's when he hit the road on what turned out to be a ten-year drunk, a period when his life was measured out in six-packs and jugs of cheap wine. Along with the drinking bouts, there were countless odd jobs (he once guarded doors in a Texas whorehouse), a number of nights in jail and a few semiserious attempts at suicide.

There was also a woman named Jane. He met her in a bar and lived with her on and off for several years. They had two things in common: both were alcoholics and both were losers. Jane was bouncing off a shattered marriage to an affluent attorney. She was about ten years older than Bukowski, at the stage of life when, as he puts it, "a woman is still nicely put together, just dangling on the edge of falling apart which is when they look the sexiest to me. "Jane was the first woman who brought him any tenderness and he warmed to it. Up to the age of 22 or 23 he had never even tried to get laid because he was squeamish about his disfigurements and after he did start pursuing women he found they were usually out to hustle him. As a result, he soaked up Jane's affection and stuck with her even after the occasional nights when she allowed herself to be picked up and taken home by other men.

Jane's drinking finally killed her, and a couple of years later, at the age of 35. Bukowski almost died himself from relentless boozing. Eleven pints of blood were pumped into him at L.A. County Hospital to save him from a bleeding ulcer. When he left the hospital, his doctors told him he would be a dead man if he touched alcohol again. It made him so nervous that he walked to the nearest bar and tossed down a few beers—a nice touch for the legend that was to follow. After a period of recuperation, he settled into a routine. At night he worked as a postal clerk at the dreary downtown post office. Then, in the early morning hours, he came home to a dingy apartment turned the radio to a classical music station, sat-down behind a battered old Royal and—energized by a combination' of whiskey, rage and desperation—wrote poems: direct, brutally honest poems tinged with his pain and hostility but stamped as well with a certain compassion and justification for life. He sent the poems out to little magazines and underground publications where, to his surprise, they began to be picked up regularly, Soon small independent publishers were bringing out collections of his work. He quickly earned a reputation as an underground poet of considerable talent and there were signs that it wouldn't end at that. In 1963, in an introduction to Bukowski's *It Catches My Heart in Its Hands,* writer and critic John William Corrington was moved to speculate that "critics at the end of our century may well claim that Charles Bukowski's work was the watershed that divided 20th-century American poetry between the Pound-Eliot-Auden period and the new time in which the human voice speaking came into its own . . . . He has replaced the formal, frequently stilted diction of the Pound-Eliot-Auden days with a language devoid of the affectations, devices and mannerisms that have taken over academic verse and packed the university and commercial quarterlies with imitations of imitations of Pound and the others . . . . What Wordsworth claimed to have done, what Rimbaud actually did do in French, Bukowski has accomplished for the English language."

Heady stuff. Meanwhile, this newly heralded genus continued to expend a sizable portion of his energies sorting mail. It wasn't until 1970, with the encouragement of his primary publisher, John Martin of Black Sparrow Press, that he finally summoned the nerve to quit the job. Panicked at giving up his security, he pounded out the first draft of his first novel, **Post Office**—a kind of *M.A.S.H.* for civil servants—in three weeks, detailing in it the brain-deadening tedium and bureaucratic insanities that had gone with the job, along with descriptions of his brief, bizarre marriage to an heiress with a Texas fortune ("There went my only chance for millions") and his relationship with the woman who bore his daughter, Marina (whom he loves, visits weekly and helps to support).

Today he earns a comfortable though not gaudy income from royalties, readings and the column "Notes of a Dirty Old Man," which he writes for the *L.A. Free Press.* The big money may yet be on the way. There's a bit of wonderment in his eyes when he says: "I'll be sitting here trying to get some work done at the typer, and somebody will call about making a movie outta some of my stuff. Then I start talking about the author's cut and two-year options and how I gotta have net, not gross, and I think to myself, Good God, what's happening to me? What the hell's going on here? Now that I've got a little bit of fame, people suddenly are coming to my door. I'm wary of it. I think I can handle it but I'm wary of it."

And what if a great deal of money does arrive?

"I would probably get the fat head and be utterly malicious and stinky. Test me. No, if you want the truth, I don't think it would get to me at this stage. I've been through too much, been toughened up for too long."

Taylor Hackford, producer of a documentary on the poet for KCET-TV, Los Angeles, and holder of the screen rights to **Post Office,** says Bukowski is filled with ambivalence about the late arrival of success. "Sometimes he feels the recognition he's finally getting is well deserved and long overdue," Hackford says, "Other times he feels like it's all a big joke someone's playing on him, like someone's going to take his

typewriter away and tell him they were just kidding. There's constant battle going on inside him between the feeling that he really is one of the best and a feeling of deep insecurity. I think he'll be all right as long as he doesn't get too far away from his typewriter. The one thing that could kill him is if he started doing a lot more readings, running around the country catching planes and staying in Holiday Inns. Readings make him nervous, so he tends to drink heavily before, during and after them, and it takes its toll. I think he recognizes this danger. In fact, he wrote a great story about it called 'This Is What Killed Dylan Thomas.' If he limits the readings and keeps the drinking under reasonable control, we're going to hear a lot more from the man in the future."

> . . . I suppose a lot of obnoxious
> characters
> work their way into
> immortality.
> I'm working on it myself.
>
> —"the painter"

Bukowski, according to Bukowski, is at his "total peak. I'm writing less but I'm writing much better. There's more care in each line. I have a lot of self-doubt, so I know I'm measuring these things right. Right now everything has come together. I'm on my way. I'm unbeatable. Tomorrow morning is something else. Who knows, it may all fall apart and I'll go mad or raving or rape a goat or something. There's always the chance that I'll end up back on skid row, drinking wine with the boys. I'd never mention that I was a poet or any of that silly-ass shit. I'd just sit there and drink with em and say. 'Well, fellas, I figured it might turn out like this.'"

The beer is disappearing rapidly and his eyes are badly bloodshot back in those deep sockets under the bushy brows. A light on a desk behind him creates a halo effect around the top of his head. The halo just doesn't fit. He looks a little liverish, but seems to he feeling fine.

I ask him how much he feels his physical appearance has affected his life.

"I don't know. I suppose it helped to make a loner out of me, and being a loner isn't a bad thing for a writer. I know the face is helping to sell books now. The shot of me they used on the cover of **Erections** has done a lot to sell that book. The face on that cover is so horrific and pasty and completely gone beyond the barrier that it makes people stop and wanna find out what the hell kinda madman this guy is. So it was good luck for me to go through a lot of the shit I went through "cause now I have this mug that sells books."

And when it comes to women . . .

"That's a delicate question—does the face scare them?"

No, aren't there a lot of women who are attracted by it now?

"Yeah, I get all sorts of remarks about it. They say things like. 'You've got a face more beautiful than Christ's' That sounds good at first, but when I think about it, Christ's face wasn't all that beautiful. But I find women like ugly faces. Yeah. I'll make that statement flatly. They wanna mother ya back to heaven. I have no complaints."

A phone call interrupts us, and from the conversation I can tell it's Linda King. "No." he tells her, "I can't come over tonight. I'm being interviewed." Glancing at me, he raises his voice to make sure I can hear him. "Yeah, this guy's here from this wild-ass, perverted publication, but he looks pretty goddamn respectable to me: ten-dollar haircut, tailored clothes, Florsheim boots. What am I telling him? A lotta lies, what the hell else? I think he believes em, too."

After he gets off the phone I suggest to him that his writing recently seems to reflect a softening in his stance toward women and ask if that has something to do with his essentially happy, if rather rocky, relationship with Linda.

He rubs his rat-colored beard. "Well, I guess I might admit to mellowing a little. I've been accused of hating women but it's not true at all. It's just that most of the women I ran into for a long time weren't exactly prizes. I'd sleep with em and when I woke up, they'd be gone with my money. If a man goes into a whorehouse, he's gonna get a whore, that's all there is to it. I met Jane when I was in my 20's and she was the first woman—the first person, for that matter—who brought me any love. It was the first time I discovered the stupid little things that people do that make them care about each other, like lying in bed together on a Sunday morning reading the paper or fixing a meal together. Gentle, corny things like that."

In an attempt to bait him a bit, I recall some contradictory statements he's made in the past about women. Like, on one hand, "women are the world's most marvelous inventions." and, on the other. "I wouldn't recommend getting involved with women to any man."

"Right. Both statements are absolutely true. No contradiction. Next question." He grins and drains his beer, knowing the evasion has succeeded. Then he decides to go on anyway. "Let me tell ya a little story, kid. Before I met Linda I went four years without a woman and I felt pretty good about it. Somehow I just reached a stage where I didn't wanna go through the strain of a relationship. I didn't wanna take the time. Women can be awfully time-consuming. And when you're a poet, they expect ya to go around spouting all-this grand, glorious, profound stuff all the time about the mean-ing of life. Well, Jesus, I'm not like that. What can I tell em? I wanna fuck em, that's all. So after they're with ya four or five days and the most profound thing you've said is, 'Hey, baby, ya forgot to flush the toilet,' they think to themselves. 'What the hell kinda poet is this?' It takes a lot outta ya putting up with that stuff. During that four-year period I just decided not to join the chase for every cunt in a skirt. I'd come home from the job and I'd have the beer and my symphony music, a place to lay down and my typewriter. I masturbated a lot and got a lotta writing done, so I guess it turned out all right. Writing, after all, is more important than any woman. But I will make this concession: jerking off runs a distant second to the real thing. When you're with a woman ya like and the sex is good, there's something that takes place beyond the act itself. Some sort of exchange of souls that makes all the trouble worthwhile—at least for the rest of the night. I mean, here ya are, masturbating, whacking away at this big ugly purple thing with the veins sticking out and fantasizing about how you're balling the daylights outta some woman, and then ya finish and go lay down on the bed and think. 'Well, that wasn't too bad'—but something's missing. It's that exchange of souls."

It seems like an appropriate time to test out how seriously he takes the image of a great lover he has fostered in his stories. I inform him that Linda had volunteered the information that "he's a very creative lover. I've stayed with him five years, and if he wasn't good I could certainly find someone else."

"Well, I'll plead guilty to that," he says matter-of-factly. "I may as well admit it. I'm a good lover. At least I was the last time I did it, which wasn't long ago. But I think Linda's probably talking about sexual exploration, working down below there with the tongue and also getting in some creative movements ya haven't tried before. It's like writing a story or a poem—ya don't wanna do it the same way every time or it gets boring. It's hard to explain . . . . It's just an instinctive thing to keep things fresh and exciting. Like maybe doing it standing up as a change of pace. I can do that with these goddamn legs of mine. Most of the rest of me is shit, but the legs are dynamite. And my balls. I have genuinely magnificent balls. No shit, if my dick was in direct proportion to my balls. I'd be one of the great all-time champion studs. But my balls aside, imagination is the key. It's a creative act."

Well, uh, Linda also said she had to teach you about oral sex.

"Huh?"

Linda said you had never practiced, uh, cunnilingus before you met her.

"Ummmmmm. Christ, she couldn't let it go at telling ya I'm a great lover, could she?" His fugitive's face registers either a scowl or a smirk, hard to tell which. "All right, that's true. when I met her one of the first things she told me was that she could tell from my stories that I had never done that. Don't ask me how she figured that out. Anyway, she said it was a deficiency in my education. We set about to correct it and we did. I covered her with the reality of my tongue, how's that? Then she told me she was afraid that I'd hafta try out my new techniques on another woman. Well, she was right about that, too. One thing it proves, though, it's never too later for an old man to learn new tricks. Another bit of Bukowski wisdom."

> . . . L.A., the greatest city in the universe. Where each man and woman had a special style and a natural cool. Even the fools had a certain grace. L.A. was the end of a dead culture crawled west to get away from itself. L.A. knew it was rotten and laughed at it. Ask Chicago, ask New York City, they still think they are alive. No good. They are fucked cuckoo. While San Francisco chokes upon the glut of artists, L.A. wheels, stands at the corner of Hollywood and Western, munching a taco and enjoying the bluff and the sun. . . .

—**"Notes of a Dirty Old Man"**

The beer is gone and Bukowski is hungry. He stands up and asks a question that comes out more as an order: "How about getting something to eat? I haven't eaten since I started drinking beer and that was quite some time ago." A few minutes later, we're weaving along Western Avenue in his blue '67 VW ("I'm gonna drive this sonuvabitch till it disintegrates"), headed, he declares, for nothing less than a Pioneer Chicken stand. "Been going there for years when I'm drunk and there's no food in the apartment. Main thing is, I hafta watch out for those red lights in the rear-view mirror. I can't afford to get picked up . . . might lose my license. Suppose they pull me over? What am I gonna tell 'em, that I'm Charles Bukowski, one of the world's greatest poets? That I have magnificent balls? Ya think the men in blue would buy that?"

A car ahead of us that had stopped for a red light fails to move when the light turns green. Bukowski unleashes a torrent out the window. "Come on, motherfuck! Move it! Get your ass moving!" The driver looks around nervously and finally takes off. "Did ya see that asshole? I'll bet he's a tourist, probably from Chicago . . . . Yeah, I love this town. Well, I don't *love*, it, but it's the only place I ever wanna live. I couldn't write anywhere else. I hope I die here. Not right away, maybe when I'm 80. That seems like a reasonable age to die. That gives me another 25 years. I can write a lot of shit in 25 years. Hey, I feel good tonight. Tonight I feel like

I might make it to 80. I have some trouble with the stomach, my liver gets overloaded and my hemorrhoids are threatening to take over the world, but what the hell. I'll make it. I'm just ornery enough to make it."

> **"Ya know, I've felt kinda unreal and weird all my life. I've always had trouble getting along with people. I've always been . . . the guy who says the wrong thing and makes people feel bad. Sometimes I feel like I'm not really a part of this world."**
> —*Charles Bukowski*

We reach Pioneer Chicken and order two shrimp dinners. Sitting at an outdoor table, eating the shrimp and soggy french fries, Bukowski turns reflective, talking without prompting about his past, speculating about the effects of his father's beatings, reminiscing about the days on the road. Drunk, tired and disheveled, he stares at a young couple walking by and then, in a confessional tone, he says: "Ya know, I've felt kinda unreal and weird all my life. I've always had trouble getting along with people. I've always been the sonuvabitch—the guy who says the wrong thing and makes people feel bad. Sometimes I feel like I'm not really a part of this world." A pause. "I say I don't like people, but really I get kinda charged up when I'm around 'em. I used to sit in my old apartment with the window open, typing and looking out at the sidewalk with people walking by. And I'd incorporate the people into my stuff. Maybe now that I've got a little success I can relax and say something nice to people once in a while instead of always being the prick." He stops, looks at me, starts to go on, then thinks better of it; perhaps he's thinking that he's already said too much. The moment of reflection passes. "Ah, hell, let's eat our shrimp and watch the broads go by."

We drive back and he parks on the street near his bungalow. Out on the sidewalk we shake hands. "Listen, kid," he says. "I don't have friends, but I do have acquaintances. So now you're an acquaintance."

"Bukowski," I say, "you're not a bad guy—for a prick."

He laughs, shakes his head and walks off toward his apartment and his solitude.

James Kingstone (review date November 1984)

SOURCE: A review of *The Bukowski/Purdy Letters,* in *Ca-*

nadian Materials for Schools and Libraries, Volume XII, No. 6, November 1984, pp. 253-54.

[*In the following review, Kingstone questions the wisdom of publishing the correspondence of these two authors.*]

The advantage of reading a writer's letters is that one sees, often quite easily, the shape of informal thought that is frequently more revealing than the author's published work. By reading diaries and letters written to close friends, private communication, we see a writer's life focused for us in sharper detail; at least, that is the idea. But I cannot help but think that the private world disclosed for this reader in *The Bukowski/Purdy Letters 1964-1974* would have been better left to the world of private correspondence. The writing is undistinguished; and, while one marvels at the spontaneity and the evolution of a friendship, the exchange of letters more often than not celebrates drinking and womanizing. The rather immature boasting by each becomes tedious, and though it echoes Hemingway and Dylan Thomas, at least with them there were letters whose critical intelligence redeemed any masculine posturing. In *Bukowski/Purdy,* one has to look very hard indeed to discover any insights into the craft of writing. Scrape away the occasional inventive misspelling or pun, and the very occasional verbal facility (as in the description of a teacher as "an upright piece of chalk"), and one is left with much that is crude and embarrassing. Four-letter-word dismissals of writers substitutes for criticism in this unfortunate publication. It is really very unfortunate, because it could have been the kind of work—it is imaginatively and cleanly bound—to provoke casual readers to search out the poetry of these two men.

I suspect the blame for this effort should be laid at the feet of the editor, Seamus Cooney, who could not have been less sensitive in urging these two men to publish their letters. They could not have imagined their letters would have been published, ever, let alone while they were still alive. The publishing of literary correspondence has become very popular recently (note the publication of *The Nabokov/Wilson Letters* and several others in the last five years), but perhaps the market has reached its saturation point. We may have reached a stage now where certain individuals feel they can pass anything off to an uncritical public, and in this particular publication we have been conned, because in the growing field of published correspondence it is certainly an aberration.

Loss Glazier (review date Fall 1985)

SOURCE: "Mirror of Ourselves: Notes on Bukowski's *Post Office,*" in *Review of Contemporary Fiction,* Vol. 5, No. 3, Fall 1985, pp. 39-42.

[*In the following favorable review, Glazier discusses the novel* Post Office, *in which he sees a cogent macrocosm of the human condition.*]

When *Post Office,* Bukowski's first published novel, came off the press in 1971, an important moment in the history of modern American literature occurred. Bukowski stood like a giant, one foot astride each of two continents: poetry and prose; pornography and belles letters; suicide and sainthood; Europe and America; the underground press and the brackish water of the literati. A truly historic first novel, *Post Office* was as definitive as a line drawn in the dirt.

Bukowski had stepped forward from the maelstrom of prophetic vision, having established himself securely by such visionary poetic works as *Flower, Fist and Bestial Wail* (1960), *Crucifix in a Deathhand* (1965), and the collection *The Days Run Away Like Wild Horses over the Hills* (1969). He was able to turn his hand to fiction with a perspective unequaled in contemporary American letters. He had been through a stripping-down that would've killed any ordinary person. And yet Bukowski, rather than being weakened by each successive defoliation, seemed to get stronger with the knowledge of what was necessary. He approached a level of immediate experience that was almost religious in nature. And when he came out of his motel room with the manuscript of *Post Office,* the essential worth of his novel was inescapable, built with a prose style that was sparse, honest, and brilliant in its Epicurean asceticism.

The setting for this visionary work is quite uncontrived. Unlike a generation of previous writers who drew their inspiration from Paris, Italy and the Riviera, Bukowski created his universe from the stuff at hand. Everything that was necessary could be found wherever he found himself: in a motel room in Los Angeles, in a cottage in Texas, sitting in his car, in the jaws of the post office. The post office represents dynamically the duality which is the relentless metronome of daily life. Here we have literacy and communication; letters are flashes of narrative whereby events are caught in brief written images sent from one person to another. Yet on the other hand, the post office is representative of another side of modern life: order, authority, bureaucracy, a methodical and corporate process of dehumanization where each person is supposed to feel enriched by the contribution he is making to the organization's goal. This point of view is established firmly before the start of the narrative in "Code of Ethics":

> Postal employees have, over the years, established a fine tradition of faithful service to the Nation, unsurpassed by other groups. Each employee should take great pride in this tradition of dedicated service. Each of us must strive to make his contribution worthwhile in the continued movement of the

Postal Service toward future progress in the public interest.

The assumptions underlying this code form the justification for the dissolution of individuality in society. Here is represented the kind of conditionality and blind obedience that makes the isolation and madness of modern life possible.

The lesson of *Post Office* lies in the cleaning up of this mess. The novel provides a clear guide to the necessary first step: realizing that there is nothing to understand. There is no *reason* for it. Those that reason are those that either contribute to the strata that distance us from humanity or that contribute equally to its power through their own act of retreating. The only way of beginning to understand our predicament is to understand that there is *no asking why*.

Bukowski opens *Post Office* with a single simple paragraph: "It began as a mistake." Henry Chinaski, Bukowski's alter ego, enters the post office quite by accident, hearing that they would hire anyone. He takes the exam and physical, and goes through the motions, finally becoming a temporary mail carrier. Life is a breeze—for the moment. The novel's action starts when he is transferred to Oakford Station and the tyrannical rule of a supervisor named Jonstone. Immediately Chinaski finds himself under the degradation of a normal, ordered world. And it's clear that this world—of bondage—was made possible only through one utterly ironic condition: man's acceptance of tyranny. "The subs themselves made Jonstone possible by obeying his impossible orders," Chinaski explains. He rebels immediately and is quashed. He persists in his rebellion and continues to be suppressed. And though at one point he is even a millionaire through marriage, the process of *Post Office* is one that continually strips Chinaski down; yet each time this occurs, he pulls himself up with purified vision.

Post Office presents man as a curiosity, blind to his responsibility for creating the process of dehumanization through his own submission to it. The inhabitants of Bukowski's universe are constantly under the thumb of this principle. They are people motivated by temper, attachment, people who are spiritually starved yet stuffed with illusions. Suffering by their own hands, these people question their lot. These are the people on Chinaski's route, caught in a self-consuming cycle between disappointment and anger. For example:

> ". . . I know you have a letter for me!"
> "What makes you say that?"
> "Because my sister phoned and said she was going to write me."
> "Lady, I don't have a letter for you."
> "I know you have! I know you have! I know it's there!"

Or, more commonly:

> I handed her mail to her.
> "BILLS! BILLS! BILLS!" she screamed. "IS THAT ALL YOU CAN BRING ME? THESE BILLS?"

Bukowski's power of straightforward "seeing" is evidenced, in the face of this hysterical loss of human dignity, by his honest reply, "'Yes, mam, that's all I can bring you.'" Or, again, in a moment of quiet emptiness:

> When Betty came back we didn't sing or laugh, or even argue. We sat drinking in the dark, smoking cigarettes, and when we went to sleep, I didn't put my feet on her body or she on mine like we used to. We slept without touching.

We had both been robbed.

These are people, like Chinaski's millionairess wife, Joyce, who have lost touch with what is real. Chinaski's value as antihero is his resiliency, his ascension from the "death" of blind obedience. He speaks no other language but the real. There is no swaying, no circumnavigating the issues. Bukowski is without sympathy in standing true to the world as it exists in front of him. We witness this when Chinaski, married to Joyce and living in Texas, experiences a rare mood of benevolence and leaves work early to do a little shopping. By the time Joyce gets home that evening, Chinaski has prepared a feast, including a plate of golden, fried-in-butter snails that repulse her immediately. Eventually, however, she tries one, then examines the others on her plate closely. Finally, she breaks:

> "They all have tiny *assholes*! It's horrible! Horrible!"
> "What's horrible about assholes, baby?"
>
> She held a napkin to her mouth. Got up and ran to the bathroom. She began vomiting. I hollered in from the kitchen:
>
> "WHAT'S WRONG WITH ASSHOLES, BABY? YOU'VE GOT AN ASSHOLE, I'VE GOT AN ASSHOLE! YOU GO TO THE STORE AND BUY A PORTERHOUSE STEAK, THAT HAD AN ASSHOLE! ASSHOLES COVER THE EARTH! IN A WAY TREES HAVE ASSHOLES BUT YOU CAN'T FIND THEM, THEY JUST DROP THEIR LEAVES. YOUR ASSHOLE, MY ASSHOLE, THE WORLD IS FULL OF BILLIONS OF ASSHOLES, THE PRESIDENT HAS AN ASSHOLE, THE CARWASH BOY HAS AN ASSHOLE, THE JUDGE AND THE MURDERER HAVE ASSHOLES."

The line that Bukowski draws in *Post Office* is one that encompasses an essential decision. Man stands at an important moment in world history and cannot seem to step forward out of sheer blindness to common, ordinary facts. Man can be seen in the birds that Bukowski sets free in *Post Office,* birds that Bukowski could no longer bear to see imprisoned. He takes the cage outside and opens the door, daring the birds to step across the line. There is a dramatic moment of hesitation while they deliberate about whether or not to go. The essential challenge of *Post Office* is before them. Their accountability for their own self-determination is placed squarely under their eyes. They fly off. When Joyce returns, she is beside herself:

> "Do you mean to say you let those birds out of the cage? Do you mean to say you really let them out of the cage?"
> "Well, all I can say is, they are not locked in the bathroom, they are not in the cupboard."
> "They'll starve out there!"
> "They can catch worms, eat berries, all that stuff."
> "They can't, they can't. They don't know how! They'll die!"
> "Let 'em learn or let 'em die."

Chinaski does not simply *express* this philosophy: his life embodies it. Taking your fate into your own hands, despite the outcome, initiates the process of restoring man's humanity.

The marriage to Joyce ends, just as do all of Chinaski's relationships in *Post Office,* just as Chinaski's association with the post office will. After a long grueling battle, there will have been enough. It will be time to look at life with clearer eyes. To make a simple statement. There is an almost mystical wisdom expressed each time Chinaski moves on.

> She even helped me pack. Folding my pants neatly into suitcases. Packing in my shorts and razor. When I was ready to leave she started crying again. I bit her on the ear, the right one, then went down the stairway with my stuff. I got into the car and began cruising up and down the streets looking for a For Rent sign.

This scene, on its own, is compelling; yet the philosophical insight comes with Chinaski's observation of his own humanness. Stripped again of everything and looking for a place to live with no previous preparation, he comments, "It didn't seem to be an unusual thing to do." Chinaski survives because he keeps his eyes on the road and refuses to wallow in any kind of self-pitying analysis.

Post Office sums up the entire human dilemma in a few simple choruses. The proof of the truth of Bukowski's vision lies in the continued popularity of *Post Office* and all of Bukowski's work, both here and abroad. There is a delicate balance that must be evaluated—between what we endure and what little ground we need to claim for ourselves. Without complex theories or expressions of insurmountable entanglements, Bukowski provides a clean and simple answer in a clear and direct style: the answer is right here. It's as easy as looking in the mirror.

Julian Smith (review date Fall 1985)

SOURCE: "Charles Bukowski and the Avante-Garde," in *Review of Contemporary Fiction,* Vol. 5, No. 3, Fall 1985, pp. 56-59.

[*In the following review, Smith discusses the humor in Bukowski's short stories.*]

What is the avant-garde? A cultural elite, making Advanced or High Art, but it is also a tradition of the untraditional. Precedents exist for virtually every avant-garde eccentricity or innovation. As Roland Barthes puts it, "The avant-garde is never anything but the progressive, emancipated form of past culture." While it may become politicized (during the Vietnam War, even "the gloriously impertinent Bukowski" was temporarily radicalized), it is typically individualist, antiformal, anarchistic. Bohemian life-styles, *épater les bourgeois,* the alienation (psychological, ethical, economic) of the artist from society: Bukowski's writing echoes all these attitudes.

Bukowski's opposition to the status quo is signaled by his language. The tough-drunk persona created in the writing is intimately linked to the way in which his fictions operate, and he shows enormous resource in working a subversive content on the linguistic level. We term "postmodern" those writers who have learned from modernism, and then added extrastylistic components. While Bukowski had to erase other voices from his work (Céline, John Fante), he rewrote Hemingway with postmodern laughter, forming an utterly distinctive writing—allusive, anarchic and miraculously entertaining.

I take Bukowski's most intense and hilarious prose to be *Erections, Ejaculations, Exhibitions and General Tales of Ordinary Madness* (1972) and the collection *Notes of a Dirty Old Man* (1969). So, I shall refer to these in discussing his fictional tactics, brilliant effects, and peculiar linguistic stew.

In common with many other writers (Ginsberg, Burroughs, Snyder), Bukowski published in underground newspapers of the 1960's and 1970's; he became a prolific contributor to his local papers, *Open City* and *L.A. Free Press,* and his fiction took its place alongside coverage of student unrest, the New Left, black power, civic and police corruption, the draft resistance, drug information, and adverts for sexual contacts and services.

Exploiting this popular platform for his writing, Bukowski's uninhibited mixture of fiction and opinion is almost impossible to read without explosive laughter on virtually every page. This is partly the result of subject matter in *Notes:* a winged baseball hero brought down to earth by women and drink; sex with a three-hundred-pound whore; the last days of Neal Cassady; boxing and racing; revolution and literature; a man who wakes to find his skin turned gold with green polka dots (recalling Kafka's *Metamorphosis*); drunkenly mistaken anal intercourse; demonology; and a grossly superb cast list of comically inept muggers, murderers, gangsters, misogynists, bums and whores, rapacious land-ladies, struggling writers, misunderstood geniuses, day laborers, perverts and other social oddballs.

This satiric critique of capitalism, bourgeois morality and conventional culture is accompanied by a deliberately disorderly syntax, a "spontaneous" typewriterese that creates its effect by a radical difference from smoother, more literary writing: ". . . balls, yes, I almost cried, but then orientated by centuries, Christ's fuck-up, every sad and ripping thing, stupid, I leaped up and checked my only unripped pants not yet ripped from falling down at the knees while drunk."

The tools in his craftsman's bag are used to create an impression of artless spontaneity. How is this textual illusion obtained? By the use of the first-person singular; a vigorous street language with no recourse to dictionaries, complex words or intellectual concepts; by the use of first names or real names as though the reader were an acquaintance; by the cultivation of a no-bullshit approach, as though the speaker were too busy telling the truth to dilute it with high cultural values; and most effectively by jokes and asides to the reader: "(by the way . . . I realize I switch from present to past tense, and if you don't like it . . . ram a nipple up your scrotum—printer: leave this in)."

Bukowski flavors the lexical stew of *Notes* with misspellings, ungrammatical constructions, sentences with no verbs, repetitions, split infinitives, much slang and swearing, sexual innuendo and other linguistic ambiguities that enable him to splice sexuality, violence, nastiness and humor. By deliberately leaving in the text the sort of grammatical confusions common in speech but usually suppressed in written English, Bukowski is indicating that he wants to align writing with *spoken* rather than *written* conventions. The typing error is evidence of oral authenticity: "She thought my poems were the greatest thing since Black, no I mean Blake—and some of them are."

Surface indications to the contrary, Bukowski's fiction addresses itself to literate readers capable of appreciating the enormous number of irreverent references to writers, composers, painters and philosophers, and its slangy departures from polite literary expression. Which is why his writing goes down so well with university audiences, even though his humor subverts their educational values.

> **Bukowski's fiction addresses itself to literate readers capable of appreciating the enormous number of irreverent references to writers, composers, painters and philosophers, and its slangy departures from polite literary expression.**
> **—*Julian Smith***

From John Fante, Bukowski took the idea that the streets of Los Angeles (not Hollywood) represented a viable fictional world; from Celine, an attitude of misanthropic extremism. But Ernest Hemingway, the most accessible modernist, provided Bukowski with a macho role model, an existential material, and an experimental style already pushed in the direction of American "speech." The aficionado of the L.A. Public Library pushed the stripped-down, denotative (classic) style of Hemingway into play, parody, and laughter. Bukowski echoed the aesthetics of the prose technician; either could have written this: "The hard life created the hard line and by the hard line I mean the true line devoid of ornament" (Bukowski, **"He Beats His Women"**).

Hemingway (perhaps one should say *Ham*ingway) stressed simplicity of expression and small, "honest" words (instead of abstractions) and action to keep the existential void at bay. As Hugh Kenner says, Hemingway's "bullfights and lion hunts were aesthetic gestures"; the Bukowski hero parallels this by going to the racetrack. This allows for a flippant treatment of existential states—exaltation and despair, hysteria and boredom. Hemingway's regard for the authenticity of words and feelings seeps through onto the Bukowski page. But Bukowski's humor makes the page more divided, fecund, ambiguous, and harder to pin down ideologically than other writers (say, Mailer) who recycle Hemingway's male mythology. How is one to read this faintly comic Hemingway echo? "I dropped my pants and shorts. She looked allright. I put the thing in. I put in what I had."

The function of his humor is sometimes to subvert cant, whole attitudes (e.g., sexism) that his stories, on another level, exploit. Sexual stereotypes—women as "all ass and breast," rapacious and available, a poor companion for the male compared to barroom buddies—hold sway throughout American fiction. At his best, Bukowski animates his stereotypes with great panache, investing "ideological unsoundness" with a liberating humor. A remarkable cultural allu-siveness sends up machismo as well as alluding to and in-voking it: "'Let's go out there and tell them to jam that horn up their ass,' said the kid, influenced by the Bukowski myth (I am really a coward) and the Hemingway thing and Humphrey B. and Eliot with his panties rolled, well. I puffed on my cigar. the horn went on."

Several Bukowski stories include fantasy dialogue with Hemingway's shade: **"The Killers"** parallels Hemingway's story of the same name; the opening of **"Stop Staring at My Tits, Mister"** parodies Hemingway in a crudely sexist mood; a rat-bearded professor bears a distinct resemblance in **"Would You Suggest Writing As a Career?"**; as a coup de grace, Henry Chinaski knocks out the aging Papa in **"Class"** ("You met a pretty good man, Mr. Hemingway").

The Hemingway legacy survives most vitally in the creation of a persona sometimes called "Bukowski" or "Henry Chinaski," what Barthes calls "a paper-author: his life is no longer the origin of his fictions but a fiction contributing to his work." Bukowski's artifice disguised as autobiography enables **"Too Sensitive"** to double-bluff the reader by end-ing on this note: "Meanwhile, I write about myself and drink too much. but you know that."

The intrusions of the author/narrator into the text are inte-gral to many Bukowski stories, not merely winking to the reader but pointing up the text's artificial, fictive status. A playfulness clearly places Bukowski in the same camp as the postmoderns: "So, reader, let's forget Mad Jimmy for a minute and get into Arthur—which is no big problem—what I mean is also the way I write: I can jump around and you can come right along it won't matter a bit, you'll see."

Surrealism and existentialism enjoyed a delayed vogue in the American avant-garde of the 1950's and 1960's (Beat writ-ers revived Artaud and Céline as major influences; *The City Lights Journal* made available the work of Michaux, Prévert, Genet, Artaud). While a rhythmic, semi-surreal language is sometimes evident, employing an illogical, dreamlike syn-tax ("but death was really boredom, death was really bore-dom, and even the tigers and ants would never know how and the peach would someday scream"), surrealism and existentialism's influence on Bukowski's fiction is most pro-ductive when reinvented, transmuted.

"The Gut-Wrenching Machine" is a comic commentary on authenticity, a concept crucial in existentialism's mythol-ogy. Criminals and tyrants supposedly live more authenti-cally (that is, unhampered by moral codes, external authorities) than the solid, law-abiding citizen. Danforth and Bagley operate a wringer, turning out sufficiently pliable human material by squeezing the guts out, fitting their cli-ents for "normal" life, the materialism of bourgeois society:

"The ones labeled 'married with family' or 'over 40' lost their guts easiest."

Surrealism survives in Bukowski's bizarre characterization, the incorporation of fantastic events into a matter-of-fact nar-rative (**"The Fuck Machine," "Six Inches"**), always accom-panied by quick-fire dialogue, endless one-liners, and a surrealism of the everyday; characters take onanistic photo-graphs, fuck the phone, and fold complaining women into walls. Sexual explicitness is constantly undermined by gro-tesque details. With unexpected language reversals, delib-erate anticlimaxes, and punchlines, Bukowski's stories point up their essential hero—the irreverent writer struggling with both the world and the word.

Self-referential stories about: being a writer on the reading circuit (**"Would You Suggest Writing As a Career?"**); a writer afflicted by minor fame (**"Great Poets Die in Steam-ing Pots of Shit"**); a writer continually interrupted in his at-tempts to complete a luridly improbable story (**"Twelve Flying Monkeys Who Won't Copulate Properly"**). Frus-trated by two strangers pissing on his porch, Crazy Jack and two friends, a phone conversation with a maudlin poet, then by strangers offering a boat trip, the vomiting writer con-cludes: "We head out to sea where Conrad made it. To hell with Conrad. I'll take coke with bourbon in a dark bedroom in Hollywood in 1970, or whatever year you read this. The year of the monkey-orgy that never happened. The motor flits and gnashes at the sea; we plunge on toward Ireland. No, it's the Pacific. We plunge on toward Japan. To hell with it."

The frisson provided by cultural reference and tough-guy language is typically irreverent, disruptive, avant-garde; for Bukowski, the pleasure of the text is always laughter.

Norman Weinstein (review date Fall 1985)

SOURCE: "*South of No North:* Bukowski in Deadly Ear-nest," in *Review of Contemporary Fiction*, Vol. 5, No. 3, Fall 1985, pp. 52-55.

[*In the following review, Weinstein examines the similari-ties in Bukowski's short story collection to the fiction of Hemingway.*]

In no other collection of Bukowski's fiction does Ernest Hemingway's ghost play such a major role. Even the book title, with that flatly articulated oxymoron reminiscent of *Men without Women* and *Winner Take Nothing*, alerts the reader to the Hemingway presence. The Bukowski/ Hemingway connection is one riddled with complex ambivalences. I trust this brief reading of *South of No North* might indicate a few dimensions of that knot.

A first reading of Bukowski's collection evoked thoughts of his consciously creating a parody of the Hemingway style. Consider this excerpt from Bukowski's **"Loneliness"**:

> "Maybe I'm no good at sex," said Edna, "maybe that's why I'm alone." She took another drink from the glass.
>
> "Each of us is, finally, alone," said Joe.
>
> "What do you mean?"
>
> "I mean, no matter how well it's going sexually or love-wise or both, the day arrives when it's over."

There is the identical sound of simply cadenced American speech bonded by conversational syntax, created through a severely limited (though far from limiting) vocabulary of the archetypal "Ordinary Joe." This likeness to Hemingway becomes even more striking when we put the above in relationship to this excerpt from Hemingway's *Death in the Afternoon:* "Madam, all stories, if continued far enough, end in death, and he is no true story teller who keeps that from you."

However hard-boiled Hemingway sounded in his bullfight epic, Bukowski is determined to outdo Papa. Bukowski's sense of competition with Hemingway's talent humorously borrows the same metaphor Hemingway uses to describe his competitive relationship to master fiction writers from the past. Here is Hemingway bragging to his publisher with mock modesty and macho abandonment: "Am a man without any ambition, except to be champion of the world, I wouldn't fight Dr. Tolstoi in a 20 round bout because I know he would knock my ears off . . . Mr. Henry James I would just thumb him once the first time he grabbed and then hit him once where he had no balls and ask the referee to stop it." Bukowski's **"Class"** is little more than the author's dream of getting into a boxing ring—literally!—with Hemingway. Of course Bukowski gleefully celebrates his raw powers: "I had Hemingway up against the ropes. He couldn't fall. Each time he started to fall forward I straightened him with another punch. It was murder. *Death in the Afternoon.*" Yet a reading of Bukowski here should transcend parody of Papa. Note the turn **"Class"** takes after the narrator knocks Hemingway out:

> I got dressed and then Ernie regained consciousness.
>
> "What the hell happened?" he asked.
>
> "You met a pretty good man, Mr. Hemingway," somebody told him.

> "You're a good man, Papa. Nobody wins them all."
> I shook his hand. "Don't blow your brains out."

Even the flippancy of the narrator's last line can't erase the sense of tender respect (rare in this book) that Bukowski feels for Papa.

"No Neck and Bad As Hell" is the other story in *South of No North* where Hemingway's ghost becomes reanimated and duels with Henry Chinaski-cum-Charles Bukowski. One of the narrator's drunken reveries provides the setting; he imagines Hemingway at his local bar saying to him:

> "You talk like a character out of early Huxley."
>
> "I think you're wrong. I'm desperate."
>
> "But," said Hemingway, "men become intellectuals in order not to be desperate."

And the verbal sparring continues until (naturally) the narrator wins. But Bukowski is willing to let Hemingway draw some blood in the fray with that stab about Bukowski's roots in Huxley.

Despite these instances of Bukowski triumphing over Hemingway, one can't help but note Bukowski's humility before the Hemingway genius in **"This Is What Killed Dylan Thomas,"** a thinly disguised account of Bukowski's first public reading in San Francisco: "We walk across the street to an Italian cafe. Marionetti is back with the guy from the *S.F. Chronicle* who wrote in his column that I was the best short story writer to come along since Hemingway. I tell him he is wrong; I don't know who is the best since Hemingway but it isn't H.C. I'm too careless. I don't put out enough effort. I'm tired."

These are the examples from *South of No North* where Hemingway is *directly* evoked in Bukowski's stories. However, the overwhelming machismo sensibility of a Hemingway constantly punctuates Bukowski's fictions. **"A Man"** is the Bukowski story which states the machismo most starkly:

> "I'm a man, baby, understand that?"
>
> "I know you're a man, George."
>
> "Here, look at my muscles!" George stood up and flexed both of his arms. "Beautiful, eh, baby? Look at that muscle! Feel it! Feel it!"
>
> Constance felt one of his arms. Then the other.
>
> "Yes, you have a beautiful body, George."

"I'm a man. I'm a dishwasher but I'm a man, a real man."

The character's assertion of masculine dignity in spite of the lowness of his occupation is another factor which links Bukowski to Hemingway. Both authors assert masculine dignity as a necessary rite-of-passage technique in order to survive integrally within an unjust and emasculating socioeconomic system. The ruthless drive to "act like a man" that all Hemingway and Bukowski characters share leads to a distrust in both authors of any political solutions. So Hemingway writes in a letter to Paul Romaine:

I'm no goddamned patriot nor will I swing to left or right.

Would as soon machine gun left, right, or center any political bastards who do not work for a living.

Bukowski voices a similar disgust in **"Politics"** where he describes his disillusionment with student politics at L.A. City College where he assumes a pro-Hitler stance with fellow students simply because he is bored with their pious and unfelt antifascist platitudes. Bukowski's cynicism about countercultural protest on the Left is brutally symbolized by red ants crawling over the tattered remains of an abandoned protest flag in **"Something about a Viet Cong Flag."**

Characters in Bukowski and Hemingway are the rugged individualists who defy the utopian schemes of all ideologues. Male character armor held firm by a swaggering boastfulness assures survival. Bukowski characteristically develops this stance in **"Bop Bop against That Curtain"**: "There weren't any public funds for playgrounds. We were so tough we played tackle football in the streets all through football season, through basketball and baseball seasons and on through the next football season. When you get tackled on asphalt, things happen. Skin rips, bones bruise, there's blood, but you get up like nothing was wrong." This could be Hemingway's Nick Adams speaking, the identical will-to-survive reinforced through a manly toughness. And it is worth remembering how Hemingway also spoke of the importance of an unhappy childhood in the making of a writer. His letters to F. Scott Fitzgerald strongly asserted the usefulness of getting "hurt" by life, of knowing how to use personal pain as a wellspring for fiction which transcends the personal.

All of this emphasis in Hemingway and Bukowski has a consequence in terms of the development of female characters. Hemingway's fictions have been expertly critiqued by a number of feminist critics (most vitally by Judith Fetterley in *The Resisting Reader*) who have accused Hemingway of having women with no human dimensions in his works. This criticism can, perhaps should, be even more ruthless in

Bukowski's case. Women characters in *South of No North* are little more than sexual fetishes, replaceable by mute mannequins if we believe the narrator in "Love for $17.50." Yet both Hemingway and Bukowski can exhibit a boyishly fetching and worshipful sentimentality toward women in their stories. Men without women, in both Hemingway's and Bukowski's worlds, seem reduced to a most base condition.

Bukowski's characters don't even attempt to understand women; the tone in these stories is antipsychological. Once again, this posture echoes Hemingway. The puzzling war between the sexes can no more be ended through psychoanalysis than through political reorganizations. The writer's job is to state honestly the facts concerning sexual warfare, neither more nor less.

Call this stance anti-intellectualism in Hemingway and Bukowski. But I would rather tag this position as a form of adolescence, what depth psychologist James Hillman labels as a fix in the "Puer-Senex" complex. There is a great deal of the eternal youth in both writers, a refusal to "grow up." Gertrude Stein never forgot twenty-three-year-old Hemingway coming into her parlor crying that he was too young to be a father to his newly born son. Bukowski and his characters live in a world without parental responsibilities, are unanchored drifters looking for singular moments of love, love which never lasts.

Is it not precisely this adolescence of vision which makes Hemingway and Bukowski the quintessential American story writers of our age?

Stan Theis (essay date Summer 1989)

SOURCE: "Bukowski's Hollywood," in *ENclitic,* Vol. 11, No. 3, Summer 1985, pp. 89-93.

[*In the following essay, Theis explores the connections between Bukowski's novel,* Hollywood, *his screenplay for the movie* Barfly, *and the author's life.*]

Even for the artist or writer who silently screams refusals to be caught, coopted, by the lures of commercial culture, the dreams of monetary success are hard to fight off. The big bucks for landing a script at a more upscale studio privy to the points where culture and cash separate and merge together, or for a book contract at one of the major publishing houses, have the power to give artists and writers a dose of schizophrenia. Ego and lust tempered by the gnawing desire for creature comforts batters the artistic temperament with a reckoning force, especially in Hollywood town where movies are the art form, where art and cash might be more incestuously connected. And this might be changing the status of the struggling culture-producer who batters away on the fringe of substantial reward in pursuit of lofty goals and untainted absolutes. With such dismal prospects for survival in a time when Gentry and working class heroes look at each other across a wider rift than ever (the lofty can't be sketched out in downtown LA lofts affordable now only by the upwardly mobile brokers of this and that commodity), the notion of the struggling artist may becoming a vanishing species in the old sense we've come to attach to it.

This paradox is what mainly propels Bukowski's latest book, *Hollywood.* The contradictions of a life style overtaken with the pursuit of success on terms not always of one's own making: this is the major concern throughout. As a successful writer of the type chronicled in these pages, is he obsessed with going back to the days of struggle because that was when the experience of being a writer was more "real," naively oblivious to the system of exchange values that engulf the lives of all writers, something that seemed so abstractly removed? Do the lures of fame mitigate against true success? Bukowski has been heaped with it in the past few years to the point of warding off all publicity comers. Can good writing/art be produced under conditions of sated security? Isn't this why the scripting arts of the film world won't allow the entry of the controversial and subversive, that by the time a subject gets framed by the studios, it ceases to be one? Or is this just a romantic illusion, sentiments expressed by outsiders who couldn't make the grade, survive in the jungle where markets are always the best arbiter of quality?

There is some Romanticism in Bukowski's book, but we can't mistake most of what he's doing for a serious investigation of the life of the writer (*his* in fact, the book's a biographical statement) in a cultural wasteland that demanded his devotion for too many years of his life. His scenario appears to be an attempt to make sense of the road he passed along to get where he is now. His main character, Henry Chinaski, is roughly the same age as Bukowski, and surely harbors similar anxieties about the occupation of writer in the land of celluloid. Chinaski is all too aware of his place in life, at age 65. He feels pressured into becoming that other kind of writer/artist, the one with a desk, agent, assignment, front money: "My fighting days were over. To think I had once weighed 144 pounds on a 6-foot frame: the grand old starving days when I was writing the good stuff." The "good stuff" is *created* under conditions of maximum deprivation and adversity, the less-than-good *produced* on the downside of recognition, when mature complacency has fought off any urge to experiment? This sort of evolution doesn't apply to Bukowski's output, but perhaps his earlier writing has the stamp of the vintage angriness we now slot him into (like we do with the raging Burroughs and Ferlinghetti during their heydays).

We already know Chinaski as Bukowski's protagonist

through several novels and the film *Barfly.* Chinaski's struggles have occupied Bukowski for quite some time in working out his designs. He has been the gladiator-man-in-the-street, raging, not so much out of excess emotion, as sheer doggedness grounded in hard-hitting speculation (like his many systems for playing the horses channeled into one simple premise: " . . . there is only one bet, and that is bet it to win; not to place or show.") He's self-absorbed in his very resistance to floating along with the norm. He possesses a praiseworthy stubbornness that often fuels the most insightful intellectual fervor, romantic or otherwise. In *Ham on Rye* ('82), about Chinaski's youth, he lays it out:

> "I could see the road ahead of me. I was poor and I was going to stay poor. But I didn't particularly want money. I didn't know what I wanted. Yes, I did. I wanted someplace to hide out, someplace where one didn't have to do anything. The thought of being something didn't only appall me, it sickened me. The thought of being a lawyer or a councilman or an engineer, anything like that, seemed impossible to me. To get married, to have children, to get trapped in the family structure. To go someplace to work every day and to return. It was impossible. To do things, simple things, to be part of family picnics, Christmas, the 4th of July, Labor Day, Mother's Day . . . was a man born just to endure those things and then die? I would rather be a dishwasher, return alone to a tiny room and drink myself to sleep."

Bukowski's vision of the right stuff (*then* at least, early in the maturing writerly ego) couldn't be further from what we imagine to be the filmmaking world's version of floating along with the norm. Romantic visionaries who cling nostalgically to an existence of enforced deprivation, of self-fulfillment through lack, of living on the seedy margins where pain and adversity catalyze the persistent flow of creative life, aren't easily tamed into Hollywood industrial slots. These diehards hang out at Al's Bar in downtown LA (at least the vintage version back in the days when Bukowski himself straddled the makeshift bar as a culture fly seeding his reputation as an anti-hero), nurturing energies for use in an appropriate moment of escape. The rest seek out the avenues of successful script placement at City Cafe (and its many pastiches throughout LA), averse to the dirt and din of seedy life that violates the respectability of the entertainment arts.

But Bukowski's *Hollywood* is also a sophisticated take on all this. That is, the novel is really about the making of the film *Barfly* ('87), a movie that perhaps can be seen as his answer, through the art of film, to questions plaguing him for so long. This may explain why, in certain ways, it doesn't really come off as a novel. It seems at times like notes toward the writing of a script, a kind of script, however, that doesn't jive with the Hollywood product. The force, of the book is not so much in a story line that pulls or drags the reader along (like a Hollywood narrative?), as it is in sheer emotional overkill nearly dumbfounding because of the accessibility of the prose. The words are sort of doled out, flowing like the conversation between pulls on a bottle of red passed around without glasses in an alley behind the local drugstore. The reader feels the back and darkside of Hollywood, the part we know is there but can never really intuit through the mask of glamor. The several cancellations of the film in progress, and bilking of the cast and crew by the producers, sheds some light on what goes on beneath the glitz, the behind-the-scenes give and take, that tells us what we already know but in a way that suggests we really might not.

The force, of the book [*Hollywood*] is not so much in a story line that pulls or drags the reader along . . . as it is in sheer emotional overkill nearly dumbfounding because of the accessibility of the prose.
—*Stan Theis*

Hollywood is a book about the making of a film which brings to bear all the ambivalences a creative person might have in negotiating for a slice of security in an alien culture. It's hardly a predictable genre. It is too reflective of itself, too multi-layered to fall into generic slots. The all-too-predictable slotting into the Hollywood machine is the occasion for most of the drama, but Chinaski's relationship to the world of filmmaking, the grit of the novel, stages a bit more than this. Chinaski has mostly disdain for the film scene, but perhaps like the author himself, immersion in the celluloid arts may indeed be another stage in the evolution of a career, a necessity which every aspiring creative person in the shadows of the studios must accept as fact. Perhaps Chinaski truly wants to invigorate the scene, change it in some way, with his ideas cultivated on the fringes, in adversity and deprivation. Because he is clearly not what they are. He's formula breaker, a category dissolver, everything we would expect to find in the makeup of the raging writer who might experiment from time to time with other life styles and media. So a big part of the work is Chinaski breaking barriers: from writing to film, from moderate to upper class living, toward drinking less and eating some "health foods." (For example, after the first day of filming, "having seen the movie made that afternoon we were now somehow different, we would never think or talk quite the same. We now knew something more but what it was seemed very vague and even perhaps a bit disagreeable.")

Chinaski is rooted in suspicion, of a type not usually found among the sort who automatically apply the precepts of good

Hollywood filmmaking. He's, not quite sure what to make of the bogus glamor and parade of false artists he comes into contact with because, for one thing, they are survivors like himself, and therefore can't be so easily and totally written off to oblivion. He finds a particular type of representative from this world, the kind who are surely not the pure machine-honed cipher, but carry a certain symptomatic disdain with them into the filmmaking trenches (and who are also victims of crossing boundaries). An identification with these types might maintain Chinaski's sanity. They, like him, are hooked on the film world, and not all that sure why. From actors to extras, financiers, producers, directors, writers, the book is a cavalcade of idiosyncracy, what we expect in Bukowski's world. One character after another sort of sneaks up on the reader and at times almost makes the drinking, brawling Chinaski look like an oasis of sanity. Francois Racine, friend and sometimes roommate of director Jon Pinchot, is "a great actor but now and then he goes crazy. He'll just forget the script and the scene he's supposed to be doing and do his thing. It's a sickness, I think. He must have done it again. He got canned." This type seems like a clone of the rebel on the outs with studios in a never ending battle for independence of vision, the likes of Dennis Hopper or Orson Welles, perhaps, the only sort we can imagine Bukowski identifying with, or even consorting with, in his flirtation with Hollywood.

Racine's firing brings him back from France and soon he and Pinchot have taken residence in, where else, the Venice ghetto, the same environs that captured Hopper's imagination. They easily acclimate to the Venetian vibes and pander their newly acquired vision of a transition life style, keeping chickens so that they can save their money for wine and cigars. They fend off young black boys from the spoils of the family business in gestures of survival burlesqued in a fashion that only Bukowski can pull off:

> *The chickens! HEGGS! All the time we eat HEGGS! Nothing but HEGGS! Poop, poop, poop! The chickens poop HEGGS! All day, all night long my job is to save the chickens from the young black boys! All the time the young black boys climb the fence and run at the chicken coop! I hit them with a long stick, I say, 'You muthafuckas you stay away from my chickens which poop the HEGGS!' I cannot think of my own life or my own death, I am always chasing these young black boys with the long stick! Jon, I need more wine, another cigar!*

He spends the remainder of his time practicing gambling on a little electric roulette wheel.

Harry Friedman is another one of these transitional figures (anti-heroes?) peopling Chinaski's universe. He's a ruthless authority figure and somewhat familiar character in the

Bukowski lexicon (conjuring "the Stone," supervisor Johnstone in **Post Office** ('71), who put the cocky Chinaski through postal hell and, like a drill sergeant, tried to break him). He's an immanent god-like figure who supervises all the wrangling desires the rest of us submit to again and again, but who seems to harbor some conflicting impulses to the point of demonstrating a disdain for what he represents. Is this a caricature of Hollywood power moguls, or the discovery of Dostoyevskyian energies derivative from the monied film scene yet blindly and obsessively devoted to its destruction? These kinds of formations are not all that alien to Bukowski's world. Friedman and Nate Fischman are the executive producers of Firepower Productions. They're new in Hollywood, outcasts in a certain sense yet penultimate members of the Club. Nobody knows quite what to make of them. They used to make exploitation films in Europe. They arrived in America almost overnight and began making scores of movies. They are hated by everyone, but they are dealers, capable of delivering product with maximum efficiency, conjuring Don De Lillo's host of caricatures who operate in seedy realms of dollar deification. Bukowski describes Friedman making an entrance at his own birthday party: "Here he came in an old suit, no necktie, top button missing from his shirt and the shirt was wrinkled. Friedman had his mind on other things besides dress. But he had a fascinating smile and his eyes looked right at people as if he were x-raying them. He had come from hell and he was still in hell and he'd put you in hell too if you gave him the slightest chance. He went from table to table, dropping small and precise sentences."

References to Friedman punctuate the novel, hearken back to the struggle of Chinaski's earlier days when he was always up against the pricks and assholes—bosses—having it in for him. Chinaski is racked by the ups and downs of film production, and all the whipping boys who put it to him over and over again. Chinaski is apprehensive about participating in a competitive (ersatzly so: ideas squelched by marketing savvy), boorish process that most often produces bad films. (One gets the feeling that had the film failed it may have been a relief for Bukowski, who then would still be able to foist a warrior Chinaski on us for a good example, a raging bohemian always trying to beat insurmountable odds)

So Bukowski's foray through tinsel town doesn't produce the easy results we might expect. In a certain sense he sets a trap for the reader. Early on we are on the lookout for some scapegoat, someone who can be blamed for sustaining a world which so magically trades off quality and dealing. We never really find one, and perhaps we never really find the hero-god either. We get a slew of characters whose motives never seem to be either as jaded or as revelatory as one might expect. Chinaski is always at odds with the powers of the film scene, implicitly expressing his superiority over what

they claim to represent, but at times comes off as a convert to it, one who after all is just like the rest, who wants a successful premiere to bank on. At one point he tells Pinchot that he wants a "white stretch limo with a chauffeur, a stock of the best wine, color tv, car phone, cigars . . . ." There's a certain sinking feeling here that lingers until the "bullshit" is over; then it's back to a Bukowski-land more familiar to his readers, one where the good and bad guys are at least somewhat recognizable.

So much of the novel ponders the status of Bukowski's readers, his fans, as if he might be trying to work out his own ambivalent relation to the film world. There are only a few moments where the film world is treated sympathetically, and we sense a great deal of worry about how his viewers/readers perceive him. Once he and his wife Sarah hustle out of a bar full of leather jackets when he is recognized and greeted lynchmob style: ". . . I can kick your ass, . . . can you still get it up? . . . can I read you one of my poems? . . . come on stay and drink with us! Be a good guy! Be like your writing, Chinaski! Don't be a prick!" A fellow has mailed an example of his poetry with the cover letter: ". . . Piss on you! You were once a great writer! Now you suck! You've sold out! My grandmother writes better shit than you do! . . . You gobble your own weenie under sky of vomit!" He receives such dispatches three or four times a month. Chinaski admits that he has a love-hate relationship with his audience.

This is so, perhaps, because he embodies, in so many ways, the true working class hero who aspired to get beyond repressive circumstances but found little to attract him in the world of tinsel. Caught between nostalgia for a vitality of lumpen life that hardly existed, and longing for the successful completion of the next stage of self-realization, he somehow wavers in a sea of bitterness, apologizing, lashing out, and oftentimes just self-destructing. There's a lot in Chinaski—and Bukowski—to identify with for many. Even the well-to-do, feeling disdain for dumb complacency, the stupid crowd, fatigue with the events of a day, can easily muster an anti-social arrogance and identify with Chinaski as he tells the world to fuck off. But maybe as he becomes too many things for too many different people, his identity is polished over with enigmatic imagery, inviting aggressive misunderstandings. Only a star in the contradictory limelight can know and explain what this is like. And each discovery of misunderstanding, excessive praise and hyperemotional attachment may force another fade into silence and obscurity to ponder one's true value. Chinaski, the man who has fought and resisted all his life, submits a silent message to be read in his absence: "Every time somebody spoke to me I felt like diving out a window or taking the elevator down. People just weren't interesting. Maybe they weren't supposed to be. But animals, birds, even, insects were. I couldn't understand it . . . I'm not happy around people and after I drink enough they seem to vanish."

Chinaski did nearly die of a hemorrhage in his early thirties from the effects of alcohol abuse, and was advised to start playing the horses instead of drinking himself to death. He was told by doctors that if he took another drink he'd soon die. He began to go to the track on a daily basis, "then, slowly, I began to drink a little again. Then I drank more. And I didn't die." Self-obsessed, detesting the culture that throws up artificial barriers and interactions between him and the outside world, does he play around with the dangerous edge in isolation, fulfilling the mandate of a working class hero who might have just won the lottery? In 1985, roughly the same time as when *Barfly* was being written, Bukowski told the *Saturday Review:* "I drink wine as I write (usually a good California wine, perhaps Gamay Beaujolais). I don't know if I write when I drink, or drink when I write . . . My routine is: at about 10 p.m., three or four nights a week, I'll open a bottle of wine and turn on the radio to classical music, and I type until two or three in the morning."

Bukowski has cultivated an image (reinforced by a media that makes sure the public won't forget the trail of alluring qualities attached to his person over the years), that can't be sullied by Hollywood or Bohemia. He's in his own camp. Witness his perennial obstinate refusal to be caught by any category or person intruding into his inviolate space, a well-deserved creation that sanctions the nature of his life-long struggle. Secure in this space of his own making, he directs his own movie, and responds to the media and public in ways we would expect from an author above the fray. There's been little need to say much, beyond the obvious and self-evident, about those works created through adversity, a life of drinking and brawling that becomes more or less imprinted on the page as fiction. *Hollywood* and *Barfly,* according to Bukowski, told it like it was and is, narrated a period of his life that until that time hadn't been written about much. It was the aesthetics of the drinking scenes in *Barfly* that he really appreciated, and there seems to be more than a little pride in having become the best alcoholic possible while still preserving his ability to write effectively. He has no regrets about any of it. In fact, he relishes the possibility of being part of the lineage of the best writer-drinkers: O'Neill, Faulkner, Hemingway, London and others. Bukowski knows the strange and desperate lives drunks live better than most. And for him, as for Chinaski, the booze can only free up the typewriter keys for better service.

Joli Funari (review date February 1990)

SOURCE: A review of *Hollywood*, in *Small Press*, Vol. 8, No. 1, p. 36.

[*In the review below, Funari provides a brief plot summary of the novel* Hollywood.]

The movie-making machinations of the title town are exposed in this thinly veiled *roman à clef* about a hard-drinking poet-novelist turned screenwriter. Presumably based on his experiences writing the movie, *Barfly,* Bukowski lays open the absurdity and egotism of the film industry from the worm's-eye view of a screenwriter.

Harry Chinanski has been asked by Jon Pinchot, a French director, to write a screenplay. Pinchot doesn't seem to care what the story is about. Neither does Chinaski; he's more concerned about where his next drink is coming from, and when. Sarah, his wife, is amenable to all this, matching her husband drink for drink and concerned only about getting home in time to feed their five cats. The couple takes a precarious journey through the land of corrupt backers and bizarre creative types where the writer "was where he belonged, in some dark corner, watching."

This novel is funny, and it moves quickly. When Chinanski isn't being updated on the movie's progress, he's playing the ponies. Alcohol and its accoutrements have as large a part as any of the characters. Nestled between the progress reports are anecdotes from Chinanski's past which are now enacted in "The Dance of Jim Beam," in part by an actress who insists he write a scene that will showcase her legs. If nothing else, the experience spawned a novel.

Gary Dretzka (review date 30 January 1994)

SOURCE: "Cries of pain from a man of letters," in *Chicago Tribune Books,* January 30, 1994, p. 7.

[*In the following review, Dretzka reviews the collection of Bukowski's letters:* Screams from the Balcony.]

Hearse, Gallows, Eros, Scimitar and Song, Harlequin, Coffin, Outsider, Black Cat Review, Wormwood Review, Windfall Press, Ole, Evidence, Choice, Mimeo Press, Klacto, Intrepid, Open City . . . Black Sparrow.

Such were the names of the little magazines, chapbooks, literary pamphlets and broadsheets that flourished in a purely non-financial sense of the word in the 1960's, before Xerox machines and desktop computers would revolutionize the way writers placed their words in front of hungry readers.

The titles roll off the tongue like poetry itself and represent, at least for Charles Bukowski—America's grand old man of letters—a neat encapsulation of his struggle to be regularly published between 1958 and 1970, the period covered in this collection of letters. Letters?. . . Cries of pain would be more like it.

The span takes us from Hearse—one of the little magazines that first printed Bukowski's poems after his 10-year break from writing—to Black Sparrow, which continues to produce lovely books from its Santa Rosa, Calif, base. It also matches the Los Angeles barfly's abject search for recognition, from actually paying to have poems reproduced, or selling them for the price of a six-pack, to becoming a columnist in L.A.'s Open City underground newspaper and finally leaving the post office to pursue a literary career at age 50.

These 350-plus pages of letters—a fraction of his actual output—tell the story of that challenge, much in the same way that Bukowski's inter novels would describe the life of Chinaski, his dirty-old-man alter ego. Full of cranky opinions, critiques and misanthropic observations, they were written to other scribes and editors who either share his dark visions or are actively working to make him a star. That many are penned under the influence, from some flophouse or lonely kitchen table, should come as no surprise to anyone familiar with Bukowski's work.

Imagine something like this brightening your mailbox: ". . . the alka seltzer's sparkling and down it goes, depressed fit of cut cat running by without a tail where it had a tail before, or my head is strung around a savage day. All that crap. Anyhow, I have been drinking too much, and on top of that—another kind of mess, and the time has gone by and I haven't done anything, I am ashamed, I am lazy, I am stupid, I am King Kong bending over for a button, I am a torn picture postcard of East Bermuda."

Bukowski writes, seemingly incessantly, as if it might help him think, or feed "the impulse to write poems," according to editor Seamus Cooney. How prolific: 10-, 12-page tomes, day after day, to a dozen or so people, commenting on everything from how the horses are running to the relative merits of the day's poets, celebrated and obscure. Some of those targeted in published critiques would take offense at the candor of this largely unknown writer.

"I began (to write) at 35," he replies. "but I knew whether I liked a poem or not and why, and men don't write with their reputations; they write, most of them, with typewriters, each time you sit down reputation is gone with yesterday's sun; every man begins even again, right now, I am very glad I do not have a hotshot reputation—it keeps me clear with myself."

Mostly, though, he writes about Buk, himself, and his personal struggles with the ladies, his editors, foremen, whiskey, bad teeth and hemorrhoids. He does this not to avoid writing poems, but in addition to turning them out, mailing them off and hoping the rejected ones are returned, since he never kept carbons.

"I think the letter is an important form. You can touch about everything as you run around. It lets you out of the straight-jacket of pure Art, and you've *got* to get out once in a while. Of course, I don't restrict myself as much in the poem as most do, but I have made this my business, this freedom with the word and idea, because . . . to be perfectly corny . . . I know I'll only be around once and I want to make it easy on myself."

Nothing elegant here, but the words reveal the life inside this one man's work, and the struggle to get other people to listen to his often discordant sounds and perhaps' dip into his skid-row milieu for a while. There isn't much irony or symbolic swordsmanship; Bukowski's view is much like that of a video camera—somewhat grainy and distorted, but full of movement and studied, self-deprecating humor.

Here, circa 1967: "I've kind of dropped out of the letter-writing phrase (sic) in order to batch up enough glue to hold myself together a bit longer, the letter-writing thing can become a trap—I started by writing one or 2, then it got to three or four, then it got to 13 or 14, and all I was doing was writing letters. now, if this were my prime purpose, fine enough, but there are other things to do along the way too like . . . inking out a sketch or catching few winners at the track, or just staring at the walls, wondering about toes and your waste, and what the game was about, there are times TIMES TO DO NOTHING, very important times, hard to get between women and jobs and sickness and and and . . . so the writing of too many letters to too many people can get like carrying 50 pound rocks back and forth during your few moments of leisure, but people will . . . think you're up light or writing President Johnson or essays for the Atlantic. me, I'm hanging onto the slippery walls."

Cooney, of Western Michigan University, did a nice job editing these often-difficult epistles (examples of the actual letters, complete with sketches and smears are included) from their much longer and messier original forms, while maintaining all their flavor and character. If you're a fan, this is a must acquisition.

My hope—beyond that president Clinton will name Bukowski Poet Laureate some April 1—is that young people, especially those attracted to the zines and poetry slams, will stumble upon this book and realize what a pure joy it is to write and receive letters as full of life and raw humanity as this. Yes, I know this is the digital age and we can call each other or correspond via something called E-mail, but many of us are old enough to remember when it was the postman who delivered the treasures of our day, and words filled the sails of our imagination.

George Stade (review date 5 June 1994)

SOURCE: "Death Comes for the Detective," in *The New York Times Book Review*, June 5, 1994, pp. 49-50.

[*In the following review, Stade provides a plot summary of Bukowski's last novel,* Pulp.]

Charles Bukowski, ur-beatnik and author of more than 40 volumes of countercultural prose and verse, finished *Pulp* shortly before he died of leukemia at the age of 73 in March. *Pulp* is a spoof of the hard-boiled detective novel, especially as perpetrated by Mickey Spillane. It does not, of course, take much to send up the hard-boiled detective novel—all you have to do is write one. The conventions by now seem to mock themselves, if you stand back a bit. But *Pulp* does more than stand back from itself.

Bukowski's hard-boiled dick is one Nick Belane, although he sometimes wonders, apropos of nothing, whether he isn't really Harry Martel, whoever he is. Business is slow, but Belane occupies himself by catching flies and drinking from the bottle he keeps in his desk, a bottle of sake. On the job he will make do with Scotch or vodka with beer chasers. ("Nice thing about being a drunk, though, you were never constipated.") He also keeps in his desk a gun, variously described as a Luger, a .45, a .32—something worth getting straight, you would think. On the wall of his office is a "fake Dali," the melting watch.

Belane rolls his own cigarettes when not smoking cigars, wears a derby, drives a Volkswagen bug, plays the horses, (disastrously), hums bits from *Carmen,* regularly humbles 300-pound tough guys and regards women with the usual mixture of misogyny and lust. ("I was always a leg man. It was the first thing I saw when I was born.") And he regards himself with the classic mixture of covert narcissism and self-pity: ("My eyes were blue and my shoes were old and nobody loved me.") Nick Belane is no intellectual, he has just failed the written part of the test for a driver's license. On the whole, the fee he charges his clients, $6 an hour, seems about right.

Apropos of nothing, business suddenly picks up. Lady Death arrives at Belane's office, a lady always "dressed to kill." She wants him to discover whether a certain Celine, who hangs around bookstores checking out the competition apparently, is *the* Celine, "France's greatest writer," who would now be a century old, way overdue for Lady Death. Then John Barton, who recommended Belane to Lady Death, calls. He hires Belane to find the Red Sparrow, not otherwise identified.

There's an insider's joke here, one of many. John Martin, longtime supporter and publisher of Bukowski's work, owns Black Sparrow Press, sometimes called the house a poet built, the poet being Bukowski. "You've got talent," says John Barton in the accents of John Martin, "It's a little raw but it's part of the charm." Much of the spoofing in *Pulp* is at the expense of Bukowski, another hard-drinking, tough-talking, horse-playing barroom brawler, and like other novelists, a species of private investigator.

A third new client, Jack Bass, hires Belane to find out whether his wife, Cindy, née Cindy Maybell, Miss Chili Cook-Off of 1980, is playing around. (She is, in a way—with Celine.)

Then there is Hal Grovers, a mortician, who is being pestered by "a hot number from outer space" named Jeannie Nitro, a body snatcher from Zoros as it turns out. Her powers are pretty much those of that other Jeannie, of television fame. Finally Celine hires Belane to prove or disprove that Lady Death is what she claims to be. (She is, as Celine finds out—the hard way.)

There's lots of fun and much ingenuity in the way each of these separate cases becomes a ratchet, a cam, a cog, a flywheel in the works of the others, one big melting watch. But about three-quarters of the way through, the fun thins out, the death-haunted atmosphere thickens and there is a sense of time running out. First Jeannie and her companions decide they will not, after all, stay to colonize Earth. "It's just too awful," she says. "Smog, murder, the poisoned air, the poisoned water, the poisoned food, the hatred, the hopelessness, everything."

Then Belane distances himself from that everything to move inexorably toward the Red Sparrow, in the way a man might move in fear and longing to embrace his own death. Belane gets "enveloped" by the Sparrow in the way a dead writer gets absorbed by his words—as printed, in this case, by Black Sparrow Press.

As parody, *Pulp* does not cut very deep. As a farewell to readers, as a gesture of rapprochement with death, as Bukowski's sendup and send-off of himself, this bio-parable cuts as deep as you would want.

Elizabeth Young (review date 17 June 1994)

SOURCE: "Bum steered," in *New Statesman and Society,* June 17, 1994, pp. 37-38.

[*Young provides a favorable review of the Bukowski anthology* Run With The Hunted: A Charles Bukowski Reader.]

Any serious reader thinks they know only too well what Charles Bukowski's work will deliver. Wet rings on bar counters; the swish of the barman's dirty cloth. Rotgut whisky and paint-stripper wine. Misanthropy. Despair. Women with big, swaying bottoms and very high heels. A touch of misogyny. Barflies, bums, floozies, the tote, the track and the betting shop. He's typing in his underwear in a low-rent room, with a filthy glass, an empty bottle and an overflowing ashtray beside him. Yes, we had him well sussed.

And so, with all due respect to this recently departed author, why read any more of the old fart's books? After all there are nearly 50 of them—poetry, short stories and novels (as well as the screenplay for **Barfly**)—with his reason for choosing one form over another often seeming to be quite arbitrary.

These were my feelings, vaguely, upon picking up **Run With The Hunted,** and seldom have smug assumptions been so suddenly and sharply rebuked. I read this at one sitting and found it to be one of the rarest of volumes—a beautifully edited anthology of a writer's work, collated by an editor profoundly sympathetic to his author's intentions.

From the vast vat of Bukowski homebrew, John Martin has distilled a cut-glass decanter of 100-proof literary perfection. That he should have been able to do so is not altogether surprising as Martin, at Black Sparrow Press, has been Bukowski's most consistent publisher and editor, as well as supporter and mentor. It was he who released Bukowski in the 1960's, at the age of 45, from 11 years of wage slavery at the post office by offering him $100 a month if he would do nothing else but write. And this Bukowski did—whether drunk or sober, rich, poor, infatuated or broken-hearted. But then Bukowski had written obsessionally for a long time before that—apart from a 10-year alcoholic hiatus during the 1950's when his liver swelled to the size of a watermelon.

This is a poignant and moving book. By the simple expedient of using extracts from Bukowski's books and poems in chronological order (corresponding to his life story) rather than in the order that they were published, Martin in effect supplies us with Bukowski's own autobiography. Born in Germany in 1920, Bukowski landed in America in infancy and spent his life in Los Angeles, a city he both loved and hated.

His childhood was blighted by a brutal father—"a cruel, shiny bastard with bad breath". In adolescence he suffered terribly from boils and acne and from the gut-churning treatments available at the time. These experiences left him feeling ugly and hopeless and he drifted into a long series of dead-end jobs, including a stint in a dog biscuit factory. At other times he existed as a Skid Row bum.

Despite his decades of devoted reading and writing, his straightforward, largely autobiographical work received little attention until his middle years, when he was discovered by a disaffected post-Beat audience of younger readers, particularly in Europe, and propelled into the spotlight. His persona became increasingly fixed and near-parodic but he did attempt to write about the cryptic, complex ways of fame with honesty and intelligence.

He noted in detail both its advantages—meeting celebrities, other writers and being showered with groupies from Planet Mensa—and its disadvantages—which were more or less identical. He tended to cling nostalgically to his old, grimy alcoholic ways until taken in hand by second wife Linda, who enabled him to die a *rich* drunken bum.

In addition to its acerbic edge, Bukowski's writing always possessed a sense of the frailty of human endeavor. Hemingway was his most obvious stylistic influence. Bukowski's was a lifelong struggle to express himself clearly, honestly and concisely. He has similarities with Henry Miller and, like Miller, has had trouble over his alleged "sexism", although much of this seems no more than normal lust accompanied by the bewilderment and irritations that attend its slaking.

Bukowski's own influence on younger writers has been subtle and pernicious. There is a hugely increased tendency to substitute personal experience for imagination in fiction. Much new fiction shows how gifted Bukowski was in shaping and organizing the original material into something far more significant than a self-obsessed diary.

John Martin has done Bukowski a great service—and a sort of disservice too. After such a brilliantly constructed anthology, who is going to read all the books? His posthumous novel **Pulp** is the first to take a non-autobiographical tack. It is modeled on the hard-boiled private-eye novels of Chandler and Hammett and is likely to divert those who appreciate that genre, and its lively collision with Bukowksi's trademark style.

Dick Lochte (review date 30 October 1994)

SOURCE: "Lady Death and Aliens from the Planet Zaros," in *Los Angeles Times Book Review,* October 30, 1994, p. 11.

[*In the following, Lochte summarizes and favorably reviews* Pulp.]

Private eye Nick Belane sits in his sleazy downtown L.A. office, alone and lonely. It's hot outside and his air conditioner is on the fritz. His rent is overdue. He looks at a fly crawling across the top of his desk. Ever since the prime of Raymond Chandler, and probably long before that, fictional private eyes have been sitting at their desks, sweating and studying flies. But *Pulp*'s Belane is a little different. A woozily parodic creation of the swirling mind of the late writer-poet Charles Bukowski, he is both earthier and more fanciful than his predecessors. And his pursuits are certainly more literary.

For example, Chandler's Philip Marlowe (in the novel *The Little Sister*) uses a swatter on his fly, then picks the insect up daintily by one wing and deposits it into a wastebasket. Belane smashes his with his bare hand and, barely pausing to wipe the result onto his pants leg, he fields a call from a client. It's Lady Death. Not some television horror movie hostess, but the genuine article. She hires Belane to find Louis-Ferdinand Celine, who has been seen at a used book store searching for Faulkner first editions. The problem is that the French novelist died back in the '60s. And if that isn't enough to make a shamus swill all the sake in his bottom desk drawer, Lady Death is just the first of a series of clients with odd requests.

There's John Barton, who hires him to get a line on the elusive Red Sparrow, whatever it may be. And entrepreneur Jack Bass, who asks him to follow Mrs. Bass, the former Miss Chili Cookoff of 1990, who he thinks may be deceiving him with another man. And, strangest of all, there 4-foot-8 Hal Grovers, who wants him to get rid of the woman who's making his life a living hell, Jeannie Nitro, who just happens to be one of six space aliens from the planet Zaros here to settle down on our browning earth.

In true detective novel tradition, the cases are related. And in his own blunt, heavy-handed manner, Belane works his way through to their solutions. This makes for a whimsical and oddly charming (a word not often used in describing Bukowski's work) spoof. The literary allusions are amusing. John Barton is a stand-in for John Martin, the owner of Black Sparrow Press, his publisher of record. Celine was a novelist whose world view and use of argot probably made him a Bukowski favorite. Two dim leg-breakers are named Dante and Fante, the former probably a reference to the poet of *Divine Comedy* fame, the later to John Fante who pioneered fictional studies of Hollywood's demimonde a bit before Bukowski. The explanation of the author's reason for depicting them as thugs I leave to better informed students of his work, along with any subtext to the rest of the cast of characters, including bookstore owner Red Kowldowsky, McKelvy the landlord and the treacherous beauty Deja Fountain.

Bukowski obviously wasn't out to bury the private detective genre with this playful pastiche. But he was toying with its conventions, with the smart talk and tough guy attitude. Probably of deeper import is the realization that, with all the boozy goofiness and slapstick whimsy of Belane's caper, this is very much an autobiographical work, a portrait of the aging author as an aging private eye, always on the case whether he is following up serious lines of inquiry or tossing away all his loot at Hollywood Park or in some dim bar.

Pulp was printed only months after his death last March at the age of 73. Though a few decades younger, Belane's sense of his own mortality is acute. Everywhere he looks he sees people and places he knew leaving the scene. And after he delivers Celine to Lady Death and she reclaims him, Belane and his client have this conversation:

> "You haven't seen the last of me," the Lady said.
>
> "Look, baby, can't we cut a deal?"
>
> "It's never been done, Belane."
>
> "Well, O.K., but how about giving me a date, your know, a D.O.D.?"
>
> "What's that?"
>
> "Date of Demise."
>
> "What good would that do?"
>
> "Lady, I could prepare myself."
>
> "Every human should anyhow, Belane."
>
> "Lady, they don't, they forget it, they ignore it or they're just too stupid to think it."

Eventually, he arrives at his moment of truth. "This can't be happening, I thought. This isn't the way it's supposed to happen." But it does, at a time when Belane has solved all of his cases. One hopes that Bukowski solved all of his, too.

Russell Harrison (essay date 1994)

SOURCE: "Sex, Women, and Irony," from *Against the American Dream: Essays on Charles Bukowski,* Black Sparrow Press, 1994, pp. 183-215.

[*In the following essay, Harrison challenges the common view of Bukowski as a chauvinist and misogynist. He illustrates his point with several selections from* Post Office, Factotem, *and* Women, *in which Bukowski ironically deconstructs the macho male image.*]

"Why can't you be decent to people?" she asked.

"Fear," I said.

No aspect of Bukowski's writing has been more sharply criticized than his portrayal of women. In response to his early work, one critic [Len Fulton] wrote (hyperbolically but with some justification):

> Bukowski's antics with women, his thoughts about them, are one vast and sniggering cliché. He has nothing to tell us about them because, I'm convinced, he knows nothing about them (e.g., "the ladies will always be the same.") and is determined at this point not to learn. They are a dirty joke to him, a dirty joke on him. Inside the web of his booze-bull-and-broad exploits lurks a demon sexual jingoist, erupting and irrupting in self-punishing concatenations; hostile, frustrated, pugilistic—fearful of the role into which (he thinks) one is cast by fate of genitalia.

Although such a characterization is no longer valid, it represents an early (and continuing) response to Bukowski's work. However, his depiction of women has changed significantly over the third of a century in which he has been writing. The crucial period for this change was the 1970's and this essay focuses on the novels written during this period; just in the seven years between *Post Office* (1971) and *Women* (1978) there was an increased subtlety of characterization, a more nuanced treatment of psychological dynamics and less reliance on stereotypes.

While I will discuss Bukowski's undeniable male chauvinism, what has become significant in his writing is the irony with which he has come to treat his protagonist's machismo, something which distinguishes him from many male American novelists of his generation. Reading Fulton's comments after reading *Women,* it becomes clear how far Bukowski has moved from his earlier position.

Kate Millett's 1970 book *Sexual Politics* provides a useful background for such a discussion. There, she places the women's movement in a historical context and develops categories for the analysis of patriarchal society's views of women in literature. She convincingly argues that women were rarely depicted objectively by modern male authors who were the prisoners of myth and of a puritanical view of sexuality in which a woman, by virtue of her interest in and enjoyment of sex was seen as perverse or defiled. Her periodization of the liberation movement is also useful. She notes that the years 1930-1960 represented a counter-revolutionary period with respect to women's liberation. This is important in any discussion of Bukowski's work because it underlines the fact that part of his boyhood, all of his adolescence, and part of his maturity took place during an era of reaction against women's gains, while his novels were

written and published in the middle of the "second wave" of women's liberation.

In his novels Bukowski has depicted a number of women through their relationships with Henry Chinaski; indeed, one of the reasons "thoughtful female readers find no chance whatsoever to positively identify with the female characters" is that women are rarely presented independent of their relationships with Chinaski. By the time Bukowski came to write *Women,* however, this had begun to change and his depiction of women and sexual relationships gradually shifted from crude descriptions of events and flat characterizations of women to fuller descriptions, more rounded characterizations and female characters who, it was suggested, had lives outside the orbit of Henry Chinaski.

In his first novel, *Post Office,* Bukowski depicts events that, but for their brevity, might suggest comparison with the most chauvinist scenes in Henry Miller:

> I think it was my second day as a Christmas temp that this big woman came out and walked around with me as I delivered letters. What I mean by big was that her ass was big and her tits were big and that she was big in all the right places. She seemed a bit crazy but I kept looking at her body and I didn't care.
>
> She talked and talked and talked. Then it came out. Her husband was an officer on an island far away and she got lonely, you know, and lived in this little house in back all by herself.
>
> "What little house?" I asked.
> She wrote the address on a piece of paper.
> "I'm lonely too," I said, "I'll come by and we'll talk tonight."
>
> I was shacked but the shackjob was gone half the time, off somewhere, and I was lonely all right. I was lonely for that big ass standing beside me.
>
> "All right," she said, "see you tonight."
>
> She was a good one all right, she was a good lay but like all lays after the 3rd or 4th night I began to lose interest and didn't go back.

Here, on the first page of Bukowski's first novel, the woman is objectified in the crudest terms, presented as mentally problematic, the aggressor and unfaithful. But even in such a crude and simplistic depiction, there are hints of a subtler dynamic: along with the woman's seemingly unambiguous infidelity, a reason for her behavior is suggested: her husband is away (i.e., withholding his affection), behavior repeated by Chinaski who soon stops seeing the woman.

A few pages further along, Chinaski encounters a woman who grabs a registered letter (without signing for it) which he then attempts to retrieve, forcing his way into the house:

"YOU HAVE NO RIGHT IN MY HOUSE! GET OUT!"
"And you have no right to rob the mails! Either give me the letter back or sign for it. Then I'll leave."

"All right! All right! I'll sign."

I showed her where to sign and gave her a pen. I looked at her breasts and the rest of her and I thought, what a shame she's crazy, what a shame, what a shame.

She handed back the pen and her signature—it was just scrawled. She opened the letter, began to read it as I turned to leave.

Then she was in front of the door, arms spread across. The letter was on the floor.

"Evil evil evil man! You came here to rape me!"

"Look lady, let me by."

"THERE IS EVIL WRITTEN ALL OVER YOUR FACE!"

"Don't you think I know that? Now let me out of here!"

With one hand I tried to push her aside. She clawed one side of my face, good. I dropped my bag, my cap fell off, and as I held a handkerchief to the blood she came up and raked the other side.

"YOU CUNT! WHAT THE HELL'S WRONG WITH YOU!"

"See there? See there? You're evil!"

She was right up against me. I grabbed her by the ass and got my mouth on hers. Those breasts were against me, she was all up against me. She pulled her head back, away from me—

"Rapist! Rapist! Evil rapist!"

I reached down with my mouth, got one of her tits, then switched to the other.

"Rape! Rape! I'm being raped!"

She was right. I got her pants down, unzipped my fly, got it in, then walked her backwards to the couch. We fell down on top of it.

She lifted her legs high.
"RAPE!" she screamed.
I finished her off, zipped my fly, picked up my mail pouch and walked out leaving her staring quietly at the ceiling . . .

Once more a woman is depicted as disturbed and aggressive—although here it is a more complicated situation; indeed, although she cries "rape!", she is shown as partially complicit and when Chinaski agrees that it is rape, we feel he doesn't really believe it, that somehow her physical aggression sanctions his sexual violence. But he does rape her, or at least I think most readers would see it that way, and such irony as there is in the passage is overshadowed by the protagonist's brutal actions and crude chauvinist language. Such language is especially evident in **Post Office** because Bukowski is nowhere near as effective in distancing himself from Chinaski as he became in the later novels.

If the writing is sometimes repetitive and unmediated in **Post Office,** this is no longer the case in **Factotum** (1975). But although Bukowski's distance from his protagonist is more evident and the writing more skillful, the underlying dynamic remains the same. On the first page of the novel, soon after his arrival in Miami, Henry Chinaski is assaulted by the siren call of a "high yellow": "*Hey, poor white trash!*" and responding, is made a fool of. Twenty-odd pages later in the first explicit sexual encounter of the novel he is literally assaulted by Martha, a fellow-lodger in his rooming house. After some brief conversation and a dance-cum-strip-tease Martha attacks:

Suddenly her eyes narrowed. I was sitting on the edge of the bed. She leapt on me before I could move. Her open mouth was pressed on mine. It tasted of spit and onions and stale wine and (I imagined) the sperm of four hundred men. She pushed her tongue into my mouth. It was thick with saliva, I gagged and pushed her off. She fell on her knees, tore open my zipper, and in a second my soft pecker was in her mouth. She sucked and bobbed. Martha had a small yellow ribbon in her short grey hair. There were warts and big brown moles on her neck and cheeks.

My penis rose; she groaned, bit me. I screamed, grabbed her by the hair, pulled her off. I stood in the center of the room wounded and terrified. They were playing a Mahler symphony on the radio. Before I could move she was down on her knees and on me again. She gripped my balls mercilessly with both of her hands. Her mouth opened, she had me; her head bobbed, sucked, jerked. Giving my balls a tremendous yank while almost biting my pecker in half she forced me to the floor. Sucking sounds filled the room as my radio played Mahler. I felt as if I were being eaten by a pitiless animal. My pecker rose, covered with spittle and blood. The sight of it threw her into a frenzy. I felt as if I was being eaten alive.

If I come, I thought desperately, I'll never forgive myself.

The last sentence is one of the funniest in all of Bukowski's writings. Rarely has the mind-body split been presented so comically. The tactic Bukowski uses is reminiscent of the effective use of humor in his social criticism (noted in the last chapter) as he treats a subject of some (psychological) weight—Chinaski's reluctance to lose control—in a comic way.

Here the male has completely lost control; while the scene is comic, it is the comic transformation of the male's ultimate nightmare: he—or at least his penis—has fallen prey to a sexually devouring woman. The depiction of a wounded and terrified Chinaski radically contravenes our traditional expectations. To appreciate how radically, we need only try to imagine Henry Miller or Norman Mailer invoking such a protagonist. Both Miller and Mailer have too much invested in maintaining the male's power to allow this much loss of control or to present what is at bottom for them a serious issue—in fact, *the* issue, as a subject for jest.

Chinaski, in a tactic not unknown in Bukowski, gives the woman money afterwards, although she hasn't mentioned payment and, indeed, seems content with the pleasure she has derived from the act itself. Commodifying the act is the male's last-gasp attempt to maintain control and escape his victimization (inherent in his being treated as an object) by reversing the roles. This passage represents something quite unusual in the presentation of a male protagonist in American fiction. Though it does not depict the woman positively, indeed not even as fully human, neither is it the language of simple chauvinism, and its significance lies as much in what it reveals about men and the masculine role as in its degradation of women. The male's loss of control and the anxiety it provokes are clear in the language. The passage is comic, but the comedy is also a defense against the anxiety occasioned by the loss of control.

In *Factotum,* Bukowski develops Chinaski's passivity, even masochism, which, along with the theme of male victimization is the virtual signature of the protagonist. This becomes obvious in his relationship with Gertrude, a young woman he meets in his St. Louis roominghouse. They become emotionally involved (though not lovers).

> Whenever I went out into the hall of the roominghouse Gertrude seemed to be standing there. She was perfect, pure, maddening sex, and she knew it, and she played on it, dripped it, and allowed you to suffer for it. It made her happy. I didn't feel too bad either. Like most men in that situation I realized that I wouldn't get anything out of her—intimate talks, exciting roller-coaster rides, long Sunday afternoon walks—until after I had made some odd promises.

Here the masochistic element, which runs like a red thread through Chinaski's relationships, appears explicitly for the first time, expressed in the passage: "She was sex . . . and allowed you to suffer for it. It made her happy. I didn't feel too bad either."

In one sense, Chinaski remains in control by denying women sex, or deeper involvement (thus expressing a sadism that we would also expect to be present), but this is not the whole story. The ambivalence of the situation is reflected in the odd construction: "allowed you to suffer." The more expected phrasing would be "made you suffer," but this is too straightforward and suggests the possibility of an open conflict whereas in the narrator's phrasing, the male is presented as totally powerless and the choice of "allowed" implies that something desirable, pleasurable, i.e., painful, is being granted, a projection of his own masochistic delight in the situation; indeed the tentativeness of Chinaski's language in the whole exchange is marked, as if he is almost pleading to be subjected to Gertrude's power.

However, this is only the opening gambit in a more complex interaction. Gertrude is interested in Chinaski and shows it. Yet Chinaski is obviously of two minds. In spite of his knowledge of the need for "some odd promises," he allows the relationship to progress, ostensible grateful for her "allow[ing] him to be warmed by a glimpse of it." One night Chinaski takes Gertrude to a bar:

> Gertrude turned her head and stared into the crowd of people. Then she looked at me.
>
> "Isn't he *handsome*?"
> "Who?"
> "That soldier over there. He's sitting alone. He sits so *straight*. And he's got all his medals on."
> "Come on, let's get out of here."
> "But it's not late."
> "You can stay."
> "No, I want to go with *you*."

"I don't care what you do."

"Is it the soldier? Are you mad because of the soldier?"

"Oh, shit!"

"It was the soldier!"

"I'm going."

I stood up at the table, left a tip and walked toward the door. I heard Gertrude behind me. I walked down the street in the snow. Soon she was walking at my side.

"You didn't even get a taxi. These high heels in the snow!"

I didn't answer. We walked the four or five blocks to the rooming house. I went up the steps with her beside me. Then I walked down to my room, opened the door, closed it, got out of my clothes and went to bed. I heard her throw something against the wall of her room.

While Gertrude is interested in Chinaski, he, needing a reason to end a difficult situation (difficult because his involvement entails vulnerability), uses the pretext of her casual remarks about the soldier to terminate the relationship. While the incident may have been used to suggest the faithlessness of women (a theme in Bukowski), the underlying cause of the break is the protagonist's failure to respond to a woman's emotional needs. What, in fact, has happened? Gertrude has become involved with Chinaski who, not interested in a deeper relationship, has nevertheless allowed Gertrude to become involved and causes her pain by his behavior. What has taken place is the reverse of what had been described in the passage quoted earlier: he has allowed her to become involved with him and makes her suffer for it. Gertrude is obviously ambivalent, too; her attraction to the soldier stems not so much from his physical attractiveness as from his "straightness": he has played the game correctly, has gotten medals to prove it, whereas the appeal of Chinaski is his refusal to play the game (which also appeals to Gertrude).

This passivity is again evident in the relationship with Laura (the first extended sexual relationship in the novel). While Chinaski initiates it, it soon becomes clear who is in control. Chinaski buys Laura four or five drinks, then tells her, "That drink was it. I'm broke."

"Are you serious?"

"Yes."

"Do you have a place to stay?"

"An apartment, two or three days left on the rent."

"And you don't have any money? Or anything to drink?"

"No."

"Come with me."

Laura, along with two other women, Grace and Jerry, is living with and being supported by Wilbur Oxnard, an eccentric millionaire who is writing an opera, *The Emperor of San Francisco*. Chinaski is accepted into the fold, ostensibly to write the libretto. At one time or another, each of the women had been Wilbur's lover, though "Grace is his main girl." Wilbur has a boat and on it, in one memorable chapter, Chinaski has sex, *seriatim,* with all three women, though Laura is *his* main woman. The situation as it develops is noteworthy because here he immediately moves in with (sort of) the first woman he meets who shows him the slightest bit of affection and who has sex with him and by virtue of his relationship with her winds up being supported by Wilbur. This complete "surrender" doesn't jibe with the independent loner image that Chinaski likes to project. That Chinaski himself recognizes this and is, momentarily, made uneasy by the developing structure of the relationship is apparent when, on the night of their first meeting they return to his apartment with liquor, food and cigarettes (charged to Wilbur): "I brought her drink and curled up next to her. I did feel foolish." It is the loss of control that is at the root of this feeling.

Throughout the book women continue to initiate relationships. The most important such relationship, with Jan Meadows, begins somewhat as the relationship with Laura began:

> We had met at an open air lunch counter—I was spending my last fifty cents on a greasy hamburger—and we struck up a conversation. She bought me a beer, gave me her phone number, and three days later I moved into her apartment.

The relationship is broken off, a good deal later there is a reconciliation, and then it ends for good. Jan precipitates both breakups, though the first time it is Chinaski who leaves. This occurs after a period in which Chinaski has been working regularly and also winning money at the track.

> The new life didn't sit well with Jan. She was used to her four fucks a day and also used to seeing me poor and humble. After a day at the warehouse, then the wild ride and finally sprinting across the parking lot and down through the tunnel, there wasn't much love left in me. When I came in each evening she'd be well into her wine.
>
> "Mr. Horseplayer," she'd say as I walked in. She'd be all dressed up; high heels, nylons, legs crossed high, swinging her foot. "Mr. Big Horseplayer. You know, when I first met you I liked the way you walked across a room. You didn't just *walk* across

a room, you walked like you were going to walk through a wall, like you owned everything, like nothing mattered. Now you get a few bucks in your pocket and you're not the same anymore. You act like a dental student or a plumber."

Whatever superficial cogency Chinaski's explanation might initially possess is demolished by the exchange that follows:
"Don't give me any shit about plumbers, Jan."
"You haven't made love to me in two weeks."
"Love takes many forms. Mine has been more subtle."
"You haven't fucked me for two weeks."

Surely Jan has a point in that the reduction in the incidence of lovemaking from about 28 times per week (!) to zero cannot be completely traced to the demands made on Chinaski's stamina by steady employment and the visits to the track (he is, after all, in his twenties); clearly Chinaski has begun to withdraw his affection from Jan, and her complaint, which his superficial riposte does nothing to answer, seems justified. Jan's focus is not so much on Chinaski's having money but on his going to the track which takes place after work and thus deprives her of his company. Chinaski, however, subtly changes the grounds of her complaint: "The arguments were always the same. I understood it too well now—that great lovers were always men of leisure. I fucked better as a bum than as a puncher of timeclocks." Again, there is an element of projection here. It is Chinaski who resents having to work whereas Jan's objection merely expresses her resentment at his neglecting her for the track; he takes his resentment out on Jan because she is an easy target. Jan has said nothing at all about the quality of their lovemaking (indeed, how could she, since there hasn't been any), only wanted to make love. What has happened has been a replay of the relationship with Gertrude: the woman has become emotionally involved with Chinaski and Chinaski has begun to withdraw from her. The result is that Jan, naturally enough, begins to seek love and affection elsewhere:

Most of the evenings fell into a pattern. She'd argue, grab her purse and be gone out the door. It was effective; we had lived and loved together for too many days. I had to feel it and feel it I did. But I always let her go as I sat helpless in my chair and drank my whiskey and tuned in the radio to a bit of classical music. I knew she was out there, and I knew there would be somebody else. Yet I had to let it happen, I had to let events take their own course.

This particular evening I sat there and something just broke in me and I got up and walked down the four flights of stairs and into the street. I walked down from Third and Union Streets to Sixth Street

and then West along Sixth toward Alvarado. I walked along past the bars and I knew she was in one of them. I made a guess, walked in, and there was Jan sitting at the far end of the bar. She had a green and white silk scarf spread across her lap. She was sitting between a thin man with a large wart on his nose, and another man who was a little humped mound of a thing wearing bifocals and dressed in an old black suit.

Jan saw me coming. She lifted her head and even in the gloom of the bar she seemed to pale. I walked up behind her, standing near her stool. "I tried to make a woman out of you but you'll never be anything but a goddamned whore!" I back-handed her and knocked her off the stool. She fell flat on the floor and screamed. I picked up her drink and finished it. Then I slowly walked towards the exit. When I got there I turned. "Now, if there's anybody here . . . who doesn't like what I just did . . . just say so."

There was no response. I guess they liked what I just did, I walked back out on Alvarado Street.

The portrayal of the male and of the psychological dynamics at work, in this passage, lies somewhere between the depictions of *Post Office* and those of *Women*. There is no irony here although there are obvious contradictions. Initially, it seems Bukowski wants the reader to see things from Chinaski's point of view. Jan's "infidelity" is being used to justify Chinaski's ending the relationship; once again, Chinaski is shown as victimized. Rhetorically, Bukowski gives Chinaski an edge (though calling Jan's behavior a "counterattack" implies that she is the original victim). He is "helpless," though this contradicts the assumption of control in "I always let her go," which is in turn trumped by "I had to let it happen . . . to let events take their own course"; this last is itself an ambivalent formulation, the redundant "own" perversely indicating the *protagonist's* control. But overall, the passage conjures up a victimized Chinaski; forced to be content with "a bit" of music. Given his unwillingness (or inability) to deal with his conflicts, Chinaski must view himself as betrayed.

It is Chinaski's contention that all women are whores or at least all the women he becomes involved with. But in reality he is almost never involved with prostitutes and Jan is not a prostitute. Chinaski feels compelled to make women into whores (in his eyes) and here we can see one reason why. His own implication in terminating relationships is disguised and evaded if women can be presented as inherently unfaithful, like prostitutes. It seems obvious that what Jan most wants here is companionship. Clearly, were sex her intent, she would hardly have chosen "a thin man with a large wart on his nose" or "a little humped mound of a thing wearing bifocals and dressed in an old black suit." If it seemed at first that it was Bukowski's purpose to justify Chinaski's behavior, he concludes by letting us see that Chinaski's inability to sustain relationships is the issue, not Jan's, although it is a nice question as to how conscious a strategy this is in *Factotum.* (It is clearly so in *Women.*)

Not too long after the incident in the bar Jan and Henry separate in an unusually abrupt way. They are drinking in their apartment: "When Jan brought the drink I drank it straight down. 'You keep the car,' I said, 'and half the money I have left is yours.'" No reason is given for Chinaski's wanting to leave, but in the preceding chapter, five pages after the incident in the bar (the exact mid-point of the novel), Chinaski has a revealing dream, which forms all of chapter 51.

Though the entire chapter is printed in italics and, after the introductory paragraph, is one long paragraph, not even being indented for dialogue, the description is quite realistic and not very dream-like (it is only the violence and possible murder that suggest a lack of reality in the event); so realistic that we can believe that Henry Chinaski, on awakening, has trouble believing it was only a dream. (And not just Henry Chinaski. Readers, too, not infrequently ignore the italics and think a murder has been committed.) In the dream Henry and Jan go to the race track at Los Alamitos. On returning to their seats after placing their bets, they find that their places in the grandstand have been taken by a *"small gray-haired man."* They had previously placed newspapers there to indicate that the seats were taken. They explain to the man that this is the custom, but he simply says, *"These seats are NOT reserved."* After that they go for a drink and Jan taunts Chinaski, saying the old man had *"called your card."* Chinaski replies, *"What can a guy do with an old man?"* to which Jan responds, *"If he had been young you wouldn't have done anything either."* When they return to where they have squeezed in beside the old man, Jan begins to flirt:

> Jan sat down next to him. Their legs were pressed together. "What do you do for a living?" Jan asked him. "Real estate. I make sixty thousand a year— after taxes." "Then why don't you buy a reserved seat?" I asked. "That's my prerogative." Jan pressed her flank against him. She smiled her most beautiful smile. "You know," she said, "you've got the nicest blue eyes?" "Uh huh." "What's your name?" "Tony Endicott." "My name is Jan Meadows. My nickname is Misty."

After this continues for a little while, Chinaski grabs the man by his shirt collar and, after a struggle, manages to push him down between the rows of the grandstand, a thirty-five foot drop.

It is, presumably, the emotions that caused such a dream, along with Jan's behavior, that prompt Chinaski to think that it's time to get out of the relationship, although we are told nothing of this. But while no explicit connection between the dream and the first break-up is made, there is an implicit connection between this dream and the final break-up between Jan and Henry at the end of the novel. After a gap of eighty pages, in which Jan has only been mentioned once, she reappears, only to disappear for good:

> The day before I had helped Jan move in with a fat real estate operator who lived on Kingsley drive. I'd stood back out of sight in the hall and watched him kiss her; then they'd gone into his apartment together and the door had closed . . . . We'd been evicted from our apartment. I had $2.08. Jan promised me she'd be waiting when my luck changed but I hardly believed that. The real estate operator's name was Jim Bemis, he had an office on Alvarado Street and plenty of cash. "I hate it when he fucks me," Jan had said. She was now probably saying the same thing about me to him.

Chinaski suggests that Jan has left him because he's down on his luck. Yet that was his situation when they met: a man spending his "last fifty cents on a greasy hamburger," whom she had to buy a beer. Hence, lack of money isn't the issue. But it's important that it seem the issue in order to reinforce Chinaski's view of women as faithless and predatory creatures drawn only by wealth. Though Chinaski doesn't actually say that that's why she's leaving him, the implication is more effective than any explicit statement could be because it is presented "objectively," solely in terms of "facts": he has no money; the real estate "operator" does; the reader draws the conclusion. (We might also wonder why, if Jan does leave him because he has no money, Chinaski earlier asserted that she liked him best as a "bum.")

Because the reasons for this—as for the earlier—break-up are not explored (and because the scene recalls Jan's behavior towards the wealthy real-estate salesman in the dream), we can see that the function of this scene is to show Jan deserting Chinaski in his hour of need, clearly a false and self-serving construction of the events, aimed at justifying Chinaski's view of women. There is yet another attempt to create sympathy for the "victimized" Chinaski when, concealed, he is described as "watch[ing]" them kiss. Why he waits around to view this moment is not hard to guess: it represents both the actual confirmation of Jan's "unfaithfulness" as well as a masochistic gratification.

In summary, we can say that in these novels women are presented as aggressive and faithless, "allowing" men to suffer, "whores" attracted to men with money. Men are shown as "helpless" creatures who not infrequently, the moment a woman becomes interested in them, move in with her. For the most part, relationships are synonymous with conflict and inevitably end in bitterness.

Bukowski's third novel, *Women* (1978), represents a change in his depiction of women and of relationships between men and women. Here such relations are the dominant theme of the novel which focuses on the interpersonal and the emotional (although fame and success are important sub-themes) as Bukowski treats such issues as the possibility of lasting relationships, sexuality and "what men want." While the protagonist of the novel continues to objectify women, it is an objectification that often subverts itself by depicting the male chauvinist ironically (this is *Women*'s real achievement). There is also, by the end of the novel an attempt to depict women sympathetically.

Historically, the novel came at the end of the second wave of women's liberation. Hence, fifteen years after its publication, *Women* can be seen as a product of the same era that saw the publication of novels like John Updike's *Couples* (1968) and Philip Roth's *Portnoy's Complaint* (1969) and as having come at the end of a twenty-year period of increased equality and sexual freedom for women. Bukowski (born in 1920, in Germany) was in a particularly ambivalent position vis-à-vis such a movement. On the one hand, he gained by the decrease in hypocrisy and the weakening of the Victorian moralism reinstituted during the reactionary period that had coincided with the formative years of his childhood and adolescence. Yet, irresistibly, the attitudes towards women and sex engendered during those years still played a role in the 1960's and 1970's, (Bukowski's forties and fifties). The two distinct dynamics produced both the chauvinism and its ironic treatment.

In the course of *Women,* according to one critic, Henry Chinaski has sex with "well over 20 women." These relationships yield a representative sample with which to analyze Bukowski's depiction of women and relationships in the late 1970's, as the liberating effects of the 1960's made their way into the general population and as Bukowski approached his 60th birthday.

Octavio Paz's delineation of the *macho* is useful in revealing how Bukowski's portrayal of men and women has changed:

> The fact is that the essential attribute of the *macho*—power—almost always reveals itself as a capacity for wounding, humiliating, annihilating . . . .
> He is power isolated in its own potency, without relationship or compromise with the outside world. He is pure incommunication, a solitude that devours itself and everything it touches.

While this is an apt characterization of the early Chinaski, it is no longer valid for the protagonist of *Women.* One important difference is Bukowski's attempt in *Women* to give us more of the feelings of both his protagonist and the women with whom he has relationships. *Women* is both an attempt to let his protagonist speak, to progress beyond the "pure incommunication. . . that devours itself and everything it touches" as well as to portray women as more than "wholly mechanical and one dimensional . . . exploitable objects." While not always successful, the attempt itself represents a profound shift in his thinking. Equally important is the extent to which Bukowski has begun consciously and consistently to treat his male protagonist ironically. Although the book is entitled *Women,* it is an ironic deconstruction of its womanizing protagonist.

The most important relationship in *Women* is that between Henry Chinaski and Lydia Vance, a sculptress. It is Bukowski's most successful attempt at presenting such a relationship in depth and (with the exception of Henry Chinaski, Sr. in *Ham On Rye*) at creating a "round" character other than the protagonist. The two meet at a poetry reading Chinaski is giving. Lydia approaches Chinaski during the break, but is repelled by his crude response: "'I'd like to rip that fringe off your jacket—we could begin there!' Lydia walked off. It hadn't worked. I never knew what to say to the ladies." At moments like these one gets the impression that Chinaski is acting according to an image he has of how men are expected to act rather than how he actually feels. Chinaski, having achieved some fame as a writer (and his writings having been misinterpreted and distorted to present an image that is more his readers' projections than the texts'), has now become a prisoner of that distortion. But even here, there is a somewhat ambivalent turn in that we would expect Chinaski, in his chauvinist mode, to want to rip off more than merely the *fringe* of the jacket. It should also be noted that this is verbal, not physical, aggression, a not unimportant distinction.

Nevertheless, taking the initiative (as—true to form—do a number of the women in *Women*) Lydia tries again, coming over to Chinaski's apartment a few days later. After a brief visit, during which Chinaski's interest in her is evident, Lydia leaves and returns two days later and asks if she can sculpt his head. They agree on an appointment for the following morning. During the first session Chinaski plays the aggressor. He grabs Lydia and after two kisses she pushes him away. The sessions continue, however, and one morning he comes over and we see a new and surprising vulnerability in Chinaski:

> "Ooooh," she said, "you've got on a new shirt!"
> It was true. I had bought the shirt because I was thinking about her, about seeing her. I knew that she

knew that, and was making fun of me, yet I didn't mind."

Sometime later they consummate the relationship. Shortly before they make love, though, Lydia tells him about herself. Her father had left her some money that "had enabled Lydia to divorce her husband. She also told me she'd had some kind of breakdown and spent time in a madhouse. I kissed her and told her that was fine." There is an irony in the last sentence of which Chinaski is not unaware. On one level, he is assuring Lydia that he is not judgmental. We are undoubtedly meant to see his response as evidence of tenderness and understanding—maturity—on his part. It may well be that. But "fine" is marked here. We would expect "all right," or something similar, a neutral and less positive characterization. On the other hand, anyone familiar with Chinaski's track record, could as easily take it to mean that it is "fine" because Chinaski needs a woman with emotional problems so that, viewing her as "crazy," there will be little chance for the real intimacy that would allow a relationship to develop. Suspicions as to Lydia's motivation (and ultimately as to her rationality) have been raised by an exchange that took place four pages earlier:

"I've heard about you," she said.
"Like what?"
"About how you throw guys off your front porch. That you beat your women."
"Beat my women?"
"Yes, somebody told me."
I grabbed Lydia and we went into our longest clinch ever.

Lydia's questionable mental state can also be seen as giving Chinaski (at least in his mind) some power in the relationship.

Before they make love, Lydia warns him:

"Listen," she said, "after you stick that thing inside me, pull it out just before you come. O.K.?"

"I understand."

I climbed on top of her. It was good. It was something happening, something real, and with a girl 20 years younger than I was and really, after all, beautiful. I did about 10 strokes—and came inside of her.

She leaped up.
"You son-of-a-bitch! You came inside of me!"

"Lydia, it's been so *long* . . . it felt so good . . . I couldn't help it."

There are several things worth noting here. Foremost, perhaps, is the humor, and irony of the scene. Lydia's instructions about Chinaski's withdrawing before he ejaculates prepare us, as in a vaudeville routine, for what happens by telegraphing the reader that something *is* going to happen. This and the tenderness in the scene before they go to bed, where she speaks intimately to Chinaski lead up to the quick climax on Chinaski's part (followed immediately by Lydia's leaping out of bed, hardly the *post coitum triste* we might expect) which makes a mockery of everything that has gone before, just because it is so thoughtless and self-involved. The humor in Chinaski's half-hearted defense—"it sneaked up on me!"—is capped by their last exchange which opposes sharply different reactions:

"Lydia, I love you."
"Get the hell away from me!"

All of this contributes to making this depiction of seduction and love so distanced and *verfremdend* and the characters so pathetic that one can see just why Bukowski's writings have often alienated readers. It is not the explicitness of his writing, since he is clearly within the boundaries of realist sexual *écriture* as it existed from the mid-1960s on in American fiction, but rather the lack of sentiment with which he handles such material. Perhaps even more than the ironic treatment of love, the ironic treatment of sex strikes a disquieting note at this point in our social history.

Yet more than simple irony is at work because in irony an identification with the character is preserved; we cannot fully appreciate the ironic situation of a protagonist unless we feel—at least to some extent—positively involved in his fate. Here, and in other passages in **Women,** the reader's identification with the protagonist is threatened. In the earlier novels there was no doubt as to whose side the implied author was taking and where the reader's sympathy was being directed. A simplistic view of "right" and "wrong" in such affairs had begun to break down in **Factotum** as, for example, the bar scene quoted earlier reveals. Now Bukowski is consciously questioning Chinaski's behavior and the male role in such situations and trying to present events from the woman's perspective as well.

The issue of fidelity has also been introduced. The view that women are inherently unfaithful, "whores," is confirmed by what Chinaski perceives as Lydia's flirtatious behavior at a party he throws where, on arriving, "she didn't speak to me but immediately sat down next to a handsome young bookstore clerk and began an intense conversation with him." Chinaski tolerates this behavior, although it clearly upsets him and, again a masochistic trait is apparent. On their first formal date Lydia and Henry drive to Venice beach. They buy food at a delicatessen and then sit on a knoll of grass overlooking the sea where they see "a tall black man," shirtless, with "a very strong muscular body" who "appeared to be in his early twenties."

> "Did you see that guy?" she asked.
> "Yes."
> "Jesus Christ, here I am with you, you're twenty years older than I am. I could have something like that. What the hell's wrong with me?"
> "Look. Here are a couple of candy bars. Take one."
> She took one, ripped the paper off, took a bite and watched the young black man as he walked along the shore.
> "I'm tired of the beach," she said, "let's go back to my place."

(The depiction of) Chinaski placatingly offering Lydia the candy bar after she has crudely insulted him is the antithesis of what we would expect from a true representative of the patriarchy. Chinaski's behavior here is quite different from his reaction to Gertrude's comment about the soldier in the bar in **Factotum**. Bukowski's skill in depicting the nuances of behavior (and to a certain extent of character as well) has increased considerably. The male is no longer imprisoned in stereotypes and stock reactions but is revealed as vulnerable at times and, at other times, as downright unattractive. He has become something quite different from "power isolated in its own potency, without relationship or compromise with the outside world," as Paz described the macho.

The break-up with Lydia is revealing. Chinaski has returned from a reading in Houston where he has had a brief affair with another woman, Laura. He had injured his leg before the trip and it has still not healed on his return to L.A. Met at the airport by Lydia, who is "horny as usual," Chinaski wonders if he can "handle" sex with his injury:

> "*What*?"
> "It's true. I don't think I can fuck with my leg the way it is."
> "What the hell good are you then?"
> "Well, I can fry eggs and do magic tricks."
> "Don't be funny. I'm asking you, what the hell good are you?"
> "The leg will heal. If it doesn't they'll cut it off. Be patient."
> "If you hadn't been drunk, you wouldn't have fallen and cut your leg. It's *always* the bottle!"
> "It's not always the bottle, Lydia. We fuck about four times a week. For my age that's pretty good."
> "Sometimes I think you don't even enjoy it."
> "Lydia, sex isn't *everything*! You are obsessed. For Christ's sake, give it a rest."
> "A rest until your leg heals? How am I going to make it meanwhile?"

> "I'll play Scrabble with you."
> Lydia screamed. She literally screamed. The car began to swerve all over the street. "YOU SON-OF-A-BITCH! I'LL KILL YOU!"

Clearly Chinaski is acting in bad faith. His injured leg has not prevented him from making love to Laura, so it cannot be the reason he doesn't make love to Lydia. Lydia is depicted as disturbed and obsessed with sex, Chinaski, as having a more balanced view. Chinaski's points are not those we associate with the typical male protagonist, who is again being subverted here. Bukowski uses Chinaski's eminently sane view of sex to gain the reader's sympathy while Lydia's compulsive demands puts her in a bad light. Yet both these positions are in turn undermined; it is clear that sex is not really the issue for either Chinaski or Lydia. The fact is, Chinaski's feelings have changed. It is a nice question, however, as to how much his bad faith causes the reader to withhold giving full credence to the otherwise sensible view he espouses of the place of sex in a relationship. But whatever we finally decide, the tone of Chinaski's argument, and the depiction of Lydia cut across our expectations in this 1970's Thurberesque "battle of the sexes."

Bukowski has begun presenting the male as he is rarely presented in American fiction (especially in what might be termed "the chauvinist tradition"); indeed, he has begun to deconstruct that tradition as we have come to associate it with Hemingway, Miller and Miller. This is effected through a character who, while on one level attempting to maintain the older image of the unreconstructed male chauvinist, on another is aware of the contradictions involved. Right after the break-up with Lydia and about to enter another relationship, he is asked:

> "But, Hank. don't forget what you told me about your women."
> "Told you what?"
> "You said, "They always come back.""
> "That's just macho talk."

Chinaski doesn't want to have sex with Lydia, but Bukowski portrays him as feeling rejected by Lydia because he "can't" have sex. Lydia is presented as a "sexaholic," completely irrational, and relentless in her demands. Previously it had been Chinaski who objectified women, saw them primarily in terms of their physical attractions, as potential objects of his sex drive, denied them mind and emotions. Here this view is projected onto Lydia, who is shown as rejecting companionship. Chinaski does not admit to the fact that it is he who makes the break here by denying her sex (as he had denied Jan sex in **Factotum**).

In the earlier novels Bukowski was content to let events speak for themselves without making much of an attempt to get at his characters' motivation. In **Women** he is trying to explain and to have his readers understand why his protagonist acts as he does, to make events intelligible. Laura (renamed "Katherine" by Chinaski for her resemblance to Katharine Hepburn), the woman with whom Chinaski *has* had sex during his trip to Houston for a poetry reading, figures in one of Chinaski's more significant relationships. Interested in understanding his protagonist, Bukowski has Chinaski trying to understand why that relationship ended. It seems to be going well when, as Chinaski puts it, he "loses her." He takes Laura to the fights and the track where she realizes that he is one of "them," "the racetrack people and the boxing crowd."

> That night she drank half a bottle of red wine, good red wine, and she was sad and quiet. I knew she was connecting me with the racetrack people and the boxing crowd, and it was true. I was with them, I was one of them. Katherine knew that there was something about me that was not wholesome in the sense of wholesome is as wholesome does. I was drawn to all the wrong things: I liked to drink, I was lazy, I didn't have a god, politics, ideas, ideals. I was settled into nothingness, a kind of non-being, and I accepted it. It didn't make for an interesting person. I didn't want to be interesting, it was too hard. What I really wanted was only a soft hazy space to live in, and to be left alone. On the other hand, when I got drunk I screamed, went crazy, got all out of hand. One kind of behavior didn't fit the other. I didn't care.
>
> The fucking was very good that night, but it was the night I lost her. There was nothing I could do about it. I rolled off and wiped myself on the sheet as she went into the bathroom. Overhead a police helicopter circled over Hollywood.

Suggestive as this passage is, it really tells us almost nothing about the emotional states of Katherine and Chinaski. Most of what Chinaski says about himself is patently false and what isn't is clearly no news to Katherine who has read his books and must, on one level, be attracted to his lifestyle. To take but one example: to call someone lazy who has worked for decades to become a successful writer is misleading and disingenuous. Chinaski has organized his life efficiently and been extremely productive. And indeed, one might also wonder why Chinaski "loses" Laura in the very night when the lovemaking was "very good." One suspects that, at the very least, something has been elided here. The naturalist profession of faith: "There was nothing I could do about it," is ultimately more faithful to Chinaski's determinist world view, but it is not particularly enlightening.

It is clear that in **Women** Bukowski wants to create a certain depth to his characters, and depicting their thoughts and feelings is one way to do this. He succeeds in this to a greater extent than he had previously. Yet, in the end, he cannot get outside the narrator, and even then rarely goes beyond superficial analysis. The first sentence of the above passage is good because it relies on description but the repetition of "wine" hints at the felt limits of description alone, because here repetition is substituting for development or qualification. There is the feeling that something more should be said to prepare us for or explain "Katherine's" mood; Bukowski senses this, otherwise there would be no impulse to repeat the fact of the wine; but owing to the limits Bukowski has—consciously or unconsciously—placed on himself, he is at a loss as to how to proceed. Giving us the Volkswagen license plate number—"TRV 469"—in the passage quoted below reflects the same dynamic. As soon as Bukowski tries to go further he inevitably has to revert to the protagonist: "I knew she was connecting me with . . ."

Once again, Chinaski implies that it is the woman who terminates the affair. Yet they continue to enjoy making love and Laura wants to continue the relationship. After the above-mentioned night of lovemaking and after the fights

> Katherine stayed 4 or 5 more days. We had reached the time of the month when it was risky for Katherine to fuck. I couldn't stand rubbers. Katherine got some contraceptive foam. Meanwhile the police had recovered my Volks. We went down to where it was impounded. It was intact and in good shape except for a dead battery. I had it hauled to a Hollywood garage where they put it in order. After a last goodbye in bed I drove Katherine to the airport in the blue Volks. TRV 469.
>
> It wasn't a happy day for me. We sat not saying much. Then they called her flight and we kissed.
>
> "Hey, they all saw this young girl kissing this old man."
> "I don't give a damn . . ."
> Katherine kissed me again.
> "You're going to miss your flight," I said.
> "Come see me, Hank. I have a nice house. I live alone. Come see me."
> "I will."
> "Write!"
> "I will . . . ."
> Katherine walked into the boarding tunnel and was gone.
> I walked back to the parking lot, got in the Volks, thinking, I've still got this. What the hell, I haven't lost anything.
> It started.

The odd juxtaposition of the last days of sex with the re-covered car, implied in the last sentence of the first paragraph, where a kind of identity is effected between the sex and the car, and then explicitly (if perhaps a bit ironically) stated in the next-to-last paragraph, underline Chinaski's dilemma when humans are objectified. Clearly there are pressures here that remain unexamined; once again Chinaski has rejected the woman but tried to hide that fact from himself. (It is more than a little reminiscent of "Bukowski's" equating the death of his first real love with the "death" of his first automobile in the poem **"I didn't want to,"** discussed above.)

After the relationship with Laura ends, a good part of **Women** concerns itself with Chinaski's string of relatively casual affairs, with no one relationship depicted as having any great significance (with the obvious exception of the relationship with Sara and with the possible exception of the relationship with Tammie) although the narrator is almost always shown as at least somewhat involved emotionally. While the depiction of intense emotional involvements is foregone, we do have a picture of sex and the American male in the 1970's, the full flowering of the "second phase" of Women's Liberation. Here again, Bukowski has done something noteworthy, not to mention out of "character." In the way that Henry Miller can be taken as representative of male attitudes of an earlier era (and Miller, too, came to a writing career late and represents attitudes characteristic of an earlier generation than the one in which he wrote, while that in which he wrote immediately succeeds an era of increased freedom for women), so Bukowski reflects those of his own era by revealing in his descriptions of sex the changes that have taken place in (sexual) relations between men and women. Miller's "I slipped it in and gave her what's what" (language that reflects the attitude of a murderer, not a lover) has been significantly transformed.

As early as **Post Office,** sexual intercourse had sometimes been depicted as problematic:

> In bed I had something in front of me but I couldn't do anything with it. I whaled and I whaled and I whaled. Vi was very patient. I kept striving and banging but I'd had too much to drink.
>
> "Sorry, baby," I said. Then I rolled off. And went to sleep.

The inability to perform, often because of drink, comes up frequently. It is the pendant to the theme of the sexually assertive woman. Indeed, the traditional view that men have more interest in sex than women is often reversed in these novels: in **Post Office,** "Joyce, my wife, was a nymph"; in **Factotum,** "You haven't fucked me for two weeks"; and in **Women,** "Lydia liked to fuck at least five times a week. I preferred three."

When Chinaski is met at the Houston airport by Joanna Dover, a woman whom he is visiting to escape from Tammie, there is no beating about the bush:

> ". . . Did I interrupt anything?"
> "No. There was a garage mechanic. But he petered out. He couldn't stand the pace."
> "Be kind to me, Joanna, sucking and fucking aren't everything."

Later, after dinner out and drinking, and then more drinking back at Joanna's place, she says:

> "Let's fuck."
> "I've drunk too much."
> "Let's go to bed."
> "I want to drink some more."
> "You won't be able to . . . "
> "I know. I hope you'll let me stay four or five days."
> "It will depend on your performance," she said.
> "That's fair enough."
>
> By the time we finished the wine I could barely make it to the bed. I was asleep by the time Joanna came out of the bathroom . . .

The affair runs its course: "I lasted five days and nights. Then I couldn't get it up anymore. Joanna drove me to the airport." The roles have been reversed; the woman is sexually the aggressor. The man, sensing his loss of control, feels exploited and resists at first by drinking himself into incapacity, and then is put out to pasture when his usefulness is gone. Looked at realistically, the reasons for the end of the relationship scarcely seem credible. Are we to believe that Chinaski only had it in him to perform for "four or five nights" and then, the first night he can't (or doesn't want to?) make love, Joanna asks him to leave? That she could go at least one night without sex was proven by her having somehow survived the first night without sex. But that is irrelevant. What is important is the way Bukowski has chosen to present the episode, his using it to undermine the traditional male role.

Chinaski's drinking had also interfered in the relationship with Lydia: "She loved sex and my drinking got in the way of our lovemaking. 'Either you're too drunk to do it at night or too sick to do it in the morning'"; later in the novel, with Cassie: "Her body was amazing, glorious, Playboy style, but unfortunately I was drunk"; or with Lilly:

> I switched off the bed lamp fast. I kissed her some more, played with her breasts and body, then went down on her. I was drunk, but I think I did O.K.

But after that I couldn't do it the other way. I rode and rode and rode. I was hard but I couldn't come. Finally I rolled off exhausted and went to sleep . . .

and Mindy: "Mindy and I finished the bottle and then went to bed. I kissed her for a while, then apologized, and drew away. I was too drunk to perform. One hell of a great lover"; and Liza:

> Without foreplay it was much more difficult but finally I got it in. I began to work. I worked and I worked. It was another hot night. It was like a recurring bad dream. I began sweating. I humped and I pumped. It wouldn't go down, it wouldn't come off. I pumped and I humped. Finally I rolled off. "Sorry, baby, too much to drink."

With Mercedes (after having "dr[u]nk and smoked [marijuana] quite a long time"):

> I pumped on and on. Five minutes. Ten minutes more. I couldn't come. I began to fail. I was getting soft. Mercedes got worried. "Make it!" she demanded. "Oh, make it, baby!" That didn't help at all. I rolled off. It was an unbearably hot night. I took the sheet and wiped off the sweat. I could hear my heart pounding as I lay there. It sounded sad. I wondered what Mercedes was thinking. I lay dying, my cock limp.

With Iris: "We drank another hour and then went to bed. I ate her up but when I mounted I just stroked and stroked without effect. Too bad."

Not infrequently sex is just work, and hard labor at that: "I began to work. I worked and I worked . . . I began sweating. I humped and I pumped . . . . I pumped and I humped"; "I pumped on and on"; "I worked and worked." And in perhaps the most excruciating sexual moment in the novel:

> I worked and I worked . . . I began to sweat. My back ached. I was dizzy, sick . . . It was agony, it was relentless work without a reward. I felt damned . . . I desperately wanted to come . . . My heart began to pound loudly. I heard my heart. I felt my heart. I felt it in my chest. I felt it in my throat. I felt it in my head. I couldn't bear it. I rolled off with a gasp.

I don't want to give the impression that this is the sole image of sex presented in the novel because it isn't. Sex is often satisfying with the same women with whom sex has been less than satisfying. But it can't be denied that all of this constitutes a distinctly unmacho (not to mention unromantic) depiction of lovemaking. The drinking can be viewed as a

means of allaying Chinaski's underlying anxiety, or as a hostile, sadistic way of hurting women by denying them the full pleasure, and intimacy, of successful lovemaking. In any event, there has been a significant amount of slippage in how much control the man has—the decision to have sex, for example, is often the woman's. It cannot be argued that it is not a different image of the male that Bukowski is giving us. The distinctly unromantic, at times alienated, light in which sex is shown offers a different picture of the man and the male role, a part of the larger change in Bukowski's depiction of men.

This deconstruction of the male protagonist in *Women,* as male, is clear from the first paragraph, indeed, from the first sentence, of the novel . . .
—*Russell Harrison*

It is in this larger change that the primary significance of the novel lies. What has happened is that the male protagonist is now being treated ironically. This irony manifests itself both generally and in small, self-deprecating comments by Chinaski, as, for example, when he remarks of himself: "Not a very well-known writer, of course, but I managed to pay the rent and that was astonishing" where the remark also serves to distance the reader from the sexual description. The male has been problematized as the protagonists of Lawrence, Miller and Hemingway had not been.

This deconstruction of the male protagonist in **Women,** as male, is clear from the first paragraph, indeed, from the first sentence, of the novel:

> I was fifty years old and hadn't been to bed with a woman for four years. I had no women friends. I looked at them as I passed them on the streets or wherever I saw them, but I looked at them without yearning and with a sense of futility. I masturbated regularly, but the idea of having a relationship with a woman—even on non-sexual terms—was beyond my imagination. I had a 6 year old daughter born out of wedlock. She lived with her mother and I paid child support. I had been married years before at the age of 35. That marriage lasted two and one half years. My wife divorced me. I had been in love only once.

Relationships with women have become problematic for Henry Chinaski. Although he has sexual relationships with twenty-odd women in the roughly six-year span of the novel, these are rarely devoid of involvement. Indeed, the depths of Chinaski's needs, the overdetermined nature of his involvement (where his complete avoidance of relationships with women then causes him to overvalue any woman, causes him, indeed, to immediately think of marriage) are often ironically mocked, as, for example, with "Katherine," with whom he had spent a night in Houston. She then visits him in L.A. In the evening of the day of her arrival, after they have made love—"It was glorious"—and before falling asleep, Chinaski muses on the day's and evening's events:

> For the first time I thought of marriage. I knew that there certainly were flaws in her that had not surfaced. The beginning of a relationship was always the easiest. After that the unveiling began, never to stop. Still, I thought of marriage. I thought of a house, a dog and a cat, of shopping in supermarkets. Henry Chinaski was losing his balls. And didn't care.

> At last I slept. When I awakened in the morning Katherine was sitting on the edge of the bed brushing those yards of red-brown hair. Her large dark eyes looked at me as I awakened. "Hello, Katherine," I said, "will you marry me?"

> "Please don't," she said, "I don't like it."
> "I mean it."
> "Oh, *shit,* Hank!"
> "What?"
> "I said, 'shit,' and if you talk that way I'm taking the first plane out."
> "All right."
> "Hank?"
> "Yes?"

> I looked at Katherine. She kept brushing her long hair. Her large brown eyes looked at me, and she was smiling. She said, "It's just *sex,* Hank, it's *just sex!*" Then she laughed. It wasn't a sardonic laugh, it was really joyful. She brushed her hair and I put my arm around her waist and rested my head against her leg. I wasn't quite sure of anything.

It is clear that Chinaski's behavior arises to a much greater extent than is usual from various "historical" psychic factors rather than from a just appreciation of the real person. Indeed, the fact that he can't use her real name, but renames her after a movie star long past *her* viability as a sex symbol, i.e., she, too, is not being viewed as she is, but as a memorial to some idealized image, indicates the extent to which Chinaski is here operating at a remove from reality.

Such scenes as this one with Katherine have an additional significance. (It is worth noting that this scene is an identical repetition—dynamically—of the scene of the beginning of his relationship with Lydia Vance.) Similar scenes, and

there are more than a few in the novel, have, in Bukowski's phrase, a "comic edge" to them, but there is also an underlying seriousness present. Here we have an absolute reversal of the scene where the woman (traditionally viewed as the romantic in such situations) falls in love and it is the man who makes (or thinks) the distinction between love and sex. Thus *Women* hardly presents a traditional male protagonist, let alone a macho. Surely the image of Chinaski, his head resting against Laura's leg, "not quite sure of anything," is a far cry from Henry Miller's descriptions, who to the best of my knowledge has never written a scene of such calm intimacy and whose descriptions of alienated sex and objectified women are too well known to require quotation. In fact, whenever, in *Women,* Chinaski attempts such a role, attempts, that is, to act "in character," he is unsuccessful. At one point in the novel, after a fight with Lydia, he goes to the track and has a good night, drinking and betting, leaving "$950 ahead." He calls Lydia from a phone booth:

> "Listen," I said, "listen, you bitch. I went to the harness races tonight and won $950. I'm a winner! I'll always be a winner! You don't deserve me, bitch! You've been playing with me! Well, it's over! I want out!. This is it! I don't need you and your goddamned games! Do you understand me? Do you get the message? Or is your head thicker than your ankles?"
> "Hank . . ."
> "Yes?"
> "This isn't Lydia. This is Bonnie. I'm baby sitting for Lydia. She went out tonight."
> I hung up and walked back to my car.

Here Chinaski and his "macho talk" are ridiculed. Such passages sabotaging the traditional male role are important evidence of a change. Moreover, Lydia's having gone out that night, rather than sitting around in her apartment, depressed, adds a nice touch, revealing her as independent. She doesn't need to rely on Chinaski for a social life.

If, in *Factotum,* the women usually initiated relationships, in *Women* they are even more assertive and not content to play their traditional roles in other ways. This reversal of traditional sexual roles and its ironic effect on the male image appear in the sphere of sexual practices as well. Traditionally, the man has been viewed as the more adventurous, the more willing to experiment, perhaps because he has also been—or at least been seen as—the more experienced. The reason for a woman's supposed lesser interest in sexual variety and experimentation might be that such an interest would suggest more prior sexual experience than society feels comfortable with her having. Here, too, things have changed in *Women:*

> We remained apart a week. Then one afternoon I

was over at Lydia's place and we were on her bed, kissing. Lydia pulled away.

"You don't know anything about women, do you?"

"What do you mean?"

"I mean, I can tell by reading your poems and stories that you just don't know anything about women."

"Tell me more."

"Well, I mean for a man to interest me he's got to eat my pussy. Have you ever eaten pussy?"

"No."

"You're over 50 years old and you've never eaten pussy?"

"No."

"It's too late."

"Why?"

"You can't teach an old dog new tricks."

"Sure you can."

"No, it's too late for you."

"I've always been a slow starter."

Lydia got up and walked into the other room. She came back with a pencil and a piece of paper. "Now, look, I want to show you something." She began to draw carefully on the paper. "Now, this is a cunt, and here is something you probably don't know about—the clit. That's where the feeling is. The clit hides, you see, it comes out now and then, it's pink and very *sensitive*. Sometimes it will hide from you and you have to find it, you just touch it with the tip of your tongue . . ."

"O.K.," I said, "I've got it."

Once again Bukowski humorously undermines a traditional image of the male: as aggressive, adventurous, experienced—that is, powerful. The scene is also effective for suggesting one reason for Lydia's attraction to Chinaski, a reason that is in direct contradiction to her statement: "Jeez, I thought you were a man, all your books . . . ." What she has sensed in him is a vulnerability and insecurity vis-à-vis women.

The effect of Bukowski's depiction of women, chauvinist though it can be, is quite different from what his predecessors and contemporaries produced. Although depicting Chinaski as sexist, Bukowski at the same time, and more tellingly, goes to great pains to undermine this position. Indeed, it would be more accurate to characterize Chinaski as "pseudo-macho." In the light of this it is useful to return to the earlier criticisms. Huffzky had written:

> In his underground society he describes a purely masculine world, in which women are hardly more than splashes of a puddle through which hardy fellows traipse, mostly drunk, or in which they wal-

low. Then afterwards: wipe off & away! Also most of the times drunk . . . . almost everything in his head is reduced to the magical actions: fuck, drink, fight: beating women . . ."

It should be clear by now that this and similar critiques concerning Bukowski's portrayal of women don't do justice to what are really complex texts. It is not a purely masculine world that Bukowski depicts. The women and relationships presented in **Women** are more than simplistic stereotypes. For example, the women presented almost always have jobs and sometimes have careers. Huffzky is, however, more justified in her criticism that "there are no women in his novels with whom a thoughtful female reader can identify positively." But this must be seen in a larger context. While Huffzky is correct in what she says about the absence of positive women characters (though there are exceptions, such as Laura in **Women**), what has to be grasped is that there are few characters generally, male or female, with whom an intelligent reader, male or female, can identify. As Bukowski remarked to Sean Penn: "Sure I make women look bad sometimes, but I make men look bad too. I make *myself* look bad." At times we may identify with certain aspects of Henry Chinaski: his anti-authoritarian stance vis-à-vis bosses and bureaucracy and his self-deprecation and irony are attractive qualities. But those are, especially in **Women,** only moments. We do not identify with Henry Chinaski in his behavior towards women.

What Bukowski has achieved here is a kind of Brechtian "Verfremdung," the "playing in quotation marks." As Brecht explained in "A Dialogue About Acting":

> Oughtn't the actor then try to make the man he is representing understandable? Not so much the man as what takes place. What I mean is: if I choose to see Richard III I don't want to feel myself to be Richard III, but to glimpse this phenomenon in all its strangeness and incomprehensibility.

In Bukowski, the reader's subjectivity has not been captured through empathy but is rather alienated and this facilitates a critical analysis of the protagonist's behavior. Reading Bukowski in this way, without any preconceptions based on a reputation that he has long outgrown, I think we can see him questioning (sometimes, granted, in spite of himself) rather than advocating, the attitudes and behavior with which he has long been (mistakenly) identified.

Robert Peters (essay date 1994)

SOURCE: "Gab Poetry, or Ducks vs. Nightingale Music: Charles Bukowski," in *Where the Bee Sucks: Workers,*

Drones, and Queens of Contemporary American Poetry, Santa Maria: Asylum Arts, 1994, pp. 56-66.

[*In the following essay, Peters discusses the elements of Bukowski's poetry.*]

I once witnessed a Charles Bukowski *first:* the debut of the great raunchy poet as actor. The vehicle, *The Tenant,* was a two character drama written by Linda King. Bukowski contributed lines of his own, better developing his own image in the play. This line was his addition, as delivered by Miss King: "You may be the greatest poet of the century, but you sure can't fuck." In a lively way *The Tenant* turns upon the problem of whether a super-poet should move in with his girlfriend, who would then, one would suppose, buy him his beer, give him bj's, and let him abuse her. The event was choice. An actor scheduled to read the Bukowski role was unable to show, so Buk took over.

There were twenty people in the well of the Pasadena Museum—sad, alas, because of the significance of the event. Bukowski, script in hand, trod the boards. The props were a telephone—used with nearly as much frequency as Barbara Stanwyck's in *Sorry, Wrong Number*; a mattress upon which King and Bukowski, scripts in hand, fell to enact their erotic comings after dismal separations. The performance, pixie-ish, included a tender moment where Bukowski acted as W.C. Fields towards a child who had a brief moment of stage glory. Needless to say, the small audience chuckled, particularly over Bukowski's Bogart-like delivery. Ms. King, with various stunning Bridget Bardot-esqueries nicely foiled the poet.

The Tenant gave Bukowski a chance, under the guise of art and aesthetic distance, to extol his stature as a poet. Buk has never been known for his reticence, and his being utterly ignored hitherto by the literary establishment hasn't affected him in the least.

I remember how zapped I was when I first read him: I was teaching at the University of California at Riverside and had been given *Crucifix in a Deathhand.* I carried the book to a string quartet concert, began reading it before the concert, experienced chills, elevations, charismatic flashes, barber pole exaltations, and fevers in the groin. I had not read such poems since discovering Dylan Thomas in the fifties. Here was something awe-thentic at last! I nudged my companion who thought I was crazy. Bukowski was unafraid of life's terror meat-slabs, and he made the angels sing.

I began to ask others if they had heard of Bukowski. Yes, he was living in a Hollywood dump, they said, dismissing him as a charlatan steeped in booze, flop-gutted, and rancid-breathed. I gave up trying to explain his impact on me. Moreover, I didn't care whether he rolled in his own puke, or swallowed pints of maiden juice. He was a super poet.

His example loosened my own writing. Lowell, Snodgrass, Wilbur, Ashbery, and Olson were dilettantes.

One afternoon, carrying a six-pack of Coors, I beat my way to Buk's door, four or five days before Christmas. He and his daughter were trimming a tree. There weren't many ornaments—half a dozen on the low branches. Bukowski asked me in. I found a man of charm—nothing of the horrible-retchable I had been led to expect. I have been a fan ever since. He, though, remembers the visit otherwise, and wrote about it in his collection **Beneath the Fortinaria.**

The appearance of **Burning in Water Drowning in Flame: Selected Poems 1955-1973** invites me to describe what I found so telling in his work and to point up what I find are unfortunate recent drifts. My remarks should dissolve some of the celebrity aura threatening his reputation. **It Catches My Heart in Its Hands** (1963) and **Crucifix in a Deathhand** (1965), two Loujon Press books, are among the dozen most beautifully printed and designed books of poetry ever. Since they are out of print, and rare, it is great to have those reprinted.

"The tragedy of the leaves" propels us into Bukowski's world: hangover, desertion by his woman, the screaming landlady, and a world that's failed him utterly. Set up for the big blubbery whine of self-pity? No! He transmutes all raunchy conditions through unusual images: "I awakened to dryness and the ferns were dead, / the potted plants yellow as corn . . . ." How well *dryness* echoes *awakened*; the latter implies a grappling with the world, moving toward insight. Compression follows:

> my woman was gone
> and the empty bottles like bled corpses
> surrounded me with their uselessness . . . .

The long vowel sounds are well-spaced, and Bukowski, sensing the positive, remarks on the sunlight brightening the landlady's note in its "fine and / undemanding yellowness." The occasion, he observes, demands "a good comedian, ancient style, a jester/ with jokes upon absurd pain." There's wisdom here: "pain is absurd / because it exists, nothing more." He believes that as a poet he is stagnant: "that's the tragedy of the dead plants." In this concluding passage note the effective slant rhymes *more* and *razor* and the repeated *dead, dead, dark,* and *stood* accompanying some monosyllabic tough nouns, *Execrating, waving,* and *screaming,* mesh, as *hall, final, hell,* and *failed* weave subtle echoes. Here he manages to be tender towards a harsh landlady:

> and I walked into a dark hall
> where the landlady stood
> execrating and final,
> sending me to hell,

waving her fat, sweaty arms
and screaming
screaming for rent
because the world had failed us
both.

Empathy is present in other poems. **"For marilyn m."** avoids sentimentality through a diction suited to the fey person Monroe was:

> . . .and we will forget you, somewhat
> and it is not kind
> but real bodies are nearer
> and as the worms pant for your bones,
> I would so like to tell you
> that this happens to bears and elephants
> to tyrants and heroes and ants
> and frogs,
> still, you brought us something,
> some type of small victory,
> and for this I say: good
> and let us grieve no more . . . .

"The life of Borodin," grandly empathetic, is effective reportage on the miserable composer's life. Wife-hounded, he slept by placing a dark cloth over his eyes. His wife lined cat boxes and covered jars of sour milk with his compositions. Nothing is overstated in this taut free-verse poem. The parallels between Bukowski's life and Borodin's are implicit.

"The twins" evokes another tremulous situation, one that a lesser poet might easily have wrecked. Here Bukowski confronts his hatred of his father, immediately after the father's death: "A father is always your master even when he's gone." To cope, the poet moves through the house stunned, then proceeds outside where he picks an orange and peels it. Common day noises of dogs and neighbors bespeak sanity. Back inside, the poet dons one of his father's suits:

> I try on a light blue suit
> much better than anything I have ever worn
> and I flap the arms like a scarecrow in the wind
> but it's no good;
> I can't keep him alive
> no matter how much we hated each other.
>
> we looked exactly alike, we could have been twins
> the old man and I: that's what they
> said. he had his bulbs on the screen
> ready for planting
> while I was lying with a whore from 3rd street.
>
> very well. grant us this moment: standing before a
> mirror
> in my dead father's suit

waiting also
to die.

The event is stark. To wear another person's clothes is, in a sense, to become that person. Bukowski's mimicry of death as scarecrow is macabre. Despite the hate, the survivor can't bring the dead man back to life.

"Old poet" treats Bukowski's distaste for aging (forty-two at the time) without a public to love his work. Finding his sexual energies diminished, he's reduced to pawing dirty pictures. He's had too much beer and has heard too much Shostakovitch. He swats "a razzing fly" and "ho, I fall heavy as thunder . . ." The downstairs tenants will assume "he's either drunk or dying." Despite his depression, every morning he packs off envelopes of poems, hoping to place them in magazines. Rejection slips annoy him briefly; but soon he's back at his typewriter:

> the editors wish to thank you for
> submitting but
> regret . . .
> down
>   down
>   down
>   the dark hall
> into a womanless hall
> to peel a last egg
> and sit down to the keys:
> click click a click,
> over the television sounds
> over the sounds of springs,
> click click a clack:
> another old poet
> going off.

"View from the screen" might easily have dissolved into narcissism; it has all the accoutrements. It shouldn't work, but it does. The death-whispers of the heron and the bone-thoughts of sea creatures dominate his universe as the poet crosses the room:

> to the last wall
> the last window
> the last pink sun
> with its arms around the world
> with its arms around me . . . .

The sun is benign. Its pinkness produces the pig-image, an unusual trope and one that eschews turning maudlin. The Platonic cave motif is obvious:

> I hear the death-whisper of the heron
> the bone-thoughts of sea-things
> that are almost rock;

this screen caved like a soul
and scrawled with flies,
my tensions and damnations
are those of a pig,
pink sun pink sun
I hate your holiness
crawling your gilded cross of life
as my fingers and feet and face
come down to this . . . .

Writing, for Bukowski, is for getting "feelings down." Now, that may sound like warmed-over Shelley. Bukowski's urge to write, prompted by a mix of sardonicism and angst, is as natural as defecation. An image allows him to translate pain into a testimony for his spirit, one fraught with "madness and terror" along "agony way." There's a time-bomb inside his chest, and if it doesn't go off as a poem it will explode in drunkenness, despair, vomiting, or rage. As long as he writes he leashes terror. **"Beans with garlic"** is about this. A terrific idea—beans as lovers! Beans as your words! Stirring them is like writing poems:

but now
there's a ticking under your shirt
and you whirl the beans with a spoon,
one love dead, one love departed
another love . . .
ah! as many loves as beans
yes, count them now
sad, sad
your feelings boiling over flame,
get this down.

"A nice day" deals with a knife the speaker carries inside him. Bukowski can't feel doom, so he goes outside "to absolutely nothing / a square round of orange zero." A woman says good morning, thereby twisting the knife:

I do notice though the sun is shining
that the flowers are pulled up on
their strings
and I on mine:
belly, bellybutton, buttocks, bukowski
waving walking
teeth of ice with the taste of tar
tear ducts propagandized
shoes acting like shoes
I arrive on time
in the blazing midday
of mourning.

The concluding pun is effective, and the lines are original. Bukowski produces (invents) his rhetoric, and this sometimes betrays him. Often, his latest voice, in the gab barfly manner, sounds like imitation Bukowski. His best poems dis-

charge energy. We are touched by a vital creative mind prizing the creative act. Nothing, not even bad booze, can diminish it. Call this *originality*; for, to paraphrase T.S. Eliot on Tennyson, Bukowski has originality in abundance.

In *At Terror Street and Agony Way* (1968) there is evidence of deterioration. Bukowski's paranoia intensifies. He's nastier than he's hitherto been. His sympathies are with outrageous, destructive folks: the guy who emasculates himself with a tin can; "the nice guy" who cuts up a woman and sends the parts to people. Bukowski senses that a sycophantic public expects outrageous cartwheels and titillations, and he obliges. There is a discernible drifting off from the earlier tender humanity. And there is a troublesome loquaciousness; the honed work of the early manner is usurped by rambling, grotty passages of prose masquerading (chopped into lengths) as poetry. And he is vicious to other poets, as he is in a parody of Michael McClure and in a tasteless piece on Jack Hirschman as narcissist Victor Vania.

"Sunday before noon," though it concludes with a funny piece of hysteria, reflects Bukowski's current narcissism:

going down
are the clocks cocks roosters?
the roosters stand on the fence
the roosters are peanutbutter crowing,
the FLAME will be high, the flame will be big,
kiss kiss kiss
everything away,
I hope it rains today, I hope
the jets die, I hope
the kitten finds a mouse, I hope
I don't see it, I hope
it rains, I hope
anything away from here,
I hope a bridge, a fish, a cactus somewhere
strutting whiskers to the noon,
I dream flowers and horses
the branches break the birds fall the buildings
burn, my whore walks across the room and
smiles at me.

There's evidence of the old originality here in the juxtaposition of peanut butter and roosters, and in the branches and birds, and in the buildings that open the poem and close it. But the stance, the narcissism of "going down," the wish to be wiped out, and to wipe out, is dull. There isn't much in life now (petulance) worth grappling for. There's a nagging tone as Bukowski slips towards the next binge:

and I got out of bed and yawned and scratched my
belly
and knew that soon   very soon   I would have to
get

very drunk again.

Isolating *soon* and *again* with extra spaces emphasizes the sterility of the writing. Ditto for the repetition of *very*. Bukowski now cracks wise with editors who reject his poems. He becomes a rhino-skinned poet s. o. b.:

> when a chicken
> catches its worm
> the chicken gets through
> and when the worm
> catches you
> (dead or alive)
> I'd have to say,
> . . . that it enjoys
> it.
>
> it's like when you
> send this poem
> back
> I'll figure
> it just didn't get
> through.
>
> either there were
> fatter worms or the chicken
> couldn't see.
>
> the next time
> I break an egg
> I'll think of
> you.
> scramble with
> fork
>
> and then turn up
> the flame
> if I
> have
> one.

This poem has an attractive petulance, and the motif of chicken, worm, egg, is original. Also the minimalist lines work well. Yet, Bukowski drifts into cuteness; the starch in the initial images is smothered under narcissism.

Particularly off-putting is Bukowski's obsession with fame. In "The difference between a bad poet and a good one is luck," he regales us with his life in Philadelphia when he was broke, trying to write, and waiting for the ultimate handout to enable him to sit around "drinking wine on credit and watching the hot pigeons suffer and fuck." He hops a train to Texas, and busted for vagrancy, is dumped off in the next town where he meets a woman who gives him so many teeth

marks he thinks he'll get cancer. In prime macho fashion, he greets a bunch of his mistress' cowboy friends:

> I had on a pair of old bluejeans, and they said
> oh, you're a writer, eh?
> and I said: well, some think so.
> and some still think so . . .
> others, of course, haven't wised up yet.
> two weeks later they
> ran me out
> of town.

He seems wistfully amused that trash men busy about their work don't know that he, Great Poet, is alive—a thought held, I would guess, by all great men who snicker in their martinis: "Oh, if they only knew how near to greatness they are banging those trash cans down there . . ." In **"Lost"** Bukowski waxes philosophical in the manner of a hip-Merwin. The Big Conclusion? "We can't win it." Who's surprised? "Just for awhile," folks, "we thought we could." This Life Significance Statement serves up duck-music as distinct from nightingale music. The loquaciousness is typical of his recent poetry. I call it *gab poetry*. The gab poem is related to Chaucer's fabliaux. Obscenities are sexual: a husband shoves a hot iron rod up his wife's lover's anus whilst the lover is taking a crap out her boudoir window; an old husband's young wife is being swyved in a tree just out of eyeshot of the old fart, standing amidst the flowers.

"Hot" is a good example of *gab poetry*. The speaker's been working at the post office, see, on a night pickup run. He knows Miriam the delicious whore is at home waiting for him, deadline 8 p.m. At the last pickup the truck stalls. Miriam is waiting. Speaker arrives late to find Miriam gone. She's left a note propped against his pillow, addressed to "son of bitch." The note is held in place by a purple teddy bear. Speaker gives the bear (heh heh) a drink and has one himself, the poem is prose cut up into boozy breath-groups. Nothing much poetically catches the ear—this is in a sense a one-shot (as in bourbon) piece.

Some poems, like **"Burn and burn and burn,"** set in bars, exude an easy cynicism. Petulance accompanies the "vomiting into plugged toilets / in rented rooms full of roaches and mice":

> well, I suppose the days were made
> to be wasted
> the years and the loves were made
> to be wasted

Instead of the Victorian Ernest Dowson's roses and lilies of rapture (and vice), vomit and plugged toilets cram Buk's wasted days.

Perhaps, if we persist, we'll find the secret of life tucked inside a plastic envelope inside a box of Bukowski Creepy-Crawly, Vomit, Crunch Cereal. Jesus Christ, says Buk, "should have laughed on the cross." There's a secret here somewhere. When Bukowski equates himself with Christ, he's maudlin:

> out of the arms of one love
> and into the arms of another
> I have been saved from dying on the cross
> by a lady who smokes pot
> writes songs and stories.
> and is much kinder than the last,
> much much kinder,
> and the sex is just as good or better.
> it isn't pleasant to be put on the cross and left
> there,
> it is much more pleasant to forget a love which
> didn't
> work
> as all love
> finally
> doesn't work . . . .

Beautiful people, says Bukowski, "don't make it . . . they die in flame . . . they commit suicide . . ." They "are found at the edge of a room / crumpled into spiders and needles and silence." They "die young / and leave the ugly to their ugly lives . . ."

One superb new poem, **"the catch,"** is as good as any Bukowski has written. Guesses are that a strange fish is a Hollow-Back June whale, a Billow-Wind sand-groper, or a Fandango Espadrille with stripes. Folks don't agree. They examine the creature; it's "grey and covered with hair / and fat." It stinks like "old socks." Joyously, the creature promenades along the pier chomping hot dogs, riding the merry-go-round, and hopping a pony. It falls into the dust. "Grop, grop," it goes. Followed by a crowd, it returns to the pier where it falls backwards and thrashes about. Somebody pours beer over its head. "Grop, grop." It dies, and people roll it into the ocean and argue further over its name.

Charles Bukowski is an easy poet to love, fear, and hate. He develops personal legends as dude, boozer, and womanizer. And he can be winsome, almost childlike. By stressing his personality I perhaps short change his poetry. It shouldn't matter that he vomits a lot, gets laid less often than he'd like, that seventy-seven new poems appeared in little magazines this year, or that he's Black Sparrow's leading commodity. Many readers prefer his fiction to his verse. The latter, I think, even with the flaws, remains a more durable art than his prose.

Robert Sward (review date March/May 1995)

SOURCE: A review of The Bukowski/Purdy Letters, A Decade of Dialogue, in *American Book Review*, Vol. 16, No. 6, March/May 1995, pp. 17-18.

[*Sward offers a short, favorable review, including some excerpts from the letters between Al Purdy and Bukowski.*]

In 1964, Canadian poet Al Purdy (author of *The Stone Bird; Sex And Death;* etc.) discovered and reviewed Charles Bukowski's **It Catches My Heart In Its Hands** for *Evidence Magazine.* Purdy mailed a copy of his review to Bukowski who responded with a letter and the correspondence that gave rise to **The Bukowski/Purdy Letters, A Decade Of Dialogue** was underway.

What was in it for Bukowski?

"Getting a letter from Purdy always got my day up off the floor. I found my life more than unappealing and his letters lent a steadiness, some hope, and some hardrock wisdom," wrote Bukowski in the book's Preface. "I wrote letters to many in those days, it was rather my way of screaming from my cage. It helped, that and the gambling, the drinking, the paintings, the poems and the short stories."

Purdy, in his Foreword to this handsomely designed Paget Press book, describes himself as "a pretty callow 45-year-old . . . with too much ego and too little talent." Purdy is by turns modest, boastful, belligerent, charming, supportive—as only a friend can be—of Bukowski's numerous ups and downs, and not at all reticent about expressing his opinions. Purdy says, for example, that the best American poets of all time are Charles Bukowski, Robinson Jeffers, and Emily Dickinson. He is unimpressed by Walt Whitman who, he says, makes him sick to his stomach. But he admires James Dickey, e.e. cummings, Ramon Guthrie and Elizabeth Bishop, poets who, Purdy says, "wrote a few poems," though they are not of the "top level."

The letters are anything but mealy mouthed and devious. Bukowski and Purdy alike delight in a cheery, take no shit-from-anybody attitude. Writing about the Black Mountain poets, who continue to be greatly esteemed in Canada, Al Purdy has this to say.

> I don't like the togetherness let's everybody pat each other of the Duncan-Creeley-Olson bunch. And I don't like their so-called poems either. And I don't like the holy attitude noli me tangere (whatever that means) of their awed disciples.

Bukowski, for his part, says little about other poets. However, he comes through loud and clear in other ways:

I live in a whorehouse district of east Hollywood. I was walking down the street today when one of the girls in a love parlor hollared, 'Hey, come on in!' I didn't even blush, man."

or,

I sit here at my small kitchen table, after shooting my mouth all night in order not to have to *listen* to the other workers, and the half pint of Cutty Sark is about gone and only 4 or 5 bottles of beer left, and soon the sun will be making it in with its mockery. Somebody sent me a roundtrip ticket to Santa Fe, and I might as well go down there for a couple of days.

Drunk again . . . fuck guilt . . .

If you like reading other peoples' mail and have a taste for Bukowski, *The Bukowski/Purdy Letters* are for you.

I've been reading Purdy for the last twenty years. What's *his* take on this exchange?

"This Buk-Purdy thing was a private correspondence, which neither of us expected to see in public, gossiping away like a dumb loudspeaker. I do confess, it makes me a little morose, the way I don't feel when I have lost myself in poems," says the Canadian who concludes his Foreword with the words: "I hope nobody likes me for it, but someone might be slightly interested."

Well, this reader likes him for it. I like in particular the sense I get of Purdy's warmth, humor, generosity and his capacity for friendship.

Imagine, two poets who never met actually writing one another, helping one another and sustaining a friendship for over twenty years!

Ameliasburgh, Ontario's Al Purdy and California-based Charles Bukowski had much in common. Exuberant, anti-academic, prolific, scarred heavyweights, survivors, veterans of innumerable brawls, literary and not-so literary. Yes, both shared an appetite and burly love for strong drink and women. And both assumed in their poems the stance of the poet as tough guy and played the part convincingly. Both shared a suspicion of nondrinkers, critics and academics. Lovers of women, both spoke of womankind in terms that might likely offend one-half the human race.

"I suppose I've been through the mill as you mention," wrote Purdy. "I've ridden the freights, been in jail a few times, done a fair amount of fucking, been unwise, silly, foolish,

cowardly, braggardly, loud, etc.—a character of excess in most ways."
What did they say about one another's work?

"I'm very like you in poems in many ways, and very unlike you in others. My so-called world-view is close to yours, tho at the same time has variations. But yours is only what I see in poems. Tho I think that must be, has to be, authentic."

Can you guess who wrote the above? A free copy of the Paget Press book to those who guess correctly.

The answer is Canada's Purdy who, by the way, comes across as more analytical, more self-conscious and oddly more "stable" than Bukowski who, from the nature of his ailments and complaints, sounds as if he were more often than not in pain and, therefore, in need of his friend's humorous advice and merry, if not raucous, consolation.

If you're looking for a rough and ready view of the 1960's and early 70's as experienced by Charles Bukowski and his Canadian counterpart, check out *The Bukowski/Purdy Letters.*

William Anthony Nericcio (review date Autumn 1995)

SOURCE: A review of *Pulp,* in *World Literature Today,* Autumn 1995, pp. 791-92.

[*Nericcio favorably reviews* Pulp, *citing a poetic essence to the novel that complements and transcends the genre it emulates.*]

"It was a hellish hot day and the air conditioner was broken. A fly crawled across the top of my desk. I reached out with the open palm of my hand and sent him out of the game." These lines are from the opening page of *Pulp,* the posthumous "last" novel by our singular American troubadour of the down-and-out. Charles Bukowski, and his words here encapsulate nicely his general concern in this novel with death. With "Lady Death," to be more specific, and to disclose also the largely allegorical structuring of the piece. With Bukowski's own recent death, it takes the reader some work to get past seeing chief protagonist Nick Belane, private dick, as a loosely sealed surrogate for the late Bukowski himself. "a loser, a dick who couldn't solve anything." Bukowski was known for taking self-deprecation to new heights: not for nothing is *Pulp* dedicated to "bad writing." Not that he did not respect his works—he did, but he did not take them so seriously that he imagined himself the grand artist. Delusions like that might get in the way of a good drink.

Pulp is "pulp fiction" with a twist. As with Quentin Tarantino's movie *Pulp Fiction,* the novel *Pulp* is as much a modest example of the genre's tawdry domain as a knowing reflection upon its obsessions. In Bukowski's pages grimy, dark potboiler meets an allegory on authoring: picture here the bastard singular issue of Mickey Spillane and Laurence Sterne, and you get a sense of Bukowski's scheme. In the end our gutter-friendly scribe hands us a "meta-pulp." This is Hammett and Chandler retooled by a Quixote-era Cervantes—a bowery Borges or skid-row Pynchon. Or, shifting medium. *Pulp* is a painting by René Magritte or Remedios Varo—on black velvet. For example, Bukowski has the private-eye patois down pat. Belane: "A dick without a gat is like a tomcat with a rubber. Or like a clock without hands." But there is a manipulative, knowing narratological savvy also in the response by the detective's antagonist. McKelvey: "Belane . . . you talk goofy."

Pulp's plot line merits recording: a shadowy figure called Lady Death hires Nick Belane ("Mr. Slow Death" to his bookie) to find a guy named Celine—yes, that Celine. Ms. Death tells Belane that Celine's been hanging around Red's bookstore . . . asking about Faulkner, McCullers [and] Charles Manson." Bukowski's Celine is a paranoid boor and gets the novel's best lines: on Thomas Mann, "This fellow has a problem . . . he considers boredom an Art"; on the *New Yorker,* "One problem there . . . they just don't know how to write"; and on writers (while fondling a signed copy of Faulkner's *As I Lay Dying*). "In the old days . . . writers' lives were more interesting than their writing. Now-a-days neither the lives nor the writing is interesting." Wit notwithstanding, Celine meets his maker soon after, again, leaving Belane free to pursue other related cases, which include space-alien bombshells, whores, bars, and red sparrows. As might be expected, Bukowski's "pulp" women are worshiped and shat upon by turns. Belane's threat here to an adulteress named Cindy Bass is typical: "You bitch . . . I'll nail your ass . . . against the wall."

As the novel muses upon death, salient and somewhat predictable reflections on Identity appear, but they are neither winded nor sour with age. Bukowski's lines are "Sartre" filtered through a pulp vein: "Was Celine Celine or was he somebody else? Sometimes I felt that I didn't even know who *I* was. All right, I'm Nicky Belane. But check this. Somebody could well out Hey . . . Harry Martell' and I'd most likely answer, 'Yeah, what is it? I mean. I could be anybody, what does it matter?'"

Bukowski accomplishes other feats with this slight novel, filled as it is with brief tips of the hat to Bukowski's life-long loves: masturbation, "loose" women, bar fights, and booze—lots of booze. Authors too are duly noted. Celine, mentioned above, comes out well. In addition, two thugs sent to rough up Belane early on are named "Dante" and

"Fante"—a salute to Italian maestro Dante Alighieri and Italian-American writer John Fante, writers divided by centuries and region who shared Bukowski's attentive eye for spiritual darkness.

The novel has its highs and lows. "I checked my desk for the luger. It was there, pretty as a picture. A nude one." As you can see, Bukowski is not always subtle. On the whole, however, his staccato prose matches the novel's spare range, yielding a minimalist homage: "It was dark in there. The tv was off. The bartender was an oily guy, looked to be 80, all white, white hair, white skin, white lips. Two other guys sat there, chalk white . . . . No drinks were showing. Everybody was motionless. A white stillness." With few words, Bukowski charts the singular contours of an eccentric cast. His neighbor the mailman, is typical: "His arms hung kind of funny. His mind too." Here readers will find less the labyrinthine literary terrain of G. K. Chesterton and more the moist, fouled corridor of Nathanael West's fiction.

Rhetorically speaking, I eschew ending reviews with loaded quotations drenched with pathos, but given Bukowski's recent exit, it seems worth forgoing any expository fastidiousness here. Nick Belane's reverie is fitting epitaph to Charles Bukowski the man and his fine last novel: "All in all, I had pretty much done what I had set out to do in life. I had made some good moves. I wasn't sleeping in the streets at night. Of course, there were a lot of good people sleeping in the streets. They weren't fools, they just didn't fit into the needed machinery of the moment."

FURTHER READING

Biography

Cherkovski, Neeli. *Hank: The Life and Times of Charles Bukowski,* New York: Random House, 1991, 337 pp.
    Cherkovski is a widely published writer, critic, and editor. Drawing from numerous interviews with Bukowski and several of the author's friends, he provides a detailed portrait of the writer's life.

Criticism

Cherkovski, Neeli. "Notes on a Dirty Old Man." *Whitman's Wild Children.* Venice, CA: The Lapis Press, 1988: 1-38.
    In his chapter on Bukowski, Cherkovski combines anecdotes of meetings with the author and criticism of his work.

Harrison, Russell. *Against the American Dream: Essays on*

Charles Bukowski. Santa Rosa, CA: Black Sparrow Press, 1994, 323 pp.

In the twelve chapters of his book, Harrison focuses in on various aspects of Bukowski's poetry and fiction.

Glover, David. "A Day at the Races: Gambling and Luck in Bukowski's Fiction." *Review of Contemporary Fiction* 5, No. 3 (Fall 1985): 32-33.

Glover examines Bukowski's use of luck as a counterpoint to the implied fatalism of his writing.

Kessler, Stephen. "Notes on a Dirty Old Man." *Review of Contemporary Fiction* 5, No. 3 (Fall 1985): 60-63.

Kessler recounts his first personal encounter with Bukowski. He provides a view of the author that suggests that the compassionate, mellow person that many

feel developed as the writer matured was under the gruff exterior all the time.

Madigan, Andrew J. "What Fame Is: Bukowski's Exploration of Self." *Journal of American Studies* Vol. 30, No. 3 (December 1996): 447-61.

Madigan explores the effect of fame on Bukowski by examining the author's treatment of the subject in his own writing.

Interviews

Penn, Sean. "Tough Guys Write Poetry." *Interview Magazine* XVII, No. 9 (September 1987): 94, 96, 98.

The interview provides a first-person account of Bukowski's opinions on a wide variety of topics.

Additional coverage of Bukowski's life and career is contained in the following sources published by Gale: *Contemporary Authors,* **Vols. 17-20R, Obituary in** *Contemporary Authors,* **Vol. 144,** *Contemporary Authors New Revisions Series,* **Vol. 40,** *Dictionary of Literary Biography,* **Vols. 5, 130, 169,** *DISCovering Authors Modules: Novelists Module, Poets Module, Major 20th-Century Writers.*

Joel and Ethan Coen
1955- and 1958-

American screenwriters; Joel directs and Ethan produces their films.

INTRODUCTION

Within a few years of the release of their first film, *Blood Simple* (1984), brothers Joel and Ethan Coen were considered successful filmmakers, although not by the usual standard of box-office popularity. Their unconventional films appeal to only a subset of the movie-going public, but critics consistently give their work serious consideration: their 1991 film, *Barton Fink,* won that year's Cannes Film Festival awards for best film, best director, and best actor. The fact that the Coens maintain the financial backing of major studios and final editing rights to their work indicates that they are respected, if not always understood, in Hollywood.

Biographical Information

The Coen brothers were born in Minneapolis, Minnesota, to two college professors: their father, Edward, taught economics, and their mother, Rena, was an art historian. Despite this background, both brothers recall their childhoods as less than intellectual. "My mother once wrote an article, 'How to Take Children to an Art Museum,'" Joel remarked in an interview, "but I don't recall her ever taking us." Instead, the brothers spent their early years engrossed in television, watching films such as *Pillow Talk* and *Boeing Boeing.* Joel began making movies at the age of eight, casting his brother and other neighborhood children in dramas and comedies shot with a Super 8 camera. Joel later pursued this interest in college, moving to New York to attend New York University's film school. Ethan, meanwhile, studied philosophy at Princeton, then also moved to New York, where he rented an apartment near Joel's and supported himself as a statistical typist for Macy's department store. Joel worked as an assistant editor and production assistant on low-budget horror films, including the cult classic *The Evil Dead,* written and directed by Sam Raimi. The brothers have said they were not exceptionally close as children, but, as Joel remarked, they "kind of rediscovered each other after college, really through making movies." In 1980, they began writing *Blood Simple.* Unable to find a studio to back the project, the brothers raised the necessary funds by selling limited partnerships in the film. Through elaborate pre-planning—storyboarding every scene and shot—and creative filmmaking techniques, they were able to produce a film that had the look of a much more expensive production.

Major Works

Blood Simple won the United States Film Festival's Grand Jury prize in 1984 and the Independent Spirit Award for best director from the Independent Film Project in 1986. Created in the *film noir* tradition, *Blood Simple* has been compared to the works of James M. Cain and Dashiell Hammett. The story is a variation on the classic lover's triangle, with a quartet of main characters. The husband, Julian Marty, hires a private detective, Visser, to kill his wife, Abby, and her lover, Ray. Visser takes the money and frames Abby for the murder of her husband. Ray discovers Julian's body and, thinking he is protecting Abby, disposes of it. Ray's subsequent cryptic comments to Abby confuse and frighten her, reinforcing the theme of paranoia that pervades the film. With their second film, *Raising Arizona* (1987), the Coens explored the genre of madcap comedy, but not without their signature quirks. The protagonists, H.I. ("Hi") and Edwina ("Ed") are a pair of losers who decide to leave the criminal life behind and pursue their idea of the American dream. Plans of raising a family are thwarted, however, with the discovery that Ed is unable to conceive. They decide to rectify the situation by stealing one of the "extra" children of unfinished furniture magnate Nathan Arizona, but their plans are complicated by H.I.'s vindictive boss and his former cellmates, recently escaped from prison. Their situation becomes still more desperate when they discover that they are the targets of a psychopathic bounty hunter, the Mad Biker of the Apocalypse, who also turns out to be H.I.'s long-lost brother. The madcap pace and excessive but bloodless violence of *Raising Arizona* prompted some critics to describe it as something like a live-action "Road Runner" cartoon. *Miller's Crossing* (1990) returns to the *film noir* genre. Tom Regan, the central character, is an adviser to the Irish Mafia, headed by Leo O'Bannion, who are entrenched in a war with the Italian mob. Tom seems to be working for Leo, but is also involved in an affair with Leo's girlfriend, Verna. That relationship in turn affects how Regan deals with a petty grifter, Bernie Bernbaum, Verna's brother. Tom keeps his plans hidden from everyone, including viewers, until the end of the story. While working on the screenplay for *Miller's Crossing,* the Coens hit a period of writer's block. This became the basis for their next film, *Barton Fink* (1991). Fink, described by many critics as a Clifford Odets-like figure, is a successful, serious Broadway playwright lured to Hollywood to write a Wallace Berry wrestling film. Obsessed with the importance of writing a story about the "common man," Fink ignores the common man, Charlie Meadows, living next door and spends much of his energy concealing his writer's block from the studio. Fink's mental deterioration, along with his obsession with "the life of the mind," caused some critics to question whether the ending of the film should be taken literally: Some suggest that the violent conclusion, in which the "common man" neighbor is revealed to be the serial killer Madman Mundt, occurs inside Fink's mind. The Coens returned to the madcap with their next film, *The Hudsucker Proxy,* coauthored by Sam Raimi. Described as a cross between a Preston Sturges and a Frank Capra film, *Hudsucker Proxy* is the story of the elevation of a likeable idiot, Norville Barnes, to the presidency of Hudsucker Industries by the movie's villain, Sid Mussburger, in an attempt to gain control of the company. Despite his limited intellect, Norville succeeds by introducing his pet project, the hula hoop. The Coens return to the themes of *Blood Simple*—mindless violence and actions based on limited knowledge—with their next film, *Fargo* (1996). In order to resolve his financial difficulties, car salesman Jerry Lundegaard hires two petty criminals, Carl Showalter and Gaear Grimsrud, to kidnap his wife so that he can collect a ransom from his wealthy father-in-law, Wade Gustafson. Things go wrong almost immediately when, in spite of Jerry's insistence on "no rough stuff," Carl and Gaear kill three people—a policeman who stops them for an improper license plate and two witnesses. Many more random and planned acts of violence punctuate the film which, unlike some earlier Coen works, is far from bloodless. The hero of the story is the very pregnant Chief of Police Marge Gunderson, who discovers Jerry's guilt and captures Gaear in the end, catching him in the act of feeding portions of his partner Carl's body through a wood chipper.

Critical Reception

Critical response to the technical aspects of the Coen brothers' films has been generally favorable, while response to the stories has been mixed. A great deal has been written about their creative process and up-front planning. Their judicious use of storyboarding to pre-plan every detail of a film before they begin is credited as one of the ways in which they are able to maintain tight budgets. Eric Pooley remarked, "When Joel and Ethan began to write *Raising Arizona,* in May 1985, they worked in a disciplined, visual way, and when they were through, the result was a lean shooting script—a blueprint with no excess. Reading the script is like watching the movie—the thing emerged so fully formed from their imaginations that little changed between typewriter and camera." Many critics have asserted that this process results in tight, integrated stories. Hal Hinson, speaking of *Blood Simple,* commented, "Everything plugs into the film's basic idea: that we are dependent in our judgments upon what our senses tell us, and that our senses lie—that in life we never really know what's going on." Tim Pulleine similarly praised the Coens' unity of story and structure: "*Miller's Crossing* assumes a precision of correspondence between content and form which is all too rare in the cinema today." The Coens have also been commended for well-written dialogue. Jeff Evans suggested that the specific choice of words for each of their characters tells viewers as much about them as the messages those words contain. Discussing the character of H.I. in *Raising Arizona,* Evans noted, "When we hear his rural, native speech layered over comically by the language of pop jargon, advertisement, cliché, we recognize the violation and ethical confusion that language can wreak on character and action." However, not all critics are as sympathetic to the Coens' concepts. As critic Richard K. Ferncase asserted, "There is something fundamentally annoying about *Blood Simple* that irritates in an incipient, barely perceptible fashion—like the pesky fly that crawls around M. Emmet Walsh's ear and temple. Garish and vacuous, *Blood Simple* is, in the final analysis, a catalogue of noir and suspense clichés, a film about unpleasant characters that is itself unpleasant to watch." Several critics have faulted the Coens for failing to present characters with whom the audience can empathize. Tad Friend concluded, "This aloofness from the viewer's sympathy is why the Coens have remained highbrow darlings and box-office lepers." John Harkness asserted that the Coens are often misinterpreted: "People think their notorious press conferences and interviews, which consist of misdirected remarks and gnomic mumbles, are a put on, but really they work to hide the fact that the brothers don't believe in much of anything—they have enormous abilities, but are sphinxes without riddles. One suspects that Ethan's comment at the Cannes press conference for *Barton Fink* that their films are just frameworks on which they can hang cheap jokes was not a joke at all. There is an emptiness at the heart of their work which can be ignored when the films are entertaining, but which shows up dreadfully when they aren't." McKinney maintained that this detachment from the characters is successful in some cases. Of *Barton Fink,* he commented, "At their most original, the Coens have exercised the darker, more difficult impulse to unite characters and audience not in the warmth of a common affirmation, but in the chill of a common alienation. It's an empathy that says not 'I recognize that man's situation and now don't feel so lonely,' but 'I recognize that man's situation and now I'm lonelier than before.'"

PRINCIPAL WORKS

Blood Simple (screenplay) 1984
Raising Arizona (screenplay) 1987
Miller's Crossing (screenplay) 1990
Barton Fink (screenplay) 1991
The Hudsucker Proxy (screenplay) 1994
Fargo (screenplay) 1996

CRITICISM

Hal Hinson (essay date March/April 1985)

SOURCE: "Bloodlines," in *Film Comment,* Vol. 21, No. 2, March/April, 1985, pp. 14-19.

[*In the following essay, which includes an interview with the Coen brothers and Barry Sonnenfeld, their cinematographer, Hinson discusses the making of* Blood Simple.]

In his novel *Red Harvest,* Dashiell Hammett wrote that after a person kills somebody, he goes soft in the head—"blood simple." You can't help it. Your brains turn to mush. All of a sudden, the blond angel whose husband you just buried starts getting strange phone calls. You reach into your pocket for your cigarette lighter—the silver-plated one the Elks gave you with your name spelled out in rope on the front—and it's not there. Your lover limps in early one morning with blood on his shirt and a .38, *your* .38, stuffed in his jeans and announces, "I've taken care of it. All we have to do now is keep our heads." Yeah. That's all. Just keep your heads. Might as well go ahead and call the cops.

For the characters in the stylish new thriller *Blood Simple,* passion, guilt, and the sight of blood on their hands causes the world to warp and distort just as Hammett said it would,

like the nightmare reflection in a fun-house mirror. The movie, which was put together on a shoe-string by Joel and Ethan Coen, a couple of movie-mad brothers from Minneapolis, has its own lurid, fun-house atmosphere. The camera swoops and pirouettes as if in a Vincente Minnelli musical; at times it scuttles just inches above the ground, at shoe-top level, crawls under tables, or bounces down hallways. Always some part of the frame is energized by an odd detail or incongruous fillip of color. Composed in phosphorescent pastels, in neon pinks and greens that stand out against the khaki-colored Texas landscapes, the movie has a kind of tawdry flamboyance that draws attention to itself, like a barfly adjusting her makeup by the light of the jukebox. *Blood Simple* is only the Coens' first movie—their contributions overlap, with Joel credited as writer-director and Ethan as writer-producer—but already they have an agile sense of visual storytelling and a playfully expressive camera style. They don't make movies like beginners.

If anything, the Coens' technique in *Blood Simple* is too brightly polished, too tightly screwed down. But their excesses come from an over-eagerness to impress, to put their talents on display. *Blood Simple* looks like a movie made by guys who spent most of their lives watching movies, indiscriminately, both in theaters and on TV, and for whom, almost through osmosis, the vocabulary and grammar of film has become a kind of instinctive second language. Made up of equal parts *film noir* and Texas Gothic, but with a hyperbolic B-movie veneer, it's a grab-bag of movie styles and references, an eclectic mixture of Hitchcock and Bertolucci, of splatter flicks and Fritz Lang and Orson Welles.

On the face of it, *Blood Simple* may appear to be more about other movies than anything else, and there is an element of movie-movie formalism in their work. But the Coens aren't interested in just recycling old movie formulas. In *Blood Simple,* the filmmakers assume that the audience grew up on the same movies they did, and that we share their sophisticated awareness of conventional movie mechanics. But the Coens don't play their quotations from old movie thrillers straight; they use our shared knowledge of movie conventions for comedy. The movie has a wicked, satirical edge—there's a devilish audacity in the way these young filmmakers use their film smarts to lure us into the movie's system of thinking, and then spring their trap, knocking us off-balance in a way that's both shocking and funny.

The basic geometry of the film is a James M. Cain triangle: husband, wife, lover. The husband, Julian Marty (Dan Hedaya), is a brooding Greek with a militant brow and a puckered chin who owns a gaudy roadside nightspot called the Neon Boot. One look at Marty, who looks like he was born to catch lead, and it's clear why his wife Abby (Frances McDormand) thinks she'd better hightail it before she uses the pearl-handled revolver he gave her as an anniversary present on him. Ray (John Getz), a drawling bartender who works for Marty, becomes involved with Abby innocently enough when she asks him to help her move out. Almost inevitably, Abby and Ray fall into the nearest motel room where a fourth figure, a slob detective named Visser (M. Emmet Walsh), catches them *in flagrante* and delivers his photographic evidence to Marty ("I know where you can get these framed"), along with his own leering account of the evening's bedroom activities, setting the film's tragic spiral of events in motion.

> **Much of the pleasure in *Blood Simple* comes from watching the filmmakers run their intricately worked-out plot through its paces. The film's narrative is never merely functional in the usual murder-mystery fashion; things don't happen in this movie just to push the plot along. Everything plugs into the film's basic idea: that we are dependent in our judgments upon what our senses tell us, and that our senses lie—that in life we never really know what's going on.**
> **—Hal Hinson**

Much of the pleasure in *Blood Simple* comes from watching the filmmakers run their intricately worked-out plot through its paces. The film's narrative is never merely functional in the usual murder-mystery fashion; things don't happen in this movie just to push the plot along. Everything plugs into the film's basic idea: that we are dependent in our judgments upon what our senses tell us, and that our senses lie—that in life we never really know what's going on. The Coens have created a world in which nothing is exactly as it seems. When Marty sees Visser's picture of Abby and Ray nestled together in bloody sheets, we assume, as Marty does, that the hired killer has done his job and the lovers are dead. It's not until the next scene, when Ray saunters into the bar and finds Marty's body, that we discover the photo was doctored. In this movie, a corpse is not always a corpse.

All the characters in *Blood Simple* are able to see only part of the whole picture. Each character has his own point of view in the film, his own version of what has happened and why. And based on the evidence before them, each one behaves appropriately. But each one is limited by his own perspective and it's what they don't know, what they *can't* see from where they stand, that keeps getting them into trouble. Only the audience is given the whole picture. But the Coens never let us relax. Just as we think were in synch with the film, they shove our assumptions back in our faces. Like their characters, we're making a mistake by believing what we see.

It's this layering of points of view, the interweaving of four versions of the same events, each one complicating and contradicting the other, that distinguishes *Blood Simple* from Lawrence Kasdan's *Body Heat* and other *film noir* retreads. It's been some time since a low-budget thriller has had this kind of narrative richness. And if at times the Coens are a little too much in love with their own cleverness, occasionally bogging the movie down with self-conscious arty flourishes, they are saved by their drive to provide low-down thrills, to surprise and delight their audience. *Blood Simple* suggests that the Coens are an anomaly on the independent film scene. They don't see a conflict between film art and film entertainment. Nor, in *Blood Simple,* do they break new aesthetic ground. First and foremost, they are entertainers.

Some critics have used this aspect of their work to dismiss *Blood Simple* either as an independent film with a conventional Hollywood heart or as just another schlocky exploitation picture with a glossy, high-art finish. They use the film's accessibility as a club to beat it over the head with, as if to imply that the things that make the movie fun to watch, that satisfy an audience, are precisely the things that compromise its artistic purity. According to this logic, *Blood Simple* is little more than an audition piece, a stepping stone to the world of big-budget studio financing.

But it's the Coens' showmanship, their desire to give the audience a cracking good ride, that gives *Blood Simple* its freshness and originality. The film is most effective when it plays as a comedy. The Coens have a sharp eye for the oddball details of the sleazy Texas milieu they've created. Their humor is droll and understated; their characters spout a kind of terse, prairie vernacular that's dead-on authentic but with a twist, like Horton Foote with a rock in his shoe.

As the scuzzy detective slithering through the movie in a beat-up VW bug, M. Emmet Walsh is a redneck variation on all the bad cops and corrupt gumshoes in the hard-boiled genre. Dressed in a canary-yellow leisure suit, his belly sagging over his western-style belt buckle, Visser is the kind of half-witted vermin who likes to torture puppies in his spare time. Walsh gives his character a mangy amorality; one look at this guy and you know he's for sale at bargain-basement prices. His performance sets a new standard for scumbag character acting.

Dan Hedaya, who plays Marty, does something that even Walsh isn't able to pull off: He shows us what a slime the guy is and still makes us feel almost sorry for what happens to him. Marty is the perpetual outsider, the one who's always put upon and misunderstood. He doesn't even talk like the others. Instead of speaking in a lazy Texas drawl, he spits his words out quickly in a tight Northeastern accent that's clenched like a fist. With his dark, swarthy looks, gold chains, and European-cut shirts, he's on the opposite end of the sleaze scale from Walsh's Visser, but their scenes together are the best in the film.

The Coens aren't as successful with their main characters: John Getz and Frances McDormand are bland and uninteresting as Ray and Abby. In *The Postman Always Rings Twice,* Frank and Cora were so hot for each other that sparks seemed to arc between them; their passion was so volatile that it almost *had* to erupt into violence. There are no comparable sexual fireworks between the lovers in **Blood Simple;** it's tepid affair, and neither character has enough vitality to engage us. It may be that the Coens have a natural talent for creating lively villains. In any case, in **Blood Simple,** the sympathetic lovers are upstaged by their loathsome adversaries. Their low-watt rapport leaves a dark, empty space at the center of the film.

The most remarkable thing about **Blood Simple** is that it's satisfying both as a comedy *and* a thriller. What the Coens have learned from Hitchcock, whose spirit hovers over the film as it does in Brian De Palma's movies, is that murder can be simultaneously tragic and comic. The moment in **Blood Simple** when the two lovers confront one another, each one convinced of the other's guilt, and from out of nowhere a rolled-up newspaper arches into the frame, hitting the screen door between them with a sickening smack, is so startlingly unexpected and yet so right, that for a moment you're not sure you actually saw it. Watching **Blood Simple,** you begin to feel uncertain even of the ground beneath your feet. They have that kind of skill.

This interview took place with Joel and Ethan Coen, and their cinematographer Barry Sonnenfeld, in an apartment on the Upper East Side of Manhattan on the afternoon of **Blood Simple**'s commercial opening in New York. All three were casually dressed and, at the beginning of the session, excitedly talking, not about their opening night, but about their upcoming lunch at the Russian Tea Room, about superagent Sam Cohn ("Does he really eat Kleenex?") and the politics of who sits where. During the interview, the Coens chainsmoked Camels out of the same pack, passing it back and forth across the glass tabletop in front of them.

[*Hal Hinson:*] *Let's start with the basics. You were both born and raised in Minneapolis?*

[Joel Coen:] Yeah. We both grew up in Minneapolis, but have lived in New York, on and off, for about ten years. I moved here to go to school at NYU and haven't really lived in Minneapolis since then, except for about a year when we were raising money for the movie. We raised a lot of the money there, although some of it came from here and New Jersey and Texas.

[Ethan Coen:] I left Minneapolis to go to school at

Princeton—I studied philosophy—and after that came to New York.

How did you become interested in film-making?

[Joel:] There were two things really. We made a lot of Super 8 movies when we were kids.

[Ethan:] They were incredibly cheesy, even by Super 8 standards.

[Joel:] We remade a lot of bad Hollywood movies that we'd seen on television. The two that were most successful were remakes of *The Naked Prey* and *Advise and Consent*—movies that never should have been made in the first place. At that time, we didn't really understand the most basic concepts of filmmaking—we didn't know that you could physically edit film—so we'd run around with the camera, editing it all in the camera. We'd actually have parallel editing for chase scenes. We'd shoot in one place, then run over to the other and shoot that, then run back and shoot at the first spot again.

Did these films have titles?

[Joel:] Yeah. The remake of *The Naked Prey* was called *Zeimers in Zambia*—the guy who played the Cornell Wilde part was nicknamed Zeimers. We had very weird special effects in that film. We actually had a parachute drop—a shot of an airplane going overhead, then a miniature, then cut to a closeup of the guy against a white sheet hitting the ground.

[Ethan:] It was hell waiting for the airplane to fly by. We were nowhere near a flight path.

This sounds amazingly sophisticated.

[Joel:] It wasn't, really. They were just hacked together. *Advise and Consent* was interesting, though, because at the time we made it we hadn't seen the original film *or* read the book. We just heard the story from a friend of ours and it sounded good, so we remade it without going back to any of the source material.

When you finally saw the original, which did you like better, your version or theirs?

[Ethan:] Well, we're big Don Murray fans, so I like the original.

[Joel:] Yeah, guys like Don Murray and the early Disney stars, you know, Dean Jones and Jim Hutton, are big favorites. Kurt Russell, too.

Sounds like you watched a lot of movies on TV.

[Ethan:] Yeah, we saw a lot of Tarzan movies and Steve Reeves muscle movies. What was that Tarzan rip-off with Johnny Sheffield?

[Joel:] *Bomba the Jungle Boy.* What's-his-name used to introduce those.

[Ethan:] Andy Devine.

[Joel:] Yeah, he had a thing called "Andy's Gang" . . .

[Ethan:] But that wasn't *Bomba,* that was a serial set in India called *Ramar.* Did you ever see *Tarzan's New York Adventure?* That's one of the greatest. And the Sixties Tarzans were kind of weird.

[Joel:] A movie like *Boeing Boeing* was big with us. And we were into movies like *That Touch of Mink, A Global Affair,* Bob Hope movies, Jerry Lewis movies, anything with Tony Curtis, *Pillow Talk.* We tried to see everything with Doris Day. Those were important movies for us. I saw *Pillow Talk* again recently. It's incredibly surreal.

[Ethan:] It's a very weird, wooden aesthetic that nobody's interested in anymore. *The Chapman Report* is great that way too.

[Joel:] What's happened is that those movies have now become TV fodder.

Did the look of those movies have anything to do with your decision to shoot **Blood Simple** *in color? It's kind of film noir, which is usually done in black-and-white.*

[Joel:] There was a big practical consideration. Since we were doing the movie independently, and without a distributor, we were a little leery of making a black-and-white movie. But we never really considered that a sacrifice. We wanted to keep the movie dark, and we didn't want it to be colorful in the . . .

[Ethan:] . . . the *That Touch of Mink* sort of way.

[Joel:] Right. What we talked about early on was having the elements of color in frame be sources of light, at least as much as possible, like with the neon and the Bud lights, so that the rest of the frame would be dark. That way it would be colorful, but not garish.

[Barry Sonnenfeld:] I think we were afraid that to shoot the film in black-and-white would make it look too "independent," too low-budget.

[Ethan:] Yeah. We wanted to trick people into thinking we'd made a real movie.

The film has been criticized for that reason.

[Joel:] Yeah, one critic said it had "the heart of a Bloomingdale's window and the soul of a résumé." I loved that review.

[Ethan:] The movie is a no-bones-about-it entertainment. If you want something other than that, then you probably have a legitimate complaint.

[Joel:] But you can't get any more independent than *Blood Simple.* We did it entirely outside of Hollywood. To take it a step further, we did it outside of any established movie company anywhere. It can't be accused of not being an independent film. It was done by people who have had no experience with feature films, Hollywood or otherwise.

[Barry:] What this writer means by independent, though, is arty or artistic. It wasn't our intention to make an art film, but to make an entertaining B movie.

Do you consider yourself linked in any way with other independent filmmakers and what they're doing?

[Ethan:] The independent movies that we see aren't really avant-garde. John Sayles is an independent filmmaker who I like. Although I haven't seen his new film, I like what Alan Rudolph does. He'll make a movie for a studio, like *Roadie* or *Endangered Species,* and then go off on his own to make a movie just for himself for $800,000.

[Joel:] Also, I like low-budget horror movies that are made independently. They're mass-audience pictures, but they're done independently. I've worked with a lot of people who've done that stuff, like Sam Raimi. Those are the kind of independent filmmakers that we feel closer to than, say, the more avant-garde artists. I liked *Stranger than Paradise,* though, which I suppose is closer to being avant-garde than we are.

[Ethan:] I think there's room for all kinds of independent movies. And whenever anyone makes a successful one, no matter what kind it is, it's good for everybody.

I think the distinction that's being made is between art and entertainment.

[Joel:] That's a distinction that I've never understood. If somebody goes out to make a movie that isn't designed primarily to entertain people, then I don't know what the fuck they're doing. I can't understand it. It doesn't make sense to me. What's the Raymond Chandler line? "All good art is entertainment and anyone who says differently is a stuffed shirt and juvenile at the art of living."

Some people see **Blood Simple** *as a shrewd maneuver to* *establish yourselves on the scene in order to launch your careers as mainstream filmmakers.*

[Ethan:] They're wrong. We made the movie because we wanted to make it, not as a stepping stone to anything else. And we prefer to keep on making this kind of movie, independently.

[Joel:] Someone in *Film Comment* said **Blood Simple** was "aggressively New Hollywood." We wanted to make this movie, and the way we did it was the only way we could have done it. The main consideration from the start was that we wanted to be left alone, without anyone telling us what to do. The way we financed the movie gave us that right.

When you were both still in school, you wrote a few feature scripts together. What were they like?

[Joel:] The first one was called *Coast to Coast.* We never really did anything with it. It was sort of a screwball comedy.

[Ethan:] It had 28 Einsteins in it. The Red Chinese were cloning Albert Einstein.

[Joel:] After that we were hired by a producer to write a script from a treatment he had. That was never produced. Then Sam Raimi, whom I worked with on *The Evil Dead,* hired us to write something with him called *The XYZ Murders.* It's just been finished. And we're writing something with him now that Ethan and I are going to do.

What movies had you worked on before **Blood Simple?**

[Joel:] I was assistant editor on a few low-budget horror films, like *Fear No Evil.* There was another one that I actually got fired from called *Nightmare,* which had a small release here in New York. And *The Evil Dead.* Those are the only three features I've worked on. *Evil Dead* was the most fun. A lot of the stuff in our film, like the camera running up on the front lawn, is attributable to Raimi, who does a lot of shaky-cam stuff.

How do you two collaborate when you're writing?

[Joel:] He does all the typing. We just sit down together and work it out from beginning to end. We don't break it up and each do scenes. We talk the whole thing through together.

[Barry:] They pace a lot. And there's a lot of cigarette smoking.

How was it determined that Joel would direct and Ethan produce?

[Ethan:] We had a thoin coss. . . . I mean a coin toss.

[Joel:] The standard answer is that I'm bigger than he is— that I can beat him up so I get to direct.

[Ethan:] It's those critical three inches in reach that make the difference.

[Joel:] To tell you the truth, the credits on the movie don't reflect the extent of the collaboration. I did a lot of things on the production side, and Ethan did a lot of directorial stuff. The line wasn't clearly drawn. In fact, the way we worked was incredibly fluid. I think we're both just about equally responsible for everything in the movie.

[Ethan:] Although, on the set, Joel is definitely the director. He's the one in charge.

[Joel:] Yeah, I did work with the actors and all that. But as far as the script and the realization, down to the tiniest details and including all the major aesthetic decisions, that's a mutual thing.

Who sets up the shots?

[Joel:] This is where it gets really fuzzy. When we're writing a script, we're already starting to interpret the script directorially. As to how we want the movie to look, even down to specific shots and the kind of coverage we want, that's worked into the writing of the script. Also, before production, Ethan, Barry, and I story-boarded the movie together.

[Ethan:] Also, at the beginning of every day, the three of us and the assistant director would have breakfast at Denny's— the Grand Slam special—and go through the day's shots and talk about the lighting.

[Joel:] On the set, we'd put it all together and look through the viewfinder. Barry might have an idea, or Ethan would come up with something different, and we'd try it. We had the freedom to do that, because we'd done so much advance work.

[Barry:] Also, on the set, we'd try to torture each other. For example, I didn't allow smoking. . .

[Ethan:] "It degrades the image."

[*Laughs.*]

[Barry:] . . . which meant that only one of them would be on the set at any time, because the other one was off having a cigarette.

The atmosphere of the film shows the influence of hard-boiled detective fiction. Have you read a lot of that stuff?

[Joel:] We read all of Cain six or seven years ago when they reissued his books in paperback. Chandler and Hammett, too. We've also pored through a lot of Cain arcana.

[Ethan:] Cain is more to the point for this story than Chandler or Hammett. They wrote mysteries, whodunits.

[Joel:] We've always thought that up at Low Library at Columbia University, where the names are chiseled up there above the columns in stone—Aristotle, Herodotus, Virgil—that the fourth one should be Cain.

[Ethan:] Cain usually dealt in his work with three great themes: opera, the Greek diner business, and the insurance business.

[Joel:] Which we felt were the three great themes of 20th-century literature.

Marty, the cuckold, seems to be lifted directly out of Cain.

[Ethan:] He is, but a little less cheerful and fun-loving.

[Joel:] They're usually greasy, guitar strumming yahoos, which of course Marty isn't. But yeah, that's where he comes from.

Why did you set the film in Texas?

[Joel:] The weather's good. And it just seemed like the right setting for a passion murder story. And people have strong feelings about Texas, which we thought we could play off of.

[Ethan:] And again, your classic *film noir* has a real urban feel, and we wanted something different.

Did you set out to create a film noir *atmosphere?*

[Joel:] Not really. We didn't want to make a Venetian-blind movie.

[Ethan:] When people call **Blood Simple** a *film noir,* they're correct to the extent that we like the same kind of stories that the people who made those movies liked. We tried to emulate the source that those movies came from rather than the movies themselves.

[Joel:] **Blood Simple** utilizes movie conventions to tell the story. In that sense it's about other movies—but no more so than any other film that uses the medium in a way that's aware that there's history of movies behind it.

How were you able to maintain such a delicate balance between the comic and the thriller elements in the story?

[Joel:] I think that gets back to Chandler and Hammett and Cain. The subject matter was grim but the tone was upbeat. They move along at a very fast pace. They're funny . . .

[Ethan:] . . . they're insanely eupeptic . . .

[Joel:] . . . and that keeps the stories from being grim. We didn't want this to be a grim movie. There's a lot of graphic violence and a lot of blood, but I don't think the movie's grim.

[Ethan:] We didn't have an equation for how to balance the blood and the gags. But there is a counterpoint between the story itself and the narrator's attitude toward the story.

[Joel:] To us it was amusing to frame the whole movie with this redneck detective's views on life. We thought it was funny, but it also relates directly to the story. It's not a one-liner kind of funny.

[Ethan:] It's easy to think that we set out to parody the *film noir* form because, on one hand, it is a thriller, and, on the other, it is funny. But certainly the film is supposed to work as a thriller and I don't think it would work as both at once.

[Joel:] Humorless thrillers—*Gorky Park,* or *Against All Odds*—are dull, flat. They take themselves too seriously in a way that undercuts the fun of the movie. We didn't really think about making the situations in the film funny. Our thinking was more like, "Well, this will be scary," and "Wouldn't it be fun if the character were like this?"

In preparing **Blood Simple,** *did you look at other movies and use them as models?*

[Joel:] *The Conformist* is one of the movies we went with Barry to see before we started shooting in terms of deciding what we wanted the visual style of the movie to be, the lighting and all that. Also, we went to see *The Third Man.*

[Barry:] Which is funny because I read that Richard Kline [the cinematographer] and Larry Kasdan went to see the same two films before they shot *Body Heat.*

[Joel:] And came up with a completely different look. We wanted a real non-diffuse image which is the kind of image that Vittorio Storaro got in *The Conformist.* But in *Body Heat* they got this over-exposed, halating image with light running through the windows. Maybe they saw a really bad print.

[Ethan:] We're also big fans of Robby Müller, particularly

The American Friend, which we've all seen a number of times. So there are a lot of points of reference. Actually, we just wanted the movie to be in focus.

Do you intend to continue your arrangement as it is at present, with Joel directing and Ethan producing, or do you want to switch it around next time?

[Ethan:] We're going to continue the same way. [To Joel] We've got to do *Boeing Boeing* credits next time [in which, to calm top-billing egos, Jerry Lewis' and Tony Curtis' names revolved on an axis].

[Joel:] We're thinking that next time we'll have it say, "Ethan and Joel Coen's *Whatever.*"

[Ethan:] No, I like "Ethan Coen presents a film by his brother Joel."

And you would like to continue working together?

[Joel:] Oh yeah. In fact the three of us do. There are certain collaborations which are really fruitful. One of them is with Sam Raimi, which we hope continues on other movies in the future. Another is with Barry.

As a result of the success you've had so far with **Blood Simple,** *are the studios beating a path to your door with offers?*

[Joel:] We're getting a lot of talk, but we don't know what it means. You spend one week in Hollywood. . . ! [*Laughs.*] People have been calling. But we'd like to continue to work as independently as possible. Not independent necessarily of the Hollywood distribution apparatus, which is really the best if you want your movie to reach a mass market. But as far as production is concerned, there's a real trade-off involved. It's true that certain movies require more money to produce right than **Blood Simple** did. But the difference with us is, while we may need more money for the next one than we did for **Blood Simple,** we're still not talking about the kind of budgets that the studios are used to working with. We did this film for a million and a half, and, for me, $3-4 million is an incredible amount of money to make a movie. And that's attainable without going to the studios.

[Ethan:] The bottom line is, even if **Blood Simple** does well, we're comfortable with the idea of making another low-budget movie.

[Joel:] Right. We're not afraid of making movies for cheap.

Barry Sonnenfeld (review date July 1985)

SOURCE: "Shadows and Shivers for *Blood Simple,*" in *American Cinematographer,* Vol. 66, No. 7, July, 1985, pp. 70-72, 74.

[*In the review below, Sonnenfeld, the cinematographer for* Blood Simple, *provides a behind-the-scenes look at low-budget production.*]

There is almost no problem in the making of a feature film that cannot be solved by throwing money at it. More lights, more time, more crew, a bigger crane, a re-shoot, can all be bought with a big time budget.

One of the challenges of shooting **Blood Simple,** a Texas murder mystery shot in Austin, Texas, was to make a $1.5 million movie look like ten times that. The money was raised over a period of almost a year in the form of a limited partnership. The director, Joel Coen, had never directed before; his younger brother, Ethan, had never produced a film (and worked as a statistical typist at Macy's to pay their rent while they raised the money). I had never looked through a 35mm camera.

The money was raised by shooting a three minute trailer of the movie, as if it was finished and about to appear in your neighborhood theater. The trailer was our selling tool. It showed prospective investors that we could make something that looked like a real film, and it was something to invest in that had a recognizable form, unlike a treatment or script, for which none of the investors had any expertise. We were so low budget that we waited until "President's Weekend," to shoot the trailer, when we could rent the 35mm camera over Washington and Lincoln's birthdays, using the camera and lights from Thursday until Tuesday and paying a one day rental charge (thank you, FERCO). I taught my cousin Kenny, a neuro-pharmacologist, how to pull focus.

Eight months after we shot the trailer, we had our money and were on our way to Austin to make our movie. **Blood Simple** is a tightly plotted murder mystery in the *film noir* tradition. The plot involves the owner of a bar who discovers that his wife is having an affair with one of his bartenders. He hires a sleazy 'good ol' boy' detective to kill his wife and bartender. The detective has a better idea. He takes a photograph of the lovers in bed, and doctors the snapshot to look like they have been shot to death. The detective presents this photo as proof of a job well done, gets paid by the husband, and then shoots him. In effect, the detective has committed the safer murder. He leaves the wife's gun, which he has stolen from her pocketbook as evidence for the police, when, he assumes, the body is discovered.

Unfortunately for everybody concerned, the lover comes to the bar that night, finds the body and the gun, and assumes that the wife committed the murder. He cleans up the mess and goes to bury the body in a field. However, he discovers that the body isn't quite dead and is forced to finish the job himself. He then goes back to the wife and says, "Don't worry, I took care of everything." She doesn't know what he's talking about, and their misunderstanding leads to mistrust, and several more murders.

Every scene in *Blood Simple* was storyboarded. The only effective way to bring a low budget film in on budget is to preplan everything. Pre-production is cheap compared to standing around the set with a crew, scratching your head, saying things like, "What would it look like if we put the camera over here?" The other reason, besides economics, that the film was storyboarded was the intricate nature of the plot. Certain visual elements repeat themselves in ironic visual ways, and these were all planned. Visual devices such as match cuts, sound overlaps, and camera-locked-down dissolves are all cheap and easy to do if they are thought about ahead of time, and tend to give a film a production value far beyond the cost of achieving these effects. There is a stretch of 20 minutes in the film with no dialogue which works totally on a visual/filmic level.

We were very lucky to have Tom Prophet as our key grip. Tom's wife felt that Los Angeles was no longer geologically sound, and convinced Tom to get out of L.A. while they could still drive out. They relocated in Austin, luckily for us. Tom taught us a lot of Hollywood high technology with his pipe dolly and other rigging devices, and we taught him some low technology as well. Joel and I decided early on that we wanted to move the camera a lot, and when the camera wasn't moving, we sometimes would dolly or raise or lower lights during the shot, so there was always some kind of apparent movement.

One of the cheap but efficient ways we moved the camera on *Blood Simple* was by dragging me around the floor hand holding an Arri BL3 while lying down on a sound blanket. This was quite effective since not only could we virtually be on the floor with the camera, the grips could actually pick up the blanket during our moving shots and turn the sound blanket into a crane. Another device we used to move the camera I believe was first used by Caleb Deschanel on *More American Graffiti* and was shown to us by Sam Raimi, who directed *Evil Dead*. This device is the 'shakicam,' and cannot be beat at any price. The 'shakicam' is a two inch by 12 foot piece of lumber with a handle at either end of its twelve foot length. The camera is then centered on the board. An Arri-2C with a Kinoptik 9.8mm lens was used. With a grip at either end, the camera was raced along the ground at full speed, approaching the fighting wife and husband. Due to the extreme wide angle lens, in a matter of a couple of seconds, the camera races from an extreme wide shot into a super close-up of the wife as she bends back and breaks her husband's finger. In effect, all the shaking of two grips, rac-

ing at top speed along rough terrain, are smoothed out by the time the shakes reach the middle of the twelve foot shakicam, and the camera seems to float. It was a very enjoyable shot to watch being made, since it looks like such a stupid idea. I would run behind the camera, not looking through the viewfinder, but still getting a sense of level and angle. I also got to yell "duck!" at the actors, since as the shakicam raced towards them, it was also rising from several inches off the ground to eye level, and the device has the stopping ability of a Boeing 747.

Another unusual and effective device we used was to lock the actress and camera to each other. For this, we used Tom's speed rail. The actress was strapped down into what looked like a torture device. The camera and I were then strapped in four feet in front of her, and the whole device was rigged with a block and tackle to a beam in our studio. We then had two backdrops built. The backdrop directly behind her, at the head of the shot, was of the back room of the bar. On the floor, we built a bed. As the contraption pivots 90 degrees on itself, the actress, in effect, leaves one scene and falls through space past a series of side lit inkies, and eventually lands on her bed, and a different location in the film. Not only is this an effective transition visually, but psychologically as well, since, at this point in the film, she's quite confused. Since the actress and camera are stationary to each other, there is almost a feeling of the two scenes floating towards her.

Originally, my thought for the lighting on *Blood Simple* was that the high contrast, *film noir* look should come from a high ratio of main light to fill light, but that the quality of the light should be softer, bounce light. However, once we started shooting, I decided a more controllable way to go was with direct fresnels. Almost every shot in the movie was lit with either an Ianiro Miser, which is similar to an inkie, but tends to have a more even field, or a 4K HMI. It was a strange combination of extremes, but it worked for us. In fact, the extremes of lighting is what I like about the technical end of the film the most. In the end, there were no soft lights, bay lights, silks, and only a rare bounce light for scenes in the bathroom.

I am proud to say that the lighting in *Blood Simple* is almost totally unmotivated. There is a lot of discussion in the industry about motivated light (seeing the light sources in the frame), as if it is more truthful, honest, or more beautiful. For *Blood Simple* the lighting was used as a psychological tool. For the film to be effective, the film had to be dark and contrasty. In fact, at the end of the film, the lighting itself becomes a character. The evil detective, in a bright bathroom, starts shooting bullets through a wall into a dark, adjoining apartment where our heroine is hiding. As each bullet slams through the common wall, light streaks through the darkened apartment at all kinds of crazy angles. By the time the detective runs out of bullets, the darkened room is sliced up into thirty tubes of light bleeding out of the six bullet holes, slicing at all kinds of angles, racing out in four or five different directions from each bullet hole. The only motivation for these crazy streams of light are twenty open face 1Ks on the other side of the wall. However the audience is affected by the scene; it is funny and terrorizing, and it works.

Joel, Ethan and I felt strongly that we wanted our blacks to be rich, with no milky quality. The entire film was shot on 5293 rated at 200, which overexposed the stock between one half and a full stop. Our printing lights were always in the very high 40's. This produced a very thick negative, and although the raw stock is overexposed, the film is printed quite dark and contrasty, and the blacks are black. The development and answer printing was done at Du Art Labs in New York. My camera reports to the lab were always the same: "Print it too dark!" Du Art did a great job.

Jane Musky was the production designer. She created sets that were terrific and laughably inexpensive. That the film came in on time and on budget was due in no small way to Deborah Reinisch, the first assistant director and a film director in her own right, and Mark Silverman, the PM/associate producer.

Harry M. Geduld (review date July/August 1985)

SOURCE: A review of *Blood Simple,* in *The Humanist,* Vol. 45, No. 4, July/August, 1985, p. 43.

[*In the following review, Geduld criticizes* Blood Simple *as lacking in creativity and unable to provide engaging characters.*]

This nasty little thriller (stylistically distinguished only by some clever uses of extreme closeups) provoked me into recalling the masterpieces of the genre, in particular Billy Wilder's 1944 adaptation of James M. Cain's *Double Indemnity.* Notwithstanding the work of Hitchcock, Wilder's film remains for me the outstanding movie example of what E. F. Bleiler has called "the inverted detective story," that narrative form in which the focus is on the criminal and on the motives and methods of his or her crime rather than on the detective. The most notable *literary* examples I know are Ira Levin's *A Kiss Before Dying* and C. S. Forester's *Payment Deferred,* both of which received less than satisfactory film treatment.

Blood Simple consists of unmistakable variations on the plot of *Double Indemnity.* Taken together, the two films explore most of the possible changes on the "eternal triangle" of hus-

band, wife, and lover. In *Double Indemnity,* it is the ruthless wife (Barbara Stanwyck) and her lover (Fred MacMurray) who plot the murder of the husband; in *Blood Simple,* the plotter is the husband, but a fourth character, a relentless investigator (a variation on Edward G. Robinson's claims manager in *Double Indemnity*), throws a monkey wrench into the machinery. Borrowings from other notable movie thrillers show up throughout. Thus, this fourth character is clearly modeled on Hank Quinlan, the corrupt cop in *Touch of Evil* (1958), and he carelessly drops his cigarette lighter at the scene of the crime—a gratuitous "quote" from Hitchcock's *Strangers on a Train* (1951).

> *Blood Simple* **has nothing to offer that hasn't been done superlatively well before.**
> —*Harry M. Geduld*

Without revealing more of the plot, suffice it to say that most of *Blood Simple*'s ingenuities are predictable and that, where *Double Indemnity* provided suspense, *Blood Simple* gives us merely shock and gore. The mounting tension and anxiety created in *Double Indemnity* depended upon our identifying with the two killers. To ensure this, Wilder first established them as fascinating characters who are suddenly, irresistibly caught up in a passionate affair. When they turned from adultery to murder, our inextricable involvement with them made us want desperately to see them succeed—so that when, for example, their getaway car failed to start, *their* panic inevitably became *ours.* By contrast, a parallel situation in *Blood Simple* evoked nothing from me but scorn for the stupidity of a murderer who would drive into the middle of a ploughed field to bury his victim, leaving half a mile of tire tracks for the police to trace. Apart from that, this character—like everyone else in *Blood Simple*—appears too "crummy" (to use a favorite word of my eight-year-old) to arouse empathy. It's impossible to get worked up over a couple of lackluster lovers, a jealous husband with a permanent scowl on his face, and a tired imitation of Orson Welles. *Blood Simple* has nothing to offer that hasn't been done superlatively well before.

Eric Pooley (review date 23 March 1987)

SOURCE: "Warped in America," in *New York,* Vol. 20, No. 12, March 23, 1987, pp. 44, 46-48.

[*In the following review, Pooley discusses the Coens' film production methods.*]

It's the last week of February, and 400 people have turned up at the Gotham theater for a screening of a comedy called

Raising Arizona. The film has excellent word of mouth, and a host of industry types, including director Jonathan Demme, are on hand to see it—but Joel Coen, 32, who directed and co-wrote the film, is not among them. Neither is his brother, Ethan, 29, who produced and co-wrote it. Instead of seeing what people think of their second movie (their first was the stylish, godless cult hit **Blood Simple**), the brothers are on their way across town, to a small screening of a film called *Evil Dead 2: Dead by Dawn.*

When the Coens slouch into the lobby before the horror film begins, a man spots them. "Hey," he says. "I thought you guys'd be at the other movie."

"Nah," says Joel, flicking some hair out of his face. "We've seen that one."

Actually, they've seen this one too. But the Coens hate to be the center of attention; and they hate watching their own movies—they waited in the lobby during a 1984 New York Film Festival screening of **Blood Simple.** And besides, *Evil Dead 2,* directed by their friend Sam Raimi, is a hoot—a series of inventive chain-sawings, shotgunnings, and battles with the demons from Beyond.

"Heh, heh, heh," laughs Joel as a man is attacked by his own severed hand.

"Heh, heh, heh," laughs Ethan.

At one point, a character looks at someone who's been beaten senseless and says, "Crazy buck's gone *blood simple.*" A few people laugh. Joel and Ethan don't—they just sit in the dark, smiling.

When **Blood Simple** was released in 1985, the lives of Joel and Ethan Coen changed in a way that many would-be filmmakers dream about while sitting over someone else's moviola. Joel, an NYU film-school graduate from suburban Minneapolis, had spent years working on the fringes of the industry—editing mad-slasher flicks like *The Evil Dead,* working on rock-video crews. Ethan, who has a philosophy degree from Princeton, had moved to New York in 1979 and got a job as a typist at Macy's. They wrote **Blood Simple** in 1980, raised $750,000 for it in 1981, shot it in 1982, edited it in 1983, searched for a distributor in 1984, and finally released it in 1985—to almost universal acclaim and a place on several ten-best lists. A taut, redemptionless tale of death and double cross at a Texas roadhouse, **Blood Simple** is funny, disturbing, and outrageously self-conscious; *New York*'s film critic, David Denby, called it "one of the most brazenly self-assured directorial debuts in American film history." Steven Spielberg asked the Coens to come for a visit. Hugh Hefner invited them to his mansion.

In another way, though, the lives of the Coen brothers didn't change at all when **Blood Simple** came out. Joel didn't cut his hair, become polite to people he didn't like, or start hanging around with Hollywood directors. Ethan still avoided parties—not because he was shy, but because he wasn't interested. The Coens remained aloof from both the big studios and the arty independent-film scene, preferring the company of directors like Raimi. "The boys"—as their friends call them—didn't want to make pictures for Spielberg, and Hefner and his mansion were a joke to them. They signed a four picture deal with an independent production company, not a studio, because the deal gave them complete creative control, and controlling the process of moviemaking was all that mattered.

"The boys live to make movies," says their friend and cinematographer, Barry Sonnenfeld. "Money isn't important to them, except to make movies. They never want to be in a position where anyone has any power to tell them what to do. They could make more by going with a studio, but I don't believe they ever will. And that's intimidating to a lot of people in the business. It's frightening that two people can be that self-contained."

In fact, it is sometimes hard to tell where one Coen ends and the other begins. "They're like identical twins," says Sonnenfeld. "Alike, but very different."

"It's the yin and yang of one being," says Raimi. Joel, with dark, deep-set eyes and an air of rude mischief, is brilliant in a quiet, absentminded, artistic way. Ethan, with finer features and an even quieter air, is brilliant in a more analytical way. Ethan reads all the time; Joel is more visual. They pace the floor in step with each other, chain-smoke the same brand (Camel Lights), and share a telepathic sense of humor—they'll laugh at a joke without bothering to say it aloud. They are, together, an autonomous filmmaking unit. "Joel is theoretically the director and Ethan is theoretically the producer," says Sonnenfeld, "but they both do everything." Sonnenfeld was talking about the Coens to actress-director Penny Marshall not long ago. "They're so easy to work with," he said. "It's like working with one person."

"Sure," said Marshall. "One of them's mute."

Now, with their second film getting great notices, the brothers seem even more intimidating: They appear capable of making any kind of movie they want. Where **Blood Simple** is dark, deliberate, and frightening, **Raising Arizona** is bright, lively, and hilarious. It's also sweet—the story of a sleepy convenience-store robber named H.I. (Nicolas Cage) and his ex-cop wife Ed (Holly Hunter) who steal a baby because, as H.I. says in his oddly formal, TV-preacher way, "Her insides were a rocky place where my seed could find no purchase." The movie is all over the place: It's full of broad physical comedy (fights that become pro-wrestling parodies, shoot-outs in supermarkets). There are scores of sight gags, comic set pieces, and memorable bit parts; there's a Mad Biker of the Apocalypse who rides his Harley from H.I.'s nightmare into reality, tries to recover the stolen child, and gets blown to pieces at the end. As writers, directors, producers, and editors, the Coens—even in humorous excess—are in complete control.

"We wanted to make something different than *Blood Simple,*" says Joel.

"After that one," says Ethan, "we were labeled *film noir.*"

"So this time," says Joel, "we wanted to make one that was—"

"*Sui generis,*" says Ethan.

In *Blood Simple,* there's a fifteen-minute stretch without a word of dialogue in which the dumb, woman-crazy bartender played by John Getz finds his boss dead and decides that his lover (the boss's wife) did it. He drives the body to a wide-open field, discovers that it is still crawling, tries to kill it with a shovel, and finally buries it alive against a soundtrack of shoveling, hard breathing, and the wretched, inhuman moans of the victim disappearing beneath the Texas dirt. Denby called it "a sequence of which Hitchcock could be proud."

"After the body was covered with dirt," says Ethan, "that was me squirming under there. I'm proud of *that.*"

In *Raising Arizona,* there's a five-minute stretch without dialogue in which a wide-open, rain-soaked field gives birth—a head pops out of the ground, a man spits mud and scum from his mouth, starts bellowing, and hauls himself out of the slime. A tall, big-bellied guy, he dives back in and pulls out his little brother, another heavy load, feet first. The two dumb jailbirds Gale and Evelle Snopes are free, having tunneled out of prison through a sewer line, and they arch their backs and howl at the clouds.

The two scenes capture the difference between the two movies: *Blood Simple* is full of dumb, mean folks heading into the ground, and *Raising Arizona* is full of dumb, well-meaning folks trying to get *off* the ground—through their dreams, through their marriages, by having (or stealing) kids. But in other ways, the movies are alike. Both are full of exhilarating camera work—giddy tracking shots that hop over drunks and climb ladders, the kind of work that has always been found, not coincidentally, in the exploitation horror flicks that the Coens love. And both are populated by those dumb folks—what the Coens call hay-seeds—rubes who blunder around without a clue as to what they're doing. Only the

Coens, in fact, ever really know what's going on in the worlds they create.

"There was a lot of talk about hayseeds on the set," says John Goodman, who plays Gale Snopes, the older brother. "We had some laughs at their expense."

"The boys move their characters around to create effects," says Sonnenfeld. "Put them where things can happen to them to scare the audience, or amuse it." As a result, they have been accused of cold, detached filmmaking—the Coens' favorite *Blood Simple* review says the film has "the heart of a Bloomingdale's window and the soul of a resumé." But the brothers do have their feeling side, and at the end of *Raising Arizona,* when H.I. has a sweet dream of the future, they produce their first truly emotional film moment—and promptly undercut it with a joke.

Sonnenfeld says, "I asked Ethan, 'Hey, did you guys really mean that stuff about love at the end?' He just gave me a look. I felt stupid for asking. And I never got the answer. They are emotionally hidden."

The Coens don't really know much about murdering people in Texas, or stealing babies in Arizona. They don't write from experience—"a movie about Minnesota people running around in snowsuits killing each other wouldn't be any fun," says Joel—and they don't research their pictures. Neither has children (Ethan is married; Joel lives with actress Frances McDormand, who is in both movies), but in *Raising Arizona,* they capture the baby-boomer's love for children and anxiety about having them: diptet shots, toddlers wrecking the mobile home, Dr. Spock's "instructions"—details that give the film richness. And in *Blood Simple,* they capture the soullessness of the best pulp fiction.

"A man crawls a mile with his brains blown out," the novelist Jim Thompson once wrote. "A man is hanged and poisoned and shot and he goes right on living." That's what *Blood Simple* is like—but the Coens hadn't read Thompson when they made the film. Somehow, growing up quietly in a placid, upper-middle-class suburb of Minneapolis, they had soaked up enough late-night dramas, James M. Cain thrillers, and tabloid headlines to fashion their very own vision. Like many suburban kids, their imaginations were fired by empty American landscapes, and by death.

"What I know about is Texas," they wrote in *Blood Simple,* even though they didn't. "And down here, you're on your own."

The Coens work out of a West 23rd Street industrial building full of printing and graphics shops. Taking the stairs to their sixth-floor room feels like a climb to the office of a private detective—dim light filters through the dust, voices are muffled behind steel doors. A body in the stairwell would not seem out of place. Their one-room office, with its dirty windows, framed portraits, and frosted-glass door, fits the picture, too, but the Coens themselves don't seem to. They are mild, inward: Joel sits, legs crossed, smokes, and talks quietly. Ethan sits, legs crossed, smokes, and talks hardly at all.

"We're not trying to educate the masses," says Joel.

"Does that make us bad people?" asks Ethan. They laugh. They hate talking film theory, like talking film technique, and love talking murder.

"Did you hear about the guy in Connecticut who put his wife in the wood chipper?" asks Joel.

"Heh, heh, heh," laughs Ethan.

"The cops said that one good rainfall would have washed her away," says Joel with satisfaction. "And they never would have found her." They pause a while and smoke in silence, pondering the cinematic possibilities.

"That was a good one," says Ethan.

"That *was* a good one," says Joel.

In the spring of 1980, Sam Raimi drove a station wagon from Detroit to New York, with the raw footage of *Evil Dead* in the backseat. He'd produced the film independently, raising money with a half-hour version he used to show (and sicken) investors. Now he was coming to edit the movie. "I'd never driven into New York before," says Raimi, "and I knew there'd be all sorts of hoodlums and bad characters about. When I pulled up to the building where the cutting room was, this guy came up to the car with long scraggly hair down his chest, looking undernourished. I thought he was trying to rip us off. That was my first meeting with Joel."

Coen had moved from Minneapolis—where his father is a University of Minnesota economics professor, his mother an art historian—to NYU in 1974. An average student in high school, he went to NYU "because it had a late application deadline—I missed all the others." After four desultory years there—"I made some movies, then some more"—he graduated and "chased a woman" to the University of Texas graduate film school in Austin. He quit after a semester, returned to New York, and took jobs as a production assistant and assistant editor.

"He was the world's worst P.A.," says Sonnenfeld, who hired him for some industrial jobs he was working on in those days. "He got three parking tickets, came late, set fire to the smoke machine." He was better in the cutting room, and

spent four months there with Raimi, editing *Evil Dead.* Soon the two of them, with Ethan, were writing scripts in the Riverside Drive apartment the Coens shared.

"Writing with them was like watching a badminton game," says Raimi. "Joel would mention a line of dialogue, and Ethan would finish the sentence. Then Joel would say the punch line, and Ethan would type it up." When things weren't clicking, they would pace, following each other in designated tracks. "I could subtly torture them," says Raimi, "by altering the speed of my pace."

At about that time, the brothers were working on a script of their own, one that took place in the barren roads and road houses Joel had seen around Austin. To raise money, they made a slick two-minute "coming attraction" trailer for a movie that didn't exist. They shot it during a long weekend— it was their first time shooting 35 mm. film. When they watched the footage the next day, Sonnenfeld thought it looked great. "But Joel only said, 'Okay, bye.' I was crushed. Later, I found out he was really excited, too. But because they don't need compliments, they don't realize other people do. That's another thing that gets people mad at them. They never notice."

Joel took the clip—a gun being loaded, a man being buried alive, gunshots being fired through a wall and light streaming through the bullet holes—to Minneapolis, where he met a fund-raiser for Hadassah, the Jewish philanthropic organization. Armed, as Sonnenfeld says, "with a list of the hundred richest Jews in town," he raised $750,000 in nine months.

When the Coens wrote their script, they had in mind the great character actor M. Emmet Walsh for the sweaty, snickering divorce detective Visser, who cracks jokes, kills, and sticks in the memory like gum to the heel of a boot. "When I read the script," says Walsh, "I said, 'This character is so much fun, I'll flesh him out and use him in an important movie six or seven years down the road.' Because no one was ever going to hear about this movie. At best, it would be the third bill at an Alabama drive-in."

Walsh met the Coens in Austin before shooting began. "These two scrawny kids. I said, 'You boys got rich parents who're puttin' up the money?' They showed me this two-minute film; I thought, What the hell is this? Then I saw the storyboards and the shooting schedule, and I realized they knew *exactly* what they were doing."

In a trailer on the set of **Raising Arizona,** Joel was about to say something to Nicolas Cage.

"Hey, Joe," said Ethan.

Joel turned to his brother. "Yeah, Eth, I know. I was gonna tell him." Ethan nodded. "And you just knew," says Sonnenfeld, who was there, "that each knew what the other was thinking. It happened literally every day."

"It's hard to figure just what Ethan's role is on the set," says Walsh, who has a fine cameo in *Raising Arizona.*

"He just smokes and whispers in Joel's ear," says John Goodman.

It's what they whisper about that counts. They talk in a film-buff's code—"Let's have a *Mean Streets* look" or "a *Love Boat* look." A spotlight that lighting designers call a "magenta kicker," the Coens refer to as "hell light."

They don't have money to spare—*Raising Arizona* was made for just $5 million—so they can't waste film on shots that won't make the final cut. The key is a long and meticulous preproduction process that begins with the script. When Joel and Ethan began to write *Raising Arizona,* in May 1985, they worked in a disciplined, visual way, and when they were through, the result was a lean shooting script—a blueprint with no excess. Reading the script is like watching the movie—the thing emerged so fully formed from their imaginations that little changed between typewriter and camera.

In August, they began the period of casting and technical preparation, which takes them almost twice as long as it takes other filmmakers. "If I were a producer," says Sonnenfeld, "I'd have my director take as much preproduction time as they do. It's the cheapest way to make movies."

In December, Joel, Ethan, and Sonnenfeld sat down with a storyboard artist to draw what the camera would see in each shot of the movie. (Another film-maker who storyboarded that obsessively was named Hitchcock.) The Coens knew 90 percent of the shots going into the session; "we wouldn't have written the scenes," says Joel, "if we didn't know how we were going to shoot them." The storyboard session defines the look of the movie, and also its pacing; it is the time when each scene is constructed shot by shot, setup by setup, and it is arguably the most creative moment in a Coen film. "By the time you get on their set," says Walsh, "they've got it worked out like a commercial shoot—preplanned to the *n*th degree. They *never* went to work without knowing what they were up to. To the point where if you made a suggestion, it almost got in the way."

"If we didn't preplan it," says Joel, "I don't think we'd be able to handle the pressure. I couldn't walk out there without knowing just what I was after. I'd flounder, and the movie would get away from me, and I'd face the horror of watching it veer off into the ditch. There's no way to stop it

at that point—it's impossible to wrestle back on course. It's got its own . . . horrible momentum." They both break into eerie laughter, the kind they spilled out during *Evil Dead 2.*

When the Coens start filming, they love to come up with cheap, jury-rigged solutions to filmmaking problems. ("A USC film graduate has to solve a problem, he calls his uncle at Universal," says Walsh. "The Coens do it themselves.") A studio would rent a huge crane to film a complicated tracking shot, but the Coens use a "shaky cam"—a camera mounted on a twelve-foot beam, Joel on one end, Ethan on the other, running the thing while the camera rolls. Or a "blankey cam"—Sonnenfeld on his belly on a blanket, dragged along while he films. The idea is to do things in the simplest, least expensive way—to get as many camera setups as possible, to allow the brothers as many editing options as possible. Judging by the result, it works. And as long as it keeps working, they'll be happy—two brothers, playing together.

"We're not really habitués of Nathan's," says Joel, eating with his brother in the Times Square hot-dog joint. "We like Flamers on 42nd Street—but that burned down—or Harvey's, the lunch counter at Woolworth's." They enjoy their dogs, though, and admire the security force. "I like a restaurant," says Joel, "where six-foot-four guards swing clubs." Then Ethan gets an idea.

"Hey," he says. "Let's go ride the elevators at the Portman."

The Mariott Marquis, the futurist-suburban atrium hotel designed by John Portman, was the object of considerable scorn when it touched down in Times Square in 1985; the Coens love the place. When the hotel opened, they would invade it to ride the glass elevators that glide up the outside of the grooved-cement shaft scaling the center of the 37-story atrium. And tonight, after Nathan's, the Coens do it again.

"Doesn't it look like a Ridley Scott set?" says Joel, referring to the *Blade Runner* director, "before decay has set in?" They're leaning against a balcony in the lobby, gazing up at the soundless elevators slipping out of sight. "Imagine what this will look like in twenty years, with a layer of grime, this obsolete vision of the future. People will say, 'What could they have been thinking of?'"

"Wouldn't this be a great place to shoot a low-budget thriller?" says Ethan.

"Let's *ride,*" says Joel.

Inside the elevator, they smile and stare down as the thing slides up 37 stories. At the top, they get out, lean over a balcony rail, and peer down at the lobby floor. "Tempted to spit?" asks Joel.

Back in the elevator, they are joined by two young brothers—perhaps eight and eleven—for the voyage back. And the two sets of brothers ride down the elevator, noses pressed to glass, happy just to be riding.

David Edelstein (essay date April 1987)

SOURCE: "Invasion of the Baby Snatchers," in *American Film,* Vol. 12, April, 1987, pp. 26-30, 56.

[*In the following essay, Edelstein describes a visit to the set of* Raising Arizona.]

If you've ever left something on the roof of a car and then realized the goof several miles down the road, you'll get a kick out of a bit in ***Raising Arizona,*** Joel and Ethan Coen's farce about a babynapping and its aftermath. What's left on the car roof is an infant, and when the awful truth is discovered, the occupants—a pair of escaped convicts—make a squealing 180-degree turn and go barreling back to where the babe has presumably landed. Cut to the infant in his carseat in the center of the blacktop, staring offscreen with gurgling, Gerber-baby glee, while, behind him, the vehicle rushes in at ninety miles an hour, screeching to a halt about an inch from his little head. And the kid is still smiling.

This is how the guys behind the ghoulish ***Blood Simple*** invade the American mainstream: The kid is so *cuuute* and the gag so felicitous that you hardly register the perversity. In ***Raising Arizona,*** a young hayseed couple—ex-con H.I. "Hi" (Nicolas Cage) and police booking officer Edwina "Ed" (Holly Hunter)—learn they cannot have a child. (As narrator Hi puts it, "Her insides were a rocky place where my seed could find no purchase.") In desperate need of a baby to complete their blissful, suburban existence, they shanghai one of the newborn Arizona quintuplets, sons of Nathan Arizona (Trey Wilson), an unpainted-furniture baron.

In a world where moviemakers often inflate themselves and their motives, Joel and Ethan Coen—thirty-two and twenty-nine, respectively, both childless but presumably fertile—take the opposite approach: They talk coolly about craftsmanship and storytelling, and little else. With ***Raising Arizona,*** the Coens say, they wanted to make a film as different from ***Blood Simple*** as possible—galloping instead of languorous, sunny instead of lurid, genial and upbeat instead of murderous and cynical.

"It's not an emotional thing at all," says Barry Sonnenfeld, their cinematographer. "Given any topic, they could write an excellent script. Topics are incredibly unimportant to them—it's structure and style and words. If you ask them

for their priorities, they'll tell you script, editing, coverage, and lighting."

When pressed for their attraction to the *subject*—babies, child-rearing, images of the family—the Coens squirm and smoke and do their best in the face of so irrelevant a question. We're in a small Greek coffee shop near Joel's Manhattan apartment, where, in less than half an hour, they have smoked three cigarettes apiece; the air in the room has grown so foggy that we seem to have drifted out to sea.

Finally, out of the cloud, Joel speaks: "You have a scene in a movie when someone gets shot, right? Bang! And the squib goes off and the blood runs down and you get a reaction, right? It's movie fodder, you know what I mean? And in a really different way, a baby's face is movie fodder. You just wanna take elements that are good fodder and do something different with them." He laughs—a reassuring laugh, like old bedsprings—and turns to his brother. "Wouldn't you say that's basically it?"

"Yeah," says Ethan, deadpan, "it's like a real cheap and shameless bid at making a *commercial* movie. We decided to sell out and that was the first decision."

If the Coens are tight-lipped and ironic with interviewers, perhaps it's because they themselves can't account for the warmth and integrity of their movie. "That's your job," suggests Ethan, helpfully.

They don't make it easy. Few journalists are allowed on the ***Raising Arizona*** set, and when I arrive, there isn't a lot to see. It's the end of a thirteen-week shoot, and all I get to watch is part of a chase scene in a supermarket: There's no dialogue, the shots have been meticulously storyboarded, and the only real challenges are those facing the special-effects people. (I spend a lot of time watching them blow popcorn and cereal out of an air cannon.)

But I'm lucky to be there at all, and it's hard to blame the Coens for their wariness of the press. No one paid any attention to them when they made ***Blood Simple*** on $1.5 million—money they raised themselves from private investors, most in the vicinity of their hometown, Minneapolis. Sometimes their crew consisted of one person, Barry Sonnenfeld. ***Raising Arizona,*** while no biblical epic, cost four times as much, sports a full roster of production assistants, and is being released by a major studio, Twentieth Century-Fox.

"The attitude on ***Blood Simple,***" says Sonnenfeld, "was 'Just go for it, 'cause if we screw it up, no one will know about it, it'll be just one more unreleased movie.' I still take chances, but there's no question we're more scared."

By this point in the shoot, however, Joel and Ethan seem

anything but antsy. (The Coens co-wrote the script; Joel is nominally the director, Ethan the co-producer with Mark Silverman.) Although I have agreed in advance not to way-lay them, they're happy to make small talk—or, in this case, baby talk.

"The babies were great," says Ethan, of the most potentially problem-ridden scene, in which Hi swipes Nathan, Jr. (T. J. Kuhn), from the nursery and accidentally liberates the other infants.

"We kept firing babies when they wouldn't behave," says Joel. "And they didn't even know they were being fired, that's what was so pathetic about it."

What gets a baby fired?

"Some of them took their first steps on the set," says Joel. "Ordinarily, you'd be pretty happy about something like that, but in this case it got them fired."

"They'd make the walk of shame," in-tones Ethan.

"The parents were horrified. One mother actually put her baby's shoes on backward so he wouldn't walk."

We're in a supermarket in Tempe, Arizona, in the middle of a long, flat stretch of shopping centers outside Phoenix. In keeping with the movie's visual motif of aggressive bad taste, the female extras shop with curlers in their hair and let out sustained shrieks; as Hi dodges their carts, a red-faced manager pulls out a shotgun and starts blasting. No babies are involved, but a pack of dogs have chased Hi into the supermarket. Early on, it's clear that if you're ever pursued by angry dogs, the absolute best move would be ducking into a supermarket—the animals don't have much traction on those shiny floors and get easily traumatized.

"This is worse than when we had babies," says Ethan. "At least with babies, you could smack them around. People are afraid to hit dogs."

The Coens remain calm, laid-back. Joel, the taller, has nearly shoulder-length hair and dangling arms; ten or fifteen years ago, the look was vintage pothead. Ethan, unshaven, lighter, and more compact, divides his gaze between the action and the floor, pacing between shots and grinding out cigarettes. Synchronicity is the key: Sonnenfeld has compared them to a two-man ecosystem; and while they do communicate through tiny signals and monosyllables, they seem to be the recipients of what Mr. Spock would term a "Vulcan mind meld."

Jim Jacks, executive producer, narrates their trademark pas de deux: "You watch Ethan walk in a circle this way and

Joel walk in a circle that way; each knows exactly where the other is and when they'll meet. Then they go to Barry."

This is also how the Coens write; they don't make films so much as pace them out. (Asked where the confidence to make movies comes from, Ethan replies, "Every little step considered one at a time is not terribly daunting.") Ethan, the more silent and cryptic of the two, majored in philosophy at Princeton, and the contrast between his placid demeanor and the nicotine-fueled churnings of his brain gives pause. The computer in his head seems to try out hundreds of moves before it ever lets him do anything.

Between setups, the brothers take turns on a decent game of Ms. Pac-Man. They're going a little stircrazy by now; Scottsdale, where they've been settled for the last few months, seems (as actress Frances McDormand puts it) like a big golf course; and the nearby desert, though magnificent, is not reliably soul-quenching.

Nicolas Cage sits in silence next to the book rack, idly flipping through magazines. On his canvas chair, a Band-Aid separates "Nic" from "olas," the offending "h" obscured. Cage is touchy about misspellings of his first name, and, in a soothing (and poetic) gesture, Ethan ministered to the hurt. That's what producers are for.

Reluctant to discuss his methods, Cage is clear about his goals. He arrives on the set with a ton of ideas; even in the uncomplicated supermarket chase, he proposes a glance at his watch during a tiny lull. Joel politely shakes off the suggestion. Their relationship has been bumpy but respectful. Cage praises the brilliant script and the Coens' professionalism, but he's clearly miffed that he couldn't bring more to the party. "Joel and Ethan have a very strong vision," he says, "and I've learned how difficult it is for them to accept another artist's vision. They have an autocratic nature."

A few minutes after the interview, Cage summons me back. "Ah, what I said about Joel and Ethan . . . with relatively new directors, that's when you find that insecurity. The more movies they make, the more they'll lighten up. The important thing is not to discourage an actor's creative flow."

Not all the actors feel their flow was dammed, however. Holly Hunter, a friend of Joel and Ethan's (inspired by her ramrod Southern tenacity, they wrote the part of Ed for her), insists she always held the reins, but could rely on Joel as a safety net. "Joel and Ethan function without their egos," she says. Then, thinking it over, she amends, "Or maybe their egos are so big they're completely secure with anybody who disagrees with them."

That sounds more like it. "You can convince Joel and Ethan

of things," says Sonnenfeld. "I find the best thing to do is bring up your point, drop it, and wait a couple of days."

The Coens radiate confidence, and you can bet their young, nonunion crew picks up on it. The set ("remarkably sex and drug free," I'm told) behaves like a winning clubhouse—kids just up from the minors who know they'll top the standings by season's end. The tone is relaxed but superefficient. In return for artistic control, the Coens are determined to stay on schedule. "They worry more about going over budget than we do," says Ben Barenholtz, who signed both to a four-picture deal with Circle Releasing Company (producers of **Blood Simple**). Fox has left them alone; the day after I arrive, executive vice-president Scott Rudin flies in to see his first set of dailies.

To say the Coens come prepared to shoot is to understate the case. The script has been rubbed and buffed, the shots storyboarded. On the set they rarely improvise; Joel insists that when you make a movie for so little money, you can't afford to mess around. It's strange, then, to hear him rhapsodize about Francis Coppola, a director who can't seem to work without a crisis, hammering out scenes and shots on the spot. "I have no idea how you can go into a movie without a finished script," Joel admits.

Sitting with Joel, Ethan, and Sonnenfeld in a Scottsdale Denny's before the next evening's shoot, the mood is as comfortable as one of those all-night bull sessions in *Diner.* The Coens aren't limo types, and it takes very little to make them happy—a pack of cigarettes, coffee, a warm Denny's. "When they're in work mode, creature comforts become minimal," says Frances McDormand, who played the heroine of **Blood Simple** and has lived with Joel for the past couple of years. (She was Holly Hunter's roommate before that, and has a brazen cameo in **Raising Arizona.**)

"They love the performance part of their job, like the minute you walk on a stage or the camera starts rolling. For them, the writing is one part of it, the budgeting and preproduction another, but it's all building toward the shoot. And then in postproduction, that's when they get to lead the artistic life: They get to stay up late and get circles under their eyes and smoke too much and not eat enough and be focused entirely on creating something. And then it starts again."

Truly, a design for living.

Joel and Ethan Coen grew up in a Jewish suburb of Minneapolis, the sons of two college professors—a father in economics, a mother in art history. (They have a sister, now a doctor.) Despite their ties to academia, they're almost perversely anti-intellectual about what they do; in fact, they insist that their home was short on high culture. Recalls Joel,

"My mother once wrote an article, 'How to Take Children to an Art Museum,' but I don't recall her ever taking us."

Instead, the children were left to their own devices, and weaned on pop culture and television; they set James M. Cain beside Aristotle, and among their most favorite film experiences, cite fifties and sixties sex comedies like *Boeing Boeing* and *Pillow Talk.* (For the record, they also love good movies.)

From the age of eight, Joel made films—remakes of pictures like *Advise and Consent*—and eventually went off to study filmmaking at New York University, where he's remembered for sitting in the back of the class and making snotty remarks. He says he learned almost nothing, but welcomed his parents' subsidy to make movies. (In his thirty-minute thesis film, *Soundings,* a woman makes love to her deaf boyfriend while verbally fantasizing about his buddy in the next room.) At Princeton, Ethan was equally out of step. After neglecting to notify the college that he planned to return from a term off, he tried to cut through the red tape with a phony doctor's excuse (from a surgeon at "Our Lady of the Eye, Ear, Nose, and Throat") that claimed he'd lost an arm in a hunting accident in his brother-in-law's living room. The school ordered him to see a shrink.

After film school, Joel worked as an editor on Sam Raimi's *The Evil Dead*—the *Don Giovanni* of hack-em-ups—and quickly struck up a friendship with Raimi, for whom he and Ethan wrote a script called *The XYZ Murders.* It was mangled and discarded by its studio, Embassy (and had a limited Columbia release as *Crime Wave*), a disaster that made the Coens more wary of dealing with major studios. "We've always let Sam make those mistakes for us," explains Joel. "'Sam', we tell him, 'you go do a movie at a studio and tell us what happens.'"

The Coens are pranksters, but colleagues also describe them as affable and generous, not to mention quick studies: They're fond of quoting entire scenes from other movies, along with lines from bad reviews. Their geniality doesn't come through in the rigid, Q & A format of interviews, though, and while promoting **Blood Simple,** their anarchic impulses came out. In their press conference at the 1985 New York Film Festival, for which **Blood Simple** had been selected, Ethan summed up their aesthetic by quoting Raimi: "The innocent must suffer, the guilty must be punished, you must drink blood to be a man."

"That's the great thing about Joel and Ethan," says Sonnenfeld. "They don't wanna be on the 'Today' show. They don't wanna be in *People.* They don't give a shit. They wanna have a good time."

My formal interviews with the Coens are, in some respects,

exercises in futility—me talking and Joel and Ethan smoking, their faces evoking Redford's response to Newman in *Butch Cassidy and the Sundance Kid:* "You just keep thinkin,' Butch. That's what you're good at." Maybe the questions are dumb, or maybe (as they insist) they're just dull guys, movies being their one step out. Perhaps they learned a lesson from their *Blood Simple* interviews. "We wince when we read ourselves in print," says Joel.

Like their movies, the Coens seem suspended between high and low impulses. Ethan studied philosophy, of course, but only "for fun"; there's something absurd, he implies, about being an intellectual in a culture this junky. Like Preston Sturges—one of their models for *Raising Arizona*—the Coens debunk all notions of aesthetic responsibility. Their movies poke fun at ideas, and their characters suffer from tunnel vision, each gripped by an obsession he or she can't be bothered to explain (nor, for that matter, can the Coens).

> The Coens insist that the last part of what they jokingly call their "Hayseed Trilogy" will be a long time in coming, but you can see what drew them to this part of the country to make their first films—the absurdity of mass-culture junkiness set against these parched, primal landscapes. Many of their gags spring from an innocent love of this culture (which they share with their characters) combined with wicked insight into its looniness.
> —*David Edelstein*

Perhaps they'd rather just listen. "Their favorite midtown lunch spot is the counter at Woolworth's," says editor Michael Miller. "They go to hear dialogue that will find its way into a script. The opening of *Blood Simple*—many of those lines they'd overheard. Their attention is never more riveted than when they're in the back seat of a taxi. I've seen Joel draw out taxi drivers in a way he doesn't draw out his friends. Once, on the way home from the airport, the driver had a ball game on—the Mets were playing someone and it was in the heat of the pennant drive—and Joel said, 'What's the game?' and the cabdriver said, 'Baseball, I think.' They loved that."

Found objects constitute much of the Coens' work. "It's not meant to be condescending," says Joel. "If the characters talk in clichés, it's because we like clichés. You start with things that are incredibly recognizable in one form, and you play with them."

The ingredients might be "movie fodder," but they resonate like crazy when the context is altered. The Coens' principal target is the way Americans conceal their self-interest behind apple-pie slogans and icons, sometimes unconsciously. At the start of *Blood Simple,* homilies about American individualism have a different kind of impact when the narrator is a killer and each character is fatally locked into his or her point of view. In *Raising Arizona,* Hi and Ed return home with the kidnaped Nathan, Jr., and a banner in the living room reads, "WELCOME HOME SON." Ed clutches the infant to her breast and weeps, "I love him *so-ho-ho-ho* much," and Hi hauls out the camera and marks the occasion with a classic family portrait.

The Coens insist that the last part of what they jokingly call their "Hayseed Trilogy" will be a long time in coming, but you can see what drew them to this part of the country to make their first films—the absurdity of mass-culture junkiness set against these parched, primal landscapes. Many of their gags spring from an innocent love of this culture (which they share with their characters) combined with wicked insight into its looniness.

A charge implicit in the backlash against *Blood Simple* was that these film-school brats were condescending to the common folk. And, during the shoot of *Raising Arizona,* a Tempe paper got hold of the script and was dismayed to find the place portrayed as a hick town, the film's set and costumes in studiously bad taste. "Of course it's not accurate," says Ethan. "It's not supposed to be. It's all made up. It's an Arizona of the mind."

All their impersonal talk of structure can't conceal the pleasure Joel and Ethan get out of cracking each other up, a pleasure that transcends their devotion to craft, their immaturity as artists. "They laugh hysterically at their own stuff," says Sonnenfeld. "The only person Joel cares about pleasing is Ethan."

"We didn't have that much to do with each other as kids," says Joel. "We kind of rediscovered each other after college, really through making movies." The joy of that rediscovery—of shared assumptions, of a cultural foundation—binds their gags together in ways they're not always conscious of. And that joy pulls us in, too. In a Joel and Ethan Coen movie, we love being in on the joke.

"They're genuinely surprised when people like their films," says Ben Barenholtz. "I remember Joel walked out of a *Blood Simple* screening and started laughing. 'They really liked it,' he said." And Barenholtz imitates Joel shrugging broadly.

I saw the shrug recently, in that same Greek coffee shop. Ethan talks about a test screening of *Raising Arizona* in Fort Worth, Texas, where a woman said, "You depicted very accurately the mentality of Texas prisoners. I ought to know. I spent eight and a half years in a Texas penitentiary. I did some things I shouldn't have."

Joel laughs and shrugs: There isn't a germ of authenticity in the prison scenes. But there's one thing he's forgetting. Mass culture penetrates prisons, too. She'd probably seen all the same movies.

David Handelman (essay date 21 May 1987)

SOURCE: "The Brothers from Another Planet," in *Rolling Stone,* May 21, 1987, pp. 59, 61, 114, 117.

[*In the following essay, Handelman provides a behind-the-scenes look at the Coen brothers at work, both on the set and during the writing process.*]

Pacing and smoking, pacing and smoking, in their rented house, Joel and Ethan Coen are waiting for the phone to ring. Every time Ethan finishes a cigarette, he mutters, "Butt me, butt me." Joel occasionally stops at the window to scream at Los Angeles, a visceral but controlled scream of rage. It is 1984; after writing the film-noir-like *Blood Simple* in 1980, raising funds for it in 1981, directing it in 1982 and editing it in 1983, the Coen brothers were broke. They flew from New York to Los Angeles with the reels of *Blood Simple,* fairly confident that the artful thriller would find a distributor.

"We brought the film around to all these different studios and had 'em bone us," Joel says today, "Sat there and listened to their garbage." During one meeting, a studio chief kept spitting sunflower-seed shells into a cuspidor behind his desk. He suddenly interrupted his barrage to ask, apropos of nothing, "Why is *Revenge of the Nerds* making so much money?" The brothers exchanged a quizzical look. On the way out, Ethan said, 'If there's anything else you want to know about the movie business feel free to call me." The executive stared at Ethan then threw his head back and screamed with laughter, slapping Ethan on the back so hard that he knocked over a chair and slammed into the wall.

This sort of encounter was typical. Hollywood was hot for the Coens—maybe they'd like to direct *Psycho III*?—but nobody wanted to distribute *Blood Simple.* The word was it was too gory to be an art film, too arty to be an exploitation film, funny but not quite a comedy.

So the brothers just hung out. They killed time concocting "thought experiments"—high-concept movies they'd have liked to see but didn't want to bother making. The most telling remnant from their stay in L.A. is a thought experiment they hatched there called *Adolf "Terry" Hitler,* which re-

writes history thusly: Hitler's parents emigrate to America at the turn of the century and head west. Young Adolf grows up and becomes a big Hollywood agent nicknamed Terry, running the Adolf Hitler Agency (AHA); he wears baggy suits and takes lunches at Mortons, waving to everyone and reading *People* magazine.

Unsurprisingly, when *Blood Simple* finally found a distributor, it was Circle Releasing, a small company based in Washington, D.C., not in the Coens' beloved Los Angeles. The studios missed out on a prestigious project, that had the critics gushing and won a Grand Jury Prize at the United States Film Festival, the independent filmmakers' equivalent of the Oscars.

These days, the Coens and Hollywood seem to have figured each other out. As soon as the studios saw the script for the brothers' second movie, *Raising Arizona,* they scrambled to buy distribution rights from Circle, and Twentieth Century Fox won out. *Arizona* reached the screen an ingeniously executed gonzo caper, starring Nicolas Cage as the petty thief H.I. McDonnough and Holly Hunter as his policewoman sweetheart, Ed. After they marry, Ed learns that she's barren, and they kidnap a quintuplet named Nathan Arizona Jr., reasoning that his parents have "more than they can handle."

Full of the same showy camera work and slightly dim characters as *Blood Simple, Raising Arizona* also tosses in slam-bang mass-appeal elements like car chases, a biker from hell and cute babies. Most critics were bowled over, calling it "a deranged fable of the New West" (*New York*) and "exuberantly-original" (*Time*). *Vanity Fair* said, "The brothers seem to be having a ball, and inviting crashers."

The biggest fear shared by Fox, Circle and the Coens was that *Arizona*—stylized, difficult to classify and lacking big-name stars—would perform like *Blood Simple,* filling a few art houses and little more. But as *Arizona* opened gradually around the country ("platformed," in movie-business lingo), the box-office returns quashed those fears. Joel, 32, and his little brother, Ethan, 29, didn't go Hollywood: they made Hollywood come to them.

The Coen brothers could be a deadpan vaudeville act performed by a two-headed creature from some low-budget sci-fi flick. Both are pencil skinny, shave only every four or five days and wear glasses and Levi's. Joel is taller, a little more sociable; he recounts tales with exuberant sound effects. Ethan is quieter, more the word man—a Scrabble fiend who has been known to bring paperback books to parties. They don't take drugs; in bars they usually order Cokes. They don't always agree, but their disagreements are never personal. A favorite pastime is testing each other on arcane trivia, like the ingredients on a ketchup bottle. When working, they often take phone calls together, finishing each other's sentences, prompting each other's anecdotes or just wallowing in protracted, nicotine-fueled pauses.

If it's a shtick, it's a twenty-four-hour-a-day one; the Coens both border on being space cadets. When Joel drives, says their cinematographer, Barry Sonnenfeld, "he literally stops at green lights and finally, for no apparent reason sees the light turn red and steps on the gas." They live as cheaply as they work, taking the subway and subsisting on coffee shop chow. Until recently, only Joel had a checking account, and neither one had a credit card. Joel still doesn't: "American Express rejected me."

The Coens grew up in Minneapolis which has a lot to do with their off-center, slowed-down sensibility. (Their parents, Ed and Rena, are college professors; their older sister, Debbie, is a doctor in Israel.) Forced to amuse themselves in America's Arctic, they warmed themselves by the TV, developing a shared taste for kitsch as they sat through hours of wooden epics on *Mel Jass' Matinee Movie.* They filmed a Super 8 make of *Advise and Consent* and originals like *Lumberjacks of the North.* "We owned a couple of plaid shirts," explains Ethan.

But Minnesota's grayness closed in. "I wanted to get as far away as possible as fast as possible," says Joel. He left for Simon's Rock College, in Massachusetts, and then studied film at New York University; Ethan went to Princeton and majored in philosophy. They hadn't hung out together much since they were kids, but around 1980 Ethan moved to an apartment in New York near his brother.

Joel had already been married and divorced ("There was no ugliness and no money," he says) and was assistant-editing slasher moves like *The Evil Dead* and *Fear No Evil.* Ethan was temping as a statistical typist at Macy's. "It was a long road that had no end," he says. So they began writing scripts nights and weekends, selling one, a black comedy called *Suburbicon.* Seeing other directors lose creative control of even low-budget movies, Joel decided to finance his first directorial effort, ***Blood Simple,*** himself; he returned to Minnesota, scraping up pledges of $550,000 from sixty-eight investors in bits as small as $5,000. (The final budget was $855,000 plus $187,000 in deferred costs.) To get by, the boys bummed endless loans from friends.

In Austin, Texas, on October 4th, 1982, they started shooting a feature film, an understandably surreal experience for two guys whose last joint effort was in Super 8. "Joel still had this film-school view" says Barry Sonnenfeld, "that he and Ethan would be up late at night making peanut-butter sandwiches for the crew." But they had something other directors didn't: a second head. Though Joel was nominally the director and Ethan the producer, it was more a tag-team

effort. They defied the adage about being in two places at once; if one wandered off, the other could be on the set checking a camera angle.

After filming, the Coens ran out of money, and during re-shoots they were forced to stand in for the actors; then, too broke to hire anyone, they edited the movie themselves, taking pseudonymous credit in the titles as Roderick Jaynes. Joel says, "We still feel a strange, juvenile thrill when that name comes on the screen, like we pulled something off."

It's the spring of 1985, and the Coens are writing ***Raising Arizona,*** holed up in the musty ground-floor Upper West Side apartment that Joel has inhabited since college.

"You wanna doughnut?" asks Ethan, offering Joel an open box of chocolate glazed. His shirt still has its Salvation Army price tag stapled to the collar.

Singing, "Papa-oom-mow-mow," Ethan pads in his stocking feet over the dusty floor to the kitchen, where the coffee water is boiling in a tin pot. Tacked to the bulletin board are a HOW TO HELP A CHOKING VICTIM poster, an autographed picture of Wink Martindale and some Polaroids a friend took of the TV when the Coens were on the *Today* show promoting ***Blood Simple.*** They sat slumped, smoking, making comments like "Ooh, that was exciting" during film clips. Off camera, Jane Pauley told Ethan he ought to be spanked.

Ethan starts his pace pattern, walking brisk laps through the kitchen into the spacious living room and out again and making occasional raspberry noises.

Joel sits, his Reebok-shod feet up on the metal desk, smoking.

Ethan, continuing to pace, asks, "Cut to the car?"

Joel says, "They're taking their car, right?"

Ethan says, "Why not his?" He halts and sits at the desk, leafing through what they've written so far: twenty-seven pages. The Coens write scripts without an outline, painting themselves in and out of corners "Wildy style." According to Joel, Mack Sennett's silent-film studio employed certified lunatics called Wildies, who would come to script meetings and blurt out crazy, non sequitur plot ideas, which Sennett would often use.

Ethan turns on the Smith-Corona portable, which buzzes. He folds his arms across the top and buries his head, as if trying to feel the words emanating from the machine.

Buzz, goes the typewriter.

Slowly, Ethan begins laughing to himself. It starts as a hiccup, grows to a wheezing heehaw and explodes into snorts.

"What?" Joel asks. "What? What?"

"As soon as he realizes they're not gonna go with him, he starts screaming. . . ."

Joel chews this over. Ethan turns off the typewriter, noodles on its plastic keys, stands up and starts pacing. Joel says, "What do you think Eeth? We barking up the wrong tree here?"

"Ah, I dunno." Ethan hiccups, cartoon style. Joel absent-mindedly opens a desk drawer. Ethan shuts it and says, "We could have him run away; he puts his head down and runs around the corner of the building, presses himself up against the wall, close-up of him like . . ." He breathes heavily. "He says, 'I won't ever run away again.'"

"You mean make him sort of a retard?" asks Joel. "Yeah," says Ethan.

Silence.

Joel starts singing, "I ain't gonna work on Maggie's faaarm no more . . ." Ethan starts pacing. The floor creaks. Outside on the street, cars pass.

"To me," Joel says, "that just wastes time."

Ethan returns from the kitchen, carrying a box of toothpicks. "You don't like it 'cause it's kind of senseless?"

"Yeah," says Joel. "When are we gonna shed some blood?"

Ethan grunts a small laugh. He reads the toothpick box. "You know what these toothpicks are made of?"

Joel gives it some consideration.

"Pine? Oak? Mahogany? I dunno."

"White birch."

"Really?"

"Yeah," says Ethan, picking up a small rubber ball and bouncing it. "What if the state trooper takes off after them?"

"Well, the chase scene I really want is where the baby gets thrown around in the car. I don't see that coming here."

Pause.

"Let's just figure out what they're doing," says Ethan.

"Yeah," says Joel, "that's what I'm trying to figure out." He stands up, jingling his key chain, and wanders over to the stereo cabinet. He picks up something lying on it. "Hey, Eeth; you know whose glove is this?"

After handing in the *Arizona* script to Circle, the brothers finally got some money, which they used to upgrade their lifestyles somewhat. Ethan moved downtown to a big sublet—more pacing space—with his girlfriend, Hilary, and traded in his tilted granny glasses for round wire rims. Joel had been dating *Blood Simple* star Frances McDormand, and she moved in with him. She redecorated the apartment in nouveau diner, disposing of Ethan's *Blood Simple* "souvenir"—a huge, bloodied wall used for the excruciating hand-stab scene.

The Coens also rented a share in a Chelsea office to force themselves to get some work done. One day in December of 1985, just before filming began on *Raising Arizona,* Ethan asked Joel, "Is it okay if I cut out early today?" Joel said, "Sure. What for?" Ethan said, "Hilary and I were thinking of going down to City Hall and getting married. Wanna come?"

"Sure" Joel said: He served as best man. Friends found out about the wedding later, on a need-to-know basis.

Vroom! Vroom! "You wanna move that muthafucka?" growls leather-clad giant Randall "Tex" Cobb from his motorcycle, leveling two prop sawed-off shotguns at a pickup truck full of spectators. The truck pulls away fast, and Tex, a former pro boxer who is playing the biker-from-hell character, Lenny Smalls, laughs uproariously. He turns to Joel and bellows, "You're working with a professional athlete. Try and keep your instructions simple."

It's February 1986, and the Coens are filming *Raising Arizona* in balmy Scottsdale. A waterworks is serving as a prison exterior, and Cobb is supposed to ride the motorcycle up to the edge of the hole from which H.I.'s prison buddies Evelle and Gale Snopes (William Forsythe and John Goodman) have escaped. But the scene has been dragging on forever, because rough guy Cobb is actually lousy on a bike and often misses his mark or stalls out.

Then on the next take the bike keeps rolling, falls in the hole and throws Cobb face down in the dirt. There's an ominous pause: if Cobb is injured, he's irreplaceable. Finally, the prostrate actor yells a muffled "Cut!" Joel grins and says "Print that take. I liked it."

The Coens seem to care most about amusing each other. After watching the rehearsal for a stunt in which Cage catches a knife with a plank, Joel calmly says, "My guess is that it won't work." Ethan replies, "That's what they said about the shuttle."

Beyond the gags, they remain inscrutable on the set. They rarely say hello to anyone, and for all the ambling, mumbling, smoking and joking, the Coens are as self-confident and focused as ace poker players. "Those boys are *absorbed*," says Holly Hunter.

They're also tense, because even before any film was shot, they'd already spent more than the entire ***Blood Simple*** budget. The friends whose careers they'd launched—co-producer Mark Silverman, cinematographer Sonnenfeld, production designer Jane Musky and associate producer and assistant director Deborah Reinisch—returned, but at substantially higher rates. The stunts, the larger cast and the better-equipped offices will eventually push costs over $5 million.

Yet the brothers' anxiety comes out in weirdly calm, wacky ways. The most demonstrative they get is when Joel remarks, "See what an incredible pain in the ass this is?" or Ethan addresses a problem by asking, "Is that, like, un-dealable-with?" Ethan keeps quitting and restarting smoking, endlessly chewing sticks of gum; Joel gets migraines, for which he pops an occasional prescription pill, and relaxes by pulling a yellow yo-yo from his pocket and "walking the dog."

During filming they maintain their telepathic rapport. "Joel and Ethan have their own language," says Hunter. "It goes with the level of concentration. Sometimes it's hard to penetrate; if I didn't know 'em, I might find it intimidating."

But they're not ego tripping; when someone can't start a prop car, Joel helps to push it. When Joel worries that a rubber stunt knife might hurt Cage, he tests it by sending Ethan a few yards away and winging it at him. Ethan plays a willing target, much like a kid obeying his big brother.

They do have their weaknesses. Although each shot has been carefully planned, Joel's instructions to actors are often as oblique as "This is an epic-romantic scene, y'know?" Fran McDormand, who plays Ed's overbearing friend Dot, says, "I can't imagine Joel ever making a movie that was actor oriented, like a *Sophie's Choice,* where you set up the camera and two actors just work together. He sets up a mood and talks about rhythm." Cage will later complain that he feels stymied—the Coens aren't taking his suggestions and at first didn't let him see the daily rushes.

Yet he plays along with every Looney Tune prank. Rehearsing the climactic fight with Tex Cobb, Cage falls on gravel and gashes his hand. He stumbles to his feet, looks around and drawls, "Can I get a Band-Aid—or at least a *"Curad?"*

Joel and Ethan double up with laughter—they've created another brother.

Although ***Blood Simple*** is generally perceived as a hit and the Coens hawked it on a grueling tour, it actually made only $5 million, less than the amount a blockbuster like *Lethal Weapon* makes its first weekend. So the brothers are understandably reluctant about hyping (or analyzing) *Arizona.* "It's always an ambition," says Joel, "no matter who you are, John Sayles or Steven Spielberg, that you want a lot of people to see your movie. I can't believe that Sayles wouldn't be happy if *Lianna* had grossed $400 million, right? But obviously his ambition isn't to go to Hollywood and make $25 million movies in a quest for that kind of gross. And I don't think our ambition is, either."

Big box office may not be their goal, but *Arizona* is making a bundle anyway and is an official entry (not in competition) at this year's Cannes Film Festival. The Coens, nonplused, are already pacing through their next script. When asked about it, Joel says, deadpan, "It's a hot, hot project."

One afternoon in April, a few weeks after the premiere of ***Raising Arizona,*** Ethan Coen is in Times Square to see a movie. Emerging into daylight, he's nearly run down by a tremendous, wailing cavalcade of Secret Service limousines, police cars and ambulances. He cocks his head and watches as sedan after sedan whizzes past. "Maybe Barry Diller is in town," he says.

Actually, it isn't the president of Fox—just the vice-president of the U.S. Ethan is happy to be outside of the limos looking in. He wanders to the subway stop and heads underground to meet up with Joel, eager to continue the private conversation that has been going on for twenty-nine years.

Tom Milne (review date Summer 1987)

SOURCE: "Hard on Little Things," in *Sight and Sound,* Vol. 56, No. 3, Summer, 1987, pp. 218-19.

[*In the review below, Milne provides a plot summary of* Raising Arizona.]

Joel Coen is an original, no doubt about that. A B-movie noir with the tang of nightmare terror, ***Blood Simple*** led one to suppose that his line of descent was by James M. Cain out of the horror comics. ***Raising Arizona*** offers no grounds for changing that view, except in suggesting that somewhere back along that heritage Antonin Artaud must have bred in the bloodlines of both the Theatre of Cruelty and the Theatre of the Absurd.

More comedy than thriller, **Raising Arizona** at first seems far removed from characteristic Cain territory, with its tale of a latter-day outlaw who decides to settle down and become an upstanding family man. It nevertheless echoes the device which Cain once described as the mainspring of his fiction: "I, so far as I can sense the pattern of my mind, write of the wish that comes true, for some reason a terrifying concept, at least to my imagination. . . I think my stories have some quality of the opening of a forbidden box."

The forbidden box opened by H.I. McDonnough (Nicolas Cage) in **Raising Arizona** is no less than the American Dream. A marvelous pre-credits sequence, executed strip-cartoon style in a series of rapid-fire tableaux, establishes Hi, a would-be outlaw branded with a Woody Woodpecker tattoo, as a sad sack criminal who gets arrested every time he attempts to rob a convenience store, then paroled because he uses empty guns for fear of hurting anyone. "I tried to stand up and fly straight," he explains mournfully, "but it wasn't easy with that sonofabitch Reagan in the White House." Emerging a three-time loser, he takes with him a wife in the shape of a policewoman (Holly Hunter) wooed and won during the three-time process of being photographed and fingerprinted.

Marriage, a home and a job follow naturally, but alas no children, since the policewoman proves barren. So what more natural in a land of consumer plenty than to steal one? Especially when newspaper accounts of the birth of quints to unpainted furniture king Nathan Arizona (Trey Wilson) feature the father's wry disclaimer, "More than we can handle!" No sooner has Hi proudly introduced his hijacked son to his new home and the mod cons of bedroom, kitchen and TV ("Two hours a day maximum, so you don't ruin your appreciation for the finer things") than the heavens open up in a storm of retribution. Turned into a sea of mud, the open ground in front of the prison heaves, and two prehistoric Frankenstein monsters erupt, turning into redneck convict escapees, former jailmates of Hi's, who elect to use his home as a hideout.

Once more poor Hi finds himself an outlaw, no longer able to accept the slobbishly amoral camaraderie of the underworld, not yet ready for the sophistications of decent society. On a visit with his wife (who proves an eager source of tips on motherhood) and bevy of children (who rampage on an orgy of destruction), Hi's boss Glen (Sam McMurray), reacting angrily to a punch on the jaw when he randily suggests a bout of wife-swapping, determines to turn Hi in as a kidnapper. Only to be forestalled when the two convicts (John Goodman, William Forsythe), reacting angrily when Hi's wife kicks them out of the house, decide to kidnap the baby themselves with a view to ransom. A Laurel and Hardy duo, surprisingly delicate in their social graces despite brutish manners, the pair haven't quite the heart to go through with it. Instead, discovering all sorts of frustrated paternal and maternal yearnings, they agonize over the advisability of leaving Nathan Junior in the getaway car while they raise finance by robbing a bank: "Suppose we go in there and get ourselves killed, it could be hours before he gets discovered."

Meanwhile, the forbidden box opened by Hi is still working its magic, and retribution is on the road in the fear-some person of the Lone Biker of the Apocalypse, a bearded aboriginal armed to the teeth and with features grimed by the fires of hell. First seen as a streak of fire burning up the highway as he shoots up wayside animals for the fun of it, the Lone Biker has accredited independent existence as Leonard Smalls (Randall "Tex" Cobb), a bounty-hunter who switches from escaped convicts to kidnaped baby; but an incredible subjective shot preceding the bike as it races at breakneck speed to a house, up a ladder and through the open window just as Hi wakes in the grip of a nightmare, establishes him as a force released by Hi's dream. Only when Hi defeats the Biker in desperate single combat, and subsequently returns the baby to its bereft parents, do the furies subside.

Raising Arizona is studded with set pieces that are wonderfully funny in their own right, like Hi's first attempt to steal the baby, only to have its siblings set up a sympathetic squall, which ends as a free-for-all of scuttling babies as, each one parked at random as another requires comfort, all five race around like demented cockroaches; or his equally frustrating attempt to steal a pack of nappies, which escalates into a balletic dance for fugitive, pursuing police, rabid dogs and vigilante gunman ("Son, you got a panty on your head," an elderly motorist interestedly remarks as the stocking-masked Hi tries to cadge an escape ride). But the reason that this *reductio ad absurdum* of Reagan's America works so beautifully is that while its characters do not bleed—the violence, with the biker finally blown into fragments, is pure *Tom and Jerry*—they have a surprisingly touching vulnerability.

The Lone Biker, so Hi's off-screen voice comments as a grenade casually demolishes a rabbit, is "especially hard on little things"; and there is a very real sense in which the characters are all children, childlike in their humors, whether these make them innocently demanding (Hi and the policewoman), irresponsible (the two convicts), naughtily spoilt (Glen and his wife), comfortably blasé (Nathan Arizona and his wife), or viciously destructive (the Lone Biker, whose secret Woody Woodpecker brand makes him Hi's long-lost brother). Mom and apple pie still rule the American dream, as one of the convicts recalls when he ticks Hi's wife off for not breast-feeding her baby ("He'll hate you for it later, that's why we wound up in prison"), and as the Lone Biker confirms through the tattoo on his arm ("Mama didn't love me"). Is the dream, on the other hand, worth standing up and flying straight for? The sting in the movie's tail is that when Hi has finally sorted himself out and joined society, his reward is a dream of future blessings in which he and his wife, now senior citizens, are surrounded by a mysterious family of children and grandchildren . . . the first generation of whom bear a suspiciously marked resemblance to wife-swapper Glen and his wife.

Rodney Hill (essay date Summer 1989)

SOURCE: "Small Things Considered: *Raising Arizona* and *Of Mice and Men*," in *Post Script,* Vol. 8, No. 3, Summer, 1989, pp. 18-27.

[*In the following essay, Hill suggests links between the themes of* Raising Arizona *and* Of Mice and Men, *comparing the psychological roles of their characters.*]

Little things mean a lot, we often hear. But the philosophy that "the best things come in small packages" is frequently rejected in America, where bigger is always called better— and where the biggest is definitely the best. Such a contradiction seems indicative of a fundamental cultural flaw: instead of embracing truly worthwhile (although perhaps small) values and goals, we adopt the more popular, less-thought-out, superficially "big" ideas. We seem to pride ourselves, as a culture, on size rather than quality: the size of our cars, our homes, and, in an era in which moviemakers often inflate themselves and their motives, even our movies. Independent filmmakers like Joel and Ethan Coen, though, seem to take the opposite approach and even to find great significance in the small things that do abound in American culture. Their first feature was itself a "small" work, a cheaply-made, modern *film noir, Blood Simple,* that quickly attracted a cult following. Its success paved the way for their mainstream comedy *Raising Arizona* which, despite its far larger budget, still has much of the small about it.

Raising Arizona is about a little man in the American scheme of things, a little man with small ambitions. H.I. McDunnough (Hi) is a small-time crook whose specialty is robbing convenience stores—seldom successfully. But what gives this far from unusual figure some resonance is the way the film connects him to one of the almost archetypal depictions of the little man in American literary history. The Coens' film is a pointed retelling of John Steinbeck's *Of Mice and Men,* a classic tale about downtrodden men who long to claim a piece of the American dream: the dimwitted Lennie Small and his smarter yet smaller companion George. Through their comic elaboration on the Steinbeck novel, the Coens have fashioned a contemporary response to the popu-

lar American gospel of bigness and success, a response that, in contrast, tells us how much those little things can really mean if only we will seek them out.

The most obvious link between *Raising Arizona* and *Of Mice and Men* occurs in the main characters of the two works. For not only is Hi a minor character on the American scene, a small-time crook, but he also has an alter ego named Leonard Smalls, whose comment, "My friends call me Lennie," forms a firm association with Steinbeck's Lennie Small. Of course, this biker-bounty hunter is hardly a pure reincarnation of Steinbeck's sympathetic Lennie; rather, the combination of Smalls and Hi, his psychological double, form a mutated, nightmarish, and more complex version of the Steinbeck character. In the novel, we might note, Lennie is not at all malicious, although his retardation causes him to do bad things without realizing the consequences of his actions. Similarly, Hi means no real harm by his hold-ups, his kidnaping of one of Nathan Arizona's "extra" babies, or even his fight with his foreman. He is simply compelled by some inner force or urge to this socially unacceptable behavior. But the Coens go a step further with their central character by concretely incarnating his asocial and potentially menacing aspect in the horrible figure of the lone biker.

Smalls is essentially a distorted, negative image of all the qualities that endear Lennie Small to Steinbeck's readers. While Small adores little, cuddly animals—in illustration of what Steinbeck called "the inarticulate and powerful yearnings of all men"—*Raising Arizona*'s Smalls, whose very name accents a multiplicity of purpose not as evident in Steinbeck's "singular" Small, is, we are told, "especially hard on little things," as we see when he kills a roadside rabbit with a hand grenade. While Steinbeck's Lennie does inadvertently injure or even kill all of his playthings, the Coens' Lennie has destruction as his *raison d'être.* These "little things," the animals, are thus central to the way the film elaborates on Steinbeck's tale, for through them it develops its own characters, setting up the entity of Hi-Smalls much as the novel defines Lennie's character. Lennie is intimately involved with animals, while Smalls compares himself to numerous creatures—a bloodhound, a pup, even a "warthog from Hell." In fact, the very source of the identification of Smalls as Hi's "other self" is a Woody Woodpecker tattoo that each possesses, a symbol simultaneously of animalism, childhood, and phallic sexuality that hints of each's full complexity. Hi's primitive behavior during his robberies—with the legs of the pantyhose slipped over his head resembling floppy rabbit ears—and his fight with his boss Glen may be partly attributed to the "big weight bearing down" from the pressures of his family and social life. For the Coens' world, just as Steinbeck's, seems to be one in which "innocent persons are sacrificed," like animals, "to the perversities of a decadent world that, because of financial or sexual obsessions, cannot allow such innocence to flourish". The escaped brothers, Gale and Evelle, suggest to Hi that the source of his marital friction (which disrupts the happy home centered on the toddler) could be financial worries. As a solution, they suggest that Hi accompany them on a bank robbery—a financial obsession threatening to Hi's newfound innocence as well as the absolute innocence symbolized in the baby. Gale and Evelle cannot know, however, that the source of the financial problem (Hi's loss of his job) was his revulsion over Glen's proposition that they engage in wife-swapping, a sexual obsession threatening to innocence, an obsession to which Hi is ultimately sacrificed by being fired. As Hi points out, "It is a tough world for little things" who are at the mercy of man's perverse, animalistic nature.

Just as the Hi-Smalls pairing forms a parallel to Lennie Small, the pairing of Hi (including the Smalls aspect of his psyche) and Ed parallels the Lennie-George combo. Hi is tall (though not bulky—that trait belongs to Smalls), irresponsible, and trying to escape a checkered past of crimes against society. Ed, however, is his opposite, with her small build, great sense of responsibility and decorated efforts as a law enforcement officer. Ed constantly has to remind Hi of the proper way in which to behave in certain situations, much as George tells Lennie what to say and do. For example, she scolds Hi for allowing two escaped convicts to intrude into their "decent" home (ironically forged by the crime of kidnaping), and she chastises his violence against Glen. In this respect Ed and Hi may be seen as the conscious and subconscious—or possibly even superego and id—the former always trying to keep the latter in check. Interestingly, Ed sometimes resembles Lennie, as her need for a child echoes his desire to tend little rabbits, and in one scene Hi becomes George; he destroys Smalls, saying, "I'm sorry," displaying the same regret with which George shoots Lennie.

Typically, such switching of characters would break down the foundation of any comparison of two works. However, in this case the interchangeability of character relationships between **Raising Arizona** and *Of Mice and Men* not only serves to underscore the existence of Ed, Hi, and Smalls (as well as George and Lennie) as small segments of one whole personality, but it also contributes to one of the Coens' strongest thematic tools: confusion of identity.

If one is to make a successful metamorphosis into a better existence, then one must first come to grips with the true nature of one's current self. The inability of **Raising Arizona**'s characters to do so, indicating the futility of their dreams, is pointed up in the numerous confusions of identity throughout the film. The hero is alternately called "H.I.," "Hi," "Daddy," "Mr. McDunnough," and "Herbert" (the name he uses to sign the letter acknowledging the confused, troubled side of his character). The validity of his mate's name is called into doubt when Hi queries, "What kind of name is

'Ed' for a pretty little thing like you?" Her reply introduces an alternate name, "Edwina," and she is later called "Mrs. McDonnough" (a title lending a false air of respect and import) and even "young Missy" (a child-like name evoking images of smallness). Ed, like Hi, is also facing a serious identity crisis: she is an officer of the law who marries an ex-con, tenders her badge, and embarks on a criminal act. Amusingly, the motif of confused identify is extended to some minor characters, such as the large, burly man in Hi's prison therapy group who, because of terrible menstrual cramps, feels trapped in a man's body.

Such ambiguous personalities are evident in *Of Mice and Men* as well, where they also indicate a reluctance or inability to engage in introspection. Lennie's surname, "Small," is obviously at odds with his physical size; it is, however, in accord with his inability to understand his environment and himself; and while Lennie may be physically strong ("Leonard" means "strong or brave as a lion"), he is not emotionally viable, nor is he brave. While there is no apparent contradiction in George Milton's name, a contradiction or confusion of identify is clear in his repeated avoidance of questions about his relationship to Lennie. Several ranch hands remark that it is odd to see two men traveling together as they do, but George insists that there is nothing strange about it at all. Dusenbury theorizes that Steinbeck points up the unusual friendship to emphasize the aloneness of the typical ranch hand. However, on the surface there is a subtly implied homosexuality, underlined by Lisca's reminder that "George" means "husbandman," in this case husband to one who is "strong or brave as a lion." More important than denying homosexuality, though, George is denying that Lennie is really his psychological twin; Lisca suggests that the Lennie-George dichotomy could be that of the unconscious and the conscious or the id and the ego. George fails to admit this relationship and the fact that they have no choice but to travel together.

While the main characters in the two works are all confused about where they stand in life, they are equally unsure of exactly what they seek. Steinbeck called his novel "a study of the dreams and pleasures of everyone in the world." Rabbits symbolize the fertile dreams of Lennie and George, but they are easily replaced with whatever suitable substitutes can be found: first with a mouse, then with a puppy, and finally with George's trip to a "cat house." In one version of his plans, George even mentions the possibility of eating some of the rabbits, an act which is paradoxically destructive of the very symbol of the dream itself.

In **Raising Arizona,** the McDunnoughs' hopes are personified in the form of a toddler who undergoes no fewer than six changes of identity, indicating the characters' lack of focus on their dreams. He is first called "Nathan, Jr., I think" by Hi. Nathan Arizona later uses the same phrase to refer to the child; and he admits that his own "name ain't Nathan Arizona," but rather Nathan Huffhines. Thus the baby becomes Nathan Huffhines, Jr., by association. Once they have him home, the McDunnoughs continue to call him "Nathan, Jr.," in private, but they subsequently label him "Hi, Jr., 'til we think of a better name," and "Ed, Jr.," in the company of others. The most brilliantly absurd confusion of identity comes when Hi tells Glen that the baby is Ed, Jr. Glen mistakes the name "Ed," normally a masculine name, to be feminine, remarking, "I thought you said it was a boy." In a line that would in most instances seem quite superfluous, Hi then has to explain that "Ed" is in this case short for "Edward," not "Edwina." As others try to horn in on the dream (just as Candy and Crooks beg to be let in on George and Lennie's dream), the child becomes Glen, Jr., and Gale, Jr. Put simply, Nathan, Jr., is all things to all people, none of whom has given serious thought to what his true goals are. The characters "suffer from tunnel vision, each gripped by an obsession he or she cannot . . . explain."

The fact that something has gone seriously awry with Hi and Ed's schemes for a family life is underscored by the paralleling of the lone biker with the gigantic rabbit in Lennie's nightmare. Just as the rabbit is a symbol of the utopian farm made monstrous in size and cruel in speech, Smalls, incarnated in Hi's first dream, clearly symbolizes an infant made monstrous and cruel, his booties dangling from his body armor and his tattoo reading, "Mama didn't love me." The cartoonish yet hellish lighting of the biker together with the woodpecker tattoo contributes to the "evil child" image, and, as Steele says of Lennie's nightmare rabbit, when one's most cherished dream turns upon one, it is indeed the death of hope.

If one's goals are unclear or badly founded, then the determination from within that is necessary to the actualization of one's dreams is absent. Therefore, working toward those aspirations becomes an impossibility, and, rather than re-evaluate the validity of his goals, that person may seek a short-cut to achievement. However, the easy way out almost always involves settling for less than the desired result. For example, Hi's holdups (significantly of convenience stores), intended as quick ways of getting cash, result in one incarceration after another. One of Hi's fellow inmates tells how, as a child, he often settled for eating sand when he could find neither meat, nor fowl, nor crawdads. He describes a disastrous attempt to cook a crawdad in a boiler, but without any water (i.e., without following the proper, time-consuming steps); instead of a crawdad lunch, he got something more closely resembling popcorn.

Attempts to reach goals too quickly are more abundantly portrayed in **Raising Arizona** as premature births. Hi is repeatedly released on parole, as the cell doors "swing wide" before he has had a chance to reform at all, before the fat man with the mop has finished cleaning the dirty floors of Hi's rambunctious mind. The escape of Gale and Evelle from prison is shown as a birth from a tunnel, each man screaming like a newborn baby, and Evelle's feet-first emergence suggests a problem with the delivery. The brothers' entrance back into society is made in a stolen station wagon—significantly a family car, the ideas of family and home being modes of cultural acceptance throughout the film—which they drive off while it is still being filled with gasoline, leaving the pump hose lying on the ground like a prematurely severed umbilical cord. Hi, in his last flight from the police, undergoes a birth from the cab/womb of his getaway truck (screaming in unison with the driver/mother), through its windshield/birth canal, and (again prematurely) into the "Ozzie and Harriet" world of a split-level ranch home. This is a world for which Hi obviously is not ready, and he must run through it since it has no place for him yet. Most importantly, Hi and Ed have "born" a baby into their world, but they have done it much too easily and prematurely. Only when Nathan, Jr., is kidnaped from them by Gale and Evelle do they admit that they never really deserved him in the first place.

This realization is the slap in the face that puts the McDunnoughs on the right track to a truly hopeful future. The lone biker arrives immediately, visible for the first time to Hi's conscious and to Ed. They are now face to face with Hi's alter ego, the biggest single obstacle barring a new life from them. Just as George kills that aspect of himself that Lennie represents, Hi must confront Smalls, the true nature which he has feared and about which he has been confused; he must either overcome this side of his psyche or be destroyed along with his dreams.

In the aftermath of their triumph over the lone biker of the apocalypse, Hi and Ed, not certain that kidnaping was not the proper solution to their problems, return Nathan, Jr., to his crib, a gesture indicating their intent to start afresh. Just as George and Lennie's retreat to the spot by the river has explicit overtones of a return to the womb and rebirth, Hi and Ed momentarily "retreat" from their mad pursuit, realize where their problems lie, and are reborn to a new way of seeing their dreams. Barth points out that the Coens' stylistic alterations of reality throughout the film work to suggest the necessity of just such a new way of perceiving.

Throughout the film, Arizona is a source of confusion, especially as used as an assumed name by Nathan Huffhines; and with its absurd juxtaposition of mass-culture junkiness with parched, primal landscapes, it has been referred to by Ethan Coen as "an Arizona of the mind." Arizona is also the American state where the characters have chosen to pursue the American dream, indicating, in the context of its symbolic use, a fundamental flaw of uncertainty in the pursuit. In the final line of dialog, Hi muses, "I don't know; maybe it was Utah." Thus he doubts the very essence of his entire struggle. Has he been on the wrong track from the beginning? He is raising Arizona as one would raise a question, and he has finally achieved the necessary level of self-examination that may make his dream a possible reality.

Thus, by borrowing Steinbeck's theme of small Americans and their misguided dreams, Joel and Ethan Coen contend that, in order to achieve true personal success, one must look beyond the cultural stereotypes of what one's goals should be and pursue instead the small, truly wonderful things in life. To the jubilant cheers of the human race found in the yodels of the closing soundtrack, Hi opens his eyes to the reality of his misdirected quest, indicating an awakening that will foster new, more realistic dreams.

Richard Jameson (review date September 1990)

SOURCE: "Chasing the Hat," in *Film Comment,* Vol. 26, No. 5, September/October, 1990, pp. 32-33.

[*Below, Jameson favorably reviews* Miller's Crossing.]

Ice dropping into a heavy-bottomed glass: cold, hard, sensuous. The first image in ***Miller's Crossing*** hits our ears before it hits the screen, but it's nonetheless an image for that. Tom Reagan (Gabriel Byrne) has traveled the length of a room to build a drink. Not that we saw him in transit, not that we yet know he is Tom Reagan, and not that we see him clearly now as he turns and stalks back up the room, a silent, out-of-focus enigma at the edge of someone else's closeup. Yet he is a story walking, as his deliberate, tangential progress, from background to middle distance and then out the side of the frame, is also a story—draining authority from the close-up Johnny Caspar (Jon Polito) who's come to insist, ironically enough, on the recognition of his territorial rights.

The place is a story, too, which we read as the scene unfolds. A private office; not Caspar's, but not Reagan's either—it's city boss Liam "Leo" O'Bannion (Albert Finney) who sits behind the camera and his big desk, listening. An upstairs office, we know from the muted street traffic (without stopping to think about why we know). Night outside, but sunlight would never be welcome, or relevant, here. A masculine space, green lampshades amid the dark luster of wood, leather, whiskey. A remote train whistle sounds, functional and intrinsically forlorn; the distance from which it reaches us locates the office in space and in history. This room exists in a city big enough to support a multiplicity of criminal fiefdoms and a political machine that rules by maintaining the balance among them, yet it is still a town whose municipal core lies within faint earshot of its outskirts. Ur-

ban dreams of empire have not entirely crowded out the memory of wilderness, of implacable places roads and railroads can't reach, even if one of them has been wishfully designated Miller's Crossing. Hence we are not entirely surprised (though the aesthetic shock is deeply satisfying) when the opening master-scene, with its magisterial interior setting and dialogue fragrant with cross purpose, gives way to a silent (save for mournful Irish melody) credit sequence in an empty forest. And then to a title card announcing, almost superfluously, "An Eastern city in the United States, toward the end of the 1920s."

It has always been one of the special pleasures of movies that they dream worlds and map them at the same time. *Miller's Crossing* dreams a beaut, no less so for the fact that Joel and Ethan Coen's film is a reverent, rigorous reimagining of the world of Dashiell Hammett, especially as limned in *The Glass Key* and *Red Harvest.* (A phrase from *Red Harvest* supplied the title of the Coens' filmmaking debut ***Blood Simple.***) The look is right, from first frame to last—even the aural "look" of that ice: this is a movie that knows what drinking is about in Hammett, what it has to do with rumination and gravity, coolheadedness and rash error, and every coloration of brown study. The mood is instinct with the private pain that separates reticence from caring and conceals itself, with desperation and anger, in seeming not to care. Even the narrative spaces are true to Hammett. There is a man named "Rug" Daniels who enters the film dead, whose murder is the least insistent and finally least significant of the film's mysteries, offhandedly explained amid the backwash from gaudier mayhem ("I don't know, just a mixup"); the cast has to wonder—though the audience need not—why Daniels' corpse should be missing his eponymous toupee. Floyd Thursby might envy a death surrounded by such perplexity and pixilation.

The terrain is worthy of mapping. But more importantly, the mapping itself becomes cinematic terrain in ***Miller's Crossing,*** each adjustment of distance and perspective invested with exquisite sensibility. Sometimes the effect is startling, like the delayed revelation that the precariously politic dialogue between Leo and Caspar, with Tom kibbitzing, also involves a fourth man: The Dane (J. E. Freeman), Caspar's partner in crime, who, though standing directly behind Caspar the entire time, is never seen by the audience till his fierce visage towers in sudden closeup several minutes into the scene. That silent detonation is the most effective shock cut since Dennis Hopper in *Blue Velvet* offered to "fuck anything that moves." But one takes no less satisfaction when, a moment later, after Caspar and The Dane's angry departure, Tom Reagan leaves off lounging at the window ledge behind his friend and boss, moves to a couch along the wall, settles in, takes a deep drink, and says, "Bad play, Leo." Ninety-nine directors out of a hundred would have played that line in closeup. Joel Coen frames Tom within enough space that we feel both director and character have a judicious respect for patterns, for the ways in which moves and designs can go wrong, and for the crisis whose resolution is going to drive Tom and Leo forever apart.

When John Wayne noticed that Dean Martin, as the drunk in need of redemption, seemed to have the ripest part in *Rio Bravo,* he asked Howard Hawks what he ought to do to hold up his own end of the screen. Hawks replied, "You look at him like he's your friend." Tom Reagan is Leo O'Bannion's friend in *Miller's Crossing,* but he has the devil's own time looking out for the interests of both of them. Johnny Caspar starts out wanting only to send a red letter to "The Schmatte," Bernie Bernbaum (John Turturro), a bookmaker who's been screwing the play every time Caspar fixes a prize-fight. Leo refuses to lift protection on Bernie, partly to insist on his own authority, but also because Bernie is the cherished brother of Verna (Marcia Gay Harden), whose dark beauty has stirred banked fires in his heart. Tom wishes his friend could keep his mind on business. He also wishes he knew what to do about the fact that he himself is secretly Verna's lover.

Reportedly, Albert Finney came late to the role of Leo, after Trey Wilson, the 43-year-old actor who played the father of the quintuplets in the Coens' *Raising Arizona,* died of a stroke. Finney's extra decade introduces an imbalance into the friendship between Tom and Leo and adjusts the nature of their rivalry for Verna; besides being a hefty powerbroker ill-made for romantic conquest, his Leo takes on the pathos of age and last options. But if Finney's Leo is less than equal on the field of love, he's more than equal as a figure of estimable regard. The screenplay obliges Leo to disappear for most of the last two-thirds of the movie; excellent player that he was, it's doubtful whether the late Wilson could have loomed so large in absentia as Finney's Leo does. The sense of rueful aspiration that drives Tom Reagan during his often mystifying maneuvers to set the cockeyed world of *Miller's Crossing* right finds expression mainly through the Irish music that marks his passage, and our memories of Leo—apart from his beefy authority and boyish candor—reverberate as a kind of music. Not only the playing of "Danny Boy" over the most audacious of the film's tour-de-force sequences (an exhilarating first-act high that would render the remainder of any other movie anticlimactic), but also the mortally wounded sighs Leo emits after learning of Tom and Verna's affair. And the way Finney gets the history of a long day and Leo's life and his friendship with Tom into responding to the offer of a late-night drink—"I wouldn't *mind.*"

That line reading is one of a thousand things to love about *Miller's Crossing,* along with a zephyr of smoke through waxed floorboards, the rubbing together of stark trees above a killing ground, the arrival of a small man to conduct the

beating a giant couldn't manage, the way men and guns fill up a nocturnal street like autumn leaves drifting. And one loves a screenplay with the fortitude to lay all its cards on the table in the first sequence and then demonstrate, with each succeeding scene, that there is still story to happen, there is still life and mystery in character, there is reason to sit patient and fascinated before a movie that loves and honors the rules of a game scarcely anyone else in Hollywood remembers anymore, let alone tries to play. Johnny Caspar is a brute posing as a philosopher, but he knows the word that fits the Coen brothers' moviemaking: "et'ics." [ethics]

One of the Coens told a *New York Times* writer that *Miller's Crossing* had its genesis in the image of a black hat coming to rest in a forest clearing, then lifting to soar away down an avenue of trees. That image accompanies the main title, a talisman of the movie's respect for enigma and dedication to the irreducible integrity of style. It also crops up verbally as a dream Tom describes to Verna—the closest he gets to sharing a confidence. Yeah, says Verna, and then you chased the hat and it changed into something else. "No," Tom says immediately, "it stayed a hat. And I didn't chase it." But one way or another, this man in grim flight from his heart, who cannot, must not "look at him like he's your friend" till the last world-closing shot of the film, chases his hat all through *Miller's Crossing.* So do the Coens. And that it doesn't change into something else is the best news for the American cinema at the dawn of the Nineties.

Tim Pulleine (review date Winter 1991)

SOURCE: "Neo-Classic Hammett," in *Sight and Sound,* Vol. 60, No. 1, Winter, 1991, pp. 64-65.

[*In the following review, Pulleine praises* Miller's Crossing *for its unity of plot and structure.*]

Blood Simple, the first feature of Joel Coen (writer-director) and his brother Ethan (writer-producer), was widely seen as updating the protocols of the school of writing most readily associated with James M. Cain. Now, after the high-pitched comic detour of *Raising Arizona,* the Coens have turned for inspiration to a different area of crime writing, the novels of Dashiell Hammett. This time they have adhered to the period of the originals: the milieu of *Miller's Crossing* is an unspecified American city during Prohibition. The makers have spoken of echoing the 'dirty town' premise of *Red Harvest,* though in fact the narrative bears a more particular resemblance to *The Glass Key.*

The plot is of a complexity that would defy any brief synopsis, but turns in outline on the attempted overthrow of the city's Irish 'boss' (Albert Finney) by his Italian arch-rival—

the former's Achilles heel being his infatuation with the sister (Marcia Gay Harden) of a double-dealing petty criminal (John Turturro)—and on the thwarting of this design by Finney's chief lieutenant (Gabriel Byrne), who has also been Harden's lover and who feigns desertion to the opposition in order to repair his mentor's fortunes.

> **For all its humor, *Miller's Crossing* contains a heart of darkness. The intimations of sado-masochistic emotion which insinuated themselves into *Blood Simple,* and were even perceptible (in a farcically distanced vein) in the no-hoper couple of *Raising Arizona,* here tend to hold sway.**
> —*Tim Pulleine*

The manner in which the densely packed storyline is negotiated, moreover, is not the delirious modernism of *Blood Simple,* but rather that of neo-classicism. Restraint is the keynote, whether in the preponderance of frequently near-static medium and close shots, the 'invisible' editing, or the restricted palette of Barry Sonnenfeld's cinematography, with its emphasis on browns and greys. This restraint might, to begin with, risk seeming artificial. But as the movie progresses, its scale gradually opens out and violent action intermittently intrudes, most astonishingly so in the set-piece in which the strains of 'Danny Boy' from Finney's horn gramophone majestically counterpoint his bloody turning of tables on the would-be assassins who have infiltrated his mansion retreat.

Despite such interventions, however, and the pattern of repetitions (only properly discernible at a second viewing) which underpins its structure, *Miller's Crossing* is elucidated pre-eminently through interchange between characters. In the manner of a Howard Hawks movie—though thankfully there is no suggestion of direct reference—it erects an exact yet invisible dramatic scaffolding, around which the participants, no matter how far removed from 'real' life, can create an illusion of independent existence.

Here Gabriel Byrne's hard-bitten insouciance, admirably offset by the bluffness of Finney, easily transcends anything this actor has previously done on the screen. And although it might be invidious to single out anyone else from an exactly balanced ensemble, J. E. Freeman, as the rival's granitic enforcer, contrives a figure from the realms of nightmare: asked whether he wants to kill a potential victim, he replies, 'For starters.'

Throughout, indeed, the pungently idiomatic dialogue invites quotation, whether it be Byrne's dismissal of a third party

as 'not a bad guy if looks, brains and personality don't count', or a bookie's comment on Byrne's lack of gambler's luck: 'If I were a horse, I'd be down on my fetlocks praying you don't bet on me'.

Yet for all its humor, *Miller's Crossing* contains a heart of darkness. The intimations of sado-masochistic emotion which insinuated themselves into *Blood Simple,* and were even perceptible (in a farcically distanced vein) in the no-hoper couple of *Raising Arizona,* here tend to hold sway. The punishment to which Byrne submits with something like complicity, in the cause of preserving Finney, becomes an expiation of his guilt at having been the older man's amorous betrayer, but also an expurgation of his feelings toward this ambiguously paternal protector. At the end, the grateful Finney's almost priest-like utterance of 'I forgive you' is met by his erstwhile protégé with, 'I didn't ask for that and I don't want it': the two men's mutual dependence is at an end. (Thematically, too, the film could be said to contain indirect echoes of Hawks.)

By this time, the explication of the intrigue behind the conspiracy, however gripping in itself, has assumed a kind of irrelevance, so that the perversity of motivation is, as it were, absorbed into the very fabric of the narrative. In consequence, *Miller's Crossing* assumes a precision of correspondence between content and form which is all too rare in the cinema today; and the resolute effacement of any authorial 'signature', such as would detract from the telling of the tale, renders the film all the more clearly the product of a (double-headed) auteur.

William Preston Robertson (essay date August 1991)

SOURCE: "What's the Goopus?" in *American Film,* Vol. 16, August, 1991, pp. 30-32, 46.

[*In the following essay, Robertson describes a day in the shooting of* Barton Fink.]

Listlessly scratching his facial stubble, Ethan Coen gazes thoughtfully out through impenetrably dark sunglasses at the path Barton Fink must traverse. Ethan glances at me, then away. A second later, he looks at me again. He gestures vaguely outward. "Gloria Swanson used to live here," he says dully. He drops his hand limply at his side and stares ahead again.

Ethan has good reason to be excited. It's "Lipnik by the Pool" Day on the set of his and his brother Joel's latest movie, *Barton Fink.* Today's the day Barton pays a home visit to Jack Lipnik, the blustery titan of Capitol Pictures, and Lipnik apoplectically fires studio toady Lou Breeze for not kissing Barton's foot, then—what the hell—congenially gets down on his knees and kisses the damn thing himself.

We are standing in the backyard of a pricey, sun-drenched stucco mansion in Beverly Hills that, despite its current ownership by a couple of psychiatrists, still retains much of the Swansonian-period opulence so vital to the 1940s-studio-mogul-at-leisure look: a stone veranda overlooking a split-level lawn with a fish pond, palm trees, huge flowering bushes and grass so compulsively groomed that incriminating footprints are left behind wherever you walk on it. Phony Greek statuary and a gazebo have been carted in for good measure. It all veritably screams "Lipnik by the Pool."

Of course, nothing screams "Lipnik by the Pool" quite like Lipnik himself. Big, tan and silver-haired, Michael Lerner, who plays Lipnik, sits over by the twinkling cerulean pool on a yellow-padded chaise with a glass pitcher full of orange juice beside him. He wears an open, heavy, beige robe and a high-waisted, belted swimsuit of some sparkly, Decoy fabric reminiscent of the '30s futuristic fashions worn by Buster Crabbe in the old *Flash Gordon* serials.

Lerner's face is pensive. Moments from now, filming will commence on the critical Barton-walks-from-the-house-down-to-the-pool shot that sets up the whole Lipnik scene, and he will throw his arm into the air in a life-embracing, Old World gesture of salutation and bellow a line of dialogue across the yard.

Joel, taller than Ethan but, like his younger brother, slouchy, comes up on my other side and stares at the mansion. A second later he gives me an insensate glance through impenetrable sunglasses, then looks at Ethan. "Eeth, you tell Bill about Gloria Swans. . . ?"

"Yeah," Ethan says.

Joel falls silent and looks back at the house.

Lipnik/Lerner throws his arm into the air with Tevye-like abandon. "Bah't!" he bellows across the yard. "So happy to see ya!"

And into this posh, glitzy setting *he* comes—moving down the stone steps, past the fish pond and flowering bushes, toward Lipnik/Lerner and the pool. At his side is actor Jon Polito, in character as that Charon of the Hollywood Hades, Lou Breeze. And before him is a big muscular guy with longish hair, harnessed into a elaborate-looking device called a Steadicam, who tiptoes delicately backward like a timid portable rocket launcher-equipped Rambo retreating in the presence of something greater than might—a good mind.

The mind belongs to a lanky man. He wears a brown, rumpled three-piece suit, black, round George S. Kaufman glasses and has a kinky-haired, mythic-sized, anvil-shaped coif with a protruding ledge that extends at least as far as his nose. His flesh is moist and pale, his cheeks peppered with five o'clock stubble. His body moves stiffly and awkwardly. His hands fidget at his chest, and his lips are pursed and crooked as they idly suck on nothing but the nectar of neurosis.

It is the eyes, however, that are the most striking. Well, OK, let's not kid ourselves—it's the mythic-sized, anvil-shaped coif that is most striking. But the eyes run a very close second. Wide and blinking frequently, they give off a stunned, vulnerable glint—not unlike the orbs of some burrowing nocturnal critter abruptly dragged from its hole by malicious children into the blinding starkness of daylight.

He is Barton Fink. Dreamer. Sufferer. Champion of the Common Man. Babe in the Woods. Fathead.

"He *looks* like a writer," someone has chuckled to me on another occasion. "He has that defensive look."

It's a fair enough statement. With his Barton Walk and his Barton Stare and his Barton Lip-Sucking Business, the extremely talented John Turturro, who plays Barton, has managed to find the fear that lurks in the heart of every writer and wears it on his shirt like the Sweat Stain of Courage to great comic effect.

Yet, there is something more at work here.

After the take, I catch sight of Turturro in conference with Joel and Ethan. The three stand in an amiable huddle, each rocking slightly from side to side, each grinning and bobbing his head in asthmatic chortling—Ethan with his curly light brown I-just-let-it-sit-there 'do, Joel with his dark Sam Elliot-manqué, Afghan-hound-from-the-wrong-side-of-the-tracks shag, and Barton/Turturro with his Stonehenge coif, more reminiscent of an insurance company's logo than something on a person's head. Three slender, fidgety, bespectacled men with unshaven faces and . . . well, somewhat interesting-looking hair.

I have seen this sight on the set many times, of course. But now, as always, I am struck by what a powerful, trenchant image it is, this prism of refracted Coen-ness, this enchanted, albeit badly warped, tailor's mirror of the artistic soul, this wacky triptych on the altar of the chuckleheaded god of cinema.

And, as always, the impression is fleeting.

As I approach the three, the sensation is not unlike walking down a hospital corridor into the emphysema ward during Clown Day. The wheezing, strangled inhalations of mirth grow louder with each step.

What's so funny this time?

The Coen brothers laugh. Oh, how they laugh.

With *Barton Fink,* their fourth movie, Joel and Ethan Coen, the writing-directing-producing Vladimir and Estragon of American cinema, scarfed a staggering trio of awards at this year's Cannes Film Festival: best director (Joel), best actor (Turturro) and the Palme d'Or for best picture. The lads who brought us *Blood Simple, Raising Arizona* and *Miller's Crossing* have created their most poignantly intimate film statement to date. But don't whip out your honker-wipers just yet. *Barton Fink* is an absurd comedy about writer's block, decapitation and the Life of the Mind.

Barton is an earnest, socially conscious playwright with a poetically turgid, Clifford Odetsian writing style whose stirring drama about fishmongers on the Lower East Side, "Bare Ruined Choir," has made him the toast of the 1941 New York theatrical season. Insecure, but headstrong about his art, Barton is now within reach of his lifelong dream to create a theater of, about and for the Common Man.

So he takes the next logical career step. He goes to Hollywood, where, under contract to Capitol Pictures, he is hired to write a Wallace Beery wrestling movie called "The Burlyman"—joining the ranks of other great literary minds of his day who, lured by the scent of moola, have been herded like cattle into Hollywood Babylon's loony, pitiless, golden corral.

Then a horrible thing happens. Barton gets creatively bollixed. Sitting at his desk, sweating in his underwear in his stiflingly hot residential-hotel room, tormented by what may be the only mosquito in hundreds of miles and watching as the wallpaper oozes sap and sloughs from the wall, Barton finds himself unable to produce a single word. Frantically dancing around the studio's madcap inquiries about his progress, desperately and vainly seeking advice from other lost-soul writers, Barton thrashes, writhes and undulates in that lonely personal hell that is the Life of the Mind.

His only refuge is a growing friendship with his next door neighbor, Charlie Meadows (John Goodman), a big, affable, self-effacing insurance salesman in whom Barton sees the quintessential Common Man and in whose quaintly simple view of life he finds peace.

Sort of. Because Charlie is not as common or simple as he seems. And he shows Barton a thing or two about hell and the life of the mind.

Like the Coens' previous movies, *Barton Fink* is an unsettling combination of the dark and the bumptious, full of wryly humorous dialogue and various trademark Coenist auteuristic obsessions. But *Barton Fink* is different from other Coen movies in that it does not play off an established film genre, as *Blood Simple* did film noir, *Raising Arizona* did baby comedies and *Miller's Crossing* did gangster melodramas (unless, of course, there's a genre of violent comedies about the creative process). No, this time out, the Coen brothers have drawn inspiration from an unlikely source: personal experience.

It was the fall of 1987 and Joel and Ethan, wearing mental loincloths, were grunting and gasping with an untitled script they were writing about gangsters in a corrupt town in 1929. Though they eventually titled the script *Miller's Crossing,* in those days they referred to it as *The Bighead,* which was their affectionate nickname for the main character, Tom, a pensive, ungarrulous Hammettian antihero trying to think his way through the chaos of a gang war.

At first, the boys were merely stymied by *The Bighead*—something about its plot being too complicated to figure out, they said. Before long, however, they would look wistfully back at their halcyon stymied days, as they came face to face with a huge case of writer's block. The Coens tried various techniques to break through their block. They tried different writing locations. (Come to think of it, that was their only technique.)

Which is how they came to visit me in my small, rundown Victorian apartment in St. Paul, Minnesota. They stayed a full week, and we mostly sat around drinking coffee from my matching Elvis Presley mugs, listening to old Clancy Brothers records, watching *Jeopardy!* every day at 4 PM and eating doughnuts. One night, however, we took a break from this grueling routine to see *Baby Boom.*

Soon after, I started to notice an improvement in the boys' attitude. They attacked their doughnuts with greater appetite. Ethan, I remember, seemed particularly taken with the *Baby Boom* theme song and began to hum it—incessantly, I thought. By the week's end, though there was no visible progress made on *The Bighead,* the elevation in the Coens' mood was palpable. They left beaming and thanking me profusely and saying that it had all been tremendously helpful.

Three weeks later, Joel and Ethan called me from New York to tell me they'd written *Barton Fink.*

When I read the script, I saw immediately that the Coens had overcome their problem in an ingenious way. They had taken their writer's block and made an effigy of it, an effigy named Barton—a neck-hanged, rag-stuffed, immolated dummy vaguely resembling themselves—to which they could then also play the angry, ululating mob that paraded it rebelliously through the streets while chanting simple but catchy slogans of humiliation. With a joyful shake of the pole, they could make the flaming effigy dance and twirl in comic mimicry of nightmarish agony. They could make him sweat in his underwear, give blood to a ravenous mosquito and stare at the walls of his room with lip-sucking, blank-minded insentience until the paper literally peeled away. They'd force him to have his brain slapped and his foot kissed by blustery studio moguls and make him open his bed-side Bible to find his own writing contained in "Genesis." They'd show him hell. What connection this had to *Baby Boom*, I had no idea.

After that, the writing on *The Bighead* flowed more freely.

And the rest, of course, is history: **Miller's Crossing** died at the box office.

It is exactly as I had imagined it: a dreary, stale-looking, for-gotten place in which not even the bright wash of kliegs can revive the color and vibrancy that have been so long dead. The wool carpet, a dull, rosy floral pattern, is threadbare from too many pacing steps. The green Deco palm-motif wallpaper, glistening in the heat with its own runny paste, shrugs and crinkles away from the wall like fungi-ravaged, water-logged flesh. The bed, thin and lumpy and springy, has a kind of Deco-jail-house look to it, with a zigzag-cornered, cheap silver-painted frame of small orbs and long bars. The only other furniture of note is a writing desk with an old-fashioned typewriter and wadded pieces of paper. Hanging on the wall above it is the only thing of real color in the room: a tinted photograph of a peach-skinned, brunette woman sitting with her back to us, staring pensively out at the inscrutable blue sea.

Barton's room.

I am standing alongside Ethan on the top step of a raised set built on a sound stage at Culver Studios. It's my first day here. Over by a wall, the weary-faced, curly gray-haired Brit-ish cinematographer Roger Deakins sits on a dolly and squints through the eyepiece of a movie camera pointed at a solitary drop of wallpaper sap drooling slowly down the faded deco palms. As Roger tracks the sluggish path of the dewy paste, Joel and other crew members stand beside him, intently watching, their gazes just discernibly edging lower and lower.

They will be filming inserts like this all week long. I wanted to come the previous week, when they were filming the cli-mactic and extremely exciting-sounding "Burning Hallway" sequence. But Ethan seemed pretty sure the fire marshal wouldn't permit it. And besides, he said, this way I'd be sure

to get to see the *goopus*—the Coens' name for the oleagi-nous wallpaper gum.

The shot ends, and everybody sits back with an audible sigh. The crew begins to reposition the camera. Joel turns lan-guidly from the wall. "Goopus, Gilbert, please," he says.

In striking contrast to Joel's shuffling torpor, Gilbert Johnquest breezes energetically onto the set. Gilbert is the *goopuser*. It is upon his shoulders solely that the responsi-bility of applying the dribbling wall paste rests. Carrying a veritable artillery of goopus-applicators, each clearly labeled according to a specific type of goopus, Gilbert intently sets about his task. Holding up a large yellow spray tank marked "Wall Sweat Goopus" Gilbert spritzes the wall, beading it with moisture. Then he picks up a hand-soap dispenser marked "Ropeus Goopus" and, cranking it, creates long, fat dribbles of translucent pasty gunk. Gilbert works with speed and precision, for time is of the essence.

Ethan leans over confidentially. "It was really cool when we were doing the scenes between Barton and Charlie," he says, his voice low. "Just before a take, someone would come in and spritz Turturro and Goodman—getting Goodman under the armpits and all. And in the background, Gilbert would be moving around, spritzing and goopusing the walls."

Gilbert brings up a plastic catsup bottle, the nozzle of which is cut to provide a thinner, more vermicelli-like strand of Ropeus Goopus. He squeezes it, and it makes a loud, em-barrassing sputter.

Joel, who has been pacing as the crew works, suddenly pipes up. "The sound of the farting goopus bottle means that Gil-bert is on the set!" he says in a high-school documentary nar-rator voice, never once losing step in his pacing.

Gilbert ignores him and continues to squeeze the bottle with flatulent vigor, just trying to get his work done. Gilbert is an artist in his own right—a painter and sculptor. It is his burden that the task of goopus application fell to him, that there is an unlucky alliteration between his name and his task and that he is on the crew of a Coen brothers movie. He is a big, lean, strapping guy, Gilbert, with long hair pulled back in a tiny samurai ponytail. He wears Bermuda shorts, darkly discolored high-top sneakers and an open, checked shirt over one of many "Gilbertville" T-shirts he acquired from a town of that same name in Iowa when he was working on *Field of Dreams*.

Next to Gilbert's high-tops is a plastic bucket with a paint brush in it. It is marked, simply and eloquently, "Goopus." Gilbert picks up the broad, goopus-sodden brush, which flops downward like a heavily salivating tongue, and looks up at an area of wallpaper that has peeled away, exposing the blank wall beneath. Gilbert gives the area a healthy slather.

Sometimes, when the Coens tire of calling for "Goopus, Gilbert," they call for "Gilbus, Goopert." Crew members who also worked on the set of *Miller's Crossing* and who used to greet each other with the oft-repeated gangster line, "What's the rumpus?," now greet each other with "What's the goopus?"

It is Gilbert's burden to bear.

Later, I find myself the only person on the set, standing in the middle of Barton's room. I stare down at Barton's writing desk, then up at the picture of the woman at the beach staring out to sea, then around at the goopus-befouled walls. Suddenly, I understand. Though *Barton Fink* is set during the bizarreness and insanity of Hollywood's golden days, Hollywood is really just a colorful backdrop that provides a few easy opportunities for some bellowing and vomiting and bluster. This goopus-stained room—*this* is what the movie is really about. *Barton Fink* is not so much about Hollywood as it is about the timeless, knuckleheaded hubris of the creative process and, in general, of any effort to try to craft sense and order out of the chaos that is life. It's not that it's a bad thing to do, really. It's just that it's . . . well, *funny*. Ah, Barton. Ah, humanity.

Joel and Ethan have told me of their plans to make a sequel to *Barton Fink,* to be called *Old Fink,* picking up the story of the great writer years after his having ratted on all of his friends to the House Un-American Activities Committee in the '50s. Middle-aged, Barton will hang out with members of the '60s youth movement. He will wear long gray sideburns and turtlenecks with big medallions. What the hair will be like no one will say—but the mind reels. Barton Fink fans will have to wait, however, just as the Coens intend to wait, for that day when John Turturro has himself achieved middle age. Such is the uncompromising gamble of creating art.

Joel walks onto the set, a paper cup of coffee in his hand. After a moment, he motions for me to follow him to a wall. "See, when it dries, it turns white like this," he says, brushing his hand lightly over milky streaks. "But sometimes if you put on a lot, it dries into this long hardened piece that you can peel right off in one chunk." He pulls a long, globby strip from the wall, then shows it to me. "It's like this weird food starch stuff," he says, turning the dried goopus like Euell Gibbons with fossilized raccoon dung on a grade-school nature walk.

I stare at the dried goopus in Joel's hand, then around at the room. "I can't believe I came all the way out here and you're just going to do inserts all week."

Joel nods, looks around, sips his coffee. "Well, not all week," he says. "Friday's 'Lipnik by the Pool' Day." He drops the dried goopus to the floor and heads off the set, into the darkness of the sound stage. "When you really should've come was last week," he says, his voice echoing from the dark. "We did the burning hallway."

John Powers (review date September 1991)

SOURCE: "Finking It," in *Sight and Sound,* Vol. 1, No. 5, September, 1991, p. 4.

[*In the following review, Powers praises* Barton Fink *but accurately predicts its box office failure.*]

Let me begin, as you secretly want me to, by boasting about the weather. The day is bright, the temperature a placid 27 degrees, and the smog's been carried up-country by the Santa Ana winds that Raymond Chandler made part of the local mythology. In short, it's one of those natty Los Angeles mornings that once prompted that Julian Temple (remember him?) to remark over brunch, "If we had days like this in London, we wouldn't have Mrs Thatcher. Yes, there's something about the sunshine that makes it possible to believe almost anything. For the last five years Twentieth Century Fox has believed that the Coen brothers, writer-director Joel and writer-producer Ethan, were destined to become Hollywood superstars.

When *Blood Simple* came out in 1984, the Coens received the kind of reviews that most young film-makers would kill for, unaware that such overpraise usually winds up killing them. But despite the critical fanfare—Joel was called the next Welles, the next Leone, the next Scorsese—the public found it slow and cold and filled with hateful characters.

Still, the industry was high on the Coens' talent and expected that their next film would prove them mainstream crowdpleasers like *Back to the Future's* Bob Zemeckis and Bob Gale. But for all its raves and saturation advertising, *Raising Arizona* enjoyed only a brief, lackluster run. And *Miller's Crossing* did even worse. After opening the New York Film Festival to the familiar gaga reviews, it was last seen limping trembling through the grass like that hare in Keats.

This pattern will continue with their new comedy, *Barton Fink,* which snatched the top prizes at Cannes (including the Palm d'Or) and has been hailed by even those critics who, like me, had savaged their earlier work for its adolescent smirkiness. *Barton Fink* has no chance of finding a large audience and for once I think it's a pity, because it's both an amusing send-up of 40s Hollywood and a sly commentary on the role of the artist. The eponymous hero is a self-absorbed, pseudo-radical 40s playwright who's hired by Hollywood to impart "that Barton Fink feeling" to a wrestling picture for Wallace Beery. Stricken by writer's block, he spends all his time looking for help; yet he's so busy blathering self-absorbedly on about the "life of the mind" and "telling the stories of the common man," that he never listens to anybody, least of all the common man.

Fink, in fact, looks like the Coens' parody of the kind of self-important message-mongering artist they absolutely refuse to be. For all their winking at the audience and taste for classic genres, they are essentially *formalists,* constructing hermetic worlds whose meanings are self-referential and profoundly abstract. (I've been told that Ethan's a great reader of Wittgenstein, but that might have been a joke.) The Coens' work exults in self-conscious plot twists and narrative echoes, recurrent imagery and running jokes, camera moves that pull you away from the action to make you admire instead the director's proficiency and cheek. Whatever ideas these brothers do have about love and loyalty, art and life, are invariably approached at the obliquest of angles.— the surest road to box office failure. *Barton Fink* makes it obvious that the Coens don't care about making popular hits.

And, for the moment anyway, Hollywood doesn't seem to mind; the Coens are still seen as hot young film-makers. Fox executives are proud to have backed a Palm d'Or winner, if only as penance for their unholy success with *Home Alone.* Besides, they feel sure that two young guys as talented and hip as Joel and Ethan Coen will eventually succumb to the inevitable—and produce a box office smash.

Richard T. Jameson (review date September 1991)

SOURCE: "What's in the Box," in *Film Comment,* Vol. 27, No. 5, September, 1991, pp. 26, 32.

[*Below, Jameson offers a mixed review of* Barton Fink.]

What's terrific about *Barton Fink* has been terrific about Joel and Ethan Coen's work since the last sequence of *Blood Simple,* when Frances McDormand did everything she could to keep a wall or a door between her and M. Emmet Walsh's implacably murderous private dick as he menaced her in a dark apartment. In the new film, the principal space is the hotel room where Barton (John Turturro), social-conscious New York playwright drafted to knock out genre scripts in 1941 Hollywood, struggles to get past FADE IN. Confronted with an epic sweep of blank page and the whining mosquito of doubt that he has anything to offer as either a spokesman for "the masses" or a proficient hack, he is opportunely di-

verted by garbled laughter/weeping/moaning coming through the wall from next-door. Into his life steps Charlie Meadows (John Goodman), hail-fellow insurance salesman, homely personification of the Common Man, and sentimental simulacrum of the Wallace Beery for whom Barton is supposed to be writing "a wrestling picture." Charlie, as he gladhandingly remarks several times, "could tell you stories," but Barton, who can't tell a story, doesn't listen. So stories come after him.

The Coens, unlike Barton Fink, know that space is a story. They map Barton's room, and Barton in it, from every conceivable angle. They know, too, that all space is interior space, and that Hollywood movies dream of worlds from inside boxes. Nicely thrown-away visual joke in a producer's outer office: Secretary sits typing under a wall-sized blowup from a desert adventure movie—a "window" on a realm of spectacle and romance—while to her left is a porthole of opaque glass holding the California sun at bay. Piquantly harrowing visual joke punctuating the entire movie: Over Barton's writing desk hangs a framed, hotel-furnished image of a young woman in a two-piece swimsuit sitting on a beach staring out to sea. The photo is small, her back is turned, the flesh she presents to us is but a pastel wash. Yet she is California, "the pictures," Life and Art, unreality and the only reality. You cannot touch her; you cannot let go of the dream of her.

Barton Fink is mesmerizingly authoritative as long as it stays within its own imaginative projection of "the life of the mind." Outside that, the movie goes askew. Not cagy-askew—like the surreal nuttiness of its deadpan proposition that there ever was such a genre as the wrestling picture— but simply off, ill-considered, wrong. One of the things the Coens get wrong is the movies themselves—their history and lore, and the accidental/inevitable conjunction of art and zeitgeist. Michael Lerner fulminates hilariously as Capitol Pictures boss Jack Lipnick, a zany conflation of Harry Cohn's brute vulgarity with Louis B. Mayer's obscene unctuousness (Tony Shaloub and Jon Polito are equally fine at catching, respectively, the manic desperation and damp acquiescence of two second-echelon execs); but Capitol, which would make sense as a version of Cohn's Columbia in the early Thirties ("We don't make B pictures here, let's put a stop to *that* rumor right now!"), bears no resemblance to Columbia or MGM or any other studio that could have had Wallace Beery under contract in 1941. John Mahoney's courtly, julep-voiced novelist-screenwriter W. P. Mayhew is the spitting image of William Faulkner (who did work on a script, the 1932 *Flesh,* featuring a wrestler role for Wallace Beery), but Mayhew, written as artist-sellout foil to Fink, is such a careless mélange of Faulkner-bio minutiae and libelous distortion that this comparatively minor character provokes major doubts about the Coens' sense of fealty to their art and forebears.

The 1941 time-frame is also at least half a decade too late to accommodate the aesthetic, political, or professional trajectory of a Barton Fink, even if Fink weren't modeled so conspicuously on *echt*-Thirties figure Clifford Odets (John Turturro uncannily succeeds in looking simultaneously like Odets *and* Ethan Coen *and* Joel Coen at any given moment). Unfortunately, the Coens appear to have hit upon 41 because it positions them, on the eve of World War II, to hazard some supremely silly historical allegory, up to and including a mind-boggling dropping of the name Hitler and a figurative Holocaust. The holocaust, small-*h*, is superb on its intrinsic terms, the consumption of the known world by the rampant solipsism of a madman—or a writer. It's also arguably a tip of the hat to Nathanael West's "burning of Los Angeles" (West is *Barton Fink's* literary godfather as Hammett was *Miller's Crossing's*, though *Fink* is closer to West's *The Dream Life of Balso Snell* than to *Day of the Locust*). But it illuminates the impending historic immolation not at all, and the Coens were feckless in even momentarily implying that it should.

Barton Fink doesn't need History to lend it scale. The only scale that matters is the awful disparity between the smudge of blood from a swatted mosquito and the surge of gore that washes Barton and the movie into madness.

Unless, of course, they were there from the start. The film begins with an injoke that's really a joke on in-ness, a slow-descending crane shot backstage at a New York theater as John Turturro's voice declaims passionate (and accurately parodied) Odets-speak; the shot eventually arrives at a closeup of Turturro—as playwright Fink (the anonymous player who exits past him had ostensibly been speaking the dialogue we heard). Everything we see and hear from then on is arguably Inside Barton Fink—projections of his paranoia and his pride, his doubts and desires, his self-inflation and self-rebuke.

Not that his various "secret sharers" are to be denied their stature. Charlie Meadows, the jolly fat man and loyal neighbor who traffics in "peace of mind . . . human contact," is also a monster named Karl Mundt who severs heads all over the U.S.A.; one of them may be in the box he gives Barton to keep for him. John Goodman's performance is twinkling, towering. Meadows comes into existence at the moment Barton needs him—something to distract him from the script he can't write. Mundt becomes a concept just in time to galvanize Fink into performing.

Someone else also leads Barton to perform. Audrey, the keeper of Bill Mayhew's writerly legend, enters Barton's bed just in time to become a blood sacrifice to his art. Judy Davis is resplendent in the role, the epitome of that neurasthenic Southern womanhood that is its own perfect parody. We can believe that Audrey writes Mayhew's (if not Faulkner's)

books; Davis visibly *tastes* language as it issues from lips drawn by weariness and wit in equal measure, tastes the words and savors every alternative meaning with a decorous sexual thrill. Her Audrey is the color of the girl in the picture. She comes into the movie pre-bled.

And leaves it shockingly too soon. An enigma hangs over the last reel of *Barton Fink*. Barton has come up against sweat-and-blood real life and been moved to write after all (a photo of Meadows/Mundt having been fitted into the corner of the beach girl's frame above his typewriter). The boorish Lipnick rejects his script and his pretensions—"You think the whole world revolves and rattles inside that little kike head of yours"—and it's the cream of at least one Coen jest that Lipnick may be right. Has Barton written "the best thing I've ever done," or merely reduced his own brief (implicitly dubious) legend to hack formula, and unsalable formula at that? The Coens rather fudge that one, but at the end of the movie Barton has the box Charlie gave him, and it may have become his. He's found the beach and the girl. "Are you in pictures?" he asks. Is he? We don't know whether he should look in the box. We don't know whether, if he does or doesn't, he could tell us stories.

Richard Grenier (review date November 1991)

SOURCE: "Hollywood's Holy Grail," in *Commentary*, Vol. 92, No. 5, November, 1991, pp. 50-53.

[*In the following excerpt, Grenier asserts that the ending of* Barton Fink *fails to live up to the promise of its beginning.*]

Barton Fink is not the story of a Jewish Galahad. Created by Joel and Ethan Coen, scripted by the two brothers working as a team, directed by Joel, produced by Ethan, *Barton Fink* is the first movie in the history of the Cannes Film Festival to win three top awards (best film, best director, best leading actor, John Turturro). With *The Fisher King* sharing the Silver Lion at Venice, it makes an impressive one-two for the new highbrow Hollywood.

Barton Fink was conceived while the Coen brothers were stricken with writer's block during the creation of *Miller's Crossing*, an ambitious and critically well-received evocation of the Chicago gangland of the 1920's. Like *Miller's Crossing, Barton Fink* is visually striking, unusually well cast, and oddly *stylized*. The Chicago mobsters of *Miller's Crossing* are mythic characters whose behavior at several points makes no sense at all, and the Hollywood denizens of *Barton Fink* are equally mythic, derived in several cases from historical characters who were rather larger than life to begin with.

Yet the Coen brothers deny that they set out to make a film about Hollywood, new or old. "We started," the brothers say, "with the idea of a big seedy hotel with John Turturro [much praised for his roles in films by Spike Lee] and John Goodman [best known for playing Roseanne Barr's husband on television's *Roseanne*]. We'd been reading a little bit about that period in Hollywood and it seemed like an amusing idea to have John Turturro as a playwright in Hollywood at that time [1941]." In early conversations, the name of Clifford Odets kept coming up, so Turturro read books about Odets and the Group Theater, and also Michael Gold's 1930 novel about the Lower East Side, *Jews Without Money,* and off they went.

For a movie in which the Coen brothers say Hollywood is a "secondary issue," "almost the cheapest part," and "not really what we were interested in," *Barton Fink* overflows with Hollywood icons and folklore. We have baroque versions of not only Clifford Odets, but MGM's Louis B. Mayer (Michael Lerner), a quintessential period film producer (Tony Shalhoub), the novelist William Faulkner during one of his filmland stints (John Mahoney), and a lady presented as Faulkner's mistress (Australia's Judy Davis from *Impromptu*). We see the old Ambassador Hotel, the old MGM lot, Culver City, eyeglasses inspired by Louis B. Mayer's, a hairdo inspired by George S. Kaufman's, a colonel's uniform made by the actual tailor who made one at the outbreak of World War II for Jack Warner. Larger than life, *Barton Fink* is also cruder than life. But if Terry Gilliam, director of *The Fisher King,* says he finds Hollywood "cynical," "awful," and "intimidating," the Coen brothers do not seem intimidated at all.

Barton Fink opens with the Broadway triumph of Barton Fink's *Bare Ruined Choirs,* a play about Fulton Street fishmongers (and a parody of Clifford Odets's *Awake and Sing!*). "Cast iron wind . . . . I'm awake for the first time in years! . . . My eyes are open now! . . . Let them sing their hearts out! . . . We'll hear from that kid, and I don't mean a postcard." The Coen brothers consider their film a comedy, and their Barton Fink tells us lugubriously that he is the playwright of the "common man," writing from "deep inner pain to ease the suffering of my fellow man," the "average working stiff," "the masses." Anguished, Barton Fink asks why the hopes and dreams of this common man should move us less than those of kings.

Signed up by one of the major film studios, Fink checks into a dilapidated, ghostly Los Angeles hotel that seems to have been inspired by the Eagles' eerie rock hit, *Hotel California* ("Welcome to the Hotel California . . . . You can check out any time you like/But you can never leave"). Actual screenwriters of the *Barton Fink* period, including Faulkner, Scott Fitzgerald, and Nathanael West, slaved away in little studio cubicles, but Barton Fink, assigned to a Wallace Beery

wrestling movie, is allowed to stay home in his rundown hotel, and there (like the Coen brothers) he gets a grand case of writer's block. He starts out: "Scene: A tenement building on Manhattan's Lower East Side. Faint traffic noise is audible." He comes to a terrible halt. The next day he adds: ". . . as are the cries of fishmongers."

Down the hall is a friendly, hearty traveling insurance salesman, a common man if ever there was one, Charlie Meadows (John Goodman), just dying to tell stories. Meadows says again and again, "I could tell you stories . . . ." These are tales which our blocked screenwriter desperately needs, but Fink always interrupts Meadows to rhapsodize on the theme of the writer's mission to serve the common man. Self-absorbed, Fink cannot listen.

His encounters with the studio brass are bizarre but quite funny; the film's most remarkable performance is by Michael Lerner as a combination of Louis B. Mayer and Columbia's Harry Cohn:

> Is that Barton Fink? Let me put my arms around this guy! The writer is king at Capital Pictures! We need more heart in the movies! The poetry of the streets! We want that Barton Fink feeling! The hopes and dreams of this wrestler! A romantic interest? Is Wally too old for a romantic interest? Is he an orphan maybe? Which is it, Bart? Orphan? Dame? I'm bigger, meaner, and louder than any other kike in this town! End of the week, Bart. We're all expecting great things.

Fink's encounters with the William Faulkner character are rather less entertaining. Timid, plain, no hand with the ladies, Barton Fink somehow manages to go to bed with Faulkner's mistress, and during their night together the camera does strange things. It dollies over to the hotel room's washbowl and goes down the drain—down, down, down— through the plumbing. After which *Barton Fink* becomes a different movie.

Is this *Barton Fink Through the Washbowl Plumbing* intended to be the Hollywood nether world? Is it a dream? The movie, from the time Fink arrives in Hollywood, has never been realistic. The vast and ghostly Hotel Earle has only two specter-like employees, and Fink and Charlie Meadows are its only guests. But when our blocked screenwriter wakes up in the morning post-plumbing, there is a sharp break. In a panic, Fink sees a flood of blood oozing from the lady he went to bed with, who is quite dead. Charlie Meadows disposes of the body for him. Fink has a story conference with the Louis B. Mayer-like studio mogul and finds him grotesque—although since the mogul was already rather grotesque the change here is less obvious than waking to find one's bedmate dead. Back at the Hotel Earle, two hard-bitten (and anti-Semitic) detectives tell Fink that Charlie Meadows, now missing, is no likable traveling salesman after all but a serial killer, "Mad Man Mundt."

In a burst, Fink finally writes a screenplay about a wrestling fishmonger, ending with the charged words, "We'll hear from that wrestler again, and I don't mean a postcard!" Our studio mogul rages at Fink for writing "a fruity movie about suffering" and announces he is going to keep him under contract but never produce any of his scripts (purgatory). And then Charlie Meadows, a/k/a Mad Man Mundt, returns. In the corridors of the Hotel Earle, ablaze with metaphoric hellfire, he guns down the police detectives, screaming, "I'll give you the life of the mind!" We never, in fact, emerge from the washbowl plumbing.

What does it all mean? Since, according to the Coen brothers, Hollywood was not what they were really interested in, the true subject of the movie, still according to the Coen brothers, can only be the relationship between the common man's playwright, Barton Fink, and a genuine common man, Charlie Meadows. Here the sanctimonious show-business leftism of the 1930's and 1940's is clearly being satirized. Written as it was by two blocked writers, *Barton Fink* seems, also, to be about the creative process. But why the blood? Why turn a gregarious, good-humored insurance salesman into a serial killer? Are these arbitrary plot devices supposed to deepen the audience's perception of "reality"?

The Coen brothers are far more guarded about their movie's meaning than was T. S. Eliot about *The Waste Land,* and no film critics I have read seem even to have noticed the through-the-washbowl-plumbing shot or the sharp change in register the shot marks. Some reviewers have merely labeled the film's ending "obscure." But it really does appear that everything after the plumbing—the bedmate dead, Charlie Meadows a serial killer, the hotel ablaze, the studio mogul threatening—is indeed a Barton Fink nightmare. It is admittedly an extensive and elaborate nightmare, taking as it does 45 minutes in a two-hour movie. But it hardly makes a satisfactory end for such a film, and it is not very funny. Which is unfortunate, because the early parts of *Barton Fink* show real talent.

When Lewis Carroll sent his Alice through the looking glass she found a droll, ironic world, still entertaining to us today. When the Coen brothers send Barton Fink through the plumbing of his seedy Los Angeles hotel, he finds flames, lurid violence. Does Barton Fink's nightmare tells us anything interesting about the creative process, Hollywood, or even Barton Fink? In *The Fisher King,* director Terry Gilliam, responsible for the amusing and imaginative animation sequences in British television's *Monty Python* series and for a number of increasingly ambitious movies (*Jabberwocky, Time Bandits, Brazil, The Adventures of*

Baron Munchausen), similarly goes overboard when he pursues deep meaning.

But nowadays—witness the awards for both the Coen brothers and Gilliam—film-festival juries are really wowed by deep meaning.

Tad Friend (interview date April 1994)

SOURCE: "Inside the Coen Heads," in *Vogue,* April, 1994, pp. 348, 350-51, 407-08.

[*In the following interview, Friend talks with the Coen brothers on the set of* The Hudsucker Proxy.]

Susan Sarandon crept up to the magnificent double doors. It was February 1993, in Wilmington, North Carolina, and she was visiting her longtime companion, Tim Robbins, who was filming **The Hudsucker Proxy.** The set's lavish scale clearly took her aback. Was this a Coen Brothers film? Weren't they supposed to be small-budget, art-house, seat-of-the-pants productions peopled with little-known character actors? She poked her head through the doorway to survey the scene: the gargantuan office, massive Art Deco fixtures, terrazzo-marbleized walls—and there, behind a huge desk, wearing a gray suit, smoking a fine cigar, and looking serenely iconic, Paul Newman.

Sarandon turned to the movie's director. "It's gorgeous!"

Joel Coen nodded, almost. Unshaven, pony-tailed, fingering a cigarette lighter like a rosary, he has a perpetual up-all-night-for-the-French-lit-exam look. His brother, Ethan, unshaven, curly-haired, and shorter, wandered out of Newman's office trailing a hand along the wall, like a kid counting his footsteps. Ethan is nominally the producer, but the brothers write and film their movies together, behaving as one brain. "Can we make the second hand go faster?" Ethan asked the special-effects gang boss, referring to the huge Hudsucker Industries clock outside Newman's window.

"Like, a hair?"

"Two hairs," Ethan said, with no change of expression. "Two hairs and a tidge." The scene depends on a certain mechanized exactitude: the synchronized movements of a ticker-tape machine, a Newton's Cradle ball-bearing game, and the clock hand. (Later, in postproduction, the Coens will have an animator paint in better, more foreboding clock-hand shadows.)

The Hudsucker Proxy, set in 1958, is a comedy about Norville Barnes (Tim Robbins), a nice cluck from Muncie,

Indiana, who comes to New York and is chewed up by the relentless engines of the city—emblematized by that sweeping clock hand. He is played for a patsy both at work and in his affair with hard-bitten reporter Amy Archer (Jennifer Jason Leigh). He triumphs by inventing the Hula-Hoop, is dragged down to the point of suicide, then triumphs again.

The assistant director shouts the ritual "Lock it up!" and everyone quiets for a take. (Ethan has been trying to get the AD to shout instead, "All aboard for hilarity!" with only mixed success.) In this scene, Norville, working in the Hudsucker mail-room, enters with a letter for the movie's villain, Sid Mussburger (Newman). Mussburger is looking to install a moron as president (thus, "proxy") so the company's stock will fall and the board can acquire a controlling interest. Norville's haplessness—he ends up rolling around trying to extricate his foot from a burning trash can—catches Mussburger's eye.

As Robbins comes in, Newman is telling an underling over the phone, "Either you get me a grade A dingdong or you can tender your key to the executive washroom." The quirky, precise language is a Coen trademark: Words like *rumpus* and *nonce* leap from their screenplays. Nicolas Cage's doleful metaphor for his wife's barrenness in **Raising Arizona**— "the doctor explained that her insides were a rocky place where my seed could find no purchase"—is classic Coens, as is the chiming consonance of **Barton Fink**'s "You're a sick fuck, Fink."

That wised-up ear is one reason Joel and Ethan have been everyone's favorite auteurs since **Blood Simple,** the film noir they shot in 1982 for a mere $855,000, and released to great acclaim in 1984. Another reason is astonishing technique: They flaunted their talents early in **Blood Simple,** when the camera glides assuredly along a bar top, approaches a sleeping drunk—and bumps up and over his head before resuming its prowl.

The Coens have since made **Raising Arizona,** a hyperactive comedy about a baby-napping; the 1930s-ish gangster film **Miller's Crossing;** and **Barton Fink,** in which a Clifford Odets-like playwright goes to Hollywood, suffers from severe writer's block, and gets entangled with a serial killer. Each is funny, weird, and masterful, yet utterly individual in tone. In an industry rife with overbudgeted disasters and studio interference, the Coens are also legendary for storyboarding their scenes down to the minutest sound effect, for adhering to the budget, for not having been spoiled by critical success, and for having always preserved the contractual right to make the movie's final cut—a right that many filmmakers work decades to achieve.

Between camera setups, I asked Joel how it felt to be filming here, at the corner of the Carolco lot's Kassar Boule-vard and Rambo Drive—a roundabout way of inquiring whether he has any concerns about selling out. None of their previous movies cost more than $9 million; *Hudsucker* is a $25 million film executive-produced by the flashy action-film maven Joel Silver (*Die Hard, Lethal Weapon*). It's their first movie with stars, their first movie with potential for real commercial success. Coen's eyes fluttered skyward at my question. "Oh ... well ... in the Disney lot they have Mickey Drive.... " The next shade of apparent boredom would be a coma.

He and Ethan went off to murmur to the actors: Joel leaning over Robbins, and Ethan sleepily lying across Newman's desk. "It was never some angst-ridden, torturous process of self-examination," Robbins said later of these discussions. "Mostly it was 'Let's do it again . . . but funnier.'"

But though low-key and seemingly open to suggestion, the Coens know exactly what they want: actors who serve the story and say the lines as written. Nicolas Cage, the star of **Raising Arizona,** called them "autocratic." "It's difficult to convey to an actor that he is just supposed to be the bad guy in a melodrama, and not, as is natural, seek to go beyond it," Joel would say later about Hudsucker.

That bad guy, Paul Newman, says Joel and Ethan "are musicians with a great sense of verbal rhythm. I'd say, 'What do you want, Stravinsky or Bach?' They usually wanted *The Rite of Spring*." Deeper questions of theme or intent were off-limits. "They call this an 'industrial comedy,'" Newman notes with amiable perplexity. "What the fuck an industrial comedy is, I have no idea."

Joel and Ethan are known to all as "the boys." They finish mumbling each other's sentences, have similar problem hair, always wear jeans and sneakers, have quick, thievish minds, and love to exchange movie dialogue (like the "You fuckin' my wife?" scene between Joe Pesci and Robert De Niro in *Raging Bull*).

They supposedly grew up in a suburb of Minneapolis with an older sister, Debbie, and two college-professor parents, and spent a lot of time with a Super 8 camera making movies like *Froggy Went A' Courtin'*, which featured road-killed frogs and toads. Both brothers are said to have married within the past year, each for the second time (Joel to Frances McDormand, star of **Blood Simple,** and Ethan to Tricia Cooke, an editor who has worked on Coen films).

Yet it's hard to imagine Joel and Ethan in a domestic context; they comprise their own private biosphere. They often seem like extremely precocious kids with an Erector set, refusing to explain to the adults just what it is that they're building. They talk in a private shorthand: a "Miles" is the faint squawk of the person at the other end of the onscreen telephone; an "ambassador" is a gesture, look, or remark that introduces you to a character's motivations; and "hubcaps" are the diminishing sounds after a big aural effect—the clatter of an ashtray after someone slams a fist on a desk. While filming *Miller's Crossing* they called the A camera "Elvis" and the viewfinder "Little Elvis," Elvis's reputed nickname for his penis. Instead of saying "that's a wrap," they'd announce "Ladies and gentlemen, Elvis has left the building."

And the Coens are a legendarily tough interview. Bored by recounting the truth, they are by turns gnomic and absurd. They told one reporter that Jennifer Jason Leigh was actually "bald as a cue ball" and wore a wig throughout filming, and that she showed no embarrassment about taking out her false teeth and swishing them around in a glass.

I first spoke with them at length in their ground-floor office on Manhattan's Upper West Side. Joel, 39, slouched on the couch smoking Camel Lights while Ethan, 36, paced in distracted loops and circles, chewing a toothpick. He would make six or seven small loops near the door photo of Kurosawa on the wall, then a long circle out of sight through the kitchen. Eventually he'd reappear and resume his tight loops, the orbiting electron to Joel's collapsed neutron.

Friends of theirs had said that Joel puts key objects in the left side of the frame, whereas Ethan favors the right, and that Joel worries more about camera angles while Ethan focuses more on the dialogue. Surely there were other, more interesting differences?

There was an excruciating silence. "No . . . nah . . . no, no, no . . . not really," Ethan finally said. "It's a terrible question, a terrible thing to do. . . ." Joel mumbled. "It's like you're on *The Dating Game*," Ethan said. "Yeah," Joel said. "You're going to find a real resistance to talking about ourselves as opposed to talking about the movies."

OK: Tim Robbins said to ask about the European critics' interpretation of the buzzing mosquito in *Barton Fink,* and how it epitomizes people over interpreting your movies.

A longer silence. "That's another thorny thing . . ." Ethan finally said. "You're getting to the nub," Joel said, as Ethan started to snicker. "On the one hand, we want to talk about the movies . . ." "But the movies speak for themselves," Ethan concluded.

I tried asking them about an idea proposed by Sam Raimi—their co-screenwriter on *Hudsucker,* the man who gave Joel his first break after NYU film school as the assistant editor of Raimi's movie *The Evil Dead,* and their close friend. Raimi had remarked that the Coens have several thematic rules: The innocent must suffer; the guilty must be punished; you must taste blood to be a man. "Joel and Ethan are play-

ing with an additional one," he'd added. "The dead must walk."

Joel and Ethan shrugged, separately. "That really applies more to *The Evil Dead* than anything else," Joel said. "I guess they applied to **Blood Simple,**" Ethan allowed. And to **Raising Arizona, Miller's Crossing, Barton Fink,** and **The Hudsucker Proxy,** I pointed out. "Yeah . . ." Joel said. "Yeah, yeah, yeah, yeah, yeah, yeah," Ethan said, gnawing a fingernail. Ethan had actually quoted Raimi's formulation to explain their own work at the New York Film Festival in 1984; now they both had deflective amnesia.

Finally, after they'd evaded the last of my questions, I said, "Well, what *should* I be asking you? This is something of a disaster."

"I thought it was going really well," said Ethan, genuinely surprised.

"Yeah," Joel said, shaking his head as if the whole thing were out of his control. "There was a picture of us in *The New York Times,* taken by a friend of ours, where we were sitting there glumly looking like we'd just ax-murdered our mother, and when my wife Fran looked at it, she said, 'Jesus, what a couple of assholes.'"

"We could never figure out how to end the movie," says Sam Raimi, who wrote **Hudsucker** with Joel and Ethan beginning in 1984, when they all shared a house in Los Angeles. "We left it two scenes from the end, with Norville up on the ledge about to jump." Raimi had always wanted to have a definite ending in mind, but Joel and Ethan were happy working without that safety net, improvising, disagreeing, letting it all hang out. (Their closed-ranks cohesion kicks in later, when they start to film.)

"I would actually throw firecrackers or ladyfingers at the boys to get them moving, to spark an idea," Raimi said. "Sometimes when Ethan was pacing, I'd move some of the objects in the room. He'd come up to these obstacles and make a hoarse barking noise—'Hunhh!' I'd like to think I was jogging him to a higher plane. When I'd suggest something they considered absurdly wrong, they'd just laugh and laugh and say 'No, no, no—you can't, because . . . because you just *can't.*' I suggested that Mussburger might turn out to be a nice guy who'd been led astray. When they broke into laughter I realized it's a film of broad strokes, of blacks and whites, and that changing Mussburger would diminish Norville's plight. But they accused me of trying to malign the film, kill them, destroy art."

Finally with a definite ending, ten years later, **The Hudsucker Proxy** is a very funny movie. When Norville says "You have a very charming wife, Sid," Mussburger replies absently, "So they tell me." (Raimi says the Coens wanted Mussburger's wife to be Jack Lemmon in drag; they settled for an actual woman.) Amy Archer says of the Hula-Hoop, "Finally there would be a thing that brought everybody in America together—even if it kept them apart, spatially." A great many stock characters turn up like old friends: haughty society wives, persnickety executive secretaries, Germanic scientists, Germanic psychiatrists, even asylum attendants carrying butterfly nets. It's not parody, exactly. The Coens use these classic totems to emphasize Norville's predicament. He's surrounded by people behaving like caricatures, like subhumans. They also use them as a flat-out gag. "Part of the fun of all those stock characters," Ethan says, "is just its stupidity."

Recognizable visual or thematic influences on *Hudsucker* include *His Girl Friday, The Front Page, Mr. Deeds Goes to Town, The Court Jester, The Fountainhead,* and *The Big Clock,* among many others. "We agreed that *Citizen Kane* had the scale and perspective we wanted," says production designer Dennis Gassner, "but we wanted to do it much better than they did it, do it the Coen way, not the Welles way." Adds Leigh, "Making the movie really brought me back to all those childhood sick days when I was home with the stomach flu. I would watch those great screwball comedies by Cukor, Sturges, and Capra and laugh and laugh until it was the next time to throw up."

The Coens pureed all these referents in their cranial Cuisinarts, then spiced in most of the recurrent Coen motifs: "howling fat men, blustery titans, violence, vomiting, and peculiar haircuts," as their friend William Preston Robertson puts it. (There is, alas, no vomiting in *Hudsucker.*) The movie has showy camera pans up the side of a building and, later, into a screaming woman's mouth (the Coen "Glottis Shot"). It has hyperrealistic sound effects, like the foreboding scrape-scrape of a sign painter as he scratches the former president's name from his office door.

It has a tour-de-force wordless montage of the Hula-Hoop being readied for production and then catching on across America, choreographed to characteristically unexpected music, in this case Khatchaturian's "Sabre Dance." This, Joel and Ethan's favorite part of the movie, is reminiscent of their other great wordless montages: the fifteen-minute section of *Blood Simple* in which the bartender buries his boss alive in an open field; the gunfight in *Miller's Crossing* that features a gangster being shot to pieces as his twitching finger continues firing his own Thompson submachine gun while "Danny Boy" floats lyrically into our ears.

What *Hudsucker* doesn't have is signposts to help the audience root for the characters. There is one appealing balcony love scene, but in their detachment the Coens seem to be laughing up their sleeves at Norville and his romance.

"It's almost axiomatic that a movie's principal characters have to be sympathetic, and that the movie has to supply moral uplift," Joel said. "People like it. But it's not interesting to us. You're not supposed to sympathize with Gabriel Byrne in *Miller's Crossing,* or with Barton Fink. John Turturro used to say that Fink is the guy who if you're invited to a party, everyone asks"—Joel adopted a tone of suspicion—"'Is Barton going to be there?' And you only sympathize with Norville in a certain way—he's an outsider, and with good reason. He's not just misunderstood." Coen gave an Arnold Horshack laugh. "People feel Jennifer is too tough in the movie, but I don't feel that at all—that's the way the movie works. People do find that distance chilly, or cold around the edges."

Other film staples the Coens find uninteresting: "A theme song sung by a pop singer just for the movie," Joel said. "A journey to self-awareness," Ethan suggested, "where you open the script and a character says, 'I thought you were feeling that I . . .'" "A tearjerker about a cancer patient," Joel said. Any story involving a triumph of the human spirit, I suggested. "Yeah, yeah," Joel said, and Ethan snorted and chuckled. The film behind their eyes dropped away, briefly.

This aloofness from the viewer's sympathy is why the Coens have remained highbrow darlings and box-office lepers. Joel Silver couldn't contain the sneer in his voice when he said of *Barton Fink,* which won the Palme d'Or at the 1991 Cannes Film Festival, "I don't think it made $5 million, and it cost $9 million to make. They've had a reputation for being weird, offcenter, inaccessible. They were having trouble getting the money for this $25 million script—people were stymied by the fact that Joel and Ethan's name was on it."

Silver, surprisingly, was a huge Coens fan, so he got involved to line up the money after the Coens had written the last two scenes and begun shopping the script in 1991. Even stranger, the Silver-Coen collaboration has gone well. At least until now. The problem, Silver said bluntly, is that "if they intend to continue making mainstream, higher-budget films, this film is going to have to deliver asses on seats." When the movie premiered at the Sundance Film Festival in late January, Silver, concerned that *Hudsucker* would "be perceived as a festival film" (i.e., an arty head-scratcher), kept telling the Coens, Robbins, and Leigh that they had to stress at the press conference that it was an accessible, straight-ahead comedy. They did so, but only dutifully.

"The pressures are very visible and very legitimate," Ethan acknowledged. "It's all money: Making more money makes it easier to get money for your next film." Joel added, "But as far as being perceived as mainstream movie-makers—that's not particularly important to us. It's not like we're doing this so we can now go do . . ." he casts about, "*Beethoven III.*"

What saves the Coens from social autism is their engaging ironic distance on their own ironic distance. The introduction to the forthcoming book version of the *Hudsucker* screenplay is a Q and A between Joel Silver and one "Dennis Jacobson, professor of cinema studies at the University of Iowa." In fact, it was written by Joel and Ethan, who always use the introductions to their published screenplays to mock themselves.

The pseudo-Silver reveals that the Coens whined a lot, seemed happiest playing with their storyboards, and hadn't wanted Paul Newman in the picture. "Their attitude, it was funny. Like it's a sin to use a movie star. God forbid somebody should actually be enticed into the theater to see one of their movies. 'No, he's too iconic.' And Tim Robbins, that whole thing—forget about it."

> DJ: Tim Robbins was not their choice either? And yet he's very good.
>
> JS: This—I found this unbelievable at the time, but this—Ethan wanted to play the part. . . . He says only he understands the character fully. . . . It was absurd, but I let him test.
>
> DJ: How was it?
>
> JS: What do you think how was it? It was goddamned embarrassing. It's—it was like the early days of talkies. Ethan is lumbering around on this pathetic little set they've mocked up, with his flat Midwestern voice, chopping the air with his hands, these stiff gestures, I mean, Richard Nixon doing a love scene. Stiffo.

And so forth. "The intros to screenplays are always some screenwriter gassing on with self-congratulation or some sort of foggy analysis of what they've just done," Joel says. "We'd rather do something that's fun to write." It's a few days later. He is sitting alone in his office with no lights on. Cigarette smoke curls up dimly through the dark afternoon.

I start to ask whether there wouldn't be some value in a clear explanation of their tenets, and then catch myself. Stupid question. "If Preston Sturges could somehow be reanimated to write a clear explanation of his working principles, his trade secrets, wouldn't you want to read that?" I ask.

Joel looks uncomfortable. "It's interesting to know that Preston Sturges had a big dog on the set that frequently barked and ruined takes. That's more interesting to me than anything Sturges could tell me about his working methods." He's aware that he sounds willfully perverse.

"What if you won an Oscar and had to make an acceptance speech? Would you riff through that emotional moment, too?"

"We'd be so mortified at the thought of having to speak in public that I doubt we'd write anything," Joel says, and laughs. "We'd probably wing it. I'm always impressed, genuinely, by graceful acceptance speeches." A long pause. "I think that sort of thing is just beyond my capabilities."

"I can't watch our old movies—I'm overcome by a fog of boredom," Ethan says. He sits alone in an armchair, willing himself to stay in one place. "I saw *Blood Simple* on TV a while ago, and I enjoyed it because it was different: They had commercials. I think all black-and-white movies should be colorized and chopped up with commercials. If you had hooked my brain up with electrodes, you'd have seen a big spike of interest when the Ty-D-Bol Man came on."

So where is the pleasure in doing what you do? He thinks for a while, making an effort, then begins pacing again, to get the thoughts flowing. "Well, in *Raising Arizona,* we blow up a car. And to be incredibly crude about it, it's just so cool to sit there and watch a car blow up. That was a peak. It gave us a deep, warm feeling of inner satisfaction."

Joel is still puzzled by the imputation of chilliness in their movies. "You can put a five-year-old up on the screen and make him cry—and that's the most cerebral, formulaic-bullshit corny manipulation, yet everyone will be crying their eyes out." He makes a "boo-hoo" sound.

"People do have a problem dealing with the fact that our movies are not straight-ahead: They would prefer that the last half of *Barton Fink* just be about a screenwriter's writing-block problems and how they get resolved in the real world, or that *Raising Arizona* just be about a couple of schmoes in a trailer park who want to have a kid—the arrival of the bounty hunter from hell interrupts the comfort level people have with their world. But we feel a strong emotional connection to those characters, we're not laughing down at them."

So the end of *Raising Arizona,* when Hi has a vision of him and his wife "suffused in a warm golden light" and in a land where "all parents are strong and wise and capable, and all children are happy and beloved," is totally serious?

Joel Coen snickers faintly, then gathers himself. "Absolutely."

John Harkness (review date August 1994)

SOURCE: "The Sphinx without a Riddle," in *Sight and Sound,* Vol. 4, No. 8, August, 1994, pp. 7-9.

[In the following negative review, Harkness suggests that the Coens tried to combine the works of Frank Capra and Preston Sturges in The Hudsucker Proxy.]

There's a fine line between homage and rip-off. The Coen Brothers' originality lies not in their stories, which are derived from any number of better-known sources, but in the sheer aplomb they bring to the film-making process, the relentless darkness of their humor and the ironic twists they give to familiar tales.

Blood Simple and **Miller's Crossing** are *film noir* plain but not simple, the latter owing so much to *The Glass Key* that it's a wonder the Hammett estate didn't sue for plagiarism. **Raising Arizona** functions simultaneously as a commentary on the baby-centric comedies of the mid-80s and a live-action realization of a Road Runner cartoon. **Barton Fink** belongs both in the writers' nightmare school of Hollywood stories and as a concurrent remake of *The Tenant* and *Repulsion*—its Palme D'Or at Cannes came the year Polanski was president of the jury, though when I interviewed jury member Alan Parker shortly thereafter, he assured me that the decision had been unanimous.

The Coens' latest, **The Hudsucker Proxy,** predates **Blood Simple** as a project. Written by the Coens and their mentor Sam Raimi (*The Evil Dead, Darkman*), eventually someone managed to get hack genius Joel Silver, producer of *Lethal Weapons* and *Predators,* to put up $40 million to finance the production of this monstrous confluence of Frank Capra and Preston Sturges. This is the funniest thing about **The Hudsucker Proxy.**

Waring Hudsucker (Charles Durning) listens to his comptroller's financial report and then launches himself from the window of the 44th floor of the Hudsucker Building at the moment when Norville Barnes (Tim Robbins) arrives to begin his career in the mailroom. A graduate of the Muncie School of Business, Barnes has dreams of making it to the top of Hudsucker Industries, a plan that will be unwittingly assisted by the machinations of the evil Sidney J. Mussberger (Paul Newman). Barnes becomes the figurehead president of the company, and begins work on his invention, which he carries drawn on a carefully maintained, well-worn piece of paper in his shoe. The film charts Barnes' rise, fall and recovery, through the travails of bad press (Jennifer Jason Leigh as a tough-talking reporter with a heart of gold), accusations of fraud, and divine intervention.

From his infelicitous name to his physical clumsiness, Norville Barnes is a Preston Sturges hero trapped in a Frank Capra story, and never should that twain meet, especially not in a world that seems to have been created by Fritz Lang—the mechanistic monstrousness of the mailroom contrasted with the Bauhaus gigantism of the corporate offices perfectly matches the boss-labor split in *Metropolis.*

The difference between Capra and Sturges is that Capra has an authentic belief in the romanticism of pure individualism. His characters are genuinely heroic battlers against the grinding power of big money and big politics. It's a faith blind to its own darkest implications that untrammeled individualism is as much a piece of the capitalist monsters as it is of the heroes, the dividing line being that the capitalists' individualism is wholly self-interested.

Sturges, on the other hand, is a romantic wiseguy. He believes in love, but only in its more bizarre and tortured forms, as in Henry Fonda's obsession with Barbara Stanwyck's card-sharp in *The Lady Eve,* or Eddie Bracken's masochistic pursuit of Betty Hutton in *The Miracle of Morgan's Creek.* Sturges is too in love with the baroque possibilities of the English language to honor the simple decency of a Jimmy Stewart in *Mr. Smith Goes to Washington.* The world created in his films is benign and harmless. His heroes do battle with their own limitations, rather than with the malevolent forces of darkness that range themselves against Capra's heroes. A Sturges hero would be eaten alive in Capra's world, which is why **Hudsucker**'s premise doesn't work. There isn't enough weird luck in the universe to save Norville Barnes from Sidney Mussberger, so the film's ending turns out to be more improbable than anything in either Sturges or Capra.

The Coens are quite different. People think their notorious press conferences and interviews, which consist of misdirected remarks and gnomic mumbles, are a put on, but really they work to hide the fact that the brothers don't believe in much of anything—they have enormous abilities, but are sphinxes without riddles. One suspects that Ethan's comment at the Cannes press conference for **Barton Fink** that their films are just frameworks on which they can hang cheap jokes was not a joke at all. There is an emptiness at the heart of their work which can be ignored when the films are entertaining, but which shows up dreadfully when they aren't.

One can easily see what the Coens are attempting here, with their extreme stylization and willingness to reduce actors to single bit players' mannerisms, but this misses the point. Directors in the 30s and 40s used the stylized performances of the great bit players as a characterological shorthand, the way Renaissance dramatists could refer to the *commedia dell'arte* and everyone would know what they meant. But the leading players were not reduced to a single trick, the way the Coens shrivel Jennifer Jason Leigh into a caricature of Katherine Hepburn's drawl and one imperious gesture. (I think Jennifer Jason Leigh may be the most talented actress in American movies today, but all I could think while watching **The Hudsucker Proxy** was that she didn't enunciate well enough to be a plausible visitor from Planet Kate, and that, to echo Addison DeWitt, she simply wasn't tall enough to make the finger to the sky salute the Coens kept asking of her.)

The Coens' fondness for extreme stylization often works. In **Blood Simple** and **Miller's Crossing,** their reduction of characters to trademark gestures and phrases is well suited to the hermetically sealed universe of *film noir.* **Raising Arizona**'s characters inhabit the same malevolently indifferent world as Wile E. Coyote, whom Nicolas Cage could play without resorting to a costume. The delirious self-absorption of the characters in **Barton Fink** emerges in their unique and completely differentiated mass of tics—it is entirely appropriate that the two least stylized players in the film would turn out to be John Goodman's serial killer and his victim, Judy Davis. **Barton Fink** can easily be seen as an opera in which everyone gets an aria, but they are all loath to sing duets.

In **The Hudsucker Proxy,** the Coens attempt to jam together two items that simply don't mix—a 30s story and characters, and a 50s setting. The styles of American film acting changed so much between the age of Gary Cooper and the age of James Dean and Marlon Brando that it's hard to realize that they were separated by only a couple of decades. The styles of urban everyman had changed, the style of supporting acting had changed, the style of dialogue had changed. The exterior assurance of the 30s stars gave way to the tortured interior anguish of the 50s Method mumblers. The first influx of New York writers, the Hechts and Perlmans and Parkers, all urban smarts, had given way to the seriousness of Inge and Williams, all anguish. The casual patter of comedies in the late 50s is a drone, not the rat-a-tat of the old newspaper comedies. In addition, 30s cinema has an intimacy that often disappears by the time the studios start filming on outdoor locations and trying to fill the CinemaScope frame. One can see why the Coens wanted a 30s-style patter and a 50s setting, for Barnes' invention is inextricably associated with the latter period, but big empty sets are not conducive to snappy dialogue, which is why there are so few laughs in *Lawrence of Arabia.*

Furthermore, the stylized acting of the 30s and 40s comedies takes place around the realistic romantic leads. It humanizes the beauty of the young Gary Cooper if his best friend is a baleful cynic like Walter Brennan. Even in Sturges' films, there is often a conventional leading man who exists as a still center around whom and to whom things happen—Joel McCrea in *Sullivan's Travels,* Henry Fonda in *The Lady Eve.* Even in *The Miracle of Morgan's Creek,* the epic degradation of Eddie Bracken's character makes us sympathetic towards him—we never perceive him, as we do Norville Barnes, as some kind of geek savant.

Part of this comes from Tim Robbins' performance, though

I don't think we can blame Robbins himself—the best performances in the Coen's films often seem to be ones that get away from the brothers' rigid conception (Goodman in **Barton Fink,** for example), and Robbins' broad mugging was probably asked for. We cannot blame an actor if his casting is a mistake from the outset. The hero is supposed to be a loveable little guy, and casting Tim Robbins as loveable or little is like casting Rip Torn as Gandhi. He towers over everyone else, and whatever Robbins' fine qualities as an actor, being loveable isn't one of them. Had he played this role earlier in his career, about the time when he was doing *Erik the Viking* and *Bull Durham,* he might have got away with it, but while Altman may have given him his two best roles—in *The Player* and *Short Cuts*—he also revealed that Robbins' great talent is an ability to inhabit the reptilian skins of men best described as cold-hearted bastards.

Capra was not an innocent film-maker, but he was a naive one, and there is no evidence that he ever doubted the peculiar American dream his films portrayed, or that he was anything but indifferent to the dark implications of his work: the way the 'little people' are subject to manipulation at the hands of capitalist media and prone to lapse into mob violence and hysteria at the drop of a hat; the way his shining heroes are self-absorbed individualists as immune to compromise as any of the heroes of writer Ayn Rand—exemplified by the arch-individualist architect in *The Fountainhead.* It seems only too appropriate that Gary Cooper, who played Capra's small-time heroes Mr. Deeds and John Doe, would later star as the overweening monumentalist in King Vidor's film adaptation of Rand's novel.

We live in an age so conscious of media manipulation and cinematic effects that it is difficult to make a film today that is not determinedly ironic about its own devices. Neo-Capra films such as Stephen Frears' *Accidental Hero* and Ivan Reitman's *Dave* cannot convince us of the reality of their worlds because the film-makers have lost that power of belief. Why else would *Accidental Hero* try so hard yet so futilely to evoke the Capra of the 30s—its huge dissolve montages come straight out of *Meet John Doe.* The Capra films still function because of their extraordinary conviction and potent performances.

Capra's great films—*Meet John Doe* and *It's a Wonderful Life*—work because their dreams cannot contain their nightmares. The Coens' strengths lie in a stylization that reduces or even eliminates the human presence from the frame, and a gallows humor they never shy away from. Their happy endings are ironic commentaries on the genres they subvert, and their world is composed only of nightmares.

Jonathan Rosenbaum (review date 1995)

SOURCE: "Crass Consciousness," in *Placing Movies: The Practice of Film Criticism,* University of California Press, 1995, pp. 248-53.

[*In the following review, Rosenbaum criticizes inconsistencies in* Barton Fink.]

I'm not one of the Coen brothers' biggest fans. I walked out of **Blood Simple,** their first feature. The main sentiment I took away from **Raising Arizona** and **Miller's Crossing**—their second and third efforts, both of which I stayed to the end of—was that at least each new Coen brothers movie was a discernible improvement over the last. **Raising Arizona** may have had some of the same crass, gratuitous condescension toward its country characters as Blood Simple but it also had a sweeter edge and more visual flair. In both craft and stylishness, **Miller's Crossing** was another step forward, and even if I never really believed in either the period ambience or the characters—the dialogue bristled with anachronisms, and Albert Finney's crime boss seemed much too blinkered and naive for someone who was supposed to be ruling a city—the film nevertheless demanded a certain attention.

On its own terms, **Miller's Crossing** was the work of a pair of movie brats (both in their midthirties) eager to show their emulation of Dashiell Hammett but, in spiky postmodernist fashion, almost totally indifferent to Hammett's own period—except for what they could skim from superficial readings of *Red Harvest, The Glass Key,* and a few secondary sources. Historical and psychological veracity consisted basically of whatever they could get away with, based on the cynical assumption that their audience was every bit as devoid of interest in these matters as they were. Unlike their earlier efforts, **Miller's Crossing** was a commercial flop—an undeserved one, given its visual distinction and its strong performances. Even if the film was soulless, it showed an obsession with its Hammett-derived male-bonding theme that suggested the Coens were aspiring to something more than crass entertainment; for better or worse, it looked like art movies were their ultimate aim.

Barton Fink confirms this impression with a vengeance. Unfortunately, the movie ultimately founders on the Coens' primary impulses, which drive them to use a festival of fancy effects; whatever their ambitions, midnight movies are still the brothers' métier. The movie's arty surface fairly screams with significance, but the stylistic devices are designed for immediate consumption rather than being part of a coherent strategy. As entertainment, **Barton Fink** is in some ways even better than **Miller's Crossing,** though also just as adolescent and much less engaging when seen a second time. Last May it received the unprecedented honor of being awarded three top prizes at the Cannes film festival—for best picture, best director, and best actor (John Turturro)—which will undoubtedly help it commercially in Europe. Whether these awards will count for much in the more hidebound United States still remains to be seen.

The president of the Cannes jury was Roman Polanski, who took the job only after demanding that he be allowed to handpick his own jury members. Considering the indebtedness of **Barton Fink** to Polanski pictures like *Repulsion, Rosemary's Baby,* and *The Tenant*—in its black humor, treatment of confinement and loneliness, perverse evocations of everyday "normality," creepy moods and hallucinatory disorientation, phantasmagoric handling of gore and other kinds of horror as shock effects, and even its careful use of ambiguous off-screen sounds—the group of awards should probably be viewed more as an act of self-congratulation than as an objective aesthetic judgment.

Nevertheless, **Barton Fink** is an unusually audacious movie for a major studio to release—not only because of its bizarre form and content, but also because the Coens had complete creative control. Whatever else they might mean, then, the Cannes prizes cannot be regarded as automatic nods to the commercial tried-and-true. In terms of overall meaning, **Barton Fink** qualifies as a genuine puzzler. Considering how transparent most commercial movies are, **Barton Fink** at least deserves credit for stimulating a healthy amount of discussion.

The title hero is a working-class Jewish playwright (Turturro) who has just scored a hit in New York with his first play, *Bare Ruined Choirs*; the year is 1941. Offered a lucrative Hollywood contract by Capitol Pictures that he reluctantly accepts—he doesn't want to compromise his passionate vision of a theater "by and for the common man"—he goes to the west coast, checks into a faded deco hotel called the Earle, and goes to see Capitol's hysterically effusive studio head Jack Lipnick (Michael Lerner), who promptly asks him to write a wrestling picture for Wallace Beery.

Alone in his squalid room at the Earle, Barton finds himself painfully blocked, unable to get beyond a few scene-setting sentences. The sound of sobbing (or is it laughing?) in the next room prompts him to phone the front desk, and a few minutes later his next-door neighbor (John Goodman)—a burly, friendly fellow who identifies himself as an insurance salesman named Charlie Meadows—pays him an apologetic visit. Barton recognizes him as exactly the kind of working stiff he's interested in writing about, and they soon become friends—though Barton is too full of himself to show much interest in learning anything about Charlie (who repeatedly announces that he has stories to tell).

Barton meets with Ben Geisler (Tony Shalhoub), the flinty producer assigned by Lipnick to the wrestling-picture project. He also meets W.P. Mayhew (John Mahoney), an alcoholic southern novelist turned screenwriter clearly modeled after William Faulkner, and Audrey (Judy Davis), Mayhew's abused secretary and mistress, whom Barton clearly takes a shine to.

Stylistically, the movie chiefly consists of three kinds of scenes. There is entertaining if obvious satire about Hollywood vulgarians (Shalhoub—who played the cabdriver in the underrated *Quick Change*—and Lerner are both very funny and effective). There are extended mood pieces involving the heat, solitude, and viscousness (peeling wallpaper with running, semenlike glue) of Barton's seedy hotel room, with frequent nods to *Eraserhead* as well as Polanski, and many repeated, obsessive close-ups of both Barton's portable typewriter and a tacky hand-colored photo of a bathing beauty framed over the desk. Finally, there are the scenes between Barton and Charlie, all of which occur in Barton's room (no other room in the hotel is ever seen) and suggest a sort of sweaty homoerotic rapport somewhat reminiscent of Saul Bellow's novel *The Victim* and the tortured male bonding in **Miller's Crossing.**

There's a certain temptation to follow **Barton Fink** simply as a midnight movie, a string of sensations that alternates among styles and moods like a kind of vaudeville. As the plot suddenly veers into outright fantasy and metaphor, incorporating other styles and moods (mainly those of arty horror films), the effect of putting one damn showstopper after another is to almost obliterate any sense of logical narrative. (Moviegoers who don't want their surprises spoiled should check out at the end of this paragraph.) We're essentially invited to take a funhouse ride through these effects rather than ponder too much what they're supposed to mean. But however much it appears to profess otherwise, **Barton Fink** is as heavily laden with "messages" as any Stanley Kramer film. Almost all of these messages, I should add, are cynical, reactionary, and/or banal to the point of stupidity.

As I see it, the messages are as follows:

1. *Socially committed artists are frauds.* Admittedly, the only one we see is Barton Fink, but the film has no interest in showing us any others. The principal model for Fink appears to be Clifford Odets (although he's given a George S. Kaufman haircut), and the film is at pains to show us that his ideas are trite, self-centered, and so limited that he ends both *Bare Ruined Choirs* and his wrestling-picture script with virtually the same corny line. We have no way of knowing whether he's genuinely talented or not, and the movie seems completely uninterested in exploring this question, except for suggesting briefly that the people who praise his play are lunkheads. When the United States suddenly enters World War II toward the end of the movie, it seems not only to catch him completely unawares but to leave him indifferent as well—certainly not the reaction of the socially committed artists the Coens appear to be modeling him after. (As

a friend has pointed out, Barton's preoccupations are about a decade off; by 1941, proletarian leftist artists were talking about fascism and the war, not about lower-east-side fishmongers.) He's an infantile sap throughout, and the movie forces us to share his consciousness in every scene.

2. *Genuine artists like William Faulkner are frauds too—at least partially.* It's true that Mayhew is meant to *suggest* Faulkner rather than duplicate him, but consider how the Coens have loaded their deck. Mayhew looks like Faulkner, and he has both a "disturbed" off-screen wife with the same name as Faulkner's disturbed wife (Estelle) and a secretary (Audrey) modeled in certain respects on Meta Carpenter, the script girl Faulkner was involved with. By contrast, Faulkner was a taciturn drunk whereas Mayhew is a loquacious loudmouth who's successively humming and belting out "Old Black Joe" both times we see him and spouts flowery rhetoric at every opportunity. Although the Coens claim not to have known this until after they wrote their script, Faulkner actually worked on a Wallace Beery wrestling picture when he first came to Hollywood (John Ford's *Flesh,* 1932), and although it's conceivable that Carpenter or other friends could have helped to write some of his scripts, the suggestion that Carpenter may have helped to write some of the novels is ridiculous and was invented for this movie only to suggest that Mayhew, like Fink, is a poseur who can't really deliver the goods. Certainly the Coens have every right to twist reality as they please, but their alterations ("Old Black Joe"?) are so crass that they tend to rebound. Considering that most audience members won't be closely acquainted with Faulkner, it's disturbing that the only point at which Mayhew and Audrey diverge incontrovertibly from their models is when both of them become victims of a mad serial killer. (Audrey "gets hers," in classic puritanical slasher style, just after she's had sex with Barton.)

3. *Hollywood producers are frauds.* As indicated above, Lipnick and Geisler are hilarious, but the laughs are easily come by, and they make it difficult to see how such people could have turned out any pictures at all, much less several beautiful ones. (For whatever it's worth, the first "Wallace Beery wrestling picture," *The Champ,* was arguably one of King Vidor's masterpieces and won Beery, who actually played a prizefighter in the film, an Oscar.) Perhaps the Coens are justified in calling attention to Hollywood bigwigs as illiterate vulgarians, but judging from an early script of **Barton Fink** that I happen to have read, they themselves don't even know how to spell such words as "choir," "playwright," and "tragedy." In short, the rhetorical power of commercial moviemaking, available to anyone with a few million dollars to spend, allows them a free ride over a lot of people's corpses—Louis B. Mayer's as well as Faulkner's and Odets's—a ride that made me slightly nauseous.

4. *The very notion of the "common man" is fraudulent.*

Charlie is introduced to us as the embodiment of this cliché, and Goodman's wonderful performance manages to encompass it without ever seeming hackneyed. But the way the movie undermines the common-man cliché is by dragging out a contemporary countercliché that's every bit as hackneyed. When Charlie turns out to be the serial killer, we are offered the revelation that people who chop off other people's heads are nice, ordinary people just like you and me—"common" folks, in fact. (This cliché is promulgated in the news as well as in movies—take those interviews with junior high school teachers about how "nice" the killers seemed to be. Mysteriously, each time the homily is trotted out, whoever's using it—in this case the Coens—seems to think it's brand new and profound.)

So judging from *Barton Fink,* what is it the Coens do believe in? Friendship, perhaps. Also, perhaps, an abstraction that the movie designates repeatedly as "the life of the mind" and that it associates with the act of creation—Barton's mind and act of creation in particular—as well as with Charlie himself. (Barton's room is clearly meant to suggest a brain, oozing fluids and all, and Charlie's climactic reappearance when the movie suddenly goes metaphorical—walking down the hotel corridor with a shotgun while the rooms on both sides of him successively burst into flames—is accompanied by his vengeful declaration, *"I'll show you 'the life of the mind!'"*)

In order to follow the Coens' shift from one metaphor to another, the wanton abandon of midnight-movie viewing becomes necessary—it might even help if you're half asleep. Ironically, Goodman's Charlie, the most multiple of all the film's metaphors, also proves to be the only real character. (Turturro's Barton seems much too simpleminded to have ever written a successful play, and his so-called struggles with writer's block, as depicted in the film, could easily have been dreamed up in Lipnick's office.)

One way of sorting much of this out is to follow the provocative suggestion of *Variety* reviewer Todd McCarthy and assume that Charlie doesn't exist at all, except as an emanation of Barton's unconscious—the "common man" his blocked imagination is screaming for. This interpretation would make the overheard sobs (or laughs) in the next room, Charlie's murderous impulses, and even the mysterious package Barton receives from Charlie all really emblems of Barton's own tortured mind; significantly, Mayhew indicates that he associates the act of writing with pleasure whereas Barton replies that *he* associates it with pain. According to this scenario, Barton murders Audrey himself because he can't bear to face the possibility of her creative mind coming to the rescue of his own on the wrestling script.

The only problems with this scenario are that it fails to account for how Barton finally breaks through his creative block—unless we view Audrey's murder as the less-than-instantaneous catalyst—and that it fails to mesh coherently with some of the other metaphors in the movie. I've been told that Deutsch and Mastrionotti, the wise-cracking anti-Semitic detectives on the killer's trail who question Barton and are ultimately killed by Charlie (one of whom is dispatched with the epithet "Heil Hitler"), are meant by the Coens to represent the Axis powers. (I suppose that makes Lipnick—whom we last see dressed as a full-fledged Army officer—the United States.) But if this is the case, the historical *and* metaphorical imaginations of the Coens must be even more threadbare and confused than I imagined. In what sense, exactly, were Hitler and Mussolini trying to track down the common man—or the life of the mind—and bring him (or it) to justice? And in what sense did this common man or life of the mind that wound up killing Hitler and Mussolini sell insurance or chop off people's heads?

A final point should be made about the broad, comic-book-style Jewish caricatures in the film—Barton, Lipnick, Geisler, and Lipnick's assistant Lou Breeze (Jon Polito). Spike Lee was lambasted on the op-ed page of *The New York Times* and by Nat Hentoff in the *Village Voice* (among other places) for Jewish caricatures in *Mo' Better Blues* which employed one of the same actors (Turturro), occupied only a fraction as much screen time, and were if anything *less* malicious than the caricatures in *Barton Fink.* So I assume the reason Lee was singled out for abuse and the Coens won't be to the same extent is that the Coens happen to be Jewish. For whatever it's worth—speaking now as a Jew myself—I don't consider any of the caricatures in either movie to be racist in themselves, and it seems to me somewhat absurd that Lee should be criticized so widely for something that the Coens do at much greater length with impunity. Being white, having the minds of teenagers, and believing that social commitment is for jerks are all probably contributing factors to this privileged treatment.

Kim Newman (review date June 1996)

SOURCE: A review of *Fargo,* in *Sight and Sound,* Vol. 6, No. 6, June, 1996, pp. 40-41.

[*Below, Newman provides a plot summary and favorable review of* Fargo.]

Minnesota. Car salesman Jerry Lundegaard, deeply in debt, goes to Fargo to meet Carl Showalter and Gaear Grimsrud, two criminals. Jerry gives them a car off his lot and arranges with them to kidnap his wife Jean. He plans to extort a million dollar ransom from his wealthy father-in-law Wade Gustafson, giving Carl and Gaear half of what he claims is only $80,000 dollars. Carl and Gaear snatch Jean but are stopped on the road near Brainerd by a policeman because the car still has dealer license plates. Gaear shoots the cop dead, then pursues and murders two passing tourists.

The heavily pregnant Brainerd police chief, Marge Gunderson, follows the trail of the killers, which takes her to Minneapolis-St Paul. Wade insists on delivering the ransom personally and is shot dead during a struggle by Carl, who, wounded and bleeding himself, discovers the size of the ransom and buries most of the money, intending to split only the original $80,000 with Gaear. Returning to their hideout, Carl finds Gaear has killed Jean out of hand. They get into an argument about the money, which winds up with Gaear taking an axe to Carl.

Jerry, having concealed Wade's body, is questioned by Marge, who thinks the killers' car might have been stolen from his lot. Jerry runs, convincing Marge of his involvement. Driving home, Marge spots the car by the hideout, and finds Gaear disposing of Jean and Carl in a wood-chipper. She shoots and then arrests the fleeing Gaear. Later, Jerry is arrested in a motel.

A quiet opening caption insists on the factual basis of *Fargo,* although it avoids prefacing the film with the most dispiriting rubric in the language, "based on a true story". We are told that something very like this impossible, *Blood Simple*-ish story did in fact happen in the Coen brothers' home state of Minnesota in 1987. The first melancholy shot of one car dragging another through a blinding white blizzard to a wonderful Carter Burwell arrangement of the hymn "The Lost Sheep' is followed by our introduction to the rubber-faced sad sack that William H. Macy makes of the protagonist Jerry Lundegaard. These images signal just how different this film will be. It's a departure, not only from the dreary parade of True Crime television movies released in the UK by Odyssey video, such as *The Amy Fisher Story,* but also from such comparable, aren't-folks-funny, talk show dramatizations as *I Love You to Death.*

We are given only telling hints of the circumstances that have brought the likeable but clearly doomed Jerry to Fargo but everything is made heart-breakingly clear by his brief telephone conversations with a bank official who needs clarification of a form Jerry has deliberately fudged to clear a loan. Later, we see his dreams die during a couple of crushing meetings with his overbearing, wealthy and subtly bullying father-in-law, to whom he has brought an investment but who is unwilling to underwrite Jerry's own involvement in the deal. "This would be a good thing for Jean and Scotty and me," Jerry claims, only to have the rich Wade snort, "Jean and Scotty never have to worry about money". Jerry is a tragic figure but also a clown (with a mouth like Joe E. Lewis').

Fargo is a further demonstration of Joel Coen's remarkable ability to mix comedy with horror. The film operates a certain double standard in its characterizations. Jean, for instance, is relegated to the status of a joke, with her squeaky voice and the slapstick inflicted on her (blindfolded by the kidnappers, she runs around like a headless chicken in the snow). She winds up casually murdered off-screen. Meanwhile, the one-scene sub-plot character of Marge Gunderson's nervy old flame, who has a disastrous reunion with the police chief in Minneapolis, segues from stooge to tragic figure when it is revealed that his story of recent widowerhood is all a fantasy.

Joel Coen has always—like his best known character Barton Fink—been open to charges of asking us to laugh at the disadvantaged provincials about whom he spins stories. He has spotlighted the redneck grunge of Texas in *Blood Simple* and the backwoods whininess of the locals in *Raising Arizona.* Here, on his home turf, he allows a great deal of regional humor, joking at the expense of 'ya ya' Scandiwegian locals who wander about with ear-flaps down through biting winds and acres of white snow. The waddling Marge, played by Joel's wife and longtime collaborator Frances McDormand, may be a maternal Columbo, whose ethnic and character quirks disguise a penetrating detective ability, but a great many other characters are amusingly dimwitted, peculiarly-accented and 'funny-looking'. These specimens range from the hooker who is cheerfully only able to remember of a client that "he wasn't circumcised" to the touchy kidnapper, Carl Showalter, who gets into a trivial and ultimately fatal argument about money just after he has squirreled away a never-to-be-reclaimed million dollars in cash.

As with *Blood Simple,* the Coens prove themselves masters of orchestrating cross-purposes plots, with half-thought-out criminal schemes going awry in ways that are surprising and yet obvious, ironic and yet horrifying. Whereas the earlier film presented a quartet of corrupt characters whose double-crosses are understood only by the audience and the dead, *Fargo* offers McDormand (incidentally, the sole survivor of *Blood Simple*'s plot) as a detective who through intuition, logic and luck does penetrate the backstory.

The real heart of the film is in Marge's understated relationship with her slobbish artist husband, Norm Gunderson, whose last-reel compromised triumph is that he sells a bird painting to be reproduced on the three-cent stamp. His tepid triumph is wearying enough to maybe make her look up that old flame, but the relationship still provides a warmth that gives her a strength none of the other characters—whose homes are seen to be stifling or freezing—can manage. Snuggling with her husband, and cheering him up by pointing out that people need small change stamps whenever the mail prices go up, Marge finally admits that she can't understand why the people whose trail she has followed have acted with such desperation. Here, with chilling but touching directness, Coen cuts his amusing but distanced conic approach and shows a heart that matches his undoubted skill.

Michael Wood (review date 20 June 1996)

SOURCE: "The Life of the Mind," in *London Review of Books,* Vol. 18, No. 12, June 20, 1996, pp. 18-19.

[In the following review, Wood expresses that, althourhg he finds the movie flawed, Fargo *is the Coens' best work since their first two films.]*

The screen shows a flat, empty road from a very low angle, a torn tire lying on it like a piece of junk sculpture. Then the towers of a city in the distance, then a set of ramshackle houses, a pasture and a farmhouse, the white screen of a drive-in, a field full of oil pumps. A drawling voice, all wide vowels and unclosed consonants, starts to philosophize. "The world is full of complainers, and the fact is, nothing comes with a guarantee . . . Something can always go wrong . . . What I know about is Texas, and down here you're on your own." These are the opening moments of **Blood Simple.** Ethan and Joel Coen's first movie, released in 1983, and they look like an agenda, an announcement of work to come. They look that way only now, though, when we have seen the later films, learned that the appearance of raw and gritty realism in that first movie was deceptive. We were never in America, only "America," a place full of stories about itself, none the less mythological because historical reality every now and then manages to catch up with it, or incorporate a piece of its gory or flamboyant action. The "down here" in the voice-over now sounds like a giveaway, since it implies an awareness of other places, even an anxiety about them, about the way Texas may look from a different region. Of course there's boasting in the claim too, in the fact that chain saw massacres, for instance, don't happen just anywhere.

Since then the Coen brothers have given us a dusty South-West (**Raising Arizona,** 1987) an unnamed Thirties Prohibition city that would look like Chicago if it looked like a city at all (**Miller's Crossing,** 1990); a Forties Hollywood that looks like Hollywood's idea of itself (**Barton Fink,** 1991) a toytown Fifties New York (**The Hudsucker Proxy,** 1993), and now a bleached-out, snow-driven Midwest, where the very names of places, for all their actual presence in the atlas, sound like a scrambled allegory. Fargo, North Dakota, Brainerd Minnesota, Bismarck, North Dakota. What happens in these far-flung settings, this dream-America, as Nabokov once called a similar country? People die a lot, often violently. They are shot in the head and in the gut, their faxes are torn away. Heads are severed. One body is tipped into an incinerator, another body is minced in a woodchipping machine. A husband arranges to have his wife and her lover killed, another husband arranges to have his wife kidnapped. Irish and Italian mobsters kill each other, and they both want to kill their Jewish competition. Even when this world turns to comedy, scheming is still an important feature: a baby is stolen, and then is stolen from those who stole it, a large manufacturing company organizes its own failure, and then fails to fail. A businessman flings himself from a window on the 44th floor (45 if you count the mezzanine, as a member of the board insists). Schemes go wrong from coast to coast, and from Texas to the Canadian border. No zone is safe. So it's not quite true that nothing comes with a guarantee. Chaos comes with a guarantee, because something can always go wrong, and always does. The dream of the cancellation of all this which ends **Raising Arizona** is not the exception that proves the rule, it is the fantasy which confirms the presumed disorder of fact. "It seemed like home," Nicolas Cage murmurs in voice-over, the camera showing an absurdly conventional family reunion set far in the future. "If not Arizona, then a land not too far away, where all parents are strong and wise and capable, and all children are happy and beloved." A pause, "I don't know. May be it was Utah."

"Things have changed," one of the hoodlums says in **Fargo,** when a little kidnapping has escalated into triple murder: a policeman blown away because he wouldn't be bribed, a young man and a young woman swiftly shot because they drove by and saw the dead policeman "Circumstances . . . Beyond the, uh, acts of God force majeure." And then later he says twice rather solemnly: "Blood has been shed." The fancy diction in the nasty situation recalls the films of Quentin Tarantino, and the actor is Steve Buscemi, who appears in a not dissimilar role in *Reservoir Dogs.* In **Fargo,** when Buscemi returns to the hideout he and his fellow hood are using, his face ripped by a gun shot, and caked with blood, he can speak only in a mangled way. He says: "You should see the other guy!"

Fargo, like *Reservoir Dogs* and *Pulp Fiction,* is dedicated to a ghastly comedy of violence, and to the suggestion that violence in life is mainly not malign and planned, but messy, like lasagne dropped all over the kitchen floor, or pathological, like a failure to distinguish between the uses of fly swatters and revolvers. But the Coen brothers are more programmatic about this suggestion than Tarantino is, and heavier in their use of it. With them it isn't really anything as soft as a suggestion, it is what the films are manifestly saying to us, and in **Fargo** particularly the expectation that things will get out of hand, that the horrific is the normal once you step into certain areas of American experience, is paired with a joky insistence on the weirdness of normality even when it's nice. The film feels a little heavy not because it's slow (although it is), but because it's edited to make us pause over its ideas: these ordinary people really are strange; these strange people really are ordinary.

The movie ends with the criminals put away and the nice dumpy couple, pregnant police chief and amiable, boring husband, watching TV in bed. She says "Heck, we're doing pretty good, Norm." He says "I love you, Margie." She says "I love you, Norm." Then they both say, one after the other. "Two more months." This is too low-key to be funny, and too tacky to be serious. The message, I think, is supposed to be that life goes on, there are good people in the world as well as psychopaths, but the whole thing feels like an unfocused spoof of ordinariness, as if dull married life was, after all, weirder than anything else. This is a subject addressed in **Barton Fink,** where the pretentious young writer, a sort of travesty of Clifford Odets, is always talking about the common man. But the pay-off there is that there aren't any common men, that the fellow Fink cast in the role turns out to be a serial killer who specialises in lopping heads off, and the best moments in the film are not its feeble gestures towards satire but its forays into apocalyptic lunacy, as when the killer runs through a burning hotel, flames leaping up all around him as if he were the master of hell, brandishing a shotgun and shouting: "Look upon me: I'll show you the life of the mind!" That movie portrays a Faulkner figure in the shape of J. P. Mayhew, a drinking Southern gentleman but it's closer here to Flannery O'Connor, the great American artist of the grotesque. She once said she didn't think that the texture of Southern life was "any more grotesque than that of the rest of the nation but it does seem evident that the Southern writer is particularly adept at recognising the grotesque." Growing up Jewish in the Midwest might not be a bad training either. In his Introduction to the screenplay of **Fargo,** Ethan Coen recalls his grandmother insistently teaching the boys a Russian phrase signifying "By your tongue you will get to Kiev;" a maxim meaning "If you don''t know, just ask." Coen is not sure how talking about Kiev was meant to work in America, but takes the proverb as looking forward to a certain extravagance of truth: "Surely young Grandma (itself a paradox) would not have believed anyone selling her that she would never in her life see Kiev, but *would* see The Jolly Troll Smorgasbord & Family Restaurant in Minneapolis."

The voice at the beginning of **Blood Simple** is that of a private detective played by M. Emmet Walsh. He is a greasy bulging fellow, whose sweaty face slides in and out of erratic smiles, as if it were made of warm wax. He drives a scruffy Volkswagen Beetle, and he seems to be just a buffoon. Then you realise he's a lethal buffoon. He's hired to kill a pair of lovers, but kills the husband who hires him instead, then tries to kill the lovers after all, and gets the man before the woman gets him. At one point there seemed to be a logic to his actions, but you lose track of it, and the movie is all the better for this: the man is like some materialisation of the crazy violence lurking everywhere in this imagined Texas, and his air of shabby incompetence makes him all the scarier when you realise he is grimly determined to bump off all the movie's principal characters if he can. He's a slob, but a slob with an iron will, and all the meanness in the world. The moment when he breaks down a wall with one hand in order to remove the knife that is pinning his other hand to a window-sill makes it clear that he is not to be taken lightly. He dies laughing, because the woman who shot him (through a door) still thinks he is her husband. Down here you're on your own, but you can still see the joke.

The things you remember from this film have to do with its cleverness, but the things are not only clever. The woman sits up in bed in front of a window, talking to her lover. When she lies down, we see the private detective's rusty Volkswagen parked outside. How long has it been there? The eeriness of its appearance, without cut or change of angle, suggests a form of magic. It has always been there, even when we couldn't see it. Or it has been conjured up just now, by the woman's talk. Craziness comes when you call it, or even think of it. A little earlier, there is what seems to be a conventional sequence of cuts from ceiling fan to a man (the husband) sitting thinking to ceiling fan again to a woman in bed in another house. What's conventional is the use of the item of furniture as a transition—think of all those chandeliers in movies which are only there to get us to another chandelier. But here the ceiling fans are different: the first, with pale wooden blades, is in the husband's office, the second, with blue metal blades, is in the lover's house. So strong is the sense of the gaze directing meanings in the movies that you can't believe a cut from a man looking at the ceiling to a ceiling fan doesn't represent what he actually sees. I had to rewind the film twice to convince myself that the fans are different. And of course, the effect is perfect, and prophetic. The man is in the other house in his angry mind, and the next time we see him he has infiltrated the house in fact.

The Coens' movies are full of touches like this. But they are not always, or even usually, as delicately connected to mood and movement. Elsewhere the cinematic swishes—the close-up on the whisky glass, the busy high-angle shots all over the place, the Hitchcockian figures cropped at the knees so that only their legs and feet are in the frame—are just cinematic swishes, signs that movie-making is going on. There is one interesting moment in **Miller's Crossing,** though, where the movie-making is not relevant but appealing for just that reason. We see a dog, and a boy, and what they are looking at: the body of a dead man slumped against a wall in an alley. There is something strange about the angle of the man's hair. Close-up of the boy, a poor-looking innocent out of a De Sica movie or a Kertesz photograph. The boy tugs at the dead man's hair, it's a wig, comes off easily. The boy and the dog scamper off. The dead man turns out to be Rug Daniels, an Irish gangster, and there are various guesses about who killed him. The mystery is finally solved, but nobody can work out why the killer would want to take the man's wig, and nobody can imagine that accident has whisked the wig away.

The woman who heroically survives the onslaught of the miasmic detective in **Blood Simple** is played by Frances McDormand, who is also a leading character in **Fargo**— Marge Gunderson, the pregnant Brainerd police chief called in when the kidnapping turns to murder. She has a wonderfully understated acting style, dominated by a level stare, which in the earlier movie means bewildered innocence, but here means crafty intelligence masquerading as northern stupidity. You can also see her in the thriller *Primal Fear,* where she plays a psychiatrist, and the stare there suggests a refusal to be bullied and an intelligence in excess of local needs. When she arrives at the scene of the triple crime in **Fargo,** she sums it up in seconds, deducing what happened exactly as we have seen it happen: "Okay, so we got a trooper pulls someone over, we got a shooting, and these folks drive by, and we got a high-speed pursuit, ends here, and this execution-type deal." All this delivered in a slow, monotonous Swedish-inflected accent; most of the people in the movie talk as if they were trying out for a Bergman film but had to do it in English, and had a vocabulary which rarely went beyond "Geez" and "Yah". When Marge has to throw up, it is not, as her colleague thinks, at the sight of the destroyed face of one of the corpses. It's morning sickness.

The screen keeps whiting out in this movie, as if the film had faded into nothing, but it's just the northern weather: pale sky, or icy mist, or a snow-storm, or a snow-covered car park. When the trooper pulls the kidnapper over, we see his prowler, lights flashing, through the iced rear window of the hoods car, it's like a ghost ship in some arctic vision. When the Buscemi character decides to bury the kidnapping money, he trudges across a field of snow, chooses a spot close to a wire fence, digs a hole, covers it over. Then he looks up: the fence stretches for miles in both directions, identical poles sticking up in unmarked snow. The effect the Coens were after, Ethan Coen says in his Introduction, was that of "the abstract landscape of our childhood—a bleak windswept tundra, resembling Siberia except for its Ford dealerships and Hardee's restaurants" What's interesting is that apart from the temperature and the coloring, the landscape also resembles that of their first two movies, **Blood Simple** and **Raising Arizona,** a world where the camera is always being used to register emptiness and flatness, and where the car and the road are almost everything. A recurring image in these films is the double yellow line down the centre of a long, flat highway: as if human beings had managed to make one tidy mark on this inhuman scene, but had messed up ev-

erything else. A stage direction in **Fargo** reads: "The police car enters with a whoosh and hums down a straight-ruled empty highway, cutting a landscape of flat and perfect white."

The other remarkable performance in this movie, apart from McDormand's, is that of William H. Macy as Jerry Lundegaard, a car salesman who owes a lot of money (he's borrowed $320,000 against a set of cars he hasn't got), and has hatched the hare-brained scheme of having his wife kidnapped and splitting the ransom money with the kidnappers. Who's going to pay the ransom? His rich and unsympathetic father-in-law. Why doesn't Jerry just ask for the money, from his wife or her father? Because they don't know he needs it, and wouldn't give it to him anyway. Macy looks amiable, nervous, grins as if in pain. He looks like a crook's idea of a trustworthy person, so deeply suspect that you realise he's never going to deceive anybody, and his helplessness, along with his pathetic belief in the possibilities of his no hope plans, almost makes you like him. The trick is that his scheme should seem close to insane (to us) and entirely plausible (to him). He doesn't know the criminals he's dealing with, and he doesn't know how much damage can result. He would be a sort of innocent if he were not so determined to be devious. The most subtle and discreet comment on what's wrong with his notions is not the series of murders he has indirectly unleashed, although that is comment enough, but the scene in which his son sobs for his stolen mother, and wonders what will happen to her. Jerry hasn't really thought about this—she was only an item in his scheme—and can't comfort his son, only offer him the weary, transparent lies he's telling everyone else.

There aren't quite enough such moments in the movie. It's very intelligent work, and its icy atmosphere tells a whole austere story in its own right. It's probably the Coens' best film since **Blood Simple** and **Raising Arizona.** But it still recycles American mythologies rather than exploring them or playing with them. When Marge has arrested the remaining criminal single-handed (the real psychopath, the one who was feeding the corpse of Buscemi to the woodchipper), she broods on the meaninglessness of it all. Five people dead now—the state trooper, the two witnesses, Buscemi and, almost incidentally, Jerry's unfortunate wife—and what for? "For a little bit of money," Marge says to the stonily silent killer. "There's more to life than a little money, you know." A little later: "I just don't understand it." It's right that Marge shouldn't understand it, of course, and that we shouldn't understand it either. But there is something too easy about this orchestration of our failure, just as there is something too easy about the movie's amazement at the ordinary. Violence is grotesque and readily stumbled into, just waiting for impatient or stupid or arrogant people. And happiness is grotesque too, picturable only as a remorseless absence of glamour. Nothing is glamorous except cold weather, and that is only glamorous to look at, since it shows the screen at its empty best.

Devin McKinney (review date Fall 1996)

SOURCE: A review of *Fargo,* in *Film Quarterly,* Fall, 1996, pp. 31-34

[*In the following review, McKinney praises some aspects of* Fargo *but asserts that the Coens condescend to the characters.*]

The Coen brothers have spent 12 years and six movies walking a tightrope of their own devising, flirting with the nihilism and ex-cathedra contempt for the poor materials of reality that are marks of the gifted undergraduate. What has saved them from hipsterism is a sense of irony that is not merely ironic, a consistent faith in the power of controlled craft to open up holes of chaos in content, and a study of the quirk so monastic and intent it yields ambiguities not retrievable by looser methods.

What also saves them is an artistic personality which, in opposition to many of their vaunted peers in the film school generation, is less a commercial trademark, a promise of the familiar, than an organizing impulse in the movies themselves. They are darker-souled than Tarantino and also less obsessed with fun at any cost, and though they are temperamentally incapable of aggressively confronting an audience as Spike Lee does, they are still too involved in the oddities of their imagination to affect the Jarmusch shrug. Nor can they be accurately described as pastiche artists, as mavens of the literary swipe and the cinematic in-joke. Certainly the comic contemplation of genre tropes is a player in their game, but they have used the in-joke (or, in polite society, intertextuality) not as a self-justifying end but as a springboard to touch depths mostly unplumbed by the purveyors of either pulp fiction or *Pulp Fiction.* Whether *Miller's Crossing* takes off from Dashiell Hammett or *Blood Simple* from James M. Cain is ultimately less important than that the Coens have twisted the various idioms into shapes peculiar to themselves, and that despite their stylistic change-ups they have, like most great film artists, been making essentially the same movie over and over again, playing variations on a theme. That their styles do not bespeak "obsessiveness" does not mean an obsession is not being worked out.

This said, the pursuit of personal themes does not ensure a straight shot to enlightenment; it may as easily as any other path yield a blind alley. *Fargo* sees the Coens plummeting unceremoniously from their tightrope, not taking a fall so much as a willed descent. Fundamentally, the film cannot be called a failure, since it is clearly the work it was meant to be, and it is if nothing else of a conceptual piece with everything they have ever done. But its very success on its own terms is disturbing because *Fargo,* in addition to being a personal work, is also a fatuous piece of nonsense, a tall cool drink of witless condescension. Coming from the Coens, it is a betrayal—of themselves, of their audience, of a human milieu.

Like each of their five previous features, *Fargo* is about the quotidian horrors visited upon those who would commit the grave error of living out not the lives they have been given but the lives they envision in their own master narratives. Minneapolis car salesman Jerry Lundegaard (William H. Macy) hires two men (the rat-like Steve Buscemi and the hulking icemonster Peter Stormare) to kidnap his wife, his hope being to extort money from his parsimonious father-in-law. Grievous violence and a strangely homiletic, Velveeta-textured variety of chaos ensue, until order pervades in the pendulous form of the seven-months-pregnant Marge Gunderson (Frances McDormand). Marge is sheriff of the little northern Minnesota town that hosted a pair of homicides related to the kidnaping; despite her chirruping mouth and eyes perpetually peeled in an avid gape, she is a self-effacing pro who will not only solve the case but face down evil and live to wonder at the saddening, mystifying inhumanity of man.

Though an opening title suggests a factual basis for the story, it hews so closely to the Coen line that its purported documentary truth becomes irrelevant after the first ten minutes. Jerry, the common-man hero of *Fargo,* is kin to the other Coen figures who did their best to hold reality hostage so that they might live a while in the cozier realm of fantasy. The master narrative is his, but—like the other characters—Jerry finds his grand designs aborted by the incompetence, conflicting motives, or undifferentiated hostility of those who will not play their parts. He and his plot hearken back to the confused scenarios of infidelity in *Blood Simple,* the bourgeois aspirations of the *Raising Arizona* hero, the machinations of an Irish mob mastermind in *Miller's Crossing,* and *Barton Fink*'s misreading of a crypto-Nazi serial killer as that grand abstraction of 30s intellectuals—the common man.

But nothing worth lingering on is ever so schematic. The mickey in such a reading of the Coens' work is that the end point of a given fantasy is not predetermined. In *Fargo,* it goes disastrously wrong; in *The Hudsucker Proxy,* it executes itself with the precision of a timepiece. In *Miller's Crossing,* it goes both right and wrong, with the Irishman scripting things perfectly but for one detail: having written himself out of the order he has obtained, he ensures his own desolation, his own surcease as the hero of the fantasy. If the dream of self-determination (and consequent control of the immediate environment) is the theme, then these are the variations, and they signal the currents of possibility, disorder, and chance that percolate below the self-possessed surfaces of what is otherwise a tightly dammed style.

Fargo, though bound to the Coens' better work by the connective tissue of thematics and a deliberate visual aesthetic, constitutes a rupture in every other way, trading dark humor for dim slapstick, a piquantly distanced observational mode for a feckless pose of sham objectivity. The film's sole claim to narrative novelty is, of course, the insertion as crimestopper and moral orderly of a pregnant woman whose singular ungainliness stems less from her physical condition than her insistence on a fanatically hearty demeanor. She is that rarest of birds in the Coen aviary, a true innocent.

The problem is that in *Fargo* the Coens do not give true innocence its dramatic or psychological credit, as they do with the corruption and inner rot that sire Jerry's scheme and predestine its abysmal end. Marge's naïveté does not come off as something which in its way is as organic and inviolable, and thus as much an expression of essential character, as the pure evil which Stormare represents and which is far easier for an artist to sell to an audience. The Coens play the character in two irreconcilable ways, first tipping their hand by scoring Marge's clever crime-scene conjectures for laughs even though they are meant to suggest a shrewdness which resides in her like the meat in a bland walnut. As written and performed, Marge is so vapid that her astute ratiocinations seem more a function of plot exigencies than any definition of persona. While promoting her homespun acumen, the Coens inflate her horsy jollity—neglecting any corners of doubt or disturbance that might lie between—and the split leaves the character not just gutted of particular qualities but grandiosely unreal, an elaborately embellished kitsch artifact. When faced with the full measure of the atrocious crimes that have been committed—that point in the story which requires her, finally, to say what she is about—she has this to say: "I don't understand it." That no ambivalence soils the virgin territory of her mind seals her fate as a character, and shows the Coens resorting to the oldest, easiest kind of positivist aphorism: ignorance is not only bliss, but grace.

Marge represents too well the north-country rabble that inhabits this snowy landscape, most of them undiscerning pods whose ordinary human specificity is buried under vacuous grins, cowtown bonhomie, and about 50 too many distended Scandinavian "yahhh"s. The "yahhh" is ubiquitous, for the screenplay sings it like a mantra; Whitman's yawp is here transmuted to a somewhat less stirring assertion of self. The fact that even the most addled Minnesotans do not sound like this is of course not to the point; that this vocal leitmotif diminishes the characters instead of particularizing them is. (The faux-literate argot of *Raising Arizona* had the opposite effect, since it signified both the absence and the unre-

ality of Hi McDonough's grand dreams without reducing him to foolishness; in the film's cartoon context, such language was a key to character as much as comedy.) The "yahhh," in fact, is what topples the Coens from their tightrope—that which spans the gulf between condescending to one's characters and magnifying one's ambivalence toward them for a larger and fuller effect.

The Coens have often been accused of condescending, but close viewing always deflected the charge. In the past they have had the nerve to burrow past condescension to discover a more complex, less comfortable empathy with their characters than fiction usually grants in our benighted time. Barton Fink, for all his blather and oblivion, was also allowed the grace of sitting on a beach, quietly contemplating his own disintegration as a poster-art beauty sat beyond his reach and a clumsy gull speared its quarry in the Pacific. There are few moments in movies that are more dispassionate, and fewer that effect such a galling, inarticulate connection to one's own cosmic loneliness.

That spin which the Coens give to our expectation of and need for empathy amounts to an existential reversal, given that empathy as a literary idea is commonly understood to be a unifying agent. "Who is that man?" becomes "I am that man." At their most original, the Coens have exercised the darker, more difficult impulse to unite characters and audience not in the warmth of a common affirmation, but in the chill of a common alienation. It's an empathy that says not "I recognize that man's situation and now don't feel so lonely," but "I recognize that man's situation and now I'm lonelier than before." So the Coens do, in some measure, recoil from Barton Fink, just as Frank Norris (and von Stroheim) recoiled from McTeague, or as any author recoils from a character who needs to learn something the author feels he already knows. But having recoiled, the Coens do not sidle back into the safety of superiority. Instead they are thrown back on the fact of despair, and with their roving camera suddenly paralyzed, they can do nothing but watch the waves.

Fargo does nothing more striking than to unite its characters in the torpor of a common idiocy, and this goes past the mere depiction of ordinary people as obtuse bunglers in the face of fleshly realities. This theme goes back a long way, and certainly in the Coen universe nearly everyone is blood simple under the facade of hauteur and self-control, save for those monstrous wild cards (M. Emmet Walsh in *Blood Simple,* John Goodman in *Fink,* Stormare in *Fargo*) who are just plain simple, the hot point of their humanity having been frozen by some ambiguous pathology. The film extends no empathy, easy or hard, to its belittled figures, and to the extent that it tries to elicit ours (Marge), it is repelled by gross caricature. (The kidnaped wife is a shrieking windup toy, and even the residual pity one feels for the hapless

Lundegaard is due more to William H. Macy's rubber mask of jovial desperation than to any overarching fear for his fate created by the Coens.) The film's failure is that it mistakes the easy return of ethnic humor for the deeper response engendered by characters who are defined in emotionally or psychologically significant ways, and that it unproblematically offers its heroine's home-and-hearth complacency—her shallows, not her depths—as proof of human substance. This is condescension if anything is.

All auteurs content themselves on occasion with skating along the thin surface of their fixations rather than engaging deeply with them and thus risking incoherence, self-indulgence, failure. For every *Persona* there is an *Hour of the Wolf,* for every *Touch of Evil* a *Mr. Arkadin.* The Coens are not yet in this company, but they are continuing to stake a piece of cinematic ground which other film-makers will find hard to share, and what they do right in *Fargo* is very right— namely, dank but pungent scenes of unexcited violence which bring in a cold air of hopelessness and are the film's only exchange with anything troubling.

But otherwise *Fargo* is troubling only in unintended ways. The ending, which finds Marge and phlegmatic hubby snugly abed with talk of postage stamps, is another of the Coens' faintly absurdist enigmas, this time lacking the potent ingredients that allowed the others to tantalize. It is in fact an upbeat variant on the ending of *Barton Fink.* Both narratives tramp through thickets of essentially unmotivated destruction to find chaos bestilled for a moment. In *Fink* the final absurdism found itself in a wordless quiet which accompanied the detritus of human violence. Here it lies in the embrace of banality as an eternal verity, the value for which Middle Americans deserve the approbation of their cultural betters: postage stamps and a baby on the way. Barton watches the ocean; Mr. and Mrs. Marge watch TV.

Jeff Evans (essay date 1996)

SOURCE: "Comic Rhetoric in *Raising Arizona,*" in *Studies in American Humor,* Vol. 4, No. 2, 1996, pp. 39-53.

[*In the essay below, Evans explores the use of language in* Raising Arizona, *suggesting that a major theme of the movie is the use of language for self-delusion.*]

Joel and Ethan Coen's film *Raising Arizona* is about the American dream and its more specific components—such as the American family and notions of community in America—filtered through the culture-clashed psyche of the 1980's. In their reinvestigation of our central cultural myth, the Coens use several rhetorics to disturb their audience's traditional assumptions about the subject: one is the primary focus of this paper, language play. At the same time, the variety and complicated interplay of the different rhetorics attest to the confusion of definitions and values at the base of the American dream(s). One such rhetoric, which will not be developed here, is the Coens' antic cinematography and editing. A second, which will serve as introduction, is their delighted interweaving of strands of different American film genres. Most genres serve as a kind of narrative shorthand, communicating through their generic conventions implied but significant narrative information: identifying chronological, geographical, and/or class setting; posing inherent cultural issues; and creating narrative patterns that work to resolve these issues. An audience often engages itself through these acts—conscious or not—of intellectual recognition, which in turn encourages it to consume—and thus sustain—the genre production. But the sheer wealth of generic referents in *Raising Arizona* is initially less pleasing than dizzying. The chase film is cinematically spanned from its early French origins and their influences on Mack Sennett and his Keystone Kops through the more recent practices of a *Bullitt* or *French Connection.* There is an insistent evocation of the road warrior movies in the character of Leonard Smalls, the "lone biker of the apocalypse." There are more specific analogues to Arthur Penn's classic of 1960's alienation, *Bonnie and Clyde,* from the spirited banjo music to the outlaw subject matter, to the dialect and regionalism, to the motif of infertility, and so on. Equally important and evocative are both films' tributary New Wave cinematography and editing that correlate *Raising Arizona* and its moral estrangement from the dominant culture with the sympathetic if dimwitted outlaw couple of Clyde and Bonnie. The Coens thus create a link between *Bonnie and Clyde,* which so profoundly spoke to the individualistic drop-out impulse of the 1960's, and their *Raising Arizona,* which has as its matrix correspondingly self-absorbed Yuppie values of the 1980's.

Most importantly, because of its subject, the American dream, and its geographical setting, the movie frequently refers visually, verbally, and structurally to the Western, with its identifying motifs of the frontier; stages of cultural development and tensions therein; and violence. Granted, some of the generic referentiality may be youthful film school exuberance in this, the Coens' second feature release. But organically the many different generic borrowings or re-renderings continually dislocate us comically as audience while placing the Coens, along with their protagonists, outside of an unquestioning or uncritical culture. Thus, our leads aspire to the vast middle-class based on such cultural premises as social progress, material success, class ascension, and growth and transformation of the individual that they are lacking in. Similarly, the audience is placed outside of the conventions and culture of the classical Hollywood film by the Coens' generic manipulations. The Coens adapt one more American film genre—the recent culture-clash comedy, like *Desperately Seeking Susan* (1985), *Something Wild* (1986), or *After Hours* (1986)—in a way that may give us a partial hold on this film that is both generically and ethically slippery. The culture-clash films develop an incongruous humor arising from the experiences of a middle-class, or even Yuppie, type suddenly confronted with life in a wilder, more marginalized environment. The Coens' twist on this new formula is to cast the marginalized types themselves as the two leads and trace their often misguided attempts to adapt to the dominant middle-class culture, values, and attitudes. Throughout the film, the Coens' use of language dramatizes and comically evaluates these aspirations.

The film's title immediately clues us to the importance of language play and control. Its verbal connotations suggest thematic issues that the film develops. The plot centers on two characters introduced immediately, an Arizona policewoman named Ed ("short for Edwinna") and H.I. McDonnough, a petty thief whose "raison d'être" is convenience stores: characters of limited education, background, and promise. The gender confusion or androgyny suggested nominally has potentially significant generic functions at the determination of the climax. Initially, though, it serves to introduce the ambiguities of self-identification and assumption of traditional roles in the American "great good place" of society. Ed and H.I. meet, their relationship grows, and he subsequently proposes marriage, all in the same police booking room. Vowing that H.I. will go straight, they marry and settle down to jobs and family life: until Ed discovers she is infertile and their recent, shallow roots in middle-classism, what H.I. had called "the salad days," wither. But spurred by characteristic American initiative gotten from watching broadcast news, they resolve to build a family and their American dream: by kidnaping one of the Arizona quintuplets just born to Mrs. Nathan Arizona. The plot—and their version of the American dream—has at its foundation a kidnaped child, thus preparing us for other ethical incongruities the Coens see in the American psychological landscape. The film's title, thus, also prepares us for motifs regarding birthing, babies, growth and development in America. It nominally suggests correspondence between an individual and her state or country and, by extension, suggests the tendency for individual dreams to mimic popularizations of national ones. "Raising," as in ascension, initiates the film's satiric depiction of the American cultural virtue of progress, improving the quality of life. But the rapid staccato pacing and editing, the often manic camera movement, the complex and frequently oppositional mise-en-scene, and the frenzied, eclectic musical score promote too the pun of razing, thus sounding a violence associated with our society and, more specifically, with attempts at class or cultural change in America. There is an alarming incidence of guns in this humorous film, with many of the characters—often photographed with an exaggerating camera lens—taking an observable delight in shooting at H.I. That H.I.'s gun is always unloaded during his robberies not only echoes the motif

of infertility, but, more importantly, it situationally and ethically sets him apart from the dominant—and dominating—society, while adding to the film's deliberate moral ambiguity. Thus, the film also suggests that violence may be a necessary antecedent to cultural change, rebirth, or a consequence of premature social birth in the 1980's.

This theme of rebirth of the American individual, capable of self-improvement, transformation, generating new identities, goes back to the roots of our cultural emigration. Thus, our kidnaped baby goes through five name changes during the course of three baby-nappings and an intended fourth, and his futures and dreams alternate accordingly. We will see that language play often keys our revaluation of such American attitudes. For example, our pronounced cultural belief in the malleability and openendedness of life in America is voiced early on as H.I. looks forward to a future with Ed, "a future that was only eight to fourteen months away." This is a good example of how the Coens use visuals to undercut or countermand the verbal rhetoric: as H.I. speaks here, he is shown musing in his prison bunk. The series of baby snatchings, which through their repetition structurally undercut the American trust in social progress, creates the loose episodic structure of the film, which climaxes with H.I. and Ed rescuing "Junior" from the "lone biker" in a Western showdown and returning him to his rightful family, thereby displaying a growth or transformation of their own. The structure—and the thematic motif of birthing, then coming of age in America—is complicated by the ethical problems of what the nature of good life in America is, another issue that links this film to the Western genre. Here, the illicit "birth" of H.I. and Ed's family coincides with two more "birthings," both strikingly visualized: the prison escape of H.I.'s fellow inmates, the Snopes brothers, and the gestation of the "lone biker of the apocalypse . . . . a man with all the powers of hell at his command," born from H.I.'s guilt-ridden conscience and criminal act: "That night I had a dream . . . ." The Coens' awareness of the fates of some of America's recent social and political dreamers, verbally echoed by H.I. here, sounds one of the tones of the film that raises it above the level of farce to treat significant cultural issues.

So the Coens' employment of various generic conventions and identifications helps signal their stance of comic incongruity toward the dream, its components, and the pursuit of it. The film title's word play alerts us to the Coens' sensitivity to language and the variety of comic treatments it offers. There are several literary allusions within the film text that further underpin our growing awareness of language flexibility and use in **Raising Arizona.** What the film centers on is a series of episodes wherein characters' basic misunderstandings of language, misappropriations of it, or ignorance of the gap between word and deed or actuality promote the Coen's running commentary on the quality and viability of the dream. The characters use language to describe or reify the dream; and they use language to desperately or pathetically or hypocritically accelerate their pursuit and achievement of it. Language is seen by them as a controlling and directive tool; but the Coens frequently show that the actual functioning and results of language work counter to this. The American Adamic impulse to name, give utterance to, create is frequent and multiplicitous, but it is not sanctified. The Word in America does not always adhere.

One category of comic rhetoric is language use that cues us, often through its banality, to popularizations or linguistic attenuations of certain cultural beliefs. Surely some of this goes back through our comic types, such as the cracker-barrel philosophers, to the proverbial type of Benjamin Franklin's vastly popular "Father Abraham" and may account in part for the Coens choosing a voice-over narrator. There is something in the American sensibility that is expeditiously addressed by quick, aphoristic, proverbial language/wisdom—rhetorically packaged and controlled. For example, the state of spiritual achievement being manifested in material success goes back through Franklin to William Bradford. And our Adams and Eves seem to be similarly guiled by the adage that more is better in America: they conceive of adding to their "family unit" while watching furniture store entrepreneur, Nathan Arizona, whose son Nathan, Jr. is the kidnaped baby, aggressively hawking his dinette, bedroom, bathroom, boudoir sets on t.v. Arizona's emotional delight in his multiple babies seems partly grounded in the virtue of material acquisitiveness that he so aggressively fosters. In a nice instance of verbal irony and confusion that sounds the falsity that the Coens often see beneath the rhetoric surrounding or describing the Dream, we learn that Nathan Arizona's original name is Nathan Huffhines, which he has changed for business reasons. But as audience, we also see and hear him proclaim his business slogan, "And if you can find lower prices anywhere my name ain't Nathan Arizona!" The complement to Nathan Arizona's confusing spiritual materialism is H.I. and Ed's equally confused belief that the material existence of a child—regardless of source or legality of origin—will beget familial happiness.

Similarly, H.I.'s language is riddled with clichés. When he confesses to the kidnaping, he says, "I crept in yon window"; penning a goodbye letter to Ed while "you and Nathan slumber . . . [he] cannot tarry"; when the couple first arrive home with the stolen baby, H.I.'s well-conditioned media impulse is to "Let's us preserve the moment in pictures!" These are minor examples among a myriad of potential ones to draw our attention to two more profound implications of H.I.'s sentimentalized speech. It is H.I.'s language that predominates throughout the film because the Coens employ H.I., somewhat unconventionally, as the voice-over narrator. He thus creates the verbal mindscape of much of the film. When we hear his rural, native speech layered over comically by the language of pop jargon, advertisement, cliché, we recognize the violation and ethical confusion that language can wreak on character and action. As they drive off with the kidnaped baby, Ed has a sudden maternal, sympathetic identification with Mrs. Nathan Arizona and her loss, but H.I. consoles her causistically, "Well now honey we been over this and over this. There's what's right and there's what's right and never the twain shall meet." The same Hallmark card sophistry applies to their initial impulse toward family: "Ed felt like having a critter was the next logical step. . . . Her point was that there was too much love and beauty for just the two of us. . . ." Thus, it is H.I.'s often muddled language and thought that contribute to the Coens' deliberate moral myopia in the film.

One of the most revealing groupings of rhetoric in the film is that comprised of the characters' usage that encourages false pride, self-delusion, or mock success—in other words, language that mimics the cultural tenet of the pursuit of success even as it misrepresents the individual's place in relation to his world or the dream. During the brief stint when H.I. attempts to go straight, we overhear a dialogue—rather monologue—from one of his machine-shop co-workers: "So we was doin' paramedical work in affiliation with the state highway system—not actually practicin', y'understand—and me and Bill's patrollin' down Nine Mile.". When we realize that the paramedical work he was engaged in—"not actually practicin"—is cleaning up after highway accidents and road kills, we sense a gap between self-image and reality. The gap is rendered comic partly by the visual incongruity—the greasy, gum-snapping, *alazon* figure verbally aspiring to a white-collar medical status. But part of it is the verbal command—or temporary suspension of disbelief—created by the anecdotalist. And finally, I think, part of the humor comes at our own expense: despite an idealism for a classless, non-elitist American society, there will always be machine operators as well as medical practitioners. Gale and Evelle Snopes, two of H.I.'s compatriots at prison, likewise assert a professional pride through their delusive language use. The two concur with the prison counselor's advice about taking on adult responsibility: "GALE: . . . sometimes your career gotta come before family. EVELLE: Work is what's kept us happy." The film recurs visually or verbally several times to these prison counseling sessions. We are thus presented with the process and results of the institutional attempt at culturally educating and transforming the individual. Having escaped from prison, the Snopes indeed set their sights on ascension and the rise of fortune in America. They invite H.I. in on a score, a bank robbery: "Come on, Hi, you're young, you got your health—what do you want with a job? . . . I know you're partial to convenience stores but, H.I., the sun don't rise and set on the corner grocery. It's like Doc Schwartz says: you gotta have a little ambition. . . . We keep goin' 'till we can retire—or we get caught. Either way we're fixed for life." Here, the language of American aphorism and initiative combine to rhetorically legitimize the future while linguistically and ethically obfuscating the means to those ends.

We see that it is frequently language—jargon acquired from our own social institutions—that is used by the characters to allow for rationalization, irresponsibility, or evasion. This in itself might counter some of the perceived condescension of the Coens to their individual characters. In a frenetic chase sequence, when H.I. awakens to the realities of middle-class life with its requisite responsibilities (the baby's dip-tet shots) and attendant hypocrisies (an offer of wife-swapping, rhetorically purified as "l'amour"), he turns back to the familiar outsider life of robbing a convenience store, this time thoughtfully remembering to steal a carton of Huggie diapers for the baby. His defense to Ed, furious at losing her recent niche in middle-class life, is a retreat into the jargon of popular psychology, "You know, honey, I'm okay you're okay?" H.I. has similarly used cliché, sentiment, and jargon to explain their early, fallow state of marriage—". . . This woman who looked as fertile as the Tennessee Valley could not bear children . . . the doctor explained that her insides were a rocky place where my seed could find no purchase"—and their subsequent failure to qualify to adopt, "It's true I've had a checkered past, but. . . . But biology and the prejudices of others conspired to keep us childless." When the escaped Snopes brothers arrive at HI and Ed's, they redefine and defend their prison breakout to the indignant Ed by manipulating correctional system jargon: "We released ourselves on our own recognizance. . . . We felt the institution no longer had anything to offer us." In a scene that visually and verbally captures some of the awkwardness brought on by sudden class change in America, the Snopes brothers rationalize their own criminal past sociologically while earnestly trying to improve the baby's future by advocating breast-feeding: "Ya don't breast feed him, he'll hate you for it later. That's why we wound up in prison. Anyway, that's what Dr. Schwartz tells us." This humorous manipulation of psychological/sociological learning becomes serious when the comic language causes us to question whether the institutions we create do serve, do nurture us.

The Coens dramatize their concerns for the abuses of language in America and entrench their themes of linguistic and cultural incongruities by several times showing elderly characters and their tenets and practices of language use as a counterpoint to the present-day babel. In one instance, the Snopes hold up an "old timer" running a country grocery store. He is instructed ". . . and don't you move till you've counted up to eight hundred and twenty-five and then backwards down to zero. I'll be back to check—see you ain't cheating." As the Snopes drive off, we hear the old-timer slowly enumerating "One one thousand, two one thousand. . . ." He does faithfully count up to eight hundred and twenty-five and back down to seven hundred and ninety-one

before he feels he has done justice to his linguistic order. But raising himself from the floor, he sees the Snopes barreling back down upon him: in their ineptitude, they had left the kidnaped baby at the scene of the crime. His faith in adherence of deed to language scared back into him, we hear the old-timer dutifully resuming his counting and prone position as the visuals stay with the fleeing Snopes.

When the Snopes arrive at their goal, their score, "a hayseed bank," they command the elderly customers, "All right you hayseeds, it's a stick-up! Everybody freeze! Everybody down on the ground!" (We've all heard this on t.v.) But another old-timer points out the impossibility of physically acting upon these linguistic directions—

> Well which is it young fella? You want I should
> freeze or get down on the ground? Mean to say,
> iffen I freeze, I can't rightly drop. And iffen I drop,
> I'm a gonna be in motion.

The resultant plot disorder comically locates the generational and cultural rift between the old-timers' literal adherence to and trust in denotative language to direct or describe action, a time when language held credence and permanence, to the Coens' present era of linguistic self-service and confusion. In the hilarious scene when the kidnaping of Nathan, Jr. has been discovered and the police and F.B.I. investigations begun, we hear a crescendo of language—that of hucksterism, evasion, retreat into institutional jargon, and self-aggrandizement—most often at the expense of language meeting humanistic needs. Emblematically here in Nathan Arizona, Sr.'s desperate and incongruous diction—exemplars, fortes, daisy farm, microbes, Yodas'n shit—we see all the characters' attempts to demonstrate knowledge of their world and capabilities to work with it through their language use and control.

The Coens cannot be unaware that their own feature-length language play links them to their characters, who try to create and control reality through their language utterance. This identification might well give rise to a sympathy, rather than condescension, toward these characters. A genuine concern for the baby's health incongruously links the outlaw Snopes brothers with the swinging middle-class types, Dot and Glen, by the shared trust in medical science verbalized and echoed in their insistence on "dip-tet shots." Each time the baby is kidnaped, the snatchers dutifully bring along his accompanying *Dr. Spock's Baby and Child Care*, which H.I. had given Ed when they first kidnaped Nathan, Jr.: "Here's the instructions." The characters want language, and want to trust language, to give them verbal instructions for assimilating into the American community.

Interestingly, in this film that is especially verbal but has as its central metaphor babies, there is also a motif of non-verbal orality. Thus, as Ed sternly reminds H.I. after his first, botched attempt at kidnaping, "Babies cry!" And at significant plot junctures in *Raising Arizona,* all of the major and supporting characters scream, cry, yell, roar, or bellow, as if regressing into an infantile, primal language state. These instances also suggest that language is not equivalent to the felt emotion or needed action of the moment. The characters explode in non-verbal utterance (sequentially, Mrs. Arizona, Mr. Arizona, H.I., Ed, the Snopes brothers) when the baby is variously kidnaped or, in the lone biker's instance, when he himself—along with his bronzed baby shoes—is about to be exploded by his hand grenade. This technique serves as another comic prod to our consciousness about the responsibility of language to articulate and shape human need and act. But it also serves as a transition to a second issue that draws together two of the rhetorics mentioned in the introduction, language and genre.

The climax of the film—H.I. and Ed recapturing Nathan, Jr. from the lone biker to return him to his rightful family—takes place in a deliberately Western setting: the wooden slatted Farmer's Bank, raised wooden sidewalks, hitching posts, a hard-packed, dusty, single, deserted, main street. With H.I. temporarily stunned, Ed advances unarmed upon the lone biker to confront him—verbally: "Gimme that baby, you warthog from hell!" The direct allusion here to Flannery O'Connor's "Revelation" once again draws attention to the self-conscious use of language throughout the film. The unlikelihood of Ed having read and recalled O'Connor aside, the inappropriateness of a literary allusion to articulate the excited emotions of a character at the story's climax sounds again the Coens' sense of discordant language use in America. But, given the setting and dramatic situation, Ed's response is also not appropriate generically. Jane Tompkins has recently argued that

> . . . because the western is in revolt against a culture, perceived as female, where the ability to manipulate symbols confers power, the western equates power with "not language." And not language it equates with being male.

In other words, H.I.'s ensuing physical confrontation with the lone biker resuscitates, albeit sentimentally and feebly, the Western's generic convention of language being associated with civilization and being a pallid substitute for (male) action. Here, at the climax, the usually loquacious H.I. is the Western protagonist standing against the landscape: taciturn, laconic, choosing to engage an objectified world physically rather than to subjectivize a world through language.

Raising Arizona, through exploration of many issues originating from the visual and verbal motifs of birth, babies, and self-articulation, is about growth, development, coming of age in America. Characters represent different stages of development, both individual and cultural, and they undergo initiations and transformations, such as of name, vocation, class. The language use in *Raising Arizona* often draws our attention comically to the cultural myths and values that are meant to guide us, to the institutions that are meant to serve us, and to a gauge by which we may measure our individual and cultural growth. Thus, we hear the communal tag phrase, "[Well,] okay then," throughout the film. That it serves variously as the legal judgment of H.I.'s parole board, as the minister's blessing of H.I. and Ed's marriage, and as a frightened store clerk's response to the demands of an armed robber reiterates the Coens' sense of language in America working to identify positive, meaningful goals and often resulting in comic confusion and incongruity instead.

This disparity between language and reality carries through to the film's coda. Here H.I. resumes his voice-over narration. Typically, voice-over gives the narrator a verbal and diegetic authority: he/she selects, arranges, and presents the narrative information. But it is unlikely by now that the audience accepts the presumed authority of H.I.'s voice-over, which has been visually undercut throughout the film as it is questioned again here. H.I.'s closing sentimental vision of the future is made suspicious by a subjective, slow-motion camera and a dreamily sanitized mise-en-scene. The visual surreality and self-consciousness create genuine doubt about H.I.'s narrative accuracy as we see him dream into being generations of family born to the infertile Ed and him. And the film ends with more ambiguity, this time linguistic. H.I. wistfully tries to enjoin his dream onto a reality when he locates his vision of the future somewhere in our frontier West, someplace ". . .that seemed real. . . . And it seemed like . . . well . . . our home. . . . If not Arizona, then a land not too far away where all parents are strong and wise and capable, and all children are happy and beloved. . . . I dunno—maybe it was Utah."

While still on the set of *Raising Arizona,* director and co-writer Joel Coen discussed the language use of his characters: "It's not meant to be condescending. . . . If the characters talk in clichés, it's because we like clichés. You start with things that are incredibly recognizable in one form, and you play with them." And this is what we have seen taking place in *Raising Arizona:* the Coens presenting the familiar icons and speech of America and then investigating them through rhetorical and generic play. If one example could approach encapsulating the Coens' explosive vision of language at odds, at work, and going in all directions at once while including their tone—antic, fond, comic—it might be Nathan Arizona, Sr.'s unwitting pun to the press and legal investigators as he looks forward to the kidnaped Nathan, Jr.'s return, "when we're a nuclear family again."

FURTHER READING

Criticism

Behrens, Michael A. "Cinema Brats: The Coens and Their Scripts." *San Francisco Review of Books* 17, No. 1 (January 1992): 25-6.
    Behrens finds the work of the Coem brothers to be guilty of the weaknesses they parody.

Ferncase, Richard K. "Neon Noir: Blood Simple." *Outsider Features: American Independent Films of the 1980s* Greenwood Press (1996): 67-76.
    Ferncase proides a mixed review of *Blood Simple* and summarizes the reactions of other critics to several of the Coen brothers' films.

Francke, Lizzie. "Hell Freezes Over." *Sight and Sound* 6, No. 5 (May 1996): 24, 26.
    Brief article in which the Coens discuss some of the recurring imagery in their films.

Holt, Linda. "I'm So Prouda You." *Times Literary Supplement* (June 14, 1996): 20.
    Holt provides a favorable review of the movie *Fargo*.

Horowitz, Mark. "Coen Brothers A-Z: The Big Two-Headed Picture." *Film Comment* 27, No. 5 (September/October 1991): 27-32.
    Humorous lexicon of terms associated with the Coen brothers and their films.

Additional coverage of the Coens' lives and careers are contained in the following source published by Gale: *Contemporary Authors*, Vol. 126.

Robert Coles

1929-

American psychiatrist, biographer, social commentator, and nonfiction writer.

The following entry presents an overview of Coles's career.

INTRODUCTION

Robert Coles' work is marked by a conception of the craft of writing as a blend of poetry, fiction, psychoanalysis, sociology, ethnography and political commentary. Trained as a psychiatrist, Coles has nurtured a life-long interest in literature and the wide range of experience for which it is often a vehicle. An equally pronounced early interest in matters of morality and spirituality have also found expression in his work, which is often based on extensive one-on-one encounters, primarily with children. In his writing his subjects do the talking, and Coles tries to bring out the inherent stories which reveal truths and realities that simple clinical facts could not. In this original manner he deals with themes rooted in concrete experience having to do with childhood, politics, ethics, spirituality and altruism. Of his work with children, Coles has said "What I do is listen . . . and try to make sense of the various contradictions and inconsistencies in their struggle for coherence." Walker Percy—an early influence, who was also a doctor and writer—has said of Coles: "Like Freud he is humble before the facts," and he "keeps his ideological spectacles in his pocket and spends his time listening to people and trying to understand them." His books are accounts of that understanding.

Biographical Information

Robert Coles was Born on October 12, 1929 in Boston, son of Sandra Young Coles and Philip Winston Coles, an engineer. His early career ambition was to be a high school English teacher and to combine literature and religion; he was influenced in this regard by Perry Miller who taught English and American literature at Harvard College and was one of Coles' thesis supervisors when he wrote on William Carlos Williams' long poem *Paterson*. Meeting Williams was a turning point. From Williams, a poet and pediatrician who would, on his house calls, sit with the children on the floor and play with them, Coles learned "how much medicine can give both moral and intellectual shape to a particular life." He subsequently completed his education at Columbia University, College of Physicians and Surgeons in 1954. After residencies in several hospitals and holding the post of chief of neuropsychiatric service at Biloxi Mississippi Air Force Base (1958-60), he married Jane Hallowell, a high-school

teacher. She was a motivating force in Coles' project of recording children's reflections on social and political issues during the troubled period of the civil rights movement of the early 1960s; a period that proved to be a crucible for the work for which he has gained fame and recognition. This resulted in his Pulitzer Prize-winning *Children of Crisis: A Study of Courage and Fear* (1967-1978). Around this time, he began his association with Harvard as a staff member, beginning as a clinical assistant 1960-62, then as a research psychiatrist in 1963, a Lecturer in General Education in 1966, and Professor of Psychiatry and Medical Humanities from 1978. In 1981, a grant from the MacArthur Foundation led to work on an international scale with *The Political Life of Children* (1986) and *The Moral Life of Children* (1986). As a professor his curriculum includes literature classes for students of medicine, law and architecture. Coles is also the author of articles, stories and poems.

Major Works

Story-telling is at the heart of Robert Coles' method, which involves finding in the words of his subjects stories that display prominent elements of human nature. This approach is first seen in his books on childhood from the *Children of Crisis* series to *The Moral Intelligence of Children* (1997), and is equally present in his biographical studies such as *Dorothy Day: A Radical Devotion* (1987), *Simone Weil: A Modern Pilgrimage* (1987) and *Anna Freud: The Dream of Psychoanalysis* (1992). Rather than presenting ideas via an analysis based on a theoretical or ideological framework, he prefers to let the ideas arise out of the people. Coles has commented on his method, saying it entails "pulling together . . . the recurrent themes and topics that [his interview subjects] bring up." What he finally presents is "a distillation and a condensation, a 'reading' of a particular life." He adds: "What a novelist does is try to highlight a certain moment. That's what I try to do too." His models are creative works of literature in which he satisfies an interest in "stories, as moral moments conveyed through the suggestive power of language," a phenomenon he explored in detail in *The Call of Stories* (1989). In his books on children, where some might find economic, social, or racial problems, Coles sees instead, "moral problems and family problems of a deep and disturbing nature." And he sees a need for a spiritual solution. As he points out, the children affected need not only economic and political support but "a moral and spiritual life they don't have. . . . that can help give them a certain kind of strength they otherwise will lack." His mentors, whether literary or in the field of psychology have also become subjects of his writing, notably *Walker Percy: An American Search* (1978), *William Carlos Williams: The Knack of Survival in America* (1975) and *Erik H. Erikson: The Growth of His Work* (1970).

Critical Reception

Critics of Coles' work have been sympathetic to the humanity with which he treats subjects that are often handled with clinical detachment. Reviewing *The Moral life of Children*, Neil Postman portrayed Coles in heroic terms: "He is to the stories that children have to tell what Homer was to the tale of the Trojan War," suggesting that Coles' strength is that he transforms his material "into a kind of narrative poetry". Jonathan Kellerman, reviewing *The Political Life of Children*, described Coles' narrative gifts as "Dickensian," adding that he is "a master chronicler, providing few answers but asking his questions so eloquently that his writings emerge as classic portrayals of social upheaval and its effect upon the young." Unlike Dickens, however, Coles avoids sentimentality in his social realism. Katherine Paterson remarked: "a reading of *The Political Life of Children* should cure any adult of a sentimental view of childhood." There have been objections to a noted tendency for whitewashing. Laura Sessions Stepp, considering *The Spiritual Life of Children* (1990), objects to Coles' approach on the grounds that "he spends relatively little time on religion's darker side, the shame and guilt too many children suffer at

the hands of know-it-all preachers and Sunday School teachers," and identifies in Coles' book what may be considered "a skewed, Pollyanna vision." In the same vein, Richard Bernstein complained that *The Moral Intelligence of Children* (1997) "is weakened by nebulousness, wordiness, by Dr. Coles's tendency to circle the issue so that he raises interesting questions but then answers them with not much more than earnest truisms." He concedes that Coles is "certainly an insightful and sensitive man," but complains that Coles is often at the center of the book, with characteristics of "strenuous modesty and self-effacement that one suspects it is a form of egoism," and he doubts that one learns anything from Coles' approach. This indeterminacy in his style has been recognized by other critics; however, some see in this a positive feature. The lack of specific and overt answers in his books, the idea that Coles poses questions remarkably well and that Coles is not prescriptive, that he doesn't offer us "pediatric prescriptions," is an admired quality. The naïveté of the Coles approach, although irritating to some, is refreshing for most critics. Francis X. Rocca, for example, praises Coles' work for being free from "the constraints of the psychoanalytic vocabulary, which cannot convey ambiguity and irony."

PRINCIPAL WORKS

Children of Crisis 5 volumes (nonfiction) 1967-1978
Erik H. Erikson: The Growth of His Work (biography) 1970
William Carlos Williams: The Knack of Survival in America (biography) 1975
Walker Percy: An American Search (biography) 1978
The Moral Life of Children (nonfiction) 1986
The Political Life (nonfiction) 1986
Dorothy Day: A Radical Devotion (biography) 1987
Simone Weil: A Modern Pilgrimage (biography) 1987
The Call of Stories (nonfiction) 1989
The Spiritual Life of Children (nonfiction) 1990
Anna Freud: The Dream of Psychoanalysis (biography) 1992
The Moral Intelligence of Children (nonfiction) 1997

CRITICISM

Melvin J. Friedman (review date Fall 1982)

SOURCE: "Robert Coles's South and Other Approaches to Flannery O'Connor," in *The Southern Literary Journal,* Vol. XV, No. 1, Fall 1982, pp. 120-129.

[*In the following review of several publications on Flannery O'Connor, Friedman explains the critical approaches that Coles takes in his* Flannery O'Connor's South.]

Robert Coles is Professor of Psychiatry and Medical Humanities at Harvard Medical School. This unorthodox title helps characterize an unconventional career, which has brought Dr. Coles from spirited civil rights marcher in the company of Martin Luther King to author of an overflowing shelf of books which may one day extend in length to Charles W. Eliot's magical five-foot shelf. Coles has in common with Eliot impeccable New England and Harvard credentials. He also has in common with him a discomfort with insularity. Trained as a child psychiatrist, Dr. Coles has crossed over to a variety of other disciplines, establishing formidable credentials as literary critic, poet, sociologist, theologian, philosopher. He is "myriad-minded," if the expression Coleridge used about Shakespeare has any meaning. His has been unfailingly a social discourse, with a distinctly humanistic cutting edge.

Coles is one of the premier intellectuals of his generation. Readers of Flannery O'Connor's correspondence, *The Habit of Being,* know how uncomfortable she was with that word and how she tortured it mercilessly until it became "interleckchul." Coles seems to enjoy playing around with the paradox, in the third part of his *Flannery O'Connor's South;* of O'Connor's being "an intellectual almost to her last breath, and at the same time she was toughly critical about certain influential intellectual assumptions" (p. 123). But he does evidence a certain discomfort and self-consciousness about his own geographical and cultural roots— which would seem to place him so far from Flannery O'Connor country. He need not have entertained any doubts. He has produced a book which almost certainly would have delighted its subject; it has the ideal mix of literary interpretation and social and theological speculation; it is agreeably modest and undogmatic; it is free of jargon and written with grace and ease. Rather than force Flannery O'Connor onto the couch and raise serious doubts about her personal life, as Josephine Hendin did in *The World of Flannery O'Connor,* Coles wisely divests himself of his psychiatric baggage and proceeds to read, listen, and search. These are three things he does very well.

Before delivering the lectures which form the basis of *Flannery O'Connor's South,* Robert Coles wrote a book about another Southern Catholic novelist, *Walker Percy: An American Search.* In this case, the pairing of author and subject seemed inspired: both Coles and Percy appeared to use medical degrees as occasions to wander off into other areas—Percy never practicing medicine, instead writing about philosophy and psychiatry on the way to becoming a novelist. The extent to which they are kindred spirits is clear from Coles's introduction which sets an autobiographical tone: "I may well be describing myself. I have no distance, certainly, on Dr. Percy's writing. . . ." "I was making a decision about that life of mine during 1960, when *The Moviegoer* appeared; I decided to stay South, to live in New Orleans upon

discharge from the air force. . . . " It is clear from his introduction that Coles is as much on an American "search" as is Percy. The word is offered also to define Coles's methodology in writing this book, as he gently removes the prefix from *research.*

Walker Percy: An American Search offers a passageway to *Flannery O'Connor's South:* "I connect Dr. Percy, maybe out of my own peculiar inclinations, with another Southerner, Flannery O'Connor. . . . " Coles's O'Connor study is also a search, as it eschews more conventional methods of literary commentary. Coles "adventures" into a geographical area, Baldwin County, Georgia, and "explores" an *oeuvre* which has abiding roots in that area. He examines O'Connor's two novels and a handful of stories in admirable detail.

Flannery O'Connor's South marks, in a certain way, the bringing together of the two strains of the New England sensibility on Southern soil, the dark side represented by Hawthorne, the light represented by Emerson. Flannery O'Connor has always come down on the side of Hawthorne, the one writer of his region she unqualifiedly admired. She mentions Emerson only twice in *The Habit of Being,* each time rather disparagingly. While acknowledging the essential presence of Hawthorne in her bleak literary endeavors, Coles seems to bring to *Flannery O'Connor's South* an Emersonian brightness and optimism.

Coles's book contains an introduction, three lengthy sections, and a brief bibliographical essay. His prefatory remarks tend to be rather personal as he sketches in the role he and his wife, "Yankee outsiders," played in the civil rights movement; the "ever so brief and restricted, but nonetheless memorable, acquaintance" (p. xix) they had with Flannery O'Connor; an intriguing comparison between the Georgia writer and the unliterary black woman (with "a storyteller's narrative urgency") who brought about the brief acquaintanceship. Coles does a good deal of listening and searching here.

When he begins to offer her works close readings he approaches them with a freshness and gentle persuasiveness absent from much O'Connor criticism. He discusses the fiction in three sections: "The Social Scene," "Hard, Hard Religion," and "A Southern Intellectual." His method is to examine a work leisurely, search out its contours, and then enlarge its frame by locating its relevance to contemporary events. Coles manages intermittently to sneak a glance at himself almost as if the discussion of an O'Connor text were part of an ongoing ritual of self-discovery.

"The Social Scene" offers a lengthy and probing analysis of "The Displaced Person." Coles, at first, seems to gnaw away at the edges of the story, but nothing he does, it turns out, is gratuitous; everything is part of a design, a stratagem. Coles treats a casual conversation between two blacks, Astor and Sulk, and the self-assured Mrs. Shortley, early in "The Displaced Person," by introducing unlikely references to existentialism, logical positivism, and Gabriel Marcel; the conversation is amusing and Coles underscores its comic aspects by bringing in his own bits of incongruity. A few pages later he offers the words of a black farmer he spoke to during his "stay South." Something resembling literary counterpoint takes place here as we are intended to measure these words against those of Astor and Sulk. He thus proves decisively that Flannery O'Connor "was always listening," as her readers have suspected for a long time. There is perhaps a trace of positivism, familiar to the social scientist, in the way Coles goes about his critical labors but he always manages a humanistic light touch. He juxtaposes and confronts scenes from literary texts with social scenes.

> **There is perhaps a trace of positivism . . . in the way Coles goes about his critical labors but he always manages a humanistic light touch.**
> **—Melvin J. Friedman**

The method serves him well in his analysis of "Everything That Rises Must Converge." Again he leisurely makes his way through the story and enlarges its frame by quoting from several of the letters in *The Habit of Being* and by drawing valuably on his own experience in the civil rights movement. At one point James Baldwin is introduced. Readers of O'Connor's letters will recall one she wrote to Maryat Lee on April 25, 1959, which began: "No I can't see James Baldwin in Georgia. It would cause the greatest trouble and disturbance and disunion." Coles indulges his fantasies, using "Everything That Rises Must Converge" and this bit of information as texts:

> Had Miss O'Connor written a different kind of story; had she, to repeat, invited James Baldwin home, to Andalusia, or better, to her mother's stately antebellum residence in downtown Milledgeville, hard by the Governor's Mansion of the old Confederacy; and had she, as a final thrust, allowed television to show all of that "carrying-on" to the public—well, she'd have become a great heroine of the early 1960s to many of us, a pronoun from which I certainly don't exclude myself. (p. 41)

The sense is, of course, that Flannery O'Connor was unimaginable in that role as heroine and indeed no amount of heroics would be allowable if it meant sacrificing the fine story we have for "a different kind."

The "Hard, Hard Religion" section offers more of the same.

This time the central texts are *Wise Blood* and "Parker's Back." The chapter is liberally sprinkled with lengthy comments and jeremiads by revivalist types who abound in Baldwin County. Coles leads into his examination of *Wise Blood* and Hazel Motes with an extended discussion of Gnosticism in its various guises and its lingering fascination for Southern evangelists. "Parker's Back" is also approached through the Gnostic heresy, with a helping hand from Walker Percy and Kierkegaard.

"A Southern Intellectual," the third part of **Flannery O'Connor's South,** begins with a discussion of the seeming contradiction in O'Connor's own nature: ". . . a woman of extraordinary intellectual depth, with a hungry mind that was willing to travel widely and deeply" (p. 111), who nevertheless seemed to feel uncomfortable with intellectuals and even assumed anti-intellectual postures (especially in *The Habit of Being*). Coles also observes that "a streak of anti-intellectualism runs through the stories, and *The Violent Bear It Away* as well" (p. 122). Sheppard in "The Lame Shall Enter First" and Rayber in *The Violent Bear It Away* receive a good deal of attention although there are also interesting side glances at Hulga in "Good Country People" and Asbury in "The Enduring Chill." Coles makes an uncommon number of personal interventions in this section, recalling his own residency in child psychiatry and dwelling on the limitations of his discipline: ". . . I am all too sadly reminded of all of us: the child psychiatrists of the twentieth century, evangelist heroes to others, and all too quickly, to ourselves" (p. 124). The raw nerves of the critic are fascinatingly on display here. This was probably the most difficult section of **Flannery O'Connor's South** for Coles to write.

The final few pages of his book offer a brief assessment of the O'Connor criticism (and related material) which has mattered to him. Coles believes that O'Connor, in substantial part, has been handsomely served by her commentators. When he introduces a negative note—"I was made uncomfortable by Ms. Hendin, as I have not been by any other O'Connor critic"—he is careful to insist that "she is a psychologically sensitive reader" (p. 164).

II

In something of an unprecedented gesture, Louisiana State University Press brought out Carol Shloss' book on Flannery O'Connor only months after Robert Coles's. Which means that the Press now has three O'Connor books in print—the third is Martha Stephens' *The Question of Flannery O'Connor.* And the record of success is notable: Coles's and Stephens' studies, in a crowded field, belong at the very top and Shloss' does not lag far behind.

Flannery O'Connor's Dark Comedies moves from a series of theoretical statements to a close reading of a handful of stories and *The Violent Bear It Away*. Carol Shloss goes through a worrying process about Flannery O'Connor's "sense of audience." She is concerned that the Georgia writer does not always anticipate "fictionally" the needs and assumptions of her "monstrous readers." Carol Shloss' uncertainties are in certain ways akin to those of Martha Stephens although they are expressed in different terms. Instead of the "tonal dilemma" which bothered Stephens, Shloss' dilemma is with reader response. Shloss feels, rightly, that the text is the proper place for communication between writer and audience. She explains this forthrightly in her first chapter:

> To require that a reader share the artist's beliefs or that he construe the meaning of a story from extrinsic commentary is to insist on bypassing the fiction as a linguistic construct with inherent meanings.

> Is the biographical information gleaned from these essays the most effective starting point of criticism? It seems better to remember that language is communal, effective to the extent that writer and reader construe it similarly. Consequently, a writer's "sacramental view" is immaterial unless it can be embodied in, that is, translated into, writing techniques that permit its discovery by readers. (p. 15)

Because Flannery O'Connor expected "anagogic" responses does not mean that readers with more secular persuasions should necessarily have them, unless a view of the sacred is "discoverable from the text itself." (p. 136)

Armed with this "irreverent" set of critical tools—she mentions several times that she offers a given interpretation even though O'Connor clearly would have been unhappy with it— she engages the fiction head on. She makes her way through a variety of rhetorical strategies while assessing individual works. She often discovers that the realistic contours and textures of the fiction remain forbiddingly at odds with the "sacramental view" O'Connor was so intent on transmitting.

Shloss comes down particularly hard on *The Violent Bear It Away*. She finds little to choose between old Mason Tarwater and Rayber "for the descriptions of both are equally alienating" (p. 96). She even suggests that young Tarwater's mission at the end of the novel "may simply be the fruit of irreversible psychological damage" (p. 85). She throws up her hands at one point and insists that "the grounds for unambiguous interpretation simply have not been firmly laid" (p. 96). She ends her discussion of *The Violent Bear It Away* by flatly asserting that it "remains a secular novel" (p. 101).

Shloss is rather more encouraging in her discussion of "The Artificial Nigger"; she feels that the epiphany experienced by Mr. Head is managed "without the heavy ambiguities that often linger in other scenes of supposed revelation" (p. 123).

(Ambiguous and unambiguous are two of her fondest words!) O'Connor admitted that "The Artificial Nigger" was her favorite story and Shloss sees in it the ideal coming together of authorial anticipation and reader response. She ends on a positive note, then, as this is the last O'Connor story discussed.

The five-page concluding chapter convincingly reiterates some of Shloss' reactions to a body of fiction which is technically accomplished and yet can be frustrating for the agnostic reader. Her final sentence places her on the side of the angels: "Even when unembellished by revealed anagogical implications, Flannery O'Connor's work retains a weight of human concern that makes the reading of the fiction a disturbing encounter, valuable to readers of any persuasion because its haunting truth rests on sharable experience rather than prohibitive religious allusion" (p. 128). Even O'Connor's staunchest supporters should find little to quarrel with in these words.

Flannery O'Connor's Dark Comedies ends with a useful chronology of the fiction and a selected bibliography. One glaring mistake in the bibliography (p. 150), which should be corrected in a second edition, is that Sally Fitzgerald appears as the editor of *The Complete Stories of Flannery O'Connor*. No editor is mentioned on the title page but if the honor is to be accorded anyone it should be Robert Giroux.

While on the subject of bibliographies, mention should be made of David Farmer's long-awaited *Flannery O'Connor: A Descriptive Bibliography*. This elegant witness to her career "includes work published both in her lifetime and posthumously—from the early contributions to journals at Georgia State College for Women, through the stories and books that formed the bulk of the canon, to *The Habit of Being* of 1979" (p. xv). Farmer seems to have managed exemplary patience, accuracy, and comprehensiveness. Aside from the expected sections describing O'Connor's books and her contributions to books and periodicals, there is a part describing her early art work—including reproductions of some of the linoleum block cartoons she did for *The Colonnade,* her college newspaper, and *The Spectrum,* her college yearbook—as well as sections listing translations of her work and film and television adaptations of it. The one omission I discovered is a Japanese translation of "Everything That Rises Must Converge," "Good Country People," and "Revelation," done by Kichinosuke Ohashi, published by Shufunotomo Company, Tokyo, in 1977, in a volume which also contains fiction by Pearl Buck and O'Connor's *bête noire* Carson McCullers. Farmer can certainly be forgiven for missing this item which could easily have been lost in the deluge of translations of American literature done by the Japanese in recent years. I am reminded, in this connection, of a line from one of John Updike's Henry Bech stories: "He

[Bech] learned that the Japanese had managed to issue more books by him than he had written."

Farmer's bibliography is of the same high quality as James L.W. West's *William Styron: A Descriptive Bibliography,* if one is to compare it with a recent effort of similar dimensions. It is a work that everyone interested in the process and product of Flannery O'Connor's art will need to have close at hand.

Another such indispensable companion piece is *Flannery O'Connor's Georgia.* This handsome volume contains a foreword by Robert Coles and an elegantly turned introduction by Barbara McKenzie—who is also responsible for the photographs (except those from the O'Connor family album) and captions. McKenzie's introductory remarks are lively, engaging, and informative. At one point she quotes a passage from *The Habit of Being* in which O'Connor roundly asserts that "photographers are the lowest breed of men." Armed with this bit of encouragement, McKenzie goes about the task of using her camera "to record the tangible dimension or physical reality of Flannery O'Connor's fiction" (p. xii). The central premise of her introduction is that O'Connor belonged to two domains: "I think the distinction between the Georgia she knew by birth and upbringing and the Georgia she chose to write about is very important" (p. xiii). The many photographs engage both settings and the captions McKenzie accompanies them with nicely work in biography and literary reference. One of these captions, placed above photographs of road signs with religious messages, reads: "The insistent signs nailed on pine trees or posts asked as well as answered questions about life and eternity, and I thought of Rufus Johnson in 'The Lame Shall Enter First,' who was destined to 'know the Bible with or without reading it'" (p. 66). These carefully chosen words suggest the extent of Barbara McKenzie's knowledge of Flannery O'Connor's work and presence.

III

The tone of Emersonian optimism I have maintained until now threatens to give way to a more Hawthornean bleakness. Lorine M. Getz's *Flannery O'Connor: Her Life, Library and Book Reviews,* while it performs several important services, has some failings. To talk first about these services. Her alphabetical list of all the volumes found in the Flannery O'Connor Collection at Georgia College is of considerable value. The reprinting of O'Connor's book reviews, an inspired gesture, makes available an ancillary, less realized side of her talent. At her best Flannery O'Connor was adept at offering the essentials of a book or a journal in a very few words; a model of its kind is a hundred-word review of Teilhard de Chardin's *The Phenomenon of Man*—the only piece she did for *The American Scholar.* The not too genial

put-down, apparent in so many of her letters, surfaces in some of the reviews, such as one of *The Georgia Review:*

> It is, apparently by design, one of the least intellectually strenuous of the college quarterlies.... It is obviously a magazine by Southerners for Southerners about Southerners. Its manner is so relaxed as to suggest genial front-porch monologues by local scholars whom it is not necessary to listen to very attentively.... Its poems are well-turned and undemanding. Its fiction, with only an occasional exception, leaves the impression that it has travelled much and been rejected many times before finding asylum here. (p. 183)

In a review of a Catholic magazine, *The Critic,* commenting on the fact that it publishes occasional poetry and fiction, O'Connor was quick to point out: "The poetry will probably be tolerated, though not read, and the fiction read but not tolerated" (p. 166). Clever and barbed turns of phrase make this "occasional prose" a useful addendum to her fictional habits.

Following the reviews Lorine Getz offers a list of books and magazines reviewed. This in turn is followed by a bibliography. Rarely have I seen so many lists and introductions! Both tend to be invariably useful but the introductions suffer from some careless writing and lapses in detail. Here is one of the typically crowded, inelegant sentences: "Whereas in her earliest days she had been raised in her father's city, surrounded by his family and under his direction, his illness with disseminated lupus effectively removed him from the financial center of the family (he had been in business as a real estate man) and his milieu was displaced for one that, while still Georgian, was less cosmopolitan, more agrarian and culturally Protestant fundamentalist" (p. 10). Here is a sentence which disturbed me for other reasons: "Several American expatriots [*sic*], including T.S. Eliot, James Joyce, Ernest Hemingway and Ezra Pound, who had fled the American scene for the European cultural and intellectual milieu, were studied for their realism, historical consciousness and naturalistic symbolism." (p. 78) Although many of Joyce's best interpreters are American, I was unaware until now that *be* was an American! The flabbiness of the vocabulary is also noteworthy: what exactly is "naturalistic symbolism?" William James is asked several times to stand in for his younger brother Henry, as on this occasion: "Flaubert, Williams [*sic*] James and their successors, Conrad, Chekhov and Joyce, became models for the Renaissance writers" (p. 78). Sentences like these mar what is otherwise a useful book.

The Flannery O'Connor Companion makes clear its intentions in the opening sentence of the preface: "*The Flannery O'Connor Companion* introduces readers to the writings—nonfiction, fiction, and letters—of Mary Flannery O'Connor

(1925-1964), a Southern, Catholic writer who died young, age thirty-nine, of lupus." Indeed it delivers what it promises, but one wonders whether we need such a "reader's guide" at this late date. First of all, we are blessed with an uncommon amount of first-rate commentary by Robert Coles, Martha Stephens, John Hawkes, Marion Montgomery, Robert Drake, Louis Rubin, Hugh Holman, Miles Orvell, Gilbert Muller, and many others. Secondly, we might address the question raised by Robert Coles in his introduction to **Flannery O'Connor's South:** "How much more critical attention can a couple of dozen stories and two quite slim novels, however brilliantly and originally crafted, manage to sustain—without some recognition from all of us that the time has come for a bit of a pause?" (p. xxiii). It is difficult, then, to welcome a book which offers an introduction subdivided into "subject matter," "O'Connor's characters," "religion," and "place"; makes its way, item by item, through her nonfiction (faithfully following the order of *Mystery and Manners*), stories, and novels; gives a complete "kaleidoscope" (Grimshaw's word) of characters from her fiction; locates her place in twentieth-century literature; and ends with a variety of appendixes and the inevitable "selected bibliography." This "programming" of Flannery O'Connor somehow goes against the grain of her own instincts; what she calls on one occasion "the devil of Educationism" seems to have found its way here. I am not faulting James A. Grimshaw who seems to have the proper credentials for his task (he was once Flannery O'Connor Visiting Professor of English at Georgia College) and to have read the work with exemplary patience. The problem is with publishers who seem committed to the format of "reader's guide" or "companion" as a saleable item for undergraduate instruction. We are in need of "skeleton keys" when confronted by difficult texts like [James Joyce's] *Finnegans Wake*, [Ezra] Pound's *Cantos*, the later verse of Mallarmé, and [Thomas Pinchon's] *Gravity's Rainbow*, but Flannery O'Connor is easily approached without them. One is tempted on this occasion to heed her advice, which we find in *Mystery and Manners*, "when anybody asks what a story is about, the only proper thing is to tell him to read the story."

There are a number of lapses in *The Flannery O'Connor Companion*. I can only offer a sampling of them here. On p. 48, the third in the series "accomplices forever" should be Mr. Shortley instead of Mrs. Shortley; Mrs. Shortley has died by this time. On p. 66, Shoat's should be Shoats'. To move along to the "kaleidoscope of characters": on p. 73, Chestney should be Chestny; on p. 74, in the description of Star Drake, the following lines from "The Comforts of Home" should probably be noted: "The girl called herself Star Drake. The lawyer had found that her real name was Sarah Ham." In the bibliography, Rose Lee Walston should be Rosa Lee Walston, McCowen should be McCown (both on p. 119), and Nathaniel West should be Nathanael West (p. 126).

Robert Coles's acknowledgement that "the time has come for a bit of a pause" does not seem to have deterred Flannery O'Connor's most recent commentators. The six words under discussion here indicate that critics are not ready as yet to declare a moratorium. Fortunately, most of these books, especially Coles's, are well worth having.

Neil Postman (review date 19 January 1986)

SOURCE: "A Singer of Their Tales," in *New York Times Book Review,* January 19, 1986, pp. 1, 28.

[*In the following review of* The Moral Life of Children *and* The Political Life of Children, *Postman demontrates how Coles goes beyond theory and facts to reveal the truth of his subjects.*]

When I was in grade school, Christmas time was a problem. We were always made to sing those mysterious carols, and although "Jingle Bells" was a piece of cake, most of the canon was fraught with danger for a Jewish boy. Harold Goldstein and I figured out a way to defend ourselves. We turned the line "Deck the halls with boughs of holly" into "Deck the halls with rows of cholly," this last word being our rhymed distortion of "challah," the delicious Jewish bread served on the Sabbath. No one actually heard us do this. We believed Christian ears would not suffer our defiance lightly, and so we silently mouthed the words rather than utter them. When we had done this, Harold and I always exchanged the kind of glance that might have passed between Kim Philby and Guy Burgess in the corridors of Whitehall.

I do not know even now if we were making a political statement, a moral statement, or just being ornery. But if Robert Coles could have observed us, *he* would know. And if he didn't, he would at least be interested in the question. For there is no one who is more interested in what children say, sing, don't say or don't sing—and why—than Robert Coles. He is to the stories that children have to tell what Homer was to the tale of the Trojan War. And in more ways than one—all of which are richly exhibited in these companion volumes.

Indeed, it would have been only slightly pretentious if he had begun either of these books with the words "I sing the wrath of children," for his matter is the political and moral anguish of youth, and his manner is that of a singer of their tales. Though he may be called a child psychiatrist, and may even wish to be so known (would Harvard University grant tenure to a singer of tales?), he is at his best when he is listening to children talk, recording their talk and then transforming their talk into a kind of narrative poetry. He characterizes his work as "documentary child psychiatry," and with impeccable academic manners acknowledges the validity of the criticism (made by a colleague) that children do not talk exactly the way they do in his books. But the criticism is irrelevant. Dr. Coles is less a documentarian than a poet, which is to say, he is after the truth, not just the facts.

His quest is to learn something significant about how the political and moral consciousness of children develops. To get at the truth, he has made several odysseys—with his family and tape recorder—to places where there are serious problems and therefore where it is to be expected that children will have plenty to say about where they stand. Thus, Dr. Coles has ended up in South Africa, Brazil, Northern Ireland, Poland, Southeast Asia, Nicaragua, French-speaking Canada and certain troubled sections of America.

His method is to get to know children, ask them significant questions and let them speak. Much of each volume is taken up with what the children say, or, more precisely, what they mean to say. Dr. Coles is reluctant to offer elaborate or even well-organized interpretations of his protocols. He distrusts much of the conceptual baggage carried about by psychologists, especially theories about how moral or political sensibility comes into being. In *The Moral Life of Children,* he contrasts the words of Lawrence Kohlberg, Harvard's leading authority on moral development, with both the words and actions of Ruby Bridges, one of the black children who, at age 6 and in the face of abusive, even violent, resistance, initiated school desegregation in New Orleans. According to Mr. Kohlberg, Ruby would not rank very high on the scale of moral maturity; indeed, at her age, she is in a "premoral" state. In Dr. Coles's view, there is less wrong with Ruby's moral condition than with Mr. Kohlberg's taxonomy. "Her prayers," Dr. Coles remarks, "her smiles, were, I suppose, mere gestures, not the careful responses of a truly reflective person—a Cambridge theorist, for example. As for many other children we knew in the South, both black and white, I doubt they would fare much better in Kohlberg's scheme of things."

This is about as nasty as Dr. Coles gets in his rebuke of theorists, but he wishes to be very clear about the limits and prejudices of theory. "Moral life" he says, "is not to be confused with tests meant to measure certain kinds of abstract (moral) thinking, or with tests that give people a chance to offer hypothetical responses to made-up scenarios." Dr. Coles gets a little help here from his friends and teachers— for example, Paul Tillich, Anna Freud and William Carlos Williams—in finding support for his neglect of theory. He quotes each of them worrying about the academic tendency to submit facts to the sovereignty of inappropriate but deified theories.

Dr. Coles is sure that what one must do first is observe, and this mostly means to listen. When one listens, he believes, theoretical frameworks often seem to lie somewhere between aridness and irrelevancy. Here, for instance, is Ruby Bridges, speaking about the crowds who converged around her, screaming her death warrant: "They keep coming and saying the bad words, but my momma says they'll get tired after a while and then they'll stop coming. They'll stay home. The minister came to our house and he said the same thing, and not to worry, and I don't. The minister said God is watching and He won't forget, because He never does. The minister says if I forgive the people, and smile at them and pray for them, God will keep a good eye on everything and He'll be our protection." In the face of such awesome piety, theory must declare itself incompetent and remain mute.

Dr. Coles is convincing on the validity of his method and the value of his material but is less so on the distinction he draws between political and moral discourse. More than once while engrossed in the angry or frightened or puzzled outpourings of the children, I was not sure which of the two books I was reading. For example, Cathy, a Roman Catholic from Northern Ireland, has been told that the answer to the trouble in Derry is to bring in a few hundred Pakistanis. Then all the Catholics and Protestants would unite to hate the "Pakis" (as they are called). "Mummy," Cathy asks, "do you mean that the only way we can be nice to each other is to have people around we can point at and not be nice to?" Later, she addresses her father: "Would Jesus stand up for them [the Protestants] today? They've been bad to us, and they still are; we're 'pigs' to them, and they say so, and we are poor, and they own everything."

> "Nowhere on the five continents I've visited in this study has nationalism failed to become an important element in the developing conscience of young people. . . ."
> —*Dr. Robert Coles*

These remarks are quoted in *The Political Life of Children,* but as Dr. Coles is well aware, it is in the nature of the issues Cathy is trying to sort out that the moral and political are inseparable. The problem, therefore, of making two books out of one requires some ingenuity. Dr. Coles tries to solve the problem by focusing on issues of "character" in *The Moral Life of Children* and issues of "nationalism", in *The Political Life of Children,* and, I suppose, he does about as well as can be expected. In explaining why he was compelled to divide his study in this way, Dr. Coles says: "Nowhere on the five continents I've visited in this study has nationalism failed to become an important element in the developing conscience of young people. . . . Who can listen to children, of any nationality, and not hear the political superego constantly exerting its requirements upon eager and vulnerable minds?"

But if one expects Dr. Coles to assume an enlightened hostility to nationalism, one is in for a surprise. He does quote an articulate Belfast doctor's denunciation of nationalism as a "virus," and, possibly, Dr. Coles is temperamentally inclined to agree. The stories the children tell, though, lead him to a different conclusion. "Nationalism," he says, "encourages social commitment to a neighborhood, a willingness to exert oneself toward civic tasks. Nationalism also energizes the entire moral life of a child, his parents, his relatives—gives them all a structure on which they can hang a range of oughts, noughts, maybes, its."

One need not agree with this or any other generalization of Dr. Coles's to rank his book as a major contribution to our understanding of how children become socialized. Readers can draw their own conclusions from what the children say. But these books, like the "Iliad," are not about conclusions. They are about the myths, prejudices, worries and observations from which children generate their opinions and loyalties. "No one teaches children sociology or psychology," Dr. Coles remarks; "yet, children are constantly noticing who gets along with whom, and why." His tales are about what they have noticed, and how it affects them.

As a consequence, the books are written in a way that does not allow for a clear characterization of Dr. Coles's position. He does not start from a given point and progress to deeper and wider insights. Rather, he circles around certain themes, sometimes appearing to make a point but then quickly moving away from it. He is, as I say, a storyteller, and, as every storyteller knows, the characters must do the speaking. One might say of Dr. Coles that his process of inquiry is his result; his method, his conclusion.

There is, however, one conclusion that a careful reader cannot fail to draw; we are all amateurs in the task of socializing our children. Parents, teachers, clerics, even Cambridge theorists, may make their plans this way and that, and according to sure-fire instructions. But the oughts, noughts, maybes and its that count most in giving shape to a child's character and political loyalties appear to come from diverse and unexpected sources. Sometimes, as in the case of Ruby Bridges, the exhortations of a minister or a mother penetrate deeply. More often, it is the stuff of ritual, movies, television, the daily news—the unsystematized material of a child's symbolic environment—that will exert the most enduring influences. And even then, with results quite unintended. For it is repeatedly documented in these books that children are not empty vessels into which the content of culture is poured. Children are as much makers as receivers.

A case in point: Dr. Coles and a 14-year-old Georgia boy

discuss the film "The Man Who Shot Liberty Valance." The boy makes it clear that his loyalties are with the John Wayne character but not with the Senator, played by James Stewart. "They want you to be on the side of that Senator," the boy says, "and I'm not on his side. I mean, he was one of the good guys; he was the good guy. But who believes anyone like him is for real?" Those of us who worry about what a sequence of "Rambo" movies holds in store for the politics and character of our youth may thus take heart.

And we may also take heart from the fact that Robert Coles always seems to be traveling somewhere in the world listening to the planet's children, doing his deeply humanistic research. And that if we put aside our theories and preconceptions, he will tell us what is on their minds, and something about how it got there.

Katherine Paterson (review date 2 February 1986)

SOURCE: "Out of the Mouths of Babes," in *Washington Post Book World,* Vol. XVI, No. 5, February 2, 1986, pp. 1, 14.

[*In the following review, Paterson considers the methods Coles uses to reveal the moral and political lives of children.*]

One of Jimmy Carter's unforgiveable mistakes as president was his revelation that he thought his 12-year-old had opinions worth listening to. The public hoot that greeted this earnest statement still echoes in negative assessments of the Carter presidency. We are a nation, you see, that sentimentalizes children or dismisses them, but we do not take them seriously. Nor do we have much regard for people who do.

The author of these two books is a notable exception to this prevalent attitude. We do respect Robert Coles. Of course, Coles is a psychiatrist with the imprimatur of Harvard University, but it is not his medical or professorial credentials that have won him respect, but his work as a social observer over the last 25 years. And though we are not inclined to pay much attention to adults who are concerned with the young, we have been compelled by the volume and integrity of his writings to notice him, despite the fact that the heart of his work is, as he himself describes it, "listening . . . then describing what has been heard—selecting the most revealing excerpts, I hope, from the endless stories children have to tell."

Children tend not to say what we want to hear when we want to hear it, but, to the patient, perceptive adult who takes them seriously, their words are eloquent, disturbing, transforming.

Most of us are not good listeners, but the moral and political life of our nation would take a giant leap forward if we were to pay close attention to this man who is.

During the past 10 years, Coles, often accompanied by his wife and sons, has been observing and listening to find out how children develop morally and politically. To do so he has revisited persons he has worked with before, but, for the first time, he has taken his work beyond the bounds of his own country, returning repeatedly to South Africa, Brazil, Northern Ireland, Poland, Nicaragua and Canada.

These two volumes on the political and moral lives of children are the result of that decade of listening, but, reading the books, it is clear that the origins of the work go back at least as far as the author's days as a psychiatric resident, because learning how to listen to children has been a long and difficult process. Often as Coles admits, his psychoanalytic training has proved a hindrance rather than a help. In his field work which developed into *Children of Crisis,* Coles met children in situations of severe stress who were apparently coping quite well. How does a psychiatrist deal with children who have none of the symptoms he has been taught to treat?

Coles says that if his wife had had her way back in 1969 the subject of the moral life of children would have been their major preoccupation all these years. "But in my mind their 'moral life' meant their psychological ways of dealing with perplexing and even dangerous circumstances. I was not ready to chronicle the moral ups and downs of these children's lives; I wanted to show (when I paid any attention at all to the moral side of things) what kind of psychological turmoil a child's conscience can incite, or indeed, constrain, dampen."

It was more than 10 years before Coles himself began actively to observe the moral life of children, though Ruby, whom he first met in New Orleans in 1961, had even then refused to fit into his psychological cubby holes. Day after day, week after week, this 6-year-old black child had walked past a line of screaming, threatening white adults to desegregate (by herself) a formerly all-white school. As a therapist, Coles kept looking for signs of the terrors he felt sure the child was experiencing. How long could she deny them? Yet Ruby endured, returning smiles for jeers, and praying for her tormentors each night before she went peacefully to sleep.

Coles's wife kept urging him to investigate this. Where did such moral strength come from? There was no proper psychological explanation. Ruby wouldn't make the first stage in psychologist Lawrence Kohlberg's scheme of moral development, but this child and other unlikely children do exist and are, as Coles makes us realize, well worth listening to. Among the children Coles came to know and marvel over are a 10-year-old Brazilian con artist whose family barely survives from one day to the next, but who has drawn the line at sexual pandering or drug dealing, and a teen-age prostitute who feeds her younger brothers and sisters and gives the rest of her earnings to a Roman Catholic orphanage.

These are children for whom morality is not discussed as an academic exercise but "who were all trying to find moral answers for themselves through the daily steps they took."

To say Coles came to know a child is to say that over a period of years he visited this child repeatedly, usually in the child's own home. Unlike most social scientists, he does not give tests or fill out questionnaires, he converses with his young subjects. Sometimes the basis for the conversation is a picture the child has painted. Thirty of these paintings are included in *The Political Life of Children,* four in *The Moral Life of Children.* Because Coles' relationship with a child goes over a period of years, he can reveal how a child's attitude and/or behavior changes as he or she grows older. In the case of Ruby she continues to grow as a thoughtful and compassionate human being; but sadly, not all the changes Coles notes in the lives of his young subjects are for the better.

That children have a political life at all is a surprise to many adults. Or if children's political concerns are acknowledged, the assumption is made that their ideas are determined by the family and community in which children live. What Coles and his wife and sons and associates began to discover as they listened to the children themselves is that while the political thoughts and actions of children are certainly influenced by the concerns of their environments, in many instances children are not simply parroting the cant of their elders but struggling with their own political concepts in the midst of influences that affect their lives.

A reading of *The Political Life of Children* should cure any adult of a sentimental view of childhood. If hearing the words of Alice, the crippled child who is a runner for a Protestant paramilitary group in Belfast doesn't do it, listening to the story of Lon, an orphaned Cambodian refugee, or studying the painting done by Hendrick, a young Afrikaner, surely will.

Late one night I kept my husband awake telling him the difference between the Polish children Coles interviewed and the Nicaraguan. All these children live in communist countries, but the Polish children without exception despised the Jaruzelski government as an interloping force in their beloved nation, whereas the children of Nicaragua, especially the poor, but also, if grudgingly, the sons and daughters of the rich, felt that the Sandinistas, for all their faults, had given back to the people the country the Samozas and their

North American allies had stolen away. "I think the president should appoint Robert Coles as National Security Adviser," I blurted out. Now, several weeks later, in the cold light of a winter morning, I still think that is one of my better ideas.

Jonathan Kellerman (review date 9 February 1986)

SOURCE: Review of *The Moral Life of Children* and *The Political Life of Children* in *Los Angeles Times Book Review,* February 9, 1986, pp. 2, 12.

[*In the following review, Kellerman looks at Coles' individual approach to child psychology and the insights it yields.*]

Trained as a pediatrician and child psychoanalyst, Robert Coles has spent his professional life exploring and illuminating the inner world of the child. In the process, he has created an impressive body of work, crowned by the Pulitzer Prize-winning, multivolume **Children of Crisis** series.

In his writings, Coles has seemingly ignored the delineation between the academic and the popular, producing books that are scholarly, yet accessible, writing with warmth, clarity and grace that set him apart in a field notorious for jargon-laden puffery. (It is no coincidence that among his major influences are doctor-novelists William Carlos Williams and Walker Percy.) More important, he is a researcher with integrity, stating his biases forthrightly (agnostic, left-leaning white liberal) and taking pains to tease out their impact upon his conclusions. And here is one psychoanalyst who eschews the protective omnipotence of the unseen interviewer: When Coles interviews a child, it is clear that two human beings are present, each influencing the other.

But what truly distinguishes this self-described "inveterate loner and wanderer" are context and scope, for Coles has traded the comforts and limitations of the psychotherapist's office for the streets and fields of America, seeking out a broad range of children—the offspring of migrants, Eskimos, Indians, the affluent—talking, playing, drawing, interpreting, in an attempt to learn how their development has been affected by the social roles assigned them through the vagaries of nature and nurture.

In The Moral Life of Children and **The Political Life of Children,** Coles' lab has been expanded to embattled societies outside the United States—Brazil, Nicaragua, Poland, South Africa, Northern Ireland and French Canada. His 35th and 36th books, respectively, they are re-analyses of data—transcripts, drawings and paintings—accumulated over two and a half decades, a final, lingering look prior to permanent deposition in the University of North Carolina library.

The Moral Life of Children is loosely constructed around a pair of mega-questions: What is morality and from whence does it spring? Coles criticizes models of moral development, such as Lawrence Kohlberg's, that too strongly correlate morality with intelligence. Quoting Percy's warning that it is possible to "get all A's and flunk life," he offers a brief sample of moral outrages committed by the highly intelligent and describes numerous instances of moral vitality displayed by the "cognitively limited."

Having found cognitive-based theories wanting, Coles searches elsewhere, exploring the psychoanalytic view of altruism as a form of masochism, but remaining clearly dissatisfied with this cynical view of the world. He finds his psychiatric training sometimes irrelevant, even obstructive because of its obsession for value-free analysis and notes "as I got nearer and nearer to becoming . . . a child psychiatrist, I heard less and less about 'character' and more and more about 'character disorders.'" Repeating Gordon Allport's caution that "no amount of psychoanalysis, even an interminable stretch of it . . . can provide a strong conscience to a person who has grown up in such a fashion as to become chronically dishonest, mean-spirited, a liar." Coles journeys into theology, social science and popular culture—one chapter is devoted to the moral images created by movies and television—but emerges with only meager clues, and in the end, settles for re-description—the terse but unilluminating assessment of character as "a moral center that was, quite simply, there."

Along the way, however, he offers a fascinating banquet of vignettes, children whose deeds, thoughts and feelings resonate with moral strength. There is Ruby, a black child, living in the New Orleans of the '50s, who braved daily threats, humiliation and danger at the hands of racist mobs in order to desegregate a school, all the while praying for her oppressors. And Hank, "from a family all too easily labeled by the likes of me, 'redneck,'" son of an abusive, hard-drinking, Klan-sympathizing father—who must undergo "dramatic moral shifts" in order to reconcile the racism he has learned at home with his personal—and moral—view of the world.

On the streets of Rio de Janeiro, Coles encounters a 17-year-old prostitute who'll do virtually anything for money but donates much of her earnings to the wretched poor and fights angrily to maintain a psychic boundary between behavior and self-concept. During a chance meeting in that same city of extremes, he comes upon 10-year-old Eduardo, a street-hustling *favelado* who, after panhandling Coles and eyeing his money, warns: "You had better hide; the whole world will be upon you—and then you'll have to beg, too!" Intrigued, the psychiatrist tracks the boy down and interviews him, discovering a slum child who, despite a daily struggle to survive, has managed to develop a fierce moral code and a trenchant philosophy of life: "We are here to stay for a while, and if we're lucky, we'll leave people behind who like us, and when our name is mentioned, they smile and clap."

In *The Political Life of Children,* Coles conceptualizes the family as a mini-state typified by a perpetual jockeying for power and suggests that nationalism results from the transfer of parental authority to the state. He criticizes the social psychology research of the '50s that found children inevitably rating political leaders as benevolent and contends that youngsters react individually and idiosyncratically, despite remaining outwardly faithful to social norms. The material he produces to back this up is by and large unsurprising—South African children on both sides of the color line, emotionally constricted youngsters in Northern Ireland struggling with religious hatred, Polish children who love their country while coldly despising their government, Nicaraguan students parroting anti-American slogans—but no less convincing and poignant for that.

Coles has an affection for Dickens, and there is a Dickensian flavor to these two books, and to some extent, to Coles' work in general. He is a master chronicler, providing few answers but asking his questions so eloquently that his writings emerge as classic portrayals of social upheaval and its effect upon the young.

New Yorker (review date 10 February 1986)

SOURCE: Review of *The Political Life of Children* and *The Moral Life of Children,* in *The New Yorker,* Vol. LXI, No. 51, February 10, 1986, p. 115.

[*The following brief review offers a concise statement of Coles' observations on the political and moral development in children.*]

These two volumes report the results of long-term surveys in the United States and nine other countries by the noted psychiatrist. Dr. Coles mentions that previous investigations of the ways in which values are transmitted through time have not been extensive, even though the subject is of considerable interest. Not surprisingly, he found that, for good or ill, children pick up political attitudes at home. Where the political scene is one of violent division, as in Northern Ireland, the child's identity is fused with group hatred. Other children—American Indians, for example—early see the political deck stacked against them. The sense of national identity is very strong in young Poles but varies with economic class among young Brazilians. Although the sources of political opinions are comparatively easy to trace, goodness—

the most fascinating of qualities—seems as unaccountable among children as it does among adults, and Dr. Coles found young people of every class and nationality whose stalwart loving-kindness is inexplicable by any system he knows.

John Leo (review date 17 March 1986)

SOURCE: "Mysteries," in *Time,* Vol. 127, No. 11, March 17, 1986, p. 81.

[*In the following review, Leo raises objections to Coles' methods of presenting his subjects and questions the importance of his findings.*]

If the world offered Oscars for interviewing children, Anna Freud would win for lifetime achievement, Art Link-letter would walk off with the trophy for most tots questioned, and Harvard Psychiatrist Robert Coles would be handsdown, standing-ovation winner of the Jean Hersholt Humanitarian Award. He might also win the Dino De Laurentiis plaque for epic production. To date, Coles has spent 28 years toting notebook, crayons and tape recorder around the world, attempting to glean moral and political insights from children, an effort that now runs to seven books and more than a million words.

What to make of this extraordinary labor? Coles is an erudite, fiercely moral man. But he is not a gifted interviewer, and, judging by his books, rapport with children does not come easily. His interviews feature the usual dutiful responses of youngsters to earnest adult interrogation. The long set speeches that his children give are cobbled together from fragments of speech, and Coles is honest enough to admit that the process is apt to make an interviewee sound like a miniature version of the author. In his pages, Coles-like Irish children offer much the same insight as Coles-like Eskimo children: there is good and bad in everyone, and that is the way of the world.

Inevitably, a million-word enterprise involves a certain amount of recycling. Ruby Bridges, the courageous black child who integrated a New Orleans school in 1960, appears in one of the five volumes of Coles' *Children of Crisis* series, in one of the two volumes of his *Women of Crisis* books and in *The Moral Life of Children.* Once again, Coles gets very little out of an extraordinary child who smiled serenely at those who spat on her and prayed each night for her tormentors. His principal reaction is bewildered admiration. A Mississippi black woman tells her daughter that people of every hue are a mixture of good and bad, and the good fights the bad in politics all the time. Coles is again deeply impressed: "Such a moral and theological analysis of political life is worthy of Reinhold Niebuhr."

Coles has a nettlesome habit of segueing into awe at the exact moment that analysis is desperately needed. He devotes 22 pages to a stoical chicano girl named Marty, whose father and brother were killed by a drunk driver. Writing of Marty and another brave child, Coles declares, "One can only try to fathom how children like those two have managed so far to do as they've done. One thereby nudges theory toward human experience, hoping that the latter brings the former to life, and the former helps arrive at a persistent, comprehensible aspect of the human scene." In other words, the development of a moral life is certainly complex and so far seems to be an unfathomable mystery.

Why this insight should require seven books is another mystery, at least for those who believe that readers are capable of arriving at non-comprehension on their own. Coles' distaste for ideas and intellectual analysis is profound and usually presented in his books along with the belief that truth will somehow radiate out of unexamined statements by children. Coles seems to think morality is the indefinable and unpredictable result of simply making decisions. A footnote says, "I can only get a bit mystical here, summon the notion of action as 'transcendence,' and, admittedly, risk murkiness and evasion." But why pass along such confusion at book length? As the author writes at one point, "I am, yet again, coming up with nothing very startling."

Kenneth L. Woodward (review date 6 September 1987)

SOURCE: "Two Paradoxical Saints," in *New York Times Book Review,* September 6, 1987, p. 10.

[*In the following review of* Dorothy Day: A Radical Devotion *and* Simone Weil: A Modern Pilgrimage, *Woodward discusses Coles' depiction of the "life of the spirit".*]

Few of us really like saints. Admire them, yes, but the demands they make on themselves inspire us to keep our distance. Simone Weil and Dorothy Day aspired to the kind of intimacy with God that is typical of saints, and each tried "to live in such a way that," as Emmanuel Cardinal Sunard of Paris said, "one's life would not make sense if God did not exist." Both women lived and identified with the underclass; both experienced religious conversions; both were thinkers who became suspicious of the intellect; both rallied against violence and war; and if either had had her way, we would all live simpler, more communitarian lives than modern nations permit. But they were very different pilgrims of the absolute. Weil was only 34 when she died of tuberculosis and self-willed malnutrition in 1943, alone and unpublished. Day, on the other hand, was an exhausted 83 when she died in 1980, attended by her daughter and grand-

child, and by her extended family of "Catholic Workers," people who remain bonded by her vision.

Neither of Robert Coles's volumes, which appear in the Radcliffe Biography series, is biography. Instead, Dr. Coles takes up certain themes and passions that preoccupied his subjects, and wrestles with them as one might do with those of any figure who has become a lifelong spiritual companion. If we come to understand Day better than Weil, it is not only because Weil's severe solitariness is so forbidding. The main reason is that Dr. Coles draws on correspondence and conversations he had with Day, including 50 hours of taped interviews conducted in the decade before her death.

There are rewards here even for those who have read Day's autobiography, *The Long Loneliness.* Under Dr. Coles's prompting, she recalls the excitement of her 20's, when she lived in Greenwich Village, wrote for leftist journals, stayed up all night talking and smoking, fell in love with several men and had an abortion. What comes across is her profound attraction to all of human experience—the pull of the sea, the ecstasies of sex, the warmth of companionship and the bliss of producing a daughter (by a common-law husband) whose birth, paradoxically, triggered her own rebirth as a rather austere Roman Catholic. "I wanted to be poor, chaste and obedient," she told Dr. Coles. "I loved the church for Christ made visible." What she didn't like was the mass of Catholics, including clergy, who accepted the church but refused to follow Jesus or refract his harsh and dangerous love. The Catholic Worker movement, which she founded with Peter Maurin, was her response.

What emerges from these conversations is a woman whose Christian spirituality was radically rooted, like the Bible, in the concrete and specific—notably in serving this drunk, that crazed drifter and all the homeless individuals who showed up daily at the Workers' houses of hospitality. She fasted and picketed against war (including American participation in both world wars) and other large social evils but she distrusted what she called "morality in the abstract," which too easily ignores the neighbor in front of us. "But for me the heart of our work is just that," she told Dr. Coles, after he reminded her of her lifelong opposition to the welfare state, "making the soup and serving it, trying to help someone get to the hospital who otherwise might not get there, because he's confused, because she's not aware she even needs to go there." The point was not to be "effective humanitarians," but to do as Jesus bade. Lest he miss the center of the Workers' life, she reminded Dr. Coles: "We pray."

Her life of prayer was concrete, too, formed by a sense of connection: daily mass with its communion of body and blood, the kneading of the rosary and above all, an almost tactile reliance on the Bible, which she read daily. The abstractions of theology put Day off. She found more of the soul in her favorite storytellers, notably Dostoyevsky, Tolstoy and Ignazio Silone, plus the lives of saints like Thérèse of Lisieux. Indeed, the only possessions she found difficult to share were her favorite books.

Day, thank God, had her vices. As Dr. Coles makes wonderfully plain, she could be a scold, and she had the spiritual sense to recognize her repeated sins of pride, which she aggravated by efforts at selflessness. In the end, Dr. Coles finds, she wisely declared a truce in her battle for spiritual perfection. What is missing from this otherwise revealing probe by Dr. Coles, whose chief professional concern has been with what he calls children of crisis, is how Day's extraordinary life affected her daughter, Tamar Teresa. Parents can pass on their faith, but even saints cannot transmit their friendship with God to the next generation.

Simone Weil, on the other hand, was a solitary spiritual migrant, cut off from the living faith of her people, the Jews, and from the sacraments of the Roman church, which she judged herself unworthy to accept. A dazzlingly brilliant student and keen social observer, her passions were of the spirit; food, she seemed to feel, was something to renounce, and marriage, she wrote, "is a consented rape. And so," she added, "is the soul's union with God."

To Dr. Coles, irony and paradox are the very conditions of life, and in Weil he finds much to try to explain. Straight off he confronts her probable suicide and links it—successfully, I think—with her lifelong aspiration to the condition of hunger, not only as a way of sharing the deprivations of those who suffer, but as a spiritual condition of those who, as she put it, are "waiting for God." Dr. Coles also focuses on Weil's evident anti-Semitism, suggesting that it was part of a more fundamental effort to assert her "independence from the conventions and constraints (the 'gravity') of this earthly life." Her Christianity is even harder to account for. Drawn to the figure of Jesus and the folk Catholicism of the poor, she nonetheless refused to accept baptism. What she took from Christianity was the cross, and with it a fierce hunger for God that allowed her to see in every enhancement of self a diminution of God. "Salvation," she declared, "is consenting to die."

Like Day, Weil understood that Christianity inverts accepted human values, and in her powerful essays she pushed paradox to its limit. Dr. Coles tries hard, but in the end he cannot bring Weil into reliable focus. No one else has, either. The chief reason is that, like Soren Kierkegaard, Weil lives essentially in her writings, and they resist commentary. Still, it is well worth having both of the Coles books for what they tell us about the life of the spirit. Together they suggest that for those who hunger for God, the hardest test may be accepting the paradox that He has "pitched his tent among us," and we are to call it "home."

Jeff Dietrich (review date 13 September 1987)

SOURCE: "Simone Fasted, Dorothy Fed," in *Los Angeles Times Book Review,* September 13, 1987, p. 23.

[*In the following review, Dietrich examines the figures at the center of Coles' biographical studies* Simone Weil: A Modern Pilgrimage *and* Dorothy Day: A Radical Devotion.]

One woman spent her entire life feeding the hungry, while the other died a premature death of voluntary starvation. Though Dorothy Day and Simone Weil were Christian mystics who developed a remarkably similar critique of modern Western culture based upon their deep spiritual integrity, they were radically different personalities, representing radically different strains of Christian spirituality.

In the tradition that he has established in such previous work as *Children of Crisis* and *Women of Crisis,* Robert Coles, Harvard psychologist and social critic, offers an illuminating perspective on the moral climate of our culture through the examination of the spiritual journeys of these two *modern saints.*

Of the two, Dorothy Day is certainly the more personally appealing, while Simone Weil is quirky and just a little neurotic. In fact, Coles admits that he wrote the book to "try to figure where (Weil) was saner than some and where she was probably a little loony."

Before she was 25, this precocious and brilliant, though little-known philosopher, had composed articles that pierced to the core of our cultural contradictions. Her work has been compared to that of Soren Kierkegaard and Jean-Paul Sartre and was to be extravagantly praised by the French existentialist Albert Camus, who likened her to Karl Marx in her analysis of oppression and economics.

Since her untimely death in 1943, Weil has steadily emerged as one of the few strong Christian voices in Western philosophical thought. It is her grounding in Christian spirituality that makes her unique and sharpens her incisive critical analysis of Western cultural modalities. Because she writes from a vantage point outside of man-made cultural constructs, she is quick to perceive the false gods of 20th-Century humanity: the idolatry of science and industrialism and the civil religion of nationalism and militarism.

During the dark days of World War II, she went so far as to write that the whole of Western culture was based on the use of force, a legacy she believed came from our Roman forebears. The conflict for Coles is that her intellectual perceptions were so precise while at he same time, she was, as already noted, "a little loony."

"She could do without sleep, without food . . . she had no sex life. It is said that she cringed when touched and, in general, she took poor care of her body."

Though her intellectual life was firmly grounded in numerous experiences in the *real world*—a year on an automobile assembly line, some months as a volunteer with the Republican forces during the Spanish Civil War, participation in labor strife and agricultural work with peasants in the fields—Simone Weil never quite fit in.

Her time in the Renault factory left her with migraines. Her experience in the Spanish Civil War ended in a freak accident: stepping in a pot of boiling oil. Even her conversion to Christianity grew out of an experience of pain: "In a wretched condition physically, I entered the little Portuguese village . . . on the very day of the festival of its patron saint. . . . The wives of the fishermen were in procession, making a tour of all the ships . . . singing ancient hymns of sadness. There the conviction bore in on me that Christianity was pre-eminently the religion of slaves, that slaves cannot help belonging to it, and I among others."

For Simone Weil her time here on earth was a time of "slavery," a time of "waiting for God" and the "liberation" that he would bring. Thus, in 1943 when she contracted tuberculosis and continued to eat no more than the rations of workers in occupied France, one cannot help wondering whether this was an act of high morality or an act of suicide, a final liberation from the awkwardness of this world into mystical union with her only true love, God.

If Simone Weil's mystical vision was based on Platonic dualism, the separation—some would call a false separation—of a divine pure spirit from an earthly, corrupt flesh, Dorothy Day's vision of mystical union is based on an embrace of the divine incarnate in the poor and suffering of the world.

Hers is a practical asceticism that finds its objective not in a nether realm but in the direct service of the poor and suffering, here and now. If Simone Weil thought of herself as a helpless slave before God, Dorothy Day thought we should "pray as if everything depended upon God and work as if everything depended upon ourselves."

We are indebted to Robert Coles for adding this unique contribution to the growing volume of literature on the life of Dorothy Day and the Catholic Worker Movement, of hospitality house and farming communes that she founded more than 50 years ago.

Dorothy Day was a socialist, a Wobbly and a bohemian. She lived in Greenwich Village in the early days of this century, and her friends and drinking companions included Eugene O'Neill, Jack Reed, Emma Goldman and Max Eastman. She had a legal husband, a common law husband, an abortion, a baby and at least one wild love affair.

Upon her conversion to Catholicism and her subsequent meeting with Peter Maurin, she founded the Catholic Worker, a movement of lay people which combined her passion for social justice and political action, with centers of service and hospitality to the poor.

Dorothy's 50 years of humble service to the poor have had an incalculable impact on Christians and non-Christians alike. The movement that she founded operates today more than 100 soup kitchens and hospitality houses throughout the country and continues to have an ongoing effect on the church that Day, unlike Weil (who never actually became a Catholic), embraced in full knowledge of its sinfulness and corruption.

What strikes one most in Coles' book may be the human, virtually sensuous quality that emerges so keenly in Day's description of the common-law husband from whom she separated when she converted to Catholicism: "I loved him for all of the things he knew and pitied him for all he didn't know. I loved him for the odds and ends I fished out of his pockets and for the sand and shells he brought in with fishing. I loved his lean cold body as he got into bed smelling of the sea, and I loved his integrity and stubborn pride."

Dorothy loved life. As she often said, "All the way to heaven is heaven." For her there was no distinction between heaven and earth. "Heaven is a banquet, and life is a banquet too, wherever a crust of bread is shared."

No doubt the living witness of Dorothy Day is more appealing to modern sensibilities than the spiritual asceticism and personal quirkiness of Simone Weil. Going to the banquet is much more fun than fasting. But it is nevertheless true that each woman draws on a deep though distinctly different spiritual integrity, a mystical sense of wholeness that sheds divine light on the brokenness and idolatry of our culture.

Fitzhugh Mullan (review date 8 May 1988)

SOURCE: Review of *Times of Surrender* in *Washington Post Book World,* Vol. XVIII, May 8, 1988, p. 11.

[*In the following review, Mullan identifies the central themes and approaches found in the essays collected in* Times of Surrender.]

In 1967 a group of medical students at the University of Chicago, hungry for relevance and frustrated with the tidy complacency of their educations, invited Robert Coles to speak to them. The young psychiatrist, already established as a writer, civil rights activist and social critic, told the students he was anxious to visit because only eight years earlier he had done his internship at the University of Chicago. He had left it for psychiatry, a course that led him ever further away from traditional biomedicine. He wanted to have a peek at his old life, he told the students, from his new one. The students, eager for the political and moral message he brought them, assured him he had made the right decision.

Times of Surrender, a selection of Coles' essays written over the subsequent 20 years, bears out the veracity of the students' judgement. There are about 40 book reviews, interviews, speeches and commentaries, all testifying to the quantity and quality of Coles' work. He writes with erudition and passion on subjects as varied as psychiatry, politics, children, minorities, religion and medicine.

The consistent and riveting theme of Coles' writing is the importance of the humanities in our lives. "The humanities do not belong to any one kind of person," he writes. "They are part of the lives of ordinary people who have their own ways of struggling for coherence, for a compelling faith, for social vision, for an ethical position, for a sense of historical perspective." It is literature in all its forms—the interview, the child's story, the poem and the novel—that preoccupies Coles. Favorite writers such as George Eliot, William Carlos Williams, Soren Kierkegaard and Walker Percy appear and reappear in these pages as do references to Hopi tales, Eskimo legends, southern country stories and ghetto jokes: "Stories connect children to the past of their parents, their people," Coles writes, "Stories also enable children to connect themselves to something even more fundamental, their very essence of talking, listening, thinking creatures, who are anxious to fit together, as best they are able whatever they learned about human experience."

For Coles the humanities are not simply culture. In the 20th century they play a more critical role—they are an antidote, a counterweight to what he calls "the conceit of theory," a widespread affliction of our times. The natural sciences, based as they are in empiricism and quantitative disciplines, underlie the technology that is all around us. The social sciences have followed in the same vein, running double time to prove that they are reputable pursuits, based on measurement and numerical proofs. Valuable as these sciences are, they are not the whole story. Novelists, poets and painters know that and they, in contrast to the scientists, tell of "times of surrender before life's thickness, its complexities, ironies, ambiguities, and its chancy nature—meaning the ever-present possibilities (for the good and bad, both) that arrive at our doorstep through luck, fate, circumstance or accident."

It is the humanities that recognize the individual and resist the tendency toward the average that is celebrated by statisticians.

This is a strange posture for a person trained in medicine and psychiatry, natural and social sciences respectively. Coles is, in truth, an anomalous scientist, lured into the practice of medicine by early encounters with the poet-physician William Carlos Williams and drawn towards psychiatry by the work of Erik Erikson. He expresses no vituperation toward the staid sciences but, rather, argues that the humanities leaven and enlighten the practice of medicine—a position that Williams, his mentor, surely would appreciate. "A sense of the complexity of human affairs, respect for human particularity, an interest in the ethical, the just and unjust sides of the social order, an awareness of life's unremitting contingencies, and an awe of the mystery that clings to us 'world without end'—these are the stuff of the humanities at their best, and ought to be, too, of the doctor's education, the doctor's everyday practicing life."

Coles writes with industrial efficiency. He tells us in an interview, **"On Medicine and Literature,"** that he turns out 800 to 1,000 words a day, five days a week, handwritten on yellow lined legal paper. This discipline, coupled with his reading, his artistry of observation and his global travels, explains his prodigious output. Occasionally his writing shows the strain of rapid production, and some sentences or ideas call out for a good editorial scrubbing. There is, too, an occasional tendency to repetition with certain works; Jeremiah from the Bible, George Eliot's *Middlemarch* and Georges Bernanos' *The Diary of a Country Priest* are cited time and again. What is really extraordinary, however, is that these essays, written as they were over two decades and intended for sundry audiences, hold together with the cogency and power of, say, a good novel.

Times of Surrender is really a mosaic of the work of a spiritual man. Christ, the Old Testament, Dorothy Day and Gandhi appear regularly on his pages. He frequently refers to agnosticism, a theme that intrigues and perturbs him. Pure religion, like pure science, does not seem to offer the answers he seeks. Rather it is the individuality, the paradox and the outright contrariness of life that keep running out in front of the mind and spirit of Robert Coles. One hopes that he will continue his chase, pausing only to scribble his three or four yellow lined pages a day.

Helen Bevington (review date 26 February 1989)

SOURCE: "You Tell Me Yours, I'll Tell You Mine," in *New York Times Book Review,* February 26, 1989, p. 38.

[*In the following review, Bevington situates* The Call of Stories *in relation to Coles' oeuvre and interests that have marked his career.*]

By now most people know Robert Coles. Or for their own sake they ought to. Becoming his patient or his student is, I suppose, the best way to go about it, though to read his books, notably the famous five-volume **Children of Crisis**, is to make him a lasting friend.

That work, which represents some 20 years Dr. Coles spent in the rural South—in Mississippi, Louisiana, Georgia, Appalachia, New Mexico, among migrants, sharecroppers, mountaineers, Indians, Chicanos—is a study of children in the midst of change, caught in the rising crisis between blacks and whites, helpless in the struggle with poverty and ignorance. It's a study of uprooted, stranded families that, to escape the misery, fled to Northern cities like New York and Chicago, where their children became ghetto children. He called the first volume **A Study of Courage and Fear,** and said of it, "I have no illusions that anything I write will make life easier or better for [them]." But nothing kept him from trying.

The present volume, **The Call of Stories,** tells its own revealing story of how his career as doctor, writer and teacher began when, as a junior at Harvard in a course in American literature, Dr. Coles was introduced to the stories and poems of the doctor-poet William Carlos Williams. The meeting was momentous; it changed his life. After writing his undergraduate thesis on the first two books of *Paterson,* and summoning up courage to send it to Williams, he was invited by that "astonishing and inspiring" doctor not only to drop over to New Jersey for a visit, but to accompany Williams on his rounds among the poor in Paterson's squalid tenements—about which the poem eloquently speaks. The result was that, instead of the English teacher Robert Coles had meant to be, he became a medical doctor, eventually a child psychiatrist, and like Williams a great storyteller.

In significant ways he reminds one of Williams, with the same moral imagination, the kindness and compassion—though without the truculent manner, the toughness, the profanity, the anger, the scorn of intellectuals that marked the man he came to revere. The main lesson Williams the doctor taught him was always to listen to his patient, not only listen to his story but confide to him one's own, since only through stories can one person fully enter another's life. Slowly, and alarmed at first at the time it took, Dr. Coles learned to let the patient be the teacher, without hurrying to a diagnosis. He took to heart what one patient, a young man who had attempted suicide, once said to him: "You tell me your story, and I'll tell you mine."

Through stories, the "call of stories"—meaning their appeal, their value, their justification—the physician seeks to heal others as himself. Dr. Coles fondly remembers Phil, a boy of 15, paralyzed by polio and deeply resentful of what had happened to him, who found in books two voices that he heard and liked, that gave him hope. Huckleberry Finn and Holden Caulfield, of *Catcher in the Rye,* became his closest friends, and Dr. Coles in turn told the boy how *Paterson* had affected him. He remembers the physicist Enrico Fermi, as he lay incurably ill and dying in the hospital where Dr. Coles was an intern and saw him daily. "Had I read *The Death of Ivan Ilych*?" Fermi asked him. The reading of books, he reflected with a smile, was keeping him alive; Tolstoy was helping him find acceptance of death.

In 1974 Dr. Coles returned to New England and to teaching, where at the Harvard Medical School he taught a course of his own invention, "Literature and Medicine." Years before, Williams had said to him, "Sure, if you could get medical students to read certain novels or short stories it might make a difference." But don't bet on it, he added. The course included stories by doctors: Williams himself, Chekhov, Walker Percy; and about doctors: *The Magic Mountain* [Thomas Mann], *Arrowsmith* [Sinclair Lewis], *Middlemarch* [George Eliot] .Since his medical students, like his patients, were forever attempting to find out what life meant and where they were headed, he continued to offer the course, reading with them the literature of pain, fatal illness, grief, reading Robert Lowell on madness, Sylvia Plath on suicide, Richard Eberhart's poem "The Cancer Cells."

Now professor of psychiatry and medical humanities at Harvard, he has branched out considerably, broadening the view, teaching seminars in "Dickens and the Law" in the Law School, Flannery O'Connor's stories of spiritual grace in the Divinity School, *The Great Gatsby* in the Business School, *All the King's Men* in the Kennedy School of Government, Ibsen's play *The Master Builder* to future architects in the Harvard School of Design. I imagine him walking into a classroom some days and looking around in bewilderment, wondering where he is, though it really doesn't matter. The same narratives succeed for all, conveying here a suggestion, there a powerful meaning to which they can respond as human beings. One of his medical students observed in surprise, "I've never thought of stories or a novel as a help in figuring out how to get through a working day."

Thus steadily in this persuasive book, Robert Coles makes clear his profound belief in the call of stories and their usefulness, their moral support. "Dr. Williams," he says in conclusion, "urges intense, searching self-scrutiny. Dr. Chekhov urges a close look not only at ourselves but at others, at the terrible contrasts of this world. . . . All in all, not a bad start for someone trying to find a good way to live this life."

Francis X. Rocca (review date March 1989)

SOURCE: Review of *Harvard Diary* and *That Red Wheelbarrow: Selected Literary Essays,* in *American Spectator,* Vol. 22, No. 3, March 1989, pp. 40-41.

[*In the following review, Rocca assesses Coles' style and approach to writing and thinking about issues covered in* Harvard Diary *and* That Red Wheelbarrow.]

A few years ago, before starting a lecture on the "Literature of Social Reflection" (a course for Harvard undergraduates that dwells on suffering and sacrifice in life and literature), Robert Coles was preempted by a prankster from the *Harvard Lampoon.* The Phool (an initiate into the *Lampoon*) walked to the front of the class and performed an uncanny imitation. He employed the professor's pacing and a characteristic mannerism, tugging at his sweater. His monologue recounted a fanciful highway pile-up, ostensibly witnessed by the professor on the way to work in a Volvo. In fact, Coles drives a BMW, but the mimic's plaintive tone, overwrought and tortured locution, and discursive remarks that combined the routine with the disastrous, were all ridiculously apt. Yet the class did not laugh. The professor walked in, obviously bewildered, and the Phool ended his bit. After a moment's silence a woman rose and proclaimed: "We love you, Dr. Coles!" The room filled with applause.

Except for practitioners of self-help quackery, Coles could be the best-known psychiatrist in America. More than twenty years ago, with a study of black and white children in the South during the civil rights movement, he began *Children of Crisis;* the best-selling series has stretched to five volumes, including *Migrants, Sharecroppers, Mountaineers and Eskimos, Chicanos, Indians;* the last one so far is *Privileged Ones,* about the children of affluence. In this Pulitzer Prize-winning series, which constitutes his major scholarly contribution, he combines techniques of ethnography, oral history, and psychoanalysis in long but readable first-person accounts, illustrated with diagnostic crayon drawings by the children. In total, Coles has written more than two dozen volumes on psychiatry, social problems, literature, and religion. And though he is nothing like the advice columnists and radio shrinks, who make casual diagnoses and prescriptions, Coles has written for their same vast audience: for instance, his recent cover story—**"Grandparents: Can They Love Too Much?"**—in the senior citizens magazine, *50 Plus.*

In an age that lacks a moral authority, Coles serves as a professional conscience of the professional class. For example, although his primary affiliation is with Harvard Medical School, he has undertaken the commendable and quixotic mission to teach *Bleak House* and *The Great Gatsby* at Harvard's law and business schools, respectively. He elicits a sense of guilt from his students and teaches them to assuage it confessionally. They can follow the example of their professor's contrition, as he expounds on his dilemmas and failings as a physician, a teacher, and a Christian.

Harvard Diary is a collection of columns that originally appeared under that title in the *New Oxford Review,* a monthly published by Roman Catholic laymen (Coles is an Episcopalian). The articles concentrate on religion and moral philosophy, through a variety of topics; exemplary lives (Dorothy Day, Edith Stein), current controversies (abortion, pornography, school prayer), and eternal questions (God's grace, wealth vs. poverty).

Throughout, Coles emphasizes the predicament of a Christian in a secular community, with inevitable political implications. He calls himself "a social conservative, a political liberal, an economic populist or egalitarian." What he is, is a conservative by temperament, with a vague sense of obligation to liberalism. He laments the vicissitudes of a market economy no less than the "spiritual poverty" that afflicts the most prosperous capitalists. On the other hand, he is frankly anti-Communist and suspects that "Christian socialism" is more socialist than Christian. And he puts no faith in liberalism as a remedy for the evils of capitalism, or as a bulwark against totalitarianism. On the so-called social issues he is less ambivalent: abortion is "an affront to the Lord"; for homosexuals to identify themselves culturally and politically by their sexuality is "abhorrent"; women should be free to raise their own children, not forced to seek respectability in careers. These are not remarkable opinions, except at Harvard.

This book is largely a jeremiad about "the modern, agnostic, liberal sensibility" (known in more polemical parlance as "secular humanism"), as codified in the social sciences—especially psychology. Coles fulminates on the distortions and abuses of that discipline as a "faith":

> The result is everywhere apparent: parents who don't dare bring up their children, from infancy on, without recourse to one expert's book, then another's; students who are mesmerized by the talk of psychological "stages" or "phases" and "behavioral patterns" and "complexes"; grown-up people who constantly talk of an "identify crisis" or a "mid-life crisis"; elderly men and women who worry about "the emotional aspects of old age," and those attending them at home or in the hospital who aim at becoming versed in steering the "dying" through *their* "stages" or "phases"...

The worst influence of this "secular idolatry" is that it distracts well-meaning clergy from spiritual duties, in order to cater to the temporal needs of their flocks.

In the moral wasteland Coles surveys, individuals stand out who have acted in fidelity to their principles, and in defiance of blatant oppression or insidious conventions; who have suffered meaningfully in service to others, or to a higher cause, or to both. These are Coles's heroes, more or less saints. They include the theologian Dietrich Bonhoeffer and the philosopher Sister Edith Stein, who were killed by the Nazis. A favorite of Coles is the mystic Simone Weil, a refugee in England during World War II, who hastened her own death from tuberculosis by choosing to eat only as much as her compatriots in occupied France. To be sure, Coles also celebrates those who lived their biblical three-score and ten, more or less, such as Dorothy Day, the founder of the *Catholic Worker,* and the theologian Reinhold Niebuhr. Yet the most inspiring stories are of those who made the supreme sacrifice, or who at least died before their time. The rapturous style in which he memorializes the fallen is reminiscent of Catholic devotion to the cultus of a martyred saint.

Coles, of course, has no hope of martyrdom. He is cursed by luck; at least he curses his own luck, continually. He decries the arrogance and selfishness of his "ilk," a recurring word by which he means, variously, "the intelligentsia," psychiatrists, "well-educated and successful Anglos," or simply the affluent. Here he would seem to be squarely in the liberal camp, but he is following an older tradition: his humility is on the authority of the Gospels. And as he envies the poor their spiritual advantages promised in the Sermon on the Mount, he must also envy the punishing respect that victims of conscience enjoy. It is not hard to think of him, who is disillusioned with his privileged circumstances and who eulogizes his heroes with such vicarious fervor, as a Walter Mitty of moralists, lapsing into fantasies of self-sacrifice and grand suffering.

> **Coles appreciates the subtlety of Dicken's social vision: that the well-off are themselves victimized and corrupted in their oppressive relationship with the oppressed.**
> —*Francis X. Rocca*

As the basis for his reflections on moral, social, and political matters, Coles prefers fiction and poetry to the cut-and-dried social sciences, because literature "does not shun or try to conceal this life's paradoxes, inconsistencies and contradictions." *That Red Wheelbarrow* is a collection of his book reviews and longer literary essays from the pages of publications as diverse as the *New England Journal of Medicine* and the *American Poetry Review.* These articles might have been compiled more selectively, to less redundant effect. Certain words, phrases, anecdotes, and quotations recur so often that they obscure what is often astute moral

reasoning. Coles espouses intellectual humility, but he has deemed it worthwhile to reprint for posterity seemingly every word of literary commentary he has published.

At his best, Coles shrewdly assesses the honesty and fairness of his favorite writers. He points out that, in *Let Us Now Praise Famous Men,* James Agee spared the impoverished tenant farmers an examination of their racism, and portrayed them as sinless. Coles appreciates the subtlety of Dicken's social vision: that the well-off are themselves victimized and corrupted in their oppressive relationship with the oppressed. And on the other hand:

> [Flannery] O'Connor knew that the poor, the uneducated, can also be thoroughly impure, as wretched spiritually as the rest of us who are far luckier. Did Christ promise every poor person admission to heaven? A socioeconomic fact become an existential one!

In the Coles literary pantheon, William Carlos Williams is the most revered. This book's title is a reference to Williams's famous poem "The Red Wheelbarrow" ("So much depends. . . "). Williams was something of a mentor to Coles; he urged the younger man to study medicine, and corresponded with him until the older man's death. Irrespective of admiration and affection, it is natural that Coles, who can sermonize broadly on the slightest pretext, devotes so much space to Williams, whose minimalist verse lends itself to the most profuse elaboration. As Bruce Bawer put it recently in the *New Criterion,* "[Williams] makes it easy for critics to look more important than the poems they're writing about."

Indeed, Coles monopolizes this book with more than his share of "Augustinian self-scrutiny," a quality that he praises in Williams, Weil, O'Connor, George Eliot, and George Orwell. These authors are the guests of a solicitous host, who nevertheless repeatedly interrupts them, and steers the conversation inevitably to himself. Throughout the book, as though anticipating this objection, he intones against "narcissism" (perhaps 100 times in 352 pages) and, almost as often, the very "scrupulosity" with which he dwells on it. In Coles's own words: "The preacher is flawed in precisely the respect he denounces during his sermons, and the doctor is ailing even as he tries to heal others."

The ailing Dr. Coles does not perform literary psychoanalysis, though we might expect him to. He vehemently disavows the practice. Several times he invokes Freud's admonition to alienists to "lay down [their] arms" on the artist's terrain. Not that Coles defends psychoanalysis under any circumstances at all; in this book he treats the practice only skeptically or derisively: by its "reductionism" it fails to comprehend human integrity, demeaning the patient and deceiving the doctor.

Instead of a distinguished practitioner of this ineffectual profession, Coles would rather be a novelist or a poet. He resents the constraints of the psychoanalytic vocabulary, which cannot convey ambiguity and irony. But his own prose, free of jargon except between ironical quotation marks, does not justify departures from the language of his discipline. He gives in to verbosity and vagueness. At his worst, he commits labored, homiletic diction: "How ought one live this particular life we happen to have, and what does it mean, actually—if anything?"

This life, in Cole's vision, is rather dismal:

> On our way to another planet or layer of the unconscious or new social structure, we of this century don't worry about the dread every man is heir to, nor do we consider envy, passion, and hate things that will always plague man, however lovingly and scientifically he is reared, and in whatever social, political, or economic system. . . . Necessarily, said Plato, the Fates can never be thwarted, and they cannot be thwarted today, even by a million computers and consulting rooms. Necessarily, says [Cormac] McCarthy, the dark is out there, waiting for each of us. Necessarily, our lot is assigned; we have to contend with our flaws, live with them, and all too often be destroyed by them.

The frequent references to Augustine are not casual after all. Though tempered by tolerance and erudition, it is mostly pessimism—which Chesterton called Luther's corruption of Augustine—that infuses these books. Coles's agonizing never reaches a conclusion. Insistently, intelligently, he disturbs middle-class complacency, but he offers no alternative, leaving the morally serious reader merely discouraged.

Most troubling is the virtual absence of humor. The painfully earnest tone is never relieved by the "mocking sense of humor with respect to itself" that Coles misses in scholarly life. His emotional range is between anxiety and resignation, with a few oscillations toward despair or ecstasy. While he tries several times to evoke the impression of Jesus "as He walked Galilee," and to contemplate the mystery of the Incarnation, Coles does not appreciate what Chesterton sensed: that "there was some one thing that was too great for God to show us when He walked upon our earth; and I have sometimes fancied that it was His mirth."

Iain Bamforth (review date 7-13 July 1989)

SOURCE: "Clinical Humanitities," in *Times Literary Supplement,* No. 4501, July 7-13, 1989, p. 752.

[*In the following review, Bamforth comments on Coles' combined concerns for medicine and literature.*]

Times of Surrender is a collection of reviews, addresses and reminiscences from the past twenty years which attests to Robert Coles's conviction that appreciation of literature is a useful adjunct to the study of medicine. Coles is Professor of Psychiatry and Medical Humanities at Harvard; literary texts have thus been his chosen means of guiding a generation of over-achieving medical students towards the ethical dilemmas awaiting them in their professional lives. Of the forty-odd essays in this collection, a large number are devoted to writers and thinkers, among them John Kennedy Toole, Georges Bernanos, Reinhold Niebuhr, Thomas Merton, Robert Jay Lifton and B. F. Skinner. Coles's stance is that of a mediator between the natural sciences and the humanities, with a sceptical interest in their hybrid, the social sciences. Although not the first commentator to notice how highly specialized dexterity may often gloss moral nullity, or to feel adrift between plodding empiricism and ballast-free theory, his advocacy of literacy for anyone with the presumption to heal and his promotion of medicine's concern for the individual share common ground with conventional wisdom and radical critiques of contemporary practices.

The professionally successful but inwardly deadened Dr. Lydgate in George Eliot's *Middlemarch* is referred to in more than one essay as an instructive object-lesson for intending doctors: self-scrutiny should precede any other kind of diagnosis. Times of surrender, Coles suggests, are moments of recognition prompted by the confrontation between doctor and patient; in effect a renunciation of clinical detachment. Throughout, he is quick to demolish the prolix and self-serving language of his profession, comparing it unfavourably with the genius for listening of William Carlos Williams, his own mentor. Its need for easy therapeutic triumphs and the swell of goal-directed categorizing in psychiatry inevitably quicken his suspicion. The considerable benefits of today's medicine, its rage to cure and its grandiose and seemingly invulnerable articles of faith may have been acquired, he tentatively implies, at an even greater cost.

All the essays have been lifted unchanged from their original settings: the uninformed reader could thus be forgiven for imagining that James Baldwin had returned to New York for good in 1977, or that Lillian Hellman was as "ethically sensitive" as Coles, in a disconcerting encomium, supposes she is. The most memorable essay is a partly autobiographical piece, "The Wry Dr. Chekhov", which tells of a young patient's death from cancer while under his care as a medical student. Her life almost depleted, the patient's quietly resigned and obliquely stated request that he read "Ward 6" fell on deaf ears. Later realization of the justness of her allusion marked a crucial formative experience for the young Coles, an insight both literary and existential into the shifting locus of pathology and the drastic role-change contemplated in Chekhov's story.

As a species, however, novelists have a remarkably broad angle of vision; Coles marginally weakens his case by the normalizing assumption that medicine and literature are indeed complementary. It might be thought, on the contrary, that doctors and writers are their own best antidote and that Coles's quest for edifying literature and exemplary lives has been highly selective. In reminding us of the key historical and etymological kinship between curing and caring as a "writing doctor" (Coles himself endorses this copywriter's tag), he lends a cautionary voice to what is otherwise understated or overlooked in a profession which tends, like many others, to talk only to itself. Coles's essays have the singular virtue of practising what they preach.

Sanford Pinsker (essay date Summer 1989)

SOURCE: "'After Such Knowledge, What Forgiveness?':
The Rise of Ethical Criticism," in *Georgia Review,* Vol. XLIII, No. 2, Summer 1989, pp. 395-405.

[*In the following essay, Pinsker considers Coles' The Call of Stories in the context of ethical criticism and moral responses to literature.*]

On Moral Fiction (1978), John Gardner's idiosyncratic, often downright cranky musing about contemporary fiction was so roundly hooted out of academe's groves that one began to wonder if he had not, in fact, hit a raw nerve. It was not only that his detractors protested far more about the book's self-serving, self-righteous moral posturing than the occasion required, but also that their attacks disguised an equally strong aversion to ethical criticism itself.

Saul Bellow—one of the few writers whom *On Moral Fiction* did not bash—takes a special pleasure in posing precisely the sort of moral questions that made the critics of Gardner's study so uncomfortable. "*Has the filthy moment come,*" Moses Herzog asks in one of his characteristically agitated mental letters, "*when moral feeling dies, conscience disintegrates, and respect for liberty, law, public decency, all the rest collapses in cowardice, decadence, blood?*" After reading the brightest and the best of contemporary literary thought, one is tempted to tell Professor Herzog that there is good news and bad news: the good news being that the apocalyptic smashup he so worried about failed to ma-

terialize; the bad news turning out to be a long patch in which value words have had to duck for cover.

Indeed, the case against ethical criticism has become so much a part of the postmodernist landscape that those who raise questions about the link between literary structures and the larger rhythms of our moral life must show a pedigree at the door or find themselves dismissed either as hopelessly naive or as potential book burners. Those *with* pedigrees, (which is to say, those who have no trouble seeing the imagination as an ideological expression of, say, one's feminism or Marxism) move easily—some would say *too* easily—from culture to cultural politics. But even these critics tend to bristle when they are lumped together under the umbrella of "moral criticism." After all, it is one thing if a literary discussion is thick with talk of "privileging and empowering," but quite another when the conversation turns to which books are good or bad for people, and why. As Christopher Clausen puts it in a pioneering study of ethical criticism well worth a second (or for most readers, a first) look: "The effort of bringing an undogmatic moral criticism back to life, or rather of showing that it was only playing dead, is worthwhile for a number of reasons. The most important for literary purposes is that we should be clearer about what we are doing when we judge a book to be well or badly written."

Clausen, it now turns out, is not the only voice out to give moral criticism a renewed vitality. Wayne Booth has made something of a career as a public speaker by addressing literary problems that most critics wouldn't touch with ten-foot vita. *The Vocation of a Teacher* is a collection of occasional pieces delivered to a wide variety of audiences—fellow teachers, graduate students, nervous freshmen, and, of course, the General Public—over the span of years between 1967 and 1988. If Booth does not always regard as an unalloyed blessing the ancient Chinese curse, "May you live in interesting times!" he does, at least, regard the interesting times of the last two decades, often fractious and increasingly divisive, as a bracing rhetorical challenge. And as any readers of Booth's earlier work (e.g., *The Rhetoric of Fiction* [1961]; *The Rhetoric of Irony* [1974]) can attest, Booth is a considerable rhetorician.

Interestingly enough, the lecture that set into motion the wheels of *The Company We Keep*—namely, a talk delivered at Hamilton College during the mid-1970's entitled "Can Art Be Bad for You?"—is not included in *The Vocation of a Teacher.* What matters, of course, is that Booth has continued to ask common-sense questions about the "kind of company we are keeping as we read or listen"—everything from "Am I willing to be the kind of person that this storyteller is asking me to be?" to "Will I accept this author among the small circle of my true friends?" For those who prefer to keep critical inquiry under tight wraps, these are dangerous questions, capable of turning a classroom discussion into a messy, altogether impressionistic affair. One might be willing to trust a Wayne Booth with such yardsticks, but not those who lack his wide reading and palpable sophistication.

Booth, however, welcomes exactly the sort of give and take feared by most critics, including those who normally side against the authoritarian. As he puts it, the aim of *The Company We Keep* is, first,

> to restore the full intellectual legitimacy of our common-sense inclination to talk about stories in ethical terms, treating the characters in them and their makers as more like people than labyrinths, enigmas, or textual puzzles to be deciphered; and, second, it aims to "relocate" ethical criticism, turning it from flat judgment for or against supposedly stable works to fluid conversation about the qualities of the company we keep—and the company that we ourselves provide.

Booth is no slouch where it comes to providing us with the best that has been thought and said about critical theory or to unloading his own ideas about such topics as narrative structure, but he knows the value of occasion and anecdote. In this sense, *The Company We Keep* is a book out to make reading a human, and humane, activity. Booth's distinctive thumbprint appears on every page, in every paragraph—always reminding us of what is at stake when we give ourselves over to a "story."

He begins with an incident that has haunted him for some twenty-five years. It began innocently enough, as members of the University of Chicago's humanities teaching staff met to discuss the books to be assigned to the next batch of entering students. Mark Twain's *Adventures of Huckleberry Finn* had been on the list for years, and there was a general assumption that it would be on the list once again. But, as Booth tells the story, "suddenly the one black member of the staff, Paul Moses, an assistant professor of art, committed what in that context seemed an outrage: an overt, serious, uncompromising act of ethical criticism."

> It's hard for me to say this [Moses began], but I have to say it anyway. I simply can't teach *Huckleberry Finn* again. The way Mark Twain portrays Jim is so offensive to me that I get angry in class, and I can't get all those liberal white kids to understand why I am angry. What's more, I don't think it's right to subject students, black or white, to the many distorted views of race on which that book is based. No, it's not the word "nigger" I'm objecting to, it's the whole range of assumptions about slavery and its consequences, and about how whites should deal with liberated slaves, and how liberated slaves should behave or will behave toward whites, good

ones and bad ones. That book is just bad education, and the fact that it's so cleverly written makes it even more troublesome to me.

Moses' response has proved as "troublesome" for Booth as *Huckleberry Finn* was, and presumably still is, for Moses. The old reasons that Booth and his shocked colleagues trotted out twenty-five years ago—that Jim is the character closest to the book's moral center, that Twain's novel is as thoroughly *anti*racist as any one might imagine—remain good arguments, but Booth is no longer of a mind that Moses breached some unstated rule of academic decorum by venting his reservations: "I shall argue . . . that Paul Moses's reading of *Huckleberry Finn,* an overt ethical appraisal, is one legitimate form of literary criticism."

Moreover, Booth is well aware that taking Moses' position seriously (despite the fact that he continues to disagree with it) has consequences—not only for small, closed-door meetings but also for classrooms, for lecture halls, for the literary profession as a whole:

> Such appraisals are always difficult and always controversial; those modern critics who banned them, at least in theory, from the house of criticism had good reason to fear what they too often spawn when practiced by zealots. Anyone who attempts to invite ethical criticism back into the front parlor, to join more fashionable, less threatening varieties, must know from the beginning that no simple, definitive conclusions lie ahead. . . . But if the powerful stories we tell each other really matter to us—and even the most skeptical theorists imply by their *practice* that stories do matter—then a criticism that takes their "mattering" seriously cannot be ignored.

In short, ethical criticism raises precisely the sort of embarrassing questions that formalist critics thought had been put to rest forever decades ago: Is this "poem" morally, politically, or philosophically sound? It is likely to work for good or ill in those who read it? Viewed in this way, ethical criticism may not be such a lonely enterprise after all, because in recent years its numbers have been swelled by feminist critics asking tough questions about a male-dominated canon and its effects on the consciousness of both men and women; by black critics whose challenges are at once more thoroughgoing and more thoughtful than Moses'; by neo-Marxists who challenge the class biases of European literary traditions; and by various religious critics who attack modern literature for its "nihilism."

Nor does it especially worry Booth that some practitioners of ethical criticism are likely to be simplistic or clumsy or just plain reductive. As long as the conversation about what we expect of a given book, and what the given book expects of *us,* remains conversation—as opposed to, say, efforts on behalf of censorship—he figures the result will be a generation of more engaged, and therefore *better,* readers.

The Company We Keep is a powerful argument, not only for its contention that literature *can* make something happen (it can, for example, teach us to "desire better desires"), but also for its abiding faith that literature can be a means of experiencing life more intimately, more deeply, more importantly, than most of us have imagined possible or permissible. Furthermore, Booth's arguments do not depend upon our agreeing with his intricate breakdowns of authors and readers (no less than three in each camp) or his distinctions between what he calls "hypocrisy downward" (in which author, reader, or both pretend to be worse off than they really are) and "hypocrisy upward," in which the claims about disinterest or unselfishness are out of kilter with their source. To be sure, Booth is as persuasive about the nuts and bolts of his mechanics of reading as he is about the more general issue of an ethics of criticism, but what matters most in *The Company We Keep* will linger long after Booth's line separating an "implied" from an "immediate" author blurs.

That we are up to our eyeballs in competing literary theories and the claims of special-interest politics is hardly as newfangled a condition as we might think. Castiglione's *The Book of the Courtier* (1528) is, among other things, a book of worries, and none pressed harder than the realization that "it is so difficult to know what true perfection is that it is well-nigh impossible; and this is due to the diversity of our judgments. . . . Everyone praises or blames according to his own opinion, always hiding a vice under the name of the corresponding virtue, or a virtue under the name of the corresponding vice." Booth's steady, gentle insistence—always buttressed by copious footnotes and elaborate bibliographies—that Don Quixote "might have been rescued by reading *Don Quixote,* that Emma Bovary's best hope would have been to read *Madame Bovary,*" is a badly needed testament to the powers that reading rightly might have for us. Reading, for Booth, remains what it has always been—namely, an intensely human activity, one in which talk about characters and even about authors quite naturally includes estimations of our approval and disapproval:

> . . . I have never come to a point of trusting him [Norman Mailer] as a friend. That is partly a matter of my disagreeing with some of his views about the kind of sympathy we should grant Gary Gilmore. But it is even more my sense of an untroubled incoherence, and hence untrustworthiness, in this career author. I know much less about the "real" [Ann] Tyler than I know about the public image "Norman Mailer," or about the career author I have met in reading most of his books. "My" Tyler's range and daring are much more limited than "my"

Mailer's, but I feel that she is giving me everything she's got, and she cares a great deal about what will become of me as I read. My Mailer, in contrast, is simply playing games with me; he does not care a hill of beans for my welfare—he would obviously be happy to sacrifice me and any other reader to further his own ends.

In Booth's eminently sensible sentences I get the point, and I can even agree with him, although I am not so sure that I would want to encourage, or to read, a handful of sophomore papers that hold forth on "their" Kafka or "their" Joyce. Moreover, I can think of authors who are good company between hard covers, but who would probably make lousy dinner companions and downright horrific weekend guests.

No one will seriously question Booth's abilities as a close, ethical reader, but there are times when one wonders if ingenuity and enthusiasm have not combined to blur his judgment. In a chapter explaining how he came to be a "lukewarm Lawrentian" (a term that the rhetorician in Booth must surely recognize as an oxymoron), Booth keeps rereading Lawrence and applying his own principles about "unreliable narrators" and "implied authors," until, one by one, the old objections to Lawrence's bombast and to the tedious—and, in my opinion, ethically dangerous—philosophizing that mars much of Lawrence's work simply drop away; and Booth finds himself

> . . . conversing with a peculiarly insistent, passionate, and wide-ranging friend, one who will respond in some interesting way to every important question I can think of. Some of our real-life friends—and they can be among our best—simply rule out certain topics from our conversation. Literary friends are like that, too. I don't expect to converse with the implied E. M. Forster about African art, let's say, or about how elementary education should be conducted. I don't converse with Jane Austen or Henry Fielding about depth psychology, and I don't talk with Henry James about metaphysics.

Quite so, Mr. Booth. One can converse with the implied D. H. Lawrence about *anything,* although I would suggest that you avoid bringing up certain topics—for example, blood consciousness, or how like-minded souls can effect a *Blutbrüderschaft.*

Booth's arguments on behalf of choosing good literary company widen considerably in Tobin Siebers' *The Ethics of Criticism,* a survey of contemporary critical theories that posits a long-standing connection between criticism and ethics. Indeed, ethical concerns become for Siebers the subtext that effectively unites widely differing theoretical schools into a hitherto unrecognized common cause. Moreover, the philosophical ground on which much of modern critical theory stands—the moral legacies of Plato, Kant, Nietzsche, and Freud—is likewise concerned with those choices that "bring the critic into a special field of action: the field of human conduct and belief concerning the human."

Granted, modern critical theory may speak in a discourse largely concerned with issues of language, but as Siebers points out, "behind its definitions lie ideals of human character":

> The slippage between the autonomy of human will, proposed within the moral philosophy of Kant, and the autonomy of language, found in the New Criticism and poststructuralist theory, proves a most fertile ground for interrogating the character of language. What is at stake . . . in ethical criticism from Plato to pluralism and the ethics of autonomy is not merely the naming of a hidden ethos. The substitution of language for the self produces its own distinct moral dilemma because it has created a view of human consciousness in which ethical reflection is always destined to fail. The character of language promoted by theory today makes extremely difficult the type of consciousness necessary to moral reflection.

For Siebers; the ethics of criticism is at once a high-stakes game *and* a study of the means by which literary criticism affects the relation between literature and human life:

> Violence is a human problem. It is never an infernal machine without a driver. It is never without a victim. If it may be called systematic, it is only so because it establishes languages and patterns of behavior that can be repeated by others.

> Literary criticism would seem far removed from such matters. Its isolation in the little rooms of academia makes it a tame occupation, and many of the dangers now associated with criticism by those in search of a vicarious thrill would be laughable, given the state of terrorism and brutality in the world, if they were not so misguided.

However, as Siebers goes on to argue, language *is* power, and as such, it is one instrument of human violence. Consequently,

> literary critics have a responsibility not only to supervise their own unjust practices as critics but to think about the ways in which language carries on the work of human prejudice, racism, sexism, classism, and nationalism.

What follows, perhaps predictably, is a tightly argued historical account that begins with Plato and makes appropriate stops to consider the contributions and failings of various critical "schools" (e.g., the Rousseauesque from Lévi-Strauss to Derrida, the Nietzschean dimensions of René Girard, and the French Freudianism of Jacques Lacan). *The Ethics of Criticism* ends with the good news about "nuclear criticism," first announced in the pages of *Diacritics* (Summer 1984), as a field uniting two aspects of ethical criticism—one that "reads other critical or canonical texts for the purpose of uncovering the unknown shapes of our unconscious nuclear fears"; and the other that "aims to show how the terms of the current nuclear discussion are shaped by literary or critical assumptions." Siebers has his quarrels with nuclear criticism, especially when it gives itself over to wholly negative representations (as he puts it, "The sentimentalist may be naive in singing songs of Melusina, but critical theorists are just as unintellectual in chanting Dies Irae"), but he also sees one clear advantage that has been conspicuously absent in most literary theories:

> Nuclear criticism . . . contains the potential to read literature not against human interests but for them. Whereas poststructuralist theory has been defined principally as linguistic, in direct opposition to psychological and anthropological issues, nuclear criticism exposes the fact that the most abstract of theoretical designs and the most simple of literary ventures conceal human interest. The central human issues, for nuclear critics, are the value of the human community and the danger of its destructive tendencies. Nuclear criticism may therefore serve a double purpose. It provides a means of reading the ethical preoccupation of those literary artists and critics who declare most zealously their antagonism to ethics, and it asserts those principles of human community and opposition to violence so vital to the discussion of nuclear issues.

Surprisingly enough, Siebers gives the last words to literature rather than to criticism—and this after some 240 densely argued, cooly disinterested pages that constitute a criticism of criticism:

> The nuclear metaphor [at the very center of the nuclear critic's panoramic vision] communicates in its care for life the wholly negative image of planetary death that literature has forever balanced with an ethical and aesthetic image of human life. To be human is to tell stories about ourselves and other human beings.

> The finally human is literature.

In important ways Irving Massey's study begins where

Siebers' ends—that is, in an effort to read Alexander Pope's teasing line, "Find you the virtue, and I'll find the Verse," against both the burdens and the benefits of a postmodernist sensibility. "Can one, then," Massey asks, "imitate virtue?" And furthermore,

> should one . . . write about vice? (This is not an idle question.) Maybe there is not even a language for the Good, since language, like image, is at least partly a form of representation. Or, at least, since the Fall, as [Walter] Benjamin would have it, language, no longer pure creative Name, is tainted, and is unable to carry the force of the Good as such. . . . The question even arises whether literature as such, which must accept pure negativity as one of its possible poles, can claim a place within a consistently ethical scheme.

In Massey's deeply personal meditations on image and desire, questions abound. Has he confused the moral with the aesthetic? Sartre, for one, would insist that he has, and furthermore, that "The real is never beautiful"—for beauty requires a detachment from the world. In short, the Good cannot either be imaged or imagined; ethics is act rather than representation. And yet, no matter how much Massey tells us—and himself—that "talk" about ethics is a sterile subject, and that virtue cannot be imitated, the nagging question remains: "What, then, is literature good for?"

Find You the Virtue seeks possible answers by pointing out how ethical concerns provide a context in which desire, image, and what Massey calls "the literary" can intersect. Here, for example, is a representative sample, taken from his discussion of Flaubert's "The Legend of Saint Julian the Hospitaler":

> The whole problem of Flaubert's tale is how the sweetness of a moral can struggle to the surface through the layer of silence that is imposed on the story by the speechless opacity of the stained glass. No image ever speaks for itself. Concepts code themselves spontaneously into images, but images do not factor themselves out into concepts. Energy is required to puncture the membrane between image and language. And in the case of "St. Julian," the moral ("Atone!") is such a cliché that one does not even think of articulating it: it can pass entirely unnoticed.

Massey draws additional illustrations from a wide range of major works: *Hamlet, Othello,* Tolstoy's "The Death of Ivan Ilych," Chekhov's "Ward 6."

Massey is, let me admit it, a difficult writer—partly because the abstract often turns abstruse and partly because his in-

dividual sentences, awash with semicolons, pack in more than the eye or head can easily hold. But that said, let me hasten to add that Massey is worth our trouble. He engages significant topics, and even more to the critical point, he brings his entire being to the enterprise:

> During periods of depression, I have sometimes had the habit of walking in Buffalo's Delaware Park. A willow tree hangs over the lake. I sometimes stop under the tree, look out through the overhanging branches, and hope that the tree is going to do something for me. On one occasion, when it did, I wrote down a comment about the experience. I repeat it here, with a partial gloss.

> "In the version of process philosophy, or Bergsonism, to which I have been committed, the ethical bonds to time and act: some defect of right haunts the pictures of the past. Yet what is love, if not an acceptance of the picture of the past, present made continuous? It lifts the baskets of the willow, and they remain in air; they become then-forevers. Through the surge of vision that moved them, all absence that might ever have been in them is obliterated."

Massey's gloss—which runs several pages—has the superficial look of an extended aside (if not of an irrelevancy), but it is not. Gradually, one begins to *see* as Massey sees, and to *understand* how the apparently disparate parts of *Find You the Virtue* comprise a vision of ethical possibility.

Granted, he is cautious, often skeptical, about easy equations between aesthetic image and human virtue. (After Auschwitz, how can one *not* be?) But a worst-case scenario and the questions it raises—e.g., "Did the Beethoven works played by the inmates of Auschwitz affect the audience of mass murderers differently from the way in which they affected the musicians?"—lead Massey to conclude:

> Even in that extreme case I would be inclined to say No. It seems that we all take pleasure to some degree in the idea of the good when we read, or when we listen to music. . . . Perhaps virtue is, after all, what everybody lusts after in books. . .

> Even in this postliterate, postaesthetic, and possibly postethical age, we all continue to seek out art, with its unnameable ethical satisfactions, ambiguous as the very status of ethics itself may be.

In many respects, Robert Coles's **The Call of Stories** is also an extended exercise in self-scrutiny, but one rendered through the voices of Coles's students as they grappled both with the works he assigned (e.g., Thomas Hardy's *Jude the*

Obscure, Flannery O'Connor's "The Artificial Nigger," Walker Percy's *The Moviegoer*) and with their often complicated reactions to them. As ***The Call of Stories*** makes clear, Coles learned to listen early—first, from parents who read *Middlemarch* or *War and Peace* aloud and gradually infected their children with the same virus for story; later, from the Dr. Ludwig who passed along this piece of invaluable advice to a young Dr. Coles just beginning to feel his way around the psychiatric wards at Massachusetts General Hospital:

"The people who come to see us" [Dr. Ludwig began, after Coles had hidden behind the word *psychodynamics* once too often] "bring us their stories. They hope they tell them well enough so that we understand the truth of their lives. They hope we know how to interpret their stories correctly. We have to remember that what we hear is *their* story."

To listen deeply was, for Ludwig, much more important than "getting a fix" on the patient or deciding on a "therapeutic agenda." While these may have value, he preferred the human being to the abstraction, the "story" to reductive formulas that rushed past it.

Still later, Dr. William Carlos Williams (Coles's mentor, both for his ideas about medicine and his ideas about art) put it this way:

"We have to pay the closest attention to what we say. What patients say tells us what to think about what hurts them: and what we say tells us what is happening to us—what we are thinking, and what may be wrong with us." A pause, then another jab at my murky mind: "Their story, yours, mine—it's what we all carry with us on this trip we take, and we owe it to each other to respect our stories and learn from them."

Granted, these comments may not carry the weight of theory that characterizes most contemporary critical discourse, but as Coles's altogether human and humanizing book goes on to demonstrate, there is important wisdom packed into a willingness to take stories seriously—those we read, as well as those our students tell us about them. In this sense, Coles's title is autobiographical: "one keeps learning by teaching fiction or poetry because every reader's response to a writer's call can have its own startling, suggesting power, as my parents tried to convey."

Like Massey, Coles falls naturally into the interrogative mode: "Ought Jude [the obscure] to haunt us in Cambridge, Massachusetts, in this century?" As it turns out, the student who posed the question meant it to be rhetorical, a way of expressing his dissatisfaction with an educational system that

asked students to write clever essays on topics such as "Discuss Jude's attitude toward education," but not to tackle tougher ethical questions. The student continued,

"I mean, why not discuss places like Oxford and Harvard? What is *our* attitude toward education? Hardy took aim at academic snobbery, and it would be great if we were asked to connect what Hardy wrote with what we see now. What's the point of reading *Jude the Obscure* if you don't stop and ask yourself about the Judes out there beyond the Harvard Yard, who might feel about us the way Jude felt when he came to Christminster? ... One way to read a novel like that is to see it as a challenge to your conscience, not just your intellect. Aren't we here to grow a little in that direction—to become self-critical as well as critical?" A long pause, and then he told me: "You don't have to answer that one."

In effect, ***The Call of Stories*** is Coles's long-delayed answer. A part of him knew then—and continues to believe now—that colleges are places that "help students learn to perform intellectual exercises." What his student dismisses so casually is both important and valuable. But who would *not* wish to see more of our students—indeed, more of *us*—read *Jude the Obscure* or *Great Expectations* in such a way that they were "not only nineteenth-century classics but urgent commentaries on twentieth-century life"?

The modest claims that Coles makes for the reading and listening he has done over the past thirty years belie the considerable impact he has had as one of our consummate teachers of literature. As he puts it, summing up: "All in all, not a bad start for someone trying to find a good way to live this life: a person's moral conduct responding to the moral imagination of writers and the moral imperative of fellow human beings in need."

I cannot help but think that the other writers I've discussed here—however different their approaches or respective vocabularies might be—would nod in agreement with Coles. But perhaps more important, I suspect that their stake in the ethics of criticism is more widely shared than even they imagine.

Herbert Mitgang (review date 21 November 1990)

SOURCE: "Thoughts on Religion From Children," in *The New York Times,* Vol. CXL, No. 48426, November 21, 1990, p. C20.

[*In the following essay, Mitgang delves into the subject of spirituality and moral questioning in children, as explored by Coles in* The Spiritual Life of Children.]

In the boldest and the most challenging of his series of books that probe the minds of children, Dr. Robert Coles turns on his tape recorder and listens to what they say about religion. It's an unchoate subject for adults and children. In *The Spiritual Life of Children* the answers are not particularly enlightening and for good reason it is hard to elicit original thoughts from the very young about religion that are not simplistic and derivative. Of course it's essential to heed the voices of children, but for the general reader wisdom doesn't necessarily come out of the mouths of babes.

The author, a professor of psychiatry and medical humanities at Harvard, deserves great respect for his pioneering work with children. To his many books and articles, he brings an inquiring and idealistic mind. The present book, he says, concludes 30 years of writing about children in various regions of the United States and in many parts of the world. In five volumes under he rubric *Children of Crisis,* he has encouraged the young to express themselves, called attention to their inner lives and made readers realize that children deserve equal consideration in society. He's on the side of the angels.

Early in his new book, Dr. Coles offers the case of an unruly 8 year-old girl he treated for two years in the 1950's at Children's Hospital in Boston. The girl, who was "utterly accepting of the Catholic Church," said that she had "bad habits" but that "the church saves me." The author searched for an explanation.

He learned that this devout youngster had seen the movie "Song of Bernadette," the film about Bernadette of Lourdes, a 19th-century French teen-age peasant whose claims of seeing visions of the Virgin Mary were met with skepticism but who was canonized in 1933. She wanted to talk about it. She accused Dr. Coles of being interested only in her problems and not her religion and told him to encourage her to discuss the movie's personal meaning. Finally, she said, "I'd like to be like Bernadette was in the movie, but you don't believe me"

As in many of the case histories in *The Spiritual Life of Children,* Dr. Coles uses this one to examine his own feelings and responses. The case of the 8 year-old does not lead to any particular conclusion about the roots of her spirituality other than the obvious influence of her devout family and her desire to emulate a heroine. A few years later, Dr. Coles recalled this white child from Boston when he was talking with black children in the South going through mobs to enter newly desegregated schools.

"At times I would still shy away from spiritual matters, try

to keep those children conversing about familial or school tensions, about this or that city's progress or seeming demise, the result of serious racial turmoil. But at other moments I would listen (with increasing patience and finally respect) to these elementary school children as they let their minds soar to heaven, descend to hell, meet with saints and sinners." He adds that these children told him they felt God was smiling down upon them as they walked through the crowd of angry whites calling them names.

What inspires children to turn to religion? Dr. Coles and his wife and sons, serving as interviewers in Northern Ireland, Poland, Nicaragua, South Africa, Brazil and in their native New England, found universal feelings about religion among children of different races and places. He says that accidents, illnesses and bad luck prompt reflection in children as they do in adults. Even for healthy children, he writes, the death of a grandparent or other person in the family circle has a powerful meaning.

In one of the most original passages in the book. Dr. Coles writes: "But less evident are the strategies boys and girls devise to accommodate a secular and familial morality, on the one hand, and the religious morality they hear espoused in churches, mosques, synagogues. The task for those boys and girls is to weave together a particular version of a morality both personal and yet tied to a religious tradition, and then (the essence of the spiritual life) ponder their moral successes and failures and, consequently, their prospects as human beings who will someday die."

In *The Spiritual Life of Children,* there is a strong moral underpinning in the adult authorities who have inspired the author: Anna Freud, Dorothy Day, Erik H. Erikson, Reinhold Niebuhr. Their comments, sprinkled through the book, help to clarify some of the opaque remarks that are made by the young children. All these role models, in their own ways, called for the need to listen instead of to lecture, to teach by example, a theme that runs throughout the book.

Of Dorothy Day, a liberal Catholic advocate of workers and the poor, Dr. Coles writes that she "often pointed out to me that at the very start of the Bible—and, indeed, of the world as the Bible presents its beginnings—there was a mixture of thought and action, of word and deed, of symbol and substance. God spoke, said, 'Let there be light,' but He also acted, breathed life into the dust."

Dr. Coles concludes, "And so it goes to this day for children, too, as they hustle their way through space and time, doing and doing and doing, but also stopping and asking and wondering, and in their own fashion declaring and affirming."

Laura Sessions Stepp (review date 23 December 1990)

SOURCE: "Faith of Our Children," in *Washington Post Book World,* Vol. XX, No. 51, December 23, 1990, p. 5.

[*In the following review, Stepp considers some of the observations on spirituality Coles elicited from children in his study of the subject in* The Spiritual Life of Children.]

During his first 25 years of interviewing and writing about children, Robert Coles managed to sidestep their persistent religious questions.

Despite hints from his young subjects that they would like to travel that road of inquiry with him, Coles focused on topics more in line with his secular training in psychiatry at Harvard. In books including the five-volume *Children of Crisis,* he produced rich documentaries of children living through desegregation, children coming to grips with their Hispanic or Native American heritage, children both blessed and cursed with wealth.

But questions such as these continued to dog him: Why, asked a boy from eastern Kentucky, did God let a coal mine collapse and kill 25 men, including his father? Is God real? asked a more well-to-do Bostonian girl. If so, what does He think we should be like?

Five years ago, Coles decided to report on such youthful spiritual struggles. He says that this is his last book about children and while I'm not sure I believe him, he has given those of us who care about the moral lives of our children a great deal to chew on.

Hundreds of children, ages 8 to 13, were interviewed at home, on long walks, in school and in Sunday School. They were, for the most part, healthy children from Christian, Jewish, Islamic, Hopi and secular families, and all had something to say about how God speaks to them and how they listen. In this book they leave no doubt that religious principles, spoken and unspoken, have helped shape their consciences and their everyday lives.

Coles, familiar with the Freudian notion that religious belief is illusion, pushed his young subjects hard to find out if they were merely mouthing the pieties they had heard from parents, teachers and clergy.

Sometimes they were. But more often they had filtered what they heard through their own personal experiences of race, gender and economic class to produce unique interpretations.

Avram, cramming for math and history tests, said his father would tell him to study until dawn if necessary. But God said, "I should keep my mind on where I was going, not just on these tests. There will be other days, not just math quiz days and history quiz days. Live for them, too, those days!"

Ginny, a 10-year-old rushing home from school, took time to help an elderly woman who was lost find her way home and then wondered if "I'd live to be old like her, and if I might meet some kid then, and she'd be like me. Maybe God puts you here and He gives you these hints of what's ahead. . . . "

This is a good news book (no pun on the Christian Gospel intended), for its children are charitable, thoughtful and likeable. Coles says he has heard his subjects be insensitive, callous and gullible, but he has chosen not to write about that. He also does not explore the turbulence and cynicism of adolescence, which might give him far different results.

He spends relatively little time on religion's darker side, the shame and guilt too many children suffer at the hands of know-it-all preachers and Sunday School teachers. For all these reasons, some critics may dismiss the book as a skewed, Pollyanna vision of what he hoped children would find in their quest for life's meaning.

Inevitably, some readers also will be put off by Coles's by now well-known writing style. In order to let people tell their own story, unimpeded by his biases, Coles allows his subjects to run on, editing them primarily for clarity. When he offers an insight or pulls together a summary he is often so profound the reader hungers for more. Reading Coles takes patience and time to pause and savor, not always easy to do in our hurried lives.

Yet to dwell on what Coles might have done differently is to shortchange what is, overall, a significant contribution to research on the psychology of children. There have been pitifully few attempts by respected scholars such as Coles to probe the spiritual life of children.

Judging by this work, that's a pity, for such efforts open a very big window into the way small people experience their world. Is the child's God dictatorial or benevolent? Is the child's favorite Bible story Moses and the Ten Commandments or the Second Coming?

Also, the spiritual conversations of children, not hardened by time or age, teach us the fundamentals of a culture. I was particularly struck by the accounts of several Islamic children, including a 13-year-old Moslem boy who dreamed frequently of battle and a very demanding Allah.

This book also reveals, in bits and pieces, Cole's own spiritual quest. When Coles was a young boy, his scientist father drove the family on Sunday to the Episcopal church and sat waiting for them in the car, reading the Sunday newspaper. As a young psychiatrist making hospital rounds in the 1950s, Coles tried unsuccessfully to make his patients' spiritual concerns fit the orthodox psychoanalysis of the time.

As the father of three boys, Coles sometimes wearied of the trite notions they learned in Sunday school but later delighted in the theological distinctions they were able to make. And as a believer in a largely secular academic community, he took comfort from his friendships with social worker Dorothy Day and novelist Walker Percy, who were both deeply spiritual people.

If indeed this is Coles's last word on children, it is a fitting conclusion, a reminder that, in order to finally understand either this author or our children, we must pay attention to their souls.

The New Yorker (review date 7 January 1991)

SOURCE: Review of *The Spiritual Life of Children*, in *The New Yorker*, Vol. LXVI, No. 47, January 7, 1991, p. 76.

[*The following brief review characterizes the method and scope of Coles' work in* The Spiritual Life of Children.]

The noted child psychiatrist, social researcher, and writer recalls that in his earlier investigations he found that children often spoke spontaneously of religion, but he didn't pursue the subject until Anna Freud suggested that he review the research he had accumulated over thirty years. Coles didn't just rework his old material. He undertook new interviews; sessions in which children drew; and group discussions on several continents, among children who were Christians, Jews, Muslims, Native Americans, and agnostics. Like adults, the children were seeking explanations of such ultimate questions as "Who made the world?" and "Why do we die?" Few accepted religion by rote; most made an intellectual effort to interpret the faith they had been taught and apply it to their own lives. Though far from uncritical, they were generous and tolerant, overflowing with desire for the good as they understood it. Perhaps children interested in religion constitute an exceptionally sensitive group; in any case, the moral attraction of Coles's subjects is irresistible.

Virginia C. Hoch (review date 26 August-2 September 1992)

SOURCE: Review of *Anna Freud: The Dream of Psychoanalysis*, in *The Christian Century*, Vol. 109, No. 25, August 26-September 2, 1992, pp. 782-84

[*In the following review, Hoch outlines the portrait of Anna Freud that emerges in Coles' biographical study.*]

The Radcliff Biographical Series highlights the contributions of women to American life and culture. Robert Coles, professor of psychiatry and medical humanities at Harvard Medical School and author of, among others, the Pulitzer Prize-winning *Children of Crisis* series, organizes his text around particular aspects of Anna Freud's life: Anna as teacher, theorist, healer, leader, idealist and writer.

He introduces her in the chapter "A Life with Children," alluding to her response to his request to write her biography: "But I don't think I'd be a good subject for a biography—not enough 'action'! You would say all there is to say in a few sentences—she spent her life with children!" Surely, as Coles points out throughout the book, that summary statement is a humble consolidation of years of intensive study, observation and practice in a field that she and her father, Sigmund, and their contemporaries developed into a viable, acceptable science.

Anna's earliest profession was that of teacher, one she claimed to continue and value throughout her life. She noted, "Teaching is not only the presentation of facts and directions about what to do, but an art, the art of exposition and persuasion—whether you can elicit from a student what an analysand of mine once called 'glad assent.'"

Her work on the psychoanalysis of children remains foundational for psychoanalytic theory and practice today. Her development of ego theory, most notably in her monumental work *The Ego and Mechanisms of Defense* built substantially upon her father's work on the ego complex some 25 years earlier.

On Anna the healer, Coles writes: "Anna Freud. . . sought to be an ally of those she treated and studied, although an ally who reserved the right to say what had to be said, an ally who would not settle for sugarcoating when bitterness had to be acknowledged in the interest of truth. . . the healer whose bemused reserve masked a maternal warmth."

By virtue of her relationship to Sigmund as well as her own integrity as an analyst, Anna became the leader of the psychoanalytic movement upon her father's death and shared her leadership with such figures as Grete Bibring, Heinz Hartmann, Karl Menninger and, later, Erik Erikson. They plied their trade and their theories against a backdrop of cynicism, ridicule, religious condemnation and world political chaos. Even so, Anna was keenly aware of the need to forge ahead and did so boldly, but with renowned tact and reserve. Her role as leader ensured her a place as a political and social activist. Bibring remarked about their activism: "Many of us were politically very active. . . . We wanted to fight for their interests [the poor]. For us psychoanalysis promises personal 'liberation' not for its own sake, but so that we could work to 'liberate' others... to help children grow up in healthier, stronger families, to improve the schools so that children were treated with respect.... I think young people sensed right away that we were on their side!"

Anna's work on *The Ego and The Mechanisms of Defense* was the paramount revelation of her idealism. Her discussion of projection as the ego's way of handing over aggressive impulses to others is the foundation for her commentary on racial and social tensions: "We find 'theys' and 'thems' to serve our purposes as repositories for everything within ourselves we don't like, have learned to fear, judge wrong or shameful. The worst in us is channeled by this mechanism, which children learn as naturally as they learn to use words." She claimed that as we identify those mechanisms at work through psychoanalysis, we can help create more inclusive and caring attitudes and behaviors around the world.

Finally, Coles documents Anna's work as a writer in references to her many professional papers, letters, books and articles, and by comments upon their enduring usefulness.

Coles's book contains several flaws: First, the flow of the early chapters is muddied frequently by unessential bracketed information. Second, Coles is writing about one of his heroines, and thus his adoration of her—"wide-eyed, openminded... earthy, detached, yet caring and responsive"—is somewhat distracting. Only in the last 50 pages of the book do we get a sense of Anna's humanity—of a woman who admitted helplessness on occasion, who could be critical of herself and others, who had psychological sore spots, and who feuded fiercely with Melanie Klein, the British psychoanalytic leader.

Third, the autobiography reveals little about Anna's childhood, and little about her psychoanalytic experience with her father, her intimacies with women, her failures and fears. It is written as a professional review of an esteemed mentor, and as such is quite exemplary. But it fails to give the reader a full account of this great woman's life. Only in the appendix do we discover some of Anna's achievements.

On the positive side, Coles shares some of Anna's unpublished letters and quotes at length from their interviews, as well as interviews with Heinz and Dora Hartmann. One develops a better sense of Anna from these quoted materials. This book is the foremost text available on Anna Freud, and as such stands as an important resource in the field of psychoanalysis.

A. J. S. (review date 1993)

SOURCE: Review of *The Spiritual Life of Children,* in *Harvard Educational Review,* Vol. 63, No. 1, 1993, pp. 121-22.

[*The following review looks at the successes of* The Spiritual Life of Children *at presenting its subject.*]

In the beginning of **The Spiritual Life of Children,** Robert Coles shares with us the difficulty he had in talking to Hopi children about matters of Hopi spirituality and theology. He attempted to interview the children during school hours, but was continually frustrated by their reluctance to discuss the subject at hand. Coles was about to give up and pack his bags when he happened to meet a Hopi mother who took the time to "educate" this renowned Harvard professor of child psychiatry and Pulitzer Prize winning author on the reasons behind the almost-mute reactions of the children to his questions. She informed Coles that the Hopi children "won't ever want to talk with you about the private events of their lives in this building. They learn how to read and write here; they learn their arithmetic here, but that is that. You are asking them about thoughts they put aside when they enter this building" (p. 24).

It is a tribute to Coles that in his genuine effort to locate the child's "geography of God's presence," he was willing to journey to a variety of physical and spiritual environments—from mosques and churches to the world of children's religious images and dreams. For instance, in the home of Sajid, a thirteen-year-old boy from Pakistan living in London, we learn about Moslem surrender and obedience. Sajid tells the author that he feels "closest" to God when he wakes up and feels that "Allah has been near me, very near. I almost want to go back to sleep so I can be nearer Him again, but I must not be greedy!" (p. 243). We meet Leah in a hospital room in Boston, courageously drawing strength from the prayers and rituals of her Jewish faith even as she submits to the disease that is about to take her life. Throughout the book, we travel into the children's world of crayon drawings to learn what Coles calls the "spiritual wakefulness" of children. For instance, responding to a verbal question, "What is your favorite Bible story?", a nine-year-old from Sweden, Josephine, insists on drawing her reply. Josephine's picture ("Jesus Helping the Leper") connects this Bible story with her own inner life more compellingly than any word-filled narrative; she has responded in a powerful, nonverbal language that Coles calls a "silent testimony."

Over the past twenty-five years, Coles has almost singlehandedly created a new methodology in an attempt to understand the inner thoughts of children. For this book, the author (along with his two sons) spent months, and in some cases years, talking to the *same* children about their religious beliefs and concepts of God. Coles is refreshingly clear on how his "talking" approach to research works. He writes:

"The point is that I let the children know as clearly as possible, and as often as necessary, what it is I am trying to learn, and how they can help me" (p. 27). This effort to establish over time a relationship based on mutual respect has resulted in a book filled with gripping children's narratives, heart-felt stories, and memorable drawings and insights that contribute to our still nascent understanding of the spiritual psychology of children. Undeniably, *The Spiritual Life of Children* is so invaluable to the field of child development precisely because the author doesn't offer us pediatric prescriptions, a new "faith development" theory, or refurbished religious education strategies. Instead, Coles simply invites the reader to listen to the voices and drawings of the children he interviewed. He passionately believes that inside these stories and creeds we might find answers to questions about our children's capacity for spirituality and religious faith.

Michelle Huneven (essay date 3 October 1993)

SOURCE: "Why Ask Why Some People Do Good?" in *Los Angeles Times Book Review,* October 3, 1993, p. 2.

[*In the following essay Huneven applies a critical eye to Coles' writing methods while citing some of the strengths of* The Call of Service.]

Robert Coles is a man of dazzling, if not overwhelming accomplishment. A pediatrician and child psychiatrist, he has published over a thousand essays and more than 50 books including biographies of Dorothy Day, Anna Freud, Simone Weil; a five-volume series on "Children in Crisis," plus one book each on the political, moral and spiritual lives of children. His latest work, *The Call of Service: A Witness to Idealism,* is a frustrating and fascinating study of how service work fits into a life.

The book opens with a conversation between Coles and his father. Laconic, conservative, himself a hard-working volunteer advocate for the elderly poor, the elder Coles warns his psychiatrist son not to delve too far into the motives of those doing service. "I don't think it matters why we do something—but it does matter a lot that what we try to do is good and right," he says. When pressed, he adds, "I frankly doubt if I could continue [volunteer activity] if I looked too hard within."

Curiously, Coles heeds his father's plea. *The Call of Service* is, as the subtitle indicates, a witnessing rather than an analysis of volunteer work. Here are dozens of interviews Coles has taped over the past four decades loosely organized and linked by what is often the most vague and discursive of commentary.

Although trained in psychoanalytic and medical thought, Coles fastidiously avoids the nomenclature and interpretations of his professions. Indeed, he actively resists anything resembling formulation lest it prove reductive; and he is hesitant to delineate even such benign categories as kinds of service (community service, charity, service to country, etc.). "I have tried to do some useful, even necessary sorting," he writes as if to apologize for the merest trace of organization, "but I hope I have left room for overlap, for a blend of motives and deeds that, properly, cautions us all against airtight conclusions and formulations."

Unfortunately, there is so much overlap and blending of motives and deeds throughout the book, it is difficult to draw any conclusions. Interviewees speak for pages, and while Coles has clearly edited out certain conversational tics, the stories, transcribed from tapes, often have the unwieldiness and dross of someone thinking out loud. Narratives burgeon out of the context Coles has given them and we, as readers, are lost.

One remembers the vivid story of Laura, a civil rights worker in Mississippi in the early 60s. Jailed, she befriends her jailer and momentarily, at least, integrates that "bastion of the segregationist power"—the county jail. One does not remember that this hilarious, telling anecdote is found under the rubric "Weariness and Resignation" in the Chapter entitled "Hazards."

Coles may justify the diffuseness of his method as an antidote to patness, but it reads exactly like undisciplined writing and poses serious difficulties to those this book might best serve: busy volunteers seeking to reflect on and contextualize their own service experiences.

Coles professes great reverence for fiction and poetry; it's a shame he has not aspired to the poet's compaction, the novelist's deftness and vividness. It is as if he sees no difference between the raw sociological data spewing from his tape recorder and the crafted stories, poems and novels of his beloved writers. A few jokes wouldn't have hurt this book, either. Even William James, who employed the prototypal patchwork of voices in *The Varieties of Religious Experience,* never resisted the impulse to amuse even as he classified and enlightened.

And yet. All this lengthy, significant objection to Coles' muzziness aside, it must be said that many of the stories in *The Call of Service* are resonant, instructive, moving. And we readers are privileged to "hear" them. And while he cannot pay equal attention to all forms of volunteer service, Coles does present a well-rounded picture of the service experience: the satisfactions and the hazards, the motivations and the consequences.

Over and over again, the stories teach that service is no hierarchy but a back-and-forth, a reciprocity in which the distinctions between teacher and pupil, giver and receiver, server and served constantly dissolves. The lives of all involved shift and change, often irrevocably. A white, well-to-do mother of a leukemic daughter drives a poor black mother and her leukemic daughter to chemotherapy treatments. Says the white woman of her passenger: "She taught me to have patience. . . . I learned to trust in each day, in my husband and my children—and in her. . . . Every time she tells me how good I've been to her, I get all teary and I tell her she's been a tremendous gift to us."

Dorothy Day, speaking of those she fed at the Catholic Worker soup kitchen states bluntly, "Our guests *are* the Catholic Worker. Without them, we'd not be here as we are."

A dying street alcoholic prays daily and at length for the staff and well being at his shelter. "I guess I'd assumed we were the ones who were doing the praying," exclaims one of the shelter workers. "Talk about arrogance!"

In two "Interludes," Coles views service from the vantage of those served. In the chapter "Doing and Learning," his Harvard students make quirky, resourceful use of Tolstoy, Hardy and George Eliot in order to shape and understand their own experiences as volunteers.

Throughout, we catch glimpses of Coles' own teachers: Poet and Dr. William Carlos Williams cautions him against sentimentality. Prof. Perry Miller reminds him that he can't feed others if he doesn't first take good care of himself. Anna Freud provides some of the psychoanalytic insight Coles himself is so loathe to articulate. Dorothy Day nudges him out of the confines of intellect and into the nitty-gritty, hands-on realm of service.

In story after story, we meet people engaged in selfless and not-so-selfless acts of giving—and receiving. Before serving cakes brought to a soup kitchen, volunteers festoon them with candles to celebrate the birthdays among the homeless and hungry. A father whose only son is born with Down's syndrome channels his rage and disappointment into working with other retarded and disabled children. And there are the intermittent appearances of Dorothy Day, to whom this book is dedicated. Beatific and industrious, Day epitomizes the humility and the pastoral, often spiritual nature of older idealism: "We feel the spirit of Christ at work—*in the work.* We are not so high on ourselves that we feel Christ is *in* us; no, we hope we are moving a bit closer to Him, to His spirit through the work we do. . . . "

How then does service fit into a life? Answers found in The Call of Service are as numerous and particular as each of the lives involved.

Robert A. Sirico (review date 15 November 1993)

SOURCE: "A Tribute to Altruism," in *Wall Street Journal,* November 15, 1993, p. A10.

[*In the following review, Sirico identifies Coles' "liberal political agenda" and comments on its manifestation in* The Call of Service.]

If it is true that much of what we do for others is for self-serving reasons, it is also true that we perform authentic acts of charity. The motivation that gives rise to charity is sometimes called idealism, or altruism; or, more picturesquely, the tug of transcendence. It is with us today as the "politics of meaning." But it has an ancient history that can clarify our current sense of charity.

When Jesus commanded his followers to love their neighbors as themselves, he did not leave self out of the equation. The love due to the self is the model of the love due others, though not the measure of it. True concern for others must be rooted in a proper appreciation for the self, even if this view of idealism leaves some romantics dissatisfied.

Robert Coles turns his attention to this topic in his latest book, *The Call of Service: A Witness to Idealism.* A Pulitzer Prize-winning psychiatrist who has worn many hats and received numerous awards and accolades, Dr. Coles is perhaps best-known for his studies on children, including *The Moral Life of Children.*

For this new book, his method was to talk to people engaged in acts of service to others—schoolteachers, Peace Corps members, soup-kitchen and shelter volunteers. One has to admire the achievement of three decades of meticulously recording conversations with a stunning array of people in and around service organizations, and classifying these for later reference. The documentation that this book offers is distinct from a statistical survey, which might be more detailed and objective yet less human and descriptive.

Many of the stories Dr. Coles has preserved are from personal interaction with early civil-rights groups: Dr. Coles volunteered as a janitor for a year at the Atlanta offices of the Student Nonviolent Coordinating Committee. At other times, he worked with Martin Luther King, was mentored by Anna Freud, made house calls with the doctor-poet William Carlos Williams, and worked closely with Dorothy Day (founder of the Catholic Worker).

Dr. Coles draws liberally from this storehouse of experiences in order to analyze the sources of people's commitment to service and the impact it has on others. The many anecdotal gems include the story of a six-year-old whose evangelical faith is a beautiful example of how to transform one's tormentor into a benefactor through virtuous example. The description of Dorothy Day's encounter with a class of Harvard freshman studying altruism offers an interesting insight into the Catholic convert.

Unfortunately, Dr. Coles is forever being stunned, amazed, enlightened or informed by the most unsuspecting sources, and it all becomes tiresome after a while. For all the tributes to altruism, the book is focused mainly on Dr. Coles, who always emerges as the humble hero.

For example, 80 of the book's approximately 85 footnotes refer to Dr. Coles's previous work, the courses he has taught or previous conversations or insights he has had.

A recurrent theme of the book is Dr. Coles being silenced by the profundities of those he records. He depicts himself as reliably teachable, a little naive, and as one who hears pearls of wisdom drop from the mouth of every drunk he meets. He should have taken the advice of his friend the poet Dr. Williams: ". . . I hope you won't get sentimental about the poor—or yourself as the one who is working with them!"

Dr. Coles's agenda is not explicit. But almost all the idealists presented here are politically correct. Mother Teresa's life service to leprosy patients, Chuck Colson's work with prison inmates, and businessman Tom Monaghan's selfless support of the anti-abortion movement are all overlooked.

And though Dr. Coles poses as the learner, it eventually becomes apparent that this student has an agenda of his own, which would be acceptable if he were more forthright about it. The liberal political agenda is implicitly put forth as the proper focus of our altruistic efforts.

One comes away from *The Call of Service* with the sense that for all the talk of high ideals and the numerous people who have them, moral ambiguity pervades the book. There is no mention of the obligation to serve others or of obedience-to-conscience. Too often the book reads like an elaborate footnote to the inane bumpersticker slogan common in university towns: "The Question is the Answer." It is gripping at first glance, yet meaningless upon reflection.

One comes away from *The Call of Service* with the sense that for all the talk of high ideals and the numerous people who have them, moral ambiguity pervades the book.
—*Robert A. Sirico*

It does little good to study ideals apart from the standards toward which they are oriented. Without standards, ideals are ultimately meaningless. The problem with Dr. Coles's

probing of idealism is that, at the end of the day, he has not told us what is right, moral or true.

Gail Russell Chaddock (review date 9 December 1993)

SOURCE: "Helping Others, Helping Ourselves," in *The Christian Science Monitor*, December 9, 1993, p. 17.

[*In the following review, Chaddock provides a brief inventory of the insights to be found in* The Call to Service.]

Robert Coles has written more than 50 books, prompting the question, does any writer have 50 books worth of wisdom to share with the world?

His latest, *The Call of Service: A Witness to Idealism,* reads less like a new venture than a gleaning through a lifetime of interviews, notebooks, and tapes for an answer to the question: Why do people serve others?

The reasons people give are as diverse as the voices in this thoughtful book: civil rights activists and sharecroppers in the Mississippi Delta in 1964, VISTA volunteers in Appalachia in the late 1960s, suburban housewives and privileged students in Boston's black neighborhoods, individuals who, for whatever reason, answered the call of service.

Some signed on to please a friend or flesh out a resume; others, out of religious conviction. For the author, service was often a means of access for his research. He got to ask questions of activists in the Student Non-Violent Coordinating Committee (SNCC) by washing dishes and sweeping floors in their Atlanta office; to black students in Boston by keeping them company during their daily bus commute to whiter, wealthier schools.

Many who served were changed by the experience. One volunteer tutor found that his tutee's need for "a kind of moral purpose that will carry him through any number of critical moments" gave him "a reason to locate more explicitly and consolidate his own moral purpose as a prelude to sharing it, however gingerly and indirectly."

Coles laces his narratives with references to loved stories and books. (The course syllabus reprinted as a footnote to Chapter 5 is worth the price of the book.)

One of startling points of this book is its frank look at the dangers of service: the endless ways to burn out, the weariness and resignation, brittle anger, arrogance, and cynicism that can grow out of "a long, tough fight, even if you win it."

The writer's advice: Stop. Take stock. Go a bit easier on yourself, be less driven, self-preoccupied, smugly self-righteous. Pay attention to what you are getting from service.

What is most memorable about this book, however, is not its generalizations or advice. It is the simple goodness that runs through the examples Coles cites.

Take Tessie, a six-year-old black girl who, escorted each day by federal marshals through abusive crowds, initiated school desegregation in New Orleans. Tessie's account of how she faced the taunts of crowds every day "turned many of my ideas and assumptions upside down," Coles writes. "Where I expected trouble, they [Tessie and her grandmother] saw great opportunity;. . . where I saw a child bravely shouldering the burden of a divided, troubled society, they saw a blessed chance for a child to become a teacher, a healer, an instrument, maybe, of the salvation of others. . . . A child's idiosyncratic and utterly spiritual notion of service was a key."

There is also the memorable voice of the author. Coles is a storyteller, and a good listener. He seems to delight in being taken by surprise and to be as interested in the insight that smashes a cherished belief as in one that confirms it.

Ed Walraven (essay date 1994)

SOURCE: "Folklore in the Writings of Robert Coles, M.D." in *Tennessee Folklore Society Bulletin*, Vol. LVI, No. 4, 1994, pp. 134-144.

[*In the following essay, Walraven examines Coles' writings for elements of folklore and shows how some of his methods and concerns resemble those of ethnography.*]

More than 30 years ago, Richard M. Dorson outlined a method of studying genuine folklore in the printed texts of American literature, a method scholars employ as an identify-and-interpret approach, with emphasis on first identifying the folklore (Dorson 1957; Stahl 1983). Dorson referred to creative writing, specifically novels, short stories, poems and/or plays. This is an approach I attempt here with what is perhaps an unconventional source of literature—the nonfiction writings of psychiatrist Robert Coles, M.D.

I come at this challenge from a variety of viewpoints that are reflective, of course, of my own experiences. First among these is the student of folklore because of my interest in oral expression. Second among these is a student of British and American literature and writing, coming from my interest in writing and the written word, as I both teach and conduct writing. As Stahl has pointed out, much can be found that

is similar between folklore and narratives that have become literature (Stahl 1983). Third among these perspectives is an interest in medicine, healing, and the medical humanities which developed in my years as a science and medicine reporter and editor.

Coles is a Harvard University professor of psychiatry and medical humanities, and is a prolific author as well. He has written or edited 50 books, including five for children. His best-known works have documented the human face—often a Southern face—of hunger, poverty, and fear. The titles of the works studied in this project reveal some of the Southern/rural flavor: *The South Goes North,* for example, or *Migrants, Sharecroppers, Mountaineers.* In addition, *Children of Crisis: A Study of Courage and Fear, The Moral Life of Children;* and *The Political Life of Children* all encompass interviews with people in stressful racial relations or economic hardship.

It may be a shaky premise that rural Southerners are prone to engage in "traditional" oral expression (maxims, similes, or other figures of speech, thoughts of the supernatural, stereotyped expressions of prejudice or hate, for example). But it seems to be a premise that generally fits my own observations and experience, and a characteristic that earned much parody at the expense of H. Ross Perot last year in his presidential bid. Therefore, one could reasonably expect to find examples of folklore in the kind of record that Coles puts down for these people.

To try to remain true to Dorson's recommended approach, I will first present the folklore that my examination finds, then an interpretation of its function. I will also describe how Coles' methodology in gathering the information was similar to that of the folklorist or ethnographer.

Traces of folklore in Coles' work often appear in a low-key fashion—figures of speech, maxims, or images included in the middle of long transcripts of narrative. There they might easily pass undetected, because they seem so natural in that oral setting. In much of the Coles work examined, such forms of folklore are simply allowed, with no analysis by Coles, to remain part of his edited transcript of the conversation. The main reason for this lack of interpretation, I believe after examining the Coles texts, is that Coles perceived them foremost as a crucial part of the way people express themselves. He simply reports them in their natural setting. In fact we are not even sure Coles recognizes them as anything other than the natural part of the language his subjects use in telling their stories. The current selective reading failed to turn up the exact term "folklore," and only one brief reference was found to "folk songs" (Coles 1967a:359). So we do not know whether he would call these utterances by the term "folklore"—or whether it would make any difference to Coles and his purpose what others may call them.

Figures of Speech

One example of a figure of speech that seems folkloric is a maxim that Coles says he commonly heard among sharecroppers and recorded in *Migrants*: "Low is de way to the upper bright world." One might translate this as the equivalent of the Biblical beatitude "blessed are the poor, for they shall enter the kingdom of Heaven." According to Coles, this is tied to the belief that poor economic circumstances among sharecroppers and hard labor in the physical life help assure one of a future place in Heaven in the afterlife (Coles 1967a:514). Having a maxim such as "Low is de way... " may give some hope, however distant, for circumstances that offer no likelihood of improving.

In another example in *Moral Life,* a boy living in the poverty-ridden favelas of Rio de Janeiro shared what he had learned from his now-absent father via his mother: "the smartest person is the one who . . . knows how to find one laugh for himself every day. One laugh is better than a lot of wine!" (Coles 1986a:104). How useful such a maxim must be for living the life of the poor, for smoothing the friction brought on by one's lot in life.

Coles, in reporting from Appalachia in *Migrants,* was able to capture another phrase with a sense of both poignancy and rustic simplicity as well as some elements of folklore. Mrs. Bowman, a Kentucky woman, described how difficult it was for her sister, Caroline—who was mentally impaired—to understand why Mrs. Bowman and her family were moving to Cleveland in hopes of a better life. The woman told Coles what happened:

> She (Caroline) gives us a look and then goes running out to where the chickens are, and then she must be upset, because she gets them (chickens) going, making a lot of noise. My mother will shake her head and say that *poor Caroline gets the chickens to do her crying for her.* [italics mine] (Coles 1967a:318)

Perhaps unknown to either Coles or the woman, the expression brushes up against several folklore motifs including the following: speaking chicken(s), Thompson's Motif B 211.3.2.1; humans teaching chickens to talk and thus having the birds tell of adultery, Motif J 1882.1; and animals speaking, sometimes at the request of humans, Motifs B 251.1.2 and B 210 ff. (Thompson 1955).

In addition, the assistance or participation of animals is a recurrent theme in folklore, especially in myths, as shown by Kluckhohn in his review of patterns from the Mediterranean basic, western Asia, and Navaho mythology: all patterns featured aid from animals as an element (Kluckhohn 1959).

Beliefs

In another instance found in Coles' *South Goes North,* a black woman who emigrated to a Boston ghetto from rural South Carolina remarked only half-jokingly to a neighbor that the Devil may own the boilers in the buildings, explaining why they can create so much heat. "Maybe up here (in the North) that can happen," she said. She also said that she would "sooner die than go down into that cellar." "I've heard about it; I've heard stories; I've heard there are so many rats down there you can't see anything but them, running all over. . . ." (Coles 1967b:10-11).

Elsewhere, Coles comes across a subject's belief in the spirits of people long dead. Interviewing an eight-year-old Hopi girl in the Southwest, Coles records this snippet of conversation from those held over a period of a number of interviews. The girl, talking about a nearby mesa where her people have lived "from the beginning of our memory" tells Coles:

> I don't know how to explain this—the Hopis are there on the mesa, their spirits. Each spirit is a soul. You can't see them, not the way you see me, and I see you. But they are there—and when we go there, we sit; and they talk to us. The wind sweeps across the mesa, and [that way we know] we've been noticed and welcomed! (Coles 1990:154)

In *The South Goes North,* Coles shares with us a family tragedy that affected a black man profoundly. The story is told by the man's daughter about the sudden death of her father's favorite sister, Leona, also one of the daughter's favorite aunts. Two days before Leona's death, the daughter said, the father had already been so psychologically affected by the event that he had

> lost his good sense and started being funny with my mother. He said Leona had suddenly turned white—that that was what had happened—she's collapsed on her face and turned white, and so naturally they won't let us see her, because she's all locked up there in the hospital with the white people, while they try to figure out what to do. (Coles 1967b:605)

This radical transformation of skin color has been previously documented as an element of African-American folklore. According to Puckett, the belief still survived among African-Americans in the mid-1920s that all humans were at first created black, but that when Cain killed Abel, Cain turned white from fear (Puckett 1926). This same sort of event manifests itself earlier in descriptions of a black Louisiana "hoodoo conjurer" who, afflicted with some disease, first has his skin become spotted, then a sort of pinkish-white (Smiley 1919). Other transformation beliefs in African-American culture were recorded by the Depression-era Louisiana Writers' Project, such as the superstitions that if a girl kisses her toe, she will become a boy, and if a person kisses his or her elbow, he or she will be able to change genders (Saxon, et al, eds., 1945).

Thompson's *Motif-Index* notes several other entries for changes of race/skin color or attempted changes. Among these are the black man who tries in vain to wash himself white (Motif J 511.1), a man who changes color through prayer (Motif V 52.11), a black man who becomes white (Motif D 57.2), a European who is transformed to black in color (Motif D 57.4), and anger turning the body black (Motif 1041.16.8).

It is possible this seed of belief may, at least in part, be behind the persistent belief that rock star Michael Jackson uses chemicals to lighten his skin, although he has consistently denied it, most widely on a prime-time television special hosted by Oprah Winfrey. Despite Jackson's publicized denials, an informal survey of two of my own college-level journalism classes within two weeks of the broadcast showed that 3 of 10 graduating seniors—supposedly those with the most training in verification and skepticism—and 11 of 34 other students in a news-content training class all believed the report of chemicals to be true or mostly true.

It is again speculation, of course, to strongly link the motifs and what the daughter described to Coles about the death of her aunt. But the existence of the motifs and the documentation of such a phenomenon circulating in African-American folklore only a few decades previous to this event both do much to argue that the father's stress-laden puzzlement over his sister's fate may have been influenced by such folklore.

Whether or not the hospital in question in Coles' account was for "whites only," as the account implies, we certainly see evidence in such circumstances of the dominant "world view" of a family from the South for whom health care, education, and other institutions have been divided along racial lines.

World Views

In the realm of world views dominated by race relations, Coles recalls in *Moral Life* a classroom discussion in Mississippi on children's opinions and views of nuclear weapons. One African-American child sincerely feared the Ku Klux Klan might come into possession of nuclear weapons. The youngster's world view, in just 10 brief years of life, had been influenced by incidents of KKK violence against blacks. He was concerned that the Klan would use anything violent to inflict terror. Nuclear bombs, the child said, were "big." Also "big" were members of the Klan: "They're big

white men, and they wear their big robes." This was not a discussion that took place in the 1950s or even the 1960s, but rather in 1983 (Coles 1986a:257-258).

Coles finds another racially-linked use of a folklore form in *Moral Life*, this time a motif for reclaiming what was lost after an apocalyptic event. Again, the discussion revolved around concern over nuclear warfare, and this time the subjects were children of the Pueblo Indian culture interviewed in 1979 and 1980:

> Maybe some of our (Pueblo) people would escape (nuclear attack), though; they'd go and hide in the caves. We know caves that the Anglos don't know. We know all the streets, and the stores, and the buildings. But we know the secret places up here, and we could just go, and hide, and wait; and then we could come out, and we would be able to keep going—we'd grow our own food, and we'd mind our own business, and not get into any big fights.

Says Coles: "I had heard such a scenario from Pueblo children years ago, though not with the atom bomb figuring in it. . . . The children, almost invariably, constructed a story quite like the one above." (Coles 1986a:253-254). Coles is his own expert witness in documenting that this scenario has been preserved and disseminated within the oral tradition of the Pueblo children over time, with the necessary elaborations to make it relevant to current times.

Storytelling

In *Migrants,* etc., it is noteworthy that Coles emphasizes the "cultural" value of the general store in Appalachia. While such an aspect is not news to many folklorists—or to those familiar with rural settings—it is interesting to see Coles recognize that such rural stores have a function well beyond that of trade and sale of merchandise: "Some stores have traditionally been, and still are, gathering places where people enjoy meeting one another, where they stand or sit and talk, where they pick guitars and sing songs . . . where they complain about things or rejoice in some good news. . . ." (Coles 1967a:326)

What function may these examples of folklore serve? This is perhaps a controversial question in itself among folklorists divided over how or whether it can be answered. One might first consider the more classical explanations of function outlined by Bascom and Herzog. These functions are: 1) revelation of human frustration and/or attempts to escape via fantasy, (Bascom 1954), and 2) smoothing of friction or dissatisfaction the individual may have in adjusting to his or her own set of circumstances (Herzog 1936). Each of these examples of folklore cited could be argued to fall within one or both of these tremendously broad function categories.

More recently, Abrahams has said that expressive folklore, "dealing as it does with the workings of social life," persists because "they (expressions) have helped to control the recurrent anxieties of the community" and provide "guidelines for behavior." Abrahams also points out that "expressive folklore is the approved and tested rhetoric of a community, its set of inherited organized techniques of control and persuasion" (Abrahams 1971). This is more well-defined that that expressed by Herzog, but still carries strong echoes of the earlier explanation, a tendency noted by Oring in his discussion of functionalism:

> Although it appears that there are serious shortcomings in the traditional functional explanations that have been offered in anthropology, sociology, and folkloristics, these functional explanations cannot be completely devoid of explanatory power. After all, we have been committed to them for decades.

Oring, however, understood that the concept of explanation should be broadened, through testable hypotheses, to fully understand the nature of the power of function in folklore (Oring 1976).

In Dorson's *Handbook of American Folklore,* Baker and Nickerson point out the role of folklore in helping college students and factory workers adjust to the seemingly unfair, illogical, insipid, subjective, restrictive hurdles to individualism and success placed in the way by the uncaring institution, be it an academy or an auto factory, and the role of initiation in helping newcomers adjust to the closed college/factory culture (Baker 1983:107-114; Nickerson 1983:121-127).

Each of the examples cited from Coles' books could be seen as functioning to provide a support system for persuading others, or even one's own self, that anxieties, tensions, friction, and dissatisfaction with one's plight in life can be handled or dealt with.

The promise of a humble and poor life on earth, to be rewarded in the "bright world"; seeing a laugh as better than wine; being too emotionally disturbed and mentally impaired to articulate sadness; seeking superstitious explanations for the death of a loved one; having a world view dominated by racial tensions can all be seen as ways of smoothing personal friction and despair. This begins to cross over into Coles' field of psychiatry.

What would have been ideal in this study would have been to have Coles conclude that these people often used tried-and-true expressive forms as a way of psychologically cop-

ing with their situation. But Coles, as we previously noted, carries out no analyses of spoken language as a coping mechanism. He does not directly refer to the use of any figure of speech, song, storytelling, or expression of a belief as a tool for psychologically coping, or as a means of expressing frustration or hostility, although the person interviewed seems to be clearly using the utterances for venting of anger, fear, or frustration, based on the context of the situation described. If such intent were confirmed, it would fit nicely into any of the explanations of function offered in the preceding discussion. But Coles the psychiatrist does not seek the counsel of folklore in discussing the people he has talked to, just as numerous folklorists often have been reluctant to seek encroachments into folklore by psychology-based inquiry.

Dundes' review of 100 years of psychological study of folklore found that while folklore "offers a socially sanctioned outlet for the expression of often taboo ideas," several key figures in folklore resisted the psychological approach, among them Stith Thompson and Richard M. Dorson, and psychologists, "for the most part, have not concerned themselves with folklore." Kluckhohn was "one of the few anthropologists sympathetic to a psychoanalytic approach to folklore" (Dundes 1991). Dundes' article does not substantially touch on any psychological approach to the use of traditional language as a coping mechanism, and thus is far beyond the point I wish to make—which is that psychologists and folklorists could have much to learn from each other, but neither seems too interested.

The examples cited here of folklore are drawn from Coles' books that contain long passages of edited transcripts of conversations Coles had. In that regard, with the exception of the editing, Coles' fieldwork methodology and that of a folklorist/anthropologist or other ethnographer seem similar. In discussing his methodology he often refers to his efforts as field work or to himself as a field worker.

These similarities in Coles' approach to fieldwork and that of a folklorist/anthropologist include the following: long-term relationships with subjects to build a base of mutual confidence; the occasional use of informants and other collaborators (often his own sons or community leaders) to identify prospective subjects and comment on data gathered; use of interviews that follow lines of inquiry, sometimes following topics on side tangents; careful recording of the spoken words; and limited post-interview analysis. Not content with the idea that children could fully verbalize the scope of their emotions, or believing they might do so equally as well through drawings, Coles collected "hundreds of children's drawings and paintings" to analyze (Coles 1990:xii). Although by no means a unique method, allowing children to express themselves through painting did allow Coles to collect children's ideas about matters under discussion when words may have been inadequate.

However, drawings are only one part of Coles' methodology of interview and observation. His methodology offers us other contact points.

To obtain these interviews, Coles did what any competent ethnographer would consider doing in similar circumstances. Instead of summoning identified subjects to his office, Coles went to them, experienced their surroundings, came to know them from their "world view." In his own words in *The South Goes North,* "I had left my world to enter their world" (Coles 1967a:39).

This is perhaps best described by his own words from *Political Life:*

> In the five volumes of *Children of Crisis* I have described in some detail how I do my work. I carry my training as a child psychiatrist to the "field," where I have conversations with children in their homes, in schools, in neighborhood situations, such as a boy's club, a girl's club, in a church, say, or other neighborhood meeting place. I don't hand out tests or questionnaires, but I am much interested in children's drawings and paintings; and so I carry paper, crayons, paints with me—and a tape recorder, which I sometimes use during a first meeting with a child, but usually keep unused until I have gotten to know the person fairly well. I tell the children that I am trying to learn about their situation: their neighborhood, their country—from those who know best, the ones who live in it. I keep coming back, in weekly, sometimes twice-weekly visits, which can last an hour, sometimes two hours or more. Most of the interviews are done in the homes, enabled by willing, indeed wonderfully hospitable parents. In the United States and in other countries, too, I have been fortunate to obtain the considerable cooperation of school authorities, and so I have been enabled to sit with groups of children in school classrooms and hold continuing discussions with them, over a period, sometimes, of months. Their parents and teachers have of course given me clues about what I might want to talk about the next time, or the time after that, with boys or girls who may be reticent one moment, voluble the next. (Coles 1986b:15)

Hours on hours of tape recordings were made. Long passages of some books are indeed devoted to what are essentially edited transcripts of the subject's side of the recorded conversation, letting those interviewed express views and emotions in their own words and at their own pace. Con-

versations that may have taken days or weeks are condensed to pages of passages, but edited to keep a train of thought intact.

Of course, such editing by Coles is not without problems, concerns, and objections, just as it would be with the folklorist/anthropologist worried that excluding certain data gives an inaccurate picture, even if to a small degree. In Coles' case, I surmise that the amount of data (remarks) edited out might be considerably more than many folklorists would consider acceptable. Coles himself notes this concern in *Moral Life:*

> I suppose this is the occasion to take up directly, and yet again, the question of authenticity. "Children don't speak the way they do in your books," I was told at a psychiatric meeting once, and I could not disagree. I have assembled remarks made by children in the course of years of acquaintance, and tried to fit them into the confines of a book. The risks are substantial: distortion of what the children have said or intended to say, the intrusion of the observer, the writer's subjectivity, if not outright bias. Under such circumstances there is a requirement of tentativeness with respect to assertations— lest a necessarily limited number of children, whose statements have been made in relatively informal moments, be turned into the vigorous spokespersons of the observer's beliefs, if not dogmas. . . . " (Coles 1986a:10)

He presents another caveat in *Political Life:*

> I am not a survey social scientist. . . . As clinicians know, patients possess within themselves many truths. . . . One can only insist on being as tentative as possible, claiming only impressions, observations, thoughts. . . . The limitations of this approach must be stressed again and again—no percentages, no statistics, no all-out conclusions. But there are a few rewards, too—those any doctor knows when he or she feels newly educated by another human being. (Coles 1986b:17)

In the references section of *The South Goes North,* Coles continues to set himself apart from social scientists. He considers that his emphasis—concentrating on the "inner life" of the people he describes—occurs "in contrast, that is, to the emphasis of a historian, or political scientist, or anthropologist 'working with' the same people or communities" (Coles 1967b:657). Folklorists, of course, may often consider themselves also to be working with the "inner life" of humans and its outward manifestations.

Those nagging concerns voiced by Coles should sound familiar to any ethnographer who worries about accuracy of data and the conclusions such data imply. But in the same passage from Coles' introduction to *Moral Life,* he balances the need for so-called experimentalists' approach to research and that of the ethnographer:

> There is a decided value to so-called objective research, to well-constructed surveys, and to tests uniformly administered. There is good reason, too, that a few of us stay around specific neighborhoods, try to figure out, no matter the hazards, just what we've heard that seems to matter for the speakers and for us who have tried to understand not only today's utterances, but many months of them, enough to enable a sense of things, a drift of things—mostly vague, but at moments as clear and resounding as a giant bell, tolling to an entire countryside, so it seems when a boy's, a girl's cri de coeur is uttered. (Coles 1986a:10)

There is a lesson in all this for the folklorist, and ethnographer, and for the professional psychiatrist, too. The lesson is that study of research in people-related disciplines can broaden each of our own professional perspectives. Psychiatrists and psychologists may be enriched to know how much of the conversation they hear harkens back to a firmly rooted oral tradition, and why. Such knowledge may even help them understand their clients and help them approach therapy from more than one or two angles. Ethnographers may be better off knowing that "field workers" in other disciplines are at work gathering types of raw data that could be useful and insightful when analyzed from an ethnographic or folkloric perspective. Such data may otherwise go wanting for such analysis if we fail to occasionally cross discipline lines and ask.

Paulina F. Kernberg (review date October 1994)

SOURCE: "A Child Analyst for All Seasons: Anna Freud," in *Contemporary Psychology,* Vol. 39, No. 10, October 1994, p. 946.

[*The following review briefly evaluates Coles' biography of Anna Freud and compares it to another work on the subject.*]

In this work, Robert Coles has undertaken to write about his experience with Anna Freud and about Anna Freud. With a sense of timing and tact, Coles sketches Anna Freud's life and work as a series of developmental profiles.

Parallels occur in the structure of this book; namely, as Anna Freud formulated her developmental lines so did Coles for-

mulate Anna Freud's biography in various lines of development: her life with children, the teacher, the theorist, the healer, the leader, the idealist, and the writer.

She would have been 99 years old in 1994; she was 31 when she became a child analyst, and she was 40 years of age when she wrote the classical *Ego and the Mechanisms of Defense* (1937). Coles attempts to capture Anna Freud's life in a succinct and poetic way with a certain protective idealization. In spite of her self-description as not being a good subject for a biography, Coles undertook this challenge and manages to present a profile of Anna Freud that speaks both to her sense of purpose and the priorities in her life. While in the midst of the most complex and abrupt changes in her familial and sociocultural circumstances, her striving for purity and clarity emerge in the evocative interchanges with the author.

The book unfolds like a story in which her being the daughter of Sigmund Freud plays an important determining factor. Two chapters begin with comments on Sigmund Freud. She was unmistakably placed in a special role in spite of her wish to be a modest and unassuming person devoted to children. An atmosphere of awe permeates most descriptions, a reverent stance that Anna Freud evoked; she transcended the conventional perspective that psychoanalysts are elitist and not involved in social issues.

Coles depicts how, as her teaching background illuminated her psychoanalytic skills, child analysis helped to illustrate and clarify her views on education with regard to empathy, concern, facilitation of autonomy, and the teacher's identification with the commitment to inquiry.

Coles uses a method similar to the one used in *The Technique of Child Psychoanalysis: Discussions With Anna Freud* by Joseph Sandler, Hansi Kennedy, and Robert Tyson (1980). She was invited to update her own views on works she had written earlier in her career. Coles asks her also to give her opinions on Coles's work with children of different ethnic and socioeconomic backgrounds. One could sense Anna Freud placed in the sphinx role when Coles writes "it was then that Anna spoke in this interesting manner, surprising to us and ever so helpful" (p. 83).

This book complements other biographies well. The polarity between Anna Freud and Coles—the former working at length with relatively few children, the latter working briefly with large numbers—reflects the ample spectrum of child analysis and its applications. The versatile role of the child analyst is beautifully represented in Anna Freud.

The book is valuable for students, to inspire them to fulfill their dreams as Anna Freud did.

Richard Bernstein (review date 27 January 1997)

SOURCE: "Making Morality a Part of Growing Up," in *New York Times Book Review,* January 27, 1997, pp. 88-9.

[*In the following review, Bernstein takes account of the qualities and failings of* The Moral Intelligence of Children.]

Robert Coles, whose voluminous writings and positions as professor of psychiatry and medical humanities at the Harvard Medical School have made his name synonymous with wisdom about children, promises to render an important service in this latest of his many books. The dust jacket phrase puts it simply: "How to raise a moral child." And Dr. Coles asserts early on that his new book deals with "how we as adults, as mothers and fathers and schoolteachers and friends, give shape to the values of children as expressed in their behavior, their conduct; how we encourage them and instruct them to uphold in daily life one or another set of beliefs."

Dr. Coles no doubt has a wealth of experience and knowledge to draw on as he sets about his task in *The Moral Intelligence of Children,* which is a sequel to highly acclaimed works of his like *The Moral Life of Children* and *The Spiritual Life of Children.* He tells many stories of encounters with young patients and their anxious parents, some of them moving and revealing and most of them illustrating Dr. Coles's main conclusion: even when children seem most in rebellion, most withdrawn, most stubbornly uncooperative, they "very much need a sense of purpose and direction in life, a set of values grounded in moral introspection—a spiritual life that is given sanction by their parents and others in the adult world."

There is, in short, wisdom in Dr. Coles's new book. But *The Moral Intelligence of Children* is weakened by nebulousness, wordiness, by Dr. Coles's tendency to circle the issue so that he raises interesting questions but then answers them with not much more than earnest truisms: be smart, be sympathetic, avoid the extremes of setting a bad moral example yourself or being so tyrannically moralistic that you squeeze the joy out of life: "Priggish, finger-pointing children (or adults) are, alas, not rare."

This advice is fine as far as it goes, but that is not very far. If you are looking for insight into the nature and origins of morality in children, or the dark side that propels some young people to be cruel or sadistic, or even what you should do if your teen-age daughter defies your moral stand and insists on having a sex life and taking drugs, this book will only partly satisfy you.

Dr. Coles begins with the concept of moral intelligence, the faculty, separate from the qualities that make one a good mathematician or lawyer, of being what he calls "a good person," somebody with "character," of being "smart" in the way one deals with others. He brings up some experiences with children: a bright little girl who cheats in class; a group of privileged, smug, ultracool teen-agers experimenting with drugs and maintaining an attitude of general disdain for their semi-absent parents; a 14-year-old girl named Delia who is pregnant and lost. "What ought to be done?" Dr. Coles then asks, and one wonders with him, what indeed?

Dr. Coles makes the important statement that "absent parents, detached parents, haunt these narratives," but he never answers his own question. Dr. Coles's central subject is, as he puts it, "the moral archeology of childhood," in which he covers the stages of moral development, from earliest infancy to adolescence, recounting therapy sessions with parents, encounters with children, discussions with his former teacher Anna Freud (toward whom his attitude is worshipful).

There are interesting and valuable passages here, especially ones that illuminate children's powerful orientation toward the creation of a moral universe for themselves, and their quickness in seeing through the usual psychologists' palaver about such things. "You can't take a breath if you're a teen-ager without someone coming at you and telling you that you're going through this 'cycle,' and you should 'share your feelings,'" one clever young women tells him.

But the problem even with these passages is that the tone is more homiletic than analytical, more earnest than shrewd. There are lengthy passages that while certainly true, do little more than evoke how interesting and wonderful the growth of a child is. "These are years of magic," Dr. Coles writes of the time when children are of the age to go to school," of the imagination stirred and fed in innumerable ways, of all that goes with a mind encouraged to explore the world, to try to make sense of it."

Dr. Coles is certainly an insightful and sensitive man, and reading his accounts of his sessions with patients, you feel you would turn to him if a child of yours needed psychiatric help. At the same time he does a great deal of talking about himself in this book, rebuking himself for his "preconceptions and blind spots and prejudices," expressing appreciation for the lifelong lessons he is always learning from the children he meets and generally striking a tone of such strenuous modesty and self-effacement that one suspects it is a form of egoism.

His concluding section, entitled "Letter to Parents and Teachers," is especially disappointing, a pastoral essay supposedly on the subject of uniting moral principles with actual behavior, but that is rambling, discursive and unfocused. Dr. Coles talks about some children's reactions to a moral parable by

Tolstoy; he remembers the way his parents tried to instill an ethical sense in him; he reflects on Ralph Waldo Emerson's remark that "Character is higher than intellect," and ends on Henry James's admonition to his nephew to above all be kind.

Nothing is objectionable here certainly. But like so much in this book, the high-mindedness of it all seems both self-serving and abstract. When you turn the final page, you feel that you have spent a couple of hundred pages with a decent, intelligent man, but you are not so sure exactly what you have learned that you didn't know before.

FURTHER READING

Criticism

Review of *The Red Wheelbarrow: Selected Literary Essays,* by Robert Coles. *The Virginia Quarterly Review* 65, No.2 (Spring 1989): 46-47.

> A short review commenting on Coles' treatment of William Carlos Williams and other literary figures.

Rochman, Hazel. Review of *The Story of Ruby Bridges,* by Robert Coles and George Ford. *Booklist* (January 15 1995): 931.

> An informative review of a children's book written by Coles about Ruby Bridges, a 6-year-old whose courage inspired Coles' early work.

Additional coverage of Coles' life and career is contained in the following sources published by Gale: *Contemporary Authors, Vols 45-48;* *Contemporary Authors New Revision Series,* Vol.32; *Something About the Author,* Vol.23.

Chester Himes
1909-1984

(Born Chester Bonar Himes) American novelist, short story writer, autobiographer, and essayist.

The following entry presents an overview of Himes's career. For further information on his life and works, see *CLC*, Volumes 2, 4, 7, 18, and 58.

INTRODUCTION

Himes was misunderstood or ignored by American reviewers during the time he wrote, and he consequently fled to Europe to seek the acceptance he failed to receive in his own country. Critics are only recently discovering the value of Himes's work and the significance of his contribution to American literature. Originally tagged as a protest writer, Himes overcame the label by tackling an unexpected genre, the detective novel. Although some considered writing in such a popular medium to be selling out, Himes overcame the criticism by infusing his crime novels with the same powerful themes and insights as his more politically oriented work. At the end of his prolific career, Himes turned to the autobiography to put his political and social observations about the absurdity of racism and race relations in a personal context.

Biographical Information

Himes was born on July 29, 1909, in Jefferson City, Missouri. His mother came from a middle-class background and had only one black grandparent. Her ancestors were house slaves and white slave owners. His father, on the other hand, was a very dark man whose ancestors had been field slaves. His father worked as a professor of mechanical arts at several black colleges in the Midwest and the South. The intraracial differences caused tension in his parents' marriage and became the basis of his semiautobiographical novel *The Third Generation* (1954). Himes had a middle-class upbringing marred by tragedy: his older brother was blinded in an accident at school, and the emotional and financial costs put a strain on the family. He himself was hurt in an elevator accident while working in a Cleveland hotel. The injury caused him back trouble for the rest of his life. Himes attended Ohio State University, but was expelled after bringing a group of students to a party at a whorehouse. He returned to his family's home in Cleveland, where he became involved in a criminal lifestyle. He was arrested three times, once for his involvement in a robbery of guns and once for passing bad checks. Both of those convictions resulted in suspended sentences. His third arrest in 1929, for robbing a

rich, white couple in their home, resulted in jail time. He was sentenced to twenty to twenty-five years in the Ohio State Penitentiary, and served seven and a half years. Himes first began writing during his time in prison. He published his first stories in African-American periodicals like *Crisis* and *Abbott's Monthly*, but his breakthrough came when *Esquire* published his "Crazy in the Stir" and "To What Red Hell." After getting out of prison, Himes married his first wife, Jean Johnson, an African-American woman whom he had known in Cleveland. After his parole was terminated in the late-1930s, Himes and his wife moved to California where he worked a series of jobs as an unskilled laborer. His first two novels are set in Los Angeles during this time period. From 1947 to 1953 Himes lived in New York City working another series of low-paying jobs. He became disillusioned at the racism and lack of opportunities in America, and at the cold reception he was receiving from American critics. His marriage dissolved and he decided to settle in Paris in 1953, with other African-American expatriates including Richard Wright. He became involved in a series of affairs with white women, finally marrying Lesley Packard, an Anglo-

Irish woman. Himes then wrote two more novels focusing on his experiences in America, *The Third Generation* and *The Primitive* (1955). In 1956, Marcel Duhamel, the creator of the popular *Serie Noire* series of crime novels, approached Himes about writing a detective novel set in Harlem. The result was *For Love of Imabelle* (1957). Himes's crime novels became best sellers in France, and in 1958 he was awarded the Grand Prix de la littérature policière for *For Love of Imabelle*. Himes suffered strokes in 1963 and 1964, which spurred him on to record the events of his life. He moved to Spain in 1969 and began to work on his autobiography. The result was a two volume work: *The Quality of Hurt* (1972) and *My Life of Absurdity* (1977). Himes left an unfinished manuscript which was published posthumously as *Plan B* (1983).

Major Works

Himes's career had three phases: his earlier short stories and what has been termed his protest novels; his detective fiction; and his autobiography. Himes's *If He Hollers, Let Him Go* (1945) tells the story of Bob Jones, a foreman in a shipyard in Los Angeles. Jones is the victim of racism. He is demoted from a position for which he is overqualified to make room for a white man, and he barely escapes lynching when a white woman lures him into a room and accuses him of rape. Himes's *Lonely Crusade* (1947) is set in 1943 and follows the efforts of Lee Gordon to organize local workers into a union. His efforts are thwarted by the corporation and by Communist forces which have infiltrated the union for their own purposes. *Cast the First Stone* (1952) is another of Himes's semi-autobiographical novels. The main character, Jim Monroe, is a white man, but seems to represent Himes as is evidenced by their similarities: both attended college, suffered a serious back injury, and were sentenced to 25 years for armed robbery. The novel focuses on the growth that Monroe experiences while in prison, and is notable for its direct treatment of homosexual relationships in prison. *The Third Generation* is about Charles Taylor, the third son of a third generation African-American family. The novel focuses on intraracial conflict resulting from color differences rather than interracial relations. Professor Taylor, Charles's father, comes from a fieldhand ancestry, and Lillian, his mother, has descended from servants. There is some white ancestry in Lillian's family, but she exaggerates her white heritage and looks down on her husband for his blackness. The novel traces the effects that the Taylors' marital troubles and Lillian's unusual obsession with her son have on Charles. *The Primitive* was Himes's last semi-autobiographical novel. It tells the story of Jesse Robinson, a struggling African-American novelist who becomes involved in an interracial relationship with a white socialite. The novel traces the stereotypes and tensions which drive such relationships to failure. *For Love of Imabelle* was the first in his detective series set in a fictional Harlem that was based on the Cleveland of Himes's youth. All of Himes's detective fiction had similar elements, including the recurring characters Grave Digger Jones and Coffin Ed Johnson. Unlike their white prototypes, Himes's detectives get hurt for real and the violence portrayed is vivid. Their role in the novels is to mediate between the white world of law enforcement and the African-American community of Harlem. As a result, they are left alienated from both worlds. The detectives' position slowly degenerates throughout the novels until they are prohibited from doing their jobs by the white detectives and their authority is threatened by a Harlem mob in the last book of the series, *Blind Man with a Pistol* (1969). Grave Digger Jones and Coffin Ed Johnson meet their demise in the novel *Plan B,* which Himes left incomplete and was published after his death. In his two-volume autobiography, Himes returned to his examination of American racism on his life. Only instead of filtering his observations through the medium of fiction, Himes wrote about the actual events of his life. He traces the effects of Jim Crowe laws and racism on his life, and the absurdity of his situation. The first volume, *The Quality of Hurt,* covers his life from birth to his departure for Europe. *My Life of Absurdity* details his experiences in Europe.

Critical Reception

Critics have only recently begun to give serious attention to Himes's work. His first novel *If He Hollers Let Him Go* received positive critical response, but *Lonely Crusade* was vilified in America. Common complaints with *Lonely Crusade* included that it was filled with hate, anti-Semitism, and smut. In France, however, *Lonely Crusade* was extremely popular, as was his detective series. Most critics see a distinct difference in what they term Himes's "serious" writing (his early novels and his autobiography) and his "popular" novels (his detective fiction), but Nora M. Alter disagrees. She asserts that, "despite the superficial genre change . . . a clear continuity can be seen in all of Himes's writing. His detective fiction does not break with his earlier politically committed works; rather, it channels the same protest in another form." As critics are beginning to re-evaluate the value of Himes's work, several positive assessments have emerged, including Himes's use of dialect and his ability to display complex interior emotions. James A. Miller says that "Himes's rendition of black vernacular is one of the best in the business." One of the most interesting comments about Himes's talent, given the sometimes dark and violent subject matter of his fiction, is his use of humor and satire. Himes's *Plan B* is generally considered inferior to his other work, and most reviewers posit that the novel is too incomplete to have been published.

PRINCIPAL WORKS

If He Hollers, Let Him Go (novel) 1945
Lonely Crusade (novel) 1947
Cast the First Stone (novel) 1952
The Third Generation (novel) 1954
The Primitive (novel) 1955
For Love of Imabelle [translated by Minnie Danzas] (novel) 1957; expanded as *La Reine des pommes*, 1958; revised English edition published as *A Rage in Harlem*, 1965
Il pleut des coup durs (novel) 1958; published as *The Real Cool Killers,* 1959
Couche dans le pain [translated by J. Herisson and H. Robillot] (novel) 1959; published as *The Crazy Kill,* 1959
Dare-dare [translated by Pierre Verrier] (novel) 1959; published as *Run Man, Run,* 1966
Tout pour plaire [translated by Yves Malartic] (novel) 1959; published as *The Big Gold Dream,* 1960
Imbroglio negro [translated by J. Fillion] (novel) 1960; published as *All Shot Up,* 1960
Ne nous enervons pas! [translated by Fillion] (novel) 1961; published as *The Heat's On,* 1966; published as *Come Back, Charleston Blue,* 1967
Pinktoes (novel) 1961
Une affaire de viol [translated by Mathieu] (novel) 1963; published as *A Case of Rape,* 1984
Retour en Afrique [translated by Pierre Sergent] (novel) 1964; published as *Cotton Comes to Harlem,* 1965
Blind Man with a Pistol (novel) 1969; published as *Hot Day, Hot Night,* 1970; translation by Henri Robillot published as *L'Aveugle au pistolet,* 1970
The Autobiography of Chester Himes, Volume I: *The Quality of Hurt* (autobiography) 1972
Black on Black: Baby Sister and Selected Writings (short stories) 1973
The Autobiography of Chester Himes, Volume II: *My Life of Absurdity* (autobiography) 1977
Plan B (novel) 1983

CRITICISM

Ralph Reckley (essay date June 1977)

SOURCE: "The Use of the Doppelganger or Double in Chester Himes' *Lonely Crusade,*" in *CLA Journal,* Vol. XX, No. 4, June, 1977, pp. 448-58.

[*In the following essay, Reckley analyzes Himes's use of doubles in his* Lonely Crusade *by looking at three of his black male characters, Lee Gordon, Lester McKinley, and Luther McGregor.*]

Chester Himes' second novel *Lonely Crusade* has not received the critical attention it merits. Critics have praised it for its protest and its naturalistic tendencies, or damned it for its Communistic implications, but so far no one has bothered to study the novel to ascertain how skillfully Himes uses doubles throughout the novel to propound his philosophy of the emasculation of the Black male. This paper, therefore, will be concerned with analyzing three of Himes' Black male characters: Lee Gordon, Lester McKinley and Luther McGregor, so that we can better understand Himes' use of doubles.

Set in Los Angeles during the war year of 1943, *Lonely Crusade* is concerned with the efforts of Lee Gordon, a college educated Black, to recruit the Black laborers of Comstock Aircraft Corporation and organize them to form a local union. His success as an organizer is impeded on the one hand by Comstock Corporation and its major shareholder-manager, Lewis Foster, who is symbolic of the socio-economic complex which discriminates against Blacks and blocks their social mobility, and on the other by the Communist and Communistic forces that would infiltrate the union for its own purposes.

In addition to Lee there are two other characters, Lester McKinley and Luther McGregor, who, in mental attitudes and social traits, act as doppelgangers or doubles to Lee. Robert Rogers, in his work, *A Psychoanalytic Study of the Double in Literature,* maintains that doubles and/or multiple characters might exist independently in a work but they are generally "fragments of some other characterological whole." Further, Rogers explains that there is doubling by division which involves "the splitting up of a recognizable, unified psychological entity into separate complementary distinguishable parts represented by seemingly autonomous characters."

Using the terms decomposition, doubling and fragmentation as synonyms (terms which will also be used in this paper as synonyms), Rogers maintains that a doppelganger might be a secret sharer or an opposing self. The secret sharer is a latent decomposition that has been "compounded and fused within the crucible of art by the catalytic heat of creative fire." According to Rogers such a double is difficult to define, not because he may exist as an independent entity, but rather because he is so deeply woven into the structure of the work that he becomes difficult to identify as a double.

The opposing self is the opposite of its double: for example, the bad self and the guardian angel, the normal self and the diabolical self. The opposing self might also symbolize possible alliances and divisions among the Id, Ego, and Super Ego.

Lester McKinley and Luther McGregor embrace Robert

Rogers' definitions of doubles because they seem to exist independently of the protagonist. They are fully aware of their environment, and psychologically they function autonomously. However, the doubling motif which girds the novel, the coupling of incidences, both internal and external, the relationship between Lee and the decompositions—their affinities and their antagonism, and the similarities of their names—all suggest that Lee Gordon is a composite character and that Lester McKinley and Luther McGregor are the components that formalize the composition of the protagonist, Lee.

While Lester and Luther are not mirror images of Lee, there is ample evidence in the novel which indicates that these three characters are bound together in more than a haphazard relationship. For example, all three are involved with Foster and Comstock Aircraft Corporation. All three are fighting the socio-economic-industrial complex. All three are boxed in by discrimination.

However, the most obvious doubling technique in the novel, one which indicates that Himes' use of doubles could have been a conscious effort, is the naming of the characters: Lee Gordon, Lester McKinley, and Luther McGregor. At once the similarity strikes the reader as more than coincidental. It becomes obvious that phonetically the names are similar, especially in the persistent use of liquids in the first names—Lee, Lester, Luther. Linguistically, it appears as though the novelist wants us to see these three figures as one composite character. The mystery surrounding McKinely's name also encourages speculation of the doubling motif in the novel. The character changes his name to Lester McKinley after he becomes an adult, an act which might imply that during his formative years he conceived of himself as Lee, for as this essay will indicate, they do have similar experiences.

One finds too, on perusing the novel, that the similitude of names blurs the characters in the reader's mind; as a result, a reader could easily mistake Lester for Luther, or Luther for Lee. This identity crisis is especially true in the case of James Lindquist, who has published recently a critical study of Himes. In his work, *Chester Himes*, Lindquist makes several references to Lester McKinley, but he accidentally refers to Lester McKinley as Luther McKinley. While Lindquist does not discuss the doubling technique in the novel, subconsciously he sees Luther and Lester as one. The fact that a critic confuses these characters suggests that there is a need to study Himes' use of the double in *Lonely Crusade*.

It was stated earlier that the minor characters are not mirror images of the protagonist but rather extensions of him. A close analysis of the experiences of the characters, Lester and Luther, in comparison with the experiences of the composite, Lee, will demonstrate their similarities (and apparent differences) by establishing how they help to complete the character of Lee.

As a youngster, Lee was informed by one of his teachers that Blacks were heathens and that many of them were cannibals. Attending a predominantly white school, Lee observed the white males to see if there were any differences between whites and blacks that would make whites superior. Finding no differences between them and him, he hid in the girls' locker room to see if they were different. The Gordons were harried out of town for their son's act.

The family moved from Pasadena to Los Angeles, but one night while Lee's father was coming home from his janitorial job, he was accidentally shot and killed by a police officer who thought that he was a burglar. The city dismissed the killing as a natural mistake, implying that all Blacks were burglars. The traumatic experiences of Lee's youth terrified him. Because of the incidents, Lee suffered from "pure and simple fear of white folks"; further, he came to the conclusion that his destiny would be governed by the whims of whites.

As a college educated adult, Lee could not find employment for which he had been trained. The constant discriminatory practices of prospective employees, despite President Roosevelt's Executive Order 8802, turned Lee Gordon into a neurotic. The protagonist describes his emotional state in this way:

> If you have never lain sleepless for seven straight nights, your navel drawing into your spine at the slightest sound, your throat muscles contracting into painful strictures, terrified by the thought of people whom you have never seen and might never see, then you would not understand. Living in the world outnumbered and outpowered by a race whom you think wants to hurt you at every opportunity.

The image presented here is one of a broken man. The sleeplessness, the contracting of the abdominal muscles, the tightness of the throat, and above all, the unknown fear of unknown people—all indicate that Lee is at the breaking point. Where Lee has reached that point Lester, his double, has passed it.

Lester McKinley's experiences parallel those of Lee's. If anything, they are more dramatic. Growing up in Georgia, Lester suffered from the same kind of racial pressures his other self, Lee, experienced. At the age of twelve he witnessed the lynching of a Black man, and from that day he had an overwhelming compulsion to kill whites. Lester attended Atlanta University and became a brilliant scholar in Latin, but his homicidal tendencies over-powered him. As a result, he left the South and moved to Albany, New York, hoping that his psychopathic inclinations would abate. Finding no respite in the North, he visited a psychiatrist who suggested that he marry a white woman and that such a union would lessen his compulsion to kill white men. Lester married a white woman and settled in California, but Lester, like Lee, could not find employment for which he had been trained. Prejudice and discrimination, combined with his compulsion to kill whites, had warped Lester's personality and rendered him insane. He had reached the stage where he was now

> Sitting in his living room, plotting the murder of Lewis Foster. McKinley knew that he was insane, but the knowledge did not terrify him because he was through fighting it. He would kill this white man he resolved, and if that didn't do any good he would kill himself.

Lee's and Lester's experiences are the same, for Lee also believed that he had been "oppressed by white people to the point of criminal compulsion." But where Lee becomes passive and internalizes his fear, Lester becomes aggressive and seeks release in the external world. (It should be noted, however, that while Lester plans murder, he never commits murder.) Lester is Lee driven to extremes by a society which humiliates and degrades him. Lindquist maintains that Lee and Lester share many impulses, but that Lee lacks Lester's craze "only because his [Lee's] despair has not yet become so deep." I contend that Lester's desperation is no greater than Lee's. Lester is Lee, a psychotic Lee who objectifies his psychopathic tendencies.

In addition to Lester's and Lee's traumatic experiences there is other evidence of doubling in their moral traits and in their social stance which yokes the two characters together. For example, both Lester and Lee are college educated, and because of their education, both have a tendency to be contemptuous of Blacks who are not educated. Both are under-employed, both are propositioned by Lewis Foster to betray the union; both refused. Both are embroiled in domestic problems because they cannot meet their obligations. And finally, both are destroyed because they refuse to be less than men in the white man's world. These parallels are not accidental. They are indicative of the doubling technique found throughout the novel.

That Lester is Lee's alter ego is exemplified in yet another manner. Lee sees himself as an honest individual surrounded by unprincipled Communists and industrialists. Lee projects this attribute of honesty to Lester. He conceives of Lester as the only source of truth in a jungle of conspirators. When attacks and counter-attacks are made by both Communists and industrialists and Lee loses his perspective, he turns to Lester. On several occasions he tries to reach McKinley because he believes that McKinley would be sympathetic and

honest. He "was positive that Lester knew the truth" and would help him to gain a new perspective of his dilemma. Lee's projecting one of his own character traits on to Lester and his expecting sympathy from Lester suggest that there is a common bond between the two characters.

Luther McGregor is the other component of the character, Lee. Where Lester is an extension of Lee, Luther becomes the opposing self. Where Lee has an affinity for Lester he despises Luther. But Luther has the intestinal fortitude to act—a quality which is lacking in Lee and to some extent in Lester.

Little is known of Luther McGregor except that he is from Mississippi where he has spent time on a chain gang. A former WPA worker, he was sunning himself on a Los Angeles beach when a rich white woman picked him up and took him home as her paramour. Another white woman, Mollie, stole him from his first lover.

McGregor is not only a gigolo, he is a card-carrying Communist and a part-time union organizer. He is neither handsome nor intelligent. Mollie refers to him as her Caliban with a pygmy brain. He is further described by the omnipotent narrator in this manner:

> Fully as tall as Lee, his six-foot height was lost in the thickness of his torso and the width of his muscular shoulders that sloped like an ape's from which hung arms a good foot longer than the average man's. His weird, long-fingered hands of enormous size and grotesque shape . . . hung placidly at his side, and his flat splayed feet seemed planted firmly in the mud. He wore a belted light-tan camel's hair overcoat over a white turtle-neck sweater above which his flat-featured African face seemed blacker than the usual connotation of the word.

Lee and Luther also differ in their racial assumptions. Lee believes his color is a handicap, and as a result, he rejects his Blackness. Luther, on the other hand, accepts himself for what he is. He takes advantage of his racial features. Arriving at the conclusion that all the white world saw in him was a "nigger," Luther becomes a professional Black who insists that whites will have to pay to exploit his Blackness. He informs Lee:

> Look, man, as long as I is black and ugly white folks gonna hate my guts. They gonna look at me and see a nigger. All of 'em Foster, and the white folks in the party and the white women in the bed, but I is always gonna make it pay off, man . . . 'Cause I is gonna be they nigger and they proof and make 'em pay for it.

Luther is also different from Lee in his attitude toward white women. Lee deserted his Black wife, Ruth, for Jackie Folks, a white friend who was really a Communist agent sent to gain his confidence and to sabotage his plans for the union. To Lee, Jackie was a lady, his "immortal woman." Luther, on the other hand, saw no saving grace in the white female. Molly, his paramour, wanted him for one reason and he realized that fact. He was her "air hammer," her "fire and bone" and steel-driving man.

On the narrative level Luther demonstrates all of the character traits Lee detests. Luther is unscrupulous. He is cunning. He is anti-social. He hates society and he doesn't hide his hate. Industry attempts to manipulate him, but he out-maneuvers industry instead. He would brutalize and/or kill anyone who threatens his well-being, and his cynical attitude towards his women borders on hate. On the psychological level, however, all of the traits that Luther exhibits are present in Lee. Although Lee does not verbalize his thoughts, his animosities towards Foster and the industrial complex are just as strong as Luther's. And like Luther, he is always thinking how he could manipulate them to his advantage. While he does not release his aggression on those whites who affront or humiliate him, he releases his hostilities on his wife by beating and raping her. He does not want to admit it, but he realizes, as Luther said, that he is just a stud and a pimp to his white lover. For even Jackie admits to Lee: "I'd be your white whore and make you a hundred thousand dollars and the proudest black man who ever lived." Physically, and on the narrative level, then, Lee and Luther appear to be different, but the psychic similarities suggest that they share, conjointly, the same thoughts, the same emotions. And it is these thoughts and emotions which suggest that Luther is a decomposition. He is Lee's opposing self.

Another suggestion of doubling is found in Luther's behavior towards Lee. Luther's familiarity with the protagonist intimates a foreknowledge of Lee. On their initial meeting Luther presents himself as though the introduction should remind Lee of past experiences. Lee's hesitation causes Luther to insist: "You know me! I'm Luther, man, I'm Luther." Luther further implies that he had known Lee for a long time. He explained that it was he who caused the union to hire Lee. When Luther drives Lee home he continues this behavior. He stalks into Lee's house and pokes around as though he lived there, as though he were Lee. Luther's acts might be attributed to his uncouthness. I suggest, however, that Luther's prescience is an indication of Himes' double motif.

Still another example of doubling is evidenced in Luther's killing of Paul Dixon. Paul and several other deputies, under the aegis of Foster, had brutally beaten Lee when he refused to accept money to betray the union. As a result of this encounter Lee wanted to kill Paul. (Lee's thoughts are conveyed to us through Ruth, his wife.) However, it is Luther who, in their second encounter with Paul, stabbed him to death when he, Luther, suspected Paul of duping them out of their fair share of the loot. In killing Paul, Luther becomes Lee's defense against external aggression in that he acts as a surrogate for Lee.

So far, we have limited our discussion to Lee and his doubles. However, in looking at the protagonist and his components, it becomes obvious that certain parallels exist between them and their creator which suggest that doubling exists between the component character and the novelist, Chester Himes.

For example, all three of the characters are emasculated and eventually destroyed either physically or psychologically. Luther McGregor is shot to death by the police, and when the novel ends policemen are about to shoot Lee Gordon. Lester McKinley, who has reached that state of complete social alienation and mental and emotional instability, literally runs from Los Angeles. Himes had the same experiences in California as his characters did. He maintains that when he went to California he was full of hopes. He had great aspirations, but race prejudice in Los Angeles prevented him from realizing his potential, and not being able to realize his goals he became bitter and frustrated. When he went to California he was emotionally stable. He states, however, that when he left he was shattered.

All three of the characters either conceived of murder or committed murder because of racial oppression. And Himes, like his creations, affirms that he not only believed himself to be capable of murder but that he might be forced to commit murder in order to defend his honor or his life. All three of the characters had stormy affairs with white women. Himes' first autobiography, *The Quality of Hurt,* seems to be concerned, for the most part, with his disastrous affairs with white women.

In addition to the similarities Himes shares with the characters in general, there are psychic features and/or social experiences that Himes shares with each of the fragmented characters. Luther, for example, is given to bursts of violent temper, a trait demonstrated in his attitude toward his paramour, Mollie, and his killing of Paul Dixon. And Himes said that while he was living in Spain, he suffered from "blind fits of rage in which it seems my brain [had] been demented." Luther spent time on a Mississippi chain gang and Himes spent time in the Ohio State Penitentiary. Like Lester, Himes had attended college, and like his intellectual double, he could not find a job for which he had been trained. (During a period of three years in California Himes says he had twenty-four jobs. Twenty-two of these assignments were as a common laborer or a domestic, and two were semi-professional.) Also like Lester, Himes suffered emotionally because of his inability to find suitable employment.

Himes states that he suffered from periods of blankness, periods during which he could not account for his actions. Lee, the protagonist of *Lonely Crusade,* suffers from like attacks. Himes was jealous of his wife's success. He says:

> It hurt me for my wife to have a better job than I did and be respected and included by her white co-workers, besides rubbing elbows with many well-to-do blacks of the Los Angeles middle-class who would not touch me with a ten-foot pole. That was the beginning of the dissolution of our marriage.

In the novel, Lee, the protagonist, and Ruth, his wife, have the self-same problem. Lee cannot find employment while his wife has a white-collar post. Because of her working with whites, Lee accuses her of conspiring with them to emasculate him. In short, Lee's marriage, like Himes', disintegrates because his spouse has a better job.

All three of the characters, individually and collectively, have experiences that parallel Himes' own experiences. Further, all three display character traits common to their creator. It is fair to conjecture, then, that the characters, individually and as a composite represent aspects of Chester Himes and that they function as surrogates for Himes. Like Richard Wright, Himes felt the need to release his aggression, but not wanting to vent his hostilities on society, he created combative characters and lived vicariously through them.

By using characters as surrogates for himself, Himes probably purged himself of those emotional tensions that plagued him. Within the novel, however, the doubling technique has other values. By creating the composite character, Himes gives us a triple view of the effects of discrimination on the Black male. Robert Rogers stated that one aspect of doubling deals with the alliances and the divisions among the Id, the Ego and the Super Ego. If we conceive of Lee as representing the Ego, the balance between the two extremes, and Luther as the Id, and Lester as the Super Ego, we might conclude that when racial pressures affect us at the primal level we could react violently as Luther McKinley did. When they affect us at the level of the higher self we could attempt to control our aggression, but in so doing, we could become psychotic as Lester McKinley did. When they affect us on the level of the ego, we could become like Lee, spiritually and physically emasculated.

Finally, the doubling technique preserves the integrity of the protagonist, Lee Gordon. Our moral sensibilities would be stunned if Lee behaved as Luther did. On the other hand, Lee would become the object of pity if he behaved as McKinley did. However, through the technique of doubling, the integrity of the protagonist is preserved and Himes still has the opportunity to bring before the reader aspects of Lee's thoughts and actions. The doubling technique results in complexity of structure in the novel. Further, it intensifies Himes' protest theme by giving us not one but three examples of the effects of racism on the Black male.

Ralph Reckley (essay date December 1977)

SOURCE: "The Oedipal Complex and Intraracial Conflict in Chester Himes' *The Third Generation,*" in *CLA Journal,* Vol. XXI, No. 2, December, 1977, pp. 275-81.

[*In the following essay, Reckley discusses the role of the Oedipal Complex and intraracial conflict in the family relationships of Himes's* The Third Generation.]

Chester Himes' novel *The Third Generation* delineates the detrimental effects of dissension on the third son of a third generation Black family. The family is that of the Taylors. Professor Taylor, a Black man whose ancestors come from the fieldhand tradition marries Lillian Manning Taylor who is descended from the body-servant tradition. The couple have three sons: Thomas, the oldest; William, the second; and Charles, the baby. The oldest son goes away to school; the second son is accidentally blinded, and as a result is placed in a special institution. The brunt of the family's feuds, therefore, falls on Charles who lives with his parents.

As Dr. Arthur P. Davis aptly states, the novel's chief concern is not with interracial protest, but rather with "discord within the Negro family caused by color differences." The intraracial conflict within the novel has its matrix in the Oedipus Complex. This paper will, in a tentative way, demonstrate that it is the Oedipus Complex operating concomitantly with the intraracial conflict that destroys the son and breaks up the family.

In psychoanalytic terms the Oedipus Complex supports the theory that the child desires sexual involvement with the parent of the opposite sex, while at the same time, experiencing a sense of rivalry with the parent of the same sex. Failure to overcome the Oedipal stage results in the child's failure to develop psychosexually into a normal adult. Freud's theory is derived from the mythical King Oedipus who, unknowingly, kills his father and marries his mother. Generally, the Oedipus Complex is associated with boys, and the female analogy is referred to as the "Electra Complex." In keeping with the title of the paper, however, the term Oedipus Complex will be used to refer to both male and female characters.

The first signs of the Oedipus complex appear in Lillian

Manning, the sixth child in a family of seven. At the age of ten, Lillian has the responsibilities of nursing her chronically ill father, Charles Manning. Because of this close relationship, she develops a fixation, which, at her father's death turns her into "a lovely lady emersed in sorrow." Even as an adult she has no lovers, no love affairs. Further, while Lillian is fantasizing about her father, she also develops the notion that she is white. In truth, she has white ancestry. Her mother, Lin Manning, is the daughter of an Irish overseer and an Indian slave. Her father, Charles, is the son of his master, Dr. Jessie Manning and a Black slave. But Lillian elaborates on these facts and romanticizes her white ancestry until:

> The resulting story was that her father was the son of Dr Manning and a beautiful octoroon, the most beautiful woman in all the state whose own father had been an English nobleman. Her mother was the daughter of a son of a United States President and an Octoroon who was the daughter of a Confederate General.

Lillian's parents punish her for telling this story to her friends and eventually she stops. As an adult, however, she revives the myth and passes it on to her children as a fact.

As an adult Lillian is lonely because young men conceive of her as "cold and unapproachable." "They were uncomfortable in her presence." Even Professor Taylor marries her by default. He goes courting her younger sister, but he becomes infatuated with Lillian's aloofness. Lillian, on the other hand, is drawn to this Black man because of his "condescending manner." She has reached that stage in which she believes she could only give herself to one she considers her inferior, and she could only give of herself "in the manner of bestowing grace."

Lillian's father-fixation and her inability to give herself to a man either physically or psychologically are indicative of her Oedipus Complex. In addition to her attitude towards her father and her belief in her white ancestry, Lillian, as a child, develops a distorted view of sex. The narrator points out:

> Once, as a little girl, when cutting through a vulgar street in niggertown, Atlanta, she had heard an obscene reference to her vagina. She had not known then what it had meant, only that it was vulgar and dirty and had filled her with horrible shame. She had never told anyone, but the feeling of shame had lingered in her thoughts like a drop of pus, poisoning her conception of sex. As she had approached womanhood, she had resolved to make her marriage immaculate.

Lillian's Oedipus Complex, her maladjusted views of sex,

and her belief in the natural superiority of her white ancestors come to a climax on her wedding night. When the couple are finally left alone to consummate the marriage, Mr. Taylor approaches his bride very gently at first, but she becomes rigid in his embrace. All she could see is a short black man whom she fears as "something inhuman." When her husband persists, Lillian procrastinates. She needs more time; the room is too shabby; she needs a light so she can see him. But Professor Taylor is not to be dissuaded. Unfortunately the defloration of his wife results in the reawakening of her father-fixation and in her hating her husband:

> The penetration chilled her body like death. For an instant the vision of her father's kindly white face, with its long silken beard flickered through her consciousness. Then her mind-closed against reality. . . .

> He struggled to . . . win her. She fought to hold herself back . . . [and] when she felt her virginity go bleeding to this vile, bestial man, she hated him.

Long after the consummation, Lillian lies hands extended (gripping the sheets) in the posture of the crucifixion. And failing to achieve either of her goals—making love to her father whom she really wants to deflower or being a perpetual married virgin—she resorts to whipping her husband psychologically because of his blackness. From her wedding night until she divorces him twenty-six years later, Lillian Manning detests her husband. She could not, as she put it, separate his sexuality from his blackness. The two were irrevocably bound together in all her thoughts of him. Professor Taylor believes that the sex act is normal between a man and his wife. But Mrs. Taylor believes her husband's desires are bestial. She refers to him as an animal, a "rapist" who does not know what marriage really is.

Although Lillian's behavior suggests that her husband is animalistic, unrefined, we have to remember that he was overly gentle in the initial stages of their relationship. Instead of revealing weaknesses in her husband, Mrs. Taylor betrays her own defects. In essence, she reveals her Oedipus Complex, for while all of her physical and psychic energy should have been engaged in the love act, she was envisioning her "father's kindly white face" and his "long, silky beard." It is in her fantasy, too, that we see the source of the racial conflict in the family. Not only is Lillian in love with her father, but she is in love with a white father. In physical appearance her husband is the exact opposite, and it seems that she could not forgive him either for his blackness or for his taking her virginity. Lillian never outgrows her father-fixation, and she never really accepts Professor Taylor as her husband.

Freud maintains that girls are generally encouraged to retain their infantile love for their fathers beyond adolescence. He further states: "And it is instructive to find out in their married life these girls are incapable of fulfilling their duties to their husbands. They make cold wives and are sexually anesthetic." Lillian typifies the cold, anesthetic wife who, because of her own sexual maladjustments and through her twisted views of her white ancestry, brings destruction to herself and her family.

Mrs. Taylor embarrasses her husband publicly and humiliates him privately. Because of her vehement quarrels with other members of the faculty and/or with her husband (there are instances when altercations with faculty members result in family feuds), and because she frequents white establishments in small southern towns, she forces her husband to move from one Black college to another. However, her greatest insults—and the reasons for almost all of their quarrels—are made in reference to her husband's color. She believes she is one thirty-second part Negro, and in her mind that is the minimum amount of black blood "a Negro could have and still remain a Negro." On the other hand, she continually reminds her husband of his cabin tradition. To her, he is nothing but a "shanty nigger"; he is from a "black and despicable brood that would never amount to anything." Sometimes she refers to him as a common nigger who is racially incapable of accomplishing great things. She alienates the children from their father by telling them: "Your father's people are black like your father and think different from us."

The strife and dissension that Lillian occasions destroy the normal operations of the Taylors' household. But what is worse than the discord is the sublimation of her affection; the love and passion that should have been devoted to her husband are lavished on her son, Charles, heightening his own Oedipus Complex.

Freud states that between the ages of three and five it is normal for the boy to hate his father and love his mother. Charles is no exception. Undoubtedly his parents' continual bickering heightens his affinity for his mother, for even at the age of six he wants to chop his father's head off. However, beyond Charles' natural affinity for his mother, there grows a deeper feeling between the parent and the child because Lillian induces it. She pets and pampers him. She encourages him to dress her hair, to manicure her nails, and to massage her feet. She even gives him a lock of her hair.

As adults, both Lillian and Charles realize that what is going on between them is not the normal mother-son relationship. Time and time again both mother and son suggest abnormal ties. For example: Lillian's love for Charles is so deep that "she was shocked by her own passionate response to his kisses." Sometimes "her love became so intense she was afraid to look at him." Even though Charles is an adult,

his mother feels that the umbilical cord still holds them together. Afraid of her own emotions, Mrs. Taylor becomes unreasonably cruel to Charles:

> There was a fury and jealousy and strong frustrations in her punishment of him. It resembled some horrible, silent ritual. At moments in her passion she felt that she would kill him. She received a vicarious pleasure. . . .

But even her punishing Charles becomes a ritual, because in a way, she is trying to punish herself for her guilty feelings.

Charles' feelings for his mother are reciprocal. At seventeen he believes that "the part of his heart which meant most to himself was dedicated to her [Lillian]. He lived for his mother." Becoming overly concerned for his mother, he wants to take her "in his arms and go out beyond the edge of life where it was dark and peaceful and they could be together and free from all the troubles they had ever known." And once when Charles suspects that he might have to marry an "ordinary colored woman," he rejects the idea because "he knew at that moment that he could never leave his mother."

Charles is so protective of his mother that on one occasion when he finds his parents fighting he knocks his father senseless, even though it is his mother who starts the quarrel. He states over and over that he hates his father, and on one occasion he implies that he wish his father were dead. Ironically, it is only at his father's death that Charles fully comprehends that he could never replace his father in his mother's life. After the physician has pronounced Professor Taylor dead, Lillian leans over and kisses her husband's lips. Charles insists that they leave the hospital, but his mother refuses. It is only then he realizes that his mother "had gone back to his father; that she would belong to his father now forever. He felt as if he had been cut in two, as if a part of himself had been severed from himself forever."

The incestuous love that Lillian Taylor lavishes on her son results in his developing a guilt-complex. Moreover, he finds it difficult to form normal relationships with women his own age. Instead, he becomes attracted to matured women, finding sexual release in whores and prostitutes who frequent the red-light district of the city. (Unfortunately his rakishness results in his contracting gonorrhea.) He becomes a compulsive thief and a habitual liar, and because of these negative traits he spends time in jail. He drinks heavily and he smokes marijuana. He harbors a deep subconscious wish to destroy himself.

According to one version of the Oedipus myth, Jocosta was present at the time Oedipus killed his father and made love to him as a reward for his patricidal act. From this account of the myth Jocosta is al least partly responsible for Oedipus' behavior. In like manner Lillian is partly responsible for Charles' maternal fixation. It is true that as a child Charles exemplifies some aspects of the Oedipus Complex, but his strong attachment for his mother becomes abnormal because she encourages it. Because she herself is attracted to her father, and therefore cannot give her love to her husband, she turns to her youngest son, Charles. Not fully conscious of her sublimation or of her hatred for her husband, she emasculates her mate by making him feel inferior because of his blackness, and she destroys her son by developing guilt feeling in him because of his incestuous love for her.

James A. Miller (review date June 1991)

SOURCE: A review of *The Collected Stories of Chester Himes,* in *The Village Voice Literary Supplement,* June, 1991, pp. 8-9.

[*In the following review, Miller favorably reviews* The Collected Stories of Chester Himes.]

Seven years after his death in Spain, Chester Himes remains as remote from American readers as he was during his lifetime. Celebrated in Europe, particularly in France, where he settled in 1953, Himes has never really been embraced by the U.S. academy, despite the efforts of Hoyt Fuller, John A. Williams, Ishmael Reed, and others. Even with the canon debates and the present ferment in African-American literary studies, Himes continues to be relegated to the periphery. His work gets one line in Houston Baker's *Blues, Ideology and Afro-American Literature: A Vernacular Theory* (though Himes's rendition of black vernacular is one of the best in the business) and but a single mention in Henry Louis Gates's *The Signifying Monkey*—even though a main character in this collection's centerpiece, "Prison Mass," is called "Signifier."

Why has Himes been so neglected? His work has often been casually lumped with that of Richard Wright as "black protest writing," but Himes simply resists literary and political classification. He always has—as *The Collected Stories of Chester Himes* makes strikingly clear.

The first such volume since *Black on Black*—Himes's own 1973 compilation of short stories, essays, and a film scenario—*The Collected Stories* (61 in all) spans over four decades of his prolific career. It begins with the first piece he published while serving time for armed robbery in the Ohio State Penitentiary during the 1930s, and continues through stories that capture the insurrectionary mood of the late 1960s. Himes seems to have taken his stories wherever he could find them; this collection demonstrates the wide range of his subjects and his extraordinary narrative gifts.

Himes first published in black periodicals like *Abbott's Monthly;* his "breakthrough" came in 1934, when *Esquire* printed **"Crazy in the Stir"** (not included in this collection) and **"To What Red Hell,"** which is based on a 1930 fire at the Ohio state pen that left more than 300 inmates dead and triggered a nine-day riot. In **"To What Red Hell,"** as in Himes's other portraits of prison life, race is often—although not always—subordinate to mood, setting, and character.

Stories like **"His Last Day"** and **"I Don't Want To Die"** have the tough, gritty feel of Cagney movies. Others, such as the melodrama of star-crossed lovers in **"Her Whole Existence,"** incorporate some of the worst clichés of popular romance. One has the impression Himes is not only developing his craft, but shrewdly judging the literary marketplace. *Esquire* did not reveal Himes's racial identity to its readers until 1936. There is certainly a difference between what he published in *Esquire* and what he wrote for black periodicals like *The Crisis, Opportunity,* and *Negro Story.*

After his parole was terminated in the late 1930s, Himes and his wife, like millions of other Americans, were lured to California by the promise of work and high wages. Twenty-three jobs (most of them as an unskilled laborer) and three years later, Himes knew the promise of American democracy was not meant for him. His stories written during this period range from sharply drawn sketches of economic desperation to wild flights of fancy and allegory.

Himes had a wicked gift for satire, a mordant sense of humor, and a highly developed sense of the absurdities of Jim Crow and American racism. In the stories from the late 1930s and early '40s, he gives full vent to his outrage. A terse, two-page tale, **"All He Needs Is Feet,"** sums up Himes's mood: Ward, a black man in Georgia, tries to yield the sidewalk to several whites—including one woman. He is assaulted by the men, the woman screams. A mob quickly forms and decides to teach Ward a lesson. They soak his feet with gasoline and burn them. Ward is subsequently arrested for assault with a deadly weapon and while he is in jail, his feet are amputated. Once released, he learns to walk on crutches and flees to Chicago. One night he goes to see a war movie, *Bataan.* At the end of the film, the American flag appears on the screen and the national anthem is played. Ward *can't* get up and is assaulted by a burly white Southerner, who explains to a policeman: "I just couldn't stand seein' that nigger sit there while they played the National Anthem—even if he din have no feet!" This is vintage Himes, the chronicler of a universe where the threat of mindless violence and absurd entrapments lurks just beneath the surface.

In the first volume of his autobiography, *The Quality of Hurt,* Himes reflected on an anthology of his short fiction planned for publication in the 1950s:

> When I read the stories again . . . they all seemed wrong and there was scarcely one that I felt proud of having written. . . . I hated the stories. I didn't want my name attached to such a collection. I wrapped them up one morning, and took them down to the bay and threw them into the sea.

The Collected Stories of Chester Himes have been floating around for some time now. I'm glad someone had the good sense to retrieve them.

Gwendoline L. Roget (review date 1992)

SOURCE: "The Chester Himes Mystique," in *African American Review,* Vol. 26, No. 3, 1992, pp. 521-23.

[*In the following review, Roget asserts that "Chester Himes's autobiography offers invaluable literary witness to the multi-faceted black experience in America and abroad."*]

Chester Himes's decision to write his autobiography was prompted by a number of exigencies, among them the need for self-validation, the need for self-knowledge and the need for self-liberation. The untimely death of his lifelong friend Richard Wright in 1960 caused Himes to become preoccupied with his own mortality. After suffering strokes in 1963 and 1964, he felt impelled to get his life on record, before it was too late. Exhibiting immense candor as well as courage, Himes, in his two-volume autobiography *The Quality of Hurt* and *My Life of Absurdity,* reviews the events of his life within the socio-cultural context of his time. He uses his autobiography to chronicle the hurt that he suffered from psychological abuse, racial discrimination, and the rejection he experienced as a writer in America.

In spite of his need to confess, Himes had an uncanny propensity for mystification which he sustains in his autobiography through the effective use of paradox, ambiguities, racial inversions, and inconsistencies. His unique ability to mystify, shock, and raise the consciousness of his reader through the use of satire and "existential contraries" was commented on by Richard Wright, who commended Himes's "rare genius" as a writer "to describe murder as personal redemption, to speak of love in terms of hate, and to use sex as a symbol of race pride." In *The Quality of Hurt* and *My Life of Absurdity,* Himes the iconoclast comes through, defiant of society's taboos and restrictions, creating his own rules in both his life and his writings, contradicting himself, and being consistent only in his inconsistency. Although he

reveals his feelings and opinions on a broad range of subjects and incidents that shaped his life, the authentic Chester Himes still eludes the reader.

The autobiography's three focal points—women, writing, and racism—are couched in paradox, ambiguities, and contradictions. Himes devoted his life to exposing "the viciousness and demoralizing consequences of racism." His diatribes against racial bigotry spared no particular group. He attacked blacks as well as whites. Although Himes was committed to social change and entente between all people, he confesses that he felt like "a pariah" among Caucasians.

This revelation is puzzling when one considers that the majority of his romantic relationships were with white women. Jean Johnson, Himes's first wife, is the only African-American woman with whom he is amorously linked in the autobiography. In his relationships with women, further contradictions and inconsistencies emerge. In *The Quality of Hurt* he postulates, "I must have been a puritan all my life. . . . I consider the sexual act private. I do not want my sexual experience to be made public." Having come to this level of understanding, he then proceeds to recount in bawdy and graphic language his sexual conquests. That the women in his life played a dominant role is substantiated by his decision to center his European experiences in the autobiography on three women in his life.

Painstakingly, Himes retraces every nuance of his feelings about being denigrated as a writer and having his works misunderstood, misinterpreted, and/or rejected in America. No matter what direction his writings took, as A. Robert Lee has astutely observed, Himes was criticized. When he wrote on black themes, as he did in *If He Hollers Let Him Go* and *Lonely Crusade,* he was criticized for being "too narrow" or "insufficiently universal." When he put race aside and used whites as his subject, as in *Cast The First Stone,* he was accused of "turning his back on his heritage." When Himes wrote on the problems facing the black middle class from within, as he did in *The Third Generation,* he was maligned as "selling out the race." When he wrote *Pinktoes* and the detective novels, he was vilified as "pandering to the tastes of the depraved." In Europe, where he would emerge as an internationally recognized writer, Himes felt immensely vindicated. Yet, while he exulted over his success and acceptance abroad, he expressed contempt for the American critics who passed over him—only to lament, "It hurt me more than I care to admit to be rejected by the American press."

Himes's journey back through his writings not only highlights the critical response to his works, but also informs readers of the genesis of his writings. He reveals how each of his major books came into being, where he was, and what he was doing during that period of his life. Moreover, the autobiographical volumes fill in the gaps and supply relevant facts about actual people alluded to in Himes's novels and describe how he actually felt during the various crisis situations in his life. In this regard, *The Quality of Hurt* and *My Life of Absurdity* are invaluable complements to his semi-autobiographical novels *The Third Generation, Cast the First Stone, The Primitive,* and *Une Affaire de Viol.*

The Quality of Hurt chronicles Himes's early years, from his birth in 1909 up to 1954 in Europe. *My Life of Absurdity* picks up the threads of his life in 1954 to follow his transcontinental experiences up to 1972. The unifying themes of the autobiography are hurt and absurdity. Although Himes states in *The Quality of Hurt* that he does not like to exhibit his wounds, in the three books that make up the volume, and in the twenty-four chapters which comprise volume two, he does just that, as he recalls the hurt of both personal and professional experiences.

Chester Himes's autobiography offers invaluable literary witness to the multi-faceted black experience in America and abroad. As long as he was physically able to do so, Himes continued to write. *The Quality of Hurt* and *My Life of Absurdity* help validate the author's self-image as an author first and foremost. His prolific output bears witness to the fact that he mastered the craft of writing. His one self-imposed exigency was that his novels should "swing." He liked to write, he said, "the way a bird sings." Yet even his style of writing was marked by his contrary personality. He could ascend to the heights of nobility, and sink to an abyss of baseness. His writing could be fastidiously rigorous or trippingly clumsy. With the stroke of a pen, he could alter his tone from lyrical to acerbic. He could reason with the cold, discerning eye of a realist, and yet emote with the maudlin sensitivity of a romantic.

Although he was outspoken on the subject of African-Americans, he took umbrage at being called a "race spokesman." In a 1972 interview with journalist Michael Mok, Himes commented that African-Americans "aren't looking for any spokesman. They can speak for themselves. The best a black writer can do is deal with subjects which are personal; so he can tell how it was for him." In his autobiography, Himes followed his own advice. His narrative continues the excellent tradition of African-American autobiography that had its inception with the slave narratives. *The Quality of Hurt* and *My Life of Absurdity* are testament to Himes's re-telling his life "in his own way." In the final lines of the autobiography he exultantly states, "For all its inconsistencies, its contradictions, its humiliations, its triumphs, its failures, its tragedies, its hurts, its ecstasies and its absurdities; that's my life—the third generation out of slavery." It is incumbent upon this generation to establish Chester Himes in his rightful place as a member of the pantheon of great writers. The recently released Paragon House paperback edition of

Himes's *The Quality of Hurt* and *My Life Of Absurdity,* by making available his autobiography once again to the American public, is a step in that direction.

Luc Sante (essay date 16 January 1992)

SOURCE: "An American Abroad," in *The New York Review of Books,* Vol. XXXIX, No. 1 and 2, January 16, 1992, pp. 8-12.

[In the following essay, Sante discusses the effects of exile, translation, and genre on Himes's work.]

There is a peculiar purgatory of esteem reserved for those American artists who have been lionized in Europe while enduring neglect at home. The obligatory jokes about Jerry Lewis aside, the history of this ambiguity stretches back to Poe and forward to such disparate figures as Nicholas Ray, David Goodis, Sidney Bechet, Samuel Fuller, Memphis Slim, Jim Thompson, Joseph Losey, and the Art Ensemble of Chicago. These writers, musicians, and film makers failed to be prophets in their own country, were recognized too late or too little, in part because they worked the side of the street deemed "popular" (although not sufficiently popular), ever a focus of American cultural insecurities. Some of them became exiles, some, like the blacklisted Losey, for explicitly political reasons.

The black jazz musicians faced these constraints in addition to a blunt racial obstruction to their careers at home, and even if their reception in France carried a hint of an exotica fetish that is merely the reverse of the racist coin, Europe at least gave them relative comfort and steadier work and an absence of Jim Crow laws. Sidney Bechet even lived to see a statue of himself erected in Nice. But for both the voluntary exiles and for those who labored in obscurity at home, the final irony of their relative success abroad was that it seemed to delay their recognition in the United States even further.

The case of Chester Himes overflows with such ironies. After his complex realist novels of race relations were met with indifference and scorn in America, he moved to France. There, his obscurity seemed total until a publisher of detective paperbacks persuaded him to attempt a crime novel set in Harlem, a milieu he, as a Midwesterner, knew only glancingly. This first effort was striking and original, and it was a roaring success in French translation. Soon he found himself famous in Europe, although inconsistently solvent. His novels did not really make him much money until two of them were used as bases for Hollywood movies, by which time he had ceased to write them. Even the success of the movies failed to make the books catch on in the United

States and, by the time Himes died, all of his work was out of print in English. It is only now, seven years after his death, that a majority of his books are again available in America, and then only after having been reprinted in England, so that some of the present American editions sport British spellings and vocabulary. Thus Himes, an important and singular African American writer, remains even posthumously an exile.

Such a fate seems all too symmetrical for Himes, whose life, professional and otherwise, was one long process of exclusion, external and internal, in which he was both subject and object. He would undoubtedly take some bitter satisfaction in this result, since the alienation that was inflicted upon him he turned into a point of pride, a weapon, and something like a cause. His work bristles with it like the quills of a porcupine.

> I was trying to say [he wrote of his novel *The End of a Primitive*] that white people who still regarded the American black, burdened with all the vices, sophistries, and shams of their white enslavers, as primitives with greater morality than themselves, were themselves idiots. . . . Obviously and unavoidably, the American black man is the most neurotic, complicated, schizophrenic, unanalyzed, anthropologically advanced specimen of mankind in the history of the world. . . . I find it very difficult to like American blacks myself; but I know there's nothing primitive about us.

His work is a rebuke to sympathy, let alone pity. His crime novels, for that matter, are anything but formulaic; they are teeming canvases of black society in which the characters are almost by definition on the wrong side of the law, all except the two black detectives whose actions are as brusque as their moral distinctions are subtle. The setting and the genre might have propelled Himes toward some far frontier of cynicism. Instead, the very inevitability of the form and the grimness of its preoccupation seemed to free him and allow him to find life and humor in every detail.

His training in division and paradox came early. A bitter racial line was present within his own family. His mother came of genteel stock and boasted of having had only one black grandparent; Himes described her as looking "like a white woman who had suffered a long siege of illness." His father was a very dark man whose parents had been slaves and who worked his way up to a position as professor of mechanical arts at various black colleges in the Midwest and South. Their marriage only barely managed to survive a continual exchange of humiliations large and small. In Himes's autobiographical novel *The Third Generation,* he imagines their wedding night: the dinginess of the "colored hotel" and the sight of his naked black body arouse her sexual terror; she

rebuffs him and goes rigid; he rapes her. The hatred born that night can do nothing but escalate.

Nevertheless, Himes's upbringing was careful and middle class, although shadowed by tragedy (an older brother was blinded by an explosion during a chemistry demonstration at school; the financial and emotional costs afterward brought the family down in the world). It was not until college that his wild streak burst out. As a freshman at Ohio State, he cut classes and hung around the poolrooms in the black part of town, and was eventually expelled for bringing a mixed-sex group of more upright students to a party in a whorehouse that turned into a brawl. He returned to Cleveland, where his family lived, and gravitated to the gambling houses and brothels along Scovil Avenue, known as the Bucket of Blood. It was there that he got his sentimental education, meeting the people, observing the capers, and absorbing the attitudes that would later turn up in his crime novels.

He was no mere onlooker, however. He went along on a robbery of guns and ammunition from a Negro YMCA and got himself arrested; a bit later he was arrested again, for passing bad checks. Both convictions resulted in suspended sentences. Himes ended the thinly fictionalized *Third Generation* at this point in the story, only he provided a climax, a melodramatic struggle for his soul in which his father is killed and the gambler and pimp who has served as his mentor meets an ambiguous fate, while his mother looks on in horror. In reality, Himes was caught after robbing a rich white couple in their home and then trying to sell the jewelry.

This time he was sentenced to twenty to twenty-five in the Ohio State Penitentiary (because, the judge charged, he had taken ten years from the lives of each of his victims). He wound up doing seven and a half, beginning in 1929, when he was nineteen years old. It was in jail that he began to write, sending his stories at first to the black newspapers and by and by to white magazines. In 1934 *Esquire* published **"To What Red Hell,"** his account of the Easter Monday Ohio State Prison fire of 1930 in which more than 330 inmates died. It remains impressive today, a sophisticated mix of reportage and impressionism:

> A variegated color pattern formed before his eyes: black smokemantled night, yellow light, red flames, gray death, crisscrossing into maggoty confusion. He ploughed through the sense of confusion, feeling that each step he took was on a different color. To his left was the white glare of the hospital corridor; gray bodies lay on the floor and white-clad convict nurses bent over them. To his right was the black confusion of the yard with bodies lying in the

semi-gloom amid the rushing, cursing convicts. At the fringe of the light smoke was a thick gray wall.

He reworked the story a bit when he incorporated it into the prison novel he wrote after his release. That the book was not published until 1952 (as *Cast the First Stone*) is to some extent a result of its low-keyed honesty; its depiction of homosexuality as pervasive, a central and unalterable fact of prison life about which his protagonist has to shed his prejudices, is as nearly nonjudgmental as was possible for its time. It was also the only thing Himes ever published that did not focus on the subject of race. The main character, Jim Monroe, is white, although he is obviously Himes in every other respect.

Himes was obsessively autobiographical. He traced the chain of his life through his novels and stories, and then recapitulated the whole thing in the two volumes of memoirs he published at the end of his writing life. His first two published novels, *If He Hollers Let Him Go* and *Lonely Crusade,* emerged from his wartime work, mostly in shipyards, in Los Angeles. The West held the promise of a new land, untainted by the racism endemic in the older states, but it actually proved worse in many ways. An unspoken but emphatic Jim Crow code was served up with a smile, governing employment, housing, hotels, restaurants, the military, and was only partly the work of the white southerners who had migrated west during the Depression.

> **Himes was obsessively autobiographical. He traced the chain of his life through his novels and stories, and then recapitulated the whole thing in the two volumes of memoirs he published at the end of his writing life.**
>
> **—Luc Sante**

In the first novel, Bob Jones is a gang foreman in a shipyard, a man too intelligent for his work who nevertheless gets knocked down in position to make way for a white man, a fascist crank. He is then teased and lured by a southern white woman who eventually maneuvers him into a room and cries rape. He narrowly avoids getting lynched. In the second book he is called Lee Gordon, and he is a union organizer at an aviation plant who has been hired for the specific task of enlisting black workers, who are suspicious or apathetic or frightened. Already embittered at the start, Gordon is further disillusioned by what he sees—not just the expected tyranny of the bosses, but the treachery within the union, particularly as practiced by the Communists. The first book is hard and fast and sure; the second sometimes drags under the weight of arguments, but the pains Himes takes with its complexities pay off. The book's melodramatic ending—

the union banner is kept aloft as bodies around it fall—is fully earned. On the other hand, while *If He Hollers Let Him Go* received good reviews, and sold modestly well, *Lonely Crusade* was reviled. "Hate runs through this book like a streak of yellow bile," said *The Atlantic; Ebony* declared that Himes was psychotic; *Commentary* compared the book to a "graffito on the walls of public toilets." Read today, the novel seems scrupulously fair; even poignantly idealistic:

> Being a Negro was a cause—yes. Thus far Luther [an amoral black Communist] had been right. But it was never a justification—never!—which was what Luther had found out in the end. Because being a Negro was, first of all, a fact. A Negro is a Negro, as a pine tree is a pine tree and a bulldog is a bulldog—a Negro is a Negro as he is an American—because he was born a Negro. He had no cause for apology or shame.

> And if because of this fact his rights were abridged, his privileges denied, and his duties rescinded, he was the object of oppression and the victim of injustice. A crime had been committed against him by sundry white people. But this did not prove that all white hands were raised against him, because he still retained the right to protest and appeal, to defend his person and his citizenship courageously, and to unceasingly demand that justice be accorded him.

Himes assumed that the attacks on his book were the work of a conspiracy led by Communists, but in fact their sources ran the ideological gamut. Their consistency in ignoring the book's claim as literature and in advancing a view of it as hate-mongering would certainly encourage conspiratorial suspicions. Himes felt as if his allotment of hope had been abruptly cut off without explanation.

For the next six years he worked at odd jobs—as estate caretaker, porter, janitor, bellhop—and in his free time reworked *Cast the First Stone* and wrote *The Third Generation,* as well as stories that used those odd jobs and their settings as material. In 1953, at the end of his rope, he sailed to France, where he took up with Richard Wright and the rest of the African American colony in Paris. Himes, never much of a joiner, soon felt alienated from his crowd. With one woman, and then another, and then a third, he moved to various European locales—the French southwest, London, Mallorca, Denmark, Holland—living in conditions seldom very much above the poverty line, even in the meagerness of postwar Europe, when the dollar was all-powerful.

Himes's response to Europe was characteristically ambivalent. In *From Harlem to Paris: Black American Writers in*

France, 1840-1980, the French literary scholar Michel Fabre points out that Himes's accounts of Europe in the 1950s and 1960s—in letters to friends, or published in American magazines like *Ebony*—are lyrical, even rhapsodic. By the time he wrote his memoirs in the 1970s, however, he had retrospectively salted his experiences in bitterness. (Then again, as Fabre also notes, an evening spent in Paris with Richard Wright and James Baldwin was remembered by Baldwin as a benevolent meeting of minds, while Himes remembered it as an angry argument.)

Himes's relations with women were even more riddled with complication. His first marriage, to a black American woman whom he had met on Scovil Avenue in Cleveland in the 1920s and wed upon his release from prison, had dissolved before he left the United States. In Paris he took up with a woman from an old New England family fleeing a bad marriage to a Dutchman, and then with a troubled young German girl; both liaisons were tortured, steeped in separate and collective misery. When Himes married again, for the second and last time, it was to Lesley Packard, an educated Anglo-Irish woman about whom little can be learned from his writings, which is perhaps, in a backhanded way, testimony to the solidity of their relationship.

In Mallorca he wrote *The End of a Primitive,* a corrosive depiction of an earlier interracial relationship (one he had, of course, and here characteristically resolved in melodramatic violence), which was published in the United States (as *The Primitive,* a telling change by his publishers) in an abridged, not to say censored, version; it has not been reprinted in America since 1971. The book was meant to be squirm-inducing, and it succeeds, for reasons that have far less to do with race than with sex. It was as if Himes had set out to write a book that would earn him the epithets that *Lonely Crusade* had undeservedly drawn; it actually is filled with bile, directed at women, or at least one in particular, Vandi Haygood, who had been acting director of the Rosenwald Foundation, which had given Himes a grant to finish his first book. She was at least as troubled as Himes was, and their affair brought out the worst in them both, leaving him to conclude that "the final answer of any black to a white woman with whom he lives in a white society is violence." By the time he wrote the book she had committed suicide. The book, he wrote, "is rather exact except that I didn't kill her. I left that for her own race to do." *The End of a Primitive* also represents Himes's most sustained attempt at literary modernism; although most of its affectations do not succeed, it does convincingly replicate the fractures and lapses caused by alcoholic blackout. Needless to say, it made him no money to speak of.

In 1956 Himes was approached by Marcel Duhamel, a former Surrealist who had created the enormously influential *Série Noire,* a regular issue of crime novels, mostly trans-

lations "de l'Américain," in a uniform edition of white-bordered black covers. Duhamel's instructions were succinct. "Make pictures," he said. "We don't give a damn who's thinking what—only what they're doing." He also gave Himes the equivalent of a thousand dollars as an advance, a larger sum than he had ever received. Soon Himes was off and running with the story. As he later recalled:

> I would sit in my room and become hysterical thinking about the wild, incredible story I was writing. But it was only for the French, I thought, and they would believe anything about Americans, black or white, if it was bad enough. And I thought I was writing realism. It never occurred to me that I was writing absurdity. Realism and absurdity are so similar in the lives of American blacks one cannot tell the difference.

The resulting book, called *La Reine des Pommes* in French and in America published first as *For Love of Imabelle* and then as *A Rage in Harlem* (he wanted to call it *The Five-Cornered Square,* the best title of them all), fully proves his point. It is a tall tale, set in a Harlem that is largely imaginary and couched in images of 1920s Cleveland, with a slang that is likewise partly dated and partly made up, and yet it is three-dimensional and ungainsayable in its poetic truth. "The Harlem of my books was never meant to be real," Himes wrote. "I never called it real; I just wanted to take it away from the white man if only in my books." The language and riotous imagination that had often been cramped by or subordinated to a mission in Himes's mainstream efforts were set free in his crime novels.

> One joker slashed the other's arm. A big-lipped wound opened in the tight leather jacket, but nothing came out but old clothes—two sweaters, three shirts, a pair of winter underwear. The second joker slashed back, opened a wound in the front of his foe's canvas jacket. But all that came out of the wound was dried printer's ink from the layers of old newspapers the joker had wrapped around him to keep warm. They kept slashing away in buck-dancing fury, spilling old clothes and last week's newsprint instead of blood.

The story—a convoluted series of con games and chases—is a toy, yet it simultaneously manages to act as a natural correlative to its setting and Himes's theme. All mystery novels are artificial. Even the best require a powerful engine of plot to get the reader over the chasms of disbelief and irrelevance. Very few succeed at making the mystery itself part of a thematic point—Hammett's *Red Harvest,* although an imperfect book, comes to mind—and even fewer incorporate their decorative excesses into a fabric of meaning. All but one or two of Himes's crime novels pull off this remarkable feat.

The French, whether for reasons of disinterested appreciation or ignoble voyeurism, made the books best sellers and Himes a celebrity, even if they failed to make him rich. It is doubtful whether such an opportunity would have been presented to Himes in America, where the idea of a black writer producing anything but "protest novels" would probably not have occurred to many publishers at the time. For Himes, being in Europe had several creative functions. Instead of being shut out by white American society he could be actively and defiantly alienated; indeed, he seemed to take a perverse pride in having lived in France for decades without learning more than the barest rudiments of the language. Exile also seems to have affected him in a way reminiscent of what Gertrude Stein meant when she insisted that being abroad purified her language: it freed his imagination from the detritus of daily contact with his subject, and allowed him to see it in a new way.

His native country repaid him by neglecting his work; even in paperback racks in black ghetto drugstores his books were outranked by the artless and viscerally potent works of Donald Goines and Iceberg Slim, a literature that now finds its echo in the rhymes of the "gangsta" rappers. Himes's work was perhaps too detached for this audience. But the detachment is as illusory as the literary quality is real. The narrative conventions of the genre forced Himes to channel all his preoccupations without betraying them, to proceed by stealth and indirection, to mask his rage as humor, to transfer his focus from himself to the diverse and particularized inhabitants of an entire teeming world, to trade his defensiveness for a gleeful assault on all fronts, and to treat social issues with an apparent insouciance that would penetrate the defenses of his readers. Popular fiction, popularly thought of as narrow, broadened Himes as a writer.

Duhamel had to talk Himes into putting some cops into his book, not surprisingly since Himes had suffered at the hands of the police and was not inclined to be sympathetic. His resulting invention, however, was memorable: the interchangeable team of Coffin Ed Johnson and Grave Digger Jones.

> Both were tall, loose-jointed, sloppily dressed, ordinary-looking dark-brown colored men. . . . They had to be tough to work in Harlem. Colored folks didn't respect colored cops. But they respected big shiny pistols and sudden death. It was said in Harlem that Coffin Ed's pistol would kill a rock and that Grave Digger's would bury it.

> They took their tribute, like all real cops, from the established underworld catering to the essential needs of the people—gamekeepers, madams, streetwalkers, numbers writers, numbers bankers. But they were rough on purse snatchers, muggers, burglars, con men, and all strangers working any racket. And they didn't like rough stuff from anybody else but themselves. "Keep it cool," they warned. "Don't make graves."

They are anything but flamboyant; they are mostly tired and often angry. Both are natives of Harlem—a place which at the time the books were written was still filling up with migrants from the South—but they are now attempting to raise their families in the quiet of suburban Queens, where they live on the same street. In Harlem everybody ducks the cops, even the pious, and everybody is scratching for money, and almost everybody is prone to violence from the strain.

> He leafed through the reports, reading charges: "Man kills his wife with an axe for burning his breakfast pork chop . . . man shoots another man demonstrating a recent shooting he had witnessed . . . man stabs another man for spilling beer on his new suit . . . man kills self in a bar playing Russian roulette with a .32 revolver . . . woman stabs man in stomach fourteen times, no reason given . . . woman scalds neighboring woman with pot of boiling water for speaking to her husband . . . man arrested for threatening to blow up subway train because he entered wrong station and couldn't get his token back. . . . Man sees stranger wearing his own new suit, slashes him with a razor. . . . Man dressed as Cherokee Indian splits white bartender's skull with homemade tomahawk . . . man arrested on Seventh Avenue for hunting cats with hound dog and shotgun . . . twenty-five men arrested for trying to chase all the white people out of Harlem—"

> "It's Independence Day," Grave Digger interrupted.

The books are all set either in vicious winter or in blazing summer. The action shifts from street to bar to poolroom to whorehouse to church to temple to undertaking parlor to barbecue restaurant to waterfront shack to Sugar Hill high-rise to rotting tenement to back alley to junkyard. The players come from every walk of Harlem life and stand in every degree of distance from the law. The few white people to be seen are usually either hustlers or corpses, with the exception of the detectives' maladroit but well-meaning superior.

As the series proceeded, Himes's imagination became increasingly apocalyptic. ***Cotton Comes to Harlem*** features a farcical recasting of Marcus Garvey's Back to Africa movement, cross-cut with an equally grandiose white racist scheme to lure black people back to the South; ***The Heat's On*** makes grim sport of the drug trade, with a rapidly proliferating cast of characters racing around in search of an elusive $3 million worth of heroin.

The last finished book in the series, *Blind Man With a Pistol,* is also the most profound. It has no plot, as such, and no center, beyond the two detectives, who for once are nearly defeated by what they face, as two criminal cases, neither of which gets solved, thread through the chaos of a summer week lit up by riots. A friend had told Himes a story about a blind man on a subway train who had gotten slapped; trying to shoot his assailant, he wound up killing a bystander. "And then I thought of some of our loudmouthed leaders urging our vulnerable soul brothers on to getting themselves killed, and thought further that all unorganized violence is like a blind man with a pistol."

What is implicit in the other books is made explicit here: Harlem itself is the main character. On 125th Street a brotherhood march, a Black Power march, and a Black Jesus ("They lynched me") march converge and then collide. The riots illustrate why the crimes are not solved: because there is no single criminal. They are the work of a system, of institutional racism that creates ghettos where crime is incubated. The series thus comes to a sweeping and appropriate conclusion, as the scope becomes panoramic. The earlier books had revolved around single cases—good stories as well as often apposite metaphors. In *Blind Man With a Pistol,* however, Himes draws back to show the interrelation of cases and conditions; they are parallel and overlapping and linked. No single story can stand alone, and no case can be wrapped up.

Still, Himes wanted to take the cycle further. In *Plan B,* which exists only in fragmentary form and has only been published in its entirety in French, he tried to depict a black revolution; one of its alternate endings has Grave Digger killing Coffin Ed, while in another they participate in kidnapping the president and vice-president. The two excerpts from *Plan B* contained in the recently published *Collected Stories* ("Tang" and "Prediction") show Himes's usual flair and caustic humor all but undone by unmediated rage. They are the product not of imagination but of powerlessness and frustration; they are, in fact, the work of that blind man with the pistol.

In between the installments of his crime series Himes published *Pinktoes,* a comedy of manners of Harlem society that has many splendid touches ("It was all for the Negro Problem. Julius was a Negro, wasn't he: and being underfoot all the time he was certainly a problem") but is just as often overemphatic and overbearing. It was originally published by the Olympia Press, the Paris-based English-language publisher of books too risqué for the standards of the US Post Office. My copy of the 1966 American paperback edition duly features quaintly leering blurbs: "A Sinerama in glori-

ous black and white . . . Rabelaisian . . . balloon-bursting." The titillation factor seems rather mild after thirty years: the contemporary reader is more likely to notice the strenuous nature of the fun, both the characters' and the author's.

Run Man Run (written in 1961, published in 1966) is a crime novel not featuring his two detectives. If the series shows Himes making triumphant use of the crime genre to explore major themes while pretending to be at play, *Run Man Run* demonstrates that he could be undermined by the constraints of formula as well. In the book, Jimmy Johnson, a porter at a Schmidt and Schindler luncheonette in midtown (Himes briefly held such a job at a Horn and Hardart), survives a wanton attack by a white detective named Walker, who, crazed by fear and whiskey, has killed two other porters. The action follows Walker and Johnson alternately as one stalks the other. Walker is the perfect white monster, the pacing is relentless, the details are telling, and the premise is obviously deeply felt. However, Himes could think of no way to end the book but by resorting to a series of utterly phony plot twists. There is, in fact, no logical ending to this traintrack of inevitability other than Johnson's death at Walker's hands. The book is an interesting case of artificiality as the result of the author's emotional involvement, rather than of hackwork or expediency.

Himes's last two books were *The Quality of Hurt* and *My Life of Absurdity,* his autobiography, volumes one and two. They are sprawling, maddening books dense with pain, anger, self-contradiction, and trivia. Himes had already worked over his childhood and troubled youth pretty well in his novels, so the reiteration as fact of those slices of his life are inevitably thin and perfunctory. The rest is mostly a writer's life, seldom good material under the best of circumstances, although Himes's has somewhat more power than most as a chronicle of racism, frustration, poverty, and thieving publishers. His relations with women are presented in claustrophobic detail, and nobody, least of all Himes himself, comes out well (with the possible exception of his second wife, who seems translucent, nearly invisible).

The first volume is painful to read, but that is in part because of the painful events Himes relates; it nevertheless conveys his wit, insight, and descriptive skill. Volume two, however, is a disaster. Evidently written when he was in failing health, it appears to be an indiscriminate regurgitation of diary material, with directions to friends' houses in the French countryside and the exact prices paid for articles of clothing given the same weight and measure as accounts of how he came to write his books or reflections on the political situation in America. It is, in addition, rife with typographical errors, errors of fact, and a variety of highly uncharacteristic misuses of language, including literal translations of French idiom that are obviously not intentional. None of this can be laid at the door of the elderly Himes, who was by then suffering from weakened eyesight and multiple sclerosis, and probably dictated the book. Rather, it seems a final indignity imposed on him by publishers, who in one guise or another had been tormenting him for more than thirty years, and at the twilight of his career chose not to assign him an editor.

But maybe Himes didn't care by then, or maybe he wanted all the raw material published without interference, displaying every wart and blotch. He had never attempted to protect his image or to present a polished front to the world, even if such had been possible, and as he got older he seemed to relish describing his worst qualities and least creditable actions. Himes often complained that white people could only appreciate books by black writers if the books contained the appropriate amount of suffering; after the early works he'd be damned if he'd give them the satisfaction, although his own suffering was indisputable. He was an original, with a prickly and ungovernable disposition, saddled with the African American writer's curse of having to be representative without having been elected. He never shirked this task, but it is significant that he did his best work under the triple cover of exile, translation, and genre.

James Robert Payne (review date Autumn 1992)

SOURCE: A review of *The Collected Stories,* in *World Literature Today,* Vol. 66, No. 4, Autumn, 1992, pp. 722-23.

[In the following review, Payne asserts that "The generously conceived and readable Collected Stories *will facilitate fuller critical response to Himes, and it should enhance his appeal to general readers."]*

After attending Ohio State University, Chester Himes involved himself with gang activity until his eight-year imprisonment. His first publication, a piece about a prison fire, appeared in *Esquire* in 1932, when the gifted African-American prose stylist and poet was in his early twenties. Like many creators of American culture, Himes has achieved substantially greater critical recognition in France than in his own country. He emigrated to France in 1953. Although Himes's best work has been stylistically compared with Hemingway, and compared with Baldwin, Hurston, and Welty for its insight, his fiction has still not received the extensive critical attention it merits. I think, however, that we are now on the verge of a clearer and fairer recognition of his achievements.

American critics and scholars are at present learning to read better and respond more sensitively to our varied texts representing the drama and ironies of race, class, and gender. Himes's fiction, effectively focused from the beginning to the end of his prolific career on race, class, and gender themes, should prove irresistibly attractive to many scholars attuned to the newer approaches. General readers, now more and more drawn to black artistry through the work of such writers as Alice Walker, Toni Morrison, and Charles Johnson, will, I believe, continue to turn to Himes, a popular writer of the previous generation whose fiction has undergone successful film adaptation since the early 1970s. The generously conceived and readable *Collected Stories* will facilitate fuller critical response to Himes, and it should enhance his appeal to general readers.

The collection opens with a brief but helpful foreword by Calvin Hernton and a very useful chronology of Himes's short fiction. It presents both his previously published works and a number of very interesting hitherto unpublished pieces, for an overall total of sixty short stories. Though a few of the stories are marked by a sketchy, inadequate development that suggests hasty composition, riches and pleasures abound.

Pleasures of course will vary from reader to reader. By having the chance to read it in the full context of his other late-1930s-to-early-1940s short fiction, I especially enjoyed an increased understanding of Himes's classic 1937 story **"Headwaiter"** (originally published as **"Salute to the Passing"**), a work which epitomizes Himes's superb mastery of nuances of class and race among black men. With stories like **"Strictly Business"** and **"Tang"** the collection allows us to see, in retrospect, how Himes rivals Nelson Algren as a fictionist of the great American urban underclass, black and white. Lone respected for his fiction of prison life, crime, and detection, Himes also demonstrates considerable power as a fictionist of black military experience, in which antagonists, as in the painful **"Christmas Gift"** and **"All He Needs Is Feet,"** tend not to be foreign enemies but rather fellow Americans. Stories such as **"A Nigger"** reveal impressive insights on male-female relationships across the color line and are especially notable for their candid and sensitive representation of complex feelings of black men. Most of Himes's stories are in a straightforward, realist-naturalist mode, with some exceptions, including the somewhat technically innovative **"Prison Mass."** *The Collected Stories* is graced with fine cover art, a portrait of Himes by Denese Morden.

Nora M. Alter (essay date 1993)

SOURCE: "Chester Himes: Black Guns and Words," in *Alteratives,* edited by Warren Motte and Gerald Prince, French Forum Publishers, 1993, pp. 11-24.

[In the following essay, Alter analyzes the role of

Gravedigger Jones and Coffin Ed as mediators between the white world of the law and the black world of the streets in Himes's detective fiction.]

Chester Himes's literary career has traditionally been divided into three distinct parts, corresponding to, and partly influenced by, the three different countries of his residence. His first writings date from between 1933 and 1953, while he was living in the United States. They include short stories, written while in prison, and, after his release, longer fictions that have been termed "protest novels." These novels offer sharp and often violent political commentaries about black life in a deeply racist white America. Though he received immediate success and publicity after his first novel, *If He Hollers Let Him Go,* his later works from this period proved too harsh for the American public and his popularity abated. When they were translated into French, however, they were received in a more positive way; in fact, *The Lonely Crusade* was chosen as one of the top five American books in France in 1952. It was in part this recognition that induced Himes to move to France in 1953. While in France, he launched the second phase of his writings, the detective fiction. Perhaps because they belong to a "popular" genre, these novels are perceived to have been motivated by the need to make money rather than by a will to make serious political statements. They were inspired in 1956 by Marcel Duhamel, editor of Gallimard's *Série Noire,* the prestigious French collection of hard-boiled mysteries. Under his guidance, during the next twelve years, Himes wrote eight detective novels set in Harlem. In 1958, he was awarded the *Grand Prix de la littérature policière.* Though achieving considerable success as a writer of *polars,* both in France and in the United States, Himes abandoned the series in 1969, moved to Spain and resumed "serious" writing, this time in the form of an autobiography. It is my contention that, despite the superficial genre change, and contrary to the prevailing opinion, a clear continuity can be seen in all of Himes's writing. His detective fiction does not break with his earlier politically committed works; rather, it channels the same protest in another form. In fact, as I shall try to show, it is this overall perspective that accounts not only for the main structural tension in the eight mysteries but also for a dramatic transformation of that tension.

There are two reasons why Himes's *Série Noire* stories are viewed as the first black detective fiction. First, their two detectives are indeed black policemen. Second, all the novels are set within the boundaries of black Harlem during the late nineteen fifties and sixties, where "anything can happen." They explore social relations of blacks and offer a vivid portrayal of racial conflict and shocking violence of power at play. Himes's Harlem, a space inhabited primarily by blacks, represents an extreme form of a society gone crazy because of racial madness: "This is Harlem. . . . Ain't no other place like it in the world. You've got to start from

scratch here, because these folks in Harlem do things for reasons nobody else in the world would think of." Particularly striking in this special place is its "otherness" of language as well as the subversion of gender and race identity by transvestites, transsexuals, albino blacks, and people who play on various gradations of "blackness" which determine social and cultural status.

To this "crazy" world, Himes brings his two hard-boiled black detectives, Coffin Ed and Gravedigger Jones (Ed Cercueil and Fossoyeur), and that insertion creates the basic structural tension in all the novels. Because of their profession, Jones and Ed are forced to mediate between the white world of law and the black world of the streets. While at the police precincts, their language is generally conventional and nonviolent, conforming to the rules of social discourse necessary for their acceptance by the white society; but once on the streets, their language and code of conduct follow a diversity of other rules prevailing in mad Harlem. Eventually, their participation in the two worlds leads to their rejection by both blacks and whites. As Coffin Ed puts it at the end of *The Heat's On:*

> What hurts me most about this business is the attitude of the public toward cops like me and Digger. Folks just don't want to believe that what we're trying to do is make a decent peaceful city for people to live in, and we're going about it the best way we know how.

But that ultimate failure only caps a dramatic evolution of their mediating function and the various strategies they adopt to fulfil it.

Initially two main strategies appear to be at their disposal for their constant move across the racial (and social) border: they can adjust their language in order to deal effectively with each group, and they can disguise their appearance in order to blend with the group or to manipulate it. But neither Coffin Ed nor Gravedigger Jones is given to disguise. Their blending ability rather stems from their indistinguishable appearance: except for Ed's scarred face (from an acid burn which melted it), they appear alike both to whites and blacks: "tall, loose-jointed, sloppily dressed, ordinary-looking dark-brown colored men." They do not play any role beyond their functional role, that of black cops. By the same token, however, they set a contrast with the other inhabitants of Harlem, who seem obsessed by disguises. *A Rage in Harlem* was originally titled *The Five Cornered Square* after a particularly gullible character who is conned by everyone and hence so square that he seems to have five corners. This Jackson is also a failure at disguises; when he tries to disguise his voice over the phone when calling his landlady, she has no trouble hearing right through his muffled voice: "I know who you is Jackson. You ain't fooling me." In contrast, Jackson's identical twin brother, Goldy, is a master at disguises and fools everybody. Goldy spends his days dressed as Sister Gabriel, much to the indignation of Jackson: "There's a law against impersonating a female." Goldy's costume allows him to move about freely and to carry out his secret activities without arousing suspicion. He lives by his "wits" not only in the world of the streets but also in the world of the cops. For Goldy, like Ed and Jones, also straddles two worlds: a criminal among Harlem blacks, he is an informer for the police. His disguise works for both roles, but, in his dealings with the detectives, he also has recourse to the second strategy: a special language adjusted to that of his interlocutors. When Jones greets him with "What's the word, Sister?" he responds with "And I saw three unclean spirits like frogs come out of the mouth of the dragon," that the black detective understands readily. In a later passage, he uses this same biblical talk to evade a white policeman for "he knew the best way to confuse a white cop in Harlem was to quote foolishly from the Bible." Eventually, it is Goldy's language that kills him and restores the social order: he "Talked himself into the grave."

No such dangers are faced by the two detectives. While indifferent to disguises, they are masters at language strategy. Though they do not yet play as central a role as they will in later novels (no doubt because Himes brought them into *A Rage in Harlem* at Duhamel's request), Ed and Jones demonstrate from the start their linguistic versatility. Jones has no problems understanding Sister Gabriel, and he controls a potentially explosive situation with a simple voice imitation trick: "'Straighten up,' he shouted in a big loud voice. And then, as if echoing his own voice, he mimicked Coffin Ed, 'Count off.'" Rather than highlighting rational deductive power as the essential function of the detective, Himes shows that rationality is itself a function of language and that it is language which determines the exercise of authority and power. As James Baldwin writes, "A language comes into existence by means of brutal necessity, and the rules of the language are dictated by what the language must convey." The power of the two detectives derives from their mastery of communication rather than from a display of brutal force. In fact, Ed and Jones are not very violent in *A Rage in Harlem:* they put their trust in words, when dealing with blacks or with whites.

To that extent, and despite its title, this first novel written in France is rather optimistic. Perhaps Himes identified his second career (a black American writer's mediation between a French white audience and a black Harlem) with the mission of his two black detectives who must similarly mediate between a white American society as represented by the police and the same black Harlem. Himes's earlier "serious" novels failed to communicate the urgency of the black problem in his own society; he might have now entertained the hope that, in France, his skills at a different form of com-

munication, adjusted to the norms of the *Série Noire's* readers, would succeed to bridge the racial and social gap. For Himes, as for many others, writing fiction and detecting may have seemed to be a similar verbal attempt to bring out a believable truth; a hopeful double undertaking.

But violence and frustration return in *The Real Cool Killers.* It opens when a white man is attacked by a black man in a bar in Harlem, then shot apparently by a group of Muslims. But Digger manages to see through their costumes and identifies them as black youths (while the white policemen remain confused and ignorant). A series of interrogations make it clear that the two black detectives have the potential to extract more information from the inhabitants of Harlem than the white authorities. Digger and Ed command respect and fear because their police badge symbolizes a white man's law, but it is only their dark color of skin that enables them to overcome suspicion and to gain some trust among the blacks. Yet, at the same time, they also generate among them a good deal of contempt and resentment. In contrast, their status as officers of the law encourages communication with white people who approve their role of protecting white society: "Maybe I can help you, the white man with the blond crew cut said to Grave Digger. 'You're a detective, aren't you?'" *The Real Cool Killers* also suggests that the two detectives are not as indistinguishable as is generally believed. In fact, Digger proves to be a better problem solver and language master, while Ed is more prone to violence: he loses his cool and shoots one of the punks. This episode provides the first instance of the blind violence that will occur with increasing frequency in Himes's detective novels, eventually dominating them. The solution of crimes will result less from deductive reasoning and language skill than from their own brutality and violence. Even Digger abandons his language skills and partakes in violence, as if contaminated by the madness of his partner and the general crazy fatality of Harlem.

This turn toward increasing violence has however a more specific reason. It is not Harlem that is changing, but Himes's vision of Harlem. And this evolution cannot be explained by the influence of changes in the detective genre. True, other contributors to the *Série Noire,* such as Chandler and Hammett, featured strong and hard-boiled detectives. But Marlowe and Sam Spade, however coarse, solve their problems through intellect and deductive reasoning. I rather believe that, on the level of the plot, the violence of Coffin Ed and Grave Digger Jones is a direct consequence of their difficult role as black detectives maintaining a white law in the black world of Harlem. As Digger explains, "colored hoodlums had no respect for colored cops unless you beat it into them or blew them away." In contrast to *A Rage in Harlem,* where they still commanded respect, in the last novel of the series, *Blind Man with a Pistol,* Jones and Ed will almost completely lose their authority among the blacks. In fact, they are threatened and attacked by a group of teenagers with a racial agenda: "'We're the law,' Coffin Ed said. . . . 'Then you're on whitey's side.'" The two detectives justify their violence against blacks—men and women—by a paradoxical double argument: their brutality is necessary to curb crime, but it is also excusable because they belong themselves to the very people they brutalize. They think that it is the only way for them to gain respect because their official title no longer holds any weight and the traditional means of questioning are no longer effective. For them, violence is an "innocent" feature of their profession as detectives in contrast to "the white men on the force who commit the pointless brutality." Yet, by the end of the series, they fail not only the citizens of Harlem who reject them, but also the white world of the police precincts which also rejects them:

> Now after twelve years as first-grade detectives they hadn't been promoted. Their raises in salaries hadn't kept up with the cost of living . . . when they weren't taking lumps from the thugs, they were taking lumps from the commissioners.

The direct cause of their failure seems to be a double alienation, from both blacks and whites. Which means that they experience a growing double gap in communication or, more generally, a double collapse of their mediating function between the two worlds.

The question is: what motivated Himes, from novel to novel, to undermine and finally negate his early trust in mediation? Was it because his own mediating function as a novelist was also progressively collapsing? A distinction must be made here between the process of mediation and its content. On the one hand, over the twelve years, Himes's novels remained successful, and the faithful French readers continued to enrich their image of Harlem. On the other hand, however, it is quite likely that Himes himself was increasingly moving away from his earlier light vision of Harlem, and his somewhat hopeful perspective on the solution of the problems of blacks in America. In other terms, I think that Himes was coming to doubt any possibility of navigating between the two incompatible worlds of white and black. The solution to divisive racism could not be found in mediating the white man's law. The strained atmosphere culminating in *Blind Man with a Pistol* testifies in that sense to Himes's growing impatience with the mounting racial tension in America and its echoes in Europe. His novels illustrate, one after another, the progression of that tension among the characters of his fictional Harlem.

A Rage in Harlem concerned itself exclusively with the lives of blacks, barely alluding to the white outside world. Then, already in *The Real Cool Killers,* racial tension becomes a mainspring of the plot. When a white man in a black bar in Harlem is believed to be murdered by a group of black punks, the white police chief is mainly afraid of racial comments; he tells Jones and Ed: "You want it said the New York City police stood by helpless while a white man got himself killed in the middle of a crowded nigger street?" Jones and Ed must solve the crime in order to preserve the face of the white police force. They are frustrated by this policy but, as Digger explains, still willing to accept it: "If you white people insist on coming up to Harlem where you force colored people to live in vice-and-crime-ridden slums, it's my job to see that you are safe." And why is this mission reserved for Jones and Ed? Because the white detectives, with a white perspective, cannot distinguish between different members of the black population: to them all blacks look, act, and think alike:

> Do I think we'll find him? Do you know who we're looking for? . . . [they are] just like eighteen thousand or one hundred and eighty thousand other colored men, all looking alike. Have you ever stopped to think there are five hundred thousand colored people in Harlem—one half of a million people with black skin. All looking alike.

They appear to them as an indistinguishable mass of blackness, invisible as individuals. To make this point clear, Himes's portrayal of Harlem characters stresses, in contrast, the gradations of skin color, clothing, body type, and other distinguishing signs that mark individual identities: "brownskin," "olivebrown," "high-yellow," and their variations. These classifications by degree of color further serve, in all of Himes's novels, to make subtle distinctions between social classes among the blacks.

In *The Crazy Kill,* the third novel of the series, the main players remain black, but a new outsider appears as the "Chink." Also, more scenes take place at the police precinct, where Ed and Digger act as mediators between blacks and whites. Only they have the authority and the ability to bring in the black mob leader Johnny and his wife, since Johnny will trust them because of their common bond of skin. In contrast, when the old black dame Mami shakes hands with the white sergeant, the latter is at a loss: "Sergeant Brody wasn't used to it. He was the law." Later, "Grave Digger saw that Brody didn't get it, so he explained." The same Brody then insults the black mobster by telling him: "'Okay, boy, you can go now.' 'Fine,' Johnny said, getting to his feet. 'Just don't call me boy.'" For Brody any black is an "other." For Ed and Jones blacks are "us": they know and understand them. Like in *A Rage in Harlem,* they have black stool pigeons, including a drug addict whom Jones and Ed manipulate by controlling when and where he will get a fix.

In *The Heat's On,* as implied in the title, racial tension is getting hotter, reaching the boiling point. The value of skin color and the mobility it affords are openly discussed. Sister Heavenly has been dyeing her skin for years to try to become white and gain respect; conversely, and more grimly, the albino Pinky is too white to be allowed to go to Africa, and, in frustration, murders his stepfather: "He said I was too white. He said all them black Africans wouldn't like colored people white as I is, and they'd kill me." Grave Digger and Coffin Ed are losing their patience with the prejudices of white society and bring up the matter of skin color to the white sergeant in the form of an innocent nursery rhyme: "'If you're white, all right,' he recited in the voice of a school boy. Coffin Ed took it up, 'If you're brown, stick around. . . .' Grave Digger capped it, 'If you're black, stand back. . . .'" Eventually, unable to control their violence, they punch a white drug dealer who has come into Harlem, cause his death, and are suspended from the force because, as they claim, "It's all right to kill a few colored people for trying to get their children an education, but don't hurt a mother-raping white punk for selling dope."

The message becomes even clearer in *Cotton Comes to Harlem.* The story now centers on an outside white man who tries to penetrate the black world of Harlem. Unlike the secret and personal motives of the Greek in *The Heat's On,* who cruised Harlem bars in order to find young black girls he wanted to beat up, Colonel Calhoun's intentions are openly social and economic from the start. He chooses Harlem as the best place from which to draw black workers and to sign them up as slaves for his cotton plantation in the South. On a parallel track, the black Reverend Deke O'Malley also plays on Harlem's poverty to try to con black families with a "Back to Africa scheme." Both O'Malley and Calhoun have chosen Harlem as the ideal hunting grounds because of the total despair of its population, cut off from any future by the whites:

> They had not found a home in America. So they looked across the sea to Africa, where other black people were both the ruled and the rulers. . . . Everyone has to believe in something; and the white people of America had left them nothing to believe in.

The rhetoric grows in speeches and impassioned pleas from all sides. Whereas the dialogue was minimal in *A Rage in Harlem,* with a focus on fast-paced action, *Cotton Comes to Harlem* subordinates the action to philosophy and commentary. The opening scene has a spokesperson for the Back to Africa movement trying to gather mass support: "These damn southern white folks have worked us like dogs for four hundred years and when we ask them to pay off, they ship us up to the North. . . . And these damn northern white folks don't want us." At which point he is silenced with machine-gun shots. Violence takes over the function of words. Yet, the attempts at communication multiply, both among the

novel's characters and from the novel to the reader. Thus Digger, departing from his role as a neutral upholder of the law, offers social commentary that expresses frustration with purely legal solutions to crimes. He tells the police sergeant, as well as the readers, that:

> We got the highest crime rate on earth among the colored people of Harlem. And there ain't but three things to do about it: Make the criminals pay for it—you don't want to do that; pay the people enough to live decently—you ain't going to do that; so all that's left is let 'em eat one another up.

Echoing Digger's inability to remain silent are the black masses who give vent to their frustrations by calling for racial violence. Passive resistance is no longer satisfactory and immediate solutions are sought. For, as Himes points out, a black man will never be able to change the color of his skin unlike a "Puerto Rican [who] becomes white enough he's accepted as white, but no matter how white a spook might become he's still a nigger."

Furthermore, it is not only in the world of Harlem that the situation is heating up. In the white world of the police precinct, intolerance has increased. Earlier efforts at masking racial prejudice or sparing the feelings of Grave Digger and Coffin Ed are given up. The atmosphere is almost as tense as that on the streets. Captain Brice blames all black men for the problem of racism and threatens: "I'll arrest every black son of a bitch in Harlem," and Coffin Ed responds: "Including me and Digger?" Brice then sends his two "ace" detectives on a virtually hopeless and fatal mission: in his mind, they have become expendable. He thus fulfills Digger's earlier prophecy that the people in Harlem "will eat one another up," including him and Ed. Because they are black, Ed and Jones are now locked outside the white police precincts and only called in when their skin color may be useful. And while they agree to stay on their jobs, it is only because of a higher duty to their own race, not because of the duty of law enforcement: "I wouldn't do this for nobody but my own black people." At the end, when Digger and Ed finally catch Calhoun, they let him go free, instead of arresting him, in return for the money he stole from the black families. For, had he been turned over to the law, the families would never have seen that money again. This illegal action is justified by the ironic ending which shows that, once back in the South, Calhoun is protected by the law from extradition since in Alabama "killing a Negro did not constitute murder."

In the last novel in the series, *Blind Man with a Pistol,* Himes's frustration leads him to innovations in structure and in content. He adds both a preface and a foreword that refer directly to violence and chaos in the entire world. Furthermore, within the body of the text, there are several authorial asides or "interludes," one of which discusses the geographical, social, economic and political features of Harlem which, though populated by blacks, is actually still owned by whites. This interlude also evokes historical figures of the Harlem Renaissance: black political leaders, intellectuals and artists. In addition, *Blind Man with a Pistol* also comments on the Detroit race riot of 1943, World War II, Dr. Martin Luther King and Malcolm X, represented in the novel by a Black Muslim character named Michael X. These insertions of fragments of History were surely intended by Himes, as a literary device, to impress on the readers that the fiction they are reading is grounded in reality and that the problems it depicts are real and urgent problems. Indeed, in a Brechtian spirit, Himes moves the readers to distance themselves from the illusion of fiction, to take over from the now ineffective detectives the function of solving problems, to realize that these problems are not simply criminal but racial and social. It is not surprising then that, after *Blind Man with a Pistol,* Himes abandons fiction writing altogether and concentrates on writing his autobiography.

The main plot illustrates the mounting tension. Following the pattern set in earlier works, violence again comes to Harlem in the form of a white man entering a black space. In this instance, he is a homosexual looking for black men to satisfy his needs. He is brutally murdered during the sexual act, though for no apparent reason. And, unlike what happened in the preceding works, this crime is never fully clarified. For finally no one really cares. An inversion of goals has occurred: instead of Harlem being a backdrop for a fictional detective story, the detective story becomes the backdrop for the real racial problems in Harlem.

Blind Man with a Pistol does suggest several solutions to the "Negro Problem," but none are very satisfactory. One is embodied by Reverend Sam, who has twelve wives and is trying to have as many children as possible in order to combat racism by increasing the black population of the earth. Another character, Dr. Mubuta, invents a longevity tonic because his "solution for the Negro problem was for Negroes to outlive the white people." For Marcus Mackenzie, the solution lies in brotherhood and interracial marriage, while for Michael X it is only through violence that white racism can be overcome. All are presented as dreamers.

Racism thus becomes the basic topic of the novel. It is dramatized in many ways. In the twelfth chapter, a racial demonstration culminates in a riot when supporters of peaceful brotherhood, very white and very black men marching arm in arm, come up against the militant separatists of Michael X. Meantime, within the police precincts the peaceful coexistence of black and white policemen has come to an end: "Yes, these black sons of bitches were going to take a lot of getting along with, the sergeant thought." No longer com-

placent, Ed and Digger can no longer operate successfully as detectives. And their lieutenant states, "Once upon a time you guys were cops—and maybe friends: now you're black racists." Grave Digger has a different but also militant view:

> But the difference is that by the time we'd fought in a jim-crow army to whip the Nazis and had come home to our native racism, we didn't believe any of that shit . . . we had learned the only difference between the homegrown racist and the foreign racist was who had the nigger.

Blind Man with a Pistol ends with a cynical dialogue between Lieutenant Anderson and Grave Digger, between white and black: "'That don't make any sense.' 'Sure don't.'" The situation has become absurd with no solution in sight.

Grave Digger Jones and Coffin Ed ultimately fail in their function as mediators. Introduced reluctantly in the first story, though with some timid optimism, they progressively realize that the black and white worlds cannot be reconciled through communication, that a hopeless violence always prevails. And they disappear. Himes himself leaves France for Spain. Tired of fiction, or as disappointed with its impact as when he left the United States for France, he turns to autobiography to tell his story: a story of frustrations. A story of his hopes and failures to write mediating fiction, to try to communicate with words the need to understand the "other" and to resist violence. He finally acknowledges that his fiction accomplished nothing against the reality of racism. Not only in Harlem, and racist America, but also, with an increasing urgency, all over the globe, including France—in short in the world transformed into a violent blind man with a pistol:

> I thought, damn right, sounds just like today's news, riots in the ghettos, war in Vietnam, masochistic doings in the Middle East. And then I thought of some of our loudmouthed leaders urging our vulnerable soul brothers on to getting themselves killed, and thought further that all unorganized violence is like a blind man with a pistol.

James Campbell (review date 24 December 1993)

SOURCE: "Himes and self-hatred," in *TLS,* No. 4734, December 24, 1993, p. 17.

[*In the following review, Campbell discusses Himes's* The Collected Stories *and* Plan B.]

Chester Himes lived a life of almost constant agitation— Harlem, Paris, Spain—settling only once: to serve seven years of a twenty to twenty-five-year sentence in the Ohio State Penitentiary, the outcome of an armed robbery staged single-handed in a prosperous white neighbourhood in Cleveland. Nineteen when he entered prison in 1929, Himes had already been a thief, a pimp, a bootlegger, and a student at the [Ohio State University]. In prison, he switched to writing fiction, publishing his first short stories in *Esquire* and the black journal, *Crisis*.

The beginning and end of Himes's fifty-year literary career (he gave up the other one) are marked out by these two books: *The Collected Stories* contains sixty stories, probably all the short pieces he ever wrote, including previously unpublished and undated material; while *Plan B* is the "unfinished masterpiece" he supposedly left behind after his death. Unfinished the novel certainly is—there could be no other explanation for its dire quality—but the publishers present it as more of an enigma than is actually the case: "After his death in 1984, a rumor persisted that [Himes] had left a final unfinished Harlem story.... *Plan B* is that novel." The very same *Plan B,* as it happens, which was published in Paris, in translation, a year before Himes died, an event described in the informative introduction by Michel Fabre and Robert Skinner. Too ill to complete the work, Himes apparently went ahead and sanctioned publication in the country where he enjoyed his greatest popularity.

Virtually all Himes's writing, especially the early and late work, is characterized by brutality, anger and self-hatred. But the honesty with which he confronts this personal turbulence makes him, at times, an engaging writer.
—James Campbell

Confusion over Himes's publishing history is excusable. He wrote about twenty books, including two volumes of autobiography, but his novels have come out at different times under different titles, and during the 1950s and 60s most of them were published first in France, where Himes wrote detective novels for Gallimard's list of thrillers, *Série Noire* (as in "film noir", of course—nothing to do with *les noirs*). In 1958, he became the first non-French author to be awarded the Grand Prix de la littérature policière (for a novel known variously as *For Love of Imabelle, A Rage in Harlem, The Five-Cornered Square* and, in French, *La Reine des Pommes*). Himes went on to write eight more thrillers, none of which enjoyed much success, at least until recently, in his own country. Although he lived in France for many years, arriving in 1953, Himes never used it as a backdrop for his longer fiction. There is a tantalizing sketch in the *Collected,* set in the Latin Quarter in Paris, but for full-

length thrills Himes always moved his imagination back to Harlem.

Virtually all Himes's writing, especially the early and late work, is characterized by brutality, anger and self-hatred. But the honesty with which he confronts this personal turbulence makes him, at times, an engaging writer. It grew out of what Himes called a "life of absurdity" (though it was not absurdity in the sense that Camus or Beckett would have recognized). "Given my disposition", he wrote in the second volume of his autobiography—which he actually called *My Life of Absurdity*—"my sensitivity toward race, along with my appetites and physical reactions and sex stimulations, my normal life was absurd." In describing his own reactions—typically to someone whom he suspects of having put him down for being black—Himes uses phrases such as "My head was throbbing like a mashed thumb ..."; or "I'd feel my brain lurch". When a friend wrote to him from home about "the most popular of the colored writers", Himes noted his response to this simple information as "What motherfucking color are writers supposed to be?" His two volume autobiography (the first instalment is *The Quality of Hurt*) is at times a catalogue of misogyny, grievance and self-aggrandizement

> Her eyes filled with conflicting emotions as she watched me go. Black pimps had taken thousands of white girls like her from the coal-mine towns of West Virginia and the little steel-mill towns of Ohio and put them to work as prostitutes in the ghettos. They liked it; they made the best whores.

Plan B has many similar passages (the introduction calls them "titillating"). The novel describes a plot by one Tomsson Black to instigate racial turmoil in America by supplying arms to blacks. Characters pop up and then disappear; plot-lines are left undeveloped; historical sketches are interleaved with contemporary events to no great effect. Even the two detectives who served Himes faithfully throughout his *Série Noire* productions, Coffin Ed Johnson and Grave Digger Jones, are sacrificed by their creator: Coffin Ed is shot by his partner, who in turn is killed by Tomsson Black.

By contrast, the very first (though not quite the earliest) story in the *Collected Stories* shows what a subtle writer Himes could be. In **"Headwaiter"**, written in prison in 1937, Dick Small performs his nightly duties in the dining-room of the Park Manor Hotel with relentless courtesy and unstoppable efficiency. With the skill of a safecracker, Himes unpicks the headwaiter's mask—applied through years of fixed smiles—to reveal not bitterness, just the desire not to emulate the cruelty of some of his customers, and the need to maintain a balancing act between genuine humanity and the humility expected of him. More than a mask, humbleness has become the man. On hearing of the death of an elderly regular,

Dick went rigid. The brown of his face tinged ashily. Then he noticed that Mrs Miller's eyes were red and swollen from crying and he upbraided himself for not having noticed immediately.

He could find no suitable words for the moment. He pitied her in a sincere, personal way, for he knew that the countess was the one person in all the world whom she considered as a friend. But he could not express his pity. He was only a head waiter.

There are many other good stories in this edition, which lacks only an editor to provide something more than the rudimentary bibliographical information given here, and to arrange the material in a way that would show the writer in the act of discovering his voice and range of techniques. By 1970, Himes's fiction-writing was tailing off, and **Plan B** seems to have been the outcome of a burst of racial fury around that date; "the most violent story I have ever attempted", he called it, suggesting that craft—together with the irony and wit and tenderness which informs Himes's best work—was not enough to give shaping sense to a life of absurdity.

Wendy W. Walters (essay date Winter 1994)

SOURCE: "Limited Options: Strategic Maneuverings in Himes's Harlem," *African American Review,* Vol. 28, No. 4, Winter, 1994, pp. 615-31.

[*In the following essay, Walters traces Himes's representation of "the absurdity of U.S. race relations" in his fiction.*]

Chester Himes, an American author who in his lifetime never found a "place" in the American literary scene, set his novels written during French expatriation in the nostalgic milieu of a Harlem he half-created in his imagination. In fiction he was able to exercise a control over U.S. racial politics which he (like most people) could never exercise in life. Himes explained the pleasure of his nostalgic literary act to John A. Williams:

> I was very happy writing these detective stories, especially the first one, when I began it. I wrote those stories with more pleasure than I wrote any of the other stories. And then when I got to the end and started my detectives shooting at some white people, I was the happiest.

Himes's detective novels allow him to control the site of nostalgia, briefly to imagine refashioning U.S. race relations and law enforcement practices. His own experiences as a black

convict in Ohio State Prison inform his authorial imagination in these novels. An emphasis present in the detective fiction, and Himes's other writings as well, is the necessity of physical safety for African Americans. Himes's two detectives, Coffin Ed Johnson and Grave Digger Jones, emerge as "the cops who should have been," the cops who could offer protection to the African American urban community. By analyzing two of Himes's detective novels, published in 1959 and 1969, we can chart the progress of these proposed heroes. In 1959 in *The Real Cool Killers* Himes constructs Coffin Ed and Grave Digger as viable folk heroes for the urban community. But by **Blind Man with a Pistol** their effectiveness as heroes is undercut by the altered socio-political landscape of U.S. race relations.

Himes's second detective novel, *The Real Cool Killers,* opens with the blues lines "I'm gwine down to de river, / Set down on de ground. / If de blues overtake me, / I'll jump overboard and drown." As a vernacular inscription, this epigram is well-suited to the themes of Himes's novel, which can be read as the ghetto's answer to white power. But the words of the blues lines imply a different and more pessimistic response to life in a racist society than the response suggested by the novel. My contention is that the characters in *The Real Cool Killers* employ specifically community-based, folk-heroic strategies of self-defense and solidarity in the face of intrusive, dominating power structures embodied by white cops. In all of his detective novels, Himes sets up Harlem as particularly unreadable and mystifying, not only to white "visitors" and cops, but also to his two heroes, Coffin Ed and Grave Digger, and even local inhabitants. What varies is the degree to which Harlem mystifies the various characters, and it is the community insiders' special skill both in reading Harlem *and* in manipulating its unreadability which allows for their self-protecting solidarity. Most governmental systems of ordering and labeling urban reality are not applicable in Himes's Harlem. When Grave Digger questions a suspect to find out an address, the evasive response he gets is, "'You don't never think 'bout where a gal lives in Harlem, 'les you goin' home with her. What do anybody's address mean up here?'" The breakdown of the ability to rely on official locating practices functions in several ways in the novel. First, it completely baffles the white cops (especially chiefs and lieutenants) and renders them ineffectual. It allows Himes to project Coffin Ed and Grave Digger as powerful inside readers of an otherwise inscrutable milieu. And it enables the residents of Harlem to manipulate the particular codes which confound white cops, in the interest of self-protection. In *The Real Cool Killers* the white cops continually express their frustration in being unable to pin down a systematic way to decipher their surroundings. Their inability to make sense of their environment is directly linked to their preconceived racist stereotypes, as is seen in the exasperated statement of one white cop to another: "'What's a name to these coons? They're always changing about.'"

The context which makes strategies of manipulation both necessary and successful is the historical presence of white law enforcement in black urban communities and the way this white presence has been seen by the residents of these communities. John W. Roberts explains that "the tremendous amount of power vested in white law enforcement officers in the late nineteenth century caused many African Americans to view them as the embodiment of the 'law' and, by extension, white power." Because these law officers were not community insiders, and only entered black neighborhoods for work, their knowledge of the territory was limited, and African Americans soon developed strategies for exploiting this white ignorance, ways of manipulating codes.

These strategies of evasion should be seen as subversive power exercised by the black Harlem residents of Himes's novels, in their manipulation of codes. This relative power is based in the underclass's superior knowledge of the minds of their oppressors. It should be readily apparent that this knowledge, coupled with behavior subversive of dominant power, calls to mind the qualities of the trickster hero of black folklore. Roberts explains that the trickster has the ability to step adeptly "inside his dupe's sense of reality and manipulate it through wit, guile, and deception to secure material rewards." It is possible in a more current context to replace *material rewards* with *personal safety*. In the context of the black ghetto, safety from abusive white law enforcement becomes a most valued commodity. Sheikh, the leader of the teenage gang The Real Cool Moslems, becomes the trickster turned badman, outlaw hero. Sheikh's skill in reading white stereotypical assumptions about black behavior enables him to baffle the cops. When his gang members question the believability of the behavioral disguise Sheikh tells them to adopt, he answers,

> "Hell, these is white cops. They believe spooks are crazy anyway. You and Sonny just act kind of simpleminded. They gonna swallow it like it's chocolate ice cream. They ain't going to do nothing but kick you in the ass and laugh like hell about how crazy spooks are. They gonna go home and tell their old ladies and everybody they see about two simpleminded spooks up on the roof teaching pigeons how to fly at night all during the biggest dragnet they ever had in Harlem. You see if they don't."

Sheikh banks on white inability to understand black behavior in addition to white racist assumptions about black intelligence. In this analysis he shows himself to be the more skilled reader of minds. In fact the cops who do confront the gang members on the roof are immediately unable to decipher even the physical scene, see only blackness and two

"tarbabies," and the sergeant even reads the scene as a "voodoo" rite in a way that specifically emphasizes an intensely mystified othering of the African American subject. It is probably not irrelevant, however, that voodoo has been seen historically by the white community not only as mystifying or inexplicable but, by extension, *powerful*. Roberts adds conjure to the trickster repertoire of means of deceiving and fooling those in power. The subversive power of this behavior can be seen in the white cops' baffled reaction and (correct) fear that they're being duped:

> "Do you think all these colored people in this neighborhood know who Pickens and the Moslems are?"

> "Sure they know. Every last one of them. Unless some other colored person turns Pickens in he'll never be found. They're laughing at us."

Recalling the novel's epigram, the blues emerge again in an analogue with roots in folk sayings: "Got one mind for the white folks see, another mind I know is me."

If Sheikh and his quasi-criminal teenage gang of Real Cool Moslems are the trickster heroes of the novel's milieu, what role is played by Coffin Ed and Grave Digger, the two black police detectives on the Harlem beat? Indeed their position as black enforcers of white police domination has caused them to be misread as excessively violent towards "their own people" and in many ways more unapologetically complicit with the white power structure than I see them as being.

I would contest a common, and reductive, view of Grave Digger and Coffin Ed as expressed by Jay R. Berry in "Chester Himes and the Hard-Boiled Tradition": "Their cultural antecedents give them the moral authority that they exercise—from folk culture they are the 'bad niggers' in the tradition of Stackalee." Central to any consideration of whether this is an accurate description of Coffin Ed and Grave Digger would be a study of the particular socio-cultural bases of the uses of the term *bad nigger*. Robert's chapter "The Badman as Outlaw Hero" is a thorough, Afrocentric revision of previous folklore scholarship on black heroic figures, and Roberts criticizes the faulty equation made by many scholars between *bad nigger* and *badman*. During slavery, "bad niggers," originally a label given by whites, "sought through open defiance, violence, and confrontation to improve their lot in slavery regardless of the consequences of their actions for the own or the slave community's welfare." The "bad nigger" does *not* have moral authority either from the black community or the white power structure; he is viewed by both as dangerous. Roberts explains the Afrocentric view of the "bad nigger": "To African Americans, individuals who acted as 'bad niggers' in their communities were not heroes, but rather individuals whose characteristic behavior threatened their abilities to maintain the value that they placed on harmony and solidarity as a form of protection against the power of the law." Coffin Ed and Grave Digger clearly do not fit this characterization, both because they care not for personal acquisitiveness and because their ultimate motivating force is based in community self-protection from an invading, threatening outside force—namely, white law enforcement. Contrary to the "bad nigger" stereotype, Coffin Ed and Grave Digger see the values of the black community as binding. In fact, Stackolee is a *badman,* celebrated by African American folk heroic balladry, not a *bad nigger,* which Roberts points out was *not* the focus for heroic folktales. Roberts explains that the badmen celebrated by balladry were outlaw folk heroes "whose characteristic behaviors were perceived as justifiable retaliatory actions" against the white power structure. While Coffin Ed and Grave Digger possess some similarities to badmen heroes of legend, they are ultimately a different modern figuration of heroism in Himes's conceptualization of their role in *The Real Cool Killers.*

Grave Digger and Coffin Ed possess some badmen-like qualities, such as their often violent and unpredictable behavior. Their guns, like those of many badmen heroes, are extremely formidable symbolic images and very real instruments of destruction known by the whole community. At least one scene in each of Himes's detective novels introduces these guns. Here is a representative example from *The Real Cool Killers:*

> Coffin Ed drew his pistol from its shoulder sling and spun the cylinder. Passing street light glinted from the long nickel-plated barrel of the special .38 revolver, and the five brass-jacketed bullets looked deadly in the six chambers.

Here the gun literally reflects the street, the life of the ghetto, and the gun's image repeats its power in the ghetto imagination when Choo-Choo, one of Sheikh's gang members, fantasizes, "'What I'd rather have me is one of those hard-shooting long-barreled thirty-eights like Grave Digger and Coffin Ed have got. Them heaters can kill a rock.'" Choo-Choo's hyperbolic description of the guns' power is tied to similarly legend-infused tales of Coffin Ed's and Grave Digger's own power, based on their quickness to use these infamous weapons. But Coffin Ed and Grave Digger play a very complex and multi-layered role in their negotiation of the city's white power structure and their relationship to the black community, and there is less ambivalence in their behavior than there is conscious manipulation and folk heroic maneuvering in a very tight space of operation. Traditional badmen are outlaws, and Coffin Ed and Grave Digger operate within the law and attempt to control outlaws. Thus, they cannot correctly be seen only as badmen heroes.

It is necessary to acknowledge their brutality, but not with-

out also seeing it as a "natural" part of the general, cartoon-like excessive violence of Himes's detective fiction as a whole. For Coffin Ed and Grave Digger, violence, or its threat (which is effective due to community knowledge of the pair's capacity to do actual violence), is what enables them to get informants to talk. As cops, Coffin Ed and Grave Digger have official *sanction* from the white police department to be excessively brutal. This caveat removes the traditional prohibition against police brutality, which in many cases is only nominal anyway. But this particular nod from their white superiors functions differently for the white cops than it does for Coffin Ed and Grave Digger. For as the chief says to Grave Digger, "'You know Harlem, you know where you have to go, who to see. . . . I don't give a goddamn how many heads you crack; I'll back you up.'" Thus, their license for brutality is based on the police department's utter reliance on them as skilled readers of Harlem's behavioral and linguistic codes.

This reliance is very much like that placed on black slave drivers during slavery. Roberts tells us that, "in the black slave driver, the masters, *from their point of view,* had an individual who could be held responsible when enslaved Africans violated the rules of the system and whose loyalty could be counted on" (italics added). While this is what plantation owners (and the white police force) *think* they are getting in a black slave driver, the actual allegiance of the black cops is elsewhere. Hence, during slavery a body of folklore emerged celebrating the driver as trickster hero, portraying "John as a talented and skillful exploiter of his exploitation by Old Master, his dupe or foil in most of the tales." The split between white perceptions of black behavior and black loyalty and the realities of that behavior and loyalty is central to an understanding of the ways that Coffin Ed and Grave Digger function as *protectors* within their community. I draw these parallels to folk culture both to locate Coffin Ed and Grave Digger within this tradition of African American folk-heroic creation, and to mark out their differences from existing or previous heroes. I see them as neither the *bad niggers* nor the *badmen* of folklore, but instead embodiments of a complex yet idealistic image of protection in the ghetto.

The Real Cool Killers opens with the murder of a white man, a "visitor" to Harlem. This fact brings the white cops to Harlem in full racist force: "'Rope off this whole goddamned area,' the sergeant said. 'Don't let anybody out. We want a Harlem-dressed Zulu. Killed a white man. . . . Pick up all suspicious persons.'" When white power in the form of armed white police officers invades the ghetto, every black person becomes a potential suspect, a potential scapegoat. And because the crime is the murder of a white man, every black person becomes a potential victim of lynching by the white mob. Himes specifically suggests this potential, again in his return to the blues, when he describes the white cops' intrusive presence swarming over the neighborhood:

[The white chief of police] turned and pointed toward a tenement building across the street. It looked indescribably ugly in the glare of a dozen powerful spotlights. Uniformed police stood on the roof, others were coming and going through the entrance; still others stuck their heads out of front windows to shout to other cops in the street. The other front windows were jammed with colored faces, looking like clusters of strange purple fruit in the stark white light.

It is essential here to relate Himes's imagery of "colored faces" to its vernacular and literary black antecedents, specifically Billie Holiday and Jean Toomer, in contrast to previous critical interpretations which have aligned Himes's imagery with European painters and writers. When we look to Jean Toomer's "Song of the Son" as a precursor for Himes's language we open up Himes's writing to the powerful allusions to slavery which enrich his meaning. The last two stanzas of Toomer's poem from *Cane* read:

> O Negro slaves, dark purple ripened plums
> Squeezed, and bursting in the pinewood air,
> Passing, before they stripped the old tree bare
> One plum was saved for me, one seed becomes
>
> An everlasting song, a singing tree,
> Caroling softly souls of slavery,
> What they were, and what they are to me,
> Caroling softly souls of slavery.

The words of Toomer's poem—"squeezed, and bursting"—suggest the violence of slavery, the pressure of exploitation; and these images resonate with the condition of impoverished blacks in modern U.S. urban ghettos.

Billie Holiday's famous blues song "Strange Fruit" articulates the image of lynching even more overtly, in a way that is crucial to Himes's own description of the relationship of white law enforcement to the black community. Her musical version of a poem by Lewis Allan, recorded 20 April 1939, has potent resonance in black culture:

> Southern trees bear a strange fruit:
> Blood on the leaves, and blood at the root.
> Black bodies swinging in the Southern breeze;
> Strange fruit hanging from the poplar trees.
> Pastoral scene of the gallant South:
> The bulging eyes and the twisted mouth.
> Scent of magnolia, sweet and fresh;
> Then the sudden smell of burning flesh.
> Here is a fruit for the crows to pluck;
> For the rain to gather, for the wind to suck;
> For the sun to rot, for the tree to drop.
> Here is a strange and bitter crop.

When seen in the context of politicized African American poetic antecedents, Himes's linguistic imagery is allowed to signify upon this verbal tradition. Singing to an urban New York audience at Cafe Society in Greenwich Village in 1939 Billie Holiday contextualizes Southern racism and oppression for the Northern audience as relevant to them. Himes uses the same metaphors for lynching as the pine-scented, squeezed-plum imagery of "Song of the Son," but substitutes for the pastoral vision of "Strange Fruit" the modern, signally urban, decaying tenement flooded with police spotlights and surrounded by uniformed white cops—perhaps urban equivalents of hooded Southern embodiments of white power. Allowing Himes's voice to resonate among Holiday's and Toomer's historicizes a critique of Southern racism by bringing it to a Northern urban context and showing the way that lynch mob "law enforcement" is replicated in the modern ghetto when a white is presumed murdered by a black.

True to the lynch mob mentality, the white cops are looking for *any* "Harlem-dressed Zulu" who can "hang" for the crime. But no criminal appears apprehendable, and the police chief is in danger of losing face before the white press. The master has been duped; he's caught unable to read the signs, solve the mystery, and appease the mob with a lynching. So he must get his hands on a black body quickly. Sonny Pickens becomes the scapegoat for the chief, who says, "'We haven't got anybody to work on but him and it's just his black ass.'" Obviously here Pickens's black ass is much less valuable in the cops' mentality than the white ass of Galen, the murdered man. And this essential unequivalence cannot be balanced. In the racial economy of 1959 one dead black ass does not equal one dead white ass—an unequal economy of bodies that becomes the central issue of Himes's detective fiction.

The Harlem milieu in which Coffin Ed and Grave Digger operate as detectives is one marked by the proliferation of (what they consider) *minor* vices like prostitution, the numbers racket, other forms of gambling, and small-scale robbery. For the most part Coffin Ed and Grave Digger allow these activities to flourish, and even develop a somewhat symbiotic relationship with their participants, who become key informers for them, people who will talk because they desire to continue operating without hassles from the law. In this way Harlem's underworld becomes part of the inner network which enables Ed's and Digger's investigative work. Historically, as institutionalized economic oppression became a more dominant factor of impoverished black urban life, such illegal activities were often a necessary part of the system by which the ghetto could continue to exist (in both the positive and the negative senses implied by such an existence). Roberts explains that

> . . . the relative absence of the [white] "law" in
> black neighborhoods allowed for the creation of a

socio-cultural environment in which certain types of illegal activities involved relatively little risk to personal well-being from the "law" while enhancing the potential for extraordinary economic gain at its expense. In addition the pervasiveness of destructive material and physical conditions in the black community attributed to the power of the "law" over the lives of African Americans created an atmosphere in which social restraints against certain types of actions which violated the law were greatly diminished.

But Roberts also importantly acknowledges that such behaviors were only accepted until they "threatened the solidarity and harmony of communal life in ways that created the *potential of external intervention*" (italics added). The danger of external intervention is the propelling force behind Coffin Ed's and Grave Digger's protective strategies.

The two detectives' roles are made complex when white people come to Harlem to support its vices, buy its citizens' bodies. When some white people in a Harlem bar question Grave Digger's "tough" police language, his response is, "I'm just a cop, if you white people insist on coming up to Harlem where you force colored people to live in vice-and-crime ridden slums, it's my job to see that you are safe.'" Digger's comment here is essential in several ways, the most obvious of which being that it names the invidious complicity of white socio-economic oppression and white participation in exploitative vice. Additionally, his comment, and others like it throughout the detective novels, implies that his job is to protect *white people.* But Digger and Ed are much more skillful readers of the particular politics of violence and law enforcement in the black ghetto, and their ultimate aim is the protection of *black people,* and especially black community security. In fact, their success in meeting this goal can be measured in part by the fact that their deeper motives are not recognized by the police force. They know that the best way to ensure the security of black bodies is by keeping the lynch mobs at bay, a goal they seek to accomplish by what may seem like a circuitous means—protecting the singular white body in Harlem. As we have seen, *one* white death in Harlem brings the cops *en masse* to the area, with unquenchable lynching fervor; one white stiff ends up equaling four black corpses and one maimed black body.

If Coffin Ed and Grave Digger use violence in their questioning procedures, their goal is to solve crimes so that white cops stay out. The complexity of Coffin Ed and Grave Digger as heroes rests in this double-edged quality of their behavior: Their violence is both directed at members of their community and used as a force to prevent the more uncontrollable violence of lynch mobs. John Cawelti, writing on "hard-boiled" detective fiction, considers that "the action of legitimized violence . . . resolves tensions between the an-

archy of individualistic impulses and the communal ideas of law and order by making the individual's violent action an ultimate defense of the community against the threat of anarchy." In their protection of the community against the anarchic forces of white law enforcement, Coffin Ed and Grave Digger are complex black heroic figures. Possessing some of the traits of the trickster, badman, and slave driver, they stand apart from all these.

> **In their protection of the community against the anarchic forces of white law enforcement, Coffin Ed and Grave Digger are complex black heroic figures. Possessing some of the traits of the trickster, badman, and slave driver, they stand apart. . . .**
> —*Wendy W. Walters*

Asked in a 1970 interview in *Le Monde* by Michel Fabre whether his black detectives are traitors to their race, Himes brought out an important issue which has special bearing on *The Real Cool Killers:*

> Cerceuil et Fossoyeur seraient des traîtres à leur race s'ils étaient les personnages réalistes. Ce qui n'est pas le cas: ils représentent le type de policier qui *devrait* exister, celui qui vit dans la communauté, la connait bien et fait respecter la loi de façon humaine. Je crois en eux. Je les ai créés: deux personnages qui seraient les ennemis des Noirs dans la réalité, mais que j'ai voulu sympathique.

> (Coffin Ed and Grave Digger would be traitors to their race if they were realistic characters. This is not the case: They represent the type of cop who *should* exist, who lives in the community, knows it well, and enforces respect for the law in a humane way. I believe in them. I created them: two people who would be enemies of Blacks in reality, but whom I intended to be sympathetic.)

Himes's statement is confusing in that it champions yet denies realism. When Fabre asks whether Coffin Ed and Grave Digger are traitors, he is speaking of their characters, not "real" black cops in general. Yet Himes does not respond *directly* to this question to discuss his *portrayal* of the cops, but instead hypothesizes that "real" black cops would be traitors. I take Himes to mean that Coffin Ed and Grave Digger are ideal types, that "real" cops who are black are necessarily traitors to their race, but that these two are sympathetic, that their allegiance is above all to their community.

In his 1963 article written for *Présence Africaine* entitled **"Harlem ou le cancer de l'Amérique,"** Himes identifies the social milieu which grounds the necessity for heroes like Coffin Ed and Grave Digger. He outlines the series of American race riots in ghettos around the country, especially Harlem and Detroit. The result of a Detroit riot in which many blacks are killed by white police is that, "en consequence, Harlem fut submergée de policiers blancs qui portaient de lourdes matraques et patrouillaient dans les rues à cheval ou à motocyclette. Les incidents succédèrent aux incidents." ("Consequently, Harlem was flooded with white policemen who carried heavy bludgeons and patrolled the streets on horseback or motorcycles. There was one incident after another.") Coffin Ed and Grave Digger, then, are created in the hope of preventing this abusive presence from invading black neighborhoods. They can be seen as artful strategizers of legal politics whose perhaps imperfect methodology of protecting one white body (their overt, white-perceived purpose) has as its goal the effective prevention of a general lynching of black bodies. While such a goal was possible to *articulate* in the U.S. racial environment of 1959, it was not possible to *realize*. Coffin Ed and Grave Digger cannot fully prevent the lynching, and innocent black citizens are killed. Ten years later, with the publication of **Blind Man With a Pistol,** Coffin Ed's and Grave Digger's strategic methodology is much less plausible even to articulate and becomes, in fact, absurd.

> A friend of mine, Phil Lomax, told me this story about a blind man with a pistol shooting at a man who had slapped him on a subway train and killing an innocent bystander peacefully reading his newspaper across the aisle and I thought, damn right, sounds just like today's news, riots in the ghettos, war in Vietnam, masochistic doings in the Middle East. And then I thought of some of our loudmouthed leaders urging our vulnerable soul brothers on to getting themselves killed, and thought further that all unorganized violence is like a blind man with a pistol.

In the ten-year span between the publication of **The Real Cool Killers** and **Blind Man With a Pistol** race relations in the U.S. had become even more volatile as white power cemented itself further. The assassinations of Martin Luther King, Jr., and Malcolm X had violently demonstrated U.S. institutional response to powerful black heroes. In his chapter "Sixties' Social Movements, the Literary Establishment, and the Production of the Afro-American Text," W. Lawrence Hogue explains that the increasing economic disparity between blacks and whites led to riots and rebellions across the nation, and the civil rights and black power struggles which "continued to undermine and bring into question the authority and legitimacy of the dominant ideological apparatus." Coffin Ed and Grave Digger, by virtue (or fault) of

their connection to this apparatus, would also meet with challenges to their previously unquestioned authority. The nationalist impulse in the black community in the 1960s saw white power as centralized and therefore fightable. Thus, in any conceptualization of two distinct sides, Coffin Ed and Grave Digger were now seen as on the wrong one.

As his preface shows, during his expatriation in Europe, Himes remained closely aware of both internal and international U.S. politics and ideology. Given the social circumstances outlined by Hogue, the creation and function of Coffin Ed and Grave Digger as ideal heroic solutions and community protectors become entirely implausible for Himes. White power and white law enforcement domination is so entrenched, and its control over the ghetto so pervasive, that the smaller scale heroism of a Coffin Ed or Grave Digger becomes ineffectual. **Blind Man,** as Himes's last completed detective novel set in Harlem, charts this landscape and demonstrates this collapse. The removal of a protective capacity in turn leads to widespread random violence throughout Harlem, a situation which allows Himes to bring forth his long-held criticisms of unorganized violence.

While **Blind Man** is less a detective story than any of Himes's previous detective fiction, there is the premise of a mystery within the novel. Like **The Real Cool Killers,** it involves a white man who lives outside Harlem, comes there to buy a black body for sex, and ends up dead on the street. As **Blind Man** progresses it becomes obvious that, if Ed's and Digger's former heroic strategies were ever viable ones, they can no longer succeed, for in 1969 the urban scene is very different from that in 1959. The corruption of the police force, previously alluded to, now works to circumscribe Ed's and Digger's behavior. Predictably, the dead white man on the street brings on the white cops in full force, and Grave Digger and Coffin Ed try futilely to protect the citizens from the ensuing lynch mob. At the scene of the crime Grave Digger says to Coffin Ed,

> "I just wish these mother-rapers wouldn't come up here and get themselves killed, for whatever reason."
>
> . . . Coffin Ed turned on [the crowd of black onlookers] and shouted suddenly, "You people better get the hell away from here before the white cops come in, or they'll run all your asses in."
>
> There was a sound of nervous movement, like frightened cattle in the dark, then a voice said belligerently, "Run whose ass in? I lives here!"
>
> "All right," Coffin Ed said resignedly. "Don't say I didn't warn you."

While Coffin Ed and Grave Digger are still following their earlier strategy of protecting Harlem citizens from the anarchic wrath of white law enforcement, the scene has changed. The unidentified belligerent voice who contests Coffin Ed's demands and who asserts his rights as a resident is the voice of a new generation which does not automatically respect either Ed's and Digger's authority or the intimidating practices of the white cops. Ed's answer back to the voice is "resigned," a new way to describe Ed's and Digger's behavior in a crowd.

The breakdown of Ed's and Digger's uncontestable heroic authority originates from two different directions. Primarily, their behavior is curtailed by the white cops who run the force. But also, this new, more militant generation of Harlem citizens has no respect for "the law" in any form. Confronting some young kids threatening another kid with violence because he is too chicken to stone the white cops, Coffin Ed and Grave Digger are neither automatically recognized nor feared. One kid challenges the once formidably terrifying Coffin Ed:

> "You scared of whitey. You ain't nothing but shit."

> "When I was your age I'da got slapped in the mouth for telling a grown man that."

> "You slap us, we waste you." . . .

> "We're the law," Coffin Ed said to forestall any more argument. Six pairs of round white-rimmed eyes stared at them *accusingly.*

> "Then you on whitey's side." . . .

> "Go on home," Grave Digger said, pushing them away, ignoring flashing knife blades. "Go home and grow up. You'll find out there ain't any other side." (italics added)

Here Coffin Ed and Grave Digger express their recognition of the pervasiveness of white power. Whitey's side is the ruling paradigm, and they do not see the nationalist moment as viable, the opponent as fightable. The younger generation of Harlem citizens, however, represents a popularized version of nationalism, which Himes's novel will ultimately critique. They at this point possess the impulse of anger toward white power, the refusal to tolerate further oppression, but they lack the organization of purpose which Himes sees as essential to revolutionary efficacy.

Himes now depicts his former heroes as laughable. Throughout the novel they are frequently described in clown-like imagery: "They looked like two idiots standing in the glare of the blazing car, one in his coat, shirt and tie, and purple shorts above gartered sox and big feet, and the other in shirtsleeves and empty shoulder holster with his pistol stuck in his belt." Their former possibly heroic stance, Himes's ideal creation of the cops who "*devrait* exister," is no longer even a viable part of the cultural imagination. Their role has been fully obviated.

Harlem, however, is still a mystified space of illogic to the white cops and to outsiders. The confused anger on the part of whites who can't understand black Harlem linguistic play ends up leading to violence in more than one scene in the novel. Toward the absurdly random end of the novel, a misunderstanding between subway riders is exacerbated by this phenomenon: "The big white man thought they were talking about him in a secret language known only to soul people. He reddened with rage." Because the white cops also fear this "secret language" they still rely on Coffin Ed's and Grave Digger's interpretive police skills, however cursory this reliance may be.

In one scene the white cops who have basically taken charge of the investigation of the white man's murder are accompanied by Ed and Digger, following the blood trail to a tenement's basement room:

> The blood trail ended at the green door.

> "Come out of there," the sergeant said.

> No one answered.

> He turned the knob and pushed the door and it opened inward so silently and easily he almost fell into the opening before he could train his light. Inside was a black dark void.

> Grave Digger and Coffin Ed flattened themselves against the walls on each side of the alley and their big long-barreled .38 revolvers came glinting into their hands.

> "What the hell!" the sergeant exclaimed, startled.

> His assistants ducked.

> "This is Harlem," Coffin Ed grated and Grave Digger elaborated:

> "We don't trust doors that open."

Here Ed and Digger are their old selves, acting in tandem, keenly reading the visual clues of the environment they know by heart. But despite their obviously superior knowledge they are not allowed to act alone, they are not allowed to *investigate.* Coffin Ed's and Grave Digger's skills in interpreting the Harlem environment lead them too close to un-covering embarrassing connections to Harlem's vice indus-try on the part of the white power structure and the deeper levels of corruption and complicity within the police force. Therefore Captain Brice and Lieutenant Anderson curtail their activity.

As Brice tells them to leave the investigation to the D.A.'s homicide bureau he asks,

> "What do you think you two precinct detectives can uncover that they can't?"

> "That very reason. It's our precinct. We might learn something that wouldn't mean a damn thing to them."

This fact, Ed's and Digger's heightened ability to decode their environment, is what makes them successful investi-gators and therefore what now makes them threatening to the white police force with something to hide. Ed and Dig-ger, over a twelve-year development as characters, have lost any earlier optimistic idealism:

> The two black detectives looked at one another. Their short-cropped hair was salted with gray and they were thicker around their middles. Their faces bore the lumps and scars they had collected in the enforcement of law in Harlem. Now after twelve years as first-grade precinct detectives they hadn't been promoted. Their raises in salaries hadn't kept up with the rise of the cost of living. They hadn't finished paying for their houses. Their private cars had been bought on credit. And yet they hadn't taken a dime in bribes. Their entire careers as cops had been one long period of turmoil. When they weren't taking lumps from the thugs, they were tak-ing lumps from the commissioners. Now they were curtailed in their own duties. And they didn't ex-pect it to change.

Thus, while Coffin Ed and Grave Digger may have begun the series with the heroic potential of ideal figures, the fur-ther institutionalization of discrimination throughout U.S. society has rendered them ineffectual. Not only has white power cemented its position, but it also acts to prevent any public discovery of its complicitous actions.

Coffin Ed's and Grave Digger's previously folk-heroic strat-egies for maintaining community security have become ab-surd. Even as they attempt to pursue their original investigation of the white man's death, they are now aware of this absurdity and identify its racial basis. Astute readers of police force ideology, Ed and Digger clearly see, and state, the racial politics behind the restraint placed on them.

When Anderson denies them access to what they know is a key suspect, Grave Digger responds,

> "Listen, Lieutenant. This mother-raping white man gets himself killed on our beat chasing black sis-sies and you want us to whitewash the investiga-tion."

> Anderson's face got pink. "No, I don't want you to whitewash the investigation," he denied. "I just don't want you raking up manure for the stink."

> "We got you; white men don't stink."

Coffin Ed's and Grave Digger's initial strategies fail as their political consciousness rises. The more they know about the inner workings of the white-run police force, the more clearly they realize that the premise of their role as detectives or investigators is flawed and ineffectual at its base.

As increasingly politically conscious readers of their racist U.S. environment, Coffin Ed and Grave Digger are quite able to *name* the culprit. What they cannot do is apprehend "him." During the course of **Blind Man** Harlem has been the scene of several riots, and the white cops have given Grave Digger and Coffin Ed the task of finding out who is the cause of these seemingly inexplicable riots—a particu-larly conservative and palliative version of law enforcement so commonly practiced by the white cops. In a crucial con-frontation with Lieutenant Anderson toward the end of **Blind Man,** Ed and Digger point the blame at the unapprehendable criminal they have been chasing their whole careers. In this key scene they are so mentally attuned to one another they speak in a close call-and-response pattern that frustrates Anderson, who exclaims,

> "All right, all right! I take it you know who started the riot."

> "Some folks call him by one name, some another," Coffin Ed said.

> "Some call him lack of respect for law and order, some lack of opportunity, some the teachings of the Bible, some the sins of their fathers," Grave Dig-ger expounded. "Some call him ignorance, some poverty, some rebellion. Me and Ed look at him with compassion. We're victims."

> "Victims of what?" Anderson asked foolishly.

> "Victims of your skin," Coffin Ed shouted brutally, his own patchwork of grafted black skin twitching with passion.

Anderson's skin turned blood red.

Ed and Digger are quite clear here on the balance of law and order on their beat: While the rioters may be black citizens, the instigator, the criminal responsible, is the white racism which causes poverty, ignorance, the hypocrisy of religion, etc. Their own alignment is clearly, as it has ever been, on the side of the victims.

Himes's writing here is at its resonant best as he focuses on the twitching patchwork of Ed's grafted skin. As any reader of the detective novels knows, Ed's face was scarred early in the series by an acid-throwing hoodlum. It is thus a sort of narrative reflection of the violence borne by these two would-be protectors and defenders against white lynch mob law enforcement, as are the other scars and marks which attest to Ed's and Digger's life work. But the pastiche of skin on Ed's face can also be seen as an aspect of the arbitrariness and absurdity of race as a determining category, of blackness as a social construct. By calling attention to the "grafted on" nature of Ed's blackness, and juxtaposing it to Anderson's white, then red face, Himes implicitly questions the absoluteness of race as a category, especially as so obviously resorted to by the white police force. In his 1969 interview with John A. Williams Himes historicizes this discussion of the "cause" of U.S. race riots:

> . . . this whole problem in America, as I see it, developed from the fact that the slaves were freed and that there was no legislation of any sort to make it possible for them to live. . . . What is it that they have in heaven—milk and honey? That some poor nigger could go and live on nothing. Just to proclaim emancipation was not enough. You can't eat it; it doesn't keep the cold weather out.

Himes makes a similar statement in an italicized "Interlude" in *Blind Man,* where Grave Digger and Coffin Ed name Lincoln as the instigator of the riots: "'*He hadn't ought to have freed us if he didn't want to make provisions to feed us.*'" Here Ed and Digger clearly provide Anderson with the singular culprit so doggedly desired by the police force, but of course he cannot be apprehended, and further, if he were, he couldn't be convicted—because he's white. Says Coffin Ed, "'Never was a white man convicted as long as he plead good intentions.'"

Blind Man ends with less resolution than any of Himes's previous detective novels, a point noted by many critics as Himes's ultimate stretching of detective fiction's generic limits. A. Robert Lee writes, "*Blind Man With a Pistol,* especially, approaches antic nightmare, a pageant of violence and unresolved plot-ends which, true to the illogic of a dream, careens into a last chapter of senseless riot." Coffin Ed and Grave Digger are reduced to the inanity of shooting at rats fleeing a burning tenement. These are crucial aspects of Himes's own long-standing political philosophies about both "senseless riot" and the absurdity of racism. Himes would write in *The Crisis* as early as 1944,

> The first step backward is riots. Riots are not revolutions. . . . Riots are tumultuous disturbances of the public peace by unlawful assemblies of three or more persons in the execution of private objects— such as race hatreds. . . . Riots between white and black occur for only one reason: *Negro Americans are firmly convinced that they have no access to any physical protection which they do not provide for themselves.* It is a well-known and established fact that this conviction is rooted in history: *Negroes in fact do not have any protection from physical injury inflicted by whites other than that which they provide for themselves.* It is a rather deadly joke among Negroes (especially since the Detroit riots) that the first thing to do in case of a race riot is not to call the police but to shoot them. . . . "Man, what you mean call the police; them the people gonna kill you."

Fourteen years before the publication of *The Real Cool Killers* Himes stated the relationship of white law enforcement to the black community. It is important to see the discourse of *protection* running throughout Himes's writings, even at this early stage.

Himes, who throughout his life was against random violence (as opposed to planned revolution), critiques the chaotic, riotous violence which erupts in Harlem at the end of *Blind Man.* In his 1970 *Le Monde* interview with Michel Fabre, Himes explains the genesis of *Blind Man:*

> Il y a plusieurs années, de nombreuses émeutes ont éclaté en Amérique, suivies d'émeutes spontanées après l'assassinat de Martin Luther King et de batailles entre les Panthères noires et la police. J'ai pensé que toute cette violence inorganisée que les Noirs déchaînent en Amérique n'était rien d'autre que des coups de feu tirés à l'aveuglette, et j'ai intitulé mon roman *Blind Man with a Pistol.* Tel était mon commentaire sur l'inefficacité de ce type de violence.

> (Several years ago, numerous riots erupted in America followed by spontaneous riots after the assassination of Martin Luther King and battles between the Black Panthers and the police. I thought that all this unorganized violence that the Blacks unleashed in America was nothing other than shots fired blindly, and I titled my novel *Blind Man With*

a Pistol. Such was my commentary on the ineffi-
cacy of this type of violence.)

While Himes had since at least 1944 seen unorganized, riotous violence as ineffective, it is important to trace out his
"call" for successful planned revolution. Edward Margolies,
in his article "Experiences of the Black Expatriate Writer:
Chester Himes," quotes from the English transcript of
Himes's *Le Monde* interview:

> I realized that subconsciously that was the point I
> had been trying to make in [***Blind Man***]. . . . I think
> there should be violence . . . because I do not be-
> lieve that anything else is ever going to improve the
> situation of the black man in America except vio-
> lence. I don't think it would have to be great shat-
> tering and shocking violence. If the blacks were
> organized and if they could resist and fight injus-
> tice in an organized fashion in America, I think that
> might be enough. Yes, I believe this sincerely.

In his representation of chaos and the inefficacies of splin-
tered popular nationalisms at the novel's close, Himes maintains a consistency with his views about the need for a more
systematic form of revolution as a means of opposing white
power. This need for violent revolution is a common line of
thought in Himes's writings, not only occasioned by particular events of the Sixties, but present within his political ideology since (or before) his 1944 *Crisis* article **"Negro
Martyrs Are Needed."** The title of the article points us toward the role of a single martyr in the revolutionary cause,
and Himes's short story **"Prediction"**—as well as the
prefigurings of his final detective novel set in the U.S., ***Plan
B.***

It is possible to see Himes's philosophies about the need for
organized violence as in some ways an inverted economy
of bodies, bearing in mind his earlier idealized construction
of Coffin Ed and Grave Digger as protectors of one white
body in order ultimately to protect many black bodies. What
happens in the economy of **"Prediction"** and **"Negro Martyrs Are Needed"** is an ideologically revolutionary inversion: One black body is martyred in the interest of creating
more white corpses. In his 1944 article Himes states, "The
first and fundamental convictions of the political tactician
fighting for the human rights of the people are: (1) Progress
can be brought about only by revolution; (2) Revolutions can
be started only by incidents; (3) incidents can be created only
by Martyrs." Himes specifically counterposes this idea of a
planned incident by a martyr to what he sees as more random, spontaneous rioting, which he condemns as ineffectual
and based in self-interest, as opposed to race betterment.
Twenty-five years later he would tell John A. Williams,

> Even individually, if you give one black one high-

powered repeating rifle and he wanted to shoot it
into a mob of twenty thousand or more white
people, there are a number of people he could destroy. Now, in my book [the uncompleted ***Plan B***],
all of these blacks who shoot are destroyed. They
not only are destroyed, they're blown apart; even
the buildings they're shooting from are destroyed,
and quite often the white community suffers fifty
or more deaths itself by destroying one black man.

There is a distinct contrast, which we should not ignore, between Himes's comments to John A. Williams, fellow black
American writer, and Michel Fabre, white French literary
critic. Though both interviews were given at about the same
time, Himes's divergent expressions of revolutionary ideology reveal both ambiguities in his own thought as well as
alterations for his perceived audiences. To Fabre he states
(assures?) that "great shattering and shocking violence" is
not necessary. Blacks should just use violence "to resist and
fight injustice in an organized fashion." His words here seem
like platitudes, as he implies a specific and localized enemy
who could be systematically resisted. The author of ***Blind
Man,*** however, knows that there is no such singular enemy.
The act of shooting a repeating rifle into a crowd of twenty
thousand, as Himes describes to Williams, is fairly "shattering and shocking violence." And the portrayal of this act in
"Prediction" emphasizes the graphic nature of the violence.
While the philosophy of limited black deaths in order to produce larger numbers of white deaths seems a reversal of the
economy of bodies in the discourse of *protection* articulated
in the detective novels, the ideological basis understands
white behavioral motivation in the same way. The white reaction to black violence against whites is one that crushes
anything in its path. This is simply a more advanced stage
of the lynch mob reactiveness of law enforcement behavior
as seen throughout the detective novels. In Himes's 1969
short story, appropriately titled **"Prediction,"** this crushing
white reaction is disembodied in the form of a tank with a
brain.

The story, which would become chapter 21 of ***Plan B,*** opens
with an all-white police parade "headed north up the main
street of the big city." Instead of the precisely locatable,
named Harlem geography of the detective novels, the incidents of **"Prediction"** and ***Plan B*** could theoretically occur in any U.S. city. The story describes an all-white scene:
white cops, white crowds, white workers, etc. "There was
only one black man along the entire length of the street at
the time, and he wasn't in sight." This unnamed man, hidden in a church with an automatic rifle, is Himes's martyr
for the cause of black liberation: "Subjectively, he had waited
four hundred years for this moment and he was not in a
hurry." Just as Lincoln was the criminal responsible for the
riots in ***Blind Man,*** historical racial oppression since slavery
is clearly the instigator of the revolution which will follow

this triggering incident. The martyr knows, however, the nature of white reaction to his planned crime—he is aware of the lynch-like fervor to follow: "He knew his black people would suffer severely for this moment of his triumph. He was not an ignorant man." The man is "consoled only by the hope that it would make life *safer* for blacks in the future. He would have to believe that the children of the blacks who would suffer now would benefit later" (italics added). Note here the presence again of the discourse of safety and protection running throughout Himes's depictions of black life in the U.S. This language exists in dialogic relationship with the language of equality, with greater emphasis on safety as the most important condition of freedom for African Americans.

When the police parade reaches a key position on the street, the black gunman opens fire and begins mowing down rows of officers. Himes's depiction of this carnage shows his writing at its maximally grotesque:

> [The commissioner] wore no hat to catch his brains and fragments of skull, and they exploded through the sunny atmosphere and splattered the spectators with goo, tufts of gray hair and splinters of bone. One skull fragment, larger than the others, struck a tall, well-dressed man on the cheek, cutting the skin and splashing brains against his face like a custard pie in a Mack Sennett comedy.

Combined with the more obvious political reasons, this level of grotesque description of white deaths caused by blacks is something Himes knew the U.S. publishing establishment—and, by extension, reading public—would reject. Discussing *Plan B* with John A. Williams he says, "I don't know what the American publishers will do about this book. But one thing I do know, Johnny, they will hesitate, and it will cause them a great amount of revulsion."

The slaughter causes general pandemonium in the crowd, with police officers firing at each other, at civilians, etc., in their frustrated confusion and inability to find the sniper. The lynch mob mentality takes hold, and

> all were decided, police and spectators alike, that the sniper was a black man for no one else would slaughter whites so wantonly. . . . in view of the history of all the assassinations and mass murders in the U.S., it was extraordinarily enlightening that all the thousands of whites caught in a deadly gunfire from an unseen assassin, white police and white civilians alike, would automatically agree that he must be black.

In an apocalyptic climax, the lynch mob itself takes the form of a technologically developed war machine, a riot tank, endowed with a brain and an eye searching, at first futilely, for the hidden sniper:

> Its telescoped eye at the muzzle of the 20-mm. cannon stared right and left, looking over the heads and among the white spectators, over the living white policemen hopping about the dead, up and down the rich main street with its impressive stores, and in its frustration at not seeing a black face to shoot at it rained explosive 20-mm. shells on the black plaster of Paris mannequins displaying a line of beachwear in a department store window.

The lynch mob law enforcement behavior has here reached its apocalyptic level of absurdity, shooting at plaster images of black bodies when it cannot find a human black body. This destructive action in turn triggers further mass hysteria and killing of vast numbers of innocent bystanders, until finally the tank demolishes the church with the sniper inside.

Even this last act, however, is not conclusive for the white mob, since it does not produce the desired black *body:* "It did not take long for the cannon to reduce the stone face of the cathedral to a pile of rubbish. But it took all of the following day to unearth the twisted rifle and a few scraps of bloody black flesh to prove the black killer had existed." When whites are killed, only a black body will appease the lynching mob, and the capturing, dead or alive, whole or in pieces, of this body becomes the all-important aim. In the breakdown of criminal apprehendability which characterizes the cementing of white hegemonic power as represented in the socio-cultural milieu of *Blind Man,* blackness is made to function as redundancy in white power relations. It is as if, after Lincoln, after four hundred years of oppression, after the ghetto, white power is still, *redundantly,* emptying its bullets into an already beaten black "opponent."

For the martyr, because of the number of whites he has killed, the exchange of his body for their deaths seems fair:

> He was ready to die. By then he had killed seventy-three whites, forty-seven policemen and twenty-six men, women and children civilians, and had wounded an additional seventy-five, and although he was never to know this figure, he was satisfied. He felt like a gambler who had broken the bank.

Himes specifically envisions this kind of murderous gamble as the key move to trigger more widespread planned violence by blacks "which will mobilize the forces of justice and carry us forward from the pivot of change to a way of existence where everyone is free."

In 1972, Himes explained his long-held belief in the necessity of violence to Hoyt Fuller: "I have always believed—

and this was from the time that *If He Hollers* . . . was published—that the Black man in America should mount a serious revolution and this revolution should employ a massive, extreme violence." Again, notice that to a black interviewer, for a piece published in *Black World,* Himes calls for "massive, extreme violence." Himes's political philosophizing moves from an assertion of defensive violence to an aggressive violence, yet all within the construct of making the U.S. ultimately a *safer* place for blacks.

Himes's literary expression of black revolutionary ideologies should be seen within a tradition—his voice obviously is not the first, nor does it stand alone. Hoyt Fuller, in his *Black World* interview, calls Himes's attention to his literary company in Sam Greenlee's *The Spook Who Sat By the Door* and another novel whose author is unnamed, *Black Commandoes.* I would historicize this revolutionary discourse further and add Sutton Griggs's *Imperium in Imperio* to the list. Griggs's novel exists as an interesting precursor for *Plan B,* since it too involves two heroes, long-time companions who disagree over particular revolutionary ideologies, with death as the result. Coffin Ed and Grave Digger play a minor role in *Plan B.* Himes states," I began writing a book called *Plan B,* about a real black revolution in which my two black detectives split up and eventually Grave Digger kills Coffin Ed to save the cause." Grave Digger is then killed by Tomsson Black. Thus, in *Plan B* we see the final role and ultimate demise of Himes's two heroes.

> **For Himes . . . white law enforcement represents the greatest threat to personal safety for impoverished African American urban dwellers.**
> **—*Wendy W. Walters***

For Himes, then, white law enforcement represents the greatest threat to personal safety for impoverished African American urban dwellers. In an environment pervaded by racial oppression the first requirement of freedom is protection from lynch mobs, and the feeling that one's body is not endangered. But over the course of Himes's writing we see this first requirement become less and less attainable. We reach what Himes always considered the absurdity of U.S. race relations.

Steven J. Rosen (essay date Summer 1995)

SOURCE: "African American Anti-Semitism and Himes's *Lonely Crusade,* in *Melus,* Vol. 20, No. 2, Summer, 1995, pp. 47-68.

[In the following essay, Rosen discusses the presence of anti-Semitism in Himes's Lonely Crusade *and its sources and implications.]*

Most critics have considered Chester Himes's second novel about racial conflict at a Los Angeles war industry plant, *Lonely Crusade,* to be his most ambitious and substantial work. However, the novel has attracted little notice since its reissue (1986), having long been unavailable after its initial publication. Were it known as it deserves, *Lonely Crusade* would still stir controversy.

Himes maintained that the Communist party—excoriated in *Lonely Crusade*—had effectively suppressed it. However, as he also acknowledged, "Everyone hated it. . . . The left hated it, the right hated it, Jews hated it, blacks hated it." According to Himes, black reviewers (such as James Baldwin) had been offended by his hero's discovery that "the black man in America . . . needed special consideration because he was so far behind." As Himes insisted, this argument for what he provocatively called "special privileges" long preceded demands for "affirmative action." *Lonely Crusade* also anticipated the controversy, occasioned nearly twenty years later by the Moynihan Report (1965), about African American matriarchy. Additionally, Himes's hero, Lee Gordon, finds black workers resistant to integration and has to explain this to a baffled white liberal; such self-segregating tendencies (as in recent proposals for all-male African American high schools) still surprise liberals.

But perhaps the most controversial topic Himes pioneered in *Lonely Crusade* was black anti-Semitism. "The conflict between Blacks and Jews," as Addison Gayle asserted in his history of the African American novel, had been "previously ignored by other black writers." In light of more recent black-Jewish conflict, Himes's treatment has proven to be very prescient.

As Himes acknowledged, *Lonely Crusade* did offend Jews, such as the *Commentary* reviewer Milton Klonsky, discussed below. Is the novel anti-Semitic? I argue that it is, but the subject is highly complicated. Himes ventured to mediate between Jewish leftists and blacks whose hostilities to Jews he thought partly irrational and partly justified. In *Lonely Crusade,* the hero explains black anti-Semitism to a sympathetic Jew puzzled and troubled by its increase. Lee Gordon cites various black complaints against Jews, which no doubt were more widespread at that time than most black leaders or Jewish liberals cared to acknowledge. But Gordon dissociates himself from some of these charges, such as ignorant exaggeration of Jewish economic power. And Himes further distances himself from black anti-Semitism by noting, in his narrative voice, his hero Lee Gordon's irrational hostility to Jews. In a talk delivered at the University of Chicago one year after *Lonely Crusade*'s disappointing reception, Himes complained of having been "reviled" for his rare "integrity" in revealing such "realities" as "paradoxical anti-Semitism" among the effects of black oppression.

In my view, *Lonely Crusade* not only, as Himes claims, depicts and deplores black anti-Semitism, it also ventilates an anti-Semitic streak that recurs in Himes's work in tandem with anxiety to assert masculinity. Himes tended to disparage Jews in order to construct his manhood—differentiating himself from those (Jews) who imputedly lacked masculinity or disrespected its significations. To locate this and other anti-Semitic tendencies in Himes means neither that he was always unsympathetic to Jews, nor that his criticisms of Jews were wholly unjustified. In my opinion, two other Himes novels that deal with Jewish characters much more incidentally (*If He Hollers Let Him Go* and especially *The Primitive*) deftly criticize a Jewish ethnocentricity that for Himes, perhaps, epitomized racism's absurdity. Dreading to seem unfair to Himes, whose early novels remain unjustly unappreciated, I focus on *Lonely Crusade,* where his critique of Jews is both most fully and rather objectionably developed. Its anticipation of current black-Jewish hostilities, together with a misleading discussion of "the question of anti-Semitism" in the foreword to the novel's 1986 edition, make the subject irresistible.

Actually, the foreword, by Graham Hodges, minimizes both sides of the issue's embarrassment: (1) the novel's irreducibly unreasonable anti-Semitism and (2) the possible justification for some African American hostility to Jews. According to Hodges,

> the portraits Himes draws of Jewish paternalism and black anti-Semitism are unflinchingly honest. Most tellingly, it is Abe Rosenberg, Ruth, and Smitty, another union organizer, that are [the main character, the African American Lee] Gordon's only true allies. At one crucial point, Lee and Rosenberg, a highly sympathetic character, engage in a fierce debate over these historic racial tensions in American history, hurling insults and stereotypes at one another until finally, like exhausted fighters, they come to recognize their ignorance and hatred by confronting them in honest discussion. . . . We come to see Lee Gordon as far less anti-Semitic than Maud, the Communist secretary.

Lonely Crusade does have an air of honesty; the main Jewish character, Rosenberg, does act benevolently. However, the confrontation Hodges describes as a mutual combat is rather a black intellectual's tirade against Jews, occasionally interrupted by a Jew who makes not one criticism of blacks (except that he is beginning to notice anti-Semitism among them). Were he tactless, Rosenberg might have answered Gordon's charges against Jews by simply reversing them—

i.e., countering gouging Jewish landlords and merchants with irresponsible black tenants and debtors, or opposing the charge that Jews pamper their children by asserting that blacks brutalize theirs. However, as Stephen Milliken observed, Rosenberg unrealistically "listens to Lee's anti-Semitic diatribes with smiling patience, responds with eager, warm understanding, indeed almost with cloying sweetness." Why did their confrontation remain more monologue than dialogue? Apparently, Himes did not want Gordon's charges against Jews effectively opposed. His hero complains about Jews, not so much to exemplify the problem of black anti-Semitism, as Himes sometimes implied, but to air Himes's own hostility. Indeed, Himes substantially reiterated his hero's complaints against Jews more than twenty years later, when interviewed by John A. Williams.

Besides misrepresenting a barely qualified attack on Jews as a "debate," Hodges ignores the novel's malicious caricature of Jewish characters. He cites one minor figure, Maud, a Communist secretary and a "self-hating" Jew, as someone whose anti-Semitism exceeds and thereby condones that of Himes's hero. But Himes significantly links her self-hatred to her typically ugly Jewish looks and mannerisms:

> She hated all Jews and all things Jewish with an uncontrollable passion as an escape from which she had become a Communist. And yet she was as Jewish in appearance as the Jewish stereotype.

Maud, a grotesque, speaks in a "usually rasping voice," and when provoked, "the stub of her missing arm jerk[s] spasmodically." Lee Gordon perceives the main Jewish character, Abe Rosenberg, similarly:

> Hearing the delayed cadence ending on a question mark, he thought "Jew," before he jerked a look down at Abe Rosenberg's bald head in the sunshine. Sitting on a disbanded wooden casing, feet dangling and his froglike body wrapped in a wrinkled tan cotton slack suit, Rosie looked the picture of the historic Semite.

Even when Gordon comes to feel "grateful" to Rosenberg, who defends him to his own cost, the Jewish Communist remains a "frogshaped" and "grotesque little man." While gentile grotesques (such as the murderous black Communist Luther MacGregor) also inhabit the novel, only its Jewish characters consistently alienate by moving and speaking oddly—Maud twitches and rasps, Abe dangles and singsongs, and another Jewish character, Benny Stone, scampers and effuses.

The first time a Jewish character, Benny Stone, saunters into view, an omniscient voice narrates: "Benny's effusive greeting brought a recurrence of the old troubling question. On what side did the Jew actually play?" This instances a third aspect of the novel's anti-Semitism. Although Himes's narrative voice sometimes dissociates itself from his hero's hostility to Jews, for instance, by calling it a "tendency to anti-Semitism," it participates in that tendency as well. Similarly, Gordon's assertions that other blacks, rightly or not, blame Jews more than he does work to substantiate and normalize his diatribe.

Altogether, the main character's tirade, the physical repulsiveness of all the Jewish characters, and the narrator's complicity in the hero's anti-Semitism establish, at the least, that Himes wanted to disabuse Jews of any presumptions upon the high regard of blacks and, more generally, to wound them in their self-esteem.

One probable reason for the novel's articulation of black anti-Semitism was Himes's desire to overcome the fear of "writing the unthinkable and unprintable." When Gordon tells Rosenberg that "the Jew . . . [has] cornered us off into squalid ghettos and beaten us out of our money," Rosenberg retorts, "Such nonsense should never be spoken." The very prohibition placed on such expressions by the Jews who comprised most of Himes's white friends and benefactors might well have conferred an allure upon them. Yet the likeliest reason that *Lonely Crusade* voiced hostility to Jews is simply that Himes felt some himself. And we can begin to locate his grievances in the complaint his protagonist produces, charges including: (1) betrayals, exploitations, and manipulations of African American causes by Communists, at a time when many Communists were Jews; (2) a Jewish tendency to ridicule blacks for gentiles (e.g., as humorists); (3) the exploitative practices of Jewish businessmen, with whom blacks had been obliged to deal preponderantly; (4) Jewish prejudice against blacks, which Gordon claims exceeds that of other whites, despite the sympathy Jews ought to feel for other oppressed people; (5) miscellaneous Jewish "manners and personal habits" the character finds "repulsive"—aside from discourtesy in money matters—chiefly mothers spoiling their sons.

Though space limits here (among other factors) preclude an adequate analysis of these complaints, it would be unfair to ignore them. So I will briefly consider the context of Gordon's charges against Jews, assess how Himes apparently felt about them, and note where they seem partially justified and where disturbingly objectionable. Significantly, one common component emerges: the (supposed) Jewish insult to black masculinity.

Communists. Like his friends Richard Wright and Ralph Ellison, Himes criticized the Communist party, chiefly for cultivating a ruthless disregard of truth and decency in its members and also for subjecting the personal and national interests of African Americans to a shifting party line, hu-

miliating in its inconsistencies and emanating, absurdly, from the Soviet Union. At that time, though few Jews were Communists, many American Communists were Jews. Still, African American contemporaries of Himes who criticized the Party did *not* tend to fault its Jewish representation. Wright's *American Hunger* focuses on the oppressive anti-intellectualism of *black* Communists; they even expel "a talented Jew" along with Wright from a theater company. Likewise, Ellison's notably unrealistic treatment of the Communist party (obscured as The Brotherhood in *Invisible Man*) may have been motivated in part by his unwillingness to seem anti-Semitic. Not without anguish, Himes overcame that inhibition. Though the most venal Communist in **Lonely Crusade** (Luther McGregor) is African American, and the most idealistic one (Rosenberg) is Jewish, Himes does relate at least some objections to Communist party culture to its heavily Jewish membership. These offenses are the Communists' inappropriate internationalism (which may mask specifically Jewish interests and sympathies); their humiliating imposition of alien discourse and values on African American members; and, most crucially, their insufficient appreciation of specifically *masculine* dignity.

Himes had already connected a tactless preoccupation with an international agenda to a putative Communist's Jewishness in his first novel, **If He Hollers Let Him Go.** When a union steward with a "big hooked nose" asks the black hero to subordinate his racial grievance for the unified fight against fascism, the latter calls the steward both "Comrade" and "Jew boy." Likewise, in **Lonely Crusade,** Lee Gordon "felt vindicated in his stand against the Communists, whose insidious urging that he become a laborer to help defeat fascism had become obnoxious." Why "insidious"? "At a party of Jewish Communists," he interprets their fervent internationalism as a covert Jewish nationalism: "Another Jew joined in the conversation. "Russia must be saved!" "For who? You Jews?" Lee asked harshly.

The prolonged, preponderant, inevitably resented influence of Jews, however benevolently motivated, not only on African American policies in the American Communist Party, but as executives in civil rights organizations such as the NAACP and the Urban League, helps explain Himes's associated hostilities to Jews and Communists. As Harold Cruse was to contend in *The Crisis of the Negro Intellectual*, it must have been galling for African American Communists to have their situation defined for them by others (many of them Jews) and to be made by the Party to speak a language of leftist jargon that alienated other African Americans. Even Mark Naison, who defends the sincere dedication of Jewish Communists to African American causes and culture, acknowledges that the party's "language and ideology, and above all its interracialism" alienated African Americans. From this perspective, one might understand the appeal of anti-Semitic language for Himes; it might seem an exquisitely iconoclastic declaration of independence, potent in its populistic appeal. (Likewise, Jesse Jackson "on one occasion" characterized his later renounced "anti-Semitic discourse" as "talking Black.")

Perhaps the chief cultural differences between Jewish Communists and black populists involved constructions of gender. In *Lonely Crusade,* a benevolent Jewish Communist, obtuse to their cultural difference, provokes one of Lee Gordon's most visceral revulsions: The "small, elderly Jewish man with a tired, seamed face and kindly eyes" takes Gordon into a bedroom at the party and shows him "a picture of a naked Negro" which Gordon mistakes for a "ballet dancer" until the Jew identifies him as a lynching victim. Shocked, nauseated, enraged, reminded that such crimes go unavenged, and confronted perhaps with a mutilated black figure of uncertain gender, Gordon's masculinity has been insulted. Significantly, he directly hears "someone . . . saying: 'There are no such things as male and female personalities. There is only one personality.'" In reaction, Gordon promptly asserts his traditionally construed masculinity:

> I like women who are women. . . . I like to sleep with them and take care of them. I don't want any woman taking care of me or even competing with me.

In *My Life of Absurdity,* Himes remarks that to enjoy his detective novels as they enjoyed their folk culture "American Blacks had to get all the protest out of their minds that the communists had filled them with." That is, they had to stop regarding themselves as suffering victims, with the attendant implication of unmanliness. Rather than "just victims," as "protest writer[s]" portrayed them, Himes wished to present black Americans as "absurd"—i.e., as capable perpetrators as well as victims of violence, humorous, extroverted, and full of *joie de vivre.* In contrast, he felt that Jewish Communists sought to politically organize African Americans through pooled self-pity, and that they demeaned black masculinity by making the lynch victim a protest logo.

Humorists. Lee Gordon complains that, to similarly demeaning effect, "the Jew will hold Negroes up for ridicule by the gentile—that in instances where the gentile is not thinking of the Negro, the Jew will call attention to the Negro as an object of scorn." Apparently, Himes felt this way himself because twenty-three years later he reiterated the charge in his Williams interview, claiming that Jews, paradoxically because of their somewhat similar status, are most likely to offend blacks. He said, "You know, some of the Jewish writers, because of the fact that they belong to a minority too, can get more offensive than the other writers do." Himes more pointedly told *Black World* editor Hoyt Fuller that a Jewish screenwriter's rejected treatment of *Cotton Comes to Harlem* was "a smart Jew-boy angle, especially of the ra-

cial scene, because he figured the Jews had a right to do so." Likewise, a Jewish fence in Himes's detective novel *The Big Gold Dream,* having through prolonged familiarity assumed the speech style of blacks, also indulges in offensive racial humor. And a Jewish junk dealer in Himes's *Cotton Comes to Harlem* tries some tactless ethnic humor while bargaining with blacks.

Himes told John Williams he once walked out of a Hollywood script conference on a film about George Washington Carver beginning with Carver ironing a shirt in his kitchen—i.e., feminized by tool and workplace. He understandably resented the traditional movie treatment of blacks as comical servants and menials, and he may have held the predominantly Jewish studio heads accountable. Likewise, while praising *Lonely Crusade'*s treatment of black-Jewish relations, Himes's admirer Ishmael Reed complained of "Jewish playwrights, cartoonists, film-makers, novelists, magazine editors and television writers [who] depict Blacks in such an unfavorable light as if to say to whites, 'we'll supply the effigy, you bring the torch.'" (Reed compared David Susskind, for "defending the troopers' actions at Attica," to Hitler.) Jews are liable to be blamed—as recently and controversially by City College professor Leonard Jeffries—for unflattering references to African Americans in the news or entertainment media. Of course, anti-Semitic exaggerations of their offenses do not absolve Jews from whatever blame their conduct may merit. However, I regard the claim that Jews have been especially prone to racist ridicule as dubious, and that gentiles have needed Jewish incitements to "scorn" African Americans as preposterous.

Businessmen. Lee Gordon's complaints about the exploitative control of black commercial life by Jewish businessmen, while not unjustified, also contain disturbing exaggerations and dangerous implications. Again, Himes later reasserted these complaints in his own voice, and again anxiety about masculine dignity attaches to the issue.

Speaking of the 1940s, Lee Gordon chiefly justifies growing African American hostility to Jews by real economic grievances:

> Most of the Negro contact with the business world is with the Jew. He buys from the Jew, rents from the Jew, most of his earnings wind up, it seems, in the Jew's pocket. He doesn't see where he's getting value in return. He pays too much rent, too much for food, and in return can't do anything for the Jew but work as a domestic or the like.

His Jewish interlocutor acknowledges that "many [Jewish businessmen] exploit Negroes" but counters that at least they give blacks commercial opportunities others deny them; Rosenberg adds that their own exclusion from gentile-dominated industry forced Jews to deal with blacks. Gordon grants that most blacks exaggerate Jewish economic power, but he insists that "many [other] Negroes [wrongly] . . . think that Jews control all the money to the world."

By sometimes differentiating his narrator's views from his hero's, as well as his hero's from those of less sophisticated African Americans (whose ideas he nonetheless needs to convey), Himes lends an interesting ambiguity to the novel's anti-Semitic expressions; and he protects himself through undermining their authority. However, since he insists on conveying (while denying) an irrational anti-Semitism he imputes to a segment of the black population less able than he to propagate their views, those views take on the pathos of suppressed thoughts struggling for expression. And, indeed, a recurrent, fundamental association of Jews with money—both as benefactors and as exploiters—functioned importantly for Himes himself.

In his Williams interview, Himes again attributed then current (1969) black hostility to Jews to economic factors. He claimed, like his character Gordon, that the real basis of black animosity to Jews was that they were formerly the only, and currently the primary, dealers of goods and services to blacks, and that they took advantage of that position. He also granted, as his character Rosenberg had asserted, that Jews had been relegated to servicing blacks by an anti-Semitic society. But Himes himself used emphatic and exaggerated language in asserting that, given the commercial ignorance of blacks,

> Jewish landlords and merchants misused them. . . .
> All businesses in the ghettoes were owned by
> Jews. . . . The black had an ingrown suspicion and
> resentment of the Jew. He realized that he was be-
> ing used in certain ways by all Jewish landlords and
> merchants. Even today a Jew will make a fortune
> out of the race problem, and this builds up a sub-
> conscious resentment—although most of the white
> people I do business with, who help me, whom I
> love and respect, are Jews. But that doesn't negate
> the fact that the Jews are the ones who had contact
> with the blacks and took advantage of them.

Some hyperbolical and mystifying aspects of Himes's language here indicate a disturbing willingness to cultivate an irrational approach to this topic. Surely Jews cannot have owned "all" the ghetto businesses. Can "all" the Jewish "landlords and merchants" have "misused" blacks? Describing black resentment of Jewish economic exploitation as "ingrown" and "subconscious" means that its existence cannot and need not be demonstrated; that it can thrive without concrete occasion; yet that releasing such resentments might constitute the African American's most essential liberation.

The degree to which Jews had controlled ghetto commerce was hotly debated in the sixties. The most widely accredited writer to deal with the topic, James Baldwin, both condemned and condoned black rage against Jewish landlords and businesses. Jewish writers commonly argued that banks, universities, market forces and other impersonal institutions and conditions actually controlled the ghetto economy. Of course, Jews were conspicuously engaged in ghetto commerce (in part because they had lived there before blacks did). Some certainly cheated blacks, and even if they did constitute a small percentage of Jewish businessmen, it does not take many instances of victimization (as with criminal violence) to stigmatize a perpetrator's group if it already carries signs of otherness. Certainly most major Jewish businesses in ghettoes were slow to employ blacks in responsible positions. And nobody likes landlords, whatever their ethnicity. So when Himes wrote **Lonely Crusade** (and later when he discussed the issue with Williams), black resentment of Jewish businessmen was both widely felt and understandable, if often disproportionate to real offenses. Hence, Himes's treatment of this conflict cannot be dismissed as unrepresentative, though its representativeness does not excuse it from criticism.

Himes's complaints about the behavior of Jewish businessmen might especially typify resentments among black creative artists. Himes hoped for work as a writer in Hollywood, but reported that Jewish employers jim-crowed and insulted him there. Today, mistrust of Jewish employers is commonly voiced among black jazz musicians and rap artists. In Spike Lee's film *Mo' Better Blues,* graceless, greedy Jewish nightclub owners apparently exploit black performers; their caricaturization provoked a controversy in which the Anti-Defamation League, Nat Hentoff, and other Jewish writers attacked Lee, who defended his Jewish characters as realistic.

In Himes's **Lonely Crusade,** unlike Lee's less complex film, the major Jewish character, the Communist Rosenberg, behaves very generously to his black friend, Gordon. And Himes himself readily acknowledged many Jewish friends and supporters. He wrote his first novel on a Rosenwald Fellowship. An element of ambivalence on this subject—i.e., a tendency to regard Jews not only as exploiters but as benefactors—might help explain why Himes describes the general black hatred of Jewish businessmen as "subconscious." The fiercely independent Himes might have resented Jewish philanthropists as much as Jewish businessmen, but also felt that it was wrong to do so.

Himes's convoluted economic connections with Jews may have predated his birth. He claimed that his "father's father was the slave blacksmith of a Jewish slaveowner, probably named Heinz, whose name he took when he was freed. That's how [he] came by the name of Himes." However,

Himes scholar Edward Margolies told me that Himes's brothers did not corroborate this claim and that both blacks and whites named Himes—none of them apparently Jewish—occupied the region of his father's forbears. From an early age, Himes seems to have found Jews risky sources of substantial funds. In 1928, having heard a chauffeur "bragging about the large sums of money his boss always kept in his house," Himes held up the boss (named Miller) and his wife in their home. (Margolies opines that the couple were Jewish.) Himes fled to Chicago, where he approached "a notorious fence called Jew Sam." Sam turned him over to the cops. Then the police "sent to Cleveland for someone to identify the jewelry, and one of the executives of the firm that insured it arrived. His name was Frieberg. Later he became a friend." Near the conclusion of his autobiography, Himes described some traveling and dining that he and his second wife, moderately prosperous at last, enjoyed in the company of his good friend and "excellent agent," Roslyn Targ, and her husband. The Targs are Jews. At the end of their trip, as both couples sat together in Himes's home,

> Roslyn began crying and said, "Chester, at last you've got your own house. I congratulate you both." We all began crying, thinking that after all these years at last I had a house when I was sixty-one years old.

My point is that Himes, who consistently associated Jews with money, blamed them when financially frustrated and bonded with them when successful.

Himes was willing to exploit, even to inculcate, a very reductive association of Jews with money in his Harlem thriller *The Big Gold Dream.* The Jewish fence, whose offensively familiar humor was cited above, is reduced to a mere stereotype through constant reference to him simply as "the Jew." Such images as "his face lit slowly with an expression of uncontainable avarice . . . saliva trickled from the corners of his mouth" make "the Jew" grotesquely greedy—but so are many of Himes's black characters. What bothers me here is that Himes's black detectives, who always speak with authority, simply reduce the Jew's meaning to money with several statements such as "in order to bring the Jew into it, there had to be money." This disturbs because the dehumanizing equation of Jews with money prompts people to take out their economic frustration on innocent Jewish scapegoats. Thus, for instance, the Nobel Prize winner Elias Canetti in *Crowds and Power* explained the Nazi persecution as a reaction to catastrophic inflation; Germans associated Jews with money and passed on the sting to them when their currency became worthless. Likewise, according to one analysis, an outburst of black anti-Semitism occurred when African Americans did not get the economic parity some expected after the achievement of civil rights legislation—not because Jews exploited blacks but because disappointment and envy required an outlet.

Himes's tendency to associate Jews with money also ramified into his gender anxiety. His very first published story, **"His Last Day,"** reciprocally relates Jewish money and black masculinity. A condemned convict, Spats, aims to walk to his death so coolly that fellow convicts will say "what a man," and he spends his last day recalling the "frightened eyes of the little Jew . . . a little tyke," i.e., *kike,* whom he had robbed. He also blames himself for trembling "just like that tyke" he had threatened with his gun. Note how the euphemistic substitution of "little tyke," for "kike" insults both the Jew's ethnicity and his masculinity. Later, Spats frightens and gyps his lawyer, a "lousy tyke fixer who [inadvertently] gave his services for nothing," by refusing to locate his cache for the lawyer's payment. Despite his bravado, Himes's convict only barely masks his "utter fear" before electrocution. And, of course, the story does not propose that blacks ought to assert their masculinity by robbing and intimidating Jews. Still, Spats's lack of remorse, his toughness, his candid irreligion—among other qualities Himes, then imprisoned for robbery, presumably admired—suggest at least some identification with the convict.

Lee Gordon also resembles Spats, Himes's first protagonist: he expresses hostility to Jews, is benefited by one he verbally abuses (rather than robs), and manfully walks to his probable death at the plot's conclusion. Gordon's characterization also reflects Himes's financial-marital crisis when he wrote *Lonely Crusade.* His promising connections with Jewish leftists in Hollywood having proven fruitless, Himes later wrote that his intense inner hurt only became consciously racial when he found he could not support his wife, i.e., fulfill his traditional economic role as a man. She "had a better job than [he] did and . . . that was the beginning of the dissolution of [their] marriage." As Himes put it, he "was no longer a husband to [his] wife; [he] was her pimp. She didn't mind, and that hurt all the more." Furthermore, it was through a relative of his wife that he got a fellowship from the Rosenwald Foundation. When Himes was broke and embarrassed before his wife, she enjoyed both a better job and better relations with Jews than he did, all of which threatened his masculinity.

Conspirators. In *Lonely Crusade,* Lee Gordon claims that Jewish prejudice against blacks exceeds that of other whites. He also insists that he "believe[s], like other Negroes, that Jews fight, and underhandedly [the African American] struggle for equality." Charges of secretive, conspiratorial opposition can hardly be disproven. But clearly, by their former substantial involvement in civil rights organizations (however disparaged as conscience money) and their still quite similar voting records (despite divergent economic interests), Jews have demonstrated far less hostility to blacks than other whites.

Here Himes might be distinguished from his character, whose paranoia on this point might be what the narrator means when he refers to Gordon's sentiments as "anti-Semitism." As noted above, a Jew, Rosenberg, proves Gordon's most devoted friend. However, Gordon also recalls an incident when a white gentile had warned him "that the Jewish people . . . were trying to get the white people to drive them from their neighborhood," lest "the property would go down." There the narrative does intimate at least one Jewish anti-black conspiracy.

Perhaps the most important aspect of Lee Gordon's charge that Jews fight blacks "underhandedly" is that such contention is unmasculine. Unlike open hostility—"fighting like a man"—secretive opposition affords no opportunity to affirm masculinity, even if defeated, through combat. This links the charge of conspiracy to Gordon's other complaints against Jews by their common insult to black manhood. Jewish Communists emasculate blacks by publicizing their victimization in lynchings. Jewish producers and entertainers present or joke about unthreatening, submissive black men. Jewish businessmen make black husbands look bad before wives they find difficult to support, lacking a Jew's economic opportunities.

Mothers. Gordon's final, apparently incidental but psychologically crucial complaint against Jews explicitly concerns gender: Jewish mothers pamper their sons. He deplores "the repulsive manner in which Jewish mothers worship their sons, making little beasts of them. I've sat on a streetcar and seen Jewish tots beat their mothers in the face. . . ." But significantly, Gordon is the novel's only character who beats an unprotesting woman, his wife, in part because she plays an excessively maternal role. In other words, the defense mechanism of projection appears to be operating in this instance of his anti-Semitism.

Himes's resentment of women clarifies his parallel resentment of Jews. As his most autobiographical novel, *The Third Generation,* reveals, Himes disastrously overidentified with his mother, a very light-skinned woman of color highly contemptuous of blacks. She both doted upon and beat him, and photos show that she kept him, her youngest child, overlong in girlish attire. Perhaps another source of gender anxiety might have been Himes's prison experience. Because he wore a back brace, he was housed with "crippled" inmates. In *Cast the First Stone,* his prison novel, the hyper-masculine hero's homoerotic love object is embittered, disabled, and effeminate.

Himes's intense identification with his mother and perhaps his prison experience disposed him to differentiate himself from women violently. His autobiographical novels, *The Primitive* and *The Third Generation,* reflect their author's woman-beating tendencies, justified as follows in *The Quality of Hurt:* "the only way to make a white woman listen is to pop her in the eye, or any woman for that matter."

The marital relationship in *Lonely Crusade* closely parallels Himes's account of his own domestic circumstances when he wrote the novel. Ruth Gordon has a better job than her husband, resulting in a sexual "impotency, that was . . . trampling down his every endowment of manhood"—though he beats and rapes her. The narrator states that Gordon's wife

> had not minded absorbing his brutality, allowing him to assert his manhood in this queer, perverted way, because all of the rest of the world denied it. But at so great a price, for it had given to her that beaten, whorish look of so many other Negro women, who no doubt did the same.

Gordon knows that it is wrong to beat his wife, but reflects, "Lord God, a man had to stand on somebody, because this was the way it was." Gordon reflects that his wife had formerly, at her first job, worked for Jewish Communists who had "wooed" her, so that he "felt that the [Jewish] Communists were taking her away from him." These Jews may pose a sexual threat, indirectly, through their ability to offer her salary and flattery. However, the Jew is feared here, not so much as a wife-seducer but as someone likely to conspire with her against her husband's desire to affirm masculinity with other men, including white men, if only through open combat against them.

Gordon is a union organizer, and when the company's WASP tycoon offers to buy him off with a high-paying job, his wife wants him to take it. But that would be "without honor." And

> he had reached the point in life where if he could not have the respect of men he did not want the rest. And if this entailed her having to work for what he would not give her in dishonor, she should at least understand that there was nothing noble in her doing so; it was only the white man's desire to deride the Negro man that had started all the lies and propaganda about the nobility and sacrifices of Negro women in the first place.

Eventually, Ruth Gordon does quit her job to repair her husband's masculine ego. But she can never bond with him in violent heroism. Nor can the Jewish Communist Rosenberg, despite pronouncing Gordon "a Negro of revolutionary potential" who will "not be afraid to die." As Gordon marches into suicidal combat against union-busting cops at the book's conclusion, his wife screams in terror, while the equally self-sacrificing and protective "Rosie" stands at her side and yells: "No, Lee! No!"

Gordon finds his wife financially superior and physically inferior. Her very supportiveness unmans him; the Jewish analogy (in Hodges's) is to "paternalism." "Little" "Rosie" likewise treats Gordon to lunch and absorbs his (verbal) abuse. When Gordon hides out, hunted and sick, Rosenberg comes to nurse him, undressing him, putting him to bed and feeding him—functions more readily associated with wives and mothers than with buddies. In short, the novel's chief Jewish character resembles the hero's wife as an oddly maternal figure. But Gordon resents their motherings. One of his pet peeves is the theory that African American society is matriarchal, which he won't accept "even if it is true," because " in a white society where the family unit of the dominant group is patriarchal, doesn't that make us something less?"

This line of thought reflects Himes's personal need to establish a masculine identity by cutting himself away from his overbearing mother. But the associated anti-Semitism and anti-feminism he sometimes expressed may not be explained so well by his personal psychology as by his intuition of how African American cultural authority would have to be communicated to a broader audience.

Himes determined that African Americans would only be respected in America by emphatically (if "absurdly") brandishing their masculinity, and that this entailed the sacrifice of their special relationship with Jews and the world view of leftist Jewish intellectuals. Blacks could bond with Jews through political argument, as Rosenberg and Gordon do in *Lonely Crusade.* But they could more readily and authoritatively bond with gentile white Americans in drinking, fast driving, brawling, shooting, and gambling—i.e., through the rituals of mainstream, masculinity-proving American culture.

> **Himes determined that African Americans would only be respected in America by emphatically (if "absurdly") brandishing their masculinity, and that this entailed the sacrifice of their special relationship with Jews and the world view of leftist Jewish intellectuals.**
>
> *—Steven J. Rosen*

Underlying the connection between Lee Gordon's hostility to Jews and to women is his attraction to a masculinity-proving ethos—a violent, straight-dealing culture shared with most American black and white men, but, he felt, neither with his wife nor with American Jews. Hence, Himes characterized the model of *Lonely Crusade*'s Rosenberg, his

friend Dan Levin, as the author of a novel "in a way a forerunner of the Jewish writer's treatment of the war theme. . . . Jewish writers never glorified war." Contrastingly, in *Lonely Crusade,* war *is* glorified in a speech by a Southern white army officer who trains black pilots; it tells them that World War II requires their fighting heroism, though formerly they have been encouraged to suffer misfortune patiently. This call to arms includes such phrases as "all of us must prove first of all that we are capable of the dignity and nobility of manhood." To Gordon, this means that "whenever a Negro came to believe that full equality was his just due, then he would have to die for it, as would any other man."

Clearly, a political rhetoric that prioritizes proving manhood poses problems. For one thing, it is dangerous. Note that it is a socially privileged male, a white Southern army officer, who asserts the need to "prove first of all that we are capable of the dignity and nobility of manhood." It was by courageously fighting for the unjust cause of slavery that Southern army officers established their iconic masculinity in American culture. Indeed, *unjust* occasions for combat (e.g. gang warfare) may facilitate proving masculinity even better than just ones. The rhetoric is also unrealistic. Himes himself lived a good long seventy-five years, rather than dying for "full . . . equality as would any other man." It is also problematic that these values exclude women and, with them, (Diaspora) Jews—not Israelis, whose combativeness Himes admired and thought American blacks should emulate. Both women and (Diaspora) Jews have generally felt—as Himes's Southern colonel said of traditional African Americans—that their group would be more harmed than helped by displays of heroic violence.

Unsurprisingly, one of *Lonely Crusade*'s most negative reviews did come from the Jewish journal *Commentary.* The review and Himes's response to it together illuminate the black/Jewish *kulturkampf* brewing then and yet to come. Both the black novelist and the Jewish reviewer (Milton Klonsky) misrepresented each other's texts and seemed most obtuse to each other when dealing with the touchy gender issue.

Complaining in *The Quality of Hurt* about the biased reception of *Lonely Crusade,* Himes said that "the writing might well have been bad, but the writing was not criticized by one review I had read." He also said the *Commentary* review most objected to his depiction of a "Christ-like Jew." Both accounts are mistaken.

The *Commentary* reviewer, who was not the only one to do so, did attack what he (wrongly) called Himes's "shabby style" and "clumsily written" novel. He found especially ludicrous Himes writing of lovers going to bed "to consummate their gender." (Might this refusal to consider the sexual act as an signification of gender typify a difference in the sexual sensibilities of Jewish and black writers?) Not above delivering a gender insult in a patronizing racial tone, Klonsky wrote that "although the author is himself a Negro, his book is so deracinated, without any of the lively qualities of the imagination peculiar to his people, that it might easily have been composed by any clever college *girl*" (emphasis added).

The reviewer also objected, not to Himes's treatment of his main Jewish character as "Christ-like," but to Rosenberg being stereotyped as a Communist and caricatured as physically repulsive. He also objected to the black and Jewish characters' discussion of "why Jews love money." (But their discussion of the domination of ghetto commerce by Jewish businessmen makes no such claim; it is hardly that crude.) While conceding that Himes might have been well-intentioned, Klonsky concluded that his "treatment here reveals a bias which is almost incredible in a book of its pretensions." That is, Himes's evident hostility to Jews was oddly incongruous with his intention to analyze and warn of black anti-Semitism.

Himes considered himself a mediator between worried Jews and blacks more anti-Semitic than he, all of whom required compassionate attention. His response to the *Commentary* review attributed Klonsky's hostility to "subconscious disturbances within the individual" and denied its "calumny"— that the book was anti-Semitic. He asserted that his hero's "self-destructive . . . anti-Semitism" resulted from "oppression." But Himes's attribution of his hero's anti-Semitism to "oppression" too thoroughly condones it. Rather than substantiate such an analysis, the novel ventilates an anti-Semitic tirade, then qualifies it (e.g., in Rosenberg's kindness and "wisdom of five thousand years"). Though this ambivalence is one of the book's many sources of interest, it does not erase its anti-Semitism.

Himes's reply to *Commentary* twice insisted that his novel's main theme was the universal one of "searching for manhood"—even, implausibly, that "this story could have been written about a Jew, a Gentile, a Chinese. . . ." And he concluded his response by repeating his Southern officer's call to masculinity-proving heroism. By insisting upon the masculinity-proving theme and its universality, Himes both assertively countered the charge of ethnic bias and, implicitly, blamed Jews like Klonsky, because they lack authority and manifest obtuseness in masculinist discourse. Indeed, most American Jews have felt proving manhood by violence to be inimical to their culture and potentially dangerous to them.

Klonsky's reply to Himes boasted of his review's having stuck it to the novelist—"It seemed to have stuck in his throat but barely grazed his mind." He otherwise refused to perpetuate the dialogue. *Commentary*'s reviewer was understandably disturbed and offended by *Lonely Crusade.* However, he grossly underestimated Himes's extremely well-written and prescient novel.

Himes's prescience consists essentially in having realized, in the heyday of Ernest Hemingway and Humphrey Bogart (and just before Jackie Robinson), that African Americans would most effectively enter the mainstream of American culture through a display of hyper-masculine endeavor: that is, in sports, in the military, in hard-driving music, perhaps in the police (like his Harlem detectives), and in other potentially heroic roles, which men (perhaps especially Southern, even racist white men) cannot help but admire. It is too bad that Himes sometimes employed Jewish characters or formulated Jewish traits as a foil to the black American masculinity he endeavored to invoke. This made Himes a disturbing exponent of African American anti-Semitism—though he remains one of its more penetrating analysts. Certainly, in encouraging discussion of this touchy and offensive topic, few set a bolder example than Chester Himes.

Robert Crooks (essay date October 1995)

SOURCE: "From the Far Side of the Urban Frontier: The Detective Fiction of Chester Himes and Walter Mosley," in *College Literature,* October, 1995, pp. 68-90.

[*In the following essay, Crooks analyzes the frontier mentality in the detective fiction of Chester Himes and Walter Mosley.*]

Frederick Jackson Turner's 1893 essay "The Significance of the Frontier in American History" marked a watershed for the European-American version of the history of North America. By 1890 the western frontier as a geographical space had disappeared, and "the frontier" as signifier was now cut adrift, its attachment to past, present, and future conceptual spaces a matter of debate. Indeed, for Turner himself the signifier slides significantly, sometimes figuring as a place where European-American settlement or colonization of North America ends, but also as a conceptual space, a shifting no-man's-land between European-and Native-American cultures, and finally, ideologically, as a "meeting point between savagery and civilization."

Other conceptual and spatial divides along ethnic and racial lines emerged almost simultaneously with the western frontier, however, and were available to absorb and transform its conceptual significance. The most obvious was that between European and African Americans embodied in the codes, economy, and practices of slavery and subsequent segregation. Such lines of segregation became particularly sharp and contested in urban settings, thanks to the close proximity of sizable communities formed along racial lines, often subject to differential treatment in terms of urban development, availability of credit, school funding, policing, and so forth. It is this urban manifestation of frontier ideology, and particularly the textual space opened up by crime fiction for an articulation of that frontier from its "other" side, that will concern me here.

Turner suggests, in an inchoate way, the need for and function of the particular ideological formation that drew a line between "white" civilization and "Indian" savagery, a term for which "black" criminal chaos could easily be substituted. Noting that there was not one frontier, but rather a trading frontier, a farming frontier, a military frontier, a railroad frontier, and so forth, he also notes that the various frontiers did not coincide geographically, nor in the economic interests that constructed them. In an attempt to account for the assumed ideological unity of the (European-American) United States, Turner maps these differences onto a progressive cultural history stretching from the savage prehistory of Indian lands in a linear development to the industrial metropolitan centers of the east. Ignoring the lack of fit between this mapping and the uneven developments of various frontiers, Turner identifies the Indians as the unifying factor that transformed the various frontiers, their regulation, and their histories into a unity by posing a "common danger" of absolute otherness.

It is difficult to reconcile this distinctive unity produced by common danger with Turner's invocation of the western frontier as the factor that transformed the European colonists into Americans: "The American frontier is sharply distinguished from the European frontier—a fortified boundary running through dense populations. The most significant thing about the American frontier is, that it lies at the hither edge of free land." On the one hand, Turner conceives of the frontier as the near edge of a wilderness of free resources, providing what he would later call a "safety valve" inhibiting the reproduction of the European class tensions between owners of the means of production and labor. In this sense the ideological work of the frontier was the production of individualism—meaning both individual liberty and individualized entrepreneurial competition—as an alternative to class politics. On the other hand, the frontier as a producer of unity is precisely a "fortified boundary" dividing "civilization" from "savage" others, a consolidating interpretation that rescues a racialized sense of national identity from the threat of anarchic individualism.

The role of individualism in this racializing and naturalizing of the frontier, translating it from a site of cultural contestation and ideological struggle into an expanding boundary of civilization, is overdetermined. First, the ideology of individualism romanticizes capitalist competition,

displacing collective machinations with an image of a "fair fight" between free individuals. Second, as Richard Slotkin points out, early frontier narratives depicted figures like Benjamin Church and Daniel Boone as "the lone white man among tribes of Indians" even though "both men dealt with the Indians as agents for large land companies." Produced by a familiar trope of individualizing the European-American self against collectivized others, the "lone white man" would be a recurring image suggesting that the struggle of European Americans against the wilderness was not even a "fair fight," but rather a heroic battle against the odds. Third, in conjunction with the representation of the far side of the frontier as vacant wilderness, capitalist competition (including that with Native Americans for land and resources) could be concealed behind images of individual entrepreneurs—whether farmers, traders, trappers, or prospectors—taming a "nature" divested even of collectivized Native American subjects, bringing it within the pale of culture. Finally, the ideology of individualism could mediate between the narratives of men against the wilderness and the experiences of the European-American colonists of the frontier as a site of ideological struggle between different cultures. A continuous stream of diatribes against "Indianization" and the motif of the "good Indian," prominent in frontier narratives from Cooper through Zane Grey to the *Daniel Boone* television series, has helped in a variety of ways to reconcile a racially defined oppression with ideologies of egalitarianism and tolerance by posing frontiersmen and Indians as individuals free to choose European-American civilization over Indian savagery.

These various meanings and functions of individualism are not mutually compatible or equally operative in every moment of discourse. Such disjunctions are a consequence of contradictions that emerge in the ideological negotiation of material encounters between cultures or emergent micro-cultures. The ability of Turner to move discursively back and forth between "Indian lands" and "free lands," or to rewrite complex modalities of capitalist competition as a progressive history inscribed seamlessly across the continent, demonstrates the possibility and necessity of evading such contradictions through the ideological isolation of discourses. In geographical terms, the western frontier was a battlefront in a territorial war that was articulated within various struggles over issues including race, the structuring of the State, and the proper use of land and resources. Because such war could not be justified according to prevailing ethics or law, it was necessary to isolate discursively the colonization of territory from the battle between civilization and savagery by converting "the idea of racial propensities into a rationale for wars of extermination."

From the European-American perspective, then, the frontier wars were not wars of conquest, for the assertion of authority by the U.S. government to make legal claim to land occupied by Native Americans was tantamount to redefining Native Americans themselves as foreign intruders to be eradicated. Through this redefinition, the "Indian Question" was discursively linked to the "Slavery Question." At the same time that the European-American frontier was being pushed westward, a new and distinctively American "science" of craniometry was developing an "objective" method for differentiating among races.

Such work in racial "science" not only helped to justify the continuation of slavery and the war on Native Americans, but also helped determine the shape of the eventual "solutions" to those problems. Though the complete extermination of Native Americans and the mass transportation of black Americans "back" to Africa had many proponents, the compromise solution was collective oppression and exploitation facilitated by racial segregation, the containment of Native Americans and Native-American culture on Reservations, and the similar containment of African Americans through various forms of segregation.

This partitioning refocused the frontier ideology, which continued to map cultural and racial divisions, but in geographical terms now denoted relatively fixed lines of defense for the purity and order of European-American culture. Such lines became particularly charged in cities like New York, Chicago, and Los Angeles, where population densities and the size of minoritized communities threaten individualist ideologies, since the collective experience of exploitation lends itself to collective resistance or rebellion. Thus the meaning of the other side of the frontier, in the shift of focus from its western to its urban manifestation, has been partly transformed: no longer enemy territory to be attacked and conquered or vacant land to be cultivated, it now constitutes in mainstream European-American ideologies pockets of racial intrusion, hence corruption and social disease to be policed and contained—insofar as the "others" threaten to cross the line.

Like the association of individualism with European-American manifest destiny, the association of black urban communities in particular with the criminal side of the urban frontier has historically been overdetermined. Many of the African Americans migrating to the cities were forced to seek housing and then to remain in the poorest areas of the cities by discriminatory practices in housing, as well as in the workplace and schools. Furthermore, as Homer Hawkins and Richard Thomas point out:

> Most northern white policemen not only believed in the inferiority of blacks but also held the most popular belief that blacks were more criminally inclined by nature than whites. . . . For decades, white officials in northern cities allowed vice and crime to go unpoliced in black neighborhoods. This non-

protection policy had the effect of controlling the development of black community by undermining the stability of black family and community life.

Police indifference to black-on-black crime has been frequently noted in all regions of the U.S. and persists to such an extent that Rita Williams exaggerates little, if at all, when she says that "African Americans know they can murder each other with impunity and absolutely no one will care."

Inadequate policing of intra-community crime, the saturation of black communities with liquor and gun stores, and gentrification supplement strategies of containment with strategies of eradication and displacement. If the war of extermination and deterritorialization goes largely unrecognized, it is because the urban frontier works more through hegemony than openly repressive force. All Americans can watch the physical and economic "self-destruction" of black communities on the nightly news, and conservative African-American intellectuals can be co-opted into chastising blacks for failing to take responsibility for "their own" problems and the disintegration of their communities Meanwhile the urban frontier serves the same purpose for capitalism as did the western frontier and the European colonial frontiers in general: the production of relatively cheap resources, including labor.

Though specific techniques of oppression and exploitation have changed, then, the frontier ideology remains largely intact, though displaced. Individualism in particular remains crucial in disguising a site of ideological struggle as a line of defense against crime and chaos or the boundary of advancing modernization or "urban renewal" or "revitalization," and for disarming collective resistance. Hegemony works through negotiation, though, and resistance does exist, in however fragmented forms. In the remainder of this essay I will consider one mode of resistance from the far side of the frontier, the emergence of African-American detective fiction, a popular form that has the capacity both to represent and enact resistance in social and literary terms.

> And it wasn't just this city. It was any city where they set up a line and say black folks stay on this side and white folks on this side, so that the black folks were crammed on top of each other—jammed and packed and forced into the smallest possible space until they were completely cut off from light and air.

Cultural historians like Slotkin and Alexander Saxton have argued persuasively that the hard-boiled American detective is a direct descendant of nineteenth-century frontier heroes like Natty Bumppo, liminal figures who crisscross the frontier, loyal to European-American society but isolated from it through their intimate involvement with Native American others. Indeed, Saxton sees the rapid emergence of the dime-novel detective in the late 1880s partly as a consequence of the closing of the frontier and a corresponding "credibility gap . . . between the occupational activities of [real contemporary miners and cowboys] and the tasks that western heroes were expected to perform." Critics of detective fiction—Cynthia Hamilton's recent *Western and Hard-Boiled Detective Fiction in America* is the most elaborate and thorough account—have likewise traced the lineage of the American adventure hero through the hard-boiled detectives of Dashiell Hammett and Raymond Chandler and beyond, without, however, paying much attention to the fate of the "frontier" in that passage.

The importance of that genealogy is indisputable, I think, particularly for considering the ideological and cultural work of hard-boiled crime fiction. The emphasis on the figure of the adventure hero, largely apart from the rest of the hard-boiled urban world, has on the other hand been something of a critical red herring encouraged by the rhetoric of the fiction itself. Hard-boiled fiction, possibly more than any popular formula, has been overwhelmingly dominated by the individualism that is crucial to frontier ideology, in that it allows recuperation of the outlaw frontier hero who, in Slotkin's suggestive reading, is represented as renewing European-American civilization through acts of violence that at once transgress and defend its symbolic and geographical boundaries. Though particular discourses do, of course, construct particular subject positions, their most important ideological work lies not in the construction of individual subjects but rather in matrices of subject relations within a conceptual space. For that reason, we need to look beyond particular characters in adventure fiction to the dynamic spaces, the intersubjective matrices, constructed by those fictions.

Given the overdetermined association of African Americans and crime in everyday life and the representations of that association as a natural result of essential racial characteristics, one might expect black crime and racial conflict to play a more central role in hard-boiled detective fiction, which more often deals with white law and white deviance. That this is not the case seems partly a consequence of the transformation of the frontier from a movable western boundary into a relatively fixed partitioning of urban space. An overt war of extermination requires that the other side be represented, if in distorted or fantasmatic form. Sustained oppression, which is a covert war of extermination largely by ideological remote control, benefits more from sanctioned ignorance. Nevertheless there are occasionally references to a racial frontier at the extreme edge of society that marks the ultimate frontier, the absolute boundary of the "order" of the familiar, as in this passage from Mickey Spillane's *One Lonely Night*:

Here was the edge of Harlem, that strange no-man's-land where the white mixed with the black and the languages overflowed into each other like that of the horde around the Tower of Babel. There were strange, foreign smells of cooking and too many people in too few rooms. There were the hostile eyes of children who became suddenly silent as you passed.

This frontier dividing Harlem from the rest of Manhattan is represented from its far side in Chester Himes's novel of the same period, *A Rage in Harlem* (also known as *For Love of Imabelle*), as Jackson, the central character, on the verge of escape after a harrowing flight from the police, suddenly realizes that he has left Harlem and is "down in the white world with no place to go . . . no place to hide himself." He turns back to face certain capture rather than go on. Himes does more than simply affirm the existence of the border, however: he explores its meaning as an ideological concept marking the exercise of white hegemony. In doing so he offers a conception of crime never more than tentatively articulated in European-American detective novels by acknowledging an "underworld" that is "catering to the essential *needs* of the people" (my emphasis), perhaps not in ideal fashion but in a manner necessitated by the character of the socioeconomic system. A good deal of criminal activity in this fiction is a result of the U.S. economy's partitioning through segregation. Crime itself, then, is a potentially resistant practice.

Viewing crime as part, rather than the breakdown, of a cultural system, Himes and, more recently, Walter Mosley construct a complex picture of crime and detection as a negotiation of cultural needs and values, operating within the black American subculture as a critique of white racial ideologies. Referring repeatedly and explicitly to the complex politics of race and class in the U.S., they seek to disentangle justice and morality from white hegemony, fighting exploitation and violence within black communities while also attacking a social system that engenders crime. In short, they resist the assimilation of the far side of the frontier as "chaos" and "evil," favoring a conception of the frontier as a site of ideological struggle for rights and privileges between two American microcultures.

The general grounds for such struggle are perhaps best summed up by Himes, commenting on "The Dilemma of the Negro Novelist in the U.S.A.": "Of course, Negroes hate white people, far more actively than white people hate Negroes. . . . Can you abuse, enslave, persecute, segregate and generally oppress a people, and have them love you for it? Are white people expected not to hate their oppressors?" Whatever differences there might be on specific details, Himes and Mosley agree in affirming the need for African-American opposition to oppression and in rejecting the privilege of white supremacist ideology to diagnose and prescribe remedies for the situation of African Americans.

Self-policing of a community, even an oppressed one, is not necessarily complicitous with the oppressive order, of course, or at least not completely so. As I indicated earlier, crime within an oppressed community may be a form of resistance, but it is also a part of the larger, macrocultural economic and social structure. In the U.S. that means crime is exploitative, for it acts out the imperatives of capitalist competition in a particularly unfettered manner. Therefore, as Manning Marable has pointed out, in relatively poor African-American communities, like those of the Himes and Mosley novels, "the general philosophy of the typical ghetto hustler is not collective, but profoundly individualistic . . . The goal of illegal work is to 'make it for oneself,' not for others. The means for making it comes at the expense of elderly Blacks, young black women with children, youths and lower-income families who live at the bottom of the working class hierarchy." It is because of their need to resist the manifestations of individualist competition as criminal entrepreneurship that Himes's police detectives and Mosley's private investigator work in their own communities.

Aside from that common ground, however, the novels of the two series differ considerably, and these differences intersect in complicated ways with the construction of the urban/racial frontier in the two series. These constructions in turn reflect the contradictions produced by ideological struggle between differing American microcultures. A dominant ideology tends to be self-sustaining, thanks to its greater access to means of reproduction like educational systems and mass communication media. Nevertheless dominance and its reproduction can never be complete, never attend adequately to every extra-cultural force operating through travel, migration and immigration, international economic transactions, and so forth, or to every gap that develops in the intra-cultural social formation through uneven development. On the other hand, the pervasiveness of dominant ideologies tends to fragment and disperse the force of other microcultural modes of ideological resistance. Resistance is therefore always under pressure, faced with an incessant need to escape from or relocate itself within a space defined by the dominant microculture.

Michel de Certeau's *Practice of Everyday Life* still offers perhaps the most exhaustive attempt to theorize this locating of resistance, by positing two logical possibilities. *Strategic* resistance finds its space outside the domain of the dominant by attaching itself to an alternative, fully constituted ideology that exists elsewhere. *Tactical* resistance, on the other hand, works within the space of the dominant, exploiting the contradictions within that space as opportunities arise, but unable to hold on to what is gained in the tactical moment. The novels of Mosley and Himes can be

usefully read as narratives representing, respectively, strategic and tactical resistance. To read the novels this way, however, also raises questions about the dichotomy de Certeau constructs, suggesting a more complicated relation between strategies and tactics.

Resistance in *representational* practices, of course, cannot operate in a straightforward manner. Fictional narratives in particular raise the question of the use of representation for resistance, since the diegetic world constructed by a narrative has an ambiguous, if necessary, relation to the world of everyday practice. Furthermore, representation of resistance need not itself be a resistant practice (mainstream media coverage of the Los Angeles uprising in 1992 offers the most blatant recent demonstration). Therefore, in what follows I will separate questions of representing resistance from the manner of representation, in this case narration.

> "Detectives Grave Digger Jones and Coffin Ed Johnson reporting for duty, General," Pigmeat muttered.

> "Jesus Christ!" Chink fumed. "Now we've got those damned Wild West gunmen here to mess up everything."

Representation and enactment of resistance to white hegemony is central to detective fiction of both Himes and Mosley. In discussing these issues, I will consider the two writers in reverse chronological order for two reasons. In terms of representation, Himes's police detectives occupy a more complex and ambiguous ideological space. In terms of enactment, Himes's formal experimentation, especially in **Blind Man With a Pistol,** possesses a more radical potential than anything in Mosley's writing to date, though the latter also suggests directions for resistance unexplored by his precursor.

Unlike detective characters ranging from Mike Hammer or Kinsey Millhone, who despite many differences all bend the law only to better uphold it, Mosley's Easy Rawlins readily and unrepentantly acknowledges having been on the "wrong" side of the law himself. His detective work is described as being for the community and outside the white system of law, often performed on a barter basis and for people who "had serious trouble but couldn't go to the police" because they themselves are already of material necessity living on the fringes, if not outside, of the law: "In my time I had done work for the numbers runners, church-goers, businessmen, and even the police. Somewhere along the line I had slipped into the role of a confidential agent who represented people when the law broke down." This strategic position of "confidential agent" is justified partly on the grounds that an African American could not both work for the police and remain part of the community. Speaking of Quinten Naylor, a black cop who figures in the second and third novels, Rawlins says that he "got his promotion because the cops thought that he had his thumb on the pulse of the black community. But all he really had was me. . . . Even though Quinten Naylor was black he didn't have sympathy among the rough crowd in the Watts community."

Within the narratives as a whole, the division between a communal African-American order and white law proves tenuous. Mosley's first three novels turn on problematic intersections of the white and black communities of Los Angeles, focusing on figures who traverse the unstable interstice between: Daphne Monet/Ruby Hanks, an African-European-American ("passing" for a "white" woman) who likes the Central Avenue jazz clubs and black lovers; Chaim Wenzler, a Jewish member of the American Communist Party who works in and for the black community; Robin Garnett, a rich young white woman who has rebelled against her family and upbringing by becoming a stripper and prostitute in Watts under the name of Cyndi Starr. And in each case, Easy Rawlins is pressed into detective work by forces from the white world as well: racketeer DeWitt Albright, who plays on Easy's need for quick mortgage money after losing a job (*Devil in a Blue Dress*); the IRS and FBI, who threaten to prosecute him for tax evasion (*Red Death*); the L.A. police, who threaten to pin a series of murders on his friend Mouse (*White Butterfly*). More important than these connections with the white community, however, is Easy Rawlins' discovery that there is no simple way to work for order and justice in his African-American community when what counts as "order" and "justice" is defined, at least in part, by a dominant white supremacist ideology. Rawlins does not share the common illusion of the privileged, that such terms can be defined outside of ideology. He observes frequently that all people act according to what they perceive to be their own best interests. That leaves open, however, the question of whether a community that is systematically disempowered by a dominant ideology can produce a coherent strategic resistance.

Mosley's second novel, *A Red Death,* addresses the question most directly. At the beginning of the story Rawlins is summoned by an IRS investigator for tax evasion. Technically the charge is valid, because Easy failed to report as income $10,000 that he acquired illegally, though in his own view legitimately in *Devil in a Blue Dress.* FBI Agent Craxton then offers to help Rawlins cut a deal with the IRS, provided that he helps them get damaging information about Chaim Wenzler, a Polish Jew who survived the Holocaust and is a member of the Communist Party in the U.S. Craxton appeals to Easy's patriotism, positing an alliance between them through an explicit statement of urban frontier logic: "the Bureau is a last line of defense. There are all sorts of enemies we have these days. . . . But the real enemies, the ones we have to watch out for, are people right here at home.

People who aren't Americans on the inside." Easy doesn't trust Craxton, insists that he will do the job only because he has no choice, and tells us that his own feelings about communism are "complex" because of the alliance between the Soviet Union and the U.S. during the war and Paul Robeson's professionally disastrous connections with Russia. However, he doesn't actually challenge Craxton's construction of the frontier between real Americans and un-Americans. Instead he dismisses the idea of communist activity in the African-American community and insists that he will help the FBI get Wenzler but won't work against his "own people."

The rest of the narrative shows that any attempt to define such an internal frontier that aligns black and white interests against a common un-American enemy leads to unresolvable contradictions. Wenzler himself proves to be a sympathetic figure who works in the black community because of the links he sees between his own experience as Jew in Poland and that of African Americans. His main activities involve charitable work that Rawlins supports and aids. Furthermore, Wenzler's connections within the black community make any attempt to isolate him as an object of investigation impossible. Partly as a result of Rawlins' work, two black women and a black minister get murdered in addition to Wenzler, and Rawlins finds himself having to investigate the Garveyite African Migration group.

In short, Easy finds no reason to aid the FBI's investigation except his own economic interests, and he feels increasingly guilty about that. What is most interesting about the novel in ideological terms, however, is the response he works out to that guilt. One might expect that, seeing the impossibility of sharing the collective interests of the white-dominated U.S. government, Rawlins would decide between the two models for African-American opposition offered by Wenzler's Communist Party and the African Migration group. Both, after all, draw upon oppositional ideological formations, one drawn along class lines, the other along racial and cultural ones. Mosley uses an appeal to individualism to validate Easy's rejection of both collective positions. In each case Easy appeals to Jackson Blue, who might be described as the paradigmatic organic intellectual of Mosley's mid-twentieth century Watts. Jackson expresses his own rejection of the Migration agenda in terms of the cultural gap between Africa and African Americans: "We been away too long, man." Shortly thereafter Easy echoes Jackson's rejection of the Migration movement himself, but with a crucial difference: "I got me a home already. It might be in enemy lands, but it's mine still and all." Unlike Jackson's argument on grounds of collective, microcultural differences, Easy appeals to the imperative of individual property interests.

Jackson rejects communism on similar grounds of an unbridgeable difference of *collective* interests. While admitting that the communist economic agenda coincides with the interests of African Americans, he reduces the question of the Communist Party in America to the blacklist, and says that whites will eventually get off the list, but the situation of blacks will remain the same. Again Easy's rejection of collective action soon follows, based again on individual interests rather than microcultural ones: "It wasn't political ideas I didn't care about or understand that made me mad. It was the idea that I wasn't, and hadn't been, my own man. . . . Like most men, I wanted a war I could go down shooting in. Not this useless confusion of blood and innocence."

The position reflected here aligns Easy with the individualist ideology that has crucially underpinned conservative frontier American politics, which helps explain why he is unable to reject the FBI's new frontier account of real and unreal Americans even though he distrusts Craxton. The positing of "American" as a collective cultural and ideological identity stands in direct contradiction with the notion that what makes one American is precisely radical "individuality." That contradiction has enabled the frontier ideology, in both its western and urban manifestations, to link an egalitarian political rhetoric with systematic aggression against Native Americans on the one hand, and the systematic underdevelopment of Black America meticulously documented by Marable on the other. Given the demand of political expediency, frontier ideology sometimes serves the establishment of national boundaries or internal partitions on the basis of an essentialist racial ideology that hierarchizes individuals by group identifications. At other times, however, and in other geographical or cultural terms, the idea that all people are free individuals is used to argue that they fall on either side of the frontier lines through their own bad choices or personal failings. The logic of individualism coupled with that of nationalism and patriotism thus permits systematic and collective cultural aggression and oppression to be passed off as a policing action against one bad Indian like Cochise or Crazy Horse or Geronimo, or as the legitimate surveillance of a dangerous black leader like Martin Luther King or Malcolm X—or a communist like Wenzler. That Easy Rawlins falls into line with the ideology that claims that he can be his own man seems to confirm the accusation made by his friend Mouse: "You learn stuff and you be thinkin' like white men be thinkin'. You be thinkin' that what's right fo' them is right fo' you." Thus it is on very shaky ground indeed that Easy chides the black police officer Quinten Naylor: "You one'a them. You dress like them and you talk like them too."

The trajectory of Easy's particular negotiation of the contradictions of American culture can be traced, I think, to a lesson he learns from DeWitt Albright in the first novel of the series: "You take my money and you belong to me. . . . We all owe out something, Easy. When you owe out then you're in debt and when you're in debt then you can't be your own man. That's capitalism." There is no necessary linkage between capitalism and white supremacist ideology, but just as racism can serve the interests of capitalism by ideologically fragmenting classes, so too can a capitalistic individualism undermine collective resistance to racism. Various sympathies notwithstanding, Easy's actions are structured by the drive to accumulate wealth, which drives wedges between him and the South Central community. At the end of *White Butterfly,* Easy announces his move to a section of West Los Angeles that "[m]iddle-class black families had started colonizing." Significantly absent from the text is the recognition of the way this geographical sectoring of classes in the capitalist metropolis splits the interests of African Americans as a minoritized community—a phenomenon well understood by Bob Jones in Himes's ***If He Hollers Let Him Go:*** "When you asked a Negro where he lived, and he said on the West Side, that was supposed to mean he was better than the Negroes who lived on the South Side; it was like the white folks giving a Beverly Hills address." Instead, Easy's casual use of the "colonizing" metaphor suggests the subordination of collective interests to the exigencies of white capitalism, which undermines strategic resistance organized around either class or community.

As police detectives, on the other hand, Chester Himes's Grave Digger Jones and Coffin Ed Johnson align themselves explicitly with the existing power structure, while nevertheless enacting a tactical resistance within that system. Although they ostensibly solve crimes, the solutions often turn out to be plausible but false ones. These solutions satisfy the white legal establishment, but also work to rid Harlem of committed criminals while sparing others, often "squares" who have gotten involved in crime through a desperate need for money, and offering them incentives to avoid further crime. Usually these fortunate survivors, like Jackson and Imabelle in ***A Rage in Harlem*** or Sissie and Sonny in ***The Real Cool Killers,*** marry at the end of the novels. In addition, Jones and Johnson's position within the law enforcement structure allows them to critique it directly, which they do most frequently by pointing out the roots of black crime in economic exploitation by whites.

Nevertheless they take their orders and carry them out. As insiders, Grave Digger and Coffin Ed cannot mount any consistent resistance to white oppression. Rather, in the way that de Certeau cogently recognizes, they seize opportunities where they arise, never working directly against the interests of the police department, but twisting situations and police procedures in such a way as to subvert them and turn them to the use of the Harlem community.

Such tactical resistance proves as difficult to define and sustain as the strategic resistance attempted by Easy Rawlins, however, and that difficulty seems implicitly addressed by a trajectory that can be traced through the Grave Digger/Coffin Ed series. The pattern involves the way in which crime and policing, the relation between the two, and between the two and the Harlem community, are conceived.

As I pointed out earlier, a passage in the first novel of the series radically defines crime not as a deviation from, but rather an integral part of the U.S. economy, catering to "essential needs" of people that are not satisfied through "legitimate" business, or at least not satisfied uniformly, given the various kinds of inequalities that are also integral to the U.S. economy and culture. And far from standing in simple opposition to one another, the police and the organized crime system are also bound by economic relations. Himes's detectives are said to take "their tribute, like all real cops," and as Coffin Ed succinctly puts it, "Crime is what pays us." Nonetheless, the novels insist on an order, a standard of tolerable or legitimate action, and that requires drawing a line, constructing a frontier. The passage on crime and the police in *A Rage in Harlem* reveals some of the contradictions that ordering raises, even within Himes's radical redefinitions:

> [Grave Digger and Coffin Ed] took their tribute, like all real cops, from the established underworld catering to the essential needs of the people—gamekeepers, madams, streetwalkers, numbers writers, numbers bankers. But they rough on purse snatchers, muggers, burglars, con men, and all strangers working any racket. And they didn't like rough stuff from anybody else but themselves.

Aside from the complicated question of what constitutes "essential needs" or legitimate access to "rough stuff," the inclusion of "strangers" in the list of those who cross the line of legitimacy is a particularly troubling one given the line drawn by whites that establishes all blacks as strangers outside Harlem. Jones and Johnson themselves, by working for the white police, make themselves strangers both in and outside Harlem. The novels themselves acknowledge this tenuous position. Early in *The Heat's On,* Coffin Ed notices residents of a white-occupied apartment building watching them, and remarks, "They think we're burglars," to which Grave Digger replies, "Hell, what else are they going to think about two spooks like us prowling about in a white neighborhood in the middle of the night?" In *Blind Man With a Pistol* a black woman appeals to the two for help when white policemen try to arrest her unjustly, and Grave Digger is forced to respond: "Don't look at me . . . I'm the law too."

Theoretically, the problem is one that de Certeau's *Practice of Everyday Life* manages consistently to evade or finesse: since even dominant cultures are riven by ambiguities and contradictions emerging in the gap between ideologies and practices, how exactly is tactical resistance to be distin-

guished from complicity, or to put in terms that Himes might more likely use, how is justice to be distinguished from injustice?

Himes's novels themselves seem aware of this problem and try to address it by gradually shifting the position of Jones and Johnson from one of tactical to one of strategic resistance. The claim that the two take their tribute from the underworld like all the rest of the cops is reversed in later novels, and in *Blind Man With a Pistol* they are described as martyrs for the cause of honesty:

> Now after twelve years as first-grade precinct detectives they hadn't been promoted. Their raises in salaries hadn't kept up with the rise of the cost of living. They hadn't finished paying off their houses. Their private cars had been bought on credit. And yet they hadn't taken a dime in bribes.

It is from this position of unshakable honesty that Coffin Ed can ask, in *The Heat's On,* "Is everybody crooked on this mother-raping earth?" The immediate point of such passages seems to be the moral superiority of the two over the rest of the police force, yet the passages also work to legitimate Jones and Johnson's access to acceptable violence in Harlem on the same moral grounds. Thus Himes emphasizes the distance Grave Digger and Coffin Ed place between themselves and the Harlem community, a distance he otherwise tries to mitigate through occasional encounters between the detectives and acquaintances from their childhood. In effect, then, the resistant position of the detectives is established in terms of the individualist ideology that Mosley resorts to, because the legitimacy of Jones and Johnson's liberties with the law rests entirely on their individual moral quality, and has nothing to do with the inadequacy of the law itself. Collective resistance to a system of law and order based on collective oppression is therefore undermined altogether and the black detective located on what has been the good white side of the frontier all along. The project of collective opposition to a white supremacist culture succumbs to the fantasy of being one's own man.

Yet neither Himes nor Mosley embraces individualism unambiguously. *Blind Man With a Pistol* maps the end of multiple trajectories of the Harlem detective series, and where the career of Jones and Johnson leads to an ideological cul de sac, the narrative turns instead back to the Harlem community itself for a model of effective resistance. Indeed, the story is one of continual frustration for Grave Digger and Coffin Ed. They are forbidden by their superiors to use their prized pistols, forbidden to solve the murders that occur, and instead ordered to determine who's responsible for a series of riots in Harlem. The detectives offer one culprit themselves—Lincoln, who "hadn't ought to have freed us if he didn't want to make provisions to feed us"—and they receive another answer from Michael X, a Black Muslim leader— "Ask your boss, if you really want to know . . . he knows." Other culprits are produced by the narrative as a whole: an earnest but stupid integrationist organizer named Marcus Mackenzie; the leader of a Black Jesus movement named Prophet Ham, whose motives seem dubious; Dr. Moore, a racketeer who uses a Black Power movement as a front; and finally, a blind man with a pistol.

This multiplication of suspects, and the failure of the detectives to narrow the list to one guilty party, as the detective formula demands, suggests that the individualist question posed is the wrong one altogether. Instead the novel suggests that riots are caused by a conjuncture of various personal interests with a general atmosphere of frustration, resentment, and hatred. The parable of the blind man with a pistol that forms the narrative's conclusion, displacing the conventional tying up of loose ends in the District Attorney's office, is important in this regard. Superficially the tale suggests that riots are caused by blind anger lashing out randomly. There is a crucial, though implicit, connection between this episode and the rest of the novel, however. Though the blind man starts shooting his pistol because of a complex misunderstanding and hits all the wrong targets, the one certain condition of possibility for the event is his fear and hatred of white people that is produced by the dominant racial ideology of the U.S. It is the same ideology that creates the crowds necessary to turn an individual cause or scam into a riot, that allows Michael X to say with confidence, "Ask your boss, he knows" who's starting the riots, and impels Grave Digger to respond, "You keep on talking like that you won't live long."

The turn away from individualist ideology, which permits right and wrong to be sorted out in terms of intrinsically good and bad guys, is manifested in other ways as well. For the first time in the series, Grave Digger and Coffin Ed have serious and repeated disagreements, not about facts or procedures in a specific case, but about their own role in general. Here's a representative passage, from a scene in which the detectives question a witness, a white woman named Anny:

> "You changed your race?" Coffin Ed interrupted.

> "Leave her be," Grave Digger cautioned.

> But she wasn't to be daunted. "Yes, but not to your race, to the human race."

> "That'll hold him."

> "Naw, it won't. I got no reverence for these white women going 'round joining the human race. It ain't that easy for us colored folks."

> "Later, man, later," Grave Digger said. "Let's stick to our business."

> "That is our business."

In this reconsideration of their business, the detectives and the narrative itself suggest that the answer to the linked problems of racism and crime may not lie with them at all, but rather in collective resistance within the black community. In the earlier *Cotton Comes to Harlem,* a back-to-Africa movement is dismissed as a scam through which hustlers con the squares of Harlem, much in the same way that the Brotherhood, Black Jesus, and Black Power movements are dismissed in *Blind Man With a Pistol.* The Black Muslims also figure briefly in *Cotton Comes to Harlem* and are not subject to the same satirical treatment, but neither are they dealt with in more than a passing way. However, Grave Digger and Coffin Ed's ultimate engagement with the Black Muslims in *Blind Man With a Pistol,* an alternative ending that immediately precedes the concluding parable, is marked by startling departures from character on the part of the detectives. For the first time in the series, their engagement with another character is free of both irony and paternalistic condescension. Having chafed at orders not to use their pistols throughout the novel, here they volunteer to surrender them as a gesture of their good will toward Michael X. And when Michael X does agree to talk to them, they listen with astonishing seriousness and humility to the man described unequivocally as "the master of the situation."

I take the gesture of offering to hand over their pistols to be particularly significant because of the way it alters the position of the detectives constructed in *A Rage in Harlem* through the words "they didn't like rough stuff from anybody else but themselves." This early position reproduces a dominant definition of legitimate access to violence. The gesture of laying down arms, while not reversing that definition, at least marks a refusal on the part of Jones and Johnson to uphold it actively.

The novel doesn't explicitly endorse the Black Muslims or lay out in any detail an effective oppositional strategy. Indeed, as I noted above, Grave Digger's last words to Michael X are a grim prediction of an imminent and violent death. In addition, sexual integration is tentatively held up earlier in the novel as the ultimate solution to racial inequality. I will not pretend to resolve the question of whether the proper form of black American resistance is tactical or strategic, terms that in this case coincide roughly with integrationist/ assimilationist and black nationalist agendas. The merits and weaknesses of each of these projects have been widely debated, and the problems are perhaps best summed up by Michele Wallace (citing Harold Cruse's *The Crisis of the Negro Intellectual*) in "Doing the Right Thing":

black political philosophy has always seesawed between an integrationist/assimilationist agenda and a cultural nationalist agenda. . . . Integrationism always ends up being an embarrassment to its black supporters because of the almost inevitable racism and bad faith of its white supporters; they are willing to "integrate" with a small portion of upper-class blacks only if the masses of poor blacks are willing to remain invisible and powerless. Cultural nationalism, on the other hand, has conventionally taken refuge in a fantasy of economic and political autonomy that far too often compounds its sins by falling into precisely the trap of bigotry and racism (against gays, women, Jews, "honkies," and others) it was designed to escape.

Aside from the problems, though, integrationism and separatism need to be seen not in simple opposition to one another, but rather in triangulation with the ideology they resist, that of old or new frontier capitalist individualism. Thus far Mosley's series, at the level of representation, has examined that triangulation and opted for individualism, viewing the collective possibilities of integration or separatism as they inevitably look from the individualist position: as individual choices amounting to something like voluntary club membership. Himes's series, on the other hand, finally leaves the triangulation as exactly that, an unresolved tension pulling the community of Harlem in different directions.

Mosley gestures toward a critique of individualism in a different way, by elaborating Easy's place within a community. His relationships with other characters like Jackson Blue, Mouse, and EttaMae are not merely glyphs that naturalize the authority of the central figure, as in most detective series, but rather change in significant connection to events of the narratives—Easy makes friends, loses them, feels the conflicts among his own various interests and ties acutely enough not to set himself on a moral pedestal. As a result those other characters attain a complex subjectivity that allows us to measure Easy's own limitations, making room for ironies at the level of textual narration if not at that of the first person narrator.

Himes's critique of individualism depends also on redefining crime again in **Blind Man With a Pistol.** Michael X implies that Harlem's crime is not a self-sustaining economy, as was suggested in **A Rage in Harlem,** and that the ultimate profit goes to the white community outside. In those terms, the irreducibly collective form of "crime," rioting, that preoccupies the novel also invalidates the individualist premises of American justice and law enforcement systems. Walter Mosley's series seems headed toward similar ends, since the historical trajectory of his series so far suggests that Easy Rawlins will eventually confront the Watts riots of 1965, just as **Blind Man With a Pistol** obviously alludes

to the Harlem riots of 1964. The difference between the two series in their relation to the individualism central to frontier ideology extends beyond representations of crime and detection or policing, however. The Harlem series and Mosley's three novels employ quite different strategies of narrational enunciation that have implications as well for their relation to the urban frontier.

> It was a Black-Art bookstore on Seventh Avenue dedicated to the writing of black people of all times and from all places. . . .
>
> "If I had read all these books I wouldn't be a cop," Coffin Ed said.

Like most kinds of fiction aimed at a mass market, detective fiction generally has been fairly conventional in most formal terms. Although the detective story trades heavily on enigmas, withheld information, misdirection, and confusion, readers can generally depend on the detective to finally put all the scattered pieces in place to construct a single, accurate account of events. Walter Mosley's novels are no exception, assuming perhaps the most common form for hard-boiled detective novels since Raymond Chandler began the Philip Marlowe series: a first-person narrative told by the detective. Though any narrative form can be manipulated to various ideological ends, this form lends itself to an individualist stance, especially in a formula where the central question might be articulated as "who has the one true version of the story?" The ideological frontiers that the detective novel generally constructs, between good and evil or justice and injustice, tend to get drawn around the figure of the narrating detective trying to negotiate a path of honesty in a corrupt world. Easy Rawlins agonizes over his own shortcomings and ethical blind spots—letting himself be manipulated into betraying his friends and community in *A Red Death,* forcing his wife to have sex against her will in *White Butterfly,* and so forth. He still seems to emerge, in his own accounts, as the most scrupulous and decent of the erring humans mired in the blindness of their cultural situations. In this respect Rawlins is hardly distinguishable from Philip Marlowe, Mike Hammer, or Kinsey Millhone, though as I suggested above, his meticulous placing within a community works against the monological form of the detective's narration, and perhaps will undermine it altogether as the series continues.

Chester Himes offers no such vision of community micro-politics, but on the other hand, he established himself as a formal innovator in the field of popular crime fiction from the beginning. In what seems an ingenious tactical response to the problem of writing novels set on the far side of the urban frontier, he rejected the convention of centering the novel in the perspective of the detectives, instead combining the narrational forms of the hard-boiled detective novel with that of criminal adventure narratives like James M. Cain's *Double Indemnity* or, to stretch definitions a bit, his own *If He Hollers Let Him Go* and *Lonely Crusade.* All the novels begin with so-called crimes and criminals, and the detectives often aren't introduced until several chapters into the narrative. Subsequently the point of view tends to shift back and forth, with some additional shifting on both sides of the law/crime divide. The limitations of each perspective are emphasized through a sprinkling of observations like "[Coffin Ed] hadn't discovered any lead to Uncle Saint, so he didn't know there were already three others dead from the caper." No single character ever acquires complete knowledge of the events of the novels. The conventional aim of the detective novel, to restore or uphold an order we are asked to accept as legitimate, and that of the conventional aim of the criminal adventure thriller, to test the order but finally to succumb or be reconciled to it, are displaced by a negotiation that never leaves an established order entirely dominant or unquestioned.

This mixing of genres tends to subvert the adamant insistence of crime fiction on the accessibility of "truth" to an individual perspective and its containment within a single coherent narrative. Such resistance to a dominant fictional mode is still limited, nonetheless, by established conventions of reading. Setting the detective story against the criminal adventure story does not simply consign meaning and truth to a site of contestation. Rather, both narrative points of view are subordinated to that of the overarching narration that assures readers of getting a true account, even if it is denied to any diegetic subject. *Blind Man With a Pistol* carries narrational innovation further, however, in a way that undermines the assurance of single, stable meaning.

As narratologists such as Seymour Chatman have argued, narrative discourse as such depends upon a double time-scheme, in which we can distinguish an order of diegetic events from the order in which those events are narrated. We need not have a complete account of the events told, but conventional narrative depends upon a stable narrational time to assure that such a complete account is available in principle. Cutting between different scenes of action, different sets of characters, different points of view, and so forth, is acceptable even without explicit transitions, so long as we have the impression that a unique spatial and temporal relation between all the events could at least possibly be reconstructed.

Blind Man With a Pistol flouts these conventions. It is impossible to tell how many riots occur, or when they occur in relation to other events of the novel. There are repetitions of names and features of characters without a clear indication in some cases of whether the same character is reappearing or whether another happens to have the same feature. There are italicized interludes whose relation to the rest of

the story seems to vary considerably. For the most part events seem organized according to a clear temporal order only within specific episodes.

This narrative disorder threatens the possibility of conventional narrative closure (aside from the fact that no closure is offered even nominally within some of the particular sub-plot sequences). If we nevertheless finish the novel and try to make sense of it, we are forced to seek some other principle of unity than temporal sequence of events connected through a limited set of characters. What offers itself instead, I think, is a thematic coherence linking various episodes. And the point of that alternative mode of coherence, I think, is that the problems of racism and oppression cannot be thought through in the personal, individualistic terms that conventional narrative offers, but rather in terms of collective practices that invisibly link disparate individual stories. In other words, a novel like *Blind Man With a Pistol* reproduces ideological linkages as rhetorical ones, and therefore renders at least potentially visible in fiction what is generally concealed in the practices of everyday life in the United States.

This is only textual play, perhaps. But the Frontier remains powerful as the text of American destiny, fixing it in a genre of expansionist adventure and natural cultural dominance. The erosion of generic boundaries may then be crucial to eroding the urban frontier. From frontier adventure tales to Proposition 187, the text of the frontier has been most effective in its capacity to construct a single cultural enemy on which to build a fantasy of a unified American people pursuing a linear national narrative. The disruption of narrative exemplified in Himes's *Blind Man With a Pistol* may offer one effective strategy for disrupting the frontier narrative itself in a way that lays bare its ideological underpinnings and internal contradictions. Mosley's digressions into the micropolitics of community and between communities pull at the seams of the detective narrative in another way, undermining the traditional generic reassurance that the good guys and bad guys can be sorted out, and disrupted order reestablished. Pursuing this trajectory, investigating the genre as much as the crimes, may lead toward and beyond the achievement of *Blind Man with a Pistol,* toward multiple stories that produce irreducibly multiple culprits. A radical rewriting of the frontier might thus be an overdue rewriting of Turner's thesis, insistently restoring the frontier's fragmentation that he was at pains to conceal.

David Cochran (essay date Autumn 1996)

SOURCE: "So Much Nonsense Must Make Sense: The Black Vision of Chester Himes," in *The Midwest Quarterly,* Vol. XXXVIII, No. 1, Autumn, 1996, pp. 11-30.

[*In the following essay, Cochran discusses the portrayal of racial tensions in Himes's fiction and states that "Himes viewed race as a dialectical relationship which progressed toward increasing absurdity."*]

In the penultimate chapter of Chester Himes's 1969 crime novel **Blind Man With A Pistol**—the last in his series of stories set in Harlem—the eponymous character makes his first appearance, shooting craps in a small gambling house on a hot summer afternoon. After losing all his money, he walks to the subway station and boards a train. An eccentric pride precludes the man from admitting his blindness to anyone, including himself, and his naturally surly temperament is exacerbated by his gambling losses. On a crowded subway car he sits across from Fat Sam, an embittered black laborer carrying on a loud and intense argument with himself. Fat Sam mistakes the blind man's unseeing gaze for a mocking stare and begins belligerently shouting at him. Unaware that he is the object of Sam's anger, the blind man pays no attention, which further infuriates Sam. When a female passenger sticks up for the blind man, he unleashes his anger at both her and Sam, saying all he wants is the money that has been taken from him. A neighboring black minister, reading the *New York Times,* puts down his paper and attempts to maintain peace, pleading "Brothers! Brothers! You can settle your differences without resorting to violence." A nearby white passenger retorts, "Violence hell! What these niggers need is discipline," to which the blind man responds, "Beware, mother-raper! Beware!" causing the preacher to quickly sit down. But both the white man and Fat Sam take offence at the warning and the white man knocks the blind man down. Getting up, the blind man states "If'n you hit me again, white folks, I'll blow you away." As the minister begs "Peace, man, God don't know no color," the blind man pulls a..45 from beneath his coat and fires, accidentally striking the minister in the heart. A woman begins screaming "BLIND MAN WITH A PISTOL" and pandemonium ensues as the blind man fires two more shots. "The second blasts were too much," Himes writes. "Everyone reacted immediately. Some thought the world was coming to an end; others that the Venusians were coming. A number of the white passengers thought the niggers were taking over; the majority of the soul people thought their time was up." Fat Sam escapes by shattering the subway's glass doors just as the train pulls into the 125th Street station. Others follow as the station landing becomes strewn with fleeing, stumbling bodies, cut by glass, screaming in panic. As the woman continues yelling "BLIND MAN WITH A PISTOL" the title character stumbles over the bodies lying about the floor, waving his gun, asking "Where? Where?"

Meanwhile, on the street above the subway station, a group of angry Harlem residents is watching the demolition of condemned slum buildings, part of an urban renewal program which has succeeded primarily in displacing the ghetto's in-habitants without providing new housing. The famous black New York City detectives, Coffin Ed Johnson and Grave Digger Jones—heroes of eight Himes novels—are standing at the intersection of Lenox Avenue and 125th Street using their signature long-barreled, nickel-plated .38-caliber pistols on .44-caliber frames to shoot rats as they flee the buildings being demolished while several white policemen stand by watching. Having long since been pulled off the case that provided the original plot for the novel—a case everyone, including the author, seems to have lost sight of—the two must vent their fury on Harlem's literal, rather than figurative, rats. Onto this scene, from out of the nearby subway entrance, bursts Fat Sam immediately followed by a crowd of running, hysterical people covered in blood. As the white policemen pull their pistols, the blind man comes stumbling up the stairs and fires his gun, hitting a white cop in the middle of the forehead, before being gunned down by the other officers. Witnessing the chaotic unfolding of events, the denizens of Harlem immediately begin crying that white cops have killed an innocent black man. Rumors spread rapidly and Harlem is quickly engulfed in a full-scale riot. When Grave Digger speaks with his commanding officer, Lieutenant Anderson, an hour later, Anderson asks, "Can't you men stop that riot?"

> "It's out of hand, boss," Grave Digger said.
> "All right, I'll call for reinforcements. What started it?"
> "A blind man with a pistol."
> "What's that?"
> "You heard me, boss."
> "That don't make any sense."
> "Sure don't."

With this incredible scene—simultaneously violent, disordered, grotesque and humorous—Himes draws his series of Harlem crime novels to its logical conclusion, as the barely controlled chaos which had permeated his world view explodes into a maelstrom of racial apocalypse. Coming in 1969, the scene contained numerous symbolic references to specific recent events as well as to more general racial tensions. A year after the assassination of Martin Luther King, Jr., Himes portrays an ineffectual, intellectual black minister pleading nonviolence and reconciliation who, ironically, is the gunman's accidental first victim. At a time when both political parties sought to outdo the other in calling for "law and order"—a racially-charged code term for cracking down on urban violence—Himes shows a white bystander scornfully declaring "what these niggers need is discipline." Fat Sam, a handyman for a white family, embittered by his low pay, demeaning work, and degrading contacts with his white employers, pathetically seeks to exert what power he can by forcing the other passengers to listen to his tirade. Outside the subway, Himes depicts the impotent anger of Harlem's black population confronting a distant, bureaucratic city government which cavalierly destroys its homes. Meanwhile, tensions with white police, the only immediate and tangible targets of the imperious city government, have reached the breaking point. Finally, the title character symbolizes the blind rage of African Americans who lash out in violence, with other blacks usually being their first victims. As Himes writes in the preface, the novel's central metaphor derived from a true incident a friend told him about, "and I thought, damn right, sounds like today's news, riots in the ghettos, war in Vietnam, masochistic doings in the Middle East. And then I thought of some of our loudmouthed leaders urging our vulnerable soul brothers on to getting themselves killed, and thought further that all unorganized violence is like a blind man with a pistol."

In the interactions between the blind man and the people he meets on the street and subway and between the residents of Harlem and the police, Himes conveys what Mikhail Bakhtin termed heteroglossia. With this concept, Bakhtin referred to the way in which discourse

> is entangled, shot through with shared thoughts, points of view, alien value judgments and accents. The word, directed toward its object, enters a dialogically agitated and tension-filled environment of alien words, value judgments and accents, weaves in and out of complex interrelationships, merges with some, recoils from others, intersects with yet a third group: and all this may crucially shape discourse, may leave a trace in all its semantic layers, may complicate its expression and influence its entire stylistic profile.

Some recent scholars of postmodern theory give a largely benign view of this concept, seeing in this heteroglossia a mélange of discourses of various racial, ethnic and other subcultures in which everyone can find his own niche. According to Jim Collins, the chorus of competing voices is so complex that the issue of power becomes problematic and the source of power, ultimately, unlocatable. But Himes's vision is much more sinister, as he sees in this cacophony of voices what Strother Martin would call "a failure to communicate" and the implications of this failure, Himes predicts, will be catastrophic. And unlike Collins, Himes firmly situates power in the distant, undemocratic, and white city government and portrays the competing discourses in Harlem as being a dialogic of the powerless.

Minority artists played a special role in the development of an emergent critical culture in the post-World War II period, since, as George Lipsitz has said, "[t]heir exclusion from political power and cultural recognition has allowed aggrieved populations to cultivate sophisticated capacities for ambiguity, juxtaposition and irony." Himes employs these artistic strategies in an effort to unmask the cultural contra-

dictions of America in the postwar period. His paradigm, though, differs in significant ways from the traditional African American worldview. As Lawrence Levine has said, historically blacks have had little understanding of and appreciation for absurdity. Normally, only those fully integrated into a system of beliefs have the luxury of being able to see it as absurd. With their history of exclusion from and struggle to gain admission into the dominant culture, black Americans have seldom viewed the social order as fundamentally meaningless, as that would similarly render their struggle meaningless.

> As an expatriate living in Europe during the height of the civil rights struggle, Himes gained enough distance from the American situation to formulate a concept of race relations that contrasted sharply with most African Americans' understanding of the issue.
> —*David Cochran*

But Himes viewed absurdity as a concept central to an understanding of race. As an expatriate living in Europe during the height of the civil rights struggle, Himes gained enough distance from the American situation to formulate a concept of race relations that contrasted sharply with most African Americans' understanding of the issue. Himes viewed race as a dialectical relationship which progressed toward increasing absurdity. As he wrote in the second volume of his autobiography:

> Racism introduces absurdity into the human condition. Not only does racism express the absurdity of the racists, but it generates absurdity in the victims. And the absurdity of the victims intensifies the absurdity of the racists, ad infinitum. If one lives in a country where racism is held valid and practiced in all ways of life, eventually, no matter whether one is a racist or a victim, one comes to feel the absurdity of life.
>
> Racism generating from whites is first of all absurd. Racism creates absurdity among blacks as a defense mechanism. Absurdity to combat absurdity.

Himes experienced the absurdity of both Southern and Northern racism. Born in 1909 in Jefferson City, Missouri, Himes spent his early years living in several Southern and border states where his father taught blacksmithing at a series of black state colleges. The family moved to Cleveland, Ohio, in 1925, where, after graduating from high school Himes began consorting with the criminal underworld. In 1928 he robbed the house of a rich white couple at gunpoint, stealing money, jewels, and a car, and fled to Chicago. Arrested in Chicago, Himes was badly beaten by two detectives—who handcuffed his feet together and his hands behind his back, hung him upside down with the cuffs on his feet draped over an open door, and then beat him around the ribs and testicles. Extradited to Cleveland, Himes was sentenced to twenty-five years in the Ohio State penitentiary.

While in prison, Himes began writing, publishing short stories in such magazines as *Esquire* in 1934. Paroled in 1936, he returned to Cleveland where he worked for the Works Progress Administration as a member of the Ohio Writer's Project. Moving to California in 1940, he worked at a variety of unskilled jobs in the booming war industries and wrote his first two novels, *If He Hollers Let Him Go* and *Lonely Crusade*. The failure of the second novel left Himes embittered and determined to leave the country at the first chance and, in 1953, he emigrated to Europe. But during his European sojourn Himes was always a stranger in a strange land, his soul seldom finding refuge. Though he lived in France for nearly two decades, he never bothered to learn the language. His relations with the community of black American artists in Paris were always strained, and he was as appalled by French racism as by American. He ran through a series of difficult relationships with white women, both American and European. And, despite his eventual success in France, he was as unable to earn an adequate living from his writing in Europe and America and, for nearly a decade and a half, lived a largely hand-to-mouth existence.

It was in 1956, during one of these many periods of dire financial straits, that Himes's friend Marcel Duhamel (who had translated *If He Hollers Let Him Go*), urged him to write a crime story. The suggestion seems much more natural now than it did to Himes at the time. Not only did Himes claim not to know how to write detective stories, but virtually no black American authors had ever used the mystery story genre. But as Duhamel remarked, Himes's prose already bore a strong resemblance to the American style of Tough-Guy detective stories. "Write like you did in the novel I translated," he told Himes. "All action. Perfect style for a detective story." Beyond Himes's personal style, the genre itself is in many ways ideally suited for minority writers. As John Reilly has written:

> Tough-Guy fiction in viewpoint or setting reflects conditions produced by the class and caste system. In the manner of Naturalism it depicts character as the product of social conditions, and from the standpoint of an outsider it provides a guide to the disorder of American civilization, making clear that the cause of it all is eventually located in the practices of the dominant class.

Finally Himes's adoption of the hard-boiled crime genre allowed him to escape the standard categorization of black writers, which fit all writing by blacks under the heading "protest." Like Ralph Ellison's Invisible Man, African American authors in the post-war period were invisible because of the dominant white culture's determination to force them into a predetermined, stereotyped mold of protest writer, a problem Himes had faced repeatedly. In the shadow of Richard Wright, black writers were expected to portray, with naturalistic despair, the effects of racism. But at the same time blacks were given only this one creative outlet, the public was growing weary of black protest novels. Himes too was dissatisfied with the form. In his autobiography he wrote:

> I had the creative urge, but the old, used forms for the black American writer did not fit my creations. I wanted to break through the barrier that labeled me as a "protest writer." I knew the life of an American black needed another image than just the victim of racism. We were more than just victims. We did not suffer, we were extroverts. We were unique individuals, funny but not clowns, solemn but not serious, hurt but not suffering, sexualists but not whores in the usual sense of the word; we had a tremendous love of life, a love of sex, a love of ourselves. We were absurd.

Ironically, only by allowing himself to be typecast as a writer within another fictional genre—one relegated to second-class citizenship in the field of literature—could Himes escape the confines of being a black writer.

The universe of Himes's Harlem crime stories is marked by chaos, ambiguity, absurdity and violence while his description of it is filled with "that bitter self-corroding irony which white people call 'Negro humor.'" Harlem's residents are so accustomed to the disorder of their surroundings that they feel comfortable in it. As Grave Digger says at one point, "so much nonsense must make sense." Even the elements themselves contribute to this sense of chaos and violence, as all of Himes's stories take place either in the oppressive heat of summer or the bitter cold of winter. In the Harlem of his crime stories, Himes found a perfect metaphor for his worldview, which he described in his autobiography.

> Some time before, I didn't know when, my mind had rejected all reality as I had known it and I had begun to see the world as a cesspool of buffoonery. Even the violence was funny. A man gets his throat cut. He shakes his head to say you missed me and it falls off. Damn reality, I thought. All of reality was absurd, contradictory, violent and hurting, It was funny, really, if I could just get the joke. And I got the handle, by some miracle.

The atmosphere of violence pervading this world is immediately apparent as virtually all of the stories open with a scene mixing chaotic and graphic violence with slapstick comedy. ***The Real Cool Killers,*** for example, begins with the only white man in a crowded bar being accosted by a diminutive patron with a knife. When Big Smiley, the bartender, comes to the aid of the white man, the small knifeman cuts his arm. Big Smiley reaches beneath the bar and pulls out a fireman's axe and swings it, cutting off the attacker's arm. "The severed arm in its coat sleeve, still clutching the knife, sailed through the air, sprinkling the nearby spectators with drops of blood, landed on the linoleum tile floor, and skidded beneath the table of a booth." When Big Smiley continues to advance on the small knifeman, he yells, "Wait a minute, you big mother-raper, till Ah finds my arm! It got my knife in his hand," before collapsing. When the white manager announces that everyone should remain calm and that the police have been called, the bar's remaining patrons stampede for the door. As soon as they exit, a hophead on the sidewalk accuses the same white patron of messing with his wife and begins pursuing him with a gun. The chase is soon joined by a gang of juvenile delinquents disguised as Arabs—the Real Cool Moslems—and a large crowd of black bystanders. Finally the white man is shot and the hopheaded gunman and the gang stand around his body laughing until the police come. Several of the other opening scenes are equally as bizarre.

These wildly absurd introductions merely foreshadow increasing violence, and chaos to come. In Himes's view, he sought to realistically portray the effects of violence. Cultural images of violent death rarely depict the effects guns, knives and other weapons have on the human body. "Even when they just say 'blown to pieces' that doesn't describe what they look like blown to pieces," he said. "When a shell hits a man in a war, bits of him fly around, half of his liver is flying through the air, and his brains are dribbling off. These are actual scenes, no one states these outright." No one except Himes, whose graphic descriptions of violence utilize grotesque metaphors and, often, slapstick comedy. One typical passage, in which a group of gunmen invade a large barbecue and opens fire, says, "There was a burst from a machine gun. A mixture of teeth, barbecued pork ribs, and human brains flew through the air like macabre birds."

Himes self-consciously sought to place his portrayal of violence in the broader context of American history and culture. "[T]here is no way," he told John Williams, "that one can evaluate the American scene and avoid violence, because any country that was born in violence and has lived in violence always knows about violence." It is, in fact, the close interrelationship between American culture and violence which has served as the basis of the large body of American hard-boiled detective novels. "'Cause no one," Himes said, "*no one,* writes about violence the way that Americans do[,] . . . for the simple reason that no one understands violence or experiences violence like the American civilians do. . . . American violence is public life, it's a public way of life, it became a form, a detective story form."

Similarly Himes plays with other icons of American culture in his portrayal of violence. Coffin Ed and Grave Digger are often viewed as fast-on-the-draw sheriffs and Harlem a dangerous frontier town. As one character says upon seeing Ed and Digger arrive on the scene of a crime, "Now we've got those damned Wild West gunmen here to mess up everything." The two mete out their own brand of frontier justice in an attempt to maintain some semblance of order amidst the daily chaos of Harlem. Their first appearance in a book is almost always immediately followed by mayhem. Arriving on the scene in ***The Real Cool Killers*** in which the crowd has just chased down and shot the white man from the bar, Ed and Digger line up the suspects. When one of the defiant Real Cool Moslems throws a bottle of ceremonial perfume at Coffin Ed—who once had a bottle of acid thrown in his face—then Ed fires off two shots, killing the perfume-thrower, injuring a woman bystander and sending the crowd into a panicked stampede, trampling the injured woman and two others.

In this case, first appearances are not deceiving. Beatings, threats and shootings provide the primary means by which Digger and Ed solve their cases. In ***A Rage in Harlem,*** they take turns slapping one suspect on the cheek. "They slapped him fast, from one to another, like batting a Ping-pong ball. Gus's head began ringing. He lost his sense of balance and his legs began to buckle. They slapped him until he fell to his knees, deaf to the world." Later in the novel, when the beautiful suspect Imabelle tries to seduce Grave Digger in order to avoid being arrested, Himes writes, "He slapped her with such savage violence it spun her out of the chair to land in a grotesque splay-legged posture on her belly on the floor. . . ."

That Himes's attitude toward his protagonists could not have been unambiguous is reflected in ***The Crazy Kill*** where Ed and Digger take the suspect Chink back to police headquarters to elicit information from him. There they beat him in the same manner the young Himes was beaten when arrested for armed robbery. Chink's ankles are cuffed together and his hands behind his back, he is hung upside down by his ankles from the top of an open door, then the two put their heels in Chink's armpits and push down. Such practices frequently lead Digger and Ed into trouble both with the Harlem community and the police hierarchy, and the two often find themselves reprimanded or suspended by the commissioner and excoriated in the press for excessive use of force. But as Ed and Digger understand, their brutal tactics are necessary for survival in the violent and bizarre world of Harlem. "They had to be tough to work in Harlem. Colored folks didn't respect colored cops. But they respected big shiny pistols and sudden death. It was said in Harlem that Coffin Ed's pistol would kill a rock and that Grave Digger's would bury it."

With this portrayal of his two detectives, Himes epitomizes a major transformation occurring in the late fifties and sixties in popular cultural images of heroes. In his study of sixties' films, Ethan Morden has discussed the "very relative morality" of the era by focusing on actor Lee Marvin. In the fifties, Marvin had been typecast as a brutal and violent heavy and then graduated to playing heroes in the sixties, though in fact his heroes are as brutal and violent as his villains had been. "In Marvin," Morden said, "we have . . . a figure to centralize the decade's growing belief in violence as an expression not of villainy but of humanity." In his discussion of Marvin's performance in *Point Blank* Morden could easily be describing Coffin Ed and Grave Digger— "There's steel in his mad, even charm in his tense. No regrets. No opinions. When you deal with cheaters and liars and 'the organization,' violence is like breathing: necessary." In the era's popular culture, perhaps only Mickey Spillane's Mike Hammer rivalled Ed and Digger for sheer brutality. But the New York City Hammer stalked was a Manichean world, with good and bad easily identifiable. Himes's heroes, on the other hand, inhabit an ambiguous and chaotic universe where values are relative and the two blunder through acting on an imperfect knowledge of good and evil. Thus while Hammer never accidentally shoots innocent bystanders, Ed and Digger frequently beat and injure the innocent along with the guilty.

What redeems these two is that they adhere to a strict code of ethics, though one that does not necessarily jibe with the law. In this sense they fit in with one of the dominant themes of American hard-boiled fiction. From Dashiell Hammett's Sam Spade to Robert Parker's Spenser, detectives have been considered heroic if, in the midst of a chaotic, violent, and morally ambiguous world, they have carved out and maintained a rigorous code of honor. The first principle of Ed's and Digger's code is absolute loyalty to each other. The two are constantly together to the point that their personalities are almost interchangeable. Distrusted by the community they serve, frequently at odds with the department hierarchy, the two realize they can absolutely count on no one but each other.

In their Sisyphean quest to maintain order in Harlem, Digger and Ed have formulated a complex code of selective law enforcement.

> They took their tribute, like all real cops, from the established underworld catering to the essential needs of the people—game-keepers, madams, streetwalkers, numbers writers, numbers bankers.

But they were rough on purse snatchers, muggers, burglars, con men, and all strangers working any racket. And they didn't like rough stuff from anybody but themselves.

As Reilly has pointed out, Ed and Digger accept organized crime because its very organization lends consistency and stability to the community. But individual crime is unpredictable and thus exacerbates the normal chaos, so it is intolerable.

The two also have a well-ordered hierarchy of crime, with drug-dealing being the most serious offense. As Digger says of pushers, "I hate this type of criminal worse than God hates sin." When the two are reprimanded for using excessive force in punching a dwarf pusher in the stomach and inadvertently killing him, the district attorney says, "You killed a man suspected of a minor crime, and not in self-defense," to which Digger relies, "You call dope peddling a minor crime? [. . .] All the crimes committed by addicts—robberies, murders, rapes. . . . All the fucked-up lives. . . . All the nice kids sent down the drain on a habit. . . . Twenty-one days on heroin and you're hooked for life. . . . Jesus Christ, mister, that one lousy drug has murdered more people than Hitler. And you call it *minor!*"

Similarly the two often reach compromises which, while technically violations of the law, more fully meet their own moral code and serve relatively to preserve order, peace and stability. In *All Shot Up,* they find the $50,000 that Harlem's corrupt political boss had stolen and, instead of returning it, send it anonymously to the New York Herald Tribune Fresh Air Fund, which sends young New York boys of all races on summer vacations in the country, and send an anonymous telegram to the crooked boss saying "Crime doesn't pay." And in *Cotton Comes to Harlem,* they force a corrupt white con man to pay an $87,000 bribe so that they can return the money to eighty-seven families that have invested $1,000 each in a crooked back-to-Africa scam.

Digger and Ed are also admirable because of their inestimable skill as cops on New York's toughest beat and the envy they have earned from other, mainly white, policemen. When they break up a potential riot in *Cotton Comes to Harlem,* Himes writes, "The white cops looked at Grave Digger and Coffin Ed with the envious awe usually reserved for a lion tamer with a cage of big cats." On occasion the two have to earn the respect of other policemen. In *All Shot Up,* at the scene of a crime, a white cop twice uses the word "nigger." Ed tells him:

> "If you use that word again I'll kick your teeth down your throat."
> The cop bristled. "Kick whose teeth—."
> He never got to finish. Coffin Ed planted a left hook

in his stomach and crossed an overhand right to the jaw.

Himes once said in an interview that "the characters in my detective stories, in order to remain credible, had to grow with the passage of time and as they did so, they developed a greater race consciousness." The major difference between Ed and Digger and the rest of the police department has always been their direct connection with the community. At one point Coffin Ed explains the difference in attitude between them and others in the department, saying:

> "Brody is a homicide man and solving murders is his business. He goes at it in a routine way like the law prescribes, and if some more people get killed while he's going about it, that's just too bad for the victims. But me and Digger are two country Harlem dicks who live in this village and don't like to see anybody get killed. It might be a friend of ours."

But over the course of the series, their affinity for the people of Harlem takes on a more specifically racial feeling. In *Cotton Comes to Harlem,* the next-to-last book in the series, Digger and Ed are deeply moved by the plight of the eighty-seven poor, black families that have put up their hard-earned money on the basis of a dream of a return to Africa. As Himes says, "Everyone has to believe in something; and the white people of America had left them nothing to believe in." The two detectives sympathize with the people taken in by the back-to-Africa movement while rejecting the movement itself, a sentiment that paralleled Himes's own. In the early sixties, Himes had become a friend of Malcolm X's. But, as Himes says:

> I agreed with everything about his program except his religion. I tried . . . to tell him that the Moslems were the first people to go into black Africa and collect the blacks whom they took to the African coasts and sold to the European slave-traders, but Malcolm saw the Moslems as the saviors of the blacks. I had been in Egypt and had seen the blacks in Cairo and Alexandria still treated as slaves, and I didn't agree with him at all. But I was all in favor of his politics.

In *Blind Man With a Pistol* Digger and Ed specifically discuss Malcolm. Ed says:

> "You know one thing, Digger. [Malcolm] was safe as long as he kept hating white folks—they wouldn't have hurt him, probably have made him rich; it wasn't until he began including them in the human race they killed him. That ought to tell you something."

> "It does. It tells me that white people don't want to be included in a human race with black people," [Digger responds].

The Harlem which Grave Digger and Coffin Ed patrol is as stylized as the Bedford-Stuyvesant in Spike Lee's 1989 film *Do the Right Thing.* As Himes writes in his autobiography, he had only lived in Harlem a brief time and so, while he knew the geography of the area, "I didn't really know what it was like to be a citizen of Harlem. . . . *The Harlem of my books was never meant to be real; I never called it real; I just wanted to take it away from the white man if only in my books.*" By lifting Harlem out of the realm of realism and into the symbolic, Himes can portray it, in Edward Margolies's words, "as the intensification, the logical absurdity, the comic horror of the black experience of America." In a typical passage, Himes captures the contradictions of black life in Harlem, wherein the widespread poverty fosters serious social problems while, at the same time, the community offers black people's only refuge from whites.

> It was a street of paradox: unwed young mothers, suckling their infants, living on a prayer; fat black racketeers coasting past in big bright-colored convertibles with their solid gold babes, carrying huge sums of money on their persons; hardworking men, holding up the buildings with their shoulders, talking in loud voices up there in Harlem where the white bosses couldn't hear them; teen-age gangsters grouping for a gang fight, smoking marijuana weed to get up their courage; everybody escaping the hot-box rooms they lived in, seeking respite in a street made hotter by the automobile exhaust and the heat released by the concrete walls and walks.

Violence permeates Himes's Harlem, both the repressive violence of the police and the violence borne of frustration that blacks practice on one another. Knifings, shootings, throat-slashings are an everyday occurrence, "because," as Grave Digger says, "these folks in Harlem do things for reasons nobody else in the world would think of. Listen, there were two hardworking colored jokers, both with families, got to fighting . . . and cut each other to death about whether Paris was in France or France was in Paris." Violence even marks Himes's description of Harlem's geography. In describing the distance between two points, he says, "It was ten minutes by foot, if you were on your way to church, about two and a half minutes if your old lady was chasing you with a razor."

In Himes's view, the violence of Harlem's residents is a pathological response to their social position. Harlemites prey on each other in wildly absurd ways and often for ridiculous reasons. Frantz Fanon described a similar tendency among colonial peoples, terming it "collective autodestruction." "While the settler or the policeman," Fanon said, "has the right the livelong day to strike the native, to insult him and to make him crawl to them, you will see the native reaching for his knife at the slightest hostile or aggressive glance cast on him by another native; for the last resort of the native is to defend his personality vis-à-vis his brother."

Himes's universe is populated with grotesque characters. As Jackson Lears has argued, a recurrent theme of modernist artists has been the belief that the commercial image of the sleek, successful twentieth-century American is neither as substantial nor as realistic as the pathetic, unfortunate and grotesque denizens of, for instance, Winesburg, Ohio, or Yoknapatawpha County, Mississippi. Similarly, black modernists in the post-World War II period faced the slick, Sidney Poitier image of the successful black integrationist, one they knew did not convey the reality of their lives. But not in their darkest nightmares could Sherwood Anderson or William Faulkner conjure up the grotesqueries of Himes's Harlem, peopled as it is with a giant albino Negro idiot, a dwarf pusher, an elderly, withered female faith healer/heroin pusher, a transvestite nun/con man/junkie who sells tickets to heaven, a ninety-year-old black Mormon with eleven wives and a brood of children who run around naked and eat from a trough, and numerous others. Even Coffin Ed is a grotesque; his face, badly scarred when a criminal threw acid in it, is now a patchwork of varicolored skin grafted from his thigh. "The result was that Coffin Ed's face looked as though it had been made up in Hollywood for the role of the Frankenstein monster." Minor characters also often have deformities or physical handicaps. In such figures Himes gave form to his thesis that American racism severely deformed black personality and culture.

Of Himes's contemporaries, perhaps only Nelson Algren consistently provided as nuanced and sympathetic a portrait of society's losers, its petty criminals and small-time con men. Moreover, Himes never romanticizes his subjects. His vision is absent any cloying populist sentimentalism about the nobility of the poor. With his naturalistic sensibility, Himes accepts the dehumanizing effects of the environment. When Lieutenant Anderson says of Harlem, "I hate to see people tearing at one another like rapacious animals," Digger responds, "Hell, what do you expect? As long as there are jungles there'll be rapacious animals."

Just as Levine has argued that slave tales were an ongoing and perceptive parody of white slave-owners' culture, so Himes's Harlem is a savage satire of American capitalist culture. As he said in a 1948 speech, blacks may have "the face of Africa, but [their] heart has the beat of Wall Street." Harlem's residents are as avaricious as the big money men on Wall Street, but the stakes they play for are smaller and the money-making schemes they engage in often do not have the official imprimatur of law. As Himes describes it:

> Looking eastward from the towers of Riverside Church, perched among the university buildings on the high banks of the Hudson River, in a valley far below, waves of gray rooftops distort the perspective like the surface of a sea. Below the surface, in the murky waters of fetid tenements, a city of black people who are convulsed in desperate living, like the voracious churning of millions of hungry cannibal fish. Blind mouths eating their own guts. Stick in a hand and draw back a nub.

That is Harlem.

Within this environment blacks have developed a vibrant economy and the requisite skills for success. As Digger once remarks, "If our people were ever let loose they'd be a sensation in the business world, with the flair they got for crooked organizing," to which Ed replies, "That's what the white folks is scared of."

In portraying Harlem as the underside of American-style capitalism, Himes offers a vision of America as being, at its base, violent, chaotic, and absurd. This view captures what Marshall Berman identified as one of the central tenets of modernism, a realization of "the destructive brutalities that bourgeois nihilism brings to life," the logical outgrowth of a world in which, as Marx wrote in *The Communist Manifesto,* "all that is solid melts into air." Just as Coffin Ed and Grave Digger struggle constantly merely to maintain some semblance of order in Harlem, so Himes depicts the "order" of the American capitalist system as a thin veneer masking a dark and nihilistic core. At the end of **Blind Man With a Pistol,** the sheen is ripped away and the chaos that has always lay just below the surface comes out in the open. Similarly, in his 1969 short story **"Prediction,"** Himes depicts a lone black gunman hiding in a church watching a parade of white policemen march by. He opens fire, and in the exchange between himself and the police department, more than seventy people are killed, the downtown area decimated and the church levelled. "In the wake of this bloody massacre," Himes writes, "the stock market crashed. The dollar fell on the world market. The very structure of capitalism began to crumble. Confidence in the capitalistic system had an almost fatal shock. All over the world millions of capitalists sought means to invest their wealth in the Communist East." In this passage Himes articulates what had been implicit throughout his crime series, a sensibility that captures, in Berman's words

> the glory of modern energy and dynamism, the ravages of modern disintegration and nihilism, the strange intimacy between them; the sense of being

caught in a vortex where all facts and values are whirled, exploded, decomposed, recombined; a basic uncertainty about what is basic, what is valuable, even what is real; a flaring up of the most radical hopes in the midst of their radical negations.

Or as the unnamed Harlem intellectual whom Himes quotes as an epigraph to **Blind Man With a Pistol** says, "Motherfucking right, it's confusing; it's a gas, baby, you dig."

FURTHER READING

Criticism

Austin, Jacqueline. "Harlem on His Mind." *The Village Voice Literary Supplement* 31, No. 19 (May 1986): 26-7.
  Austin discusses Himes' Harlem Thrillers.

Brunet, Elena. Review of *Cotton Comes to Harlem,* by Chester Himes. *Los Angeles Times Book Review* (11 December 1988): 14.
  Praises Himes's *Cotton Comes to Harlem* for "vividly

bring[ing] to life the streets of Harlem and delv[ing] into the minds of criminal and policemen with equal expertise."

Diawara, Manthia. "*Noir* by *Noirs:* Towards a New Realism in Black Cinema." *African American Review* 27, No. 4 (Winter 1993): 525-37.
  Discusses how Himes's *A Rage in Harlem* and contemporary black films that "participate in the discourse of *film noir . . .* force the audience to reexamine the genre and its uses by Black filmmakers."

Fabre, Michel. "Chester Himes's Ambivalent Triumph." In his *From Harlem to Paris: Black American Writers in France, 1840-1980,* pp. 215-37. Urbana, IL: University of Illinois Press, 1991.
  Analyzes Himes's relationship with France during his years of exile there.

Newton, Adam Zachary. "From Exegesis to Ethics: Recognition and Its Vicissitudes in Saul Bellow and Chester Himes." *The South Atlantic Quarterly* 95, No. 4 (Fall 1996): 979-1007.
  Discusses the relationship between Himes's *If He Hollers Let Him Go* and Saul Bellow's *The Victim.*

Additional coverage of Himes's life and career is contained in the following sources published by Gale: *Black Literature Criticism; Black Writers,* **Vol. 2;** *Contemporary Authors,* **Vol. 25-28R, 114;** *Contemporary Authors New Revision Series,* **Vol. 22;** *Dictionary of Literary Biography,* **Vols. 2, 76, 143;** *DISCovering Authors Modules: Multicultural; Major Twentieth-Century Writers.*

Langston Hughes

1902-1967

(Full name James Mercer Langston Hughes) American poet, dramatist, novelist, nonfiction, and short story writer.

The following entry presents an overview of Langston Hughes's career through 1995. For further information on his life and works, see *CLC,* Volumes 1, 5, 10, 15, 35, and 44.

INTRODUCTION

Langston Hughes is one of the best known African-American writers of the twentieth century and a figure at the forefront of the Harlem Renaissance. Through his poetry Hughes expressed the voice of many African Americans, capturing the language, experiences and strength of common people. While Hughes is known as the poet laureate of Harlem, he has also been recognized for his depictions of the African-American struggle in his prose, plays, and literature for children.

Biographical Information

Hughes was born February 1, 1902, in Joplin, Missouri. While he was an infant his parents split and he moved to Lawrence, Kansas where he was cared for by his grandmother. His mother worked in Kansas City as an actress and his father practiced law in Mexico. When Hughes's grandmother died he moved briefly to Illinois before settling in Cleveland, Ohio where he attended Central High School. There he ran on the track team and was the class poet, publishing poems in the school newspaper. After he graduated he lived for a year with his father in Mexico and then attended Columbia University for one year. Hughes took various jobs and traveled the world. In 1926 he published his first book of poems *The Weary Blues.* He attended Lincoln University in Pennsylvania, earning a B.A. in 1929. In 1930 his first novel *Not Without Laughter* won the Harmon gold medal for literature and Hughes decided to pursue a career in writing. He lectured across the country and lived in New York City, writing prolifically. Throughout the 1930s Hughes became involved with the political Left and in 1953 he was investigated by the Senate subcommittee chaired by Joseph McCarthy for his alleged involvement in selling books to libraries abroad. Hughes died in New York City May 22, 1967.

Major Works

Hughes published works in many genres but was primarily

known as a poet. He published his first collection of poems *The Weary Blues* in 1926, containing one of his most famous poems "The Negro Speaks of Rivers." Other important volumes of poetry are *Fine Clothes for the Jews* (1927), *Montage of a Dream Deferred* (1951), *Selected Poems of Langston Hughes* (1959), and *Ask Your Mama: 12 Moods for Jazz* (1961). In his poetry Hughes renders the voices, experiences, emotions, and spirit of African Americans. In his attempt to capture the lives of everyday African Americans he deals with subjects like prostitution, racism, lynchings, and teenage pregnancy. Hughes is well known for the influence of jazz and bebop music in his poetry, both as a subject matter and as a structure. Critics have noted his skill in imitating the sound, cadence, and rhythms of the blues style as well as capturing the humor, despair, and loneliness depicted in the music. Hughes's most famous fiction involved a character named Jesse B. Semple, often called Simple. These short stories provided Hughes with another opportunity to showcase the problems facing African Americans. In Hughes's many plays he captures the vernacular of African Americans and is able to employ such innovative techniques as theatre-in-the-round and audience participation.

Critical Reception

Throughout his career, Hughes encountered mixed reactions to his work. Many black intellectuals denounced him for portraying unsophisticated aspects of lower-class life, claiming that his focus furthered the unfavorable image of African Americans. However, other critics have noted the uneven quality of his writing. Critics agree that Hughes is at his best when he depicts the everyday experiences of African Americans and that these depictions are often their best in his most simple and direct poetry. Critics also praise Hughes's innovative ability to imitate the sounds and the mood of jazz and the blues. Reviewing *Fine Clothes for the Jews,* Julia Peterkin writes, "He has taken the joys and woes of dishwashers and bell-hops, crap-shooters and cabaret girls, broken women and wandering men, and, without losing their strong racial flavor, he has molded them into swift patterns of musical verse." Later in life, Hughes was criticized for failing to address controversial issues and to reflect the more militant fight for civil rights. However, later critics note that Hughes remained constant in his focus on the problems of racism and the failure of African Americans to realize the American Dream. James Presley argues that Hughes promoted the idea that "the Negro's bed has been lined with injustices, but eventually the American Dream will triumph."

PRINCIPAL WORKS

The Weary Blues (poetry) 1926
Fine Clothes to the Jew (poetry) 1927
Not Without Laughter (novel) 1930
Dear Lovely Death (poetry) 1931
The Negro Mother and Other Dramatic Recitations (poetry) 1931
The Dream Keeper and Other Poems (poetry) 1932
Scottsboro Limited: Four Poems and a Play in Verse (poetry and drama) 1932
Popo and Fifina: Children of Haiti [with Arna Bontemps] (juvenilia) 1932
A Negro Looks at Soviet Central Asia (nonfiction) 1934
The Ways of White Folks (short stories) 1934
Mulatto (drama) 1935
Little Ham (drama) 1936
When the Jack Hollers [with Arna Bontemps] (drama) 1936
Don't You Want to Be Free? (drama) 1938
A New Song (poetry) 1938
The Big Sea: An Autobiography (autobiography) 1940
Shakespeare in Harlem [with Robert Glenn] (poetry) 1942
Freedom's Plow (poetry) 1943
Jim Crow's Last Stand (poetry) 1943
Lament for Dark Peoples and Other Poems (poetry) 1944
Fields of Wonder (poetry) 1947
One-Way Ticket (poetry) 1949

Troubled Island (libretto) 1949
Simple Speaks His Mind (short stories) 1950
Montage of a Dream Deferred (poetry) 1951
Laughing to Keep from Crying (short stories) 1952
The First Book of Negroes (juvenilia) 1952
Simple Takes a Wife (short stories) 1953
The Glory Round His Head (libretto) 1953
Famous American Negroes (juvenilia) 1954
The First Book of Rhythms (juvenilia) 1954
The First Book of Jazz (juvenilia) 1955
The Sweet Flypaper of Life [with Roy DeCarava] (nonfiction) 1955
The First Book of the West Indies (juvenilia) 1956
I Wonder As I Wander: An Autobiographical Journey (autobiography) 1956
A Pictorial History of the Negro in America [with Milton Meltzer] (nonfiction) 1956
Simple Stakes a Claim (short stories) 1957
Simply Heavenly (drama) 1957
Famous Negro Heroes of America (juvenilia) 1958
Tambourines to Glory (novel) 1958
Selected Poems of Langston Hughes (poetry) 1959
The First Book of Africa (juvenilia) 1960
The Best of Simple (short stories) 1961
Ask Your Mama: 12 Moods for Jazz (poetry) 1961
The Ballad of Brown King (libretto) 1961
Fight for Freedom: The Story of the NAACP (nonfiction) 1962
Something in Common and Other Stories (short stories) 1963
Tambourines to Glory (drama) 1963
The Prodigal Son (drama) 1965
Simple's Uncle Sam (short stories) 1965
The Panther and the Lash: Poems of Our Times (poetry) 1967
Black Magic: A Pictorial History of the Negro in American Entertainment [with Milton Meltzer] (nonfiction) 1967
Black Misery (nonfiction) 1969
Good Morning Revolution: Uncollected Social Protest Writings by Langston Hughes (nonfiction) 1973
The Collected Poems of Langston Hughes (poetry) 1994
The Sweet and Sour Animal Book (juvenilia) 1994

CRITICISM

James Presley (essay date Autumn 1963)

SOURCE: "The American Dream of Langston Hughes," in *Southwest Review,* Vol. 48, No. 4, Autumn, 1963, pp. 380-86.

[*In the following essay, Presley looks at the theme of the American dream in Hughes's poetry, drama, prose, and nonfiction.*]

One summer in Chicago when he was a teen-ager Langston Hughes felt the American Dream explode in his face; a gang of white youths beat him up so badly that he went home with blacked eyes and a swollen jaw.

He had been punished for cutting through a white neighborhood in the South Side on his way home from work. That night as he tended his injuries young Hughes must have mused disturbed thoughts about fulfilment of his American dream of freedom, justice, and opportunity for all.

A few years after that traumatic Chicago afternoon Hughes inaugurated a prolific and versatile writing career. Over the four decades separating then and now, his reaction to the American Dream has been one of his most frequently recurring themes. For many years Hughes, often hailed as "the poet laureate of the Negro people," has been recognized by white critics as an author-poet of the protest genre. Others, more conservative and denunciatory, have assailed Hughes as radical and leftist, to mention the more polite language. In both instances the critics referred to Hughes's treatment of imperfections in the American Dream that we, as a nation, hold so dear.

The American Dream may have come dramatically true for many, Hughes says, but for the Negro (and other assorted poor people) the American Dream is merely that—a dream. If the critics and would-be censors had read further they would have noted that for Hughes the American Dream has even greater meaning: it is the *raison d'être* of this nation. Nevertheless, Hughes was still a regular target for right-wing barbs as recently as the 1960's, having been anathema to the right wing for decades.

Long before the Chicago summer during World War I Hughes had experienced the plight of the Negro in America. Although he was not born in the South where conditions probably were worse, the boy Langston had faced the practical prejudices of the Middle West and the North. In Topeka, Kansas, he was to have been dispatched across town to a Jim Crow school, but his determined mother complained so vigorously to the school board that Hughes was enrolled, the only Negro pupil, in the elementary school nearest his home. And there the American Dream of equal treatment for everyone shone through almost perfectly. But a shadow fell: while most of the teachers were kind to him, one kept referring to his color in the classroom. On occasions when the teacher had singled him out for his brownness, several of his classmates would climax the day by throwing stones or epithets at him. There was a great stain on the American Dream.

All was not stain, though. While one teacher exercised her prejudices and some classmates poked fun and more tangible objects at him, other classmates championed his cause. Con-

sequently the youth Langston was never completely alienated, and despite his poverty and darkness in a sea of white he was to know that there were others who believed in equality and justice for him too. Later on, in integrated Cleveland, Ohio, he was named poet of his high school class. Ever since those moments out of a sensitive childhood the future poet has maintained his faith in the American Dream, while confirming his enmity to the stifling and transmogrification of it. In pursuing the Dream, Hughes has followed a course very similar to that of the American Negro in general: the Dream is fine—if realized.

Langston Hughes was born February 1, 1902, at Joplin, Missouri. The three races of America—Indian, Negro, and Caucasian—contributed to his bloodlines: slaves, warriors, planters. His cultural heritage was a proud and lively one. His earliest memories were of his grandmother, a copper-skinned woman of strong Indian ancestry, sitting on the same platform with President Theodore Roosevelt at a public commemoration of the Harper's Ferry raid. She was the last surviving widow of John Brown's historic raid. Her husband, a free Negro, had been one of the first to die in the raid. Young Langston at an early age learned to prize freedom highly.

As a child of separated parents Hughes grew up in many different places in the heartland of America—Kansas, Illinois, Ohio, Missouri, Colorado—and began his globetrotting life with a visit to his father in Mexico where the elder Hughes had fled to escape Jim Crow.

After an interlude at Columbia University in the early 1920's Hughes signed on a freight steamer and saw Africa and Europe. In 1925 he worked for Dr. Carter G. Woodson, editor of *Journal of Negro History,* and in 1926 his first book of poetry, **The Weary Blues,** appeared. As a student at Lincoln University that year he won the Witter Bynner undergraduate poetry prize; he graduated from Lincoln in 1929.

As the depression reached its depth in the early 1930's he had to scratch for new means of earning his living, but he found the perfect way by making poetry pay: he organized a public reading tour of the South. Subsequent travels in the 1930's took him around the world in connection with a movie-making project which never made it to the screen. A Negro company had gone to Russia to film *Porgy and Bess* under the auspices of the Soviet government. Hughes went as a writer. When the Soviets delayed and delayed so that the movie was never made Hughes converted the opportunity into one to see as much as he could of Russia. When the Spanish Civil War broke out a few years later Hughes covered it for the Baltimore *Afro-American.* By the time the realities of World War II reached America, Hughes was in his forties and an established Harlem figure busily producing volumes and volumes of poetry, newspaper columns, anthologies, books for juveniles, novels, short stories, and plays.

As might be expected Hughes has written most frequently, though not exclusively, of Negro characters. Consequently the importance of the color line in America is frequently reflected in his work. The effect of the color line on the American Dream is therefore an integral part of his protest. In one of his biographies for young people, *Famous Negro Music Makers* (1961), Hughes quotes musician Bert Williams as saying: "It is not a disgrace to be a Negro, but it is very inconvenient." In viewing the string of "inconveniences" vitally affecting the dignity of black Americans Hughes voices his reactions to shriveled freedom, dwarfed equality, and shrunken opportunity—blemishes on the essential ingredients of the American Dream. His poetry and prose echo protest and, usually, hope.

Two poems especially reflect his theme of protest and hope. **"Let America Be America Again,"** published in *Esquire* and in the International Worker Order pamphlet *A New Song* (1938), pleads for fulfilment of the Dream that never was. It speaks of the freedom and equality which America boasts, but never had. It looks forward to a day when "Liberty is crowned with no false patriotic wreath" and America is "that great strong land of love." Hughes, though, is not limiting his plea to the downtrodden Negro; he includes, as well, the poor white, the Indian, the immigrant—farmer, worker, "the people" share the Dream that has not been. The Dream still beckons. In **"Freedom's Plow"** he points out that "America is a dream" and the product of the seed of freedom is not only for all Americans but for all the world. The American Dream of brotherhood, freedom, and democracy must come to all peoples and all races of the world, he insists.

Almost invariably Hughes reflects hope, for that is part of his American Dream. However, some of his poems, apparently written in angry protest, are content to catch the emotion of sorrow in the face of hopelessness and gross injustice. One of his most biting is a verse in *Jim Crow's Last Stand* (1943). Aimed at southern lynch law which had just taken the lives of two fourteen-year-old Negro boys in Mississippi, and dedicated to their memory, the poem cried that **"The Bitter River"** has

> . . . *strangled my dream:*
> *The book studied—but useless,*
> *Tools handled—but unused,*
> *Knowledge acquired but thrown away,*
> *Ambition battered and bruised.*

In one of his children's poems, **"As I Grow Older,"** the poet looks at the Dream again. He had almost forgotten his dream; then it reappeared to him. But a wall rose—a high, sky-high wall. A shadow: he was black. The wall and the shadow blot-

ted out the dream, chasing the brightness away. But the poet's dark hands sustain him.

> *My dark hands!*
> *Break through the wall!*
> *Find my dream!*
> *Help me to shatter this darkness,*
> *To smash this night,*
> *To break this shadow*
> *Into a thousand lights of sun,*
> *Into a thousand whirling dreams*
> *Of sun!*

On a similar theme, one of the concluding poems in his child's book, *The Dream Keeper* (1932), treats of the Dream. In **"I, Too,"** the "darker brother" of America eats in the kitchen when company calls. But tomorrow, he says, he'll eat at the table; nobody will dare tell him to eat in the kitchen then.

> *Besides,*
> *They'll see how beautiful I am*
> *And be ashamed—*
> *I, too, am America.*

In *Montage of a Dream Deferred* (1951) Hughes might have been thinking of the wall which blackness had erected in the child's poem. *Montage's* background is Harlem. There is a wall about Harlem, and the American Dream, as a reality, exists outside Harlem. Harlem (and, one can just as well add, the world of the American Negro) is a walled-in reality where dreams are deferred. The faded Dream pierces black New Yorkers to their hearts. Things which "don't bug . . . white kids" bother Harlemites profoundly. White boys cling to the stimulating dream that any American may grow up to be President of the United States. The Negro boy knows better. He also knows that the liberty and justice of the Pledge to the Flag are inherent rights only of white folks. Even in Harlem, the capital of the North which Hughes once described in a novel as "mighty magnet of the colored race," the American Dream is frayed and ragged.

Probably the greatest portion of Hughes's poetry does not refer specifically to the American Dream, despite the habit of many critics' labeling him a protest writer primarily. But in *Ask Your Mama: 12 Moods for Jazz* (1961) he returns to the Dream, in jazz tempo with barbs appropriate for a dream too long deferred. With an impish introduction of the melody "Dixie" in the background, the poet combines dreams and nightmares to produce a mural of black power in the South; he dreams the Negroes have voted the Dixiecrats out of office. As a result Martin Luther King becomes governor of Georgia and high posts go to other Negro patriots. The remainder of the passage reflects the opposite of the southern power structure for the past hundred years or so. Negroes relax on the verandas of their mansions while their white sharecroppers sweat on the plantations. The reverse pattern of historical reality is carried out even to the extent of Negro children having white mammies, of which there are Mammy Faubus, Mammy Eastland, and Mammy Patterson. (And, if he had written later, Mammy Wallace, one thinks.) The patronizing air of the plantation white bourbon is reproduced as the poet notes that the "*dear darling old white mammies*" are sometimes even buried with the family!

But the grandiose dream sequence, itself reflecting how one-sided the American Dream has been in the South, is short-lived. The poet returns to the pessimistic here and now. The Negro can't keep from losing, even when he's winning, he moans in blues tempo. *Ask Your Mama* relates to the vast spectrum of the American Dream, as it affects Negroes. There are the hardships of blockbusting, or integrating a white residential area, the bitterness of Negro artists, the stereotyped attitudes of whites toward Negroes, the hope of a better material world for ambitious Negroes, and the eternal suspicions cast upon any Negro who does anything worthwhile or, often, anything that is ordinary for white folks to do.

As effectively as Hughes's poetry presents the unfulfilled fraction of the American dreamers, the Simple stories of his prose elaborate the most telling criticism of racial discrimination. Social criticism and humor travel hand in hand as his character, Jesse B. Semple, depicts the America of discrimination in an intimate, personal manner. Although Simple, as his friends call him, lives in Harlem, the loquacious Negro comments pithily on prejudice he has experienced in the South and in the Army. Jim Crow is his personal devil.

One of the several features of American life that especially disturbs Simple is that Jim Crow gives little or no respite to the Negro. Even a foreigner just off the boat from Europe can Jim Crow the Negro who has been following the Dream for generations. "He *starts* on top of my head," moans Simple. Jim Crow is the despoiler of the American Dream, and Simple reserves his most stinging venom for the southern way.

In a piece, **"Jim Crow's Funeral"** from the book *Simple Stakes a Claim* (1957), one of three books filled with Simple stories, the Harlemite preaches Jim Crow to his reward. He summarizes his emotions:

> It gives me great pleasure, Jim Crow, to close your funeral with these words—as the top is shut on your casket and the hearse pulls up outside the door— and Talmadge, Eastland, and Byrnes wipe their weeping eyes—and every coach on the Southern

Railroad is draped in mourning—as the Confederate flag is at half-mast—and the D.A.R. has fainted—*Jim Crow, you go to hell!*

Jesse B. Semple is a bitter man much of the time. He has been segregated, underpaid, underhoused. When a Negro experiences injustice anywhere, North or South, Simple feels it too. In one selection Simple refers to Jim Crow and lynching of Negroes in the South. "But these are *Christian* white folks that does such things to me," he says. "At least, they call themselves Christians. . . . They got more churches down South than they got up North. They read more Bibles and sing more hymns." Another time Simple pleads for a game preserve for Negroes, where the government would protect them from lynching and beatings. "Colored folks rate as much protection as a buffalo, or a deer," Simple says somberly.

Eventually Simple discusses all aspects of the social system which frustrates completion of the American Dream. The white folks who say they love the Negro people do not really know how the Negro lives in America, he says. They haven't slept in colored hotels or eaten in colored restaurants, they haven't sent their children to a segregated Negro school, and they haven't used a Jim Crow toilet in a bus station. "White folks has got a theoretical knowledge of prejudice. I want them to have a real one," Simple says. "I know I am equal. What I want is to be *treated* equal." Therein he touches the heart of the failure of the American Dream to date: the transition from theory to practice has not been made. White folks, insists Simple, would not put up with Jim Crow if they had experienced the unique system themselves. They need to know what it means to Negroes.

Despite the many crosses the Negro has to bear, though, he is durable, Simple believes. In **"Radioactive Red Caps"** Simple discusses the atomic bomb and his expectation of living through a nuclear war. "If Negroes can survive white folks in Mississippi," he said, "we can survive anything."

Hughes's other prose—his novels and short stories, his juvenile histories and biographies, his two autobiographical books—is less laden with reflections on the American Dream deferred, though his personal accounts, *The Big Sea* (1940) and *I Wonder as I Wander* (1956) draw in some detail his encounters with Jim Crow and even with threats of violence as a result of his being on the darker side of the color line in the South. Of his plays, his earliest, **"Mulatto"** (1931), deals intimately with the Negro end of miscegenation on a southern plantation. The play concerns the consequences which follow relentlessly and brutally when a planter's mulatto son asserts himself as the Colonel's heir. The results are tragic; the Dream is squashed. Hughes's history of the NAACP, *Fight for Freedom* (1962), of course, is directly concerned with that organization's attempts to realize the American Dream for all Negroes.

Among his novels, *Not Without Laughter* (1930) indicates the effect of the American Dream on the boy Sandy, growing up in a small Midwestern town. The boy Sandy, as perhaps the boy Langston might have done years before, contemplates the color situation in America. "Being colored is like being born in the basement of life, with the door to the light locked and barred—and the white folks live upstairs," Sandy thinks. It was a white folks' world, Sandy was inclined to believe; it was one in which an unhappy run-in with a Southern white cost him his job in a hotel. An ambitious lad, Sandy wanted to be a railroad engineer when he grew up, but his aunt told him there were no colored engineers.

The characters in *Not Without Laughter* display divergent views toward white people. Tempy, Sandy's aunt, tries to emulate whites. His other aunt, Harriett, hates them. His grandmother retreats to religion, waiting for the other world to relieve her of the burden of this world's shattered Dream. Sandy's mother, Annjee, is long-suffering but hopeful. His father, Jimboy, echoes the anguish of being Negro in a white-dominated world. One of Sandy's light friends, Buster, intends to realize the Dream by passing for white when he grows up and leaves town. Yet Sandy does not single out any one view of his relatives and seize it as his own. His view of the American Dream comes empirically, as he sees (as did Langston Hughes) that there is both good and bad emanating from the white society. Sandy's eyes are wide open, and busily recording.

The boy Sandy doubtless views the Dream as Hughes had. Sandy saw the evils behind the Dream's façade, but he also knew of the good there. In spite of his sorrows and hardships Sandy had hope, pride, and ambition. He had the will to fight on, to achieve his dream. Hope is implicit in most of Hughes's work. In one of his short stories from *Laughing to Keep from Crying* (1952), **"One Friday Morning,"** in which a Negro girl has been deprived of an art prize because of race prejudice, her sympathetic Irish teacher urges the girl to keep faith. Speaking of the obstacles which the Irish had to overcome after they came to America and were discriminated against, the teacher says: " . . . we didn't give up, because we believed in the American dream, and in our power to make that dream come true." The theme is a recurring one with Hughes: the Negro's bed has been lined with injustices, but eventually the American Dream will triumph.

Throughout Hughes's life—and his literary expression—the American Dream has appeared as a ragged, uneven, splotched, and often unattainable goal which often became a nightmare, but there is always hope of the fulfilled dream

even in the darkest moments. During World War II Hughes, commenting on the American Negroes' role in the war, recognized this. " . . . we know," he said in a 1943 speech reprinted in *The Langston Hughes Reader* (1958),

> that America is a land of transition. And we know it is within our power to help in its further change toward a finer and better democracy than any citizen has known before. The American Negro believes in democracy. We want to make it real, complete, workable, not only for ourselves—the fifteen million dark ones—but for all Americans all over the land.

The American Dream is bruised and often made a travesty for Negroes and other underdogs, Hughes keeps saying, but the American Dream does exist. And the Dream *must* be fulfilled. In one of his verses he put it more plainly. He might have been speaking to his harshest political critics or to the white youths who beat him up on that long-ago summer day in Chicago.

> *Listen, America—*
> *I live here, too.*
> *I want freedom*
> *Just as you.*

Rita B. Dandridge (essay date December 1974)

SOURCE: "The Black Woman as a Freedom Fighter in Langston Hughes's *Simple Uncle Sam*," in *CLA Journal*, Vol. 18, No. 2, pp. 273-83.

[*In the following essay, Dandridge explores the portrayal of women as active civil rights freedom fighters in* Simple Uncle Sam.]

Despite her historical significance, the black woman as a fighter for the liberation of her people from racial injustice is just beginning to emerge as an important character in the literature of black American writers. She appears as a devoted Negro maid who becomes a revolutionary killer in Ed Bullins' play, "The Gentleman Caller" (1968). In Ted Shine's play, "Contribution" (1968), Mrs. Love, who is in her seventies, befriends whites opposed to the black man's struggle for freedom and then poisons them by putting "special seasoning" in the food she gives them. Nettie McCray's play, "Growin' into Blackness" (1969), introduces Pearl, an articulate black nationalist, who urges her girlfriends to fight against the genocidal tactics of the white man by having babies in order to build a strong black nation for the future. The final pages of Ernest Gaines' novel, *The Autobiogra-*

phy of Miss Jane Pittman (1971), focus on Miss Jane, a one-hundred-and eight-year-old ex-slave, who protests with others in her community the jailing of a black girl who drank from a water fountain intended for whites only.

Although the black woman as a freedom fighter has begun to get her due in the literature of black American writers, the most strikingly realistic descriptions of black female freedom fighters remain those of Langston Hughes in *Simple's Uncle Sam.* This is no accident because Hughes was consciously aware of the important role of the black female freedom fighter to whom he has paid tribute in several of his works. He includes a biographical sketch of Harriet Tubman, whom he calls "the Moses of her people," in *Famous American Negroes* (1954). Biographical sketches of Harriet Tubman and Ida B. Wells appear among those of advocates of freedom in *Famous Negro Heroes of America* (1958). In *Fight for Freedom* (1962), he weaves biographical sketches of Daisy Bates and Lillie Jackson into the historical narrative of the NAACP. In 1967, he dedicated his last volume of verse, *The Panther and the Lash,* to Rosa Parks, who, in refusing to give up her seat on a bus to a white man, precipitated the boycott of the Montgomery buses in 1955.

Aware then of the black woman's historical significance, Hughes was able in his fiction to show that black women, no less than black men, have fought racial injustice in a variety of ways. We see this particularly in his novel, *Simple's Uncle Sam,* where the female relatives of the main character, Jesse B. Semple (commonly called Simple), include an accommodationist, a non-violent integrationist, and a militant black nationalist. The tactics they employ as freedom fighters enable Joyce, the accommodationist; Lynn Clarisse, the non-violent integrationist; and Minnie, the militant nationalist; to function as counterparts to Booker T. Washington, Martin Luther King and Malcolm X, respectively. By including the stratagems used by these females, Hughes is able to bring into focus the various approaches to racial equality taken by black men and black women for more than half of the twentieth century.

Simple's wife, Joyce, is the first female freedom fighter encountered in *Simple's Uncle Sam.* She is a modern, urban counterpart of Booker T. Washington, the leading spokesman of his race at the turn of the twentieth century. Seeking to transcend the limited existence imposed upon her as a poor black woman living in the ghetto of Harlem, Joyce uses Washington's accommodationist approach to racial justice. She diligently prepares herself by hard work and self-help to be accepted by white America. She educates herself, saves her money to buy a home and tries to get her black neighbors to better themselves. By her actions she closely resembles Washington, who believed in and lived by his saying that "Brains, property, and character for the Negro will settle the question of civil rights. The best course to pursue in regard to the civil rights bill in the South is to let it alone; let it alone and it will settle itself."

Both Washington and Joyce stress the importance of an education related to the world in which they live. Not wanting to be an illiterate in a society of literate men, Washington taught himself how to read and write, went to free schools when he was not working in the salt furnaces and coal mines of West Virginia and then worked his way through Hampton Institute, where he received a liberal education. As an educator at Tuskegee Institute, he prepared his Southern black students to meet the challenge of their rural environment by training them to be farmers, craftsmen and teachers. An urbanite, living within the cultural capital of America, Joyce educates herself by developing her aesthetic interest. Despite her job outside the home and her numerous household chores, she still finds time to read librettos of operas and then drags Simple downtown to Carnegie Hall to operatic performances. She also attends lectures on various subjects and takes an avid interest in painting. Though Washington emphasized the practical and utilitarian aspect of education while Joyce stresses the aesthetic, both are similar in that they apply themselves to acquire the knowledge which will enable them to make a meaningful adjustment in their surroundings and win the respect of the larger environment.

For Joyce, as it was for Washington, an education includes developing character. She is particularly anxious to improve the behavior of her neighbors, the "unurbanized Negroes" who have migrated to Harlem from the South, just as Washington was interested in improving the morals of the rural Southern black who lacked standards by which to mold his character. She reminds Simple that "To act right yourself is not enough. You must also help others to act right". Weary of the "unurbanized Negro ... throwing garbage out the window, sweeping trash in the street, fussing on the stoop, and cussing on the corner," Joyce joins the women's auxiliary of the Urban League, "which has done much to help transpose the rural Negro to big-city ways". She spends long hours in the library gathering information for her Club's project on "how to take the country out of the Negro," and after completing her library research, she solicits Simple's aid in forming a Block Club to keep her block in Harlem clean. Joyce's efforts to improve the social behaviour of her neighbors parallel Washington's attempts to socially uplift blacks by emphasizing cleanliness, good conduct, self-discipline and respectability, all of which, he felt, are necessary for the black man to be accepted by white America.

The extreme manifestation of Joyce's desire to overcome racial inequality is her adept managing of household finances. Just as Washington cautioned blacks to be thrifty, Joyce urges Simple not to spend so much money for beer, and she refuses to include as little as a dollar in the budget for his beer habit. Instead, she saves her money for a home in the suburbs—a home away from the rat-infested tenements of black Harlem, a home with "wall-to-wall carpets and a chandelier . . . a porch and a porch swing . . . ". She tells Simple that "America has got two cultures, which should not be divided as they now is, so let's leave Harlem". Similar to Washington, Joyce looks upon the acquisition of property as a means of advancing her social status, and her emphasis on thrift to improve her living condition echoes Washington's insistence that the advancement of the black man in various areas of life depends upon his economic progress.

As an accommodationist constantly improving herself and trying to get others to do the same in order to be accepted by the white world, Joyce, as Washington was, is a very tactful person, careful to avoid any friction between the two races. On the delicate issue of mixed marriage, for instance, she is quick to voice her dislike for marriages between blacks and whites: "It is living in sin for a colored man to marry anybody related to Talmadge, Eastland, Wallace, Sheriff Clark, and Satan—and all white folks bears kinship". Her professed opposition to intermarriages seems a modern version of the firm stand against the socializing of the two races held by Washington in his Atlanta Exposition Address. Washington said, "In all things that are purely social we can be as separate as the fingers, yet one as the hand in all things essential to mutual progress." Even Simple fails to understand the reasoning of his wife, who gives money to CORE and the NAACP and "Yet get mad when she sees integration [a mixed couple] in action". He is unaware that Joyce's motive for working behind the scenes (as Washington often did) donating money to end segregation and her refusal to condone a defiant display of race mixing are to avoid any public indiscretion that would bring disagreement between the races. Though a very proud woman, she is yet a paradoxical one who, similar to Washington, implies by her actions that the policy of conciliation will gain more for her race in the long run than anything else and that upward striving rather than social conflict is the key to racial justice.

Hughes's second female freedom fighter is Lynn Clarisse, Simple's cousin and a counterpart of Martin Luther King, who was catapulted into national prominence as a civil rights leader in the middle 1950's when he successfully organized and led a boycott of the segregated buses of Montgomery, Alabama. Both Lynn Clarisse and King have middle-class backgrounds. Lynn Clarisse is the daughter of a wealthy Virginia mortician; King was the son of a respected and well-to-do Georgia preacher. Both are products of elite Southern black colleges. Lynn Clarisse is a Fisk University student; King matriculated at Morehouse. More important to this discussion, however, is that, in briefly depicting her as a female King, Hughes appropriately draws Lynn Clarisse from the mass of black college students who were influenced by King and protested in the early 1960's, via sit-ins, freedom rides

and mass marches their dissatisfaction with the progress of desegregation in Southern facilities.

Similar to King, Lynn Clarisse firmly believes in equal justice for black and white Americans and employs the tactic of non-violent persuasion to achieve this end. She participates in freedom rides, one of which in Alabama leaves her with a broken shoulder and scarred neck, after she is beaten with a policeman's billy club (p. 84). Despite the temporary setbacks of her struggle for racial justice, Lynn Clarisse, like King, who was a victim of threats, beatings and mob violence, never allows her courage to dissipate. She steels herself to meet the challenge of the next demonstration. In this novel, she looks forward to protesting against the South's denial of political rights to blacks by participating non-violently in voter registration drives.

Lynn Clarisse's passive endurance of the blows inflicted upon her in the Alabama freedom ride and her benevolent desire to face the possibility of similar harassment in a voter registration drive call to mind the two sources which inspired King as a freedom fighter—Gandhi's passive resistance and Christian motivation. By manifesting goodwill and brotherly love in her non-violent struggle for freedom, Lynn Clarisse, similar to King, is able to dramatize the grievances of her race, show the wrongdoings of white Southern racists against blacks to be unjustifiable and allow her oppressors ample opportunity to correct their wrongdoings. Her willingness to suffer the pain inflicted upon her by white racists suggests a faith in man similar to that held by King, who said, "There is within human nature something that can respond to goodness." Moreover, by holding no grudges against those who mistreat her, she gives direction to what Martin Luther King considered to be the ultimate solution to racism:

> Desegregation will break down the legal barriers and bring men together physically, but . . . fears, prejudice, pride and irrationality, which are barriers to a truly integrated society . . . will be removed only as men [black and white] are possessed by the invisible law which etches on their hearts the conviction that all men are brothers and that love is mankind's most potent weapon for personal and social transformation.

When Lynn Clarisse goes to New York City for a cultural visit during the summer, it becomes evident that her freedom of movement there is what she has been fighting for in the South. She independently moves into Greenwich Village and becomes an accepted resident there. She freely associates with all the artists "white and colored, and the *jazz* peoples and the writers". She takes advantage of the opportunity to see her people perform in plays which, she says, "will hardly be touring down South". Her unhampered mobility in the large city, which she has never visited before, seems intended by Hughes to be representative of the black man's ultimate exemption from the restrictions placed on his civil rights which Martin Luther King dreamed of.

Lynn Clarisse is succeeded by Minnie, the most developed of the three females and a counterpart of Malcolm X, the self-appointed black nationalist spokesman, who emerged during the militant black liberation movement of the 1960's exhorting black Americans to unite in fighting for the common goal of liberation and the control of the economic, social and political forces in their communities. Minnie and Malcolm have similar backgrounds preceding their conversions to militant activism. An illiterate Southern transplant who migrates North looking for freedom, Minnie discovers that once in Harlem, the black Mecca, she is still a victim of racial oppression and can find employment involving only menial tasks. The young Malcolm, ill-prepared to do more than servant's work, also migrated to Harlem, via Boston, after living in Lansing, Michigan, where his family originally moved from Omaha, Nebraska, in search of freedom, but where his father was allegedly murdered by white racists and his mother was declared insane by white welfare agents and the courts. Seeking a way to cope with the difficult circumstances of life, Minnie eventually becomes a hustler, who lives off the money she sweet-talks from her various Harlem boyfriends and works only when it is necessary "to keep her head above water". A clever and conniving woman, she maintains friendship with one man until his money runs out, and then she leaves him and searches for another "kind of lifeboat or lifeguard." By fleecing her unsuspecting boyfriends for survival, Minnie is comparable to Malcolm, who, discovering himself to be a victim of racial oppression while living in Harlem, economically exploited blacks as a thief, pimp, and dope peddler. Trying to keep up her courage, Minnie frequents bars and drinks heavily, just as Malcolm stayed high on narcotics. Both emulate whites, who instill in them the values of a racist society: Minnie crowns her head with an expensive blond wig, which she thinks makes her look like a movie star, and Malcolm wore his hair processed. Observing Minnie closely and disgustingly, her cousin, Simple, concludes that she is "a disgrace to the race."

After spending six years of a ten-year term in jail, where he discovered Allah and the religion of Islam, and after living a few years in Detroit as a Black Muslim minister, Malcolm undergoes a second transformation; he becomes a militant black nationalist. Comparably, Minnie undergoes metamorphosis after living in Harlem for ten years, where she becomes more and more disillusioned and frustrated by the unfulfilled promises of freedom. She ceases being a helpless character and explodes into a militant activist. In their new roles as black nationalists, Malcolm and Minnie wear their hair *au natural* (an affirmation of their true and beautiful black selves), and both become concerned with the oppressive conditions of the black community. Both attack the most visible sign of white oppression in Harlem—the policeman. Malcolm opposed policemen who perpetuate social degradation by accepting graft from persons involved in gambling, prostitution, and dope peddling. During a Harlem riot protesting the killing of a fifteen-year-old black boy by a white policeman, Minnie attacks a white cop beating a defenseless old black man who does not move on fast enough when ordered to. Though she accidentally receives a head wound from a flying bottle not meant for her and is taken to Harlem Hospital to be treated, she later tells her friends that "It is a good thing that bottle struck me down, or I would of tore that cop's head every way but loose."

Minnie believes in being non-violent "when the other parties are non-violent, too, . . . " but says, "I did not come to Harlem to look a white army of white cops in the face and let them tell me I can't be free in my own black neighborhood on my own black street in the very year when the Civil Rights Bill says *you shall be free*." She implies that the use of violence is necessary to achieve justice for the black man when the tactic of non-violence fails, and in this respect she echoes Malcolm, who said:

> I *am* for violence if non-violence means we continue postponing a solution to the American black man's problem—just to *avoid* violence. I don't go for non-violence if it means a delayed solution. To me a delayed solution is a non-solution. Or I'll say it another way. If it must take violence to get the black man his human rights in this country, I'm *for* violence . . . no matter what the consequences, no matter who was hurt by the violence.

Similar to Malcolm, Minnie is willing to lay her life on the line for freedom. She says, 'I would gladly die for freedom and come back to haunt white folks."

Not only does Minnie want police brutality stopped in her community, but she also wants political oppression to cease. She and Malcolm X consider the chief political opponents to the progress of the blackman's freedom to be Negroes acting as political stooges for a corrupt democracy. Showing scorn for such persons, Malcolm said:

> So America's strategy is the same strategy as that which was used in the past by the colonial powers: divide and conquer. She plays one Negro leader against the other. She plays one Negro organization against the other. She makes us think we have different objectives, different goals. As soon as one Negro says something, she runs to this Negro and asks him what do you think about what he said. Why anybody can see through that today—except some of the Negro leaders.

Minnie censures Negro leaders who cater to the whims of whites by "advising Harlem to go slow" in attaining its freedom. Unalterably opposed to the stratagem of gradualism advocated by some Negro leaders, she attacks these leaders by first pointing out that whites never told her to go slow at cotton-picking time:

> When I was down South picking cotton, didn't a soul tell me to go slow and cool it. "Pick more! Pick more! Can't you pick a bale a day? What's wrong with you?" That's what they said. Did not a soul say, "Wait, don't over-pick yourself." Nobody said slow down in cotton-picking days. So what is this here now? When Negroes are trying to get something for themselves, I must wait, *don't demonstrate*? I'll tell them big shots. How you sound?

And then she says that whites were never told to go slow when they brought harm to blacks:

> Did not a soul tell that man who shot Medgar Evers in the back with a bullet to be cool. Did not a soul say to them hoodlums what slayed them three white and colored boys in Mississippi to cool it. Now they calling me hoodlums up here in Harlem for wanting to be free. Hoodlums? Me, a hoodlum? Not a soul said "hoodlums" about them night riders who ride through the South burning black churches and lighting white crosses. Not a soul said "hoodlums" when the bombs went off in Birmingham and blasted four little Sunday School girls to death, little black Sunday School girls. Not a soul said "hoodlums" when they tied an auto rim to Emmet Till's feet and throwed him in that Mississippi River, a kid just fourteen years old. . . . Yet them that's supposed to be my leaders tell me, "Give up! Don't demonstrate! Wait!" To tell the truth, I believe my own colored leaders is ashamed of me. So how are they going to lead anybody they are ashamed of? Telling me to be cool. Huh! I'm too hot to be cool— so I guess I will just have to lead my own self— which I will do. I will lead myself.

The militant tone, historical references and informal and impromptu style of Minnie's speech are immediately recognized as characteristics of Malcolm's discourses. And her decision to lead herself is a helpful pointer to Malcolm's idea that Negroes should seek political freedom by organizing independent political parties because the capitalist parties and the two-party system, which put Negro stooges in office, are their enemies. But more significantly, her decision to lead herself is a reminder of the self-help tenet of Malcolm's black nationalist philosophy: "A race of people is like an individual man; until it uses its own talent, takes

pride in its own history, expresses its own culture, affirms its own selfhood, it can never fulfill itself."

Langston Hughes's brief descriptions of Joyce, Lynn Clarisse, and Minnie attest to his social awareness that the black woman has not sat on the sidelines during the black liberation struggles of the twentieth century, but has been actively engaged in the fight for her race's freedom. His inclusion of female figures, instead of male ones to serve as counterparts to Washington, King and Malcolm X, enables him to make amends for the oversight of black writers in general who have failed to depict the black woman as a freedom fighter and to assert with a non-chauvinist attitude that the female is just as much needed as the male is in the liberation struggles. Moreover, since Hughes severs his females from the traditional role of black matriarch and engages them in battles for racial justice, they give solidarity to the freedom struggles and aid in creating a sense of urgency to the appeals of the freedom fight. As a social commentator, carefully observant of and objectively reporting on the racial situation in America, Hughes deserves a round of applause for his treatment of the black female freedom fighter who unquestionably represents a powerful force in past, present and future struggles for racial equality in America.

John O. Hodges (essay date Fall 1986)

SOURCE: "'Wondering About the Art of the Wanderer': Langston Hughes and His Critics," in *The Langston Hughes Review,* Vol. 5, No. 2, Fall, 1982, pp. 19-23.

[*In the following excerpt, Hodges explores the issue of consistency in Hughes's writing, and critical reaction to his work.*]

> Me, I always been all tangled up in life—
> which ain't always as sanitary as we might
> like it to be . . .
>
> *The Sweet Flypaper of Life*

One of the most prolific and versatile writers of the twentieth century, James Mercer Langston Hughes, produced, during his literary career of over forty-five years, a corpus as impressive in its range as in its sheer quantity. He experimented in all the major forms of literary art, from poetry to the novel and from autobiography to literary criticism. Perhaps it should not be at all surprising that such an enormous and multifarious body of literature would, in turn, generate a body of criticism equally as diverse and varied in its range. Countee Cullen and James Baldwin criticized Hughes for failing to exercise discipline and control in certain of his writings, while Sterling Brown and Richard Wright praised him for his versatility and range. To some of his contemporaries Hughes was "the poet laureate of the Negro people"; to a few others, "the poet low rate of Harlem."

These kind of contradictory antithetical comments on Hughes are not uncommon, and are quite often expressed by the same critic viewing his work at different times. What this reveals, it seems to me, is something about the elusiveness of an individual whose writing often exhibited a surface simplicity that belied its true complexity. In fact, the more one learns about Hughes, both through his corpus and through critics' views of his works, the more one finds how truly enigmatic and paradoxical he really was.

The elusiveness of Hughes may be attributed, at least in part, to the same reason that he has not, heretofore, enjoyed the critical success of a Richard Wright or a Ralph Ellison. It is difficult for critics to point to a single work as providing the key to Hughes's art, in the same way that we may point to *Native Son* or *Black Boy* in the case of Wright, or *Invisible Man* in the case of Ellison. To which work do we turn as providing the key to Langston Hughes—*The Weary Blues* or *The Panther and the Lash, The Big Sea* or *I Wonder as I Wander?* Nor can Hughes be identified, definitely, with any period, theme, or character—although there have been some rather interesting claims made in this regard.

Critics, of course, who make a business of attempting to find connecting threads in the fabric of an author's work, may view this as disconcerting and frustrating news. But Hughes's corpus does not lend itself to any such neat critical formulae. The comment by the narrator in DeCarava's and Hughes's *The Sweet Flypaper of Life,* accounting for why her house is not as clean and orderly as her neighbor's, may well have expressed Hughes's own view of his literary career: "Me, I always been all tangled up in life—which ain't always as sanitary as we might like to be." Thus, as the late George Kent once surmised: "[U]pon entering the universe of Langston Hughes, one leaves at its outer darkness that *type of rationality* whose herculean exertions are for absolute resolution of contradiction and external imposition of symmetry."

J. Saunders Redding, who, as Faith Berry claims in an article in this issue, was generally favorable of Hughes's work, nevertheless found, in 1951, that Hughes's penchant for experimentation seemed to be at the heart of his failure to settle on a unique idiom and voice in his writing. Thus, he says:

> it seems to me that Hughes does have a too great concern for perpetuating his reputation as an 'experimenter.' That he was this cannot be denied. . . . But experimentation is for something: it leads to or produces a result. One would think that after twenty-five years of writing, Hughes has long since

found his form, his idiom and his proper, particular tone. If he has, let him be content with the apparatus he has fashioned, and let him go on now to say the things which many readers believe he, alone of American poets, was born to say.

What Redding intends as a criticism of Hughes could be taken as a compliment. It is not so much that Hughes had not found "his own idiom or tone," as it is that he realized no one single tone or idiom could adequately portray the lives of those "up today and down tomorrow, working this week and fired the next, beaten and baffled, but determined not to be wholly beaten. . . ." What was needed was a flexible and dynamic idiom and tone to deal with the many inconsistencies, paradoxes, and wide mood swings in the lives of the people he celebrates in his various writings.

The forty-five years plus of Hughes's literary career stretched from the Harlem Renaissance, through the Depression, the McCarthy era, and the period of Civil Rights and protest. These were years of such great change and upheaval, with a number of countervailing forces at work, that it was nigh impossible to adopt a consistent tone or voice throughout the entire period. His contribution lies, therefore, not so much in any kind of unified vision his writing may or may not evince, but, rather, in the relevance of that vision for the climate of the times. It may be said of Hughes what DuBois once said of himself: that he "flew round and round with the *Zeitgeist,* waving [his] pen and lifting faint voices to explain, expound and exhort. . . ." It is precisely Hughes's attempt to fashion a special tone and idiom, in short, to adapt his art in response to the issues appropriate to the prevailing climate that presents his critics with such a challenge. How different, in tone and theme, for example, is *The Weary Blues,* his first published book of poetry from *The Panther and The Lash,* his last.

When we turn to Hughes's own literary theory, we find even less evidence of a consistent or unified vision. Although Hughes seemed certain that the Black artist needed to assume a social role, he seemed less certain about how this task was to be undertaken. As Baldwin has suggested, Hughes found "the war between his social and artistic responsibilities all but irreconcilable." There remained in Hughes's poetry and fiction as well as in his own literary theory something of what DuBois spoke of as double consciousness. He seemed to be uncertain about the role of the black writer at once as an artist and as a propagandist for social reform for his race. This has led Hughes to appear, at times, to contradict himself. In his famous manifesto of 1926, **"The Negro Artist and the Racial Mountain,"** he could advocate a self-conscious black art in his advice to the young poet who wanted to be considered a writer, not just a Negro writer. Yet by the late 1950s, he had begun to modify his position. He would now claim that

Color had nothing to do with writing as such. So I would say, in your mind don't be a *colored* writer even when dealing in racial material. Be a writer first / Like an egg: egg; then an Easter egg, the color applied.

Wilson Moses, writing in the Spring 1985 issue of *The Langston Hughes Review,* speaks to the matter of inconsistency between Hughes's thought and his actions, when he says that, "at times, like most artists, Hughes did not heed his own advice. Like the very artists he had criticized, Hughes could stumble into some of the pitfalls of Western artistic consciousness." And Aaron Gresson, writing in the same issue, speaks more pointedly of seemingly contradictions in Hughes's critical theory:

> Hughes . . . sometimes talked as if race were primary and, at others, as if it were secondary. Hence, he writes, "Be a writer first, colored second." And further: "*Step outside yourself,* then look back and you will see how human, yet how beautiful and black you are. How very black—even when you're integrated."

How can we account for this apparent about face? Could it be that in the years between 1926 and 1960, the time between these two statements, Hughes had become much more aware of the white audience's influence on black art?

More and more, Hughes seemed to have realized the pressure of racial prejudice at work in the literary marketplace. But, to his credit, it was a position that he came to only after his own financial situation had begun to deteriorate. (Hughes, for example, depended wholly on his publications and lectures for his livelihood.) So, the latter statement comes more as a concession than as a deeply felt aesthetic principle. He noted, for instance, that in the late 1950s there was no black publishing company. When Johnson Publications began to publish works on black American life, Hughes would see this as a step in the right direction that would ultimately lead to greater freedom for the black artist.

But the impact of Hughes's financial problems on the quantity and quantity of works produced from the 1930s on is an issue to which critics need to give even greater consideration. If, indeed, there is a decline in his artistic vision during this period, as some have claimed, to what extent could this be attributed to Hughes's concern with achieving commercial success? There is little doubt that during the decades of the 1940s and 1950s, Hughes kept at least one eye focused squarely on the literary marketplace, as is revealed in the interesting exchange of letters with his life-long friend and confidant, Arna Bontemps. In his letter to Bontemps of July 17, 1954, for example, Hughes notes, in regard to his second autobiography, *I Wonder,* that "if publishers want a really documented book, they ought to advance some documented money—enough to do nothing else for two or three years." Here, as elsewhere in the *Letters,* he reiterates his determination not to become a "literary sharecropper for short rations."

We know, of course, that throughout Hughes's career, he, not unlike any other professional writer, was called upon to make concessions to publishers and agents. Concessions are not unusual in the publishing business. But one wonders, in Hughes's case, if the extra-literary considerations—whether financial, as with the production of the play *Mulatto* (1935), or political, as with the publication of *First Book of Negroes* (1952)—seriously impaired his vision or weakened his voice as a writer with an avowed strong social commitment. Though the issue is still open for debate, Faith Berry's publication of Hughes's uncollected protest writings has gone a long way toward resolving the issue in his favor.

The point I am making here is that Hughes's works, perhaps more so than those of any other writer, must be examined in their proper historical context. I take it that Richard Barksdale has something of this in mind when he observes that Hughes's "was a poet who immersed himself in the contemporary and current and often wrote poems to explicate social and emotional reactions." Whether or not this characteristic was a major failing in Hughes's writing is a question on which there is not likely to be any unanimity of opinion. But Hughes's voice was strongest, it seems to me, when he not only reported on the issues of his day but also attempted to analyze and shape them. This is why I think his social protest writings should be given greater consideration.

As I stated above, critics themselves often speak of his work with a certain ambivalence, offering different interpretations depending on their own perspective and on the historical climate at the time. To this, the articles in this issue by Berry, Harper, and Rampersad give powerful testimony, though it may or may not be a claim that any of them is prepared to make.

Faith Berry points out that Saunders Redding was one of Hughes's most consistent critics and often praised his writings in the pages of the *Afro-American* and other publications. But, as Berry goes on to say, this did not mean that Redding could applaud all of Hughes's efforts. He found, for example, that Hughes could, at times, be "jejune and iterative," as in his volume of poetry, *One Way Ticket.* Certainly, much of Reddings' ambivalence toward *Montage* is evident when he says that Hughes's "images are again quick, vibrant and probing, but they no longer educate. They probe into old emotions and experiences with fine sensitiveness . . . but they reveal nothing new." It is this kind of thoroughgoing criticism of Hughes, by one who had long carefully charted his growth and development, that lends valuable insights into the man and his art.

Akiba Harper focuses on the interesting relationship between Hughes, the spokesman for the common man, and DuBois, the apostle of high culture. Indeed, that these two individuals, so different in outlook and temperament, could meet on mutual terms of admiration is a credit to the magnanimity of both. Harper argues that DuBois praised much of Hughes's poetry and was willing to defend him, as he did at least on one occasion, in the pages of the *Crisis*. And Hughes's own high regard for DuBois and his book *The Souls of Black Folk* is clearly stated in **The Big Sea.** She is careful, however, to focus her discussion on the years from 1923 to 1933, for some years later there seems to be some evidence, according to Rampersad and others, of a rift in their relationship.

Rampersad treats what is perhaps the most problematic aspect of Hughes's literary career: "socialist" writings and his relationship to left-wing critics. His relationship with these critics was a puzzling one. Originally, Rampersad observes, *The Liberator* rejected all of Hughes's works, and they did not appear in any major white leftist publication until his reputation was firmly established. This reveals more about those critics than about Hughes himself. It seems clear that they had their own axes to grind. But what is even more puzzling and disturbing is Hughes's reaction to their criticism of his work. Why, for example, did he not include some of the pieces in his **Selected Poems?** And why did he omit Robeson and DuBois from his **First Book of Negroes** (1952)?

These and other similar questions are raised in these papers. Indeed, the best works of criticism on Hughes will seek answers to certain questions while posing a number of others. But it is only in this way that we may begin to approach an understanding of an individual for whom wondering while wandering was both act and art.

Arnold Rampersad (essay date Fall 1986)

SOURCE: "Langston Hughes and His Critics on the Left," in *The Langston Hughes Review,* Vol. 5, No. 2, Fall, 1986, pp. 34-40.

[*In the following essay, Rampersad argues that the Leftist critics failed Hughes.*]

Radicalism is one of the main points of pressure in Langston Hughes's reputation, like—for example—the question of whether or not he believed in God, or whether or not he was a communist. The matter of radicalism has left a specific wound, one never to be healed completely, on his reputation. His virtual surrender before Senator Joseph McCarthy's committee lingers uncomfortably in the mind, as well as his omission of W.E.B. DuBois and Paul Robeson from certain of his writings later in his life, in the aftermath of his encounter with McCarthy. My purpose here is to look at one aspect of Hughes and radicalism between roughly the start of his adult career and 1940, the year of his autobiography **The Big Sea.** That aspect concerns Hughes's reception by literary critics of the left. How was he treated by them? Did this reception have an impact on his work? In trying to answer these basic questions, perhaps we can learn something more about the art of Langston Hughes, as well as something more about the practice of literary criticism among certain radicals.

If this analysis involves the adverse criticism of some literary figures on the left at one point in Hughes's career, I hope it will not be construed as an attack upon leftist critics in general, or—even more undeserved—an attack upon progressivism or radical socialism in general. Certainly that is not my purpose here.

The approval of the left was something Langston Hughes craved virtually from the start of his writing career. In **The Big Sea,** he claimed that he was introduced to the left by his Jewish classmates at Central High School in Cleveland between 1916 and 1920. They "lent me *The Gadfly* and *Jean-Christophe* to read, and copies of the *Liberator* and the *Socialist Call.* They were almost all interested in more than basketball and the glee club. They took me to hear Eugene Debs. And when the Russian Revolution broke out, our school almost held a celebration." What these young leftists thought of Hughes's poetry in the *Central High School Monthly* is impossible to say; however, the three short stories he either published in the *Monthly* or wrote about this time (**"Those Who Have No Turkey," "Seventy-five Dollars,"** and **"Mary Winosky")** show unmistakably the influence of socialist passion and even of socialist logic. Together, they depict human beings oppressed by hunger, poverty, war, and urban impersonalism. Clearly, from the outset of his literary career Hughes identified the function of the artist with a certain socialist outlook and conscience.

Hughes remembered sending poems from Cleveland to Floyd Dell at the *Liberator,* which had revived *Masses* magazine (banned during the war and edited previously by Dell, Max Eastman, and John Reed). "I learned from [the *Liberator*] the revolutionary attitude toward Negroes," he said of the magazine. "Was there not a Negro on its staff?" The Negro was Claude McKay—but McKay did not join the *Liberator* staff until April 1921, some months *after* Hughes left Central High. The dates here are important. All evidence indicates that Hughes did not begin to break into predominantly white magazines until *after* his success with W. E. B. DuBois,

Jessie Fauset, and A.G. Dill's *Brownies' Book* and *Crisis* magazine—or until after the middle of 1921. The point here is that Hughes probably did not try the *Liberator* before he had reached a certain proficiency as a poet. The leftists at the *Liberator,* however, made clear what they thought of his work by rejecting all of it; although Dell once wrote to say he liked one poem most of all, he added that "none moves us deeply." Either young Langston Hughes was offering them unusually poor verse, or the *Liberator* editors could not recognize good poetry that was different. In some respects, this is the recurring puzzle arising from Hughes's relationship to his critics on the left.

For whatever reason, Hughes did not publish in a socialist magazine until 1924, when his verse appeared in A. Philip Randolph and Chandler Owen's *Messenger: The World's Greatest Negro Monthly.* But when we recognize that the poetry and fiction in the *Messenger,* unlike its editorials and essays, were ideologically indistinguishable from, say, the *Crisis* or *Opportunity,* we see that Hughes's debut in a bona fide radical journal came only in March 1925, after four years of publishing. In March 1925, the Communist *Workers Monthly* brought out three of his poems, followed by others the following month. Did Hughes's poetry suddenly improve? Or was the *Workers Monthly* simply getting on the Hughes bandwagon? After all, March 1925 saw the appearance of Alain Locke's edition of the historic special number of the *Survey Graphic* that became *The New Negro.* From that point, Langston Hughes was a poet of some note. We come perhaps upon an unfortunate truth about so many radical socialist magazines in the twenties and thirties and perhaps always; they seem to be almost incapable, in general, of recognizing and nurturing young talent independent of the bourgeois magazines they scorn. Established names can be drawn to the leftist journals; for reasons that are probably not hard to understand, the journals themselves often seem incapable of growing their own.

If at the heart of this disturbing thought is the attitude of many radical critics to the artist, then Hughes's experience with his first book, **The Weary Blues,** is a case in point. *New Masses,* the successor to *Masses* and the *Liberator,* appeared on the scene in 1926, only months after the publication of **The Weary Blues.** Reviewing the book in October, the radical poet James Rorty opened his essay by reviling the "white, death-house silence" of greedy capitalistic New York, a silence "that aches to be filled." As blacks poured into Harlem, "the sharp Jews and Nordics who run the cabarets have found a new decoy—painted black—and how it does pay!" Blacks are Broadway, there is a "Negro renaissance," and "New York is amused. But how about the Negro in all this? I, for one, am sick of black-face comedians, whether high-brow or low-brow. I am sick of the manumitted slave psychology. . . . I want the Negroes to stop entertaining the

whites and begin to speak for themselves. I am waiting for a Negro poet to stand up and say 'I—I am *not* amused.'"

> Langston Hughes doesn't say anything like this. Nothing as bitter, nothing as masterful, nothing as savage. Why not? . . . Are Negroes really savages? One hopes so, but one doubts. . . . Nevertheless, Hughes is a poet, with a curiously firm and supple style, half naive and half sophisticated, which is on the whole more convincing than anything which has yet appeared in Negro poetry.

Quoting **"When Sue Wears Red"** in its entirety, Rorty called it startlingly effective. However, when the persona in another poem mourns, "I am afraid of this civilization— / So hard, / So strong, / So cold," Rorty attacked: "I hope and trust Hughes doesn't mean this. If he does, I'd rather have Garvey, who may not be intelligent, but who at least seems more angry than afraid." We see in Rorty's review certain admirable traits of the radical reviewer, especially its decisive penetration of dishonesty in the national culture. However, there are other, less admirable aspects to note. In poetry, the quiet voice is mistrusted; irony is almost treasonable. "I am afraid of this civilization," the poem says—so Rorty deduces that the poet himself must be afraid. Mood and tone must exist not subtly but under a glaring political spotlight, because—apparently—the reader cannot be trusted to notice their deviant aspects. And no matter how radical the author is, seldom is he or she radical enough. The reviewer's radicalism overwhelms the poet—and often overwhelms poetry itself. Rorty's review takes up two columns of equal length, but one is finished and the other in its tenth line before the name Langston Hughes is mentioned. We are past line thirty of the second column before the first word of poetry is quoted; and the last comment is a reprimand. One wonders how, under such harsh conditions, *any* poetry gets written.

As far as I know, **Fine Clothes to the Jew,** published the following year, was not reviewed immediately in the radical press. Considering the drubbing that Hughes received in the black press for the volume, perhaps that is well. (Later, however, the book was reviewed by the left; we shall see how.)

Published in 1930, **Not Without Laughter** drew one private response from the left on which I would like to concentrate here. On March 14, 1931, an American radical, Agnes Smedley, wrote to Hughes from Shanghai about his novel. To Smedley, **Not Without Laughter** was a good book, but one with a central failing: "It still does not picture the existence of your people." Hughes must "show us the fate of the Negro masses. Such a fate is not happy—but is beaten and debased by [the] condition of beastly subjection. Try to show us in the life of Negro proletarians . . . men who work . . . and are defeated and must be defeated until they organise and fight on a revolutionary basis." In Hughes's depictions of blacks singing and dancing, "I feel too much technique of writing, too much colour photography shown on a broad screen. The picture has value only if shot through with something that explains the cause. I cannot get my hands on you and explain what I mean—but your book lacks intensity. . . . There was great suffering, perhaps hopes, dreams that were smashed,—and we get but a faint idea of it. If *Not Without Laughter* is partly autobiographical, she continued, then it is clear that "you were always on the outer edge of your class—of the working class. In other words, of petty bourgeois up-bringing, and later, an intellectual."

It is obvious that Smedley, who had never met Hughes, evidently could tell something startlingly accurate about his background through a radical Marxist analysis of his fiction; the radical critique certainly can be penetrating. And her criticism, like most radical criticism, was linked to genuine political problems. For example, Smedley's last words in her letter were not about literary theory, but about life and death: "Ten days ago the Chinese authorities arrested 23 more Communists, among them 4 more left writers; they made them dig their own graves, and then mowed them down with machine guns." Still we must ask, was her criticism of Hughes and *Not Without Laughter* justified? How does it jibe with the tremendous groundswell of applause from all the black reviewers, who hailed the book as a landmark in its representation of the ordinary truths of black life. These reviewers may have been bourgeois, but even the most bourgeois of blacks have been hypersensitive about the depiction of the race and politics, of accommodationism and resistance.

In any event, by the time Smedley wrote her letter in 1931 Hughes was at the start of a tremendous swing to the left, one that would result in the composition of some of the most radical pieces of verse ever penned by an American. So complete was his transformation that when he received in 1933 his most thorough literary examination from a leftist point of view, by Lydia Filatova in an article in *International Literature,* "LANGSTON HUGHES: American Writer," he came away, in her final analysis, with flying colors—but not before sharp rebukes for his previous work. So sharp, in fact, that one wonders about Lydia Filatova's candor, for want of a better word—not the first or last time one is forced to ask this question about radical socialist critics. In the Harlem Renaissance, and in particular in his landmark essay **"The Negro Artist and the Racial Mountain,"** Hughes had advanced "a theory of bourgeois estheticism, the right of the artist to hold aloof from social themes, to be indifferent to the day's racial and social problems." This is a bizarre reading of an essay that asserts the power of racial feeling in the face of the black and the white bourgeoisie. To facilitate her reading, however, Filatova cites as its title not **"The Negro Artist and the Racial Mountain,"** which

was how it was called from its first appearance in the *Nation* in 1926, but simply "The Negro Artist."

In *The Weary Blues,* according to Filatova, Hughes "almost ignores the question of racial oppression." When he acknowledges racial oppression, he fails to understand it from a class point of view. More often, however, he "shuns reality and varnishes it with romantic illusions. Tomorrow is to bring liberation; but the poet's dreams about the better future are hazy and nebulous. His protest against the surrounding realities is an abstract one. It resolves itself into a vague striving toward sunshine, toward the exotic." In *Fine Clothes to the Jew,* Hughes is not yet "a revolutionary artist," but gives promise of "future growth." One should notice the five poems quoted or mentioned by Filatova. Not one poem is in the blues form; in fact, in reviewing a book defined by the blues, the word "blues" is never even mentioned. Yet we note that the black reading public took deeply to heart certain racial poems in *The Weary Blues* and what Hughes did there and in *Fine Clothes* with the blues form was certainly revolutionary from an artistic and social—and political—point of view. As for the poems about religion in the latter volume, Filatova writes inexplicably: "The soporific action of religion, with its gospel of non-resistance, largely accounts for the difficulty of spreading Communism among the masses of Negro toilers. Hughes in religious ecstasy complains to heaven, sings about white wings of angels, and seeks solace in prayer."

In *Not Without Laughter,* Hughes "breaks with the Harlem tradition. He now becomes a realistic writer." But he is "still swayed by the theory that the Negroes can attain social equality only through education, through demonstrating the creative abilities of the Negro people. Hughes still fails to see the illusory nature of such theories, that the real cause of racial inequality is capitalism, and that only through revolutionary struggle against the capitalist system will the Negro gain complete emancipation. Culture and talent will not solve the problem." He also fails to see whites as other than "an undifferentiated hostile mass," and ignores the class issue.

Needless to say, Filatova took Hughes's most recent poetry (for example, **"Good Morning Revolution," "Goodbye Christ," "Letter to the Academy," "An Open Letter to the South,"** and **"Tom Mooney"**) as evidence of his emancipation as a writer. "His new poetical *credo* is the total negation of his former creative position." There was, however, one "blot" on Hughes's recent revolutionary record—*Popo and Fifina,* the children's book set in Haiti and written with Arna Bontemps. "Does this soothing syrup," Filatova asks, "represent the author's conception of children's literature? Does the method of the complete elimination of contradictions of life, such varnishing of reality, help to forge fighters for communism, to increase the membership of the Negro

Komsomol? Works of this kind detract from the revolutionary value and importance of Hughes's creative work."

Hughes evidently accepted, at this point in his career, Filatova's analysis of his work. To his friend and collaborator Prentiss Taylor, he sent home a solemn pledge: "Never must mysticism or beauty be gotten into any religious motive when used as a proletarian weapon." When he sent his poems home to his publisher Blanche Knopf and her advisor, Carl Van Vechten, he assured them that the verse had been vetted in Moscow—and presumably found radically kosher. Blanche Knopf refused to publish the collection, and Van Vechten concurred: "The revolutionary poems seem very weak to me: I mean very weak on the lyric side. I think in ten years, whatever the social outcome, you will be ashamed of these." He did not like Diego Rivera's radical politics, he insisted, but he admired Rivera's revolutionary murals. Hughes's radical verses, however, were "lacking in any of the elementary requisites of a work of art."

I do not believe that Hughes was ever ashamed of having written those poems, but it is at least interesting that his *Selected Poems,* which he chose himself, would contain not one of the poems in the radical collection.

The year 1938 saw two significant efforts by Hughes in radical literature. The first was *Don't You Want to be Free?,* a play produced by the Harlem Suitcase Theatre, which he founded that year, and the second was the appearance of a collection of radical poems, *A New Song.* In a review of the play, at least one leftist critic showed not only broad understanding of the nature of literature, but also a degree of sympathetic insight into Hughes's aims and ability as an artist.

Writing in the *Crisis* (no radical journal!) about *Don't You Want to be Free?,* the white leftist poet Norman Macleod went to the heart of the dilemma—as he saw it—facing Hughes as a black writer who wanted to speak at one and the same time on behalf of his race and on behalf of the left. Citing two lines in which blacks say, "Let the black boy swing / But the white folks die," and contrasting the statement to Hughes's more universal socialist aims expressed forcefully elsewhere in the play, Macleod saw it as exemplifying "the unresolved conflict in Langston Hughes's writing. He *feels* the Negro as his race, but only *thinks* himself (at least, in this work) a member of a white and black working class. And because of this, the scenes which are treated poetically and which deal primarily with the problems that are purely 'race' are moving and good entertainment as well. In the later scenes which introduce argument he is not as good."

Perhaps because he was writing for the *Crisis,* perhaps because his own attitude toward the left was changing, Macleod concluded that Hughes should stick more to writing that de-

rived from his "feeling," rather than to writing that derived from his "thinking." Hughes, he declared, "is essentially a poet—a very fine poet with an ear for racial rhythms and folk speech—and it is as a poet we like him most—whether or not his poetry appears in a novel or in a play or in a poem makes little difference."

The same year, 1938, Hughes's *A New Song* appeared. The poems were published by the International Workers Order, the well-organized and widely influential Communist-organized benevolent association which had also sponsored the Harlem Suitcase Theatre. Like the play, the appearance of *A New Song* followed a sharp revival of Hughes's own radicalism after months in war-torn Spain. Obviously Hughes was not yet "ashamed" of the poems, as Van Vechten had said he would be. Mike Gold, a lion of the literary far left in America, wrote an introduction to this collection of radical verse. In these poems, which were the fruit of a decade of experiment and radical experience, Gold saw no "unresolved conflict" (to quote Macleod). "Many young writers have lost their way in this period, mistaking some dazzling skyrocket of a aesthetic theory for a star," Gold declared. But not Langston Hughes. "He has expressed the hopes, the dreams, and the awakening of the Negro people. He has done it naturally, like a bird in the woods; but in choosing this theme, he has been led on and on, until he has also become a voice crying for justice for all humanity. The Negroes are enslaved, but so are the white workers, and the two are brothers in suffering and struggle. This is his message today."

> In *The New Republic,* the black radical Richard Wright praised Hughes as a "cultural ambassador" and for having carried on "a manly tradition" when other writers "have gone to sleep at their posts."
> —*Arnold Rampersad*

Written hardly one year later, however, Hughes's autobiography *The Big Sea* documents a strange turn of events—strange even if one considers the demands of bourgeois is publishers. Walt Carmon, once an editor at *New Masses* and a friend to Hughes in Moscow, was shocked to notice "not a single mention of a radical publication you've written for or a single radical you have met or has meant anything to you." In *The New Republic,* the black radical Richard Wright praised Hughes as a "cultural ambassador" and for having carried on "a manly tradition" when other writers "have gone to sleep at their posts." But in using the term "ambassador," Wright invited recollection of the opening of his "Blueprint for Negro Writing," where he had scorned past black writers as the "prim and decorous ambassadors," The "artistic ambassadors" of the race, "who went a-begging to white America . . . in the knee-pants of servility." And in the *Ne-*

gro *Quarterly,* Ralph Ellison, then also a radical, complained that "too much attention is apt to be given to the aesthetic aspects of experience at the expense of its deeper meanings," and questioned whether the style was appropriate to "the autobiography of a Negro writer of Hughes's importance."

Why did the bottom fall out, as it were, of Hughes's radical aesthetic? For possibly many reasons, including events on the international scene, notably the disastrous (certainly for the American left) Nazi-Soviet pact of non-aggression. One thing is clear, however; Hughes owed very little or nothing to literary critics from the left. Scholar-critics, either as writers or in teaching, should never forget that they perform a vital function in the literary process, even if artists sometimes ungratefully regard us as parasites. In this case, on the other hand, the leftist critics in general performed weakly where Hughes was concerned because their reviews were generally poor in quality—reductive, intolerant, and philistine. I need only add here the obvious: Marxist criticism has come a long way since the twenties and thirties; as a reminder of what Hughes experienced, however, if one looks at much Soviet literary criticism today, one would probably conclude that, at least in some quarters, it has not yet come far enough.

Under the communist aesthetic as interpreted by these reviewers, the greatest of Hughes's poems, which all have to do with race—**"The Negro Speaks of Rivers,"** or **"Mother to Son,"** or **"The Weary Blues,"** or **"Jazzonia,"** or **"Dream Variation"**—could not have been written. What the left took to be petty bourgeois ambivalence was Hughes's continual attempt to arbitrate between rage at racism, on one hand, and the uncontaminated love of his people, on the other. In the most radical work, the process of arbitration is shortcircuited; rage is shaped according to ideology, and what often results is not a poem but ideology tempered and sharpened into slogans. In the process, much is lost, including Hughes's essential identity. Only Hughes could have written **"The Negro Speaks of Rivers"** but—given the right mixture of radical rage and literary adroitness on the part of a writer—**"Good Morning Revolution"** could have been written by almost anyone. Many literary radicals, especially those who are also back or who are interested in recruiting blacks, have not learned how to deal with the theoretical problem behind this last statement. The problem, however, is mainly theirs, and not Langston Hughes's.

Mary Beth Culp (essay date Fall 1987)

SOURCE: "Religion in the Poetry of Langston Hughes," in *Phylon,* Vol. 48, No. 3, pp. 240-45.

[*In the following essay, Culp asserts that Hughes's poetry emphasizes the diverse role that religion plays in the Afri- can- American community.*]

Langston Hughes lived basically in terms of the external world and in unison with it, making himself one with his people and refusing to stand apart as an individual. His poetry reflects collective states of mind as if they were his own, merging the poet's personality with his racial group. He assumes various personae—sometimes he is the spirit of his race, at other times he is a spittoon polisher, a black mother, a prostitute, a black man without job or money—but there is a commonality among the various experiences presented in his poems which gives them a kind of consistent persona.

As a folklorist Hughes sought to capture the essence of every aspect of black culture, including its religion. Religious feeling is always interdependent with racial feeling in his poetry. He views religion in the larger context of black culture, presenting it variously as a source of strength for the oppressed, an opiate of the people, the religion of slavery, and an obstacle to emancipation. When asked in an interview about his own religious views, Hughes responded:

> I grew up in a not very religious family, but I had a foster aunt who saw that I went to church and Sunday School . . . and I was very much moved, always, by the, shall I say, the rhythms of the Negro church . . . of the spirituals . . . of those wonderful old-time sermons. . . . There's great beauty in the mysticism of much religious writing, and great help there—but I also think that we live in a world . . . of solid earth and vegetables and a need for jobs and a need for housing . . .

In his autobiography *The Big Sea,* Hughes describes his "conversion" at the age of thirteen. It happened on a hot night during a revival meeting at his aunt's church in Lawrence, Kansas. Hughes and another boy were waiting alone on the mourner's bench to see the light of Jesus, while "the building rocked with prayer and song." Finally the other boy whispered to Langston, "God damn! I'm tired o'sitting here. Let's get up and be saved," and he went forward. Langston waited in vain to see Jesus, but finally, amid the praying and sobbing and singing of the congregation he, too, went forward, "to save further trouble." Hughes concludes his description of this incident as follows:

> That night, for the last time in my life, but one . . . I cried. I cried, in bed alone, and couldn't stop. I buried my head under the quilts, but my aunt heard me. . . . She . . . told my uncle I was crying because the Holy Ghost had come into my life, and because I had seen Jesus. But I was really crying because I couldn't bear to tell her that I had lied, that I had deceived everybody in the church, that I

hadn't seen Jesus, and that now I didn't believe there was a Jesus any more, since he didn't come to help me.

In the only poem in which Hughes speaks of religion in his own voice and not that of a persona of his people, he states:

> In an envelope marked:
> *Personal*
> God addressed me a letter.
> In an envelope marked:
> *Personal*
> I have given my answer.

In the remainder of his more than sixty poems containing religious references, Hughes captures the essence of religious feeling in the black culture through his use of language, rhythm, and form. The simplest of these is a group of six lyrics and songs composed between 1926 and 1964, celebrating the story of the Christ Child. Another group, including **"Judgment Day"** (1927); **"Prayer Meeting"** (1923); **"Sinner"** (1927) and **"Acceptance"** (1957) reflect the simple faith of blacks in settings reminiscent of Hughes's childhood experiences. **"Judgment Day"** dramatizes the imagination of a simple black person whose soul has gone "flyin' to de stars and moon / A shoutin' God I's comin' soon!"

Among Hughes's poems which suggest that religion has been valuable to black people in toughening a certain life force within, one of the most popular is **"The Negro Mother"** (1931). The archetypal speaker says:

> I am the one who labored as a slave, Beaten and mistreated for the work that I gave

> Three hundred years in the deepest South: But God put a song and a prayer in my mouth. God put a dream like steel in my soul.

Here the religion of the slavemasters has become resolution in the mind of the slaves.

Other of Hughes's poems with religious references are predominantly celebrations of life, short though it may be. These include **"Sylvester's Dying Bed"** (1931); **"Saturday Night"** (1926); **"Fire"** (1927); and **"Sunday by the Combination"** (1951), all concerning good-timing sinners who lived robustly until "the Lawd put out the light." In **"Madam and the Number Writer"** (1943) Hughes's well-known character Madame Alberta K. Johnson whimsically swears off playing the numbers in Harlem in favor of heaven's "golden streets / Where the number not only / Comes out— but repeats!" In **"Tambourines"** (1959) the speaker celebrates life with "A gospel shout / And a gospel song: / Life is short / *But God is long*!"

The influence of jazz is seen in many of these poems. There is a similarity between religious exaltation and the exaltation of human nature that finds an outlet in jazz. Wagner has pointed out that "in both establishments [church and dance hall] the shouts and rhythms are the same and human beings find means of release and forgetfulness, whether profane or sacred."

Perhaps the most powerful of Hughes's poems with a religious reference, however, are those which use Christ as a central figure. In the poetry of Hughes, as well as other black poets, Christ is sometimes white, symbolizing the oppressors and acting as their accomplice; at other times he is black, the image and friend of the lynched Negro, and one who suffers with him. With the black-white Christ symbol black poets have represented the contradictory elements of the religion of whites which was passed on to the slaves.

In the original version of **"A New Song"** (1932) the poet expresses regret that the Negro has never really shared in the Christian community; he denies that Christ's sacrifice took place on behalf of black people, and asserts that the blacks must redeem themselves.

> Bitter was the day
> When . . .
> . . . only in the sorrow songs
> Relief was found—
> Yet no relief,
> But merely humble life and silent death
> Eased by a Name
> That hypnotized the pain away—
> O, precious Name of Jesus in that day!
>
> That day is past.
>
> I know full well now
> Jesus could not die for me—
> That only my own hands,
> Dark as the earth,
> Can make my earth-dark body free.

"Goodbye, Christ!" (1933) spurns the Christ of white supremacy and reflects an attraction to Communist ideology, although Hughes later declared he had never shared the views expressed in this poem.

> Listen, Christ,
> You did alright in your day, I reckon—
> But that day's gone now.
> They ghosted you up a swell story, too,
> Called it Bible—
> But it's dead now.
> The popes and the preachers've

Made too much money from it.
They've sold you to too many
Kings, generals, robbers, and killers—

Goodbye,
Christ Jesus Lord God Jehova,
Beat it on away from here now.
Make way for a new guy with no religion at all—
A real guy named
Marx Communist Lenin Peasant Stalin Worker
ME.

As a result of this poem the poet was barred from speaking at a Los Angeles YMCA in 1935, was picketed by the America First Party while speaking at Wayne State University in 1942, and fifteen years later was still explaining that the poem was an "ironic protest against racketeering in the churches."

In other poems, Christ is seen as the archetype of suffering blacks. A comparison between the fate of Jesus and the revilement of black people appears in Hughes's poetry both early and late. In **"Ma Lord"** (1927) an anthropomorphic Christ is pictured. The second stanza reads:

Ma Lord knowed what it was to work
He knowed how to pray
Ma Lord's life was trouble, too
Trouble ever day.

The fusion of Christ and black people has a long tradition, reinforced by the influence of black ministers who drew comparisons between Christ's martyrdom and the debasement of black people. In his short story **"Big Meeting"** Hughes describes a typical sermon in which this identification is apparent. The sermon on the crucifixion is divided into three parts. In the first, the preacher talks about the power of the lowly, represented by Christ; then about the ability of a man to stand alone like Jesus, who told his weakening disciples to "sleep on." The congregation chants, "sleep on, sleep on." The second part of the sermon turns to images of violence. The minister recalls that Jesus "saw the garden alive with men carrying lanterns and swords and staves, and the mob was everywhere." Other images of violence which the preacher supplies are *handcuffs, prisoner, chains, trail, lies.* Then the minister closes the gap between Christ and the congregation. The picture of the crucified Jesus is finished:

Mob cussin' and hootin' my Jesus! Umn!
The spit of the mob in His face! Umn!
His body hangin' on the cross! Umn!

That's what they did to my Jesus!
They stoned Him first, they stoned Him!

Called Him everything but a child of God.
Then they lynched him on the cross.

The word *mob* begins the Negro identification with Christ; the word *lynched* seals it. The sermon is almost a poem itself. In it one can see the "rhythms of the Negro church" to which Hughes referred in the interview cited.

The poem which is the strongest statement of this theme is **"Christ in Alabama"** (1931).

Christ is a nigger,
Beaten and black
Oh, bare your back!

Mary is His mother:
Mammy of the South,
Silence your mouth.

God is His father:
White Master above
Grant Him your love.

Most holy bastard
Of the bleeding mouth,
              Nigger Christ
              On the cross
              Of the South.

Hughes's first reading of the poem at the University of North Carolina on November 21, 1931, caused threats of violence from whites. The poem itself was written to protest violence against blacks which was weighing heavily on Hughes's mind. While on his reading tour of the South, he had learned that a recent graduate of Hampton Institute had been beaten to death by an Alabama mob for parking his car in a white parking lot. In the same week he learned of the death of Juliette Derricotte of Fisk University, who had been involved in an automobile accident in Georgia and had been refused treatment in a white hospital. In addition, the Scottsboro case had affected Hughes deeply. Nine Negro youths were in Kilby prison in Alabama, accused of raping two white prostitutes in a coal car traveling through the state. In his autobiography *I Wonder as I Wander,* Hughes describes these events and their repercussions in his typical low-key, wry manner. He relates the reaction of a local politician in Chapel Hill to the poem: "It's bad enough to call Christ a bastard . . . but to call Him a nigger—that's too much!" In an article in the Atlanta World of December 18, 1931, Hughes said of the poem:

Anything which makes people think of existing evil conditions is worthwhile. Sometimes in order to attract attention somebody must embody these ideas in sensational forms. I meant my poem to be a protest against the domination of all stronger peoples over weaker ones.

The word *protest* may have diminished the artistic merit of the poem in the eyes of many. Although Jean Wagner considers it "shocking rather than profound," James Emanuel thinks it noteworthy for the economy of its phrasing and its acrostic flair.

A less shocking poem using the crucifixion theme is **"The Ballad of Mary's Son"** (1954), which merges the persons of "Mary's boy," a young black man lynched during the Passover, and Christ, "Mary's son," in a shared spiritual tragedy. The first two stanzas establish the relationship:

> It was in the Spring
> The Passover had come.
> There was feasting in the streets and joy.
> But an awful thing
> Happened in the Spring—
> Men who knew not what they did
> Killed Mary's Boy.
>
> He was Mary's Son,
> And the Son of God was He—
> Sent to bring the whole world joy.
> There were some who could not hear,
> And some were filled with fear—
> So they built a cross
> For Mary's Boy.

Perhaps Hughes's finest poem using the crucifixion theme is **"Song for a Dark Girl,"** written in 1927.

> Way Down South in Dixie
> (Break the heart of me)
> They hung my black young lover
> To a cross roads tree.
>
> Way Down South in Dixie
> (Bruised body high in air)
> I asked the white Lord Jesus
> What was the use of prayer.
>
> Way Down South in Dixie
> (Break the Heart of me)
> Love is a naked shadow
> On a gnarled and naked tree.

In this poem, protest has given way to grief. The irony of the gay Dixieland tune juxtaposed on the heartbreaking refrain gives the poem impact, as does its simple imagery and symbolism. In the first stanza the black young lover is the Christ figure, hung to a *cross roads* (divided for emphasis) tree. In the second stanza the speaker addresses the white Christ, expressing the frustration of the black religious experience in America. In the third stanza the two Christ figures, representing love, are fused into "a naked shadow / On a gnarled and naked tree."

In these poems, as in all his works, Langston Hughes's primary purpose was to reveal the folk expression of his people in all its diversity. He shows the folk inside and outside the church, happy and sad, in states of grace and of sin. Although he wrote with emotional strength of the oppression of his people, he was primarily a folklorist who created his art out of the stuff of common black experience. Arna Bontemps has rightly called him a minstrel and a troubadour in the classic sense.

Steven C. Tracy (essay date September 1988)

SOURCE: "'Midnight Ruffles of Cat-Gut Lace': The Boogie Poems of Langston Hughes," in *CLA Journal,* Vol. 32, No. 1, September, 1988, pp. 55-68.

[*In the following essay, Tracy analyzes Hughes's use of the boogie-woogie form in five poems from* Montage of a Dream Deferred.]

The influence of the blues tradition on Langston Hughes's poetry is by now an oft-discussed and readily accepted fact, although the depth and breadth of his employment of the tradition has not often been discussed with a similar depth and breadth. A close examination of a related sequence of Hughes's blues poems offers the opportunity to explore his fusion of oral and written traditions and to examine his tremendous skills as a literary-jazz improviser. That is not to suggest that Hughes's poems are spontaneous creations. Improvisation is normally thought of as a spontaneous act, but the jazz or blues musician's improvisations are in fact bounded by several things: the musician's "vocabulary"—style, patterns, techniques, and riffs; the accepted conventions of the specific genre (even if those conventions are deliberately violated, they are, in a large sense, at work); and the boundaries of the individual piece being performed. For example, boogie-woogie pianist Pete Johnson, in his 1947 version of "Swanee River Boogie," performs the melody of the song to a boogie-woogie beat, thereafter improvising solos built around the song's chord changes, the boogie-woogie beat, and variations on the melody of the piece, combined with his arsenal of boogie-woogie riffs and performed in his inimitable style. Hughes, in his 1951 collection, ***Montage of a Dream Deferred,*** generated a set or sequence of six "boogie" poems—**"Dream Boogie," "Easy Boogie," "Boogie 1 a.m.," "Lady's Boogie," "Nightmare Boogie,"** and **"Dream Boogie: Variation"**—that have in common much more than the "boogie" of the titles. The poems comprise an intricate series of interwoven "improvisations" over a set boogie-woogie rhythm, with Hughes modulating and modifying rhythm, words, imagery, moods, and themes, and constructing a complex interrelationship between music, the musical instrument, the performance, and a set of attitudes exemplified by them.

A close examination of a related sequence of Hughes's blues poems offers the opportunity to explore his fusion of oral and written traditions and to examine his tremendous skills as a literary-jazz improviser.
—*Steven C. Tracy*

Structurally, Hughes's six boogie poems share the exciting, rushing rhythms of boogie-woogie: Hughes at work on his poems, pounding out rhythms on his typewriter keyboard. Briefly, boogie-woogie is a form of Afro-American music, normally performed on the piano, that emerged as a recognizable genre in the 1920s. As blues researcher Karl Gert zur Heide points out, "the theme of boogie is the blues, some features derive from ragtime, and the rhythmic interplay of both hands can be traced back to African roots." In boogie-woogie, the improvisations executed by the pianist's right hand on the treble keys of the piano are set off against the ostinato or repeated phrases of the left hand on the bass keys. Characteristically boogie-woogie follows the twelve-bar blues chord change pattern—in the key of C, CFC GFC—employing a repeated bass pattern recognizable most often for its eight beats to the bar and performed at a medium-to-fast tempo that builds an explosive drive and swing appropriate to the dance step after which it was named. Besides identifying a dance step and a type of music, however, the term "boogie" functions in other contexts: to boogie is to raise a ruckus or act wildly or uninhibitedly; it also has sexual connotations:

> I'm gonna pull off my pants and keep on my shirt,
> I'm gonna get so low you think I'm in the dirt.
> I'm gonna pitch a boogie-woogie,
> Gonna boogie-woogie all night long.

In this tune, singer Big Bill Broonzy has taken a boogie-woogie beat suitable for dancing and provided both the "wild acting" and sexual connotations that go with it. In the tradition, the word carried these connotations, and typically Hughes tried to capture the ambience of the tradition.

Hughes demonstrated his knowledge of boogie-woogie in *The First Book of Jazz,* in which he and his coauthors identified among the outstanding exponents of boogie-woogie "Pinetop" Smith, Jimmy Yancy, Meade Lux Lewis, Albert Ammons, and Pete Johnson—all important and generally recognized masters. It was the spirited, exuberant, danceable, and often rhythmically complex and intricate music of performers like those men that provided the basis for Hughes's boogie poem rhythms and the connotations of the word and the tradition that he tried to capture in his poems.

Hughes obviously wanted us to hear the boogie rhythms in these poems: the first four poems in the boogie sequence ("Dream," "Easy," "1 a.m.," and "Lady's") are very "aural"; the words "hear" and "heard" are employed repeatedly, both in a question—

> Ain't you heard
> The boogie-woogie rumble
> Of a dream deferred?

and an assertion—

> I know you've heard
> The boogie-woogie rumble
> Of a dream deferred.

The incessant rhythm and rumbling of boogie-woogie becomes in the poems symbolic of the dream he had delineated in his earlier poem **"Dream Variations"**:

> To fling my arms wide
> In some place of the sun,
> To whirl and to dance
> Till the white day is done
> Then rest at cool evening
> Beneath a tall tree
> While night comes on gently,
>   Dark like me—
> That is my dream!

Hughes is trying to get black people to recognize that the deferment of that dream is a large part of their lives, both by questioning and by asserting the "obvious." If they hadn't heard that boogie-woogie rumble, they could certainly hear it in the rhythms of Hughes's poems; for example, if one were to treat **"Dream Boogie,"** the first poem of the sequence and therefore a prototype for the other poems in the sequence, as if it were a lyric to be sung to boogie-woogie music, and identify the beats and chord changes as they relate to the words, the annotation would look as follows:

> C
> 1 2 34 567 8
> Good morning, daddy!
>
> 1 2 34 5 67
> Ain't you heard

8 12   34   56
The boogie-woogie rumble

7 8 12   34   56 7 8
Of a dream deferred?

F
1234   567
Listen closely:

8   12   34   5678
You'll hear their feet

C
1 2 3 4 5 6 7 8
Beating out and beating out a—

You think
It's a happy beat?

G
1 2 3 4 5 6 7 8
Listen to it closely:

F
1 2 3 4 5 6 78
Ain't you heard

C
1   2   3 4 5 6 7 8
Something underneath like a—

What did I say?
Sure,
I'm happy!
Take it away!

Hey pop!
Re-bop!
Mop!

Y-e-a-h!

What Hughes has done is create a twelve-line, twelve-bar boogie-woogie poem, annexing an exclamatory "tag" ending like those occasionally employed in music. Here, though, Hughes has manipulated the form and rhythm: stanzas two and three are jarred by the dramatic insertion of disturbing questions that achieve their impact by rewording the line we would expect in the normal rhythm and progression of thoughts into a question. Thus, in stanza two, "Beating out and beating out a happy beat" becomes:

Beating out and beating out—

You think
It's a happy beat?

Just as Hughes shifts to the interrogative and separates those questions from their normal stanzaic group, he just as surely upsets the boogie-woogie rhythm, eventually violating even the rhyming pattern in stanza three. This is significant because stanza three draws on the first two stanzas for a repetition of important lines: "Listen closely" of stanza two becomes "Listen to it closely" (Hughes employs a common characteristic of blues lyrics, building slightly modulated lines around loose formulaic patterns) in stanza three, while "Ain't you heard" of stanza one is lifted verbatim. Stanza three, however, becomes deliberately vague—"Something underneath"—in order to force the audience to answer the subsequent question, "What did I say?" By upsetting the rhythm and asking the questions, Hughes highlights the disparity between the rumbling seriousness of the deferred dream and the superficial happiness of the beat or performance. To this masterful maneuvering of the idiom Hughes annexes the "tag" ending—in jazz and blues a four-bar section appended to the end of a tune that repeats a phrase, offers a final comment, or indicates that the performance is about to end—often for those dancing to the performance. Hughes's seven-line ending contrasts once again the happiness of the words/music performance with the underlying problem. In light of the dramatic irony with which Hughes dealt with the subject earlier, this return to the facade of carefree happiness adds psychological complexity to the poem. Hughes felt that blacks needed to recognize the reality of deferred dreams, as he has forced in stanza three, but in stanza four he emphasizes the need to retain the spirit of cultural expression and the usefulness of the elaborate role-playing that provided blacks with the opportunity for advances, while whites concentrate on the superficial happy roles that blacks played.

The boogie rhythms extend to other poems in the sequence, although the twelve-bar progression is not necessarily present in any of them. **"Easy Boogie," "Nightmare Boogie,"** and **"Dream Boogie: Variation"** could theoretically fit into the twelve-bar pattern annotated with the variations above. One indication that they may not have been intended to fit into the twelve-bar pattern is the presence, in **"Easy Boogie,"** of the line "Riffs, smears, breaks" between stanzas two and three, which seems to indicate an instrumental break that would not be characteristic in a standard twelve-bar blues—the breaks would come between the twelve-bar verses. This underscores the importance of "hearing" the boogie-woogie rhythm and spirit of the performance as opposed to following a predetermined structure. **"Lady's Boogie"** and **"Boogie 1 a.m."** reemphasize the distinction, each of them eight-line poems (with an additional mock-jive exclamation in the former) in boogie rhythm. These poems, then, are tied together by the rhythm and spirit of boogie-woogie—a rhythm and spirit that Hughes clearly intended for us to hear.

The poems, of course, have other features in common besides boogie-woogie rhythm. The first four poems in the sequence all employ black jive slang: in **"Dream Boogie"** he uses "Daddy!" and "Hey pop! Re-hop! Mop! Y-e-a-h!"; in **"Easy Boogie"** he uses "Hey, Lawdy, Mama!"; in **"Boogie 1 a.m."** he uses "Daddy!"; and in **"Lady's Boogie"** he employs the phrase "Be-Bach!" Coupled with the boogie rhythms this plying of black speech demonstrates the influence of oral culture on Hughes's work, giving the distinctively black flavor to the poems necessary to suggest encoded messages appropriate to a segregated group of people. Music critic John McDonough has pointed out the usefulness of slang code words:

> There is a fraternal link that always seems to bond together those who would challenge or otherwise separate themselves from the mainstream of social custom. Sometimes the trappings and devices of such brotherhood are enjoyed for their own sake— a sort of college game without substance. But more commonly, they have a very specific and necessary function. In a hostile and crowded world, such devices identify each member to the other. It may be a handshake, a secret word or phrase, gesture or symbol. In short, a lexicon of code words that separate the true believers from the indifferent or unfriendly.

Hughes doesn't employ code words that whites are unlikely to understand, but the words are readily identifiable with black culture, and by doing so he intimates that his message is directed at blacks and, to a great measure, originates with them.

This slang also helps call attention to the similarities and contrasts of the poems. Both **"Dream Boogie"** and **"Boogie 1 a.m.,"** for example, are narrated by women, as indicated by the address "Daddy." This address, along with "Papa," is common in the blues songs of females and in black culture in general, but the term of address would not be used by a male; "Daddy-o" would be used, but not simply "Daddy." This use of a female speaker, which is also prevalent in Hughes's blues poems, is important in that it indicates that the ideas are not necessarily identifiable with a single viewpoint: that of the black male Hughes. The suggestion is that the problems of blacks connected with deferred dreams is not simply an intricate artistic stance of the author, but the representative stance of sensitive blacks, both male and female, who, especially in terms of the sexual theme of the poems, will be creating future generations.

"Dream Boogie" is a poem of beginnings: besides being the first poem of the sequence, it is the poem that greets at the beginning of the day and poses the nagging and disconcerting questions dealt with repeatedly in the other poems. It is appropriate that this is the first poem in the sequence, since upon awakening one would have the best chance of recalling dreams, and awakening from the fantasy/dream world to reality would accentuate the disparity between those two worlds. In **"Dream Boogie"** the speaker asks questions, in contrast to **"Boogie 1 a.m.,"** a poem of conclusion that addresses the listener at day's end—"Good evening, Daddy"— and asserts that the listener is aware of the rumblings of the dream deferred, presumably after day-long contact with the white-controlled world.

Similarly, **"Easy Boogie,"** the second poem of the sequence, and **"Lady's Boogie,"** the fourth, are related. In contrast to **"Dream Boogie,"** in **"Easy Boogie"** a man addresses a woman—"Hey, Lawdy Mama!" The speaker associates the recognition of the steady beat of the dream deferred with the vitality of the sexual act:

> Hey, Lawdy Mama!
> Do you hear what I said?
> Easy like I rock it
> In my bed!

This sexual vitality, implicit in the word "boogie," as already pointed out, is also linked with the soul's aspirations through the repetition of sentence construction:

> Down in the bass
> That easy roll
> Rolling like I like it
> In my soul.

The souls' dreams are seen as vital, lively, and life-giving. Thus through the repetition of phrases and structures, Hughes expands the importance of his words beyond their initial or superficial meanings.

"Lady's Boogie" exposes the superficial concerns of a posturing "lady" who

> ain't got boogie-woogie
> On her mind.

Viewed in comparison to **"Easy Boogie,"** the sexual connotation is at work here, suggesting a sexually ineffectual or inhibited person and connecting that to the inability to hear the beat of the dream deferred. Hughes suggests that the "Lady" has not listened, and could be successful if she did:

> But if she was to listen
> I bet she'd hear

Way up in the treble
The tingle of a tear.

However, the final exclamation ("Be-Bach!") suggests that her pretense makes a mockery of her own people's language in combining the phrase be-bop with the classical composer from another culture, mocking the pretension of her position and making it seem ludicrous.

"Easy Boogie" and **"Lady's Boogie"** also begin to deal with the relationships between the performer/creator, his instrument, and his creation, as they relate to the underlying desires and feelings of blacks. Although the "boogie-woogie rumble of a dream deferred" played "underneath" on the bass keys of a piano had already been introduced in **"Dream Boogie," "Easy Boogie"** further connects the bass rumble with something "down," something "underneath," something sexual, something elemental. It is the walking bass of solidarity:

Down in the bass
That steady beat
Walking, walking, walking
Like marching feet.

This solidarity is connected, through repetition and parallel sentence structure, with the feeling of the soul:

Down in the bass
that steady roll,
Rolling like I like it
In my soul.

Conversely, **"Lady's Boogie"** deals with the speaker's attitude toward a woman who has allowed the pretensions of "society" to interfere with her realizations about the problems of her people. This woman's mind is linked to the notes played in the treble on the piano:

See that lady
Dressed so fine
She ain't got boogie-woogie
On her mind—

But if she was to listen
I bet she'd hear
Way up in the treble
The tingle of a tear.

Once again the lines relate through their parallel structures: the lady whose pretensions prevent her from "hearing," being aware; who concentrates on appearances rather than sounds, messages; who doesn't listen to the agent that would "enlighten" her, the treble improvisations; whose mind refuses her emotional involvement with the boogie-woogie

message. Hughes is, in effect, replicating the amazing dexterity and remarkable rhythmic diversity of the boogie-woogie pianist: he is combining the rumbling, infectious bass beat and rhythm with treble variations and improvisations, relating the former to the "soul" and action, and the latter to the mind and thought of the "movement" to foster awareness of the problems of black people in terms of the deferred dream. The staccato alliteration is particularly effective in **"Lady's Boogie," "Boogie 1 a.m."** ("trilling the treble"), and **"Dream Boogie: Variation"** ("tinkling treble"), particularly when picked out over the momentum of the rolling bass.

These treble and bass patterns are used to introduce and indeed are a part of the compelling unifying image of the poems:

Trilling the treble
And twining the bass
Into midnight ruffles
of cat-gut lace.

Here the right-hand treble notes and the left-hand bass notes are united in performance, just as the mind and soul or thought and feeling of blacks are meant to be united in a common cause: the recognition of the dream deferred and the organization into a unified front to confront the problems of blacks in America. Hughes did not want to overemphasize the bass/sex/soul of the second poem of the sequence, **"Easy Boogie"**; neither did he want to concentrate exclusively on the treble/inhibitions/mind of the fourth poem, **"Lady's Boogie."** It was the poem in between, **"Boogie 1 a.m.,"** that presented the "unified sensibility" for which Hughes aimed and that combined the bass and treble into a single compelling image.

The image itself at once suggests several things: ruffles and lace both suggest the delicate trimming of clothing; however, to be ruffled is to become disturbed, and to ruffle is to cause disturbances, as in water; the lace becomes something to hold things together in light of the "cat-gut" prefix. All these combine to suggest a decorative appearance tied to an underlying disquietedness. The "midnight" of "midnight ruffles" identifies the revelation as a black one and places the revelation at nighttime—the time of dreams and nightmares.

A variation of the image returns in **"Nightmare Boogie,"** which follows **"Lady's Boogie"** and, with **"Dream Boogie: Variation,"** helps emphasize the dream theme at the end of the sequence. **"Nightmare Boogie"** deals with the collective loss of black identity:

I had a dream
and I could see
a million faces
black as me!

A nightmare dream:
Quicker than light
All them faces
Turned dead white!

This sentiment is a magnification of the problem recognized in **"Lady's Boogie,"** where the "lady" has lost the ability to hear and understand cultural messages. In **"Nightmare"** Hughes identifies the instantaneous loss of black identity as a phenomenon that occurred more quickly than it could be recognized, more quickly than it could be exposed, thus stressing the urgency of black identity, pride, and unity. What is important here is that the first four lines have a direct parallel relationship to lines five through eight: the dream of line one is the nightmare of line five; the seeing of line two is the revelation of line six; the faces of lines three and seven and the colors of lines four and eight define whether the event was a dream or a nightmare. At the climax of the metamorphosis from black to white, from dream to nightmare, Hughes eschews a smooth transition, generating a "whirling" midnight incantation, as if awakening to a real solution:

Boogie-woogie,
Rolling bass,
Whirling treble
Of cat-gut lace.

This variation on the lines of **"Boogie 1 a.m."** labels the dream deferred as a nightmare that leads to a racial identity, resolvable only by hearing and understanding the "message" of boogie-woogie.

In contrast to the nightmare of the dream deferred, the black pride/identity "movement," the marching, walking feet of **"Dream Boogie"** and **"Easy Boogie,"** is a whirling awakening to a new dream, which forms a very natural sequence to **"Dream Boogie: Variation"**—the final poem of the entire sequence—and a counterpoint to "Dream Boogie," the first. Whereas **"Dream Boogie"** is an upbeat, urgent poem, **"Variation"** is much more sad and subdued: the portrait of the boogie-woogie pianist, performing his music, his piano screaming for him under his lone stomping feet, his eyes misting at the prospect of having missed his chance at freedom. Here, however, the "midnight ruffles of / cat-gut lace" of the **"Boogie 1 a.m."** quatrain, and the "Whirling treble / of cat-gut lace" of the **"Nightmare Boogie"** quatrain become "High noon teeth / In a midnight face," identifying the central idea and image of the poems with the actual facial features and identity of the performer, the creator, the one closest to the music itself. Hughes is emphasizing here how easy it is for an individual to fail to recognize the dream deferred, the nightmare as it relates to the individual himself. The final image is not the jive-talking, energetic persona of **"Dream Boogie"**; it is the embodiment of the boogie-woogie tradition, alone and too late, playing the wistful boogie of freedom deferred.

By varying and manipulating the rhythm, words, imagery, moods, and themes of these poems, Hughes has illuminated the issue of the dream deferred from different emotional perspectives. By employing folk culture so well, he in effect gives his poems traditional authority, makes them unadulteratedly black, and establishes a continuity that makes them seem to express the ideas of the people for the people.

Arnold Rampersad (essay date 1989)

SOURCE: "Langston Hughes and Approaches to Modernism in the Harlem Renaissance," in *The Harlem Renaissance: Revaluations,* Garland Publishing, 1989, pp. 49-72.

[*In the following essay, Rampersad argues that Hughes's use of the blues form in his poetry places him in the modernist tradition.*]

In 1936, certainly after the end of the Harlem Renaissance, one highly literate young black student, a junior at Tuskegee Institute, saw no connection between modernism and black American verse even as he recognized a link between modernism and black culture. "Somehow in my uninstructed reading of Pound and Eliot," he later wrote, "I had recognized a relationship between modern poetry and jazz music, and this led me to wonder why I was not encountering similar devices in the work of Afro-American writers." In 1936, however, the youth came across a poem by a young black Communist based in Chicago, published in *New Masses.* Although the poem "was not a masterpiece," he would write, at last "I found in it traces of the modern poetic sensibility and techniques that I had been seeking."

The student was Ralph Ellison; the Communist poet, Richard Wright. The point is that Ellison, following the Harlem Renaissance, could see nothing of literary modernism in its writing, but had to depend for a glimpse of modernism in black poetry on a writer who not only had nothing to do with either Harlem or its Renaissance, but would the following year, 1937, dismiss virtually all of black writing. "Generally speaking," Wright declared (without offering an exception), "Negro writing in the past has been confined to humble novels, poems, and plays, prim and decorous ambassadors who went a-begging to white America." Wright knew well that ambassadors speak typically in archaic, sanctioned formulae; in general, they initiate nothing, make nothing new.

The writers of the Harlem Renaissance apparently had not responded to Emerson's primal dictum that "the experience of each new age requires a new confession, and the world seems always waiting for its poet." Or had they? Let us resolve modernism into a series of questions aimed at these writers. Did they sense some historic shift in the world that justified Pound's famous charge to writers to "Make it new!"? Did they perceive a crisis of expression, a need to, again in Pound's words, "resuscitate the dead art / Of poetry?" Had blacks made a pact with Walt Whitman, as Pound had done ("I make a pact with you, Walt Whitman— / I have detested you long enough")? Did they perceive the modern dominance of science and technology as requiring a self-preserving, adaptive response by art, in order to make something, in Frost's phrase, of "a diminished thing?" Did they recognize a crisis in the loss of prestige by religion? Or were the black writers of the Harlem Renaissance merely, as Ellison and Wright would have us believe, dull and uninspired imitators of mediocre white writers?

I would argue that writers such as Jean Toomer, Countee Cullen, Langston Hughes, Claude McKay, Wallace Thurman, Richard Bruce Nugent, and Zora Neale Hurston were as aware as anyone else about the pressure of the modern on their lives and their art. Of course, to be aware of a situation does not mean that one acts responsibly; to act responsibly does not guarantee success. My purpose here is to look at some of the ways in which black writers engaged or failed to engage various compelling aspects of the age in which they lived. Perhaps we can thus learn something about the Renaissance, and perhaps even about modernism itself.

The movement toward the modern in black letters began, in fact, a generation before the Harlem school, when Afro-American poetry was dominated by the work, in standard English but more popularly in dialect form, of Paul Laurence Dunbar. By 1900 (he would die six years later) Dunbar's poetry enjoyed a national vogue; as a boy, for example, William Carlos Williams read the black poet as a matter of course. To Dunbar himself, however, and to at least one other black writer, James Weldon Johnson, dialect poetry, and thus Afro-American poetry, was a dead art. In it, "darkies" most often either sang, danced, ate, and stole comically, or they mourned some minor loss pathetically. Dunbar's verse led William Dean Howells to note "a precious difference of temperament between the races which it would be a great pity to lose," and to see "the range between appetite and emotion, with certain lifts far beyond and above it," as the range of the black race. Such a reaction made Dunbar despair, without showing him a way out of his dilemma. "He sang of life, serenely sweet, / With, now and then, a deeper note," he wrote once about himself. "He of love when earth was young, / And Love, itself, was in his lays. / But ah, the world, it turned to praise / A jingle in a broken tongue."

The first step in the resuscitation of black poetry came late in the summer of 1900, when Dunbar's friend and admirer

James Weldon Johnson at last read the work of a white writer who had died during the previous decade. "I was engulfed and submerged by the book, and set floundering again," Johnson later recalled in his autobiography, *Along This Way:*

> I got a sudden realization of the artificiality of conventionalized Negro dialect poetry: of its exaggerated geniality, childish optimism, forced comicality and mawkish sentiment. . . . I could see that the poet writing in the conventionalized dialect, no matter how sincere he might be, was dominated by his audience; that his audience was a section of the white American reading public; that when he wrote he was expressing what often bore little relation, sometime no relation at all, to actual Negro life; that he was really expressing only certain conceptions about Negro life that his audience was willing to accept and ready to enjoy; that, in fact, he wrote mainly for the delectation of an audience that was an outside group. And I could discern that it was on this line that the psychological attitude of the poets writing in the dialect and that of the folk artists faced in different directions; because the latter, although working in the dialect, sought only to express themselves for themselves, and to their *own group.*

Thus Johnson laid bare the central dilemma facing not merely Dunbar but all black writers in America. The white poet was, of course, Walt Whitman, with whom Johnson made a pact more than a dozen years before Pound did. Neither Johnson nor Pound, however, would have been sensitive to Whitman had it not been for altering social and historical conditions that first gradually, then torrentially, made Whitman's insights into social meaning and poetic form shine forth. For Pound, the twin factors were, perhaps, science and technology, on one hand, and the Great War on the other. I suspect that in 1900, when Johnson first read Whitman, science meant relatively little to him as a threat, and the Great War was still more than a dozen years away. Or was it? For blacks, there was another great war, one that saw in the 1890s (the "nadir" of Afro-American history, as Rayford Logan has called it) racial segregation and black disfranchisement made law by the Supreme Court and enforced brutally by the Ku Klux Klan. In *Along This Way,* Johnson's discussion of *Leaves of Grass* follows immediately on his horrified recollection of the fourth major race riot in the history of blacks in New York, occurring in 1900 and capping a decade in which almost 1700 blacks had been lynched, "numbers of them with a savagery that was satiated with nothing short of torture, mutilation, and burning alive at the stake." This was for blacks the "Great War," compared to which their involvement in the later carnage in Europe was almost a form of affirmative action—affirmative action with a vengeance, if you will. Every major American war from the Revolution to Vietnam, it must be remembered, has led to a material *advance* in the freedom of black Americans.

That this pressure had its effect on poetic form among blacks is independently demonstrated in the sometime poetry of the scholar-turned-protagonist, W.E.B. DuBois. In DuBois's verse we see rage against racism making the tropes of traditional poetic discourse impossible, and pushing his pen, willy-nilly, toward free verse and liberated rhyme in a series of poems, such as "A Litany of Atlanta," "The Burden of Black Women," "Song of the Smoke," and "Prayers of God," published in the first two decades of this century. When the war in Europe came, it only added to the pressure toward the modern. "We darker men said," DuBois wrote in his essay "The Souls of White Folk," "This is not Europe gone mad; this is not aberration nor insanity; this is Europe; this seeming Terrible is the real soul of white culture,—stripped and visible today. This is where the world has arrived—these dark and awful depths and not the shining and ineffable heights of which it boasted."

By this time, at least one younger black writer had taken black poetry closer to the modern. In 1912 Fenton Johnson's first book of verse, *A Little Dreaming,* was conventional and included both a long poem in blank verse and Dunbaresque dialect verse. Within two or three years, however, he had completely renovated his sense of poetry. In *Visions of Dusk* (1915) and *Songs of the Soil* (1916) he not only adopted free verse but altered his ways of viewing civilization itself. Instead of glorifying white high culture, Fenton Johnson spurned it, as Pound would do in writing of Europe as "an old bitch gone in the teeth," and "a botched civilization." Unlike Pound, however, Fenton Johnson did so from an unmistakably racial perspective:

> I am tired of work; I am tired of building up some body else's
>   civilization.
> Let us take a rest, M'Lissy Jane.
> I will go down to the Last Chance Saloon, drink a gallon or
>   two of gin, shoot a game or two of dice and sleep the
>   rest of the night on one of Mike's barrels.
> You will let the old shanty go to rot, the white people's
>   clothes turn to dust, and the Cavalry Baptist Church
>   sink to the bottomless pit. . . .
> Throw the children into the river; civilization has given us
>   too many. It is better to die than it is to grow up and
>   find out that you are colored.

> Pluck the stars out of the heavens. The stars mark our
>   destiny. The stars marked my destiny.
> I am tired of civilization.

In "The Banjo Player," the speaker wanders the land playing "the music of the peasant people." He is a favorite in saloons and with little children. "But I fear that I am a failure. Last night a woman called me a troubadour. What is a troubadour?" "The Scarlet Woman," who possesses "a white girl's education and a face that enchanted the men of both races," spurns classical mythic language and enters a bordello for white men: "Now I can drink more gin than any man for miles around. Gin is better than all the water in Lethe."

Fenton Johnson was so close to the center of the Chicago manifestation of modernism, which is to say the center of literary modernism except for wherever Ezra Pound happened to be at the moment, that it is unclear how much he owes to the more famous poets he resembles in his work— Carl Sandburg, whose groundbreaking *Chicago and Other Poems* appeared in 1916, and Edgar Lee Masters in his *Spoon River Anthology* (1915). Johnson published in Harriet Monroe's *Poetry* magazine and at least one other important modernist outlet, *Others.* One point must be noted, however, about the work thus far of Fenton Johnson, James Weldon Johnson, and DuBois. For all its incipient modernism, their verse betrays no sign of any specific innovative formal influence by the culture, or subculture, they championed. Indignation at the treatment of blacks moved them to change as poets; black culture itself did not. This was the crucial hurdle facing would-be black modernists.

Yet another poet to balk at the highest fence was Claude McKay, the Jamaican-born writer who first gained notice in the United States in 1917, when he published two sonnets in *Seven Arts* magazine. Subsequent publications in *Pearson's,* Max Eastman's *Liberator* (where he would serve as an associate editor), and the leading black journals, such as the radical socialist *Messenger* and DuBois's *Crisis,* as well as in prestigious English publications, such as C.K. Ogden's *Cambridge Magazine,* made him for a while the most respected of Afro-American *versifiers.* Two volumes of verse, *Spring in New Hampshire* (London, 1920), with an introduction by I.A. Richards, and *Harlem Shadows* (Harcourt, Brace, 1922) anchored his reputation. For black Americans, however, McKay's single most impressive publication was not one of his lyric evocations of nature but a sonnet published in 1919, following perhaps the bloodiest summer of anti-black riots since the end of the Civil War. In "If We Must Die," McKay implored his readers not to die "like hogs / Hunted and penned in an inglorious spot" but to "nobly die, / So that our precious blood may not be shed / In vain." Even if death is certain, "Like men we'll face the murderous, cowardly pack, / Pressed to the wall, dying, but fighting back."

With McKay and "If We Must Die," we come not only directed to the Harlem school but also to one of its principal tensions—that between radicalism of political and racial thought, on the one hand, and, on the other, a bone-deep commitment to conservatism of form. As a poet, McKay was absolutely ensnared by the sonnet, which—for all the variety possible within its lines—is perhaps the most telling sign of formal conservatism in the writing of poetry in English. Perhaps no greater tension exists in a brief Afro-American text than that between the rage of "If We Must Die" and the sonnet form. McKay used the form again and again to write some of the most hostile verse in Afro-American letters, as in "To the White Fiends" ("Think you I am not a fiend and savage too? / Think you I could not arm me with a gun / And shoot down ten of you for every one / Of my black brothers murdered, burnt by you?" and in **"The White House,"** or **"Tiger,"** where "The white man is a tiger at my throat, / Drinking my blood as my life ebbs away, / And muttering that his terrible striped coat / Is Freedom's."

McKay was not alone in his commitment to conservative forms even in the postwar modernist heyday. If the work of Countee Cullen, a far younger writer, was more varied than McKay's, his formal conservatism was as powerful. Cullen's idols were John Keats ("I cannot hold my peace, John Keats; / There never was a spring like this"), and A.E. Housman, still alive but moribund surely when one considers the distance between his blue remembered hills and the steamy streets of Harlem. And unlike McKay, who wrote of both race and "universal" topics without a sense of contradiction, Cullen resented the inspiration that came from racial outrage. In a novel, *One Way to Heaven* (1932), he satirized a black woman who insists upon teaching her students verse by Langston Hughes. "While her pupils could recite like small bronze Ciceros, 'I Too Sing America'," the narrator jibes, "they never had heard of 'Old Ironsides,' 'The Blue and the Gray,' or 'The Wreck of the Hesperides.' They could identify lines from Hughes, Dunbar, Cotter, and the multitudinous Johnsons, but were unaware of the contributions of Longfellow, Whittier, and Holmes to American literature." Elsewhere he ridicules a poem by a so-called "Negro poet." "Taken in a nutshell," a character explains scornfully, "it means that niggers have a hell of a time in this God-damned country. That's all Negro poets write about." In perhaps his best-known couplet, Cullen lamented "this curious thing: / To make a poet black, and bid him sing!"

Exactly why McKay and Cullen stuck by conservative forms in the midst of a decade of change is too complicated a question to answer here. But we might take note of one or two points. If McKay was a radical socialist and an anti-modernist, he was in line with a tradition of taste among great radicals from Marx to Lenin, who fomented revolution but clung to the classics like bourgeois intellectuals. "I am unable to consider the productions of futurism, cubism, expressionism and other isms," Lenin wrote privately somewhere. "I do not understand them. I get no joy from them." In addition, McKay was in line with the very philosophy of Marxism, which defines the world in a way diametrically opposed to modernism; Marxism and modernism are poles apart.

Langston Hughes, in opening his *Nation* essay in 1926, **"The Negro and the Racial Mountain,"** bluntly attacked Cullen's dilemma without naming him. He wrote about a black friend, a writer, who wished to be known not as a Negro poet, but as a poet. "Meaning subconsciously," Hughes wrote, "'I would like to be white.'" Cullen might have defended himself by quoting T.S. Eliot on tradition—or, if you permit an anachronism—by quoting Ralph Ellison, who would distinguish between (on one hand) his ancestors—T.S. Eliot and Hemingway, above all, who strongly influenced him, and (on the other) his family, such as Richard Wright and Langston Hughes, who apparently influenced him not at all. But Cullen was not Eliot nor could ever be. Eliot spoke up for the power of dead poets on aesthetic grounds, but the choice of white ancestors over black relatives cannot ever be, to say the least, a purely aesthetic matter. In addition, one must be wary of the motives of anyone, of any color, who exalts his ancestors at the expense of his family.

Let us turn from the most conservative members of the Harlem school to probably the *least* conservative according to modernist standards—Jean Toomer and Richard Bruce Nugent. Toomer's *Cane,* a pastiche of fiction, poetry, drama, and hieroglyphics published in 1923, has been hailed almost invariably as the greatest single document of the Renaissance. Bruce Nugent's published work in the 1920s was scant but very striking, especially the hallucinogenic, stream-of-consciousness story "Smoke, Lilies and Jade," which was too quickly compared by at least one review of *FIRE*!! magazine, where it first appeared in 1926, to *Ulysses.* Is it significant that Toomer and Nugent, the most modernist of the black writers, were also probably the least racial either personally or in their writing? From the start, Nugent seemed to consider race a great irrelevancy. And while Jean Toomer's *Cane* is saturated with a concern for race and the complex fate of being black in America, even as his book was appearing the extremely light-skinned Toomer was vehemently denying that he was a Negro—an attitude that only intensified over the years as his writing became more modernist and purged of the racial theme. Bruce Nugent, one black modernist, says that race doesn't matter; Toomer, another, says that race doesn't matter as long as nobody calls him black. Are we to conclude, then, that modernism and black racial feeling, with its political consequences, are incompatible?

It might be useful here to look at the work of Melvin B. Tolson, who began writing at the tail end of the Renaissance with a limited sense of the modern, but grew to be acclaimed as the first authentic black modernist poet. Tolson was the author of *A Gallery of Harlem Portraits,* posthumously published but in manuscript form by 1931; the Marxist-influenced *Rendezvous with America* (1944); and a deeply modernist *Libretto for the Republic of Liberia* (1953), among other works. Beginning with the sense of the modern derived from Edwin Arlington Robinson and Carl Sandburg, Tolson repudiated their blending of free verse, highly accessible language, and folk references in order to master the most complex version of modernism. The result was poetry beyond the ability of all but a few readers to understand, let alone enjoy. This new poetry, however, tremendously excited those privileged few, including the reformed racist Allen Tate, who in 1931 refused to attend a dinner for Langston Hughes and James Weldon Johnson in Nashville because they were black, but lived to write an introduction in 1953 to *Librello for the Republic of Liberia.* Tolson not only showed a "first rate intelligence at work from first to last," Tate marveled, but for "the first time, it seems to me, a Negro poet has assimilated completely the full poetic language of his time, and by implication, the language of the Anglo-American tradition." As if that were not praise enough, William Carlos Williams found a place of honor for Tolson, and Allen Tate, in the fourth book of *Paterson:*

> —and to Tolson and to his ode
> and to Liberia and to Allen Tate
> (give him credit)
> and to the South generally
>
> **"Selah!"**

Thus encouraged, Tolson deepened his commitment to modernism with *Harlem Gallery: Book I. The Curator* (1965). In his introduction to the book, however, Karl Shapiro questioned Tate's statement that Tolson was indebted to white modernist masters and their special language. "*Tolson writes in Negro,*" Shapiro declared. Let me quote some lines from the first stanza of the book:

> Lord of the House of Flies,
>   jaundiced-eyed, synapses purled,
> wries before the tumultuous canvas,
>   *The Second of May—*
>   by Goya:
>   the dagger of Madrid
>   vs.
>   the scimitar of Murat.
> In Africa, in Asia, on the Day
> of Barricades, alarm birds bedevil the Great White
> World, a Burdian's ass—not Balaam's—between
> oats
> and hay.

Any Negro who speaks naturally like this is probably wearing a straightjacket. In its stated themes, the poem justifies Tolson's continuing sense of himself as a champion of his fellow blacks and their history; in its full language, it repudiates that sense. A while ago, Toomer and Nugent led me to *ask* whether modernism can be compatible with strong racial feeling. Tolson leads me to *understand* that complex modernism cannot be so compatible. Racial feeling, which is spurious unless accompanied by a deep sense of political wrong, demands an accessible art; the more pervasive the political wrong, the more accessible must be the art. Melvin Tolson may be on his way to Mount Olympus, but only at the expense of his people and their common poets, washed up on the shores of oblivion while the mighty modernist river rolls by.

When we drive by the scene of an accident, we feel the pain of broken bones and flowing blood. We tremble, but we drive on, unscathed and unstained. Are all of us integral victims of the accident of modernism (which followed the accident of World War I)? Or are some of us only rubbernecking? Must we assume that what is modern for the white goose is also modern for the black gander, that the dominant quality of white life in the twentieth century, as perceived by certain great white poets, is the same as the dominant temper for black? Or that the white quality is something to which blacks should have *aspired* (a tragic attitude, but one to which Jean Toomer, I think, succumbed)? Nor is this a matter of black and white alone. Robert Frost, to my mind, achieved unquestioned greatness swimming against the tide of modernism, ridiculing free verse, gentrifying run-down forms, forging out of a mixture, in which New England regionalism played a very strong part, both a critique of modernism and a body of work beyond easy category.

The major meditative poem by a black writer of the decade, Arna Bontemps's "Nocturne at Bethesda," reveals a black poet "flying low, / I thought I saw the flicker of a wing / Above the mulberry trees; but not again. / Bethesda sleeps. This ancient pool that healed / A host of bearded Jews does not awake. . . . " "Nocturne at Bethesda" is the black counterpart to Wallace Stevens's magnificent "Sunday Morning," in which Stevens dwells on the crisis of spirituality but denies transcendent religion in favor of a future of hedonism: "Supple and turbulent, a ring of men / Shall chant in orgy on a summer morn / Their boisterous devotion to the sun, / Not as a god, but as a god might be, / Naked among them, like a savage source," In "Nocturne at Bethesda," Arna Bontemps, who never outgrew completely the lugubriousness of his Seventh Day Adventism, nevertheless also looks to a new day beyond religion: "Yet I hope, still I long to live. / If there can be returning after death / I shall come back. But it will not be here; / If you want me you must search for me / Beneath the palms of Africa."

The finest black poet of the decade, Langston Hughes, rejected metaphysics and superstition altogether; loyal to perhaps the essential modernist criterion, Hughes for the most part looked not before and after, but at what *is*. Hughes went in the only direction a black poet could go and still be great in the 1920s: he had to lead blacks, in at least one corner of their lives—in his case, through poetry—into the modern world. His genius lay in his uncanny ability to lead by following (one is tempted to invoke Eliot's image of the poet's mind as a platinum filament), to identify the black modern, recognize that it was not the same as the white modern, and to structure his art (not completely, to be sure, but to a sufficient extent for it to be historic) along the lines of that black modernism.

Hughes went in the only direction a black poet could go and still be great in the 1920s: he had to lead blacks, in at least one corner of their lives—in his case, through poetry—into the modern world.
—*Arnold Rampersad*

Modernism began for Hughes on January 1919, a month short of his seventeenth birthday, when the Cleveland Central High School *Monthly,* in which he had been publishing undistinguished verse for more than a year, announced a long poem "in free verse"—apparently the first in the history of the magazine. **"A Song of the Soul of Central"** ("Children of all people and all creeds / Come to you and you make them welcome") indicates that Hughes had made his individual pact with Walt Whitman. With Whitman's influence came a break with the genteel tyranny of rhyme and the pieties of the Fireside poets and the majority of black versifiers. Already conscious of himself as a black, however, Hughes could not accept, much less internalize, a vision of the modern defined largely by the fate of Europe after the war. Sharing little or nothing of J. Alfred Prufrock's sense of an incurably diseased world, Hughes looked with indifference on the ruined splendors of the waste land. In practice, modernism for him would mean not Pound, Eliot, or Stevens, but Whitman, Vachel Lindsay, and, above all, Sandburg. The last became "my guiding star." Hughes, however, did not remain star-struck for long; within a year or so he had emancipated himself from direct influence. In one instance, where the well-meaning Sandburg had written: "I am the nigger / Singer of Songs, / Dancer," Hughes had responded with the more dignified (though not superior) **"Negro":** "I am the Negro: / Black as the night is black, / Black like the depths of my Africa."

The key to his release as a poet was his discovery of the significance of race, as well as other psychological factors (beyond our scope here) that amount to a final admission of his aloneness in the world, with both factors combining to make Hughes dependent on the regard of his race as practically no other black poet has been. He responded by consciously accepting the challenge of Whitman and Sandburg but also by accepting as his own special task, within the exploration of modern democratic vistas in the United States, the search for a genuinely Afro-American poetic form. At the center of his poetic consciousness stood the black masses,

> Dream-singers all,
> Story-tellers,
> Dancers,
> Loud laughers in the hands of Fate—
> My people.

Or, as he soon more calmly, and yet more passionately, would express his admiration and love:

> The night is beautiful,
> So the faces of my people.
>
> The stars are beautiful,
> So the eyes of my people.
>
> Beautiful, also, is the sun
> Beautiful, also, are the souls of my people.

Before he was nineteen, Hughes had written at least three of the poems on which his revered position among black readers would rest. The most important was **"The Negro Speaks of Rivers"** ("I've known rivers: / I've known rivers ancient as the world and older than the flow of human blood in human veins. / My soul has grown deep like the rivers.") **"When Sue Wears Red"** drew on the ecstatic cries of the black church to express a tribute to black woman unprecedented in the literature of the race.

> When Susanna Jones wears red
> Her face is like an ancient cameo
> Turned brown by the ages.
>
> Come with a blast of trumpets,
> Jesus! . . .

The third major poem of this first phase of Hughes's adult creativity was **"Mother to Son,"** a dramatic monologue that reclaimed dialect (Dunbar's "jingle in a broken tongue") for the black poet ("Well, son, I'll tell you: / Life for me ain't been no crystal stair. / It's had tacks in it, / And splinters"). With this poem and the resuscitation of dialect, Hughes came closer than any of the poets before him to what I have identified as the great hurdle facing the committed black poet—how to allow the race to infuse and inspire the very form of a poem, and not merely its surface contentions. Until this step could be taken, black poetry would remain antiquarian, anti-modern.

To a degree greater than that of any other young black poet, however, Hughes trained himself to be a modern poet—I am conscious here of Pound's words on the general subject, and on Eliot in particular. His high school, dominated by the children of east European immigrants, and where he was class poet and editor of the yearbook, was a training ground in cosmopolitanism. Mainly from Jewish classmates, "who were mostly interested in more than basketball and the glee club," he was introduced to basic texts of radical socialism. Although at 21 he began his first ocean voyage by dumping overboard a box of his books, the detritus of his year at Columbia (he saved only one book—*Leaves of Grass:* "That one I could not throw away"), it was not out of ignorance of what they might contain. "Have you read or tried to read," he wrote in 1923 to a friend, "Joyce's much discussed 'Ulysses'?" By the age of 23 he could speak both French and Spanish. In 1923 he was writing poems about Pierrot (a *black* Pierrot, to be sure), after Jules Laforgue, like Edna St. Vincent Millay in *Aria da Capo,* and another young man who would soon concede that he was a poet manqué and turn to fiction to confront the gap between lowly provincialism and modernism—William Faulkner. If Hughes went to Paris and Italy without finding the Lost Generation, at least he was able in 1932 to assure Ezra Pound (who had written to him from Rappallo to complain about the lack of instruction in African culture in America) that "Many of your poems insist on remaining in my head, not the words, but the mood and the meaning, which, after all, is the heart of a poem."

Hughes also shared with white modernists, to a degree far greater than might be inferred from his most popular poems, an instinct toward existentialism in its more pessimistic form. One poem, written just before his first book of poems appeared in 1926, suggests the relative case with which he could have taken to "raceless" modernist idioms. From **"A House in Toas"**:

> Thunder of the Rain God
> And we three
> Smitten by beauty.
> Thunder of the Rain God:
> And we three
> Weary, weary.
> Thunder of the Rain God
> And you, she and I
> Waiting for the nothingness. . . .

Hughes, however, had already committed himself to a very different vision of poetry and the modern world, a vision rooted in the modern black experience and expressed most powerfully and definitively in the music called blues. What is the blues? Although W.C. Handy was the first musician to popularize it, notably with *St. Louis Blues,* the form is so deeply based in the chants of Afro-American slave labor, field hollers, and sorrow songs as to be ancient and comprises perhaps the greatest art of Africans in North America. Oral and improvisational by definition, the blues nevertheless has a classical regimen. Its most consistent form finds a three-line stanza, in which the second line restates the first, and the third provides a contrasting response to both. "The blues speak to us simultaneously of the tragic and the comic aspects of the human condition," Ralph Ellison has written; they must be seen "first as poetry and as ritual," and thus as "a transcendence of those conditions created within the Negro community by the denial of social justice." "It was a language," Samuel Charters asserts in *The Legacy of the Blues,* "a rich, vital, expressive language that stripped away the misconception that the black society in the United States was simply a poor, discouraged version of the white. It was impossible not to hear the differences. No one could listen to the blues without realizing that there were two Americas."

A long brooding on the psychology of his people, and a Whitmanesque predisposition to make the native languages of America guide his art, led Hughes early in 1923 to begin his greatest single literary endeavor: his attempt to resuscitate the dead art of an American poetry and culture by invoking the blues (exactly as George Gershwin, the following year, would try to elevate American music in his *Rhapsody in Blue*). If Pound had looked in a similar way, at one point, to the authority of the Provincial lyric of the middle ages, Hughes could still hear the blues in night clubs and on street corners, as blacks responded in art to the modern world. At the very least, Pound and Hughes (and Whitman) shared a sense that poetry and music were intimately related. To Hughes, black music at its best was the infallible metronome of racial grace: "Like the waves of the sea coming one after another, always one after another, like the earth moving around the sun, night, day—night, day—night, day—forever, so is the undertow of black music with its rhythm that never betrays you, its rooted power." In the blues, in its mixture of pain and laughter, its lean affirmation of humanity in the face of circumstance, all in a secular mode (no "shantih, shantih" here; no brand plucked from the "burning!"), he found the tone, the texture, the basic language of true black modernism. A line from the epigraphic note to the volume says it all: "The mood of the *Blues* is almost always despondency, but when they are sung people laugh."

Over a period of five years, starting some time around 1922, he slowly engaged the blues as a literary poet, first describing the blues from a distance, then enclosing the blues within a traditional poem, as he did in the prizewinning **"The Weary Blues"** ("Droning a drowsy syncopated tune, / Rocking back and forth to a mellow croon, / I heard a Negro play"), until, at last, in his most important collection, *Fine Clothes to the Jew* (1927), he proposed the blues exclusively on its own terms by writing in the form itself, alone. Thus he acknowledge at last the full dignity of the people who had invented it.

Savagely attacked in black newspapers as "about 100 pages of trash [reeking] of the gutter and sewer," containing "poems that are insanitary, insipid, and repulsing," this book nevertheless was Hughes's greatest achievement in poetry, and remarkable by almost any American standard, as the literary historian Howard Mumford Jones recognized in a 1927 review. "In a sense," Jones wrote of Hughes, "he has contributed a really new verse form to the English language."

More important, blues offered, in a real sense, a new mode of feeling to the world (Eudora Welty has reminded us that literature teaches us how to feel) and a new life to art. To probe this point we would have to make a fresh reading of art and culture in the 1920s, for which I do not have the time or, truly, the skills. But instead of dismissively talking about the jazz age we would have to see that 1920, when the first commercial recording of a black singer, Mamie Smith's *Crazy Blues,* appeared, was perhaps as important a year for some people (certainly the millions of blacks who bought blues records in the decade, and the millions of whites down to our day who would thereafter sing and dance to the blues and its kindred forms) as was 1922, the year of Eliot's *The Waste Land,* for other people. We would see Gershwin's *Rhapsody in Blue,* premiered at Paul Whiteman's concert "An Experiment in Modern Music" in New York in 1924, as a modern American landmark that is in fact an alternative to the spirit of European modernism. We might go further, not simply to the work of other musicians such as Stravinsky and Bartok and Aaron Copeland but also to the work of writers like Faulkner, whose genius was emancipated in *The Sound and the Fury,* I would suggest, by a balance between the modernism of Joyce, which dominates the first section of the novel, and the counter-modernism of the blues, which dominates the last in spite of the religious overtones there, and in spite of Faulkner's ultimate unwillingness to take on the consciousness of a black character whose life is informed by the blues. To me, it is instructive that Joycean technique facilitates the utterance of the idiot, Benjy, but that the blues temper informs the most affirmative section of the book, that dominated by black Dilsey Gibson and her people ("they endured").

Far from suggesting that only Langston Hughes in the Harlem Renaissance discovered the black modern, I see the whole Harlem movement as struggling toward its uncovering. Why? Because it was inescapable; it was what the masses lived. In one sense, reductive no doubt, the Harlem Renaissance was simply an attempt by the artists to understand blues values and to communicate them to the wider modern world.

Finally, I would suggest that this question of modernism, and Hughes's place in it, needs to be seen in the context not merely of Harlem but of international cultural change in the twentieth century. By the age of twenty-one, he belonged already to an advanced guard of writers, largely from the yet unspoken world outside Europe and North America, that would eventually include Neruda of Chile, the young Borges of Argentina (who translated **"The Negro Speaks of Rivers"** in 1931), Garcia Lorca of Spain (see his "El Rey de Harlem"), Jacques Roumain of Haiti (see his poem "Langston Hughes"), Senghor of Senegal (who would hail Hughes in 1966 as the greatest poetic influence on the *Negritude* movement), Césaire of Martinique, Damas of French Guyana, and Guillen of Cuba (who freely asserted in 1930 that his first authentically Cuban or "Negro" poems, the eight pieces of *Molivos de Son,* were inspired by Hughes's visit to Havana that year). To these names should be added painters such as Diego Rivera, following his return from Paris in 1923, and his friends Orozco and Siquieros.

The collective aim of these writers and artists was to develop, even as they composed in the languages and styles of Europe and faced the challenge of European modernism, an aesthetic tied to a sense of myth, geography, history, and culture that was truly indigenous to their countries, rather than merely reflective of European trends, whether conservative or avant-garde. Finally, let me suggest that Hughes's virtual precedence of place among them has less to do with his date of birth or his individual talent than with the fact that he was the poetic fruition of the Afro-American intellectual tradition, where these questions of race and culture and this challenge to civilization had long been debated, and under the harshest social conditions. In 1910, after all, when DuBois founded *Crisis* magazine, he gave it a challenging subtitle—but one he had already used for an even earlier publication. He called it "A Record of the Darker Races."

Herman Beavers (essay date 1992)

SOURCE: "Dead Rocks and Sleeping Men: Aurality in the Aesthetic of Langston Hughes," in *The Langston Hughes Review,* Vol. 11, No. 1, 1992, pp. 1-5.

[*In the following essay, Beavers argues that Hughes's role was to amplify the voice of African Americans.*]

In his 1940 autobiography, *The Big Sea,* Langston Hughes discusses the circumstances that lead him, at the puerile age of 19, to the creation of his poem, **"The Negro Speaks of Rivers."** The poem came into being during a trip to Mexico, Hughes writes, "when [he] was feeling very bad. Thus, he connects poetic inspiration and emotional turbulence, both of which stemmed from his attempt to understand his father's self-hatred. He relates, "All day on the train I had been thinking about my father and his strange dislike of his own people. I didn't understand it because I was a Negro, and I liked Negroes very much." What is striking about the end of this passage is that one finds Hughes adopting a posture both inside and outside the race: he does not make a statement of self-love (e.g. I like myself), rather he indicates through a kind of reflexivity, that he has self-worth. In short, he is unable to articulate self-valuation, he can only construct his positionality as the mirror opposite of his father's racial feeling. But then Hughes shifts the subject and recalls that "one of the happiest jobs [he] ever had," was the time he spent working behind the soda fountain of a refreshment parlor, in "the heart of the colored neighborhood" in Cleveland. He offers this description:

> People just up from the South used to come in for ice cream and sodas and watermelon. And I never tired of *hearing* their talk, *listening* to thunderclaps of their laughter, to their troubles, to their discussions of the war and the men who had gone to Europe from the Jim Crow South, their complaints over the high rent and the long overtime hours that brought what seemed big checks, until the weekly bills were paid. (my emphasis)

I quote this passage at length to point to the disjointed quality Hughes's narrative assumes. In one chapter, we find the self-hatred of his father, his own admiration for the recuperative powers of newly arrived Southern blacks, and the act of composing a famous poem. The elements that form Hughes's account can be read, at least on a cursory level, as an attempt to demonstrate that his "best poems were written when [he] felt the worst." This notwithstanding, what I would like to propose is that we can place the poem into an aesthetic frame that brings these three disparate elements into a more geometrical alignment.

Hughes's autobiographical account can be found in the middle of a chapter entitled, "I've Known Rivers." Having established his father as someone he neither understands nor wishes to emulate, the autobiography paints the older man as an outsider, not only geographically, but spiritually as well. That Hughes would discuss his father in relation to such an important poem, alludes to body travel of a different sort than that which he undertakes in this chapter of his autobiography. Moving further away from Cleveland, the geographical space where he encountered the individuals he describes as "the gayest and bravest people possible . . . ", Hughes elides the distance his father has put between himself and other blacks. He resists the impulses that lead to the latter's self-imposed exile: he is immersed in a vernacular moment and simultaneously peripheral to that moment. What differentiates the younger Hughes is that he listens to the voices of the folk and is "empowered rather than debilitated" by what he hears.

In composing the poem, Hughes looks at "the great muddy river flowing down toward the heart of the South" (*The Big Sea*). While he suggests that it is his gaze—looking out of the train window at the Mississippi—that initiates composition, I would assert that what catalyzes his act of writing is the act of recovering the spoken word. A point emphasized, moreover, by the fact that he recounts a moment where he is listener rather than speaker.

Later in the autobiography, Hughes relates, in much less detail, the events which lead to his poem, **"The Weary Blues."** There, he states, simply: "That winter, I wrote a poem called **"The Weary Blues,"** about a piano-player I heard in Harlem. . . . " Again, Hughes's poetic composition moves forward from an aural moment where, as with **"The Negro Speaks of Rivers,"** he is an outsider. Arnold Rampersad alludes to this when he observes:

> . . . [I]n his willingness to stand back and record, with minimal intervention as a craftsman, aspects of the drama of black religion or black music, Hughes had clearly shown already that he saw his *own art as inferior* [my emphasis] to that of either black musicians or religionists . . . At the heart of his sense of inferiority . . . was the knowledge that he stood to a great extent *outside* the culture he worshiped.

Rampersad concludes that Hughes's sense of alienation resulted from the fact that "his life had been spent away from consistent, normal involvement with the black masses whose affection and regard he craved."

This trajectory repeats itself in **"The Weary Blues."** Rampersad intimates as much in his description of the poem's inception: "And then one night in March [of 1922], in a little cabaret in Harlem, he finally *wrote himself and his awkward position accurately into a poem* [my emphasis]." This assessment calls our attention to an important consideration, namely, that Hughes's aural aesthetic employs the externality he felt in the African American community. That he was a writer and not a musician, preacher, or dancer meant that his artistic project was to record artistic expression, to amplify the African American vernacular speech event for the rest of the world to hear. Further, Hughes's sense that his literary representation of the folk was inferior, mere imitation, in turn means that he was positioned, as artist, at a distance from the "real source," almost as if he were a loudspeaker serving as a medium through which sound travels, rather than the source itself. In becoming comfortable with this role, Hughes traversed repeatedly the conceptual distance necessary to create authentic representations of black speech. Hence, as he achieved a greater place among the African American intellectual elite, the distance increased between him and the masses he sought to portray. Nonetheless, as his aesthetic sensibility crystallized, his conceptual movement was *toward* them.

This is evidenced by the fact that Hughes's Simple character resulted from a conversation he shared with a factory worker and his girlfriend in a Harlem bar in 1943. Intrigued as he listened to the exchange, Hughes used the qualities he discerned from the conversation to create the character, who first appeared in his column for *The Chicago Defender*. Constructed as a dialogue between a narrator speaking in standard English and Jesse B. Semple (or Simple), who spoke in a more colorful, Southern idiom, the columns work out Hughes's passionate desire to honor the self-redemptive power found in the African American community. Thus, Simple became a vehicle for giving voice to the nature of his artistic project; indeed, it is he who articulates the necessity, as if it were a constant reminder to Hughes, to listen "eloquently."

If the ability to "listen eloquently" characterizes Hughes's attempts to celebrate "the folk," one also finds him creating stories that illustrate the ways that African American culture is objectified because people, particularly whites, fail to understand what African American voices articulate. In Hughes's collection of stories, *The Ways of White Folks,* for example, we find stories like **"Slaves on the Block,"** where the Carraways are described as "people who went in for Negroes." When their maid's nephew, Luther, arrives at their home, they are immediately attracted to him as the ultimate exotic. Michael Carraway, as one who thinks "in terms of music," exclaims, "He's 'I Couldn't Hear Nobody Pray.'" Not only does Hughes suggest that Carraway confuses physicality and spirituality, but the song title signals his lack of aural dexterity as well.

> **[O]ne . . . finds [Hughes] creating stories that illustrate the ways that African American culture is objectified because people, particularly whites, fail to understand what African American voices articulate.**
> **—Herman Beavers**

In **"The Blues I'm Playing,"** Mrs. Ellsworth takes on the role of benefactress for Oceola, a young black woman who is a gifted pianist. However, the investment leads her to believe that she can dictate what her protégé will play. Indeed, she can only "hear" Oceola when she plays classical music, despite the fact that she also plays the blues and spirituals. Tension develops between the two when the older woman,

"really [begins] to hate jazz, especially on a grand piano." In short, Oceola is mute unless she capitulates to Mrs. Ellsworth's belief that classical music is "superior" to vernacular musical expression.

What both these stories suggest, through their dramatization of white aural incompetence, is that African American culture is self-constituted, discursive, and regenerative. In each, Hughes is positioned at the nexus of the two cultures to mediate the events, to encode what one reads in the stories as aural incompetence. At the end of "The Blues I'm Playing," Mrs. Ellsworth claims that marriage will "take all the music" out of Oceola. The latter responds by playing the blues, which symbolizes her rejection of what Hughes suggests is the bourgeoisie's inclination to compartmentalize experience in order to create art.

Herein lies an important consideration: that Hughes's aesthetic works out a trope that brings internality and externality into a state of opposition. One sees an example of how this unfolds in **"The Weary Blues."** The speaker in the poem documents the experience of listening to a piano player in Harlem play the blues. Steven Tracy's compelling argument asserts that the piano player and speaker are united by the performance.

I would like to argue to the contrary however. In my view, the poem works out Hughes's apprehension, his feeling that his ability to understand the emotions that generated this form of artistic expression was not on a par with the expression itself. This is indicated by the last line of the poem, where the speaker notes that the piano player "slept like a rock or a man that's dead." The key word here is "or," for it denotes the imprecision of the speaker's understanding. What the blues articulates is the simultaneous presence of the "tragic and comic aspects of the human conditions." Thus, the blues in the poem is not the conventional "either/or" condition configured within the Cartesian construct. Rather, the piano player, by metaphorizing loneliness has already chosen self-recovery. The poem's last line, then, ignores the blues performer's ability to articulate pain and likewise to subsume it. That the speaker and the piano player never meet, or as Tracy asserts, "strike up a conversation, share a drink, or anything else," suggests that the experience does not rupture the speaker's externality. He never enters that space whereby the piano player is speaking for him, giving utterance to his loneliness. Finally, at no point in time does the speaker in the poem insert himself into the lyrics.

What this implies is that **"The Weary Blues"** can also be read as an anti-Jazz Age poem. That is, a case can be made in which we need not equate the speaker in the poem with Hughes at all. While Hughes obviously had a strong desire to "link the lowly blues to formal poetry," locking him into the poem ignores its efficacy as cultural commentary. Given the increasing number of whites traveling to Harlem to be entertained in clubs like The Cotton Club, the poem can be seen as an attempt on Hughes's part to warn the community that African American expression was being appropriated by mainstream culture.

The poem's structure enables this reading, if only because the speaker "quotes" the lyrics, but never allows his own voice to give way to them. Moreover, the speaker is "Down on Lenox Avenue . . . " which also, interestingly enough, marks the location of the Cotton Club and thus implies travel from downtown Manhattan. The I/he dichotomy Hughes establishes never collapses, which means that we can read the exteriority of the speaker as that which pertains to someone being entertained, who will leave Harlem after the performance is over. In this respect, the "or" in the last line calls our attention to the slippage that occurs when an understanding of the blues is lacking. That the speaker utters the possibility that the piano player has killed himself illustrates his failure to realize that the blues is performed reflection and not a preface to suicidal behavior.

If we return to the moment in his autobiography where Hughes is headed to Mexico towards his father, what is clear is that he circumvents his father's hatred of blacks by reconstituting the aural joy he feels in their midst. In short, Hughes's aesthetic rests on his need to assure his readership that if his writing spoke, both to and for them, it was because he took great pains to hear them. In his multifarious roles as poet, fiction writer, autobiographer, and columnist, Langston Hughes relates to the African American community as a speaker to be sure, but here the term is dualistic: the term alludes to the act of writing as both composition and amplification. As the Rampersad biography makes very clear, Hughes never elevated books over spoken forms of eloquence and his passion for writing flowed naturally from the fact that he seized every opportunity to posit himself as a listener. *The Big Sea* begins, after all, with Hughes standing on the deck of the *S.S. Malone* (his pseudonym for the freighter, *West Hesseltine*) and throwing books into the sea. [B]ooks had been happening to me," he writes, "I was glad they were gone." What this suggests is that Hughes never wanted to subordinate experience to literacy; books could not replace the value of improvisation. Although their disappearance from his life was temporary, one can imagine that that movement, like so many others in Hughes's life, led him towards what he so dearly loved to do: put his ear to the wind and serve as a witness for all there was to hear.

Dolan Hubbard (essay date Spring 1992)

SOURCE: "Symbolizing America in Langston Hughes's 'Fa-

ther and Son,'" in *The Langston Hughes Review,* Vol. 11, No.1, Spring, 1992, pp. 14-20.

[*In the following essay, Hubbard discusses Hughes's observations on the mulatto and the culture of race as depicted in the short story "Father and Son."*]

Langston Hughes was haunted by a sense of literal *kinship* between black and white Americans. His preoccupation shows up in much of his writing, even in the poem **"I, Too"** with its arresting second line that glosses the experience of blacks in America: "I am the darker brother." This ancient and just claim for recognition and acceptance is rooted in the poet's own biography. On his maternal side, Hughes inherited an enhanced perspective of what it means to be loved in a mixed marriage, wherein the claims of family take precedence over artificial claims such as those of race. His great grandfather, Captain Ralph Quarles, was a white plantation owner who fell in love with Lucy Langston, a slave woman of Indian descent. Quarles had received her as chattel on a promissory note for money borrowed by her former owner, but he soon freed her. The two subsequently lived as a married couple on his Louisa County, Virginia, plantation (such a marriage, of course, was technically illegal). Quarles acknowledged paternity of their four children (unlike the iconoclastic patriarch in Hughes's literary productions), and sent them North to school where they were enrolled in Oberlin College. As a result of Quarles breaking with the accepted code of conduct for slaveholding whites, the entire family was ostracized. When Lucy Langston and Ralph Quarles died, they were buried as husband and wife, side by side on the farm. Their children proved to be even more active in resisting the expectations of a slave society. Charles Langston (1817-1892), Hughes's grandfather, distinguished himself as an abolitionist, educator, and reformer; John Mercer Langston (1829-1897), his renowned uncle, distinguished himself as educator, diplomat, and politician. As a descendent of arguably one of the more prominent black families in nineteenth-century America, Langston Hughes accepted his racial duality as a historical fact, that he did not necessarily reject, but he continually explored the ambiguities of his dual ancestry. These factors help account for Hughes's fascination with the "mulatto" and his unusual treatment of mixed-race characters in his texts.

For over a quarter of a century, Langston Hughes presented the mulatto theme in four different genres, in treatments varying in length from a twelve-line poem to a full-length Broadway play. Reduced to its simplest level, the "tragic mulatto" theme as depicted in American fiction and drama presents a character of a dual ancestry (usually the offspring of a white father and a black mother), who suffers because of difficulties arising from his or her biracial background. In **"Cross"**, his first statement on the as yet unresolved American melodrama of family and race, Hughes renders in three quatrains the mulatto's complaint, his victimization as a result of his divided inheritance:

> My old man's a white old man
> And my old mother's black,
> If I ever cursed my white old man
> I take my curses back.
>
> If I ever cursed my black old mother
> And wished she were in hell,
> I am sorry for that evil wish
> And now I wish her well.
>
> My old man died in a fine big house,
> My ma died in a shack.
> I wonder where I'm gonna die,
> Being neither white nor black?

(*Selected Poems*)

Unlike Jean Toomer and Georgia Douglas Johnson, who celebrated the mulatto as *both* white *and* black, Langston Hughes generally portrays the mulatto character as lamenting that he is *neither* white *nor* black, which actually fits the dominant ideology better. Hughes's glory, as was the glory of Charles Chesnutt and Paul Laurence Dunbar, was his wish and determination to be *American.* However, Hughes, unlike Chesnutt, Dunbar and Thomas Nelson Page, is not trapped by an outmoded romanticism. He advances a bold idea that America is far richer and more vibrant as a result of her encounter with Africa.

"**Father and Son,**" the last story in *The Ways of White Folks* (1934), is the American tragedy of color caste told against the background of an ostensibly idyllic South. Set on the Norwood plantation in south Georgia in the 1930s, "**Father and Son**" is replete with the classic picture of plantation geography: the Big House, Quarters, and hard working, singing blacks. Somewhat God-like, Colonel Tom Norwood, the patriarch, proudly surveys all that he sees, for all within his purview is his—grounds, buildings, and five children (one dead) by his faithful black mistress of 30 years. Trouble in paradise takes the form of his youngest son—the spitting image of the Colonel—who returns home from Atlanta where he is a student at a black college. Bert Lewis returns to claim title to what he rightfully feels is his: the Norwood name and the rights and privileges attached to it. Try as she might, the despairing mother cannot keep the peace between the self-righteous, stubborn father and the equally stubborn son, who resents the Colonel for refusing to acknowledge him.

Bert Norwood, the intrepid protagonist, is one of a number of complex characters whom Hughes had portrayed, along with Roy Williams in "**Home,**" and Oceola Jones in "**The Blues I'm Playing.**" They resist definitional certainty in that they do not conform to the stereotype of the submissive, fawning "darky." In these three stories, Hughes engaged in a prolonged brooding over the fascinating spectacle of socially constructed existence.

The larger than life struggle between father and son is reinforced by a deeper realism which sees beyond and beneath the exterior world to the hidden reality which is the essence of things. The essence of things refers to the elemental human emotions rendered on an epic scale in white and black, dramatized against the background of fratricidal violence that bathes the beauty of an agrarian South in blood. Ostensibly, Hughes attacks the romantic vision of a verdant South, in which the Civil War is a noble and just cause. The apologists for this ideology do not acknowledge the violence that it takes to make the system work for the few while the many suffer in silence. Against the backdrop of an outdated economic system, one that no longer can sustain itself, Hughes presents us with something else—the denial of kin (whose antecedents have Biblical overtones). The unrecognized son insists on a right to his patrimony, his claim of identity with his father whose racist ideology conflicts with his tabooed interracial desire. Hughes looks behind the stereotype to demystify the mulatto. But the focus of the violence seems to be a family drama, amplified to represent on a larger scale an American tragedy.

The thirty-year relationship between the Colonel and Bert's mother fall outside the boundary that the society deems socially acceptable. It is not sanctioned by official institutions—economic, political, religious; which is to say, it is rendered invisible. Colonel Norwood, regardless of his social standing, does not change the status of his five children by his black mistress. They are black and inferior. It is precisely because of this lineage system, which can be described as *descending* miscegenation, that the black child inherits a patrimony of failure.

The Colonel cannot publicly acknowledge his black children; to do so would be tantamount to undermining the credibility of the system that empowers him, and which has shaped his image of himself. With a novel twist, Hughes asserts that the fight for the body obscures the real fight—the bastard son's fight for acknowledgment and family. In his adamant denial of any such acknowledgment or identity, the father uses racial rather than family identity as prima-facie evidence of separation. This choice then translates into control of the "black" body as is evident in the Colonel's unmerciful beating of the then 14-year-old Bert for calling him "Papa" in front of his white friends. And the Colonel repeats his threat of beating his now 20-year-old, athletically-gifted son for forgetting his place.

The fight for the body, for the text is the matrix within which all other terms are fleshed and shaped, as the Colonel is acutely aware with his references to Cora about Bert's being "your" not "our" son. In addition, the fight for the body is made manifest in the Colonel's condescending remarks to Cora about *his* educating *her* children. The implication is that he, the Lord of the land, gives and can take away as he closed the only public school in the county for black children once Cora's children graduated. That he sends Cora's black children to college in Atlanta is socially acceptable, as they attend segregated and inferior black institutions. Bert's fight for the text—his refusal to be a *white folks'* nigger—makes him appear, at best, indecently arrogant and, at worst, incurably mad. In a contemplative moment on the train ride home in the Jim Crow car, Bert ponders what it means to be black and the difference between his and his family's response to race:

> "It's hell," Bert thought.
> Not that Cora's other kids had found it hell. Only he had found it so, strangely enough. "The rest of 'em are too dumb, except little Sallie [two years behind him in college], and she don't say nothing— but it's hell to her, too, I reckon." the boy thought to himself as the train rocked and rumbled over the road. "Willie [the oldest] don't give a damn so long as his belly's full. And Bertha's got up North away from it all. I don't know what she really thought. . . . But I wish it hadn't happened to me."

The 'it' refers to Bert's acute self-consciousness which, like the mute red-headed baby in the story by the same name, is a synecdoche for the silent black subject trapped in history. One aspect of the racial text imposed on people such as Bert by whites who control the modes of production is a denial of their biracial and bicultural identity. The American racial text does not acknowledge the possibility of a person's being both black and white; it denies any family continuity between the races.

Hughes argues that white men's control of textuality constitutes one of the primary causes of the patrimony of failure. Forced to read texts written by powerful white men, blacks are forced to become characters in those texts. And since the texts written by these men assert as fact what blacks know to be fiction, not only do blacks lose the power that comes from authoring; more significantly, they are forced to deny their own reality and to commit in effect a kind of psychic suicide. Three manifestations of this psychic suicide are: first, the mother's sexual politics to make the quality of life better for her children; second, the nauseating subservience of Bert's oldest brother, Willie, who obediently knows his place; and third, the sister who moved to Chicago to escape from this repressive lifestyle. There is tremendous pressure on them to forget rather than remember the terror that

is history. One sees the genesis of the blues in the circumscribed lives of these minor characters.

Determined not to be a "*white folks'* nigger", the rejected Bert engages in a time honored ritual of trying to displace the father. The mother tries to keep the peace between father and son. The father, for all of his supercilious posturing, finds himself rootless in spirit at the height of what should be his finest hour: the return home of his handsome and debonaire son who is the "spittin' image" of the Colonel. It is ironic that he, one of those who walks proudly in the light, now finds himself walking in the dark. For the better part of the day, Colonel Norwood remains sequestered in his library. In a curious reversal, he finds himself in exile on his own plantation as he experiences the impotence of power. The grotesque emerges in an unexpected form. To maintain his power, prestige, and privilege, Colonel Norwood, who fancies himself a benevolent patriarch, dons his demonic mask. As an archetype of his class, he is orgiastic in his exercise of power. The Lord of the land had become so rich on the backs of his black workers that he could command the "body politic." He sets in motion the legal machinery and public opinion that leads to the death of one son by suicide and the hanging of the other by an enraged mob.

In a variation on the freedom-restraint, flight-pursuit motif that is a recurrent theme in nineteenth-century Southern fiction, Hughes shows how both the father and son take turns being pursuer and pursued. On the day of Bert's homecoming, the secretly proud father retreats to his library, presumably containing many of the great books of western culture, yet he is not inclined to share the culture which he venerates. On another level, as the last of the white Norwoods, the Colonel is engaged in a flight from the new economic reality. He is at the mercy of economic forces that stand ready to gobble him up, as is evident by his concern for the depressed cotton market and the encroachment of industrial capitalism.

With an heightened self-consciousness, Bert returns home to engage in two struggles: the pursuit of that which he can never have—the Norwood name, and the struggle to free himself from being an object possessed or owned by another. Unlike his sister who is two years behind him in college, Bert refuses to suppress his natural personality in his quest for an autonomous self or quietly to accept definitional certainty as a silent subject. In these two interconnected yet distinct struggles, Bert shares the latter with all other black people, while the former stands reserved for those of white patriarchy who want to claim their ancestry. Boldly asserting his claim for full recognition of his bloodlines, Bert terrorizes the black community. The price they pay for his unrelenting quest for freedom is that they live in increased fear for their welfare. In Bert, Hughes anticipates Wright's nihilistic anti-hero, Bigger Thomas.

In **"Father and Son,"** Hughes subverts the romance; the expected closure does not occur. Although there are no white heirs, Bert, the prince charming cannot win a bride and live happily ever after in this Eden kept beautiful by the hard working sons and daughters of Africa. Instead of the suave prince charming, wooing and winning a bride, there are the tragic consequences of filial rejection; Bert kills his gun-toting father with his bare hands in the twilight darkness of the library. He slays no dragons; he wins no honor that is socially approved; he does not become the lord of the estate. Instead of a happily married couple, there is the image of the embittered mother. Cora re-visions history as she redeems the good name of her soon-to-be-dead son. In her monologue directed at the dead man on the floor, she confronts the fiction of race:

> "Colonel Tom, you hear me? You said he was ma boy, ma bastard boy. I heard you. But he's your'n too—out yonder in the dark runnin'—from your people."

Cora's lamentation over the imminent death of their son for killing his white father locates her at the intersection of subject and history—a ritual of pain that involves her rebuking the "white-male-is-norm ideology". Speaking as a lover and mother who bore the now dead Colonel five children, she questions her relation to the material conditions that define her and her existence. Like her hunted son, she finds herself at odds with language that arbitrarily privileges her blackness over her humanness.

That there is no romantic interest for the socially accomplished Bert speaks to the ideology that governs the patrimony of failure. Hughes understood that to destroy a people, you first destroy the men. This accounts, in large part, for the absence of stable family relationships in the short fiction of Langston Hughes. Lifting the veil on an ostensibly idyllic South, Hughes reminds us that the practical effect of the patrimony of failure is continued economic and social polarization.

To restate this observation from another angle of vision, Hughes rewrites Booker T. Washington's speech at the Atlanta Cotton States and International Exposition (18 September 1895) in which Washington accepted social and legal segregation but promised racial friendship and cooperation. A people cannot work their way up from slavery if they adhere to an ideology of accommodation, the handmaiden of industrial capitalism in the United States. While he would disagree with the ideology that informs their vision, Hughes would agree with the Agrarians on our need to be careful of an uncritical worship of material progress as an end in

itself. From this perspective, Hughes in **"Father and Son"** gives us a stunning example of one mode of American modernism.

Christopher C. DeSantis (essay date Spring 1993)

SOURCE: "Rage, Repudiation, and Endurance: Langston Hughes's Radical Writings," in *The Langston Hughes Review,* Vol. XII, No. 1, Spring, 1993, pp. 31-9.

[*In the following essay, DeSantis reveals the ways racial injustice and violence influenced Hughes's writings in the 1930s and 1940s.*]

In **The Big Sea** Langston Hughes laments the close of the 1920s and the first years of the 1930s as the end of the period known as the Harlem Renaissance, a cultural movement of international significance which generated an outpouring of African American art, literature, and criticism. The final chapters of Hughes's autobiography strike a tone of sadness, markedly different from the lively prose describing the writer's early years in vibrant Harlem. Hughes writes: "The generous 1920s were over. And my twenties almost over. I had four hundred dollars and a gold medal." It is fitting that Hughes chose to mention his financial status in closing. With the Depression looming darkly over America, the hands of patrons who sustained many artists during the Harlem Renaissance were withdrawn. The prizes offered to promising writers by African American journals were fewer, and the stipends for submissions were of lesser amounts. Nevertheless, armed with the four hundred dollars that came with the 1931 Harmon Award ("Four hundred dollars! I had never had a job that paid more than twenty-two dollars a week."), Hughes scoffed at the national economic crisis: ". . . I'd finally and definitely made up my mind to continue being a writer—and to become a professional writer, making my living from writing."

While Hughes was able to adhere to his goal of writing for a living, writing was certainly not the most pressing thing on his mind. The end of the Harlem Renaissance saw an increase in racial violence and economic hardship for the black masses in America. The beatings, lynchings and daily humiliation of segregation which African Americans suffered in the South and elsewhere outraged Hughes. As a member of the African American community Hughes accepted the responsibility to speak out against these injustices in his writing and to fight them in his daily life, at whatever cost to his own personal welfare. The body of writing which resulted from these turbulent years contains the most searing, ironic, and powerful poetry and prose that Hughes ever wrote. Often overlooked by readers and critics, Hughes's radical writings assume great significance when viewed in the context of the ever-increasing racial tensions we are witnessing in the 1990s. It is my intent here to re-introduce some of these works to readers and critics, lest we forget the powerful and far-reaching significance of Langston Hughes's famous question, "What happens to a dream deferred?"

The Scottsboro incident of 1931 set the tone for much of Hughes's radical poetry and prose that would emerge in the following years. The incident involved nine African American teenagers who were jailed in Scottsboro, Alabama, for allegedly raping two white prostitutes in an open railroad freight car. After a trial in Scottsboro, eight of the youths were sentenced to the electric chair and the ninth to life imprisonment. In *I Wonder as I Wander* Hughes reveals that Ruby Bates, one of the white women involved in the incident, later recanted her rape testimony and admitted that she fabricated the entire story. Arnold Rampersad notes in his biography of Hughes that whereas the NAACP hesitated to react to the indictment against the Scottsboro youths, "the International Labor Defense, the legal defense arm of the Communist Party, threw its energies into appealing the case and mobilizing public support for the defendants." Taking the Scottsboro incident very much to heart, Hughes embraced the Communist Party as the only entity which seemed able, or at least willing, to help the nine youths. Though Hughes never formally joined the Communist Party, Rampersad found evidence to suggest that he served as honorary president of the League of Struggle for Negro Rights, an organization formed by the Communist Party to "bring the race problem into sharper relief."

While Hughes was physically active lecturing and fund-raising on behalf of the youths involved in the Scottsboro Case, he also took a firm stand on the incident in his writing. Two searing essays responded to the call of the nine teenagers imprisoned in the State Penitentiary at Kilby, Alabama. The first, **"Southern Gentlemen, White Prostitutes, Mill-Owners, and Negroes,"** strikes a tone of disgust and defiance as Hughes poses a challenge to the African American community at large and specifically to the black leaders of the NAACP involved with the incident:

> But back to the dark millions—black and half-black, brown and yellow, with a gang of white fore-parents—like me. If these twelve million Negro Americans don't raise such a howl that the doors of Kilby Prison shake until the 9 youngsters come out . . . , then let Dixie justice (blind and syphilitic as it may be) take its course, and let Alabama's Southern gentlemen amuse themselves burning 9 young black boys till they're dead in the State's electric chair. (*Good Morning Revolution*)

Hughes ends the essay in mock prayer, signifying the bitter irony of the Scottsboro Case in particular and the hypocriti-

cal structures of the southern white social order in general: "Dear Lord, I never knew until now that white ladies (the same color as Southern gentlemen) traveled in freight trains . . . Did you, world? . . . And who ever heard of raping a prostitute?"

Hughes's second essay on the Scottsboro incident, **"Brown America in Jail: Kilby,"** was written after Hughes paid a visit to the Scottsboro youths while on a speaking tour through the South. Though eager to cheer the young men with some of his more humorous poems, Hughes notes in *I Wonder as I Wander* that the atmosphere in the prison had a feeling of desperation: "The youngest boy, Andy Wright, smiled. The others hardly moved their heads. Then the minister prayed, but none of the boys kneeled or even changed positions for his prayer. No heads bowed." The essay is marked throughout by a tone of profound sadness and bitterness. Although one of the women involved in the Scottsboro incident recanted her rape testimony under oath, the youths remained in the "death house" of the prison. Where Hughes's first Scottsboro essay struck a tone of defiance and projected hope for justice, the second essay conveys the seeming futility of challenging a brutal and apparently hopeless racial situation in Alabama:

> For a moment the fear came: even for me, a Sunday morning visitor, the doors might never open again. WHITE guards held the keys. (The judge's chair protected like Pilate's.) And I'm only a nigger. Nigger. Niggers. Hundreds of niggers in Kilby Prison. Black, brown, yellow, near-white niggers. The guards, WHITE. Me—a visiting nigger (*Good Morning Revolution*)

Although the tone of the essay is decidedly desperate, Hughes recognizes the Communist Party and a number of revolutionary writers for their interest in helping to change the racial situation in America. Through sarcasm Hughes drives the point home, further strengthening his ties with people and organizations which would prove to shape the nature of his writings in the years preceding the McCarthy hearings:

> (Keep silent, world. The State of Alabama washes its hands.) Eight brown boys condemned to death. No proven crime! Farce of a trial. Lies. Laughter. Mob. Music. Eight poor niggers make a country holiday. (Keep silent, Germany, Russia, France, young China, Gorki, Thomas Mann, Romain Rolland, Theodore Dreiser. Pilate washes his hands. Listen Communists, don't send any more cablegrams to the Governor of Alabama. Don't send any more telegrams to the Supreme Court. What's the matter? What's all this excitement about, over eight young niggers? Let the law wash its hands in peace.)

Although at the time of the Scottsboro incident Hughes had achieved a certain degree of fame and was traveling around the country on a successful speaking tour, he realized that celebrity status was no protection against the bloody wrath of racial discrimination. A decade after the Scottsboro case, this proved equally true. **"Roland Hayes Beaten (Georgia: 1942),"** was written after the world-famous singer walked into a shoe store in Georgia, his home state, and was brutally beaten by a white store clerk. The beating occurred in 1942, during a war which was supposedly being fought to rid the world of racial supremacy, and in which many black soldiers saw active duty. In the poem Hughes addresses the theme of African Americans rising up against the oppression of whites, a theme that would become prevalent in much of his post-Scottsboro writings. He does not focus on details of Hayes's bloody beating here. The power of the poem lies in the juxtaposition of humanity and nature. The comparison plays off of the stereotypical meek, humble, and accommodating nature of African Americans:

> Negroes,
> Sweet and docile,
> Meek, humble, and kind:
> Beware the day
> They change their minds!
>
> Wind
> In the cotton fields,
> Gentle breeze:
> Beware the hour
> It uproots trees!

(*Selected Poems*)

In the poem Hughes alludes to the dispossessed slaves in the Southern fields (the wind; transient and dynamic) and to the plantation overseers (the trees; established and static). Through this analogy Hughes suggests that the same oppression and brutality which resulted in slave revolts exists still, and will be dealt with in a similar manner. Fury will not sprout from the meek and humble, but rather from the oppressed, the brutalized and the displaced. Hughes's message is clear, and the clarity gains passion and fury when we consider other radical writings—often overlooked by readers and critics—written during his distinguished career.

In a scathing essay addressed to the leaders and educators of African American colleges throughout the nation, Hughes asserted that white people could no longer be blamed exclusively for the propagation of Jim Crow ethics and practices. **"Cowards from the Colleges,"** first published in *The Crisis* in 1934, marked a turning point in Hughes's writing. Though he still concerned himself with documenting folk mannerisms, patterns of speech, and ways of life of common black people, Hughes perceived in the educated black elite an invidious pattern of behavior that seemed to encourage rather than ameliorate the social codes that served to keep the African American community in the margins of American society: "To combine these charges very simply: Many of our institutions apparently are not trying to make men and women of their students at all—they are doing their best to produce spineless Uncle Toms, uninformed, and full of mental and moral evasions" (*Good Morning Revolution*). In backing up his assertions, Hughes cites two incidents in which blatant racism was glossed over by college administrators worried about the possible danger of offending white patrons of the college. The first incident concerned Juliette Derricotte, the dean of women at Fisk University, who died after an automobile accident because she was refused treatment by white Georgia hospitals. The second incident involved the football coach of Alabama's A&M Institute at Normal, who was beaten to death by a mob in Birmingham while attempting to see his team play. Outraged by the two incidents which occurred during the same weekend, students at Hampton, where Hughes was lecturing at the time, attempted to band together and protest the racial violence. Citing the school's policy of "moving slowly and quietly, and with dignity," Major Brown, the dean of men at Hampton, and an African American, effectively killed the protest. Hughes writes:

> On and on he talked. When he had finished, the students knew quite clearly that they could not go ahead with their protest meeting. (The faculty had put up its wall.) They knew they would face expulsion and loss of credits if they did so. The result was that the Hampton students held no meeting of protest over the mob-death of their own alumnus, nor the death on the road . . . of one of the race's finest young women. The brave and manly spirit of that little group . . . was crushed by the official voice of Hampton speaking through its Negro Major Brown. (*Good Morning Revolution*)

Hughes's anger at some of the black leaders and institutions of higher learning did not, of course, go unexpressed in his poetry. Although some of the intellectuals in Harlem during the Renaissance found books such as *The Weary Blues* and *Fine Clothes to the Jew* disturbing because of their glamorization of the black working class, those texts did not offend nearly so much as the more radical verse Hughes wrote in the 1930s. **"To Certain Negro Leaders,"** a poem first published in *New Masses*, addresses in sparse and angry language the bitter frustrations Hughes attempted to document in **"Cowards from the Colleges"**:

> Voices crying in the wilderness,
> At so much per word
> From the white folks:
> "Be meek and humble,

All you niggers,
And do not cry
Too loud."

(*Good Morning Revolution*)

Hughes cryptically posits here the dangerous ramifications white patronage and philanthropy pose to African American institutions. Money becomes a shackle to the receiving institutions; the maker of the gift holds the power to tighten it at will. Hughes arrived at these conclusions through his bitter experiences with Charlotte Mason during the Harlem Renaissance. When Hughes expressed a desire to try different things with his poetry, Mason's patronage was quickly, and finally, withdrawn.

The hypocrisy which seemed to fester behind philanthropic fronts troubled Hughes long after the end of the Harlem Renaissance and the largesse of wealthy patrons who supported it. Addressing the first American Writers' Congress in 1935, Hughes called on African American writers to expose these hypocrisies through their novels, stories, poems, and articles:

> The lovely grinning face of Philanthropy—which gives a million dollars to a Jim Crow school, but not one job to a graduate of that school; which builds a Negro hospital with second-rate equipment, then commands black patients and student-doctors to go there whether they will or no; or which, out of the kindness of its heart, erects yet another separate, segregated, shut-off, Jim Crow Y.M.C.A.
> (*Good Morning Revolution*)

Hughes believed in the transformative powers of the written word, and cautioned writers about using their art for purposes other than social change. This rhetoric, of course, was first espoused by Hughes during the Harlem Renaissance. In **"The Negro Artist and the Racial Mountain,"** published in 1926, Hughes called for the formation of a "racial art" which would lead to the creation of a distinct black aesthetic. He denounced writers who believed their art came first, their race second. More significant here, Hughes believed in a social force inherent in art, and considered it a basic duty of black artists to channel this force toward social change. At his speech before the first American Writers' Congress in 1935, Hughes called on black writers to fulfill this basic duty:

> Sure, the moon still shines over Harlem. Shines over Scottsboro. Shines over Birmingham, too, I reckon. Shines over Cordie Cheek's grave, down South. Write about the moon if you want to. Go ahead. This is a free country. But there are certain very practical things American Negro writers can do. And must do. There's a song that says, "the time

ain't long." That song is right. Something has got to change in America—and change soon. We must help that change to come. The moon's still shining as poetically as ever, but all the stars on the flag are dull. (And the stripes, too).

(*Good Morning Revolution*)

Hughes's poems of this period, while adhering to the basic artistic ideals established in the 1920s, were far removed from the optimism generated by the artists of the Harlem Renaissance. With the Depression came more hunger, more oppression, and more racial violence. These facets of American life were certainly not new to Hughes, but there seemed during this period to be something more evil and more dangerous with which African Americans had to contend. Not content to see the African American community merely endure, Hughes felt that revolution was a necessary end:

> I am so tired of waiting,
> Aren't you,
> For the world to become good
> And beautiful and kind?
> Let us take a knife
> And cut the world in two-
> And see what worms are eating
> At the rind.

(*Good Morning Revolution*)

With Hughes's disgust at the generally bleak state of life in America came a profound mistrust of religion, particularly directed at those people who used Christianity as a cloak behind which to hide their oppressive actions. **"Goodbye, Christ"** most explicitly conveys Hughes's attitude at the time. Where the call for revolution was softened by imagery in **"Tired,"** here Hughes unleashes words of anger and bitterness which make clear his political posture:

> Listen, Christ,
> You did alright in your day, I reckon—
> But that day's gone now.
> They ghosted you up a swell story, too,
> Called it Bible—
> But it's dead now.
> The popes and the preachers've
> Made too much money from it.
> They've sold you to too many.

(*Good Morning Revolution*)

In the poem Hughes examines, or rather obliterates, the tenets set forth in a supposedly Christian country. If a majority of Americans do indeed call themselves Christians, why then do we witness so much suffering, so much oppression? During the time in which the poem was written Hughes made a journey to the Soviet Union and saw Socialism working, whereas in America, Christianity had failed. Though resources in the Soviet Union were meager, Hughes notes the fact that "white and black, Asiatic and European, Jew and Gentile stood alike as citizens on an equal footing protected from racial inequalities by the law" (*Good Morning Revolution*). Hughes thus called for a rethinking of dominant American beliefs and an acceptance of the tenets of Marxism:

> Goodbye,
> Christ Jesus Lord God Jehovah,
> Beat it on away from here now.
> Make way for a new guy with no religion at all—
> A real guy named
> Marx Communist Lenin Peasant Stalin Worker
> ME. . . .

> (*Good Morning Revolution*)

The trip to the Soviet Union obviously had a profound affect on much of Hughes's writing during this period. A little more than a decade after the visit, Hughes wrote a series of articles addressing his experiences. These pieces appeared in Hughes's weekly **"Here To Yonder"** column in the *Chicago Defender,* an influential African American newspaper. Though the anger and bitterness evident in his 1930s writings lost intensity as Hughes moved into the 1940s, his vision of humanity remained unchanged. Indeed, the first article in the series deals mainly with the humanitarian aspects of the Soviet Union:

> There is one country in the world that has NO Jim Crow of any sort, NO UNEMPLOYMENT of any sort, NO PROSTITUTION or demeaning of the human personality through poverty, NO LACK OF EDUCATIONAL FACILITIES for all of its young people, and NO LACK OF SICK CARE or dental care for everybody. That country is the Soviet Union. (*Good Morning Revolution*)

Hughes was not completely unrealistic or idealistic about the Soviet Union, and was quick to point out that it was not a paradise. He recognized the meagerness of resources to be a serious problem, but found the Soviet way of life and governance to be ultimately superior to that in America: "[The] steps toward an earthly paradise reach higher today on the soil of the Soviet Union than they do anywhere else in this troubled world. And the future of the Soviet Union is based on more concrete modern social achievements than that of any other existing state." Hughes bases this assertion on many factors, one of the most important being the position of women in the Soviet Union. He was very much impressed that prostitution had been wiped out, linking the demeaning profession to capitalism and greed: "In many great cities of the capitalist world, I have seen poor girls of high school age selling their favors as cheaply as a pair of stockings. . . . During the American depression, the streets of our big cities were full of such women. Poverty, the economic root of prostitution, is gone in the Soviet Union" (86). Where the general welfare of the people in the Soviet Union seemed superior to that in America, however, Hughes found that the Soviet people did not enjoy the freedom of speech which was largely taken for granted in the United States. Heads of government were assured of not being ridiculed publicly, for the price of denouncing a public official was often a rather stiff prison sentence. Hughes both lamented and praised the Soviet newspapers for not printing crime news or racially derogatory statements: "Nice juicy murders and big black brutes are both missing from their pages. Soviet headlines are not as exciting in a sensational way as ours."

Despite its faults, however, Hughes saw in the Soviet Union a degree of hope which seemed sadly absent in America. While the African American community was still suffering the same violence and oppression it had endured for years, followers of the Soviet doctrines seemed infinitely better off. Hughes addresses this idea in **"Lenin,"** one of his last poems to endorse Communism:

> Lenin walks around the world.
> Frontiers cannot bar him.
> Neither barracks nor barricades impede.
> Nor does barbed wire scar him.
>
> Lenin walks around the world.
> Black, brown, and white receive him.
> Language is no barrier.
> The strangest tongues believe him.
>
> Lenin walks around the world.
> The sun sets like a scar.
> Between the darkness and the dawn
> There rises a red star.

> (*Good Morning Revolution*)

Although Hughes ultimately abandoned his support of Communism shortly after **"Lenin"** was written, his love for the Soviet Union and its people remained. Arnold Rampersad has noted that Hughes's renunciation of Communism did not result in a break with all organizations on the Left, and that Hughes continued to support groups that fell under the scrutiny of Joseph McCarthy's investigations. Retaining these ties, it seems, made Hughes amply suspect. On March 26, 1953, Hughes appeared before McCarthy's Senate Permanent Sub-Committee on Investigations to explain and account for this "anti-American," radical past. At the hearing Hughes offered a prepared statement which effectively repudiated his radical writings and saved him from serious charges by the Committee. When asked by Roy Cohn, the head examiner, to describe the time period in which he sympathized with the Soviet form of government and when that period ended, Hughes replied:

> There was no abrupt ending, but I would say, that roughly the beginnings of my sympathies with Soviet ideology were coincident with the Scottsboro case, the American depression, and that they ran through for some 10 or 12 years or more, certainly up to the Nazi-Soviet Pact, and perhaps, in relation to some aspects of the Soviet ideology, further, because we were allies, as you know, with the Soviet Union during the war. So some aspects of my writing would reflect that relationship, that war relationship.

When further questioned by Cohn as to what exactly caused his change in ideology, Hughes offered an answer which amply satisfied the Committee:

> The Nazi-Soviet Pact was, of course, very disillusioning . . . and then further evidences of, shall we say, spreading imperialist aggression. My own observations in 1931-32, as a writer, which remained with me all the time, of the lack of freedom of expression in the Soviet Union for writers, which I never agreed with before I went there or afterward—those things gradually began to sink in deeper and deeper. And then, in our own country, there has been, within the last 10 years, certainly within the war period, a very great increase in the rate of acceleration of improvement in race relations.

In closing, Hughes was asked if he was in any way mistreated by the staff or the committee involved with the investigation. His reply could only have served to warm the hearts of the very people who had caused him much pain: "I must say that I was agreeably surprised at the courtesy and friendliness with which I was received. . . . [Senator Dirksen] was, I thought, most gracious and in a sense helpful in defining for me the area of this investigation; and the young men who had to interrogate me, of course, had to interrogate me."

Rampersad has demonstrated that by cooperating with McCarthy and the Committee, Hughes was choosing the lesser of two evils: "He could defy the body and destroy much of his effectiveness in the black world. Or he could co-operate, draw the disapproval, even the contempt, of the white left, but keep more or less intact the special place he had painstakingly carved out within the black community." Given Hughes's love for his community which he had held since he began writing, Rampersad suggests that the choice

was perhaps easy to make. Although Hughes repudiated a body of writing that was so important to a turbulent period in his life, the choice allowed him to continue doing what he loved best. After the hearing he resumed the admirable task of making a living as a writer, perhaps subconsciously secure in the fact that his writings, including the ones he apparently repudiated, were tucked safely away in the archives of universities across the country.

Edward Mullen (essay date Fall 1993)

SOURCE: "Langston Hughes in Mexico and Cuba," in *Latin American Literature and Arts,* Vol. 47, Fall, 1993, pp. 23-27.

[*In the following essay, Mullen argues that Hughes's experiences in Mexico and Cuba had a significant influence on his writing and identity.*]

In his introduction to *Do the Americas Have a Common Literature?* (Duke University Press, 1990), Gustavo Pérez Firmat underscores the fact that the field of inter-American literary studies is something of a terra incognita. The occasion of the quincentenary, in which so much writing has been directed toward the theme of the identity of the Americas, seems a particularly appropriate juncture to fill in some of the open critical space to which Pérez Firmat refers. The shaping of the American identity has been marked in no small degree by a relatively constant set of discoveries carried out by writers from both sides of the border, from the period of Conquest to the present day. It is no surprise that Robert E. Spiller, in his classic *The Cycle of American Literature,* credits Columbus's letter of 1493 to the Royal Treasurer of Spain describing his discovery as the earliest genuinely American text. In fact, a list of North American writers who have traveled to Latin America reads like a veritable *Who's Who* of North American literature: James Fenimore Cooper, Herman Melville, Henry Wadsworth Longfellow, William Cullen Bryant, John Dos Passos, Ernest Hemingway, Willa Cather, Katherine Anne Porter, and William Styron.

To this impressive list should be added the name of Langston Hughes. It is one of those curious paradoxes that in many ways define North American literature that the best known, if not the most prolific black American writer of the twentieth century, was more familiar in Latin America at the time of his death than he was in his native country. The case of Hughes serves not only as a paradigm of the African American literary experience, which has been deeply shaped by influences outside of the United States (one recalls the cases of Richard Wright, James Baldwin, and Chester Himes, all of whom flourished in Paris), but also demonstrates the deeply rooted interconnections among writers of the black diaspora.

Much as did his spiritual *compadre,* Manuel Zapata Olivella, Hughes spent much of his life as a writer, both searching for and sharing his sense of selfhood and blackness with other writers. It was, in particular, first his travels to Mexico and then to Cuba that were to prove most significant in his formation as a writer and that would equip him with both the linguistic skills and the personal connections to share his developing sense of a genuine black folk aesthetic. Between 1907 and 1934, for example, Hughes journeyed to Mexico four times, accumulating almost two years in Toluca and Mexico City. These travels were crucial in shaping his notions of race and class—elements so essential in his poetics. Ironically, his discovery of Spanish American literature was due, in part, to the fact that his father, an embittered Afro-American attorney, had selected Mexico as his place of self-imposed exile. James Hughes—aloof and uncaring toward his son—was particularly contemptuous of black American culture. Langston's first trip to Mexico, which took place when he was five, was a fleeting experience, marked only by an earthquake, and recalled in his autobiography, *The Big Sea.* He returned in 1919 to spend a summer with his father, a summer, he wrote in the book, that was "the most miserable I've ever known," spent in brooding isolation in Toluca. Lured by the prospect of securing money to attend Columbia University, Hughes again returned to see his father in the summer of 1920. This was a period of increasing racial awareness for the young Hughes, who had read W.E.B. DuBois's *The Souls of Black Folk* (1903) and was aware of Marcus Garvey's "Back to Africa" movement. It was en route to Mexico City that he composed his most often anthologized poem. **"A Negro Speaks of Rivers."** After crossing the border, he penned the following telling comments in his journal: "But here nothing is barred from me. I am among my own people, for . . . Mexico is a brown man's country. Do you blame them for fearing a 'gringo' invasion, with its attendant horror of colored hatred.

Hughes spent the year teaching English in a small business college, learning Spanish, and writing about his experiences. From a literary standpoint, it was an extremely productive period in his life. He published three short prose sketches in a journal recently founded by Dr. W.E.B. Dubois, *The Brownies Book.* **"Mexican Games,"** his first essay published in an American magazine, appeared in January 1921. It was followed in April by **"In a Mexican City,"** a description of market day in Toluca, and in December by **"Up to the Crater of an Old Volcano,"** an account of a trip to Xinantécatl, near Toluca. The same month *Crisis* published a very brief note, **"The Virgin of Guadalupe."**

During his weekend trips to Mexico City, he met the young poet Carlos Pellicer, who was a member of an important literary coterie known as the *Contemporáneos* ("Contemporaries"). Pellicer had a deep affinity with Hughes and his poetry. He was, at the time of their meeting, himself actively engaged as a writer in the quest for a genuine Mexican folk aesthetic based on the rediscovery of the country's indigenous past. Pellicer would be one of the few Mexican poets to write about Africa. "Surgente fin" ("Surging End"), a poem written in the 1960s, deals with the primordial ties between Africa and Mexico. It was through Pellicer that Hughes met the playwright and poet Xavier Villaurrutia (1902-1950) and the essayist Salvador Novo (1904-1973). Villaurrutia published translations of four of Hughes's poems in the important journal *Contemporáneos* in the fall of 1931 and wrote poems about racial tensions in the United States, "North Carolina Blues," which he dedicated to Hughes. Novo also identified Hughes in an essay on Afro-American poetry—one of the first such assessments of its kind—in the same issue of *Contemporáneos.*

When Hughes returned to Mexico in December 1934 to settle his father's estate, he was already an established writer. By now, he had published the basic document of his aesthetic, **"The Negro Artist and the Racial Mountain"** in the *Nation* (1926) and two major books of poetry. *The Weary Blues* (1926) and *Fine Clothes to the Jew* (1927)— which would find particular resonance in Latin America. This, his final extended stay in Mexico, lasted some six months, during which he met writers and artists such as Luis Cardoza y Aragón, Rufino Tamayo, and Nellie Campobello.

He had become a familiar figure among the Mexican literati, who were fascinated with both the content and form of his poetry and had begun to view him as a genuine spokesman for the black proletariat. Translations of his poetry and prose were to appear in Mexico with regularity up until the time of his death. Mexico was a place special to Hughes, but unlike writers such as Katherine Anne Porter and Malcolm Lowry, whose experiences in Mexico inspired much of their writing, apart from his early stories for children, which he had published in the *Brownies Book,* he wrote little about Mexico. Hughes's Mexican audience, while almost always appreciative, often misread him. Salvador Novo felt that his blues poems would soon be subsumed into a more universalist aesthetic, while Rafael Lozano, one of his earliest translators, cast him as the embodiment of a black artistic primitiveness. The thesis that primitive peoples (translate: blacks and Native Americans) were more directly in touch with nature and their feelings was widespread during the 1920s and 1930s. Thus, Lozano wrote: "Langston Hughes's poetry is highly spontaneous. . . . It is a primitive composition, like all of the poetry of his race, which expresses itself, like jazz music, with his own slightly syncopated rhythm.

While his contact with Mexico certainly had a profound shaping influence on Hughes, it would be his travels to the Caribbean and Cuba, in particular, that would prove to be most significant. Hughes traveled to Cuba on three separate occasions, in 1927, 1930, and 1931. His first trip took place in July 1927, when he went to Havana as a crew member on a freighter. The trip, a brief and unpleasant one, was later recalled in his short story **"Power White Faces"** which deals with racial discrimination in the brothels of Havana. In February 1930, he spent two weeks in Havana in search of a black composer to collaborate with him on an opera commissioned by his patron, Charlotte Mason. He arrived on February 25, 1930, with a letter of introduction from Miguel Covarrubias, whom he had met in Harlem, and who had done illustrations for **The Weary Blues,** and went directly to meet José Antonio Fernández de Castro, the editor of the influential newspaper *El Diario de la Marina*. The latter, a white patron of the arts, who had a strong interest in black culture, had published the first Spanish translation of a poem by Hughes (**"I, Too"**) in the Cuban journal *Social* in 1928.

In March 1930 Fernández de Castro published an essay "Introducing Langston Hughes" in the *Revista de la Habana*. The Cuban's comments, essentially a paraphrase of Carl Van Vechten's preface to **The Weary Blues,** "Introducing Langston Hughes to the Reader," stress in particular Hughes's sense of racial pride:

> In the lyrical works of L.H.—as in those of Countee Cullen. Walter F. White. Jessie Fauset. Claude McKay, to name only the most representative black writers in the United States—a vigorous racial pride is evident, a combativeness unknown until the present by the intellectual writers of that race. His technique is modern and with this sensitivity he achieves very personal touches which make him stand out as unique in the complicated panorama of contemporary poetic production in the United States. L.H., during his recent visit to Cuba, was received and entertained by representatives of our young intellectuals, and by distinguished and important black Cubans.

Fernández de Castro introduced Hughes to a group of Afro-Cuban writers—Nicolás Guillén, Reginio Pedroso, and Gustavo Urrutia—who toured the poet around Havana's centers of black culture. While Hughes was dazzled by the *son,* an African-based song-dance form, his hosts were equally startled by his questions about race and the social status of blacks. Guillén interviewed Hughes and published the text of his "Conversation with Langston Hughes" in the literary supplement "Ideales de una raza" of the newspaper *Diario de la Marina* on March 9, 1930. This meeting led to a long and fruitful friendship which was later renewed in Spain during the Civil War. The interview is an important document, inasmuch as it signals the deep affinities between the two in regard to their attitudes toward black artistic consciousness. Here Hughes confesses that it was during his early visit to Africa that he had become conscious of his role as a poet: "I knew then that I had to be their friend, their voice, their poet. My only ambition is to be the poet of the blacks, the black poet." Guillén replied: "I understand. And I feel that the poem with which Hughes opens his first volume of verse, rises from the depths of my own soul: I am black, black as the night, black as the depths of my Africa.'"

As critics have been careful to point out, Hughes's meeting with Guillén was to have a profound effect on the young Guillén, who was still in a formative stage as a writer. The early 1930s was a critical period in Caribbean letters as writers struggled with the fundamental problematic of the time: how to express the region's unique cultural heritage within the framework of a universalist Eurocentric aesthetic. While white writers such as Ramón Guirao and Juan Marinello wanted to posit black culture as an alternative to white neo-colonialism, their project failed, projecting at best a picturesque but external view of black culture. One month after Hughes's departure, Guillén published eight powerful dialect poems under the title *Motivos de son (Son Motifs)* in the *Diario de la Marina*. Similar in theme to Hughes's **The Weary Blues** and making strong use of neo-African musical forms, they were the object of immediate and often vitriolic critical reaction. In a letter to Hughes. Guillén said that they had "created a scandal," while Gustavo Urrutia wrote that Guillén was writing "the best kind of Negro poetry we ever had; indeed, we had no Negro poems at all in Cuba before the new work." The poems were later translated by Hughes and appeared in *Cuba Libre: Poems by Nicolás Guillén* (1948), the first book-length translation of Guillén into English.

In the spring of 1931, with the money he had received from the Harmon Gold Award for Literature, Hughes made a trip to Cuba and Haiti, accompanied by his friend, Zell Ingram. By now, he was a well-known figure in Cuban artistic circles. In fact, Hughes had already published a short note on the black Cuban sculptor, Ramos Blanco in *Opportunity* a year earlier and had done translations of poetry by Guillén and Pedroso and of an essay by Urrutia. As with his earlier experiences in Mexico, Hughes captured his impressions of Cuba both in poetry and prose. For example, he published a somewhat stylized reflection on Cuban high life called **"Havana Dreams"** in *Opportunity* in June 1933 and dedicated several pages of **I Wonder as I Wander,** describing racial discrimination in Havana. He also wrote a short story **"Little Old Spy,"** in which he depicted the racist policies of the Machado dictatorship. In May 1931, Hughes published **"To the Little Fort, San Lázaro, on the Ocean Front Havana"** in *New Masses*. A bitter attack on economic imperialism, the poem prefigures the radical assault on society that Guillén would undertake in *West Indies Ltd.* (1934) and, at the same time, vaguely evokes the poetry of Hughes's Mexican friend Carlos Pellicer.

While Mexico and Cuba were important points of contact for Langston Hughes, they are only pieces of a larger literary mosaic to which Hughes is linked. He spent time, for example, in Spain during the Civil War and was an accomplished translator of Federico García Lorca and Gabriela Mistral. In the area of hemispheric literary interrelationships, however, he remains a singular figure, one who was able to convey a sense of what it meant to be black in America to a white Hispanic audience while supplying a voice to Afro-Hispanic writers (Guillén, Zapata Olivella) to articulate their own vision of black Hispanic culture. It is no coincidence that Hughes appears as a character in Manuel Zapata Olivella's epic novel *Changó, el gran putas* (*Changó, the Big Mother,* . . . 1983), which is perhaps the most important work written about the black experience in the New World to date by an Afro-Hispanic writer.

Anne Borden (essay date Fall 1994)

SOURCE: "Heroic 'Hussies' and 'Brilliant Queers': Genderracial Resistance in the Works of Langston Hughes," in *African American Review,* Vol. 28, No. 3, Fall, 1994, pp. 333-45.

[*In the following essay, Borden examines how freely Hughes discusses gender and race relations in his works.*]

In his writings, Langston Hughes explores the convergence of race and gender in Black men's and women's lives, questioning binary constructions of identity and exploring sensuality in relation to social change. These are the pages, as bell hooks suggests, that lay marked on bedside tables, that become worn with searching fingers, that represent something other than "the Langston Hughes most folks read or remember." They are poems and stories that deal with love among Black men and women, nature, romantic quandary, mother-daughter and father-son relations, friendship, and silences. In discussing Black male and female identity, Hughes speaks of the ways gender uniquely colors these experiences. He writes in a manner which could be described as *genderracial,* emphasizing how gender and racial identity are intertwined.

In an often cited passage from **"The Negro Artist and Racial Mountain,"** Hughes comments, "One of the most promising of the young Negro poets said to me once, 'I want to be a poet, not a Negro poet.' . . . I was sorry the young man said that, for no great poet has ever been afraid of being him-

self. And I doubted then, that, with his desire to run away spiritually from his race, this boy would ever be a great poet." To Hughes, identity is inseparable from, and indeed central to, one's artistry. His work is strengthened by a poetic imagination which enters the consciousness of those with varying experiences. Hughes's images are at times disturbing, also comforting, alternately sad and joyous, and directly connected to his identity as a Black man who heard the voices of many—white and of Color, male and female, gay and straight, within and without himself.

Suggesting a useful approach to Hughes's genderracial concerns, Frances Beale's 1970 essay "Double Jeopardy: To Be Black and Female" comments on the tendency of social movements to privilege one liberation struggle over another in their vision of change. She cites the women's movement's dismissal of Black women's concerns in their drive to advance the status of white women, and Black Power's assertion of Black "manhood" through the subordination of Black women. And she queries, "Are there any parallels between this struggle and the movement on the part of Black women for *total emancipation*?"

Deborah King expands on Beale and borrows from W.E.B. Du Bois's theory of double consciousness to describe Black women's "multiple consciousness." She concurs that "the gender-only perspective alone is insufficient for understanding Black female oppression" and asserts a form of consciousness which occupies a "both/and holistic orientation", a consciousness which she identifies as polyrhythmic. Drawing connections between African and African American expressive art forms and Black consciousness, King explains: "For Black women, the interrelationship among strips of strong contrast in multiple, counter rhythms which produces music, . . . dance or quilts replicates the interdependence of individuals and other elements of the cosmos, all of which have strong, contrasting natures in an ever-changing yet stable whole."

> **Gender and race converge for Hughes's female characters, who confront genderracial myths in their exploration of identity.**
>
> —*Anne Borden*

Gender and race converge for Hughes's female characters, who confront genderracial myths in their exploration of identity. bell hooks notes that Hughes often invokes the voice of a Black woman, and that he appears "comfortable in this fictive transvestism." In **"Southern Mammy Sings,"** Hughes takes on a female voice to contrast the genderracial stereotype of the "mammy" with the reality of Black domestic work:

Miss Gardner's in her garden
Miss Yardman's in her yard
Miss Michaelmas is at de mass
And I am gettin' tired!
  Lawd!
I am gettin' tired!

The form of the poem indicates the blues as the musical form representative of a Black woman's experience working in white folks' kitchens, contrasting sharply with the images of the cheerful, singing "mammy" seen in the minstrel show or on the big screen, and in literature.

In **"Ruby Brown,"** Black domestic work is contrasted with the work of Black female prostitutes. A young woman, sitting on the backporch of her white employer, polishing the silver, is struck by two questions:

What can a colored girl do
On the money from a white woman's kitchen?
And ain't there any joy in this town?

The economic realities of sex work are reflected in Ruby Brown's decision to work in prostitution. She searches for joy among her sisters and brothers in "the sinister shuttered houses of the bottoms." Her motives for becoming a prostitute reflect tragic economic need, not "looseness" or moral corruption on her part. Hughes writes:

. . . the white men,
Habitués of the high shuttered houses,
Pay more money to her now
Than they ever did before,
When she worked in their
kitchens.

Like **"Ruby Brown,"** Hughes's novel *Not Without Laughter* explores the ways in which economic and social conditions influence the identities of Black women, embodying polyrhythm and resistance. In this work, Hughes acknowledges male perspective through the character Sandy. A young boy, Sandy remains distant and curious throughout most of the book, constantly reconciling his view of the world around him with the views of the women who raise him. Gender, race, and class converge in the dialogues among the women, which Sandy often overhears, being a quiet boy, in their kitchen conversations. His mother Anjee works as a domestic, and his grandmother Hagar takes in washing from local whites. His Aunt Harriet, once fired from a kitchen job for breaking a glass pitcher, rebels against the traditionally ascribed "respectable" occupations for Black women; she works as a carnival dancer, a blues singer, and a prostitute at different points in the story. A third sister, Tempy, is a middle-class homemaker who avoids her family in her attempt to establish herself in the middle class.

The perspectives of the four women coexist in Sandy's consciousness. There is no clear-cut right or wrong; their realities survive in the flashes of joy and conflict that make up family. Despite varying views and lifestyles, a spirit of collectivity is maintained; a polyrhythmic quality such as that which King describes suffuses the novel. The movement of Sandy among the households of Hagar, Tempy, Harriet, and Anjee signifies dialogue among them. For instance, when Harriet moves away from home to work in a bordello, Sandy becomes a liaison between the worlds of Hagar and the highly religious Harriet. Upon visiting the bordello with word that Hagar has taken ill, he realizes his aunt is still much the same woman as before: "Presently, Harriet appeared in a little pink wash dress, such as a child wears, the skirt striking her just above the knees. She smelled like cashmere-bouquet soap, and her face was not yet powdered, nor her hair done up, but she was smiling broadly, happy to see her nephew, as her arms went around his neck."

This greeting, not unlike other family greetings, signifies the wholeness of Harriet's experience, in which her occupation plays but one part. While Harriet prepares herself to leave with Sandy, the young boy waits in the parlor, among the empty bottles and ashtrays. As he waits, women's voices are heard from upstairs: "'Can I help you, girlie? Can I lend you anything? Does you need a veil?'" This dialogue offers humanity to the race, class, and gender identity of Harriet and her co-workers; it resists genderracial stereotypes and explores the commonalities between the world of Harriet and the other women in her family.

Similarly, the **"Madam"** series of poems reflects genderracial resistance in Black women's lives. The series focuses on the life of Madam Alberta K. Johnson, a Black woman surviving in the city, who asserts her pride in part by taking the name *Madam* when negotiating with her landlord, the census taker, her employer, and the reader. Addressing the reader, she comments:

I do cooking,
Day's work, too!
Alberta K. Johnson—
Madam to you.

Like **"Southern Mammy Sings,"** the **"Madam"** series describes the gender, race, and class concerns Black women face in domestic work. In **"Madam and Her Madam,"** Madam recounts an incident in which she responds to being overworked by her employer:

I said, Madam,
Can it be
You trying to make a
Pack-horse out of me?

She opened her mouth
She cried, Oh, no!
You know, Alberta,
I love you so!

This passage speaks to the convergence of race, class, and gender in Black women's dealings with white women. While the narrator's name is Madam Alberta K. Johnson, her employer insists on referring to her by her first name only, while Madam must refer to her employer as "Madam." The fact that Madam is overworked and exploited by her employer, yet her employer claims to "love" her, points to the historic relationship between white and Black women of racist *and* sexist oppression. Though both Madam and her employer share a subordinate, female status, the oppressions heaped upon Madam are in no way lessened by the fact that her oppressor is a woman. In fact, by calling her out of her name, Madam's female employer is attempting to *negate* Madam's status as a "real" woman. The response which Madam recounts is not surprising:

I said, Madam,
That may be true—
But I'll be dogged
If I love you!

The speaker rejects the mythic relationship between white and Black women and instead asserts her own reality to the reader. The poem simultaneously identifies gender-racial myths about relations between white and Black women, and gives voice to Black female resistance.

Hughes demonstrates that the oppressions of Black women and men are linked because of race, but are manifested in gender-specific ways. In **"Mulatto"** and **"Father and Son,"** the image of the "loose black woman" used to justify rape by white men is connected with the label of "bastard" pinned on children of white fathers, and with the use of the image of Black men as sexual beasts to justify lynching.

"Mulatto" addresses the consciousness of a white male plantation owner, as felt by a Black boy:

What's a body but a toy?
Juicy bodies
Of nigger wenches
Blue black
Against black fences.
O, you little bastard boy,
What's a body but a toy?

As a means of survival, the boy finds himself pondering the oppressor's-eye-view of his mother. He risks, in such intimacy, the internalization of genderracial myths which would contribute to his own oppression of Black women and self-destructive behaviors. The poem actively resists this internalization of myths when the boy shouts, "*I am your son, white man!*", rejecting the myths used to justify the rape of his mother and the economic exploitation of both mother and son.

In addressing the sexual exploitation of Black women by white men, Hughes explores the use of gender stereotypes as a means of reinforcing racial oppression. In **"Father and Son,"** Coralee Lewis comes to live in the "big house" of the plantation upon which she and her family work for one Colonel Norwood. Her second son by Colonel Norwood, Bert, resists the label of "bastard" his father has pinned on him. As a small child he refers to Colonel Norwood as "Papa," despite his father's repeated warnings and beatings. Returning home from college one summer, he confronts his father, who will send him to college yet won't allow him to enter through the front of the house. The confrontation climaxes when Bert kills his father in self-defense. As her son is chased by a vicious mob, Miss Lewis holds the dead Colonel Norwood in her arms, screaming:

"You said he warn't your'n—Cora's po' little yellow bastard. But he is your'n, Colonel Tom, and he's runnin' from you. . . . You can't fool me—You ain't never been so still like this before—you's out yonder, runnin' ma boy! Colonel Thomas Norwood runnin' ma boy through de fields in de dark, runnin' ma po' helpless Bert through de fields in de dark for to lynch him and to kill him. . . . God damn you, Tom Norwood! . . . . God damn you!"

The oppression of Coralee and her son are linked because of racism, but are manifested in gender-specific ways. Coralee is left penniless, because "the dead man left no heirs." Her association with Colonel Norwood is negated by the white community's view of her as "loose" and unworthy. The *lynching* of Bert and his brother, which ends the story, is a white response to Bert's rebellion against the role ascribed to him as a "nigger" and a "bastard"; it is justified by whites through the myth that Black men are beasts.

Hughes's exploration of Black male identity emphasizes the convergence of gender and race in threatening Black male survival. Responding to the 1931 Scottsboro case, in which one young Black man was given a life sentence and eight others were sentenced to the electric chair for the alleged rape of two white women, Hughes wrote:

BLACK BOYS IN A SOUTHERN JAIL.
WORLD, TURN PALE!

8 black boys and one white lie.
Is it much to die?

In asking *"Is it much to die?"* Hughes confronts white notions of the value of Black male life, discussing how one's very personhood and survival are political acts. Elsewhere in the poem, he likens the struggle of the Scottsboro Boys to those of great political martyrs such as John Brown and Christ. Similarly, **"Christ in Alabama"** juxtaposes Black male experience with a cultural symbol of political martyrdom, exposing the hypocrisy of racist white Christians:

> Most holy bastard
> Of the bleeding mouth
> Nigger Christ—
> On the cross
> Of the South.

Hughes's anti-lynching writing contrasts white-created images of white piety with the reality of racist brutality against Black people. In **"Silhouette,"** Hughes contrasts the genderracial myth of gentle, swooning white ladies with the reality of their role in the barbarous act of lynching:

> Southern gentle lady
> Do not swoon
> They've hung a black man
> In the dark of the moon.
> They've hung a black man
> To a roadside tree
> In the dark of the moon
> For the world to see
> How Dixie protects
> Its white womanhood.

Not limiting himself to the overt, Hughes comments on the sexualization of racist power by liberals as well as lynch mobs, often with a mordant humor. For example, **"Slave on the Block"** chronicles a Greenwich Village couple's fascination with racial exoticism. Hughes begins, "They were people who went in for Negroes—Michael and Anne—the Caraways." Artists, they are forever seeking entrance into the "jungle life" of Negroes, voying at Negro speakeasies, trying to speak, paint, and learn Negro ways, yet are perplexed, for "as much as they loved Negroes, Negroes didn't seem to love Michael and Anne." The sexual shade of their desire to possess Blackness is exemplified in Anne's motivation to use a young Black man in one of her paintings:

> She wanted to paint him now representing to the full the soul and sorrow of his people. She wanted to paint him as a slave about to be sold. And since slaves in warm climates had no clothes, would he please take off his shirt. . . . Before luncheon Michael came in, and went into rhapsodies over Luther on the box without a shirt, about to be sold into slavery.

In addition to exploring whites' genderracial stereotypes, Hughes also comments on gender issues within the Black community—specifically, the ways in which gender affects the struggle to maintain community in racist society. His work contributes to African American dialogue on gender, often in the context of racism and economic class oppression. In **Montage of a Dream Deferred** Hughes uses jazz and blues forms to punctuate a series of dialogues among Black men and women on gender issues. For instance, in **"Sister,"** a young man issues a concerned complaint about his sister's affair with a married man:

> That little Negro's married and got a
> kid.
> Why does he keep foolin' around
> Marie? . . .
> Why don't she get a boy-friend
> I can understand—some decent
> man?

to which a mother's voice replies:

> Did it ever occur to you, boy,
> *that a woman does the best she can?*

and, in response, a man sitting on the stoop comments:

> *So does a man.*

In **"Same in Blues,"** Hughes again expresses gender dialogue in the Black community, focusing on the frustration a man feels at not being able to fulfill the male-ascribed role of provider, because of racial and economic conditions:

> Lulu said to Leonard
> I want a diamond ring.
> Leonard said to Lulu
> You won't get a goddamn thing!
>
> There's a certain
> amount of nothing
> *in a dream deferred.*
>
> Daddy, daddy, daddy,
> All I want is you.
> You can have me, baby—
> but my lovin' days is through.
>
> A certain
> amount of impotence
> *in a dream deferred.*

Leonard wishes to fulfill a masculine role in his relationship, yet he is disempowered because of racism. The second italicized remark expresses feelings of inadequacy and hopelessness caused by this awareness: "You can have me, baby," he states, "but my lovin' days is through."

Male withdrawal from feeling as an expression of hopelessness is challenged by Hughes's female characters. In **"Hard Daddy,"** Hughes invokes the blues to discuss a woman's frustration with her man's response to her tears:

> I cried on his shoulder but
> He turned his back on me.
> Cried on his shoulder but
> He turned his back on me.
> He said a woman's cryin'
> Never gonna bother me.

Though the characters act in typically gender-ascribed ways, Hughes adds a twist at the end of the poem as the female character rebels against her man's hardness with her own fury:

> I wish I had wings to
> Fly like the eagle flies. . . .
> I'd fly on ma man an'
> I'd scratch out both his eyes.

The destructive potential of masculine and feminine social constructs is addressed in Hughes's work, yet it is not always broken down into a male-female dichotomy, or even into simple notions of the masculine and the feminine. Rather, Hughes identifies a subversive strength in the feminine and a vulnerability intrinsic to masculinity. At times in his work, gender is left entirely ambiguous, broadening the scope of discussion to include masculine and feminine conflicts within one's self.

Hughes's unapologetic discussion of such topics as homosexuality, teenage pregnancy, and prostitution—which earned him the title of "the poet low rate of Harlem" in the *Chicago Whip* and "The Sewer Dweller" in the *Amsterdam News*—promotes dialogue on taboo genderracial issues. Hughes demonstrates polyrhythmic consciousness by placing opposing views together in dialogue. Commonly, there is no clear "right" or "wrong" character; rather, the reader is invited to view the conflict through numerous perspectives simultaneously.

In discussing the genderracial concerns of gay Blacks, for example, Hughes explores racial realities and gender constructs in the Black community which contribute to homophobia. In **"Blessed Assurance,"** Hughes invokes an ironic sympathy with a father who worries that his son is "turning into a queer," while bringing to light contradictions in the father's wishes that his son were more "masculine." The father, John, worries that homosexuality will compound the young man's oppression as a Negro:

He was a brilliant queer, on the Honor Role in high school, and likely to be graduated in the spring at the head of the class. But the boy was colored. Since colored parents always like to put their best foot forward, John was more disturbed about his son's transition than if they had been white. Negroes had enough crosses to bear.

The text is sympathetic to John's concerns, while discussing a personal, gendered concern: John doesn't want his boy to look like a "sissy" in front of John's friends. It is significant that Hughes uses the term *queer* to define Delly, particularly when he continues, "If only Delly were not such a sweet boy—no juvenile delinquency, no stealing cars, no smoking reefers ever. He did chores without complaint. He washed dishes too easily. . . . "

John's concern that his son's homosexuality will further impede the boy's survival intertwines with his gender-located embarrassment and personal privileging of heterosexually ascribed styles of masculinity. The ironic twist of Delly's academic and personal success suggests that in breaking from traditional styles of masculinity—sexually and socially—Delly avoids certain traps which defer dreams for young boys trying to fit into "proper" gender roles. By examining the contradictions of John's wishes for his son, Hughes contributes to dialogue on homosexuality as a spring point for genderracial reform. Thus, **"Blessed Assurance"** works to move homosexuality out of the realm of the dangerous and deviant in our minds, and creates dialogue on its possible uses in promoting positive social change.

Similarly, **"Café: 3 A.M."** resists stereotypes of gay identity. Reprinted in several gay and lesbian anthologies, the poem discusses police violence against homosexuals:

> Detectives from the vice squad
> With weary sadistic eyes
> Spotting fairies.
> *Degenerates,*
> some folks say.
>
> But God, Nature,
> or somebody
> made them that way.
>
> Police lady or Lesbian
> Over there?
> *Where?*

"Café" advocates greater understanding of gays and lesbians and, on second glance, also explores the label *deviant* in the context of multiple consciousness. One might interpret Hughes's "*Degenerates*" as the police themselves, huddled off in a corner, waiting to strike, scoping out their victims on the basis of appearance. Yet we reconcile our-selves—"somebody / made them that way"—wanting to un-derstand the intricate gut machinery of the Other, to get to the roots of homophobic violence, or to get to the root of gaiety if we are straight. The last stanza further deepens this double reading of the poem, adding a poly-rhythmic feel to the identity of a café dweller. By asking whether she is a "Lesbian" *or* a "police lady," Hughes invokes the ironic sen-timent that, of course, she *could* be *both;* and he questions what this identity would mean to her, to her co-workers, to the gay community.

In **"Café,"** Hughes set forth the complex rhythm of multiple consciousnesses and oppressions to illuminate our moral di-lemmas. Several of Hughes's works comment on moral judg-ments against women in many facets of female sexuality, addressing the ways in which women are judged by their sexual behavior. Sexuality is a necessary battleground for those who are marginalized and abused because of their sex or gender; as African American gay poet Essex Hemphill notes, the erogenous zones are far from "demilitarized" in a sexist society. For many women, sexuality becomes a means of expression, and often it is the form of our expres-sion which is taken most seriously.

Hughes's **"Ballad of the Girl Whose Name Is Mud"** evokes the voice of a whispering gossip who disapproves of a girl who dated "a no-good man." The last stanza gives voice to the experience of the "hussy" herself, through gos-sip:

> . . . The hussy's telling everybody—
> Just as though it was no sin—
> That if she had a chance
> *She'd do it agin*'!

The "hussy" rejects gender constructs, which tell her she should be remorseful; instead, she shocks those around her by stating that "*she'd do it agin*'!" This type of resistance, grounded solidly in the societal notion that women express themselves primarily through their sexuality, portrays female sexual identity much as Black male identity is portrayed in **"Scottsboro,"** as a political act. Similar sentiments recur in **"S-sss-ss-sh!,"** which discusses unmarried, probably teen-age, pregnancy. Hughes contrasts the natural imagery of birth with disapproval by family and neighbors:

> The baby came one morning
> Almost with the sun.
>
> *The neighbors—*
> *And its grandma—*
> *Were outdone*!
>
> But mother and child

Thought it fun.

In simultaneously enacting several views of the birth, **"Sh-sss-ss-sh!"** promotes dialogue on gender issues in a polyrhythmic way. It interrogates our notions of female shame in an age when unmarried pregnancy held greater stigma than it does today.

As Sandra M. Gilbert and Susan Gubar have suggested in their analysis of women writers, Hughes lends a subversive quality to his "mad women." Imagery of nakedness is heavy in Hughes's discussion of women's identity struggles, sug-gesting an awareness of women's sexuality as a site of re-sistance. The sharp and mysterious **"Strange Hurt,"** describes a female who seeks out storms from shelter, "fi-ery sunshine" from shade. Hughes concludes:

> In months of snowy winter
> When cozy houses hold,
> She'd break down doors
> To wander naked
> In the cold.

In **"March Moon,"** Hughes uses irony to break down con-structions of female sexuality, while connecting it with broad issues of power and inequality. The social construction of female shame is addressed through an ironic examination of the bright bare moon:

> The moon is naked.
> The wind has undressed the moon.
> The wind has blown all the cloud-garments
> Off the body of the moon
> And now she's naked.
> Stark naked.
>
> But why don't you blush,
> O shameless moon?
> Don't you know
> It isn't nice to be naked?

As a poem about women, **"March Moon"** unveils the con-struction of female shame which represses female expres-sion—sexually, spiritually, and intellectually. **"March Moon"** exposes the fallacy of "niceness" that clenches our desires, prefiguring Audre Lorde's comment that, "as women, we have come to distrust that power which rises from our deepest and non-rational thought. We have been warned against it all our lives by the male world . . . The fear of our desires keeps them suspect and indiscriminately powerful."

Constructing naked space as a moment of potential power, **"Strange Hurt"** and **"March Moon"** speak to the need to break down oppressive social constructs, and addresses the power of expressing our desires without shame. In a Black gay context, particularly in the age of AIDS, the need to express desire has a particular resonance. Many feel the need to emphasize the erotic as a means of broad social comment on gender, race, and class oppression. Essex Hemphill connects the devaluation of erotic experience with narrow constructs of femininity and masculinity. In **"Heavy Breathing,"** he comments on the "threadbare masculinity" he has "outgrown":

> At the end of the heavy breathing
> the funerals of my brothers
> force me to wear
> this scratchy black suit.
> I should be naked,
> seeding their graves.

Hemphill blends images of tragedy and injustice with nakedness, sensual yearning. Similarly, Brad Johnson's "Protest Poem" discusses a veteran's yearning:

> i would like to become
> a soldier and fight
> my way to the finest
> guerrilla i could find,
> lick the musky sweat
> from his body
> and let him make love
> to me. . . .

Johnson's poem invokes the sensual to signify greater struggle. He suggests that to love another man is to cross a battlefield, and that love among Black men is, as Joseph Beam comments, "*the* revolutionary act."

Read in the context of Hemphill's and Johnson's work, Hughes's **"I Loved My Friend"** contributes to a genderracially resistant Black male identity. The poem embodies a soft blue atmosphere of melancholy tenderness, of loss:

> I loved my friend.
> He went away from me.
> There's nothing more to say.
> The poem ends, soft as it began.
> I loved my friend.

By naming his love, sexual or otherwise, for a Black man, Hughes simultaneously confronts a racist culture that treats Black people as objects of fear and scorn, and resists gender constructs which forbid the articulation of love between men. **"I Loved My Friend"** directly challenges racism and sexism in whites and internalized racism and sexism in the self.

Occupying marginal spaces within the Black community as gays and within the gay community as Blacks, Black gay artists offer a unique viewpoint on genderracial constructs of Black identity. Arguably less inhibited by the constraints of heterosexual gender roles in expressing love for members of the same sex, writers such as Hemphill and Johnson challenge genderracial self-hatred which contributes to destruction of Black male pride and community. Marlon Riggs comments on his development of Black male pride as a Black gay man:

> I was blind to my brother's beauty/my own
> but now I see.
> Deaf to the voice that believed
> we were worth wanting/loving
> each other.
> Now I hear.

Vega writes of his romantic connection with another Black man as a source of strength in the face of racism and homophobia:

> You precious gem
> black pearl that warms the heart
> symbol of ageless wisdom,
> I derive strength
> from the touch of your hand.

Like Vega, Hughes uses erotic experience as a touchstone for gender, race, and class concerns. "In Hughes's work," bell hooks remarks, "sexual passion is always mediated by issues of materiality, class position, poverty"; gender, race, and class conflict "disrupts, perverts and distorts sexuality." Social concerns and sexual expression are inextricably linked as Hughes inquires into the nature of power, meditates on hope, and envisions social transformation through his use of sensual imagery.

In "The Uses of the Erotic: The Erotic as Power," Audre Lorde discusses the potential power of sensuality in transforming conceptions of reality imposed upon us by "racist, patriarchal, and anti-erotic society." She observes some of the ways in which the erotic frees us to explore our own capacity for joy. Once this joy is actualized through the erotic, we can no longer settle for anything less in the full spectrum of our lives. Lorde comments:

> In the way my body stretches to music and opens
> into response, hearkening to its deepest rhythms, so
> every level upon which I sense also opens to the
> erotically satisfying experience, whether it is danc-
> ing, building a bookcase, writing a poem, examin-
> ing an idea. [It] is a measure of the joy which I
> know myself to be capable of feeling. And that deep
> and irreplaceable knowledge . . . comes to demand

from all my life that it be lived within the knowledge that such satisfaction is possible.

The bridge which connects dream and vision with the material and political is, Lorde asserts, "formed by the erotic—the sensual—those physical, emotional and psychic expressions of what is deepest and strongest and richest within us, being shared, the passions of love in its deepest meaning." Hughes's **"Fulfillment"** has particular resonance in this context:

> The earth-meaning
> Like the sky-meaning
> Was fulfilled.
>
> We got up
> And went to the river,
> Touched silver water,
> Laughed and bathed
> In the sunshine.

Hughes's sensual vision can be compared to the jazz music he so loved, transcending the barriers of beauty, creating new vision, stretching the limitations of rational thought. Like the soothing confusion of Thelonius Monk's arrangements, Hughes's poetic sensualism moves from the rushing within our heads, our dreams, to the articulation of those dreams in talk and, eventually, reality. Like Lorde's, Hemphill's, and Vega's, this dialogue on interpersonal sensual relationships broadens to include larger social relations and issues of power and inequality, and addresses social change through the exploration of yearning.

Many of Hughes's poems which explore erotic experience comment on personal relations and broad social struggle simultaneously. The poem **"Desire"** uses erotic imagery to address many types of desire:

> Desire to us
> Was like a double death,
> Swift dying
> Of our mingled breath. . . .

Of what desire is Hughes speaking? The mention of mingled breath may hearken sexual imagery, but Hughes simultaneously addresses greater struggle:

> Evaporation
> Of an unknown strange perfume
> Between us quickly
> In a naked
> Room.

Thus this poem about a brief sexual encounter also expresses the desire to understand the death following any brief spell of harmony. Hughes intertwines moments of hope with its absence, personal dreams with sociopolitical reality. We do not know what perfume seeps into these moments with hope, allowing us to dream, or why it is so often that chaos emerges from the ensuing silence.

Similarly, in **"Demand,"** Hughes inquires into the nature of hope, addressing "the dream" almost aggressively:

> Listen!
> Dear dream of utter aliveness—
> Touching my body of utter death—
> Tell me, O quickly! dream of aliveness,
> The flaming source of your bright
>   breath.

"Demand" contemplates how to move dreams out of the realm of fantasy. The dream of utter aliveness touches the speaker's body when it is feeling close to death. The poem suggests that, if we knew the flaming source that breathes life into hopeless souls, it would be the source of our deepest power.

In **"Daybreak in Alabama"** Hughes suggests that human language limits our articulation of dreams, that it is too tethered to social hierarchy. Yet still he struggles with words as he ponders their limitations, using words to describe the music he wants to write. He contrasts natural images of the South—"the scent of pine needles / And the smell of red clay after rain"—with dreamlike visions:

> Of black and white black white black people
> And I'm gonna put white hands
> And black hands and brown and yellow hands
> And red clay earth hands in it
> Touching everyone with kind fingers. . . .

In disrupting race and gender classifications, Hughes breaks down hierarchical barriers and allows readers to envision Alabama transmuted from its reality of hunger and small hard hate, of "mixing blood and rain," to a blending of people in touch and kindness—race, gender, and class hierarchy transformed. This contrasting imagery sounds a blue note, a powerful space on the page, where laughter and tears meet.

"Joy" alludes to such a place of power, again through the use of sensual imagery:

> I went to look for Joy
> Slim, dancing Joy,
> Gay, laughing Joy,
> Bright-eyed Joy—
> And I found her
> Driving the butcher's cart

In the arms of the butcher boy!

The speaker is at once dismayed and pleased to find Joy "in the arms of the butcher boy." Joy is demystified, found amidst the chaotic harmony of city streets and work, in the space we occupy between barbarism and tender hope. The poem asserts that joy exists all around us in our ability to love and dream. Here, as in his well-known **"Harlem,"** the dream is a human right, a daily act of resistance.

Anticipating the current rediscovery of Hughes's work by Black gay artists, **"Old Walt"** examines poet Walt Whitman's life through the lens of Hughes's experience. Isaac Julien's film *Looking for Langston,* a meditation on Hughes and the Black gay artists' tradition, transposes Hughes and Black gay life much in the manner which Hughes transposes Whitman and his own artistic searching:

> Old Walt Whitman
> Went finding and seeking,
> Finding less than sought
> Seeking more than found,
> Every detail minding
> Of the seeking or the finding.
>
> Pleasured equally
> In seeking as in finding
> Each detail minding,
> Old Walt went seeking
> And finding.

bell hooks writes that "it is [the] evocation of pleasure that is seductive, that suggests the poem is about sensuality and desire." The overlapping of desire and discovery points to the interaction between the two realms. In this search we see the yearning bringing finding and the finding spurring yearning; dreams and their actualization are spun together.

As artists, both Hughes and Whitman act as visionaries in unique ways, transcending social constructs momentarily through the poetic imagination. Hughes uses this dreamspace to inquire into the nature of power, eventually interrogating his own role in the creative process. As we have seen, Hughes, in **"The Negro Artist and the Racial Mountain,"** demonstrated his awareness of his role as a Negro writer, and made inquiry into his own identity and the power in that role. In **"To Artina,"** he problematizes his relationship as writer with his poetic subject through the use of romantic, sensual imagery:

> I will take your heart.
> I will take your soul out of your body
> As though I were God.
> I will not be satisfied
> With the little words you say to me.

> I will not be satisfied
> With the touch of your hand
> Nor the sweet of your lips alone.

If we view "I" as the writer and "you" as the poetic subject, the poem stands as a reminder of the limits of poetic omniscience. It is this final ellipse—"I will take your heart for mine. / I will take your soul. / I will be God when it comes to you"—that signifies the power differential between writer and subject. Recognizing the role of one's own (multiple) consciousness in informing one's perspective on poetic subjects dissipates some of the "Godly" qualities of this omniscience. In recognizing distance, the writer's work is strengthened through a direct dialogue with the subject, centered in identity.

Hughes's discussion of identity focuses not only on his own role as a writer but on the role of literature in social transformation. In **"Long Trip,"** which was written at sea, the sea, writing, and reading are connected. The writer observes that

> The sea is a wilderness of waves,
> A desert of water.
> We dip and dive,
> Rise and roll,
> Hide and are hidden
> On the sea.

Here, as in **"Daybreak in Alabama,"** Hughes uses contrasting images to disrupt traditional imagery. Immersed in the shadowy sun glow beneath the surface, writers (and readers) "dip and dive," an image suggestive, as in **"Old Walt,"** of searching. Hughes juxtaposes seemingly binary images, to blur the disparity between them:

> Day, night
> Night, day,
> The sea is a desert of waves,
> A wilderness of water.

Through writing, Hughes takes his readers to places of vision, where traditional social constructs have been momentarily neutralized. It is significant that Hughes came to this space with a radical creativity centered in consciousness and identity. Hughes's genderracial dialogue offers an exciting contribution to discussion of the convergence of gender, race, and class in forming identity and envisioning social change through transcendent sensual imagery. In discussing Hughes's work, and the work of other authors, past and present, we must move beyond our reticence to speak of sex, gender, and race as informing their works. By exploring gender and race as inseparable players in the construction of identity, and by examining the interrogation of power through visionary fictions, we begin a new and rewarding dialogue on the poetic word.

Henry Taylor (review date 25 December 1994)

SOURCE: "He Heard America Jiving," *in New York Times Book Review,* Vol. XCIX, No. 52, December 12, 1994, p. 15.

[*In the following review of* The Collected Poems of Langston Hughes, *Taylor states that the quality of the poems is uneven but the book gives a clear picture of Hughes.*]

It is the rare poet whose words enter the culture with the apparent durability of, say, "a dream deferred." Lorraine Hansberry's play *A Raisin in the Sun,* Sara Lawrence-Lightfoot's book *I've Known Rivers*—the titles are phrases from the pen of Langston Hughes, and so is "black like me." To lodge such fragments so broadly and deeply requires not only a gift for poetry but also an unusual affinity with the language of popular speech and song. This gift and this affinity Langston Hughes had, along with an intense if scattered energy that kept him working all his adult life on a variety of projects in prose and verse—essays, columns, librettos, fiction, songs and, most important to him and to most of his readers, poems.

"**The Negro Speaks of Rivers,**" first published in 1921, when Hughes was 19, is still among his best-known poems, though vintage Hughes verse continued to appear; his last volume, *The Panther and the Lash,* was published shortly after his death in 1967. Dozens of Hughes's poems are in the mode of "**Motto,**" first collected in *Montage of a Dream Deferred* (1951):

> I play it cool
> *And dig all jive.*
> That's the reason
> *I stay alive.*
>
> *My motto,*
> *As I live and learn,*
> *is:*
>
> Dig And Be Dug
> In Return.

This has the almost anonymous authenticity to which some fine poetry aspires. Its rhythm is memorable and lively. It does what it sets out to do. Many of Hughes's poems display greater ambition, and some of them fulfill it, but he may have been most consistently at his best in short poems embodying brief moments of deeply compassionate wit. Much

of the time, his poems moved to blues and jazz rhythms, with which Hughes experimented more rewardingly than any other important poet of this century. Sometimes he would point in some self-conscious way to the technical aspects of a poem, using over emphatic capital letters or marginalia. But when the words and rhythms were allowed merely to do their work, they were often convincing and haunting.

Langston Hughes is one of the essential figures in American literature. His career is much larger than the body of his poetry alone. By his work and example, he has enriched our lives; as Gwendolyn Brooks once put it, he "made us better people." His stature demands a collection like this. It is edited by Arnold Rampersad, the Woodrow Wilson Professor of Literature at Princeton University, whose two-volume life of Hughes is among the most absorbing and well-written literary biographies of recent years, and David Roessel, who teaches English at Princeton. They say they have attempted to assemble "all the poems of Hughes published in his lifetime." (This statement is followed a few sentences later by the merciful qualification that they "have excluded as juvenilia" Hughes poems written in high school or college.) Along with a useful chronology of Hughes's life and 77 pages of scholarly notes, *The Collected Poems of Langston Hughes* gathers 860 poems, some 280 of which Hughes published in periodicals but did not choose to include in books.

It should surprise absolutely no one, then, that a great many of these poems are not good. A mere syllable or two might make the difference between the poem nourished by a light touch and the poem stifled under a heavy hand. Hughes's ear for the difference was not always reliable, but most of the time he could recognize extreme cases of ineptitude while assembling a collection. Here is a typical quatrain—the fourth—from "**Give Us Our Peace,**" which Hughes published in The Chicago Defender in 1945, but did not subsequently include in a collection:

> *Give us a peace that is not cheaply used,*
> *A peace that is no clever scheme,*
> *A people's peace for which men can enthuse,*
> *A peace that brings reality to our dream.*

In sharp contrast, here is the opening quatrain of "**Cross,**" which was published 20 years earlier in the N.A.A.C.P. magazine, *The Crisis,* and then in the collections *The Weary Blues* (1926) and *Selected Poems* (1959):

> My old man's a white old man
> *And my old mother's black.*
> If ever I cursed my white old man
> *I take my curses back.*

These two examples demonstrate, among other things, that frequent repetition is as subject to clumsiness and grace as anything else. In the first, "a" and "peace" appear four times each, to tiresome effect. In the shorter second example, "my" and "old" appear four times each without redundancy. But it would be foolish to conclude simply that Hughes sometimes had the good luck to score such direct hits as the opening of **"Cross."** Hughes was a skilled technician, but he worked quickly and threw himself feverishly into each poem while it was in process. Only later, and not quite dependably, did he come to see whether he had been successful or not. Many fine poets—Wordsworth is a stunning example— have worked this way.

The Collected Poems of Langston Hughes is divided by decades, from the 1920's through the 1960's, with a couple of appendixes: 42 mostly polemical poems, mostly written in the 40's, circulated to newspapers by The Associated Negro Press, and 33 poems for children. Mr. Rampersad and Mr. Roessel have made every effort to arrange the poems chronologically in order of publication, except for those collected in *Montage of a Dream Deferred* and *Ask Your Mama: 12 Moods for Jazz* (1961), which are presented as Hughes arranged them. It would have been extremely cumbersome to preserve the arrangement of poems in other volumes, since some of the poems appear in as many as four collections. The notes make it possible to distinguish between the previously collected and previously uncollected poems.

However, if the integrity of individual collections is of necessity destroyed here, the editors have restored in large measure the feel of the life that gave rise to the poems. It has long been recognized that Hughes believed strongly in the usefulness of poetry as polemic; this collection makes even clearer his willingness to put his name to doggerel, as well as to inspired poetry, for the sake of a cause he believed in. It also helps to clarify some of the pressures to which he reacted at various times; in the 50's, for example, he was careful to omit most of his more radically Communist verse from *Selected Poems.* It is extremely useful to have those poems here.

Plenty of readers will wish that more of these poems could have been better than they are; yet it seems impossible to wish that Hughes could have been anyone but who he was. From the beginning of his career to the end of it, Hughes spoke out clearly and courageously for racial justice. His range of tone was broad, from loving portrayal of brave people living private lives to heavy-handed but sometimes hilarious daydreams turning Orval Faubus and James O. Eastland into stick figures Mammy Faubus and Mammy Eastland. There was a great deal of anger in between, and pain, but somehow Hughes kept these emotions within the bounds of an amazingly generous heart.

Veronica Chambers (review date 12 February 1995)

SOURCE: A review of *The Sweet and Sour Animal Book* and *Black Misery*, in *New York Times Book Review*, February 12, 1995, p. 18.

[*In the following review, Chambers discusses the appeal of Hughes's simple language and life experiences in three books for children.*]

Langston Hughes (1902-67) was able to turn sophisticated and complex ideas into very simple language. A lifelong fan of jazz and blues, Hughes shared with musicians the gift of flow. His words could ride above you, breeze by or lift you like Aladdin's magic carpet. He often wrote in the AAB style of blues lyricists: the first line repeated for emphasis, the third line providing the payoff or switch. One of my favorite verses from *Blues Montage* goes:

> *Baby, baby, please don't snore so loud.*
> *Baby, baby, please don't snore so loud.*
> *You just a lil' bit of woman . . .*
> *But you sound like a great big crowd.*

In the literary world, poetry with simple rhymes is almost always looked down upon. In his lifetime, Hughes was often derided as not holding African-American arts and letters up to "intellectual" standards. Children, however, love a good rhyme. So it seems only natural that at some point in a 40-year career, which produced books of poetry, plays, novels and short stories. Hughes wrote for children, giving them just a simple but seductive taste of the blues.

The Sweet and Sour Animal Book, is an alphabet primer for the very young. A "lost" manuscript completed in 1936, according to George P. Cunningham, a scholar who contributed the afterword, it was rejected by publishers repeatedly and rediscovered only recently among Hughes's papers at Yale's Beinecke Rare Book Library by Nancy Toff, executive editor of children's books at Oxford University Press. From Ape to Zebra, the short poems reflect Hughes's childlike wonder as well as his sense of humor:

> What use
> Is a goose
> *Except to quackle?*
>
> If a goose
> Can't quackle
> *She's out of whackle.*

Always, Hughes's poetry tells children that there is no identity better than their own:

> *Newt,*

Newt, Newt,
What can you be?

Just
A salamander, child,
That's me!

This edition of **The Sweet and Sour Animal Book** is especially charming because of the illustrations by students in the lower grades at the Harlem School of the Arts. Though Langston Hughes was born in Joplin, Mo., Harlem was the mecca where he spent most of his adult life.

Hughes's childhood years and his love of Harlem are the subject of Floyd Cooper's book. *Coming Home: From the Life of Langston Hughes,* which begins with one of Hughes's poems **"Hope"**:

Sometimes when I'm lonely,
Don't know why,
Keep thinkin' I won't be lonely,
By and by.

Mr. Cooper's illustrations balance the sad stories of Hughes's childhood. The colors are warm and vivid and the artist offers a vibrant picture of the community that surrounds Hughes's family. This is a book that will no doubt touch many young readers, because in the text Mr. Cooper is honest about Hughes's difficult childhood. He grew up in Kansas, living with his grandmother Mary Langston. His father lived in Mexico because he could not practice law in the United States. His mother was an actress who pursued stardom in Kansas City. Throughout his childhood, the young poet-to-be dreamed of living with his parents, a dream that never came true.

His constant search for "home" was somewhat satisfied after he went to live with friends of the family whom he called Auntie and Uncle Reed. Hughes found another "home" in a Baptist church, with its singing and swinging and festive atmosphere. He wasn't particularly religious, but he liked being in that warm, musical place where everyone was referred to as "brother" and "sister."

But above all, Langston Hughes found "home" in Harlem, and the black community there would inspire much of his work. This is the first book Floyd Cooper has written, and his text is as inviting as his illustrations.

Black Misery, the last book that Langston Hughes wrote before his death in 1967, was originally published in 1969. It is the least elaborate of these three books, published in small format and illustrated with simple but beautiful drawings by Arouni, an artist and book designer. But the sharpness of the text, and the way it reverberates event today, will be as powerful to an adult as to a child.

> "Misery is when you heard on the radio that the neighborhood you live in is a slum but you always thought it was home . . . Misery is when you can see all the other kids in the dark but they claim they can't see you."

The language is as skeletal and yet as monumental as a dinosaur's bones. Langston Hughes tells us what black misery is, even while the alchemy of his writing turns that misery into literature.

FURTHER READING

Criticism

Anderson, Sherwood. "Paying for Old Sins." *The Nation* 139, No. 360 (11 July 1934): 49-50.
> Considers *The Ways of White Folks* a worthwhile book but believes Hughes's writing is hurt by his hatred for whites.

Davis, Thadious M. "Reading the Woman's Face in Langston Hughes's and Roy De Carava's *Sweet Flypaper of Life." The Langston Hughes Review* XII, No. 1 (Spring 1993) 22-8.
> Discusses the role of change in *Sweet Flypaper of Life.*

Dodson, Owen. "Carousels and Rain." *Poetry* 71 (1948): 279-81.
> Favorably reviews *Fields of Wonder.*

Evans, Nicholas M. "Langston Hughes as Bop Ethnographer in 'Trumpet Player: 52nd Street'." *Library Chronicle of the University of Texas* 24, No. 1-2 (1994): 119-35.
> Analyzes Hughes's portrayal of the jazz subculture in his poetry.

Ford, Karen Jackson. "Do Right to Write Right: Langston Hughes's Aesthetics of Simplicity." *Twentieth Century Literature* 38, No. 4 (Winter 1992): 436-56.
> Argues that Hughes's strength lies in his simple poems.

Harper, Donna Akiba Sullivan. "'The Apple of His Eye': Dubois on Hughes." *The Langston Hughes Review* 5, No. 2 (Fall 1986): 29-33.
> Argues that DuBois was impressed with Hughes because Hughes portrayed life truthfully.

Hutchinson, George B. "Langston Hughes and the 'Other' Whitman." In *The Continuing Presence of Walt Whitman:*

The Life after the Life, edited by Robert K. Martin, pp. 16-27. Iowa City: University of Iowa Press, 1992.
  Chronicles the influence of Walt Whitman on Hughes.

McLaren, Joseph. "Early Recognitions: Duke Ellington and Langston Hughes in New York, 1920-1930." In *The Harlem Renaissance: Revaluations,* edited by Amritjit Singh, William S. Shiver, and Stanley Brodwin, pp. 195-208. New York: Garland Publishing, 1989.
  Compares the careers of jazz musician Duke Ellington and Hughes, arguing that they fit into both "high" and "low" art.

Neal, Larry. "Langston Hughes: Black America's Poet Laureate." In *American Writing Today,* edited by Richard Kostelanetz, pp. 61-72. Troy, New York: Whitston Publishing Co., 1991.
  Provides an overview of Hughes's poetry.

Peterkin, Julia. "Negro Blue and Gold." *Poetry* 31 (October 1927): 44-7.
  Praises the rhythms and diversity of subjects in *Fine Clothes for the Jew.*

Sanders, Leslie Catherine. "'Also Own the Theatre': Representation in the Comedies of Langston Hughes." *The Langston Hughes Review* 11, No. 1 (Spring 1992): 6-13.
  Chronicles the difficulties Hughes faced in presenting his vision of African-America on stage.

Shields, John P. "'Never Cross the Divide': Reconstructing Langston Hughes's *Not Without Laughter.*" *African American Review* 28, No. 4 (1994): 601-13.
  Illustrates how Hughes altered *Not Without Laughter* to meet with the approval of his patron Charlotte Mason.

Walker, Alice. "Turning into Love: Some Thoughts on Surviving and Meeting Langston Hughes." *Callaloo* 12, No. 4 (Fall 1989): 663-66.
  Discusses the impact Walker's friendship with Hughes had on her career.

White, Jeannette S. and Clement A. White. "Two nations, One Vision. America's Langston Hughes and Cuba's Nicolás Guillén: Poetry of Affirmation: A Revolution." *The Langston Hughes Review* XII, No. 1 (Spring 1993): 42-50.
  Compare the works of Hughes and Nicolás Guillén, arguing that Hughes served as a muse for Guillén.

Additional coverage of Hughes's life and career is contained in the following sources published by Gale: *Authors and Artists for Young Adults,* Vol. 12; *Black Literature Criticism; Black Writers,* Vol. 1; *Concise Dictionary of American Literary Biography, 1929-1941; Contemporary Authors,* Vols. 1-4 (rev. ed.), 25-28 (rev. ed.); *Contemporary Authors New Revision Series,* Vols. 1, 34; *Children's Literature Review,* Vol. 17; *DISCovering Authors; DISCovering Authors Modules; Drama Criticism,* Vol. 3; *Dictionary of Literary Biography,* Vols. 4, 7, 48, 51, 86; *Junior DISCovering Authors; Major Authors and Illustrators for Children and Young Adults; Major 20th-Century Writers; Poetry Criticism,* Vol. 1; *Something about the Author,* Vol. 4, 33; *Short Story Criticism,* Vol. 6; and *World Literature Criticism.*

Joyce Carol Oates
1938-

American novelist, short story writer, poet, literary critic, essayist, nonfiction writer, and dramatist.

The following entry presents criticism on Oates's career through 1995. For further information on her life and works, see *CLC,* Volumes 1, 2, 3, 6, 9, 11, 15, 19, 33, and 52.

INTRODUCTION

One of the United States's most prolific and versatile contemporary writers, Oates has published, since the start of her award-winning literary career in 1963: more than twenty novels; hundreds of short stories in both collections and anthologies; nearly a dozen volumes of poetry; several books of nonfiction, literary criticism, and essays; and many theatrical dramas and screenplays. In the words of novelist John Barth, "she writes all over the aesthetical map." Writing in a dense, elliptical, almost neutral style that ranges from realistic to naturalistic to surrealistic, Oates concentrates on the spiritual, sexual, and intellectual malaise of modern American culture in her fiction, exposing darker aspects of the human condition. Her tragic and violent plots abound with incidents of rape, incest, murder, mutilation, child abuse, and suicide, and her protagonists often suffer as a result of the conditions of their social milieu or their emotional weaknesses. Although her works in other genres address similar issues, most critics concur that her short fiction best conveys the urgency and emotional power of her principal themes. Assessing her own fiction, Oates remarked, "I do not think my work is grim. It is more of a real picture, grim for some people, triumphant for others. The drama of our lives."

Biographical Information

Born June 16, 1938, in Lockport, New York, the daughter of a tool-and-die designer and homemaker, Oates was raised on her grandparents's farm in Erie County—later represented in much of her fiction as Eden County. A bookish, serious child, she first submitted a novel to a publisher at the age of fifteen. Oates attended Syracuse University on a scholarship and graduated Phi Beta Kappa in 1960; the following year she earned a master's degree at the University of Wisconsin and married Raymond Smith, a former English professor. From 1962 to 1968 the couple lived in Detroit, where Oates taught at the University of Detroit and published her first novels, short story collections, and poetry. She also witnessed the 1967 race riots, which inspired her National Book Award-winning novel *them* (1969). Shortly thereafter, Oates

accepted a teaching position at the University of Windsor, Ontario, staying until 1978, when she was named a writer-in-residence at Princeton University; she joined the faculty there as a professor in 1987. Despite the responsibilities of an academic career, Oates has actively pursued writing, publishing an average of two books a year in various genres since the publication of her first book, the short story collection *By the North Gate* (1963). Her early novels consistently earned nominations for the National Book Award, while her short fiction won several individual O. Henry Awards and the O. Henry Special Award for Continuing Achievement in both 1971 and 1986. A poet of some merit, and a regular contributor of essays and stories to scholarly journals, periodicals, and anthologies, Oates also is a respected literary critic whose work presents logical, sensitive analyses of a variety of topics. In 1987 she published the widely admired nonfiction study *On Boxing,* which led to at least one television appearance as a commentator for the sport. During the 1990s Oates gained additional recognition as a dramatist for producing many plays off-Broadway and at regional theaters, including *The Perfectionist* (1995), which was nominated by the American Theatre Critics Association for best new play in 1994.

Major Works

With Shuddering Fall (1964), Oates's first novel, foreshadows her preoccupation with violence and darkness, describing a destructive romance between a teenage girl and a thirty-year-old stock car driver that ends with his death by accident. Oates's best known and critically acclaimed early novels form an informal trilogy exploring three distinct segments of American society: *A Garden of Earthly Delights* (1967) chronicles the life of a migrant worker's daughter in rural Eden County; *Expensive People* (1967) exposes the superficial world of suburbia; and *them* presents the violent, degrading milieu of an inner-city Detroit family. Oates's novels of the 1970s explore American people and cultural institutions, combining social analysis with vivid psychological portraits of frustrated characters ranging from a brilliant surgeon (*Wonderland*, 1971), a young attorney (*Do with Me What You Will*, 1973), and the widow of a murdered conservative politician (*The Assassins*, 1975), to religious zealots (*Son of the Morning*, 1978) and distinguished visiting poets and feminist scholars (*Unholy Loves*, 1979). Her short stories of this period, most notably in *Marriages and Infidelities*, (1972), and *Where Are You Going, Where Have You Been?*, (1974), considered by many to be her best work, concern themes of violence and abuse between the sexes. "Where Are You Going, Where Have You Been," for instance, tells of the sexual awakening of a romantic girl by a mysterious man, Alfred Friend; this story is considered a masterpiece of the modern short form and was adapted for film. Her novels of the early 1980s—*Bellefleur* (1980), *A Bloodsmoor Romance* (1982), and *Mysteries of Winterthurn* (1984)—exploit the conventions of nineteenth-century Gothic literature as they examine such sensitive issues as crimes against women, children, and the poor, and the influence of family history on shaping destiny; likewise, many of her short stories rely on gothic elements (*Haunted*, 1994; *First Love*, 1996). Most of Oates's fiction of the 1980s features more explicit violence than does her earlier fiction, which tends more toward psychological afflictions but psychological obsessions nevertheless persist. In *Marya* (1986), for example, a successful academic searches for her alcoholic mother who had abused her as a child, and in *You Must Remember This* (1987), a former boxer commits incest with his niece during the McCarthyist 1950s. Oates's works of the 1990s continue to address relations between violence and such cultural realities of American society as racism (*Because It Is Bitter, and Because It Is My Heart*, 1990), affluence (*American Appetites*, 1989), alienation (*I Lock the Door upon Myself*, 1990), poverty (*The Rise of Life on Earth*, 1991), classism (*Heat*, 1992), sexual-political power dynamics (*Black Water*, 1992), feminism (*Foxfire*, 1993), success (*What I Lived For*, 1994), serial killers (*Zombie*, 1995), and familial implosion (*We Were the Mulvaneys*, 1996). The series of mysteries published under the pseudonym of Rosamond Smith—*Lives of the Twins* (1988), *Soul/Mate* (1989), *Nemesis* (1990), *Snake Eyes* (1992), and *You Can't Catch Me* (1995)—concern the psychopathic exploits of aberrational academics.

Critical Reception

Critics hold diverse opinions about Oates's work, particularly about her repeated use of graphic violence, which some have called a "distorted" vision of American life. Eva Manske has summarized the general view: "Some of her novels and stories are rather shrill in depicting the human situation, remain melodramatic renderings of everyday life, highly charged with unrelenting scenes of shocking, random violence, or madness and emotional distress that Oates chronicles as dominant elements of experience in the lives of her characters." Many other scholars, however, have identified the naturalistic influence of American writers, William Faulkner, Theodore Dreiser, and James T. Farrell, to justify the violence of her narratives. Despite the general disregard of Oates as a feminist writer, a number have defended the feminist sensibility underlying much of her fiction; "her works actively challenge restrictive gender ideology," according to Marilyn C. Wesley. Janis P. Stout found that "by compelling the reader to experience the inadequacies and injustices of the past through a technique of heightened realism, [Oates] does become a voice of feminist awareness." Although some critics have dismissed her gothic fiction as whimsical, others have suggested that it invigorates the gothic literary tradition, particularly feminist critics who often have likened Oates's ghosts to the cultural status of "invisible woman," as Cara Chell has pointed out. Scholars also have observed the symbolic value of "place" in Oates's fiction, both literally and figuratively. Margaret Rozga has shown how the Midwestern settings of Oates's fiction "can be places of refuge or places of terror"; on the other hand, Sally Robinson has contended that her "voyeuristic technique has risks, for it can place the writer (and the reader) in a comfortable position *above* those whose sad lives seem to compel Oates's attention." Ironically, Oates's prolificity often has aroused more suspicion than praise; her response: "perhaps critics (mainly male) who charged me with writing too much are secretly afraid that someone will accuse them of having done too little with their lives."

PRINCIPAL WORKS*

By the North Gate (short stories) 1963
With Shuddering Fall (novel) 1964
Upon the Sweeping Flood and Other Stories (short stories) 1966

Expensive People (novel) 1967

A Garden of Earthly Delights (novel) 1967

Women in Love and Other Poems (poetry) 1968

Anonymous Sins and Other Poems (poetry) 1969

them (novel) 1969

Love and Its Derangements: Poems (poetry) 1970

Ontological Proof of My Existence (drama) 1970

The Wheel of Love and Other Stories (short stories) 1970

Wonderland (novel) 1971

The Edge of Impossibility: Tragic Forms in Literature (criticism) 1972

Marriages and Infidelities (short stories) 1972

Angel Fire (poetry) 1973

Do with Me What You Will (novel) 1973

Dreaming America (poetry) 1973

The Hostile Sun: The Poetry of D. H. Lawrence (criticism) 1973

The Goddess and Other Women (short stories) 1974

The Hungry Ghosts: Seven Allusive Comedies (short stories) 1974

Miracle Play (drama) 1974

New Heaven, New Earth: The Visionary Experience in Literature (criticism) 1974

Where Are You Going, Where Have You Been?: Stories of Young America (short stories) 1974

The Assassins: A Book of Hours (novel) 1975

The Fabulous Beasts (poetry) 1975

The Poisoned Kiss and Other Stories from the Portuguese (short stories) 1975

The Seduction and Other Stories (short stories) 1975

Childwold (novel) 1976

Crossing the Border: Fifteen Tales (short stories) 1976

†*Triumph of the Spider Monkey: The First Person Confessions of the Maniac Bobby Gotteson as Told to Joyce Carol Oates* (novella) 1976

Night Side: Eighteen Tales (short stories) 1977

Season of Peril (poetry) 1977

All the Good People I've Left Behind (short stories) 1978

Son of the Morning (novel) 1978

The Stepfather (poetry) 1978

Women Whose Lives Are Food, Men Whose Lives Are Money: Poems (poetry) 1978

Cybele (novel) 1979

Unholy Loves (novel) 1979

Bellefleur (novel) 1980

The Lambe of Abyssalia (short stories) 1980

Three Plays (drama) 1980

Angel of Light (novel) 1981

Celestial Timepiece (poetry) 1981

Contraries: Essays (essays) 1981

A Sentimental Education: Stories (short stories) 1981

A Bloodsmoor Romance (novel) 1982

Invisible Woman: New and Selected Poems, 1970-1972 (poetry) 1982

The Luxury of Sin (poetry) 1983

The Profane Art: Essays and Reviews (essays) 1983

Last Days: Stories (short stories) 1984

Mysteries of Winterthurn (novel) 1984

Solstice (novel) 1985

Marya: A Life (novel) 1986

Wild Nights (short stories) 1985

Raven's Wing: Stories (short stories) 1986

Artist in Residence [with Eileen T. Bender] (nonfiction) 1987

On Boxing (nonfiction) 1987

You Must Remember This (novel) 1987

The Assignation: Stories (short stories) 1988

Lives of the Twins [as Rosamond Smith] (novel) 1988

(Woman) Writer: Occasions and Opportunities (essays) 1988

American Appetites (novel) 1989

Soul/Mate [as Rosamond Smith] (novel) 1989

The Time Traveler (poetry) 1989

Because It Is Bitter, and Because It Is My Heart (novel) 1990

I Lock the Door upon Myself (novel) 1990

Nemesis [as Rosamond Smith] (novel) 1990

In Darkest America: Two Plays (drama) 1991

I Stand Before You Naked (drama) 1991

The Rise of Life on Earth (novel) 1991

Twelve Plays (drama) 1991

Black Water (novel) 1992

Heat: And Other Stories (short stories) 1992

Snake Eyes [as Rosamond Smith] (novel) 1992

Where Is Here?: Stories (short stories) 1992

Foxfire: Confessions of a Girl Gang (novel) 1993

Haunted: Tales of the Grotesque (short stories) 1994

What I Lived For (novel) 1994

The Perfectionist and Other Plays (drama) 1995

Will You Always Love Me? (short stories) 1995

You Can't Catch Me [as Rosamond Smith] (novel) 1995

Zombie (novel) 1995

First Love: A Gothic Tale (novella) 1996

We Were the Mulvaneys (novel) 1996

*Dates of dramas refer to first publication.

†This work also was adapted as a play in 1985.

CRITICISM

Ellen Joseph (review date 25 October 1964)

SOURCE: "Growing up Assured," in *The Sunday Herald Tribune Book Week*, October 25, 1964, pp. 21, 23.

[*In the following review, Joseph comments on the plot, themes, and characters of* With Shuddering Fall.]

The enthusiasm that greeted Joyce Carol Oates last year upon the publication of her first volume, a collection of short stories called **By the North Gate,** clearly was not misplaced.

Her new book, a novel titled **With Shuddering Fall,** is set in the same world as the stories, a world of harsh weather, gratuitous destruction, inarticulate men without the veneer of culture facing the extreme experiences of life.

The central figures are Karen Herz, the beautiful 17-year-old daughter of a dominating but indulgent farmer, and the racing car driver Shar, who encounters Karen when he comes to attend the death of his demented father in a junk-filled cabin on the edge of the Herz property. From their meeting follow rape, car-wreck, murderous confrontations, enraged lovemaking, the death of a rival driver, miscarriage, race-riot, suicide and insanity.

This list indicates the external events of the story. What it fails to indicate is that Miss Oates, although her action scenes are vivid and intense, is not at all interested in shock value but in why her characters communicate with violence, how these events drive them to new realizations and growth. The struggle to become a woman, to develop from a "brutal, clever child" into a man, is her theme.

Karen is the catalyst for the change in Shar. Although she came into his life as the chance object of the "deadly whimsical range of his desire," she forces him to lose "the simplicity of vision, and simplicity of emotion" that "had always been essential in his life" and to gain ultimately the ability to make choices. As Karen knows, "His life was an accident . . . but his death wasn't—he made his death for himself! He was a man!"

Karen starts out with out such simplicity and shows finally no clear evidence of womanhood. In contrast to Shar, who tries to win her and make sense of his life "through violence, a communion of pain," she uses the weapon of "silent, limp passivity." This passivity grows out of the same condition that, despite the more obvious reasons Karen has for wanting Shar's death, is the most powerful source of her refusal to reciprocate his love: so precarious a sense of her own identity, of the reality of her existence, that she cannot give herself to anyone for fear of being lost. When at the end she returns to her family, neither Karen nor the reader is convinced that she will be able to maintain the conviction that now "She understood them, she was with them and at the same time a little apart from them, and had not lost herself in the experience."

Through Karen and Shar Miss Oates raises questions about the effects of stepping out of established roles, about guilt, love and hate, sanity. But in the same way that she sometimes makes Karen's figure overly vague in her attempt to

convey the dream-like, foggy state that illustrates Karen's unsureness of who she is, she occasionally, in her attempt to show her characters' search for meaning, burdens actions or states of mind with labels that ring of academic explication. More importantly, she causes the reader to question her judgment in making the character who bears the greatest weight so young and unformed.

Nonetheless, a young, soul-searching heroine at the center of cataclysmic events is part of a tradition that goes back to Richardson's *Clarissa.* And **With Shuddering Fall** is a traditional novel. Although Shar, at least at first, has all the marks of the modern hero—living by the mystique of speed, measuring events not in terms of external values but by his own physical being, functioning in a completely irrational environment—the general movement in the story is Karen's, from a rejection of society, through a period of suffering, to reconciliation. The virtues of the work are traditional, too. The prose is clear, unmannered, intelligent, with metaphors acting as signposts, and details always illuminating.

Elizabeth Janeway (review date 10 September 1967)

SOURCE: "Clara the Climber," in *The New York Times Book Review,* September 10, 1967, pp. 5, 63.

[*In the review below, Janeway draws thematic parallels between* A Garden of Earthly Delights *and Theodore Dreiser's fiction.*]

This isn't the best book that Joyce Carol Oates is going to write, but if you want to see a big, solid talent getting under way, I suggest you read [**A Garden of Earthly Delights.**]

Miss Oates's approach to fiction is more like Dreiser's than that of anyone else I can think of. She is as absorbed in the interaction between individual Americans and the society they live in as he was. Her writing is clumsy in places, as his was (though less clumsy in language), inhabited by strong, vivid characters—ordinary, unromantic, but thoroughly alive. There are passages that could be cut and pages, contrariwise, that want fleshing out with action. But when Miss Oates is good she is very, very good; and she is good often enough in the right way and in the right places to prove that she knows what she is doing. I found a distinct advance in her work over her deservedly praised volume of short stories, **Upon the Sweeping Flood.**

This is the story of Clara Walpole, who was born sometime in the twenties someplace in Arkansas in the back of a truck used for transporting migrant workers from one picking job to another. Clara's mother, Pearl, and her father, Carleton, were among the 30 workers riding the truck. For Carleton's hill farm in Kentucky had contrived to slide away from him under a load of debt. In the rain, on the slick road-surface, the truck collided with a car.

Breughel might have painted the scene with which the book opens—men standing around in the rain, talking, watching, waiting; excited children making a holiday of the accident; the tilted truck and, nosed against it, the car it had struck, with a frightened man trapped inside and, pounding on it with her fists, a screaming woman far gone in rage and pregnancy, so out of control that her anger was felt as sacred. This was Clara's mother. Clara was born half an hour later, under a canvas to keep out the rain, with some of the other travelling women for midwives. This is obviously the kind of scene that could be written to shock, but it isn't. Very much like Dreiser here, Miss Oates's honest grip on reality makes us feel but not flinch. The scene carries immense authority. It is heavy with the weight of human experience.

Clara grows up "travelling in the season." She is her father's favorite. As her mother sinks into withdrawn apathy, she is the only member of the family with enough grasp on life to be able to reverse the process of degradation and move out of the migratory ghetto. Clara is tough, as she must be to escape from a society that not only denies its children any ties (like schooling) with the world outside, but also rips apart that fundamental human unit, the family. Clara, however, somehow knows that the outer world can be reached, and she possesses the drive, will and native intelligence to get out into it. Her mother fades into passive madness, and dies in childbirth. Her stepmother deteriorates from a pretty girl into a malicious slattern. Her father is pushed toward bouts of uncontrolled violence. But Clara is a survivor, and when she sees a chance, she escapes.

She escapes via a man. Again, her native wit is good enough for her to find a man who will give her a chance and set her on her way. Lowry is not at all a beneficent figure. He helps Clara for his own complicated personal reasons. But he is an excellent choice for a savior. He takes Clara as far as she can go in her first giant stride toward a life in the world, and helps her to set up on her own and find her way toward independence.

Ironically, it is a very middle-class independence that Clara wants and finds, and which fails her in the end. Miss Oates seems determined to show us that if anything is better than the fragmented, torturing limbo of life in the migrant workers' camps, middle-class materialism and morality are still not good enough. Though Clara continues to fight and connive her way up the social scale, she ends not too differently from her own mother, while her father's purposeless violence reappears in her son.

Here again are Dreiserian echoes. The human being bends to the force of fate, but there is nothing mystic or supernatural about this destiny: we can see it everywhere around us in the ordinary life of mankind. Neither self-knowledge nor will can defeat the grubby gods of the everyday world where weakness, ignorance and failure wait for everyone.

If I have made Miss Oates's book and her thesis sound dreary, I have not done them an injustice. This is, in a way, a dreary book despite its excellences; dreary, powerful, determined, limited and true. How much dreariness one will put up with for the sake of truth depends on the reader. I believe that *A Garden of Earthly Delights* is a prime example of that banal description, "a book worth reading." It gives much more than it asks. Still, I suspect that Miss Oates's work is more dogged, determined and dreary than it need be; that her aims will stand forth more clearly when she loosens her grip on her characters and situations. For there is a feeling here of too much control.

Heaven knows, a writer needs self-confidence and authority to tackle a Dreiserian theme today. But the reader comes to feel, as Clara's story develops, not merely that Miss Oates knows what she is doing, but that she knows it too well. By excluding alternatives, her knowledge becomes a limiting and confining force. Perhaps Clara is doomed—but should the reader already sense this two-thirds (or less) of the way through the book? To see vital, attractive, energetic Clara cut down by the limits that society places on her could provoke a true feeling of tragedy; but not if one expects it; not if her choices are foreclosed in advance; not (in short) if one feels that the author, rather than life, is denying Clara her full scope.

Fiction and sociology run into each other these days, reaching for the same material. Sociology's facts can be fascinating and highly instructive, nor need they differ from the material of fiction: The *American Journal of Sociology,* for instance, recently carried a study of "the cocktail lounge," which offers a firm briefing on new courting patterns. What the novelist brings to this common ground is not the ability to collect case histories, but rather a training in how to relate them to an over-all pattern of behavior; in how to process data by a more daring and multilayered technique than social scientists allow themselves. Fictional characters stand for more than themselves, but not because they typify conditions. Rather, they present an aspect of absolute truth.

My quarrel with Miss Oates centers here, for I think she is generalizing too timidly from her enormously valuable social material. Clara bursts out of her background, surprising, willful, strong, earthy and decisive. When the author is describing her as if she were a case history, Clara is granted wildness and freedom: her autonomy. Miss Oates should not let her fictionalizing trap Clara in a preordained fate. That is not its function. Fiction should not pull facts toward truth by chopping off the extremes of possibility and denying them in advance. When it generalizes properly, it does so by accepting all potentialities, all extremes and working toward a meaning from them.

I honor Miss Oates's talent, her courage, her industry and her approach to describing a social world. I want only to beg her to remember how large and astonishing that world can be. It is the reach as well as the solidity of Dreiser's characters (and of Dostoevsky's, for that matter) which reconciles readers to occasional bumpy trips through dreary landscapes. Still, it is a considerable compliment to Miss Oates's talent that one argues for her characters against their author.

R. V. Cassill (review date 3 November 1968)

SOURCE: "Journey to the End of Suburban Night," in *Washington Post Book World,* November 3, 1968, p. 5.

[*Below, Cassill calls* Expensive People *"a prophetic novel," alluding to several literary precedents.*]

The question is no longer whether Miss Oates is a very good writer—she is, indeed—but just how far and high she can thrust the trajectory of brilliant accomplishment she has begun. It appears to me that her gifts are at least equal to those of the late Flannery O'Connor. If she is not absolutely more serious than Nabokov—whose *Lolita* this present novel resembles in its virtuosity—she is more obviously "ours" and therefore to be taken more seriously by us. Everything she touches turns to such blistering gold that sometimes I suspect she must have had Rumpelstiltskin in to help her spin it in the night.

Expensive People contains and exploits a little of everything. It is satire, confession, dream, report on suburbia, gothic tale in contemporary dress, with even some touches of the pop novel thrown in to show that the author can find a valid use for the screech of that untuned fiddle, too. But though her technique is eclectic, parodistic, sheer magpie, her bits of everything are fused into a prophetic novel as singular in effect as the night cry of a hurt animal.

The Ancient Mariner who narrates this journey to the end of the suburban night is Richard Everett, carrying 250 pounds of glutton's fat on his bones, eighteen years old, and looking back from the far side of precocity at his pre-pubescent years and at a murder he committed then. Precocity is the theme his confessions elaborate upon, and not the good old tame *dementia praecox* of the clinicians, either, but the

fated precocity of children at the end of an age that has exhausted its possibilities and parceled out its vision in cubes of knowledge that don't even have to be dispensed through schools anymore.

Poor Richard's parents are either disastrously mismatched or perfectly matched for disaster. His mother, Nadya or Natasha or just plain Nancy according to the *persona* she assumes, is a novelist with the kind of small, esoteric reputation that helps not at all in her suburban manipulations and ambitions. She claims to be of immigrant Russian ancestry, but one of her short stories discovered and read by her prodigious son hints of a more uncanny origin—as if she had been born, really, from her own bad dreams. In spite of her fictional sensibilities, she conducts her social life, parenthood and numerous adulteries with the crude, unillumined remainder of her nature.

Apparently this fey woman married Elwood Everett exactly so he would carry her into the "heaven" of suburban affluence. "I am Natasha Everett and I am out of history. . . . I'm clean of its stink," she cries to one of her former friends, who has showed up to rebuke her for backsliding from Bohemia. Another literary lover complains that her husband "is not contemporary with me. That man is out of Charles Dickens." ("He is not out of Dickens but out of Proust, you bastard," says Nadya.)

The author sees Elwood Everett as being out of Sinclair Lewis, though the qualities of Babbitt are mostly insulation or camouflage for a core of power and cunning that gives Everett the power to match Nadya's enormities with moral atrocities of his own. At one point he can display a sort of malodorous saintliness, begging his son not to let on to mother that they know about her adulterous connections. Nevertheless, even his attempts at cultural self-improvement or parental kindness are soured by purposeful bad timing. He seems to use bad timing to trip others up, the better to clamber over them.

In spite of such vigorous characterization of the parents, the story remains Richard's. He, after all, must not only endure them and attempt to arbitrate between them. He must love them, too, because the blindness of their greed makes them his children. He must, somehow, atone for them in a godless universe where atonement is almost literally unthinkable. So the primary task they have bequeathed him might be called a theological one, on top of the emotional knots they have bound him with. His exquisitely tormented intellect mistrusts theology. Hence his choice of composing a memoir as a device for justifying himself and his family, making the tiny world of a book to serve as a screen against the horrors of existence. His memoir is not art, but refuge, he suggests.

Perhaps it will seem a *tour de force* to assign to a child such vocabulary and perception as Miss Oates does. It is her reckless wager that he will seem not less but more a child because of the purity with which he registers those contradictions that adults blur as the price of survival.

Richard Everett is childlike enough when he buys the murder weapon—a rifle with a telescopic sight—and finds the telescope the most interesting thing about it. "It brought them [some working men] to me in a kind of haze, not quite real but not imaginary either, and it pleased me to think of how they existed both for themselves and for me, their spy." The unselfishness of his motives for the killing is also—almost unbearably—childlike. To accommodate the thought of murder, we need to believe in motives formed of unambivalent passion or calculated interest. Miss Oates gives a real turn of the screw in showing how ethereal the killer's choice may be.

In reading the novel you will find that Richard Everett is no mere artifice by which the author cloaks her own voice and observations of the life of our times. I called this a prophetic novel precisely because she shows with such devastating clarity the moral and intellectual burdens this phase of the civilization has discharged on its precocious children. A gluttonous civilization whose only uncanceled hope of salvation is finally sniffed out by the narrator: He will eat himself to death, like an uncle of his mother's who killed himself with gluttony to shame his gluttonous family.

Janis P. Stout (essay date May/June 1983)

SOURCE: "Catatonia and Femininity in Oates's *Do with Me What You Will*," in *International Journal of Women's Studies,* Vol. 6, No. 3, May/June, 1983, pp. 208-15.

[*In the following essay, Stout discusses the motif of passivity in* Do with Me What You Will *as a key element of stereotypical femininity.*]

Despite her involvement with women characters and the unsparing accuracy with which she has depicted their lives, Joyce Carol Oates is not generally regarded as a feminist writer. One of her more thoroughgoing critics has observed that Oates actually "appears impervious to feminist and liberationist ideas." That appearance derives, in part, from Oates's stance vis a vis historic time and from her tone in speaking out of that stance. Poised at the threshold of social change, she chooses to look back at the gloomy interior or sideways at others poised on that threshold. She does not map out visionary vistas of the future or sound a summons to the bold to make that future real. Nor does she speak of the past, with its institutionalized modes of feminine sub-

servience, with loud and obvious denunciation. Instead, even when her works are experimental and strange in their forms and effects, she writes fundamentally as a realist. But it is precisely this scrupulous realism in depicting women's lives that makes Oates's fiction finally a feminist document. By intensifying and magnifying the realism of her female characters' lives to the point where realism breaks into surrealism, she compels the reader to experience and acknowledge the inadequacies and injustices of the past and so to acknowledge the need for change.

Oates's method in her novel **Do With Me What You Will** (1973) is precisely this explosion of realism into a surrealism that, like the satire of a Swift or a Pope, convinces by appalling. It is the classic *reductio ad absurdum.* Its object is one of the more traditional stereotypes of femininity, the old notion that women are inherently docile or passive, with its corollary that indeed they ought to be so: the perfectly feminine woman is perfectly passive or acceptant. Making her modest proposal very quietly but unflinchingly, Oates delineates a heroine who embodies this passivity—as well as a yet more brittle stereotype of perfect womanhood, physical beauty—and, by the very clarity and extremity of that depiction, makes her character's feminine perfection into disease and deformity. She shows that in its purest expression passivity is not an ideal quality but an enforced denial of the self tantamount to a fixation upon death.

The central character of the novel, Elena, is so blighted by her extraordinary beauty and by her own interiorizing of others' demands for passive accommodation that she becomes, at times, a virtual nullity. She almost ceases to exist as a separate person, moving, instead, in a fog of dullness and unassertiveness so dense that she scarcely experiences even her own bodily sensations. She merely accepts the imprints of others and echoes their wishes. At times of stress she reaches the perfection of this accommodating passivity by lapsing into catatonia, a state of suspended animation in which, like a very good little girl, she ceases to assert (or even to record) her own being. Catatonia, then, the perfection of passivity, becomes at once the perfection of Elena's femininity and the exposure of that stereotype as a fraud.

Elena's peculiar passivity, and the anxieties she tries to stifle by means of her quiescence, derive most obviously from an early childhood trauma of being kidnapped and grossly neglected by her estranged, mentally-ill father. The father continually urges her to be obedient and quiet and praises her when she makes no disturbance. His assurances of his love imply that it is conditional upon her being submissive: "'And the way you obeyed me! . . . I'll always love my good little girl, my sweet beautiful daughter. . . .'" He wants her to be a perpetual child and "never grow into a woman," a thought he finds "shocking, ugly." Indeed, he finds it preferable to think of her "perfect in death"—the ultimately passive state.

Elena readily accepts the social quiescence her father urges on her. Apparently it is a role naturally congenial to her. She obediently crawls under the schoolyard fence as soon as he approaches her and tells her to come away. She repeats words that he urges her to say and does not "resist" when he insists she must go to the bathroom during a filling station stop in their flight. At times, however—and this will prove very significant—she uses this very passivity as a means of escape or disguised resistance. When her father tries to distract her from the distress of being kidnapped from school by giving her a present, she "did not seem to know what to do with it," and when he wipes her nose after telling her she "mustn't cry" she "didn't resist, but did not seem to notice." Most tellingly, she uses a quiescence like the stasis of death to withdraw from unwanted gestures of affection: "*the fingers reached out to touch me, the right side of my face. That side went stiff. He stroked my face and like magic my face went stiff.*" Indeed, her quiet passivity nearly brings her to death, as she obeys her father so well that she remains unnoticed in their room, grossly neglected, and when found is not only filthy and vermin-ridden but dehydrated and nearly starved.

When Elena is rescued from her father, her aggressive mother, Ardis, reinforces the message of docility, praising her for being "very good" in that she "never resisted" the doctors and nurses. Like her father, Elena's mother forces her into expressions of love which she obediently mouths although "the air at the back of her mouth" was "almost gagging her." Elena is being taught to associate love with fear, and to use expressions of love as means of escaping disapproval. In this, as in other ways, Elena says what she senses that others expect. Her mother and father have both taught her that lesson, but the readiness with which she accedes to their pressure indicates an inherent tendency to submissiveness. Oates is not clear as to whether such a tendency is peculiar to Elena or is a natural trait of women. But she is clear that the trait is reinforced by social conditioning and that this kind of submissiveness must be overcome if a woman is to achieve personhood.

If Elena's experience with her father is more traumatic, leaving anxieties from which she never fully recovers, her life with her mother is finally more baleful. Ardis's role as a model and the fact that she is overwhelmingly domineering make it difficult for Elena to judge and resist her. Ardis actively instills in Elena an urge toward statis, or nonbeing, as a positive value. She extols deathlike sleep, "absolute unconsciousness," as the "most important thing in life" and insists that a state of stony immobility is the highest value, the "*center of the world.*" Later, preparing Elena for an arranged marriage, Ardis urges her, "*Think of statues, the famous statues made of stone, Elena, think of how perfect they are, the peace in them.*" Again, Elena appropriates the lesson without question: "*I looked down upon my own body and saw*

that it had gone into stone, and the folds of my dress had become the creased folds of a gown. Such a body does not even need a head."

Ardis's lessons in immobility begin early. Even in childhood Elena is employed as a fashion model, with her mother functioning as her manager. In modelling, Elena's two most destructive and most stereo-typically feminine qualities, her extraordinary beauty and her extraordinary passivity, coalesce. She is, of course, a very good model—a virtual statue. She can sit under the lights "not seeing anything, not moving her face, not even sniffing, hardly breathing." She is perfectly malleable, perfectly submissive to the male authority figures who "propped her up onto stools, tilted her face, shaped a smile with their fingers." With her mother praising her as a "very good little girl to sit so still" and the photographers echoing her father's insistence on immobility—they tell her "*Don't move. Don't blink. Be good.*"—it is little wonder that Elena is suicidally good at modelling. She so perfects the art of sitting still that she sits open-eyed under the lights until her eyes are burned.

Elena's early passivity and immobility culminate in her first catatonic fit. She has been taunted by girls at school who, knowing she was afraid of the dark, threatened to turn off the lights in the school basement. Worse yet in Elena's mind, "*they said the boys were hiding down there.*" In response, Elena falls into a sort of catatonia. As her principal reports it to Ardis, "*she seemed to become paralyzed.*" In the school nurse's office she lies utterly still, hearing and feeling but giving no sign of sentience. "*I couldn't talk,*" she recalls. "*I couldn't move.*" Typically, Ardis acts protective in the presence of others, but when they are alone accuses Elena of disgraceful and rebellious behavior. She threatens her with being given back to her father or with being sold by means of a newspaper ad "*a bad girl is for sale.*" A number of elements coalesce in the incident: Elena's fear of the unknown, of death and of darkness; her fear of males; her father's role as both a threat and a refuge; her use of immobility, a death-like state, as an escape from anxieties too potent for her to handle through her usual methods of repression and concealment. Even more significantly, she unconsciously uses immobility as a means of asserting her will.

During adolescence, Elena remains uncannily beautiful and is thus, to her mother, highly marketable in marriage. But Elena is scarcely aware of Ardis's manipulations and in fact remains very frightened of males. When an incident of sexual aggression occurs at school, she evades her anxiety, avoids acknowledging it or tracing its origins, by again lapsing into a catatonic state: "she seemed to go dead, all sensation flowed out of her, her brain went dead, black." Nevertheless, her extreme beauty and radical passiveness—so extreme that she is often scarcely aware of what goes on around her, and thus appears radically innocent as well—attract the attention of Marvin Howe, a more potent, powerful, and wealthy man than Ardis had dared to hope for. The attraction is so unlikely that Ardis accuses her, once more, of subversively manipulating it, of playing her own ambitious game. Ardis is wrong, of course; Elena has not asserted herself at all. She has only sat quiescently by while her mother strove to arrange a marriage to a small-time night club operator, and her very lack of active playing for attention has drawn Howe. But once again her static passivity has functioned, unintentionally, as a means of asserting herself and thwarting her mother. At the end of the book it will function that way intentionally.

The patterns set in Elena's childhood and adolescence determine the quality of her adult life and her marriage to Marvin Howe. To some extent she functions in a normal upper-middle-class wifely way, giving dinner parties and attending functions with her husband, taking evening classes (when he "lets" her). But at the same time, conditioned by her mother's teachings and by her own anxieties to regard immobility as a refuge and a goal, she maintains a passivity resembling numbness. She bows her head "submissively" to receive Howe's gift of a necklace; she feels her self to "belong to" him. Clearly, Elena's passivity is a kind of death, a state almost of suspended animation. A woman who has difficulty focussing on simple events, so unalert that she fails to notice her own mother at a party and so pliant that she shapes her speech according to what is the "right," or expected, answer, appears merely defective. But for Howe, Elena's passivity is the essence of her femininity. Not only does it mean that she never causes friction by opposing his will, but it becomes for him an aspect of her fascinating otherness. Her blank unawareness is a radical innocence in which he can bury the torments of his own sense of guilt and corruption. He wants to "give" her everything, he says, and finds gratification in her mere acceptance of what he gives. Like her extreme beauty—which is also a kind of frozen death, "a substitute for existence"—Elena's passivity is the perfection of a stereotyped femininity. It is the reduction of a person to the status of a statue, a beautiful and immobile object to be possessed and admired.

It is clear, however, that Elena herself feels trapped and dissociated from a sense of self by her perfect playing of the feminine role. She has moments in which the banality of her life strikes her with a peculiar intensity. To stifle the anxieties produced by this sense of emptiness, she develops a fetish of counting—the number of boats on the lake, the number of trees she passes when walking, etc. Indeed, Elena feels her femaleness itself as an enslaving determinant that can never be escaped. When she hears, in casual party conversation, that in cadavers "the womb remains when all the other organs have disappeared," she is panic-stricken but, properly reticent, hides her response—"*I was very cold but I didn't shiver.*" That is, she holds herself still, statue-like.

Disguising her feelings reinforces the pattern of immobility.

Once again, as in her childhood and adolescence, Elena's habit of repression or denial culminates in a catatonic trance. Following a particularly empty exercise in social role-playing as she walks toward her husband's office, she stops to look at a statue of the nuclear family—for her a source of repression and control—and falls into immobility. Statues in general represent for Elena a kind of perfection through absolute withdrawal; the association was made explicit for her when her mother likened her to a beautiful statue and commended that state as the highest aspiration, a state when she would be "at the center, the center where everything is at peace." Now, needing peace, unable to confront her husband with the truth of her half-unrecognized dissatisfaction, she "stands without moving . . . posture unbreakable; backbone like steel." Projecting herself into the "perfect hardness" of the statue, she is "happy" that "everything has come to rest, in perfection it comes to rest, permanent." She is now "beyond anyone's touch," safe from the treacherous surging of human emotions. But of course her state is not perfection at all but "something wrong with her." As the man who will become her lover, Jack Morrissey, views her at this point (at the end of a long second section of the novel which leads up to the same moment as the first section), she appears "*sick*" with "dead-white skin," "trapped in a kind of stasis."

> **Oates shows clearly that the structure of traditional expectations in which 20th-century women find themselves is a smothering constriction denying them the possibility of a self-fulfilling life.**
> —*Janis P. Stout*

Before going on to look at Elena's emergence from self-nullification into self-realization, it would be well to summarize what Oates has done with the motif of passivity. At the point at which both the first and the second parts of the novel end, Elena's frozen stasis before the statue, the novel has described an elaborate *reductio ad absurdum* of traditional assumptions made about women. It has taken the stereotyped idea that passivity is one of the basic traits of the truly feminine character—a plausible enough idea, since women are not only "biologically receptive rather than aggressive" but "schooled in passivity"—and has created a character in whom both passivity and physical beauty, another requisite of the ideal female, reach their apotheosis. But the radical perfection of these traits does not amount to perfection of the individual, after all, but to extreme neurosis and a kind of living death, that is, to the destruction of the individual. When Elena is most passive, she is simply catatonic, lost in unawareness of either the outer world or her own self. The implication is clear: to idealize a stereotyped passive femininity is to idealize defect and self-destruction. Oates shows clearly that the structure of traditional expectations in which 20th-century women find themselves is a smothering constriction denying them the possibility of a self-fulfilling life. In order to reach selfhood, Elena must break out of the constraints of this traditional structure. And Elena, for all her strangeness, is a character emblematic of womankind.

It is largely through her affair with Jack Morrissey that Elena will move towards healing and authentic selfhood. But to understand that change, we need to look again at her marriage to Marvin Howe, specifically at the patterns of their sexual relationship. For Elena, that relationship is a void; it scarcely exists. Just as she deadened herself to her father's caresses long ago, so she now goes "into stone" with Howe, withdrawing herself from the experience of making love with him so that she "felt nothing." She exercises no volition in their lovemaking whatever:

> . . . she waited to accept him, she waited. She would go perfectly still inside his embrace, opening to him, his terrible frantic, helpless energy.

> This either did or did not happen.

Tolerating sex with neither aversion nor pleasure, she "obeys and is very still, unresisting," the epitome of the woman-as-receiver. Afterward, when Howe asks if she loves him, she answers yes and wonders if that is "the word he wanted." Her own feelings are irrelevant; or rather, she has none. To Howe, this passive acceptance seems wonderfully feminine, his ardor is as extreme as it is controlling: "Kissing loving worshipping her: lie still."

At first it is much the same with Jack Morrissey. Elena says what she thinks he wants to hear, and she understands that one of the things Jack most loves about her is her fear of his moodiness. Her overall feeling about their fragmentary times together is one of being domineered.

> *I want you this way and from you I want this and*
> *this and not that*
> *And I want it now*
> *And I forbid you to . . .*

Sex with Jack is still only an acceptance of his passion; she "felt nothing." But on a particularly agitated day, when he makes love to her urgently and clumsily in the front seat of his car, she experiences orgasm for the first time. It is a joltingly intense experience, as terrible as it is pleasurable.

> The sensation in her had now become terrible, spasm upon spasm localized in one part of her body, which she had to fight to control—but she could not

control it, it was so brutal and muscular . . . She clutched at him, trying not to scream, and she felt how wildly, helplessly they struggled, how viciously her body grabbed at him in its agony to keep him with her, to force him again and again into her.

Now, for the first time, she realizes her sexuality as her own deepest self, not merely the passive acceptance of another's passion.

Elena's sexual awakening is not merely a statement of a hapless Sleeping Beauty's summons to awareness by the transcendent male. For one thing, Jack has had many previous opportunities to work a phallic regeneration and has not done so. For another the sexual awakening is not an answer to Elena's problem of coming to active selfhood, but only the beginning of an answer. The sexual episode when she first experiences orgasm has been immediately preceded by Elena's calling into consciousness and into speech certain buried memories of her father, in particular the memory of an incident in which she saw a wild dog or wolf eat a snake on the threshold of her room. She confronts the association of sexuality with horror and cruelty which has troubled her for so long and goes on to assert that, despite the torment her father caused her and despite his manipulative demands that she express a love she didn't feel, she really did, in her own way, love him. Thus she brings to consciousness, so that she can cope with them, some of her most deeply buried neuroses. In the wake of this powerful moment of release and healing, when she and Jack make love, he momentarily behaves with an uncharacteristic "gentleness" that involves deferring to her will: "he asked her if she wanted him to stop." In response, she "pressed herself toward him" and "gripped him"; for the first time she takes the initiative in a sexual experience.

Following her awakening to the autonomy of her sexual self, Elena regresses into self-denial. She awakens the next day thinking "*This is the last time I will sleep here,*" that is, in Howe's bed. But instead of making a decisive step she falls into a period of vacillation between melancholic lassitude and unprecedented self-assertion (she attends an unruly political meeting that she knows neither Howe nor Morrissey would have approved her attending). Unable to force herself to an independent definition of her life, she surrenders all volition by abasing herself before Howe and confessing her affair. But the process has been begun. After a period of withdrawal from Howe—actually a mental collapse, a "self-dissolving nullity" during which her stasis and unawareness are not so total as in her period of catatonia but much more prolonged—she asserts her independence and leaves him.

Elena's decision to shape her own life involves a determination that she "would not be solved," she would not be treated as a passing problem to be disposed of by someone else. That is, she would no longer be passive, no longer be contained by the hands or the mind of another, as she had often felt herself to be. Accordingly, for the first time in her life, she assumes deliberate control of her actions. First she faces the fact of financial necessity and takes up the money Howe has tossed her, which she wanted to decline. Then she has her luxuriant hair cut short, an outward sign of her change in self, and travels back to Detroit to find Jack Morrissey.

The novel ends with a virtual kidnapping, a parallel to the kidnapping with which it opens. Elena goes to Jack's apartment and asks him to see her for only a minute. When he refuses to come out, she goes back to the street and waits there, willing him to come down to her. At this point, in direct contrast to her passive drifting through most of the novel, she has taken control of the situation and is forcing it toward its resolution. Yet the interesting point is that Elena's decisive act is presented largely in terms of the same character traits we have seen all along. She walks away from the door of the Morrisseys' apartment "as if hypnotized." She lets her hair blow "helplessly." She stands "motionless . . . suspended . . . waiting, frozen." After all, she is still the same person. She has not severed herself from her past and adopted a new and alien set of characteristics, but has gained impetus and control for that familiar self. She had learned to use her self and her past toward her own ends. In quietly waiting for Jack, who finally appears in his characteristic impatient rush, she is utilizing in a volitional way that very passiveness which before had been an abdication of volition. She is bending her essential femininity toward the "masculine" act of directing and controlling an action.

This kind of totality in the acceptance of the self and the direction of the self-as-given toward a chosen goal is, for Oates, the achievement of selfhood. She does not demand that women sever themselves from their conditioning and triumphantly create whole new modes of being for themselves. The kind of liberation and heroism required for such a free-wheeling and active transformation is, she believes, very rare. Instead, Oates affirms the validity of a quieter kind of triumph, the act of integration involved when repressed, deadened women like Elena are able to recognize and redirect the selves that experience in a real and hostile world has created for them.

Cara Chell (essay date 1985)

SOURCE: "Un-Tricking the Eye: Joyce Carol Oates and the Feminist Ghost Story," in *The Arizona Quarterly,* Vol. 41, No. 1, 1985, pp. 5-23.

[*In the essay below, Chell examines* Mysteries of Winterthurn *for the diverse ways that Oates uses conventions of the ghost story to indicate feminist concerns.*]

Joyce Carol Oates has matured into writing feminist fiction. She says (or has said) she isn't doing that: "I am very sympathetic with most of the aims of feminism, but cannot write feminist literature because it is too narrow, too limited." However, while some critics may have defined feminist literature narrowly (insisting on only sympathetic female—not sympathetic male—characters, for example), feminist literature covers as breathtaking a range as feminists, or as women, do themselves. Joyce Carol Oates is writing it. Her discussions of being a "(woman) writer" include recognition of the difficulties specific to a female writer. She is continually "insulted" by "sexist" (her words) questions like "Why is your writing so violent?" *A Bloodsmoor Romance* (1982) is obviously "a feminist romance with a lot of axes to grind" and *Mysteries of Winterthurn* (1984) is a thematically sophisticated feminist novel in which Oates explores what it means, as in the title of her recent book of poetry [*Invisible Woman*], to be literally or figuratively an "invisible woman."

In *Bellefleur* (1980), *A Bloodsmoor Romance,* and *Mysteries of Winterthurn,* Oates combines nineteenth-century forms and a unity of place. In the latest and perhaps most challenging of these three, *Mysteries of Winterthurn,* Oates uses these methods and her raised consciousness to place a chilling portrayal of family violence—with women and children as a traditional patriarch's most ravaged victims—squarely in the middle of an equally chilling portrayal of the society that creates, condones, and makes invisible such violence. In this novel, Oates also writes a biting parody of the cautionary tale, which she describes in **"At Least I Have Made a Women of Her"** as a story where "the only admirable *female* is a *lady.* . . . Bodies scarcely exist but clothes are everywhere in evidence. . . . Here is a world of female delusion in which individuality is dissolved into types, and the *eye's reading of the face is never to be corrected.*" Oates uses the past to reflect upon the present, to write her revenge on the cautionary tales of men like Hawthorne (her Hester's victimization is even more obvious, and while her narrator blames the victim, Oates does not). If many of Oates's former mentors have been male, the influences on this most recent work are female. *Mysteries of Winterthurn* owes much to both Charlotte and Emily Brontë; her contemporary use of the nineteenth-century detective novel is much like Diane Johnson's *The Shadow Knows*; her eighteenth-century protagonists are vivid reminders of Charlotte Perkins Gilman's in *The Yellow Wallpaper,* and Oates's version of hell housed in Winterthurn's Hotel Paradise, complete with Dr. Wilts's fatalistic soliloquy, is reminiscent of Djuna Barnes's *Nightwood*.

Oates writes about the invisibility of women within the

framework of a philosophical novel that has its intellectual roots in the psychology and pragmatism of William James and C. S. Pierce. The novel's progress is contemporaneous with James's career, and the protagonist, Xavier Kilgarvan, follows the pattern of the early twentieth-century intelligentsia in thinking about the "true." Oates makes clear that truth happens to an idea, that circumstances become true (Emerson's "I make my circumstances" is engraved on Kilgarvan's card), that to cling to an absolute idea is foolish. To emphasize this point, she uses all the cards she holds: she writes a ghost story/detective novel, with classical mythic allusions, plots borrowed from standard classic texts, class wars, and racial and religious prejudices, ghosts, magic, angels. Sarcasm and humor hide the fury in the story line, as in much of contemporary women's fiction and poetry. Oates, in borrowing, or rereading, to use Adrienne Rich's better word, these methods, is making the same discoveries other feminist writers are making: "Aristotle and his logician heirs tell you that nothing can be true and untrue at the same time," states Alicia Ostriker in *Writing Like a Woman.* "Such is the foundation of all rationality. One of the many pleasant results of experiencing a myth for yourself is that it shows you where Aristotle is wrong."

Oates uses two techniques (favorites of Henry James and Edith Wharton and thus appropriate to the novel's period) to clarify her vision of the relationship of pragmatism to the invisibility of women: the unreliable narrator and the ghost story. The supernatural becomes a tool that Oates uses to reveal the victimization of some of her women characters and the tool through which she allows them some form of vindication, although a still invisible form, not public. Oates forces the reader to "see" that in the context of the novel (while the foolish narrator is worried about what is "natural," "true," and "real") what is actually real are the deeds of ghostlike cherubs. By creating a ghost story that her narrator does not want to believe and by forcing the reader to believe it, Oates sets the much-vaunted "reality" of her pompous, presumably masculine, narrator on its head. Her central symbol is a trompe l'oeil mural of the Madonna and Child intended as a prized possession of a patriarchal dynasty. The trick is turned on the patriarchs; ultimately, the ghosts and the women survive.

Mysteries of Winterthurn is feminist fiction in that it "corrects" "the eye's reading of the face" and makes visible—through use of the invisible—the historical, stereotypical absurdities about women still believed as "true" by twentieth-century male novelists and their culture. Oates claims, "the most celebrated of twentieth-century writers have presented Woman through the distorting lens of sexist imagination. . . . The paradox with which the feminist critic or sympathizer must contend is this: that revolutionary advances in literature often fail to transcend deeply conservative and stereotypical images of women, as if, in a sense, the nine-

teenth century were eerily superimposed upon even the most defiantly inventive literary 'visions' of the twentieth century." To correct this fearful refusal of the (male) modernists, Oates steps back into the nineteenth century with an ironic (often sarcastic) eye and imposes her own re-vision on the cautionary tale to show the raw, violent misuse of women by men that stereotypes masked. Her pragmatic ghosts outdo the flesh-and-blood sophists defending values concerning sex, class, and race that upper-class, patriarchal, white society sees as "rational" and "true." Her point is that those stereotypes are only "true" within a white, upper-class masculine view which makes invisible any other views. Take away the patriarchal prejudice, and other interpretations become visible and equally true. In reading *Mysteries of Winterthurn,* the reader who holds racist, sexist, or classist beliefs must come to feel as foolish as the foolish narrator.

As if to make sure that her audience understands her point, Oates breaks her coherent whole, *Mysteries of Winterthurn: A Novel,* into three stories that develop thematically, telling of three separate investigations by the detective Xavier Kilgarvan into mysteries all occurring in his hometown, involving his kin, and spanning his youth, young adulthood, and early middle age. All three are unsolved in the traditional sense—not given visible, public solution and punishment. Where punishment is accomplished, the reader knows it to be unjust. The stories, **"The Virgin in the Rose-Bower; or, the Tragedy of Glen Mawr Manor," "Devil's Half-Acre; or, the Mystery of the 'Cruel Suitor,'"** and **"The Blood-stained Bridal Gown; or, Xavier Kilgarvan's Last Case,"** show by their vivid titles the unity that Oates maintains. All three, with some variation, involve cruel crimes against women, but each ends with different responses by women directly or indirectly involved. Those primarily affected are the Kilgarvan sisters, Georgina, Perdita, and Thérèse, daughters of Judge Erasmus Kilgarvan, and five working-class women whom the reader comes to know only as victims of brutal sex crimes done by a particularly foppish, demented young ruling-class heir, Valentine Westergaard. Xavier is a cousin of the Kilgarvan sisters and a member of Valentine's social set. Oates's unreliable narrator follows the pattern set by that century's society; for the most part, he blames the victim for the crime. Even though society does look for a scapegoat to punish, people believe that chambermaids seduced their employers, butchered factory girls wantonly accepted the attentions of upper-class gentlemen and deserved their fates, even if that includes rape and dismemberment, "suffragettes" asked for rape and mutilation by foolishly speaking in public places.

Crimes against women are most fully revealed in the first of the three murders, **"The Virgin in the Rose-Bower."** This story introduces the prototypical patriarch, Erasmus Kilgarvan, whose death shortly before the time period of the novel's action sets off many of the subsequent events. In the important chapter describing the judge's funeral, "The Keening," the narrator tells the history of the man he sees as an upstanding citizen, a man of superior intellect, and a county judge who believed that "he was ordained by God, as well as by the State, in his judicial role." Reading between the lines actually given by the narrator (lines like "*why,* and how, a man of such superior intelligence and proven canniness . . . chanced to marry not one, but two women of *inferior mettle*. . . . [women with] *an hereditary malaise,* in virulent union with *female pathology of an undefined sort,*" the reader gradually sees that Erasmus is a wife beater of the first magnitude, both of his wives eventually dying of his abuse, the first, Vivian Battenberg, "ending in . . . virtual disappearance, or 'fading away,'" the second, Hortense Spies, eventually poisoning herself with arsenic paste.

The narrator blames both women and dutifully reports the opinions of Dr. Colney Hatch, the society doctor, about the two women's failings. Oates is particularly revealing (and her use of her narrator is particularly sarcastic) in her vivid description of the insidious conditions women must combat in the society she describes. Dr. Hatch, for example, says as he looks from across the room at the ill Georgina, "Congestion in the head is most likely a consequence of congestion in the bowels, . . . both being symptoms of an overwrought nature, in the female sex in particular. . . . Thinking, reading, writing, etc.,—these place an inordinate strain on the system, and bring about any number of disorders." The entire second story of **"The Cruel Suitor"** shows a society quick to blame the victim for the patriarchy's crimes. Even the narrator admits that during the trial of Valentine Westergaard, "the roles of *murderer* and *victim* were, by shrewd degrees, reversed." Westergaard is found innocent of murder of the many women who, he said, "unmanned" him, who were "unclean" and "*so determined to provoke manly rage* in their thrashings and sobbings and bloody discharges!" After Xavier proves satisfactorily (to the narrator, the reader, and most of the town) that Valentine viciously seduced and sadistically murdered the young women, at the trial Westergaard himself manages to induce a "reasonable doubt" in the minds of the jurors by declaring he was haunted.

If the first two mysteries are particularly feminist in the disclosing of vulnerable positions of women in society, the third mystery further develops Oates's theme. In **"The Blood-stained Bridal Gown,"** while there is a woman victim—Perdita, victim of rape—the murder victims are Perdita's husband, mother-in-law, and the woman who appears to be her husband's lover, all vested members of the patriarchy. The dead are virtually hacked apart by axes and the bodies of the two apparent lovers are strewn with hearts. It is in this part of the novel that the subtleties of Oates's plot begin to convince the reader that women are not always pas-

sive victims and begin to give a more realistic view of women, if not a Utopian one.

The element of the supernatural enters the plot with the very first mystery and continues throughout the three stories, although with varying implications. What is most significant, perhaps, is where the original—and "real" in terms of believability in the context of the novel—ghosts come from. In the plot of the novel, the chief victim of Erasmus's cruelty is his oldest daughter, Georgina, the outlines of whose life Oates models after Emily Dickinson. That cruelty becomes evident only as the plot of the novel unfolds and as the element of the supernatural becomes explained.

The obvious mystery of the first segment of the novel is the death of an infant and the resulting insanity of its mother, Abigail Whimbrel, Georgina's cousin, after they sleep in the "Honeymoon Room" at Glen Mawr Manor, the ceiling of which is painted with the trompe l'oeil mural. The Madonna and Child of the painting are accompanied by a troop of angels or cherubs. The reader soon realizes, although the narrator is reluctant to admit to the obvious, that the murder of the infant and the molesting of the mother is done by the mural's angels, who come off of their ceiling, viciously nurse at Abigail's breast and eat away at the infant's head and body. Perdita, the youngest Kilgarvan daughter, explains to the young Xavier when he stands in the room after the crime, stares at the painting, and feels a red water drop, a tear drop or a blood drop, fall from one of the painted angel's eyes. She says, "angels *may* turn demon, with the passage of time,—if starved of the love that is their sustenance."

Perdita's explanation points to the heart of the original crime. Young Xavier soon finds, in the attic above the painted ceiling, the corpses of five infants, semimummified and still with the wire that strangled them around their necks. Two things become obvious to the reader: that the killer angels are perhaps the "representatives" of the strangled infants and that the infants' mother was Georgina. All the clues—Georgina's sometimes mad behavior, her periodic bouts of sickness and of wearing eccentric clothing, her near-hysteria over the proposal of a gentleman suitor—now clearly point to the chief crime of the original mystery: the judge's repeated incestuous "use" of Georgina, her subsequent pregnancies, and the bizarre behavior she resorts to to hide the crimes and their results. Without the actions of the angel-demons, the infants' corpses never would have been found.

So, the supernatural comes into Oates's narrative in part as a way of revealing the crimes of the patriarchy. She uses three kinds of supernatural forces that develop in the course of the novel. In the first mystery, the first type is those agents (and forces) beyond or outside of the tangible, beyond what the patriarchal world sees as "rational," "true," "natural": the avenging angels in Georgina's house. Oates makes the reader believe in this first type by inserting action done by super-natural forces into the narrative right before the reader's very eyes, so to speak. Therefore, the reader is forced to acknowledge the reality of the supernatural, even while the narrator is reluctant to reveal events without rational explanation. This kind of supernatural agent or occurrence includes, of course, the angel-demons from the trompe l'oeil painting, and parts of the other two stories: an experience Xavier has in quicksand, where he is lured by a now-you-see-it, now-you-don't lavender glove and teased by butterflies the reader suspects may be angel-demons, and, in the third story, a ghost Letitia Bunting sees. Whether or not the narrator is willing, these supernatural elements are real phenomena seen by real characters in the novel. Oates presents two other kinds of supernatural agents. The second are historical tales of the supernatural, told mainly in the second story, such as that of "Bishop" Elias Fenwick, a mad religious fanatic who is supposed to haunt the Devil's Half-Acre. Oates gives no evidence to support or deny this sort of ghost story, although it makes sense in the context of the narrative to see the person who "became" this ghost as the victim of class struggle. The third kind of ghost, which Oates begins to use in the second story and develops with more complexity in the third, is either an ironic excuse for sadistic acts, in the case of Valentine Westergaard, or a complex metaphor/excuse for psychologically determined acts that the late twentieth century would define as insane.

Part of what makes the supernatural in Oates's story a vehicle for her feminist message is that the existence of these agents is denied by the "rational" members of the ruling patriarchy, but is freely admitted by some women, some children, and by some members of the working class in Winterthurn, who, the Editor's Notes admit, were "perhaps far more sensitive,—nay, altogether more astute, in comprehending Evil." Lucas Kilgarvan, the disinherited toymaker brother of Judge Erasmus Kilgarvan and the father of Xavier, who is presented by Oates as a highly sympathetic character, one of several representative "good" men, defends the likelihood of this sort of ghost to Xavier," for where rank injustice has been perpetrated, and the Law is of no avail, shall not a man's spirit seek some manner of balance, or restitution?—or the meager solace of revenge, in committing mischief?"

In the case of the "actual" supernatural, rather than the historical or the psychological, in **"The Virgin in the Rose-Bower"** these forces act out the "meager solace of revenge" for themselves and the victim. In **"The Cruel Suitor,"** the "actual" supernatural becomes an educational agent for Xavier, convincing him of his own fallibility. In this second story the supernatural is also twisted into a psychological excuse for evil done to the victims. By the conclusion of the novel, **"The Bloodstained Bridal Gown,"** when the victim metamorphoses into the agent of her own wrath, she no

longer needs an avenging angel. By then, the reader must decide whether or not the supernatural is merely a twisted excuse for uncondonable evil, is a justified psychological rationale for uncontrollable behavior, or is yet some third more haunting and unexplainable force.

However the supernatural is interpreted throughout the three stories, Oates uses it to reveal the true plight of her women characters, to allow her women to be (more or less) survivors and, in a sense, vindicated victors, although they *seem*—in their visible actions—to be only victims in their "real" world. In **Mysteries of Winterthurn,** her spinsters and fallen women might have been written to illustrate feminist theories about reality versus myth. Oates's angels in the house do not quietly knit; they are powerful, viciously angry, supernatural forces who avenge themselves and their mother. In fact, the angel in the house myth becomes one of the key ironies of the novel, since the angels or cherubs are, throughout, the actual supernatural forces and, simultaneously, the interchangeable symbol for the "demonic" and powerful side of angry, victimized women. Oates's closely textured writing links the "angels" and "angel-demons" of the painting with the judge's view, symbolic of the patriarchy's view: "Give Woman wings & she is either angel or beast."

> **Oates presents the supernatural as representative of the immediate powerlessness of the invisible person in society. The supernatural, here, is the place where the invisible female or child becomes relatively visible—even if not literally visible to all eyes—and powerfull.**
> **—Cara Chell**

In the world of Winterthurn, the visible is "male." The "female" is invisible. In fact, Xavier's progress toward an acknowledgment of chaos, of the imagination, of the supernatural, makes him both stereotypically feminine and invisible; he becomes a "phantom," "silent as a ghost," and "possessed of nearly as much power as if he were invisible." So, Oates presents the supernatural as representative of the immediate powerlessness of the invisible person in society. The supernatural, here, is the place where the invisible female or child becomes relatively visible—even if not literally visible to all eyes—and powerful. And, in fact, the representatives of the patriarchy seem to at least unconsciously admit this power of the former victim. Valentine Westergaard for a time worries that "little Trixie, or Molly, or Emmie, or all three, or indeed, *all,* have quite bested me, in exacting their revenge from beyond the grave *in this odious wise!*" Combining the detective novel and the ghost story gives Oates two vehicles for showing how women are invisible in this society. In fact, she makes a point reminiscent of Susan Glaspell's in "Trifles." Women, both directly involved and not, repeatedly tell authorities about the angel-demons and about the identity of the Cruel Suitor, but their knowledge is dismissed as trifling. So, since patriarchal authorities will not give validity to women's testimony, in Joyce Carol Oates's city of Winterthurn, women have supernatural forces to listen to them and act for them. The angel-demons symbolize women's sometimes invisible, sometimes evil strength, demonstrating how the victim vindicates herself, in admirable and not-so-admirable ways. Georgina and Perdita are examples of this power. Each of them has, first, a supernatural way to some type of survival, and, second, a "real" way.

Georgina is the most invisible of the sisters, partly because she is the most victimized by her father, and perhaps partly because she is a poet, since during her lifetime her poetry is read by few people and is inaccessible even to those few. The real Georgina is almost completely invisible and ghost-like. The townspeople call her "the Blue Nun" (Oates's use of a nun being both sadly ironic considering Georgina's nonvirginal state and a stock convention of ghost stories in general). Characters describe her resemblance to a "'life statue' from the nearby cemetery [which] had roused itself," to a nun and a witch. They call her "haunting." She is quite literally veiled throughout her section of the novel (a choice of clothing considered by the narrator and the townspeople as discreet and appropriate). Her least action, such as coming to a store very early in the morning, is seen as *"exposing* herself to all manner of gossip and speculation" (emphasis supplied). What she does not expose, and what Winterthurn chooses to ignore, are her father's terrible crimes. Her "illnesses" are regarded as eccentricities and she is faulted for her camouflage: "There were periods when she seemed to affect a deliberate carelessness in her toilet, and in her apparel, wearing dresses that hung on her like sacks, as if to disguise her inordinate thinness; and to refute the very notion of feminine responsibility."

Georgina accepts, with almost astonishingly little protest, her society's view of her and her father's treatment of her, like the Iphigenia who is her model. She even accepts her father's dictum that she should stop publishing her poetry (although she does not stop writing it), since the poetry offends her society, which defines it as "strident," with "rude jarring images, and dashed-off lines; a penchant for the sickly, the morbid, the willfully unfeminine."

In Oates's feminist plot, Georgina's vindication, both supernatural and "real," is appropriate to her trials. The supernatural element of her vindication is illuminated by consideration of Oates's use of Iphigenia as Georgina's chosen pen name. That name is not only particularly suited to Georgina's personal history, but it also implies that in choosing it, Georgina shows an understanding of patriarchal society and of the lack of matriarchal authority in that society. The myth of Iphigenia and her parents Agamemnon and Clytemnestra, a myth Oates has used before as the basic plot of *Angel of Light,* points to a possible interpretation of the demon-angels' actions and Georgina's supernatural vindication. Oates may mean the demon-angels to be acting as the avenging Furies, creatures on wing defending matriarchal power and—in Georgina's case—avenging their mother. That Georgina was in some way aware of the angels and their actions, and that she related them to the judge's crimes, is apparent in one of her poems:

> Know, Sweet Babe—
> Thy Father's hand—
> Rudders—all thou fearest—
> 'Tis of Him—of HIM—
> (& not of ME—)
>   These Seraphim sing—
> Thou hearest—!

Poetry is Georgina's "real world" vindication. If the angel-demons or Furies try to take care of her enemies, Georgina takes care of herself through her art. With it she makes herself visible and defines herself, in creating at least a spiritual link with other people that circumstances make impossible for her physically to accomplish. Georgina's own theory of poetry, that "all poetry was, in a sense, *translation,* or *artful rendering,* of the Unknown depths of passion, into the Known strictures of language," allows the supposition that Georgina put a considerable amount of her own emotion (emotion that certainly wasn't or couldn't be displayed) into her poetry. That she created for herself such an outlet despite her circumstances is a victory. Of course, the critical popularity of her poems, edited and published after her death by Clarice, and the financial security they afforded her half-sisters, gives to Georgina another, though posthumous, form of vindication. Perdita is "invisible" in less dramatically significant ways than Georgina. Since she is alive throughout the novel's three parts, being a slightly younger contemporary of Xavier, we see her as a battered child, as a young woman very susceptible to the dictates of her society yet with the ability to see through them, and then as a young, childless wife who is confined by the expectations of her priggish husband and mother-in-law. Perdita is one of the many women in the novel who have basic intelligence and good sense (although not Georgina's creativity) but whose capabilities are totally ignored and are therefore invisible. Early in the story, Xavier realizes Perdita is "no faery child, but a very real young girl" and during the course of the novel, Oates demonstrates to the reader just how a "very real young girl" would view the society in which she is trapped. Perdita has the good sense to realize, for example, that if she had a "stake" she would rather bet on horses to make her fortune than to marry. The narrator says that the "impetuous young woman" was heard to remark, "If gambling be a sin against God . . . is it not a far more grievous sin to gamble one's very *self*, than merely with money?" Perdita, in fact, at least in part through her instruction by her sister Thérèse ("my Angel Thérèse") knows of the "dread Abyss" that separates men and women in the custom of their society, which considers "*Woman is all that man is* not: *Woman is not all that Man* is.*"

This separation across the abyss seems to symbolize, in Perdita's mind, the impossibility of acting on her intensely sexual nature. Perdita and Xavier are passionately attracted to each other, but until Perdita finally makes her ultimate rebellion from her society, she is not free at all to act on that passion, although she honestly admits her feelings to Xavier, shocking Xavier and almost shocking the reader, given the context of the narrator who continuously implies that she should be keeping those passions invisible.

The confinements that finally drive Perdita to her rebellion Oates buries in the narrator's prose, graphically demonstrating how Perdita's needs are invisible to society and how her actions are "exposed" only insofar as they are scandalous. In a lengthy parenthetical phrase, for example, the narrator details Perdita's unsuccessful attempt to adopt an infant, her desire to personally manage her Iphigenia royalties (a desire thwarted by her husband), and her joining "a ladies' cycling club, with the brazen intention of bicycling in Juniper Park, in a veritable army of bright-colored stockings, tam-o'-shanters, and bloomers!—this caprice being cut short, as one might imagine, when Reverend Bunting was informed by a parishioner." Perdita's attempt to keep the infant is made especially poignant by Xavier's discovery that Perdita baptized the child "Iphigenia" and that, despite the "tearful protestations, and threats the unhappy woman made *against her own life,*" Reverend Bunting and Dr. Hatch "had concurred in their judgment that to provide costly medical treatment for the piteous thing, and, as it were, 'nurse' it along, would be contrary to God's will . . . [and therefore] the foundling was allowed most mercifully to expire."

In this novel Oates uses chapter titles to great effect, and also causes her narrator—through the device of Xavier's "detecting"—to reveal chronological events in highly significant ways. Therefore, it is easy to make a case for the fact that the child Iphigenia's death or murder (part of the terrible strand of children's deaths and murders that runs through this novel) is the final horror that caused Perdita's rebellion. Oates tells the story of the infant's death in the chapter titled "The Betrothal," where Xavier discovers evidence of Perdita's love for him and visits Perdita to find her wearing, instead of her wedding ring, an antique ruby ring she took from Xavier when they were children. At this point in the narrative, the reader, although not the narrator or Xavier, finds the title of this story, **"The Bloodstained Bridal**

Gown," and many other clues beginning to add up to the possible (although never completely clear) solution of the murders: that Perdita and Xavier planned the murder of Harmon Bunting, Letitia Bunting, and Amanda Poindexter, and that Xavier, disguised as "the Red-Haired Specter" carried out the gruesome ax murders. Perdita's being found in her bridal gown raving about rape makes sense in the context of her finally acting on (even if in an extreme way) her passion for Xavier.

Oates's supernatural and "real" methods in Perdita's rebellion and vindication merge more in her twentieth-century story than in Georgina's nineteenth-century one. In Perdita's story the ghostly element is tied to the psychological. If **"The Virgin in the Rose-Bower"** is a ghost story told in the manner of Henry James or Edith Wharton with at least the possibility of "real" ghosts, **"The Bloodstained Bridal Gown"** is more a ghost story told in the manner of Shirley Jackson's *The Haunting of Hill House*—there are ghostly occurrences, but the agents are ultimately flesh-and-blood people acting under peculiar psychological motives.

The ghostly agent in Perdita's story is Xavier, who acts in alcohol-induced trances from which he awakens with total amnesia. For a period of time before the murders, Xavier "visits" (much like the ghostly Catherine in *Wuthering Heights*) Perdita's window as a "demon," a "most diabolical agent, in that his countenance seemed *angelic!*" By the end of the story, Xavier and the careful reader realize that he has committed the murders so that he and Perdita can be together; he even confesses to a friend (but not to the authorities) that he worked "in order to *consummate* a secret design" (emphasis supplied). The "real" part of Perdita's rebellion and vindication is in her method of escape. By her participation in the "secret design" (which, incidentally, is never "proven" in the narrative, but which makes sense given the clues Oates provides and given Xavier's chivalrous reluctance to discuss the plan), Perdita achieves both her freedom and the object of her passion. After a suitable period of what the narrator describes as an almost comatose convalescence from her rape by the red-haired specter, Perdita reappears in Winterthurn on her bicycle, wearing bloomers, kissing Xavier in public. Eventually she marries him and has a child.

Assuming that she did assist Xavier in the crime, there is a certain poetic justice in her posing as the upper-class victim of the murderer's rape. Perhaps Oates intends the reader to see Perdita as deliberately playing the role of woman as hapless victim—a part so believable to patriarchal authorities that it would remove her from investigation as the possible murderer. Whether or not Perdita is completely posing as a victim or whether she is truly driven nearly mad by the murders and Xavier's rape is left appropriately open to question. Throughout the novel it is clear that women like

Georgina and Perdita do well even to be half-rebels; that their society has so indoctrinated them to accept blame and guilt for acts they did not do, any escape at all is heroic.

It might be argued that Oates's picture of the vindicated or the victorious, of the nonvictim, is not very encouraging if the best she can do is show us an Emily Dickinson recluse or an accomplice to an ax murderer. And that may be an argument worth making. But given the psychological history of both Georgina and Perdita, a case can be made for Oates's doing well with the task she set herself. Both women are corrupted by the patriarchy, but they are far from being total, passive victims. They cannot (and cannot be expected to) escape from patriarchal corruption, but what they accomplish—from poetry to hauntings to actual refusal to accept corruption—is by no means meager. And, Oates gives the reader the third sister, Thérèse, who understands very well how the patriarchy protects itself; she tells Xavier of his naïve mistakes. Thérèse, too, may be guilty. There are clues in the novel that point to the possibility of her acting out perverse behavior or participating in the planning of crimes. But Thérèse is at least a more moderate victor than the violent Perdita or the recluse Georgina. With the financial security provided by her own work and by Iphigenia's poems, and freed of the judge, Thérèse is a successful version of the woman Georgina tried to be: a respected teacher at that same girls' school Georgina had to resign from, a well-dressed woman who even surprises people with experimentation like the "permanent wave," and (appropriate to the heterosexual world of the novel) the companion and eventually wife of the kind, gentle headmaster of the boys' school, a man much like the suitor Georgina was forced to refuse. In fact, Thérèse thinks while comparing the headmaster to Xavier, he "seemed in some obscure wise less *manly,* as he was the more *human!*"

Nevertheless, Oates is very much the realist—or the naturalist—even when entering into the world of the ghost story and the detective novel. *Mysteries of Winterthurn* climaxes, in fact, with a vision of hell called "the Hotel Paradise," with yet another "angel-child, a cherub, amazingly blighted by the hand of his Maker, as if in wrath, or in violent whimsy" and with the death of a renegade rebel from the patriarchal class in despair over his inability to protect the woman he loves, who is black, and their child, this angel. Obviously, the society Oates depicts is corrupt. While she steps forward to identify female victims within a society that victimizes nearly all of its members, she does not pretend to offer redemption. Her hero can become enlightened during his discovery of the patriarchy's crimes. He cannot find solutions. In fact, innocence lost means only that he, too, is corrupt. Xavier's journey haunts him with the knowledge that "there is, after all, no innocence in Mankind; *but only degrees and refinements of guilt.*"

Carol A. Martin (essay date Summer 1987)

SOURCE: "Art and Myth in Joyce Carol Oates's 'The Sacred Marriage,'" in *The Midwest Quarterly,* Vol. XXVIII, No. 4, Summer, 1987, pp. 540-52.

[*Below, Martin analyzes "The Sacred Marriage" as a parable of the transformative power of art, highlighting the influence of ancient myths about art on the narrative's development.*]

> Art is magnificent, divine, because it records the struggles of exceptional men to order their fantasies, their doubts, even their certainties, into an external structure that celebrates the life force itself, the energy of life, as well as the simple fact that someone created it—and especially the fact that you, the audience, are sharing it.
>
> **("Transformations")**

This affirmation of the nature and power of art, made by Joyce Carol Oates in an interview in 1972, just before the publication of her collection of short stories, *Marriages and Infidelities,* provides a hint to the meaning of the opening story in that collection, **"The Sacred Marriage,"** a story that one critic called "bewilderingly evocative," but that can be understood in terms of Oates's theory of the power of art. A testimony to the transforming power of art and the artist, the story is in keeping with Oates's practice of reworking—or "re-imagining" as Oates herself calls it—the stories of earlier artists. In this volume alone she has several stories whose titles give the clue to their predecessors: **"The Metamorphosis"** (Kafka), **"The Lady with the Pet Dog"** (Chekhov), **"The Turn of the Screw"** (Henry James), and **"The Dead"** (James Joyce). Eileen Bender connects **"The Sacred Marriage"** with James's "The Aspern Papers," but the protagonists in the two stories, as Bender seems to recognize, are significantly different. The re-imagining in **"The Sacred Marriage"** is not, in fact, of any fairly recent story, but of an ancient myth, and, as with the other stories mentioned above, the title of the story makes the connection explicit.

Features of this myth, which involves a young woman's marriage to a god and the attendant practice of sacred prostitution, are recorded in several places in James G. Frazer's *The Golden Bough,* but especially in a section titled "The Sacred Marriage." There Frazer describes a series of rituals involving the marriage of humans with divinities: "the custom of marrying gods either to images or to human beings was widespread among the nations of antiquity." In some versions of this myth, a young woman married to a god is destined to remain, physiologically, a virgin for the rest of her life. In other versions, the young woman has been married to a mortal, often for some time, has known no man but her husband, and is married to the god only ceremonially and temporarily, as in the Dionysiac festivals in Athens. In still other versions, the young woman married to the god preserves her virginity only in a figurative sense, for she prostitutes herself to the god's worshippers. "In Africa, and sometimes if not regularly in India, the sacred prostitutes attached to temples are regarded as the wives of the god, and their excesses are excused on the ground that the women are not themselves, but that they act under the influence of divine inspiration." All these rituals had some connection with fruitfulness of vine or field and ultimately with continued life, often by seeing the people and crops as participating in the immortal life of the god through the sacred marriage or divine prostitution. "In their licentious intercourse at the temples the women, whether maidens or matrons or professional harlots, imitated the licentious conduct of a great goddess of fertility for the purpose of ensuring the fruitfulness of fields and trees, of man and beast; and in discharging this sacred and important function the women were probably supposed . . . to be actually possessed by the goddess." The vision was homeopathic, involving a union, an identification of deity, man, and the natural world.

In Oates's **"The Sacred Marriage,"** the wife of the artist-deity, a poet named Connell Pearce, recently dead, invites his worshippers to their bed, the bed she had shared with her husband, a bed in a room still filled with his photographs. Pearce's autobiographical note, part of a collection of "religious parables and riddles," is discovered late in the story by the one man the reader actually sees sharing the bed. It makes the plot clear, both to the reader and to this man: "Let us imagine X, the famous Spanish novelist. . . . X is about to die and wants to write the novel of his own life, extended beyond his life. In Madrid he selects a certain woman. He is a noble, dying old man, she is a very beautiful young woman. *She* is worthy of being his wife. And therefore he marries her, and she nurses him through his last illness, buries him, and blesses all the admirers of his art who come to her, for she alone retains X's divinity. *Her body. Her consecration.* A multitude of lovers come to her, lovers of X, and she blesses them without exception, in her constant virginity."

The correspondences to *The Golden Bough* in title and plot line are accompanied by other similarities as well. The name of Connell Pearce's wife is *Emilia*; she lives in the house she and Pearce bought on *Lydia* Street. Frazer mentions one "Aurelia Aemilia," who was involved in devotional prostitution, as testified by "a Greek inscription found at Tralles in Lydia, which proves that the practice of religious prostitution survived in that country as late as the second century of our era." And it may be a coincidence, or it may be Oates's playfulness that one of the worshipful scholars who comes to Lydia Street is named "Felix Frazer." (Perhaps Oates too has contrived a mystique of names like Connell Pearce's "mystique of places—even the names of places.")

The story is told from the perspective of another worshipful scholar, Howard Dean, whose reflections and whose letter to the widow make it clear that only lovers of Pearce, only those whom Pearce had inspired, may come to his shrine. Howard is surprised that a "coldly opportunistic" acquaintance from Harvard who had wanted to obtain Pearce's papers had never had his several letters answered, while Howard Dean's own shamelessly worshipful letter received an instant reply; he wonders: "How had his single letter, written feverishly, with an almost adolescent yearning, managed to get through to Pearce's widow?" The parts of his letter that he recalls in his reverie answer that question: your husband's first book "changed my life"; "your husband has partly created me"; Connell Pearce "has managed to create a sense of destiny, personal destiny, out of this chaos, and he has made us see that it is not sentimental to believe in something, that it is not simply the pious who have hope of being saved. . . ."

That such a high purpose for art—to create a sense of destiny, to create order and unity out of chaos—is Oates's belief is clear in interviews and articles, given or written close to the time **"The Sacred Marriage"** was first published, in *Southern Review* in summer 1972. Challenging the myth of the isolated artist, Oates argued that "Creative work, like scientific work, should be greeted as a communal effort—an attempt by an individual to give voice to many voices" (**"The Myth"**). In an interview published in late 1972, she affirmed that "Art should be for the entire species, ultimately, aimed toward an elevation of other people through an extension of their latent sympathies." And in an another interview, published just before the appearance of **"The Sacred Marriage,"** she described art as a way of "transcribing dreams" but in such a way that the "private" dream is made public. This is in fact what poet Connell Pearce's art had said to Howard Dean, as he explains in his letter to Emilia:

> There is a prose-poem of your husband's that contains the lines, *We woke out of adolescence to discover that there is nothing private in the senses. Why not die, then? We are on exhibit. But, why not live? We are not doomed to private fates.* When I first read these lines I felt a tremendous shock. I can't explain my feeling. I don't know if I brought this feeling to the poem, which exposed it, or if the poem—I mean, your husband—entirely created it as I read.

It is, in Oates's theory, the power of Art that produces this inexplicable "feeling" of fusion, wherein the artist, the reader, and the work itself cannot be separated, where all are creative forces. Her views are not simply parallel or anticipatory developments in accord with "reader-response" or "aesthetics of reception" criticism such as Wolfgang Iser, Hans Robert Jauss, and others were producing at the same time and since. They are, of course, similar, but Oates's view of the artist's role gives the artist a primary function in what she sees as, potentially, a whole new world-view.

In her essay, **"New Heaven and Earth,"** published in November 1972, Oates calls for an end to the "Cartesian dualism—I/It." She sees the need "to recognize that our minds belong, quite naturally, to a collective 'mind,' a mind in which we share everything that is mental, most obviously language itself, and that the old boundary of the skin is no boundary at all but a membrane connecting the inner and outer experiences of existence." This, she affirms, "has always been a mystical vision." Here, as elsewhere, she connects the writer and the mystic, two who express this vision, who move toward and who help others move toward self-transcendence.

Insofar as Howard Dean feels this bond between himself and Connell Pearce, he has achieved some measure of self-transcendence, though his achievement is incomplete. The possibility that Howard *could* achieve transcendence led him to be chosen by Emilia as one of the few scholars allowed to visit the "sacred place" that is Connell Pearce's home and to have Pearce's mysterious origins explained by the priestess-queen in charge, who talks about Pearce with "an artless regality, as if she were in charge of a historical site, in charge of the careful recitation of events now past" (20). Such "careful recitation" is suggestive of the importance attached to language in ancient and modern religious ritual. From Howard's point of view, he "had not deserved this place, but he had come here innocently, without selfishness or design." However, until the end of the story, Howard does not fully realize the nature of his bond with Pearce, not the role of Emilia in that bond. At first he had thought of Emilia as one "like the other women Pearce had loved and brought into his life. But she had no reality for Howard, who had hardly thought of her until today: she was simply a presence, a medium between himself and the dead poet." His dismissive "simply" would deny the special mediating role of the woman in fertility cults like that of Dionysus: "Dionysus is a woman's god in the fullest sense of the word, the source of all woman's sensual and transcendent hopes, the center of her whole existence. It was to women that he was first revealed in his glory, and it was women who propagated his cult and brought about its triumph." It was through women that men were enabled to approach the god [Kerenyi, *Archetypal Image of Indestructible Life,* 1976].

Judith Ochshorn in *The Female Experience and the Nature of the Divine* observes that in the Sacred Marriage recorded of the ruler Dumuzi in Mesopotamia "as in all other instances, it was the goddess Inanna who selected him for 'the godship of the land.'" In Oates, the initiates are selected by Emilia, but she herself was chosen, for her beauty, by Connell Pearce. Here perhaps the story is closer to the

Dionysian rites and beliefs of Greece and Asia Minor; the god "compels" the women followers to join him, he is an irresistible force. Likewise, as Emilia says of Pearce, "any woman would have loved him"; when Pearce selected her, she "had no choice. I had to go with Connell," just as the women of Dionysian rite, inspired, frenzied, have no choice but to worship—like Emilia, often against the "rational" opposition of their families, as Euripedes' *Bacchae* illustrates.

Like most, perhaps all, religious cults involving sacred prostitution, the Dionysian cult is a fertility cult, in which "In the form of an animal the god suffered the extreme reduction, a cruel death, but he, indestructible *zoë* . . . escaped— to Thetis, to the Muses, or however this was expressed mythologically" (Kerenyi). Paradoxical elements are combined: death and rebirth, *eros* and *thanatos.* The followers of Connell Pearce mate with the priestess-widow in the room in which Pearce loved and died; in Pearce's death, Howard felt "as if part of himself had died" and yet Pearce too had "helped [Howard] mature. By dying, Pearce had shown him the way to die—otherwise death might have seemed to Howard unimaginable." By making death "imaginable"—by creating an image of death, and of rebirth—Connell Pearce, the embodiment of Art, enables others to live; this, however, Howard at first does not comprehend.

As a new initiate, Howard does not yet understand that Pearce represents the indestructible force of Art, which will enable him and other chosen ("not many") worshippers to live. Before he read of Pearce's death "Howard had been aware of Connell Pearce at a distance, living out a parallel life, a presence, not ghostly but very solid, substantial, the kind of transparent substance Howard had once attributed to God. So long as Pearce lived, there had been a kind of promise. . . . But Pearce had died." The knowledge to which Howard comes in the painful course of events on Lydia Street is the knowledge that "Pearce was not dead but still alive, more powerful than Howard." After this realization, Howard finds the parable of "X" in which the endurance of the artist is explained in terms of the Sacred Marriage. The connection between the artist's life and the life of the race— its survival and growth—is the central argument of an article Oates published in January 1973: "If art has any general evolutionary function, it must be to enhance the race, to work somehow toward an essential unity and harmony—survival and growth—and perhaps an integration of the human world with the natural world" (**"The Unique/Universal"**). Fertility myths, with their center in death and rebirth, provide an emblem, in **"The Sacred Marriage,"** for this unity and harmony, both within the human world and between the human and the natural.

The story begins with an emphasis on fertility images and the power of nature. As Howard drives toward the Pearce home, he looks out across fields that "were the same, uniform, dull, sweet green. A kind of paradise. Another world." The fields are green, but it is autumn, the harvest time when the ancient Sacred Marriage was usually enacted. His state replicates that of the new worshipper of Dionysus, who must leave the city and the mundane: "Rarely out of the city, rarely out of his routine of work, he felt a little giddy with the excitement of the trip, like a child. He wanted to see everything." In this new world, at the top of the ridge, he feels a strange sense of power ("he believed he could gaze right across the valley to the top of the mountain range, eyeing it levelly, in a sense as an equal"), as well as a sense of "constant, whimsical danger." He begins to abandon his usual self; his consciousness is altered: the landscape is "hypnotic"; as he sees the "fierce little plunging streams of water" he "felt he was being hypnotized and this thought somehow pleased him"; the garden of Pearce's home is "dusty, dreamy, hypnotic as the valley." Nature and humanity mingle. When he first sees Emilia, she is emerging from the house and going into the garden. Meeting her later, he notices her hair, which "curved in curls and tendrils," and her "leaf-colored green" dress.

In the context of such images, the look of Pearce's eyes in his portrait, "all iris, as if blinded by a tremendous light or a deluge of sights," can be seen as an allusion to the blinding flash of Zeus, which destroyed Dionysus' mother Semele and gave him a first birth. And as the worshippers of Dionysus often sense the presence of the god, so Emilia seems to be both listening to Howard and "to something else—a voice in her head, perhaps." In the barn (the Pearce home is on a farm), which "seemed unhuman, holy," Howard senses a presence, "glancing up at the shadowy hayloft, and behind him at the opened door, as if he expected someone to be watching."

Paradoxically, Howard's strongest moment of connection with Pearce and "the woman who had been married to him"—at the grave, where Howard feels "with an almost violent certitude that he had come to the right place"—is followed shortly by his losing sight of Pearce; he begins to see Emilia, "only *her,* her self," and interprets his attraction in conventional terms of "falling in love." Forgetting Pearce, he does not hear or understand Emilia's message, which is central in this parable of Art: "If Connell touched someone with his fingertips he would know that person . . . he could absorb that person. . . . You felt a jolt, like a small electric shock, go through you and into him, passing out of you and into him, permanently. . . . That way he brought many different people into him, into his life. He told me that he had lived through many different people." This to Howard is inexplicable, and Emilia's touch leads to his selfish desire for exclusive possession. He *becomes* selfish and designing, desiring Emilia not as the specially chosen priestess of Art, but as a potential faculty wife in Madison, Wisconsin. Hence his shock when another initiate appears, and his apostasy: "A

living woman was worth more than a dead man's novel, any dead man's novel or his poetry or any poetry. That was a fact."

Like Pentheus in his devotion to "fact" Howard is nearly destroyed, because, in seeking to remove Emilia from the sacred surroundings, he would violate the vision of unity in Pearce's poems by an assertion of his individual ego, of possessiveness, of personal power. In various essays, Oates condemns this possessiveness, this competitive selfishness: the "myth of the isolated artist," for instance, gives rise to "a society obsessed with adolescent ideas of being superior, of conquering, of destroying" (**"The Myth"**). One recalls Pearce's phrase about "working out of adolescence to discover there is nothing private in the senses."

This rise of the competitive self in Howard, a self that wishes Emilia to belong to him and to turn away all other worshippers of Pearce, is akin to the attitude of the "coldly opportunistic" professor from Harvard. That Howard should have such a feeling is incomprehensible to Emilia, who naively asks, of Howard and the new arrival, Felix, "the two of you can work in the same room, can't you? Is that too difficult, for scholars?"

> If "The Sacred Marriage" is a parable of the power of art, "working together in the same room" is clearly a metaphor for the unity that, in Oates's vision, great art provides. It is a unity in which the art itself never dies, in which the individual ego is transcended by the sense of community.
> —*Carol A. Martin*

If **"The Sacred Marriage"** is a parable of the power of art, "working together in the same room" is clearly a metaphor for the unity that, in Oates's vision, great art provides. It is a unity in which the art itself never dies, in which the individual ego is transcended by the sense of community. The poet Connell Pearce has become a kind of savior, demonstrating even how to transcend death. In dying, it seemed, to Emilia, "as if he were making up his own death, like a poem." This "poem" enables his followers to experience death without dying, as the followers of the god in the Sacred Marriage experienced godhead. In the twentieth century, art replaces religion to provide this "identifying" experience. Citing a statement by Picasso that "is so true that no one can really add to it," Oates says: "Painting isn't an aesthetic operation, it's a form of magic designed as a mediator between the strange, hostile world and us, a way of seizing the power by giving form to our terrors as well as our desires" (**"Transformations"**).

Howard's departure in the darkness of midnight is a departure in despair, but it carries with it the seeds of rebirth. Though he considers the possibility that he could drive off the steep roads and die, he does not want to die. Becoming an "ordinary man" again means here giving up the opportunism and possessiveness that had led to his despair. In a final epiphany, as the sun rises, he is infused with a sense of renewal: "the same marvelous energy he had felt upon first seeing those piles of Pearce's" manuscripts infuses him, and he drives "all day with a passion he could barely contain." With the dawn, Howard comes to accept his "mission," his "sacred obligation," to bring Pearce, the embodiment of Art in this religious parable and riddle, to the world's attention. By the end of the story, Howard has come to realize the sacred nature of art, and its transcendence of self, and the reader has come to understand what perhaps Oates meant in speaking of this collection of stories: "Some are conventional marriages of men and women, others are marriages in another sense—with a phase of art, with something that transcends the limitations of the ego. . . ."

"The Sacred Marriage," then, is an appropriate opening story in a volume that includes so many of Oates's "re-imaginings," for it is a celebration of the "magic" of art, of its transforming power. Using an ancient and widespread myth, Oates affirms the artist in the role of the divine bringer of new life to the human and natural worlds.

G. J. Weinberger (essay date Summer 1988)

SOURCE: "Who Is Arnold Friend? The Other Self in Joyce Carol Oates's 'Where Are You Going, Where Have You Been?,'" in *American Imago*, Vol. 45, No. 1, Summer, 1988, pp. 205-15.

[*In the following essay, Weinberger analyzes the* doppelgänger *motif in "Where Are You Going, Where Have You Been?," highlighting its implications about violence and sexuality.*]

When Connie faces Arnold Friend, she faces her other self, in Oates's treatment of the *Doppelgänger* motif, which informs such well-known works as Poe's "William Wilson," Melville's "Bartleby the Scrivener," Crane's "The Bride Comes to Yellow Sky," and Conrad's "The Secret Sharer," among many others. The principal outward difference between these and Oates's version, Connie's *alter ego* being of the opposite sex and extremely threatening, results from Arnold Friend's representing not only a protagonist's mythic, irrational side (one of several characteristics he shares with his literary forerunners), but also a cluster of insights into the violence and sexuality of adulthood. His indeterminate age, somewhere between eighteen and thirty, emphasizes the transition which Connie must undergo, one reflected in the future-past duality inherent in the title of the story.

We first see Connie at home, an ordinary middle-class setting, complete with a mother who runs the household and nags, an older "maiden" sister, and an uninvolved father who appears only to work, eat, read the newspaper, and sleep. Together, these people drive away, out of the story, to a conventional Sunday barbecue. Connie's father, like her friend's father who chauffeurs the girls to the shopping plaza, "never bothered to ask what they had done." The father's lack of involvement allows Connie a relative degree of freedom. No one ever asks, "Where are you going, Where have you been?"

The house and the domestic environment represent the known, the rationally apprehensible, much like the law in "Bartleby." Within this environment, Connie is a conventional adolescent girl. She is vain and messy, and bears herself differently at home and abroad. She and her mother share the occasional good moment as a reprieve from the usual arguments, which also serve to set limits for Connie. She may tell a fib here and there but she gets home shortly after 11 P.M. Connie is additionally controlled by her mother's constantly comparing her to her sister June and by June's working at her high school. But while she may have little power at home, Connie certainly does have some—over boys. This too is conventional, especially in view of the relative maturation of the sexes, and represents her first tentative experiments with adulthood. Connie is on the threshold: her hair and her walk both attract attention and she is willing to assume risks, "ducking fast across the busy road" to the hamburger drive-in "where the older kids hung out." On the night Connie meets Eddie, she and her friend run across the highway "breathless with daring," to a world of bright lights and music.

There is popular music everywhere in this story. Music is the medium through which adolescents attempt to derive the meaning of life and it is in a music-induced trance-like state that Connie later sees Arnold Friend. Music takes on an almost religious significance—"the music that made everything so good: the music was always in the background, like music at a church service; it was something to depend upon"—and Wegs [in *Journal of Narrative Technique* 5 (1975)] sees a grotesque religious parody in the entire drive-in episode. But Bob Dylan, to whom the story is dedicated, and whom Urbanski [in *Studies in Short Fiction* 15 (1978)] acknowledges as one "who contributed to making music almost religious in dimension among the youth," does not write typically adolescent music. His work often deals with types of evil ("Blowin' in the Wind," "The Masters of War"), sexuality ("Lay Lady Lay"), or change ("The Times They Are a' Changing"). Thematically, then, the music points at the serious world beyond adolescence, even if the drive-in crowd listens merely to amplified sound. In its loudness, accompanied by bright lights, it has elements of orgiastic abandon. After the drive-in episode, when she is back at the plaza, amid shops (symbols of commerce, of order), Connie is too far away to hear the music.

The function of the drive-in episode is not limited to introducing the music and bright lights and the almost cinematic effect of unreality which results. More important is Connie's seeing the shaggy-haired boy who later reappears as Arnold Friend, just as the vacuous smile of the hamburger boy atop the bottle-shaped drive-in building reappears as Arnold Friend's dangerous smile. The black-haired boy is merely a boy uttering an adolescent, would-be *macho* remark, but he provides the impetus to the rest of the story, involving Connie's trance, wherein she has her vision of the evil and often irrational world of adulthood to which she crosses over. To put it in R. D. Laing's terms, her "earliest phantasies are experienced in sensations: later, they take the form of plastic images and dramatic representations."

Significantly, when the boy in the golden car tells Connie, "Gonna get you, baby," Eddie, Connie's companion, does not notice. Eddie's being presented as an individual promising no particularly perceptive gifts—"He sat backwards on his stool, turning himself jerkily around in semi-circles and then stopping and turning again, and after a while he asked Connie if she would like something to eat"—is important because it leaves Connie as the only person who notices the boy and hears his remark; this accords with the element of private vision shared by many protagonists in *Doppelgänger* stories. Thus, for instance, William Wilson is surprised that the officials at his school remain unaware of his double's designs; the lawyer in "Bartleby" must consult his assistants to validate his perceptions of his recalcitrant copyist; and Conrad's captain wonders if Leggatt is visible only to him.

Arnold Friend does not exist—which makes him no less "real," since "phantasy is a mode of experience" (Laing). "He" is simply Connie's projected other self, depicted in Oates's way, with a heavy emphasis on evil, violence, and the threat of rape (if not death) which Connie must acknowledge. As Arnold Friend tells her, "This is your day set aside for a ride with me and you know it." The cost of refusal is failure to attain adulthood, as illustrated by the twenty-four-year-old June who works as a school secretary, still lives at home, and who obediently, and inappropriately dressed, goes to the family barbecue. To warn Connie against such a refusal is the function of Ellie Oscar. With his radio and sunglasses, and his readiness to employ violence, Ellie is an extension of Arnold Friend, but he also represents the alternative to him. His clothes, for example, and his general vapidity attest to a forty-year-old perpetual adolescence which is underscored by the sexlessness of his neuter name. His status is illustrated by Arnold Friend's telling Connie that

Ellie will sit in the back seat during their ride, in the role of child *vis-à-vis* the two "adults." Ellie apparently understands only when spoken to in adolescent clichés. In the extraordinary paragraph near the end of the story, when Arnold tells him off with an extensive series of clichés, there appears a further purpose: a kind of exorcism of these phrases for the benefit of Connie, who is leaving behind the world where they are commonly heard.

Connie's refusal to participate in the family barbecue shows her growing sense of power and independence and, more important, leaves her at home alone, a situation emphasized by her mother's "Stay home alone then." Of course, it also leaves her more vulnerable: " . . . at adolescence we observe relative ego weakness due to the intensification of the drives, as well as absolute ego weakness due to the adolescent rejection of parental ego support" (Blos, *The Adolescent Passage* [1979]). The daydreams, the music, and all the rest follow—

> Connie sat with her eyes closed in the sun, dreaming and dazed with the warmth about her as if this were a kind of love, the caresses of love, and her mind slipped over onto thoughts of the boy she had been with the night before and how nice he had been, how sweet it always was, not the way someone like June would suppose but sweet, gentle, the way it was in movies and promised in songs; and when she opened her eyes she hardly knew where she was, the back yard ran off into the weeds and a fence-like line of trees and behind it the sky was perfectly blue and still. The asbestos "ranch house" that was now three years old startled her—it looked small. She shook her head as if to get awake.

Then, after turning on the radio, "to drown out the quiet," and paying close attention to the music, as instructed by the disc jockey, she

> bathed in a glow of slow-pulsed joy that seemed to rise mysteriously out of the music itself and lay languidly about the airless little room, breathed in and breathed out with each gentle rise and fall of her chest.

Her entry into her trance—or her dream—is followed immediately by the car coming up the driveway.

The ambiguity of the passage where Connie enters her trance, which leaves room for other interpretations of this story (such as Wegs's and Urbanski's), is strongly reminiscent of the questions Hawthorne leaves us with regarding the consciousness of Young Goodman Brown in the forest. More important, however, is that Connie is alone, a prerequisite for facing one's other self. Thus, William Wilson and his double speak to each other only when they are alone together; the lawyer ensconces Bartleby on his side of the folding doors in his office; the captain takes the unusual step of going on watch and is therefore alone to receive Leggatt; and Crane's Potter, who in the company of his new bride comes upon the rampaging Scratchy Wilson, "exhibited an instinct to at once loosen his arm from the woman's grip."

The creation of Arnold Friend in Connie's mind is made possible by her reaching the appropriate time in her life. In this regard, Arnold Friend's name—"a friend"—as a common slang expression for the menstrual period, supports the theme of impending adulthood. Arnold's form, as noted earlier, is borrowed from the shaggy-haired boy in the drive-in; however, unlike the boys she knows, Arnold Friend, who is not a boy, is beyond Connie's control, although, because of his "source," he looks conventional enough:

> She recognized most things about him, the tight jeans that showed his thighs and buttocks and the greasy leather boots and the tight shirt, and even that slippery friendly smile of his, that sleepy dreamy smile that all the boys used to get across ideas they didn't want to put into words.

The adolescent boy's conventionally displayed sexuality here is serious beyond anything in Connie's prior experience. She recognizes no pattern: " . . . all these things did not come together." Arnold Friend does not stop at slippery smiles. He is all too willing to put the matter into words: and, unlike Bartleby, Scratchy Wilson, or Leggatt, he is not affected by the world of order. As Connie soon learns, he is beyond the control of police or parents.

Arnold is unable to enter the house which represents Connie's old environment as well as order, like the shops at the plaza, but only for as long as Connie does not attempt to use the telephone. Besides, he does not have to enter: "I ain't made plans for coming in that house where I don't belong but just for you to come out to me, the way you should." In other words, Connie is expected to step into adulthood voluntarily. Certainly, her merely material home (she has lived in it only during her adolescence, between the ages of twelve and fifteen) is no match for the forces of adulthood: "I mean, anybody can break through a screen door and glass and wood and iron or anything else if he needs to, anybody at all, and specially Arnold Friend."

The kinship between this "friend" and Connie—her name signifies constancy to the process of growth to adulthood—is actually established early in the story. The curious phrasing of Connie's mother's chiding her daughter, "Stop gawking at yourself. Who are you?", is directly related to Connie's first words to Arnold: "Who the hell do you think you are?"; both depict attempts to discover an emerging or new identity, in acknowledgment that adolescence "is essentially a time of personal discovery." Likewise, Connie's wishing her mother dead and her telling friends that her mother sometimes makes her want to throw up, represents not only conventional adolescent jargon and escapism, but also her preparing to leave her childhood (and her dependence on her mother) behind. Arnold Friend's threat later in the story that her family may be harmed reflects her adolescent hostility and symbolizes her unconscious knowledge that in her passage to adulthood the old ties must become as dead for her. This is underlined shortly thereafter in Connie's realization, "I'm not going to see my mother again. . . . I'm not going to sleep in my bed again."

Connie's appearance early on also foreshadows her transition from adolescence to adulthood: "She wore a pull-over jersey blouse that looked one way when she was at home and another way when she was away from home. Everything about her had two sides to it, one for home and one for everywhere that was not home. . . ." Moreover, her "trashy daydreams" which her mother complains about hail from a realm of feeling and darkness with which Connie is as yet unacquainted:

> But all the boys fell back and dissolved into a single face that was not even a face but an idea, a feeling, mixed up with the urgent insistent pounding of the music and the humid night air of July. Connie's mother kept dragging her back to the daylight by finding things for her to do. . . .

In a similar passage, when Connie agrees to spend the evening with Eddie, she goes with him, "her face gleaming with a joy that had nothing to do with Eddie or even this place; it might have been the music."

The "tiny metallic world" of Arnold Friend's sunglasses which mirror everything in miniature, and in which Connie sees her blouse reflected, is related to the mirror at the end of "William Wilson" and to the place in "The Secret Sharer" where the captain and Leggatt rest on opposite ends of the skylight, creating a mirror image of each other. At first inscrutable, Arnold Friend without his sunglasses is spectral, qualities designed to heighten the sense of unreality—"he came from nowhere and belonged nowhere" (like Bartleby)—which in turn is supported by references to the possibility of his wearing a wig and by our being told unequivocally that "His whole face was a mask."

Because Connie is not an initiate into the secrets of the world which Arnold Friend represents, she appears briefly unable to read what is clearly written on his car: his name, the numerological "secret code," and, around a dent on the left rear fender, "DONE BY A CRAZY WOMAN DRIVER." This last inscription is important because it hints at the essentially anti-woman attitude of the adult world. Women are not, and are not allowed to be, in control. They are its quintessential victims, even if the violence is occasionally masked. As Arnold Friend tells Connie, "I am always nice at first, the first time"; but later, when she is unable to call her mother, Connie "felt her breath jerking back and forth in her lungs as if it were something Arnold Friend were stabbing her with again and again with no tenderness." When she looks at the car again, she notices on the front fender the inscription "MAN THE FLYING SAUCERS," an obsolete adolescent expression, clearly pointing to Connie's leaving the world she has known. Significantly, she looks at the inscription "for a while as if the words meant something to her that she did not yet know."

Connie's formal initiation begins when Arnold Friend draws his X-sign in her direction, at which moment the music from inside the house and from the car blend together. As the encounter proceeds, it becomes more and more apparent that Arnold exists only in Connie's imagination. She never turns down his invitation to go for a ride: she gives no answer the first time and says "I don't know" the second. At first, Arnold appears to be an inch or two taller than Connie, but it becomes evident that later that they are of equal height. He knows everything about Connie—her name, her friends' names, who she was with the night before, where her family is, what they are wearing, what they are doing—because he is she. Thus, while it is tempting to think of Arnold Friend as Satan, unable to cross the threshold uninvited, Connie is actually face to face with a part of herself. Potential adulthood has always been part of Connie's make-up, as it is of every adolescent: Arnold Friend tells her, "Sure you saw me before. . . . You just don't remember," and, "I know everybody." After the blending of the music, and after his voice, orchestrated by Connie, has, in fact, become the voice of the disc jockey, she becomes dizzy, sees him in a blur, and "had the idea that he had driven up the driveway all right but had come from nowhere before that and belonged nowhere and that everything about him and even about the music that was so familiar to her was only half real."

Arnold Friend's voice, at various times monotone, lilting, or chanting, is related to music; and like music, it serves to link adolescent pop culture in general with the threatening adult world. Thus, when he asks here, "Don't you know who I am?" she hears him sound like "a hero in a movie" speaking too loudly. Soon after, when Connie has begun to accept the inevitability of her change of world, he uses "a gentle-loud voice that was like a stage voice" to tell her, "This place you are now—inside your daddy's house—is nothing but a cardboard box I can knock down any time. You know that and always did know it."

This decisive insight on Connie's part—since she *is* Arnold Friend—follows closely Arnold's telling her "It's all over for

you here," her necessarily fruitless attempt to cry out for and phone her mother—what could she possibly say to her?—and her dawning awareness: " . . . deep inside her brain was something like a pinpoint of light that kept going and would not let her relax." The change is immediate—when Arnold Friend runs his fingernail down the screen the noise does not make Connie shiver, "as it would have the day before"—and leads to Arnold's penultimate voice:

> His words were not angry but only part of an incantation. The incantation was kindly. "Now, come out through the kitchen to me, honey, and let's see a smile, try it, you're a brave, sweet little girl and now they're eating corn and hot dogs cooked to bursting over an outdoor fire, and they don't know one thing about you and never did and honey, you're better than them because not a one of them would have done this for you."

Realizing then, if only in a hazy way, that each person must undergo the rites of passage alone, with only one's other self to help, Connie, brushing the hair out of her eyes in order to see more clearly, crosses the threshold and goes out into the sunlight, into the vast, threatening adult world. The last paragraph in the story reiterates the uncaring nature of the world. As soon as it becomes apparent that Connie is leaving the house, Arnold Friend falls back on a cliché, "My sweet little blue-eyed girl," mouthing it with "a half-sung sigh that had nothing to do with her brown eyes."

Gerald Early (essay date Fall 1988)

SOURCE: "The Grace of Slaughter: A Review-Essay of Joyce Carol Oates's *On Boxing*," in *The Iowa Review*, Vol. 18, No. 3, Fall, 1988, pp. 173-86.

[*In the essay below, Early meditates on the themes of* On Boxing *in literary and critical contexts, contrasting the spectacle of boxing with wrestling.*]

> *Boxing ain't the noblest of the arts. . . .*
>   —middleweight champion Harry Greb, whose loss to Tiger Flowers in 1926 permitted the first black ever to hold the middleweight title

> *God didn't make the chin to be punched.*
>   —Ray Arcel, boxing trainer who numbered among his students the legendary Roberto Duran

> *At that time [Georges] Carpentier was only 14½ years old and I, 21 years old. So his first fight was with Georges Salmon at the Cafe de Paris, Maison*

Laffitte, and he was making good until the 11th round then he blew up. That was really because he was inexperienced on the square circle. . . . but again he was knocked down several times after the 10th round so I said to Deschamps [Carpentier's manager] to stop it. He said No. So I jumped into the ring and stopped it, picking little Georges up in my arms and took him to his corner amidst the cheers of the crowd. He was always game to the toes.

—Black American fighter Bob Scanlon recounting the beginning of his friendship with French champion Georges Carpentier

Part One: "THE PANTING PURSUIT OF DANGER . . ."

I

Joyce Carol Oates's **On Boxing** seems a sort of culmination or at least a reexamination of several ideas she expressed in her early novel, **With Shuddering Fall** (1964). That book dealt with a character named Shar Rule (the name itself speaks volumes), who is a professional racing car driver. The similarity between a jockey, a boxer, a racing car driver, and a bull fighter regarding the nature of their individuality, the brinkmanship of their sadistic/masochistic occupations, the charged, exaggerated mythic version of their masculinity and the troubling and troubled voyeurism they incite is surely clear enough and is precisely what attracts Oates to athletics: wrath, the ambivalent, oxymoronic iconography of masculine toughness as male suffering, and the pure anxiety inherent in the ritual of male slaughter. When she wrote passages like these:

Max could feel the beauty of Shar's experience in his imagination, while Shar felt it in his very body. At a certain point the speed became his body: he was one with it.

From time to time, he had toyed with the idea that spectators did not really come to see drivers be killed, as most people thought, nor did they come— as Max told him—because they wanted to share in the skill and triumph, they came to share the speed, the danger, the occasional deaths—with exultation, maybe, but with something more than that—to force themselves into the men who represented them down on the track. . . . they gave up their identities to risk violence, but they were always cheated because the violence, when it came, could not touch them. (ellipsis mine)

One can see it is not a very far distance for her to travel to this closure:

One of the paradoxes of boxing is that the viewer inhabits a consciousness so very different from that of the boxer as to suggest a counter-world. "Free" will, "sanity," "rationality"—our characteristic modes of consciousness—are irrelevant, if not detrimental, to boxing in its most extraordinary moments. Even as he disrobes himself ceremonially in the ring the great boxer must disrobe himself of both reason and instinct's caution as he prepares to fight.

Boxing and auto-racing are not simply unintelligible; they are anti-intelligible, activities akin to vision quests on the part of the men who participate in them. (" . . . [boxing is] obliquely akin to those severe religions in which the individual is both 'free' and 'determined' . . . " Oates writes.) They wish to find their spiritual selves by being in an activity that is relentlessly, ruthlessly physical but they wish to prove their goodness (i.e. their worth) in an activity that is so self-centered yet so self-annihilating that it can only be considered evil. George S. Bernard, a Catholic priest, argues that very point—the iniquity of being a boxer—in his *The Morality of Boxing,* and it seems a reasonable assertion because boxing poses, on a metaphysical level, such an uncomplex ethical proposition: beat your opponent until you have weakened him and then, when he is weak and helpless, beat him all the more fiercely in a contrived contest of fictive grievances that prides itself on being without mercy. The spectators are not simply a world apart, they are a morality apart; for the sports of boxing and auto-racing turn morality on its head by permitting acts to take place that are so dangerous (high-speed racing and hitting another without malice and not in self-defense) that they are banned outside of certain sacred spaces. It is not simply the thrill of "taboo breaking," as Oates states in **On Boxing,** that makes boxing attractive; it is the fact that the audience recognizes boxing as an attack, a frontal assault upon the very nature of taboo. The death of one of the participants is often wished so that the harsh justice of the taboo itself is made not intelligible but less a cause of distress, more rich as a result of having been empowered by human sacrifice. So death hovers near a certain masculine drama that for the audience may make death frightening but will also make it alluring, electric because it hovers so close to a pointless, intelligible, nearly existential, and very simple, even vulgar excellence. As another character in **With Shuddering Fall** expresses himself:

Why should anything be safe? . . . Look at them all, Shar and the other drivers—their hands all blisters and eyes burnt, cars about ready to explode or fall apart—wheels, axles, anything—but they love it all the way! A man puts in years out on the track—in ten minutes he gets that much living out of it. (ellipsis mine)

And in the later book:

> If boxing is a sport it is the most tragic of all sports because more than any other human activity it consumes the very excellence it displays—its drama is this very consumption. . . . the punishment—to the body, the brain, the spirit—a man must endure to become even a moderately good boxer is inconceivable to most of us whose idea of personal risk is largely ego-related or emotional. (ellipsis mine)

Shar, like a tragic young boxer, dies young, in a literal flame of glory (his car crashes in his attempt to go too fast), consumed by the very instrument that made him great. What is it in sport generally that appeals but that universal morbidity of the instant tragedy of youth used up? (Even in less dangerous sports such as baseball one feels a great loss when a pitcher like Tom Seaver retires, the golden arm that once brought him fame now all used up by the very act, the very motion that the arm used to achieve its fame in the first place, "the unnatural act," as former Oakland A's pitcher Mike Norris called it. One wonders if it is only in sex and athletics that we demand the "unnatural act" as a display of skill and a presentation of excitation.) "All athletes age rapidly but none so rapidly and so visibly as the boxer," writes Oates. Yet their rapid aging is very much akin to those illicit and disreputable members of society to whom they are constantly compared: prostitutes. And while all athletes are viewed with a certain distinct distrust and disdain which, I think, arises from the immense and intense adulation they generate, no athlete is held quite as lowly as the boxer. British novelist and former fighter Johnny Morgan, in *The Square Jungle,* constantly makes the analogy between boxers and whores. And in Roman times, as historian Michael Grant points out, gladiators were placed in the same class as women for hire. To sell one's body in performance in order to give pleasure to others ultimately saps the body, perhaps because the body's integrity has been denied. Perhaps the body is simply stupefied by its inability to be thrilled by the thrilling anymore.

At one point in the early novel, after a race Shar wins by performing a maneuver which kills another driver, two characters shout at each other: "Shar is filled with life!" "Shar is filled with death!" and perhaps it is this essential ambiguity which surrounds the prizefighter as much as it does the racing car driver that Oates finds so absorbing: Is he filled with life, or is he an angel of death, he who by his life says that life is impossible, that only the pursuit of death is real?

II

There is no sport that, like [boxing], promotes the spirit of aggression in the same measure, demands

determination quick as lightning, educates the body for steel-like versatility. If two young people fight out a difference of opinion with their fists, it is no more brutal than if they do so with a piece of ground iron. . . . But above all, the young and healthy boy has to learn to be beaten.
—Adolf Hitler

Hitler liked boxing because it resisted rationality, because its participants were forced to resist rationality. Perhaps that is why many writers have been attracted to it as well (although this difference must be understood: that Hitler worshipped boxing for its psychotic potential in much the same way a murderer worships the purity of his mayhem; Hitler's love of boxing was simply the display of a very depraved infantile taste but it should serve as a sufficient warning to all who find boxing a seduction). Unlike football, basketball, and especially baseball, boxing cannot be understood through numbers. Its statistics mean nothing; a boxer's record tells no story of the achievements of a career. As Robert Coover showed in his brilliant baseball novel, *The Universal Baseball Association, Inc., J. Henry Waugh, Prop.,* baseball's story can be unfolded through the maze of the purity of its mathematics. Boxing's change of rules in the late nineteenth century, which changed it from being a bareknuckle sport of indeterminate length to a gloved sport of timed rounds and rest periods and eventually of bouts of a finite length, was the only concession that boxing made to rationality, to the science and technology of the day. Those changes made boxing more palatable to modern audiences by making it more systematic and schematic but only better to exemplify and symbolize the irrationality of the Spenserian struggle of existence. Boxing can only be understood through story: the oral tradition of eyewitnesses or the journalistic narratives of reporters. It is a misnomer to call boxing a "science." Boxing does not seek knowing, a truth in its action. It does not seek to explain nature in the way baseball and football can and do. It is, in fact, an action that is meant to be nature itself. Boxing is always seeking its text (like Ishmael Reed's "jes grew") and the ambiguity of the magnitude of its tales. Boxing is anti-science. It is our ancient epic sung to honor a misty past of slaves and warrior-kings and the personification of brute force.

Oates wishes to do for boxing and the boxer what [Roland] Barthes says the wrestler himself does for wrestling and for himself . . . make boxing an intelligible spectacle.

—*Gerald Early*

There is an obvious similarity between Oates's *On Boxing* and Roland Barthes's famous essay, "The World of Wrestling," indeed, a series of similarities of such a strong nature that one might say that Barthes's essay begat Oates's book, not simply inspired it, but actually provided the method and language to make it possible. To say this is to pay tribute to Oates's work, to its savvy and cunning, by acknowledging that it can be placed side-by-side with Barthes's paradigmatic essay. Oates's book is the first on the sport of boxing (and there have been many written of various quality) which has, consciously I believe, emulated Barthes or a Barthes-like approach: the photos, which comment on and supplement the text without pulling the reader into the worlds of biography or history, into individual personalities or social movements, are certainly something that Barthes would have done had he written a book on boxing. The photos suggest a pure world of boxing inhabited only by boxers. " . . . boxing is not a metaphor for life but a unique, closed, self-referential world . . . " writes Oates. Naturally, in one sense, this is a fiction: for the boxer's world is something quite else than a world of himself and others like him or simply the world of his exploits (and to talk of a boxer occupying a "world" brings to mind the question Amiri Baraka asked many years ago about the title of a jazz musician's album; does the boxer really have a world or does he simply occupy a very traditional and related room in a masculine complex? Is he next door to the gloried discipline of the marine or perhaps the psychosis of the street corner gang leader?) Oates so powerfully evokes this world, this fiction, that the work does not explicate or justify boxing in the end but actually *summons* it forth. Oates wishes to do for boxing and the boxer what [Roland] Barthes says the wrestler himself does for wrestling and for himself (which may explain why there have been fewer books written on professional wrestling than on professional boxing): make boxing an intelligible spectacle. In this regard, Oates is the true deconstructionist; Barthes is simply a reporter describing a sport that deconstructs itself. Of course, boxing can be deconstructed like wrestling, like any combat sport (when will someone tackle Bruce Lee and Mas Oyama's *This is Karate*?); indeed, boxing is a sport that makes its need and its enticement to be deconstructed, to be decoded in some wizardly fashion, so obvious as to be nearly one of its conceits. "That no other sport can elicit such *theoretical* anxiety," writes Oates, "lies at the heart of boxing's fascination for the writer" (emphasis hers).

Barthes writes (in one of the few instances in his essay that he mentions boxing) that "a boxing-match is a story which is constructed before the eyes of the spectator." Oates writes: "Each boxing match is a story—a unique and highly condensed drama without words." Barthes argues that "wrestling is the spectacle of excess," that is, in fact, its virtue. Oates says that boxing is excess because it violates the taboo against violence, that as a public spectacle "it is akin to pornography" (pornographic films and stage acts I assume she means), which, I might add, means that it is, for Oates, one of the theaters in a complex of entertainments of excess. But it is the naturalism of pornography and boxing that in some sense makes them inferior to professional wrestling as excess. As Barthes writes: "[In wrestling] it no longer matters whether the passion is genuine or not. What the public wants is the image of passion, not passion itself." It is the literalness of boxing and pornography that makes them imperfect because it is that literalness, which is so much, in one sense, the expression of the innocence of the child's literalness turned to the willful immorality of the adult's reductionism, that ultimately deadens the senses. Real blood generously displayed reduces the ability to be awed by the sight of blood just as real sex copiously produced reduces the ability to appreciate the act of sex. It is this naturalism that tends to reduce every fight to being exactly every other fight that boxing as a social phenomenon tries to overcome by insisting that the fighter become a personality. (Naturalism is the horror of anonymity in modern society.) Boxing is, like wrestling, about showmanship. And the greatest showman and boxer in the history of the sport was Muhammad Ali, who made fights something other than what they were; he made them, for both the blacks and whites who watched them, the metaphors they wished the fights to be, principally the battle of good against evil. It is not an accident that boxing's greatest showman was heavily influenced by a professional wrestler, Gorgeous George. Ali made boxing deal with the one moral issue that fascinates Americans: is a black man good or evil, which is the same as asking if he is real or not? Oates's and Barthes's discussions reach a certain critical juncture when they discuss almost in complementary fashion the very essence of sport and naturalistic expression. First, Barthes:

> Wrestling is the only sport which gives such an externalized image of torture. But here again, only the image is involved in the game, and the spectator does not wish for the actual suffering of the contestant; he only enjoys the perfection of an iconography.

And Oates responds:

> Unlike pornography (and professional wrestling) boxing is altogether real: the blood shed, the damage suffered, the pain (usually suppressed or sublimated) are unfeigned. Not for hemophobics, boxing is a sport in which blood becomes quickly irrelevant. The experienced viewer understands that a boxer's bleeding face is probably the least of his worries.

Ali, like the good wrestler, made the audience care about his injuries: first, the issue of whether he could stand pain when he was unpopular and then, later, the issue of whether he was absorbing too much pain when he was popular. Ali made the moral relevance of injuries an issue, perhaps the only fighter in the history of the sport to do so without having to die in the ring. One remembers his fight with Bob Foster because it was the first time he was ever cut across the brow in the ring. The first Norton bout stands out because he suffered a broken jaw, the first Frazier fight because he was knocked down. It is the very fact that professional wrestling does not demand the realism of boxing that makes it a protest against violence. Showing violence as fakery, as parody, as comedy reveals wrestling's inner wish to say that violence is utterly impossible as a real act, utterly unbearable. Of course, wrestling is only this protest *theoretically* and in actual fact a good many wrestlers are injured every year. Even faked violence can be dangerous which makes the contemplation of real violence all the more frightening. Finally, Barthes argues that "in wrestling . . . Defeat is not a conventional sign, abandoned as soon as it is understood; it is not an outcome, but quite the contrary, it is a duration, a display, it takes up the ancient myths of public Suffering and Humiliation." And Oates makes nearly an identical observation about boxing: "Boxing is about being hit rather than it is about hitting, just as it is about feeling pain, if not devastating psychological paralysis, more than it is about winning." What is interesting here is that both assert that boxing and wrestling, symbolic violence and naturalistic violence, are not really competitive ventures in the sense that we normally think professional sport is: they are both elaborate statements about withstanding, not necessarily to overcome, but simply for the reality of enduring. Boxing and wrestling, we learn from Oates and Barthes, are the only activities in modern American and European societies that give us the enactment, the drama of shame without guilt.

Despite being a text that I think in many challenging ways carries on a dialogue with Barthes's essay, *On Boxing* occupies its own space. It is, to be sure, not the first non-fiction book on the sport to be written by a prominent literary person (although it is the first, to my knowledge, to have been written by a woman). But it is clearly not intended to present the author as George Plimpton (*Shadow-Box*): the bumbling, well-meaning journalist who cannot get out of the way of the stage; nor is it in the guise of Norman Mailer (*The Fight* and other works), the hot male predator, haunted by Hemingway, trying desperately to make the act of writing a book a blood sport. The book is neither bumbling innocence, sham egoism, nor hot competitive drive. The book is, at last, not Liebling (*The Sweet Science*), the worldly-wise intellectual in the low-life jungle. It does not slum or try to show boxing as being picturesque. It celebrates neither inadvertence nor its own prowess. *On Boxing* is a cool book. It is a book about the audience, about the voyeur and what he or she sees at a boxing match and how he or she is, in effect, what he or she sees.

During the past two or three years, quite a few books on box-

ing have been published, including the autobiographies of Angelo Dundee (his first) and Jake LaMotta (his second), biographies of Joe Louis, Jack Johnson, and Sugar Ray Leonard, a history of bareknuckle prizefighting in America, and an inside look at boxing as a business. It is not my contention that Oates's book is the best of the lot. Which book is the best has a great deal to do with what the reader wishes to know about boxing and the format he or she finds most stimulating. I do believe that *On Boxing* is a quite sophisticated book, possibly one of the most sophisticated books to have been published on the sport. It is the most critically alert.

Part Two: " . . . IS THE PURSUIT OF LIFE ITSELF."

III

To be a man, the male must be able to face the threat of masculinity within himself by facing it in others like himself.
—Walter Ong

You no longer have to come from the ghetto to know how to fight. People with a good upbringing are now learning to box. They're looking at it as an art, rather than as a kill-or-be-killed type of thing.
—Michael Olajide, middleweight contender

Any man with a good trade isn't about to get knocked on his butt to make a dollar.
—boxing promoter Chris Dundee

"The referee makes boxing possible." This statement alone may be worth the price of admission, the price of the book. There are, in essence, two types of statements in *On Boxing*: those like the above that are brilliant and unquestionable and those like the following: "[Boxing] is the only human activity in which rage can be transposed without equivocation into art," which are brilliant but debatable. Oates's accomplished analysis of the role of the referee explains not only why a fight is bearable but why a fight is actually taking place. The fight is an act of hope, a plea that warring sides, through the active presence of a disinterested but compassionate non-combatant, can be reconciled not only to each other but to the restless, self-destructive nature within ourselves. Prizefighting is about man's preoccupation with trying to live in an adversarial Eden, a world that loves and hates him, made by a God that both comforts and ignores. As Oates writes: " . . . love commingled with hate is more powerful than love. Or hate." With the presence of the referee, modern prizefighting is the irrationality of pure force confronting the humane conscience of the modern world.

The second quotation is a bit problematic; the rage in boxing, after all, is not genuine but rather fictive, and the viewer hardly knows its source or its objective. The boxer himself may not know either. It is the fact that rage in boxing is completely fake in the enactment of the contest itself that makes this statement troublesome. Boxing seems to say that the articulation of real rage in our society is utterly impossible unless, of course, it is utterly pointless which is what the contrivance of the boxing match means. The true art form of rage is the duel of which boxing is the modern rationalization: why fight to the death for honor when one can fight to the maiming for money? And suddenly the burden of masculine expendability as sport and performance fell upon the lower classes. The possible art forms of rage (with equivocation) are revolution or rebellion which are about the only worthwhile vessels for the obsessions of the poor. Of course, boxing has always been popular—television ratings tell us that—but cover articles such as the one in the British fashion magazine, *The Face,* and Oates's own piece on Bellows's boxing pictures in *Art and Antiques* lead us to believe that it is fashionable (in other words, hip) in the way that Michael Olajide says it is, although few middle-class persons in their right minds are going to perform such a sport for a living. And if it is fashionable, can the rage (pun intended) possibly be real? On the whole, **On Boxing** is a series of tableaus that offers perhaps some of the most stunning surfaces imaginable about boxing. There are penetrating discussions on machismo, on boxing as the sport that is not a sport, on time and the prize ring.

But while I find Oates's book impressive, it does have its weaknesses. The section on writers and prizefighting, for instance, does not mention one black writer. And it must be remembered that blacks have had an enormous influence on American popular culture through the sport of prizefighting. To be sure, no major black writer has written a full-length treatise, fiction or non-fiction, on boxing, but there have been several important essays produced by the likes of Amiri Baraka, Eldridge Cleaver, Richard Wright, Jervis Anderson, Larry Neal, and others. Also, two of the most important scenes in all of American literature which involve fights were written by blacks: Frederick Douglass's fight with Covey, the slavebreaker, in the 1845 edition of Douglass's *Narrative,* and the battle royal scene in Ralph Ellison's *Invisible Man.* It would have been of some interest to hear what Oates had to say about them. Such a discussion would have given statements like "the history of boxing—of fighting—in America is very much one with the history of the black man in America," a bit more validity.

Generally, the writing about race is the least persuasive in the book and might have been jettisoned without hurting the work as a whole. Ethnicity and boxing, ethnicity and American sports is simply too complex a topic to be handled well in the short space that Oates gives herself. I think her refusal to see boxing as a metaphor hurts her discussion here as well. At some point in American social and political his-

tory Jack Johnson, Joe Louis, and Muhammad Ali (the three most important blacks of the twentieth century) ceased to be men in the American mind (both black and white), they even ceased to be fighters in the ordinary sense and became something quite legendary but also something specifically inhuman. Once blacks became a force in boxing, the sport automatically became a metaphor. Indeed, what is race in America but the Melvillian doubloon hammered in our consciousness that bedevils us endlessly and turns anything it shines upon into a metaphor as well.

Some minor quarrels: 1) Her statement that "the bare knuckle era . . . was far less dangerous for fighters" is simply not true. Fewer punches were thrown under London Prize Ring Rules but the wrestling, cross buttocks, gouging, spiking, scratching, biting, pulling, and poking left the old bruisers more disfigured than modern fighters usually are. Besides, it must be remembered that audiences in the eighteenth and nineteenth centuries were a good deal more bloodthirsty than audiences today (after all, for a good part of their history, bareknucklers had to compete against public executions as a form of popular entertainment), the fights were a great deal longer, and medical care for injured fighters was quite primitive, to say the least. 2) Her assertion that "boxing is contrary to nature" does not take into account the fact that virtually *all* sports are contrary to nature. Boxing is not special in this regard: running a 26-mile marathon, balancing oneself on an elevated balance beam, or not flinching while trying to hit a 95-mph fastball are all acts that are contrary to nature. 3) "Baseball, football, basketball—these quintessentially American pastimes are recognizably sports because they involve play; they are games. One *plays* football, one doesn't *play* boxing," writes Oates (emphasis hers). There are two responses to this: on the one hand, certain sports, like football, have a certain limited *playing* sphere. Professional football player Curtis Greer put it this way in explaining why he chooses to continue to play despite a bad knee: "It's not like baseball, basketball, golf, or tennis, a sport that you can continue as a recreation once you retire. When you leave football, you just can't go up to the rec center and get into a game." So the play element in all sports cannot be characterized in the same way. Moreover, there are several different types of boxing: sparring, exhibition matches, as well as competitive fighting for titles and the like. Some non-serious boxing does involve an element of play. Sometimes sparring is serious and sometimes there are other things going on. Exhibition matches are almost never serious. So to say that one cannot play boxing is not quite true; it depends on how competitive the participants wish the bout to be and precisely what is at stake. I remember as a child a game played among black boys called "slap-to-the-head" in which both participants, laughing most of the time, would, with open hands, cuff each other lightly on the head to see who had the fastest hands. It seemed a more physical demonstration of "the dozens," for it was considered in quite bad form

("You're nothing but a chump!") if one got angry at being shown up at this. Yet it was a purposeful display of one's boxing abilities.

Her criticism of the arguments for the abolition of boxing are sometimes telling but ultimately not as compelling as other parts of the book. Doubtless, no sport compromises the humanity of its participants as much as boxing and it is hard, in the end, to overcome the frightening and bitter impact of that truth. Oates's position, if I might be so bold as to attempt a summary, is that of distressed ambivalence about boxing as a sort of tragic romantic rite of male expendability, a position that I have a great deal of sympathy for as I once occupied it myself. But, finally, I believe it a bit too disingenuous, too self-consciously self-defensive, a strategically convenient stalking ground. There is a tendency, when one occupies this position, to assume that the whole business of boxing, to borrow Richard D. Altick's words, will cause "a delicious *frisson* rather than a shudder." She likens the arguments concerning the existence of boxing to those over the morality of abortion, an apt analogy but an incomplete one, for the arguments about boxing can, with profit, be likened to other important historical debates as well: to debates over slavery before the Civil War, over prostitution during the white slavery/reformist era of the late nineteenth and early twentieth centuries, over Prohibition during both the nineteenth and the twentieth centuries, debates which greatly shaped our national character.

On Boxing is a book with an incredible amount of intense energy, compassionate yet relentlessly scrutinizing. One is often moved by passages because the author herself is moved. Boxing is, at last, not only our national sport of utter heartbreak but of how *sometimes* heartbreak is heroically endured by the boxer and even by the audience. Oates tells her part of the story of grace through slaughter (is boxing Puritan, as Oates suggests?) with astonishing compulsion and an extraordinary sense of humane concern. To be sure, Oates's book does not have the investigative detail and narrative exactitude of Barney Nagler's *James Norris and the Decline of Boxing* or Thomas Hauser's *The Black Lights,* the chatty coziness and insider's view of A. J. Liebling's *The Sweet Science,* Trevor Wignall's earlier book with the same title, or Fred Dartnell's *Seconds Outs*; and it lacks the historical guile and wit of the volumes by Pierce Egan on eighteenth- and nineteenth-century boxing and the books by Nat Fleischer on the history of black boxing. Nevertheless, it possesses a certain critical audacity that none of these books comes close to having. It makes up in critical height what it lacks in the kind of width we have become accustomed to boxing books having. Jose Torres's biography of Mohammad Ali and Floyd Patterson's pieces in *Sports Illustrated* and *Esquire* are still necessary reading for anyone who wants to understand this sport, but so is Oates's work as well. She has established the possibility and the necessity of our best

writers writing about sport in a way that is finally free of sentiment, romance, and a deadening and juvenile yearning for the purer (whiter?) past. She has freed us from reading the intellectual's entrapment of writing about boxing as if it were the fulfillment of a masculine golden dream of wonder or as if it can only produce a text that is nothing more than a *j'accuse* writ with orgiastic eloquence. Along with Hauser's *The Black Lights,* Oates's work is one of the more absorbing texts that I have come across on this topic in quite some time.

Margaret Rozga (essay date 1990)

SOURCE: "Threatening Places, Hiding Places: The Midwest in Selected Stories by Joyce Carol Oates," in *Midwestern Miscellany,* Vol. XVIII, 1990, pp. 34-44.

[*Below, Rozga discusses the significance of Midwestern setting in Oates's short fiction, focusing on her representations of Madison, Wisconsin, and Detroit, Michigan.*]

Joyce Carol Oates has employed numerous settings for her short fiction over the course of her twenty-five years as a publishing writer. Frequently she has chosen to set her stories in the location where she herself resided at the time of the story's composition. Thus having grown up in rural New York state, Oates often used rural settings for her earliest stories. But these rural settings are generic rather than specific; no actual places are named. Several early reviewers compared her settings and her characters to those of William Faulkner. Oates did, in fact, at first begin to establish her own fictional territory, Eden County.

Oates moved on, however, to graduate school at the University of Wisconsin in Madison and later to teach at the University of Detroit. When she chose to write stories set in these locales, she did not fictionalize in the same way. Instead in this later group of stories, she names the actual cities, and, moreover, she names specific streets and sites in those cities. Despite this move toward the more realistic, place continues to play a symbolic function in her fiction. The economic and racial tensions that characterized the historic Detroit in the 1960's become important in Oates' fiction as reflections of widespread disintegration, personal as well as social. What Detroit means and what Oates has made of that meaning are perhaps fairly widely known through the reputation of her award winning novel *them* and through one of her most frequently anthologized stories, **"How I Contemplated the World from the Detroit House of Correction and Began My Life Over Again."** In this last named work, the city itself functions as the chief antagonist, a degree of intense emphasis on place not equalled in many of the other stories. Nevertheless, something remains of that sense of place as working against the character's search for personal meaning and purpose.

With Madison, Wisconsin, and Detroit, Michigan, in particular, Oates suggests that the academic atmosphere in the one case and the social upheaval in the other inhibit the individual. In the academic atmosphere of Madison, Oates' protagonists take refuge in the intellectual and stunt their emotional growth. On the other hand, characters cast adrift in the social disintegration of Detroit experience such tumultuous and twisted emotion that their power of understanding on an intellectual level is overwhelmed. Only those are "saved" who find the equivalent of Madison in Detroit's universities or, what is more usual, find refuge in Detroit's suburbs.

Four stories illustrate with particular clarity how these Midwestern cities can be places of refuge or places of terror: **"Expense of Spirit," "Sacred Marriage," "How I Contemplated the World from the Detroit House of Correction,"** and **"The Dead."** Reference to a fifth story, **"The Lady With the Pet Dog,"** may help in maintaining a balanced view. Though Oates looks critically at the cities in her Midwestern experience and fiction, she does not resort to stereotypes. The Midwest is not ridiculed as the ignorant, uncultured provinces. Unlike the famous Chekhov story to which hers is a counterpart, Oates's story has no wretched violins, no ugly grey fences. Ohio, the home of Oates's Anna, is not the S—- of Chekhov's heroine. The twentieth century American Midwest poses different challenges.

The challenge of Madison, Wisconsin, is to maintain a sense of wholeness in an atmosphere that may encourage intellectual development but does so in a way detrimental to the person. **"The Expense of Spirit,"** from Oates's first collection of short stories, *By the North Gate,* is set at a graduate student party in Madison. It shows how grotesque human behavior can become when characters are isolated from ordinary human responsibilities and pursue intellectual goals to the neglect of other aspects of development. Leo Scott, surveying the apartment where the party is being held, wonders, "What would become of them all? Would leaving college jolt them overnight into becoming American citizens, thinking of house payments and cars and church—for the children, of course—and supermarket stamps to paste in books?"

At the present time of the story, the characters face no such worries. Leo, in particular, has taken refuge in his role as scholar. The role, however, is not enough to protect him from the very real pain of his wife's leaving him. He goes to the party, desperate to find her, but instead is brought face to face with himself. The noise at the party escalates from the playing of "soft, thin, effeminate pieces" by Ravel on the piano to the drunken rebuff Gordie hurls at Leo, "What the

hell are you looking at? I hate your goddam face!" As more people arrive and more quarrels erupt, it is clear that behind the intellectual pretensions, chaos reigns.

In the midst of this din, Leo loses his hold on the personal image with which he had come to the party, "Watching himself in the mirror as he shaved, he had prepared his expression for his friends: he would appear to them as fresh, happy, perhaps even innocent." In the midst of the confusion of attempted comfort and actual hostility at the party, Leo cannot long maintain that pose. Later he will turn to an external embodiment of the image of innocence in his student, Miss Edwards.

In the meantime, Leo locates another image for himself. He sees "exotic masks on one wall—three in a row. One of them reminded Leo of himself: a thin, drawn, dissipated face, with a sardonic grin implying a constantly present sense of irony that had choked off all other emotions, even self-pity." As with the pose of innocence, however, Leo's attempt at the ironic or sophisticated cracks as soon as it is challenged. Leo attempts to banter with Claude, but Claude cuts Leo off, "If I were you I would not make qualitative judgments on anyone else. You are not the man for it." There is no irony in Leo's reply: "What does that mean?" Leo is angry enough to pour his beer over Claude's head, but he cannot bring himself to act at all. He cannot fulfill either of the images he picks out for himself. He is neither the innocent, nor is he the sophisticated ironist.

At this point, again with an escalation of noise and "commotion," the two people arrive who fulfill these images. Miss Edwards, Leo's student, is only seventeen, and she exclaims in her excitement at being included in "faculty" circles. The graduate students all laugh at her naivete about their status. Jason, the Black graduate student who has brought her to the party, is from the start the ironist Leo would like to be. He explains to the girl the reason for the laughter in such a way so as to establish his own control over the situation: "'Oh, ain't she a princess!' he cried. 'Thinkin' they let the faculty teach ones young as her. Honey, it's dirt cheap labor that teaches you—ain't they 'splained that in the catalogue?'" Leo attaches himself to the couple who represent the combination of innocence and irony he believes could save him from painful realities, even from himself. He finds some respite, at least temporarily, in Miss Edwards' chatter and in Jason's vodka.

The whole party, in fact, then centers itself about Jason and Miss Edwards and, for a time, tones down. Miss Edwards is allowed a long monologue on topics ranging from her excitement at being at the university to her belief in equality. When she finishes, the cynicism of the group, and the noise, begin to reassert themselves. Someone claps; Marty sticks out his tongue and says, "Christ." Leo thinks again of his wife, of her in their bedroom mirror, but he cannot even imagine his reflection in that mirror, a sign of his growing realization that their marriage is over. Someone then brings home to Leo a cruel but accurate reflection. In a game of charades, the imitator wails, "But where's my wife?" Leo is again paralyzed. Only Miss Edwards can respond; without any hesitation, she slaps the person playing charades and flees from the party. In her innocence, she knows her only possible response to such cruelty is to flee before she gets caught up in the larger charade of the party itself.

Jason and Leo follow after her, but as much a part of the Madison academic scene as they are, they bring chaos with them. The three struggle together, break free and struggle again. In a description that shows how he has internalized the noisy atmosphere of the party, Leo feels his "mind had emptied and was buzzing hollowly." Leo's final position is desperate. He falls "to his knees in the cold street and embracing their legs, their bodies, as if he were terrified they might leave him." Leo holds on to Jason and Miss Edwards as images of the self he thinks he needs to be to survive. The innocent can reject and flee from the ugly; the sophisticate can laugh it off. Leo can really do neither. The party at Madison presents a challenge to his sense of identity that he cannot meet. Whatever success he may have as a student and as a teacher does not translate into an ability to relate effectively with others.

Howard Dean in **"Sacred Marriage"** [in *Marriages and Infidelities*] has advanced somewhat further in his academic career, but he has not advanced at all in an ability to come to terms with himself, and he is perhaps even further behind Leo in understanding others. When he fails in the end, defeated by a dead man, in both academic and human terms, he invents a self-protective purpose with which to shield himself from the failure, and he hurries back to Madison where his illusion may survive.

The illusion with which he concludes is the illusion with which he begins. Dean invests the dead poet Connell Pearce with power over him. In his initial letter to Pearce's widow Emilia, Dean had written, "Your husband has partly created me. Without his work I would not be the person I am." But what sort of person is Dean, the scholar, the academic? Gradually, enough of his past is revealed that we have an impression. Dean admits to being frightened sometimes by his fiancee "who had not exactly promised she would marry him," and frightened even of "her little girl, whose stepfather he might well become." He feels that love is a "mysterious process. He had always felt himself apart from it, baffled and unable to control it."

On the other hand, the poet whom he studies and whom he claims has shaped his life is the epitome of control. Pearce had even planned a very effective means to protect himself

from scholars like Dean and Felix Fraser who arrives shortly after Dean himself. The main purpose of Pearce's marriage to Emilia seems to have been to leave behind a guardian of his unfinished work. So Dean concludes when he discovers Pearce's notes for a religious parable: "He is a noble, dying old man, she is a very beautiful young woman. *She* is worthy of being his wife. And therefore he marries her and she nurses him through his last illness, buries him, and blesses all the admirers of his art who come to her, for she alone retains X's divinity."

The critic is aghast to find out the poet has been one step ahead of him and that he is just living out the story that the writer created. He is even more disturbed to find out that Emilia will live out the part created for her, though she seems to be unaware of how she is playing a part. She has no intention of marrying Dean despite their affair. Dean, in his depression, thinks that his is a "joke of a life." The self-examination, however, is all too short-lived. As he returns to the Midwest, he discards any disturbing thoughts and puts himself back in line with the life and goals he held before his experience in the exotic-sounding Mouth-of-Lowmoor, West Virginia:

> The sun rose. The fog burned away. Howard's depression burned away, gradually, and by the time he came to the Ohio state line at Marietta it was nearly gone. He felt instead the same marvelous energy he had felt upon first seeing those piles of Pearce's unpublished, unguessed-at-works. That was real. Yes, that was real, and whatever had happened to Howard was not very real. . . ."

Thus Howard Dean seems to be concluding with a retreat into his academic role and a retreat from confrontation with himself and all his fears.

Torborg Norman [in *Isolation and Contact,* 1984] advances the argument that Howard Dean leaves Pearce's home with enough insight to enter into a meaningful marriage with his previously feared fiancee back in Madison. Norman writes that "the real art in the Oatesian sense would lie in the transformation of the nervous fiancee to dream lover." However desirable such a transformation might be, Howard Dean's concluding thoughts seem to preclude that happening. He resolves instead "to bring Connell Pearce to the world's attention: that was his mission, the shape of his life." The fiancee has no explicit place in his concluding thoughts. He is going back to Madison as a place of narrow refuge.

Detroit presents quite a different kind of challenge to one's sense of identity and search for a full life. The narrator/protagonist in **"Unmailed, Unwritten Letters"** [in *The Wheel of Love*] is perhaps the first to define the problem posed by Detroit: "In Detroit the multiplication of things is brutal. I think it broke me down. Weak, thin, selfish, a wreck, I have become oblivious to the deaths of other people." Another fragmented narrative, also in *The Wheel of Love,* Oates' third collection of short stories, further develops this definition of Detroit. Detroit is the place of impending storms, threatening apocalypse because it presents more disorder than anyone can comprehend or deal with. Most people respond by shutting out whatever would disturb their superficial peace. The young narrator/protagonist, however, is driven by the atmosphere of the city to search for something she cannot quite name. She catalogues the weather in such a way so as to suggest some of the forces at work: "small warnings of frost, soot warnings, traffic warnings, hazardous lake conditions for small craft and swimmers, restless Negro gangs, restless cloud formations, restless temperature aching to fall out the very bottom of the thermometer or shoot up over the top and boil everything over in red mercury." The social climate, as well as the actual weather, is the disturbing quality about Detroit; social cohesion is tragically lacking. The undercurrent in Detroit's weather is the discontent of those who do not partake in the city's wealth. The narrator, a suburbanite herself, is made to feel the wrath of the dispossessed when she is beaten by Princess and Dolly in the lavatory of the Detroit House of Correction. Princess and Dolly typify the city which is dirty and dangerous and poor, except for Hudson's Department Store and Cobo Hall, "that expensive tomb."

In the suburbs, on the other hand, is the boredom and vacuity of those with abundant possessions. Separated from the dirt and disorder of the city, suburbanites feel safe. Some of the narrator's thoughts capture and exaggerate this attitude. As she listens to the maid vacuum the carpet in her parents' room, for example, she thinks, "a vacuum cleaner's roar is a sign of all good things." Beneath the clean surface, however, all is not perfectly in order. Some of the suburban young people shoplift, do poorly in school, or drift into the city, like the narrator, vaguely searching for more substantive reality. But they are inarticulate about what they seek. The narrator cannot answer the question posed by Clarita, the nondescript, city-conditioned woman who presents herself to the narrator, saying, "I never can figure out why girls like you bum around down here. What are you looking for anyway?"

Whatever she seeks, what the narrator finds is abuse, violence and the rage of those kept from the good of suburban cleanliness. Princess and Dolly who beat her, help her understand the meaning of her experience. The moment of insight comes through with her switch from third to first person: "Why is she beaten up? Why do they pound her, why such hatred? Princess vents all the hatred of a thousand silent Detroit winters on her body, the girl whose body belongs to me, fiercely she rides across the Midwestern plains on this girl's tender bruised body ... revenge on the op-

pressed minorities of America! revenge on the slaughtered Indians! revenge on the female sex, on the male sex, revenge on Bloomfield Hills, revenge, revenge. . . ."

Though she has this moment of insight, the young narrator is unable to carry the weight she feels thrown at her. She cannot resolve the contradictions and discrepancies in the society represented by Detroit and its suburbs. She can only follow her parents back to Bloomfield Hills and to her pink bedroom where she weeps, haunted by the memory of what she experienced in the city. She is at the end similar to Leo Scott in "Expense of Spirit," clinging desperately to fragments, the illusion of a place of refuge having been destroyed. The image of her Detroit lover now superimposes itself on the presence of her father. Though she abandons the third person stance she has used for much of the story, her use of the first person does not carry with it any assurance of her personal stability or triumph. She weeps because the "God in gold and beige carpeting" has no power to rescue or pull her world together into a coherent whole.

The brutal climate of Detroit reaches a deathly point in Oates' "The Dead" [in *Marriages and Infidelities*]. In this story Oates makes Detroit a place of literal death—the place where the student Emmett Norlan was beaten by the police during an anti-war demonstration and dies later in the hospital of liver failure; "he just disintegrated. . . ." It is the place where Ilena Williams' marriage dies, unable to survive the strain of her infidelity and her husband's bullying. It is the place where values die. Father Hoffman, head of the English Department at the small Catholic university in Detroit where Ilena taught is "a little corrupt in his academic standards: the Harvard years had been eclipsed long ago by the stern daily realities of Detroit." His corruption costs Ilena her job. She is fired for refusing to agree to grant a degree to a master's candidate who cannot name a poem. She has enough sense of value left to be "astonished" that "anyone would allow him to teach English anywhere." But the institutional and personal corruption around her takes its toll.

Ilena finds herself consuming whatever drugs she can get hold of. Her personal problems are intertwined with the larger social problems of Detroit. Ilena perceives the connection in these terms: "The marriage had been dwindling all during the Detroit years—1965-1967—and they both left the city shortly before the riot, which seemed to Ilena, in her usual poetic, hyperbolic, pill-sweetened state, a cataclysmic flowering of their own hatred." She seems aware of her exaggeration, and, at least as it applies to her marriage, other evidence in the story provides a more sober view. When, for example, her husband reacts scornfully to the idea of having children because, "You don't bring children into the world to fix up a rotten marriage," Ilena thinks that she had not known it was rotten, "exactly." It may also be that the cause and effect work as well in the opposite direction, the negative despairing attitude prevalent in the city twisting the emotions of the characters and thus blighting their marriage.

At any rate, Ilena is able to survive the Detroit experience. Her artistic sense, and some distance from the city, allow her to survive both the personal and the social disorder. Drawing on the experience, she writes a novel, *Death Dance*. Though she considers it her weakest novel, it becomes a best seller and frees her from financial worries. More important, the act of writing keeps her suicidal thoughts at bay. She survives well enough to return to Detroit and re-encounters the faculty at her former university. Finally in the arms once again of her former lover, she is brought to a vision of a clean slate, if not a new start. Echoing the ending of James Joyce's story "The Dead," Oates concludes with Ilena hearing "beyond the man's hoarse, strained breathing the gentle breathing of the snow, falling shapelessly upon them all."

If Detroit and Madison represent a Midwestern threat and a Midwestern avoidance of reality in particularly extreme and grotesque form, Ohio represents the Midwest in a more moderate way. Oates chooses Ohio as the twentieth century American counterpart to Anton Chekhov's provincial Russian town S——, each place depicted in the respective author's version of **"The Lady With the Pet Dog."** Oates does not make Ohio the obvious object of ridicule as Chekhov does with S——. Chekhov shows the stiffness and rigidity of nineteenth century Russia ensconced in S——. The orchestra playing at the theatre where Gurov meets Anna again is wretched; obvious badges indicate rank of patrons at the theatre; Anna's house is protected by an ugly grey fence studded with nails. But in Oates, the lovers meet again at a concert and no comment is made on the quality of the music performed. The middle-class status of Oates's Anna can be inferred from her large house, her leisure time and her husband's preoccupation with his work, but aside from knowing he has "business friends" and "a future" we do not get any specific indications of rank. Her house is large and rambling, and, if it symbolizes anything, it is a quality opposite to that of the house of Chekhov's Anna. It symbolizes a society, a way of life in which lack of structure becomes an obstacle to finding oneself. At least this is Anna's perception: "her spirit detached itself from her and drifted about the rooms of the large house she lived in with her husband, a shadow-woman delicate and imprecise. There was no boundary to her, no edge."

The Ohio setting of this story, then, shows the Midwest as more amorphous, without the specific threat of one-dimensional, academic distortion or the emerging hostility of deprived classes. This story, like **"The Dead,"** offers some contrast between the Midwest and the Northeast. Oates's Anna meets her lover on Cape Cod, where she stays in another rambling house, that of her family which supplies her with no better sense of identity than the house of her husband. But amid the noise of the beach, she is defined by the man who will be her lover in the sketch he does of Anna as the lady with the pet dog. Anna carries the sketch and the newly awakened sense of self back to Ohio where she furtively and anxiously re-examines it, trying to make sense of the two halves of her life. She does not find it easy to come to terms with herself, and before she does she flirts with suicide. Finally she sees in her lover the possibility of maintaining a sense of individuality while being in love. Though she seems to find the most successful resolution of these characters, she does not face the test of jeering pseudo-friends, as did Leo Scott in **"Expense of Spirit,"** or the disintegrating social fabric of Detroit in **"The Dead."** For Oates, Ohio is neither the threat nor the place of escape that Detroit or Madison seem to be.

The facts Oates presents about Detroit and Madison—Woodward and Livernois Avenues, State Street, the anti-war demonstrations and the 1967 riot—are specifically and literally true in a way her portrayal of earlier fictional settings is not. But Oates draws out the symbolic dimension of the facts to create in these Midwestern stories a picture of a society with fatal divisions between the intellectual and the emotional, the rich and the poor, the young and questioning and the older and more established. Her protagonists are sharply and sometimes painfully aware of the divisions. A few, like Anna in **"The Lady With the Pet Dog,"** may find a measure of personal happiness, but the search for personal identity and a meaningful life is difficult for all of them. When such complications as a distorted, one-dimensional academic milieu or a disorienting social upheaval are added, the struggle defies success and Oates's characters do well to cling to their choices or imagine a new beginning as best they can.

Marilyn C. Wesley (essay date Winter 1990)

SOURCE: "The Transgressive Heroine: Joyce Carol Oates's 'Stalking'," in *Studies in Short Fiction*, Vol. 27, No. 1, Winter, 1990, pp. 15-20.

[*In the essay below, Wesley explains how Oates's fiction challenges gender ideology by describing the characterization of the protagonist of "Stalking."*]

Although Joyce Carol Oates has frequently been labeled a non-feminist and criticized for the passivity of her female characters, her works actively challenge restrictive gender ideology. A case in point is the Oatesian figure I will define as the transgressive heroine, whose murderous early debut is the short story **"Swamps,"** the first story in Oates' first collection, and whose continuing truculent influence is felt in the Kalistruck heroines of *The Goddess and Other*

Women, in the powerful women of *Bellefleur,* and in the wilful artist of *Solstice,* and who is most fully present as the protagonist of the 1972 short story **"Stalking."**

A previous stage in the evolution of the transgressive heroine is the figure of the *anti-hero*—the protagonist who is "not simply a failed hero but a social misfit, graceless, weak, and often comic, the embodiment of ineptitude and bad luck in a world apparently made for others"—a commonplace in our contemporary literature. "The Hero, who once figured as Initiate, ends as Rebel or Victim," Ihab Hassan explains [in *Radical Innocence,* 1961]. The presentation of this anti-hero places him in counter-relation to the social structure which produces him. Oates' transgressive works, however, recognize the impossibility of the superimposition of an imaginary counter-structure. While the anti-hero, like Ralph Ellison's "invisible man," stages his protest by defining a metaphoric space of freedom and moving outside the system, the transgressive protagonist, unable to dream of lighting out for any territory, however surreal, repeatedly inscribes her discomfort from within. The victimization and ineffective rebelliousness of Oates' transgressive heroines serve to illuminate and interrogate the system which creates them.

Transgression, Michel Foucault argues [in *Language, Counter-Memory, Practice,* 1977], implies an operation more complex than the antithesis of two terms: its purpose, like the repeated violations perpetrated by Oates' transgressive protagonists, is to reveal the dysfunctional interaction between the terms:

> Transgression, then, is not related to the limit as black to white, the prohibited to the lawful, the outside to the inside, or as the open area of a building to its exposed spaces. Rather, their relationship takes the form of a spiral which no simple infraction can exhaust.

Exhibiting such transgression articulates the terms and questions the limits they impose.

In **"Stalking,"** Gretchen, the protagonist, is female—a fact which forces us from the outset to recast the convention of the anti-hero as a problem of gender. Our first glimpse of her indicates her problematic situation:

> She is dressed for the hunt, her solid legs crammed into old blue jeans, her big, square, strong feet jammed into white leather boots that cost her mother forty dollars not long ago, but are now scuffed and filthy with mud. Hopeless to get them clean again, Gretchen doesn't give a damn.

Gretchen is uncomfortably suspended between contradictory ascriptions of gender. Unlike the male anti-hero whose failure is marked by weakness, the transgressive heroine suffers from inappropriate strength. Like the ugly step-sister at the royal ball, she cannot contract her foot to any comfortable relation to the feminine apparel whose value is defined by the social system and promoted by her mother, and hence cannot claim her feminine reward. Her size, her shape, and her manner violate clear demarcation between conventional masculine and feminine identification, an interpretation reinforced by this detailed description of Gretchen's face:

> She has untidy, curly hair that looks like a wig set loosely on her head. Light brown curls spill out everywhere, bouncy, a little frizzy, a cascade, a tumbling of curls. Her eyes are deep set, her eyebrows heavy and dark. She has a stern, staring look, like an adult man. Her nose is perfectly formed, neat and noble. Her upper lip is long, as if it were stretched to close with difficulty over the front teeth. She wears no make-up, her lips are perfectly colorless, pale, a little chapped, and they are usually held tight, pursed tightly shut. She has a firm, rounded chin. Her facial structure is strong, pensive, its features stern and symmetrical as a statue's, blank, neutral, withdrawn. Her face is attractive. But there is a blunt, neutral, sexless stillness to it, as if she were detached from it and somewhere else, uninterested.

The face is, of course, no less coded than the foot. We are used to intimately observed catalogues of features in literature. What is remarkable about the use of the tradition in this story is that Oates rarely employs her gaze in this exhaustive fashion. She sketches her characters by a brief mention of their hair color and then, typically, looks through their eyes at the closely observed world around them rather than into their eyes like a rapt admirer. The function of this sustained description is keyed to the problematics of gender. The hair suggests the familiar associations of female sexuality; but although as a turbulent "cascade," it evokes abundant "nature," which usually signifies feminine sensuality, the suggestion of wig-like appearance quickly undercuts this automatic ascription. Perhaps Gretchen is neither natural nor sensual. In effect, this description invokes the literary code of femininity only to revoke it—a strategy immediately employed again in the next two sentences, where the eyebrows are emphasized as dark and thick, a feature conventionally expressive of masculinity. And, in fact, the eyes, those symbolic windows to essence, return not the modest glance of a woman expected in this context but the provocative stare of "an adult man." Further, this contradiction of femininity is at least a partly willful undertaking of Gretchen herself. Such is the message of the mouth, which has deliberately refused the application of the cosmetic allure of color and is "pursed" in tight rejection. The cumulative effect of this manner of presentation is summarized in the climactic series of adjectives, "blunt, neutral, sexless." Gretchen's statue-like physiognomy, as Oates orchestrates its "meaning," is a complex field of reference upon which is played out the repudiation of conventional femininity.

For Gretchen is, without doubt, an "anti-heroine." At thirteen years of age, her size-fourteen body is evidently "graceless." She is a clear "misfit" in a "world apparently made for others," a world whose gender requirements are garishly evident in the people, objects, and decor of the shopping mall Gretchen visits:

> Dodi's Boutique is decorated in silver and black. Metallic strips hang down from a dark ceiling, quivering. Salesgirls dressed in pants suits stand around with nothing to do except giggle with one another and nod their heads in time to the music amplified throughout the store. . . . "WCKK. Radio Wonderful. . . ."

> "Need any help?" the girl asks. She has long swinging hair and a high-shouldered, indifferent, bright manner.

Gretchen's actions in the story rebel against the alienating strictures of a system that would define her in terms—artificial, commercially attractive, thoughtlessly benign—that are appropriate to the stylized world of the salesgirl. In one store, Gretchen shoplifts a tube of pale pink lipstick, "Spring Blossom," which she takes into the "Ladies Room" to examine, destroy, and discard. As if to underscore her rejection, she also breaks the toilet into which she tosses the pilfered lipstick. And in Dodi's Boutique, Gretchen takes several dresses into the changing cubicle. She muddies one with her boots; she deliberately tears out the zipper of another.

What changes the focus of this story from Gretchen as a rebel-victim to Gretchen as a transgressive protagonist is the intriguing contest central to the action. Gretchen is not merely out shopping on a November Saturday afternoon; she is engaged in hunting down an imaginary antagonist who leads her from an open field into the mall, through several stores, and home again. "The Invisible Adversary," a male figure, is the conscious target of Gretchen's hostility throughout the story: *"You'll be sorry for that, you bastard." "You'll regret this." "You'll get yours."* Gretchen's "stalking" maneuvers finally force the Adversary out onto the highway, where he is struck by a car. He is "limping like an old man" as they both return to Gretchen's home. The story ends with Gretchen watching television: "If the Adversary comes crawling behind her, groaning in pain, weeping, she won't even bother to glance at him."

The sequence of events and attitudes demands that the reader determine who or what the Adversary represents and what his function is in the story. The thematic contest that engages Gretchen, we have already discovered, is the struggle for and against gender identity. Certainly this projection acts out a role in that struggle. In a review of a biography of Carl Jung, Oates indicates her extensive knowledge and admiration of Jungian theory, so we may identify the Adversary as an animus figure, that personification of the masculine component of a woman's unconscious typically projected in dreams and fantasies. The Jungian objective is the integration of all the unconscious elements of the personality, but what is most striking in Gretchen's story is the violence with which she strives to destroy and reject what Jung understood as her masculine nature.

The text suggests only two coded means to gender production, which do not appear to intersect. The woman may participate in the endless replication of the feminine body and her domestic accouterments through purchase encoded in the capitalistic system and epitomized in the reiterated "family rooms" Gretchen sees displayed at the furniture store:

> She wanders through Sampson Furniture. . . . a ritual with her. Again she notices the sofa that is like the sofa in their family room at home. . . . All over the store there are sofas, chairs, tables, beds. . . . People stroll around them, in and out of little displays, displays meant to be living rooms, dining rooms, bedrooms, family rooms. . . . It makes Gretchen's eyes squint to see so many displays: like seeing the inside of a hundred houses.

Gretchen herself participates directly in the practice of a masculine code of aggression:

> Some boys are fooling around in front of the record store. One of them bumps into Gretchen and they all laugh as she is pushed against a trash can. "Watch it, babe!" the boy sings out. Her leg hurts. Gretchen doesn't look at them but, with a cold, swift anger, her face averted, she knocks the trash can over onto the sidewalk. Junk falls out. The can rolls. Some women shoppers scurry to get out of the way and the boys laugh.

That the seemingly desultory destructiveness is really constitutive is evident in the emphatic differentiation in this encounter between the powerful males and the victimized female "babe," between the forceful Gretchen imitating the masculine mode and the flustered powerless women. Further, Gretchen's general anger and resultant vandalism are codified in the story as components of the ritualized stalking, hunting, and killing—activities of the primitive male hero. But Gretchen is not a hero, although it is her masculine capacity for anger and physical strength that compromises her participation in the feminine world "apparently made for others."

In the same way that she has tried to feminize her large feet by stuffing them into the feminine white boots purchased by her mother, only to finally react by desecrating them when the transformation proved inadequate and incompatible, Gretchen responds with distressed ambivalence to the gender definitions of her shopping-center world. Rather than embracing her masculine capabilities to define herself as a rebel contradicting, negating, restrictive feminine identification, Gretchen becomes a transgressor. Instead of claiming, like the "invisible man," some free but lunatic space outside the arena of constricting definition—the open field of the "Invisible Adversary" at the beginning of this story, for example—Gretchen compulsively enters and re-enters the mall, where she is repeatedly attracted to its signifying objects. She reaches for the lipstick and the dresses again and again, only to destroy them out of frustration at their lack of congruence with her own requirements. By fantasizing the destruction of her masculine capabilities, Gretchen reveals a maladaptive complicity with a code of feminine definition which will confine her to the characteristic but ineffective rage that her story presents.

"Stalking" illustrates the transgressive "spiral" which by repeatedly desecrating limitation exposes it to examination and interrogation. Underlying the concept of the transgressive heroine is the assumption that a rule which is "transgressed" is not destroyed but merely violated. Such violation calls attention to conditions that provoke defiance—a gender ideology which supports economic rather than human development in this case—at the same time that it underscores their continuing existence. The repetition of this maneuver produces not reform, but the possibility of reform. "Transgression," according to Foucault, "carries the limit right to the limit. . . ; transgression forces the limit to face the fact of its imminent disappearance. . . ." The transgressive heroine of Oates' fiction, a female protagonist who repeatedly violates the forms of gender stricture without personally solving the social problem of gender restriction, promotes feminist reform, understood as literary challenge to patriarchal ideology.

Joyce Carol Oates with students at Bellarmine College (interview date Fall 1990)

SOURCE: "An Interview with Joyce Carol Oates," compiled by David Y. Todd, in *Gettysburg: The Gettysburg Review*, Vol. 6, No. 2, Spring, 1993, pp. 291-99.

[*In the following interview, compiled from various question-and-answer sessions during the fall of 1990 while Oates visited at Bellarmine College, Oates addresses influences, her writing habits, the recurrence of violence in her work, and her personal literary philosophy.*]

Joyce Carol Oates was born in Lockport, New York, in 1938. She earned a B.A. from Syracuse University and an M.A. from the University of Wisconsin. Since 1978 she has taught at Princeton University and, with her husband, Raymond Smith, she runs the Ontario Review Press. Oates has published more than forty books of fiction, poetry, criticism, plays, and essays, and her novel *them* won the National Book Award in 1970. Recent works include a long essay, *On Boxing* (1988), the novels *You Must Remember This* (1987), *American Appetites* (1989), *Because It Is Bitter, and Because It Is My Heart* (1990), and *Black Water* (1992), and short fiction collections *The Assignation* (1988) and *Heat and Other Stories* (1991). In a review of her novel *Bellefleur* (1980), John Gardner wrote: "Oates's vision is huge, well-informed and sound. . . . By one two-page thunderstorm she makes the rest of us novelists wonder why we left the farm." In the fall of 1990, Oates visited Bellarmine College in Louisville, Kentucky, where she read from her poetry, answered questions from the audience, and later met with a small group of students and teachers at the college library. This interview was compiled from those question-and-answer sessions and from a later conversation near the end of Oates's visit to Louisville.

[*Interviewer:*] *You began publishing fiction in college, before you went to graduate school. In those early years, were there certain authors you admired or thought of as teachers?*

[Oates:] Thomas Mann was one. I studied him in my early twenties. He seems not much read today, but I've gone back and reread *Doctor Faustus* and certain of the shorter works, which I like very much.

What about Chekhov, Faulkner?

Certainly I read them, and Hemingway, Fitzgerald, Dostoevski, the Brontës, and many others in high school. I've always tried to read widely.

Any recurring favorites?

I often mention Thoreau. I frequently teach him, and recently I did the introduction to the Princeton University Press edition of *Walden*.

Do you ever go back and reread you own novels or stories?

Rarely.

Your novel **Wonderland,** *first published in 1971, was re-*

published in 1973, with a different ending. Why? Do you often want to change something after it has been published?

No. It must have been the case that I hadn't exorcised certain unconscious issues in the first version of **Wonderland.** The writing of any intensely felt work, especially one so lengthy as a novel, is very much a matter of emotions only dimly comprehended, let alone controlled. I felt a strong need to rewrite the ending, which I did, about a year after the original writing; after that, it was laid to rest. But the question is a provocative one: should one rewrite, after publication? Should one revise one's earlier self? We know that writers as varied as Marianne Moore, Robert Lowell, Auden, Yeats revised earlier work, but not always fruitfully.

My characters have a way of living on in my own mind, though of course I should be realistic and acknowledge that they are fictional constructs, imaginary. Still, I sometimes get a second chance to inhabit them, for instance in writing a screenplay for a novel. (I've recently done the screenplay for **Because It Is Bitter, and Because It Is My Heart,** which is scheduled to be directed by Lawrence Schiller.)

What did you think of the movie that was made from your story, "Where Are You Going, Where Have You Been?"

Smooth Talk was based on the story but it also was expanded. I was invited to write the screenplay, but I was doing a novel, and so a very gifted screenwriter named Tom Cole did the script. It contains the same story but is basically different. Much of the emotion of the movie had to do with the mother's relationship with her daughter, and my story has virtually nothing of that. I thought the film was extremely well done, under Joyce Chopra's direction. Laura Dern was brilliant. Movies and books are autonomous; the movie is its own artwork, and the book or short story is its own. I don't think a book can, or should, be faithfully treated in a movie; I don't think you should criticize a film for not being a book.

The very short stories in **The Assignation** *are intriguing: some of them seem to end so abruptly. How did you conceive that collection?*

I've written many conventional short stories and wanted to experiment with structure. I call these miniature narratives—quicksilver movements of plot without psychological development. Character development interests me, of course, elsewhere.

There is a broad range of voices in the collection. For example, in **"Fin de Siecle"** *you have a drug dealer telling how he and his cronies go to the home of an old rich doctor and murder him.*

I'm not sure where that came from! I was in Los Angeles when I wrote that story. I seemed to pick up a throb and beat in the air, a sort of L.A. voice. . . . It's playful, and lethal.

When you start to write a scene, do you know whether it is going to end up as a story or a novel?

I start with intense emotion. I evoke form to contain it. The memory or emotion is like a little seed. If the work is a novel, I put maps or charts on the wall to aid me in writing it. I need to get the emotion out of myself into another form. I rewrite constantly; I have to keep working with the emotion until it becomes formally disciplined, in a way "history." And I can't write a novel unless I know the precise ending: where the people are, what they are saying, the literal words. I aim for that, always have it in mind. So the sentences of a work are meditations upon this ending.

Which is not to say that this is the only way to write; there are at least two basic ways. James Joyce was very schematic, intellectual, always knew exactly what he was doing, where he was going. D. H. Lawrence, a writer of equal genius, wrote spontaneously. In a letter to a friend he once said, "I'm on page 250 of a novel [*Women in Love*] and I don't know what it's about." When he finished a novel, he would sometimes start again and rewrite the whole thing.

But I always have a sense of what I am going to do. I never start writing until I've thought it through completely. It is as though there is this great, imaginative pool in which we all are living, as if all of us are part of this pool of consciousness we share because we're human beings. Some people dip into it and write a poem or play, or paint canvases. It's something we share. To me it is all the same consciousness or imagination, and the forms vary.

Do you go through stages when you write only poetry or only fiction, or do you shift around? And when you do finish a longer piece—say a play or a novel—how do you deal with that sense of loss, walking away from those characters?

I can only do one thing at a time. When I work on a novel, all my effort goes to that. It is as though my heart were beating its blood into it.

I have especially enjoyed the series of long novels you started with **Bellefleur,** *particularly* **A Bloodsmoor Romance,** *and each time you publish a new novel, I wonder if it is going to be the next one in that group. Do you plan to write any more of those?*

I tend to oscillate between periods of realism and periods of surrealism. I had become interested in history going back to the 1950s and moving up, and did a good deal of research for *You Must Remember This.* I became deeply involved in the McCarthy era and its power in the popular culture. At the time, I had been too young to know what was going on, but I came to see parallels between the 1950s and the 1980s, having to do with race relations and other issues. *Bellefleur* goes back before the "United States" existed, the French colonial period. Then with *Mysteries of Winterthurn,* I got as far as the presidency of Theodore Roosevelt. The next novel ends with the election of Franklin Roosevelt.

Where do you find this wealth of people to write about?

I suppose most writers are simply very attentive to the world. Certainly I find people mysterious; the phenomenon of human personality.

It seems that violence occurs frequently in your fiction. Do you think it is so common a part of human existence?

Obviously! However, I tend to write about the consequences of violence. Often I focus on victims of it, women and children. It's not that I am writing about violence in itself. I write about the effects of violent events on real human beings and families. Naturally, since I am an American writer, I write about things that happen in America.

Well, at the end of the title story of **The Assignation,** *for example, your third-person narrator suddenly uses the pronoun "I" to indicate, perhaps, that he is someone outside watching a woman go through her solitary actions. It is terrifying: we don't know what's going to happen to her.*

In retrospect, perhaps one concludes that this man has invented the story. He might be imagining her going through these things, but while you read it you think she is in control, in her room, changing clothes, doing the little things we all do when we think we are unobserved. Then at the end you realize somebody is watching. Perhaps something will happen to her. As, perhaps, someday, to us.

Did you know, the whole time you were writing the story, that you were writing it from that man's perspective?

Certainly. Also, I am always rewriting.

Is that a hard process for you?

Like crawling over broken glass. It is tormenting, but worth it, as training is for an athlete. I spend a lot of time revising, a process that mesmerizes me.

You had two short plays, **Tone Clusters** *and* **The Eclipse,** *under the title* **In Darkest America,** *premiere together at Actor's Theatre of Louisville in 1990. You spoke rather joyously then of the process of having the editor there hack away at your work, spoke gratefully of his contribution. Are you similarly disposed toward the editors publishing your fiction?*

The two are completely different. A novel is sheerly language. I have been writing fiction for so long that I think I know how to edit it. But theater is another sphere, visual and three-dimensional, with a director, actors, set design. For me it is a collaborative enterprise. I've worked with Martin Scorsese, and, with plays, people ask me, "Aren't you upset to give up control over your writing?" A naive question—if I wanted to keep control, I wouldn't have anything to do with films or theater. The idea is to give up one's autonomy and work with others.

And it is exciting. When I worked with Actor's Theatre, I started with a script perhaps forty-five pages long. The assistant artistic director Michael Dixon is totally professional; has done this many times: it was his task to tighten my play, to make it as dramatic as possible. (This was my strategy, too, for *The Assignation*—write stories as tightly as possible without surrendering vital information.) When I was working with him, Michael would call me up, and we would frequently have conferences of maybe an hour. He might say, "Now, on page fourteen, we can cut that speech because it's repeated, in a sense, on page eighteen."

When you write something like a long description of a room, do you ever worry that it might not be necessary to the plot, or to the theme or characters?

If you took the descriptions that are so lyrical and beautifully written out of Dickens, or out of *Moby Dick,* or out of Dostoevski, you might tighten the prose, but you would lose so much. I admire the descriptive voice, and I read many writers—Henry James, John Updike, and others—for what we call "voice." Updike's novel *Rabbit at Rest,* for instance, has many "digressive" passages that do not move the plot forward; they represent John Updike looking at and describing the world. Some people have complained they are slow, but in many ways I like those the best, more than the plot, which somebody else might say is more important.

Do you still feel, as you have written elsewhere, that the novelist's obligation is to attempt "the sanctification of the world?"

Probably I was speaking idealistically. That is a high motive. I think you find it in some of the very best writers, certainly in the best poetry. Walt Whitman was sanctifying the world. And I think of Mark Twain's line: "persons attempting to find a moral in [this narrative] will be banished." But there is a moral in *Huckleberry Finn.* He was a very moral writer, but there is a kind of modesty in people like Twain. They don't want to sound like the Moral Majority or fundamentalist Christians or something. But I just love to describe things. Really, I love to look at nature and urban scenes and describe them. If they are "ugly" things, that so-called ugliness can be interesting.

I am sure your husband supports your work, but does he also serve as a first critic? Do you involve him in your writing?

No. I learned not long ago from Elmore Leonard, an old friend of mine, that his wife reads everything he writes as he writes it. If he has ten pages, she reads them. She is the first and, to him, the most important critic. Joan Didion and John Gregory Dunne, who have been married a long time, read each other's work. But I have never had that relationship with anybody. I don't have that temperament. I feel I must do it myself. I get impatient if people tell me something is good, when I know I can make it better. You have to be careful taking advice from people who like you: they want you to be happy. They also want you to like *them,* and that is dangerous because they probably won't tell the truth. More importantly, they probably don't know enough. I have the sense that I am alone as a writer. I have to be accountable to my own work and its integrity.

Does your teaching at Princeton affect how you write?

My work as a teacher does not have any influence on my writing. The two activities are completely different. And I am not influenced by my students, though I have been influenced in subject matter by things that have happened at Princeton. Generally, the imaginative fuel, the power or adrenaline that you need to write, comes from some other, deeper source. It isn't usually social or professional. It is hard for me to be influenced by the stories I hear. People will tell me an anecdote and say, "There's a novel for you." That is like showing you a picture of someone and saying, "Fall in love." You can't fall in love looking at a picture! It has to be something so deep and powerful, inchoate, intangible. So those two parts of my life are unrelated but compensatory. My writing is lonely, intensive, and frustrating: I live constantly with failure; I feel I am failing, that there is an abyss between the inner vision and the actual work I am doing every day. When I am done with a novel, I feel I have raised it up to a level of integrity. But when I am working through the days and hours, it is mainly in terms of failure. Nothing is ever good enough, so I have to do it over. And over.

But when I leave that behind, leave my house and drive to the university, things become normal and positive. I love teaching, and I like my colleagues at Princeton. I think I would be very lonely and unhappy if I had my writing exclusively—it is like drawing a rake through your brain!

Some writers say they work at a set time every day. Do you regiment yourself in that way?

Not really. Mornings, and nights. As late as possible, when it's quiet.

What sort of effect does your reading have on your writing? Do you ever worry about other voices coming in?

No, it's hard to be influenced. I assign my students exercises occasionally—write a paragraph in the style of Faulkner or Hemingway. They learn it is really not so easy. You can write parody, but to do it so you have really absorbed the rhythms is hard. Certain writers are inimitable—Dylan Thomas, Emily Dickinson, Melville. Any poet who gets drawn into Thomas's orbit never returns. Sylvia Plath was influenced by Dickinson to some extent, but she was strong enough to avoid disaster. Faulkner has had an invidious effect on many writers. What you learn from reading is a magnanimity of spirit and some sense of the disparity of voices. Women who read books by other women learn there are subjects they can write about well, which some generations ago they may have felt belonged only to men. It is more the sense that they can do it, rather than anything on a verbal level.

I read fairly constantly. I am doing a project for Oxford University Press, the *Oxford Book of American Short Stories,* which begins with Washington Irving. So I am doing a lot of rereading and new reading in classic American short stories. I started with "Rip Van Winkle," and recently I have been discovering a writer named William Austin. He was just as famous as Irving in his time, but I had never heard of him.

Do you ever think about the Nobel Prize? Time magazine has referred to you as the perennial American candidate. What do you think when you hear that?

One night about eight years ago, the telephone rang at eleven o'clock. It was a woman from the *Philadelphia Inquirer* and she said, "Joyce Carol Oates, you're going to win the Nobel Prize! It just came in on the wire." I said, skeptically, "Oh, really." She said, "It's you, or Doris Lessing has been mentioned too, but it's going to be a woman." She wanted an interview, as if this was a real scoop. I said, "Why don't we wait?" The next day, Milosz won, and I was supposedly a runner-up. How hard to take such rumors seriously!

Looking at another side of recognition or awards, do you have any hopes for the effect your work might have? For example, **them** *won the National Book Award. Are you ever consciously trying to drive some social issue more into popular consciousness?*

Yes, I think so. I really wrote **them** to understand what had happened in Detroit, the Detroit riots. I was teaching there and had been looking at some of the root causes of this malaise, and at violence. I wanted to look around and talk to people. It's partly that the writer wants to learn, and partly that the writer hopes to illuminate some individual hearts. I don't have a great hope as, say, Harriet Beecher Stowe did, that she could change millions of lives. I think most writers just want to touch individual people.

Do you have a system for picking your titles? Hemingway said he listed possible titles for A Farewell to Arms *and then eliminated them.*

I have never done anything that methodical. My method is more intuitive, or a sudden illumination. I cannot let the work go until I get the right title, though. Sometimes the title has come long before I started the work. Sometimes it comes when I am in the middle. Sometimes after. I suppose I do have literary allusions. I had wanted to use **Because It Is Bitter, and Because It Is My Heart** because it is a line from a Stephen Crane poem that I was very struck by as an undergraduate. That was decades ago, and I always thought I would use it in some way, but I never had the novel before that would be quite appropriate for it.

Do the critics ever help you in your writing?

By the time criticism appears, the book has already been done for a couple of years, usually, so it cannot help with that book. I was very moved, to the point of tears, by some of the response of blacks to **Because It Is Bitter,** which has many black characters in it. I had thought they might feel I was trespassing on their territory because I wrote about black families from within. But the response was very warm. I felt that was very generous, beyond criticism. Henry Louis Gates, Jr. wrote a long essay review on the novel for *The Nation.*

Graham Greene once talked about a "ruling passion, that gives to a shelf of novels the unity of a system." Do you feel there is a recurrent theme in your work?

Probably my general theme is the subject of power in society, how power is an issue in politics, let's say. It seems that is what I'm writing about a good deal of the time, though I am not that conscious of it, because I am mainly writing about men and women and young people as I get caught up in the stories of families. But when I stand back, I realize I am probably writing about the struggle of various groups for political power and for defining themselves. I do have a lot of stories and novels that end with young people dissociating themselves from the past and achieving some kind of liberation: for instance, going away to college, leaving home. If the past has been somewhat negative, then they define a new future for themselves. That is a theme I have noticed in my work, because I did that myself. I left my hometown, a very small place where the opportunities were narrow, es-

pecially for women. When I left for college and went to graduate school and so forth, it seemed like an archetypal trajectory that men and women were going through in my generation. Men had always been doing it, then women were starting to.

Some critics have commented on a darkness in your fiction. But I do not think you paint a grim picture of the world.

No, I don't think so. As I say, I have novels that end with the liberation of a young person. **You Must Remember This** concludes with a young girl going away to college. **Bellefleur** ends with young people leaving their homes, which were very confining. I do not think my work is grim. It is more of a real picture, grim for some people, triumphant for others. The drama of our lives.

Sally Robinson (review date Summer 1992)

SOURCE: "Heat and Cold: Recent Fiction by Joyce Carol Oates," in *Michigan Quarterly Review,* Vol. XXXI, No. 3, Summer, 1992, pp. 400-14.

[*In the following review, Robinson surveys the themes and storytelling techniques of* The Rise of Life on Earth, I Lock My Door Upon Myself, *and* Heat and Other Stories, *focusing on representations of 'otherness' in her fiction.*]

To read Joyce Carol Oates is to be placed in the uncomfortably fascinating position of voyeur. From the early novels **them** and **Wonderland** to her most recent fiction, Oates has specialized in a narrative technique that intrudes upon the private pains and pleasures—but mostly pains—of Others. Her narratives often explore the dynamics of a voyeurism in which subject and object confront one another across a gulf of social difference. In some cases, the confrontation takes place between characters in the story; in others, Oates stages a confrontation between the reader and the object of that reader's gaze. In her preface to **them** (1969), Oates thematizes her relation to the underprivileged lives she narrates. Confessing that she has appropriated the story of a former student and, in the process, has become fascinated with the "various sordid and shocking events of slum life," she describes how the intrusion cuts both ways: "Their lives pressed upon mine eerily, so that I began to dream about them instead of about myself, dreaming and redreaming their lives. Because their world was so remote from me it entered me with tremendous power . . . " In the process of envisioning the "remote" Other, the writer is pressed to confront the security of her own position. While every writer is, in some sense, a voyeur, Oates's fiction foregrounds the political valences of a voyeurism in which a prying observer seeks the "sordid."

Oates's politically charged negotiation of the writer's position vis-à-vis the Others on whom she trains her gaze situates her within the context of postmodernism. While her fondness for realist modes of representation might place her outside the parameters of postmodern fiction as it has generally been theorized, her sustained exploration of the politics of representing Otherness has much in common with a certain contemporary problematic. Oates's work participates in what Linda Hutcheon, in *The Politics of Postmodernism,* notes as "a general cultural awareness of the existence and power of systems of representation which do not *reflect* society so much as *grant* meaning and value within a particular society." Like the postmodern anthropologist who questions the position from which she represents the Others of Western culture, Oates's fiction raises questions about the politics of representations. Such questioning can produce a sharp critique of our assumptions about social positions as guarantors of knowledge, security, and power. But a voyeuristic narrative technique has risks, for it can place the writer (and the reader) in a comfortable position *above* those whose sad lives seem to compel Oates's attention. Some of those risks become apparent in the short novel *The Rise of Life on Earth* in which Oates revisits Detroit and the world of *them.* In sharp contrast, *I Lock My Door Upon Myself* successfully engages the problems of granting meaning and value to an "alien" life. In *Heat and Other Stories,* Oates employs a wide range of voices in what I see as a sustained exploration of the connections between narrative perspective and social position.

The Rise of Life on Earth is the story of a young woman named Kathleen whose life is marked by abuse: beat to a pulp by her drunken father, shuffled from one foster home to another, Kathleen dreams of being a nurse. When she tones down her aspirations to become a nurse's aide, Kathleen meets a young intern, Orson Abbot, who uses her body as a passive and inert receptacle—for his semen, his drug-induced fantasies and recollections, his verbal and physical battering. But this is only part of Kathleen's story of abuse, for she is not an "innocent" victim. We learn that she, not her father, has killed her younger sister, that she has set a fatal fire at her foster home, and that she indulges in a series of random murders at the various hospitals and clinics where she works. As if this unrelentingly bleak life pattern is not enough, Oates has Kathleen give herself an abortion—with a surgical knife.

The plot of this story is troubling, but what strikes me as even more troubling is that the narrative voice participates in a de-humanization of Kathleen; placing her beyond the realm of human motive, intention, and even consciousness, the narrator seems as disgusted with Kathleen's "cow-like" physicality as Orson Abbot is. Descriptions of her, from the first page on, paint a subhuman creature:

Kathleen Hennessy with her pie-shaped face, pie-shaped maturing breasts, her pale, plump, soft, seemingly textureless flesh like that of a mollusk pried from its shell . . . and her recessed eyes that were darkly bright and alert, though betraying no expression; her delicate complexion riddled with tiny pimples like buckshot. There was something unsettlingly adult in her stoic resistance to pain and such extremes of discomfort and physical humiliation she was obliged to bear at the hands of the hospital staff, and something precocious about her small, pert, moist, pink rosebud of a mouth, a miniature mouth, that reminded observers of a part of the female anatomy that is private and should not be exposed to casual eyes.

The image of the mollusk is perfectly appropriate for Kathleen, as is the final comment about the private being exposed to casual eyes, which predicts Orson's reduction of Kathleen to a "cunt." Kathleen is exposed again and again in this story, and nothing much causes her to "betray expression." She has no memory and no volition; even her acts of violence are beyond her conscious control and calculation. She seems the human form sprung out of the non-human muck at the birth of the world, as described in the science textbook from which the story takes its title. As the narrator tells us at the end of the story, Kathleen is to continue life through a "succession of robot-selves."

The narrator's objectification, and de-humanization, of Kathleen is an example of the voyeurism that places the reader *above* the "sordid" details Oates narrates. This is a painful story, and as I began the last chapter knowing that Kathleen would methodically perform the abortion on herself, I did not want to read on. The novel is not a tract on the importance of safe and legal abortion, for Oates does not moralize here—nor does she give any motivation for Kathleen's action. When, at the end, the narrator tells us that Kathleen does not contest the "price of her freedom," I am left baffled, for "freedom" does not seem to enter into the picture at all. Indeed, Kathleen has treasured the thought of her pregnancy, the only event in her life that prompts any response in Kathleen's consciousness—except for her almost religious devotion to her nursing duties.

My problems with this novel are political rather than aesthetic: Oates's representation of Kathleen so totally objectifies her that it confirms, rather than questions, middle-class attitudes toward the urban poor. The reader of this story becomes fully complicit in this objectification of Kathleen and I see nothing in the story that would prompt a questioning of the narrator's (or reader's) position in relation to her. Aesthetically, this story is admirable for the rich texture of Oates's prose. She deftly captures the kind of trance-like quality of Kathleen's engagement with the world, crafting sentences that unfold and circle, sometimes for pages. The description of Kathleen's response to the hospital's instructions for handwashing procedures conveys a rapture:

> Just as years before in an interlude in her life now virtually forgotten Kathleen Hennessy as a child of eleven had come to unexpected bloom in a ward at Children's Hospital so now as a young woman of nineteen did she come to a yet more radiant bloom as a nurse's aide at Detroit Metropolitan Hospital where she was trained in such matters as *handwashing procedures* which came to fascinate her to the point very nearly of trance as if she believed that such procedures as instructed by her superiors were clues to a fundamental principle of the universe both the human world so difficult to comprehend let alone negotiate and the world beyond the human hitherto wholly incomprehensible, unfathomable thus in a sort of waking trance a small pinched smile on her face eyes lowered as if in tremulous reverence she obeyed every commandment of such matters as *handwashing procedures*—

While a sentence like this might not appeal to all readers, I find it hypnotically rhythmic. But as much as I am carried away by Oates's language here, this virtuoso performance does not shake my uncomfortable feeling that Oates's New Directions audience is being invited to fetishize this entirely alien and utterly frightening life. To fetishize an Other means to see that Other only as a negative reflection of the Self, making difference a confirmation of identity.

I Lock My Door Upon Myself shares with the other novel a hypnotic prose style, but here the story is told through the mediating consciousness of the protagonist's granddaughter, who experiences a complicated identification with her grandmother Calla: "She was my mother's mother but not my grandmother in any terms I can comprehend and if her mad blood courses through me now I have no knowledge of it and am innocent of it." In the process of telling Calla's story, the narrator questions her own role in imagining that story and asks: "how can I speak of that woman let alone speak for her who scarcely knew her?" The narrator's account of Calla's life is punctuated by unanswered questions that all point to the narrator's concern that she is appropriating Calla's story for her own purposes. These questions, in other words, signal the story's exploration of the politics of representation: Who speaks? From what position? In whose interests?

The narrator worries that in speaking *for* Calla, she is not allowing Calla to speak for herself. As the title of the novel makes clear, Calla is protective of her secret lives and desires, and the narrator is self-conscious about violating those secrets. This novel can be called metafictional in the sense

that it explicitly thematizes the problems I have noted in the narrative stance of *The Rise of Life on Earth*. Published by the Ecco Press in a series of "fictions in imaginative collaboration with works of art," the story's inspiration comes from a painting by the nineteenth-century German artist Fernand Khnopff. It is easy to see why the painting, and especially the title, intrigued Oates. The story she weaves around this painting of a dreamy woman subtly and powerfully explores the gulf between public and private selves— or, more precisely, between a woman's self-representation and the world's representation of her.

This is the story of a woman whose "wildness" is always the object of public scrutiny. Orphaned when young, Calla dreams her way through life until she is asked to marry George Freilicht. She neither consents nor refuses, but seems, instead, to allow herself to be passively carried along on the waves of others' desires. But Calla keeps herself distant from the marriage, her husband, and later her children, continuing to live a private life separate from the public one. Her "nocturnal selves" are more real than her daytime self. To stress this division, Oates gives her protagonist both a public and a private name; she refers to herself as "Calla," while everyone else except the narrator uses her legal name, "Edith." She meets and falls in love with Tyrell Thompson, an itinerant black water diviner, and proceeds to scandalize her family and the community. Significantly, it is only to Tyrell that Calla tells her "real" name. The love affair ends in typical Oates fashion, in violence: the two lovers go over a waterfall in a rowboat. Tyrell is killed and Calla locks herself into her room, leaving the house only for funerals, and living out the remainder of her life, fifty-five years, in almost complete solitude.

This story is rich in the tradition of Faulkner: complex psychological dynamics and mysteries become the subject of an awed scrutiny on the part of the narrating consciousness. The narrator merges with Calla, as indicated by the frequent italicized passages that signal a confusion between the two. The most striking of these is repeated several times, and hints at the story's exploration of regions of experience beyond conventional language: *"If this is a dream it is not my dream for how should I know the language in which to dream it."* Calla's dream and the narrator's dream are one because, as the granddaughter explains, *"we are linked by blood and blood is memory without language."* The narrator stumbles over describing Calla in conventional terms, noting that such phrases as "unnatural mother" and "white trash" do not get at the heart of what Calla is. In the process of telling the story of Calla's unconventional life, the narrator experiences outrage at others' failure to understand her grandmother: *"And that's the insult of it, how always it comes back to a woman being a 'good' mother in the world's eyes or a 'bad' mother, how everything in a woman's life is funneled through her body between her legs."*

In the "world's eyes" Calla's complex reality is reduced to her failure to confirm that world's assumptions about what a woman is or should be; her desires, her specificity, and her point of view are denied by an objectifying gaze. It is the difference between the "world's eyes" and the narrator's eyes which suggests that Oates is critiquing the type of narrative perspective she employs in *The Rise of Life on Earth.* I am not claiming that Oates engages in self-criticism here, nor am I suggesting that *I Lock My Door Upon Myself* is a better book in the "disinterested" terms of aesthetic evaluation, for I have little faith in the validity of such terms. What I am arguing is that *I Lock My Door Upon Myself* effectively comments on what I see as the politically problematic representation in *The Rise of Life on Earth* of the "unknown" underclasses as subhuman. Whereas Kathleen is positioned as the disempowered *object* of a knowing and superior gaze, Calla and the narrator merge into a complex double *subject* of the narrative. I am reminded here of Christa Wolf's *The Quest for Christa T,* another novel in which a female narrator considers the complex personal and political implications of telling another woman's story.

Voyeurism depends on distance and difference and, thus, can be seen as opposing identification, which works through closeness and the bridging of difference. In *The Rise of Life on Earth,* the narrative voice probes Kathleen's consciousness from a distance, constructing her as the Other, the "not-me." In *I Lock My Door Upon Myself,* Oates's use of a questioning, fully participating narrator facilitates an identification that bridges the gap between Self and Other. Despite Calla's mystery, then, she is not positioned as alien or Other. In *Heat and Other Stories,* Oates experiments with a variety of narrative forms and modes of address and, as we've come to expect from Oates, the stories construct many different worlds. The collection is divided into three sections. In the first, Oates trains her lens on the lives of privileged people who confront an otherness imposed on their lives. In the vein of her recent novel *American Appetites,* these first eight stories sketch a violent underside to lives whose glittering surfaces are fragile. The characters who inhabit these slick worlds hover on the verge of revelation, but never quite get there. While these stories thematize confrontations between self and other, subject and object, security and violence, the narrative tone seems deliberately cold and even indifferent. Whereas the narrative voice in *The Rise of Life on Earth* is clinical, these narrators appear indifferent toward the lives under scrutiny. While the protagonist of the novel is objectified by the narrator, these characters do not seem to compel Oates's interest enough to be held up as alien or exotic objects. In the second section, where Oates focuses on the lives of America's urban and rural underclasses, the stories have a strikingly different tone. Part of the difference can be accounted for by her use of first-person narration in many of the stories, but I think there is something else going on here. What I see in the contrast between the two sets

of stories is a difference in perspective based on social class and position. Working under the reasonable but unprovable assumption that Oates's imagined audience is comprised mainly of middle-class readers, we can come to the tentative conclusion that the characters in the first set of stories are not constructed as Others because they lack "difference." I suspect that, for Oates, these characters are too much like "us" to be the proper objects of a voyeuristic gaze, even if the narrative perspective is distanced from the lives it narrates. Foreclosing on both voyeuristic engagement and identification, these stories thematize, rather than enact, the problematics of storytelling that I am arguing place Oates in a postmodern context. In the third section, Oates moves into more eerie, less "naturalistic" terrain, where the confrontation with Otherness is displaced onto another plane entirely.

In the first story, **"House Hunting,"** Oates offers a metaphor for the dynamics of reading. Joel, the central character, expresses an uncomfortable excitement about entering the lives and homes of others, guided by a woman who has the "key" to them all:

> She had the key to every lock; only let her fit it into the door and the door opened and she led her client inside: Mr. Collier, who was made to feel uncharacteristically passive, helpless. He didn't like the feeling. Then again, he did like it; there was something intimate and brazen, heady, as if with the air of the forbidden, about being led by a woman he didn't know into the houses of people he didn't know, escorted through rooms in which strangers lived their secret lives. The first several minutes were the most acute; he felt shy, absurdly ill at ease, excited. As if he was being brought to a test of some kind, a challenge or a riddle, and would not be equal to it.

This is the "challenge" that Oates mounts for her readers in these stories, which all have something of an "air of the forbidden." But Joel, like other characters in the first group of stories, fails to take up the challenge. He searches for meaning in empty houses, seeking to work through his grief over his wife's unsuccessful pregnancy. Imagining that the attic of one particularly decrepit house might be the "place of revelation," he finds, instead, "nothing in this room but the space itself," and the narrator asks: "But what otherwise might there have been? What had he hoped to see?"

Joel's life is without "purpose," and the story ends with his having acquired only the vaguest sense of renewed power and energy through his exploration. **"House Hunting"** is one of the few stories in *Heat* which does not culminate in an act of physical violence. **"Shopping,"** one of the best stories, is another. A ritual trip to a high-class suburban mall becomes the occasion for a woman's freeing herself from her tyrannical daughter. Mrs. Dietrich, divorced from her husband and living the life of the wealthy suburban matron, lives through her teenaged daughter Nola, whose birth is the signal event of Mrs. Dietrich's life: "She told no one, but she knew the baby would be a girl. It would be herself again, reborn and this time perfect." Clichéd as this may sound, the story goes far beyond the ordinary in painting Mrs. Dietrich as the conventional woman whose experience becomes, in Oates's subtle tones, unconventional, miraculous, and violent.

The rarified atmosphere of the mall—"the air is fresh and tonic"—reassures Mrs. Dietrich who attempts to keep the immanent violence of her relationship with Nola at bay. The product of her body has betrayed her, and violence erupts. Mrs. Dietrich is forced to confront her separateness from Nola and, in the process, the daughter becomes an alien being:

> Seeing Nola now, Mrs. Dietrich is charged with hurt, rage; the injustice of it, she thinks, the cruelty of it, and why, and why? And as Nola glances up, startled, not prepared to see her mother in front of her, their eyes lock for an instant and Mrs. Dietrich stares at her with hatred. Cold calm clear unmistakable hatred. She is thinking, Who are *you*? What have I to do with *you*? I don't know *you*, I don't love *you*, why should I?

Mrs. Dietrich's sense of "injustice" is purely personal, and does not extend to the bag lady she and Nola see in the mall. Refusing to let this woman's presence detract from the pleasure of "serious shopping," Mrs. Dietrich has no qualms about flaunting her privilege and spending her money. While Mrs. Dietrich fails to analyze the huge gulf between herself and this woman—and Nola spouts some obligatory outrage over the woman while spending over $200 on a designer jacket—the reader is left to contemplate the jarring effect of a contemporary world where Lord & Taylor coexists side-by-side with the disenfranchised. Mrs. Dietrich will return to her suburban home, and Nola to her prep school in Maine, neither of them having been much affected by the experience.

Mrs. Dietrich's desire to hide the messy emotional outbursts which end the story links **"Shopping"** with **"Passion."** In this story, the main character suffers from *lack* of passion, a lack brought home to him by his ex-wife's suicide. Dennis might well stand in for the narrative voice in many of these first eight stories, as well as for the characters who fail at naming and understanding their experiences. The lack of language with which to articulate sudden emotional turbulence seems to afflict the privileged characters in all of these stories. Remembering his ex-wife's accusation that he lacks

"passion," Dennis associates this lack with a failure of language: "In his professional life he was a man of infinite tact, intelligence, presence; in his private life, he had always seemed to himself mysteriously undefined." A recurring dream strikes Dennis "as an image of his predicament, yet to have defined that predicament, to have given it a precise vocabulary: this was a task seemingly beyond him." Ironically, it is in investigating Rona's suicide that Dennis begins to experience "passion." But this, too, remains "undefined," and the story ends with Dennis tottering on the edge of a revelation, not knowing what to do with that passion: "It frightened him, the emotion he felt—its crudeness, violence. He wondered was it passion. He wondered was it anything to which he might give a name."

In **"Knife"** and **"The Boyfriend,"** acts of physical violence seem to force the victim to some kind of revelation; but that revelation is so vaguely drawn as to leave the reader with a sense of dissatisfaction. I say this in an analytic rather than judgmental spirit, for Oates seems to purposefully structure these narratives around an anti-climax. In **"Knife,"** Harriet and her daughter Bonnie are home alone, when two men break into the house. Disappointed with the lack of material possessions, one of them rapes Harriet. The two intruders mock Harriet's privilege, the rapist threatening her verbally as well as physically: " 'You think you're hot shit, don't you? People like you'." During the attack, Harriet wonders, "Is this rape? *This*?—as the man pried her legs apart, poked himself against her." Her primary response is shame, humiliation, and worry that the police and her husband will blame her. Finally she decides to tell her husband about the rape—but only because she fears that keeping it inside will turn her "into a religious lunatic." The story ends: "And what would happen, as a consequence, would happen." The narrative voice here seems apathetic, as if Harriet's experience does not qualify as significant. Is it because an experience as violent as rape fails to shake Harriet enough? Is Oates suggesting that Harriet "deserves" the rape, as a punishment for her uninteresting and complacent life? Is violence, for Oates, the only way to find meaning, and then only if one acts violently in return?

Some of these questions find tentative answers in **"Naked,"** one of the most compelling stories of the collection. The story is the proverbial nightmare of naked exposure made real: the unnamed protagonist finds herself completely naked, entirely vulnerable, and miles from her home. Enjoying an afternoon in a "suburban wildlife preserve [!]", the woman is attacked by a vicious group of black children, who take her clothes in what the woman feels is an outrageously unprovoked act of cruelty. Her outrage is accompanied by her shame; she obsessively focuses on avoiding having to make a police report, for she fears appearing as a racist.

The oft-repeated litany, "I am not a racist," punctuates this profound exploration of the woman's subjective and social position. She alternates between thinking of her attackers as "savages" who threaten to "devour her alive: set upon her like ravenous animals, tear the flesh from her bones with their teeth and eat," and thinking that she "deserves" the attack because of "the unwanted but undeniable privilege of her white skin." Oates subtly challenges this woman's secure conviction that she harbors no racist sentiments and, simultaneously, challenges her readers to place themselves in the woman's position.

> [S]he was a woman in no way racially prejudiced who had grown up with blacks, gone to school with blacks, Chinese, Hispanics, and other minorities, as they were familiarly called, and she was determined to instill in her children the identical unjudging uncensorious liberalism her parents had quite consciously instilled in her. So it did not strike her, as perhaps it should have, upon occasion at least, that these minorities might look upon her as conspicuously different from themselves and that, against the grain of all that was reasonable, charitable, and just, they might wish to do so and take satisfaction in it.

Underneath this lovely liberalism we glimpse an absolute failure to see beyond a certain point of view—and, perhaps worse, a willed ignorance about the possibility that the "Other" might *have* a point of view that could be trained on the self. Here, Oates delivers a ringing indictment of a certain self-congratulatory liberalism, but, at the same time, manages to elicit sympathy for the woman who is, after all, the victim of a violent attack. Making her way home through the treacherous terrain hidden behind the clean surfaces of suburbia, the woman "was excited and yet dreamy too: standing for a long purposeless moment staring at the debris of strangers, wondering at lives parallel to her own yet unknown to her." Stripped of the trappings of her "civilized" existence, and forced to face the "wildlife" that infiltrates suburbia, she ponders her own vulnerability. The story transforms this woman from subject into object of a voyeuristic gaze, and Oates stresses the woman's fear that she might function as the raw material for someone else's story: "She would become a story, a fiction."

The second section of *Heat* challenges the subjective positions articulated in the first: here, the reader enters the idiosyncratically-drawn private worlds of underprivileged folks. In **"Heat,"** two uncannily alike twins are brutally murdered by a man who might or might not be "simpleminded." The narrator is a former classmate of the twins, Rhea and Rhoda, who works to fill in the gaps of the story, to invent the murder because "I wasn't there, but some things you know." This story differs from others in this section, in that the violence remains untold, "the door was shut, the shade on the window was drawn," and the reader joins in the narrator's morbid fascination with inventing the details of the murder. Closed doors and drawn shades are appropriate metaphors for a voyeuristic narrative—not unlike the cinematic technique of that master of voyeurism, Alfred Hitchcock. The grisly details of the murder remain unspoken, but the narrator hints that the crime has a lurid sexual component. This becomes particularly clear when the narrator, years later, thinks back to Rhea and Rhoda while having sex in close proximity to the scene of the murder. Her (and our) voyeuristic fascination with this crime is in sharp contrast to the indifference that marks Oates's representation of Harriet's rape.

A number of the stories in this part of *Heat* explore the difficulties of the story-teller's position, her precarious relationship to her material. In **"The Buck,"** the narrator confesses to an obsession with the story of an elderly woman who, in trying to save the life of a buck shot by a hunter, dies, her body literally merging with the buck's in a frozen tableau. In intimate relation to her readers, the narrator says: "Each time I tell this story . . . I think that maybe *this* telling will make a difference. *This* time a secret meaning will be revealed, as if without my volition, and I will be released." The meaning the narrator finds is the meaning she creates, in weaving for Melanie Snyder a life marked by sexual and familial repression. Because of the way the story is framed it is clear that Oates is commenting here on the dynamics of storytelling, implicating herself and the reader, as well as her narrator, in a kind of voyeuristic exercise in which Melanie is explicitly framed as the object of a probing gaze.

While the narrator in **"The Buck"** might be seen as the author's surrogate, Oates plays the part of ventriloquist in **"White Trash,"** a story guaranteed to raise the hackles of a politically sensitive white, middleclass reader—a reader not unlike the woman in **"Naked."** Here, we have a first-person narrator, who, despite her direct address of the reader, nevertheless reveals herself to be painfully vulnerable to that reader's gaze. One of four stories in *Heat* which equivocates over the question of rape versus consensual sex, **"White Trash"** is the story of another Melanie, a self-styled "white trash" woman who fetishizes a black jazz pianist, Mayweather Smith. The story virtually drips with the erotic energy of Melanie whose sexuality can only be characterized as masochistic. Referring to herself as both "I" and "Melanie," the narrator is split between subject and object, a split that seems entirely appropriate to her experiences. Watching and listening to Mayweather, Melanie plots his seduction, "thinking, Mmmmm, Melanie, you're the luckiest woman alive." As a backdrop to the present action, which includes a sexual encounter through which Mayweather appears to take out his resentment of white supremacy on the pathetic target of Melanie's skinny body, Melanie relates a tale of abuse at the hands of various (white) lovers and an uncaring medical establishment. The two trade stories about injustices in the world, Melanie's about the loss of a baby and Mayweather's about his baby brother killed by white police on the streets of Cleveland. No sentimentalist, however, Oates does not allow these characters to find an artificial solace in each other's arms. The sexual encounter is violent and unsettling in its depiction of racial and sexual dynamics—unsettling, precisely, to the reader whose voyeuristic gaze witnesses the event and is denied an easy answer to the questions the story raises.

> **. . . Oates's voyeuristic imagination, like Hitchcock's perhaps, inevitably seeks out the shocking and sordid.**
> —*Sally Robinson*

The stories in *Heat* are unrelentingly violent. In **"Sundays in Summer,"** a young boy jumps off a bridge and is gored by a cable in the water. **"Leila Lee"** ends with a son frenetically killing his father with an axe. **"The Swimmers"** contains a shooting, and **"Getting to Know All About You"** a brutal beating. In **"Hostage,"** a young girl is saved from being molested by an itinerant, who is then repeatedly stabbed by her rescuer. **"Yarrow"** ends with one cousin mowing down another in his car on an icy road. In **"Craps"** and **"Death Valley,"** the second appearing to be a retelling of the first, young women are subject to violent sexual attacks by men, and in the second, the man fantasizes about the woman killing him with a razor. Why is Oates so fascinated by violence, so drawn to scenes of blood and carnage? What pleasure does she expect her readers to get from this violence, from a complicity in morbid fascination? I confess that I do not have answers to these questions, except to say that Oates's voyeuristic imagination, like Hitchcock's perhaps, inevitably seeks out the shocking and sordid.

"Getting to Know All About You" provides a breath of fresh air, for here, Oates gives us a welcome touch of humor, despite the story's depiction of a family inches away from disaster. In love with her mother Trix, the narrator lovingly renders that mother's idiosyncratic speech. Judith is an intelligent, alienated adolescent girl, whose narration of her family's deterioration is haunted by her sense of guilt over "spying" on her colorful parents. Her brother Wesley speaks of the "politics of this family," epitomized by the disproportion of "before" and "after" photographs in the family album—before the children's births and after. (Trix refuses to be called "Mother," claiming that it's an "absurd definition.") Oates gives her readers a voyeuristic look into this "dysfunctional" family, the story's humor punctuated with the pathos of an impossible dream. The seemingly invincible Trix— who refers to turning thirty as "peeking over the edge into the abyss," and insists that drinking alone is "like, you know, making love alone. It lacks class"—regales the reader with

her rich language and her indomitable spirit. But, lest the reader forget that this is an Oates story, Trix ends up in the state mental hospital and Darrell on the lam from the police. If Judith and Wesley fear that they have violated the norms of privacy, and even decency, in "spying" on their parents—they blame themselves for what happens to Trix and Darrell—then the reader shares in that fear. This story explicitly comments on the dynamics of voyeurism, suggesting that looking into others' windows, uninvited, might have dire consequences for the object of the gaze.

The stories in the brief last section of *Heat* signal new territory for Oates, where the ordinary becomes alien and terrifying. These stories, in their exploration of a dark subterranean beneath the veneer of family life, cover the kind of ground that David Lynch investigates in his films. In **"Twins"** and **"Why Don't You Come Live With Me It's Time"** Oates again employs the perspective of daughters who inquire into, but do not solve, the riddles of family legend. In the first, the girl's father, Lee, is haunted by his vanished twin brother, Les. Obsessed with finding Les, Lee struggles to maintain an identity separate from his twin, but ends up being eclipsed and destroyed. The daughter-narrator, in her turn, is haunted by her dead father, and ends by wondering: "Is this common? Will it get worse? Is it something you can die of?" **"Why Don't You Come Live With Me It's Time,"** an intriguing and engaging story, begins where **"Twins"** leaves off, with the narrator seeing her dead grandmother in her mirror. The story represents the grown woman's attempt to differentiate herself from her grandmother. In the process she comes to understand that her grandmother, whom she adores, has a perspective (and life) of her own. This story contains a nightmare-like sequence, in which Claire imagines her grandmother spiking her oatmeal with glass. Claire fears sleep and identifies with her grandmother's insomnia—"but no one made the connection between her and me. Our family was that way: worrying that one weakness might find justification in another and things would slip out of containment and control," not unlike the family in **"Getting to Know All About You."**

In **"Family,"** a strange tale of a world and a family that has survived some kind of industrial or nuclear disaster, Oates forays into science fiction territory. The story is partially a cautionary tale about the hazards of a world drunk on its own technological progress. It is also a story about the violence of families, transported to an appropriately horrific setting. Babies eat mothers, mothers kill babies, fathers mysteriously disappear—but the family stubbornly holds its ground, despite the death of the world around it. Here Oates explores a postmodern terrain where an alien reality has an uncanny similarity to the lived reality of American society. Like Margaret Atwood's *The Handmaid's Tale* and some of Angela Carter's fantastic novels, this story chills because, despite its science fiction tenor, it seems all too familiar.

The story is told from the point of view of a family member who describes, but does not analyze, the gradual deterioration of life in "the valley." The story begins with a shocking description of industrial pollution and contamination as sublime:

> The days were brief and attenuated and the season appeared to be fixed—neither summer nor winter, spring nor fall. A thermal haze of inexpressible sweetness (though bearing tiny bits of grit or mica) had eased into the valley from the industrial regions to the north. . . . Above the patchwork of excavated land bordering our property—*all* of which had formerly been our property in Grandfather's time: thousands of acres of fertile soil and open grazing land—a curious fibrillating rainbow sometimes appeared, its colors shifting even as you stared, shades of blue, turquoise, iridescent green, russet red, a lovely translucent gold that dissolved to moisture as the thermal breeze stirred, warm and stale as an exhaled breath.

The family seems hypnotized by this "inexpressible sweetness" and they display a frightening ability to adapt to an increasingly poisonous environment. Part of that adaptation includes forgetting life as it used to be; memories vanish, words evaporate, vocabulary changes, and the "new" world replaces the old. At the end of the story, a post-apocalypse spring is born, and the family debates "abolishing the calendar entirely and declaring this the First Day of Year One, and beginning Time anew." This frightening tale warns against complacency and accommodation. It works.

"Ladies and Gentleman:" is also a nightmare tale that critiques the progress-oriented pulse of a society that finds it easier to forget the past than to deal with it. This is satire on the model of "A Modest Proposal" and, along with the science fiction feel of **"Family,"** suggests that Oates is once again experimenting with new modes. The story takes the form of a speech by the captain of a boat to a group of aging men and women who are being put out to pasture by their greedy children and grandchildren. The reader is made to feel trapped along with the passengers en route to The Island of Tranquility where they will be left to die. The captain suggests that "we" are being punished for failing to grant "our" children identities of their own: "Ladies and gentlemen, you rarely stopped to consider your children as other than *your* children, as men and women growing into maturity distinct from you."

These last two stories mark a departure from what I have been arguing is Oates's place within the postmodern questioning of the politics of representation. Interestingly, in terms of their anti-realist mode, these two stories seem to point toward the possibility of Oates moving more fully and explicitly into the postmodern. Indeed, Oates has entered this terrain before, with her revisions of romance form in *Mysteries of Winterthurn* and *A Bloodsmoor Romance* and with the meta-fictional and meta-historical *Bellefleur*. Joyce Carol Oates, of course, is not a writer who bows to critical or generic orthodoxy, and it is difficult to place her within any one strain of contemporary fiction. A writer of stunning range and imaginative reach, Oates, in my view, is most interesting when she leaves safe ground to explore the complex psychological and political dynamics of storytelling. This exploration is what makes *I Lock My Door Upon Myself* not only the best of the three books, but a very good book indeed. *Heat and Other Stories,* as a collection, raises a number of interesting questions about Oates's position in relation to the lives and worlds she constructs. That the stories about privileged characters utilize a different narrative voice and stance than the stories of the underprivileged suggests that Oates is fully aware of the complicated ways in which fiction engages questions of social position. If, in scrutinizing the Others of American society, she forces her readers to confront their own comfortable subjective positions, then she has accomplished a great deal. The white, middle-class characters in *Heat* are subtly displaced from their empowered positions, both by the intrusion of Otherness and uncertainty into their worlds, and by Oates's disinterested narrators who frame these characters as unworthy of reader empathy or identification. My discomfort with *The Rise of Life on Earth* stems from my sense that Oates is appropriating a "sordid and shocking" life from a voyeuristic distance that leaves her readers safe and secure in their position above that life. Perhaps other readers will see what I have missed in this novel, for Oates does not strike me as a writer who unthinkingly represents *any* life. In her famous Balzacian desire to "put the whole world into a book," Oates just might revisit Kathleen's story and tell it from Kathleen's perspective. Whatever she does next, even readers who are ambivalent about Joyce Carol Oates can at least be sure that she will continue to shock—and to surprise.

Marilyn C. Wesley (essay date Summer 1992)

SOURCE: "The Transgressive Other in Joyce Carol Oates's Recent Fiction," in *Critique: Studies in Contemporary Fiction,* Vol. XXXIII, No. 4, Summer, 1992, pp. 255-62.

[*In the following essay, Wesley surveys Oates's later fiction to describe the function of "the transgressive other" in her narrative technique.*]

According to Tony Tanner [in *Adultery in the Novel,* 1979], "Very often the novel writes of contracts but dreams of transgressions," a paradoxical statement well illustrated in the fiction of Joyce Carol Oates. Although Oates has been thought of primarily as a realist, even a moralist, her work may often be understood with respect to its dialectic *with* the text, its superimposition of a narrative leveled against the text itself to decenter the social codes through which it is organized. This radical contradiction is regularly mounted by the intriguing and anti-social character that I designate as the *transgressive other*, who is defined by a narrative position in contrapuntal relation to domestic norms and standards of communicability within which the text is located. The most famous example of this "transgressive other" is Arnold Friend in Oates's frequently anthologized short story, **"Where Are You Going, Where Have You Been?"** but other such figures are a recurrent device throughout her career and a dominant feature in her most recent novels.

In **"Where Are You Going, Where Have You Been?"** [in *The Wheel of Love*] fifteen-year-old Connie is engaged in the tentative process of defining herself through a counter-ideology—made up of popular music, shopping center trinkets, and youthful sexuality—that opposes the belief system of her parents and her "plain" and "steady" twenty-four-year-old sister until mock-heroic Arnold Friend introduces her to the unapprehended corollary to heady independence: that in abandoning family norms she also loses family protection. To read the moral of this story as a disparagement of tasteless teenage defiance is entirely possible. In fact, critics generally interpret **"Where Are You Going, Where Have You Been?"** as Connie's initiation into evil, and in the ending of the story they discover Connie's capitulation to the shallow values of a debased culture. Her own commentary on the story in a review of the film based on it shows that Oates is also particularly concerned with the ending, specifically with the reversal in the movie version of the text's "unfilmable" last paragraph. In Joyce Chopra's adaptation, Connie is saved from the murder that is her probable fate after the conclusion of the story; at the end of the film she returns to her family, "rejecting the 'trashy dreams' of her pop-teen culture." In Oates's version, however, Connie does not return to her family nor abandon her adolescent impetus toward freedom; although she will probably be raped and killed, the diction of light and open space of the final words of the story implies positive value in "the vast sunlit reaches of the land . . . Connie had never seen before and did not recognize except to know that she was going to it."

That Arnold, the probable rapist and killer, is a diabolic figure and a depraved lunatic is indisputable. As Oates reports, she based him on a "tabloid psychopath" whose "specialty was the seduction and occasional murder of teenage girls," but that he is also somehow useful, even appealing, is the clear implication of the surprising tone of the ending of the story. Arnold's positive function, I believe, is that he openly confronts the codes of the family. Although he himself has no genuine identity (he borrows his artificial form from a humorous pastiche of teenage styles and slogans), he forces Connie into a recognition of the necessary displacement of the unexamined forms of "family" that both define and confine her:

> "The place where you come from ain't there any more, and where you had in mind is cancelled out. This place you are now—inside your daddy's house—is nothing but a cardboard box I can knock down any time. You know that and you always did know it. You hear me?"

That Arnold has a positive function as the transgressive other to the text of the American family is demonstrated by the fact that similar figures of limit and challenge are a constant feature throughout Oates's oeuvre. Max, the manipulative esthete of **With Shuddering Fall** (1964); Richard Everett, the matricidal memoirist of **Expensive People** (1968); Trick Monk, the trickster foil of the protagonist in **Wonderland** (1971); Hugh Petrie, the nihilistic cartoonist of **The Assassins** (1975); Bobbie Gotteson, the "Maniac" of **The Triumph of the Spider Monkey** (1976); Fitz John Kasch, the post-romantic central consciousness of **Childwold** (1976); Alexis Kessler, the narcissistic composer of **Unholy Loves** (1979); Sheilah Trask, the "dark" opposite of Monica Jensen of **Solstice** (1985); and Maxmilian Fein, the demonic father-lover of **Marya** (1985) are key examples. What these characters have in common is their opposition to the norms of community and comprehensibility that the texts seem to endorse.

This use of a "transgressive other" to the text as a projection of deviation—a struggle within the text against its own limits of consciousness—is a prominent feature of Oates's most recent fiction, in which the story and status of such an opposing figure is foregrounded. Three important works published in 1989 and 1990—**American Appetites, Soul/Mate,** and **Because It Is Bitter, and Because It Is My Heart**—mark the emergence of this narrative pattern and its related themes as Oates's central preoccupation at this time.

Soul/Mate is a revealing example of this tendency. Not only does the plot concern the actions and motivations of an extreme "other," a "psychopath" in the tradition of Arnold Friend, but the genre of the work and even the designation of the author emphasize the thematics of "otherness." **Soul/Mate,** a "psychothriller" according to the book jacket, a genre Oates reserves for the consideration of the otherness themes of "identity, twins and doubling," is the second of her novels to be published under the pseudonym Rosamond Smith. "I wanted a fresh reading; I wanted to escape from my own identity," Oates explained, and in a discussion of Romain Gary's *nom de plume*, she posited the writer's need for "an erasure of the primary self" so that "another (hitherto undiscovered?) self may be released." This employment of an alternative authorial "other" strongly suggests the desire to test the ideological limits of "Joyce Carol Oates," a writer by now established in a particular tradition.

The structure and meaning of the novel also underscore this concern for the evasion of bounds. The two main characters of the work are Dorothea Deverell, a decorous and passive art historian approaching middle age and Colin Asch, a waif-like and appealing serial killer. Written from the third-person limited-omniscient point of view, the chapters of *Soul/Mate* alternate between the perspectives of Dorothea and Colin to produce the effect that these characters do indeed mirror one another despite their differences in style. "[O]ur lives are . . . parallel," he . "[T]heir predicaments were identical," she observes at a crucial point; "they were united in their desperation to escape." And, in fact, Colin does serve as the agent of Dorothea's unacknowledged wishes. Standing between her and future fulfillment as the director of the prestigious Brannon Institute and the wife of her lover Charles Carpenter are two impediments—Dorothea's slanderous enemy Roger Krauss, who favors another candidate for the appointment that she has been promised, and Mrs. Agnes Carpenter, Charles's alcoholic wife. By garroting Krauss and drowning Agnes, Colin clears the way for the happiness that is Dorothea's implicit fate at the conclusion of the novel.

That Colin is Dorothea's psychological other is obvious. Where she is methodical, he is manic. Where she is self-doubting, he is narcissistic. Where she is self-abnegating, he is wildly paranoid. Where she resolutely denies, he perversely accepts. Where her personal relationships are mired in "stasis," his intimate connections are resolved through deadly action. But the otherness Colin represents has a social dimension as well. While Dorothea is preternaturally sensitive to the nuances and codes of her group, Colin's self-absorption radically distorts his ability to decipher even rudimentary gestures. This is dramatically demonstrated in the first of the murders the book details:

> [D]riving out of Fort Lauderdale in the red '87 Mustang with the sliding sun roof the woman had given him, which she surely wouldn't call the police to get returned . . . he happened to see, one lane over to the right, one car length ahead, a car he thought at first to be identical with his, lipstick-red, two-door coupe . . . but it turned out to be a Toyota of about that year, and what drew his attention to it like a magnet was it had a sliding sun roof too *and the roof was partway open and there was a hand stuck through it wriggling the fingers to taunt him.*
>
> *Or was it a signal?*

Cornering the driver in a rest stop men's room, Colin demands to know the meaning of the taunting wave. Explain-

ing that he was stretching to try to keep awake, the man insists that Colin has "misread" him. Colin, however, stubbornly adhering to his own deadly misinterpretation, accuses the unfortunate motorist of having tendered a "false signal" and kills him for the crime of deceptive discourse.

A novel, of course, is made meaningful insofar as it may be read with regard to the codes and systems it invokes. But recognizable patterns of language and culture are consistently obliterated in Colin's perversions of communication and understanding. It is pertinent that Colin is presented as the anti-author of a kind of parody of the novel. In the "Blue Ledger" Colin sets down aphoristic interpretations of his own experiences—the initials of his victims, the money he has received from them, and the coded notation of their deaths. Significantly, the codes employed involve reversal. The moment of Agnes Carpenter's murder, for example, is recorded with her initials inverted as *C.A.88104am.* In the denouement of *Soul/Mate* another meaningful reversal occurs to contradict symbolically the communicative function of the text: instead of preserving his journal, before his suicide, Colin carefully feeds it page by page into the fire.

This transgressive other represents, then, a dislocation of basic patterns of meaning. In his "Blue Ledger" Colin carefully records Blakean comments that outline the collapse of organizational categories:

> Thus "praise" and "blame" are equally unmerited.
>
> Thus "he" (agent) and "it" (action) are falsely separated.
>
> Thus even the most general time demarcations—"past," "present," "future"—are invalid.
>
> For in the Blue Room (which at certain times Colin Asch was privileged to enter [through the act of murder]) all things become one. The fierce blue light erases all shadow. There is no gravity, no weight. Not even "up" and "down."

The dissolution of contradictories characteristic of Colin's "Blue Room" posits an alternative to the opposed terms—for example, good/bad, male/female—upon which communities and texts are structured, an alternative, in his case, both attractive and deadly. At once "angel boy" and "devil twin," Colin is the intermediary between two universes of meaning—that of social repression but semantic order and that of freedom but incoherence. *Soul/Mate* suggests, therefore, that the very oppositions that make meaning possible—the arrangements from which civilization emerges—also make it destructive or impossible in the social or family experience of many of Oates's characters. Again, Colin's story provides the example.

The motivation for Colin's deviance is the extreme freedom realized in the dramatic loss of his parents in an automobile accident in which they were both drowned:

> The boy managed to get out and swim to the surface, but his father and mother were trapped inside the car, in only about eight feet of water, so the boy tried to save them diving back down trying to get the doors of the car open, trying to pull his mother free and then his father. . . . [A]nd it was said that Colin had gone mad in those minutes, that his mind had simply shattered.

Colin's subsequent actions are attempts to resolve his complex reactions to this experience. His rage at his mother's abandonment finds expression in his brutal treatment of women. Significantly, he fantasizes drowning Hartley, one of his lovers, in shallow water, and he does dispatch Agnes in this fashion. His equally powerful love for his lost mother is expressed through his adoring fixation on Dorothea, who, as Hartley reminds him, "looks old enough almost to be your mother." Colin chooses to murder Agnes Carpenter rather than Charles Carpenter, his rival for Dorothea's affections, because he imagines Dorothea and Charles can replace his lost parents: "It would be the most natural thing in the world; older childless couples often take up younger unattached men. A kind of spiritual adoption. 'You will never be lonely again.'" And when Colin finally kidnaps her, even obtuse Dorothea is aware that together they seem to be enacting "a grotesque parody of domesticity." The conclusion of the novel finds Dorothea and Charles together about to embark on their marriage in a new house. Oates's most uncharacteristically unambiguous ending sets this recovery of familial arrangement against the disorder Colin has introduced.

Similar domestic resolutions counter the appeal of disorder in both *American Appetites* and *Because It Is Bitter, and Because It Is My Heart.* In the first novel, a staid middle-aged man accidentally, but with much provocation and passion, kills his wife during a vituperative drunken argument. The book is structured around the complicated issue of his guilt; and during the course of his attenuated trial, the defendant himself experiences the emotional state of otherness. "It seems so easy, somehow," Ian McCullough musingly remarks to his lawyer. "Crossing over. . . . To what's on the other side." When the scandal first hits the newspapers, the lawyer suggests that Ian move into the Sheraton Inn under a false identity to avoid publicity. During this interval, Ian experiences an alternative self, the "Jonathan Hamilton" who signed the guest register. He wears a "pair of plastic clip-on lenses, dark green" to "give substance to his incognito." He makes minor adjustments to his appearance and discovers in his assumed alter ego interests and attitudes he had not previously acknowledged in himself. But this dark liberation, which is the substance of the plot, is countered by the ironic

frame of the novel. *American Appetites* commences, as does *Soul/Mate* with the domestic ceremony of an elaborate dinner party. It concludes with another dinner party. So despite the introduction of the theme of transgressive otherness, the frame of the book attempts to rectify the deviation that has been the central preoccupation of the novel. Despite McCullough's cataclysmic experience, the only substantial change in the structure of his world is the woman who officiates at the consistent dinner, an undeviating ceremony of communal regularity at either end of an attenuated exploration of violent alternative.

In *Because It Is Bitter, and Because It Is My Heart,* young Iris Courtney moves from the failed family of her working-class background into an upper-class family of inherited wealth and academic stature at the conclusion. This novel also endeavors to contain in domestic resolution the deviation from social order that consumes Iris throughout the novel. For the plot of *Because It Is Bitter, and Because It Is My Heart* concerns her experience and pursuit of otherness. In an uncharacteristic gesture of chivalric bravado, a young black boy accidentally murders the retarded and repulsive Red Garlock who has been sexually menacing Iris. His differing race and his antisocial crime situate Jinx Fairchild as a fascinating "transgressive other," a "soul-mate" with whom Iris is obsessed throughout her life.

Different in plots and even in the class levels of social experience addressed, these three recent works are similar in their presentation of equivocally appealing otherness that violently controverts social/textual standards and in their attempts to contain that appeal within a recuperated domesticity asserted in the endings of the novels. These works of the transgressive other oscillate between the complicated advantages and disadvantages of dual alternatives: painful and radical freedom and stifling necessary order. But the transparent gestures of containment that frame or conclude these narratives do not stabilize the radical contradictions set in motion by the texts.

Soul/Mate, American Appetites, and *Because It Is Bitter, and Because It Is My Heart* exaggerate a philosophic basis in productive contradiction—a constant challenge of conventions and limits—that has been present throughout Oates's career. The introduction of her 1981 book of essays collected under the title *Contraries* states, for example, that "the seven essays in this volume, written over a period of approximately twenty years . . . were originally stimulated by feelings of opposition. . . ." But this practice has been a source of confusion for Oates's audience. In 1979 Linda Wagner surveyed the unpredictable variability in critical response to Oates's works [in *Critical Essays on Joyce Carol Oates,* 1979], and Joanne Creighton noted [in *Joyce Carol Oates,* 1973] that readers have often been unable to relate the deterministic expectations invoked by Oates's generally naturalistic techniques to "a modernist formulation" of her "visionary perspective." Generally misread and frequently condemned, Oates has never abandoned the interrogations of the social assumptions and novelistic practices in which her fiction is rooted, and her most recent novels propound again the insistent dialectical stance epitomized by her series of "transgressive others." The effect of these provocative works is the assertion of the existence of alternatives just outside the reach of ordinary experience, while the ambiguous treatment of the figures and contexts of such alternatives acknowledges both their genuine threat and their ultimate value.

Eva Manske (essay date 1992)

SOURCE: "The Nightmare of Reality: Gothic Fantasies and Psychological Realism in the Fiction of Joyce Carol Oates," in *Neo-Realism in Contemporary American Fiction,* edited by Kristiaan Versluys, Rodopi, 1992, pp. 131-43.

[*Below, Manske details conventions of Gothicism and realism in Oates's fiction, emphasizing the breadth and violence of her representation of American life.*]

"All art is autobiographical. It is the record of an artist's psychic experience, his attempt to explain something to himself: and in the process of explaining it to himself, he explains it to others." This statement by Joyce Carol Oates comes from her introduction to a collection of contemporary American short fiction which she edited under the title *Scenes From American Life.* While the title of the short story collection could easily serve as a very general description of Ms. Oates' own wide ranging, prolific oeuvre—an exploration of widely differing scenes from American life—her conviction that all art is autobiographical leaves the critic baffled and wondering when looking at her impressive output of novels and short stories which are dominated by traumatic experiences and obsessions, violent themes and conflicts. Although one does not know how much of her fiction is, in fact, autobiographical, there are recurrent places, settings, events, experiences, memories and insights into peoples' feelings that seem to suggest that Joyce Carol Oates makes extensive use of her own psychic experience. With her haunting tales about ordinary people, whose lives often turn into nightmares, she is indeed attempting to explain a troubled experience and bitter sense of American life to herself and to others.

Since the start of her literary career in 1963, Joyce Carol Oates has published more than twenty novels, hundreds of short stories (many of them collected in prize-winning collections and anthologies), half a dozen volumes of poetry, several books of literary criticism and essays, theatre plays and screenplays, earning her a reputation as one of the most prolific and gifted "serious" writers who, in the words of her contemporary John Barth, "writes all over the aesthetical map."

Although most critics agree that Joyce Carol Oates has given readers nothing less than a modern panorama of American life that Lee Milazzo in his recent collection of *Conversations with Joyce Carol Oates* compares to the cyclorama, a form of visual entertainment popular in the 19th century that "allowed eager viewers to see both the overall contours and specific details of great historical (and sometimes contemporary) events", not all critics agree on the literary merits of this oeuvre. To quote one of the more hostile critics: in his review of Oates' novel *Solstice,* titled "Joyce Carol Oates on Automatic Pilot", Jonathan Yardley writes:

> Of all the idiocies on the contemporary American literary scene, surely none is more idiotic than the persistent rumour that the next American to receive the Nobel Prize for Literature will be Joyce Carol Oates . . . To be sure, were writers to be recognized solely for their productivity, then certainly Oates would get all the prizes; they'd have to invent new ones just for her . . . Writers, reviewers and readers gaze at her in awe: she is, in the words they occasionally apply reverently to her, "a writing machine". It seems not to have occurred to anyone, that writing is like anything else: if it is done too hastily and too profusely, it almost inevitably is done badly.

While this is a highly unfair and, all in all, unjustified judgment (and most other critics provide a more balanced and sensitive critical evaluation of her work), there is undoubtedly an uneven quality to her fiction. Some of her novels and stories are rather shrill in depicting the human situation, remain melodramatic renderings of everyday life, highly charged with unrelenting scenes of shocking, random violence, of madness and emotional distress that Oates chronicles as dominant elements of experience in the lives of her characters.

> **Some of her novels and stories are rather shrill in depicting the human situation, remain melodramatic renderings of everyday life, highly charged with unrelenting scenes of shocking, random violence, of madness and emotional distress. . . .**
>
> **—Eva Manske**

"Typical activities in Oates' novels", says one reviewer, "are arson, rape, riot, mental breakdown, murder (plain and fancy, with excursions into patricide, matricide, uxoricide, mass filicide), and suicide" [*Hudson Review* 25 (Spring 1972)]. And S. K. Oberbeck stated in a meanwhile often quoted observation on her fiction [in *Washington Post Book World* (17 September 1971)]: to read Oates "is to cross an emotional minefield, to be stunned to the soul by multiple explosions . . . "

Despite these sensational and melodramatic traits of her fiction that some readers see as shortcomings, Oates is a serious and intellectual writer whose explicit commitment to art as "moral, educative, illustrative" informs her unrelenting attempts to lead her readers to a more profound "sense of the mystery and the sanctity of the human predicament".

In that sense her novels do much more than merely chronicle the horrors of a time wasted by wars, political assassinations, social riots, random violence and the psychic shocks of people paralyzed by their fear of being powerless to change their lives or things around them. Although these are recurring themes especially in her fiction of the sixties and seventies, her recent novels (**Marya: A Life,** 1986; **You Must Remember This,** 1987; **Because It Is Bitter, and Because It Is My Heart,** 1990) are efforts to not only raise the consciousness of ordinary people to the realization of the destruction of their lives, but—in her own words—attempts to "show us how to get through and transcend pain" and, furthermore, attempts to encourage her readers to affirm life and give meaning to it.

Again and again, Oates stresses the fact that her writing is "about the mystery of human emotions" and that at the same time her fiction is concerned with " . . . the moral and social conditions of my generation." It is important for the critical understanding of her fiction to respect her commitment to literature as a communal effort and her own responsibility and obligation as a writer in providing a "voice of the communal consciousness of our culture."

Oates refuses to accept the often stated verdict that today the novel has lost its power to interpret life and that realistic fiction has lost its ability to render convincingly contemporary experience and to make sense of human life in contemporary culture. Quite to the contrary, she insists on "the power of narrative fiction to give coherence to jumbled experience and to bring about a change of heart." Her novels and short fiction reveal a distinctive blend of a compelling hallucinatory but at the same time realistic rendition of the special time and place she is writing about with her intense and often haunting psychological depiction of characters and her complex propositions about the nature of human personality. This is her way of realizing her aim:

I still feel my own place is to dramatize the night-

mares of my time and (hopefully) to show how some individuals find a way out, awaken, come alive, move into the future. I think that art, especially prose fiction, is directly connected with culture, with society; that there is no 'art for art's sake' and never was, but only art as a more conscious, formal expression of a human communal need, in which individuals seem to speak individually but are, in reality, only giving voice and form to the intangible that is in the air around them. . . . Surely, the whole era participates in every creative act, an isolated individual's statement of hopelessness, voiced to no one at all, or a writer's published, distributed and advertised books. It is really all one event, with a multitude of aspects.

Not only does she admit a somewhat old-fashioned and seemingly outmoded "laughably Balzacian ambition to get the whole world into a book", but when faced with criticism [in *Conversations with Joyce Carol Oates,* 1989] that her fiction was "a charnel house of Gothic paraphernalia: blood, fire, insanity, anarchy, lust, corruption, death by bullets, death by cancer, death by plane crash, death by stabbings, beatings, crime, riot, and even unhappiness", Oates coolly explained: "A writer's job, ideally, is to act as the conscience of his race. People frequently misunderstand serious art because it is often violent and unattractive. I wish the world were a prettier place, but I wouldn't be honest as a writer, if I ignored the actual conditions around me."

Underlining the responsibility of the artist "to bear witness—in an almost religious sense—to certain things, including the experience of the concentration camps . . . the experience of suffering, the humiliation of any forms of persecution", she sees herself as a medium who takes in and gives shape to the stimuli coming from her culture. She applauds works like Harriette Arnow's neglected novel *The Dollmaker* which she praised because it showed the power "to deal with the human soul, caught in the stampede of time, unable to gauge the profundity of what passes over it, like the characters of certain plays of Yeats who live through terrifying events but who cannot understand them; in this way history passes over most of us. Society is caught in a convulsion whether of growth or of death, and ordinary people are destroyed. They do not, however, understand that they are destroyed."

This is a revealing statement with respect to her own portrayal of characters who all yearn for control over their lives but are often hopelessly caught in the stampede of time and history, in their own destructive dreams, passions and ambitions, in heartbreaking confusion and painful inarticulateness. So it is not surprising that Oates sees the role of the artist and writer also as a kind of Cassandra: "It may be, his role, his function, is to articulate the very worst, to force into consciousness the most perverse and terrifying possibilities of the epoch, so that they can be dealt with and not simply feared." Almost all of her novels focus obsessively on "the very worst . . . and the most terrifying possibilities of the epoch", presenting a nightmare of reality in a wide variety of styles, genres, fictional techniques and narrative experiments. Although Oates is sceptical of metafiction and of most of the flamboyant experimentation that characterizes postmodern fiction, she should not be dismissed as a traditional or conventional writer. Presenting herself as a storyteller whose work appeals to general readers as well as to more "literary" ones, she adapts her style to the subject she is exploring and uses a keen visual sense which allows readers to "see" individuals and events depicted in her fiction in a new, startling and often shocking light.

While drawing heavily on her childhood experience—growing up in a small town in upstate New York in a working class family that suffered from the grim economic conditions of the Depression years of the 1930s—Oates has written not only about the rural setting of this harsh and grim landscape. She wrote about the big city—most memorably about the violent urban slums of Detroit between the 1930s and the 1960s (*them*, 1969; *Wonderland*, 1971; *Do With Me What You Will*, 1973), about the emptiness and sterility of suburban life (*Expensive People*, 1968) and of the academic setting (*Unholy Loves*, 1979; *Solstice*, 1985; *Marya: A Life*, 1986) and political novels set in Washington D.C. (*The Assassins: A Book of Hours*, 1975; *Angel of Light*, 1981). In recent years Oates has published a cycle of novels that could be called "experimental genre novels" beginning with *Bellefleur* (1980) and followed by *The Bloodsmoor Romance* (1982) and *Mysteries of Winterthurn* (1984). In these novels Oates presents "America as viewed through the prismatic lens of its most popular genres". These novels deal in genre form with 19th-century and early 20th-century America: a family saga, a romance, a detective mystery and a Gothic horror. The novels are, in Oates' words, "post-modernist in conception but thoroughly serious in execution. Primarily, each novel tells a story I consider uniquely American and of our time. The characters . . . are both our ancestors and ourselves."

In these novels—which are a startling departure from her usual mode of writing—Oates makes explicit and extensive use of the Gothic tradition in American literature and she described her novels appropriately as " 'Gothic' with a capital-letter G." Greg Johnson states in his study on Oates' fiction (*Understanding Joyce Carol Oates*, 1987) that in these books "she combines her usual psychological realism with a free-wheeling, explicit use of fantasy, fairy tales, horror stories, and other Gothic elements; the central settings of all three novels, for instance, include a huge forbidding mansion and such assorted horrors as a female vampire (*Bellefleur*) and a painting which comes to life and murders a couple on their honeymoon (*Mysteries of Winterthurn*)."

But although Oates claims that her intention was "to 'see' the world in terms of heredity and family destiny and the vicissitudes of time (for all five novels are secretly fables of the American family); to explore historically authentic crimes against women and children, and the poor; to create and to identify with heroes and heroines whose existence would be problematic in the clinical, unkind, and one might almost say, fluorescent-lit atmosphere of present-day fiction," and that therefore she had to resort to the outright Gothic, she links this to her desire to present a convincing psychological portrait of characters and a sweeping social and historical picture. "If Gothicism has the power to move us (and it certainly has the power to fascinate the novelist) it is only because its roots are in psychological realism. Much of *Bellefleur* is a diary of my own life, and the lives of the people I have known." It is significant that she intended her novel *Bellefleur* as "a critique of America, but it is in the service of a vision of America that stresses, for all its pessimism, the ultimate freedom of the individual.

In that sense, she herself admits that her genre novels are more than mere Gothic stories and that the imaginative construction of a Gothic novel involves the systematic transposition of realistic social and historical as well as psychological and emotional experiences into Gothic elements and structures. The reader familiar with the Gothic novels of the 18th and 19th centuries will recognize in Oates novel *Bellefleur*, e.g., themes, obsessions and actions which were the stock-in-trade of the tales of terror. The mysterious and cruel events have a distinctly Gothic flavour to them. But one has to agree with John Gardner's observation who in his review of the novel [in *New York Times Book Review* (20 July 1980)] states: "What we learn, reading *Bellefleur*, is that Joyce Carol Oates is essentially a realist. She can write persuasively of out-of-the-body experiences because she believes in them. But she does not really believe in a brutal half-wit boy who can turn into a dog, a man who is really a bear, vampires or mountain gnomes. . . . Miss Oates believes in these legendary characters only as symbols; and the problem is that they are not symbols of the same class as those she has been using for years, the symbols provided by the world as it is. . . . The only really frightening scenes in *Bellefleur* deal with real-world atrocities . . . and these scenes in fact come nowhere near the horror of scenes in earlier novels by Miss Oates. . . . What drives Miss Oates' fiction is her phobias: that is, her fear that normal life may suddenly turn monstrous. Abandoning verisimilitude for a different mode (the willing suspension of disbelief), she loses her ability to startle us with sudden nightmare."

In that respect, her novels set in the contemporary America are more convincing, although in her attempt to convey the nightmare of everyday reality she makes extensive use of Gothic elements there, too. Her fiction often displays the kind of extreme psychological intensity and outright horror of events and emotions that result in disturbing, vicious and often disgusting scenes of violence. As Oates commented, "gothic with a small-letter 'g' suggests a work in which extremes of emotion are unleashed"—and this could be applied to almost all her fiction. Her characters—be they rich or poor, uneducated or cultured—"live within a psychological pressure-cooker, responding to intense personal and societal conflicts which lead almost inevitably to violence."

This recurrent violence as well as such traditionally Gothic elements as extreme personal isolation, violent physical and psychological conflicts and symbolic actions, melodramatic and passionate circumstances and events, or painful psychic states like loss of identity, emotional turmoil, suicide, rape, murder, incest or the psychological explorations of madness and insanity, are in Oates' words "a fairly realistic assessment of modern life."

Throughout her fiction these Gothic elements and fantasies have the larger function of expanding the thematic range and suggestiveness in conveying the atmosphere of public and private American life in the past and today. Already at the beginning of the 1970s Alfred Kazin noted in his essay on Oates' fiction [in his *Bright Book of Life,* 1973] that Oates showed in her novel ***them*** a particular sensitivity to individual lives helplessly flying off the wheel of American gigantism, and that more than most other women writers Joyce Carol Oates seemed "entirely open to social turmoil, to the frighteningly undirected and misapplied force of the American powerhouse."

Kazin rightly compares her in her instinct for and her imaginative recreation of the "melodrama" of Detroit in the 1960s to earlier writers like Theodore Dreiser (who wrote about Chicago), or Stephen Crane and John Dos Passos (who wrote about New York). But Oates is clearly different from these forerunners and her depiction of life in contemporary America is concerned with an unrelenting perception of the sheer chaos of life. Her special concern seems to be an insistence on the fact that the real American tragedy of today is the failure of people to find a language for expressing what is happening to them. This view of literature as silent tragedy that Oates noted already as praiseworthy in Arnow's novel, is also evident in her own fiction. Many of her characters move through a world that they perceive as wholly physical, and her books are packed with descriptions of this overwhelming material and physical reality. A kind of obsessive patience seems to guide her when she follows her characters through the immense factuality of contemporary existence, tracing with insight and compassion their moving around, their thinking and feeling. A density of detail marks her description of the often unconscious reactions of her characters that she explores in shockingly monstrous and violent scenes or in the everyday routines and stifling experience of a boring uneventful life.

The exploration of the inner world of women is for many readers her most memorable and fascinating contribution to the fictional exploration of a social and individual context. Women's fear of violence and damage dominates the fiction. But even more disturbing is the confusion and ignorance and heightened sense of helplessness and terror her female characters feel concerning the possibility of control over their lives. This lack of control is also expressed in the terror of the body that many of her women experience—fear of their own bodies and of men's bodies. This extends to the depiction of sexual relationships and female sexuality in general. Sexual relationships are often experienced by her female characters as threatening, and sex is described as a brutal assault on the female body, in a language that by now has become familiar: grinding, driving hardness. Sexual relationships are often bordering on incest and thus are guilt-ridden and destructive. In these imaginative renderings of female psychology and women's responses to the outer world as well as to their inner world her women suffer intensely. In many cases Oates shows that the response to existence pushes her female characters into psychic nightmares or over the edge into mental breakdown and death. Often their only form of protest is a complete breakdown or even self-destruction. Often there seems to be no relief of the feelings of despair and hopelessness, no salvation or transcendence of the unbearable pain, suffering and humiliation. Nor is the family a source of comfort and strength.

Though there are a number of tough women in her novels (mostly women coming from a working class background, as e.g. in ***them, Childwold, A Garden of Earthly Delights***), they never really succeed in understanding themselves or transcend the limits of self. They merely survive. Diminished in their response by poverty, ignorance and confusion, they turn to dreams as compensation for a troubling, boring, often unbearable life. They try to escape their everyday reality by seeing themselves as characters in movies, in TV series, in magazines and romantic fiction or even as disembodied people in mirrors—reflections of a self that they want to escape. Dreams become their reality. Victims of the media and their messages which tell them that success lies in improving their appearances, they are desperately trying to change (in most cases they change make-up, hair styles, clothes as an attempt of changing their lives and personalities!). Oates shows that in fact these women are trapped in physical and social surroundings from which they cannot escape. One is reminded of her early statement that "the greatest realities are physical and economic: all the subtleties of life come afterward. Intellectuals have forgotten, or else they never understood, how difficult it is to make one's way up from a low economic level, to assert one's will in a great crude way. It's so difficult. You have to go through it. You have to be poor."

Thus she shows her characters as products of their economic, social and cultural realities as well as victims of their own personalities. They desperately try to escape from these grim realities that they find themselves in, but they are repeatedly defeated and this defeat characterizes some traits of her tragic concept of human existence. While readers may be repelled and shocked by her often naturalistic descriptions of these lives, one has to concede that they are part of a closely observed American reality: her characters are locked in history and in a recognizable time and place in American culture, and they are vulnerable to this time, place and culture.

Her concern with these intensely felt nightmarish conditions of the present, with all the anxiety, paranoia, dislocation and explosive conflicts that come out of frustration, of boredom and bitter desperation, is connected with a subtle and convincing exploration of the psychological aspects of her characters' reactions. It is above all this psychological realism in the detailed and compelling presentation of individuals in the midst of various kinds of emotional and psychological upheaval that characterizes the by now familiar "Oates effect", haunting the reader of her fiction.

It is only in recent novels that Oates transcended these fatalistic and grim attitudes. After her detour into the fantastic world of the 19th century genre novels, her books of the late 1980s return to the territory that she has explored before and whose voices she knows perfectly: the world of lower class families in rural upstate New York and the world of academia. *Marya: A Life* can serve as an example for the changes and the possible transcendence of the violent clash and intense conflict between the individual and the surrounding society. We have again in the scenes of life that the individual chapters present, the usual shocking brutal events: the book opens with a violent chapter in which the eight-year old Marya is forced by her alcoholic mother to look at her murdered father in the city morgue and later she is abandoned by her mother and left with relatives who barely tolerate her. Marya is molested by her cousin and suffers sexual abuse, she is nearly gang-raped during her farewell party before leaving for college, in college she suffers from extreme isolation. . . . But what emerges in the course of these frightening events and experiences is an unusual and strong person, a woman who is able to break out of the economic and social conditions that determined her before. She is able to escape from the suffocating climate and to find in the life of an academic and a writer a way to become, in Oates' words "an Amazon of a sort, a warrior woman, making her own way, confident and assured."

In the end Marya is determined to face a confrontation with her mother, and though Oates does not show this meeting in her novel and her heroine knows that this meeting will cut her life in two, Oates has presented her in a way that makes not only intellectual emancipation possible but also a kind of emotional maturing that goes beyond the suffering, the ignorance and the numbness that so many women in her novels have to endure.

In this sense Oates shows that some people are able to find a way out of the nightmare of their terrifying experience of reality—that they are indeed able "to awaken, come alive, move into the future".

Eleanor J. Bader (review date Winter 1993-94)

SOURCE: "A Working-Class Sorority," in *Belles Lettres: A Review of Books by Women,* Vol. 9, No. 2, Winter, 1993-94, p. 15.

[*In the review below, Bader elucidates the feminist themes of* Foxfire, *noting the questions raised by the text.*]

The place is Hammond, New York, far upstate, near Canada. For five girls—Legs Sadovsky, Goldie Siefried, Lana Maguire, Rita O'Hagan, and Maddy Wirtz—working class kids from the shabby, hopeless section of town, the truth is indisputable: "We didn't belong and never would."

Foxfire, the girl gang they create in 1953, is their antidote, their way of thumbing their noses at the teachers, bosses, upper-class students, landlords, and politicians who disdain them. The brainchild of Legs, Foxfire starts as a tiny, secret society and gradually evolves into a complex organization dedicated to exacting justice for the disenfranchised, especially women. Maddy, alternately known as Maddy-monkey and killer, chronicles the group's development; Oates's novel [*Foxfire: Confessions of a Girl Gang*] is written as an expanded version of Maddy's notes.

This journal-of-sorts reveals the inner workings of a protofeminist support or consciousness raising group. But Foxfire is also the stuff of every adolescent girl's dreams: a brash, inventive sorority out of adult earshot and adult control. Unlike Margaret Atwood's *Cat's Eye,* which testifies to the meanness of many girl-children, Foxfire members are there for one another, bolstering each other through exhilarating antics born of revenge and the quest for recognition. In a world that treats them badly, Foxfire provides sisterhood and, in so doing, transforms each of the group's members.

Although Foxfire's mission constantly changes during its three-year history, its philosophy grows out of theories developed by Legs, their first-in-command. One of her precepts involves men, and their relationship to the women of Foxfire. Maddy discusses Legs's beliefs in her record book:

"They hate us, y'know?—the sons of bitches. It's all of them: men. It's a state of undeclared war, them hating us no matter our age or who the hell we are but nobody wants to admit it, not even us," she'd rant. She'd get so worked up there was no reasoning with her and it made us nervous 'cause like I said (and this is true right up to the present time in America) there are things you don't want to think about if you're female, say you're a young girl or a woman you're female and that isn't going to change, right?

At first, Foxfire's goal is to publicize the sexually harassing behavior of a high school math teacher. Painting public denunciations of him for all to see, they embarrass him into leaving town. Then, they beat up a salesman who attempts to force Maddy into a sexual encounter. As things escalate, Foxfire's actions take on bigger and bigger proportions, culminating in a final plan to kidnap a rich corporate executive and collect a $1 million ransom.

Like *Thelma and Louise* and other examples of this genre, Foxfire's perfect crime turns out to be flawed. As one thing after another goes wrong, the crime not only gets bungled, but Foxfire, itself, disintegrates. While Maddy survives the group's decline, and eventually goes on to get a college degree and a "respectable" job, several members of the gang end up in jail and some, including Legs, disappear. To her credit, Oates allows a thread of ambiguity to emerge. Is Legs dead or did she escape? Might she have assumed a new identity and still be out there, somewhere, fomenting feminist revolution?

Oates has written a dazzling, if unsettling, novel that looks at questions of leadership, loyalty, and sexual identity through the lens of the mid-1950s. Although the book sidesteps lesbianism, Oates's touch is light enough to be opaque: how the sexual tension between characters gets resolved is left to each reader's imagination. Again, one wonders: Did they? Could they? Might they later? Although I closed the book saddened that Foxfire did not last, permanence did not much matter to Legs or the women in her entourage. "Like a flame is real enough, isn't it, while it's burning?" she once asked. "Even if there's a time it goes out?"

Foxfire's flame, short-lived and brilliant, teaches the women of Hammond that it is possible to fight injustice and sexism. Together, the sisterhood they create transforms a tiny piece of small-town America and reminds us, 40 years later, that in unity there is strength. *Que viva,* sisters.

James Carroll (review date 16 October 1994)

SOURCE: "He Could Not Tell a Lie," in *The New York Times Book Review,* October 16, 1994, p. 7.

[*In the following review, Carroll assesses* What I Lived For, *finding that "the structure of this straightforward mystery is transformed into art of another order entirely, an exemplary work of moral investigation."*]

John Gardner once said that a novel is a vivid and continuous dream. In **What I Lived For,** Joyce Carol Oates has written a vivid and continuous nightmare: a savage dissection of our national myths of manhood and success, a bitter portrait of our futile effort to flee the weight of the past, a cold-eyed look at our loss of community and family, a shriek at the monsters men and women have become to each other and a revelation of our desolate inner lives. **What I Lived For** is an American "Inferno."

The novel is set in Union City, a fictional place on the New York shores of Lake Erie, something like Buffalo. It tells the story of Jerome (Corky) Corcoran, a two-bit politician and businessman. Though the book opens with the murder of Corky's father in 1959, the bulk of the action takes place over one long weekend in 1992. A lost weekend, it begins when Corky learns that his lover, Christina Kavanaugh, has been conducting their affair with the permission of her crippled husband, a discovery that shatters Corky's ego and sets him ricocheting all over the city, from one reversal to another, following a zigzag course through layers of social class, racial division, political machination and economic distress.

Ms. Oates has constructed a complex plot, with the apparent suicide of a young black woman, Marilee Plummer, at its center. Corky was acquainted with Marilee, and she was a friend of his grown stepdaughter, Thalia. But she was also involved somehow with Corky's mentor, the Mayor, Oscar Slattery, and with Corky's best friend, the Mayor's son and the local Congressman, Vic Slattery. The novel derives its thumping energy from Corky's inept, drunken, miserable effort to find out the truth of what happened to Marilee, and he does. But in Ms. Oates's boldly inventive narrative, the structure of this straightforward mystery is transformed into art of another order entirely, an exemplary work of moral investigation.

The novel unfolds through Corky's interior monologue, which gives the story its form, punch, immediacy and meaning. Ms. Oates has created a pithy, original voice for her protagonist, a kind of scat prose that is poignant, often hilarious, always credible. She begins by giving us a man's habits of perception and ends by giving us his soul. The effect of this device is to make even crucial turns of the plot available to the reader only indirectly. To Corky's clouded and increasingly panicked mind, the other characters are as elusive as shadows on the wall of a cave—and that is how they appear to the reader. "What's it mean, Corky hasn't a clue," Ms. Oates writes early on. "He's not a guy comfortable inside his own head." But before long the reader is. And soon—here is one of the novel's marvels of subtlety—we know by implication and suggestion more about "what's it mean" than Corky does.

I confess that because the bound galleys touted *What I Lived For*" as a daring portrait of male sexuality, I brought a suspension of disbelief to the novel somewhat unwillingly. Could the ever-versatile Joyce Carol Oates successfully ground a major work in the befuddled inner life of a middle-aged, urban, male Irish Catholic? I wondered. And, sure enough, Corky's lusty frenzy at first seemed created according to an abstract, wholly pejorative idea of American maleness, one rooted in the pages of *Playboy* (a magazine to which, in fact, Corky makes steady reference).

Was it Corky who had shaped his attitudes and self-image according to the hackneyed, pathetic Hefner ideal—or was it Ms. Oates, an author taking aim at a straw manhood? The early sex scenes between Christina and Corky, for example, are written with a euphemistic and puerile gusto—"Corky's body flames up, he turns to ashes"—and read like clips from a skin magazine's fantasy page. I might have more quickly trusted Ms. Oates's sardonic purpose, her skewering of the *Playboy* myth, but I was thrown off by the publisher's note that first serial rights of this novel were sold, lo and behold, to *Playboy.* Who's being had here? Hugh Hefner or me? But that uncertainty was quickly resolved as the consciousness of Corky Corcoran asserted itself, an irresistible accumulation of fragmentary thoughts, feelings and sensations, all rendered with such skill that the world of the novel was soon brought exactly to life.

When he was 11 years old, Corky witnessed the murder of his father. He hadn't actually seen the faces of the killers, but the police knew who they were and told the boy to identify them anyway. His family wanted him to do it, and surely so did the ghost of his father. But young Corky could not, and that inability comes to seem the very definition of failure, haunting him as an adult and putting him, on the cursed weekend of the novel's action, in mortal danger. "And why wasn't he strong enough, why wasn't it in him. To identify his father's murderers with a simple lie." Especially him, for whom deception of self and others has become a way of life.

The answer to that question is the resolution of the novel, a ringing affirmation of the most basic law of private and public morality and also of fiction: that character is destiny. To follow the drama of Corky Corcoran's tour through the circles of contemporary America's hell is to move from the pity one feels at witnessing the acute suffering of the damned to the fear one feels on realizing that this doom belongs to all of us. The catharsis Ms. Oates achieves in this novel springs from the recognition—ours, not Corky's—that this blind, drunken, skittish human pinball game has in fact been an arrow-straight moral odyssey, aimed at the truth. The boy who doomed himself by refusing to lie has become a man whose commitment to that most basic virtue may not have been entirely lost. When it threatens to cost him everything, we are heartbroken and we are thrilled.

In her 24th novel, Joyce Carol Oates has written an engrossing, moving study of desperate, lonely and lost souls, of America itself in the midst of its decline. One may approach *What I Lived For,* as I did, with a certain skepticism, but in the reading it grows and grows, accumulating authority, picking up pace and finally leaving the reader awed—at this writer's achievement, yes, but also, and more forcefully, at the surviving human capacity for doing what is right.

Steven Marcus (review date 8 October 1995)

SOURCE: "American Psycho," in *The New York Times Book Review,* October 8, 1995, p. 13.

[*Below, Marcus links the main character of* Zombie *with the recurrent theme of violence in Oates's fiction, faulting the novel's premise.*]

Divided into 57 mini-chapters, composed with typographical tics and oddities (many capitalized words, phrases and sentences; italics, ampersands and so forth), featuring crude and often pointless line drawings, *Zombie* is Joyce Carol Oates's effort to dramatize, in diarylike form, the psychotic, monstrous consciousness of a serial murderer. This creature is simultaneously intensely self-absorbed and extremely depersonalized and derealized. He speaks of himself indiscriminately in the first and third persons and uses his initials to refer to himself most of the time. Apart from his recurrent obsessions and fantasies, he is unable to retain either conscious inner stability or a reliably steady or coherent sense of the outside world.

Many of the details of *Zombie* owe much to the story of Jeffrey Dahmer, who committed a large number of homosexual murders in Milwaukee. Dahmer dismembered the bodies of his victims, saved some of their body parts and other grisly souvenirs, tried cannibalism on at least one occasion, was finally apprehended in 1991, convicted of 16 murders and was himself killed in prison.

In another sense, *Zombie* represents the continuation of Ms. Oates's longstanding interest in the extreme, the gruesome, the bizarre and violent in American life. In particular, it is a continuation of the kind of thing she created in *Black Wa-*

ter in 1992. That equally short novel consisted entirely of a dramatization of the tortured consciousness of a character modeled on Mary Jo Kopechne as she was drowning. Ms. Oates's considerable facility in transforming what is excruciatingly painful, awful to imagine and difficult to contemplate into rapid, fluent and easy-to-read prose is a characteristic attribute of the traditional Gothic literary imagination—whose resources and conventions Ms. Oates continues to draw on in this updated, post-modern variant of the genre.

The narrator of *Zombie*—the work is really an extended dramatic monologue—is one Quentin P——, 31 years old, son of an established academic family living in a Michigan university town, where he is himself a semipermanent, part-time community college student. He has recently been convicted of a homosexual misdemeanor involving an assault on a black minor and has been sentenced to probation. He visits his entirely uninterested probation officer at apparently casual intervals; he is also in private therapy (paid for by his father) and group therapy (paid for by the state)—to both of which he is grotesquely impervious and cunningly adaptive. He is on prescribed medications, as well as on whatever other substances he can pick up on the street. He works part time as a caretaker at a rooming house for students at the state university (where his father is a professor of science). He exists in a haze of fantasies blurred by drugs and alcohol and by his inherent mental condition of violent and frenzied desires, thoughts and obsessions, expressed largely through dissociated snatches and shards of language. As far as possible he makes no "EYE CONTACT with anybody."

His major obsession has to do with his unappeasable need to create for himself a zombie. He has planned and tried to do this through performing ice-pick lobotomies on his victims, who, he insanely concludes, will then become slaves, utterly empty mentally and evacuated humanly, the perfectly void objects for his sadistic compulsion to anally penetrate, violate and harm other men. They will love what he, their "Master," does to them. They will be at once passive entities to be abused and injured, and cuddly teddy bears for him to play and sleep with. There are pages and pages of this, but almost none of it is quotable in this publication. It is quite horrible and almost equally tedious because of its nonincremental and unremitting repetitiveness.

In this evil project he has failed numerous times. His hardware-store ice pick invariably inflicts too much destruction upon the brains of his partly drugged victims, and they invariably die. He disposes of the bodies in a variety of unimaginative ways and has never been caught—indeed, until the very end of the novella he has never even been suspected of anything really predatory. It helps that his victims have—until the exception at the end—regularly been socially marginal nonwhite males, vagrants, pickups at gay bars or wanderers loitering for a hitch at freeway entrances, people who will never be missed because they have already effectively disappeared from social connectedness.

But Joyce Carol Oates has something more in mind than the representation of a monstrous consciousness and individual being. In some unmistakable general sense, her murderous narrator is supposed to signify for us a number of important tendencies and truths about contemporary American society. His effort to create zombies is derived from the irreversible psychosurgical procedure that was routinely performed during the 1940's and 50's, before the invention of powerful psychotropic drugs, on thousands of unfortunate Americans judged to be psychotic, dangerous or incompetent. In a similar sense, we are suddenly informed late in the novel that his father's scientific mentor, who won the Nobel Prize, has been disclosed to have conducted, during the 1950's, "RADIATION EXPERIMENTS" for the Atomic Energy Commission, leading a team of scientists in feeding radioactive milk to retarded children and exposing the testicles of prisoners to "ionizing radiation." In other words, Ms. Oates's aberrant protagonist seems to be, on one side, little more than an individualized and monomaniacally focused version of what American society itself is capable of on its legitimate scientific and medical side. Similarly, the liberal, therapeutic culture in which the narrator, his family and everyone else in the work is immersed—"*Remember nobody's judging anybody else. That's the bottom line, guys*"—is as inane, phony and ultimately abhorrent as the old punitive culture that the contemporary ethos of nonjudgmental therapy and undiscriminating sympathetic acceptance has largely replaced, with exceptionally indifferent success. Moreover, the narrator lives on fast food, washed down with seas of intoxicants, incessantly watches television and trips out on whatever drugs happen to be handy—just like enough of the rest of America to permit one to entertain the inference that there is something representative about his deranged behavior. This dreadful creature is presented to us as not simply living in mainstream America and as not merely being affected by the culture but as in some sense an embodiment of it, as containing and conveying its truth if not its very essence.

There is something meretricious and all too easy about this proposition and the narrative that carries it. Certainly America is a violent society, and just as certainly the medical profession, including psychiatry, has perpetrated its due share of shameful cruelties and callousness. Fast food is pretty awful on any number of counts, and television seems largely produced for an audience of moderately brain-damaged viewers. But to go on and imply that America today is functionally the social equivalent or cultural analogue of a psychotic monster and serial murderer is to make an insupportable allegorical suggestion. Hitler's Germany and Stalin's gulag were societies that were largely dominated by homicidal, monstrous and indeed psychotic practices and justifications. America today, for all the violence and brutality we have come both to fear and sometimes to deny, has not quite yet descended into collective madness.

The creation of monsters in literature belongs to a long and important tradition. From Frankenstein's creature to Dostoyevsky's underground man to Kafka's Gregor Samsa, to such less impressive characters as Humbert and John Fowles's collector, monstrous beings—characters considered by themselves or by others as monstrous or murderous—have often conveyed something important to us about our humanity; the term monster itself derives etymologically from a word that signifies "warning." Sometimes, as in *Frankenstein,* we learn that the monster is more human than his human creator; sometimes, as in Kafka, we learn that his ordinary human existence as a traveling salesman in a lower-middle-class family is so dehumanizing that his metaphoric insectlike existence has turned him into a literal monstrous insect. And sometimes, as in Fowles's strange novel, the monster remains a mystery.

But what Joyce Carol Oates means to tell us is far too simple. A dozen serial murderers do not by themselves certify a monstrous social world or culture—although they're surely sufficient to cause one to think gravely about any world that in part creates them and whose material helps furnish the contents of their demented minds. The idea of this narrative—that the uncaught serial killer is somehow peculiarly representative of our current condition—is more interesting than its execution, which, like the writing in which it is embodied, is fluid, fluent, inflated and, finally, neither convincing in itself nor successfully dramatized as fiction.

FURTHER READING

Criticism

Daly, Brenda. "Marriage as Emancipatory Metaphor: A

Woman Wedded to Teaching and Writing in Oates's *Unholy Lives.*" *Critique: Studies in Contemporary Fiction* XXXVII, No. 4 (Summer 1996): 270-88.

> Examines the significance of community—both feminist and ideal—in Oates's fiction, particularly the academic novel *Unholy Lives,* likening teaching and writing to marriage.

Garner, Dwight. "When Bad Things Happen." *Washington Post Book World* (22 September 1996): 4.

> Favorable review of *We Were the Mulvaneys,* observing that "rarely has [Oates's] gift for broad, galloping narrative been this much on display."

Gates, David. "American Gothic." *The New York Times Book Review* 101 (15 September 1996): 11.

> Assesses the gothic element of *First Love* and the "family" theme of the "richly observed and engagingly peopled" novel *We Were The Mulvaneys.*

Showalter, Elaine. "Joyce Carol Oates's 'The Dead' and Feminist Criticism." *Faith of a (Woman) Writer* Greenwood Press (1988): 13-19.

> Showalter demonstrates how "The Dead" comments on the relation of women's writing to contemporary feminist criticism and the female literary tradition.

Strandberg, Victor. "Six, Violence, and Philosophy in *You Must Remember This.*" *Studies in American Fiction* 17, No. 1 (Spring 1989): 3-17.

> Strandberg outlines the philosophic contraries of Oates's dialectic between violence and control represented in *You Must Remember This,* focusing on various relationships among the characters.

Tompkins, Cynthia. A review of *Zombie,* by Joyce Carol Oates. *World Literature Today* 70, No. 3 (Summer 1996): 693.

> Praises *Zombie* on several points, noting that "Oates's uncanny ability to portray striking personalities may be the secret to her prolific career."

Additional coverage of Oates's life and career is contained in the following sources published by Gale: *Authors and Artists for Young Adults,* Vol. 15; *Authors In The News,* Vol. 1; *Bestsellers,* 89:2; *Concise Dictionary of American Literary Biography,* 1968-1988; *Contemporary Authors,* Vols. 5-8, rev. ed.; *Contemporary Authors New Revision Series,* Vols. 25, 45; *DISCovering Authors; DISCovering Authors: British; DISCovering Authors: Canadian; DISCovering Authors: Most-studied Authors Module, Novelist Module, Popular Fiction and Genre Authors Module; Dictionary of Literary Biography,* Vols. 2, 5, 130; *Dictionary of Literary Biography Yearbook,* 1981; *Major Twentieth-Century Writers; Short Story Criticism,* Vol. 6; and *World Literature Criticism.*

Julia O'Faolain

1932-

English-born Irish short novelist, short story writer, editor, and translator.

The following entry presents an overview of O'Faolain's career. For further information on her life and works, see *CLC*, Volumes 6, 19, and 47.

INTRODUCTION

The daughter of Irish writers Eileen and Sean O'Faolain, Julia O'Faolain has had to carve out her own niche in the literary world. She has developed a unique style with an international scope which has garnered her a reputation as a powerful and intelligent writer. With satirical wit and dark humor, she explores cultural attitudes and themes related to sexuality, male-female relationships, Catholicism, and politics, particularly as these issues concern female characters attempting to establish their identities.

Biographical Information

O'Faolain was born on June 6, 1932, in London, England. Her parents were strong advocates of Irish nationalism. They spoke Gaelic in their house and adopted the Gaelic version of their surname. Eileen, a writer of children's stories, kept Julia home from school until the age of eight and used her as an audience for her children's stories. The stories were fantasy-filled tales which led O'Faolain to talk of leprechauns and fairies when she entered school. After being ridiculed for her fanciful imagination, Julia began to look incredulously at anything fantastic in nature, including religion. It was this analytical outlook that O'Faolain later brought to bear in her writing. O'Faolain attended University College in Dublin where she received both a bachelor and a masters degree in the Arts. She also did graduate study at Universita di Roma and the Sorbonne, University of Paris. The fact that she has lived all over the world helps her to set her fiction in various international locales and still evoke a sense of place. O'Faolain married Lauro Martines, a teacher and historian, with whom she edited *Not in God's Image* (1973).

Major Works

O'Faolain's collection, *We Might See Sights! and Other Stories* (1968) has stories set in Ireland and Italy. The stories explore such topics as hypocritical cultural attitudes and young females discovering their sexuality. Many of the pieces in her second collection, *Man in the Cellar* (1974),

examine the power struggles between men and women, including the title story which depicts an English woman who chains her Italian husband in the cellar and attempts to convince him of the inequities in their marriage. The collection *Daughters of Passion* (1982) contains female protagonists whose identities are shaped by men and characters who adopt political views that suit their immediate purposes. O'Faolain's first novel, *Godded and Codded* (1971), is a story of sexual awakening. It centers on an Irish graduate student who travels to Paris to free herself from the stifling atmosphere of her family life. Related with bawdy humor, the novel details her sexual adventures and satirizes various character types among expatriates in Paris. In *Women in the Wall* (1975), O'Faolain builds her fictional tale around a historical figure, but O'Faolain takes artistic license with the details of the story. The novel, set in sixth-century Gaul, is based on Queen Radegunda, a Frankish saint. The main character of the novel, Radegunda, was forced to marry the king who slaughtered her family. She longed to enter a religious life without men and political turmoil. Her husband consented to let her leave and she founded the Convent of the Holy Cross. The story revolves around the reasons Radegunda and two other women have for entering the spiritual life of the convent and the role of women in medieval society. In *No Country for Young Men* (1980), O'Faolain addresses the issues of Irish nationalism to explicate the destructive, cyclical pattern of her country's history. She follows three generations of a family involved in Ireland's political troubles to develop several themes, including the influence of traditional myths and political tensions on how women are viewed in Ireland and the dubious values sometimes related to patriotism. *The Obedient Wife* (1982) is set in Los Angeles and centers on an unhappily married woman whose husband encourages her to see other men while he is away on business. O'Faolain explores the conflicts between Catholic values and personal needs through the woman's romantic relationship with a priest. O'Faolain once again switches locales in *The Irish Signorina* (1984). Set in an Italian villa, the novel concerns a young Irish woman who visits the Cavalcanti family, for whom her mother used to work as an au pair. Her mother, now dead, had never really let go of Italy or the Cavalcanti family. Ann explores her mother's past and develops her own relationship with the family. In this novel, O'Faolain develops a comparison between romanticism and rationalism and explores differing philosophies of life and love. *The Judas Cloth* (1992) focuses on Rome, the Catholic Church, and Pope Pius IX. It follows the lives of three young men as they struggle with their identities. Also significant in O'Faolain's career is her work on *Not in God's Image*. She co-edited the book which documents the place of women in Western civilization.

Critical Reception

Critics first looked for comparisons between O'Faolain's work and that of her parents. However, she soon garnered a reputation on her own merits and for her own unique talents. J. R. Frakes asserts that "she does not write like her father. And maybe, if [*Three Lovers*] is a fair harbinger, she'll become the family member whose name is used for identification." Reviewers point out how her international background affects the scope of her work and sets her apart from other Irish writers. Complaints about O'Faolain's fiction include a sense of incompleteness, where story lines are left hanging, and an occasional sense of preachiness. Many reviewers laud her use of satire and the intelligence she brings to her writing. Alan Ross says, "Julia O'Faolain has all the essential gifts—a sense of high comedy, fastidiousness of language and feeling, intellectual control over widely-ranging scraps of knowledge—and she uses them with the lightest of touches." One of O'Faolain's strongest gifts is her ability to expose and bring things to their essential level. Ann Owens Weekes states, "When I first read her work, I was struck by the acid intelligence that strips away layers of tradition, affection, and affectation, exposing an often grotesque core." Reviewers often point out the allusive nature of O'Faolain's work, which recalls images from ancient myth and history. Her work is often cited in feminist criticism for its honest portrayal of the role of women in society and women's struggle to define her identity. She is also praised for her deft handling of sensitive political issues, a topic usually considered the territory of male writers.

PRINCIPAL WORKS

We Might See Sights! and Other Stories (short stories) 1968
Godded and Codded (novel) 1971; republished as *Three Lovers,* 1971
Not in God's Image: Women in History from the Greeks to the Victorians [editor with Lauro Martines] (essays) 1973
Man in the Cellar (short stories) 1974
Women in the Wall (novel) 1975
Melancholy Baby and Other Stories (short stories) 1978
No Country for Young Men (novel) 1980
Daughters of Passion (short stories) 1982
The Obedient Wife (novel) 1982
The Irish Signorina (novel) 1984
The Judas Cloth (novel) 1992

CRITICISM

Alan Ross (review date November 1970)

SOURCE: "Carry on Codding," in *London Magazine,* Vol. 10, No. 8, November, 1970, pp. 109-10.

[*In the following excerpt, Ross praises O'Faolain's* Godded and Codded.]

A dotty Irishman, holed up in the jungles of Paris, is one of the chief characters in Julia O'Faolain's first novel *Godded and Codded. . . .* [T]his is an immensely stylish and richly allusive performance. . . . Though not exactly original in its account of the wayward affair between a sexy Irish student from the bogs and a wily, Arab revolutionary, *Godded and Codded* has so many incidental pleasures that its fairly routine plot about sexual awakening scarcely matters. In a beautifully suggested Paris of cold lodgings, hot passions, trees, restaurants, abortion wards and tutelary roués, among whom the Irish innocents flounder in a haze of romantic longing and booze, enough comes through about living, learning and loving for the odd confusions and self-indulgences to seem irrelevant. Julia O'Faolain has all the essential gifts—a sense of high comedy, fastidiousness of language and of feeling, intellectual control over widely-ranging scraps of knowledge—and she uses them with the lightest of touches.

J. R. Frakes (review date 13 June 1971)

SOURCE: "Judas-Hole Vision of Hell," in *Book World,* June 13, 1971, p. 2.

[*In the following review, Frakes lauds O'Faolain's* Three Lovers.]

It's reassuring to know that the coming-of-age process still flourishes in Paris—it gives one a sense of continuity and tradition. At twenty-two, Sally Tyndal flies from drowsy Dublin to the seedy banks of the Seine, equipped with a scholarship, a suppurating Catholic conscience, and a determination to lose her Gaelic identity as a "late virgin" and "a mental amorist." And she does indeed lose it—over and over again. Thus the dreary title of this fast, funny, and cruel novel, [*Three Lovers*]. Lover #1 is Mesli, an Algerian revolutionary, medical student, and male chauvinist, who impregnates Sally, thus setting both the plot and the passions spinning. He also, not so incidentally, considers Camus a sell-out. Lover #3, Raimondo Lupino, "extinct, bizarre, touching and finished," an Italian count and antiquarian, undertakes to complete Sally's education, and the book ends with a tarnished heroine trusting herself to his horny hands.

But Lover #2 is the "boyo" you won't forget—Fintan McCann, mad painter from Limerick, fierce and hairy "verbal onanist," lecher, opportunist, and raunchy sentimentalist. "I bite therefore I am," he boasts. Clown and conniver, victim and rebel, provincial and cosmopolite (who refuses to learn French in hopes of protecting himself by incomprehension), McCann is a flaming compound of Leopold Bloom, Gulley Jimson, and Sebastian Dangerfield. Shelves of books should be written about this man, who gives us dozens of reasons to cherish him, my own favorite being his reaction to spring: "I hate the blooming, foaming, egg-laying, seed-sprouting season."

The jauntiness and verve of this book are packed hard with wit, with tingling imagery ("Holy Mother, the sheets are like seaweed": ". . . a nose like a delft pepper-pot, shiny with blackheads"), and with a worldliness that costs more than sophistication. But all is not glitter and bounce: The abortion scene is as heavy as the ones in *End of the Road* and *Play It As It Lays,* and I'll match the harrowing visit to a dying woman in a French convent and Sally's benumbing return to Dublin for Christmas with any other judas-hole visions of hell you choose.

To anticipate your inquiries—yes, Julia O'Faolain is Sean's daughter. No, she does not write like her father. And maybe, if this uncompromising novel is a fair harbinger, she'll become the family member whose name is used for identification.

Lalage Pulvertaft (review date 4 April 1975)

SOURCE: "Under Orders," in *Times Literary Supplement,* No. 3813, April 4, 1975, p. 353.

[*In the following review, Pulvertaft praises "the clear, tough style" of O'Faolain's* Women in the Wall, *but complains that the author imposes modern prejudices on the story.*]

The Queen Radegund of history, patron saint of prisoners and captives, was born in 518, and as a young girl captured by, and forced to marry, the Frankish king Clotair. She later escaped to God, and founded the monastery of the Holy Cross, where she became famous for her visions, tended the sick, and lived as an ordinary nun, handing the running of the place over to St Agnes.

In *Women in the Wall* Julia O'Faolain uses the history of Queen Radegund to try to answer fundamental questions about women's role in society, and to discover the reasons behind vocations. In the process, as she admits, she does some violence to history, imagining Radegund to have been involved in a political plot to put an orthodox Christian

prince on the throne in order to combat disorder and Arianism. A sub-plot involves Ingunda, the imagined daughter of Agnes by the poet-priest Fortunatus, who, horrified at the discovery of her true parentage, has herself walled-up to expiate her mother's sin. Although this practice is of doubtful historical validity, it here serves well as a symbol for the buried individuality of womankind. Ingunda is accidentally killed as a result of Radegund's involvement in power politics, Agnes turns anchoress, and the monastery is handed over to a cynical woman who will comply with the state's orders to achieve personal ambition.

The story itself works well. It is written in a clear, tough style, and the men and women convince as living people as well as in the sharply contrasting attitudes they represent. Miss O'Faolain, however, judges the past with the prejudices of modern psychology and political theory. She therefore leaves out of account the one explanation for people's actions which was most demonstrably obvious to their fellows: the remarkable change that the Christian faith brought about in some of those who practiced it. In those early days, Christianity was still its true radical self, and its uncomfortable saints were more aware of the guidance of the Holy Spirit than that of Rome. St Cesarius, whose Rule the real Radegund adopted, said:

> A man worships that on which his mind is intent during prayer. Whoever in his prayers thinks of public affairs . . . worships them rather than God.

Miss O'Faolain's characters see the truth in flashes. Ingunda recognizes that God has withdrawn because she has "rubbed out her true self". Agnes knows her real sin is not the paltry one of having slept with Fortunatus, but the large one of failing to have the guts to save herself and her child. However, in her fashionable wish to explain visions as sexuality, vocations as perverted power mania, Miss O'Faolain misses the nub of the matter: that God, through Christ, had challenged women as well as men to be individuals, even if this meant attacking the institutions of society. We might, today, blame Radegund for having accepted the traditional female role in binding up the wounds inflicted by men's violence and ambition: we could hardly accuse her of a desire for personal power.

Margaret Ferrari (review date 30 August 1975)

SOURCE: A review of *Women in the Wall,* in *America,* Vol. 133, No. 5, August 30, 1975, pp. 99-100.

[*In the following review, Ferrari lauds O'Faolain's* Women in the Wall *as "engrossing for its historical detail, its present relevance and its strikingly powerful style."*]

Julia O'Faolain's *Women in the Wall* is an impressive, exciting historical novel. Reading this taut story from beginning to end, the reader is left with a feeling that a fragment of history, the sixth century, the very beginning of the dark ages, has been illuminated brilliantly.

The title refers to a group of women, royal and otherwise, who leave the world to establish one of the few refuges for women in an endangered time. The novel drifts easily and clearly back and forth in time, shaped by the interactions within the convent and the political action outside the convent walls. Three of the convent's 200 women, Radegunda, Agnes and Ingunda, are pivotal in the novel.

The story centers around Radegunda, a mystical, almost saintly ex-queen whose bloody, frightening past is elicited from her by a poet-biographer, Fortunatus. In her pre-convent days, when she was 11, her family was massacred by King Clotair, and seven years later she was forced to marry him. When, after fourteen years of marriage, her husband murdered her brother, she longed for a world of reversed values, a religious life without men and without murder. Her husband granted her request and she founded the convent. Her position as queen in the story leaves her close to the sources of power and political struggle, and her position as an all-but-declared living saint and mystic make her representative of a curiously engrossing brand of Christianity.

Agnes is also very important in the story. Her reasons for entering the convent are at best confused. Radegunda essentially forces Agnes' decision when she tells her that "natural love is cursed by the curse God put on our first parents. Sexual love is linked with death." Agnes' conviction that certain people were happy in the world seemed weak against the queen's reverberating energy. So Agnes enters the convent, and becomes its abbess at Radegunda's will. And it is out of Agnes' conflict between the world's pleasures and the convent's spiritual austerity that her greatest crisis arises and brings to the fore the novel's third important woman. Agnes conceives a child with Fortunatus, the poet-biographer soon to become a priest and eventually a bishop. Though her relationship with this man never flourishes humanly and supportively, Agnes bears their daughter, Ingunda. After initially farming her out to a peasant family to be cared for, Agnes brings the child back to be raised in the convent.

Ingunda is lonely for her peasant family and feels out of place with the high-born daughters in the convent. She becomes an anchoress, burying herself out of guilt and sadness in a space in a brick wall smaller than the shallowest closet, with a slit large enough only to pass food through. She emerges some years later, a staring-eyed, gaunt, almost bodyless creature, when a group of invading barbarians tear down her wall and lance what is left of the creature inside it.

This story, shaped around two decades of convent life in a period previously thought unimportant, and around three central women seeking a life away from men and at the same time attracted to them, is particularly pertinent today because it reverberates subtly but clearly with the struggle of many women now to define the place men should have in their lives.

Women in the Wall is an austere, mind-impacting novel that I have not stopped talking about since I started reading it. It is engrossing for its historical detail, its present relevance and its strikingly powerful style.

Ann Weekes (essay date Spring 1986)

SOURCE: "Diarmuid and Gráinne Again: Julia O'Faolain's *No Country for Old Men*," in *Eire-Ireland,* Spring, 1986, pp. 89-102.

[*In the following essay, Weekes traces how O'Faolain's* No Country for Old Men *portrays the relationship between women and the political situation in Ireland.*]

Seeking a theoretical model for feminist criticism, Elaine Showalter proposes the Ardener model of intersecting circles representing male and female spheres, a crescent of each sphere free from the intersecting circle. The male crescent, though not experienced by women, is known, because male culture dominates and represents itself. The female or "wild" crescent, the area "spatially, experientially," and "metaphysically" outside the male sphere has been "muted" both in language and power and must, therefore, be examined in an attempt to represent the whole human experience. Showalter asks feminist critics of women's writing to explore this crescent, to reveal the muted plot, the "undercurrent" flowing beneath a text which must participate simultaneously in the dominant culture. As we might expect, the perspective from the "wild" crescent varies from that of the dominant sphere: Carol Gilligan asserts that a different moral perspective is an important result of women's early training in, to use Showalter's term, the "wild" sphere. From studies she conducted on females in different stages of moral development, Gilligan concludes that women tend to base their moral judgments on concern for responsibility, nonviolence, consequence, and context; the model of human moral development, however, sets judgment based on abstract codes of rights or principles as the highest level of human moral development. Based only on the male model of moral development, the model disregards the female process as either deviant or undeveloped. But, Gilligan argues, acceptance rather than exclusion of the female model will result in a more complete, balanced model of human moral development. By and large, however, the female model has not been incorporated: lip-service is paid to the values of caring, but nations and political parties openly pursue only principles. Culture, of which legend and myth are an early and persistent element, seems to authenticate this system of moral dominance. Recognizing the problem, women writers have attempted to develop revisionist versions of ancient myths. As Susan Gubar writes, referring specifically to the Persephone myth, "Writers who are convinced that gender definitions reflect and enforce the terrible recurrence of . . . myth," must rewrite myth to evade it. But such revision can be more than evasion: In the revaluation of social, political, and economical values that Alicia Ostriker sees as one of the tasks of the revisionists, the "wild" crescent, or the other model of human moral development, with all its restrictions and all its possibilities, can be presented as, if not a substitute model, at least an equally viable one.

Julia O'Faolain is one of several contemporary Irish women writers who are attempting a revision of Irish myths, history, cultural and political attitudes. Apparently telling a tale of the sequence of Irish "Troubles" in *No Country for Young Men,* O'Faolain uncovers a destructive pattern that, despite its inevitable trail of personal and political disaster, persists through myth and history into the present time. O'Faolain's central character, Gráinne O'Malley, alerts the reader to O'Faolain's myth, when she tells the American film-maker James Duffy that she is named after the central figure in the Diarmuid and Gráinne legend. According to Eóin Neeson's rendering of the legend, Fionn Mac Cumhal, the general of the Fianna warriors in Ireland, decided to assuage his loneliness by marrying Gráinne, the beautiful daughter of King Cormac. But Gráinne, reluctant to marry the aged Fionn because she loved Diarmuid, one of Fionn's young warriors, put *geasa,* similar to obligations of honor in an Arthurian legend, on Diarmuid, and he was obliged to flee with her. Furious, Fionn sent hosts of the Fianna after the runaway lovers, to battle the forces supporting Diarmuid and Gráinne. Much land was destroyed and many lives lost before Fionn, aided by magic, succeeded in killing Diarmuid. Still desiring Gráinne's favors, Fionn remained away from the Fianna pleading his cause. When, for the sake of her children, Gráinne finally consented to return with Fionn to the Fianna, Oisin, bitter at the destruction, blamed, not Fionn for what he had wrought, but Gráinne.

Order then is restored to the Fianna when Gráinne foregoes her own desires and accepts the principle of conquest. As a woman, Gráinne is related to Ireland. Indeed, a modified version of the sexual paradigm of territorial conquest that Annette Kolodny "unearths" in American "herstory" and literature could also be used to describe Ireland, "Mother Ireland" and "the Old Woman"—hence a less sexual figure than the young America—in much of Gaelic and Anglo-Irish literature. As a source of disorder, Gráinne, in both the myth and O'Faolain's novel, is related to that aspect of the coun-

try that resists control. Gráinne O'Malley, however, does not capitulate in order to restore the "order" derived from male principles; in this, O'Faolain's novel proves more optimistic than the controlling myth.

O'Faolain's novel moves between the Civil War in 1922 and the "Troubles" of divided Ireland, in 1979. The central characters are part of a political dynasty—a frequent occurrence in Irish politics, the de Valéra and Cosgrave families are examples—founded by the hero Owen O'Malley in 1922. The 1916 Rebellion is over, but the Irish imagination is still fired by the idealism of those heroes whose execution turned their minority cause into a popular one. O'Faolain's work probes the source of the political conflict in the Republic of Ireland today, a conflict that was born in 1922 when some members of the Irish government repudiated the Treaty signed by their representatives in England. These members and their followers, insisting they were following the principles of the executed heroes, took up arms against the Treaty forces, thus beginning a protracted and deadly civil war. Owen O'Malley was such a man. American money and sympathy had flowed to the revolutionaries following the 1916 executions; such money, coming generally from Americans of Irish descent, was available as long as England was seen as the enemy. Irish Americans, however, might falter at the idea of financially assisting Irishmen to kill Irishmen. Men like O'Faolain's Sparky Driscoll were sent to Ireland from the American aid societies to monitor the situation and to recommend groups for financial support. Winning Sparky over to the antitreaty cause is, therefore, very important to Owen O'Malley. In 1922, after months of fighting, the country exhausted and success remote, the leaders of the antitreaty party agreed to rejoin the government they had abandoned, but some of their followers refused to accept their decision and resorted to guerrilla attacks against both the Republic and the Six Counties. These men, the Irish Republican Army, have been sporadically active since 1922, and, when trouble flared again in the 1960s over reforms in the Six Counties, the IRA received a much-needed transfusion of purpose and men.

Judith Clancy, sister-in-law to the dead Owen O'Malley, links the two periods. Her release from the convent where she has spent more than fifty years into the care of her nephew and niece, Michael and Gráinne O'Malley, triggers the plot. Owen Roe O'Malley, son of Owen, uncle of both Gráinne and Michael, now a member of the present Irish government, worries that "mad" Aunt Judith may reveal something, never specified but perhaps best left hidden, to James Duffy, an American film-maker recording stories of the early troubles. Indeed James's quest is clandestine: His employers desire a propaganda film to increase American financial contributions to the "Banned Aid" society that seeks to undermine both the Six County state and the Republic, and which has been condemned by the government of the Republic. Judith who, we are told, often refers to her memory as a bog, "referring as much to its power of suction as to its unfathomable layers," is thus linked with the sources of disorder who may disrupt the established pattern.

Judith first introduces us to a pattern which should remind the reader of the Gráinne myth. As Gráinne was condemned for the disorder that followed Fionn's pursuit of his desire, so women have been condemned throughout Irish history. Judith thinks back to her history lessons: All Ireland's troubles, the girls were told, were due to the "frail morals" of a woman. It is worth examining the facts from which this principle of Irish history is derived. In the 1100s, when Ireland was torn with internecine struggle, one Diarmuid Mac Murrogh, king of Leinster, carried off Dervorgilla, wife of the Lord of Brefni. Like the mythic Gráinne, Dervorgilla invited the handsome Diarmuid, and although peace was finally declared, a deadly feud ensued between the rival lovers. When fighting broke out again in 1166, Ó Ruairc repaid the trespass, by allying with Mac Murrogh's rebellious chiefs, invading Mac Murrogh's land, and forcing him into exile. Mac Murrogh, accompanied by his beautiful daughter Eva, took refuge in England, where he appealed for Henry II's aid in restoring his kingdom. Eva became the "matrimonial prize" of Strongbow, the soldier who conducted the invasion of Ireland. Thus began the long history of English involvement in Irish affairs. Of Dervorgilla we know no more, but history, as Judith Clancy notes, holds her responsible for Ireland's fate, as if historians like myth-makers believed in woman's magic, irresistible lure. The struggles for land and women are curiously linked and similar in their destructiveness: Fionn devastated the land in order to attain the young Gráinne; O Ruairc seized Mac Murrogh's land because the later had taken his beautiful, presumably young, wife; Mac Murrogh exchanged his young daughter for repossession of his land. Seizure or exchange of land and of women is balanced, suggesting an equality between the two commodities. If we substitute Ireland's symbolic name for the land, we have violent exchanges of old women for young women, and vice versa.

In myth and in history adherence to principle allows men to follow a particular course without consideration of its effect on the community, on women and the common people. Adherence is made easier, is in a measure justified, if women or the people are seen as inferior to the leaders. In 1979 Gráinne O'Malley realizes that most Irish men still think of women as chattel, though this basic notion is disguised in the 20th century by sentimental, romantic, or "realistic" rationalizations. The androcentric pagan religion and Fianna warriors are represented in the 20th century by the equally androcentric Christian religion and the Irish Republican movement. The priests and the warriors define women. Judith remembers the priest, home from World War I, counselling the young girls to go forth as inspirations, lamps held up to light men's ways. Proud of their virtue, the girls fully realize that such virtue can only be preserved by ignorance. "Eve's sin"—desiring knowledge and naming things—must be avoided at all costs. From Virginia Woolf to Simone de Beauvoir, 20th century writers have revealed the limitations and distortions of this vision of woman as man's inspiration, but in 1916, this was the picture that inspired such idealists as Patrick Pearse. In its asexuality, this ideal is linked to the ideal of the land as the "old woman."

Owen Roe, son of a warrior and himself a warrior-in-waiting, sees, not the angel in the house, but the debased earth goddess. Sexual relations to Owen Roe are simply necessary animal functions; the creation of an emotional or intellectual relationship with one's sex partner is, he thinks, an artificial, female, and unnecessary structure. Gráinne asks him why he broke off their brief affair: was she too demanding? the wrong partner? Because he likes "bed," Owen Roe answers, is no reason to think that he spends his time thinking about it. "Bed's simple really," he asserts. Women mess things up by making a "production" about "bed." It is all the nuns' fault, he continues; convent girls end up believing they have "the holy grail" between their legs, "and some knight is going to come and find it." Women and sex are a means to physical pleasure for Owen Roe; he has no objection to their receiving the same from him, but rational discussion of sex and emotions, implying, as it may, a woman's ability to objectivize, and exposing, as it may, Owen Roe's fears and ignorance, is apparently unthinkable. Later that night, reflecting on why neither passionate men, like Owen Roe, nor frigid men like her husband, Michael, can discuss sex, Gráinne concludes that the church is responsible: "Monastic tradition described woman as a bag of shit and it followed that sexual release into such a receptacle was a topic about as fit for sober discussion as a bowel movement." Although Gráinne's summary seems closer to Owen Roe's views than to those of the romantic priest, both are similar in their refusal to acknowledge sexual relationships, a refusal that may have at its source the superstitious fear of woman's lure.

Owen Roe's perspective is more pervasive in a secular world than that of the priest. Sensing Gráinne's discontent and aware of the deterioration of their marriage, Michael O'Malley thinks he "Didn't fuck her enough. Women wanted it . . . because it confirmed their sense of themselves . . . Basic creatures really." Again, Michael tells Duffy that women masquerade, "being ashamed of their essential function." Like Owen Roe, then, Michael thinks that frequent sex should keep a woman happy, but he also realizes that since he cannot, or is unwilling to, satisfy Gráinne, she does need another relationship. At this point, Michael acts as do women Gilligan has studied in the second, immature, phase of female moral development. Michael has accepted the code of mutual caring, but the balance is undermined because one partner, Michael in this case, is in a position of psychological dependence. Needing Gráinne, he tricks her into returning to him when he takes their Great-Aunt Judith into their home. Desolate, not at the idea of Gráinne's infidelity, but at her leaving and disturbing his rhythm, Michael wonders could she not have got the sex she needed in Ireland? Must she go to America for that? Michael's Grandfather Owen O'Malley explained his opinions to another American, the Republican fundraiser, Sparky Driscoll, in 1922:

> "The 'people' are clay. You can do what you like in their name but, as Aristotle said of men and women, the formative idea comes from the male and the clay is female; passive, mere potentiality. The clay here is the people who has no self and no aspiration towards determining anything at all until we infuse it into them. We are their virile soul. We are they."

Woman is not a creature with an individual destiny: defined either as inspiration, source of physical satisfaction, or as clay, the necessary intermediary between a great man and his descendants, she is in every instance seen only as she relates to man.

Accepting these definitions is destructive to women. In 1922, Judith Clancy adopts the angel myth and forcefully pushes knowledge of sex away, repressing it along with other forbidden knowledge in the unfathomable layers of her bog-like mind. She realizes that her sister, Kathleen, is more attracted to Sparky Driscoll than to her fiancé, Owen O'Malley. Sparky constantly reminds Judith of animals, whereas she sees the ascetic, priest-like Owen as incorruptible. Appalled, however, when she finds her own body betraying her by responding to Sparky's kiss, ashamed when she remembers an image of dogs coupling as Sparky warns her that Owen may be a homosexual and therefore not an appropriate husband for Kathleen, Judith represses both knowledge and emotion. In every vision of physical attraction, Judith sees animals: Sparky looks at Kathleen with "dog's eyes"; he is a "ferret" who summons "the worst, most buried filth." Alarmed at her own response, fearing that Kathleen will leave Owen and go with Sparky to America, and fearing also that Sparky will upset Owen's plans by reporting negatively on Owen's decision to fight the Treaty and thus cause Owen to lose the American funds he needs to carry on the fight, Judith kills Sparky. Judith has responded as much to her emotional as to her political convictions. Her intellectual acceptance of the priest's definition of woman and her repression of the evidence of her emotions necessitates acceptance of sex as "buried filth." The text often comments ironically on itself: Owen Roe tells Gráinne, referring, he thinks, to Aunt Judith's secret, but also, of course, to her repressed sexuality, "Even harmless secrets . . . because of being hidden, breed maggots." Judith's saving action can-

not, of course, be acknowledged—this would certainly dry up American funds—so Judith is spirited into a convent by Owen O'Malley and Sparky's murder is blamed on forces of the British crown. Judith's madness is the result of accepting male definition and of acting in the male mode—of being willing to sacrifice for the sake of Owen's principle, not only Kathleen, Sparky, and the Irish people in war, but also her own imminent sexuality. Deprived of her family, her freedom, her future, and almost of her memory—for Owen prescribes electric shock to soothe her—Judith herself becomes one of the sacrifices on the altar of Owen's ambitions.

The Diarmuid and Gráinne myth is reenacted in Kathleen's life with only a depressing variation. Engaged to Owen O'Malley, whom prison has made "cold as ice" and "A machine run on will power"—a man who cares for causes, not people—Kathleen is in love not only with Sparky Driscoll, but with the possibility of another life created by herself and for herself. She resolves to go to America with Sparky to escape the war Owen is determined to unleash and to build this new life. When Judith, to forestall this impulse of disorder, kills Sparky, she ironically helps deprive Kathleen of a self-created life, a life the mythic Gráinne experienced, at least for a time.

From this point on, Kathleen appropriately disappears from O'Faolain's text, defined only by her male relatives—even her wedding is a blank in Judith's memory. Absence from the text, indeed, is a recurrent motif in the stories surveyed: Gráinne disappears from Fianna legends once she acquiesces to Fionn's wishes; Dervorgilla disappears from "his story" once she returns to Ó Ruairc from Mac Murrogh. Years later, when Judith complains to Owen of his locking her away in a convent, causing her to disappear, Owen retorts: "What's wrong with being here? . . . You should see poor Kathleen struggling with the kids. She looks ten years older than you do." Judith asks whether Kathleen is "still pretty," and Owen replies, "Kathleen . . . is the mother of six children with another on the way." As for her happiness, Owen says, "She has her children. She knows she is useful." Owen Roe later confirms this picture of Kathleen as a tired, disillusioned woman whose single importance was to be the "clay" that O'Malley molded, the potentiality from which HE created his political descendants. Like Gráinne, Kathleen ends her life caring for the man who destroyed her personal happiness and nurturing warriors who will preserve his destructive vision.

The Diarmuid and Gráinne myth spins out finally in the 1979 story of Gráinne O'Malley, Michael O'Malley, and James Duffy. Married to the alcoholic Michael when little more than a romantic school-girl, Gráinne has never had a satisfying sexual relationship. She left Michael hoping to save her "unsuccessful, comfortable marriage," and she returns to him hoping to spark some life into both Michael and the marriage. But Michael apparently lost both his voice and his interest in sex in the brawl following his renunciation of Theo—the one woman for whom he'd ever felt passion—because of her unsuitability to be the wife of an O'Malley. Weary of her half life, Gráinne turns to Owen Roe, looking, as she remembers, "for more than sex, or more through sex." But Owen Roe, as noted earlier, responds only physically. A year after the brief affair, he strides into Gráinne's life again to warn her to dismiss James, her American friend who is probing too deeply into Judith's memory. Gráinne consents on the condition that Owen Roe stop taking her son Cormac to Republican gatherings. His refusal makes Gráinne realize that he would sacrifice Cormac's safety to his own political ambitions. Seeing Gráinne's distress at his "lethal" selfishness and the danger this poses for Cormac, Owen Roe seeks to calm her: "Silly Gráinne," he smiles, and reaches for her breast, "cupping it with authority." Owen Roe's reaction is a "natural" result of his definition of women: comfort a woman sexually, he assumes, and one will also soothe away the irritating questions, questions he believes to be his prerogative rather than Gráinne's. Gráinne responds at the level Owen Roe has assigned her: like an animal protecting her young, she bites his hand and continues to do so even after she tastes his blood. He, in turn, slaps her face back and forth, in a brutal, irrational fury that continues after she releases his hand. "Mad harridan," he cries as he slaps her. Indeed, in his terms, Gráinne is mad—mad to resist the pattern which the powerful males will impose, mad to resist the physical comfort these males may grant.

This resistance is Gráinne's first real step towards freedom: the earlier flight and return to Michael were false moves, ultimately ineffectual. She continues to resist by seeing James and by exploring the bog-like depths of Judith's memory. Traditional roles are reversed in James and Gráinne's relationship. Gráinne feels her body to be inferior in beauty to James's "gorgeous" body; she delights in sensations she had never dreamed of, in making love for her pleasure. James is horrified at Gráinne's insistence on secrecy, despite her delight in and love for him. This secrecy seems to make him "a nineteenth-century whore," "a promenading penis," and "a secret sex object." Like both the mythic Gráinne and Kathleen, Gráinne decides to go away with her lover, realizing that Michael's dependence will not change and that she cannot save Cormac. Considering her responsibilities and the consequences, Gráinne makes a moral choice. But the forces of order, Owen Roe and the Irish police, aided unknowingly, but appropriately, by Owen Roe's retarded disciple, Patsy Flynn, combine to forestall Gráinne's departure. Flynn, Judith's successor in the new "old" pattern, condemns sexuality as Judith had done. As Judith responded, against her wishes, to Sparky's kiss, so Patsy, as he lies in wait to kill the "Californicator," feels the emotion of James and Gráinne "locked into his own, maddeningly, like the pedal of someone's bike getting locked into yours." Political concerns, however, outweigh the unusual emotional involvement for Patsy: to preserve the honor of the O'Malley family and to safeguard the dynasty set up by Owen O'Malley for his heirs, Owen Roe and Cormac, Patsy kills James. Having said goodbye to Michael and Cormac, Gráinne is left standing alone, waiting unknowingly for the dead James. The text, not the woman, then disappears.

To return to an earlier point—Owen O'Malley's yoking of women, land, and the people—Irishmen see woman, not as an equal but different principle, but as deviant. This deviancy asserts itself in action disruptive to the established, male pattern, hence must be repressed in the interest of order. This same order extends to nature, which man cultivates or tames. We first meet the young Judith Clancy as she contemplates, from the rigorously ordered garden of the convent, the less tamed aspects of nature.

> This region [the bog] was as active as a compost heap and here the millennial process of matter recycling itself was as disturbing as decay in a carcass. Phosphorescent glowings, said to come from the chemical residue of bones, exhaled from its depths. "Bog" was the Gaelic word for "soft" and this one had places into which a sheep or a man could be sucked without trace.

> The bog was pagan and the nuns saw in it an image of fallen nature. It signified mortality, they said, and the sadness of the flesh, for it had once been the hunting ground of pre-Christian warriors, a forest which had fallen, become fossilized and was now dug for fuel.

Similar in its relation to Showalter's "wild" area of female experience, the bog, in its peripheral position between culture and totally untamed nature, also resembles the area that Sherry Ortner finds assigned to women "outside and around" male culture. The danger of the bog is stressed repeatedly: Owen Roe, Cormac's political mentor, also initiates Cormac in the "risky" sport of riding on the bog. Dealing with Owen Roe, Gráinne thinks, is as dangerous as walking across a bog: "You never knew when the ground might give way under your feet." In its ability to swallow men, the bog symbolizes the male fear of the female, "fallen nature," or the trap of sexuality in the nuns' eyes. The bog, however, *is* essential. It provides the commonest and cheapest source of fuel for Judith Clancy's class. Men cut into it and take its peat to their homes as a source of cooking and heat. And it is more than this. Trying to explain the Southern Irish attitude to the IRA, Gráinne tells James:

> "We double think. In practical terms we're dead against them, but in some shady, boggish areas of our minds, there's an unregenerate ghost groaning

'Up the rebels.' Most of us keep the ghost well suppressed, but children, drunks, unemployable men,
and emotional misfits can become possessed by it."

In its ability to preserve and regurgitate often contradictory
materials, the bog also symbolizes Judith's memory. Whatever its meaning, symbolic or natural, the bog, despite its
essential role, is potentially a source of disorder, a constant
threat to the established order.

The common people also threaten the established order. In
1922, Sparky Driscoll and the Clancy family, except Judith,
plead with Owen O'Malley not to destroy the material improvement the people have achieved as a result of their successful struggle against Britain. But O'Malley is unwilling
to give up the principle of a wholly free Ireland. The people,
he says, are not the best judges; he dismisses their right to
self-determination and to a better life, asserting that the
people must "be goaded for their own good." Judith realizes, many years later, that Owen, like Fionn, could not distinguish what was good for the country from what was good
for himself. Michael, too, realizes that his grandfather, who
"helped forge change through violence, ended his days
guarding the outcome from any further change." For, realizing the time was not yet ripe, Owen O'Malley cynically
preserved a status quo contrary to his ideals, but beneficial
to both himself and his heirs. Owen Roe swings full circle:
as Owen O'Malley's pragmatism guided him from his principles into a successful career of compromise, so Owen Roe
lives this compromise, but works towards the ideal of the
dead Owen. Gráinne realizes that Owen Roe, too, cares nothing for individual human beings, but will risk Cormac's life
and another civil war, believing the ensuing chaos may bring
him to power. The same arrogance that allows these men to
dictate women's actions also abrogates the rights of an entire nation, decreeing bloodshed and violence to restore a
principle they believe in, thus confusing in their madness the
country with themselves.

> **The madness that forces women to act
> against their best judgments and against
> their best interests is, in *No Country for
> Young Men*, associated with the political
> confusion that has affected Ireland for over
> sixty years.**
> —*Ann Weekes*

The madness that forces women to act against their best
judgments and against their best interests is, in *No Country
for Young Men,* associated with the political confusion that
has affected Ireland for over sixty years. The possibility of
immediate change is remote, but there are some optimistic
glimmerings in O'Faolain's work. In a work that emphasizes

the preservative power of the bog, we might expect Judith's
memories to be preserved, and we are given strong suggestions that she has taped, and so preserved them. In another
instance of intertextual commentary, Owen Roe tells Gráinne
referring to the 1922 troubles—but the remark ironically applies to Judith's secret—that "In memory as in matter, Nothing . . . is lost. It comes back in another form."

But O'Faolain offers more than symbolic hope, based on the
laws of nature. In the final revision of the myth, Gráinne is
brought to the point of awareness. Despite the loss of James,
Gráinne has experienced existential freedom: "fatigue, habit,
heritage," she realizes, are merely illusionary stakes which
she can thrust aside any time she wants to. Return to Michael
and her old pattern is not inevitable. The text falls from
Gráinne, not she from the text. When the voices cease to define her, she, and the country by implication, can proceed
to define herself. Re-creating, or re-assembling myth and history from her "crescent," O'Faolain has, like the bog, transformed and preserved the material. The "phosphorescent
glowings" come, not from the "chemical residue of bones,"
but from the artistic distillation and purification of history.
For, as O'Faolain's text preserves the truth about the fictional
O'Malley family, so the myths and texts of history have preserved, albeit in scattered formations, the truths of the past.
O'Faolain challenges her readers to a new beginning, then,
not through the traditional Irish way of physical revolution,
but through textual revolution. The "glowings" are uncertain; Gráinne stands alone, but male history itself *is*,
O'Faolain shows, a record of the consequences of following principle at the expense of community. A wider perspective in general leads to a wider level of tolerance; faint as
they are, O'Faolain's "glowings" suggest the benefit to the
Irish people in political leaders' abandoning the predominantly male model of human judgment and establishing instead a wider model, one that incorporates both male and
female moral perspectives. Incorporating the vision of the
Gráinnes and the Kathleens, this wider model might eventually incorporate the vision of the majority of the Irish
people, north and south, Protestant and Catholic. But it is
the women who will have to effect the change: being largely
unaware of the injustice and danger inherent in a pattern
which benefits them, men will act only when women place
a compelling vision of human harmony before them—a vision which, if clearly seen, may finally prove as irresistible
as and may, indeed, be Gráinne's ancient *geis*.

T. Patrick Hill (review date 2 May 1987)

SOURCE: A review of *The Irish Signorina*, in *America*, Vol.
156, No. 17, May 2, 1987, p. 371.

[*In the following excerpt, Hill states that "In* The Irish Signorina, *Julia O'Faolain has written a novel of beginnings and no endings so that a pervasive incompleteness to both character and plot takes a heavy toll on the reader, but especially on the work itself."*]

As usual, the news from Ireland is both good and bad. First the bad news. In **The Irish Signorina,** Julia O'Faolain has written a novel of beginnings and no endings so that a pervasive incompleteness to both character and plot takes a heavy toll on the reader, but especially on the work itself. Anne Ryan, the signorina of the title, comes to Italy at the invitation of the ailing Marchesa Cavalcanti. Her arrival would set the stage for the unraveling of a family mystery and personal self-discovery. Of sorts.

Anne's mother, whose recent death prompted the Marchesa's invitation, had lived 20 years earlier as an aupair in the Cavalcanti villa in Tuscany. Suddenly, under a cloud of embarrassment, she was forced to return to Ireland. There she had married a dull but apparently devoted Irishman, an officer in the Irish army, who had subsequently been killed while dismantling an I.R.A. bomb. Growing up alone with her mother, Anne comes to realize that she had never fully left Italy or the Cavalcanti family. Something, someone, unnamed, held her mother so fast as to cast an unending shadow of regret and nostalgia.

Whether Anne exorcises these ghosts or deepens the shadows is a matter of guess work. For it is not so much a mystery as the plot itself that unravels before the reader. Neither Anne's stilted affair with Guido, the scion of the Cavalcanti clan, nor her contrived involvement in the dark side of contemporary Italian politics, nor, for that matter, the Marchesa's melodramatic death-bed revelations about Anne, can rescue what refuses to be rescued. "Is this novel a tragedy?" one might ask. Yes and no. . . .

Ann Owens Weekes (essay date 1991)

SOURCE: "Julia O'Faolain: The Imaginative Crucible," in *Irish Women Writers: An Uncharted Tradition,* University Press of Kentucky, 1991, pp.174-90.

[*In the following essay, Owens Weekes discusses O'Faolain's deconstruction of ancient Irish myths and tradition.*]

Probably all parents influence their children more than the children care to admit. Some of their values are imbibed like milk; others sour mind and heart and are rejected. Occasionally we are mature enough to examine our opinions apart altogether from the emotional moss they have gathered through parental association. Writers, more than other people, mine the source of their own reactions, or maybe they just seem

to do so because they write of this activity. Certainly Julia O'Faolain has frequently considered the influences of her writer parents, Sean and Eileen O'Faolain, on her own work. Her father, she believes, is an incurable romantic: indeed both her parents reacted romantically and enthusiastically to the birth of the fledgling Irish state. They Gaelicized their names, spoke the Gaelic language at home, and embraced the original principles of de Valera's republicans. Although he would become as disillusioned with the Republic as with the older empire, Sean attempted to expose his own children to "the romantic Ireland of his youth . . . which did and didn't exist." Eileen too led her daughter to and, as happens, away from romantic Ireland. A writer of children's stories, Eileen kept the child Julia home from school until she was eight, audience for Eileen's own work. When Julia finally did go to school, the "pookas, leprachauns, magic coaches, fairy forts" of her mother's stories were more real than the "angels and demons" the nuns invoked. Ridiculed after rashly exposing her credulity, O'Faolain notes that she "determined never to be caught out again and started casting a cold eye on the devils and angels too." Neither was the growing girl unaware of her father's conflicts with church and state; indeed a desire to be on his side, whatever that was, probably nurtured her resistance to and criticism of authoritarian control. Summing up her reactions to her parents' commitments, O'Faolain notes: "He and Eileen, a pair of reluctantly disillusioned romantics, made romanticism impossible for me."

> **Valuing and employing the detachment of the eighteenth-century writers she admires, O'Faolain is a long way stylistically from her father [Sean O'Faolain] or indeed from her Gaelic-Irish predecessors Kate O'Brien and Mary Lavin.**
> —*Ann Owens Weekes*

The reader of Julia O'Faolain's work readily consents to the truth of this statement. Valuing and employing the detachment of the eighteenth-century writers she admires, O'Faolain is a long way stylistically from her father or indeed from her Gaelic-Irish predecessors Kate O'Brien and Mary Lavin. When I first read her work, I was struck by the acid intelligence that strips away layers of tradition, affection, and affectation, exposing an often grotesque core. O'Faolain's kinship with Swift and Edgeworth . . . is evident here. It is impossible to remain passive when faced with O'Faolain's vivid and exuberant grotesques: John Mellors, for example, finds **"Man in the Cellar,"** an early short story, "brilliantly disturbing"; Robert Hogan finds the same text "horrific." The no-holds-barred approach to sensitive political topics, to male territory in fact, also seems closer to the Anglo-Irish writers Somerville and Ross than to O'Faolain's Gaelic female predecessors. Finally, O'Faolain's cosmopolitan lifestyle—Irish herself and married to an Italian-American, she lives in London and Los Angeles—along with her nonromantic tendencies allow her to view her various societies with detachment and a cold eye for pretense, the same cold eye Molly Keane turns on the past. Indeed a hilarious bedroom scene in an early O'Faolain story **"A Pot of Soothing Herbs"** anticipates Keane's equally preposterous, ridiculous, and pathetic scene in *Good Behaviour.*

But if Sean and Eileen were partially responsible for the substitution of an analytical rather than a romantic perspective, the early romantic deposits were not without effect. Just as the bog of the epigraph swallows, preserves, and transforms the forest, so the mind swallows, preserves, and transforms the deposits of childhood. Indeed the nuns are rightly wary, for the legends of the pagan past dwell as certainly in the imaginative crucible of the collective memory of the nation as does the forest in the bog. All the old Fenian legends, all the old historical fictions, and all the more recent romantic tales (perhaps close to those Eileen and Sean told their children) of "raids, curfews, and dancing in mountain farmhouses with irregular soldiers who were sometimes shot a few hours after the goodnight kiss" collect in, transform, and infect the national consciousness.

This collection and preservation is, short of catastrophic occurrences, as inevitable as the process of nature. But if we accept the myths and legends passively, then they, like the bog, will contain and transform us, making of us mythic fuel with which to warm a future generation. Reacting against such passivity, O'Faolain the nonromantic declares an interest in demystifying, not mystifying. "Myths like lego constructions, can be taken apart: a double bonus for the writer, the magnifying effect of invoking myth in the first place, plus the energy involved in revoking its agreed values. Destruction releases energy." This, then, is often the O'Faolain project, similar to that Alicia Ostriker associates with the revisionist poets, of treating "existing texts as fence posts surrounding the terrain of mythic truth but by no means identical to it." O'Faolain does not limit her deconstruction to ancient or Irish tales but dismembers fictions of history and of contemporary culture alongside those of legend. Indeed one could argue that contemporary myths are more pernicious in an age or country that ignores history; consequently O'Faolain subjects both the macho Italian and the romantic Hollywood images to the same penetrating scrutiny she turns on traditional myths. Aiming to expose the cage "of assumptions," the mythic, national, religious, and familial bonds which too often imprison a people, O'Faolain releases the confined energy, the alternate materials repressed by these central cultural assumptions.

The early story mentioned already, **"A Pot of Soothing Herbs,"** enacts the problems facing the writer who would find her own voice despite restrictive traditional patterns.

The protagonist of the story, Sheila, is depicted as attempting to understand both her own and her country's approach to sexuality, to experience. The story is prompted by the mother's anger at Sheila's spending the night with a fast crowd. She little knows that Sheila's detested virgin status was unthreatened when she shared a bed with the homosexual Aiden and the lovers, the Anglo-Irish Rory and the English Claudia. To protect Sheila, Aiden had placed a "barricade" of pillows down the bed; Sheila had lain between pillows and wall, bitterly aware that Aiden's hand, reaching under the pillows to grasp hers, was extended only in a "fraternal" clasp. Neither was her knowledge of the mechanics of love increased: her head prudently covered by Aiden, Sheila intuited the activity of Rory and Claudia only by "the heavings of the mattress." Sheila tries to understand why her mother, who with her peers thrills to tales of remembered romance and adventure "as if sex, in Ireland, were the monopoly of the over-fifties," should upbraid her so. And revealing the scars the national contradiction has cut through her own psyche, she ponders why she has been unable to make love for the experience only as would, she thinks, the rational eighteenth-century fictional figures she admires.

> **Myths like lego constructions, can be taken apart: a double bonus for the writer, the magnifying effect of invoking myth in the first place, plus the enery involved in revoking its agreed values. Destruction releases energy.**
> —*Julia O'Faolain*

Sheila accurately defines part of her problem as a retreat behind the covers of language. Wanting to explore and to analyze her situation, she immediately, almost instinctively it seems, protects her privacy with a humorous, self-deprecating reference to "the Irish." Abruptly, jerkily, the narrative halts, as the narrator attempts to probe and justify her rhetoric: "It is typical of us to say 'the Irish' instead of 'I': a way of running for tribal camouflage. I am trying to be honest here, but I can't discard our usual rituals. In a way, that would be more dishonest. It would mean trying to talk like someone else: like some of my friends, sheep in monkeys' clothing, who chatter cynically all day in pubs, imitating the tuneful recusancy of a Brendan Behan." Caught between the Scylla of regurgitating the familiar words, the phrases of another time that define and disguise her, and the Charybdis of a new style also alien to her, Sheila stumbles, one moment falling into the romantic traps of her parents' generation, the next into the cynical ones of her peers'. Her identity shaped by styles that seem alien, Sheila's position is similar to though more extreme than that of the diver in the Adrienne Rich poem referred to in chapter 1: the mermaid "whose dark hair / streams black, the merman in his armored body.

It is as if language shapes Sheila, not she it. Considering her refusal to make love with the elegant Robert, she notes, "I only know that I am attracted where I sense tensions and dissatisfactions—I prefer the fat, panting Hamlet to Hotspur." She thus resorts to the abstractions of literature to explain her refusal. Later, feeling sympathy toward the upset party-giver, Edna, Sheila looks back to the solitary figure: "But he was an unappetising sight: mouth caked with the black lees of Guinness, sparse, pale stubble erupting on his chin, and a popped button on his chest revealing the confirmation medal underneath." In this instance Sheila resorts to specific language as if she observes only the negative outward aspect, which apparently marks her as an objective, even cynical, observer. But the rhetoric is deceptive: Sheila is a romantic. The outward appearance and the confirmation medal are potent, not because Sheila is modern, in search only of experience, but because these aspects of Edna effectively neutralize her potentially romantic reactions.

In linking the myth of Cuchulain, the stories of Sheila's parents, and the story of Edna, the text suggests an equivalence in all three situations. As Sheila leaves the party with Aiden and Rory, Edna, the grandson of a 1916 hero, attempts to detain her, brandishing his grandfather's gun and threatening Aiden and Rory. Removing the gun, Rory pushes it barrel-down into a pot of geraniums, admonishing, "Steady, now, fellow, steady! Remember that old Irish hero, Cuchulain, whose weapon used to get out of control and had to be put in a pot of soothing herbs? I think that's what *we* need here." Ribald weapon jokes pervade the saga of Cuchulain. One story tells how Aife, a woman warrior, defeats Cuchulain and smashes his "weapon." All she leaves him, it concludes, is "a part of his sword no bigger than a fist." Another story tells of the king's calming of Cuchulain's war-fever by standing the maidens of Ulster naked between the mad warrior and the city. On seeing the maidens, the saga continues, Cuchulain quivers in shame and is quelled finally when the warriors of King Conor plunge him into three vats of cold water. The warrior Cuchulain, like the warrior Edna who wears the confirmation medal of a soldier of Christ, becomes a figure of comic impotence rather than one of romantic potency.

The Cuchulain/Edna gloss colors the evocative, stirring stories of the parents. When Edna's gun is first mentioned, Sheila wonders whether guns are "dangerous after three generations." The answer is obviously no, as Edna, armed with the weapon of the 1916 warrior, becomes a figure of bathos rather than power, his weapon, like Cuchulain's, immobilized. The tales of the troubles can also be seen as brandished leftover weapons that retain their power only when unquestioned, when not put to the test. O'Faolain's linking of the 1916 heroes and Cuchulain is not simply humorous. A statue of the mythic hero adorns the general post office in Dublin, center of the 1916 resis-tance—Cuchulain, the warrior, was the inspiration of this resistance.

The tales the parents tell—like those they are based on—belong to the fantasy world of myth. Although Sheila suggests this, she fails to realize it, perhaps because, dreamily confusing life and art, her mental life like that of the young Elizabeth Bowen has been shaped so much by tale. Characters from life are seen as characters from fiction; fictional or historical characters are replaced by those from life. Thus Sheila sees the tortured, insecure Aiden as Hamlet but replaces Yeats's Maud Gonne and Proust's Odette de Crécy with Claudia Rain. Her mother's upbraiding sounds like a "foreign language" because, misreading her parents' tales for reality, Sheila has mistaken their values. Their talk, like that of all the Irish she identifies initially, "is not about activity. It is about talk." Retreating behind the barrier of language, Sheila is concealed but is also unable to pierce the barrier, to uncover the activity hidden by language. Like the barricade that Aiden erected, the language of Irish myth effectively conceals experience, ironically projecting a romantic image rather than the "fraternal" clasp with which Aiden penetrated the pillows.

In *No Country for Young Men,* O'Faolain uncovers multiple layers of myth—ancient, historical, and contemporary—and, enacting in the development of her novel the preservation and transformation of these deposits, tests the myths. Further, *No Country for Young Men* suggests that a nation's cultural myths are differently received by men and women. The title revises the Yeatsian myth of an Ireland exuberant with life and rejecting its "aged monuments." The young, not the old, are threatened in O'Faolain's Ireland, a country that, *pace* Yeats, valorizes history, or a particular version of history, rather than humanity. Indeed by aligning himself in "Sailing to Byzantium" with Oisin, Yeats collaborates with a figure that is negative in both O'Faolain's novel and her personal pantheon. The poet of the Fianna, Oisin, like Yeats, sought a nonhuman land, a land of eternal—static—youth, and released in his poems the myths that would shackle future generations.

Concentrating on the two recent sequences of Troubles, those of the 1920s and 1970s, O'Faolain traces a pattern that reaches back through Irish history into Irish myths and is ultimately destructive. Cuchulain of **"A Pot of Soothing Herbs"** was merely sterile, a domesticated hero in a particular tribe, but Fionn, whose myth shadows *No Country for Young Men,* and his warrior Fianna were a group of fighting men, not part of any tribe but lending their services where needed. Grainne O'Malley, the protagonist in O'Faolain's novel, alerts the reader to the myth when she tells the American filmmaker James Duffy that she is named after the central figure in the Diarmuid and Grainne legend. According to legend, Fionn Mac Cumhall, the general of the

Fianna warriors, decided to assuage his loneliness by marrying Grainne, the beautiful daughter of King Cormac. But Grainne, reluctant to marry the aged Fionn because she loved Diarmuid, one of Fionn's young warriors, put a *geasa* (similar to an Arthurian obligation of necessity and of honor) on Diarmuid, and the lovers fled together. Furious, Fionn pursued them with hosts of the Fianna. Years of war ensued; men and land were destroyed before Fionn succeeded through magic in killing Diarmuid. But the Fianna was still demoralized, for its leader remained away wooing the reluctant Grainne. Finally, for the sake of her children, Grainne returned with Fionn to the warriors. Oisin, Fionn's son and Yeats's model, bitter at the destruction, blamed not Fionn for the indulgence, despite honor and duty, of his whim, but Grainne. The myth itself, despising the obvious logic of the events it recounts, thus concludes with an irrational masculinist interpretation.

The restoration of order to the Fianna, then, depends on Grainne—whose name, as Grainne O'Malley notes, means love—forgoing her own desires and accepting the principle of conquest. As a woman, Grainne (of myth and of O'Faolain's novel) is related to Ireland—"Mother Ireland," "the old woman," or "Dark Rosaleen" in much Irish literature. Exemplifying in miniature the intoxicating and addictive power of national myth, O'Faolain has a young warrior sing "Dark Rosaleen" at the Clancy house during the civil war. When "in the last verses, the softer sentiment disappeared and menace pounded on alone," a listener remembers, "the boy had caught the mockers in his cadences. Rapt, they nodded to his beat and even the Da [who loathes the violence] applauded." Jennifer Johnston too, as we shall see, considers this mindless, emotional espousing of war disguised as love to be a form of intoxication. The image of Ireland as injured woman whose wounds call her sons or lovers to war is not unlike the sexual paradigm of territorial conquest that Annette Kolodny "unearths" in American "herstory," and O'Faolain's and Johnston's work suggests a universality in this pattern. The Irish mythmakers, whether lauding mythical or historical Irish leaders, pictured Ireland as a woman constantly in need of male protection and represented woman on her own, Ireland or Grainne without a lord or without the one "righteous" lord, as a source of disorder.

When O'Faolain's novel opens in the 1920s, Ireland and the Irish women have little choice but to submit to the demands of the competing forces of warriors. But within the country, as within women themselves, uncertainty, perhaps the residue of another order, stirs. This potential disruption is configured initially in the person of Judith Clancy, Grainne's great-aunt and the connecting link between each period. We first meet her as a young woman contemplating the untamed aspects of nature from the rigorously ordered garden of her convent school:

> This region [the bog] was as active as a compost heap and here the millennial process of matter recycling itself was as disturbing as decay in a carcass. Phosphorescent glowings, said to come from the chemical residue of bones, exhaled from its depths. "Bog" was the Gaelic word for "soft" and this one had places into which a sheep or a man could be sucked without trace.

> The bog was pagan and the nuns saw in it an image of fallen nature. It signified mortality, they said, and the sadness of the flesh, for it had once been the hunting ground of pre-Christian warriors, a forest which had fallen, become fossilized and was now dug for fuel.

A natural palimpsest, the bog can be read both as the repository of a nation's culture and as an archetypal feminine place. In the latter context the bog becomes a particularizing of that peripheral area assigned to women "outside and around" male culture and of the "wild" area, the crescent of female culture unknown to men. In its ability to devour men, the bog is also symbolic of the ancient male fear of the female, a fear perhaps of the older matriarchal tradition of the great goddess discussed in chapter 4. Here too Irish myth is relevant: the depiction in Irish legends of the overthrow of female oppressors by male heroes—Queen Maeve, for example, by Cuchulain—can also be read, as are many of the myths of the Near East, as a reenactment of the overthrow of the goddess.

No Country for Young Men presents Owen Roe O'Malley as heir to this militant political tradition. Son of the "hero" Owen O'Malley who fought the British government in the early 1920s and then his own countrymen when they accepted the treaty negotiated with England, Owen Roe is a devious politician. The first Owen arrogantly refused to accept his government's and his people's wishes and, like his mythic ancestor Fionn, insisted on fighting a war that would devastate his country. Carrying on the tradition of the poet Oisin, Michael O'Malley, Owen's grandson and Grainne's husband, writes the revisionist history of the first Owen. Owen Roe also contributes to the glorification of his father, expecting to inherit the mantle of Owen's political office and willing, like his ancestor, to plunge the country into civil war again if this would achieve his goal. Intent, like Oisin, on squashing the potentially disrupting female account, Owen Roe attempts to have Grainne silence Judith—the reservoir of the secrets of 1920.

But Judith and Grainne O'Malley are linked by Grainne's sympathy for her aunt and also referentially to bog images. Grainne, for example, thinks that "dealing with Owen Roe was like walking across a bog. You never knew when the ground might give way under your feet." She worries that

Owen Roe takes her son riding on the bog, her concern extending both to the mythological bog of Irish history and the physical bog of Calary. To be pulled into the bog is to accept the myths passively, to be shaped by them; to explore the bog, while still dangerous, is to question the history, the myths, to take control of one's own life. Throughout the text Judith's memory is described and portrayed as having the boglike power of absorbing, concealing for years, and regurgitating. Although James wishes to exploit Judith's memory and Owen Roe wishes to suppress it, it is appropriately Grainne who will explore that female place, crucible of individual and racial memory.

Within the bog of the Irish communal memory O'Faolain traces the patterns of the Diarmuid and Grainne myth in the male and female imaginations. The mythic triangle is represented in the 1920 grouping of Owen O'Malley, founder of the political dynasty; Kathleen Clancy, the woman he marries; and Sparky Driscoll, the American fund-raiser. Kathleen wishes to go away with Sparky, but her young sister Judith, who admires Owen, kills the outsider to prevent his interference with Owen's plans. The young Kathleen has loved Owen, but years in prison have made him, as Kathleen tells Judith, "cold as ice. A machine run on will power," a man who cares for causes rather than people. From the boglike depths of Judith's mind, whence most of the 1922 story comes, we are allowed to see that Kathleen is correct, that Owen is another Fionn. Determined to ignore the treaty that the legitimate representatives of the Irish party have signed, Owen, to advance his own political future, fights on despite the people's desire for peace. Explaining his stance to Sparky, who opposes fighting against the people's wishes, Owen says, "The people are clay. You can do what you like in their name but, as Aristotle said of men and women, the formative idea comes from the male and the clay is female: passive, mere potentiality. The clay here is the people who has no self and no aspiration towards determining anything at all until we infuse it into them. We are their virile soul. We are they." This convenient rationalization allows Owen to act as Fionn, to ignore the resistance of women, people, and country in pursuit of individual desire.

O'Faolain suggests that just as the bog accretes materials through the centuries so too does the history of Ireland. Laid down over mythic layers, Irish history is affected by them. In 1922 we see the young Judith Clancy remembering the history lesson: "the frail morals of a woman were first responsible for bringing the English to Ireland in 1169—so women bore inherited guilt." Irish women thus carry a double load—the fall of "mankind" and the fall of Ireland. Given the placement of this wry reflection in a narrative overtly demonstrating the manipulation and reinterpretation of recent Irish history, the reader naturally reconsiders the events that led to Ireland's "fall," to "her" being "possessed" by an alien warrior. In the 1150s the woman in question,

Dervorgilla, was married to the Lord of Brefni whose political rival was Diarmuid MacMurragh, Lord of Leinster. Dervorgilla left Brefni for MacMurragh, and though she did return, Brefni never forgave Diarmuid for the loss of face. In the course of the 1160s' internecine feuding, Brefni took the opportunity to invade Diarmuid's land. Diarmuid was forced to flee to England, where he sought Henry II's help and proffered his daughter, Eve, as gift to Strongbow, leader of the revenge expedition. Thus began the English occupation.

Like Oisin of old, historians, Judith notes, blame Dervorgilla for the devastation wrought by her jealous lovers on country and people. Imaginative patterns, especially those that justify particular courses, change very slowly. The Aristotelian principles that Owen quotes simply justify manipulating human beings in general and women in particular for his own benefit. Control is obviously necessary, the interpretations imply: witness what unfettered women, Grainne and Dervorgilla, wrought. The ascetic Irish Catholic church, Grainne O'Malley realizes, adds its layer to the justification. Considering why neither frigid men like her husband Michael nor virile ones like her former lover Owen Roe can discuss sex, Grainne blames the church. "Monastic tradition described woman as a bag of shit and it followed that sexual release into such a receptacle was a topic about as fit for sober discussion as a bowel movement." The legends of Ireland's ascetic monks—St. Kevin of Glendalough, for example—do indeed suggest the righteousness of the saint's disposing of, killing, woman, the fallen temptress.

The blame assigned, myth- and history-makers write Grainne and Dervorgilla out of their texts. O'Faolain, however, delves into the bog of Judith's memory to uncover the fate of her female characters. A quick learner, the young Judith absorbs all the lessons. She knows woman's duty, a duty reinforced in her school days by the warrior/priest home from World War I who counsels the girls to go forth as inspirations, lamps held up to light men's ways. Virtue, he tells the girls, can only be preserved by ignorance. "Desiring knowledge—Eve's sin—and naming things" are prime threats to their virtue, they (unlike Elizabeth Bowen's Lois) obediently believe.

Inspired by this ideal, Judith admires what she sees as Owen's ascetic purity, what Kathleen sees as death-giving ice. When Kathleen confesses to Judith that she loves the American, Sparky Driscoll, Judith even thinks in Owen's idiom: "Sparky was a spoiler and a giver of bad advice. In Kathleen he had found soil only too receptive." Judith sets the two men up as good and evil, and Sparky "proves" her hypothesis when he kisses her, for her body behaves so wildly she wonders if she is mad. Seeing her own response as wild, Judith sees it as disordered, as the problem of women in fact, the problem of Grainne, of Dervorgilla, and of her sister, Kathleen. Ironically, then, her reaction to

Sparky's kiss does not confirm her own and other women's sexuality but the ascetics' lessons, and the experience of her own body is discarded in favor of the authority of the fathers. Whether the early church fathers really believed female sexuality was evil matters little now. They promoted this useful idea and, as Phyllis Chesler shows in *Women and Madness,* psychiatrists and psychologists have continued to treat female sensuality as unfeminine and deviant, recognizing in it a threat to established institutions. Having adopted the male paradigm of the good woman's asexuality, Judith sees her own reaction as a response to evil. So when Sparky would interfere with Owen's plans for war, Judith is in her own mind justified in killing the evil opponent of good.

Her psyche self-repressed, Judith is forced by Owen into a convent, where electric shock is administered to quiet the dangerous memory. But the recollections surge back, and Judith tells Owen she fears for her sanity, for not even her confessor believes her story. Fearful lest anyone should, Owen, unaware of the irony, calms Judith: the priest, he suggests, "probably thinks it's sex. . . . Half the women in here are probably suffering from suppressed sex." But although Judith's adoption of the male paradigm with its subsequent repression of forbidden knowledge has driven her to the verge of madness, O'Faolain suggests a triumph. Judith does recover her story, for the bog is a potent preserver, as the "phosphorescent glowings," Judith's story in O'Faolain's work, attest.

If madness threatens Judith for accepting definitions other than those of her own psyche and her own intelligence, then deletion, another kind of madness, is Kathleen's fate, as it was Grainne's. In Judith's memory, in the bog of Irish history, no trace of Kathleen arises after her marriage but those registered by her male relatives. Years after 1922 Owen attempts to prevent Judith's leaving her convent: "What's wrong with being here? . . . You should see poor Kathleen struggling with the kids. She looks ten years older than you do." Judith asks if Kathleen is "still pretty" and if she is happy. Owen retorts, "Kathleen . . . is the mother of six children with another on the way." As for her happiness, "she has her children. She knows she is useful." Owen Roe confirms this picture to Grainne many years later. Repressive marriage, then, even more than convent life, effectively negates the independent woman, neutralizes her sense of self, her sensuality, and indeed, from a male perspective, effectively solves the problem of women's disorder. Kathleen's sole purpose, a private one, is to give birth to the clay that O'Malley has infused.

In the final triad of Grainne, Michael, and James, O'Faolain takes her characters to the point of awareness but does not define, finish, or circumscribe their story. Married to Michael when she was little more than a romantic schoolgirl, Grainne has been sacrificed, albeit happily and ignorantly, to protecting the O'Malley name from the scandal her alcoholic, free-living husband might attract. Ensconced by his powerful family in a "safe" job, Michael continues his drinking and offers Grainne only a half life. Weary of this, Grainne turns to Owen Roe, not so much for erotic gratification but for "more through sex." In the tradition of the lusty warriors of myth, however, Owen Roe takes his sexual affairs lightly: "Your trouble," he tells Grainne after the affair, "was scruples. Making mountains out of molehills. . . . The wrong woman for a politician. Do you know that the Sicilians say 'politics is sweeter than sex'? Yes. Well, no reason not to combine them—until one starts to threaten the other. That happens when the woman—it's always the woman—makes a big production out of going to bed. Bed's simple really." Grainne reflects, "He talked with assurance, driving, mashing up things—love, politics—the way a garbage-disposer mashes them to unrecognizable, recyclable, grey fritters." The bog transforms but does not destroy. Owen Roe destroys. His linguistic destruction is paralleled by his and Owen O'Malley's refusal to recognize sensuousness and their consequent violation and attempted annihilation of women's sexuality—Owen O'Malley by incarcerating Judith in a convent and by treating Kathleen as a "mode of production," and Owen Roe by his exploitation of women's bodies.

With the foreigner, James Duffy, however, Grainne establishes a fulfilling sexual relationship, one which Owen Roe sees as a threat to his political empire. By making this relationship primarily sexual (therefore ultimately limited), O'Faolain stresses the importance of responding to sensual needs so long denied women in Ireland. The warrior figure has not improved through the centuries: Cuchulain, the mythic hero of the 1916 Irish Republican Army, killed his only son rather than risk his own boasting honor; Fionn tricked Grainne into living with him by promising to protect her children; Grainne O'Malley promises to stop seeing James Duffy in return for Owen Roe's promise not to take her son, Cormac, to dangerous republican gatherings. When Owen Roe refuses, Grainne, like her namesake and like Kathleen, decides to escape with James. Once again, as in the case of Judith and Sparky, the irrational interferes on the side of the law. Patsy Flynn, whose madness is evident in his acute sexual suppression, kills James, much as Judith did Sparky, to preserve the O'Malley name and hence dynasty that is threatened equally by the outsider's sensuousness and by his political stance. But indeed sensuousness is political in Ireland. It is not a quality to be associated with mythical, historical, or fictional heroes, neither with Fionn nor Cuchulain, nor with, for example, Cuchulain's symbolic successor, Patrick Pearse, or Fionn's fictional successors, Owen and Owen Roe O'Malley.

Yet Grainne is not absorbed as her physical and mythical ancestors were. As she shares a drink with Michael, who is deeply enmeshed in her life, Grainne feels that he is trying to "web her in." "Fate, he was implying, fatigue, habit, heritage, were stakes planted around her, holding her there, limiting her choices. Poor Michael, she thought, how wrong he was. She could go anytime she liked." What Grainne intuits here is the existential freedom Stephen Dedalus achieved when he thrust aside nets of country, religion, and family. But these stakes, though unfairly binding, are powerful, and the sexual relationship with James, like that of a later O'Faolain heroine with her foreign lover in *The Obedient Wife,* is ultimately a poor thing compared to the deep, twisted relationship Grainne has with her husband. O'Faolain sees no need to supply defining endings: the text leaves Grainne searching for James, whose body has been absorbed in another bog, the river Liffey. She may act on her existential realization, or like Carla in the later work, she may return to Michael. If the latter occurs, the text of Judith's memory awaits her. What seems important, however, is that the writer releases her character, refuses to constrict her as did the myth- and history-makers. The text, as one observer notes, falls from Grainne, not she from the text.

Seeing myth as limiting, O'Faolain naturally offers no alternative tale, no simple equation of current female liberation with mythical and historical incarceration. Indeed she expresses deep fear of "myth-mongers, whether religious or political." Believing that they alone have the answers to the great questions makes them, she thinks, "dangerous, and in the end unlovable." Grainne and Michael's bonds, woven over fifteen years, are elastic enough to take the strain of Grainne's defection. More independent than her ancestors, Grainne O'Malley can seize more freedom than they could. But as mythical and historical patterns cut their own shape in a nation's imagination, so long-standing relationships cut their patterns in individual imaginations. For Julia O'Faolain sees human beings as essentially social creatures.

The bond between Grainne and Michael unites their individual psyches. Returning to her home early in the novel, having left Michael for several months, Grainne feels "bereft" at finding an empty house. "Why wasn't Michael home?" she wonders. "She had a physical illusion that she would be whole again only when she held him in her arms. Did that merely mean that he was to her as routine was to laboratory mice?" Michael too, when he suspects Grainne will leave him, agonizes at the idea of a break in their pattern. Another O'Faolain character, Una of **"The Man in the Cellar,"** tries to explain the "fetid bubble of dependence and rancour" that traps her with the wife-beating Carlo: "Between a man and a woman who are deeply involved sexually—atrocious injuries can be forgiven." (The text does not, of course, suggest that Una should remain trapped; having escaped, she attempts to explain why she remained there so long.) The intimate marital relationship, it appears, carves its pattern

as indelibly on individuals as does the mythic pattern on a nation.

Despite the mutual bruising endemic to long-standing relationships, the union itself is usually seen as positive in O'Faolain's work. In *The Obedient Wife,* O'Faolain depicts an Italian family temporarily residing in Los Angeles. Carla has taken a lover while her husband works and plays in Italy, and she must decide whether to remain with this considerate lover or to return to Italy to her chauvinistic husband. Reluctantly deciding in favor of her husband, when—and because—he hurries from Italy to persuade her, Carla accuses her lover, Leo, of having no real need of her: "You're invulnerable, strong, fenced in. You believing Christians have an enormous ego, massive pride. I imagine it comes from the notion that your first duty is to save your own soul—that's breathtaking egoism, after all, and yet you learn it as a duty, a maxim and foundation-stone to your moral system.

Although the strands are very twisted and although the sacrifice of the individual is rejected, the O'Faolain novel ultimately valorizes communal over individual values. This, I think, separates O'Faolain from those Anglo-Irish ancestors to whom I linked her earlier—Maria Edgeworth, Somerville and Ross, and Molly Keane. This valorization contrasts too, as we shall see, with the heroines in the later Jennifer Johnston novels, heroines who believe that the communal relationship is subordinate to that soul-saving activity of writing or painting. O'Faolain's Carla refuses to stay with Leo because his "giving" does not bring them close: "Fighting and wounding," Carla asserts, do engender a human empathy. "A flowing together takes place. It's not just rational. It's more intimate, almost tangible. I can't explain it in words. Lots of life evades words, Leo, but you live by them." Life, O'Faolain reminds us constantly, cannot be separated into the isolated compartments of logic or art.

Like a crucible, then, the bog melds a nation's myths and history into national imaginative patterns. All elements are preserved within this reservoir, though they are transformed by contact with each other and by time. Thus the top layers of the palimpsest show traces of the earlier writing: the great Danu is not only preserved, but she has acted throughout the centuries so that the comic Maeve, the warrior queen whom Cuchulain fights; the repressed Grainnes and Dervorgillas; and the Judiths, Kathleens, and latter-day Grainnes all bear her mark. Recall Sheila's early plaint: "The depressing thing about our talk is that it is not about activity. It is about talk." Exactly. So the literature, the stories of the historians, the myths—all the shaping material is ultimately not the reality of the past situations but the talk, the words, the literature about the material. And O'Faolain's texts, along with those of other contemporary women writers, add a new reviving, ameliorating, restorative layer to the palimpsest, a layer which not only alters the future but which also restructures the literary past. This is the optimism of O'Faolain's essentially comic image. In the feast that ends comedy, that harmonizes without the domination of any single melody, the contradictory visions of Cuchulain and Emer, Fionn and Grainne, Grainne and Michael coexist and temper each other. As I have noted elsewhere, the unexplained geasas may be nothing more than the harmony of opposites. But what more could we ask? The magic does not simply belong to a golden age. As O'Faolain detects the "phosphorescent glowings," the traces of her characters in the bog of Judith's mind, so we too can uncover our history in the bog of national literature and myth. In a typical O'Faolain irony, Owen Roe, the suppressor and distorter of history, observes: "In memory as in matter, Nothing . . . is lost. It comes back in another form."

Thomas R. Moore (essay date March 1991)

SOURCE: "Triangles and Entrapment: Julia O'Faolain's *No Country for Young Men,* in *Colby Quarterly,* Vol. XXVII, No. 1, March, 1991, pp. 9-16.

[*In the following essay, Moore analyzes the triangular relationships at work in O'Faolain's* No Country for Young Men.]

An exploration of the triangular relationships among the characters in Julia O'Faolain's 1980 novel *No Country for Young Men* reveals a paradigm of control and entrapment of women throughout Irish history. O'Faolain, who has published several other novels and short stories, also co-edited with her husband in 1973 a collection of readings concerned with the historical position of women, *Not in God's Image: Women in History from the Greeks to the Victorians.* In *No Country for Young Men* she details "how devastating to a society the mistreatment of women, the misuse of their energies and gifts, really is." Political intrigue, Irish nationalism, social commentary, clever mystery, and abundant literary and mythological allusions flesh out the narrative, but O'Faolain's primary focus is the women.

The novel comprises two interwoven plots, one in 1922, the second fifty years later. The first concerns Irish-American Sparky Driscoll, murdered by young Judith Clancy to protect American funding for the IRA; the second deals with Grainne O'Malley, Judith's grand-niece, and her affair with James, a Californian visiting Ireland to tape political reminiscences for a film. The two time periods interweave throughout the novel, intersecting at the climax as Judith witnesses James's murder. An overlayment of French critic René Girard's theory of "triangular desire" brings into focus the forces at play in the triangular relationships in the novel.

In the opening essay of his critical study, *Deceit, Desire, and the Novel: Self and Other in Literary Structure,* Girard sets forth the energies at work on fictional characters and the objects—or persons—they desire. Since Don Quixote (one of his primary illustrations) pursues the perfect chivalric existence represented by Amadis of Gaul, "he has surrendered to Amadis the individual's fundamental prerogative: he no longer chooses the objects of his own desire—Amadis must choose for him." This model of chivalry which Don Quixote aspires to is what Girard terms "the *mediator* of desire. Chivalric existence is the imitation of Amadis in the same sense that Christianity is the imitation of Christ." In Girard's schema Don Quixote and Amadis are connected by a horizontal line indicating Don Quixote's (the subject's) desire to attain Amadis' (the object's) perfect chivalric nature. But above this horizontal line "radiating toward both the subject and the object" is the mediator, the model of chivalric existence. Girard sets out this three-part system as a triangle, cautioning that "the triangle has no reality whatever, it is a systematic metaphor."

Flaubert's Emma Bovary is Girard's other primary illustration. Emma pursues a conception of a romantic heroine which, as Girard says, has been created by "the second-rate books which she devoured in her youth [which] have destroyed all her spontaneity." She is similar to "the *vaniteux*—vain person—[who] cannot draw his desires from his own resources":

> A vaniteux will desire any object so long as he is convinced that it is already desired by another person whom he admires. The mediator here is a *rival,* brought into existence as a rival by vanity, and that same vanity demands his defeat.

The intensity of the subject's desire for the object is governed by "the imaginary desire which he attributes to his rival." Girard's theory of mimetic desire does not require that the mediator be a rival, but, as in the cases of Don Quixote and Emma Bovary, simply a desired end. If the subject and mediator are rivals for the object, Girard terms this "internal mediation." Conversely, external mediation is "when the distance is sufficient to eliminate any contact between the two spheres of *possibilities* of which the mediator and the subject occupy the respective centers."

The three points of Girard's "'triangular' desire" metaphor are always subject, object, and mediator. Spontaneity, another key term in his system, is the opposite of vanity. A spontaneous character is unfettered by an outside desire—he has retained his individuality and his freedom to choose (Don Quixote and Emma Bovary have relinquished both) and would be excluded from Girard's system.

O'Faolain immediately suggests her focus on triangular relationship in choosing to name her central character Grainne. Daughter of Cormac, King of Ireland, Grainne was the "object" of the rivalry between Diarmuid and Finn. In *Grania,* Lady Gregory's play based on the myth, Finn in his old age desires the youthful Grania, and Diarmuid and Grania must flee to escape him. Diarmuid, however, faithful to Finn, swears "It is not as wife I will bring her" and that he will "show respect to her till such time as [Finn's] anger will have cooled." Diarmuid in his perfect youthfulness possesses what Finn desires, and Finn in his pursuit of Grania has forfeited his freedom to choose, a pattern of internal mediation according to Girard's model: Finn the subject, Diarmuid the mediator and rival, Grania the object. In 1880 Lady Gregory married Sir William Gregory, thirty years her senior. Critic Mary Fitzgerald points out that the Grainne myth "had such strong autobiographical significance for its author that she did not allow its production during her lifetime" and that the play "contains some of her most lyric speeches and an intimate understanding of the complexities of love between the young and old."

In Act II of *Grania,* seven years after the couple has fled, Grania says to Diarmuid: "It was not love that brought you to wed me in the end" but "jealousy, jealousy of the King of Foreign, that wild dark man, that broke the hedge between us and levelled the wall." Girard points out that "Jealousy and envy imply a third presence: object, subject, and a third person toward whom the jealousy or envy is directed. These two 'vices' are therefore triangular." Girard explores this further, noting that "like all victims of internal mediation, the jealous person easily convinces himself that his desire is spontaneous," whereas in reality "true jealousy is infinitely more profound and complex; it always contains an element of fascination with the insolent rival." We see a direct illustration of this dynamic of triangular forces when Grania explains to Diarmuid, following the fight with the King of Foreign by the pool, that "it was not till you saw another man craving my love, that the like love was born in yourself." In the same speech Grania goes on to explain to Diarmuid that if they return home their love "will be kept kindled for ever" by his hearing kings' sons saying "'It is no wonder Diarmuid to have gone through his crosses for such a wife!'" and by her overhearing "their sweethearts saying: 'I would give the riches of the world, Diarmuid to be my own comrade.'" We sense Lady Gregory's acute insight into all four of these triangular situations (ordered here as subject/object/mediator): Finn/Grania/Diarmuid, Diarmuid/Grania/the King of Foreign, Diarmuid/Grania/jealous admirers, and Grania/ Diarmuid/jealous admirers.

In *No Country for Young Men* we see Grania's namesake, Grainne O'Malley, in three relationships, each time occupying a different position in Girard's metaphorical triangle. First, in the Grainne/Thea/Michael triangle which is played out in Rome, Grainne assumes the role of the mediator (and

eventually rival), with Thea as subject and Michael as object. Thea wants Michael so she can "marry up" the way several of her friends have, but Michael hesitates, knowing his father will disinherit him if he marries below himself socially. Michael says, "He'd cut me off. We've got to move warily." When Thea turns to Grainne for advice, it becomes clear to Thea that, cousin of Michael's or not, Grainne has become a rival. Thea, the "brassy, disillusioned shopgirl," can never, even with her "readiness to adapt," become acceptable to Michael's family. Grainne becomes both rival and mediator as "the trio" dines out "almost nightly," and Grainne senses she may "be being backed into the role of predatory little deb who swipes the heroine's man." Thea wishes to imitate Grainne, the model of the socially acceptable and thus marriageable woman, in the way Emma Bovary wishes to imitate her model of the romantic heroine engendered by her reading of those "second-rate books."

Although Grainne becomes the rival of Thea for Michael, Thea and Grainne could not exchange their respective positions of subject and mediator. Not only does Thea not represent Grainne's desired image, but even in their courtship there is little sexual energy between Michael and Grainne; Michael substitutes drink for sex. Later Grainne recalls that "sex had been of such minimal importance in her marriage" and is stunned to learn, when Thea and her Columbian lover visit Dublin, that with Thea "Michael, in that department, was memorable." Something is amiss with Michael in his near incestuous marriage, in his inept fathering of Cormac, and in his sexuality as well: it was the episode of his "buggering a sheep" on the monastery farm when he was a schoolboy that had persuaded his father to send him "to Rome to have his voice trained for the Grand Opera."

In the second triangular situation, Grainne's pursuit of James, she becomes the subject, James the object, and the mediator her vision of the "free" woman (at first represented by her friend, Jane, Director of the Halfway House for Battered Wives in London) whom she wants to imitate in the same way Don Quixote attempted to imitate Amadis of Gaul. She had run off to London to be free: "Grainne was certainly not the cart-horse breed. Bad at pulling burdens, she'd slipped her harness five months back and left for London with their son, Cormac, leaving Michael to dry out alone." She had freed herself of Catholicism and had entered willfully into an affair with her cousin Owen Roe, one of O'Faolain's vain, brutal males like Fintan McCann from her early short story, **"Turkish Delight,"** who "collects scalps" and "doesn't even *like* the women he takes to bed!" At the rendezvous at the cottage James tells Grainne: "So you propose a double bind. Like your namesake did to that poor guy she forced to run off with her. In the Celtic saga. What's his name?"

O'Faolain reminds us of the myth of Grainne and Diarmuid at this moment of incipient lovemaking because it is just such a "bind" of love and commitment that Grainne is bent upon avoiding: she wants James (the Girardian "object") only insofar as he represents freedom and temporary sensuality. Her mediator is that free woman, not sexual interdependence. Feminist critic Ann Weekes points out in a discussion of the novel that Grainne's fury at Owen Roe's advances is her "first real step towards freedom" and that she continues "to resist the pattern which the powerful males will impose" and "to resist the physical comfort these males may grant" by continuing to see James. It is clear, as Weekes also mentions, that "traditional roles are reversed in James and Grainne's relationship." It is Grainne whose fingers are "rough" "like sandpaper" and James whose flesh is "fluidly perfect," unlike the situations Grainne is used to where "*she* is the desirable one to whom *they* were beholden."

The third positioning of Grainne in the metaphor of triangular desire is as object, desired by James. A mediator similar to Grainne's ideal of freedom is at work here since James is also fleeing a static marriage, "a box" he calls it, which he would need "a powerful spring" to escape from. O'Faolain's epistolary portrait of James is clearly derisive in its focus upon his self-absorption and his hypocritical concern for his wife. Therese, "the older woman" who "had got him to bed, to the registry office and through his Ph.D.," fears it is her "lumpy thighs" that have driven James off. James is being, in his own words, "a selfish and insensitive bastard," and the letters strike at Therese's fears of her waning sexual attractiveness with the animal imagery he uses to describe the affair with Grainne: "I am like a dog barking at a door behind which he smells a bitch on heat: glaze-eyed, hot-tongued, maddened." Later Grainne is "like some piece of animal bait with which Ireland trapped me." We have silence from Therese. O'Faolain includes only one letter from her before James's letters begin with the news of his affair with Grainne.

By observing Grainne in the three corners of Girard's triangle, her cage and her struggle to free herself come into clearer focus. She moves from corner to corner—from mediator to subject to object—but spontaneity eludes her. She sees beyond; she cannot get beyond. And in another triangular relationship in the novel a curious interplay of forces emerges.

In 1922 both Judith and Kathleen (Judith's sister) respond sexually to Sparky Driscoll, Kathleen willingly, Judith reluctantly. Kathleen falls in love with Sparky: "I'm in love for the first time" (thereby setting up yet another triangle of Kathleen/Owen/Sparky), and Judith is overcome when Sparky kisses her: "Her body was behaving wildly. Were they both mad?" And it is Judith as temptress and self-sacrificial savior, acting spontaneously and outside of Girardian triangular forces, who murders Sparky to keep him from going back to cut off American funds for the IRA. Judith retains her spontaneity, "saves" Ireland, but sacrifices herself in the process—another long-suffering Irish heroine, like O'Casey's Juno Boyle or Synge's Maurya in *Riders to the Sea*. Ann Weekes sees Judith's decision here and other such self-defeating acts as a "madness" which is "associated with the political confusion that has affected Ireland for over sixty years." And it is Sparky, ironically, who reminds Judith that her namesake "is the sacrificial Judith of the Bible."

In the story from the Apocrypha the biblical Judith, beautiful and "dressed in her gayest clothes" (Judith 10:3), tricks the Assyrian enemy, King Holophernes, into believing he may seduce her. While he sleeps in his tent, she murders him:

> She went to the bed-rail beside Holophernes' head and took down his sword, and stepping close to the bed she grasped his hair. "Now give me strength, O Lord, God of Israel, "she said; then she struck at his neck twice with all her might, and cut off his head.

Likewise, Judith Clancy leads Sparky to believe he may seduce her. Alone with Judith in the Devereux mansion during the storm, Sparky touches her, his fingers playing "on the base of her neck, curling and uncurling her short, escaping hair." Then Judith, temptress and savior like her namesake, takes the bayonet Sparky had removed from the wall and drives "the blade up under his rib cage, through the pit of his stomach and into the woodwork on the back of the divan." The executions fuse in both method and motive here, the Israelite Judith believing "The Lord will deliver Israel by my hand" (8:33), Judith Clancy believing she will deliver Ireland by keeping Sparky from "going back to America to cut off their only source of arms."

In the Kathleen/Owen/Sparky triangle Judith is afraid that Kathleen and Sparky's attraction for each other will provoke a fight between Owen and Sparky. Easily jealous, Owen believes Kathleen was dancing with Sparky in their clandestine visit to the Devereux Estate. However it is difficult to separate love from politics here, to set out cleanly the operative forces in this triangle. Judith herself says in answer to Grainne's question about the bad feelings between Owen and Sparky: "Politics? Oh. I suppose it came into it. What didn't it come into in those days? But no, I can't remember exactly." Judith's bog-like memory tenaciously keeps its secrets, "its unfathomable layers" revealing only occasional "phosphorescent glowings." And Sparky's death defuses the triangle.

Memory, a controlling motif throughout the novel, becomes mediator in a triangular relationship of Judith as subject and "empowerment" as object. If Judith can integrate her memory of 1921 with her present, she will reassemble her divided world. As the novel advances, Judith's memory, "shocked" into disarray, becomes progressively more lucid. Early in the narrative, "memory" is obscure, is polluted. As Michael walks Judith home from the convent they pause at the canal (where Judith will later see James murdered), and Judith comments that it "Looks dirty." Michael replies that it is "Polluted . . . like memory's stream." Mary, the present maid, becomes Bridie of 1921, further signaling Judith's two worlds. Her will to fuse these two worlds, to reassemble events, is clear when she tells Grainne "I'm seeking a memory" as she jabs at the cushion (Sparky) with Cormac's hockey stick (the bayonet). But at the end Judith wrongly believes that "she [is] in command of her faculties" as she relates James's murder to the unbelieving Owen Roe. Too terrifying for her to bring to her consciousness, the horror of Sparky's murder remains a dream, "dirty in her mind . . . like a stain . . . in the long Irish twilight." Her quest for memory, for empowerment, is as futile as Don Quixote's quest for chivalric perfection.

No Country for Young Men portrays what has become an expectation in Irish literature: women capable of sacrifice and men disabled by drink or jingoism. Eamonn, Judith's brother, is killed in the fighting in 1919; Owen O'Malley, "who doesn't really like women at all," is devoured by his patriotism; Michael is a drunk, incapacitated as husband, father, or provider; Owen Roe brutalizes women and manipulates Cormac for political ends; drunken, smelly Pasty Flynn, "invigorated" by death and caught once putting "bombs in post boxes," is an assassin; and even James is ineffectual, lost, wavering between his wife and his mistress. It is the women who act: Judith bayonets Sparky; Grainne tries to leave, first her marriage, then Ireland. Yet both women are undone by the men and their politics.

No Country for Young Men portrays what has become an expectation in Irish literature: women capable of sacrifice and men disabled by drink or jingoism.
—Thomas R. Moore

Another Irish heroine, Deirdre, "object" in a triangular affair, makes the hard decision to return to Ireland after fleeing with her lover, Naisi. In Synge's *Deirdre of the Sorrows* she says: "It's seven years we've had a life was joy only, and this day we're going west, this day we're facing death, maybe, and death should be a poor, untidy thing, though it's a queen that dies." Like Grania in the myth, Deirdre has married against the wishes of the King, and like Grania she must return home to face him. The mythical Grania is, as Ann Weekes puts it, "condemned for the disorder that followed Fionn's pursuit of his desire" just as "women have been condemned throughout Irish history." Few of O'Faolain's characters, male or female, operate outside of Girard's triangle

of forces; few have retained their "spontaneity"—the freedom to choose—and those who have are thwarted. Judith is forced into a convent by the men after she kills Sparky Driscoll; Grainne is defeated at the end by Patsy spying from the jakes and by her son Cormac who runs off to alert Michael.

Cormac, as noted earlier, carries the name of the mythological Grainne's father, Cormac Mac Art, who, in the Ossianic Cycle, had appointed Finn chief of the Fenians. In accordance with the myth O'Faolain suggests a father/son role exchange in the last scene as Cormac assumes control of the family; he races to fetch his father in the Heraldry Commission; he gives Michael "a chance" to dissuade Grainne, then himself makes the final plea: "You can't just leave us." Michael, chewing peppermints to cover his midday drinking, is silent until Grainne has left, and, as if to underscore the shift to ages in this final scene, Cormac says his mother is "behaving as people near *his* age were expected to behave." The son becomes father; paternal control is reasserted.

Girard feels it is "the simultaneous presence of external and internal mediation in the same work [that] seems to us to confirm the unity of novelistic literature." Both are evident in *No Country for Young Men,* and the structure of the novel is highlighted by the overlayment of Girard's triangle. But the "'triangular' desire" motif also brings into focus the suffocating interdependence of the ineffectual Irish man and the male-dependent Irish woman. The triangular forces become a cage, entrapping and preserving the characters like Heaney's "little adulteress" in his poem "Punishment" who is uncovered in the bog and who, like Judith, is a "poor scapegoat." Judith, entombed in her bog-like memory, is suspended in a similar stasis in time. Grainne attempts to leave—she does leave Cormac and Michael in the final scene of the novel—but the ending is ambiguous. It is Judith who sees James's car slide into the water, who sees Patsy bang with a spade or an oar "the hands of the chap who is trying to clamber out" as Owen Roe interrogates her about the ancient murder of Sparky Driscoll. James's murder and Sparky's murder coincide at the apex of the novel and are alone observed by Judith, and, true to O'Faolain's depiction of Judith throughout, no one believes her this time either: "'Bonkers!' [Owen Roe] mouthed 'Harmless.'" She is not a "vainteuse" confined by forces of triangular desire, but is preserved, cloistered by the men who have electroshocked her memory from her, the "young men" of the novel's title.

"Sailing to Byzantium," from which O'Faolain shapes the line for her title, depicts Yeats's image of escape from modern confusion and disorder, where ". . . all neglect / Monuments of unageing intellect," to a country of high artistic integrity, the sort of escape from a chaotic present that O'Faolain's characters are unable to effect. They have given up their individual wills: the men to Ireland and to drink, the women to Ireland and the men. Judith's ideal, indeed the one she murders for, is an Ireland run by young men. She tells Sparky:

> "Kathleen's fellow, Owen, will be in the Dail for sure. It'll be a country run by young men."
> "What about the women? They'll have a say now too, won't they?"
> She shrugged. "The men in this country would never let women have a say."

No Country for Young Men is a gloomy depiction of the energies at work in contemporary Ireland, and a superimposition of Girard's triangular forces on the novel only gives Ann Weekes's feminist reading increased validity. At the end we are left with the hollow sound of Grainne's boots "clumping" along the canal, like the sound of Nora's door slamming, but we wonder if Grainne will get beyond "the old place," their rendezvous spot, where James lies dead and mutilated in his car.

Laura B. Vandale (essay date March 1991)

SOURCE: "Woman Across Time: Sister Judith Remembers," in *Colby Quarterly*, Vol. XXVII, No. 1, March, 1991, pp. 17-26.

[*In the following essay, Vandale traces how "Through Judith [in O'Faolain's* No Country for Young Men] *we see how the lives of women in Ireland have been, are, and no doubt will continue to be affected by war, politics, men, and the Church."*]

No Country for Young Men by Julia O'Faolain, "one of the most accomplished Irish writers of her generation" is, as Jay Halio has described, "a darkly comic stor[y] concerned with the position of women." Dark in that it certainly has its share of death and mystery, the novel nevertheless retains a twisted touch of comedy, which challenges the readers' emotions; we laugh sometimes only because otherwise we would cry. This sense of painful comedy is embodied by the women characters throughout the story. For, despite a title which might lead one to believe otherwise, *No Country for Young Men* is unavoidably about Irish women. In particular, it is about Judith Clancy, the old mad nun great-aunt of Grainne and Michael. Through Judith we see how the lives of women in Ireland have been, are, and no doubt will continue to be affected by war, politics, men, and the Church. What sets Judith apart from other women is that she has dared act on her own initiative—refusing to be completely squelched by the limitations generally placed on women—and has suffered punishment for doing so for the rest of her life. Furthermore,

Judith is symbolic of Ireland itself, bringing to mind the Caitlin Ni Houlihan/Shan von Vocht myth. Although Ireland ultimately controls her behavior, Judith never loses her passionate love for it; indeed, she lets nothing stand between her and what she believes to be the good of Ireland and its people.

A cross-generational story, *No Country for Young Men* employs old Judith's amazingly lucid flashbacks of her youth to tell essentially two stories at once. In the one we have a young Judith surrounded by political upheaval in the troubled Ireland of the 1920s. Through her associations with Owen, her sister's revolutionary fiancé, and Sparky Driscoll, an American IRA supporter come to evaluate the situation and drum up funds back in the States, Judith is entrenched in the fight for a free Republic. In the other "present-tense" story, the aging Sister Judith finds herself removed from her familiar convent surroundings and placed in the home of her great-niece Grainne and family. Another "American for the Irish cause," James Duffy happens to enter Judith's life and—along with Grainne—works towards uncovering some of the unclear details of past IRA actions. The two stories, seemingly completely independent of one another except for Judith's existence in both, are actually intricately interconnected as we read of generations of deceptive, volatile relationships and the parallel deaths of two relatively innocent young American observers.

Essentially it is Judith, the link between past and present, about whom Ann Weekes writes when she says, "The madness that forces women to act against their best judgments and against their best interests is, in *No Country for Young Men,* associated with the political confusion that has affected Ireland for over sixty years." Operating within this political confusion, Judith would probably not agree that she acted at all against her best judgment or interest when she killed Sparky Driscoll. She was doing what she thought necessary not only to protect Owen's political and marital position but also to protect her sister from the winsome ways of the persuasive young American. But subconsciously, on an emotional level somewhere beneath her fiery exterior, Judith is obviously bothered by what she has done, for she represses the entire event—not to mention much of the history of that time—and only remembers many years later through the constant jarring of her memory by practically everyone she encounters. In her position as a woman, her rash behavior is seen as madness; madness, however, was not what caused Judith to kill Sparky. His death was the result of a blurred definition of "acting in the best interest," which grew out of that chaos commonly called politics.

Whether or not she consciously recognizes it, Judith's entire life has been influenced and shaped by politics, although in an interview with James Duffy Judith says, "Politics? Ah, I'd be no help to you there. . . . They kept me in the dark.

I'd be no help to you about politics." The "political confusion" Weekes refers to was unavoidable to a girl of seventeen whose family thrived on the turmoil:

> What bound the family together was their Republicanism. In the yard, behind the family pub, a coal pile and stacked porter barrels provided a ladder for quickly scaling the back wall in time of need. Unknown young men came and went unquestioned, sleeping on the kitchen settle or in the guest bedroom, Kathleen's *fiancé,* Owen, was active. Eamonn, their elder brother, had been killed when Judith was fifteen. Seamus too was with the lads. Only their father held back. . . . What difference was it going to make if and when they got their Republic? he asked. . . . But he was over-ruled in his own house.

For the young Judith, political unrest was so much a part of her daily repast that she failed to see any of it as "politics"; at the Clancys', "patriotic" support was a common fact of life.

But Judith wants more than token patriotism. Rather than passively standing aside observing and serving the flow of the men and weapons through their doors, as Kathleen did, Judith is infected with the spirit of the men. Sparky himself calls her a revolutionary, and, although she never openly agrees with him, the reader has the privilege of access to Judith's inner thoughts: "[After the signing of the treaty] Owen came home to find the house full of Free Staters with only Judith—who wasn't revealing her opinions—a secret diehard." Her political views have been especially shaped by Owen, whom she unadmittedly, and no doubt unintentionally, adores. Her adoration encourages thoughts most "unfeminine," as she acknowledges that "She was viscerally on Owen's side. The clash of wills excited her." This political fervor appears to have survived the years of electrotherapy, for even as a daft old woman her political stance remains firm. When Cormac, Grainne's son, questions Judith about the IRA, she confesses that as a nun she cannot make a monetary donation to the Army, but she does still support the revolutionary group. When Cormac pushes her about concern over the methods of the IRA and the fact that "The Church condemns wars which cannot be won since they expose people to needless suffering," Judith changes the subject rather than have her opinion altered by her supposed devotion to the Church. Her IRA ties are none too subtle; exhausted by an encounter with drunken Michael, old Judith must be carried up the stairs, but as she is she sings a fight song from somewhere deep in her past:

> "But the boys of Kilmichael were ready,
> And met them with powder and shot,
> And the Irish Republican Army

> Made bits of the whole shaggin' lot!"

Judith may sing her song from days gone by, but Cormac's hitting her up for a donation to the IRA is evidence that the song is not exactly anachronistic. Her life and associations intertwining the past with the present, Judith is the link between the political unrest of the 1920s and that of the 1970s, the two periods in which the action of the novel takes place. Sadly, she is witness to the fact that there have been few important changes in the political situation of Ireland during that time. Even as adolescent Judith permitted her emotions to be overrun by her political convictions, in typical IRA fashion, so do the youth of Ireland sixty years later. Time has not changed the fact that, even for women, it is nearly impossible to be Irish and not be political in some way, whether or not one chooses to act on those beliefs and ideals.

Politics cannot be separated from two other aspects of Judith's life which are mentioned early in the novel as the cause of strains in her family: sex and war. In her youth Judith cannot escape the impact that the closely intertwined forces of war and men (who are representative of sex) thrust on her life. Because her mother died while Judith was still quite young, she has not had much female influence in her life—other than her older sister Kathleen—but has been molded by the men surrounding her, by Seamus and Sparky as well as Owen. The younger of two daughters and sent away to school for many years, Judith has not had to endure quite the same male oppression as Kathleen; yet she is still well aware that, as a female, certain expectations and limitations are placed on her. Her home was male-dominated, and devoid of motherly influence:

> Home was male territory. Judith's sister, Kathleen, struggled without hope. . . . The house was full of men's boots, smells of unemptied chamber-pots, a clutter of unassigned hats and macintoshes. . . . On the chimney-piece there had once been china figures but the maids had done for them. Their mother's collection of Waterford glass had gone the same way.

Judith has been raised in an atmosphere which hints at the convention that she is supposed to be something lesser because of her womanhood. Her father reinforces the notion that even God feels this way about women when he says, "What do you need . . . tormenting Almighty God? Don't you think he has better things to do than to listen to the ulagoanings of females?"

In the convent schools Judith has, from an early age, been "reminded that it was an Irishwoman's frail morals which led to the English first coming [to Ireland] in 1169. Women bore inherited guilt." Thus girls are expected to be pure and holy and virtuous, as if this will somehow make up for all the wrongs committed by women through the centuries. They are indoctrinated with the confusing knowledge that they must remain in their places as women; otherwise their powerful influence over men might be damaging. Judith recalls the reaction she and her fellow convent girls had to the visitation of one particularly teary priest: "'My darling and beautiful and pure and innocent little girls,' said the priest, and a ripple of nervous hilarity ran from bench to bench. 'How can I ever tell you the joy it brings to my heart to see innocence abloom today in this ancient, holy and sacred land of ours?'" Weeping all the while as though in pain, he went on to talk to them about the danger of "Eve's sin," desiring knowledge. In the end the girls were "alight with vanity at the effect their feminine virtue had seemed to have on him, a ruined creature but martial, holy, and moreover male."

With this kind of repressed background it is no wonder that Judith "carefully kept herself from knowing about soppy things like love and courting" and is painfully aware of how "truly shameful . . . mention of sexual matters" would be. She is embarrassed by Sparky's forward manner and unsure of what to make of him when he shows her some attention:

> "[Kathleen]'s pretty," [Sparky] acknowledged now, "but you're more beautiful. Will be."
>
> [Judith] didn't believe she'd heard him right. *Her?*
>
> "Didn't you know?"
>
> She blushed and hated him.
>
> "I'm sorry."
>
> "What for?" she had to ask.
>
> "Dragging you out of childhood."
>
> "You have no small opinion of yourself!" There was a supply of such remarks.
>
> "You see, it's happened," he teased, "you're flirting."
>
> The impudence! But she wouldn't believe him. Redheads were rarely beautiful.

It is Sparky again who later torments her with talk of sex, bringing to her mind images which frighten her and cause her to run off, leaving him behind. He knows her naiveté and insists on capitalizing on it:

> "Why are you frightened of sex, Judith? You're a

country girl, after all," said Sparky. "You must have seen animals."

> "Stop. I won't listen." But he was blocking the path. . . .
>
> "Why are you so prudish?" he asked. "A revolutionary should be able to look at things the way they are. . . ."

Revolutionary or not, Judith denies any attraction to men, chides Kathleen for her behavior towards Sparky, and is furious with herself when she discovers she has little control over her own physical reaction to the American when he kisses her. She eventually comes to an acceptance that Sparky belongs lumped into the general category of unreliable men:

> She finally decided that poor Sparky Driscoll had a deformed mind and that she should empty her own of the bilge he had poured into it. Men were unstable creatures. . . . it could be unsafe to come too close to them and this wasn't only true of the American.

For all their instability, however, Judith seems resigned to the fact that the men are the ones making the decisions regarding her country. We might believe that she has been convinced by Owen's declaration that "the formative idea comes from the male and the clay is female: passive, mere potentiality. . . . *We* are their virile soul." Time stands still for Owen in regard to women. He thinks of them only in relation to their usefulness for men; his big hope is that the "ancestral virtue" of "maidenly modesty" would flourish in the "new, free and Gaelic Ireland." Judith apparently acquiesces to this idea of male dominance when in a conversation with Sparky she talks of the future leadership of Ireland and comments:

> "Kathleen's fellow, Owen, will be in the Dail for sure. It'll be a country run by young men."
>
> "What about the women? They'll have a say now too, won't they?"
>
> She shrugged. "The men in this country would never let women have a say."

Yet it is precisely this restriction that Judith, whether consciously or not, fights so forcefully. She refuses to play by the rules and stand along the sidelines cheering on the boys. Whether it was the influence of all the men in her life, or the lack of a mother to discourage "inappropriate" behavior, or a subconscious rebellion against the upbringing of the convent, Judith is stimulated by the idea of the war and energized to the point of wanting to fight herself. After the Treaty has been signed, she experiences a sense of regret:

> Judith did not want the Treaty to hold. This was wrong of her for war was a means and not an end. To want it to go on was wicked—but she did want it to. She had grown up in the expectation that it would be her adulthood, her confirmation as a person. And now, when she was ready to join in it, it had stopped.

Seamus is one of the few who is aware that there are indeed women who share Judith's passion; in response to a sharp remark uttered by Judith, he exclaims, "Jesus . . . the women in this country are fire-eaters. You'd be afraid to be alone with one on a dark night." He is the one who recognizes Judith's need for revolutionary involvement, and he teaches her how to charge with a bayonet:

> Judith had insisted on using a hay-fork. She attacked the bolster with such vigour that Seamus said he'd let her have a try with a real bayonet as soon as he could get his hands on one. It was a pity women weren't being armed, he said. It might calm them down to do a bit of real fighting. As it was, they had no outlet and were a sight more blood-thirsty than the lads.

During that restlessness of her seventeenth year, Judith is involved in her own personal revolt—against her approaching "womanness"—as well as in the political one. She equates her own developing self with sex, as something that should be suppressed: "Judith never reached the stage of being vain since she never discovered whether she was plain or pretty. She had a suspicion that she might be about to blossom, but put off the moment by slouching and wearing unbecoming clothes." Judith takes pleasure at being thought a tomboy for wearing bits of "masculine gear" and enjoys her time spent with the "boys." She resents Sparky for always being the one to remind her that she is actually an attractive young woman, and for responding to her as such. Judith would much rather spend her time charging the bolster with her hayfork in defense of the Republic of Ireland than playing the silly games men and women seem destined to play.

The confusion caused by these two intertwining and destructive forces—her passion for Ireland and her passion against her sexual awakening and attraction to men—ultimately overwhelms Judith, and she reacts by killing Sparky. Not only does he taunt her physically and emotionally, but also politically, which simply breaks the final thread of Judith's already tenuous self-control. He begins arguing with her against Owen's cause and in favor of the new Irish government, claiming that a revolution at this point would lack all justification: "She walked agitatedly away from him. Why

wasn't Owen here? This man could convince anyone. He was convincing *her.* What hope had Owen's party with a man like this going back to America tonight to cut off their only source of arms?" So when Sparky, having no idea of Judith's emotional instability at this point nor of her practice with the hayfork, hands her a bayonet from the wall with the challenge: "Here, feel it. Weigh it. Imagine you're driving it into the guts of a real man. You wouldn't do it. Your nerve would fail you. I know," Judith meets him on his own terms. Sparky obviously *didn't* know what he was talking about; he had no idea that Judith's devotion to Owen and the fight for Ireland was enough to drive her to murder.

Ironically, Judith sacrifices her future on behalf of a man who cannot even thank or respect her for it. In Owen's opinion women have no place in the war; rather they belong in the "domestic sphere," to which he later confines his own wife. The general assumption is that "women's role was more of a back-up one, wasn't it, in the old Republican movement?" as the Reverend Mother queries Michael when he picks Judith up at the convent. Judith's superior doubts that Judith could have been truly "active" before entering the convent—although she has been told Judith was—because "active" was not something women did. Even Judith, during her disturbed years and having little recollection of the past, oscillates between memories of having contributed something to the Republican movement and the feeling that she must have played no part at all. In a visit with Owen about ten years after entering the convent, she confronts him with what she believes have been less-than-satisfactory political results from the movement:

> "It's funny," she said. "When the fighting was on, even during the Civil War, we felt the future was ours. If the past was as bad as ours was, then we had to own the future. It was our due, inevitable, do you remember, Owen? Ours!" She let her eyes shine out at him with irony. Judith was twenty-eight that year. She had recovered from years of almost catatonic silence. "*You got your future!*"

And years later in a conversation with Cormac she begins to talk about what "we" were fighting for, then corrects herself to say that "they" were fighting for a new Ireland, as if the war were something she had observed but not in which she had participated.

Ultimately, though, it is Judith's participation, her "accepting male definition and . . . acting in the male mode" which leaves her mad and commits her to the convent. She is punished for stepping out of bounds, not only those of femininity but also those of political correctness. The crime is not so much that she killed Sparky, but that she did not disguise the murder as an accident. It was more than convenient for the IRA to have Sparky out of the way. What could not become public was that he had been killed by those he was supposedly there to assist. So, although Judith thought she was doing something to assist Owen, she only succeeded in getting herself locked up for the rest of her life. Her punishment for "acting in the male mode" is living in a place where there are no men, where she must redirect her dedication for her country towards a life in the Church.

The irony of Judith—a nun without any definite faith in God—is richly symbolic of a Catholic Ireland without any definite faith in the Church. The Irish in *No Country for Young Men* display a lack of adherence to a pronounced faith, despite how much the Church dictates their lives, especially the women.
                                    —*Laura B. Vandale*

We have hints throughout the story that Judith did not choose her vocation, but the reason behind her forced participation in convent life is not revealed until near the end of the book. Devotion to God really had nothing to do with her becoming a nun. Strangely, in a book which is centered around the life of a nun, there is a blatant absence of God in the novel. The irony of Judith—a nun without any definite faith in God—is richly symbolic of a Catholic Ireland without any definite faith in the Church. The Irish people in *No Country for Young Men* display a lack of adherence to a pronounced faith, despite how much the Church dictates their lives, especially the women. As Judith is eventually rejected by the Church, so the Irish people seem to feel abandoned by God. They have turned their sights towards other rewards, as Michael suggests when he calls the people of Dublin "success-worshippers, as materialistic as the inhabitants of any other city." Owen Roe further claims that the Church no longer has any power and that the country is run by the Catholic laymen, rather than Church officials. The Church is present yet essentially powerless in Ireland, and present but essentially meaningless to Judith.

Resonating with Owen Roe's claim of the ineffectiveness of the Church is the speech by Sister Mary Quinn, one of the new "modern" nuns, professionally styled and tailor-dressed. In defense of changes taking place in the convent and as encouragement to other nuns to follow suit in her "dynamic commitment" to change, she says, "The Church . . . is a living organism. An organism which fails to adjust to change risks being fossilized and ultimately exterminated." As part of this change, the young nuns are to move to poor parts of cities and find work there. Some of them are assigned to look after the "oldies" who "may be more of a hindrance than a help in the society to which [they] are returning." But Sister Judith is a "special" case, and we see her practically re-

jected by the Church. The Reverend Mother justifies sending Judith away into the arms of not-overly-welcoming relatives with,

> "Now that we are going public, it would jeopardize the impact of our overall effort if. . . . Can you imagine Sister Judith Clancy who, as we all know, regrettably—well, she's seventy-five and a *bad* seventy-five and there are things distressing to consider which must be considered nonetheless. . . . You do know that her delusions are not all religious?"

Judith is abandoned on the premise that she might damage the Church's image—an argument coming from one who has supposedly vowed to put aside "worldly things," like catering to others' opinions. Michael refers to Judith as a repudiated bride of Christ, and Grainne certainly sees Judith's removal as a betrayal when she says to James,

> "From what I can make out, she seems to have had an appalling life."
>
> "Why? Because she was a nun? But mustn't that have been a free choice?"
>
> ". . . It wasn't her having gone into the convent I meant but the fact that she then had to come out. Imagine: after fifty-five years! The monastic alternative was never gay but used to be reliable. Repudiation was never in the contract when you became a bride of Christ. If Jesus is a Judas . . . then. . . ."

No one is more distressed or confused by the staggering changes in her life than Judith herself. Although she sometimes considered God a "fair-ground trickster" playing with her mind, she had become relatively comfortable in her life as "an abducted bride" of Christ and does not follow the new routine in the new place. Grasping for something recognizable, she asks Grainne for her habit, not realizing she's not worn one for six months, since the sisters abandoned them. Her disrupted life "back in the world" has left her feeling as isolated as ever, if not even more so:

> Sister Judith felt she was living behind a sheet of glass. A shroud. Some insulating chemical. She was cut off and had no rights. No place of her own. No privacy. Words dripped away, rolled, disappeared, like beads from a broken rosary. She was getting too tired to try and find the right ones for what she felt. . . . Judith wished she was dead herself. She nearly was. Diminished. Isolated. Glassed in. Glassed out.

Judith fears that she is an "uncharitable old thing. And

proud" and that now she must be doing her Purgatory on earth for sins committed during her life.

But what are these great sins for which Judith is paying? When the men were rewarded for so-called revolutionary killings and made heroes of, it is patently unjust that Judith receives a life sentence in the convent for a killing that protected the cause. Here is something more than merely a political cover-up. In addition to Judith's being the archetype of the struggle of Irish women, she ultimately symbolizes Ireland itself. The country has a long history of conflict and disruption, political confusion and emotional turmoil, and people acting out of passion rather than in their own best interests. And, in spite of the attempts to hold women responsible for all of Ireland's problems, there really is no definite source of blame for Ireland's incessant violence. As Judith feels she is serving time for something she does not completely understand, so are the Irish still paying a price for inherited conflicts. Judith demonstrates the destructive pattern of which her country is also a victim: haunted by the past, bewildered by the present, and uncertain of the future. Like Judith's mind with its "power of suction" and "unfathomable layers," Ireland's history is a bog, composed of centuries-old layers of peace and strife, and sucking up generations in its never-ending quest for some sort of stability.

As a representative of her country, Judith additionally invokes the portrayal of Ireland in Irish folklore. While the characters of Grainne and Kathleen redact the Grainne-Diarmuid tale, Judith's presentation in the novel reminds us of the legend of Caitlin Ni Houlihan/Shan von Vocht. Judith, the displaced old woman taken into the O'Malley household for shelter, elicits the memory of the Shan von Vocht in Yeat's "Cathleen Ni Hoolihan." She brings to the family tales of the past, of fighting and death of a time gone by. She is "Mother Ireland," a figure who somehow does not quite fit into the current times; Cormac labels her "one of the dead generations." Like Yeats's Old Woman, Judith's heart is not quiet and she is troubled by too many strangers in the house. She has visions of men who have died and men who will die. And she herself is responsible for two men who, although not Irish, die as a result of their associations with her. Judith appears to be harmless, helpless old woman, but she is cursed and carries death with her as a burden of her past history.

Because of the construction of the novel, Judith, the dried up old hag, is simultaneously the dynamic young figure of Caitlin Ni Houlihan. As a vibrant, passionate young woman she symbolizes the "magic, irresistible lure" described in the old myth. Kathleen's statement "[Sparky]'s starry-eyed about Holy Ireland. Caitlin Ni Houlihan . . . has yer man's interest" is loaded with implications of Judith as Caitlin once we discover Sparky's attraction to the younger sister. This Caitlin Ni Houlihan, however, struggles against any attraction men may have for her, perhaps because of her superstitious fear of the luring power of a woman. Yet, intentionally or not, she does finally lead a young man to his death for the sake of the Ireland she loves.

In their youth, Judith, Owen, and the rest of the "revolutionaries" cling to an idyllic image of a united Ireland where differences are forgotten and peace replaces violence as the common fare. They are willing to attain this dream through fighting, the only way they know to make themselves noticed. W. B. Yeats wrote that Ireland is "no country for old men," but O'Faolain argues further that neither is it a country for young men. Hopeful for their futures while they are young, they live to see visions erased as the violence persists, but the united Republic never emerges. If death does not take them first, as in the case of Judith's brothers, political moves come to determine their lives, as happened to Owen, who was raised into a position of political success while lowering Judith into the void of electroshock and lost memories.

Yet Judith, not a man at all, survives with her revolutionary drives intact. Despite her shattered hopes and disturbed mental state, the forces of war, politics, the Church, and male domination cannot suppress Judith's spirit. Although she has paid the price for her youthful "rash behavior, we are left with the sense that, if she were to go back to her seventeenth year, Judith would repeat her performance. For such "repeated performances," are embedded in Ireland's history. The rashness of youth is juxtaposed with the confused identity of old age. Finally, the painful irony lies in the possibility that Judith is indeed "Mother Ireland." A not too hopeful picture is painted of a fractured Ireland, a country which, like Judith, is caught between the struggles of past and present, aware that its young men have died before, but unable to control the events leading them once again down the path towards devastation.

David Gilmore (review date 25 September 1992)

SOURCE: "A Question of Infallibility," in *Times Literary Supplement,* No. 4669, September 25, 1992, p. 24.

[*In the following review, Gilmore praises O'Faolain's* The Judas Cloth *as "[a] powerful, original and intelligent novel."*]

As I began reading **The Judas Cloth,** I could not help recalling Lampedusa's remarks on the beginnings of Scott's novels: each was "veramente insopportabile", he declared, an endless parade of people and places too often and too meticulously described. But as I read on, I remembered his observation that, after page 100, "one realizes that the faces and places have remained imprinted on one's memory. . . . And the drama is described in masterly fashion: the psychology of the characters is solid, the action alive and rapid."

These judgments might fairly be applied to Julia O'Faolain's immense work, although the action is occasionally held up by the complexities of nineteenth-century papal finance. A powerful, original and intelligent novel, *The Judas Cloth* is spread over a giant canvas, centred on Rome but stretching to Bologna and later to Paris. The papal city, bewildered by the challenges of nationalism and revolution, is vividly evoked: a sinister place of intrigue and corruption, of denunciations and anonymous letters, a city of blackmail and "ancient odours", where Jesuit priests instruct children to spy for God. The fetid atmosphere is curiously reminiscent of the Vienna of *Measure for Measure.*

From this world, at first seemingly over-peopled by aspiring monsignori and cardinals with similar names, the author pulls three young men and interweaves their lives with that of the besieged Church. Prospero, the son of a liberal count, ends up among the most intransigent of the Ultramontane bishops. Flavio, streetwise orphan, discovers that he is the son of his mother's brother and inherits the dukedom of his nominal father. And Nicola, another supposed orphan who spends much of his time ruminating on the identity of his parents, eventually finds his mother but refuses to reveal himself. It would be too operatic, he decides, too like *Figaro.* As for his father, he speculates about various people, including a cardinal, a Bonaparte and his mother's uncle, before he finally finds out.

The novel's real protagonist, however, seldom appears in the flesh. He is Pope Pius IX, the hope of the liberals at his election in 1846, the despair of all liberal Catholics soon afterwards. The author takes us through those fateful years of disastrous decisions which have bedevilled Catholicism ever since: the dogma of the Immaculate Conception, the Syllabus of Errors, the final megalomaniac proclamation of infallibility. She gives Prospero the role of defending it all—"See how pernicious freedom is! The faithful have a right to be protected against errors which could make them lose their souls"—but she has no sympathy with his leader.

Described by her publishers as an ex-Catholic who "still sees Irish Catholicism as the root of her writing", O'Faolain is neutral on the politics of the Risorgimento: no romantic enthusiasm for the nationalists, no (Harold) Actonian nostalgia for the Bourbons, and certainly no support for the temporal power. Her compassion is for the Catholic moderates, who lost out then as they have lost so often since, for the men who believed there must be an alternative to that persistent denial of the modern world. "Repeated prohibitions to think", declares Cardinal Amandi shortly before his murder, "will not defeat modern science nor put out its light."

The novel ends among the embers of the Paris Commune, but its climax occurs just before, at the Vatican Council, where the elections to the commissions have been rigged and the Pope is forcing the dissentient bishops into line. Nicola, who was a protégé of Amandi, is now titular Bishop of Trebizond and is dismayed by the infallibility debate. He retains a respect for truth, has led a largely blameless life—a single afternoon of youthful love resulting in a boy, adopted by Flavio—and cannot stomach the evils of papal politics. But at this moment he discovers, to his understandable horror, that Pius, whom he now scarcely accepts as his spiritual father, turns out to be his human father as well. As fictional coincidences go—and there are many in this book— this may be stretching things. It is certainly too much for Nicola, who begins to go to pieces, although it is not until he has been caught up in the savagery of the Commune that he finally pulls off his cassock, the "Judas cloth", and renounces the Church. Our last sight of him is in layman's clothes, at his father's funeral, rejecting the handshake of Bishop Prospero.

Antoinette M. Mastin (essay date December 1994)

SOURCE: "Stephen Dedalus in Paris?: Joycean Elements in Julia O'Faolain's *Three Lovers*," in *Colby Quarterly,* Vol. XXX, No. 4, December, 1994, pp. 244-51.

[*In the following essay, Mastin analyzes Fintan McCann from O'Faolain's* Three Lovers *as a refiguration of James Joyce's Stephen Dedalus.*]

In his now famous vehement interchange with Davin in James Joyce's *A Portrait of the Artist as a Young Man,* Stephen Dedalus declares that "Ireland is the old sow that eats her farrow." Fifty-some years later, in the world reflected in Julia O'Faolain's *Three Lovers,* Ireland continues to evoke the same criticism and be wrapped in the same strictures. When O'Faolain's Fintan McCann sees the "squat little map" of Ireland on a letter addressed to him, he sees a "foetally folded Ireland, stretching out embryo arms" to his Paris haven, threatening to consume him in its "all-devouring Irish muck." For O'Faolain's characters, Ireland is not just the "old sow that eats her farrow," it is even more inimical, a "suppurating womb of a place, [a] soggy bog of lies and loneliness." Stephen's misogynist image is here replaced by one that carries particular poignancy in a country where abortion and contraception are illegal and where a mother's life is secondary to her child's. This image suggests a land that not only destroys its people but that also jeopardizes its reproductive future. In O'Faolain's fictional world there is no easy escape from Ireland's "embryo arms."

Published in 1970 as **Godded and Codded,** Julia O'Faolain's first novel was republished in the United States in 1971 under the title **Three Lovers.** In this work O'Faolain has transformed the character of Stephen Dedalus into one Fintan McCann, an Irish painter in Paris, and thus adds an interesting coda to Joyce's *Portrait*. While Fintan is not an exact replica of Stephen, as the Irish artist in Paris he does re-enact a significant part of Stephen's quest to "forge in the smithy of [his] soul the uncreated consciousness" of the Irish race. Fintan makes no bones about his reasons for leaving Ireland: "I don't have to remind you that there's hardly an Irish artist left at home, yez missed the boat badly with a number now dead and have a lamentable record generally for yer treatment of those of us living abroad." Joyce would heartily concur.

Stephen Dedalus' Ireland flung nets of "nationality, language, [and] religion" at the souls of Ireland's citizens to hold them "back from flight." For O'Faolain, as well, the religious net, in the form of Irish Catholicism, is one of the most repressive that threatens Irish men and women. As Seamus Deane has noted, Catholicism "disallows life, it disavows freedom and it is a friend to imperial oppression and an enemy to the desire for liberation that even a maimed nationalism retains."

Fintan does not fare very well in Paris because he is unable to fly high enough to escape the nets of language, religion, and nationality. For this thirty-five year old Irish artist, Paris initially represents freedom: "There was Paris for you. You could yell your frigging head off and who gave a damn." Yet he carries with him the mannerisms and belief system of Ireland, "partly a countryman's habit." His own weapons are those with which Stephen Dedalus armed himself as he went forth on his journey: "silence, exile, and cunning." Fintan is "an odd creature: a mixture of ingenious cunning and naïveté." Steeped in neo-colonialism, he is determined to escape colonial domination, to throw off the mores of a post-colonial society.

What is troublesome and somewhat ironic from the perspective of **Three Lovers** is that Fintan's refusal to take on the dominant Irish male role of colonial hegemony leaves him in an ambivalent position with Irish women. None of the Irish women Fintan encounters are able to respond to him appropriately and recognize a masculine presence not built on domination and usurpation, the acceptable norms of masculine behavior for characters living in Ireland's neo-colonial society. As he himself tells Sally Tyndal, the female protagonist of the novel: "I'm harmless and who thinks the better of me? Tell me that now. Honestly. You make use of me, right? 'Poor Fintan, a harmless, decent skin' can be

called in to decant another man's bottle. That's about all he's good for." Sally admits that she does not think of Fintan as "a man. Men are the enemy." Instead she wants their relationship to be filial: "Let's be brother and sister like the pair in the old fairy story who lay in the wood comforting each other and for whom the birds made a coverlet of leaves." Sally is willing to share a bed with Fintan but not have sex. As Fintan tells "Miss Tyndal, I'm not a conventional man," she seems further perplexed. In effect, she becomes Fintan's Emma Cleary.

The women Fintan ends up involved with are all Irish, just as repressed as he is, and they ironically judge him by the standards set up by a patriarchal, post-colonial society. It is Fintan, nonetheless, who tries to point out to Sally that Irish patriarchy places her in a secondary, subservient role. He tries to make Sally recognize the myopic manner in which she views her Algerian revolutionary lover Mesli. As she continues to tease Fintan, he recounts that:

> They used to make a holy man, a hermit usually, anyway a sex-starved poor bastard, sleep with a pointed breasted virgin. . . . The virgin was risked to test the man's resistance. *His* virtue was judged in the morning by *her* condition. A favorite game of the early Celtic church we're told. They did it in Glendalaugh to St. Kevin if I remember aright and he threw her over a cliff. The point was she didn't count. The matter at issue was *his* sanctity.

The role of colonizer and colonized is played out in relationships in the novel, with men typically being the colonizer. However, to underscore how Ireland has warped her children, O'Faolain includes the attempted seduction of Fintan by Letty, an Anglo-Irish friend of Sally's mother, thereby reversing the usual male/female patterns established in the novel. Full of bathos, this episode's subtext nonetheless personifies Letty's position as colonizer and Fintan's as the colonized. The Anglo, or British, part of Letty's heritage is emphasized in this scene. She becomes England, the usurping aggressor, and Fintan becomes identified as the passive colonized Irish, "a servant of . . . . [t]he imperial British state," as Stephen Dedalus remarks of himself. As England then, Letty quite literally sucks the life from Fintan through oral sex. Having unwittingly been lured into the position of sharing a bed with Letty, he is left helpless as she takes full advantage of the situation:

> [T]o his horror [he] felt her reach for his penis. . . . He tried to remove her hand but it was firmly clamped and it would be ludicrous to wrestle with her. . . . Stiffly, he lay with hands plastered to his sides. Suddenly, Letty put her head beneath the sheets, dived, dolphin-like, doubling on herself. He felt her satiny breasts against his things and—Oh,

Holy Saint Michael-Mary-Joseph-and-Patrick! No 'No, Letty,' he implored, pinned by her considerable weight . . . 'Come up outa that! STOP! For God's sake stop that! Stop, stop. STOP!' Vice, he thought. THIS IS VICE! Evil. Of the Devil. Wrong. Why is she doing it? . . .

Damning and humiliating me. . . . The whoor of hell, he thought. . . . Head back, teeth bared like a mad horse's, released, overwhelmed and limp, he lay staring sightlessly at the ceiling.

Fintan is heir to rather disquieting relationships with women, seeing them, as Stephen Dedalus tends to do, as saints, virgins, or whores.

As he reflects on the one-sided sexual encounter with Letty, Fintan berates her: "Damn and blast her, wasn't it because he liked and respected her that he couldn't . . . because with some whore he might, oh he might have enjoyed the plunge into debauchery and the rich, boiling cauldron of the rabid flesh. With some she-devil whom afterwards he could deny himself, some lost—though recuperable—creature who would burn him clean." Fintan can only think of Letty, in her role as seductress, as a whore from Hell, rather than as a lonely woman who finds him sexually attractive. He must invoke the power of Catholic saints to protect himself from the evil power attributed to sex. When he thinks of his other lover, a woman in Dublin whom he may have impregnated, he castigates himself endlessly about the episode. "Ah, the flesh was weak, the foul treacherous flesh, pale and harmless without, rabid-red within." But then, the woman becomes the temptress, the whore figure from Joycean days, "so beguiling, mindless, kittenish, wanton." Progressively the image of woman as saint creeps into Fintan's mind, and he inevitably experiences the guilt bequeathed by Catholicism, "the supplementary guilt at leading another soul astray." On the other hand he calls Sally "Saint Sally," and the reader suspects that part of the reason for Fintan's exile to Paris is to get away from the young Irish woman whom he suspects is now pregnant. Unable to deal with this guilt, Fintan decides to try to avoid women and takes to telephoning them, in lieu of meeting them face to face, as a distorted means of self-defense. "A telephone call? Wasn't it the very instrument of spiritual communication? It disembodied, as no convent grills could do. Dante would have hailed Beatrice on the phone if he'd had the convenience of it." While Fintan can see the marginalization of women in Irish society, he can't consistently extricate himself from the webs that ensnare him in the same knee-jerk repressive response to women.

The confusing and contradictory image of woman, both as virgin and as temptress, that the Catholic church inevitably sets up for its flock, catches Fintan in a net that is thickened by his practical relationship with the church. Ironically, Fintan is on a "bishop's scholarship to study at the School of Art" in Paris. This scholarship has been awarded by a country that had removed all nude sculptures from its principal art gallery, the Municipal Gallery. Even in art, as in Irish life, sexuality is masked and suppressed. When Fintan takes part in an art session, paints a rather blasphemous Madonna figure, and gives the artist the status of "seer," a clerical/biblical role and one that Stephen Dedalus shares, the session is abruptly terminated by an Irish priest, "a member of some Irish Arts Committee," who tries to re-establish the status quo. Fintan finds himself caught in the snare of Irish censorship. Paralleling Sally's father, the clergy serve as the parental figures who apply the cosmetic of silence and conformity to deny and thwart the realities of Fintan's attempted nonconformity. Fintan's exile and freedom are threatened by the loss of his scholarship. If he fails in his artistic endeavors, he will have to "teach drawing in a monks' school down the country." In the end, as he sees the clergy closing in, as it were, Fintan decides to flee Paris for another European haven, leaving an anonymous guest with a hurley stick at his art exhibition to remark that he had enough material to do a thesis "to the effect that the worst thing that could have happened to Ireland was the coming of St. Patrick."

The art exhibition reverberates with the emotional turmoil and montage effect created in the "Circe" chapter of *Ulysses* when Stephen smashes a lamp. Fintan attempts to paint a picture of the Madonna, never one that he can envision without getting lost in a labyrinth of emotion, and in his mind it is replaced with images of Sally's aborted fetus and his guilt at assisting her with the abortion. The images of woman as saint and as whore become fused in his drunken stupor. Feeling the claustrophobic inhibitions of Ireland closing in on him, unable to smash any lamps and free himself from the ghosts that haunt him, Fintan flees Paris for Barcelona. Like Stephen Dedalus, he is also haunted by his relationship with his mother, similarly associating her with washing and with the domestic sphere, and within his equally ambiguous feelings toward her.

His mother had washed for him once. Poor Ma. Poor stranger. He thought of her with—Christ, to be truthful nothing. Not even guilt, though he was good at that, more with a sort of wonder that she should exist: feeling of the be-gilled and agile fish for an amoeba. Did I, with my fins and mouth and speed and lively eye, come out of you? And what can I do for you? . . . You had a deadening life and, as we were eight, it was one-eighth my fault.

Although the allusion to eight children may remind us of the Dedalus family and Stephen's mother's hard life in Drumcondra, it also underscores that little has changed since Joyce wrote *Portrait*. Irish women, burdened with too many children, with no control over their reproductive futures, have bleak lives.

Fintan McCann's inclusion in this narrative does more than simply allow O'Faolain to add an interesting coda, *A Portrait of the Artist as a Young Man in Paris,* or to provide the needed peer mentor for Sally as the female protagonist. Additionally, Fintan throws the reader back into the images of colonial Ireland that Joyce painted. The stifling air of Dublin's capital carries itself to Paris in the person of the Irish Ambassador with the "thin gombeen man's face," the Irish priest who stops Fintan's art exhibit, and the "rosarybeads of green Connemara marble" hanging in the apartment of Shewawn Donnelly to exclude men and sex. The reader finds in these Joycean comparisons that post-colonial Ireland and her citizens act and think very much like their predecessors. The yoke of England may be gone, but the legacy of colonialism lingers on. Fintan McCann finds it impossible to fly free of the nets described by Stephen, and there is still no room for the Irish artist in Ireland. Fintan reminds us that "He'd never used a real handkerchief or a flush lavatory," while Joyce would have reminded us that the lavatory was an English invention, and an English word.

However, to trace the Joycean influences in O'Faolain's work is not to suggest that she, or other Irish women writers, write in the shadow of Joyce, but rather to suggest, as Elaine Showalter and Adrienne Rich do, that women writers (re)Joyce, translating, adapting, and expanding Joyce to fit their stories, and even filling in the gaps in stories, whether those gaps be caused by gender, culture, or other realities. As Catherine Stimpson points out:

> The fact that Stephen Dedalus is male is no mere contingency but a crucial element of his identity—his relations to literature, country, and church; his relationships to others. A portrait of the artist as a young Catholic woman in late nineteenth-century Ireland might have a family likeness to Joyce's work, but at most only a family likeness. What, for example, would her dreams be of priesthood? Delirious fantasies?

Conscious, then, of Joyce's literary innovations and thematic concerns, O'Faolain forges her own novel's course by doing more than just filling in the gender gaps that a mere re-writing of *A Portrait of the Artist as a Young Woman* might entail, such as the possible re-visioning of Emma Cleary as Sally Tyndal, or of Stephen as a female sensibility.

The portraiture of Fintan is, in many ways, a portrait of Sally's male counterpart, "whelped by the same Holy Mum," Catholic Ireland, as Fintan notes, and it adds contrast to a novel whose emphasis falls heavily on exploring the impact of post-colonial Ireland on its women. By re-visioning Joyce,

O'Faolain takes advantage of the vehement outspoken voice of Stephen Dedalus wrestling with the nets of cultural repression to provide her female protagonist Sally Tyndal with a needed mouthpiece, a voice that can see the nets and name their oppressive, stifling reality. Sally is unable to give voice to her repression throughout much of the novel, so colonized is she by Irish patriarchal hegemony that she can only speak to herself or Fintan McCann and not to her oppressors. With Stephen Dedalus' character, Joyce provided an Irish male voice capable of producing, in Seamus Deane's view, "a native statement free of the trappings and prevalent ideological assumptions of the colonizer." In choosing to adapt this voice for her purposes, O'Faolain is neither myopic nor repetitious. Nor is she reticent to employ formal Joycean structures, including interior monologue, pastiche, propaganda, and a myriad of literary allusions, for her contemporary perspective on Ireland. After all, "Words," she tells the reader, "words were [Fintan's] strength."

O'Faolain weaves an intricate narrative web where Cromwell, the Shan Van Vocht, the Famine, Simone DeBeauvoir, Sleeping Beauty, Alice in Wonderland, Sweet Afton cigarettes, the Brontë characters of Heathcliff and Rochester, and Camus are beaded into an intricate web of meaning, the slightest touch of any strand producing a reverberation of narrative significance. For example, invoking the winged man of mythology, Stephen Dedalus' namesake, O'Faolain intertwines the image of flight with an Alice-in-Wonderland reference to remind the reader that the nets O'Faolain's characters have flung at them are decidedly male. These nets and webs have not been spun by Penelope. As Sally dreams, she remembers that it is her colonized Algerian lover, inseparable in identity and value from her Father, symbol of puritanism, xenophobia, and authoritarianism, who

> was pulling me into a mile-deep well—like Alice falling. I was happy until I noticed the bottom crawling with reptiles. I'm petrified by snakes, I suppose because we have none in Ireland. I kicked him away and began to soar. I could fly but, as I was reaching the top, the power left me and I began to fall again. At the last moment I saved myself from the reptiles who were spitting white poison from below. I started to rise but again, as I was gaining confidence that I'd made a getaway, I began to fall. And so on: up and down. . . .

O'Faolain shows the interconnection between repressive Irish Catholicism and sexual relations, and the inevitable guilt that haunts both Sally and Fintan regarding sex. Both genders' view of each other is distorted, most especially when it comes to sexual relationships. Sally struggles to get away from the "all-devouring Irish muck" of Irish Catholicism, which "equates sex with shame," yet sees herself as a "sort of mud creature . . . whose native habitat is a swamp of undefined guilt." While Sally finally breaks free from the grips of these repressive nets, Fintan is not so successful.

If indeed Seamus Deane is right, and all of Joyce's novels "formally . . . enact the liberation of a voice from paralysis, silence, suppression," then the many Joycean elements in O'Faolain's *Three Lovers* can be attributable, in part, to her desire to enact that same liberation. Ultimately, however, O'Faolain elects not to rewrite Joyce totally; instead she agrees with him that there is no room for the male artist in Ireland and leaves Fintan McCann very much as Joyce left Stephen Dedalus in both *Portrait* and *Ulysses,* walking off in search of a self that never seems to achieve self-actualization. We remember Stephen's parting words to Cranly in *Portrait:* "I will try to express myself in some mode of life or art as freely as I can and as wholly as I can, using for my defense the only arms I allow myself to use—silence, exile, and cunning." Those weapons are not enough for O'Faolain's Dedalus to battle through the nets of language, religion, and nationality. Indeed, in many ways, they seem to have made him even more vulnerable. Suspicious and cunning like Stephen, Fintan "would not try a new language [French]. He had come [to Paris] to be alone. Incomprehension was to have protected him. Or so he had planned it." Like Stephen, who declares to Cranly at the end of *Portrait* that he does "not fear to be alone or to be spurned for another or to leave whatever I have to leave," Fintan initially thinks that he too can survive alone without human intercourse. However, when he recognizes that "no one had accepted him into the fellowship of ordinariness," Fintan discovers that he misses that "fellowship and the odd bit of friendly contact he could get in tearooms at home," and he pines for a woman's affection. At first, his sometime Irish drinking companion's rechristening of Fintan as "Singularis McCann . . . the boar who lived apart from the herd" does not perturb him. However, by the end of the novel Condon's appellation serves to haunt the artist as he flees Paris, alone and exiled once more.

When it comes to the woman artist (Sally is after all a writer, although not an active one in this book), O'Faolain holds out more hope. Although she too has walked away from Ireland, Sally demonstrates that she can cut through the nets of cultural patriarchy. She breaks away from silence, marginality, and oppression. Unlike Fintan, Sally is able to let go of her Irish identity, and in so doing is liberated to an embryonic state of growth. "She would nurse herself" later to a level of maturity and peace. The end of the novel leaves the reader with a glimpse of Sally in the process of reassembling the "ragwoman's barrow of oddments" into something acceptable to herself, although not to Ireland. In contrast, our last word from Fintan, that with a cryptic lack of specificity echoes *Portrait*'s closing paragraph, is a note on his door that reads: "Gone to Barcelona."

FURTHER READING

Criticism

Hargreaves, Tamsin. "Women's Consciousness and Identity in Four Irish Women Novelists." In *Cultural Contexts and Literary Idioms in Contemporary Irish Literature,* edited by Michael Kenneally, pp. 290-305. Gerrards Cross: Colin Smythe, pp. 1988.

> Analyzes the search for identity and existential meaning found in classic fairy tales and the work of Julia O'Faolain, Edna O'Brien, Molly Keane, and Jennifer Johnston.

"Subjection and Seclusion." *The Economist* 246, No. 6756 (17 February 1973): 107.

> The review gives credit to the talents of O'Faolain and fellow editor Lauro Martines for making *Not in God's Image* "a source-book on the history of women . . . [which] stands in a class quite of its own."

Additional coverage of O'Faolain's life and career is contained in the following sources published by Gale Research: *Contemporary Authors,* Vol. 81-84; *Contemporary Authors Autobiography Series,* Vol. 2; *Contemporary Authors New Revision Series,* Vol. 12; *Dictionary of Literary Biography,* Vol. 14; *Major Twentieth-Century Writers.*

☐ Contemporary
Literary Criticism

Indexes

Literary Criticism Series
Cumulative Author Index
Cumulative Topic Index
Cumulative Nationality Index
Title Index, Volume 108

How to Use This Index

The main references

Camus, Albert
1913-1960 ...... **CLC 1, 2, 4, 9, 11, 14,
32, 69; DA; DAB; DAC; DAM DRAM,
MST, NOV; DC2; SSC 9; WLC**

list all author entries in the following Gale Literary Criticism series:

BLC = Black Literature Criticism
CLC = Contemporary Literary Criticism
CLR = Children's Literature Review
CMLC = Classical and Medieval Literature Criticism
DA = DISCovering Authors
DAB = DISCovering Authors: British
DAC = DISCovering Authors: Canadian
DAM = DISCovering Authors Modules
  DRAM = dramatists; **MST** = most-studied
  authors; **MULT** = multicultural authors; **NOV** =
  novelists; **POET** = poets; **POP** = popular/genre
  writers; **DC** = Drama Criticism
HLC = Hispanic Literature Criticism
LC = Literature Criticism from 1400 to 1800
NCLC = Nineteenth-Century Literature Criticism
PC = Poetry Criticism
SSC = Short Story Criticism
TCLC = Twentieth-Century Literary Criticism
WLC = World Literature Criticism, 1500 to the Present
WLCS = World Literature Criticism Supplement

The cross-references

See also CA 89-92; DLB 72; MTCW

list all author entries in the following Gale biographical and literary sources:

AAYA = Authors & Artists for Young Adults
AITN = Authors in the News
BEST = Bestsellers
BW = Black Writers
CA = Contemporary Authors
CAAS = Contemporary Authors Autobiography Series
CABS = Contemporary Authors Bibliographical Series
CANR = Contemporary Authors New Revision Series
CAP = Contemporary Authors Permanent Series
CDALB = Concise Dictionary of American Literary Biography
CDBLB = Concise Dictionary of British Literary Biography

DLB = Dictionary of Literary Biography
DLBD = Dictionary of Literary Biography Documentary Series
DLBY = Dictionary of Literary Biography Yearbook
HW = Hispanic Writers
JRDA = Junior DISCovering Authors
MAICYA = Major Authors and Illustrators for Children and Young Adults
MTCW = Major 20th-Century Writers
NNAL = Native North American Literature
SAAS = Something about the Author Autobiography Series
SATA = Something about the Author
YABC = Yesterday's Authors of Books for Children

Literary Criticism Series
Cumulative Author Index

Abasiyanik, Sait Faik 1906-1954
See Sait Faik
See also CA 123
Abbey, Edward 1927-1989 .... **CLC 36, 59**
See also CA 45-48; 128; CANR 2, 41
Abbott, Lee K(ittredge) 1947- .... **CLC 48**
See also CA 124; CANR 51; DLB 130
Abe, Kobo 1924-1993**CLC 8, 22, 53, 81; DAM NOV**
See also CA 65-68; 140; CANR 24, 60; DLB 182; MTCW
Abelard, Peter c. 1079-c. 1142 ...... **CMLC 11**
See also DLB 115
Abell, Kjeld 1901-1961 .... **CLC 15**
See also CA 111
Abish, Walter 1931- .... **CLC 22**
See also CA 101; CANR 37; DLB 130
Abrahams, Peter (Henry) 1919- ....**CLC 4**
See also BW 1; CA 57-60; CANR 26; DLB 117; MTCW
Abrams, M(eyer) H(oward) 1912- ... **CLC 24**
See also CA 57-60; CANR 13, 33; DLB 67
Abse, Dannie 1923-..**CLC 7, 29; DAB; DAM POET**
See also CA 53-56; CAAS 1; CANR 4, 46; DLB 27
Achebe, (Albert) Chinua(lumogu) 1930-**C L C 1, 3, 5, 7, 11, 26, 51, 75; BLC; DA; DAB; DAC; DAM MST, MULT, NOV; WLC**
See also AAYA 15; BW 2; CA 1-4R; CANR 6, 26, 47; CLR 20; DLB 117; MAICYA; MTCW; SATA 40; SATA-Brief 38
Acker, Kathy 1948-........................... **CLC 45**
See also CA 117; 122; CANR 55
Ackroyd, Peter 1949- .... **CLC 34, 52**
See also CA 123; 127; CANR 51; DLB 155; INT 127
Acorn, Milton 1923- ....**CLC 15; DAC**
See also CA 103; DLB 53; INT 103
Adamov, Arthur 1908-1970**CLC 4, 25; DAM DRAM**
See also CA 17-18; 25-28R; CAP 2; MTCW
Adams, Alice (Boyd) 1926-**CLC 6, 13, 46; SSC 24**
See also CA 81-84; CANR 26, 53; DLBY 86; INT CANR-26; MTCW
Adams, Andy 1859-1935 .... **TCLC 56**
See also YABC 1
Adams, Douglas (Noel) 1952- .... **CLC 27, 60; DAM POP**
See also AAYA 4; BEST 89:3; CA 106; CANR 34, 64; DLBY 83; JRDA
Adams, Francis 1862-1893 .... **NCLC 33**
Adams, Henry (Brooks) 1838-1918 **TCLC 4, 52; DA; DAB; DAC; DAM MST**
See also CA 104; 133; DLB 12, 47
Adams, Richard (George) 1920-**CLC 4, 5, 18; DAM NOV**

See also AAYA 16; AITN 1, 2; CA 49-52; CANR 3, 35; CLR 20; JRDA; MAICYA; MTCW; SATA 7, 69
Adamson, Joy(-Friederike Victoria) 1910-1980 **CLC 17**
See also CA 69-72; 93-96; CANR 22; MTCW; SATA 11; SATA-Obit 22
Adcock, Fleur 1934- ....**CLC 41**
See also CA 25-28R; CAAS 23; CANR 11, 34; DLB 40
Addams, Charles (Samuel) 1912-1988**CLC 30**
See also CA 61-64; 126; CANR 12
Addams, Jane 1860-1935 .... **TCLC 76**
Addison, Joseph 1672-1719 .... **LC 18**
See also CDBLB 1660-1789; DLB 101
Adler, Alfred (F.) 1870-1937 .... **TCLC 61**
See also CA 119; 159
Adler, C(arole) S(chwerdtfeger) 1932-..**C L C 35**
See also AAYA 4; CA 89-92; CANR 19, 40; JRDA; MAICYA; SAAS 15; SATA 26, 63
Adler, Renata 1938-...................... **CLC 8, 31**
See also CA 49-52; CANR 5, 22, 52; MTCW
Ady, Endre 1877-1919 .... **TCLC 11**
See also CA 107
A.E. 1867-1935 .... **TCLC 3, 10**
See also Russell, George William
Aeschylus 525B.C.-456B.C. ..**CMLC 11; DA; DAB; DAC; DAM DRAM, MST; DC 8; WLCS**
See also DLB 176
Africa, Ben
See Bosman, Herman Charles
Afton, Effie
See Harper, Frances Ellen Watkins
Agapida, Fray Antonio
See Irving, Washington
Agee, James (Rufus) 1909-1955 **TCLC 1, 19; DAM NOV**
See also AITN 1; CA 108; 148; CDALB 1941-1968; DLB 2, 26, 152
Aghill, Gordon
See Silverberg, Robert
Agnon, S(hmuel) Y(osef Halevi) 1888-1970 **CLC 4, 8, 14; SSC 29**
See also CA 17-18; 25-28R; CANR 60; CAP 2; MTCW
Agrippa von Nettesheim, Henry Cornelius 1486-1535 .... **LC 27**
Aherne, Owen
See Cassill, R(onald) V(erlin)
Ai 1947- .... **CLC 4, 14, 69**
See also CA 85-88; CAAS 13; DLB 120
Aickman, Robert (Fordyce) 1914-1981 .**C L C 57**
See also CA 5-8R; CANR 3
Aiken, Conrad (Potter) 1889-1973**CLC 1, 3, 5, 10, 52; DAM NOV, POET; SSC 9**

See also CA 5-8R; 45-48; CANR 4, 60; CDALB 1929-1941; DLB 9, 45, 102; MTCW; SATA 3, 30
Aiken, Joan (Delano) 1924- .... **CLC 35**
See also AAYA 1; CA 9-12R; CANR 4, 23, 34, 64; CLR 1, 19; DLB 161; JRDA; MAICYA; MTCW; SAAS 1; SATA 2, 30, 73
Ainsworth, William Harrison 1805-1882 **NCLC 13**
See also DLB 21; SATA 24
Aitmatov, Chingiz (Torekulovich) 1928-**C L C 71**
See also CA 103; CANR 38; MTCW; SATA 56
Akers, Floyd
See Baum, L(yman) Frank
Akhmadulina, Bella Akhatovna 1937-**CLC 53; DAM POET**
See also CA 65-68
Akhmatova, Anna 1888-1966**CLC 11, 25, 64; DAM POET; PC 2**
See also CA 19-20; 25-28R; CANR 35; CAP 1; MTCW
Aksakov, Sergei Timofeyvich 1791-1859 **NCLC 2**
Aksenov, Vassily
See Aksyonov, Vassily (Pavlovich)
Aksyonov, Vassily (Pavlovich) 1932-**CLC 22, 37, 101**
See also CA 53-56; CANR 12, 48
Akutagawa, Ryunosuke 1892-1927 **TCLC 16**
See also CA 117; 154
Alain 1868-1951 .... **TCLC 41**
Alain-Fournier .... **TCLC 6**
See also Fournier, Henri Alban
See also DLB 65
Alarcon, Pedro Antonio de 1833-1891**NCLC 1**
Alas (y Urena), Leopoldo (Enrique Garcia) 1852-1901 .... **TCLC 29**
See also CA 113; 131; HW
Albee, Edward (Franklin III) 1928-**CLC 1, 2, 3, 5, 9, 11, 13, 25, 53, 86; DA; DAB; DAC; DAM DRAM, MST; WLC**
See also AITN 1; CA 5-8R; CABS 3; CANR 8, 54; CDALB 1941-1968; DLB 7; INT CANR-8; MTCW
Alberti, Rafael 1902-........................... **CLC 7**
See also CA 85-88; DLB 108
Albert the Great 1200(?)-1280 ...... **CMLC 16**
See also DLB 115
Alcala-Galiano, Juan Valera y
See Valera y Alcala-Galiano, Juan
Alcott, Amos Bronson 1799-1888 ....**NCLC 1**
See also DLB 1
Alcott, Louisa May 1832-1888 . **NCLC 6, 58; DA; DAB; DAC; DAM MST, NOV; SSC 27; WLC**
See also AAYA 20; CDALB 1865-1917; CLR 1, 38; DLB 1, 42, 79; DLBD 14; JRDA;

MAICYA; YABC 1

Aldanov, M. A.
  See Aldanov, Mark (Alexandrovich)

Aldanov, Mark (Alexandrovich) 1886(?)-1957
  TCLC 23
  See also CA 118

Aldington, Richard 1892-1962 .... **CLC 49**
  See also CA 85-88; CANR 45; DLB 20, 36, 100,
  149

Aldiss, Brian W(ilson) 1925- . **CLC 5, 14, 40;**
  DAM NOV
  See also CA 5-8R; CAAS 2; CANR 5, 28, 64;
  DLB 14; MTCW; SATA 34

Alegria, Claribel 1924-**CLC 75; DAM MULT**
  See also CA 131; CAAS 15; DLB 145; HW

Alegria, Fernando 1918- .... **CLC 57**
  See also CA 9-12R; CANR 5, 32; HW

Aleichem, Sholom .... **TCLC 1, 35**
  See also Rabinovitch, Sholem

Aleixandre, Vicente 1898-1984 ... **CLC 9, 36;**
  DAM POET; PC 15
  See also CA 85-88; 114; CANR 26; DLB 108;
  HW; MTCW

Alepoudelis, Odysseus
  See Elytis, Odysseus

Aleshkovsky, Joseph 1929-
  See Aleshkovsky, Yuz
  See also CA 121; 128

Aleshkovsky, Yuz .... **CLC 44**
  See also Aleshkovsky, Joseph

Alexander, Lloyd (Chudley) 1924- .. **CLC 35**
  See also AAYA 1; CA 1-4R; CANR 1, 24, 38,
  55; CLR 1, 5, 48; DLB 52; JRDA; MAICYA;
  MTCW; SAAS 19; SATA 3, 49, 81

Alexander, Samuel 1859-1938 .... **TCLC 77**

Alexie, Sherman (Joseph, Jr.) 1966-**CLC 96;**
  DAM MULT
  See also CA 138; DLB 175; NNAL

Alfau, Felipe 1902- .... **CLC 66**
  See also CA 137

Alger, Horatio, Jr. 1832-1899 .... **NCLC 8**
  See also DLB 42; SATA 16

Algren, Nelson 1909-1981 .... **CLC 4, 10, 33**
  See also CA 13-16R; 103; CANR 20, 61;
  CDALB 1941-1968; DLB 9; DLBY 81, 82;
  MTCW

Ali, Ahmed 1910- .... **CLC 69**
  See also CA 25-28R; CANR 15, 34

Alighieri, Dante
  See Dante

Allan, John B.
  See Westlake, Donald E(dwin)

Allan, Sidney
  See Hartmann, Sadakichi

Allan, Sydney
  See Hartmann, Sadakichi

Allen, Edward 1948- .... **CLC 59**

Allen, Paula Gunn 1939- .... **CLC 84; DAM**
  MULT
  See also CA 112; 143; CANR 63; DLB 175;
  NNAL

Allen, Roland
  See Ayckbourn, Alan

Allen, Sarah A.
  See Hopkins, Pauline Elizabeth

Allen, Sidney H.
  See Hartmann, Sadakichi

Allen, Woody 1935- **CLC 16, 52; DAM POP**
  See also AAYA 10; CA 33-36R; CANR 27, 38,
  63; DLB 44; MTCW

Allende, Isabel 1942- . **CLC 39, 57, 97; DAM**
  MULT, NOV; HLC; WLCS
  See also AAYA 18; CA 125; 130; CANR 51;

DLB 145; HW; INT 130; MTCW

Alleyn, Ellen
  See Rossetti, Christina (Georgina)

Allingham, Margery (Louise) 1904-1966**C L C**
  19
  See also CA 5-8R; 25-28R; CANR 4, 58; DLB
  77; MTCW

Allingham, William 1824-1889 ...... **NCLC 25**
  See also DLB 35

Allison, Dorothy E. 1949- .... **CLC 78**
  See also CA 140

Allston, Washington 1779-1843 .... **NCLC 2**
  See also DLB 1

Almedingen, E. M. .... **CLC 12**
  See also Almedingen, Martha Edith von
  See also SATA 3

Almedingen, Martha Edith von 1898-1971
  See Almedingen, E. M.
  See also CA 1-4R; CANR 1

Almqvist, Carl Jonas Love 1793-1866 **N C L C**
  42

Alonso, Damaso 1898-1990 .... **CLC 14**
  See also CA 110; 131; 130; DLB 108; HW

Alov
  See Gogol, Nikolai (Vasilyevich)

Alta 1942- .... **CLC 19**
  See also CA 57-60

Alter, Robert B(ernard) 1935- .... **CLC 34**
  See also CA 49-52; CANR 1, 47

Alther, Lisa 1944- .... **CLC 7, 41**
  See also CA 65-68; CANR 12, 30, 51; MTCW

Althusser, L.
  See Althusser, Louis

Althusser, Louis 1918-1990 .... **CLC 106**
  See also CA 131; 132

Altman, Robert 1925- .... **CLC 16**
  See also CA 73-76; CANR 43

Alvarez, A(lfred) 1929- .... **CLC 5, 13**
  See also CA 1-4R; CANR 3, 33, 63; DLB 14,
  40

Alvarez, Alejandro Rodriguez 1903-1965
  See Casona, Alejandro
  See also CA 131; 93-96; HW

Alvarez, Julia 1950- .... **CLC 93**
  See also CA 147

Alvaro, Corrado 1896-1956 .... **TCLC 60**

Amado, Jorge 1912- **CLC 13, 40, 106; DAM**
  MULT, NOV; HLC
  See also CA 77-80; CANR 35; DLB 113;
  MTCW

Ambler, Eric 1909- .... **CLC 4, 6, 9**
  See also CA 9-12R; CANR 7, 38; DLB 77;
  MTCW

Amichai, Yehuda 1924- .... **CLC 9, 22, 57**
  See also CA 85-88; CANR 46, 60; MTCW

Amichai, Yehudah
  See Amichai, Yehuda

Amiel, Henri Frederic 1821-1881 ....**NCLC 4**

Amis, Kingsley (William) 1922-1995**CLC 1, 2,**
  3, 5, 8, 13, 40, 44; DA; DAB; DAC; DAM
  MST, NOV
  See also AITN 2; CA 9-12R; 150; CANR 8, 28,
  54; CDBLB 1945-1960; DLB 15, 27, 100,
  139; DLBY 96; INT CANR-8; MTCW

Amis, Martin (Louis) 1949- **CLC 4, 9, 38, 62,**
  101
  See also BEST 90:3; CA 65-68; CANR 8, 27,
  54; DLB 14; INT CANR-27

Ammons, A(rchie) R(andolph) 1926-**CLC 2, 3,**
  5, 8, 9, 25, 57, 108; DAM POET; PC 16
  See also AITN 1; CA 9-12R; CANR 6, 36, 51;
  DLB 5, 165; MTCW

Amo, Tauraatua i

See Adams, Henry (Brooks)

Anand, Mulk Raj 1905- .. **CLC 23, 93; DAM**
  NOV
  See also CA 65-68; CANR 32, 64; MTCW

Anatol
  See Schnitzler, Arthur

Anaximander c. 610B.C.-c. 546B.C.**CMLC 22**

Anaya, Rudolfo A(lfonso) 1937- ..... **CLC 23;**
  DAM MULT, NOV; HLC
  See also AAYA 20; CA 45-48; CAAS 4; CANR
  1, 32, 51; DLB 82; HW 1; MTCW

Andersen, Hans Christian 1805-1875**NCLC 7;**
  DA; DAB; DAC; DAM MST, POP; SSC
  6; WLC
  See also CLR 6; MAICYA; YABC 1

Anderson, C. Farley
  See Mencken, H(enry) L(ouis); Nathan, George
  Jean

Anderson, Jessica (Margaret) Queale 1916-
  CLC 37
  See also CA 9-12R; CANR 4, 62

Anderson, Jon (Victor) 1940- ..**CLC 9; DAM**
  POET
  See also CA 25-28R; CANR 20

Anderson, Lindsay (Gordon) 1923-1994**C L C**
  20
  See also CA 125; 128; 146

Anderson, Maxwell 1888-1959**TCLC 2; DAM**
  DRAM
  See also CA 105; 152; DLB 7

Anderson, Poul (William) 1926- ...... **CLC 15**
  See also AAYA 5; CA 1-4R; CAAS 2; CANR
  2, 15, 34, 64; DLB 8; INT CANR-15;
  MTCW; SATA 90; SATA-Brief 39

Anderson, Robert (Woodruff) 1917-**CLC 23;**
  DAM DRAM
  See also AITN 1; CA 21-24R; CANR 32; DLB
  7

Anderson, Sherwood 1876-1941**TCLC 1, 10,**
  24; DA; DAB; DAC; DAM MST, NOV;
  SSC 1; WLC
  See also CA 104; 121; CANR 61; CDALB
  1917-1929; DLB 4, 9, 86; DLBD 1; MTCW

Andier, Pierre
  See Desnos, Robert

Andouard
  See Giraudoux, (Hippolyte) Jean

Andrade, Carlos Drummond de .... **CLC 18**
  See also Drummond de Andrade, Carlos

Andrade, Mario de 1893-1945 .... **TCLC 43**

Andreae, Johann V(alentin) 1586-1654**LC 32**
  See also DLB 164

Andreas-Salome, Lou 1861-1937 ... **TCLC 56**
  See also DLB 66

Andress, Lesley
  See Sanders, Lawrence

Andrewes, Lancelot 1555-1626 .... **LC 5**
  See also DLB 151, 172

Andrews, Cicily Fairfield
  See West, Rebecca

Andrews, Elton V.
  See Pohl, Frederik

Andreyev, Leonid (Nikolaevich) 1871-1919
  TCLC 3
  See also CA 104

Andric, Ivo 1892-1975 ....**CLC 8**
  See also CA 81-84; 57-60; CANR 43, 60; DLB
  147; MTCW

Androvar
  See Prado (Calvo), Pedro

Angelique, Pierre
  See Bataille, Georges

Angell, Roger 1920- .... **CLC 26**

See also CA 57-60; CANR 13, 44; DLB 171
Angelou, Maya 1928-**CLC 12, 35, 64, 77; BLC; DA; DAB; DAC; DAM MST, MULT, POET, POP; WLCS**
  See also AAYA 7, 20; BW 2; CA 65-68; CANR 19, 42; DLB 38; MTCW; SATA 49
Anna Comnena 1083-1153 .... **CMLC 25**
Annensky, Innokenty (Fyodorovich) 1856-1909
  TCLC 14
  See also CA 110; 155
Annunzio, Gabriele d'
  See D'Annunzio, Gabriele
Anodos
  See Coleridge, Mary E(lizabeth)
Anon, Charles Robert
  See Pessoa, Fernando (Antonio Nogueira)
Anouilh, Jean (Marie Lucien Pierre) 1910-1987
  CLC 1, 3, 8, 13, 40, 50; DAM DRAM; DC 8
  See also CA 17-20R; 123; CANR 32; MTCW
Anthony, Florence
  See Ai
Anthony, John
  See Ciardi, John (Anthony)
Anthony, Peter
  See Shaffer, Anthony (Joshua); Shaffer, Peter (Levin)
Anthony, Piers 1934- ..... **CLC 35; DAM POP**
  See also AAYA 11; CA 21-24R; CANR 28, 56; DLB 8; MTCW; SAAS 22; SATA 84
Antoine, Marc
  See Proust, (Valentin-Louis-George-Eugene-) Marcel
Antoninus, Brother
  See Everson, William (Oliver)
Antonioni, Michelangelo 1912- .... **CLC 20**
  See also CA 73-76; CANR 45
Antschel, Paul 1920-1970
  See Celan, Paul
  See also CA 85-88; CANR 33, 61; MTCW
Anwar, Chairil 1922-1949 .... **TCLC 22**
  See also CA 121
Apollinaire, Guillaume 1880-1918**TCLC 3, 8, 51; DAM POET; PC 7**
  See also Kostrowitzki, Wilhelm Apollinaris de
  See also CA 152
Appelfeld, Aharon 1932- .... **CLC 23, 47**
  See also CA 112; 133
Apple, Max (Isaac) 1941-............. **CLC 9, 33**
  See also CA 81-84; CANR 19, 54; DLB 130
Appleman, Philip (Dean) 1926-........ **CLC 51**
  See also CA 13-16R; CAAS 18; CANR 6, 29, 56
Appleton, Lawrence
  See Lovecraft, H(oward) P(hillips)
Apteryx
  See Eliot, T(homas) S(tearns)
Apuleius, (Lucius Madaurensis) 125(?)-175(?)
  CMLC 1
Aquin, Hubert 1929-1977 .... **CLC 15**
  See also CA 105; DLB 53
Aragon, Louis 1897-1982 ..**CLC 3, 22; DAM NOV, POET**
  See also CA 69-72; 108; CANR 28; DLB 72; MTCW
Arany, Janos 1817-1882 .... **NCLC 34**
Arbuthnot, John 1667-1735 .... **LC 1**
  See also DLB 101
Archer, Herbert Winslow
  See Mencken, H(enry) L(ouis)
Archer, Jeffrey (Howard) 1940- ..... **CLC 28; DAM POP**
  See also AAYA 16; BEST 89:3; CA 77-80;

CANR 22, 52; INT CANR-22
Archer, Jules 1915- ....**CLC 12**
  See also CA 9-12R; CANR 6; SAAS 5; SATA 4, 85
Archer, Lee
  See Ellison, Harlan (Jay)
Arden, John 1930-**CLC 6, 13, 15; DAM DRAM**
  See also CA 13-16R; CAAS 4; CANR 31; DLB 13; MTCW
Arenas, Reinaldo 1943-1990 .**CLC 41; DAM MULT; HLC**
  See also CA 124; 128; 133; DLB 145; HW
Arendt, Hannah 1906-1975 .... **CLC 66, 98**
  See also CA 17-20R; 61-64; CANR 26, 60; MTCW
Aretino, Pietro 1492-1556 .... **LC 12**
Arghezi, Tudor ....**CLC 80**
  See also Theodorescu, Ion N.
Arguedas, Jose Maria 1911-1969 **CLC 10, 18**
  See also CA 89-92; DLB 113; HW
Argueta, Manlio 1936- .... **CLC 31**
  See also CA 131; DLB 145; HW
Ariosto, Ludovico 1474-1533 .... **LC 6**
Aristides
  See Epstein, Joseph
Aristophanes 450B.C.-385B.C.**CMLC 4; DA; DAB; DAC; DAM DRAM, MST; DC 2; WLCS**
  See also DLB 176
Arlt, Roberto (Godofredo Christophersen) 1900-1942**TCLC 29; DAM MULT; HLC**
  See also CA 123; 131; HW
Armah, Ayi Kwei 1939-**CLC 5, 33; BLC; DAM MULT, POET**
  See also BW 1; CA 61-64; CANR 21, 64; DLB 117; MTCW
Armatrading, Joan 1950- .... **CLC 17**
  See also CA 114
Arnette, Robert
  See Silverberg, Robert
Arnim, Achim von (Ludwig Joachim von Arnim) 1781-1831 ...... **NCLC 5; SSC 29**
  See also DLB 90
Arnim, Bettina von 1785-1859 .... **NCLC 38**
  See also DLB 90
Arnold, Matthew 1822-1888**NCLC 6, 29; DA; DAB; DAC; DAM MST, POET; PC 5; WLC**
  See also CDBLB 1832-1890; DLB 32, 57
Arnold, Thomas 1795-1842 .... **NCLC 18**
  See also DLB 55
Arnow, Harriette (Louisa) Simpson 1908-1986
  CLC 2, 7, 18
  See also CA 9-12R; 118; CANR 14; DLB 6; MTCW; SATA 42; SATA-Obit 47
Arp, Hans
  See Arp, Jean
Arp, Jean 1887-1966 ....**CLC 5**
  See also CA 81-84; 25-28R; CANR 42
Arrabal
  See Arrabal, Fernando
Arrabal, Fernando 1932-.... **CLC 2, 9, 18, 58**
  See also CA 9-12R; CANR 15
Arrick, Fran ....**CLC 30**
  See also Gaberman, Judie Angell
Artaud, Antonin (Marie Joseph) 1896-1948
  TCLC 3, 36; DAM DRAM
  See also CA 104; 149
Arthur, Ruth M(abel) 1905-1979 ...... **CLC 12**
  See also CA 9-12R; 85-88; CANR 4; SATA 7, 26
Artsybashev, Mikhail (Petrovich) 1878-1927
  TCLC 31

Arundel, Honor (Morfydd) 1919-1973**CLC 17**
  See also CA 21-22; 41-44R; CAP 2; CLR 35; SATA 4; SATA-Obit 24
Arzner, Dorothy 1897-1979 .... **CLC 98**
Asch, Sholem 1880-1957 .... **TCLC 3**
  See also CA 105
Ash, Shalom
  See Asch, Sholem
Ashbery, John (Lawrence) 1927-**CLC 2, 3, 4, 6, 9, 13, 15, 25, 41, 77; DAM POET**
  See also CA 5-8R; CANR 9, 37; DLB 5, 165; DLBY 81; INT CANR-9; MTCW
Ashdown, Clifford
  See Freeman, R(ichard) Austin
Ashe, Gordon
  See Creasey, John
Ashton-Warner, Sylvia (Constance) 1908-1984
  CLC 19
  See also CA 69-72; 112; CANR 29; MTCW
Asimov, Isaac 1920-1992 **CLC 1, 3, 9, 19, 26, 76, 92; DAM POP**
  See also AAYA 13; BEST 90:2; CA 1-4R; 137; CANR 2, 19, 36, 60; CLR 12; DLB 8; DLBY 92; INT CANR-19; JRDA; MAICYA; MTCW; SATA 1, 26, 74
Assis, Joaquim Maria Machado de
  See Machado de Assis, Joaquim Maria
Astley, Thea (Beatrice May) 1925- ...**CLC 41**
  See also CA 65-68; CANR 11, 43
Aston, James
  See White, T(erence) H(anbury)
Asturias, Miguel Angel 1899-1974 **CLC 3, 8, 13; DAM MULT, NOV; HLC**
  See also CA 25-28; 49-52; CANR 32; CAP 2; DLB 113; HW; MTCW
Atares, Carlos Saura
  See Saura (Atares), Carlos
Atheling, William
  See Pound, Ezra (Weston Loomis)
Atheling, William, Jr.
  See Blish, James (Benjamin)
Atherton, Gertrude (Franklin Horn) 1857-1948
  TCLC 2
  See also CA 104; 155; DLB 9, 78, 186
Atherton, Lucius
  See Masters, Edgar Lee
Atkins, Jack
  See Harris, Mark
Atkinson, Kate ....**CLC 99**
Attaway, William (Alexander) 1911-1986
  CLC 92; BLC; DAM MULT
  See also BW 2; CA 143; DLB 76
Atticus
  See Fleming, Ian (Lancaster)
Atwood, Margaret (Eleanor) 1939-**CLC 2, 3, 4, 8, 13, 15, 25, 44, 84; DA; DAB; DAC; DAM MST, NOV, POET; PC 8; SSC 2; WLC**
  See also AAYA 12; BEST 89:2; CA 49-52; CANR 3, 24, 33, 59; DLB 53; INT CANR-24; MTCW; SATA 50
Aubigny, Pierre d'
  See Mencken, H(enry) L(ouis)
Aubin, Penelope 1685-1731(?)............... **LC 9**
  See also DLB 39
Auchincloss, Louis (Stanton) 1917-**CLC 4, 6, 9, 18, 45; DAM NOV; SSC 22**
  See also CA 1-4R; CANR 6, 29, 55; DLB 2; DLBY 80; INT CANR-29; MTCW
Auden, W(ystan) H(ugh) 1907-1973**CLC 1, 2, 3, 4, 6, 9, 11, 14, 43; DA; DAB; DAC; DAM DRAM, MST, POET; PC 1; WLC**
  See also AAYA 18; CA 9-12R; 45-48; CANR

5, 61; CDBLB 1914-1945; DLB 10, 20;
MTCW

Audiberti, Jacques 1900-1965**CLC 38; DAM DRAM**
See also CA 25-28R

Audubon, John James 1785-1851 .. **NCLC 47**

Auel, Jean M(arie) 1936-**CLC 31, 107; DAM POP**
See also AAYA 7; BEST 90:4; CA 103; CANR 21, 64; INT CANR-21; SATA 91

Auerbach, Erich 1892-1957 .... **TCLC 43**
See also CA 118; 155

Augier, Emile 1820-1889 .... **NCLC 31**

August, John
See De Voto, Bernard (Augustine)

Augustine, St. 354-430 .... **CMLC 6; DAB**

Aurelius
See Bourne, Randolph S(illiman)

Aurobindo, Sri 1872-1950 .... **TCLC 63**

Austen, Jane 1775-1817 **NCLC 1, 13, 19, 33, 51; DA; DAB; DAC; DAM MST, NOV; WLC**
See also AAYA 19; CDBLB 1789-1832; DLB 116

Auster, Paul 1947- .... **CLC 47**
See also CA 69-72; CANR 23, 52

Austin, Frank
See Faust, Frederick (Schiller)

Austin, Mary (Hunter) 1868-1934 . **TCLC 25**
See also CA 109; DLB 9, 78

Autran Dourado, Waldomiro
See Dourado, (Waldomiro Freitas) Autran

Averroes 1126-1198 .... **CMLC 7**
See also DLB 115

Avicenna 980-1037 .... **CMLC 16**
See also DLB 115

Avison, Margaret 1918- **CLC 2, 4, 97; DAC; DAM POET**
See also CA 17-20R; DLB 53; MTCW

Axton, David
See Koontz, Dean R(ay)

Ayckbourn, Alan 1939- **CLC 5, 8, 18, 33, 74; DAB; DAM DRAM**
See also CA 21-24R; CANR 31, 59; DLB 13; MTCW

Aydy, Catherine
See Tennant, Emma (Christina)

Ayme, Marcel (Andre) 1902-1967 ..... **CLC 11**
See also CA 89-92; CLR 25; DLB 72; SATA 91

Ayrton, Michael 1921-1975 .... **CLC 7**
See also CA 5-8R; 61-64; CANR 9, 21

Azorin .... **CLC 11**
See also Martinez Ruiz, Jose

Azuela, Mariano 1873-1952 . **TCLC 3; DAM MULT; HLC**
See also CA 104; 131; HW; MTCW

Baastad, Babbis Friis
See Friis-Baastad, Babbis Ellinor

Bab
See Gilbert, W(illiam) S(chwenck)

Babbis, Eleanor
See Friis-Baastad, Babbis Ellinor

Babel, Isaac
See Babel, Isaak (Emmanuilovich)

Babel, Isaak (Emmanuilovich) 1894-1941(?)
TCLC 2, 13; SSC 16
See also CA 104; 155

Babits, Mihaly 1883-1941 .... **TCLC 14**
See also CA 114

Babur 1483-1530 .... **LC 18**

Bacchelli, Riccardo 1891-1985 .... **CLC 19**
See also CA 29-32R; 117

Bach, Richard (David) 1936- **CLC 14; DAM NOV, POP**
See also AITN 1; BEST 89:2; CA 9-12R; CANR 18; MTCW; SATA 13

Bachman, Richard
See King, Stephen (Edwin)

Bachmann, Ingeborg 1926-1973 .... **CLC 69**
See also CA 93-96; 45-48; DLB 85

Bacon, Francis 1561-1626 .... **LC 18, 32**
See also CDBLB Before 1660; DLB 151

Bacon, Roger 1214(?)-1292 .... **CMLC 14**
See also DLB 115

Bacovia, George .... **TCLC 24**
See also Vasiliu, Gheorghe

Badanes, Jerome 1937- ....**CLC 59**

Bagehot, Walter 1826-1877 .... **NCLC 10**
See also DLB 55

Bagnold, Enid 1889-1981 ...... **CLC 25; DAM DRAM**
See also CA 5-8R; 103; CANR 5, 40; DLB 13, 160; MAICYA; SATA 1, 25

Bagritsky, Eduard 1895-1934 .... **TCLC 60**

Bagrjana, Elisaveta
See Belcheva, Elisaveta

Bagryana, Elisaveta ....**CLC 10**
See also Belcheva, Elisaveta
See also DLB 147

Bailey, Paul 1937- ....**CLC 45**
See also CA 21-24R; CANR 16, 62; DLB 14

Baillie, Joanna 1762-1851 .... **NCLC 2**
See also DLB 93

Bainbridge, Beryl (Margaret) 1933-**CLC 4, 5, 8, 10, 14, 18, 22, 62; DAM NOV**
See also CA 21-24R; CANR 24, 55; DLB 14; MTCW

Baker, Elliott 1922- ....**CLC 8**
See also CA 45-48; CANR 2, 63

Baker, Jean H. .... **TCLC 3, 10**
See also Russell, George William

Baker, Nicholson 1957- . **CLC 61; DAM POP**
See also CA 135; CANR 63

Baker, Ray Stannard 1870-1946 .... **TCLC 47**
See also CA 118

Baker, Russell (Wayne) 1925- .... **CLC 31**
See also BEST 89:4; CA 57-60; CANR 11, 41, 59; MTCW

Bakhtin, M.
See Bakhtin, Mikhail Mikhailovich

Bakhtin, M. M.
See Bakhtin, Mikhail Mikhailovich

Bakhtin, Mikhail
See Bakhtin, Mikhail Mikhailovich

Bakhtin, Mikhail Mikhailovich 1895-1975
CLC 83
See also CA 128; 113

Bakshi, Ralph 1938(?)- ....**CLC 26**
See also CA 112; 138

Bakunin, Mikhail (Alexandrovich) 1814-1876
NCLC 25, 58

Baldwin, James (Arthur) 1924-1987**CLC 1, 2, 3, 4, 5, 8, 13, 15, 17, 42, 50, 67, 90; BLC; DA; DAB; DAC; DAM MST, MULT, NOV, POP; DC 1; SSC 10; WLC**
See also AAYA 4; BW 1; CA 1-4R; 124; CABS 1; CANR 3, 24; CDALB 1941-1968; DLB 2, 7, 33; DLBY 87; MTCW; SATA 9; SATA-Obit 54

Ballard, J(ames) G(raham) 1930-**CLC 3, 6, 14, 36; DAM NOV, POP; SSC 1**
See also AAYA 3; CA 5-8R; CANR 15, 39; DLB 14; MTCW; SATA 93

Balmont, Konstantin (Dmitriyevich) 1867-1943
TCLC 11
See also CA 109; 155

Balzac, Honore de 1799-1850**NCLC 5, 35, 53; DA; DAB; DAC; DAM MST, NOV; SSC 5; WLC**
See also DLB 119

Bambara, Toni Cade 1939-1995 **CLC 19, 88; BLC; DA; DAC; DAM MST, MULT; WLCS**
See also AAYA 5; BW 2; CA 29-32R; 150; CANR 24, 49; DLB 38; MTCW

Bamdad, A.
See Shamlu, Ahmad

Banat, D. R.
See Bradbury, Ray (Douglas)

Bancroft, Laura
See Baum, L(yman) Frank

Banim, John 1798-1842 .... **NCLC 13**
See also DLB 116, 158, 159

Banim, Michael 1796-1874 .... **NCLC 13**
See also DLB 158, 159

Banjo, The
See Paterson, A(ndrew) B(arton)

Banks, Iain
See Banks, Iain M(enzies)

Banks, Iain M(enzies) 1954- .... **CLC 34**
See also CA 123; 128; CANR 61; INT 128

Banks, Lynne Reid .... **CLC 23**
See also Reid Banks, Lynne
See also AAYA 6

Banks, Russell 1940- .... **CLC 37, 72**
See also CA 65-68; CAAS 15; CANR 19, 52; DLB 130

Banville, John 1945- .... **CLC 46**
See also CA 117; 128; DLB 14; INT 128

Banville, Theodore (Faullain) de 1832-1891
NCLC 9

Baraka, Amiri 1934-**CLC 1, 2, 3, 5, 10, 14, 33; BLC; DA; DAC; DAM MST, MULT, POET, POP; DC 6; PC 4; WLCS**
See Jones, LeRoi
See also BW 2; CA 21-24R; CABS 3; CANR 27, 38, 61; CDALB 1941-1968; DLB 5, 7, 16, 38; DLBD 8; MTCW

Barbauld, Anna Laetitia 1743-1825**NCLC 50**
See also DLB 107, 109, 142, 158

Barbellion, W. N. P. .... **TCLC 24**
See also Cummings, Bruce F(rederick)

Barbera, Jack (Vincent) 1945- .... **CLC 44**
See also CA 110; CANR 45

Barbey d'Aurevilly, Jules Amedee 1808-1889
NCLC 1; SSC 17
See also DLB 119

Barbusse, Henri 1873-1935 .... **TCLC 5**
See also CA 105; 154; DLB 65

Barclay, Bill
See Moorcock, Michael (John)

Barclay, William Ewert
See Moorcock, Michael (John)

Barea, Arturo 1897-1957 .... **TCLC 14**
See also CA 111

Barfoot, Joan 1946- .... **CLC 18**
See also CA 105

Baring, Maurice 1874-1945 .... **TCLC 8**
See also CA 105; DLB 34

Barker, Clive 1952- .... **CLC 52; DAM POP**
See also AAYA 10; BEST 90:3; CA 121; 129; INT 129; MTCW

Barker, George Granville 1913-1991 **CLC 8, 48; DAM POET**
See also CA 9-12R; 135; CANR 7, 38; DLB 20; MTCW

Barker, Harley Granville
See Granville-Barker, Harley
See also DLB 10

Barker, Howard 1946- .... **CLC 37**
  See also CA 102; DLB 13
Barker, Pat(ricia) 1943- .... **CLC 32, 94**
  See also CA 117; 122; CANR 50; INT 122
Barlow, Joel 1754-1812 .... **NCLC 23**
  See also DLB 37
Barnard, Mary (Ethel) 1909- .... **CLC 48**
  See also CA 21-22; CAP 2
Barnes, Djuna 1892-1982**CLC 3, 4, 8, 11, 29;**
  SSC 3
  See also CA 9-12R; 107; CANR 16, 55; DLB
  4, 9, 45; MTCW
Barnes, Julian (Patrick) 1946-**CLC 42; DAB**
  See also CA 102; CANR 19, 54; DLBY 93
Barnes, Peter 1931- .... **CLC 5, 56**
  See also CA 65-68; CAAS 12; CANR 33, 34,
  64; DLB 13; MTCW
Baroja (y Nessi), Pio 1872-1956**TCLC 8; HLC**
  See also CA 104
Baron, David
  See Pinter, Harold
Baron Corvo
  See Rolfe, Frederick (William Serafino Austin
  Lewis Mary)
Barondess, Sue K(aufman) 1926-1977 **CLC 8**
  See also Kaufman, Sue
  See also CA 1-4R; 69-72; CANR 1
Baron de Teive
  See Pessoa, Fernando (Antonio Nogueira)
Barres, Maurice 1862-1923 .... **TCLC 47**
  See also DLB 123
Barreto, Afonso Henrique de Lima
  See Lima Barreto, Afonso Henrique de
Barrett, (Roger) Syd 1946- .... **CLC 35**
Barrett, William (Christopher) 1913-1992
  CLC 27
  See also CA 13-16R; 139; CANR 11; INT
  CANR-11
Barrie, J(ames) M(atthew) 1860-1937 **T C L C**
  2; DAB; DAM DRAM
  See also CA 104; 136; CDBLB 1890-1914;
  CLR 16; DLB 10, 141, 156; MAICYA;
  YABC 1
Barrington, Michael
  See Moorcock, Michael (John)
Barrol, Grady
  See Bograd, Larry
Barry, Mike
  See Malzberg, Barry N(athaniel)
Barry, Philip 1896-1949 .... **TCLC 11**
  See also CA 109; DLB 7
Bart, Andre Schwarz
  See Schwarz-Bart, Andre
Barth, John (Simmons) 1930-**CLC 1, 2, 3, 5, 7,**
  9, 10, 14, 27, 51, 89; DAM NOV; SSC 10
  See also AITN 1, 2; CA 1-4R; CABS 1; CANR
  5, 23, 49, 64; DLB 2; MTCW
Barthelme, Donald 1931-1989**CLC 1, 2, 3, 5, 6,**
  8, 13, 23, 46, 59; DAM NOV; SSC 2
  See also CA 21-24R; 129; CANR 20, 58; DLB
  2; DLBY 80, 89; MTCW; SATA 7; SATA-
  Obit 62
Barthelme, Frederick 1943- .... **CLC 36**
  See also CA 114; 122; DLBY 85; INT 122
Barthes, Roland (Gerard) 1915-1980**CLC 24,**
  83
  See also CA 130; 97-100; MTCW
Barzun, Jacques (Martin) 1907- ...... **CLC 51**
  See also CA 61-64; CANR 22
Bashevis, Isaac
  See Singer, Isaac Bashevis
Bashkirtseff, Marie 1859-1884 .... **NCLC 27**
Basho

See Matsuo Basho
Bass, Kingsley B., Jr.
  See Bullins, Ed
Bass, Rick 1958-...............................**CLC 79**
  See also CA 126; CANR 53
Bassani, Giorgio 1916-.........................**CLC 9**
  See also CA 65-68; CANR 33; DLB 128, 177;
  MTCW
Bastos, Augusto (Antonio) Roa
  See Roa Bastos, Augusto (Antonio)
Bataille, Georges 1897-1962 ....**CLC 29**
  See also CA 101; 89-92
Bates, H(erbert) E(rnest) 1905-1974**CLC 46;**
  DAB; DAM POP; SSC 10
  See also CA 93-96; 45-48; CANR 34; DLB 162;
  MTCW
Bauchart
  See Camus, Albert
Baudelaire, Charles 1821-1867 **NCLC 6, 29,**
  55; DA; DAB; DAC; DAM MST, POET;
  PC 1; SSC 18; WLC
Baudrillard, Jean 1929- .... **CLC 60**
Baum, L(yman) Frank 1856-1919 ... **TCLC 7**
  See also CA 108; 133; CLR 15; DLB 22; JRDA;
  MAICYA; MTCW; SATA 18
Baum, Louis F.
  See Baum, L(yman) Frank
Baumbach, Jonathan 1933- .... **CLC 6, 23**
  See also CA 13-16R; CAAS 5; CANR 12;
  DLBY 80; INT CANR-12; MTCW
Bausch, Richard (Carl) 1945-................**CLC 51**
  See also CA 101; CAAS 14; CANR 43, 61; DLB
  130
Baxter, Charles (Morley) 1947- **CLC 45, 78;**
  DAM POP
  See also CA 57-60; CANR 40, 64; DLB 130
Baxter, George Owen
  See Faust, Frederick (Schiller)
Baxter, James K(eir) 1926-1972 ....**CLC 14**
  See also CA 77-80
Baxter, John
  See Hunt, E(verette) Howard, (Jr.)
Bayer, Sylvia
  See Glassco, John
Baynton, Barbara 1857-1929 .... **TCLC 57**
Beagle, Peter S(oyer) 1939- .... **CLC 7, 104**
  See also CA 9-12R; CANR 4, 51; DLBY 80;
  INT CANR-4; SATA 60
Bean, Normal
  See Burroughs, Edgar Rice
Beard, Charles A(ustin) 1874-1948 **TCLC 15**
  See also CA 115; DLB 17; SATA 18
Beardsley, Aubrey 1872-1898 .... **NCLC 6**
Beattie, Ann 1947-**CLC 8, 13, 18, 40, 63; DAM**
  NOV, POP; SSC 11
  See also BEST 90:2; CA 81-84; CANR 53;
  DLBY 82; MTCW
Beattie, James 1735-1803 .... **NCLC 25**
  See also DLB 109
Beauchamp, Kathleen Mansfield 1888-1923
  See Mansfield, Katherine
  See also CA 104; 134; DA; DAC; DAM MST
Beaumarchais, Pierre-Augustin Caron de 1732-
  1799 .... **DC 4**
  See also DAM DRAM
Beaumont, Francis 1584(?)-1616**LC 33; DC 6**
  See also CDBLB Before 1660; DLB 58, 121
Beauvoir, Simone (Lucie Ernestine Marie
  Bertrand) de 1908-1986**CLC 1, 2, 4, 8, 14,**
  31, 44, 50, 71; DA; DAB; DAC; DAM MST,
  NOV; WLC
  See also CA 9-12R; 118; CANR 28, 61; DLB
  72; DLBY 86; MTCW

Becker, Carl (Lotus) 1873-1945 ..... **TCLC 63**
  See also CA 157; DLB 17
Becker, Jurek 1937-1997 .... **CLC 7, 19**
  See also CA 85-88; 157; CANR 60; DLB 75
Becker, Walter 1950- .... **CLC 26**
Beckett, Samuel (Barclay) 1906-1989 **CLC 1,**
  2, 3, 4, 6, 9, 10, 11, 14, 18, 29, 57, 59, 83;
  DA; DAB; DAC; DAM DRAM, MST,
  NOV; SSC 16; WLC
  See also CA 5-8R; 130; CANR 33, 61; CDBLB
  1945-1960; DLB 13, 15; DLBY 90; MTCW
Beckford, William 1760-1844 .... **NCLC 16**
  See also DLB 39
Beckman, Gunnel 1910- .... **CLC 26**
  See also CA 33-36R; CANR 15; CLR 25;
  MAICYA; SAAS 9; SATA 6
Becque, Henri 1837-1899 .... **NCLC 3**
Beddoes, Thomas Lovell 1803-1849 **NCLC 3**
  See also DLB 96
Bede c. 673-735 .... **CMLC 20**
  See also DLB 146
Bedford, Donald F.
  See Fearing, Kenneth (Flexner)
Beecher, Catharine Esther 1800-1878 **N C L C**
  30
  See also DLB 1
Beecher, John 1904-1980 .... **CLC 6**
  See also AITN 1; CA 5-8R; 105; CANR 8
Beer, Johann 1655-1700 .... **LC 5**
  See also DLB 168
Beer, Patricia 1924-................................**CLC 58**
  See also CA 61-64; CANR 13, 46; DLB 40
Beerbohm, Max
  See Beerbohm, (Henry) Max(imilian)
Beerbohm, (Henry) Max(imilian) 1872-1956
  TCLC 1, 24
  See also CA 104; 154; DLB 34, 100
Beer-Hofmann, Richard 1866-1945**TCLC 60**
  See also CA 160; DLB 81
Begiebing, Robert J(ohn) 1946- .... **CLC 70**
  See also CA 122; CANR 40
Behan, Brendan 1923-1964 **CLC 1, 8, 11, 15,**
  79; DAM DRAM
  See also CA 73-76; CANR 33; CDBLB 1945-
  1960; DLB 13; MTCW
Behn, Aphra 1640(?)-1689**LC 1, 30; DA; DAB;**
  DAC; DAM DRAM, MST, NOV, POET;
  DC 4; PC 13; WLC
  See also DLB 39, 80, 131
Behrman, S(amuel) N(athaniel) 1893-1973
  CLC 40
  See also CA 13-16; 45-48; CAP 1; DLB 7, 44
Belasco, David 1853-1931 .... **TCLC 3**
  See also CA 104; DLB 7
Belcheva, Elisaveta 1893- .... **CLC 10**
  See also Bagryana, Elisaveta
Beldone, Phil "Cheech"
  See Ellison, Harlan (Jay)
Beleno
  See Azuela, Mariano
Belinski, Vissarion Grigoryevich 1811-1848
  NCLC 5
Belitt, Ben 1911- .... **CLC 22**
  See also CA 13-16R; CAAS 4; CANR 7; DLB
  5
Bell, Gertrude 1868-1926 .... **TCLC 67**
  See also DLB 174
Bell, James Madison 1826-1902 ... **TCLC 43;**
  BLC; DAM MULT
  See also BW 1; CA 122; 124; DLB 50
Bell, Madison Smartt 1957-...... **CLC 41, 102**
  See also CA 111; CANR 28, 54
Bell, Marvin (Hartley) 1937-**CLC 8, 31; DAM**

POET
See also CA 21-24R; CAAS 14; CANR 59; DLB 5; MTCW

Bell, W. L. D.
See Mencken, H(enry) L(ouis)

Bellamy, Atwood C.
See Mencken, H(enry) L(ouis)

Bellamy, Edward 1850-1898 .... **NCLC 4**
See also DLB 12

Bellin, Edward J.
See Kuttner, Henry

Belloc, (Joseph) Hilaire (Pierre Sebastien Rene Swanton) 1870-1953 **TCLC 7, 18; DAM POET**
See also CA 106; 152; DLB 19, 100, 141, 174; YABC 1

Belloc, Joseph Peter Rene Hilaire
See Belloc, (Joseph) Hilaire (Pierre Sebastien Rene Swanton)

Belloc, Joseph Pierre Hilaire
See Belloc, (Joseph) Hilaire (Pierre Sebastien Rene Swanton)

Belloc, M. A.
See Lowndes, Marie Adelaide (Belloc)

Bellow, Saul 1915-**CLC 1, 2, 3, 6, 8, 10, 13, 15, 25, 33, 34, 63, 79; DA; DAB; DAC; DAM MST, NOV, POP; SSC 14; WLC**
See also AITN 2; BEST 89:3; CA 5-8R; CABS 1; CANR 29, 53; CDALB 1941-1968; DLB 2, 28; DLBD 3; DLBY 82; MTCW

Belser, Reimond Karel Maria de 1929-
See Ruyslinck, Ward
See also CA 152

Bely, Andrey .... **TCLC 7; PC 11**
See also Bugayev, Boris Nikolayevich

Benary, Margot
See Benary-Isbert, Margot

Benary-Isbert, Margot 1889-1979 ... **CLC 12**
See also CA 5-8R; 89-92; CANR 4; CLR 12; MAICYA; SATA 2; SATA-Obit 21

Benavente (y Martinez), Jacinto 1866-1954 **TCLC 3; DAM DRAM, MULT**
See also CA 106; 131; HW; MTCW

Benchley, Peter (Bradford) 1940-. **CLC 4, 8; DAM NOV, POP**
See also AAYA 14; AITN 2; CA 17-20R; CANR 12, 35; MTCW; SATA 3, 89

Benchley, Robert (Charles) 1889-1945**T C L C 1, 55**
See also CA 105; 153; DLB 11

Benda, Julien 1867-1956 .... **TCLC 60**
See also CA 120; 154

Benedict, Ruth (Fulton) 1887-1948 **TCLC 60**
See also CA 158

Benedikt, Michael 1935- .... **CLC 4, 14**
See also CA 13-16R; CANR 7; DLB 5

Benet, Juan 1927- .... **CLC 28**
See also CA 143

Benet, Stephen Vincent 1898-1943 . **TCLC 7; DAM POET; SSC 10**
See also CA 104; 152; DLB 4, 48, 102; YABC 1

Benet, William Rose 1886-1950 ... **TCLC 28; DAM POET**
See also CA 118; 152; DLB 45

Benford, Gregory (Albert) 1941-..... **CLC 52**
See also CA 69-72; CAAS 27; CANR 12, 24, 49; DLBY 82

Bengtsson, Frans (Gunnar) 1894-1954**T C L C 48**

Benjamin, David
See Slavitt, David R(ytman)

Benjamin, Lois
See Gould, Lois

Benjamin, Walter 1892-1940 .... **TCLC 39**

Benn, Gottfried 1886-1956 .... **TCLC 3**
See also CA 106; 153; DLB 56

Bennett, Alan 1934-**CLC 45, 77; DAB; DAM MST**
See also CA 103; CANR 35, 55; MTCW

Bennett, (Enoch) Arnold 1867-1931**TCLC 5, 20**
See also CA 106; 155; CDBLB 1890-1914; DLB 10, 34, 98, 135

Bennett, Elizabeth
See Mitchell, Margaret (Munnerlyn)

Bennett, George Harold 1930-
See Bennett, Hal
See also BW 1; CA 97-100

Bennett, Hal ....**CLC 5**
See also Bennett, George Harold
See also DLB 33

Bennett, Jay 1912- ....**CLC 35**
See also AAYA 10; CA 69-72; CANR 11, 42; JRDA; SAAS 4; SATA 41, 87; SATA-Brief 27

Bennett, Louise (Simone) 1919-**CLC 28; BLC; DAM MULT**
See also BW 2; CA 151; DLB 117

Benson, E(dward) F(rederic) 1867-1940 **TCLC 27**
See also CA 114; 157; DLB 135, 153

Benson, Jackson J. 1930- ....**CLC 34**
See also CA 25-28R; DLB 111

Benson, Sally 1900-1972 ....**CLC 17**
See also CA 19-20; 37-40R; CAP 1; SATA 1, 35; SATA-Obit 27

Benson, Stella 1892-1933 .... **TCLC 17**
See also CA 117; 155; DLB 36, 162

Bentham, Jeremy 1748-1832 .... **NCLC 38**
See also DLB 107, 158

Bentley, E(dmund) C(lerihew) 1875-1956 **TCLC 12**
See also CA 108; DLB 70

Bentley, Eric (Russell) 1916- ....**CLC 24**
See also CA 5-8R; CANR 6; INT CANR-6

Beranger, Pierre Jean de 1780-1857**NCLC 34**

Berdyaev, Nicolas
See Berdyaev, Nikolai (Aleksandrovich)

Berdyaev, Nikolai (Aleksandrovich) 1874-1948 **TCLC 67**
See also CA 120; 157

Berdyayev, Nikolai (Aleksandrovich)
See Berdyaev, Nikolai (Aleksandrovich)

Berendt, John (Lawrence) 1939- ......**CLC 86**
See also CA 146

Berger, Colonel
See Malraux, (Georges-)Andre

Berger, John (Peter) 1926- .... **CLC 2, 19**
See also CA 81-84; CANR 51; DLB 14

Berger, Melvin H. 1927-.....................**CLC 12**
See also CA 5-8R; CANR 4; CLR 32; SAAS 2; SATA 5, 88

Berger, Thomas (Louis) 1924-**CLC 3, 5, 8, 11, 18, 38; DAM NOV**
See also CA 1-4R; CANR 5, 28, 51; DLB 2; DLBY 80; INT CANR-28; MTCW

Bergman, (Ernst) Ingmar 1918- **CLC 16, 72**
See also CA 81-84; CANR 33

Bergson, Henri 1859-1941 .... **TCLC 32**

Bergstein, Eleanor 1938- ....**CLC 4**
See also CA 53-56; CANR 5

Berkoff, Steven 1937- ....**CLC 56**
See also CA 104

Bermant, Chaim (Icyk) 1929- .... **CLC 40**
See also CA 57-60; CANR 6, 31, 57

Bern, Victoria
See Fisher, M(ary) F(rances) K(ennedy)

Bernanos, (Paul Louis) Georges 1888-1948 **TCLC 3**
See also CA 104; 130; DLB 72

Bernard, April 1956- .... **CLC 59**
See also CA 131

Berne, Victoria
See Fisher, M(ary) F(rances) K(ennedy)

Bernhard, Thomas 1931-1989 **CLC 3, 32, 61**
See also CA 85-88; 127; CANR 32, 57; DLB 85, 124; MTCW

Bernhardt, Sarah (Henriette Rosine) 1844-1923 **TCLC 75**
See also CA 157

Berriault, Gina 1926- .... **CLC 54**
See also CA 116; 129; DLB 130

Berrigan, Daniel 1921-.........................**CLC 4**
See also CA 33-36R; CAAS 1; CANR 11, 43; DLB 5

Berrigan, Edmund Joseph Michael, Jr. 1934-1983
See Berrigan, Ted
See also CA 61-64; 110; CANR 14

Berrigan, Ted .... **CLC 37**
See also Berrigan, Edmund Joseph Michael, Jr.
See also DLB 5, 169

Berry, Charles Edward Anderson 1931-
See Berry, Chuck
See also CA 115

Berry, Chuck .... **CLC 17**
See also Berry, Charles Edward Anderson

Berry, Jonas
See Ashbery, John (Lawrence)

Berry, Wendell (Erdman) 1934- **CLC 4, 6, 8, 27, 46; DAM POET**
See also AITN 1; CA 73-76; CANR 50; DLB 5, 6

Berryman, John 1914-1972**CLC 1, 2, 3, 4, 6, 8, 10, 13, 25, 62; DAM POET**
See also CA 13-16; 33-36R; CABS 2; CANR 35; CAP 1; CDALB 1941-1968; DLB 48; MTCW

Bertolucci, Bernardo 1940- .... **CLC 16**
See also CA 106

Berton, Pierre (Francis De Marigny) 1920- **CLC 104**
See also CA 1-4R; CANR 2, 56; DLB 68

Bertrand, Aloysius 1807-1841 .... **NCLC 31**

Bertran de Born c. 1140-1215 .... **CMLC 5**

Besant, Annie (Wood) 1847-1933 ..... **TCLC 9**
See also CA 105

Bessie, Alvah 1904-1985 .... **CLC 23**
See also CA 5-8R; 116; CANR 2; DLB 26

Bethlen, T. D.
See Silverberg, Robert

Beti, Mongo ...... **CLC 27; BLC; DAM MULT**
See also Biyidi, Alexandre

Betjeman, John 1906-1984 **CLC 2, 6, 10, 34, 43; DAB; DAM MST, POET**
See also CA 9-12R; 112; CANR 33, 56; CDBLB 1945-1960; DLB 20; DLBY 84; MTCW

Bettelheim, Bruno 1903-1990 .... **CLC 79**
See also CA 81-84; 131; CANR 23, 61; MTCW

Betti, Ugo 1892-1953 .... **TCLC 5**
See also CA 104; 155

Betts, Doris (Waugh) 1932- ...... **CLC 3, 6, 28**
See also CA 13-16R; CANR 9; DLBY 82; INT CANR-9

Bevan, Alistair
See Roberts, Keith (John Kingston)

Bialik, Chaim Nachman 1873-1934 **TCLC 25**

Bickerstaff, Isaac

Author Index

See Swift, Jonathan
Bidart, Frank 1939- .... **CLC 33**
    See also CA 140
Bienek, Horst 1930- .... **CLC 7, 11**
    See also CA 73-76; DLB 75
Bierce, Ambrose (Gwinett) 1842-1914(?)
    **TCLC 1, 7, 44; DA; DAC; DAM MST; SSC
    9; WLC**
    See also CA 104; 139; CDALB 1865-1917;
    DLB 11, 12, 23, 71, 74, 186
Biggers, Earl Derr 1884-1933 .... **TCLC 65**
    See also CA 108; 153
Billings, Josh
    See Shaw, Henry Wheeler
Billington, (Lady) Rachel (Mary) 1942- **C L C
    43**
    See also AITN 2; CA 33-36R; CANR 44
Binyon, T(imothy) J(ohn) 1936- ...... **CLC 34**
    See also CA 111; CANR 28
Bioy Casares, Adolfo 1914-1984 **CLC 4, 8, 13,
    88; DAM MULT; HLC; SSC 17**
    See also CA 29-32R; CANR 19, 43; DLB 113;
    HW; MTCW
Bird, Cordwainer
    See Ellison, Harlan (Jay)
Bird, Robert Montgomery 1806-1854 **NCLC 1**
Birney, (Alfred) Earle 1904-1995 **CLC 1, 4, 6,
    11; DAC; DAM MST, POET**
    See also CA 1-4R; CANR 5, 20; DLB 88;
    MTCW
Bishop, Elizabeth 1911-1979 **CLC 1, 4, 9, 13,
    15, 32; DA; DAC; DAM MST, POET; PC
    3**
    See also CA 5-8R; 89-92; CABS 2; CANR 26,
    61; CDALB 1968-1988; DLB 5, 169;
    MTCW; SATA-Obit 24
Bishop, John 1935- .... **CLC 10**
    See also CA 105
Bissett, Bill 1939- .... **CLC 18; PC 14**
    See also CA 69-72; CAAS 19; CANR 15; DLB
    53; MTCW
Bitov, Andrei (Georgievich) 1937- ... **CLC 57**
    See also CA 142
Biyidi, Alexandre 1932-
    See Beti, Mongo
    See also BW 1; CA 114; 124; MTCW
Bjarme, Brynjolf
    See Ibsen, Henrik (Johan)
Bjornson, Bjornstjerne (Martinius) 1832-1910
    TCLC 7, 37
    See also CA 104
Black, Robert
    See Holdstock, Robert P.
Blackburn, Paul 1926-1971 .... **CLC 9, 43**
    See also CA 81-84; 33-36R; CANR 34; DLB
    16; DLBY 81
Black Elk 1863-1950 **TCLC 33; DAM MULT**
    See also CA 144; NNAL
Black Hobart
    See Sanders, (James) Ed(ward)
Blacklin, Malcolm
    See Chambers, Aidan
Blackmore, R(ichard) D(oddridge) 1825-1900
    TCLC 27
    See also CA 120; DLB 18
Blackmur, R(ichard) P(almer) 1904-1965
    CLC 2, 24
    See also CA 11-12; 25-28R; CAP 1; DLB 63
Black Tarantula
    See Acker, Kathy
Blackwood, Algernon (Henry) 1869-1951
    TCLC 5
    See also CA 105; 150; DLB 153, 156, 178

Blackwood, Caroline 1931-1996 **CLC 6, 9, 100**
    See also CA 85-88; 151; CANR 32, 61; DLB
    14; MTCW
Blade, Alexander
    See Hamilton, Edmond; Silverberg, Robert
Blaga, Lucian 1895-1961 .... **CLC 75**
Blair, Eric (Arthur) 1903-1950
    See Orwell, George
    See also CA 104; 132; DA; DAB; DAC; DAM
    MST, NOV; MTCW; SATA 29
Blais, Marie-Claire 1939- **CLC 2, 4, 6, 13, 22;
    DAC; DAM MST**
    See also CA 21-24R; CAAS 4; CANR 38; DLB
    53; MTCW
Blaise, Clark 1940- .... **CLC 29**
    See also AITN 2; CA 53-56; CAAS 3; CANR
    5; DLB 53
Blake, Fairley
    See De Voto, Bernard (Augustine)
Blake, Nicholas
    See Day Lewis, C(ecil)
    See also DLB 77
Blake, William 1757-1827 . **NCLC 13, 37, 57;
    DA; DAB; DAC; DAM MST, POET; PC
    12; WLC**
    See also CDBLB 1789-1832; DLB 93, 163;
    MAICYA; SATA 30
Blasco Ibanez, Vicente 1867-1928 **TCLC 12;
    DAM NOV**
    See also CA 110; 131; HW; MTCW
Blatty, William Peter 1928- **CLC 2; DAM POP**
    See also CA 5-8R; CANR 9
Bleeck, Oliver
    See Thomas, Ross (Elmore)
Blessing, Lee 1949- .... **CLC 54**
Blish, James (Benjamin) 1921-1975 . **CLC 14**
    See also CA 1-4R; 57-60; CANR 3; DLB 8;
    MTCW; SATA 66
Bliss, Reginald
    See Wells, H(erbert) G(eorge)
Blixen, Karen (Christentze Dinesen) 1885-1962
    See Dinesen, Isak
    See also CA 25-28; CANR 22, 50; CAP 2;
    MTCW; SATA 44
Bloch, Robert (Albert) 1917-1994 .... **CLC 33**
    See also CA 5-8R; 146; CAAS 20; CANR 5;
    DLB 44; INT CANR-5; SATA 12; SATA-Obit
    82
Blok, Alexander (Alexandrovich) 1880-1921
    TCLC 5; PC 21
    See also CA 104
Blom, Jan
    See Breytenbach, Breyten
Bloom, Harold 1930- .... **CLC 24, 103**
    See also CA 13-16R; CANR 39; DLB 67
Bloomfield, Aurelius
    See Bourne, Randolph S(illiman)
Blount, Roy (Alton), Jr. 1941- .... **CLC 38**
    See also CA 53-56; CANR 10, 28, 61; INT
    CANR-28; MTCW
Bloy, Leon 1846-1917 .... **TCLC 22**
    See also CA 121; DLB 123
Blume, Judy (Sussman) 1938- ... **CLC 12, 30;
    DAM NOV, POP**
    See also AAYA 3; CA 29-32R; CANR 13, 37;
    CLR 2, 15; DLB 52; JRDA; MAICYA;
    MTCW; SATA 2, 31, 79
Blunden, Edmund (Charles) 1896-1974 **C L C
    2, 56**
    See also CA 17-18; 45-48; CANR 54; CAP 2;
    DLB 20, 100, 155; MTCW
Bly, Robert (Elwood) 1926- **CLC 1, 2, 5, 10, 15,
    38; DAM POET**

See also CA 5-8R; CANR 41; DLB 5; MTCW
Boas, Franz 1858-1942 .... **TCLC 56**
    See also CA 115
Bobette
    See Simenon, Georges (Jacques Christian)
Boccaccio, Giovanni 1313-1375 .. **CMLC 13;
    SSC 10**
Bochco, Steven 1943- .... **CLC 35**
    See also AAYA 11; CA 124; 138
Bodenheim, Maxwell 1892-1954 .... **TCLC 44**
    See also CA 110; DLB 9, 45
Bodker, Cecil 1927- .... **CLC 21**
    See also CA 73-76; CANR 13, 44; CLR 23;
    MAICYA; SATA 14
Boell, Heinrich (Theodor) 1917-1985 **CLC 2,
    3, 6, 9, 11, 15, 27, 32, 72; DA; DAB; DAC;
    DAM MST, NOV; SSC 23; WLC**
    See also CA 21-24R; 116; CANR 24; DLB 69;
    DLBY 85; MTCW
Boerne, Alfred
    See Doeblin, Alfred
Boethius 480(?)-524(?) .... **CMLC 15**
    See also DLB 115
Bogan, Louise 1897-1970 . **CLC 4, 39, 46, 93;
    DAM POET; PC 12**
    See also CA 73-76; 25-28R; CANR 33; DLB
    45, 169; MTCW
Bogarde, Dirk .... **CLC 19**
    See also Van Den Bogarde, Derek Jules Gaspard
    Ulric Niven
    See also DLB 14
Bogosian, Eric 1953- .... **CLC 45**
    See also CA 138
Bograd, Larry 1953- .... **CLC 35**
    See also CA 93-96; CANR 57; SAAS 21; SATA
    33, 89
Boiardo, Matteo Maria 1441-1494 .... **LC 6**
Boileau-Despreaux, Nicolas 1636-1711 **LC 3**
Bojer, Johan 1872-1959 .... **TCLC 64**
Boland, Eavan (Aisling) 1944- .. **CLC 40, 67;
    DAM POET**
    See also CA 143; CANR 61; DLB 40
Bolt, Lee
    See Faust, Frederick (Schiller)
Bolt, Robert (Oxton) 1924-1995 ..... **CLC 14;
    DAM DRAM**
    See also CA 17-20R; 147; CANR 35; DLB 13;
    MTCW
Bombet, Louis-Alexandre-Cesar
    See Stendhal
Bomkauf
    See Kaufman, Bob (Garnell)
Bonaventura .... **NCLC 35**
    See also DLB 90
Bond, Edward 1934- **CLC 4, 6, 13, 23; DAM
    DRAM**
    See also CA 25-28R; CANR 38; DLB 13;
    MTCW
Bonham, Frank 1914-1989 .... **CLC 12**
    See also AAYA 1; CA 9-12R; CANR 4, 36;
    JRDA; MAICYA; SAAS 3; SATA 1, 49;
    SATA-Obit 62
Bonnefoy, Yves 1923- .. **CLC 9, 15, 58; DAM
    MST, POET**
    See also CA 85-88; CANR 33; MTCW
Bontemps, Arna(ud Wendell) 1902-1973 **C L C
    1, 18; BLC; DAM MULT, NOV, POET**
    See also BW 1; CA 1-4R; 41-44R; CANR 4,
    35; CLR 6; DLB 48, 51; JRDA; MAICYA;
    MTCW; SATA 2, 44; SATA-Obit 24
Booth, Martin 1944- .... **CLC 13**
    See also CA 93-96; CAAS 2
Booth, Philip 1925- .... **CLC 23**

See also CA 5-8R; CANR 5; DLBY 82

Booth, Wayne C(layson) 1921- .... **CLC 24**
See also CA 1-4R; CAAS 5; CANR 3, 43; DLB 67

Borchert, Wolfgang 1921-1947 .... **TCLC 5**
See also CA 104; DLB 69, 124

Borel, Petrus 1809-1859 .... **NCLC 41**

Borges, Jorge Luis 1899-1986 **CLC 1, 2, 3, 4, 6, 8, 9, 10, 13, 19, 44, 48, 83; DA; DAB; DAC; DAM MST, MULT; HLC; SSC 4; WLC**
See also AAYA 19; CA 21-24R; CANR 19, 33; DLB 113; DLBY 86; HW; MTCW

Borowski, Tadeusz 1922-1951 .... **TCLC 9**
See also CA 106; 154

Borrow, George (Henry) 1803-1881 **NCLC 9**
See also DLB 21, 55, 166

Bosman, Herman Charles 1905-1951 . **T C L C 49**
See also Malan, Herman
See also CA 160

Bosschere, Jean de 1878(?)-1953 ... **TCLC 19**
See also CA 115

Boswell, James 1740-1795 . **LC 4; DA; DAB; DAC; DAM MST; WLC**
See also CDBLB 1660-1789; DLB 104, 142

Bottoms, David 1949- .... **CLC 53**
See also CA 105; CANR 22; DLB 120; DLBY 83

Boucicault, Dion 1820-1890 .... **NCLC 41**

Boucolon, Maryse 1937(?)-
See Conde, Maryse
See also CA 110; CANR 30, 53

Bourget, Paul (Charles Joseph) 1852-1935 **TCLC 12**
See also CA 107; DLB 123

Bourjaily, Vance (Nye) 1922- .... **CLC 8, 62**
See also CA 1-4R; CAAS 1; CANR 2; DLB 2, 143

Bourne, Randolph S(illiman) 1886-1918 **TCLC 16**
See also CA 117; 155; DLB 63

Bova, Ben(jamin William) 1932- ..... **CLC 45**
See also AAYA 16; CA 5-8R; CAAS 18; CANR 11, 56; CLR 3; DLBY 81; INT CANR-11; MAICYA; MTCW; SATA 6, 68

Bowen, Elizabeth (Dorothea Cole) 1899-1973 **CLC 1, 3, 6, 11, 15, 22; DAM NOV; SSC 3, 28**
See also CA 17-18; 41-44R; CANR 35; CAP 2; CDBLB 1945-1960; DLB 15, 162; MTCW

Bowering, George 1935- .... **CLC 15, 47**
See also CA 21-24R; CAAS 16; CANR 10; DLB 53

Bowering, Marilyn R(uthe) 1949- ... **CLC 32**
See also CA 101; CANR 49

Bowers, Edgar 1924- .... **CLC 9**
See also CA 5-8R; CANR 24; DLB 5

Bowie, David .... **CLC 17**
See also Jones, David Robert

Bowles, Jane (Sydney) 1917-1973 **CLC 3, 68**
See also CA 19-20; 41-44R; CAP 2

Bowles, Paul (Frederick) 1910-1986 **CLC 1, 2, 19, 53; SSC 3**
See also CA 1-4R; CAAS 1; CANR 1, 19, 50; DLB 5, 6; MTCW

Box, Edgar
See Vidal, Gore

Boyd, Nancy
See Millay, Edna St. Vincent

Boyd, William 1952- .... **CLC 28, 53, 70**
See also CA 114; 120; CANR 51

Boyle, Kay 1902-1992 **CLC 1, 5, 19, 58; SSC 5**
See also CA 13-16R; 140; CAAS 1; CANR 29,

61; DLB 4, 9, 48, 86; DLBY 93; MTCW

Boyle, Mark
See Kienzle, William X(avier)

Boyle, Patrick 1905-1982 .... **CLC 19**
See also CA 127

Boyle, T. C. 1948-
See Boyle, T(homas) Coraghessan

Boyle, T(homas) Coraghessan 1948- **CLC 36, 55, 90; DAM POP; SSC 16**
See also BEST 90:4; CA 120; CANR 44; DLBY 86

Boz
See Dickens, Charles (John Huffam)

Brackenridge, Hugh Henry 1748-1816 **N C L C 7**
See also DLB 11, 37

Bradbury, Edward P.
See Moorcock, Michael (John)

Bradbury, Malcolm (Stanley) 1932- **CLC 32, 61; DAM NOV**
See also CA 1-4R; CANR 1, 33; DLB 14; MTCW

Bradbury, Ray (Douglas) 1920- **CLC 1, 3, 10, 15, 42, 98; DA; DAB; DAC; DAM MST, NOV, POP; SSC 29; WLC**
See also AAYA 15; AITN 1, 2; CA 1-4R; CANR 2, 30; CDALB 1968-1988; DLB 2, 8; MTCW; SATA 11, 64

Bradford, Gamaliel 1863-1932 ...... **TCLC 36**
See also CA 160; DLB 17

Bradley, David (Henry, Jr.) 1950- .. **CLC 23; BLC; DAM MULT**
See also BW 1; CA 104; CANR 26; DLB 33

Bradley, John Ed(mund, Jr.) 1958- .. **CLC 55**
See also CA 139

Bradley, Marion Zimmer 1930- **CLC 30; DAM POP**
See also AAYA 9; CA 57-60; CAAS 10; CANR 7, 31, 51; DLB 8; MTCW; SATA 90

Bradstreet, Anne 1612(?)-1672 **LC 4, 30; DA; DAC; DAM MST, POET; PC 10**
See also CDALB 1640-1865; DLB 24

Brady, Joan 1939- .... **CLC 86**
See also CA 141

Bragg, Melvyn 1939- .... **CLC 10**
See also BEST 89:3; CA 57-60; CANR 10, 48; DLB 14

Braine, John (Gerard) 1922-1986 **CLC 1, 3, 41**
See also CA 1-4R; 120; CANR 1, 33; CDBLB 1945-1960; DLB 15; DLBY 86; MTCW

Bramah, Ernest 1868-1942 .... **TCLC 72**
See also CA 156; DLB 70

Brammer, William 1930(?)-1978 .... **CLC 31**
See also CA 77-80

Brancati, Vitaliano 1907-1954 .... **TCLC 12**
See also CA 109

Brancato, Robin F(idler) 1936- .... **CLC 35**
See also AAYA 9; CA 69-72; CANR 11, 45; CLR 32; JRDA; SAAS 9; SATA 23

Brand, Max
See Faust, Frederick (Schiller)

Brand, Millen 1906-1980 .... **CLC 7**
See also CA 21-24R; 97-100

Branden, Barbara .... **CLC 44**
See also CA 148

Brandes, Georg (Morris Cohen) 1842-1927 **TCLC 10**
See also CA 105

Brandys, Kazimierz 1916- .... **CLC 62**

Branley, Franklyn M(ansfield) 1915- **CLC 21**
See also CA 33-36R; CANR 14, 39; CLR 13; MAICYA; SAAS 16; SATA 4, 68

Brathwaite, Edward Kamau 1930- **CLC 11;**

DAM POET
See also BW 2; CA 25-28R; CANR 11, 26, 47; DLB 125

Brautigan, Richard (Gary) 1935-1984 **CLC 1, 3, 5, 9, 12, 34, 42; DAM NOV**
See also CA 53-56; 113; CANR 34; DLB 2, 5; DLBY 80, 84; MTCW; SATA 56

Brave Bird, Mary 1953-
See Crow Dog, Mary (Ellen)
See also NNAL

Braverman, Kate 1950- .... **CLC 67**
See also CA 89-92

Brecht, (Eugen) Bertolt (Friedrich) 1898-1956 **TCLC 1, 6, 13, 35; DA; DAB; DAC; DAM DRAM, MST; DC 3; WLC**
See also CA 104; 133; CANR 62; DLB 56, 124; MTCW

Brecht, Eugen Berthold Friedrich
See Brecht, (Eugen) Bertolt (Friedrich)

Bremer, Fredrika 1801-1865 .... **NCLC 11**

Brennan, Christopher John 1870-1932 **T C L C 17**
See also CA 117

Brennan, Maeve 1917- .... **CLC 5**
See also CA 81-84

Brent, Linda
See Jacobs, Harriet

Brentano, Clemens (Maria) 1778-1842 **N C L C 1**
See also DLB 90

Brent of Bin Bin
See Franklin, (Stella Maraia Sarah) Miles

Brenton, Howard 1942- .... **CLC 31**
See also CA 69-72; CANR 33; DLB 13; MTCW

Breslin, James 1930-1996
See Breslin, Jimmy
See also CA 73-76; CANR 31; DAM NOV; MTCW

Breslin, Jimmy .... **CLC 4, 43**
See also Breslin, James
See also AITN 1

Bresson, Robert 1901- .... **CLC 16**
See also CA 110; CANR 49

Breton, Andre 1896-1966 **CLC 2, 9, 15, 54; PC 15**
See also CA 19-20; 25-28R; CANR 40, 60; CAP 2; DLB 65; MTCW

Breytenbach, Breyten 1939(?)- . **CLC 23, 37; DAM POET**
See also CA 113; 129; CANR 61

Bridgers, Sue Ellen 1942- .... **CLC 26**
See also AAYA 8; CA 65-68; CANR 11, 36; CLR 18; DLB 52; JRDA; MAICYA; SAAS 1; SATA 22, 90

Bridges, Robert (Seymour) 1844-1930 **T C L C 1; DAM POET**
See also CA 104; 152; CDBLB 1890-1914; DLB 19, 98

Bridie, James .... **TCLC 3**
See also Mavor, Osborne Henry
See also DLB 10

Brin, David 1950- .... **CLC 34**
See also AAYA 21; CA 102; CANR 24; INT CANR-24; SATA 65

Brink, Andre (Philippus) 1935- **CLC 18, 36, 106**
See also CA 104; CANR 39, 62; INT 103; MTCW

Brinsmead, H(esba) F(ay) 1922- ...... **CLC 21**
See also CA 21-24R; CANR 10; CLR 47; MAICYA; SAAS 5; SATA 18, 78

Brittain, Vera (Mary) 1893(?)-1970 **CLC 23**
See also CA 13-16; 25-28R; CANR 58; CAP 1;

MTCW

Broch, Hermann 1886-1951 .... **TCLC 20**
  See also CA 117; DLB 85, 124

Brock, Rose
  See Hansen, Joseph

Brodkey, Harold (Roy) 1930-1996 ... **CLC 56**
  See also CA 111; 151; DLB 130

Brodsky, Iosif Alexandrovich 1940-1996
  See Brodsky, Joseph
  See also AITN 1; CA 41-44R; 151; CANR 37;
    DAM POET; MTCW

Brodsky, Joseph 1940-1996 **CLC 4, 6, 13, 36,**
  100; PC 9
  See also Brodsky, Iosif Alexandrovich

Brodsky, Michael (Mark) 1948- .... **CLC 19**
  See also CA 102; CANR 18, 41, 58

Bromell, Henry 1947- .... **CLC 5**
  See also CA 53-56; CANR 9

Bromfield, Louis (Brucker) 1896-1956 **TCLC
  11**
  See also CA 107; 155; DLB 4, 9, 86

Broner, E(sther) M(asserman) 1930- **CLC 19**
  See also CA 17-20R; CANR 8, 25; DLB 28

Bronk, William 1918- .... **CLC 10**
  See also CA 89-92; CANR 23; DLB 165

Bronstein, Lev Davidovich
  See Trotsky, Leon

Bronte, Anne 1820-1849 .... **NCLC 4**
  See also DLB 21

Bronte, Charlotte 1816-1855 **NCLC 3, 8, 33,**
  58; DA; DAB; DAC; DAM MST, NOV;
  WLC
  See also AAYA 17; CDBLB 1832-1890; DLB
    21, 159

Bronte, Emily (Jane) 1818-1848 **NCLC 16, 35;**
  DA; DAB; DAC; DAM MST, NOV, POET;
  PC 8; WLC
  See also AAYA 17; CDBLB 1832-1890; DLB
    21, 32

Brooke, Frances 1724-1789 .... **LC 6**
  See also DLB 39, 99

Brooke, Henry 1703(?)-1783 .... **LC 1**
  See also DLB 39

Brooke, Rupert (Chawner) 1887-1915 **TCLC
  2, 7; DA; DAB; DAC; DAM MST, POET;**
  WLC
  See also CA 104; 132; CANR 61; CDBLB
    1914-1945; DLB 19; MTCW

Brooke-Haven, P.
  See Wodehouse, P(elham) G(renville)

Brooke-Rose, Christine 1926(?)- ...... **CLC 40**
  See also CA 13-16R; CANR 58; DLB 14

Brookner, Anita 1928- **CLC 32, 34, 51; DAB;**
  DAM POP
  See also CA 114; 120; CANR 37, 56; DLBY
    87; MTCW

Brooks, Cleanth 1906-1994 .... **CLC 24, 86**
  See also CA 17-20R; 145; CANR 33, 35; DLB
    63; DLBY 94; INT CANR-35; MTCW

Brooks, George
  See Baum, L(yman) Frank

Brooks, Gwendolyn 1917- **CLC 1, 2, 4, 5, 15,**
  49; BLC; DA; DAC; DAM MST, MULT,
  POET; PC 7; WLC
  See also AAYA 20; AITN 1; BW 2; CA 1-4R;
    CANR 1, 27, 52; CDALB 1941-1968; CLR
    27; DLB 5, 76, 165; MTCW; SATA 6

Brooks, Mel .... **CLC 12**
  See also Kaminsky, Melvin
  See also AAYA 13; DLB 26

Brooks, Peter 1938- .... **CLC 34**
  See also CA 45-48; CANR 1

Brooks, Van Wyck 1886-1963 .... **CLC 29**

See also CA 1-4R; CANR 6; DLB 45, 63, 103

Brophy, Brigid (Antonia) 1929-1995 . **CLC 6,**
  11, 29, 105
  See also CA 5-8R; 149; CAAS 4; CANR 25,
    53; DLB 14; MTCW

Brosman, Catharine Savage 1934- ..... **CLC 9**
  See also CA 61-64; CANR 21, 46

Brother Antoninus
  See Everson, William (Oliver)

The Brothers Quay
  See Quay, Stephen; Quay, Timothy

Broughton, T(homas) Alan 1936- ..... **CLC 19**
  See also CA 45-48; CANR 2, 23, 48

Broumas, Olga 1949- .... **CLC 10, 73**
  See also CA 85-88; CANR 20

Brown, Alan 1951- .... **CLC 99**

Brown, Charles Brockden 1771-1810 **NCLC
  22**
  See also CDALB 1640-1865; DLB 37, 59, 73

Brown, Christy 1932-1981 .... **CLC 63**
  See also CA 105; 104; DLB 14

Brown, Claude 1937- .. **CLC 30; BLC; DAM
  MULT**
  See also AAYA 7; BW 1; CA 73-76

Brown, Dee (Alexander) 1908- .. **CLC 18, 47;**
  DAM POP
  See also CA 13-16R; CAAS 6; CANR 11, 45,
    60; DLBY 80; MTCW; SATA 5

Brown, George
  See Wertmueller, Lina

Brown, George Douglas 1869-1902 **TCLC 28**

Brown, George Mackay 1921-1996 **CLC 5, 48,**
  100
  See also CA 21-24R; 151; CAAS 6; CANR 12,
    37, 62; DLB 14, 27, 139; MTCW; SATA 35

Brown, (William) Larry 1951- .... **CLC 73**
  See also CA 130; 134; INT 133

Brown, Moses
  See Barrett, William (Christopher)

Brown, Rita Mae 1944- **CLC 18, 43, 79; DAM
  NOV, POP**
  See also CA 45-48; CANR 2, 11, 35, 62; INT
    CANR-11; MTCW

Brown, Roderick (Langmere) Haig-
  See Haig-Brown, Roderick (Langmere)

Brown, Rosellen 1939- .... **CLC 32**
  See also CA 77-80; CAAS 10; CANR 14, 44

Brown, Sterling Allen 1901-1989 **CLC 1, 23,**
  59; BLC; DAM MULT, POET
  See also BW 1; CA 85-88; 127; CANR 26; DLB
    48, 51, 63; MTCW

Brown, Will
  See Ainsworth, William Harrison

Brown, William Wells 1813-1884 .. **NCLC 2;**
  BLC; DAM MULT; DC 1
  See also DLB 3, 50

Browne, (Clyde) Jackson 1948(?)- .... **CLC 21**
  See also CA 120

Browning, Elizabeth Barrett 1806-1861
  **NCLC 1, 16, 61, 66; DA; DAB; DAC; DAM
  MST, POET; PC 6; WLC**
  See also CDBLB 1832-1890; DLB 32

Browning, Robert 1812-1889 **NCLC 19; DA;**
  DAB; DAC; DAM MST, POET; PC 2;
  WLCS
  See also CDBLB 1832-1890; DLB 32, 163;
    YABC 1

Browning, Tod 1882-1962 .... **CLC 16**
  See also CA 141; 117

Brownson, Orestes (Augustus) 1803-1876
  NCLC 50

Bruccoli, Matthew J(oseph) 1931- .... **CLC 34**
  See also CA 9-12R; CANR 7; DLB 103

Bruce, Lenny .... **CLC 21**
  See also Schneider, Leonard Alfred

Bruin, John
  See Brutus, Dennis

Brulard, Henri
  See Stendhal

Brulls, Christian
  See Simenon, Georges (Jacques Christian)

Brunner, John (Kilian Houston) 1934-1995
  CLC 8, 10; DAM POP
  See also CA 1-4R; 149; CAAS 8; CANR 2, 37;
    MTCW

Bruno, Giordano 1548-1600 .... **LC 27**

Brutus, Dennis 1924- ... **CLC 43; BLC; DAM
  MULT, POET**
  See also BW 2; CA 49-52; CAAS 14; CANR 2,
    27, 42; DLB 117

Bryan, C(ourtlandt) D(ixon) B(arnes) 1936-
  CLC 29
  See also CA 73-76; CANR 13; INT CANR-13

Bryan, Michael
  See Moore, Brian

Bryant, William Cullen 1794-1878 . **NCLC 6,
  46; DA; DAB; DAC; DAM MST, POET;**
  PC 20
  See also CDALB 1640-1865; DLB 3, 43, 59

Bryusov, Valery Yakovlevich 1873-1924
  TCLC 10
  See also CA 107; 155

Buchan, John 1875-1940 .... **TCLC 41; DAB;**
  DAM POP
  See also CA 108; 145; DLB 34, 70, 156; YABC
    2

Buchanan, George 1506-1582 .... **LC 4**

Buchheim, Lothar-Guenther 1918- .... **CLC 6**
  See also CA 85-88

Buchner, (Karl) Georg 1813-1837 . **NCLC 26**

Buchwald, Art(hur) 1925- .... **CLC 33**
  See also AITN 1; CA 5-8R; CANR 21; MTCW;
    SATA 10

Buck, Pearl S(ydenstricker) 1892-1973 **CLC 7,
  11, 18; DA; DAB; DAC; DAM MST, NOV**
  See also AITN 1; CA 1-4R; 41-44R; CANR 1,
    34; DLB 9, 102; MTCW; SATA 1, 25

Buckler, Ernest 1908-1984 .... **CLC 13; DAC;**
  DAM MST
  See also CA 11-12; 114; CAP 1; DLB 68; SATA
    47

Buckley, Vincent (Thomas) 1925-1988 **CLC 57**
  See also CA 101

Buckley, William F(rank), Jr. 1925- **CLC 7, 18,
  37; DAM POP**
  See also AITN 1; CA 1-4R; CANR 1, 24, 53;
    DLB 137; DLBY 80; INT CANR-24; MTCW

Buechner, (Carl) Frederick 1926- **CLC 2, 4, 6,
  9; DAM NOV**
  See also CA 13-16R; CANR 11, 39, 64; DLBY
    80; INT CANR-11; MTCW

Buell, John (Edward) 1927- .... **CLC 10**
  See also CA 1-4R; DLB 53

Buero Vallejo, Antonio 1916- ..... **CLC 15, 46**
  See also CA 106; CANR 24, 49; HW; MTCW

Bufalino, Gesualdo 1920(?)- .... **CLC 74**

Bugayev, Boris Nikolayevich 1880-1934
  See Bely, Andrey
  See also CA 104

Bukowski, Charles 1920-1994 **CLC 2, 5, 9, 41,
  82, 108; DAM NOV, POET; PC 18**
  See also CA 17-20R; 144; CANR 40, 62; DLB
    5, 130, 169; MTCW

Bulgakov, Mikhail (Afanas'evich) 1891-1940
  TCLC 2, 16; DAM DRAM, NOV; SSC 18
  See also CA 105; 152

Bulgya, Alexander Alexandrovich 1901-1956
TCLC 53
See also Fadeyev, Alexander
See also CA 117

Bullins, Ed 1935- ... **CLC 1, 5, 7; BLC; DAM
DRAM, MULT; DC 6**
See also BW 2; CA 49-52; CAAS 16; CANR
24, 46; DLB 7, 38; MTCW

Bulwer-Lytton, Edward (George Earle Lytton)
1803-1873 .... **NCLC 1, 45**
See also DLB 21

Bunin, Ivan Alexeyevich 1870-1953 **TCLC 6;
SSC 5**
See also CA 104

Bunting, Basil 1900-1985 ..... **CLC 10, 39, 47;
DAM POET**
See also CA 53-56; 115; CANR 7; DLB 20

Bunuel, Luis 1900-1983 .. **CLC 16, 80; DAM
MULT; HLC**
See also CA 101; 110; CANR 32; HW

Bunyan, John 1628-1688 ... **LC 4; DA; DAB;
DAC; DAM MST; WLC**
See also CDBLB 1660-1789; DLB 39

Burckhardt, Jacob (Christoph) 1818-1897
NCLC 49

Burford, Eleanor
See Hibbert, Eleanor Alice Burford

**Burgess, Anthony CLC 1, 2, 4, 5, 8, 10, 13, 15,
22, 40, 62, 81, 94; DAB**
See also Wilson, John (Anthony) Burgess
See also AITN 1; CDBLB 1960 to Present; DLB
14

Burke, Edmund 1729(?)-1797 **LC 7, 36; DA;
DAB; DAC; DAM MST; WLC**
See also DLB 104

Burke, Kenneth (Duva) 1897-1993 **CLC 2, 24**
See also CA 5-8R; 143; CANR 39; DLB 45,
63; MTCW

Burke, Leda
See Garnett, David

Burke, Ralph
See Silverberg, Robert

Burke, Thomas 1886-1945 .... **TCLC 63**
See also CA 113; 155

Burney, Fanny 1752-1840 .... **NCLC 12, 54**
See also DLB 39

Burns, Robert 1759-1796 .... **PC 6**
See also CDBLB 1789-1832; DA; DAB; DAC;
DAM MST, POET; DLB 109; WLC

Burns, Tex
See L'Amour, Louis (Dearborn)

Burnshaw, Stanley 1906- .... **CLC 3, 13, 44**
See also CA 9-12R; DLB 48

Burr, Anne 1937- .... **CLC 6**
See also CA 25-28R

Burroughs, Edgar Rice 1875-1950 . **TCLC 2,
32; DAM NOV**
See also AAYA 11; CA 104; 132; DLB 8;
MTCW; SATA 41

Burroughs, William S(eward) 1914-1997 **CLC
1, 2, 5, 15, 22, 42, 75; DA; DAB; DAC;
DAM MST, NOV, POP; WLC**
See also AITN 2; CA 9-12R; 160; CANR 20,
52; DLB 2, 8, 16, 152; DLBY 81; MTCW

Burton, Richard F. 1821-1890 .... **NCLC 42**
See also DLB 55, 184

Busch, Frederick 1941- ..... **CLC 7, 10, 18, 47**
See also CA 33-36R; CAAS 1; CANR 45; DLB
6

Bush, Ronald 1946- .... **CLC 34**
See also CA 136

Bustos, F(rancisco)
See Borges, Jorge Luis

Bustos Domecq, H(onorio)
See Bioy Casares, Adolfo; Borges, Jorge Luis

Butler, Octavia E(stelle) 1947- **CLC 38; DAM
MULT, POP**
See also AAYA 18; BW 2; CA 73-76; CANR
12, 24, 38; DLB 33; MTCW; SATA 84

Butler, Robert Olen (Jr.) 1945- **CLC 81; DAM
POP**
See also CA 112; DLB 173; INT 112

Butler, Samuel 1612-1680 .... **LC 16**
See also DLB 101, 126

Butler, Samuel 1835-1902 . **TCLC 1, 33; DA;
DAB; DAC; DAM MST, NOV; WLC**
See also CA 143; CDBLB 1890-1914; DLB 18,
57, 174

Butler, Walter C.
See Faust, Frederick (Schiller)

Butor, Michel (Marie Francois) 1926- **CLC 1,
3, 8, 11, 15**
See also CA 9-12R; CANR 33; DLB 83; MTCW

Butts, Mary 1892(?)-1937 .... **TCLC 77**
See also CA 148

Buzo, Alexander (John) 1944- .... **CLC 61**
See also CA 97-100; CANR 17, 39

Buzzati, Dino 1906-1972 .... **CLC 36**
See also CA 160; 33-36R; DLB 177

Byars, Betsy (Cromer) 1928- .... **CLC 35**
See also AAYA 19; CA 33-36R; CANR 18, 36,
57; CLR 1, 16; DLB 52; INT CANR-18;
JRDA; MAICYA; MTCW; SAAS 1; SATA
4, 46, 80

Byatt, A(ntonia) S(usan Drabble) 1936- **C L C
19, 65; DAM NOV, POP**
See also CA 13-16R; CANR 13, 33, 50; DLB
14; MTCW

Byrne, David 1952- .... **CLC 26**
See also CA 127

Byrne, John Keyes 1926-
See Leonard, Hugh
See also CA 102; INT 102

Byron, George Gordon (Noel) 1788-1824
**NCLC 2, 12; DA; DAB; DAC; DAM MST,
POET; PC 16; WLC**
See also CDBLB 1789-1832; DLB 96, 110

Byron, Robert 1905-1941 .... **TCLC 67**
See also CA 160

C. 3. 3.
See Wilde, Oscar (Fingal O'Flahertie Wills)

Caballero, Fernan 1796-1877 .... **NCLC 10**

Cabell, Branch
See Cabell, James Branch

Cabell, James Branch 1879-1958 .... **TCLC 6**
See also CA 105; 152; DLB 9, 78

Cable, George Washington 1844-1925 **T C L C
4; SSC 4**
See also CA 104; 155; DLB 12, 74; DLBD 13

Cabral de Melo Neto, Joao 1920- ... **CLC 76;
DAM MULT**
See also CA 151

Cabrera Infante, G(uillermo) 1929- **CLC 5, 25,
45; DAM MULT; HLC**
See also CA 85-88; CANR 29; DLB 113; HW;
MTCW

Cade, Toni
See Bambara, Toni Cade

Cadmus and Harmonia
See Buchan, John

Caedmon fl. 658-680 .... **CMLC 7**
See also DLB 146

Caeiro, Alberto
See Pessoa, Fernando (Antonio Nogueira)

Cage, John (Milton, Jr.) 1912- .... **CLC 41**
See also CA 13-16R; CANR 9; INT CANR-9

Cahan, Abraham 1860-1951 .... **TCLC 71**
See also CA 108; 154; DLB 9, 25, 28

Cain, G.
See Cabrera Infante, G(uillermo)

Cain, Guillermo
See Cabrera Infante, G(uillermo)

Cain, James M(allahan) 1892-1977 **CLC 3, 11,
28**
See also AITN 1; CA 17-20R; 73-76; CANR 8,
34, 61; MTCW

Caine, Mark
See Raphael, Frederic (Michael)

Calasso, Roberto 1941- .... **CLC 81**
See also CA 143

Calderon de la Barca, Pedro 1600-1681 . **L C
23; DC 3**

Caldwell, Erskine (Preston) 1903-1987 **CLC 1,
8, 14, 50, 60; DAM NOV; SSC 19**
See also AITN 1; CA 1-4R; 121; CAAS 1;
CANR 2, 33; DLB 9, 86; MTCW

Caldwell, (Janet Miriam) Taylor (Holland)
1900-1985 **CLC 2, 28, 39; DAM NOV, POP**
See also CA 5-8R; 116; CANR 5

Calhoun, John Caldwell 1782-1850 **NCLC 15**
See also DLB 3

Calisher, Hortense 1911- **CLC 2, 4, 8, 38; DAM
NOV; SSC 15**
See also CA 1-4R; CANR 1, 22; DLB 2; INT
CANR-22; MTCW

Callaghan, Morley Edward 1903-1990 **CLC 3,
14, 41, 65; DAC; DAM MST**
See also CA 9-12R; 132; CANR 33; DLB 68;
MTCW

Callimachus c. 305B.C.-c. 240B.C. **CMLC 18**
See also DLB 176

Calvin, John 1509-1564 .... **LC 37**

Calvino, Italo 1923-1985 **CLC 5, 8, 11, 22, 33,
39, 73; DAM NOV; SSC 3**
See also CA 85-88; 116; CANR 23, 61; MTCW

Cameron, Carey 1952- .... **CLC 59**
See also CA 135

Cameron, Peter 1959- .... **CLC 44**
See also CA 125; CANR 50

Campana, Dino 1885-1932 .... **TCLC 20**
See also CA 117; DLB 114

Campanella, Tommaso 1568-1639 ...... **LC 32**

Campbell, John W(ood, Jr.) 1910-1971 **C L C
32**
See also CA 21-22; 29-32R; CANR 34; CAP 2;
DLB 8; MTCW

Campbell, Joseph 1904-1987 .... **CLC 69**
See also AAYA 3; BEST 89:2; CA 1-4R; 124;
CANR 3, 28, 61; MTCW

Campbell, Maria 1940- .... **CLC 85; DAC**
See also CA 102; CANR 54; NNAL

Campbell, (John) Ramsey 1946- **CLC 42; SSC
19**
See also CA 57-60; CANR 7; INT CANR-7

Campbell, (Ignatius) Roy (Dunnachie) 1901-
1957 .... **TCLC 5**
See also CA 104; 155; DLB 20

Campbell, Thomas 1777-1844 .... **NCLC 19**
See also DLB 93; 144

Campbell, Wilfred .... **TCLC 9**
See also Campbell, William

Campbell, William 1858(?)-1918
See Campbell, Wilfred
See also CA 106; DLB 92

Campion, Jane .... **CLC 95**
See also CA 138

Campos, Alvaro de
See Pessoa, Fernando (Antonio Nogueira)

Camus, Albert 1913-1960 **CLC 1, 2, 4, 9, 11, 14,**

32, 63, 69; DA; DAB; DAC; DAM DRAM, MST, NOV; DC 2; SSC 9; WLC
See also CA 89-92; DLB 72; MTCW

Canby, Vincent 1924- .... **CLC 13**
See also CA 81-84

Cancale
See Desnos, Robert

Canetti, Elias 1905-1994**CLC 3, 14, 25, 75, 86**
See also CA 21-24R; 146; CANR 23, 61; DLB 85, 124; MTCW

Canin, Ethan 1960- .... **CLC 55**
See also CA 131; 135

Cannon, Curt
See Hunter, Evan

Cape, Judith
See Page, P(atricia) K(athleen)

Capek, Karel 1890-1938 ... **TCLC 6, 37; DA; DAB; DAC; DAM DRAM, MST, NOV; DC 1; WLC**
See also CA 104; 140

Capote, Truman 1924-1984**CLC 1, 3, 8, 13, 19, 34, 38, 58; DA; DAB; DAC; DAM MST, NOV, POP; SSC 2; WLC**
See also CA 5-8R; 113; CANR 18, 62; CDALB 1941-1968; DLB 2; DLBY 80, 84; MTCW; SATA 91

Capra, Frank 1897-1991 .... **CLC 16**
See also CA 61-64; 135

Caputo, Philip 1941- .... **CLC 32**
See also CA 73-76; CANR 40

Caragiale, Ion Luca 1852-1912 ...... **TCLC 76**
See also CA 157

Card, Orson Scott 1951-**CLC 44, 47, 50; DAM POP**
See also AAYA 11; CA 102; CANR 27, 47; INT CANR-27; MTCW; SATA 83

Cardenal, Ernesto 1925- .... **CLC 31; DAM MULT, POET; HLC**
See also CA 49-52; CANR 2, 32; HW; MTCW

Cardozo, Benjamin N(athan) 1870-1938
TCLC 65
See also CA 117

Carducci, Giosue (Alessandro Giuseppe) 1835-1907 .... **TCLC 32**

Carew, Thomas 1595(?)-1640 .... **LC 13**
See also DLB 126

Carey, Ernestine Gilbreth 1908- ...... **CLC 17**
See also CA 5-8R; SATA 2

Carey, Peter 1943- .... **CLC 40, 55, 96**
See also CA 123; 127; CANR 53; INT 127; MTCW; SATA 94

Carleton, William 1794-1869 .... **NCLC 3**
See also DLB 159

Carlisle, Henry (Coffin) 1926- .... **CLC 33**
See also CA 13-16R; CANR 15

Carlsen, Chris
See Holdstock, Robert P.

Carlson, Ron(ald F.) 1947- .... **CLC 54**
See also CA 105; CANR 27

Carlyle, Thomas 1795-1881 .. **NCLC 22; DA; DAB; DAC; DAM MST**
See also CDBLB 1789-1832; DLB 55; 144

Carman, (William) Bliss 1861-1929 **TCLC 7; DAC**
See also CA 104; 152; DLB 92

Carnegie, Dale 1888-1955 .... **TCLC 53**

Carossa, Hans 1878-1956 .... **TCLC 48**
See also DLB 66

Carpenter, Don(ald Richard) 1931-1995**C L C 41**
See also CA 45-48; 149; CANR 1

Carpentier (y Valmont), Alejo 1904-1980**CLC 8, 11, 38; DAM MULT; HLC**

See also CA 65-68; 97-100; CANR 11; DLB 113; HW

Carr, Caleb 1955(?)- .... **CLC 86**
See also CA 147

Carr, Emily 1871-1945 .... **TCLC 32**
See also CA 159; DLB 68

Carr, John Dickson 1906-1977 .... **CLC 3**
See also Fairbairn, Roger
See also CA 49-52; 69-72; CANR 3, 33, 60; MTCW

Carr, Philippa
See Hibbert, Eleanor Alice Burford

Carr, Virginia Spencer 1929- .... **CLC 34**
See also CA 61-64; DLB 111

Carrere, Emmanuel 1957- .... **CLC 89**

Carrier, Roch 1937-**CLC 13, 78; DAC; DAM MST**
See also CA 130; CANR 61; DLB 53

Carroll, James P. 1943(?)- .... **CLC 38**
See also CA 81-84

Carroll, Jim 1951- .... **CLC 35**
See also AAYA 17; CA 45-48; CANR 42

Carroll, Lewis ...... **NCLC 2, 53; PC 18; WLC**
See also Dodgson, Charles Lutwidge
See also CDBLB 1832-1890; CLR 2, 18; DLB 18, 163, 178; JRDA

Carroll, Paul Vincent 1900-1968 ...... **CLC 10**
See also CA 9-12R; 25-28R; DLB 10

Carruth, Hayden 1921- **CLC 4, 7, 10, 18, 84; PC 10**
See also CA 9-12R; CANR 4, 38, 59; DLB 5, 165; INT CANR-4; MTCW; SATA 47

Carson, Rachel Louise 1907-1964 .. **CLC 71; DAM POP**
See also CA 77-80; CANR 35; MTCW; SATA 23

Carter, Angela (Olive) 1940-1992 **CLC 5, 41, 76; SSC 13**
See also CA 53-56; 136; CANR 12, 36, 61; DLB 14; MTCW; SATA 66; SATA-Obit 70

Carter, Nick
See Smith, Martin Cruz

Carver, Raymond 1938-1988**CLC 22, 36, 53, 55; DAM NOV; SSC 8**
See also CA 33-36R; 126; CANR 17, 34, 61; DLB 130; DLBY 84, 88; MTCW

Cary, Elizabeth, Lady Falkland 1585-1639
LC 30

Cary, (Arthur) Joyce (Lunel) 1888-1957
TCLC 1, 29
See also CA 104; CDBLB 1914-1945; DLB 15, 100

Casanova de Seingalt, Giovanni Jacopo 1725-1798 .... **LC 13**

Casares, Adolfo Bioy
See Bioy Casares, Adolfo

Casely-Hayford, J(oseph) E(phraim) 1866-1930
TCLC 24; BLC; DAM MULT
See also BW 2; CA 123; 152

Casey, John (Dudley) 1939- .... **CLC 59**
See also BEST 90:2; CA 69-72; CANR 23

Casey, Michael 1947- .... **CLC 2**
See also CA 65-68; DLB 5

Casey, Patrick
See Thurman, Wallace (Henry)

Casey, Warren (Peter) 1935-1988 ..... **CLC 12**
See also CA 101; 127; INT 101

Casona, Alejandro .... **CLC 49**
See also Alvarez, Alejandro Rodriguez

Cassavetes, John 1929-1989 .... **CLC 20**
See also CA 85-88; 127

Cassian, Nina 1924- .... **PC 17**

Cassill, R(onald) V(erlin) 1919- ... **CLC 4, 23**

See also CA 9-12R; CAAS 1; CANR 7, 45; DLB 6

Cassirer, Ernst 1874-1945 .... **TCLC 61**
See also CA 157

Cassity, (Allen) Turner 1929- .... **CLC 6, 42**
See also CA 17-20R; CAAS 8; CANR 11; DLB 105

Castaneda, Carlos 1931(?)- .... **CLC 12**
See also CA 25-28R; CANR 32; HW; MTCW

Castedo, Elena 1937- .... **CLC 65**
See also CA 132

Castedo-Ellerman, Elena
See Castedo, Elena

Castellanos, Rosario 1925-1974**CLC 66; DAM MULT; HLC**
See also CA 131; 53-56; CANR 58; DLB 113; HW

Castelvetro, Lodovico 1505-1571 .... **LC 12**

Castiglione, Baldassare 1478-1529 ..... **LC 12**

Castle, Robert
See Hamilton, Edmond

Castro, Guillen de 1569-1631 .... **LC 19**

Castro, Rosalia de 1837-1885**NCLC 3; DAM MULT**

Cather, Willa
See Cather, Willa Sibert

Cather, Willa Sibert 1873-1947 **TCLC 1, 11, 31; DA; DAB; DAC; DAM MST, NOV; SSC 2; WLC**
See also CA 104; 128; CDALB 1865-1917; DLB 9, 54, 78; DLBD 1; MTCW; SATA 30

Cato, Marcus Porcius 234B.C.-149B.C.
CMLC 21

Catton, (Charles) Bruce 1899-1978 ..**CLC 35**
See also AITN 1; CA 5-8R; 81-84; CANR 7; DLB 17; SATA 2; SATA-Obit 24

Catullus c. 84B.C.-c. 54B.C. .... **CMLC 18**

Cauldwell, Frank
See King, Francis (Henry)

Caunitz, William J. 1933-1996 .... **CLC 34**
See also BEST 89:3; CA 125; 130; 152; INT 130

Causley, Charles (Stanley) 1917- .... **CLC 7**
See also CA 9-12R; CANR 5, 35; CLR 30; DLB 27; MTCW; SATA 3, 66

Caute, (John) David 1936- ..... **CLC 29; DAM NOV**
See also CA 1-4R; CAAS 4; CANR 1, 33, 64; DLB 14

Cavafy, C(onstantine) P(eter) 1863-1933
TCLC 2, 7; DAM POET
See also Kavafis, Konstantinos Petrou
See also CA 148

Cavallo, Evelyn
See Spark, Muriel (Sarah)

Cavanna, Betty .... **CLC 12**
See also Harrison, Elizabeth Cavanna
See also JRDA; MAICYA; SAAS 4; SATA 1, 30

Cavendish, Margaret Lucas 1623-1673**LC 30**
See also DLB 131

Caxton, William 1421(?)-1491(?) .... **LC 17**
See also DLB 170

Cayrol, Jean 1911- .... **CLC 11**
See also CA 89-92; DLB 83

Cela, Camilo Jose 1916-**CLC 4, 13, 59; DAM MULT; HLC**
See also BEST 90:2; CA 21-24R; CAAS 10; CANR 21, 32; DLBY 89; HW; MTCW

Celan, Paul .... **CLC 10, 19, 53, 82; PC 10**
See also Antschel, Paul
See also DLB 69

Celine, Louis-Ferdinand**CLC 1, 3, 4, 7, 9, 15,**

47
See also Destouches, Louis-Ferdinand
See also DLB 72
Cellini, Benvenuto 1500-1571 .... **LC 7**
Cendrars, Blaise 1887-1961 ..... **CLC 18, 106**
See also Sauser-Hall, Frederic
Cernuda (y Bidon), Luis 1902-1963 **CLC 54;
DAM POET**
See also CA 131; 89-92; DLB 134; HW
Cervantes (Saavedra), Miguel de 1547-1616
**LC 6, 23; DA; DAB; DAC; DAM MST,
NOV; SSC 12; WLC**
Cesaire, Aime (Fernand) 1913- . **CLC 19, 32;
BLC; DAM MULT, POET**
See also BW 2; CA 65-68; CANR 24, 43;
MTCW
Chabon, Michael 1963- .... **CLC 55**
See also CA 139; CANR 57
Chabrol, Claude 1930- .... **CLC 16**
See also CA 110
Challans, Mary 1905-1983
See Renault, Mary
See also CA 81-84; 111; SATA 23; SATA-Obit
36
Challis, George
See Faust, Frederick (Schiller)
Chambers, Aidan 1934- .... **CLC 35**
See also CA 25-28R; CANR 12, 31, 58; JRDA;
MAICYA; SAAS 12; SATA 1, 69
Chambers, James 1948-
See Cliff, Jimmy
See also CA 124
Chambers, Jessie
See Lawrence, D(avid) H(erbert Richards)
Chambers, Robert W. 1865-1933 ... **TCLC 41**
Chandler, Raymond (Thornton) 1888-1959
TCLC 1, 7; SSC 23
See also CA 104; 129; CANR 60; CDALB
1929-1941; DLBD 6; MTCW
Chang, Eileen 1921- .... **SSC 28**
Chang, Jung 1952- .... **CLC 71**
See also CA 142
Channing, William Ellery 1780-1842 . **N C L C
17**
See also DLB 1, 59
Chaplin, Charles Spencer 1889-1977 **CLC 16**
See also Chaplin, Charlie
See also CA 81-84; 73-76
Chaplin, Charlie
See Chaplin, Charles Spencer
See also DLB 44
Chapman, George 1559(?)-1634 **LC 22; DAM
DRAM**
See also DLB 62, 121
Chapman, Graham 1941-1989 .... **CLC 21**
See also Monty Python
See also CA 116; 129; CANR 35
Chapman, John Jay 1862-1933 .... **TCLC 7**
See also CA 104
Chapman, Lee
See Bradley, Marion Zimmer
Chapman, Walker
See Silverberg, Robert
Chappell, Fred (Davis) 1936- ..... **CLC 40, 78**
See also CA 5-8R; CAAS 4; CANR 8, 33; DLB
6, 105
Char, Rene(-Emile) 1907-1988 **CLC 9, 11, 14,
55; DAM POET**
See also CA 13-16R; 124; CANR 32; MTCW
Charby, Jay
See Ellison, Harlan (Jay)
Chardin, Pierre Teilhard de
See Teilhard de Chardin, (Marie Joseph) Pierre

Charles I 1600-1649 .... **LC 13**
Charriere, Isabelle de 1740-1805 ... **NCLC 66**
Charyn, Jerome 1937- .... **CLC 5, 8, 18**
See also CA 5-8R; CAAS 1; CANR 7, 61;
DLBY 83; MTCW
Chase, Mary (Coyle) 1907-1981 .... **DC 1**
See also CA 77-80; 105; SATA 17; SATA-Obit
29
Chase, Mary Ellen 1887-1973 .... **CLC 2**
See also CA 13-16; 41-44R; CAP 1; SATA 10
Chase, Nicholas
See Hyde, Anthony
Chateaubriand, Francois Rene de 1768-1848
NCLC 3
See also DLB 119
Chatterje, Sarat Chandra 1876-1936(?)
See Chatterji, Saratchandra
See also CA 109
Chatterji, Bankim Chandra 1838-1894 **NCLC
19**
Chatterji, Saratchandra .... **TCLC 13**
See also Chatterje, Sarat Chandra
Chatterton, Thomas 1752-1770 . **LC 3; DAM
POET**
See also DLB 109
Chatwin, (Charles) Bruce 1940-1989 **CLC 28,
57, 59; DAM POP**
See also AAYA 4; BEST 90:1; CA 85-88; 127
Chaucer, Daniel
See Ford, Ford Madox
Chaucer, Geoffrey 1340(?)-1400 **LC 17; DA;
DAB; DAC; DAM MST, POET; PC 19;
WLCS**
See also CDBLB Before 1660; DLB 146
Chaviaras, Strates 1935-
See Haviaras, Stratis
See also CA 105
Chayefsky, Paddy .... **CLC 23**
See also Chayefsky, Sidney
See also DLB 7, 44; DLBY 81
Chayefsky, Sidney 1923-1981
See Chayefsky, Paddy
See also CA 9-12R; 104; CANR 18; DAM
DRAM
Chedid, Andree 1920- .... **CLC 47**
See also CA 145
Cheever, John 1912-1982 **CLC 3, 7, 8, 11, 15,
25, 64; DA; DAB; DAC; DAM MST, NOV,
POP; SSC 1; WLC**
See also CA 5-8R; 106; CABS 1; CANR 5, 27;
CDALB 1941-1968; DLB 2, 102; DLBY 80,
82; INT CANR-5; MTCW
Cheever, Susan 1943- .... **CLC 18, 48**
See also CA 103; CANR 27, 51; DLBY 82; INT
CANR-27
Chekhonte, Antosha
See Chekhov, Anton (Pavlovich)
Chekhov, Anton (Pavlovich) 1860-1904 **TCLC
3, 10, 31, 55; DA; DAB; DAC; DAM
DRAM, MST; SSC 2, 28; WLC**
See also CA 104; 124; SATA 90
Chernyshevsky, Nikolay Gavrilovich 1828-1889
NCLC 1
Cherry, Carolyn Janice 1942-
See Cherryh, C. J.
See also CA 65-68; CANR 10
Cherryh, C. J. .... **CLC 35**
See also Cherry, Carolyn Janice
See also DLBY 80; SATA 93
Chesnutt, Charles W(addell) 1858-1932
TCLC 5, 39; BLC; DAM MULT; SSC 7
See also BW 1; CA 106; 125; DLB 12, 50, 78;
MTCW

Chester, Alfred 1929(?)-1971 .... **CLC 49**
See also CA 33-36R; DLB 130
Chesterton, G(ilbert) K(eith) 1874-1936
TCLC 1, 6, 64; DAM NOV, POET; SSC 1
See also CA 104; 132; CDBLB 1914-1945;
DLB 10, 19, 34, 70, 98, 149, 178; MTCW;
SATA 27
Chiang Pin-chin 1904-1986
See Ding Ling
See also CA 118
Ch'ien Chung-shu 1910- .... **CLC 22**
See also CA 130; MTCW
Child, L. Maria
See Child, Lydia Maria
Child, Lydia Maria 1802-1880 .... **NCLC 6**
See also DLB 1, 74; SATA 67
Child, Mrs.
See Child, Lydia Maria
Child, Philip 1898-1978 .... **CLC 19, 68**
See also CA 13-14; CAP 1; SATA 47
Childers, (Robert) Erskine 1870-1922 **T C L C
65**
See also CA 113; 153; DLB 70
Childress, Alice 1920-1994 **CLC 12, 15, 86, 96;
BLC; DAM DRAM, MULT, NOV; DC 4**
See also AAYA 8; BW 2; CA 45-48; 146; CANR
3, 27, 50; CLR 14; DLB 7, 38; JRDA;
MAICYA; MTCW; SATA 7, 48, 81
Chin, Frank (Chew, Jr.) 1940- .... **DC 7**
See also CA 33-36R; DAM MULT
Chislett, (Margaret) Anne 1943- ...... **CLC 34**
See also CA 151
Chitty, Thomas Willes 1926- .... **CLC 11**
See also Hinde, Thomas
See also CA 5-8R
Chivers, Thomas Holley 1809-1858 **NCLC 49**
See also DLB 3
Chomette, Rene Lucien 1898-1981
See Clair, Rene
See also CA 103
Chopin, Kate **TCLC 5, 14; DA; DAB; SSC 8;
WLCS**
See also Chopin, Katherine
See also CDALB 1865-1917; DLB 12, 78
Chopin, Katherine 1851-1904
See Chopin, Kate
See also CA 104; 122; DAC; DAM MST, NOV
Chretien de Troyes c. 12th cent. - .. **CMLC 10**
Christie
See Ichikawa, Kon
Christie, Agatha (Mary Clarissa) 1890-1976
**CLC 1, 6, 8, 12, 39, 48; DAB; DAC; DAM
NOV**
See also AAYA 9; AITN 1, 2; CA 17-20R; 61-
64; CANR 10, 37; CDBLB 1914-1945; DLB
13, 77; MTCW; SATA 36
Christie, (Ann) Philippa
See Pearce, Philippa
See also CA 5-8R; CANR 4
Christine de Pizan 1365(?)-1431(?) ...... **LC 9**
Chubb, Elmer
See Masters, Edgar Lee
Chulkov, Mikhail Dmitrievich 1743-1792 **LC 2**
See also DLB 150
Churchill, Caryl 1938- ..... **CLC 31, 55; DC 5**
See also CA 102; CANR 22, 46; DLB 13;
MTCW
Churchill, Charles 1731-1764 .... **LC 3**
See also DLB 109
Chute, Carolyn 1947- .... **CLC 39**
See also CA 123
Ciardi, John (Anthony) 1916-1986 . **CLC 10,
40, 44; DAM POET**

See also CA 5-8R; 118; CAAS 2; CANR 5, 33; CLR 19; DLB 5; DLBY 86; INT CANR-5; MAICYA; MTCW; SATA 1, 65; SATA-Obit 46

Cicero, Marcus Tullius 106B.C.-43B.C. **CMLC 3**

Cimino, Michael 1943- .... **CLC 16**
See also CA 105

Cioran, E(mil) M. 1911-1995 .... **CLC 64**
See also CA 25-28R; 149

Cisneros, Sandra 1954-**CLC 69; DAM MULT; HLC**
See also AAYA 9; CA 131; CANR 64; DLB 122, 152; HW

Cixous, Helene 1937-......................... **CLC 92**
See also CA 126; CANR 55; DLB 83; MTCW

Clair, Rene .... **CLC 20**
See also Chomette, Rene Lucien

Clampitt, Amy 1920-1994 ..... **CLC 32; PC 19**
See also CA 110; 146; CANR 29; DLB 105

Clancy, Thomas L., Jr. 1947-
See Clancy, Tom
See also CA 125; 131; CANR 62; INT 131; MTCW

Clancy, Tom .... **CLC 45; DAM NOV, POP**
See also Clancy, Thomas L., Jr.
See also AAYA 9; BEST 89:1, 90:1

Clare, John 1793-1864 **NCLC 9; DAB; DAM POET**
See also DLB 55, 96

Clarin
See Alas (y Urena), Leopoldo (Enrique Garcia)

Clark, Al C.
See Goines, Donald

Clark, (Robert) Brian 1932-............. **CLC 29**
See also CA 41-44R

Clark, Curt
See Westlake, Donald E(dwin)

Clark, Eleanor 1913-1996 .... **CLC 5, 19**
See also CA 9-12R; 151; CANR 41; DLB 6

Clark, J. P.
See Clark, John Pepper
See also DLB 117

Clark, John Pepper 1935-......**CLC 38; BLC; DAM DRAM, MULT; DC 5**
See also Clark, J. P.
See also BW 1; CA 65-68; CANR 16

Clark, M. R.
See Clark, Mavis Thorpe

Clark, Mavis Thorpe 1909- .... **CLC 12**
See also CA 57-60; CANR 8, 37; CLR 30; MAICYA; SAAS 5; SATA 8, 74

Clark, Walter Van Tilburg 1909-1971**CLC 28**
See also CA 9-12R; 33-36R; CANR 63; DLB 9; SATA 8

Clarke, Arthur C(harles) 1917-**CLC 1, 4, 13, 18, 35; DAM POP; SSC 3**
See also AAYA 4; CA 1-4R; CANR 2, 28, 55; JRDA; MAICYA; MTCW; SATA 13, 70

Clarke, Austin 1896-1974 ....**CLC 6, 9; DAM POET**
See also CA 29-32; 49-52; CAP 2; DLB 10, 20

Clarke, Austin C(hesterfield) 1934-**CLC 8, 53; BLC; DAC; DAM MULT**
See also BW 1; CA 25-28R; CAAS 16; CANR 14, 32; DLB 53, 125

Clarke, Gillian 1937-......................... **CLC 61**
See also CA 106; DLB 40

Clarke, Marcus (Andrew Hislop) 1846-1881 **NCLC 19**

Clarke, Shirley 1925- .... **CLC 16**

Clash, The
See Headon, (Nicky) Topper; Jones, Mick;

Simonon, Paul; Strummer, Joe

Claudel, Paul (Louis Charles Marie) 1868-1955 **TCLC 2, 10**
See also CA 104

Clavell, James (duMaresq) 1925-1994**CLC 6, 25, 87; DAM NOV, POP**
See also CA 25-28R; 146; CANR 26, 48; MTCW

Cleaver, (Leroy) Eldridge 1935- ..... **CLC 30; BLC; DAM MULT**
See also BW 1; CA 21-24R; CANR 16

Cleese, John (Marwood) 1939- ....**CLC 21**
See also Monty Python
See also CA 112; 116; CANR 35; MTCW

Cleishbotham, Jebediah
See Scott, Walter

Cleland, John 1710-1789 .... **LC 2**
See also DLB 39

Clemens, Samuel Langhorne 1835-1910
See Twain, Mark
See also CA 104; 135; CDALB 1865-1917; DA; DAB; DAC; DAM MST, NOV; DLB 11, 12, 23, 64, 74, 186; JRDA; MAICYA; YABC 2

Cleophil
See Congreve, William

Clerihew, E.
See Bentley, E(dmund) C(lerihew)

Clerk, N. W.
See Lewis, C(live) S(taples)

Cliff, Jimmy ....**CLC 21**
See also Chambers, James

Clifton, (Thelma) Lucille 1936- **CLC 19, 66; BLC; DAM MULT, POET; PC 17**
See also BW 2; CA 49-52; CANR 2, 24, 42; CLR 5; DLB 5, 41; MAICYA; MTCW; SATA 20, 69

Clinton, Dirk
See Silverberg, Robert

Clough, Arthur Hugh 1819-1861 ... **NCLC 27**
See also DLB 32

Clutha, Janet Paterson Frame 1924-
See Frame, Janet
See also CA 1-4R; CANR 2, 36; MTCW

Clyne, Terence
See Blatty, William Peter

Cobalt, Martin
See Mayne, William (James Carter)

Cobb, Irvin S. 1876-1944 .... **TCLC 77**
See also DLB 11, 25, 86

Cobbett, William 1763-1835 .... **NCLC 49**
See also DLB 43, 107, 158

Coburn, D(onald) L(ee) 1938- .... **CLC 10**
See also CA 89-92

Cocteau, Jean (Maurice Eugene Clement) 1889-1963**CLC 1, 8, 15, 16, 43; DA; DAB; DAC; DAM DRAM, MST, NOV; WLC**
See also CA 25-28; CANR 40; CAP 2; DLB 65; MTCW

Codrescu, Andrei 1946-**CLC 46; DAM POET**
See also CA 33-36R; CAAS 19; CANR 13, 34, 53

Coe, Max
See Bourne, Randolph S(illiman)

Coe, Tucker
See Westlake, Donald E(dwin)

Coen, Ethan 1958- .... **CLC 108**
See also CA 126

Coen, Joel 1955- .... **CLC 108**
See also CA 126

Coetzee, J(ohn) M(ichael) 1940- **CLC 23, 33, 66; DAM NOV**
See also CA 77-80; CANR 41, 54; MTCW

Coffey, Brian
See Koontz, Dean R(ay)

Cohan, George M(ichael) 1878-1942**TCLC 60**
See also CA 157

Cohen, Arthur A(llen) 1928-1986 **CLC 7, 31**
See also CA 1-4R; 120; CANR 1, 17, 42; DLB 28

Cohen, Leonard (Norman) 1934- **CLC 3, 38; DAC; DAM MST**
See also CA 21-24R; CANR 14; DLB 53; MTCW

Cohen, Matt 1942-...................**CLC 19; DAC**
See also CA 61-64; CAAS 18; CANR 40; DLB 53

Cohen-Solal, Annie 19(?)- ....**CLC 50**

Colegate, Isabel 1931- ....**CLC 36**
See also CA 17-20R; CANR 8, 22; DLB 14; INT CANR-22; MTCW

Coleman, Emmett
See Reed, Ishmael

Coleridge, M. E.
See Coleridge, Mary E(lizabeth)

Coleridge, Mary E(lizabeth) 1861-1907**TCLC 73**
See also CA 116; DLB 19, 98

Coleridge, Samuel Taylor 1772-1834**NCLC 9, 54; DA; DAB; DAC; DAM MST, POET; PC 11; WLC**
See also CDBLB 1789-1832; DLB 93, 107

Coleridge, Sara 1802-1852 .... **NCLC 31**

Coles, Don 1928- ....**CLC 46**
See also CA 115; CANR 38

Coles, Robert (Martin) 1929- .... **CLC 108**
See also CA 45-48; CANR 3, 32; INT CANR-32; SATA 23

Colette, (Sidonie-Gabrielle) 1873-1954**T C L C 1, 5, 16; DAM NOV; SSC 10**
See also CA 104; 131; DLB 65; MTCW

Collett, (Jacobine) Camilla (Wergeland) 1813-1895 ....**NCLC 22**

Collier, Christopher 1930-..................**CLC 30**
See also AAYA 13; CA 33-36R; CANR 13, 33; JRDA; MAICYA; SATA 16, 70

Collier, James L(incoln) 1928-**CLC 30; DAM POP**
See also AAYA 13; CA 9-12R; CANR 4, 33, 60; CLR 3; JRDA; MAICYA; SAAS 21; SATA 8, 70

Collier, Jeremy 1650-1726 .... **LC 6**

Collier, John 1901-1980 ....**SSC 19**
See also CA 65-68; 97-100; CANR 10; DLB 77

Collingwood, R(obin) G(eorge) 1889(?)-1943 **TCLC 67**
See also CA 117; 155

Collins, Hunt
See Hunter, Evan

Collins, Linda 1931- ....**CLC 44**
See also CA 125

Collins, (William) Wilkie 1824-1889**NCLC 1, 18**
See also CDBLB 1832-1890; DLB 18, 70, 159

Collins, William 1721-1759 . **LC 4, 40; DAM POET**
See also DLB 109

Collodi, Carlo 1826-1890 ....**NCLC 54**
See also Lorenzini, Carlo
See also CLR 5

Colman, George
See Glassco, John

Colt, Winchester Remington
See Hubbard, L(afayette) Ron(ald)

Colter, Cyrus 1910- ....**CLC 58**
See also BW 1; CA 65-68; CANR 10; DLB 33

Colton, James
See Hansen, Joseph
Colum, Padraic 1881-1972 .... **CLC 28**
See also CA 73-76; 33-36R; CANR 35; CLR 36; MAICYA; MTCW; SATA 15
Colvin, James
See Moorcock, Michael (John)
Colwin, Laurie (E.) 1944-1992 **CLC 5, 13, 23, 84**
See also CA 89-92; 139; CANR 20, 46; DLBY 80; MTCW
Comfort, Alex(ander) 1920- **CLC 7; DAM POP**
See also CA 1-4R; CANR 1, 45
Comfort, Montgomery
See Campbell, (John) Ramsey
Compton-Burnett, I(vy) 1884(?)-1969 **CLC 1, 3, 10, 15, 34; DAM NOV**
See also CA 1-4R; 25-28R; CANR 4; DLB 36; MTCW
Comstock, Anthony 1844-1915 ...... **TCLC 13**
See also CA 110
Comte, Auguste 1798-1857 .... **NCLC 54**
Conan Doyle, Arthur
See Doyle, Arthur Conan
Conde, Maryse 1937- ...... **CLC 52, 92; DAM MULT**
See Boucolon, Maryse
See also BW 2
Condillac, Etienne Bonnot de 1714-1780 **LC 26**
Condon, Richard (Thomas) 1915-1996 **CLC 4, 6, 8, 10, 45, 100; DAM NOV**
See also BEST 90:3; CA 1-4R; 151; CAAS 1; CANR 2, 23; INT CANR-23; MTCW
Confucius 551B.C.-479B.C. . **CMLC 19; DA; DAB; DAC; DAM MST; WLCS**
Congreve, William 1670-1729 **LC 5, 21; DA; DAB; DAC; DAM DRAM, MST, POET; DC 2; WLC**
See also CDBLB 1660-1789; DLB 39, 84
Connell, Evan S(helby), Jr. 1924- **CLC 4, 6, 45; DAM NOV**
See also AAYA 7; CA 1-4R; CAAS 2; CANR 2, 39; DLB 2; DLBY 81; MTCW
Connelly, Marc(us Cook) 1890-1980 .. **CLC 7**
See also CA 85-88; 102; CANR 30; DLB 7; DLBY 80; SATA-Obit 25
Connor, Ralph .... **TCLC 31**
See also Gordon, Charles William
See also DLB 92
Conrad, Joseph 1857-1924 **TCLC 1, 6, 13, 25, 43, 57; DA; DAB; DAC; DAM MST, NOV; SSC 9; WLC**
See also CA 104; 131; CANR 60; CDBLB 1890-1914; DLB 10, 34, 98, 156; MTCW; SATA 27
Conrad, Robert Arnold
See Hart, Moss
Conroy, Donald Pat(rick) 1945- **CLC 30, 74; DAM NOV, POP**
See also AAYA 8; AITN 1; CA 85-88; CANR 24, 53; DLB 6; MTCW
Constant (de Rebecque), (Henri) Benjamin 1767-1830 .... **NCLC 6**
See also DLB 119
Conybeare, Charles Augustus
See Eliot, T(homas) S(tearns)
Cook, Michael 1933- .... **CLC 58**
See also CA 93-96; DLB 53
Cook, Robin 1940- .... **CLC 14; DAM POP**
See also BEST 90:2; CA 108; 111; CANR 41; INT 111
Cook, Roy

See Silverberg, Robert
Cooke, Elizabeth 1948- .... **CLC 55**
See also CA 129
Cooke, John Esten 1830-1886 .... **NCLC 5**
See also DLB 3
Cooke, John Estes
See Baum, L(yman) Frank
Cooke, M. E.
See Creasey, John
Cooke, Margaret
See Creasey, John
Cook-Lynn, Elizabeth 1930-.. **CLC 93; DAM MULT**
See also CA 133; DLB 175; NNAL
Cooney, Ray .... **CLC 62**
Cooper, Douglas 1960- .... **CLC 86**
Cooper, Henry St. John
See Creasey, John
Cooper, J(oan) California .... **CLC 56; DAM MULT**
See also AAYA 12; BW 1; CA 125; CANR 55
Cooper, James Fenimore 1789-1851 **NCLC 1, 27, 54**
See also AAYA 22; CDALB 1640-1865; DLB 3; SATA 19
Coover, Robert (Lowell) 1932- **CLC 3, 7, 15, 32, 46, 87; DAM NOV; SSC 15**
See also CA 45-48; CANR 3, 37, 58; DLB 2; DLBY 81; MTCW
Copeland, Stewart (Armstrong) 1952- **CLC 26**
Coppard, A(lfred) E(dgar) 1878-1957 **TCLC 5; SSC 21**
See also CA 114; DLB 162; YABC 1
Coppee, Francois 1842-1908 .... **TCLC 25**
Coppola, Francis Ford 1939- .... **CLC 16**
See also CA 77-80; CANR 40; DLB 44
Corbiere, Tristan 1845-1875 .... **NCLC 43**
Corcoran, Barbara 1911- .... **CLC 17**
See also AAYA 14; CA 21-24R; CAAS 2; CANR 11, 28, 48; DLB 52; JRDA; SAAS 20; SATA 3, 77
Cordelier, Maurice
See Giraudoux, (Hippolyte) Jean
Corelli, Marie 1855-1924 .... **TCLC 51**
See also Mackay, Mary
See also DLB 34, 156
Corman, Cid .... **CLC 9**
See also Corman, Sidney
See also CAAS 2; DLB 5
Corman, Sidney 1924-
See Corman, Cid
See also CA 85-88; CANR 44; DAM POET
Cormier, Robert (Edmund) 1925- **CLC 12, 30; DA; DAB; DAC; DAM MST, NOV**
See also AAYA 3, 19; CA 1-4R; CANR 5, 23; CDALB 1968-1988; CLR 12; DLB 52; INT CANR-23; JRDA; MAICYA; MTCW; SATA 10, 45, 83
Corn, Alfred (DeWitt III) 1943- .... **CLC 33**
See also CA 104; CAAS 25; CANR 44; DLB 120; DLBY 80
Corneille, Pierre 1606-1684 .... **LC 28; DAB; DAM MST**
Cornwell, David (John Moore) 1931- **CLC 9, 15; DAM POP**
See also le Carre, John
See also CA 5-8R; CANR 13, 33, 59; MTCW
Corso, (Nunzio) Gregory 1930- .... **CLC 1, 11**
See also CA 5-8R; CANR 41; DLB 5, 16; MTCW
Cortazar, Julio 1914-1984 **CLC 2, 3, 5, 10, 13, 15, 33, 34, 92; DAM MULT, NOV; HLC; SSC 7**

See also CA 21-24R; CANR 12, 32; DLB 113; HW; MTCW
CORTES, HERNAN 1484-1547 .... **LC 31**
Corwin, Cecil
See Kornbluth, C(yril) M.
Cosic, Dobrica 1921- .... **CLC 14**
See also CA 122; 138; DLB 181
Costain, Thomas B(ertram) 1885-1965 . **C L C 30**
See also CA 5-8R; 25-28R; DLB 9
Costantini, Humberto 1924(?)-1987 **CLC 49**
See also CA 131; 122; HW
Costello, Elvis 1955- .... **CLC 21**
Cotes, Cecil V.
See Duncan, Sara Jeannette
Cotter, Joseph Seamon Sr. 1861-1949 **T C L C 28; BLC; DAM MULT**
See also BW 1; CA 124; DLB 50
Couch, Arthur Thomas Quiller
See Quiller-Couch, Arthur Thomas
Coulton, James
See Hansen, Joseph
Couperus, Louis (Marie Anne) 1863-1923 **TCLC 15**
See also CA 115
Coupland, Douglas 1961- **CLC 85; DAC; DAM POP**
See also CA 142; CANR 57
Court, Wesli
See Turco, Lewis (Putnam)
Courtenay, Bryce 1933- .... **CLC 59**
See also CA 138
Courtney, Robert
See Ellison, Harlan (Jay)
Cousteau, Jacques-Yves 1910-1997 . **CLC 30**
See also CA 65-68; 159; CANR 15; MTCW; SATA 38
Cowan, Peter (Walkinshaw) 1914- .... **SSC 28**
See also CA 21-24R; CANR 9, 25, 50
Coward, Noel (Peirce) 1899-1973 **CLC 1, 9, 29, 51; DAM DRAM**
See also AITN 1; CA 17-18; 41-44R; CANR 35; CAP 2; CDBLB 1914-1945; DLB 10; MTCW
Cowley, Malcolm 1898-1989 .... **CLC 39**
See also CA 5-8R; 128; CANR 3, 55; DLB 4, 48; DLBY 81, 89; MTCW
Cowper, William 1731-1800 . **NCLC 8; DAM POET**
See also DLB 104, 109
Cox, William Trevor 1928- .... **CLC 9, 14, 71; DAM NOV**
See also Trevor, William
See also CA 9-12R; CANR 4, 37, 55; DLB 14; INT CANR-37; MTCW
Coyne, P. J.
See Masters, Hilary
Cozzens, James Gould 1903-1978 **CLC 1, 4, 11, 92**
See also CA 9-12R; 81-84; CANR 19; CDALB 1941-1968; DLB 9; DLBD 2; DLBY 84; MTCW
Crabbe, George 1754-1832 .... **NCLC 26**
See also DLB 93
Craddock, Charles Egbert
See Murfree, Mary Noailles
Craig, A. A.
See Anderson, Poul (William)
Craik, Dinah Maria (Mulock) 1826-1887 **NCLC 38**
See also DLB 35, 163; MAICYA; SATA 34
Cram, Ralph Adams 1863-1942 ..... **TCLC 45**
See also CA 160

Crane, (Harold) Hart 1899-1932 **TCLC 2, 5;
    DA; DAB; DAC; DAM MST, POET; PC
    3; WLC**
    See also CA 104; 127; CDALB 1917-1929;
    DLB 4, 48; MTCW
Crane, R(onald) S(almon) 1886-1967**CLC 27**
    See also CA 85-88; DLB 63
Crane, Stephen (Townley) 1871-1900 **T C L C
    11, 17, 32; DA; DAB; DAC; DAM MST,
    NOV, POET; SSC 7; WLC**
    See also AAYA 21; CA 109; 140; CDALB 1865-
    1917; DLB 12, 54, 78; YABC 2
Crase, Douglas 1944- .... **CLC 58**
    See also CA 106
Crashaw, Richard 1612(?)-1649 .... **LC 24**
    See also DLB 126
Craven, Margaret 1901-1980 . **CLC 17; DAC**
    See also CA 103
Crawford, F(rancis) Marion 1854-1909**TCLC
    10**
    See also CA 107; DLB 71
Crawford, Isabella Valancy 1850-1887**NCLC
    12**
    See also DLB 92
Crayon, Geoffrey
    See Irving, Washington
Creasey, John 1908-1973 .... **CLC 11**
    See also CA 5-8R; 41-44R; CANR 8, 59; DLB
    77; MTCW
Crebillon, Claude Prosper Jolyot de (fils) 1707-
    1777 .... **LC 28**
Credo
    See Creasey, John
Credo, Alvaro J. de
    See Prado (Calvo), Pedro
Creeley, Robert (White) 1926-**CLC 1, 2, 4, 8,
    11, 15, 36, 78; DAM POET**
    See also CA 1-4R; CAAS 10; CANR 23, 43;
    DLB 5, 16, 169; MTCW
Crews, Harry (Eugene) 1935- **CLC 6, 23, 49**
    See also AITN 1; CA 25-28R; CANR 20, 57;
    DLB 6, 143; MTCW
Crichton, (John) Michael 1942-**CLC 2, 6, 54,
    90; DAM NOV, POP**
    See also AAYA 10; AITN 2; CA 25-28R; CANR
    13, 40, 54; DLBY 81; INT CANR-13; JRDA;
    MTCW; SATA 9, 88
Crispin, Edmund .... **CLC 22**
    See also Montgomery, (Robert) Bruce
    See also DLB 87
Cristofer, Michael 1945(?)-.... **CLC 28; DAM
    DRAM**
    See also CA 110; 152; DLB 7
Croce, Benedetto 1866-1952 .... **TCLC 37**
    See also CA 120; 155
Crockett, David 1786-1836 .... **NCLC 8**
    See also DLB 3, 11
Crockett, Davy
    See Crockett, David
Crofts, Freeman Wills 1879-1957 .. **TCLC 55**
    See also CA 115; DLB 77
Croker, John Wilson 1780-1857 ..... **NCLC 10**
    See also DLB 110
Crommelynck, Fernand 1885-1970 . **CLC 75**
    See also CA 89-92
Cronin, A(rchibald) J(oseph) 1896-1981**C L C
    32**
    See also CA 1-4R; 102; CANR 5; SATA 47;
    SATA-Obit 25
Cross, Amanda
    See Heilbrun, Carolyn G(old)
Crothers, Rachel 1878(?)-1958 ...... **TCLC 19**
    See also CA 113; DLB 7

Croves, Hal
    See Traven, B.
Crow Dog, Mary (Ellen) (?)- .... **CLC 93**
    See also Brave Bird, Mary
    See also CA 154
Crowfield, Christopher
    See Stowe, Harriet (Elizabeth) Beecher
Crowley, Aleister .... **TCLC 7**
    See also Crowley, Edward Alexander
Crowley, Edward Alexander 1875-1947
    See Crowley, Aleister
    See also CA 104
Crowley, John 1942- .... **CLC 57**
    See also CA 61-64; CANR 43; DLBY 82; SATA
    65
Crud
    See Crumb, R(obert)
Crumarums
    See Crumb, R(obert)
Crumb, R(obert) 1943- .... **CLC 17**
    See also CA 106
Crumbum
    See Crumb, R(obert)
Crumski
    See Crumb, R(obert)
Crum the Bum
    See Crumb, R(obert)
Crunk
    See Crumb, R(obert)
Crustt
    See Crumb, R(obert)
Cryer, Gretchen (Kiger) 1935- .... **CLC 21**
    See also CA 114; 123
Csath, Geza 1887-1919 .... **TCLC 13**
    See also CA 111
Cudlip, David 1933- .... **CLC 34**
Cullen, Countee 1903-1946**TCLC 4, 37; BLC;
    DA; DAC; DAM MST, MULT, POET; PC
    20; WLCS**
    See also BW 1; CA 108; 124; CDALB 1917-
    1929; DLB 4, 48, 51; MTCW; SATA 18
Cum, R.
    See Crumb, R(obert)
Cummings, Bruce F(rederick) 1889-1919
    See Barbellion, W. N. P.
    See also CA 123
Cummings, E(dward) E(stlin) 1894-1962**CLC
    1, 3, 8, 12, 15, 68; DA; DAB; DAC; DAM
    MST, POET; PC 5; WLC 2**
    See also CA 73-76; CANR 31; CDALB 1929-
    1941; DLB 4, 48; MTCW
Cunha, Euclides (Rodrigues Pimenta) da 1866-
    1909 .... **TCLC 24**
    See also CA 123
Cunningham, E. V.
    See Fast, Howard (Melvin)
Cunningham, J(ames) V(incent) 1911-1985
    CLC 3, 31
    See also CA 1-4R; 115; CANR 1; DLB 5
Cunningham, Julia (Woolfolk) 1916-**CLC 12**
    See also CA 9-12R; CANR 4, 19, 36; JRDA;
    MAICYA; SAAS 2; SATA 1, 26
Cunningham, Michael 1952- .... **CLC 34**
    See also CA 136
Cunninghame Graham, R(obert) B(ontine)
    1852-1936 .... **TCLC 19**
    See also Graham, R(obert) B(ontine)
    Cunninghame
    See also CA 119; DLB 98
Currie, Ellen 19(?)- .... **CLC 44**
Curtin, Philip
    See Lowndes, Marie Adelaide (Belloc)
Curtis, Price

See Ellison, Harlan (Jay)
Cutrate, Joe
    See Spiegelman, Art
Cynewulf c. 770-c. 840 .... **CMLC 23**
Czaczkes, Shmuel Yosef
    See Agnon, S(hmuel) Y(osef Halevi)
Dabrowska, Maria (Szumska) 1889-1965**CLC
    15**
    See also CA 106
Dabydeen, David 1955- .... **CLC 34**
    See also BW 1; CA 125; CANR 56
Dacey, Philip 1939- .... **CLC 51**
    See also CA 37-40R; CAAS 17; CANR 14, 32,
    64; DLB 105
Dagerman, Stig (Halvard) 1923-1954 **T C L C
    17**
    See also CA 117; 155
Dahl, Roald 1916-1990**CLC 1, 6, 18, 79; DAB;
    DAC; DAM MST, NOV, POP**
    See also AAYA 15; CA 1-4R; 133; CANR 6,
    32, 37, 62; CLR 1, 7, 41; DLB 139; JRDA;
    MAICYA; MTCW; SATA 1, 26, 73; SATA-
    Obit 65
Dahlberg, Edward 1900-1977 .. **CLC 1, 7, 14**
    See also CA 9-12R; 69-72; CANR 31, 62; DLB
    48; MTCW
Daitch, Susan 1954- .... **CLC 103**
    See also CA 161
Dale, Colin .... **TCLC 18**
    See also Lawrence, T(homas) E(dward)
Dale, George E.
    See Asimov, Isaac
Daly, Elizabeth 1878-1967 .... **CLC 52**
    See also CA 23-24; 25-28R; CANR 60; CAP 2
Daly, Maureen 1921- .... **CLC 17**
    See also AAYA 5; CANR 37; JRDA; MAICYA;
    SAAS 1; SATA 2
Damas, Leon-Gontran 1912-1978 ..... **CLC 84**
    See also BW 1; CA 125; 73-76
Dana, Richard Henry Sr. 1787-1879**NCLC 53**
Daniel, Samuel 1562(?)-1619 .... **LC 24**
    See also DLB 62
Daniels, Brett
    See Adler, Renata
Dannay, Frederic 1905-1982 . **CLC 11; DAM
    POP**
    See also Queen, Ellery
    See also CA 1-4R; 107; CANR 1, 39; DLB 137;
    MTCW
D'Annunzio, Gabriele 1863-1938**TCLC 6, 40**
    See also CA 104; 155
Danois, N. le
    See Gourmont, Remy (-Marie-Charles) de
Dante 1265-1321 .... **CMLC 3, 18; DA; DAB;
    DAC; DAM MST, POET; PC 21; WLCS**
d'Antibes, Germain
    See Simenon, Georges (Jacques Christian)
Danticat, Edwidge 1969- .... **CLC 94**
    See also CA 152
Danvers, Dennis 1947- .... **CLC 70**
Danziger, Paula 1944- .... **CLC 21**
    See also AAYA 4; CA 112; 115; CANR 37; CLR
    20; JRDA; MAICYA; SATA 36, 63; SATA-
    Brief 30
Da Ponte, Lorenzo 1749-1838 .... **NCLC 50**
Dario, Ruben 1867-1916 .... **TCLC 4; DAM
    MULT; HLC; PC 15**
    See also CA 131; HW; MTCW
Darley, George 1795-1846 .... **NCLC 2**
    See also DLB 96
Darwin, Charles 1809-1882 .... **NCLC 57**
    See also DLB 57, 166
Daryush, Elizabeth 1887-1977 ..... **CLC 6, 19**

See also CA 49-52; CANR 3; DLB 20

Dashwood, Edmee Elizabeth Monica de la Pasture 1890-1943
See Delafield, E. M.
See also CA 119; 154

Daudet, (Louis Marie) Alphonse 1840-1897
NCLC 1
See also DLB 123

Daumal, Rene 1908-1944 .... **TCLC 14**
See also CA 114

Davenport, Guy (Mattison, Jr.) 1927-**CLC 6, 14, 38; SSC 16**
See also CA 33-36R; CANR 23; DLB 130

Davidson, Avram 1923-
See Queen, Ellery
See also CA 101; CANR 26; DLB 8

Davidson, Donald (Grady) 1893-1968**CLC 2, 13, 19**
See also CA 5-8R; 25-28R; CANR 4; DLB 45

Davidson, Hugh
See Hamilton, Edmond

Davidson, John 1857-1909 .... **TCLC 24**
See also CA 118; DLB 19

Davidson, Sara 1943- .... **CLC 9**
See also CA 81-84; CANR 44

Davie, Donald (Alfred) 1922-1995 **CLC 5, 8, 10, 31**
See also CA 1-4R; 149; CAAS 3; CANR 1, 44; DLB 27; MTCW

Davies, Ray(mond Douglas) 1944- ... **CLC 21**
See also CA 116; 146

Davies, Rhys 1903-1978 .... **CLC 23**
See also CA 9-12R; 81-84; CANR 4; DLB 139

Davies, (William) Robertson 1913-1995 **C L C 2, 7, 13, 25, 42, 75, 91; DA; DAB; DAC; DAM MST, NOV, POP; WLC**
See also BEST 89:2; CA 33-36R; 150; CANR 17, 42; DLB 68; INT CANR-17; MTCW

Davies, W(illiam) H(enry) 1871-1940**TCLC 5**
See also CA 104; DLB 19, 174

Davies, Walter C.
See Kornbluth, C(yril) M.

Davis, Angela (Yvonne) 1944- **CLC 77; DAM MULT**
See also BW 2; CA 57-60; CANR 10

Davis, B. Lynch
See Bioy Casares, Adolfo; Borges, Jorge Luis

Davis, Gordon
See Hunt, E(verette) Howard, (Jr.)

Davis, Harold Lenoir 1896-1960 ..... **CLC 49**
See also CA 89-92; DLB 9

Davis, Rebecca (Blaine) Harding 1831-1910
TCLC 6
See also CA 104; DLB 74

Davis, Richard Harding 1864-1916**TCLC 24**
See also CA 114; DLB 12, 23, 78, 79; DLBD 13

Davison, Frank Dalby 1893-1970 .... **CLC 15**
See also CA 116

Davison, Lawrence H.
See Lawrence, D(avid) H(erbert Richards)

Davison, Peter (Hubert) 1928- .... **CLC 28**
See also CA 9-12R; CAAS 4; CANR 3, 43; DLB 5

Davys, Mary 1674-1732 .... **LC 1**
See also DLB 39

Dawson, Fielding 1930- .... **CLC 6**
See also CA 85-88; DLB 130

Dawson, Peter
See Faust, Frederick (Schiller)

Day, Clarence (Shepard, Jr.) 1874-1935
TCLC 25
See also CA 108; DLB 11

Day, Thomas 1748-1789 .... **LC 1**
See also DLB 39; YABC 1

Day Lewis, C(ecil) 1904-1972.. **CLC 1, 6, 10; DAM POET; PC 11**
See also Blake, Nicholas
See also CA 13-16; 33-36R; CANR 34; CAP 1; DLB 15, 20; MTCW

Dazai, Osamu .... **TCLC 11**
See also Tsushima, Shuji
See also DLB 182

de Andrade, Carlos Drummond
See Drummond de Andrade, Carlos

Deane, Norman
See Creasey, John

de Beauvoir, Simone (Lucie Ernestine Marie Bertrand)
See Beauvoir, Simone (Lucie Ernestine Marie Bertrand) de

de Beer, P.
See Bosman, Herman Charles

de Brissac, Malcolm
See Dickinson, Peter (Malcolm)

de Chardin, Pierre Teilhard
See Teilhard de Chardin, (Marie Joseph) Pierre

Dee, John 1527-1608 .... **LC 20**

Deer, Sandra 1940- .... **CLC 45**

De Ferrari, Gabriella 1941- .... **CLC 65**
See also CA 146

Defoe, Daniel 1660(?)-1731 **LC 1; DA; DAB; DAC; DAM MST, NOV; WLC**
See also CDBLB 1660-1789; DLB 39, 95, 101; JRDA; MAICYA; SATA 22

de Gourmont, Remy(-Marie-Charles)
See Gourmont, Remy (-Marie-Charles) de

de Hartog, Jan 1914-........................... **CLC 19**
See also CA 1-4R; CANR 1

de Hostos, E. M.
See Hostos (y Bonilla), Eugenio Maria de

de Hostos, Eugenio M.
See Hostos (y Bonilla), Eugenio Maria de

Deighton, Len .... **CLC 4, 7, 22, 46**
See also Deighton, Leonard Cyril
See also AAYA 6; BEST 89:2; CDBLB 1960 to Present; DLB 87

Deighton, Leonard Cyril 1929-
See Deighton, Len
See also CA 9-12R; CANR 19, 33; DAM NOV, POP; MTCW

Dekker, Thomas 1572(?)-1632 ..**LC 22; DAM DRAM**
See also CDBLB Before 1660; DLB 62, 172

Delafield, E. M. 1890-1943 .... **TCLC 61**
See also Dashwood, Edmee Elizabeth Monica de la Pasture
See also DLB 34

de la Mare, Walter (John) 1873-1956**TCLC 4, 53; DAB; DAC; DAM MST, POET; SSC 14; WLC**
See also CDBLB 1914-1945; CLR 23; DLB 162; SATA 16

Delaney, Franey
See O'Hara, John (Henry)

Delaney, Shelagh 1939-**CLC 29; DAM DRAM**
See also CA 17-20R; CANR 30; CDBLB 1960 to Present; DLB 13; MTCW

Delany, Mary (Granville Pendarves) 1700-1788
LC 12

Delany, Samuel R(ay, Jr.) 1942-**CLC 8, 14, 38; BLC; DAM MULT**
See also BW 2; CA 81-84; CANR 27, 43; DLB 8, 33; MTCW

De La Ramee, (Marie) Louise 1839-1908
See Ouida

See also SATA 20

de la Roche, Mazo 1879-1961 .... **CLC 14**
See also CA 85-88; CANR 30; DLB 68; SATA 64

De La Salle, Innocent
See Hartmann, Sadakichi

Delbanco, Nicholas (Franklin) 1942- **CLC 6, 13**
See also CA 17-20R; CAAS 2; CANR 29, 55; DLB 6

del Castillo, Michel 1933- .... **CLC 38**
See also CA 109

Deledda, Grazia (Cosima) 1875(?)-1936
TCLC 23
See also CA 123

Delibes, Miguel .... **CLC 8, 18**
See also Delibes Setien, Miguel

Delibes Setien, Miguel 1920-
See Delibes, Miguel
See also CA 45-48; CANR 1, 32; HW; MTCW

DeLillo, Don 1936- **CLC 8, 10, 13, 27, 39, 54, 76; DAM NOV, POP**
See also BEST 89:1; CA 81-84; CANR 21; DLB 6, 173; MTCW

de Lisser, H. G.
See De Lisser, H(erbert) G(eorge)
See also DLB 117

De Lisser, H(erbert) G(eorge) 1878-1944
TCLC 12
See also de Lisser, H. G.
See also BW 2; CA 109; 152

Deloney, Thomas 1560-1600 .... **LC 41**

Deloria, Vine (Victor), Jr. 1933- ..... **CLC 21; DAM MULT**
See also CA 53-56; CANR 5, 20, 48; DLB 175; MTCW; NNAL; SATA 21

Del Vecchio, John M(ichael) 1947- .. **CLC 29**
See also CA 110; DLBD 9

de Man, Paul (Adolph Michel) 1919-1983
CLC 55
See also CA 128; 111; CANR 61; DLB 67; MTCW

De Marinis, Rick 1934- .... **CLC 54**
See also CA 57-60; CAAS 24; CANR 9, 25, 50

Dembry, R. Emmet
See Murfree, Mary Noailles

Demby, William 1922-. **CLC 53; BLC; DAM MULT**
See also BW 1; CA 81-84; DLB 33

de Menton, Francisco
See Chin, Frank (Chew, Jr.)

Demijohn, Thom
See Disch, Thomas M(ichael)

de Montherlant, Henry (Milon)
See Montherlant, Henry (Milon) de

Demosthenes 384B.C.-322B.C. ...... **CMLC 13**
See also DLB 176

de Natale, Francine
See Malzberg, Barry N(athaniel)

Denby, Edwin (Orr) 1903-1983 .... **CLC 48**
See also CA 138; 110

Denis, Julio
See Cortazar, Julio

Denmark, Harrison
See Zelazny, Roger (Joseph)

Dennis, John 1658-1734 .... **LC 11**
See also DLB 101

Dennis, Nigel (Forbes) 1912-1989 .... **CLC 8**
See also CA 25-28R; 129; DLB 13, 15; MTCW

Dent, Lester 1904(?)-1959 .... **TCLC 72**
See also CA 112; 161

De Palma, Brian (Russell) 1940- ...... **CLC 20**
See also CA 109

De Quincey, Thomas 1785-1859 .... **NCLC 4**
  See also CDBLB 1789-1832; DLB 110; 144
Deren, Eleanora 1908(?)-1961
  See Deren, Maya
  See also CA 111
Deren, Maya 1917-1961 .... **CLC 16, 102**
  See also Deren, Eleanora
Derleth, August (William) 1909-1971**CLC 31**
  See also CA 1-4R; 29-32R; CANR 4; DLB 9;
  SATA 5
Der Nister 1884-1950 .... **TCLC 56**
de Routisie, Albert
  See Aragon, Louis
Derrida, Jacques 1930- .... **CLC 24, 87**
  See also CA 124; 127
Derry Down Derry
  See Lear, Edward
Dersonnes, Jacques
  See Simenon, Georges (Jacques Christian)
Desai, Anita 1937-**CLC 19, 37, 97; DAB; DAM
  NOV**
    See also CA 81-84; CANR 33, 53; MTCW;
    SATA 63
de Saint-Luc, Jean
  See Glassco, John
de Saint Roman, Arnaud
  See Aragon, Louis
Descartes, Rene 1596-1650 .... **LC 20, 35**
De Sica, Vittorio 1901(?)-1974 .... **CLC 20**
  See also CA 117
Desnos, Robert 1900-1945 .... **TCLC 22**
  See also CA 121; 151
Destouches, Louis-Ferdinand 1894-1961**C L C
  9, 15**
    See also Celine, Louis-Ferdinand
    See also CA 85-88; CANR 28; MTCW
de Tolignac, Gaston
  See Griffith, D(avid Lewelyn) W(ark)
Deutsch, Babette 1895-1982 .... **CLC 18**
  See also CA 1-4R; 108; CANR 4; DLB 45;
  SATA 1; SATA-Obit 33
Devenant, William 1606-1649 .... **LC 13**
Devkota, Laxmiprasad 1909-1959 . **TCLC 23**
  See also CA 123
De Voto, Bernard (Augustine) 1897-1955
  TCLC 29
  See also CA 113; 160; DLB 9
De Vries, Peter 1910-1993 **CLC 1, 2, 3, 7, 10,
  28, 46; DAM NOV**
    See also CA 17-20R; 142; CANR 41; DLB 6;
    DLBY 82; MTCW
Dexter, John
  See Bradley, Marion Zimmer
Dexter, Martin
  See Faust, Frederick (Schiller)
Dexter, Pete 1943- ... **CLC 34, 55; DAM POP**
  See also BEST 89:2; CA 127; 131; INT 131;
  MTCW
Diamano, Silmang
  See Senghor, Leopold Sedar
Diamond, Neil 1941-......................... **CLC 30**
  See also CA 108
Diaz del Castillo, Bernal 1496-1584 ... **LC 31**
di Bassetto, Corno
  See Shaw, George Bernard
Dick, Philip K(indred) 1928-1982**CLC 10, 30,
  72; DAM NOV, POP**
    See also CA 49-52; 106; CANR 2, 16; DLB 8;
    MTCW
Dickens, Charles (John Huffam) 1812-1870
  **NCLC 3, 8, 18, 26, 37, 50; DA; DAB; DAC;
  DAM MST, NOV; SSC 17; WLC**
    See also CDBLB 1832-1890; DLB 21, 55, 70,

159, 166; JRDA; MAICYA; SATA 15
Dickey, James (Lafayette) 1923-1997 **CLC 1,
  2, 4, 7, 10, 15, 47; DAM NOV, POET, POP**
    See also AITN 1, 2; CA 9-12R; 156; CABS 2;
    CANR 10, 48, 61; CDALB 1968-1988; DLB
    5; DLBD 7; DLBY 82, 93, 96; INT CANR-
    10; MTCW
Dickey, William 1928-1994 .... **CLC 3, 28**
  See also CA 9-12R; 145; CANR 24; DLB 5
Dickinson, Charles 1951- .... **CLC 49**
  See also CA 128
Dickinson, Emily (Elizabeth) 1830-1886
  **NCLC 21; DA; DAB; DAC; DAM MST,
  POET; PC 1; WLC**
    See also AAYA 22; CDALB 1865-1917; DLB
    1; SATA 29
Dickinson, Peter (Malcolm) 1927-**CLC 12, 35**
  See also AAYA 9; CA 41-44R; CANR 31, 58;
  CLR 29; DLB 87, 161; JRDA; MAICYA;
  SATA 5, 62, 95
Dickson, Carr
  See Carr, John Dickson
Dickson, Carter
  See Carr, John Dickson
Diderot, Denis 1713-1784 .... **LC 26**
Didion, Joan 1934-**CLC 1, 3, 8, 14, 32; DAM
  NOV**
    See also AITN 1; CA 5-8R; CANR 14, 52;
    CDALB 1968-1988; DLB 2, 173; DLBY 81,
    86; MTCW
Dietrich, Robert
  See Hunt, E(verette) Howard, (Jr.)
Dillard, Annie 1945-.. **CLC 9, 60; DAM NOV**
  See also AAYA 6; CA 49-52; CANR 3, 43, 62;
  DLBY 80; MTCW; SATA 10
Dillard, R(ichard) H(enry) W(ilde) 1937-
  CLC 5
    See also CA 21-24R; CAAS 7; CANR 10; DLB
    5
Dillon, Eilis 1920-1994 .... **CLC 17**
  See also CA 9-12R; 147; CAAS 3; CANR 4,
  38; CLR 26; MAICYA; SATA 2, 74; SATA-
  Obit 83
Dimont, Penelope
  See Mortimer, Penelope (Ruth)
Dinesen, Isak .... **CLC 10, 29, 95; SSC 7**
  See also Blixen, Karen (Christentze Dinesen)
Ding Ling ....**CLC 68**
  See also Chiang Pin-chin
Disch, Thomas M(ichael) 1940- ... **CLC 7, 36**
  See also AAYA 17; CA 21-24R; CAAS 4;
  CANR 17, 36, 54; CLR 18; DLB 8;
  MAICYA; MTCW; SAAS 15; SATA 92
Disch, Tom
  See Disch, Thomas M(ichael)
d'Isly, Georges
  See Simenon, Georges (Jacques Christian)
Disraeli, Benjamin 1804-1881 ....**NCLC 2, 39**
  See also DLB 21, 55
Ditcum, Steve
  See Crumb, R(obert)
Dixon, Paige
  See Corcoran, Barbara
Dixon, Stephen 1936- .... **CLC 52; SSC 16**
  See also CA 89-92; CANR 17, 40, 54; DLB 130
Doak, Annie
  See Dillard, Annie
Dobell, Sydney Thompson 1824-1874 **N C L C
  43**
    See also DLB 32
Doblin, Alfred .... **TCLC 13**
  See also Doeblin, Alfred
Dobrolyubov, Nikolai Alexandrovich 1836-1861

NCLC 5
Dobson, Austin 1840-1921 .... **TCLC 79**
  See also DLB 35; 144
Dobyns, Stephen 1941-........................**CLC 37**
  See also CA 45-48; CANR 2, 18
Doctorow, E(dgar) L(aurence) 1931- **CLC 6,
  11, 15, 18, 37, 44, 65; DAM NOV, POP**
    See also AAYA 22; AITN 2; BEST 89:3; CA
    45-48; CANR 2, 33, 51; CDALB 1968-1988;
    DLB 2, 28, 173; DLBY 80; MTCW
Dodgson, Charles Lutwidge 1832-1898
  See Carroll, Lewis
  See also CLR 2; DA; DAB; DAC; DAM MST,
  NOV, POET; MAICYA; YABC 2
Dodson, Owen (Vincent) 1914-1983 **CLC 79;
  BLC; DAM MULT**
    See also BW 1; CA 65-68; 110; CANR 24; DLB
    76
Doeblin, Alfred 1878-1957 .... **TCLC 13**
  See also Doblin, Alfred
  See also CA 110; 141; DLB 66
Doerr, Harriet 1910- .... **CLC 34**
  See also CA 117; 122; CANR 47; INT 122
Domecq, H(onorio) Bustos
  See Bioy Casares, Adolfo; Borges, Jorge Luis
Domini, Rey
  See Lorde, Audre (Geraldine)
Dominique
  See Proust, (Valentin-Louis-George-Eugene-)
  Marcel
Don, A
  See Stephen, Leslie
Donaldson, Stephen R. 1947- **CLC 46; DAM
  POP**
    See also CA 89-92; CANR 13, 55; INT CANR-
    13
Donleavy, J(ames) P(atrick) 1926-**CLC 1, 4, 6,
  10, 45**
    See also AITN 2; CA 9-12R; CANR 24, 49, 62;
    DLB 6, 173; INT CANR-24; MTCW
Donne, John 1572-1631**LC 10, 24; DA; DAB;
  DAC; DAM MST, POET; PC 1**
    See also CDBLB Before 1660; DLB 121, 151
Donnell, David 1939(?)- .... **CLC 34**
Donoghue, P. S.
  See Hunt, E(verette) Howard, (Jr.)
Donoso (Yanez), Jose 1924-1996**CLC 4, 8, 11,
  32, 99; DAM MULT; HLC**
    See also CA 81-84; 155; CANR 32; DLB 113;
    HW; MTCW
Donovan, John 1928-1992 .... **CLC 35**
  See also AAYA 20; CA 97-100; 137; CLR 3;
  MAICYA; SATA 72; SATA-Brief 29
Don Roberto
  See Cunninghame Graham, R(obert) B(ontine)
Doolittle, Hilda 1886-1961**CLC 3, 8, 14, 31, 34,
  73; DA; DAC; DAM MST, POET; PC 5;
  WLC**
    See also H. D.
    See also CA 97-100; CANR 35; DLB 4, 45;
    MTCW
Dorfman, Ariel 1942- ...... **CLC 48, 77; DAM
  MULT; HLC**
    See also CA 124; 130; HW; INT 130
Dorn, Edward (Merton) 1929- ... **CLC 10, 18**
  See also CA 93-96; CANR 42; DLB 5; INT 93-
  96
Dorsan, Luc
  See Simenon, Georges (Jacques Christian)
Dorsange, Jean
  See Simenon, Georges (Jacques Christian)
Dos Passos, John (Roderigo) 1896-1970 **C L C
  1, 4, 8, 11, 15, 25, 34, 82; DA; DAB; DAC;**

DAM MST, NOV; WLC
See also CA 1-4R; 29-32R; CANR 3; CDALB
1929-1941; DLB 4, 9; DLBD 1, 15; DLBY
96; MTCW

Dossage, Jean
See Simenon, Georges (Jacques Christian)

Dostoevsky, Fedor Mikhailovich 1821-1881
**NCLC 2, 7, 21, 33, 43; DA; DAB; DAC;
DAM MST, NOV; SSC 2; WLC**

Doughty, Charles M(ontagu) 1843-1926
TCLC 27
See also CA 115; DLB 19, 57, 174

Douglas, Ellen .... **CLC 73**
See also Haxton, Josephine Ayres; Williamson,
Ellen Douglas

Douglas, Gavin 1475(?)-1522 .... **LC 20**

Douglas, Keith (Castellain) 1920-1944 **T C L C
40**
See also CA 160; DLB 27

Douglas, Leonard
See Bradbury, Ray (Douglas)

Douglas, Michael
See Crichton, (John) Michael

Douglas, Norman 1868-1952 .... **TCLC 68**

Douglass, Frederick 1817(?)-1895 **NCLC 7, 55;
BLC; DA; DAC; DAM MST, MULT; WLC**
See also CDALB 1640-1865; DLB 1, 43, 50,
79; SATA 29

Dourado, (Waldomiro Freitas) Autran 1926-
CLC 23, 60
See also CA 25-28R; CANR 34

Dourado, Waldomiro Autran
See Dourado, (Waldomiro Freitas) Autran

Dove, Rita (Frances) 1952- **CLC 50, 81; DAM
MULT, POET; PC 6**
See also BW 2; CA 109; CAAS 19; CANR 27,
42; DLB 120

Dowell, Coleman 1925-1985 .... **CLC 60**
See also CA 25-28R; 117; CANR 10; DLB 130

Dowson, Ernest (Christopher) 1867-1900
TCLC 4
See also CA 105; 150; DLB 19, 135

Doyle, A. Conan
See Doyle, Arthur Conan

Doyle, Arthur Conan 1859-1930 **TCLC 7; DA;
DAB; DAC; DAM MST, NOV; SSC 12;
WLC**
See also AAYA 14; CA 104; 122; CDBLB 1890-
1914; DLB 18, 70, 156, 178; MTCW; SATA
24

Doyle, Conan
See Doyle, Arthur Conan

Doyle, John
See Graves, Robert (von Ranke)

Doyle, Roddy 1958(?)- .... **CLC 81**
See also AAYA 14; CA 143

Doyle, Sir A. Conan
See Doyle, Arthur Conan

Doyle, Sir Arthur Conan
See Doyle, Arthur Conan

Dr. A
See Asimov, Isaac; Silverstein, Alvin

Drabble, Margaret 1939- **CLC 2, 3, 5, 8, 10, 22,
53; DAB; DAC; DAM MST, NOV, POP**
See also CA 13-16R; CANR 18, 35, 63; CDBLB
1960 to Present; DLB 14, 155; MTCW;
SATA 48

Drapier, M. B.
See Swift, Jonathan

Drayham, James
See Mencken, H(enry) L(ouis)

Drayton, Michael 1563-1631 .... **LC 8**

Dreadstone, Carl
See Campbell, (John) Ramsey

Dreiser, Theodore (Herman Albert) 1871-1945
**TCLC 10, 18, 35; DA; DAC; DAM MST,
NOV; WLC**
See also CA 106; 132; CDALB 1865-1917;
DLB 9, 12, 102, 137; DLBD 1; MTCW

Drexler, Rosalyn 1926- .... **CLC 2, 6**
See also CA 81-84

Dreyer, Carl Theodor 1889-1968 ...... **CLC 16**
See also CA 116

Drieu la Rochelle, Pierre(-Eugene) 1893-1945
TCLC 21
See also CA 117; DLB 72

Drinkwater, John 1882-1937 .... **TCLC 57**
See also CA 109; 149; DLB 10, 19, 149

Drop Shot
See Cable, George Washington

Droste-Hulshoff, Annette Freiin von 1797-1848
NCLC 3
See also DLB 133

Drummond, Walter
See Silverberg, Robert

Drummond, William Henry 1854-1907 **T C L C
25**
See also CA 160; DLB 92

Drummond de Andrade, Carlos 1902-1987
CLC 18
See also Andrade, Carlos Drummond de
See also CA 132; 123

Drury, Allen (Stuart) 1918- .... **CLC 37**
See also CA 57-60; CANR 18, 52; INT CANR-
18

Dryden, John 1631-1700 **LC 3, 21; DA; DAB;
DAC; DAM DRAM, MST, POET; DC 3;
WLC**
See also CDBLB 1660-1789; DLB 80, 101, 131

Duberman, Martin (Bauml) 1930- ...... **CLC 8**
See also CA 1-4R; CANR 2, 63

Dubie, Norman (Evans) 1945- .... **CLC 36**
See also CA 69-72; CANR 12; DLB 120

Du Bois, W(illiam) E(dward) B(urghardt) 1868-
1963 **CLC 1, 2, 13, 64, 96; BLC; DA; DAC;
DAM MST, MULT, NOV; WLC**
See also BW 1; CA 85-88; CANR 34; CDALB
1865-1917; DLB 47, 50, 91; MTCW; SATA
42

Dubus, Andre 1936- **CLC 13, 36, 97; SSC 15**
See also CA 21-24R; CANR 17; DLB 130; INT
CANR-17

Duca Minimo
See D'Annunzio, Gabriele

Ducharme, Rejean 1941- .... **CLC 74**
See also DLB 60

Duclos, Charles Pinot 1704-1772 .... **LC 1**

Dudek, Louis 1918- .... **CLC 11, 19**
See also CA 45-48; CAAS 14; CANR 1; DLB
88

Duerrenmatt, Friedrich 1921-1990 **CLC 1, 4,
8, 11, 15, 43, 102; DAM DRAM**
See also CA 17-20R; CANR 33; DLB 69, 124;
MTCW

Duffy, Bruce (?)- .... **CLC 50**

Duffy, Maureen 1933- .... **CLC 37**
See also CA 25-28R; CANR 33; DLB 14;
MTCW

Dugan, Alan 1923- .... **CLC 2, 6**
See also CA 81-84; DLB 5

du Gard, Roger Martin
See Martin du Gard, Roger

Duhamel, Georges 1884-1966 .... **CLC 8**
See also CA 81-84; 25-28R; CANR 35; DLB
65; MTCW

Dujardin, Edouard (Emile Louis) 1861-1949

TCLC 13
See also CA 109; DLB 123

Dulles, John Foster 1888-1959 .... **TCLC 72**
See also CA 115; 149

Dumas, Alexandre (Davy de la Pailleterie)
1802-1870 ... **NCLC 11; DA; DAB; DAC;
DAM MST, NOV; WLC**
See also DLB 119; SATA 18

Dumas, Alexandre 1824-1895 **NCLC 9; DC 1**
See also AAYA 22

Dumas, Claudine
See Malzberg, Barry N(athaniel)

Dumas, Henry L. 1934-1968 .... **CLC 6, 62**
See also BW 1; CA 85-88; DLB 41

du Maurier, Daphne 1907-1989 **CLC 6, 11, 59;
DAB; DAC; DAM MST, POP; SSC 18**
See also CA 5-8R; 128; CANR 6, 55; MTCW;
SATA 27; SATA-Obit 60

Dunbar, Paul Laurence 1872-1906 . **TCLC 2,
12; BLC; DA; DAC; DAM MST, MULT,
POET; PC 5; SSC 8; WLC**
See also BW 1; CA 104; 124; CDALB 1865-
1917; DLB 50, 54, 78; SATA 34

Dunbar, William 1460(?)-1530(?) .... **LC 20**
See also DLB 132, 146

Duncan, Dora Angela
See Duncan, Isadora

Duncan, Isadora 1877(?)-1927 .... **TCLC 68**
See also CA 118; 149

Duncan, Lois 1934- .... **CLC 26**
See also AAYA 4; CA 1-4R; CANR 2, 23, 36;
CLR 29; JRDA; MAICYA; SAAS 2; SATA
1, 36, 75

Duncan, Robert (Edward) 1919-1988 **CLC 1,
2, 4, 7, 15, 41, 55; DAM POET; PC 2**
See also CA 9-12R; 124; CANR 28, 62; DLB
5, 16; MTCW

Duncan, Sara Jeannette 1861-1922 **TCLC 60**
See also CA 157; DLB 92

Dunlap, William 1766-1839 .... **NCLC 2**
See also DLB 30, 37, 59

Dunn, Douglas (Eaglesham) 1942- **CLC 6, 40**
See also CA 45-48; CANR 2, 33; DLB 40;
MTCW

Dunn, Katherine (Karen) 1945- .... **CLC 71**
See also CA 33-36R

Dunn, Stephen 1939- .... **CLC 36**
See also CA 33-36R; CANR 12, 48, 53; DLB
105

Dunne, Finley Peter 1867-1936 ...... **TCLC 28**
See also CA 108; DLB 11, 23

Dunne, John Gregory 1932- .... **CLC 28**
See also CA 25-28R; CANR 14, 50; DLBY 80

Dunsany, Edward John Moreton Drax Plunkett
1878-1957
See Dunsany, Lord
See also CA 104; 148; DLB 10

Dunsany, Lord .... **TCLC 2, 59**
See also Dunsany, Edward John Moreton Drax
Plunkett
See also DLB 77, 153, 156

du Perry, Jean
See Simenon, Georges (Jacques Christian)

Durang, Christopher (Ferdinand) 1949- **C L C
27, 38**
See also CA 105; CANR 50

Duras, Marguerite 1914-1996 **CLC 3, 6, 11, 20,
34, 40, 68, 100**
See also CA 25-28R; 151; CANR 50; DLB 83;
MTCW

Durban, (Rosa) Pam 1947- .... **CLC 39**
See also CA 123

Durcan, Paul 1944- **CLC 43, 70; DAM POET**

See also CA 134

Durkheim, Emile 1858-1917 .... **TCLC 55**

Durrell, Lawrence (George) 1912-1990 **C L C
1, 4, 6, 8, 13, 27, 41; DAM NOV**
See also CA 9-12R; 132; CANR 40; CDBLB
1945-1960; DLB 15, 27; DLBY 90; MTCW

Durrenmatt, Friedrich
See Duerrenmatt, Friedrich

Dutt, Toru 1856-1877 .... **NCLC 29**

Dwight, Timothy 1752-1817 .... **NCLC 13**
See also DLB 37

Dworkin, Andrea 1946- .... **CLC 43**
See also CA 77-80; CAAS 21; CANR 16, 39;
INT CANR-16; MTCW

Dwyer, Deanna
See Koontz, Dean R(ay)

Dwyer, K. R.
See Koontz, Dean R(ay)

Dye, Richard
See De Voto, Bernard (Augustine)

Dylan, Bob 1941- .... **CLC 3, 4, 6, 12, 77**
See also CA 41-44R; DLB 16

Eagleton, Terence (Francis) 1943-
See Eagleton, Terry
See also CA 57-60; CANR 7, 23; MTCW

Eagleton, Terry .... **CLC 63**
See also Eagleton, Terence (Francis)

Early, Jack
See Scoppettone, Sandra

East, Michael
See West, Morris L(anglo)

Eastaway, Edward
See Thomas, (Philip) Edward

Eastlake, William (Derry) 1917-1997 . **CLC 8**
See also CA 5-8R; 158; CAAS 1; CANR 5, 63;
DLB 6; INT CANR-5

Eastman, Charles A(lexander) 1858-1939
TCLC 55; DAM MULT
See also DLB 175; NNAL; YABC 1

Eberhart, Richard (Ghormley) 1904- **CLC 3,
11, 19, 56; DAM POET**
See also CA 1-4R; CANR 2; CDALB 1941-
1968; DLB 48; MTCW

Eberstadt, Fernanda 1960- .... **CLC 39**
See also CA 136

Echegaray (y Eizaguirre), Jose (Maria Waldo)
1832-1916 .... **TCLC 4**
See also CA 104; CANR 32; HW; MTCW

Echeverria, (Jose) Esteban (Antonino) 1805-
1851 .... **NCLC 18**

Echo
See Proust, (Valentin-Louis-George-Eugene-)
Marcel

Eckert, Allan W. 1931- .... **CLC 17**
See also AAYA 18; CA 13-16R; CANR 14, 45;
INT CANR-14; SAAS 21; SATA 29, 91;
SATA-Brief 27

Eckhart, Meister 1260(?)-1328(?) ... **CMLC 9**
See also DLB 115

Eckmar, F. R.
See de Hartog, Jan

Eco, Umberto 1932- **CLC 28, 60; DAM NOV,
POP**
See also BEST 90:1; CA 77-80; CANR 12, 33,
55; MTCW

Eddison, E(ric) R(ucker) 1882-1945 **TCLC 15**
See also CA 109; 156

Eddy, Mary (Morse) Baker 1821-1910 **T C L C
71**
See also CA 113

Edel, (Joseph) Leon 1907-1997 .. **CLC 29, 34**
See also CA 1-4R; 161; CANR 1, 22; DLB 103;
INT CANR-22

Eden, Emily 1797-1869 .... **NCLC 10**

Edgar, David 1948-... **CLC 42; DAM DRAM**
See also CA 57-60; CANR 12, 61; DLB 13;
MTCW

Edgerton, Clyde (Carlyle) 1944- ...... **CLC 39**
See also AAYA 17; CA 118; 134; CANR 64;
INT 134

Edgeworth, Maria 1768-1849 ....**NCLC 1, 51**
See also DLB 116, 159, 163; SATA 21

Edmonds, Paul
See Kuttner, Henry

Edmonds, Walter D(umaux) 1903-... **CLC 35**
See also CA 5-8R; CANR 2; DLB 9; MAICYA;
SAAS 4; SATA 1, 27

Edmondson, Wallace
See Ellison, Harlan (Jay)

Edson, Russell .... **CLC 13**
See also CA 33-36R

Edwards, Bronwen Elizabeth
See Rose, Wendy

Edwards, G(erald) B(asil) 1899-1976 **CLC 25**
See also CA 110

Edwards, Gus 1939- .... **CLC 43**
See also CA 108; INT 108

Edwards, Jonathan 1703-1758 ..... **LC 7; DA;
DAC; DAM MST**
See also DLB 24

Efron, Marina Ivanovna Tsvetaeva
See Tsvetaeva (Efron), Marina (Ivanovna)

Ehle, John (Marsden, Jr.) 1925- ...... **CLC 27**
See also CA 9-12R

Ehrenbourg, Ilya (Grigoryevich)
See Ehrenburg, Ilya (Grigoryevich)

Ehrenburg, Ilya (Grigoryevich) 1891-1967
CLC 18, 34, 62
See also CA 102; 25-28R

Ehrenburg, Ilyo (Grigoryevich)
See Ehrenburg, Ilya (Grigoryevich)

Eich, Guenter 1907-1972 ....**CLC 15**
See also CA 111; 93-96; DLB 69, 124

Eichendorff, Joseph Freiherr von 1788-1857
NCLC 8
See also DLB 90

Eigner, Larry .... **CLC 9**
See also Eigner, Laurence (Joel)
See also CAAS 23; DLB 5

Eigner, Laurence (Joel) 1927-1996
See Eigner, Larry
See also CA 9-12R; 151; CANR 6

Einstein, Albert 1879-1955 .... **TCLC 65**
See also CA 121; 133; MTCW

Eiseley, Loren Corey 1907-1977 .... **CLC 7**
See also AAYA 5; CA 1-4R; 73-76; CANR 6

Eisenstadt, Jill 1963- .... **CLC 50**
See also CA 140

Eisenstein, Sergei (Mikhailovich) 1898-1948
TCLC 57
See also CA 114; 149

Eisner, Simon
See Kornbluth, C(yril) M.

Ekeloef, (Bengt) Gunnar 1907-1968 **CLC 27;
DAM POET**
See also CA 123; 25-28R

Ekelof, (Bengt) Gunnar
See Ekeloef, (Bengt) Gunnar

Ekelund, Vilhelm 1880-1949 .... **TCLC 75**

Ekwensi, C. O. D.
See Ekwensi, Cyprian (Odiatu Duaka)

Ekwensi, Cyprian (Odiatu Duaka) 1921- **CLC
4; BLC; DAM MULT**
See also BW 2; CA 29-32R; CANR 18, 42; DLB
117; MTCW; SATA 66

Elaine .... **TCLC 18**

See also Leverson, Ada

El Crummo
See Crumb, R(obert)

Elder, Lonne III 1931-1996 .... **DC 8**
See also BLC; BW 1; CA 81-84; 152; CANR
25; DAM MULT; DLB 7, 38, 44

Elia
See Lamb, Charles

Eliade, Mircea 1907-1986 .... **CLC 19**
See also CA 65-68; 119; CANR 30, 62; MTCW

Eliot, A. D.
See Jewett, (Theodora) Sarah Orne

Eliot, Alice
See Jewett, (Theodora) Sarah Orne

Eliot, Dan
See Silverberg, Robert

Eliot, George 1819-1880 **NCLC 4, 13, 23, 41,
49; DA; DAB; DAC; DAM MST, NOV; PC
20; WLC**
See also CDBLB 1832-1890; DLB 21, 35, 55

Eliot, John 1604-1690 .... **LC 5**
See also DLB 24

Eliot, T(homas) S(tearns) 1888-1965 **CLC 1, 2,
3, 6, 9, 10, 13, 15, 24, 34, 41, 55, 57; DA;
DAB; DAC; DAM DRAM, MST, POET;
PC 5; WLC 2**
See also CA 5-8R; 25-28R; CANR 41; CDALB
1929-1941; DLB 7, 10, 45, 63; DLBY 88;
MTCW

Elizabeth 1866-1941 .... **TCLC 41**

Elkin, Stanley L(awrence) 1930-1995 **CLC 4,
6, 9, 14, 27, 51, 91; DAM NOV, POP; SSC
12**
See also CA 9-12R; 148; CANR 8, 46; DLB 2,
28; DLBY 80; INT CANR-8; MTCW

Elledge, Scott .... **CLC 34**

Elliot, Don
See Silverberg, Robert

Elliott, Don
See Silverberg, Robert

Elliott, George P(aul) 1918-1980 .... **CLC 2**
See also CA 1-4R; 97-100; CANR 2

Elliott, Janice 1931- .... **CLC 47**
See also CA 13-16R; CANR 8, 29; DLB 14

Elliott, Sumner Locke 1917-1991 ..... **CLC 38**
See also CA 5-8R; 134; CANR 2, 21

Elliott, William
See Bradbury, Ray (Douglas)

Ellis, A. E. .... **CLC 7**

Ellis, Alice Thomas .... **CLC 40**
See also Haycraft, Anna

Ellis, Bret Easton 1964- .. **CLC 39, 71; DAM
POP**
See also AAYA 2; CA 118; 123; CANR 51; INT
123

Ellis, (Henry) Havelock 1859-1939 **TCLC 14**
See also CA 109

Ellis, Landon
See Ellison, Harlan (Jay)

Ellis, Trey 1962- .... **CLC 55**
See also CA 146

Ellison, Harlan (Jay) 1934-... **CLC 1, 13, 42;
DAM POP; SSC 14**
See also CA 5-8R; CANR 5, 46; DLB 8; INT
CANR-5; MTCW

Ellison, Ralph (Waldo) 1914-1994 **CLC 1, 3,
11, 54, 86; BLC; DA; DAB; DAC; DAM
MST, MULT, NOV; SSC 26; WLC**
See also AAYA 19; BW 1; CA 9-12R; 145;
CANR 24, 53; CDALB 1941-1968; DLB 2,
76; DLBY 94; MTCW

Ellmann, Lucy (Elizabeth) 1956- ...... **CLC 61**
See also CA 128

Ellmann, Richard (David) 1918-1987 **CLC 50**
    See also BEST 89:2; CA 1-4R; 122; CANR 2,
    28, 61; DLB 103; DLBY 87; MTCW
Elman, Richard 1934- .... **CLC 19**
    See also CA 17-20R; CAAS 3; CANR 47
Elron
    See Hubbard, L(afayette) Ron(ald)
Eluard, Paul .... **TCLC 7, 41**
    See also Grindel, Eugene
Elyot, Sir Thomas 1490(?)-1546 .... **LC 11**
Elytis, Odysseus 1911-1996 **CLC 15, 49, 100;**
    DAM POET; PC 21
    See also CA 102; 151; MTCW
Emecheta, (Florence Onye) Buchi 1944-**C L C**
    14, 48; BLC; DAM MULT
    See also BW 2; CA 81-84; CANR 27; DLB 117;
    MTCW; SATA 66
Emerson, Mary Moody 1774-1863 **NCLC 66**
Emerson, Ralph Waldo 1803-1882 . **NCLC 1,**
    38; DA; DAB; DAC; DAM MST, POET;
    PC 18; WLC
    See also CDALB 1640-1865; DLB 1, 59, 73
Eminescu, Mihail 1850-1889 .... **NCLC 33**
Empson, William 1906-1984 **CLC 3, 8, 19, 33,**
    34
    See also CA 17-20R; 112; CANR 31, 61; DLB
    20; MTCW
Enchi Fumiko (Ueda) 1905-1986 ..... **CLC 31**
    See also CA 129; 121
Ende, Michael (Andreas Helmuth) 1929-1995
    CLC 31
    See also CA 118; 124; 149; CANR 36; CLR
    14; DLB 75; MAICYA; SATA 61; SATA-
    Brief 42; SATA-Obit 86
Endo, Shusaku 1923-1996 **CLC 7, 14, 19, 54,**
    99; DAM NOV
    See also CA 29-32R; 153; CANR 21, 54; DLB
    182; MTCW
Engel, Marian 1933-1985 .... **CLC 36**
    See also CA 25-28R; CANR 12; DLB 53; INT
    CANR-12
Engelhardt, Frederick
    See Hubbard, L(afayette) Ron(ald)
Enright, D(ennis) J(oseph) 1920-**CLC 4, 8, 31**
    See also CA 1-4R; CANR 1, 42; DLB 27; SATA
    25
Enzensberger, Hans Magnus 1929- . **CLC 43**
    See also CA 116; 119
Ephron, Nora 1941- .... **CLC 17, 31**
    See also AITN 2; CA 65-68; CANR 12, 39
Epicurus 341B.C.-270B.C. .... **CMLC 21**
    See also DLB 176
Epsilon
    See Betjeman, John
Epstein, Daniel Mark 1948- .... **CLC 7**
    See also CA 49-52; CANR 2, 53
Epstein, Jacob 1956- .... **CLC 19**
    See also CA 114
Epstein, Joseph 1937- .... **CLC 39**
    See also CA 112; 119; CANR 50
Epstein, Leslie 1938- .... **CLC 27**
    See also CA 73-76; CAAS 12; CANR 23
Equiano, Olaudah 1745(?)-1797**LC 16; BLC;**
    DAM MULT
    See also DLB 37, 50
ER .... **TCLC 33**
    See also CA 160; DLB 85
Erasmus, Desiderius 1469(?)-1536 ...... **LC 16**
Erdman, Paul E(mil) 1932- .... **CLC 25**
    See also AITN 1; CA 61-64; CANR 13, 43
Erdrich, Louise 1954- ..... **CLC 39, 54; DAM**
    MULT, NOV, POP
    See also AAYA 10; BEST 89:1; CA 114; CANR

41, 62; DLB 152, 175; MTCW; NNAL;
    SATA 94
Erenburg, Ilya (Grigoryevich)
    See Ehrenburg, Ilya (Grigoryevich)
Erickson, Stephen Michael 1950-
    See Erickson, Steve
    See also CA 129
Erickson, Steve 1950- .... **CLC 64**
    See also Erickson, Stephen Michael
    See also CANR 60
Ericson, Walter
    See Fast, Howard (Melvin)
Eriksson, Buntel
    See Bergman, (Ernst) Ingmar
Ernaux, Annie 1940- .... **CLC 88**
    See also CA 147
Eschenbach, Wolfram von
    See Wolfram von Eschenbach
Eseki, Bruno
    See Mphahlele, Ezekiel
Esenin, Sergei (Alexandrovich) 1895-1925
    TCLC 4
    See also CA 104
Eshleman, Clayton 1935- .... **CLC 7**
    See also CA 33-36R; CAAS 6; DLB 5
Espriella, Don Manuel Alvarez
    See Southey, Robert
Espriu, Salvador 1913-1985 .... **CLC 9**
    See also CA 154; 115; DLB 134
Espronceda, Jose de 1808-1842 ..... **NCLC 39**
Esse, James
    See Stephens, James
Esterbrook, Tom
    See Hubbard, L(afayette) Ron(ald)
Estleman, Loren D. 1952-**CLC 48; DAM NOV,**
    POP
    See also CA 85-88; CANR 27; INT CANR-27;
    MTCW
Euclid 306B.C.-283B.C. .... **CMLC 25**
Eugenides, Jeffrey 1960(?)- .... **CLC 81**
    See also CA 144
Euripides c. 485B.C.-406B.C.**CMLC 23; DA;**
    DAB; DAC; DAM DRAM, MST; DC 4;
    WLCS
    See also DLB 176
Evan, Evin
    See Faust, Frederick (Schiller)
Evans, Evan
    See Faust, Frederick (Schiller)
Evans, Marian
    See Eliot, George
Evans, Mary Ann
    See Eliot, George
Evarts, Esther
    See Benson, Sally
Everett, Percival L. 1956- .... **CLC 57**
    See also BW 2; CA 129
Everson, R(onald) G(ilmour) 1903-..**CLC 27**
    See also CA 17-20R; DLB 88
Everson, William (Oliver) 1912-1994 **CLC 1,**
    5, 14
    See also CA 9-12R; 145; CANR 20; DLB 5,
    16; MTCW
Evtushenko, Evgenii Aleksandrovich
    See Yevtushenko, Yevgeny (Alexandrovich)
Ewart, Gavin (Buchanan) 1916-1995**CLC 13,**
    46
    See also CA 89-92; 150; CANR 17, 46; DLB
    40; MTCW
Ewers, Hanns Heinz 1871-1943 ..... **TCLC 12**
    See also CA 109; 149
Ewing, Frederick R.
    See Sturgeon, Theodore (Hamilton)

Exley, Frederick (Earl) 1929-1992 **CLC 6, 11**
    See also AITN 2; CA 81-84; 138; DLB 143;
    DLBY 81
Eynhardt, Guillermo
    See Quiroga, Horacio (Sylvestre)
Ezekiel, Nissim 1924- .... **CLC 61**
    See also CA 61-64
Ezekiel, Tish O'Dowd 1943- .... **CLC 34**
    See also CA 129
Fadeyev, A.
    See Bulgya, Alexander Alexandrovich
Fadeyev, Alexander .... **TCLC 53**
    See also Bulgya, Alexander Alexandrovich
Fagen, Donald 1948- .... **CLC 26**
Fainzilberg, Ilya Arnoldovich 1897-1937
    See Ilf, Ilya
    See also CA 120
Fair, Ronald L. 1932- .... **CLC 18**
    See also BW 1; CA 69-72; CANR 25; DLB 33
Fairbairn, Roger
    See Carr, John Dickson
Fairbairns, Zoe (Ann) 1948- .... **CLC 32**
    See also CA 103; CANR 21
Falco, Gian
    See Papini, Giovanni
Falconer, James
    See Kirkup, James
Falconer, Kenneth
    See Kornbluth, C(yril) M.
Falkland, Samuel
    See Heijermans, Herman
Fallaci, Oriana 1930- .... **CLC 11**
    See also CA 77-80; CANR 15, 58; MTCW
Faludy, George 1913- .... **CLC 42**
    See also CA 21-24R
Faludy, Gyoergy
    See Faludy, George
Fanon, Frantz 1925-1961**CLC 74; BLC; DAM**
    MULT
    See also BW 1; CA 116; 89-92
Fanshawe, Ann 1625-1680 .... **LC 11**
Fante, John (Thomas) 1911-1983 .... **CLC 60**
    See also CA 69-72; 109; CANR 23; DLB 130;
    DLBY 83
Farah, Nuruddin 1945- **CLC 53; BLC; DAM**
    MULT
    See also BW 2; CA 106; DLB 125
Fargue, Leon-Paul 1876(?)-1947 ... **TCLC 11**
    See also CA 109
Farigoule, Louis
    See Romains, Jules
Farina, Richard 1936(?)-1966 .... **CLC 9**
    See also CA 81-84; 25-28R
Farley, Walter (Lorimer) 1915-1989 **CLC 17**
    See also CA 17-20R; CANR 8, 29; DLB 22;
    JRDA; MAICYA; SATA 2, 43
Farmer, Philip Jose 1918- .... **CLC 1, 19**
    See also CA 1-4R; CANR 4, 35; DLB 8;
    MTCW; SATA 93
Farquhar, George 1677-1707 ... **LC 21; DAM**
    DRAM
    See also DLB 84
Farrell, J(ames) G(ordon) 1935-1979 **CLC 6**
    See also CA 73-76; 89-92; CANR 36; DLB 14;
    MTCW
Farrell, James T(homas) 1904-1979**CLC 1, 4,**
    8, 11, 66; SSC 28
    See also CA 5-8R; 89-92; CANR 9, 61; DLB 4,
    9, 86; DLBD 2; MTCW
Farren, Richard J.
    See Betjeman, John
Farren, Richard M.
    See Betjeman, John

Author Index

Fassbinder, Rainer Werner 1946-1982**CLC 20**
See also CA 93-96; 106; CANR 31
Fast, Howard (Melvin) 1914- **CLC 23; DAM NOV**
See also AAYA 16; CA 1-4R; CAAS 18; CANR 1, 33, 54; DLB 9; INT CANR-33; SATA 7
Faulcon, Robert
See Holdstock, Robert P.
Faulkner, William (Cuthbert) 1897-1962**CLC 1, 3, 6, 8, 9, 11, 14, 18, 28, 52, 68; DA; DAB; DAC; DAM MST, NOV; SSC 1; WLC**
See also AAYA 7; CA 81-84; CANR 33; CDALB 1929-1941; DLB 9, 11, 44, 102; DLBD 2; DLBY 86; MTCW
Fauset, Jessie Redmon 1884(?)-1961**CLC 19, 54; BLC; DAM MULT**
See also BW 1; CA 109; DLB 51
Faust, Frederick (Schiller) 1892-1944(?) **TCLC 49; DAM POP**
See also CA 108; 152
Faust, Irvin 1924- ....**CLC 8**
See also CA 33-36R; CANR 28; DLB 2, 28; DLBY 80
Fawkes, Guy
See Benchley, Robert (Charles)
Fearing, Kenneth (Flexner) 1902-1961 **CLC 51**
See also CA 93-96; CANR 59; DLB 9
Fecamps, Elise
See Creasey, John
Federman, Raymond 1928- ....**CLC 6, 47**
See also CA 17-20R; CAAS 8; CANR 10, 43; DLBY 80
Federspiel, J(uerg) F. 1931- ....**CLC 42**
See also CA 146
Feiffer, Jules (Ralph) 1929- .....**CLC 2, 8, 64; DAM DRAM**
See also AAYA 3; CA 17-20R; CANR 30, 59; DLB 7, 44; INT CANR-30; MTCW; SATA 8, 61
Feige, Hermann Albert Otto Maximilian
See Traven, B.
Feinberg, David B. 1956-1994 ....**CLC 59**
See also CA 135; 147
Feinstein, Elaine 1930- ....**CLC 36**
See also CA 69-72; CAAS 1; CANR 31; DLB 14, 40; MTCW
Feldman, Irving (Mordecai) 1928- .....**CLC 7**
See also CA 1-4R; CANR 1; DLB 169
Felix-Tchicaya, Gerald
See Tchicaya, Gerald Felix
Fellini, Federico 1920-1993 ....**CLC 16, 85**
See also CA 65-68; 143; CANR 33
Felsen, Henry Gregor 1916- ....**CLC 17**
See also CA 1-4R; CANR 1; SAAS 2; SATA 1
Fenno, Jack
See Calisher, Hortense
Fenton, James Martin 1949- ....**CLC 32**
See also CA 102; DLB 40
Ferber, Edna 1887-1968..............**CLC 18, 93**
See also AITN 1; CA 5-8R; 25-28R; DLB 9, 28, 86; MTCW; SATA 7
Ferguson, Helen
See Kavan, Anna
Ferguson, Samuel 1810-1886 ....**NCLC 33**
See also DLB 32
Fergusson, Robert 1750-1774 ....**LC 29**
See also DLB 109
Ferling, Lawrence
See Ferlinghetti, Lawrence (Monsanto)
Ferlinghetti, Lawrence (Monsanto) 1919(?)-**CLC 2, 6, 10, 27; DAM POET; PC 1**
See also CA 5-8R; CANR 3, 41; CDALB 1941-

1968; DLB 5, 16; MTCW
Fernandez, Vicente Garcia Huidobro
See Huidobro Fernandez, Vicente Garcia
Ferrer, Gabriel (Francisco Victor) Miro
See Miro (Ferrer), Gabriel (Francisco Victor)
Ferrier, Susan (Edmonstone) 1782-1854 **NCLC 8**
See also DLB 116
Ferrigno, Robert 1948(?)-..................**CLC 65**
See also CA 140
Ferron, Jacques 1921-1985 ....**CLC 94; DAC**
See also CA 117; 129; DLB 60
Feuchtwanger, Lion 1884-1958 ....**TCLC 3**
See also CA 104; DLB 66
Feuillet, Octave 1821-1890 ....**NCLC 45**
Feydeau, Georges (Leon Jules Marie) 1862-1921 ....**TCLC 22; DAM DRAM**
See also CA 113; 152
Fichte, Johann Gottlieb 1762-1814 **NCLC 62**
See also DLB 90
Ficino, Marsilio 1433-1499 ....**LC 12**
Fiedeler, Hans
See Doeblin, Alfred
Fiedler, Leslie A(aron) 1917- . **CLC 4, 13, 24**
See also CA 9-12R; CANR 7, 63; DLB 28, 67; MTCW
Field, Andrew 1938-..........................**CLC 44**
See also CA 97-100; CANR 25
Field, Eugene 1850-1895 ....**NCLC 3**
See also DLB 23, 42, 140; DLBD 13; MAICYA; SATA 16
Field, Gans T.
See Wellman, Manly Wade
Field, Michael ....**TCLC 43**
Field, Peter
See Hobson, Laura Z(ametkin)
Fielding, Henry 1707-1754 **LC 1; DA; DAB; DAC; DAM DRAM, MST, NOV; WLC**
See also CDBLB 1660-1789; DLB 39, 84, 101
Fielding, Sarah 1710-1768 ....**LC 1**
See also DLB 39
Fierstein, Harvey (Forbes) 1954-....**CLC 33; DAM DRAM, POP**
See also CA 123; 129
Figes, Eva 1932-................................**CLC 31**
See also CA 53-56; CANR 4, 44; DLB 14
Finch, Anne 1661-1720 ....**LC 3; PC 21**
See also DLB 95
Finch, Robert (Duer Claydon) 1900-**CLC 18**
See also CA 57-60; CANR 9, 24, 49; DLB 88
Findley, Timothy 1930-. **CLC 27, 102; DAC; DAM MST**
See also CA 25-28R; CANR 12, 42; DLB 53
Fink, William
See Mencken, H(enry) L(ouis)
Firbank, Louis 1942-
See Reed, Lou
See also CA 117
Firbank, (Arthur Annesley) Ronald 1886-1926 **TCLC 1**
See also CA 104; DLB 36
Fisher, M(ary) F(rances) K(ennedy) 1908-1992 **CLC 76, 87**
See also CA 77-80; 138; CANR 44
Fisher, Roy 1930-...............................**CLC 25**
See also CA 81-84; CAAS 10; CANR 16; DLB 40
Fisher, Rudolph 1897-1934 . **TCLC 11; BLC; DAM MULT; SSC 25**
See also BW 1; CA 107; 124; DLB 51, 102
Fisher, Vardis (Alvero) 1895-1968 ......**CLC 7**
See also CA 5-8R; 25-28R; DLB 9
Fiske, Tarleton

See Bloch, Robert (Albert)
Fitch, Clarke
See Sinclair, Upton (Beall)
Fitch, John IV
See Cormier, Robert (Edmund)
Fitzgerald, Captain Hugh
See Baum, L(yman) Frank
FitzGerald, Edward 1809-1883 ....**NCLC 9**
See also DLB 32
Fitzgerald, F(rancis) Scott (Key) 1896-1940 **TCLC 1, 6, 14, 28, 55; DA; DAB; DAC; DAM MST, NOV; SSC 6; WLC**
See also AITN 1; CA 110; 123; CDALB 1917-1929; DLB 4, 9, 86; DLBD 1, 15, 16; DLBY 81, 96; MTCW
Fitzgerald, Penelope 1916- ... **CLC 19, 51, 61**
See also CA 85-88; CAAS 10; CANR 56; DLB 14
Fitzgerald, Robert (Stuart) 1910-1985**CLC 39**
See also CA 1-4R; 114; CANR 1; DLBY 80
FitzGerald, Robert D(avid) 1902-1987**CLC 19**
See also CA 17-20R
Fitzgerald, Zelda (Sayre) 1900-1948**TCLC 52**
See also CA 117; 126; DLBY 84
Flanagan, Thomas (James Bonner) 1923-**CLC 25, 52**
See also CA 108; CANR 55; DLBY 80; INT 108; MTCW
Flaubert, Gustave 1821-1880**NCLC 2, 10, 19, 62, 66; DA; DAB; DAC; DAM MST, NOV; SSC 11; WLC**
See also DLB 119
Flecker, Herman Elroy
See Flecker, (Herman) James Elroy
Flecker, (Herman) James Elroy 1884-1915 **TCLC 43**
See also CA 109; 150; DLB 10, 19
Fleming, Ian (Lancaster) 1908-1964 .**CLC 3, 30; DAM POP**
See also CA 5-8R; CANR 59; CDBLB 1945-1960; DLB 87; MTCW; SATA 9
Fleming, Thomas (James) 1927- ....**CLC 37**
See also CA 5-8R; CANR 10; INT CANR-10; SATA 8
Fletcher, John 1579-1625 ....**LC 33; DC 6**
See also CDBLB Before 1660; DLB 58
Fletcher, John Gould 1886-1950 ....**TCLC 35**
See also CA 107; DLB 4, 45
Fleur, Paul
See Pohl, Frederik
Flooglebuckle, Al
See Spiegelman, Art
Flying Officer X
See Bates, H(erbert) E(rnest)
Fo, Dario 1926- ....**CLC 32; DAM DRAM**
See also CA 116; 128; MTCW
Fogarty, Jonathan Titulescu Esq.
See Farrell, James T(homas)
Folke, Will
See Bloch, Robert (Albert)
Follett, Ken(neth Martin) 1949- .....**CLC 18; DAM NOV, POP**
See also AAYA 6; BEST 89:4; CA 81-84; CANR 13, 33, 54; DLB 87; DLBY 81; INT CANR-33; MTCW
Fontane, Theodor 1819-1898 ....**NCLC 26**
See also DLB 129
Foote, Horton 1916-**CLC 51, 91; DAM DRAM**
See also CA 73-76; CANR 34, 51; DLB 26; INT CANR-34
Foote, Shelby 1916-**CLC 75; DAM NOV, POP**
See also CA 5-8R; CANR 3, 45; DLB 2, 17
Forbes, Esther 1891-1967 ....**CLC 12**

See also AAYA 17; CA 13-14; 25-28R; CAP 1; CLR 27; DLB 22; JRDA; MAICYA; SATA 2

Forche, Carolyn (Louise) 1950- **CLC 25, 83, 86; DAM POET; PC 10**
See also CA 109; 117; CANR 50; DLB 5; INT 117

Ford, Elbur
See Hibbert, Eleanor Alice Burford

Ford, Ford Madox 1873-1939**TCLC 1, 15, 39, 57; DAM NOV**
See also CA 104; 132; CDBLB 1914-1945; DLB 162; MTCW

Ford, Henry 1863-1947 .... **TCLC 73**
See also CA 115; 148

Ford, John 1586-(?) .... **DC 8**
See also CDBLB Before 1660; DAM DRAM; DLB 58

Ford, John 1895-1973 .... **CLC 16**
See also CA 45-48

Ford, Richard .... **CLC 99**

Ford, Richard 1944- .... **CLC 46**
See also CA 69-72; CANR 11, 47

Ford, Webster
See Masters, Edgar Lee

Foreman, Richard 1937- .... **CLC 50**
See also CA 65-68; CANR 32, 63

Forester, C(ecil) S(cott) 1899-1966 .. **CLC 35**
See also CA 73-76; 25-28R; SATA 13

Forez
See Mauriac, Francois (Charles)

Forman, James Douglas 1932- .... **CLC 21**
See also AAYA 17; CA 9-12R; CANR 4, 19, 42; JRDA; MAICYA; SATA 8, 70

Fornes, Maria Irene 1930- .... **CLC 39, 61**
See also CA 25-28R; CANR 28; DLB 7; HW; INT CANR-28; MTCW

Forrest, Leon 1937- ....**CLC 4**
See also BW 2; CA 89-92; CAAS 7; CANR 25, 52; DLB 33

Forster, E(dward) M(organ) 1879-1970 **C L C 1, 2, 3, 4, 9, 10, 13, 15, 22, 45, 77; DA; DAB; DAC; DAM MST, NOV; SSC 27; WLC**
See also AAYA 2; CA 13-14; 25-28R; CANR 45; CAP 1; CDBLB 1914-1945; DLB 34, 98, 162, 178; DLBD 10; MTCW; SATA 57

Forster, John 1812-1876 .... **NCLC 11**
See also DLB 144, 184

Forsyth, Frederick 1938-**CLC 2, 5, 36; DAM NOV, POP**
See also BEST 89:4; CA 85-88; CANR 38, 62; DLB 87; MTCW

Forten, Charlotte L. .... **TCLC 16; BLC**
See also Grimke, Charlotte L(ottie) Forten
See also DLB 50

Foscolo, Ugo 1778-1827 .... **NCLC 8**

Fosse, Bob .... **CLC 20**
See also Fosse, Robert Louis

Fosse, Robert Louis 1927-1987
See Fosse, Bob
See also CA 110; 123

Foster, Stephen Collins 1826-1864 . **NCLC 26**

Foucault, Michel 1926-1984 . **CLC 31, 34, 69**
See also CA 105; 113; CANR 34; MTCW

Fouque, Friedrich (Heinrich Karl) de la Motte 1777-1843 .... **NCLC 2**
See also DLB 90

Fourier, Charles 1772-1837 .... **NCLC 51**

Fournier, Henri Alban 1886-1914
See Alain-Fournier
See also CA 104

Fournier, Pierre 1916- .... **CLC 11**
See also Gascar, Pierre
See also CA 89-92; CANR 16, 40

Fowles, John 1926-**CLC 1, 2, 3, 4, 6, 9, 10, 15, 33, 87; DAB; DAC; DAM MST**
See also CA 5-8R; CANR 25; CDBLB 1960 to Present; DLB 14, 139; MTCW; SATA 22

Fox, Paula 1923- .... **CLC 2, 8**
See also AAYA 3; CA 73-76; CANR 20, 36, 62; CLR 1, 44; DLB 52; JRDA; MAICYA; MTCW; SATA 17, 60

Fox, William Price (Jr.) 1926- .... **CLC 22**
See also CA 17-20R; CAAS 19; CANR 11; DLB 2; DLBY 81

Foxe, John 1516(?)-1587 .... **LC 14**

Frame, Janet 1924-**CLC 2, 3, 6, 22, 66, 96; SSC 29**
See also Clutha, Janet Paterson Frame

France, Anatole .... **TCLC 9**
See also Thibault, Jacques Anatole Francois
See also DLB 123

Francis, Claude 19(?)- ....**CLC 50**

Francis, Dick 1920-**CLC 2, 22, 42, 102; DAM POP**
See also AAYA 5, 21; BEST 89:3; CA 5-8R; CANR 9, 42; CDBLB 1960 to Present; DLB 87; INT CANR-9; MTCW

Francis, Robert (Churchill) 1901-1987 . **C L C 15**
See also CA 1-4R; 123; CANR 1

Frank, Anne(lies Marie) 1929-1945**TCLC 17; DA; DAB; DAC; DAM MST; WLC**
See also AAYA 12; CA 113; 133; MTCW; SATA 87; SATA-Brief 42

Frank, Elizabeth 1945- ....**CLC 39**
See also CA 121; 126; INT 126

Frankl, Viktor E(mil) 1905-1997 ......**CLC 93**
See also CA 65-68; 161

Franklin, Benjamin
See Hasek, Jaroslav (Matej Frantisek)

Franklin, Benjamin 1706-1790 .. **LC 25; DA; DAB; DAC; DAM MST; WLCS**
See also CDALB 1640-1865; DLB 24, 43, 73

Franklin, (Stella Maraia Sarah) Miles 1879-1954 .... **TCLC 7**
See also CA 104

Fraser, (Lady) Antonia (Pakenham) 1932- **CLC 32, 107**
See also CA 85-88; CANR 44; MTCW; SATA-Brief 32

Fraser, George MacDonald 1925- ...... **CLC 7**
See also CA 45-48; CANR 2, 48

Fraser, Sylvia 1935- ....**CLC 64**
See also CA 45-48; CANR 1, 16, 60

Frayn, Michael 1933-**CLC 3, 7, 31, 47; DAM DRAM, NOV**
See also CA 5-8R; CANR 30; DLB 13, 14; MTCW

Fraze, Candida (Merrill) 1945- ....**CLC 50**
See also CA 126

Frazer, J(ames) G(eorge) 1854-1941**TCLC 32**
See also CA 118

Frazer, Robert Caine
See Creasey, John

Frazer, Sir James George
See Frazer, J(ames) G(eorge)

Frazier, Ian 1951- ....**CLC 46**
See also CA 130; CANR 54

Frederic, Harold 1856-1898 ....**NCLC 10**
See also DLB 12, 23; DLBD 13

Frederick, John
See Faust, Frederick (Schiller)

Frederick the Great 1712-1786 .... **LC 14**

Fredro, Aleksander 1793-1876 ....**NCLC 8**

Freeling, Nicolas 1927- ....**CLC 38**
See also CA 49-52; CAAS 12; CANR 1, 17,

50; DLB 87

Freeman, Douglas Southall 1886-1953**T C L C 11**
See also CA 109; DLB 17

Freeman, Judith 1946- .... **CLC 55**
See also CA 148

Freeman, Mary Eleanor Wilkins 1852-1930 **TCLC 9; SSC 1**
See also CA 106; DLB 12, 78

Freeman, R(ichard) Austin 1862-1943**T C L C 21**
See also CA 113; DLB 70

French, Albert 1943- .... **CLC 86**

French, Marilyn 1929-**CLC 10, 18, 60; DAM DRAM, NOV, POP**
See also CA 69-72; CANR 3, 31; INT CANR-31; MTCW

French, Paul
See Asimov, Isaac

Freneau, Philip Morin 1752-1832 .... **NCLC 1**
See also DLB 37, 43

Freud, Sigmund 1856-1939 .... **TCLC 52**
See also CA 115; 133; MTCW

Friedan, Betty (Naomi) 1921- .... **CLC 74**
See also CA 65-68; CANR 18, 45; MTCW

Friedlander, Saul 1932- .... **CLC 90**
See also CA 117; 130

Friedman, B(ernard) H(arper) 1926-.**CLC 7**
See also CA 1-4R; CANR 3, 48

Friedman, Bruce Jay 1930- ...... **CLC 3, 5, 56**
See also CA 9-12R; CANR 25, 52; DLB 2, 28; INT CANR-25

Friel, Brian 1929- .... **CLC 5, 42, 59; DC 8**
See also CA 21-24R; CANR 33; DLB 13; MTCW

Friis-Baastad, Babbis Ellinor 1921-1970**CLC 12**
See also CA 17-20R; 134; SATA 7

Frisch, Max (Rudolf) 1911-1991**CLC 3, 9, 14, 18, 32, 44; DAM DRAM, NOV**
See also CA 85-88; 134; CANR 32; DLB 69, 124; MTCW

Fromentin, Eugene (Samuel Auguste) 1820-1876 ....**NCLC 10**
See also DLB 123

Frost, Frederick
See Faust, Frederick (Schiller)

Frost, Robert (Lee) 1874-1963**CLC 1, 3, 4, 9, 10, 13, 15, 26, 34, 44; DA; DAB; DAC; DAM MST, POET; PC 1; WLC**
See also AAYA 21; CA 89-92; CANR 33; CDALB 1917-1929; DLB 54; DLBD 7; MTCW; SATA 14

Froude, James Anthony 1818-1894**NCLC 43**
See also DLB 18, 57, 144

Froy, Herald
See Waterhouse, Keith (Spencer)

Fry, Christopher 1907- **CLC 2, 10, 14; DAM DRAM**
See also CA 17-20R; CAAS 23; CANR 9, 30; DLB 13; MTCW; SATA 66

Frye, (Herman) Northrop 1912-1991**CLC 24, 70**
See also CA 5-8R; 133; CANR 8, 37; DLB 67, 68; MTCW

Fuchs, Daniel 1909-1993 .... **CLC 8, 22**
See also CA 81-84; 142; CAAS 5; CANR 40; DLB 9, 26, 28; DLBY 93

Fuchs, Daniel 1934- .... **CLC 34**
See also CA 37-40R; CANR 14, 48

Fuentes, Carlos 1928-**CLC 3, 8, 10, 13, 22, 41, 60; DA; DAB; DAC; DAM MST, MULT, NOV; HLC; SSC 24; WLC**

See also AAYA 4; AITN 2; CA 69-72; CANR 10, 32; DLB 113; HW; MTCW

Fuentes, Gregorio Lopez y
See Lopez y Fuentes, Gregorio

Fugard, (Harold) Athol 1932-CLC **5, 9, 14, 25, 40, 80; DAM DRAM; DC 3**
See also AAYA 17; CA 85-88; CANR 32, 54; MTCW

Fugard, Sheila 1932- .... **CLC 48**
See also CA 125

Fuller, Charles (H., Jr.) 1939-CLC **25; BLC; DAM DRAM, MULT; DC 1**
See also BW 2; CA 108; 112; DLB 38; INT 112; MTCW

Fuller, John (Leopold) 1937- .... **CLC 62**
See also CA 21-24R; CANR 9, 44; DLB 40

Fuller, Margaret .... **NCLC 5, 50**
See also Ossoli, Sarah Margaret (Fuller marchesa d')

Fuller, Roy (Broadbent) 1912-1991CLC **4, 28**
See also CA 5-8R; 135; CAAS 10; CANR 53; DLB 15, 20; SATA 87

Fulton, Alice 1952- .... **CLC 52**
See also CA 116; CANR 57

Furphy, Joseph 1843-1912 .... **TCLC 25**

Fussell, Paul 1924- .... **CLC 74**
See also BEST 90:1; CA 17-20R; CANR 8, 21, 35; INT CANR-21; MTCW

Futabatei, Shimei 1864-1909 .... **TCLC 44**
See also DLB 180

Futrelle, Jacques 1875-1912 .... **TCLC 19**
See also CA 113; 155

Gaboriau, Emile 1835-1873 .... **NCLC 14**

Gadda, Carlo Emilio 1893-1973 .... **CLC 11**
See also CA 89-92; DLB 177

Gaddis, William 1922- CLC **1, 3, 6, 8, 10, 19, 43, 86**
See also CA 17-20R; CANR 21, 48; DLB 2; MTCW

Gage, Walter
See Inge, William (Motter)

Gaines, Ernest J(ames) 1933- CLC **3, 11, 18, 86; BLC; DAM MULT**
See also AAYA 18; AITN 1; BW 2; CA 9-12R; CANR 6, 24, 42; CDALB 1968-1988; DLB 2, 33, 152; DLBY 80; MTCW; SATA 86

Gaitskill, Mary 1954- .... **CLC 69**
See also CA 128; CANR 61

Galdos, Benito Perez
See Perez Galdos, Benito

Gale, Zona 1874-1938TCLC **7; DAM DRAM**
See also CA 105; 153; DLB 9, 78

Galeano, Eduardo (Hughes) 1940- .. **CLC 72**
See also CA 29-32R; CANR 13, 32; HW

Galiano, Juan Valera y Alcala
See Valera y Alcala-Galiano, Juan

Gallagher, Tess 1943- ...... CLC **18, 63; DAM POET; PC 9**
See also CA 106; DLB 120

Gallant, Mavis 1922- ... CLC **7, 18, 38; DAC; DAM MST; SSC 5**
See also CA 69-72; CANR 29; DLB 53; MTCW

Gallant, Roy A(rthur) 1924- .... **CLC 17**
See also CA 5-8R; CANR 4, 29, 54; CLR 30; MAICYA; SATA 4, 68

Gallico, Paul (William) 1897-1976 ..... **CLC 2**
See also AITN 1; CA 5-8R; 69-72; CANR 23; DLB 9, 171; MAICYA; SATA 13

Gallo, Max Louis 1932- .... **CLC 95**
See also CA 85-88

Gallois, Lucien
See Desnos, Robert

Gallup, Ralph

See Whitemore, Hugh (John)

Galsworthy, John 1867-1933TCLC **1, 45; DA; DAB; DAC; DAM DRAM, MST, NOV; SSC 22; WLC 2**
See also CA 104; 141; CDBLB 1890-1914; DLB 10, 34, 98, 162; DLBD 16

Galt, John 1779-1839 .... **NCLC 1**
See also DLB 99, 116, 159

Galvin, James 1951- .... **CLC 38**
See also CA 108; CANR 26

Gamboa, Federico 1864-1939 .... **TCLC 36**

Gandhi, M. K.
See Gandhi, Mohandas Karamchand

Gandhi, Mahatma
See Gandhi, Mohandas Karamchand

Gandhi, Mohandas Karamchand 1869-1948 TCLC **59; DAM MULT**
See also CA 121; 132; MTCW

Gann, Ernest Kellogg 1910-1991 ...... **CLC 23**
See also AITN 1; CA 1-4R; 136; CANR 1

Garcia, Cristina 1958- .... **CLC 76**
See also CA 141

Garcia Lorca, Federico 1898-1936TCLC **1, 7, 49; DA; DAB; DAC; DAM DRAM, MST, MULT, POET; DC 2; HLC; PC 3; WLC**
See also CA 104; 131; DLB 108; HW; MTCW

Garcia Marquez, Gabriel (Jose) 1928-CLC **2, 3, 8, 10, 15, 27, 47, 55, 68; DA; DAB; DAC; DAM MST, MULT, NOV, POP; HLC; SSC 8; WLC**
See also AAYA 3; BEST 89:1, 90:4; CA 33-36R; CANR 10, 28, 50; DLB 113; HW; MTCW

Gard, Janice
See Latham, Jean Lee

Gard, Roger Martin du
See Martin du Gard, Roger

Gardam, Jane 1928- .... **CLC 43**
See also CA 49-52; CANR 2, 18, 33, 54; CLR 12; DLB 14, 161; MAICYA; MTCW; SAAS 9; SATA 39, 76; SATA-Brief 28

Gardner, Herb(ert) 1934- .... **CLC 44**
See also CA 149

Gardner, John (Champlin), Jr. 1933-1982 CLC **2, 3, 5, 7, 8, 10, 18, 28, 34; DAM NOV, POP; SSC 7**
See also AITN 1; CA 65-68; 107; CANR 33; DLB 2; DLBY 82; MTCW; SATA 40; SATA-Obit 31

Gardner, John (Edmund) 1926-CLC **30; DAM POP**
See also CA 103; CANR 15; MTCW

Gardner, Miriam
See Bradley, Marion Zimmer

Gardner, Noel
See Kuttner, Henry

Gardons, S. S.
See Snodgrass, W(illiam) D(e Witt)

Garfield, Leon 1921-1996 .... **CLC 12**
See also AAYA 8; CA 17-20R; 152; CANR 38, 41; CLR 21; DLB 161; JRDA; MAICYA; SATA 1, 32, 76; SATA-Obit 90

Garland, (Hannibal) Hamlin 1860-1940 TCLC **3; SSC 18**
See also CA 104; DLB 12, 71, 78

Garneau, (Hector de) Saint-Denys 1912-1943 TCLC **13**
See also CA 111; DLB 88

Garner, Alan 1934-CLC **17; DAB; DAM POP**
See also AAYA 18; CA 73-76; CANR 15, 64; CLR 20; DLB 161; MAICYA; MTCW; SATA 18, 69

Garner, Hugh 1913-1979 .... **CLC 13**

See also CA 69-72; CANR 31; DLB 68

Garnett, David 1892-1981 .... **CLC 3**
See also CA 5-8R; 103; CANR 17; DLB 34

Garos, Stephanie
See Katz, Steve

Garrett, George (Palmer) 1929-CLC **3, 11, 51**
See also CA 1-4R; CAAS 5; CANR 1, 42; DLB 2, 5, 130, 152; DLBY 83

Garrick, David 1717-1779 ....LC **15; DAM DRAM**
See also DLB 84

Garrigue, Jean 1914-1972 .... CLC **2, 8**
See also CA 5-8R; 37-40R; CANR 20

Garrison, Frederick
See Sinclair, Upton (Beall)

Garth, Will
See Hamilton, Edmond; Kuttner, Henry

Garvey, Marcus (Moziah, Jr.) 1887-1940 TCLC **41; BLC; DAM MULT**
See also BW 1; CA 120; 124

Gary, Romain .... **CLC 25**
See also Kacew, Romain
See also DLB 83

Gascar, Pierre .... **CLC 11**
See also Fournier, Pierre

Gascoyne, David (Emery) 1916- .... **CLC 45**
See also CA 65-68; CANR 10, 28, 54; DLB 20; MTCW

Gaskell, Elizabeth Cleghorn 1810-1865NCLC **5; DAB; DAM MST; SSC 25**
See also CDBLB 1832-1890; DLB 21, 144, 159

Gass, William H(oward) 1924-CLC **1, 2, 8, 11, 15, 39; SSC 12**
See also CA 17-20R; CANR 30; DLB 2; MTCW

Gasset, Jose Ortega y
See Ortega y Gasset, Jose

Gates, Henry Louis, Jr. 1950- CLC **65; DAM MULT**
See also BW 2; CA 109; CANR 25, 53; DLB 67

Gautier, Theophile 1811-1872 .. NCLC **1, 59; DAM POET; PC 18; SSC 20**
See also DLB 119

Gawsworth, John
See Bates, H(erbert) E(rnest)

Gay, Oliver
See Gogarty, Oliver St. John

Gaye, Marvin (Penze) 1939-1984 ..... **CLC 26**
See also CA 112

Gebler, Carlo (Ernest) 1954- .... **CLC 39**
See also CA 119; 133

Gee, Maggie (Mary) 1948- .... **CLC 57**
See also CA 130

Gee, Maurice (Gough) 1931- .... **CLC 29**
See also CA 97-100; SATA 46

Gelbart, Larry (Simon) 1923- .... CLC **21, 61**
See also CA 73-76; CANR 45

Gelber, Jack 1932- .... CLC **1, 6, 14, 79**
See also CA 1-4R; CANR 2; DLB 7

Gellhorn, Martha (Ellis) 1908- .. CLC **14, 60**
See also CA 77-80; CANR 44; DLBY 82

Genet, Jean 1910-1986CLC **1, 2, 5, 10, 14, 44, 46; DAM DRAM**
See also CA 13-16R; CANR 18; DLB 72; DLBY 86; MTCW

Gent, Peter 1942- .... **CLC 29**
See also AITN 1; CA 89-92; DLBY 82

Gentlewoman in New England, A
See Bradstreet, Anne

Gentlewoman in Those Parts, A
See Bradstreet, Anne

George, Jean Craighead 1919- .... **CLC 35**
See also AAYA 8; CA 5-8R; CANR 25; CLR 1;

DLB 52; JRDA; MAICYA; SATA 2, 68

George, Stefan (Anton) 1868-1933 **TCLC 2, 14**
See also CA 104

Georges, Georges Martin
See Simenon, Georges (Jacques Christian)

Gerhardi, William Alexander
See Gerhardie, William Alexander

Gerhardie, William Alexander 1895-1977
CLC 5
See also CA 25-28R; 73-76; CANR 18; DLB 36

Gerstler, Amy 1956- .... **CLC 70**
See also CA 146

Gertler, T. .... **CLC 34**
See also CA 116; 121; INT 121

Ghalib .... **NCLC 39**
See also Ghalib, Hsadullah Khan

Ghalib, Hsadullah Khan 1797-1869
See Ghalib
See also DAM POET

Ghelderode, Michel de 1898-1962 **CLC 6, 11;**
DAM DRAM
See also CA 85-88; CANR 40

Ghiselin, Brewster 1903- .... **CLC 23**
See also CA 13-16R; CAAS 10; CANR 13

Ghose, Zulfikar 1935- .... **CLC 42**
See also CA 65-68

Ghosh, Amitav 1956- .... **CLC 44**
See also CA 147

Giacosa, Giuseppe 1847-1906 .... **TCLC 7**
See also CA 104

Gibb, Lee
See Waterhouse, Keith (Spencer)

Gibbon, Lewis Grassic .... **TCLC 4**
See also Mitchell, James Leslie

Gibbons, Kaye 1960- **CLC 50, 88; DAM POP**
See also CA 151

Gibran, Kahlil 1883-1931 . **TCLC 1, 9; DAM**
POET, POP; PC 9
See also CA 104; 150

Gibran, Khalil
See Gibran, Kahlil

Gibson, William 1914- .. **CLC 23; DA; DAB;**
DAC; DAM DRAM, MST
See also CA 9-12R; CANR 9, 42; DLB 7; SATA 66

Gibson, William (Ford) 1948- ... **CLC 39, 63;**
DAM POP
See also AAYA 12; CA 126; 133; CANR 52

Gide, Andre (Paul Guillaume) 1869-1951
TCLC 5, 12, 36; DA; DAB; DAC; DAM
MST, NOV; SSC 13; WLC
See also CA 104; 124; DLB 65; MTCW

Gifford, Barry (Colby) 1946- .... **CLC 34**
See also CA 65-68; CANR 9, 30, 40

Gilbert, Frank
See De Voto, Bernard (Augustine)

Gilbert, W(illiam) S(chwenck) 1836-1911
TCLC 3; DAM DRAM, POET
See also CA 104; SATA 36

Gilbreth, Frank B., Jr. 1911- .... **CLC 17**
See also CA 9-12R; SATA 2

Gilchrist, Ellen 1935- **CLC 34, 48; DAM POP;**
SSC 14
See also CA 113; 116; CANR 41, 61; DLB 130; MTCW

Giles, Molly 1942- .... **CLC 39**
See also CA 126

Gill, Patrick
See Creasey, John

Gilliam, Terry (Vance) 1940- .... **CLC 21**
See also Monty Python
See also AAYA 19; CA 108; 113; CANR 35;

INT 113

Gillian, Jerry
See Gilliam, Terry (Vance)

Gilliatt, Penelope (Ann Douglass) 1932-1993
CLC 2, 10, 13, 53
See also AITN 2; CA 13-16R; 141; CANR 49;
DLB 14

Gilman, Charlotte (Anna) Perkins (Stetson)
1860-1935 .... **TCLC 9, 37; SSC 13**
See also CA 106; 150

Gilmour, David 1949- .... **CLC 35**
See also CA 138, 147

Gilpin, William 1724-1804 .... **NCLC 30**

Gilray, J. D.
See Mencken, H(enry) L(ouis)

Gilroy, Frank D(aniel) 1925- .... **CLC 2**
See also CA 81-84; CANR 32, 64; DLB 7

Gilstrap, John 1957(?)- .... **CLC 99**
See also CA 160

Ginsberg, Allen 1926-1997 **CLC 1, 2, 3, 4, 6, 13,**
36, 69; DA; DAB; DAC; DAM MST,
POET; PC 4; WLC 3
See also AITN 1; CA 1-4R; 157; CANR 2, 41,
63; CDALB 1941-1968; DLB 5, 16, 169;
MTCW

Ginzburg, Natalia 1916-1991 **CLC 5, 11, 54, 70**
See also CA 85-88; 135; CANR 33; DLB 177;
MTCW

Giono, Jean 1895-1970 .... **CLC 4, 11**
See also CA 45-48; 29-32R; CANR 2, 35; DLB
72; MTCW

Giovanni, Nikki 1943- **CLC 2, 4, 19, 64; BLC;**
DA; DAB; DAC; DAM MST, MULT,
POET; PC 19; WLCS
See also AAYA 22; AITN 1; BW 2; CA 29-32R;
CAAS 6; CANR 18, 41, 60; CLR 6; DLB 5,
41; INT CANR-18; MAICYA; MTCW; SATA
24

Giovene, Andrea 1904- .... **CLC 7**
See also CA 85-88

Gippius, Zinaida (Nikolayevna) 1869-1945
See Hippius, Zinaida
See also CA 106

Giraudoux, (Hippolyte) Jean 1882-1944
TCLC 2, 7; DAM DRAM
See also CA 104; DLB 65

Gironella, Jose Maria 1917- .... **CLC 11**
See also CA 101

Gissing, George (Robert) 1857-1903 **TCLC 3,**
24, 47
See also CA 105; DLB 18, 135, 184

Giurlani, Aldo
See Palazzeschi, Aldo

Gladkov, Fyodor (Vasilyevich) 1883-1958
TCLC 27

Glanville, Brian (Lester) 1931- .... **CLC 6**
See also CA 5-8R; CAAS 9; CANR 3; DLB 15,
139; SATA 42

Glasgow, Ellen (Anderson Gholson) 1873(?)-
1945 .... **TCLC 2, 7**
See also CA 104; DLB 9, 12

Glaspell, Susan 1882(?)-1948 .... **TCLC 55**
See also CA 110; 154; DLB 7, 9, 78; YABC 2

Glassco, John 1909-1981 .... **CLC 9**
See also CA 13-16R; 102; CANR 15; DLB 68

Glasscock, Amnesia
See Steinbeck, John (Ernst)

Glasser, Ronald J. 1940(?)- .... **CLC 37**

Glassman, Joyce
See Johnson, Joyce

Glendinning, Victoria 1937- .... **CLC 50**
See also CA 120; 127; CANR 59; DLB 155

Glissant, Edouard 1928- . **CLC 10, 68; DAM**

MULT
See also CA 153

Gloag, Julian 1930- .... **CLC 40**
See also AITN 1; CA 65-68; CANR 10

Glowacki, Aleksander
See Prus, Boleslaw

Gluck, Louise (Elisabeth) 1943- **CLC 7, 22, 44,**
81; DAM POET; PC 16
See also CA 33-36R; CANR 40; DLB 5

Glyn, Elinor 1864-1943 .... **TCLC 72**
See also DLB 153

Gobineau, Joseph Arthur (Comte) de 1816-
1882 .... **NCLC 17**
See also DLB 123

Godard, Jean-Luc 1930- .... **CLC 20**
See also CA 93-96

Godden, (Margaret) Rumer 1907-... **CLC 53**
See also AAYA 6; CA 5-8R; CANR 4, 27, 36,
55; CLR 20; DLB 161; MAICYA; SAAS 12;
SATA 3, 36

Godoy Alcayaga, Lucila 1889-1957
See Mistral, Gabriela
See also BW 2; CA 104; 131; DAM MULT;
HW; MTCW

Godwin, Gail (Kathleen) 1937- **CLC 5, 8, 22,**
31, 69; DAM POP
See also CA 29-32R; CANR 15, 43; DLB 6;
INT CANR-15; MTCW

Godwin, William 1756-1836 .... **NCLC 14**
See also CDBLB 1789-1832; DLB 39, 104, 142,
158, 163

Goebbels, Josef
See Goebbels, (Paul) Joseph

Goebbels, (Paul) Joseph 1897-1945 **TCLC 68**
See also CA 115; 148

Goebbels, Joseph Paul
See Goebbels, (Paul) Joseph

Goethe, Johann Wolfgang von 1749-1832
NCLC 4, 22, 34; DA; DAB; DAC; DAM
DRAM, MST, POET; PC 5; WLC 3
See also DLB 94

Gogarty, Oliver St. John 1878-1957 **TCLC 15**
See also CA 109; 150; DLB 15, 19

Gogol, Nikolai (Vasilyevich) 1809-1852 **NCLC**
5, 15, 31; DA; DAB; DAC; DAM DRAM,
MST; DC 1; SSC 4, 29; WLC

Goines, Donald 1937(?)-1974 **CLC 80; BLC;**
DAM MULT, POP
See also AITN 1; BW 1; CA 124; 114; DLB 33

Gold, Herbert 1924- .... **CLC 4, 7, 14, 42**
See also CA 9-12R; CANR 17, 45; DLB 2;
DLBY 81

Goldbarth, Albert 1948- .... **CLC 5, 38**
See also CA 53-56; CANR 6, 40; DLB 120

Goldberg, Anatol 1910-1982 .... **CLC 34**
See also CA 131; 117

Goldemberg, Isaac 1945- .... **CLC 52**
See also CA 69-72; CAAS 12; CANR 11, 32;
HW

Golding, William (Gerald) 1911-1993 **CLC 1,**
2, 3, 8, 10, 17, 27, 58, 81; DA; DAB; DAC;
DAM MST, NOV; WLC
See also AAYA 5; CA 5-8R; 141; CANR 13,
33, 54; CDBLB 1945-1960; DLB 15, 100;
MTCW

Goldman, Emma 1869-1940 .... **TCLC 13**
See also CA 110; 150

Goldman, Francisco 1955- .... **CLC 76**

Goldman, William (W.) 1931- ...... **CLC 1, 48**
See also CA 9-12R; CANR 29; DLB 44

Goldmann, Lucien 1913-1970 .... **CLC 24**
See also CA 25-28; CAP 2

Goldoni, Carlo 1707-1793 **LC 4; DAM DRAM**

Goldsberry, Steven 1949- .... **CLC 34**
See also CA 131
Goldsmith, Oliver 1728-1774**LC 2; DA; DAB; DAC; DAM DRAM, MST, NOV, POET; DC 8; WLC**
See also CDBLB 1660-1789; DLB 39, 89, 104, 109, 142; SATA 26
Goldsmith, Peter
See Priestley, J(ohn) B(oynton)
Gombrowicz, Witold 1904-1969**CLC 4, 7, 11, 49; DAM DRAM**
See also CA 19-20; 25-28R; CAP 2
Gomez de la Serna, Ramon 1888-1963**CLC 9**
See also CA 153; 116; HW
Goncharov, Ivan Alexandrovich 1812-1891 **NCLC 1, 63**
Goncourt, Edmond (Louis Antoine Huot) de 1822-1896 .... **NCLC 7**
See also DLB 123
Goncourt, Jules (Alfred Huot) de 1830-1870 **NCLC 7**
See also DLB 123
Gontier, Fernande 19(?)- .... **CLC 50**
Gonzalez Martinez, Enrique 1871-1952 **TCLC 72**
See also HW
Goodman, Paul 1911-1972 ...... **CLC 1, 2, 4, 7**
See also CA 19-20; 37-40R; CANR 34; CAP 2; DLB 130; MTCW
Gordimer, Nadine 1923-**CLC 3, 5, 7, 10, 18, 33, 51, 70; DA; DAB; DAC; DAM MST, NOV; SSC 17; WLCS**
See also CA 5-8R; CANR 3, 28, 56; INT CANR-28; MTCW
Gordon, Adam Lindsay 1833-1870 **NCLC 21**
Gordon, Caroline 1895-1981**CLC 6, 13, 29, 83; SSC 15**
See also CA 11-12; 103; CANR 36; CAP 1; DLB 4, 9, 102; DLBY 81; MTCW
Gordon, Charles William 1860-1937
See Connor, Ralph
See also CA 109
Gordon, Mary (Catherine) 1949-**CLC 13, 22**
See also CA 102; CANR 44; DLB 6; DLBY 81; INT 102; MTCW
Gordon, N. J.
See Bosman, Herman Charles
Gordon, Sol 1923- .... **CLC 26**
See also CA 53-56; CANR 4; SATA 11
Gordone, Charles 1925-1995**CLC 1, 4; DAM DRAM; DC 8**
See also BW 1; CA 93-96; 150; CANR 55; DLB 7; INT 93-96; MTCW
Gore, Catherine 1800-1861 .... **NCLC 65**
See also DLB 116
Gorenko, Anna Andreevna
See Akhmatova, Anna
Gorky, Maxim 1868-1936**TCLC 8; DAB; SSC 28; WLC**
See also Peshkov, Alexei Maximovich
Goryan, Sirak
See Saroyan, William
Gosse, Edmund (William) 1849-1928**TCLC 28**
See also CA 117; DLB 57, 144, 184
Gotlieb, Phyllis Fay (Bloom) 1926- .. **CLC 18**
See also CA 13-16R; CANR 7; DLB 88
Gottesman, S. D.
See Kornbluth, C(yril) M.; Pohl, Frederik
Gottfried von Strassburg fl. c. 1210-. **CMLC 10**
See also DLB 138
Gould, Lois .... **CLC 4, 10**
See also CA 77-80; CANR 29; MTCW

Gourmont, Remy (-Marie-Charles) de 1858-1915 .... **TCLC 17**
See also CA 109; 150
Govier, Katherine 1948- .... **CLC 51**
See also CA 101; CANR 18, 40
Goyen, (Charles) William 1915-1983**CLC 5, 8, 14, 40**
See also AITN 2; CA 5-8R; 110; CANR 6; DLB 2; DLBY 83; INT CANR-6
Goytisolo, Juan 1931- . **CLC 5, 10, 23; DAM MULT; HLC**
See also CA 85-88; CANR 32, 61; HW; MTCW
Gozzano, Guido 1883-1916 .... **PC 10**
See also CA 154; DLB 114
Gozzi, (Conte) Carlo 1720-1806 .... **NCLC 23**
Grabbe, Christian Dietrich 1801-1836**NCLC 2**
See also DLB 133
Grace, Patricia 1937- .... **CLC 56**
Gracian y Morales, Baltasar 1601-1658**LC 15**
Gracq, Julien .... **CLC 11, 48**
See also Poirier, Louis
See also DLB 83
Grade, Chaim 1910-1982 .... **CLC 10**
See also CA 93-96; 107
Graduate of Oxford, A
See Ruskin, John
Grafton, Garth
See Duncan, Sara Jeannette
Graham, John
See Phillips, David Graham
Graham, Jorie 1951- .... **CLC 48**
See also CA 111; CANR 63; DLB 120
Graham, R(obert) B(ontine) Cunninghame
See Cunninghame Graham, R(obert) B(ontine)
See also DLB 98, 135, 174
Graham, Robert
See Haldeman, Joe (William)
Graham, Tom
See Lewis, (Harry) Sinclair
Graham, W(illiam) S(ydney) 1918-1986**CLC 29**
See also CA 73-76; 118; DLB 20
Graham, Winston (Mawdsley) 1910- **CLC 23**
See also CA 49-52; CANR 2, 22, 45; DLB 77
Grahame, Kenneth 1859-1932**TCLC 64; DAB**
See also CA 108; 136; CLR 5; DLB 34, 141, 178; MAICYA; YABC 1
Grant, Skeeter
See Spiegelman, Art
Granville-Barker, Harley 1877-1946**TCLC 2; DAM DRAM**
See also Barker, Harley Granville
See also CA 104
Grass, Guenter (Wilhelm) 1927-**CLC 1, 2, 4, 6, 11, 15, 22, 32, 49, 88; DA; DAB; DAC; DAM MST, NOV; WLC**
See also CA 13-16R; CANR 20; DLB 75, 124; MTCW
Gratton, Thomas
See Hulme, T(homas) E(rnest)
Grau, Shirley Ann 1929- .. **CLC 4, 9; SSC 15**
See also CA 89-92; CANR 22; DLB 2; INT CANR-22; MTCW
Gravel, Fern
See Hall, James Norman
Graver, Elizabeth 1964- .... **CLC 70**
See also CA 135
Graves, Richard Perceval 1945- .... **CLC 44**
See also CA 65-68; CANR 9, 26, 51
Graves, Robert (von Ranke) 1895-1985 **CLC 1, 2, 6, 11, 39, 44, 45; DAB; DAC; DAM MST, POET; PC 6**

See also CA 5-8R; 117; CANR 5, 36; CDBLB 1914-1945; DLB 20, 100; DLBY 85; MTCW; SATA 45
Graves, Valerie
See Bradley, Marion Zimmer
Gray, Alasdair (James) 1934- .... **CLC 41**
See also CA 126; CANR 47; INT 126; MTCW
Gray, Amlin 1946- : .... **CLC 29**
See also CA 138
Gray, Francine du Plessix 1930- ..... **CLC 22; DAM NOV**
See also BEST 90:3; CA 61-64; CAAS 2; CANR 11, 33; INT CANR-11; MTCW
Gray, John (Henry) 1866-1934 ...... **TCLC 19**
See also CA 119
Gray, Simon (James Holliday) 1936- **CLC 9, 14, 36**
See also AITN 1; CA 21-24R; CAAS 3; CANR 32; DLB 13; MTCW
Gray, Spalding 1941-**CLC 49; DAM POP; DC 7**
See also CA 128
Gray, Thomas 1716-1771**LC 4, 40; DA; DAB; DAC; DAM MST; PC 2; WLC**
See also CDBLB 1660-1789; DLB 109
Grayson, David
See Baker, Ray Stannard
Grayson, Richard (A.) 1951- .... **CLC 38**
See also CA 85-88; CANR 14, 31, 57
Greeley, Andrew M(oran) 1928- ..... **CLC 28; DAM POP**
See also CA 5-8R; CAAS 7; CANR 7, 43; MTCW
Green, Anna Katharine 1846-1935 **TCLC 63**
See also CA 112; 159
Green, Brian
See Card, Orson Scott
Green, Hannah
See Greenberg, Joanne (Goldenberg)
Green, Hannah 1927(?)-1996 .... **CLC 3**
See also CA 73-76; CANR 59
Green, Henry 1905-1973 .... **CLC 2, 13, 97**
See also Yorke, Henry Vincent
See also DLB 15
Green, Julian (Hartridge) 1900-
See Green, Julien
See also CA 21-24R; CANR 33; DLB 4, 72; MTCW
Green, Julien .... **CLC 3, 11, 77**
See also Green, Julian (Hartridge)
Green, Paul (Eliot) 1894-1981**CLC 25; DAM DRAM**
See also AITN 1; CA 5-8R; 103; CANR 3; DLB 7, 9; DLBY 81
Greenberg, Ivan 1908-1973
See Rahv, Philip
See also CA 85-88
Greenberg, Joanne (Goldenberg) 1932- **CLC 7, 30**
See also AAYA 12; CA 5-8R; CANR 14, 32; SATA 25
Greenberg, Richard 1959(?)- .... **CLC 57**
See also CA 138
Greene, Bette 1934- .... **CLC 30**
See also AAYA 7; CA 53-56; CANR 4; CLR 2; JRDA; MAICYA; SAAS 16; SATA 8
Greene, Gael .... **CLC 8**
See also CA 13-16R; CANR 10
Greene, Graham (Henry) 1904-1991**CLC 1, 3, 6, 9, 14, 18, 27, 37, 70, 72; DA; DAB; DAC; DAM MST, NOV; SSC 29; WLC**
See also AITN 2; CA 13-16R; 133; CANR 35, 61; CDBLB 1945-1960; DLB 13, 15, 77,

100, 162; DLBY 91; MTCW; SATA 20

Greene, Robert 1558-1592 .... **LC 41**

Greer, Richard
  See Silverberg, Robert

Gregor, Arthur 1923- .... **CLC 9**
  See also CA 25-28R; CAAS 10; CANR 11;
  SATA 36

Gregor, Lee
  See Pohl, Frederik

Gregory, Isabella Augusta (Persse) 1852-1932
  TCLC 1
  See also CA 104; DLB 10

Gregory, J. Dennis
  See Williams, John A(lfred)

Grendon, Stephen
  See Derleth, August (William)

Grenville, Kate 1950- .... **CLC 61**
  See also CA 118; CANR 53

Grenville, Pelham
  See Wodehouse, P(elham) G(renville)

Greve, Felix Paul (Berthold Friedrich) 1879-
  1948
  See Grove, Frederick Philip
  See also CA 104; 141; DAC; DAM MST

Grey, Zane 1872-1939 .. **TCLC 6; DAM POP**
  See also CA 104; 132; DLB 9; MTCW

Grieg, (Johan) Nordahl (Brun) 1902-1943
  TCLC 10
  See also CA 107

Grieve, C(hristopher) M(urray) 1892-1978
  CLC 11, 19; DAM POET
  See also MacDiarmid, Hugh; Pteleon
  See also CA 5-8R; 85-88; CANR 33; MTCW

Griffin, Gerald 1803-1840 .... **NCLC 7**
  See also DLB 159

Griffin, John Howard 1920-1980 .... **CLC 68**
  See also AITN 1; CA 1-4R; 101; CANR 2

Griffin, Peter 1942- .... **CLC 39**
  See also CA 136

Griffith, D(avid Lewelyn) W(ark) 1875(?)-1948
  TCLC 68
  See also CA 119; 150

Griffith, Lawrence
  See Griffith, D(avid Lewelyn) W(ark)

Griffiths, Trevor 1935- .... **CLC 13, 52**
  See also CA 97-100; CANR 45; DLB 13

Griggs, Sutton Elbert 1872-1930(?)**TCLC 77**
  See also CA 123; DLB 50

Grigson, Geoffrey (Edward Harvey) 1905-1985
  CLC 7, 39
  See also CA 25-28R; 118; CANR 20, 33; DLB
  27; MTCW

Grillparzer, Franz 1791-1872 .... **NCLC 1**
  See also DLB 133

Grimble, Reverend Charles James
  See Eliot, T(homas) S(tearns)

Grimke, Charlotte L(ottie) Forten 1837(?)-1914
  See Forten, Charlotte L.
  See also BW 1; CA 117; 124; DAM MULT,
  POET

Grimm, Jacob Ludwig Karl 1785-1863**NCLC
  3**
  See also DLB 90; MAICYA; SATA 22

Grimm, Wilhelm Karl 1786-1859 .... **NCLC 3**
  See also DLB 90; MAICYA; SATA 22

Grimmelshausen, Johann Jakob Christoffel von
  1621-1676 .... **LC 6**
  See also DLB 168

Grindel, Eugene 1895-1952
  See Eluard, Paul
  See also CA 104

Grisham, John 1955- ..... **CLC 84; DAM POP**
  See also AAYA 14; CA 138; CANR 47

Grossman, David 1954- .... **CLC 67**
  See also CA 138

Grossman, Vasily (Semenovich) 1905-1964
  CLC 41
  See also CA 124; 130; MTCW

Grove, Frederick Philip .... **TCLC 4**
  See also Greve, Felix Paul (Berthold Friedrich)
  See also DLB 92

Grubb
  See Crumb, R(obert)

Grumbach, Doris (Isaac) 1918-**CLC 13, 22, 64**
  See also CA 5-8R; CAAS 2; CANR 9, 42; INT
  CANR-9

Grundtvig, Nicolai Frederik Severin 1783-1872
  NCLC 1

Grunge
  See Crumb, R(obert)

Grunwald, Lisa 1959- .... **CLC 44**
  See also CA 120

Guare, John 1938- . **CLC 8, 14, 29, 67; DAM
  DRAM**
  See also CA 73-76; CANR 21; DLB 7; MTCW

Gudjonsson, Halldor Kiljan 1902-
  See Laxness, Halldor
  See also CA 103

Guenter, Erich
  See Eich, Guenter

Guest, Barbara 1920- .... **CLC 34**
  See also CA 25-28R; CANR 11, 44; DLB 5

Guest, Judith (Ann) 1936- .**CLC 8, 30; DAM
  NOV, POP**
  See also AAYA 7; CA 77-80; CANR 15; INT
  CANR-15; MTCW

Guevara, Che .... **CLC 87; HLC**
  See also Guevara (Serna), Ernesto

Guevara (Serna), Ernesto 1928-1967
  See Guevara, Che
  See also CA 127; 111; CANR 56; DAM MULT;
  HW

Guild, Nicholas M. 1944- .... **CLC 33**
  See also CA 93-96

Guillemin, Jacques
  See Sartre, Jean-Paul

Guillen, Jorge 1893-1984 .... **CLC 11; DAM
  MULT, POET**
  See also CA 89-92; 112; DLB 108; HW

Guillen, Nicolas (Cristobal) 1902-1989 .**C L C
  48, 79; BLC; DAM MST, MULT, POET;
  HLC**
  See also BW 2; CA 116; 125; 129; HW

Guillevic, (Eugene) 1907- .... **CLC 33**
  See also CA 93-96

Guillois
  See Desnos, Robert

Guillois, Valentin
  See Desnos, Robert

Guiney, Louise Imogen 1861-1920 **TCLC 41**
  See also CA 160; DLB 54

Guiraldes, Ricardo (Guillermo) 1886-1927
  TCLC 39
  See also CA 131; HW; MTCW

Gumilev, Nikolai Stephanovich 1886-1921
  TCLC 60

Gunesekera, Romesh 1954- .... **CLC 91**
  See also CA 159

Gunn, Bill .... **CLC 5**
  See also Gunn, William Harrison
  See also DLB 38

Gunn, Thom(son William) 1929-**CLC 3, 6, 18,
  32, 81; DAM POET**
  See also CA 17-20R; CANR 9, 33; CDBLB
  1960 to Present; DLB 27; INT CANR-33;
  MTCW

Gunn, William Harrison 1934(?)-1989
  See Gunn, Bill
  See also AITN 1; BW 1; CA 13-16R; 128;
  CANR 12, 25

Gunnars, Kristjana 1948- .... **CLC 69**
  See also CA 113; DLB 60

Gurdjieff, G(eorgei) I(vanovich) 1877(?)-1949
  TCLC 71
  See also CA 157

Gurganus, Allan 1947-..**CLC 70; DAM POP**
  See also BEST 90:1; CA 135

Gurney, A(lbert) R(amsdell), Jr. 1930- .**C L C
  32, 50, 54; DAM DRAM**
  See also CA 77-80; CANR 32, 64

Gurney, Ivor (Bertie) 1890-1937 ... **TCLC 33**

Gurney, Peter
  See Gurney, A(lbert) R(amsdell), Jr.

Guro, Elena 1877-1913 .... **TCLC 56**

Gustafson, James M(oody) 1925- .. **CLC 100**
  See also CA 25-28R; CANR 37

Gustafson, Ralph (Barker) 1909- .... **CLC 36**
  See also CA 21-24R; CANR 8, 45; DLB 88

Gut, Gom
  See Simenon, Georges (Jacques Christian)

Guterson, David 1956- .... **CLC 91**
  See also CA 132

Guthrie, A(lfred) B(ertram), Jr. 1901-1991
  CLC 23
  See also CA 57-60; 134; CANR 24; DLB 6;
  SATA 62; SATA-Obit 67

Guthrie, Isobel
  See Grieve, C(hristopher) M(urray)

Guthrie, Woodrow Wilson 1912-1967
  See Guthrie, Woody
  See also CA 113; 93-96

Guthrie, Woody .... **CLC 35**
  See also Guthrie, Woodrow Wilson

Guy, Rosa (Cuthbert) 1928- .... **CLC 26**
  See also AAYA 4; BW 2; CA 17-20R; CANR
  14, 34; CLR 13; DLB 33; JRDA; MAICYA;
  SATA 14, 62

Gwendolyn
  See Bennett, (Enoch) Arnold

H. D. .... **CLC 3, 8, 14, 31, 34, 73; PC 5**
  See also Doolittle, Hilda

H. de V.
  See Buchan, John

Haavikko, Paavo Juhani 1931- .. **CLC 18, 34**
  See also CA 106

Habbema, Koos
  See Heijermans, Herman

Habermas, Juergen 1929-............... **CLC 104**
  See also CA 109

Habermas, Jurgen
  See Habermas, Juergen

Hacker, Marilyn 1942- .**CLC 5, 9, 23, 72, 91;
  DAM POET**
  See also CA 77-80; DLB 120

Haggard, H(enry) Rider 1856-1925**TCLC 11**
  See also CA 108; 148; DLB 70, 156, 174, 178;
  SATA 16

Hagiosy, L.
  See Larbaud, Valery (Nicolas)

Hagiwara Sakutaro 1886-1942**TCLC 60; PC
  18**

Haig, Fenil
  See Ford, Ford Madox

Haig-Brown, Roderick (Langmere) 1908-1976
  CLC 21
  See also CA 5-8R; 69-72; CANR 4, 38; CLR
  31; DLB 88; MAICYA; SATA 12

Hailey, Arthur 1920-**CLC 5; DAM NOV, POP**
  See also AITN 2; BEST 90:3; CA 1-4R; CANR

2, 36; DLB 88; DLBY 82; MTCW

Hailey, Elizabeth Forsythe 1938- .... **CLC 40**
See also CA 93-96; CAAS 1; CANR 15, 48;
INT CANR-15

Haines, John (Meade) 1924- .... **CLC 58**
See also CA 17-20R; CANR 13, 34; DLB 5

Hakluyt, Richard 1552-1616 .... **LC 31**

Haldeman, Joe (William) 1943- .... **CLC 61**
See also CA 53-56; CAAS 25; CANR 6; DLB
8; INT CANR-6

Haley, Alex(ander Murray Palmer) 1921-1992
CLC 8, 12, 76; BLC; DA; DAB; DAC;
DAM MST, MULT, POP
See also BW 2; CA 77-80; 136; CANR 61; DLB
38; MTCW

Haliburton, Thomas Chandler 1796-1865
NCLC 15
See also DLB 11, 99

Hall, Donald (Andrew, Jr.) 1928- **CLC 1, 13,**
37, 59; DAM POET
See also CA 5-8R; CAAS 7; CANR 2, 44, 64;
DLB 5; SATA 23

Hall, Frederic Sauser
See Sauser-Hall, Frederic

Hall, James
See Kuttner, Henry

Hall, James Norman 1887-1951 ..... **TCLC 23**
See also CA 123; SATA 21

Hall, (Marguerite) Radclyffe 1886-1943
TCLC 12
See also CA 110; 150

Hall, Rodney 1935- .... **CLC 51**
See also CA 109

Halleck, Fitz-Greene 1790-1867 .... **NCLC 47**
See also DLB 3

Halliday, Michael
See Creasey, John

Halpern, Daniel 1945- .... **CLC 14**
See also CA 33-36R

Hamburger, Michael (Peter Leopold) 1924-
CLC 5, 14
See also CA 5-8R; CAAS 4; CANR 2, 47; DLB
27

Hamill, Pete 1935- .... **CLC 10**
See also CA 25-28R; CANR 18

Hamilton, Alexander 1755(?)-1804 **NCLC 49**
See also DLB 37

Hamilton, Clive
See Lewis, C(live) S(taples)

Hamilton, Edmond 1904-1977 .... **CLC 1**
See also CA 1-4R; CANR 3; DLB 8

Hamilton, Eugene (Jacob) Lee
See Lee-Hamilton, Eugene (Jacob)

Hamilton, Franklin
See Silverberg, Robert

Hamilton, Gail
See Corcoran, Barbara

Hamilton, Mollie
See Kaye, M(ary) M(argaret)

Hamilton, (Anthony Walter) Patrick 1904-1962
CLC 51
See also CA 113; DLB 10

Hamilton, Virginia 1936- .... **CLC 26; DAM**
MULT
See also AAYA 2, 21; BW 2; CA 25-28R;
CANR 20, 37; CLR 1, 11, 40; DLB 33, 52;
INT CANR-20; JRDA; MAICYA; MTCW;
SATA 4, 56, 79

Hammett, (Samuel) Dashiell 1894-1961 **C L C**
3, 5, 10, 19, 47; SSC 17
See also AITN 1; CA 81-84; CANR 42; CDALB
1929-1941; DLBD 6; DLBY 96; MTCW

Hammon, Jupiter 1711(?)-1800(?) . **NCLC 5;**

BLC; DAM MULT, POET; PC 16
See also DLB 31, 50

Hammond, Keith
See Kuttner, Henry

Hamner, Earl (Henry), Jr. 1923- ...... **CLC 12**
See also AITN 2; CA 73-76; DLB 6

Hampton, Christopher (James) 1946- **CLC 4**
See also CA 25-28R; DLB 13; MTCW

Hamsun, Knut .... **TCLC 2, 14, 49**
See also Pedersen, Knut

Handke, Peter 1942- **CLC 5, 8, 10, 15, 38; DAM**
DRAM, NOV
See also CA 77-80; CANR 33; DLB 85, 124;
MTCW

Hanley, James 1901-1985 ..... **CLC 3, 5, 8, 13**
See also CA 73-76; 117; CANR 36; MTCW

Hannah, Barry 1942- .... **CLC 23, 38, 90**
See also CA 108; 110; CANR 43; DLB 6; INT
110; MTCW

Hannon, Ezra
See Hunter, Evan

Hansberry, Lorraine (Vivian) 1930-1965 **CLC**
17, 62; BLC; DA; DAB; DAC; DAM
DRAM, MST, MULT; DC 2
See also BW 1; CA 109; 25-28R; CABS 3;
CANR 58; CDALB 1941-1968; DLB 7, 38;
MTCW

Hansen, Joseph 1923- .... **CLC 38**
See also CA 29-32R; CAAS 17; CANR 16, 44;
INT CANR-16

Hansen, Martin A. 1909-1955 .... **TCLC 32**

Hanson, Kenneth O(stlin) 1922- .... **CLC 13**
See also CA 53-56; CANR 7

Hardwick, Elizabeth 1916- .... **CLC 13; DAM**
NOV
See also CA 5-8R; CANR 3, 32; DLB 6; MTCW

Hardy, Thomas 1840-1928 **TCLC 4, 10, 18, 32,**
48, 53, 72; DA; DAB; DAC; DAM MST,
NOV, POET; PC 8; SSC 2; WLC
See also CA 104; 123; CDBLB 1890-1914;
DLB 18, 19, 135; MTCW

Hare, David 1947- .... **CLC 29, 58**
See also CA 97-100; CANR 39; DLB 13;
MTCW

Harewood, John
See Van Druten, John (William)

Harford, Henry
See Hudson, W(illiam) H(enry)

Hargrave, Leonie
See Disch, Thomas M(ichael)

Harjo, Joy 1951- .... **CLC 83; DAM MULT**
See also CA 114; CANR 35; DLB 120, 175;
NNAL

Harlan, Louis R(udolph) 1922- .... **CLC 34**
See also CA 21-24R; CANR 25, 55

Harling, Robert 1951(?)- .... **CLC 53**
See also CA 147

Harmon, William (Ruth) 1938- .... **CLC 38**
See also CA 33-36R; CANR 14, 32, 35; SATA
65

Harper, F. E. W.
See Harper, Frances Ellen Watkins

Harper, Frances E. W.
See Harper, Frances Ellen Watkins

Harper, Frances E. Watkins
See Harper, Frances Ellen Watkins

Harper, Frances Ellen
See Harper, Frances Ellen Watkins

Harper, Frances Ellen Watkins 1825-1911
TCLC 14; BLC; DAM MULT, POET; PC
21
See also BW 1; CA 111; 125; DLB 50

Harper, Michael S(teven) 1938- ... **CLC 7, 22**

See also BW 1; CA 33-36R; CANR 24; DLB
41

Harper, Mrs. F. E. W.
See Harper, Frances Ellen Watkins

Harris, Christie (Lucy) Irwin 1907- . **CLC 12**
See also CA 5-8R; CANR 6; CLR 47; DLB 88;
JRDA; MAICYA; SAAS 10; SATA 6, 74

Harris, Frank 1856-1931 .... **TCLC 24**
See also CA 109; 150; DLB 156

Harris, George Washington 1814-1869 **N C L C**
23
See also DLB 3, 11

Harris, Joel Chandler 1848-1908 ... **TCLC 2;**
SSC 19
See also CA 104; 137; DLB 11, 23, 42, 78, 91;
MAICYA; YABC 1

Harris, John (Wyndham Parkes Lucas) Beynon
1903-1969
See Wyndham, John
See also CA 102; 89-92

Harris, MacDonald .... **CLC 9**
See also Heiney, Donald (William)

Harris, Mark 1922- .... **CLC 19**
See also CA 5-8R; CAAS 3; CANR 2, 55; DLB
2; DLBY 80

Harris, (Theodore) Wilson 1921- ...... **CLC 25**
See also BW 2; CA 65-68; CAAS 16; CANR
11, 27; DLB 117; MTCW

Harrison, Elizabeth Cavanna 1909-
See Cavanna, Betty
See also CA 9-12R; CANR 6, 27

Harrison, Harry (Max) 1925- .... **CLC 42**
See also CA 1-4R; CANR 5, 21; DLB 8; SATA
4

Harrison, James (Thomas) 1937- **CLC 6, 14,**
33, 66; SSC 19
See also CA 13-16R; CANR 8, 51; DLBY 82;
INT CANR-8

Harrison, Jim
See Harrison, James (Thomas)

Harrison, Kathryn 1961- .... **CLC 70**
See also CA 144

Harrison, Tony 1937- .... **CLC 43**
See also CA 65-68; CANR 44; DLB 40; MTCW

Harriss, Will(ard Irvin) 1922- .... **CLC 34**
See also CA 111

Harson, Sley
See Ellison, Harlan (Jay)

Hart, Ellis
See Ellison, Harlan (Jay)

Hart, Josephine 1942(?)- **CLC 70; DAM POP**
See also CA 138

Hart, Moss 1904-1961 **CLC 66; DAM DRAM**
See also CA 109; 89-92; DLB 7

Harte, (Francis) Bret(t) 1836(?)-1902 **TCLC 1,**
25; DA; DAC; DAM MST; SSC 8; WLC
See also CA 104; 140; CDALB 1865-1917;
DLB 12, 64, 74, 79; SATA 26

Hartley, L(eslie) P(oles) 1895-1972 **CLC 2, 22**
See also CA 45-48; 37-40R; CANR 33; DLB
15, 139; MTCW

Hartman, Geoffrey H. 1929- .... **CLC 27**
See also CA 117; 125; DLB 67

Hartmann, Sadakichi 1867-1944 ... **TCLC 73**
See also CA 157; DLB 54

Hartmann von Aue c. 1160-c. 1205 **CMLC 15**
See also DLB 138

Hartmann von Aue 1170-1210 ...... **CMLC 15**

Haruf, Kent 1943- .... **CLC 34**
See also CA 149

Harwood, Ronald 1934- .... **CLC 32; DAM**
DRAM, MST
See also CA 1-4R; CANR 4, 55; DLB 13

Hasek, Jaroslav (Matej Frantisek) 1883-1923
  TCLC 4
  See also CA 104; 129; MTCW
Hass, Robert 1941- ... **CLC 18, 39, 99; PC 16**
  See also CA 111; CANR 30, 50; DLB 105;
  SATA 94
Hastings, Hudson
  See Kuttner, Henry
Hastings, Selina .... **CLC 44**
Hathorne, John 1641-1717 .... **LC 38**
Hatteras, Amelia
  See Mencken, H(enry) L(ouis)
Hatteras, Owen .... **TCLC 18**
  See also Mencken, H(enry) L(ouis); Nathan,
  George Jean
Hauptmann, Gerhart (Johann Robert) 1862-
  1946 .... **TCLC 4; DAM DRAM**
  See also CA 104; 153; DLB 66, 118
Havel, Vaclav 1936- ... **CLC 25, 58, 65; DAM
  DRAM; DC 6**
  See also CA 104; CANR 36, 63; MTCW
Haviaras, Stratis .... **CLC 33**
  See also Chaviaras, Strates
Hawes, Stephen 1475(?)-1523(?) .... **LC 17**
Hawkes, John (Clendennin Burne, Jr.) 1925-
  CLC 1, 2, 3, 4, 7, 9, 14, 15, 27, 49
  See also CA 1-4R; CANR 2, 47, 64; DLB 2, 7;
  DLBY 80; MTCW
Hawking, S. W.
  See Hawking, Stephen W(illiam)
Hawking, Stephen W(illiam) 1942- **CLC 63,
  105**
  See also AAYA 13; BEST 89:1; CA 126; 129;
  CANR 48
Hawthorne, Julian 1846-1934 .... **TCLC 25**
Hawthorne, Nathaniel 1804-1864 **NCLC 39;
  DA; DAB; DAC; DAM MST, NOV; SSC
  3, 29; WLC**
  See also AAYA 18; CDALB 1640-1865; DLB
  1, 74; YABC 2
Haxton, Josephine Ayres 1921-
  See Douglas, Ellen
  See also CA 115; CANR 41
Hayaseca y Eizaguirre, Jorge
  See Echegaray (y Eizaguirre), Jose (Maria
  Waldo)
Hayashi Fumiko 1904-1951 .... **TCLC 27**
  See also CA 161; DLB 180
Haycraft, Anna
  See Ellis, Alice Thomas
  See also CA 122
Hayden, Robert E(arl) 1913-1980 **CLC 5, 9,
  14, 37; BLC; DA; DAC; DAM MST,
  MULT, POET; PC 6**
  See also BW 1; CA 69-72; 97-100; CABS 2;
  CANR 24; CDALB 1941-1968; DLB 5, 76;
  MTCW; SATA 19; SATA-Obit 26
Hayford, J(oseph) E(phraim) Casely
  See Casely-Hayford, J(oseph) E(phraim)
Hayman, Ronald 1932- .... **CLC 44**
  See also CA 25-28R; CANR 18, 50; DLB 155
Haywood, Eliza (Fowler) 1693(?)-1756 **LC 1**
Hazlitt, William 1778-1830 .... **NCLC 29**
  See also DLB 110, 158
Hazzard, Shirley 1931- .... **CLC 18**
  See also CA 9-12R; CANR 4; DLBY 82;
  MTCW
Head, Bessie 1937-1986 .. **CLC 25, 67; BLC;
  DAM MULT**
  See also BW 2; CA 29-32R; 119; CANR 25;
  DLB 117; MTCW
Headon, (Nicky) Topper 1956(?)- .... **CLC 30**
Heaney, Seamus (Justin) 1939- **CLC 5, 7, 14,**

**25, 37, 74, 91; DAB; DAM POET; PC 18;
  WLCS**
  See also CA 85-88; CANR 25, 48; CDBLB
  1960 to Present; DLB 40; DLBY 95; MTCW
Hearn, (Patricio) Lafcadio (Tessima Carlos)
  1850-1904 .... **TCLC 9**
  See also CA 105; DLB 12, 78
Hearne, Vicki 1946- .... **CLC 56**
  See also CA 139
Hearon, Shelby 1931- .... **CLC 63**
  See also AITN 2; CA 25-28R; CANR 18, 48
Heat-Moon, William Least .... **CLC 29**
  See also Trogdon, William (Lewis)
  See also AAYA 9
Hebbel, Friedrich 1813-1863 **NCLC 43; DAM
  DRAM**
  See also DLB 129
Hebert, Anne 1916- **CLC 4, 13, 29; DAC; DAM
  MST, POET**
  See also CA 85-88; DLB 68; MTCW
Hecht, Anthony (Evan) 1923- **CLC 8, 13, 19;
  DAM POET**
  See also CA 9-12R; CANR 6; DLB 5, 169
Hecht, Ben 1894-1964 .... **CLC 8**
  See also CA 85-88; DLB 7, 9, 25, 26, 28, 86
Hedayat, Sadeq 1903-1951 .... **TCLC 21**
  See also CA 120
Hegel, Georg Wilhelm Friedrich 1770-1831
  NCLC 46
  See also DLB 90
Heidegger, Martin 1889-1976 .... **CLC 24**
  See also CA 81-84; 65-68; CANR 34; MTCW
Heidenstam, (Carl Gustaf) Verner von 1859-
  1940 .... **TCLC 5**
  See also CA 104
Heifner, Jack 1946- .... **CLC 11**
  See also CA 105; CANR 47
Heijermans, Herman 1864-1924 .... **TCLC 24**
  See also CA 123
Heilbrun, Carolyn G(old) 1926- .... **CLC 25**
  See also CA 45-48; CANR 1, 28, 58
Heine, Heinrich 1797-1856 .... **NCLC 4, 54**
  See also DLB 90
Heinemann, Larry (Curtiss) 1944- ... **CLC 50**
  See also CA 110; CAAS 21; CANR 31; DLBD
  9; INT CANR-31
Heiney, Donald (William) 1921-1993
  See Harris, MacDonald
  See also CA 1-4R; 142; CANR 3, 58
Heinlein, Robert A(nson) 1907-1988 **CLC 1, 3,
  8, 14, 26, 55; DAM POP**
  See also AAYA 17; CA 1-4R; 125; CANR 1,
  20, 53; DLB 8; JRDA; MAICYA; MTCW;
  SATA 9, 69; SATA-Obit 56
Helforth, John
  See Doolittle, Hilda
Hellenhofferu, Vojtech Kapristian z
  See Hasek, Jaroslav (Matej Frantisek)
Heller, Joseph 1923- **CLC 1, 3, 5, 8, 11, 36, 63;
  DA; DAB; DAC; DAM MST, NOV, POP;
  WLC**
  See also AITN 1; CA 5-8R; CABS 1; CANR 8,
  42; DLB 2, 28; DLBY 80; INT CANR-8;
  MTCW
Hellman, Lillian (Florence) 1906-1984 **CLC 2,
  4, 8, 14, 18, 34, 44, 52; DAM DRAM; DC 1**
  See also AITN 1, 2; CA 13-16R; 112; CANR
  33; DLB 7; DLBY 84; MTCW
Helprin, Mark 1947- **CLC 7, 10, 22, 32; DAM
  NOV, POP**
  See also CA 81-84; CANR 47, 64; DLBY 85;
  MTCW
Helvetius, Claude-Adrien 1715-1771 . **LC 26**

Helyar, Jane Penelope Josephine 1933-
  See Poole, Josephine
  See also CA 21-24R; CANR 10, 26; SATA 82
Hemans, Felicia 1793-1835 .... **NCLC 29**
  See also DLB 96
Hemingway, Ernest (Miller) 1899-1961 **C L C
  1, 3, 6, 8, 10, 13, 19, 30, 34, 39, 41, 44, 50,
  61, 80; DA; DAB; DAC; DAM MST, NOV;
  SSC 25; WLC**
  See also AAYA 19; CA 77-80; CANR 34;
  CDALB 1917-1929; DLB 4, 9, 102; DLBD
  1, 15, 16; DLBY 81, 87, 96; MTCW
Hempel, Amy 1951- .... **CLC 39**
  See also CA 118; 137
Henderson, F. C.
  See Mencken, H(enry) L(ouis)
Henderson, Sylvia
  See Ashton-Warner, Sylvia (Constance)
Henderson, Zenna (Chlarson) 1917-1983 **S S C
  29**
  See also CA 1-4R; 133; CANR 1; DLB 8; SATA
  5
Henley, Beth .... **CLC 23; DC 6**
  See also Henley, Elizabeth Becker
  See also CABS 3; DLBY 86
Henley, Elizabeth Becker 1952-
  See Henley, Beth
  See also CA 107; CANR 32; DAM DRAM,
  MST; MTCW
Henley, William Ernest 1849-1903 .. **TCLC 8**
  See also CA 105; DLB 19
Hennissart, Martha
  See Lathen, Emma
  See also CA 85-88; CANR 64
Henry, O. .... **TCLC 1, 19; SSC 5; WLC**
  See also Porter, William Sydney
Henry, Patrick 1736-1799 .... **LC 25**
Henryson, Robert 1430(?)-1506(?) ..... **LC 20**
  See also DLB 146
Henry VIII 1491-1547 .... **LC 10**
Henschke, Alfred
  See Klabund
Hentoff, Nat(han Irving) 1925- .... **CLC 26**
  See also AAYA 4; CA 1-4R; CAAS 6; CANR
  5, 25; CLR 1; INT CANR-25; JRDA;
  MAICYA; SATA 42, 69; SATA-Brief 27
Heppenstall, (John) Rayner 1911-1981 **C L C
  10**
  See also CA 1-4R; 103; CANR 29
Heraclitus c. 540B.C.-c. 450B.C. .... **CMLC 22**
  See also DLB 176
Herbert, Frank (Patrick) 1920-1986 **CLC 12,
  23, 35, 44, 85; DAM POP**
  See also AAYA 21; CA 53-56; 118; CANR 5,
  43; DLB 8; INT CANR-5; MTCW; SATA 9,
  37; SATA-Obit 47
Herbert, George 1593-1633 ..... **LC 24; DAB;
  DAM POET; PC 4**
  See also CDBLB Before 1660; DLB 126
Herbert, Zbigniew 1924- ... **CLC 9, 43; DAM
  POET**
  See also CA 89-92; CANR 36; MTCW
Herbst, Josephine (Frey) 1897-1969 **CLC 34**
  See also CA 5-8R; 25-28R; DLB 9
Hergesheimer, Joseph 1880-1954 ... **TCLC 11**
  See also CA 109; DLB 102, 9
Herlihy, James Leo 1927-1993 .... **CLC 6**
  See also CA 1-4R; 143; CANR 2
Hermogenes fl. c. 175- .... **CMLC 6**
Hernandez, Jose 1834-1886 .... **NCLC 17**
Herodotus c. 484B.C.-429B.C. .... **CMLC 17**
  See also DLB 176
Herrick, Robert 1591-1674 **LC 13; DA; DAB;**

DAC; DAM MST, POP; PC 9
See also DLB 126
Herring, Guilles
See Somerville, Edith
Herriot, James 1916-1995 **CLC 12; DAM POP**
See also Wight, James Alfred
See also AAYA 1; CA 148; CANR 40; SATA 86
Herrmann, Dorothy 1941- .... **CLC 44**
See also CA 107
Herrmann, Taffy
See Herrmann, Dorothy
Hersey, John (Richard) 1914-1993 **CLC 1, 2, 7, 9, 40, 81, 97; DAM POP**
See also CA 17-20R; 140; CANR 33; DLB 6; MTCW; SATA 25; SATA-Obit 76
Herzen, Aleksandr Ivanovich 1812-1870 **NCLC 10, 61**
Herzl, Theodor 1860-1904 .... **TCLC 36**
Herzog, Werner 1942-....................... **CLC 16**
See also CA 89-92
Hesiod c. 8th cent. B.C.- .... **CMLC 5**
See also DLB 176
Hesse, Hermann 1877-1962 **CLC 1, 2, 3, 6, 11, 17, 25, 69; DA; DAB; DAC; DAM MST, NOV; SSC 9; WLC**
See also CA 17-18; CAP 2; DLB 66; MTCW; SATA 50
Hewes, Cady
See De Voto, Bernard (Augustine)
Heyen, William 1940-.................. **CLC 13, 18**
See also CA 33-36R; CAAS 9; DLB 5
Heyerdahl, Thor 1914- .... **CLC 26**
See also CA 5-8R; CANR 5, 22; MTCW; SATA 2, 52
Heym, Georg (Theodor Franz Arthur) 1887-1912 .... **TCLC 9**
See also CA 106
Heym, Stefan 1913- .... **CLC 41**
See also CA 9-12R; CANR 4; DLB 69
Heyse, Paul (Johann Ludwig von) 1830-1914 **TCLC 8**
See also CA 104; DLB 129
Heyward, (Edwin) DuBose 1885-1940 **TCLC 59**
See also CA 108; 157; DLB 7, 9, 45; SATA 21
Hibbert, Eleanor Alice Burford 1906-1993 **CLC 7; DAM POP**
See also BEST 90:4; CA 17-20R; 140; CANR 9, 28, 59; SATA 2; SATA-Obit 74
Hichens, Robert (Smythe) 1864-1950 . **TCLC 64**
See also CA 162; DLB 153
Higgins, George V(incent) 1939- **CLC 4, 7, 10, 18**
See also CA 77-80; CAAS 5; CANR 17, 51; DLB 2; DLBY 81; INT CANR-17; MTCW
Higginson, Thomas Wentworth 1823-1911 **TCLC 36**
See also DLB 1, 64
Highet, Helen
See MacInnes, Helen (Clark)
Highsmith, (Mary) Patricia 1921-1995 **CLC 2, 4, 14, 42, 102; DAM NOV, POP**
See also CA 1-4R; 147; CANR 1, 20, 48, 62; MTCW
Highwater, Jamake (Mamake) 1942(?)- **C L C 12**
See also AAYA 7; CA 65-68; CAAS 7; CANR 10, 34; CLR 17; DLB 52; DLBY 85; JRDA; MAICYA; SATA 32, 69; SATA-Brief 30
Highway, Tomson 1951- **CLC 92; DAC; DAM MULT**

See also CA 151; NNAL
Higuchi, Ichiyo 1872-1896 .... **NCLC 49**
Hijuelos, Oscar 1951- **CLC 65; DAM MULT, POP; HLC**
See also BEST 90:1; CA 123; CANR 50; DLB 145; HW
Hikmet, Nazim 1902(?)-1963 .... **CLC 40**
See also CA 141; 93-96
Hildegard von Bingen 1098-1179 . **CMLC 20**
See also DLB 148
Hildesheimer, Wolfgang 1916-1991 ..**CLC 49**
See also CA 101; 135; DLB 69, 124
Hill, Geoffrey (William) 1932- **CLC 5, 8, 18, 45; DAM POET**
See also CA 81-84; CANR 21; CDBLB 1960 to Present; DLB 40; MTCW
Hill, George Roy 1921- .... **CLC 26**
See also CA 110; 122
Hill, John
See Koontz, Dean R(ay)
Hill, Susan (Elizabeth) 1942- . **CLC 4; DAB; DAM MST, NOV**
See also CA 33-36R; CANR 29; DLB 14, 139; MTCW
Hillerman, Tony 1925- ..**CLC 62; DAM POP**
See also AAYA 6; BEST 89:1; CA 29-32R; CANR 21, 42; SATA 6
Hillesum, Etty 1914-1943 .... **TCLC 49**
See also CA 137
Hilliard, Noel (Harvey) 1929- .... **CLC 15**
See also CA 9-12R; CANR 7
Hillis, Rick 1956- .... **CLC 66**
See also CA 134
Hilton, James 1900-1954 .... **TCLC 21**
See also CA 108; DLB 34, 77; SATA 34
Himes, Chester (Bomar) 1909-1984 **CLC 2, 4, 7, 18, 58, 108; BLC; DAM MULT**
See also BW 2; CA 25-28R; 114; CANR 22; DLB 2, 76, 143; MTCW
Hinde, Thomas .... **CLC 6, 11**
See also Chitty, Thomas Willes
Hindin, Nathan
See Bloch, Robert (Albert)
Hine, (William) Daryl 1936-.............. **CLC 15**
See also CA 1-4R; CAAS 15; CANR 1, 20; DLB 60
Hinkson, Katharine Tynan
See Tynan, Katharine
Hinton, S(usan) E(loise) 1950- **CLC 30; DA; DAB; DAC; DAM MST, NOV**
See also AAYA 2; CA 81-84; CANR 32, 62; CLR 3, 23; JRDA; MAICYA; MTCW; SATA 19, 58
Hippius, Zinaida .... **TCLC 9**
See also Gippius, Zinaida (Nikolayevna)
Hiraoka, Kimitake 1925-1970
See Mishima, Yukio
See also CA 97-100; 29-32R; DAM DRAM; MTCW
Hirsch, E(ric) D(onald), Jr. 1928-..... **CLC 79**
See also CA 25-28R; CANR 27, 51; DLB 67; INT CANR-27; MTCW
Hirsch, Edward 1950- .... **CLC 31, 50**
See also CA 104; CANR 20, 42; DLB 120
Hitchcock, Alfred (Joseph) 1899-1980 **CLC 16**
See also AAYA 22; CA 159; 97-100; SATA 27; SATA-Obit 24
Hitler, Adolf 1889-1945 .... **TCLC 53**
See also CA 117; 147
Hoagland, Edward 1932-................... **CLC 28**
See also CA 1-4R; CANR 2, 31, 57; DLB 6; SATA 51
Hoban, Russell (Conwell) 1925- . **CLC 7, 25;**

DAM NOV
See also CA 5-8R; CANR 23, 37; CLR 3; DLB 52; MAICYA; MTCW; SATA 1, 40, 78
Hobbes, Thomas 1588-1679 .... **LC 36**
See also DLB 151
Hobbs, Perry
See Blackmur, R(ichard) P(almer)
Hobson, Laura Z(ametkin) 1900-1986 **CLC 7, 25**
See also CA 17-20R; 118; CANR 55; DLB 28; SATA 52
Hochhuth, Rolf 1931-...**CLC 4, 11, 18; DAM DRAM**
See also CA 5-8R; CANR 33; DLB 124; MTCW
Hochman, Sandra 1936- .... **CLC 3, 8**
See also CA 5-8R; DLB 5
Hochwaelder, Fritz 1911-1986 **CLC 36; DAM DRAM**
See also CA 29-32R; 120; CANR 42; MTCW
Hochwalder, Fritz
See Hochwaelder, Fritz
Hocking, Mary (Eunice) 1921-.......... **CLC 13**
See also CA 101; CANR 18, 40
Hodgins, Jack 1938- ....**CLC 23**
See also CA 93-96; DLB 60
Hodgson, William Hope 1877(?)-1918 **T C L C 13**
See also CA 111; DLB 70, 153, 156, 178
Hoeg, Peter 1957- .... **CLC 95**
See also CA 151
Hoffman, Alice 1952- ... **CLC 51; DAM NOV**
See also CA 77-80; CANR 34; MTCW
Hoffman, Daniel (Gerard) 1923- **CLC 6, 13, 23**
See also CA 1-4R; CANR 4; DLB 5
Hoffman, Stanley 1944- .... **CLC 5**
See also CA 77-80
Hoffman, William M(oses) 1939- ...... **CLC 40**
See also CA 57-60; CANR 11
Hoffmann, E(rnst) T(heodor) A(madeus) 1776-1822 .... **NCLC 2; SSC 13**
See also DLB 90; SATA 27
Hofmann, Gert 1931- .... **CLC 54**
See also CA 128
Hofmannsthal, Hugo von 1874-1929 **TCLC 11; DAM DRAM; DC 4**
See also CA 106; 153; DLB 81, 118
Hogan, Linda 1947-... **CLC 73; DAM MULT**
See also CA 120; CANR 45; DLB 175; NNAL
Hogarth, Charles
See Creasey, John
Hogarth, Emmett
See Polonsky, Abraham (Lincoln)
Hogg, James 1770-1835 .... **NCLC 4**
See also DLB 93, 116, 159
Holbach, Paul Henri Thiry Baron 1723-1789 **LC 14**
Holberg, Ludvig 1684-1754 .... **LC 6**
Holden, Ursula 1921- .... **CLC 18**
See also CA 101; CAAS 8; CANR 22
Holderlin, (Johann Christian) Friedrich 1770-1843 .... **NCLC 16; PC 4**
Holdstock, Robert
See Holdstock, Robert P.
Holdstock, Robert P. 1948-................ **CLC 39**
See also CA 131
Holland, Isabelle 1920- .... **CLC 21**
See also AAYA 11; CA 21-24R; CANR 10, 25, 47; JRDA; MAICYA; SATA 8, 70
Holland, Marcus
See Caldwell, (Janet Miriam) Taylor (Holland)
Hollander, John 1929-........... **CLC 2, 5, 8, 14**
See also CA 1-4R; CANR 1, 52; DLB 5; SATA 13

Hollander, Paul
  See Silverberg, Robert
Holleran, Andrew 1943(?)- .... **CLC 38**
  See also CA 144
Hollinghurst, Alan 1954- .... **CLC 55, 91**
  See also CA 114
Hollis, Jim
  See Summers, Hollis (Spurgeon, Jr.)
Holly, Buddy 1936-1959 .... **TCLC 65**
Holmes, Gordon
  See Shiel, M(atthew) P(hipps)
Holmes, John
  See Souster, (Holmes) Raymond
Holmes, John Clellon 1926-1988 ..... **CLC 56**
  See also CA 9-12R; 125; CANR 4; DLB 16
Holmes, Oliver Wendell, Jr. 1841-1935**T C L C
  77**
  See also CA 114
Holmes, Oliver Wendell 1809-1894 **NCLC 14**
  See also CDALB 1640-1865; DLB 1; SATA 34
Holmes, Raymond
  See Souster, (Holmes) Raymond
Holt, Victoria
  See Hibbert, Eleanor Alice Burford
Holub, Miroslav 1923- .... **CLC 4**
  See also CA 21-24R; CANR 10
Homer c. 8th cent. B.C.- ... **CMLC 1, 16; DA;
  DAB; DAC; DAM MST, POET; WLCS**
  See also DLB 176
Honig, Edwin 1919-........................... **CLC 33**
  See also CA 5-8R; CAAS 8; CANR 4, 45; DLB
  5
Hood, Hugh (John Blagdon) 1928-**CLC 15, 28**
  See also CA 49-52; CAAS 17; CANR 1, 33;
  DLB 53
Hood, Thomas 1799-1845 .... **NCLC 16**
  See also DLB 96
Hooker, (Peter) Jeremy 1941- .... **CLC 43**
  See also CA 77-80; CANR 22; DLB 40
hooks, bell .... **CLC 94**
  See also Watkins, Gloria
Hope, A(lec) D(erwent) 1907- ...... **CLC 3, 51**
  See also CA 21-24R; CANR 33; MTCW
Hope, Brian
  See Creasey, John
Hope, Christopher (David Tully) 1944- **C L C
  52**
  See also CA 106; CANR 47; SATA 62
Hopkins, Gerard Manley 1844-1889 ..**N C L C
  17; DA; DAB; DAC; DAM MST, POET;
  PC 15; WLC**
  See also CDBLB 1890-1914; DLB 35, 57
Hopkins, John (Richard) 1931-...........**CLC 4**
  See also CA 85-88
Hopkins, Pauline Elizabeth 1859-1930**T C L C
  28; BLC; DAM MULT**
  See also BW 2; CA 141; DLB 50
Hopkinson, Francis 1737-1791 .... **LC 25**
  See also DLB 31
Hopley-Woolrich, Cornell George 1903-1968
  See Woolrich, Cornell
  See also CA 13-14; CANR 58; CAP 1
Horatio
  See Proust, (Valentin-Louis-George-Eugene-)
  Marcel
Horgan, Paul (George Vincent O'Shaughnessy)
  1903-1995 .... **CLC 9, 53; DAM NOV**
  See also CA 13-16R; 147; CANR 9, 35; DLB
  102; DLBY 85; INT CANR-9; MTCW;
  SATA 13; SATA-Obit 84
Horn, Peter
  See Kuttner, Henry
Hornem, Horace Esq.

  See Byron, George Gordon (Noel)
Horney, Karen (Clementine Theodore
  Danielsen) 1885-1952 .... **TCLC 71**
  See also CA 114
Hornung, E(rnest) W(illiam) 1866-1921
  TCLC 59
  See also CA 108; 160; DLB 70
Horovitz, Israel (Arthur) 1939-**CLC 56; DAM
  DRAM**
  See also CA 33-36R; CANR 46, 59; DLB 7
Horvath, Odon von
  See Horvath, Oedoen von
  See also DLB 85, 124
Horvath, Oedoen von 1901-1938 ... **TCLC 45**
  See also Horvath, Odon von
  See also CA 118
Horwitz, Julius 1920-1986 .... **CLC 14**
  See also CA 9-12R; 119; CANR 12
Hospital, Janette Turner 1942- .... **CLC 42**
  See also CA 108; CANR 48
Hostos, E. M. de
  See Hostos (y Bonilla), Eugenio Maria de
Hostos, Eugenio M. de
  See Hostos (y Bonilla), Eugenio Maria de
Hostos, Eugenio Maria
  See Hostos (y Bonilla), Eugenio Maria de
Hostos (y Bonilla), Eugenio Maria de 1839-1903
  TCLC 24
  See also CA 123; 131; HW
Houdini
  See Lovecraft, H(oward) P(hillips)
Hougan, Carolyn 1943-....................... **CLC 34**
  See also CA 139
Household, Geoffrey (Edward West) 1900-1988
  CLC 11
  See also CA 77-80; 126; CANR 58; DLB 87;
  SATA 14; SATA-Obit 59
Housman, A(lfred) E(dward) 1859-1936
  **TCLC 1, 10; DA; DAB; DAC; DAM MST,
  POET; PC 2; WLCS**
  See also CA 104; 125; DLB 19; MTCW
Housman, Laurence 1865-1959 .... **TCLC 7**
  See also CA 106; 155; DLB 10; SATA 25
Howard, Elizabeth Jane 1923-..... **CLC 7, 29**
  See also CA 5-8R; CANR 8, 62
Howard, Maureen 1930-......... **CLC 5, 14, 46**
  See also CA 53-56; CANR 31; DLBY 83; INT
  CANR-31; MTCW
Howard, Richard 1929- .... **CLC 7, 10, 47**
  See also AITN 1; CA 85-88; CANR 25; DLB 5;
  INT CANR-25
Howard, Robert E(rvin) 1906-1936 **TCLC 8**
  See also CA 105; 157
Howard, Warren F.
  See Pohl, Frederik
Howe, Fanny 1940- .... **CLC 47**
  See also CA 117; CAAS 27; SATA-Brief 52
Howe, Irving 1920-1993 .... **CLC 85**
  See also CA 9-12R; 141; CANR 21, 50; DLB
  67; MTCW
Howe, Julia Ward 1819-1910 .... **TCLC 21**
  See also CA 117; DLB 1
Howe, Susan 1937- .... **CLC 72**
  See also CA 160; DLB 120
Howe, Tina 1937- .... **CLC 48**
  See also CA 109
Howell, James 1594(?)-1666 .... **LC 13**
  See also DLB 151
Howells, W. D.
  See Howells, William Dean
Howells, William D.
  See Howells, William Dean
Howells, William Dean 1837-1920**TCLC 7, 17,

41**
  See also CA 104; 134; CDALB 1865-1917;
  DLB 12, 64, 74, 79
Howes, Barbara 1914-1996 .... **CLC 15**
  See also CA 9-12R; 151; CAAS 3; CANR 53;
  SATA 5
Hrabal, Bohumil 1914-1997 .... **CLC 13, 67**
  See also CA 106; 156; CAAS 12; CANR 57
Hsun, Lu
  See Lu Hsun
Hubbard, L(afayette) Ron(ald) 1911-1986
  CLC 43; DAM POP
  See also CA 77-80; 118; CANR 52
Huch, Ricarda (Octavia) 1864-1947**TCLC 13**
  See also CA 111; DLB 66
Huddle, David 1942- .... **CLC 49**
  See also CA 57-60; CAAS 20; DLB 130
Hudson, Jeffrey
  See Crichton, (John) Michael
Hudson, W(illiam) H(enry) 1841-1922**T C L C
  29**
  See also CA 115; DLB 98, 153, 174; SATA 35
Hueffer, Ford Madox
  See Ford, Ford Madox
Hughart, Barry 1934- .... **CLC 39**
  See also CA 137
Hughes, Colin
  See Creasey, John
Hughes, David (John) 1930- .... **CLC 48**
  See also CA 116; 129; DLB 14
Hughes, Edward James
  See Hughes, Ted
  See also DAM MST, POET
Hughes, (James) Langston 1902-1967**CLC 1,
  5, 10, 15, 35, 44, 108; BLC; DA; DAB;
  DAC; DAM DRAM, MST, MULT, POET;
  DC 3; PC 1; SSC 6; WLC**
  See also AAYA 12; BW 1; CA 1-4R; 25-28R;
  CANR 1, 34; CDALB 1929-1941; CLR 17;
  DLB 4, 7, 48, 51, 86; JRDA; MAICYA;
  MTCW; SATA 4, 33
Hughes, Richard (Arthur Warren) 1900-1976
  CLC 1, 11; DAM NOV
  See also CA 5-8R; 65-68; CANR 4; DLB 15,
  161; MTCW; SATA 8; SATA-Obit 25
Hughes, Ted 1930-**CLC 2, 4, 9, 14, 37; DAB;
  DAC; PC 7**
  See also Hughes, Edward James
  See also CA 1-4R; CANR 1, 33; CLR 3; DLB
  40, 161; MAICYA; MTCW; SATA 49; SATA-
  Brief 27
Hugo, Richard F(ranklin) 1923-1982 **CLC 6,
  18, 32; DAM POET**
  See also CA 49-52; 108; CANR 3; DLB 5
Hugo, Victor (Marie) 1802-1885**NCLC 3, 10,
  21; DA; DAB; DAC; DAM DRAM, MST,
  NOV, POET; PC 17; WLC**
  See also DLB 119; SATA 47
Huidobro, Vicente
  See Huidobro Fernandez, Vicente Garcia
Huidobro Fernandez, Vicente Garcia 1893-
  1948 .... **TCLC 31**
  See also CA 131; HW
Hulme, Keri 1947- .... **CLC 39**
  See also CA 125; INT 125
Hulme, T(homas) E(rnest) 1883-1917 **T C L C
  21**
  See also CA 117; DLB 19
Hume, David 1711-1776 .... **LC 7**
  See also DLB 104
Humphrey, William 1924-1997 .... **CLC 45**
  See also CA 77-80; 160; DLB 6
Humphreys, Emyr Owen 1919- .... **CLC 47**

See also CA 5-8R; CANR 3, 24; DLB 15
Humphreys, Josephine 1945- ..... **CLC 34, 57**
See also CA 121; 127; INT 127
Huneker, James Gibbons 1857-1921**TCLC 65**
See also DLB 71
Hungerford, Pixie
See Brinsmead, H(esba) F(ay)
Hunt, E(verette) Howard, (Jr.) 1918- . **CLC 3**
See also AITN 1; CA 45-48; CANR 2, 47
Hunt, Kyle
See Creasey, John
Hunt, (James Henry) Leigh 1784-1859**NCLC 1; DAM POET**
Hunt, Marsha 1946- .... **CLC 70**
See also BW 2; CA 143
Hunt, Violet 1866-1942 .... **TCLC 53**
See also DLB 162
Hunter, E. Waldo
See Sturgeon, Theodore (Hamilton)
Hunter, Evan 1926- . **CLC 11, 31; DAM POP**
See also CA 5-8R; CANR 5, 38, 62; DLBY 82; INT CANR-5; MTCW; SATA 25
Hunter, Kristin (Eggleston) 1931- ... **CLC 35**
See also AITN 1; BW 1; CA 13-16R; CANR 13; CLR 3; DLB 33; INT CANR-13; MAICYA; SAAS 10; SATA 12
Hunter, Mollie 1922- .... **CLC 21**
See also McIlwraith, Maureen Mollie Hunter
See also AAYA 13; CANR 37; CLR 25; DLB 161; JRDA; MAICYA; SAAS 7; SATA 54
Hunter, Robert (?)-1734 .... **LC 7**
Hurston, Zora Neale 1903-1960**CLC 7, 30, 61; BLC; DA; DAC; DAM MST, MULT, NOV; SSC 4; WLCS**
See also AAYA 15; BW 1; CA 85-88; CANR 61; DLB 51, 86; MTCW
Huston, John (Marcellus) 1906-1987**CLC 20**
See also CA 73-76; 123; CANR 34; DLB 26
Hustvedt, Siri 1955- .... **CLC 76**
See also CA 137
Hutten, Ulrich von 1488-1523 .... **LC 16**
See also DLB 179
Huxley, Aldous (Leonard) 1894-1963 **CLC 1, 3, 4, 5, 8, 11, 18, 35, 79; DA; DAB; DAC; DAM MST, NOV; WLC**
See also AAYA 11; CA 85-88; CANR 44; CDBLB 1914-1945; DLB 36, 100, 162; MTCW; SATA 63
Huxley, T. H. 1825-1895 .... **NCLC 67**
See also DLB 57
Huysmans, Charles Marie Georges 1848-1907
See Huysmans, Joris-Karl
See also CA 104
Huysmans, Joris-Karl .... **TCLC 7, 69**
See also Huysmans, Charles Marie Georges
See also DLB 123
Hwang, David Henry 1957- ... **CLC 55; DAM DRAM; DC 4**
See also CA 127; 132; INT 132
Hyde, Anthony 1946- .... **CLC 42**
See also CA 136
Hyde, Margaret O(ldroyd) 1917- .... **CLC 21**
See also CA 1-4R; CANR 1, 36; CLR 23; JRDA; MAICYA; SAAS 8; SATA 1, 42, 76
Hynes, James 1956(?)- .... **CLC 65**
Ian, Janis 1951- .... **CLC 21**
See also CA 105
Ibanez, Vicente Blasco
See Blasco Ibanez, Vicente
Ibarguengoitia, Jorge 1928-1983 ..... **CLC 37**
See also CA 124; 113; HW
Ibsen, Henrik (Johan) 1828-1906 **TCLC 2, 8, 16, 37, 52; DA; DAB; DAC; DAM DRAM,**

MST; DC 2; WLC
See also CA 104; 141
Ibuse Masuji 1898-1993 .... **CLC 22**
See also CA 127; 141; DLB 180
Ichikawa, Kon 1915- .... **CLC 20**
See also CA 121
Idle, Eric 1943- .... **CLC 21**
See also Monty Python
See also CA 116; CANR 35
Ignatow, David 1914- .... **CLC 4, 7, 14, 40**
See also CA 9-12R; CAAS 3; CANR 31, 57; DLB 5
Ihimaera, Witi 1944- .... **CLC 46**
See also CA 77-80
Ilf, Ilya .... **TCLC 21**
See also Fainzilberg, Ilya Arnoldovich
Illyes, Gyula 1902-1983 .... **PC 16**
See also CA 114; 109
Immermann, Karl (Lebrecht) 1796-1840 **NCLC 4, 49**
See also DLB 133
Inchbald, Elizabeth 1753-1821 ...... **NCLC 62**
See also DLB 39, 89
Inclan, Ramon (Maria) del Valle
See Valle-Inclan, Ramon (Maria) del
Infante, G(uillermo) Cabrera
See Cabrera Infante, G(uillermo)
Ingalls, Rachel (Holmes) 1940- .... **CLC 42**
See also CA 123; 127
Ingamells, Rex 1913-1955 .... **TCLC 35**
Inge, William (Motter) 1913-1973 **CLC 1, 8, 19; DAM DRAM**
See also CA 9-12R; CDALB 1941-1968; DLB 7; MTCW
Ingelow, Jean 1820-1897 .... **NCLC 39**
See also DLB 35, 163; SATA 33
Ingram, Willis J.
See Harris, Mark
Innaurato, Albert (F.) 1948(?)- .. **CLC 21, 60**
See also CA 115; 122; INT 122
Innes, Michael
See Stewart, J(ohn) I(nnes) M(ackintosh)
Innis, Harold Adams 1894-1952 .... **TCLC 77**
See also DLB 88
Ionesco, Eugene 1909-1994**CLC 1, 4, 6, 9, 11, 15, 41, 86; DA; DAB; DAC; DAM DRAM, MST; WLC**
See also CA 9-12R; 144; CANR 55; MTCW; SATA 7; SATA-Obit 79
Iqbal, Muhammad 1873-1938 .... **TCLC 28**
Ireland, Patrick
See O'Doherty, Brian
Iron, Ralph
See Schreiner, Olive (Emilie Albertina)
Irving, John (Winslow) 1942-**CLC 13, 23, 38; DAM NOV, POP**
See also AAYA 8; BEST 89:3; CA 25-28R; CANR 28; DLB 6; DLBY 82; MTCW
Irving, Washington 1783-1859. **NCLC 2, 19; DA; DAB; DAM MST; SSC 2; WLC**
See also CDALB 1640-1865; DLB 3, 11, 30, 59, 73, 74; YABC 2
Irwin, P. K.
See Page, P(atricia) K(athleen)
Isaacs, Susan 1943- .... **CLC 32; DAM POP**
See also BEST 89:1; CA 89-92; CANR 20, 41; INT CANR-20; MTCW
Isherwood, Christopher (William Bradshaw) 1904-1986 .... **CLC 1, 9, 11, 14, 44; DAM DRAM, NOV**
See also CA 13-16R; 117; CANR 35; DLB 15; DLBY 86; MTCW
Ishiguro, Kazuo 1954- **CLC 27, 56, 59; DAM**

NOV
See also BEST 90:2; CA 120; CANR 49; MTCW
Ishikawa, Hakuhin
See Ishikawa, Takuboku
Ishikawa, Takuboku 1886(?)-1912 **TCLC 15; DAM POET; PC 10**
See also CA 113; 153
Iskander, Fazil 1929- .... **CLC 47**
See also CA 102
Isler, Alan (David) 1934- .... **CLC 91**
See also CA 156
Ivan IV 1530-1584 .... **LC 17**
Ivanov, Vyacheslav Ivanovich 1866-1949 **TCLC 33**
See also CA 122
Ivask, Ivar Vidrik 1927-1992 .... **CLC 14**
See also CA 37-40R; 139; CANR 24
Ives, Morgan
See Bradley, Marion Zimmer
J. R. S.
See Gogarty, Oliver St. John
Jabran, Kahlil
See Gibran, Kahlil
Jabran, Khalil
See Gibran, Kahlil
Jackson, Daniel
See Wingrove, David (John)
Jackson, Jesse 1908-1983 .... **CLC 12**
See also BW 1; CA 25-28R; 109; CANR 27; CLR 28; MAICYA; SATA 2, 29; SATA-Obit 48
Jackson, Laura (Riding) 1901-1991
See Riding, Laura
See also CA 65-68; 135; CANR 28; DLB 48
Jackson, Sam
See Trumbo, Dalton
Jackson, Sara
See Wingrove, David (John)
Jackson, Shirley 1919-1965 . **CLC 11, 60, 87; DA; DAC; DAM MST; SSC 9; WLC**
See also AAYA 9; CA 1-4R; 25-28R; CANR 4, 52; CDALB 1941-1968; DLB 6; SATA 2
Jacob, (Cyprien-)Max 1876-1944 .... **TCLC 6**
See also CA 104
Jacobs, Harriet 1813(?)-1897 .... **NCLC 67**
Jacobs, Jim 1942- .... **CLC 12**
See also CA 97-100; INT 97-100
Jacobs, W(illiam) W(ymark) 1863-1943 **TCLC 22**
See also CA 121; DLB 135
Jacobsen, Jens Peter 1847-1885 ..... **NCLC 34**
Jacobsen, Josephine 1908- .... **CLC 48, 102**
See also CA 33-36R; CAAS 18; CANR 23, 48
Jacobson, Dan 1929- .... **CLC 4, 14**
See also CA 1-4R; CANR 2, 25; DLB 14; MTCW
Jacqueline
See Carpentier (y Valmont), Alejo
Jagger, Mick 1944- .... **CLC 17**
Jahiz, Al- c. 776-869 .... **CMLC 25**
Jakes, John (William) 1932- .. **CLC 29; DAM NOV, POP**
See also BEST 89:4; CA 57-60; CANR 10, 43; DLBY 83; INT CANR-10; MTCW; SATA 62
James, Andrew
See Kirkup, James
James, C(yril) L(ionel) R(obert) 1901-1989 **CLC 33**
See also BW 2; CA 117; 125; 128; CANR 62; DLB 125; MTCW
James, Daniel (Lewis) 1911-1988
See Santiago, Danny

See also CA 125

James, Dynely
See Mayne, William (James Carter)

James, Henry Sr. 1811-1882 .... NCLC 53

James, Henry 1843-1916 **TCLC 2, 11, 24, 40, 47, 64; DA; DAB; DAC; DAM MST, NOV; SSC 8; WLC**
See also CA 104; 132; CDALB 1865-1917; DLB 12, 71, 74; DLBD 13; MTCW

James, M. R.
See James, Montague (Rhodes)
See also DLB 156

James, Montague (Rhodes) 1862-1936 **T C L C 6; SSC 16**
See also CA 104

James, P. D. .... **CLC 18, 46**
See also White, Phyllis Dorothy James
See also BEST 90:2; CDBLB 1960 to Present; DLB 87

James, Philip
See Moorcock, Michael (John)

James, William 1842-1910 .... **TCLC 15, 32**
See also CA 109

James I 1394-1437 .... **LC 20**

Jameson, Anna 1794-1860 .... **NCLC 43**
See also DLB 99, 166

Jami, Nur al-Din 'Abd al-Rahman 1414-1492 **LC 9**

Jammes, Francis 1868-1938 .... **TCLC 75**

Jandl, Ernst 1925- .... **CLC 34**

Janowitz, Tama 1957- ... **CLC 43; DAM POP**
See also CA 106; CANR 52

Japrisot, Sebastien 1931- .... **CLC 90**

Jarrell, Randall 1914-1965 **CLC 1, 2, 6, 9, 13, 49; DAM POET**
See also CA 5-8R; 25-28R; CABS 2; CANR 6, 34; CDALB 1941-1968; CLR 6; DLB 48, 52; MAICYA; MTCW; SATA 7

Jarry, Alfred 1873-1907 . **TCLC 2, 14; DAM DRAM; SSC 20**
See also CA 104; 153

Jarvis, E. K.
See Bloch, Robert (Albert); Ellison, Harlan (Jay); Silverberg, Robert

Jeake, Samuel, Jr.
See Aiken, Conrad (Potter)

Jean Paul 1763-1825 .... **NCLC 7**

Jefferies, (John) Richard 1848-1887 **NCLC 47**
See also DLB 98, 141; SATA 16

Jeffers, (John) Robinson 1887-1962 **CLC 2, 3, 11, 15, 54; DA; DAC; DAM MST, POET; PC 17; WLC**
See also CA 85-88; CANR 35; CDALB 1917-1929; DLB 45; MTCW

Jefferson, Janet
See Mencken, H(enry) L(ouis)

Jefferson, Thomas 1743-1826 .... **NCLC 11**
See also CDALB 1640-1865; DLB 31

Jeffrey, Francis 1773-1850 .... **NCLC 33**
See also DLB 107

Jelakowitch, Ivan
See Heijermans, Herman

Jellicoe, (Patricia) Ann 1927- .... **CLC 27**
See also CA 85-88; DLB 13

Jen, Gish .... **CLC 70**
See also Jen, Lillian

Jen, Lillian 1956(?)-
See Jen, Gish
See also CA 135

Jenkins, (John) Robin 1912- .... **CLC 52**
See also CA 1-4R; CANR 1; DLB 14

Jennings, Elizabeth (Joan) 1926-. **CLC 5, 14**
See also CA 61-64; CAAS 5; CANR 8, 39; DLB 27; MTCW; SATA 66

Jennings, Waylon 1937- .... **CLC 21**

Jensen, Johannes V. 1873-1950 ...... **TCLC 41**

Jensen, Laura (Linnea) 1948- .... **CLC 37**
See also CA 103

Jerome, Jerome K(lapka) 1859-1927 **TCLC 23**
See also CA 119; DLB 10, 34, 135

Jerrold, Douglas William 1803-1857 **NCLC 2**
See also DLB 158, 159

Jewett, (Theodora) Sarah Orne 1849-1909 **TCLC 1, 22; SSC 6**
See also CA 108; 127; DLB 12, 74; SATA 15

Jewsbury, Geraldine (Endsor) 1812-1880 **NCLC 22**
See also DLB 21

Jhabvala, Ruth Prawer 1927- **CLC 4, 8, 29, 94; DAB; DAM NOV**
See also CA 1-4R; CANR 2, 29, 51; DLB 139; INT CANR-29; MTCW

Jibran, Kahlil
See Gibran, Kahlil

Jibran, Khalil
See Gibran, Kahlil

Jiles, Paulette 1943- .... **CLC 13, 58**
See also CA 101

Jimenez (Mantecon), Juan Ramon 1881-1958 **TCLC 4; DAM MULT, POET; HLC; PC 7**
See also CA 104; 131; DLB 134; HW; MTCW

Jimenez, Ramon
See Jimenez (Mantecon), Juan Ramon

Jimenez Mantecon, Juan
See Jimenez (Mantecon), Juan Ramon

Joel, Billy .... **CLC 26**
See also Joel, William Martin

Joel, William Martin 1949-
See Joel, Billy
See also CA 108

John of the Cross, St. 1542-1591 .... **LC 18**

Johnson, B(ryan) S(tanley William) 1933-1973 **CLC 6, 9**
See also CA 9-12R; 53-56; CANR 9; DLB 14, 40

Johnson, Benj. F. of Boo
See Riley, James Whitcomb

Johnson, Benjamin F. of Boo
See Riley, James Whitcomb

Johnson, Charles (Richard) 1948- **CLC 7, 51, 65; BLC; DAM MULT**
See also BW 2; CA 116; CAAS 18; CANR 42; DLB 33

Johnson, Denis 1949- .... **CLC 52**
See also CA 117; 121; DLB 120

Johnson, Diane 1934- .... **CLC 5, 13, 48**
See also CA 41-44R; CANR 17, 40, 62; DLBY 80; INT CANR-17; MTCW

Johnson, Eyvind (Olof Verner) 1900-1976 **CLC 14**
See also CA 73-76; 69-72; CANR 34

Johnson, J. R.
See James, C(yril) L(ionel) R(obert)

Johnson, James Weldon 1871-1938 **TCLC 3, 19; BLC; DAM MULT, POET**
See also BW 1; CA 104; 125; CDALB 1917-1929; CLR 32; DLB 51; MTCW; SATA 31

Johnson, Joyce 1935- .... **CLC 58**
See also CA 125; 129

Johnson, Lionel (Pigot) 1867-1902 **TCLC 19**
See also CA 117; DLB 19

Johnson, Mel
See Malzberg, Barry N(athaniel)

Johnson, Pamela Hansford 1912-1981 **CLC 1, 7, 27**

See also CA 1-4R; 104; CANR 2, 28; DLB 15; MTCW

Johnson, Robert 1911(?)-1938 .... **TCLC 69**

Johnson, Samuel 1709-1784 **LC 15; DA; DAB; DAC; DAM MST; WLC**
See also CDBLB 1660-1789; DLB 39, 95, 104, 142

Johnson, Uwe 1934-1984 .. **CLC 5, 10, 15, 40**
See also CA 1-4R; 112; CANR 1, 39; DLB 75; MTCW

Johnston, George (Benson) 1913- .... **CLC 51**
See also CA 1-4R; CANR 5, 20; DLB 88

Johnston, Jennifer 1930- .... **CLC 7**
See also CA 85-88; DLB 14

Jolley, (Monica) Elizabeth 1923- **CLC 46; SSC 19**
See also CA 127; CAAS 13; CANR 59

Jones, Arthur Llewellyn 1863-1947
See Machen, Arthur
See also CA 104

Jones, D(ouglas) G(ordon) 1929- ..... **CLC 10**
See also CA 29-32R; CANR 13; DLB 53

Jones, David (Michael) 1895-1974 **CLC 2, 4, 7, 13, 42**
See also CA 9-12R; 53-56; CANR 28; CDBLB 1945-1960; DLB 20, 100; MTCW

Jones, David Robert 1947-
See Bowie, David
See also CA 103

Jones, Diana Wynne 1934- .... **CLC 26**
See also AAYA 12; CA 49-52; CANR 4, 26, 56; CLR 23; DLB 161; JRDA; MAICYA; SAAS 7; SATA 9, 70

Jones, Edward P. 1950- .... **CLC 76**
See also BW 2; CA 142

Jones, Gayl 1949- ...... **CLC 6, 9; BLC; DAM MULT**
See also BW 2; CA 77-80; CANR 27; DLB 33; MTCW

Jones, James 1921-1977 ...... **CLC 1, 3, 10, 39**
See also AITN 1, 2; CA 1-4R; 69-72; CANR 6; DLB 2, 143; MTCW

Jones, John J.
See Lovecraft, H(oward) P(hillips)

Jones, LeRoi .... **CLC 1, 2, 3, 5, 10, 14**
See also Baraka, Amiri

Jones, Louis B. .... **CLC 65**
See also CA 141

Jones, Madison (Percy, Jr.) 1925- .... **CLC 4**
See also CA 13-16R; CAAS 11; CANR 7, 54; DLB 152

Jones, Mervyn 1922- .... **CLC 10, 52**
See also CA 45-48; CAAS 5; CANR 1; MTCW

Jones, Mick 1956(?)- .... **CLC 30**

Jones, Nettie (Pearl) 1941- .... **CLC 34**
See also BW 2; CA 137; CAAS 20

Jones, Preston 1936-1979 .... **CLC 10**
See also CA 73-76; 89-92; DLB 7

Jones, Robert F(rancis) 1934- .... **CLC 7**
See also CA 49-52; CANR 2, 61

Jones, Rod 1953- .... **CLC 50**
See also CA 128

Jones, Terence Graham Parry 1942- **CLC 21**
See also Jones, Terry; Monty Python
See also CA 112; 116; CANR 35; INT 116

Jones, Terry
See Jones, Terence Graham Parry
See also SATA 67; SATA-Brief 51

Jones, Thom 1945(?)- .... **CLC 81**
See also CA 157

Jong, Erica 1942- **CLC 4, 6, 8, 18, 83; DAM NOV, POP**
See also AITN 1; BEST 90:2; CA 73-76; CANR

26, 52; DLB 2, 5, 28, 152; INT CANR-26; MTCW

Jonson, Ben(jamin) 1572(?)-1637 .. **LC 6, 33; DA; DAB; DAC; DAM DRAM, MST, POET; DC 4; PC 17; WLC**
See also CDBLB Before 1660; DLB 62, 121

Jordan, June 1936- .... **CLC 5, 11, 23; DAM MULT, POET**
See also AAYA 2; BW 2; CA 33-36R; CANR 25; CLR 10; DLB 38; MAICYA; MTCW; SATA 4

Jordan, Pat(rick M.) 1941- .... **CLC 37**
See also CA 33-36R

Jorgensen, Ivar
See Ellison, Harlan (Jay)

Jorgenson, Ivar
See Silverberg, Robert

Josephus, Flavius c. 37-100 .... **CMLC 13**

Josipovici, Gabriel 1940- .... **CLC 6, 43**
See also CA 37-40R; CAAS 8; CANR 47; DLB 14

Joubert, Joseph 1754-1824 .... **NCLC 9**

Jouve, Pierre Jean 1887-1976 .... **CLC 47**
See also CA 65-68

Jovine, Francesco 1902-1950 .... **TCLC 79**

Joyce, James (Augustine Aloysius) 1882-1941 **TCLC 3, 8, 16, 35, 52; DA; DAB; DAC; DAM MST, NOV, POET; SSC 3, 26; WLC**
See also CA 104; 126; CDBLB 1914-1945; DLB 10, 19, 36, 162; MTCW

Jozsef, Attila 1905-1937 .... **TCLC 22**
See also CA 116

Juana Ines de la Cruz 1651(?)-1695 ..... **LC 5**

Judd, Cyril
See Kornbluth, C(yril) M.; Pohl, Frederik

Julian of Norwich 1342(?)-1416(?) .... **LC 6**
See also DLB 146

Juniper, Alex
See Hospital, Janette Turner

Junius
See Luxemburg, Rosa

Just, Ward (Swift) 1935- .... **CLC 4, 27**
See also CA 25-28R; CANR 32; INT CANR-32

Justice, Donald (Rodney) 1925- .. **CLC 6, 19, 102; DAM POET**
See also CA 5-8R; CANR 26, 54; DLBY 83; INT CANR-26

Juvenal c. 55-c. 127 .... **CMLC 8**

Juvenis
See Bourne, Randolph S(illiman)

Kacew, Romain 1914-1980
See Gary, Romain
See also CA 108; 102

Kadare, Ismail 1936- .... **CLC 52**
See also CA 161

Kadohata, Cynthia .... **CLC 59**
See also CA 140

Kafka, Franz 1883-1924 **TCLC 2, 6, 13, 29, 47, 53; DA; DAB; DAC; DAM MST, NOV; SSC 5, 29; WLC**
See also CA 105; 126; DLB 81; MTCW

Kahanovitsch, Pinkhes
See Der Nister

Kahn, Roger 1927- .... **CLC 30**
See also CA 25-28R; CANR 44; DLB 171; SATA 37

Kain, Saul
See Sassoon, Siegfried (Lorraine)

Kaiser, Georg 1878-1945 .... **TCLC 9**
See also CA 106; DLB 124

Kaletski, Alexander 1946- .... **CLC 39**
See also CA 118; 143

Kalidasa fl. c. 400- .... **CMLC 9**

Kallman, Chester (Simon) 1921-1975 **CLC 2**
See also CA 45-48; 53-56; CANR 3

Kaminsky, Melvin 1926-
See Brooks, Mel
See also CA 65-68; CANR 16

Kaminsky, Stuart M(elvin) 1934- ..... **CLC 59**
See also CA 73-76; CANR 29, 53

Kane, Francis
See Robbins, Harold

Kane, Paul
See Simon, Paul (Frederick)

Kane, Wilson
See Bloch, Robert (Albert)

Kanin, Garson 1912- .... **CLC 22**
See also AITN 1; CA 5-8R; CANR 7; DLB 7

Kaniuk, Yoram 1930- .... **CLC 19**
See also CA 134

Kant, Immanuel 1724-1804 ..... **NCLC 27, 67**
See also DLB 94

Kantor, MacKinlay 1904-1977 .... **CLC 7**
See also CA 61-64; 73-76; CANR 60, 63; DLB 9, 102

Kaplan, David Michael 1946- .... **CLC 50**

Kaplan, James 1951- .... **CLC 59**
See also CA 135

Karageorge, Michael
See Anderson, Poul (William)

Karamzin, Nikolai Mikhailovich 1766-1826 **NCLC 3**
See also DLB 150

Karapanou, Margarita 1946- .... **CLC 13**
See also CA 101

Karinthy, Frigyes 1887-1938 .... **TCLC 47**

Karl, Frederick R(obert) 1927- .... **CLC 34**
See also CA 5-8R; CANR 3, 44

Kastel, Warren
See Silverberg, Robert

Kataev, Evgeny Petrovich 1903-1942
See Petrov, Evgeny
See also CA 120

Kataphusin
See Ruskin, John

Katz, Steve 1935- .... **CLC 47**
See also CA 25-28R; CAAS 14, 64; CANR 12; DLBY 83

Kauffman, Janet 1945- .... **CLC 42**
See also CA 117; CANR 43; DLBY 86

Kaufman, Bob (Garnell) 1925-1986 . **CLC 49**
See also BW 1; CA 41-44R; 118; CANR 22; DLB 16, 41

Kaufman, George S. 1889-1961 **CLC 38; DAM DRAM**
See also CA 108; 93-96; DLB 7; INT 108

Kaufman, Sue .... **CLC 3, 8**
See also Barondess, Sue K(aufman)

Kavafis, Konstantinos Petrou 1863-1933
See Cavafy, C(onstantine) P(eter)
See also CA 104

Kavan, Anna 1901-1968 .... **CLC 5, 13, 82**
See also CA 5-8R; CANR 6, 57; MTCW

Kavanagh, Dan
See Barnes, Julian (Patrick)

Kavanagh, Patrick (Joseph) 1904-1967 **CLC 22**
See also CA 123; 25-28R; DLB 15, 20; MTCW

Kawabata, Yasunari 1899-1972 **CLC 2, 5, 9, 18, 107; DAM MULT; SSC 17**
See also CA 93-96; 33-36R; DLB 180

Kaye, M(ary) M(argaret) 1909- .... **CLC 28**
See also CA 89-92; CANR 24, 60; MTCW; SATA 62

Kaye, Mollie

Kaye, M(ary) M(argaret)
See Kaye, M(ary) M(argaret)

Kaye-Smith, Sheila 1887-1956 .... **TCLC 20**
See also CA 118; DLB 36

Kaymor, Patrice Maguilene
See Senghor, Leopold Sedar

Kazan, Elia 1909- .... **CLC 6, 16, 63**
See also CA 21-24R; CANR 32

Kazantzakis, Nikos 1883(?)-1957 **TCLC 2, 5, 33**
See also CA 105; 132; MTCW

Kazin, Alfred 1915- .... **CLC 34, 38**
See also CA 1-4R; CAAS 7; CANR 1, 45; DLB 67

Keane, Mary Nesta (Skrine) 1904-1996
See Keane, Molly
See also CA 108; 114; 151

Keane, Molly .... **CLC 31**
See also Keane, Mary Nesta (Skrine)
See also INT 114

Keates, Jonathan 19(?)- .... **CLC 34**

Keaton, Buster 1895-1966 .... **CLC 20**

Keats, John 1795-1821 . **NCLC 8; DA; DAB; DAC; DAM MST, POET; PC 1; WLC**
See also CDBLB 1789-1832; DLB 96, 110

Keene, Donald 1922- .... **CLC 34**
See also CA 1-4R; CANR 5

Keillor, Garrison .... **CLC 40**
See also Keillor, Gary (Edward)
See also AAYA 2; BEST 89:3; DLBY 87; SATA 58

Keillor, Gary (Edward) 1942-
See Keillor, Garrison
See also CA 111; 117; CANR 36, 59; DAM POP; MTCW

Keith, Michael
See Hubbard, L(afayette) Ron(ald)

Keller, Gottfried 1819-1890 **NCLC 2; SSC 26**
See also DLB 129

Kellerman, Jonathan 1949- ... **CLC 44; DAM POP**
See also BEST 90:1; CA 106; CANR 29, 51; INT CANR-29

Kelley, William Melvin 1937- .... **CLC 22**
See also BW 1; CA 77-80; CANR 27; DLB 33

Kellogg, Marjorie 1922- .... **CLC 2**
See also CA 81-84

Kellow, Kathleen
See Hibbert, Eleanor Alice Burford

Kelly, M(ilton) T(erry) 1947- .... **CLC 55**
See also CA 97-100; CAAS 22; CANR 19, 43

Kelman, James 1946- .... **CLC 58, 86**
See also CA 148

Kemal, Yashar 1923- .... **CLC 14, 29**
See also CA 89-92; CANR 44

Kemble, Fanny 1809-1893 .... **NCLC 18**
See also DLB 32

Kemelman, Harry 1908-1996 .... **CLC 2**
See also AITN 1; CA 9-12R; 155; CANR 6; DLB 28

Kempe, Margery 1373(?)-1440(?) .... **LC 6**
See also DLB 146

Kempis, Thomas a 1380-1471 .... **LC 11**

Kendall, Henry 1839-1882 .... **NCLC 12**

Keneally, Thomas (Michael) 1935- **CLC 5, 8, 10, 14, 19, 27, 43; DAM NOV**
See also CA 85-88; CANR 10, 50; MTCW

Kennedy, Adrienne (Lita) 1931- ..... **CLC 66; BLC; DAM MULT; DC 5**
See also BW 2; CA 103; CAAS 20; CABS 3; CANR 26, 53; DLB 38

Kennedy, John Pendleton 1795-1870 **NCLC 2**
See also DLB 3

Kennedy, Joseph Charles 1929-

See Kennedy, X. J.
See also CA 1-4R; CANR 4, 30, 40; SATA 14, 86

Kennedy, William 1928- .. **CLC 6, 28, 34, 53; DAM NOV**
See also AAYA 1; CA 85-88; CANR 14, 31; DLB 143; DLBY 85; INT CANR-31; MTCW; SATA 57

Kennedy, X. J. .... **CLC 8, 42**
See also Kennedy, Joseph Charles
See also CAAS 9; CLR 27; DLB 5; SAAS 22

Kenny, Maurice (Francis) 1929- ..... **CLC 87; DAM MULT**
See also CA 144; CAAS 22; DLB 175; NNAL

Kent, Kelvin
See Kuttner, Henry

Kenton, Maxwell
See Southern, Terry

Kenyon, Robert O.
See Kuttner, Henry

Kerouac, Jack .... **CLC 1, 2, 3, 5, 14, 29, 61**
See also Kerouac, Jean-Louis Lebris de
See also CDALB 1941-1968; DLB 2, 16; DLBD 3; DLBY 95

Kerouac, Jean-Louis Lebris de 1922-1969
See Kerouac, Jack
See also AITN 1; CA 5-8R; 25-28R; CANR 26, 54; DA; DAB; DAC; DAM MST, NOV, POET, POP; MTCW; WLC

Kerr, Jean 1923- .... **CLC 22**
See also CA 5-8R; CANR 7; INT CANR-7

Kerr, M. E. .... **CLC 12, 35**
See also Meaker, Marijane (Agnes)
See also AAYA 2; CLR 29; SAAS 1

Kerr, Robert .... **CLC 55**

Kerrigan, (Thomas) Anthony 1918-**CLC 4, 6**
See also CA 49-52; CAAS 11; CANR 4

Kerry, Lois
See Duncan, Lois

Kesey, Ken (Elton) 1935- **CLC 1, 3, 6, 11, 46, 64; DA; DAB; DAC; DAM MST, NOV, POP; WLC**
See also CA 1-4R; CANR 22, 38; CDALB 1968-1988; DLB 2, 16; MTCW; SATA 66

Kesselring, Joseph (Otto) 1902-1967**CLC 45; DAM DRAM, MST**
See also CA 150

Kessler, Jascha (Frederick) 1929-........**CLC 4**
See also CA 17-20R; CANR 8, 48

Kettelkamp, Larry (Dale) 1933- ...... **CLC 12**
See also CA 29-32R; CANR 16; SAAS 3; SATA 2

Key, Ellen 1849-1926 .... **TCLC 65**

Keyber, Conny
See Fielding, Henry

Keyes, Daniel 1927-**CLC 80; DA; DAC; DAM MST, NOV**
See also CA 17-20R; CANR 10, 26, 54; SATA 37

Keynes, John Maynard 1883-1946 **TCLC 64**
See also CA 114; DLBD 10

Khanshendel, Chiron
See Rose, Wendy

Khayyam, Omar 1048-1131**CMLC 11; DAM POET; PC 8**

Kherdian, David 1931-...................... **CLC 6, 9**
See also CA 21-24R; CAAS 2; CANR 39; CLR 24; JRDA; MAICYA; SATA 16, 74

Khlebnikov, Velimir .... **TCLC 20**
See also Khlebnikov, Viktor Vladimirovich

Khlebnikov, Viktor Vladimirovich 1885-1922
See Khlebnikov, Velimir
See also CA 117

Khodasevich, Vladislav (Felitsianovich) 1886-1939 .... **TCLC 15**
See also CA 115

Kielland, Alexander Lange 1849-1906**T C L C 5**
See also CA 104

Kiely, Benedict 1919- .... **CLC 23, 43**
See also CA 1-4R; CANR 2; DLB 15

Kienzle, William X(avier) 1928- ..... **CLC 25; DAM POP**
See also CA 93-96; CAAS 1; CANR 9, 31, 59; INT CANR-31; MTCW

Kierkegaard, Soren 1813-1855 ...... **NCLC 34**

Killens, John Oliver 1916-1987 .... **CLC 10**
See also BW 2; CA 77-80; 123; CAAS 2; CANR 26; DLB 33

Killigrew, Anne 1660-1685 .... **LC 4**
See also DLB 131

Kim
See Simenon, Georges (Jacques Christian)

Kincaid, Jamaica 1949- .. **CLC 43, 68; BLC; DAM MULT, NOV**
See also AAYA 13; BW 2; CA 125; CANR 47, 59; DLB 157

King, Francis (Henry) 1923-**CLC 8, 53; DAM NOV**
See also CA 1-4R; CANR 1, 33; DLB 15, 139; MTCW

King, Martin Luther, Jr. 1929-1968 **CLC 83; BLC; DA; DAB; DAC; DAM MST, MULT; WLCS**
See also BW 2; CA 25-28; CANR 27, 44; CAP 2; MTCW; SATA 14

King, Stephen (Edwin) 1947-**CLC 12, 26, 37, 61; DAM NOV, POP; SSC 17**
See also AAYA 1, 17; BEST 90:1; CA 61-64; CANR 1, 30, 52; DLB 143; DLBY 80; JRDA; MTCW; SATA 9, 55

King, Steve
See King, Stephen (Edwin)

King, Thomas 1943- .... **CLC 89; DAC; DAM MULT**
See also CA 144; DLB 175; NNAL; SATA 96

Kingman, Lee .... **CLC 17**
See also Natti, (Mary) Lee
See also SAAS 3; SATA 1, 67

Kingsley, Charles 1819-1875 .... **NCLC 35**
See also DLB 21, 32, 163; YABC 2

Kingsley, Sidney 1906-1995 .... **CLC 44**
See also CA 85-88; 147; DLB 7

Kingsolver, Barbara 1955-**CLC 55, 81; DAM POP**
See also AAYA 15; CA 129; 134; CANR 60; INT 134

Kingston, Maxine (Ting Ting) Hong 1940-**CLC 12, 19, 58; DAM MULT, NOV; WLCS**
See also AAYA 8; CA 69-72; CANR 13, 38; DLB 173; DLBY 80; INT CANR-13; MTCW; SATA 53

Kinnell, Galway 1927- **CLC 1, 2, 3, 5, 13, 29**
See also CA 9-12R; CANR 10, 34; DLB 5; DLBY 87; INT CANR-34; MTCW

Kinsella, Thomas 1928- .... **CLC 4, 19**
See also CA 17-20R; CANR 15; DLB 27; MTCW

Kinsella, W(illiam) P(atrick) 1935- **CLC 27, 43; DAC; DAM NOV, POP**
See also AAYA 7; CA 97-100; CAAS 7; CANR 21, 35; INT CANR-21; MTCW

Kipling, (Joseph) Rudyard 1865-1936 **T C L C 8, 17; DA; DAB; DAC; DAM MST, POET; PC 3; SSC 5; WLC**

See also CA 105; 120; CANR 33; CDBLB 1890-1914; CLR 39; DLB 19, 34, 141, 156; MAICYA; MTCW; YABC 2

Kirkup, James 1918- .... **CLC 1**
See also CA 1-4R; CAAS 4; CANR 2; DLB 27; SATA 12

Kirkwood, James 1930(?)-1989 .... **CLC 9**
See also AITN 2; CA 1-4R; 128; CANR 6, 40

Kirshner, Sidney
See Kingsley, Sidney

Kis, Danilo 1935-1989 .... **CLC 57**
See also CA 109; 118; 129; CANR 61; DLB 181; MTCW

Kivi, Aleksis 1834-1872 .... **NCLC 30**

Kizer, Carolyn (Ashley) 1925-**CLC 15, 39, 80; DAM POET**
See also CA 65-68; CAAS 5; CANR 24; DLB 5, 169

Klabund 1890-1928 .... **TCLC 44**
See also DLB 66

Klappert, Peter 1942- .... **CLC 57**
See also CA 33-36R; DLB 5

Klein, A(braham) M(oses) 1909-1972**CLC 19; DAB; DAC; DAM MST**
See also CA 101; 37-40R; DLB 68

Klein, Norma 1938-1989 .... **CLC 30**
See also AAYA 2; CA 41-44R; 128; CANR 15, 37; CLR 2, 19; INT CANR-15; JRDA; MAICYA; SAAS 1; SATA 7, 57

Klein, T(heodore) E(ibon) D(onald) 1947-**CLC 34**
See also CA 119; CANR 44

Kleist, Heinrich von 1777-1811 **NCLC 2, 37; DAM DRAM; SSC 22**
See also DLB 90

Klima, Ivan 1931- .... **CLC 56; DAM NOV**
See also CA 25-28R; CANR 17, 50

Klimentov, Andrei Platonovich 1899-1951
See Platonov, Andrei
See also CA 108

Klinger, Friedrich Maximilian von 1752-1831 **NCLC 1**
See also DLB 94

Klingsor the Magician
See Hartmann, Sadakichi

Klopstock, Friedrich Gottlieb 1724-1803 **NCLC 11**
See also DLB 97

Knapp, Caroline 1959-...................... **CLC 99**
See also CA 154

Knebel, Fletcher 1911-1993 .... **CLC 14**
See also AITN 1; CA 1-4R; 140; CAAS 3; CANR 1, 36; SATA 36; SATA-Obit 75

Knickerbocker, Diedrich
See Irving, Washington

Knight, Etheridge 1931-1991 **CLC 40; BLC; DAM POET; PC 14**
See also BW 1; CA 21-24R; 133; CANR 23; DLB 41

Knight, Sarah Kemble 1666-1727 .... **LC 7**
See also DLB 24

Knister, Raymond 1899-1932 .... **TCLC 56**
See also DLB 68

Knowles, John 1926- .. **CLC 1, 4, 10, 26; DA; DAC; DAM MST, NOV**
See also AAYA 10; CA 17-20R; CANR 40; CDALB 1968-1988; DLB 6; MTCW; SATA 8, 89

Knox, Calvin M.
See Silverberg, Robert

Knox, John c. 1505-1572 .... **LC 37**
See also DLB 132

Knye, Cassandra

See Disch, Thomas M(ichael)

Koch, C(hristopher) J(ohn) 1932- ... **CLC 42**
 See also CA 127

Koch, Christopher
 See Koch, C(hristopher) J(ohn)

Koch, Kenneth 1925- .... **CLC 5, 8, 44; DAM POET**
 See also CA 1-4R; CANR 6, 36, 57; DLB 5; INT CANR-36; SATA 65

Kochanowski, Jan 1530-1584 .... **LC 10**

Kock, Charles Paul de 1794-1871 .. **NCLC 16**

Koda Shigeyuki 1867-1947
 See Rohan, Koda
 See also CA 121

Koestler, Arthur 1905-1983 **CLC 1, 3, 6, 8, 15, 33**
 See also CA 1-4R; 109; CANR 1, 33; CDBLB 1945-1960; DLBY 83; MTCW

Kogawa, Joy Nozomi 1935- .. **CLC 78; DAC; DAM MST, MULT**
 See also CA 101; CANR 19, 62

Kohout, Pavel 1928- .... **CLC 13**
 See also CA 45-48; CANR 3

Koizumi, Yakumo
 See Hearn, (Patricio) Lafcadio (Tessima Carlos)

Kolmar, Gertrud 1894-1943 .... **TCLC 40**

Komunyakaa, Yusef 1947- .... **CLC 86, 94**
 See also CA 147; DLB 120

Konrad, George
 See Konrad, Gyoergy

Konrad, Gyoergy 1933- .... **CLC 4, 10, 73**
 See also CA 85-88

Konwicki, Tadeusz 1926- .... **CLC 8, 28, 54**
 See also CA 101; CAAS 9; CANR 39, 59; MTCW

Koontz, Dean R(ay) 1945- ..... **CLC 78; DAM NOV, POP**
 See also AAYA 9; BEST 89:3, 90:2; CA 108; CANR 19, 36, 52; MTCW; SATA 92

Kopit, Arthur (Lee) 1937- **CLC 1, 18, 33; DAM DRAM**
 See also AITN 1; CA 81-84; CABS 3; DLB 7; MTCW

Kops, Bernard 1926- .... **CLC 4**
 See also CA 5-8R; DLB 13

Kornbluth, C(yril) M. 1923-1958 .... **TCLC 8**
 See also CA 105; 160; DLB 8

Korolenko, V. G.
 See Korolenko, Vladimir Galaktionovich

Korolenko, Vladimir
 See Korolenko, Vladimir Galaktionovich

Korolenko, Vladimir G.
 See Korolenko, Vladimir Galaktionovich

Korolenko, Vladimir Galaktionovich 1853-1921 .... **TCLC 22**
 See also CA 121

Korzybski, Alfred (Habdank Skarbek) 1879-1950 .... **TCLC 61**
 See also CA 123; 160

Kosinski, Jerzy (Nikodem) 1933-1991 **CLC 1, 2, 3, 6, 10, 15, 53, 70; DAM NOV**
 See also CA 17-20R; 134; CANR 9, 46; DLB 2; DLBY 82; MTCW

Kostelanetz, Richard (Cory) 1940- .. **CLC 28**
 See also CA 13-16R; CAAS 8; CANR 38

Kostrowitzki, Wilhelm Apollinaris de 1880-1918
 See Apollinaire, Guillaume
 See also CA 104

Kotlowitz, Robert 1924- .... **CLC 4**
 See also CA 33-36R; CANR 36

Kotzebue, August (Friedrich Ferdinand) von 1761-1819 .... **NCLC 25**

See also DLB 94

Kotzwinkle, William 1938- ..... **CLC 5, 14, 35**
 See also CA 45-48; CANR 3, 44; CLR 6; DLB 173; MAICYA; SATA 24, 70

Kowna, Stancy
 See Szymborska, Wislawa

Kozol, Jonathan 1936- .... **CLC 17**
 See also CA 61-64; CANR 16, 45

Kozoll, Michael 1940(?)- .... **CLC 35**

Kramer, Kathryn 19(?)- .... **CLC 34**

Kramer, Larry 1935- **CLC 42; DAM POP; DC 8**
 See also CA 124; 126; CANR 60

Krasicki, Ignacy 1735-1801 .... **NCLC 8**

Krasinski, Zygmunt 1812-1859 .... **NCLC 4**

Kraus, Karl 1874-1936 .... **TCLC 5**
 See also CA 104; DLB 118

Kreve (Mickevicius), Vincas 1882-1954 **TCLC 27**

Kristeva, Julia 1941- .... **CLC 77**
 See also CA 154

Kristofferson, Kris 1936- .... **CLC 26**
 See also CA 104

Krizanc, John 1956- .... **CLC 57**

Krleza, Miroslav 1893-1981 .... **CLC 8**
 See also CA 97-100; 105; CANR 50; DLB 147

Kroetsch, Robert 1927- **CLC 5, 23, 57; DAC; DAM POET**
 See also CA 17-20R; CANR 8, 38; DLB 53; MTCW

Kroetz, Franz
 See Kroetz, Franz Xaver

Kroetz, Franz Xaver 1946- .... **CLC 41**
 See also CA 130

Kroker, Arthur (W.) 1945- .... **CLC 77**
 See also CA 161

Kropotkin, Peter (Aleksieevich) 1842-1921 **TCLC 36**
 See also CA 119

Krotkov, Yuri 1917- .... **CLC 19**
 See also CA 102

Krumb
 See Crumb, R(obert)

Krumgold, Joseph (Quincy) 1908-1980 **C L C 12**
 See also CA 9-12R; 101; CANR 7; MAICYA; SATA 1, 48; SATA-Obit 23

Krumwitz
 See Crumb, R(obert)

Krutch, Joseph Wood 1893-1970 ...... **CLC 24**
 See also CA 1-4R; 25-28R; CANR 4; DLB 63

Krutzch, Gus
 See Eliot, T(homas) S(tearns)

Krylov, Ivan Andreevich 1768(?)-1844 **N C L C 1**
 See also DLB 150

Kubin, Alfred (Leopold Isidor) 1877-1959 **TCLC 23**
 See also CA 112; 149; DLB 81

Kubrick, Stanley 1928- .... **CLC 16**
 See also CA 81-84; CANR 33; DLB 26

Kumin, Maxine (Winokur) 1925- **CLC 5, 13, 28; DAM POET; PC 15**
 See also AITN 2; CA 1-4R; CAAS 8; CANR 1, 21; DLB 5; MTCW; SATA 12

Kundera, Milan 1929- .. **CLC 4, 9, 19, 32, 68; DAM NOV; SSC 24**
 See also AAYA 2; CA 85-88; CANR 19, 52; MTCW

Kunene, Mazisi (Raymond) 1930- .... **CLC 85**
 See also BW 1; CA 125; DLB 117

Kunitz, Stanley (Jasspon) 1905- **CLC 6, 11, 14; PC 19**

See also CA 41-44R; CANR 26, 57; DLB 48; INT CANR-26; MTCW

Kunze, Reiner 1933- .... **CLC 10**
 See also CA 93-96; DLB 75

Kuprin, Aleksandr Ivanovich 1870-1938 **TCLC 5**
 See also CA 104

Kureishi, Hanif 1954(?)- .... **CLC 64**
 See also CA 139

Kurosawa, Akira 1910- **CLC 16; DAM MULT**
 See also AAYA 11; CA 101; CANR 46

Kushner, Tony 1957(?)- **CLC 81; DAM DRAM**
 See also CA 144

Kuttner, Henry 1915-1958 .... **TCLC 10**
 See also Vance, Jack
 See also CA 107; 157; DLB 8

Kuzma, Greg 1944- .... **CLC 7**
 See also CA 33-36R

Kuzmin, Mikhail 1872(?)-1936 ...... **TCLC 40**

Kyd, Thomas 1558-1594 **LC 22; DAM DRAM; DC 3**
 See also DLB 62

Kyprianos, Iossif
 See Samarakis, Antonis

La Bruyere, Jean de 1645-1696 .... **LC 17**

Lacan, Jacques (Marie Emile) 1901-1981 **CLC 75**
 See also CA 121; 104

Laclos, Pierre Ambroise Francois Choderlos de 1741-1803 .... **NCLC 4**

La Colere, Francois
 See Aragon, Louis

Lacolere, Francois
 See Aragon, Louis

La Deshabilleuse
 See Simenon, Georges (Jacques Christian)

Lady Gregory
 See Gregory, Isabella Augusta (Persse)

Lady of Quality, A
 See Bagnold, Enid

La Fayette, Marie (Madelaine Pioche de la Vergne Comtes 1634-1693 .... **LC 2**

Lafayette, Rene
 See Hubbard, L(afayette) Ron(ald)

Laforgue, Jules 1860-1887 **NCLC 5, 53; PC 14; SSC 20**

Lagerkvist, Paer (Fabian) 1891-1974 **CLC 7, 10, 13, 54; DAM DRAM, NOV**
 See also Lagerkvist, Par
 See also CA 85-88; 49-52; MTCW

Lagerkvist, Par .... **SSC 12**
 See also Lagerkvist, Paer (Fabian)

Lagerloef, Selma (Ottiliana Lovisa) 1858-1940 **TCLC 4, 36**
 See also Lagerlof, Selma (Ottiliana Lovisa)
 See also CA 108; SATA 15

Lagerlof, Selma (Ottiliana Lovisa)
 See Lagerloef, Selma (Ottiliana Lovisa)
 See also CLR 7; SATA 15

La Guma, (Justin) Alex(ander) 1925-1985 **CLC 19; DAM NOV**
 See also BW 1; CA 49-52; 118; CANR 25; DLB 117; MTCW

Laidlaw, A. K.
 See Grieve, C(hristopher) M(urray)

Lainez, Manuel Mujica
 See Mujica Lainez, Manuel
 See also HW

Laing, R(onald) D(avid) 1927-1989 .. **CLC 95**
 See also CA 107; 129; CANR 34; MTCW

Lamartine, Alphonse (Marie Louis Prat) de 1790-1869 **NCLC 11; DAM POET; PC 16**

Lamb, Charles 1775-1834 ..... **NCLC 10; DA;**

DAB; DAC; DAM MST; WLC
See also CDBLB 1789-1832; DLB 93, 107, 163;
SATA 17
Lamb, Lady Caroline 1785-1828 ...**NCLC 38**
See also DLB 116
Lamming, George (William) 1927- **CLC 2, 4, 66; BLC; DAM MULT**
See also BW 2; CA 85-88; CANR 26; DLB 125;
MTCW
L'Amour, Louis (Dearborn) 1908-1988 . **C L C 25, 55; DAM NOV, POP**
See also AAYA 16; AITN 2; BEST 89:2; CA 1-4R; 125; CANR 3, 25, 40; DLBY 80; MTCW
Lampedusa, Giuseppe (Tomasi) di 1896-1957 **TCLC 13**
See also Tomasi di Lampedusa, Giuseppe
See also DLB 177
Lampman, Archibald 1861-1899 ...**NCLC 25**
See also DLB 92
Lancaster, Bruce 1896-1963 .... **CLC 36**
See also CA 9-10; CAP 1; SATA 9
Lanchester, John .... **CLC 99**
Landau, Mark Alexandrovich
See Aldanov, Mark (Alexandrovich)
Landau-Aldanov, Mark Alexandrovich
See Aldanov, Mark (Alexandrovich)
Landis, Jerry
See Simon, Paul (Frederick)
Landis, John 1950- .... **CLC 26**
See also CA 112; 122
Landolfi, Tommaso 1908-1979 ....**CLC 11, 49**
See also CA 127; 117; DLB 177
Landon, Letitia Elizabeth 1802-1838 . **N C L C 15**
See also DLB 96
Landor, Walter Savage 1775-1864 **NCLC 14**
See also DLB 93, 107
Landwirth, Heinz 1927-
See Lind, Jakov
See also CA 9-12R; CANR 7
Lane, Patrick 1939- .... **CLC 25; DAM POET**
See also CA 97-100; CANR 54; DLB 53; INT 97-100
Lang, Andrew 1844-1912 .... **TCLC 16**
See also CA 114; 137; DLB 98, 141, 184;
MAICYA; SATA 16
Lang, Fritz 1890-1976 .... **CLC 20, 103**
See also CA 77-80; 69-72; CANR 30
Lange, John
See Crichton, (John) Michael
Langer, Elinor 1939- .... **CLC 34**
See also CA 121
Langland, William 1330(?)-1400(?) ... **LC 19; DA; DAB; DAC; DAM MST, POET**
See also DLB 146
Langstaff, Launcelot
See Irving, Washington
Lanier, Sidney 1842-1881 ..... **NCLC 6; DAM POET**
See also DLB 64; DLBD 13; MAICYA; SATA 18
Lanyer, Aemilia 1569-1645 .... **LC 10, 30**
See also DLB 121
Lao Tzu .... **CMLC 7**
Lapine, James (Elliot) 1949- .... **CLC 39**
See also CA 123; 130; CANR 54; INT 130
Larbaud, Valery (Nicolas) 1881-1957 **TCLC 9**
See also CA 106; 152
Lardner, Ring
See Lardner, Ring(gold) W(ilmer)
Lardner, Ring W., Jr.
See Lardner, Ring(gold) W(ilmer)
Lardner, Ring(gold) W(ilmer) 1885-1933

TCLC 2, 14
See also CA 104; 131; CDALB 1917-1929;
DLB 11, 25, 86; DLBD 16; MTCW
Laredo, Betty
See Codrescu, Andrei
Larkin, Maia
See Wojciechowska, Maia (Teresa)
Larkin, Philip (Arthur) 1922-1985**CLC 3, 5, 8, 9, 13, 18, 33, 39, 64; DAB; DAM MST, POET; PC 21**
See also CA 5-8R; 117; CANR 24, 62; CDBLB 1960 to Present; DLB 27; MTCW
Larra (y Sanchez de Castro), Mariano Jose de 1809-1837 .... **NCLC 17**
Larsen, Eric 1941- .... **CLC 55**
See also CA 132
Larsen, Nella 1891-1964**CLC 37; BLC; DAM MULT**
See also BW 1; CA 125; DLB 51
Larson, Charles R(aymond) 1938- ... **CLC 31**
See also CA 53-56; CANR 4
Larson, Jonathan 1961-1996 .... **CLC 99**
See also CA 156
Las Casas, Bartolome de 1474-1566... **LC 31**
Lasch, Christopher 1932-1994 .... **CLC 102**
See also CA 73-76; 144; CANR 25; MTCW
Lasker-Schueler, Else 1869-1945 ... **TCLC 57**
See also DLB 66, 124
Laski, Harold 1893-1950 .... **TCLC 79**
Latham, Jean Lee 1902- .... **CLC 12**
See also AITN 1; CA 5-8R; CANR 7; MAICYA;
SATA 2, 68
Latham, Mavis
See Clark, Mavis Thorpe
Lathen, Emma .... **CLC 2**
See also Hennissart, Martha; Latsis, Mary J(ane)
Lathrop, Francis
See Leiber, Fritz (Reuter, Jr.)
Latsis, Mary J(ane)
See Lathen, Emma
See also CA 85-88
Lattimore, Richmond (Alexander) 1906-1984 **CLC 3**
See also CA 1-4R; 112; CANR 1
Laughlin, James 1914- .... **CLC 49**
See also CA 21-24R; CAAS 22; CANR 9, 47;
DLB 48; DLBY 96
Laurence, (Jean) Margaret (Wemyss) 1926-1987 .. **CLC 3, 6, 13, 50, 62; DAC; DAM MST; SSC 7**
See also CA 5-8R; 121; CANR 33; DLB 53;
MTCW; SATA-Obit 50
Laurent, Antoine 1952- .... **CLC 50**
Lauscher, Hermann
See Hesse, Hermann
Lautreamont, Comte de 1846-1870**NCLC 12; SSC 14**
Laverty, Donald
See Blish, James (Benjamin)
Lavin, Mary 1912-1996**CLC 4, 18, 99; SSC 4**
See also CA 9-12R; 151; CANR 33; DLB 15;
MTCW
Lavond, Paul Dennis
See Kornbluth, C(yril) M.; Pohl, Frederik
Lawler, Raymond Evenor 1922- .... **CLC 58**
See also CA 103
Lawrence, D(avid) H(erbert Richards) 1885-1930**TCLC 2, 9, 16, 33, 48, 61; DA; DAB; DAC; DAM MST, NOV, POET; SSC 4, 19; WLC**
See also CA 104; 121; CDBLB 1914-1945;
DLB 10, 19, 36, 98, 162; MTCW
Lawrence, T(homas) E(dward) 1888-1935

TCLC 18
See also Dale, Colin
See also CA 115
Lawrence of Arabia
See Lawrence, T(homas) E(dward)
Lawson, Henry (Archibald Hertzberg) 1867-1922 .... **TCLC 27; SSC 18**
See also CA 120
Lawton, Dennis
See Faust, Frederick (Schiller)
Laxness, Halldor .... **CLC 25**
See also Gudjonsson, Halldor Kiljan
Layamon fl. c. 1200- .... **CMLC 10**
See also DLB 146
Laye, Camara 1928-1980 .. **CLC 4, 38; BLC; DAM MULT**
See also BW 1; CA 85-88; 97-100; CANR 25;
MTCW
Layton, Irving (Peter) 1912-**CLC 2, 15; DAC; DAM MST, POET**
See also CA 1-4R; CANR 2, 33, 43; DLB 88;
MTCW
Lazarus, Emma 1849-1887 .... **NCLC 8**
Lazarus, Felix
See Cable, George Washington
Lazarus, Henry
See Slavitt, David R(ytman)
Lea, Joan
See Neufeld, John (Arthur)
Leacock, Stephen (Butler) 1869-1944**TCLC 2; DAC; DAM MST**
See also CA 104; 141; DLB 92
Lear, Edward 1812-1888 .... **NCLC 3**
See also CLR 1; DLB 32, 163, 166; MAICYA;
SATA 18
Lear, Norman (Milton) 1922- .... **CLC 12**
See also CA 73-76
Leavis, F(rank) R(aymond) 1895-1978**CLC 24**
See also CA 21-24R; 77-80; CANR 44; MTCW
Leavitt, David 1961- ...... **CLC 34; DAM POP**
See also CA 116; 122; CANR 50, 62; DLB 130;
INT 122
Leblanc, Maurice (Marie Emile) 1864-1941 **TCLC 49**
See also CA 110
Lebowitz, Fran(ces Ann) 1951(?)-**CLC 11, 36**
See also CA 81-84; CANR 14, 60; INT CANR-14; MTCW
Lebrecht, Peter
See Tieck, (Johann) Ludwig
le Carre, John .... **CLC 3, 5, 9, 15, 28**
See also Cornwell, David (John Moore)
See also BEST 89:4; CDBLB 1960 to Present;
DLB 87
Le Clezio, J(ean) M(arie) G(ustave) 1940- **CLC 31**
See also CA 116; 128; DLB 83
Leconte de Lisle, Charles-Marie-Rene 1818-1894 .... **NCLC 29**
Le Coq, Monsieur
See Simenon, Georges (Jacques Christian)
Leduc, Violette 1907-1972 .... **CLC 22**
See also CA 13-14; 33-36R; CAP 1
Ledwidge, Francis 1887(?)-1917 .... **TCLC 23**
See also CA 123; DLB 20
Lee, Andrea 1953-**CLC 36; BLC; DAM MULT**
See also BW 1; CA 125
Lee, Andrew
See Auchincloss, Louis (Stanton)
Lee, Chang-rae 1965- .... **CLC 91**
See also CA 148
Lee, Don L. ....**CLC 2**
See also Madhubuti, Haki R.

Lee, George W(ashington) 1894-1976**CLC 52; BLC; DAM MULT**
See also BW 1; CA 125; DLB 51

Lee, (Nelle) Harper 1926-.. **CLC 12, 60; DA; DAB; DAC; DAM MST, NOV; WLC**
See also AAYA 13; CA 13-16R; CANR 51; CDALB 1941-1968; DLB 6; MTCW; SATA 11

Lee, Helen Elaine 1959(?)- .... **CLC 86**
See also CA 148

Lee, Julian
See Latham, Jean Lee

Lee, Larry
See Lee, Lawrence

Lee, Laurie 1914-1997 **CLC 90; DAB; DAM POP**
See also CA 77-80; 158; CANR 33; DLB 27; MTCW

Lee, Lawrence 1941-1990 .... **CLC 34**
See also CA 131; CANR 43

Lee, Manfred B(ennington) 1905-1971**CLC 11**
See also Queen, Ellery
See also CA 1-4R; 29-32R; CANR 2; DLB 137

Lee, Shelton Jackson 1957(?)-**CLC 105; DAM MULT**
See also Lee, Spike
See also BW 2; CA 125; CANR 42

Lee, Spike
See Lee, Shelton Jackson
See also AAYA 4

Lee, Stan 1922- .... **CLC 17**
See also AAYA 5; CA 108; 111; INT 111

Lee, Tanith 1947-............................... **CLC 46**
See also AAYA 15; CA 37-40R; CANR 53; SATA 8, 88

Lee, Vernon .... **TCLC 5**
See also Paget, Violet
See also DLB 57, 153, 156, 174, 178

Lee, William
See Burroughs, William S(eward)

Lee, Willy
See Burroughs, William S(eward)

Lee-Hamilton, Eugene (Jacob) 1845-1907 **TCLC 22**
See also CA 117

Leet, Judith 1935-............................... **CLC 11**

Le Fanu, Joseph Sheridan 1814-1873**NCLC 9, 58; DAM POP; SSC 14**
See also DLB 21, 70, 159, 178

Leffland, Ella 1931- .... **CLC 19**
See also CA 29-32R; CANR 35; DLBY 84; INT CANR-35; SATA 65

Leger, Alexis
See Leger, (Marie-Rene Auguste) Alexis Saint-Leger

Leger, (Marie-Rene Auguste) Alexis Saint-Leger 1887-1975 **CLC 11; DAM POET**
See also Perse, St.-John
See also CA 13-16R; 61-64; CANR 43; MTCW

Leger, Saintleger
See Leger, (Marie-Rene Auguste) Alexis Saint-Leger

Le Guin, Ursula K(roeber) 1929- **CLC 8, 13, 22, 45, 71; DAB; DAC; DAM MST, POP; SSC 12**
See also AAYA 9; AITN 1; CA 21-24R; CANR 9, 32, 52; CDALB 1968-1988; CLR 3, 28; DLB 8, 52; INT CANR-32; JRDA; MAICYA; MTCW; SATA 4, 52

Lehmann, Rosamond (Nina) 1901-1990**CLC 5**
See also CA 77-80; 131; CANR 8; DLB 15

Leiber, Fritz (Reuter, Jr.) 1910-1992 **CLC 25**
See also CA 45-48; 139; CANR 2, 40; DLB 8;

MTCW; SATA 45; SATA-Obit 73

Leibniz, Gottfried Wilhelm von 1646-1716**LC 35**
See also DLB 168

Leimbach, Martha 1963-
See Leimbach, Marti
See also CA 130

Leimbach, Marti .... **CLC 65**
See also Leimbach, Martha

Leino, Eino .... **TCLC 24**
See also Loennbohm, Armas Eino Leopold

Leiris, Michel (Julien) 1901-1990 ..... **CLC 61**
See also CA 119; 128; 132

Leithauser, Brad 1953- .... **CLC 27**
See also CA 107; CANR 27; DLB 120

Lelchuk, Alan 1938- .... **CLC 5**
See also CA 45-48; CAAS 20; CANR 1

Lem, Stanislaw 1921- .... **CLC 8, 15, 40**
See also CA 105; CAAS 1; CANR 32; MTCW

Lemann, Nancy 1956- .... **CLC 39**
See also CA 118; 136

Lemonnier, (Antoine Louis) Camille 1844-1913 **TCLC 22**
See also CA 121

Lenau, Nikolaus 1802-1850 .... **NCLC 16**

L'Engle, Madeleine (Camp Franklin) 1918- **CLC 12; DAM POP**
See also AAYA 1; AITN 2; CA 1-4R; CANR 3, 21, 39; CLR 1, 14; DLB 52; JRDA; MAICYA; MTCW; SAAS 15; SATA 1, 27, 75

Lengyel, Jozsef 1896-1975 .... **CLC 7**
See also CA 85-88; 57-60

Lenin 1870-1924
See Lenin, V. I.
See also CA 121

Lenin, V. I. .... **TCLC 67**
See also Lenin

Lennon, John (Ono) 1940-1980 . **CLC 12, 35**
See also CA 102

Lennox, Charlotte Ramsay 1729(?)-1804 **NCLC 23**
See also DLB 39

Lentricchia, Frank (Jr.) 1940- .... **CLC 34**
See also CA 25-28R; CANR 19

Lenz, Siegfried 1926- .... **CLC 27**
See also CA 89-92; DLB 75

Leonard, Elmore (John, Jr.) 1925-**CLC 28, 34, 71; DAM POP**
See also AAYA 22; AITN 1; BEST 89:1, 90:4; CA 81-84; CANR 12, 28, 53; DLB 173; INT CANR-28; MTCW

Leonard, Hugh .... **CLC 19**
See also Byrne, John Keyes
See also DLB 13

Leonov, Leonid (Maximovich) 1899-1994 **CLC 92; DAM NOV**
See also CA 129; MTCW

Leopardi, (Conte) Giacomo 1798-1837**NCLC 22**

Le Reveler
See Artaud, Antonin (Marie Joseph)

Lerman, Eleanor 1952- .... **CLC 9**
See also CA 85-88

Lerman, Rhoda 1936- .... **CLC 56**
See also CA 49-52

Lermontov, Mikhail Yuryevich 1814-1841 **NCLC 47; PC 18**

Leroux, Gaston 1868-1927 .... **TCLC 25**
See also CA 108; 136; SATA 65

Lesage, Alain-Rene 1668-1747 .... **LC 28**

Leskov, Nikolai (Semyonovich) 1831-1895 **NCLC 25**

Lessing, Doris (May) 1919-**CLC 1, 2, 3, 6, 10, 15, 22, 40, 94; DA; DAB; DAC; DAM MST, NOV; SSC 6; WLCS**
See also CA 9-12R; CAAS 14; CANR 33, 54; CDBLB 1960 to Present; DLB 15, 139; DLBY 85; MTCW

Lessing, Gotthold Ephraim 1729-1781 **LC 8**
See also DLB 97

Lester, Richard 1932-......................... **CLC 20**

Lever, Charles (James) 1806-1872 . **NCLC 23**
See also DLB 21

Leverson, Ada 1865(?)-1936(?) .... **TCLC 18**
See also Elaine
See also CA 117; DLB 153

Levertov, Denise 1923-**CLC 1, 2, 3, 5, 8, 15, 28, 66; DAM POET; PC 11**
See also CA 1-4R; CAAS 19; CANR 3, 29, 50; DLB 5, 165; INT CANR-29; MTCW

Levi, Jonathan .... **CLC 76**

Levi, Peter (Chad Tigar) 1931- .... **CLC 41**
See also CA 5-8R; CANR 34; DLB 40

Levi, Primo 1919-1987 . **CLC 37, 50; SSC 12**
See also CA 13-16R; 122; CANR 12, 33, 61; DLB 177; MTCW

Levin, Ira 1929-...........**CLC 3, 6; DAM POP**
See also CA 21-24R; CANR 17, 44; MTCW; SATA 66

Levin, Meyer 1905-1981 . **CLC 7; DAM POP**
See also AITN 1; CA 9-12R; 104; CANR 15; DLB 9, 28; DLBY 81; SATA 21; SATA-Obit 27

Levine, Norman 1924-......................... **CLC 54**
See also CA 73-76; CAAS 23; CANR 14; DLB 88

Levine, Philip 1928- .. **CLC 2, 4, 5, 9, 14, 33; DAM POET**
See also CA 9-12R; CANR 9, 37, 52; DLB 5

Levinson, Deirdre 1931- .... **CLC 49**
See also CA 73-76

Levi-Strauss, Claude 1908- .... **CLC 38**
See also CA 1-4R; CANR 6, 32, 57; MTCW

Levitin, Sonia (Wolff) 1934- .... **CLC 17**
See also AAYA 13; CA 29-32R; CANR 14, 32; JRDA; MAICYA; SAAS 2; SATA 4, 68

Levon, O. U.
See Kesey, Ken (Elton)

Levy, Amy 1861-1889 .... **NCLC 59**
See also DLB 156

Lewes, George Henry 1817-1878 ... **NCLC 25**
See also DLB 55, 144

Lewis, Alun 1915-1944 .... **TCLC 3**
See also CA 104; DLB 20, 162

Lewis, C. Day
See Day Lewis, C(ecil)

Lewis, C(live) S(taples) 1898-1963**CLC 1, 3, 6, 14, 27; DA; DAB; DAC; DAM MST, NOV, POP; WLC**
See also AAYA 3; CA 81-84; CANR 33; CDBLB 1945-1960; CLR 3, 27; DLB 15, 100, 160; JRDA; MAICYA; MTCW; SATA 13

Lewis, Janet 1899-............................... **CLC 41**
See also Winters, Janet Lewis
See also CA 9-12R; CANR 29, 63; CAP 1; DLBY 87

Lewis, Matthew Gregory 1775-1818**NCLC 11, 62**
See also DLB 39, 158, 178

Lewis, (Harry) Sinclair 1885-1951 . **TCLC 4, 13, 23, 39; DA; DAB; DAC; DAM MST, NOV; WLC**
See also CA 104; 133; CDALB 1917-1929; DLB 9, 102; DLBD 1; MTCW

Lewis, (Percy) Wyndham 1882(?)-1957 **TCLC 2, 9**
See also CA 104; 157; DLB 15

Lewisohn, Ludwig 1883-1955 .... **TCLC 19**
See also CA 107; DLB 4, 9, 28, 102

Lewton, Val 1904-1951 .... **TCLC 76**

Leyner, Mark 1956- .... **CLC 92**
See also CA 110; CANR 28, 53

Lezama Lima, Jose 1910-1976 **CLC 4, 10, 101; DAM MULT**
See also CA 77-80; DLB 113; HW

L'Heureux, John (Clarke) 1934- ...... **CLC 52**
See also CA 13-16R; CANR 23, 45

Liddell, C. H.
See Kuttner, Henry

Lie, Jonas (Lauritz Idemil) 1833-1908(?) **TCLC 5**
See also CA 115

Lieber, Joel 1937-1971 .... **CLC 6**
See also CA 73-76; 29-32R

Lieber, Stanley Martin
See Lee, Stan

Lieberman, Laurence (James) 1935- **CLC 4, 36**
See also CA 17-20R; CANR 8, 36

Lieksman, Anders
See Haavikko, Paavo Juhani

Li Fei-kan 1904-
See Pa Chin
See also CA 105

Lifton, Robert Jay 1926- .... **CLC 67**
See also CA 17-20R; CANR 27; INT CANR-27; SATA 66

Lightfoot, Gordon 1938- .... **CLC 26**
See also CA 109

Lightman, Alan P(aige) 1948- .... **CLC 81**
See also CA 141; CANR 63

Ligotti, Thomas (Robert) 1953- **CLC 44; SSC 16**
See also CA 123; CANR 49

Li Ho 791-817 .... **PC 13**

Liliencron, (Friedrich Adolf Axel) Detlev von 1844-1909 .... **TCLC 18**
See also CA 117

Lilly, William 1602-1681 .... **LC 27**

Lima, Jose Lezama
See Lezama Lima, Jose

Lima Barreto, Afonso Henrique de 1881-1922 **TCLC 23**
See also CA 117

Limonov, Edward 1944- .... **CLC 67**
See also CA 137

Lin, Frank
See Atherton, Gertrude (Franklin Horn)

Lincoln, Abraham 1809-1865 .... **NCLC 18**

Lind, Jakov .... **CLC 1, 2, 4, 27, 82**
See also Landwirth, Heinz
See also CAAS 4

Lindbergh, Anne (Spencer) Morrow 1906- **CLC 82; DAM NOV**
See also CA 17-20R; CANR 16; MTCW; SATA 33

Lindsay, David 1878-1945 .... **TCLC 15**
See also CA 113

Lindsay, (Nicholas) Vachel 1879-1931 **TCLC 17; DA; DAC; DAM MST, POET; WLC**
See also CA 114; 135; CDALB 1865-1917; DLB 54; SATA 40

Linke-Poot
See Doeblin, Alfred

Linney, Romulus 1930- .... **CLC 51**
See also CA 1-4R; CANR 40, 44

Linton, Eliza Lynn 1822-1898 .... **NCLC 41**

See also DLB 18

Li Po 701-763 .... **CMLC 2**

Lipsius, Justus 1547-1606 .... **LC 16**

Lipsyte, Robert (Michael) 1938- **CLC 21; DA; DAC; DAM MST, NOV**
See also AAYA 7; CA 17-20R; CANR 8, 57; CLR 23; JRDA; MAICYA; SATA 5, 68

Lish, Gordon (Jay) 1934- ... **CLC 45; SSC 18**
See also CA 113; 117; DLB 130; INT 117

Lispector, Clarice 1925-1977 .... **CLC 43**
See also CA 139; 116; DLB 113

Littell, Robert 1935(?)- .... **CLC 42**
See also CA 109; 112; CANR 64

Little, Malcolm 1925-1965
See Malcolm X
See also BW 1; CA 125; 111; DA; DAB; DAC; DAM MST, MULT; MTCW

Littlewit, Humphrey Gent.
See Lovecraft, H(oward) P(hillips)

Litwos
See Sienkiewicz, Henryk (Adam Alexander Pius)

Liu E 1857-1909 .... **TCLC 15**
See also CA 115

Lively, Penelope (Margaret) 1933- . **CLC 32, 50; DAM NOV**
See also CA 41-44R; CANR 29; CLR 7; DLB 14, 161; JRDA; MAICYA; MTCW; SATA 7, 60

Livesay, Dorothy (Kathleen) 1909- **CLC 4, 15, 79; DAC; DAM MST, POET**
See also AITN 2; CA 25-28R; CAAS 8; CANR 36; DLB 68; MTCW

Livy c. 59B.C.-c. 17 .... **CMLC 11**

Lizardi, Jose Joaquin Fernandez de 1776-1827 **NCLC 30**

Llewellyn, Richard
See Llewellyn Lloyd, Richard Dafydd Vivian
See also DLB 15

Llewellyn Lloyd, Richard Dafydd Vivian 1906-1983 .... **CLC 7, 80**
See also Llewellyn, Richard
See also CA 53-56; 111; CANR 7; SATA 11; SATA-Obit 37

Llosa, (Jorge) Mario (Pedro) Vargas
See Vargas Llosa, (Jorge) Mario (Pedro)

Lloyd Webber, Andrew 1948-
See Webber, Andrew Lloyd
See also AAYA 1; CA 116; 149; DAM DRAM; SATA 56

Llull, Ramon c. 1235-c. 1316 .... **CMLC 12**

Locke, Alain (Le Roy) 1886-1954 .. **TCLC 43**
See also BW 1; CA 106; 124; DLB 51

Locke, John 1632-1704 .... **LC 7, 35**
See also DLB 101

Locke-Elliott, Sumner
See Elliott, Sumner Locke

Lockhart, John Gibson 1794-1854 .. **NCLC 6**
See also DLB 110, 116, 144

Lodge, David (John) 1935- **CLC 36; DAM POP**
See also BEST 90:1; CA 17-20R; CANR 19, 53; DLB 14; INT CANR-19; MTCW

Lodge, Thomas 1558-1625 .... **LC 41**

Loennbohm, Armas Eino Leopold 1878-1926
See Leino, Eino
See also CA 123

Loewinsohn, Ron(ald William) 1937- **CLC 52**
See also CA 25-28R

Logan, Jake
See Smith, Martin Cruz

Logan, John (Burton) 1923-1987 .... **CLC 5**
See also CA 77-80; 124; CANR 45; DLB 5

Lo Kuan-chung 1330(?)-1400(?) .... **LC 12**

Lombard, Nap
See Johnson, Pamela Hansford

London, Jack .. **TCLC 9, 15, 39; SSC 4; WLC**
See also London, John Griffith
See also AAYA 13; AITN 2; CDALB 1865-1917; DLB 8, 12, 78; SATA 18

London, John Griffith 1876-1916
See London, Jack
See also CA 110; 119; DA; DAB; DAC; DAM MST, NOV; JRDA; MAICYA; MTCW

Long, Emmett
See Leonard, Elmore (John, Jr.)

Longbaugh, Harry
See Goldman, William (W.)

Longfellow, Henry Wadsworth 1807-1882 **NCLC 2, 45; DA; DAB; DAC; DAM MST, POET; WLCS**
See also CDALB 1640-1865; DLB 1, 59; SATA 19

Longley, Michael 1939- .... **CLC 29**
See also CA 102; DLB 40

Longus fl. c. 2nd cent. - .... **CMLC 7**

Longway, A. Hugh
See Lang, Andrew

Lonnrot, Elias 1802-1884 .... **NCLC 53**

Lopate, Phillip 1943- .... **CLC 29**
See also CA 97-100; DLBY 80; INT 97-100

Lopez Portillo (y Pacheco), Jose 1920- . **CLC 46**
See also CA 129; HW

Lopez y Fuentes, Gregorio 1897(?)-1966 **CLC 32**
See also CA 131; HW

Lorca, Federico Garcia
See Garcia Lorca, Federico

Lord, Bette Bao 1938- .... **CLC 23**
See also BEST 90:3; CA 107; CANR 41; INT 107; SATA 58

Lord Auch
See Bataille, Georges

Lord Byron
See Byron, George Gordon (Noel)

Lorde, Audre (Geraldine) 1934-1992 **CLC 18, 71; BLC; DAM MULT, POET; PC 12**
See also BW 1; CA 25-28R; 142; CANR 16, 26, 46; DLB 41; MTCW

Lord Houghton
See Milnes, Richard Monckton

Lord Jeffrey
See Jeffrey, Francis

Lorenzini, Carlo 1826-1890
See Collodi, Carlo
See also MAICYA; SATA 29

Lorenzo, Heberto Padilla
See Padilla (Lorenzo), Heberto

Loris
See Hofmannsthal, Hugo von

Loti, Pierre .... **TCLC 11**
See also Viaud, (Louis Marie) Julien
See also DLB 123

Louie, David Wong 1954- .... **CLC 70**
See also CA 139

Louis, Father M.
See Merton, Thomas

Lovecraft, H(oward) P(hillips) 1890-1937 **TCLC 4, 22; DAM POP; SSC 3**
See also AAYA 14; CA 104; 133; MTCW

Lovelace, Earl 1935- .... **CLC 51**
See also BW 2; CA 77-80; CANR 41; DLB 125; MTCW

Lovelace, Richard 1618-1657 .... **LC 24**
See also DLB 131

Lowell, Amy 1874-1925 .... **TCLC 1, 8; DAM**

POET; PC 13
See also CA 104; 151; DLB 54, 140
Lowell, James Russell 1819-1891 .... **NCLC 2**
See also CDALB 1640-1865; DLB 1, 11, 64,
79
Lowell, Robert (Traill Spence, Jr.) 1917-1977
**CLC 1, 2, 3, 4, 5, 8, 9, 11, 15, 37; DA; DAB;
DAC; DAM MST, NOV; PC 3; WLC**
See also CA 9-12R; 73-76; CABS 2; CANR 26,
60; DLB 5, 169; MTCW
Lowndes, Marie Adelaide (Belloc) 1868-1947
TCLC 12
See also CA 107; DLB 70
Lowry, (Clarence) Malcolm 1909-1957**TCLC
6, 40**
See also CA 105; 131; CANR 62; CDBLB
1945-1960; DLB 15; MTCW
Lowry, Mina Gertrude 1882-1966
See Loy, Mina
See also CA 113
Loxsmith, John
See Brunner, John (Kilian Houston)
Loy, Mina .... **CLC 28; DAM POET; PC 16**
See also Lowry, Mina Gertrude
See also DLB 4, 54
Loyson-Bridet
See Schwob, (Mayer Andre) Marcel
Lucas, Craig 1951- .... **CLC 64**
See also CA 137
Lucas, E(dward) V(errall) 1868-1938 **T C L C
73**
See also DLB 98, 149, 153; SATA 20
Lucas, George 1944- .... **CLC 16**
See also AAYA 1; CA 77-80; CANR 30; SATA
56
Lucas, Hans
See Godard, Jean-Luc
Lucas, Victoria
See Plath, Sylvia
Ludlam, Charles 1943-1987 .... **CLC 46, 50**
See also CA 85-88; 122
Ludlum, Robert 1927-**CLC 22, 43; DAM NOV,
POP**
See also AAYA 10; BEST 89:1, 90:3; CA 33-
36R; CANR 25, 41; DLBY 82; MTCW
Ludwig, Ken .... **CLC 60**
Ludwig, Otto 1813-1865 .... **NCLC 4**
See also DLB 129
Lugones, Leopoldo 1874-1938 .... **TCLC 15**
See also CA 116; 131; HW
Lu Hsun 1881-1936 .... **TCLC 3; SSC 20**
See also Shu-Jen, Chou
Lukacs, George .... **CLC 24**
See also Lukacs, Gyorgy (Szegeny von)
Lukacs, Gyorgy (Szegeny von) 1885-1971
See Lukacs, George
See also CA 101; 29-32R; CANR 62
Luke, Peter (Ambrose Cyprian) 1919-1995
CLC 38
See also CA 81-84; 147; DLB 13
Lunar, Dennis
See Mungo, Raymond
Lurie, Alison 1926- .... **CLC 4, 5, 18, 39**
See also CA 1-4R; CANR 2, 17, 50; DLB 2;
MTCW; SATA 46
Lustig, Arnost 1926-........................... **CLC 56**
See also AAYA 3; CA 69-72; CANR 47; SATA
56
Luther, Martin 1483-1546 .... **LC 9, 37**
See also DLB 179
Luxemburg, Rosa 1870(?)-1919 ..... **TCLC 63**
See also CA 118
Luzi, Mario 1914-............................... **CLC 13**

See also CA 61-64; CANR 9; DLB 128
Lyly, John 1554(?)-1606**LC 41; DAM DRAM;
DC 7**
See also DLB 62, 167
L'Ymagier
See Gourmont, Remy (-Marie-Charles) de
Lynch, B. Suarez
See Bioy Casares, Adolfo; Borges, Jorge Luis
Lynch, David (K.) 1946- .... **CLC 66**
See also CA 124; 129
Lynch, James
See Andreyev, Leonid (Nikolaevich)
Lynch Davis, B.
See Bioy Casares, Adolfo; Borges, Jorge Luis
Lyndsay, Sir David 1490-1555 .... **LC 20**
Lynn, Kenneth S(chuyler) 1923-....... **CLC 50**
See also CA 1-4R; CANR 3, 27
Lynx
See West, Rebecca
Lyons, Marcus
See Blish, James (Benjamin)
Lyre, Pinchbeck
See Sassoon, Siegfried (Lorraine)
Lytle, Andrew (Nelson) 1902-1995 ... **CLC 22**
See also CA 9-12R; 150; DLB 6; DLBY 95
Lyttelton, George 1709-1773 .... **LC 10**
Maas, Peter 1929- .... **CLC 29**
See also CA 93-96; INT 93-96
Macaulay, Rose 1881-1958 .... **TCLC 7, 44**
See also CA 104; DLB 36
Macaulay, Thomas Babington 1800-1859
NCLC 42
See also CDBLB 1832-1890; DLB 32, 55
MacBeth, George (Mann) 1932-1992**CLC 2, 5,
9**
See also CA 25-28R; 136; CANR 61; DLB 40;
MTCW; SATA 4; SATA-Obit 70
MacCaig, Norman (Alexander) 1910-**CLC 36;
DAB; DAM POET**
See also CA 9-12R; CANR 3, 34; DLB 27
MacCarthy, (Sir Charles Otto) Desmond 1877-
1952 .... **TCLC 36**
MacDiarmid, Hugh**CLC 2, 4, 11, 19, 63; PC 9**
See also Grieve, C(hristopher) M(urray)
See also CDBLB 1945-1960; DLB 20
MacDonald, Anson
See Heinlein, Robert A(nson)
Macdonald, Cynthia 1928- .... **CLC 13, 19**
See also CA 49-52; CANR 4, 44; DLB 105
MacDonald, George 1824-1905 .... **TCLC 9**
See also CA 106; 137; DLB 18, 163, 178;
MAICYA; SATA 33
Macdonald, John
See Millar, Kenneth
MacDonald, John D(ann) 1916-1986 **CLC 3,
27, 44; DAM NOV, POP**
See also CA 1-4R; 121; CANR 1, 19, 60; DLB
8; DLBY 86; MTCW
Macdonald, John Ross
See Millar, Kenneth
Macdonald, Ross .... **CLC 1, 2, 3, 14, 34, 41**
See also Millar, Kenneth
See also DLBD 6
MacDougal, John
See Blish, James (Benjamin)
MacEwen, Gwendolyn (Margaret) 1941-1987
CLC 13, 55
See also CA 9-12R; 124; CANR 7, 22; DLB
53; SATA 50; SATA-Obit 55
Macha, Karel Hynek 1810-1846 ....**NCLC 46**
Machado (y Ruiz), Antonio 1875-1939**T C L C
3**
See also CA 104; DLB 108

Machado de Assis, Joaquim Maria 1839-1908
TCLC 10; BLC; SSC 24
See also CA 107; 153
Machen, Arthur .... **TCLC 4; SSC 20**
See also Jones, Arthur Llewellyn
See also DLB 36, 156, 178
Machiavelli, Niccolo 1469-1527**LC 8, 36; DA;
DAB; DAC; DAM MST; WLCS**
MacInnes, Colin 1914-1976 .... **CLC 4, 23**
See also CA 69-72; 65-68; CANR 21; DLB 14;
MTCW
MacInnes, Helen (Clark) 1907-1985 **CLC 27,
39; DAM POP**
See also CA 1-4R; 117; CANR 1, 28, 58; DLB
87; MTCW; SATA 22; SATA-Obit 44
Mackay, Mary 1855-1924
See Corelli, Marie
See also CA 118
Mackenzie, Compton (Edward Montague)
1883-1972 .... **CLC 18**
See also CA 21-22; 37-40R; CAP 2; DLB 34,
100
Mackenzie, Henry 1745-1831 .... **NCLC 41**
See also DLB 39
Mackintosh, Elizabeth 1896(?)-1952
See Tey, Josephine
See also CA 110
MacLaren, James
See Grieve, C(hristopher) M(urray)
Mac Laverty, Bernard 1942-............. **CLC 31**
See also CA 116; 118; CANR 43; INT 118
MacLean, Alistair (Stuart) 1922(?)-1987**C L C
3, 13, 50, 63; DAM POP**
See also CA 57-60; 121; CANR 28, 61; MTCW;
SATA 23; SATA-Obit 50
Maclean, Norman (Fitzroy) 1902-1990 . **C L C
78; DAM POP; SSC 13**
See also CA 102; 132; CANR 49
MacLeish, Archibald 1892-1982**CLC 3, 8, 14,
68; DAM POET**
See also CA 9-12R; 106; CANR 33, 63; DLB
4, 7, 45; DLBY 82; MTCW
MacLennan, (John) Hugh 1907-1990 **CLC 2,
14, 92; DAC; DAM MST**
See also CA 5-8R; 142; CANR 33; DLB 68;
MTCW
MacLeod, Alistair 1936-**CLC 56; DAC; DAM
MST**
See also CA 123; DLB 60
Macleod, Fiona
See Sharp, William
MacNeice, (Frederick) Louis 1907-1963**C L C
1, 4, 10, 53; DAB; DAM POET**
See also CA 85-88; CANR 61; DLB 10, 20;
MTCW
MacNeill, Dand
See Fraser, George MacDonald
Macpherson, James 1736-1796 .... **LC 29**
See also DLB 109
Macpherson, (Jean) Jay 1931- .... **CLC 14**
See also CA 5-8R; DLB 53
MacShane, Frank 1927-..................... **CLC 39**
See also CA 9-12R; CANR 3, 33; DLB 111
Macumber, Mari
See Sandoz, Mari(e Susette)
Madach, Imre 1823-1864 ....**NCLC 19**
Madden, (Jerry) David 1933-....... **CLC 5, 15**
See also CA 1-4R; CAAS 3; CANR 4, 45; DLB
6; MTCW
Maddern, Al(an)
See Ellison, Harlan (Jay)
Madhubuti, Haki R. 1942- **CLC 6, 73; BLC;
DAM MULT, POET; PC 5**

See also Lee, Don L.
See also BW 2; CA 73-76; CANR 24, 51; DLB 5, 41; DLBD 8

Maepenn, Hugh
See Kuttner, Henry

Maepenn, K. H.
See Kuttner, Henry

Maeterlinck, Maurice 1862-1949 .... **TCLC 3; DAM DRAM**
See also CA 104; 136; SATA 66

Maginn, William 1794-1842 .... **NCLC 8**
See also DLB 110, 159

Mahapatra, Jayanta 1928- .... **CLC 33; DAM MULT**
See also CA 73-76; CAAS 9; CANR 15, 33

Mahfouz, Naguib (Abdel Aziz Al-Sabilgi) 1911(?)-
See Mahfuz, Najib
See also BEST 89:2; CA 128; CANR 55; DAM NOV; MTCW

Mahfuz, Najib .... **CLC 52, 55**
See also Mahfouz, Naguib (Abdel Aziz Al-Sabilgi)
See also DLBY 88

Mahon, Derek 1941- .... **CLC 27**
See also CA 113; 128; DLB 40

Mailer, Norman 1923-**CLC 1, 2, 3, 4, 5, 8, 11, 14, 28, 39, 74; DA; DAB; DAC; DAM MST, NOV, POP**
See also AITN 2; CA 9-12R; CABS 1; CANR 28; CDALB 1968-1988; DLB 2, 16, 28; DLBD 3; DLBY 80, 83; MTCW

Maillet, Antonine 1929- .... **CLC 54; DAC**
See also CA 115; 120; CANR 46; DLB 60; INT 120

Mais, Roger 1905-1955 .... **TCLC 8**
See also BW 1; CA 105; 124; DLB 125; MTCW

Maistre, Joseph de 1753-1821 .... **NCLC 37**

Maitland, Frederic 1850-1906 .... **TCLC 65**

Maitland, Sara (Louise) 1950- .... **CLC 49**
See also CA 69-72; CANR 13, 59

Major, Clarence 1936- **CLC 3, 19, 48; BLC; DAM MULT**
See also BW 2; CA 21-24R; CAAS 6; CANR 13, 25, 53; DLB 33

Major, Kevin (Gerald) 1949-.. **CLC 26; DAC**
See also AAYA 16; CA 97-100; CANR 21, 38; CLR 11; DLB 60; INT CANR-21; JRDA; MAICYA; SATA 32, 82

Maki, James
See Ozu, Yasujiro

Malabaila, Damiano
See Levi, Primo

Malamud, Bernard 1914-1986**CLC 1, 2, 3, 5, 8, 9, 11, 18, 27, 44, 78, 85; DA; DAB; DAC; DAM MST, NOV, POP; SSC 15; WLC**
See also AAYA 16; CA 5-8R; 118; CABS 1; CANR 28, 62; CDALB 1941-1968; DLB 2, 28, 152; DLBY 80, 86; MTCW

Malan, Herman
See Bosman, Herman Charles; Bosman, Herman Charles

Malaparte, Curzio 1898-1957 .... **TCLC 52**

Malcolm, Dan
See Silverberg, Robert

Malcolm X .... **CLC 82; BLC; WLCS**
See also Little, Malcolm

Malherbe, Francois de 1555-1628 .... **LC 5**

Mallarme, Stephane 1842-1898 **NCLC 4, 41; DAM POET; PC 4**

Mallet-Joris, Francoise 1930- .... **CLC 11**
See also CA 65-68; CANR 17; DLB 83

Malley, Ern

See McAuley, James Phillip

Mallowan, Agatha Christie
See Christie, Agatha (Mary Clarissa)

Maloff, Saul 1922- .... **CLC 5**
See also CA 33-36R

Malone, Louis
See MacNeice, (Frederick) Louis

Malone, Michael (Christopher) 1942-**CLC 43**
See also CA 77-80; CANR 14, 32, 57

Malory, (Sir) Thomas 1410(?)-1471(?)**LC 11; DA; DAB; DAC; DAM MST; WLCS**
See also CDBLB Before 1660; DLB 146; SATA 59; SATA-Brief 33

Malouf, (George Joseph) David 1934-**CLC 28, 86**
See also CA 124; CANR 50

Malraux, (Georges-)Andre 1901-1976**CLC 1, 4, 9, 13, 15, 57; DAM NOV**
See also CA 21-22; 69-72; CANR 34, 58; CAP 2; DLB 72; MTCW

Malzberg, Barry N(athaniel) 1939-....**CLC 7**
See also CA 61-64; CAAS 4; CANR 16; DLB 8

Mamet, David (Alan) 1947-**CLC 9, 15, 34, 46, 91; DAM DRAM; DC 4**
See also AAYA 3; CA 81-84; CABS 3; CANR 15, 41; DLB 7; MTCW

Mamoulian, Rouben (Zachary) 1897-1987 **CLC 16**
See also CA 25-28R; 124

Mandelstam, Osip (Emilievich) 1891(?)-1938(?) **TCLC 2, 6; PC 14**
See also CA 104; 150

Mander, (Mary) Jane 1877-1949 ... **TCLC 31**

Mandeville, John fl. 1350- .... **CMLC 19**
See also DLB 146

Mandiargues, Andre Pieyre de .... **CLC 41**
See also Pieyre de Mandiargues, Andre
See also DLB 83

Mandrake, Ethel Belle
See Thurman, Wallace (Henry)

Mangan, James Clarence 1803-1849**NCLC 27**

Maniere, J.-E.
See Giraudoux, (Hippolyte) Jean

Manley, (Mary) Delariviere 1672(?)-1724 **L C 1**
See also DLB 39, 80

Mann, Abel
See Creasey, John

Mann, Emily 1952- .... **DC 7**
See also CA 130; CANR 55

Mann, (Luiz) Heinrich 1871-1950 ... **TCLC 9**
See also CA 106; DLB 66

Mann, (Paul) Thomas 1875-1955 **TCLC 2, 8, 14, 21, 35, 44, 60; DA; DAB; DAC; DAM MST, NOV; SSC 5; WLC**
See also CA 104; 128; DLB 66; MTCW

Mannheim, Karl 1893-1947 .... **TCLC 65**

Manning, David
See Faust, Frederick (Schiller)

Manning, Frederic 1887(?)-1935 ... **TCLC 25**
See also CA 124

Manning, Olivia 1915-1980 .... **CLC 5, 19**
See also CA 5-8R; 101; CANR 29; MTCW

Mano, D. Keith 1942- .... **CLC 2, 10**
See also CA 25-28R; CAAS 6; CANR 26, 57; DLB 6

Mansfield, KatherineTCLC 2, 8, 39; DAB; SSC 9, 23; WLC**
See also Beauchamp, Kathleen Mansfield
See also DLB 162

Manso, Peter 1940- .... **CLC 39**
See also CA 29-32R; CANR 44

Mantecon, Juan Jimenez

See Jimenez (Mantecon), Juan Ramon

Manton, Peter
See Creasey, John

Man Without a Spleen, A
See Chekhov, Anton (Pavlovich)

Manzoni, Alessandro 1785-1873 .... **NCLC 29**

Mapu, Abraham (ben Jekutiel) 1808-1867 **NCLC 18**

Mara, Sally
See Queneau, Raymond

Marat, Jean Paul 1743-1793 .... **LC 10**

Marcel, Gabriel Honore 1889-1973 . **CLC 15**
See also CA 102; 45-48; MTCW

Marchbanks, Samuel
See Davies, (William) Robertson

Marchi, Giacomo
See Bassani, Giorgio

Margulies, Donald .... **CLC 76**

Marie de France c. 12th cent. - .... **CMLC 8**

Marie de l'Incarnation 1599-1672 ...... **LC 10**

Marier, Captain Victor
See Griffith, D(avid Lewelyn) W(ark)

Mariner, Scott
See Pohl, Frederik

Marinetti, Filippo Tommaso 1876-1944**TCLC 10**
See also CA 107; DLB 114

Marivaux, Pierre Carlet de Chamblain de 1688-1763 .... **LC 4; DC 7**

Markandaya, Kamala .... **CLC 8, 38**
See also Taylor, Kamala (Purnaiya)

Markfield, Wallace 1926- .... **CLC 8**
See also CA 69-72; CAAS 3; DLB 2, 28

Markham, Edwin 1852-1940 .... **TCLC 47**
See also CA 160; DLB 54

Markham, Robert
See Amis, Kingsley (William)

Marks, J
See Highwater, Jamake (Mamake)

Marks-Highwater, J
See Highwater, Jamake (Mamake)

Markson, David M(errill) 1927- ...... **CLC 67**
See also CA 49-52; CANR 1

Marley, Bob .... **CLC 17**
See also Marley, Robert Nesta

Marley, Robert Nesta 1945-1981
See Marley, Bob
See also CA 107; 103

Marlowe, Christopher 1564-1593**LC 22; DA; DAB; DAC; DAM DRAM, MST; DC 1; WLC**
See also CDBLB Before 1660; DLB 62

Marlowe, Stephen 1928-
See Queen, Ellery
See also CA 13-16R; CANR 6, 55

Marmontel, Jean-Francois 1723-1799 . **LC 2**

Marquand, John P(hillips) 1893-1960**CLC 2, 10**
See also CA 85-88; DLB 9, 102

Marques, Rene 1919-1979 ..... **CLC 96; DAM MULT; HLC**
See also CA 97-100; 85-88; DLB 113; HW

Marquez, Gabriel (Jose) Garcia
See Garcia Marquez, Gabriel (Jose)

Marquis, Don(ald Robert Perry) 1878-1937 **TCLC 7**
See also CA 104; DLB 11, 25

Marric, J. J.
See Creasey, John

Marryat, Frederick 1792-1848 .... **NCLC 3**
See also DLB 21, 163

Marsden, James
See Creasey, John

Marsh, (Edith) Ngaio 1899-1982 **CLC 7, 53; DAM POP**
See also CA 9-12R; CANR 6, 58; DLB 77; MTCW

Marshall, Garry 1934- .... **CLC 17**
See also AAYA 3; CA 111; SATA 60

Marshall, Paule 1929-**CLC 27, 72; BLC; DAM MULT; SSC 3**
See also BW 2; CA 77-80; CANR 25; DLB 157; MTCW

Marsten, Richard
See Hunter, Evan

Marston, John 1576-1634**LC 33; DAM DRAM**
See also DLB 58, 172

Martha, Henry
See Harris, Mark

Marti, Jose 1853-1895**NCLC 63; DAM MULT; HLC**

Martial c. 40-c. 104 .... **PC 10**

Martin, Ken
See Hubbard, L(afayette) Ron(ald)

Martin, Richard
See Creasey, John

Martin, Steve 1945- .... **CLC 30**
See also CA 97-100; CANR 30; MTCW

Martin, Valerie 1948- .... **CLC 89**
See also BEST 90:2; CA 85-88; CANR 49

Martin, Violet Florence 1862-1915 **TCLC 51**

Martin, Webber
See Silverberg, Robert

Martindale, Patrick Victor
See White, Patrick (Victor Martindale)

Martin du Gard, Roger 1881-1958 **TCLC 24**
See also CA 118; DLB 65

Martineau, Harriet 1802-1876 .... **NCLC 26**
See also DLB 21, 55, 159, 163, 166; YABC 2

Martines, Julia
See O'Faolain, Julia

Martinez, Enrique Gonzalez
See Gonzalez Martinez, Enrique

Martinez, Jacinto Benavente y
See Benavente (y Martinez), Jacinto

Martinez Ruiz, Jose 1873-1967
See Azorin; Ruiz, Jose Martinez
See also CA 93-96; HW

Martinez Sierra, Gregorio 1881-1947**TCLC 6**
See also CA 115

Martinez Sierra, Maria (de la O'LeJarraga) 1874-1974 .... **TCLC 6**
See also CA 115

Martinsen, Martin
See Follett, Ken(neth Martin)

Martinson, Harry (Edmund) 1904-1978**C L C 14**
See also CA 77-80; CANR 34

Marut, Ret
See Traven, B.

Marut, Robert
See Traven, B.

Marvell, Andrew 1621-1678**LC 4; DA; DAB; DAC; DAM MST, POET; PC 10; WLC**
See also CDBLB 1660-1789; DLB 131

Marx, Karl (Heinrich) 1818-1883 . **NCLC 17**
See also DLB 129

Masaoka Shiki .... **TCLC 18**
See also Masaoka Tsunenori

Masaoka Tsunenori 1867-1902
See Masaoka Shiki
See also CA 117

Masefield, John (Edward) 1878-1967**CLC 11, 47; DAM POET**
See also CA 19-20; 25-28R; CANR 33; CAP 2; CDBLB 1890-1914; DLB 10, 19, 153, 160;

MTCW; SATA 19

Maso, Carole 19(?)- .... **CLC 44**

Mason, Bobbie Ann 1940-**CLC 28, 43, 82; SSC 4**
See also AAYA 5; CA 53-56; CANR 11, 31, 58; DLB 173; DLBY 87; INT CANR-31; MTCW

Mason, Ernst
See Pohl, Frederik

Mason, Lee W.
See Malzberg, Barry N(athaniel)

Mason, Nick 1945- .... **CLC 35**

Mason, Tally
See Derleth, August (William)

Mass, William
See Gibson, William

Masters, Edgar Lee 1868-1950 **TCLC 2, 25; DA; DAC; DAM MST, POET; PC 1; WLCS**
See also CA 104; 133; CDALB 1865-1917; DLB 54; MTCW

Masters, Hilary 1928- .... **CLC 48**
See also CA 25-28R; CANR 13, 47

Mastrosimone, William 19(?)- .... **CLC 36**

Mathe, Albert
See Camus, Albert

Mather, Cotton 1663-1728 .... **LC 38**
See also CDALB 1640-1865; DLB 24, 30, 140

Mather, Increase 1639-1723 .... **LC 38**
See also DLB 24

Matheson, Richard Burton 1926- ..... **CLC 37**
See also CA 97-100; DLB 8, 44; INT 97-100

Mathews, Harry 1930- .... **CLC 6, 52**
See also CA 21-24R; CAAS 6; CANR 18, 40

Mathews, John Joseph 1894-1979 .. **CLC 84; DAM MULT**
See also CA 19-20; 142; CANR 45; CAP 2; DLB 175; NNAL

Mathias, Roland (Glyn) 1915- .... **CLC 45**
See also CA 97-100; CANR 19, 41; DLB 27

Matsuo Basho 1644-1694 .... **PC 3**
See also DAM POET

Mattheson, Rodney
See Creasey, John

Matthews, Greg 1949- .... **CLC 45**
See also CA 135

Matthews, William 1942- .... **CLC 40**
See also CA 29-32R; CAAS 18; CANR 12, 57; DLB 5

Matthias, John (Edward) 1941- .... **CLC 9**
See also CA 33-36R; CANR 56

Matthiessen, Peter 1927-**CLC 5, 7, 11, 32, 64; DAM NOV**
See also AAYA 6; BEST 90:4; CA 9-12R; CANR 21, 50; DLB 6, 173; MTCW; SATA 27

Maturin, Charles Robert 1780(?)-1824**N C L C 6**
See also DLB 178

Matute (Ausejo), Ana Maria 1925- .. **CLC 11**
See also CA 89-92; MTCW

Maugham, W. S.
See Maugham, W(illiam) Somerset

Maugham, W(illiam) Somerset 1874-1965 **CLC 1, 11, 15, 67, 93; DA; DAB; DAC; DAM DRAM, MST, NOV; SSC 8; WLC**
See also CA 5-8R; 25-28R; CANR 40; CDBLB 1914-1945; DLB 10, 36, 77, 100, 162; MTCW; SATA 54

Maugham, William Somerset
See Maugham, W(illiam) Somerset

Maupassant, (Henri Rene Albert) Guy de 1850-1893**NCLC 1, 42; DA; DAB; DAC; DAM**

MST; SSC 1; WLC
See also DLB 123

Maupin, Armistead 1944-**CLC 95; DAM POP**
See also CA 125; 130; CANR 58; INT 130

Maurhut, Richard
See Traven, B.

Mauriac, Claude 1914-1996 .... **CLC 9**
See also CA 89-92; 152; DLB 83

Mauriac, Francois (Charles) 1885-1970**C L C 4, 9, 56; SSC 24**
See also CA 25-28; CAP 2; DLB 65; MTCW

Mavor, Osborne Henry 1888-1951
See Bridie, James
See also CA 104

Maxwell, William (Keepers, Jr.) 1908-**CLC 19**
See also CA 93-96; CANR 54; DLBY 80; INT 93-96

May, Elaine 1932- .... **CLC 16**
See also CA 124; 142; DLB 44

Mayakovski, Vladimir (Vladimirovich) 1893-1930 .... **TCLC 4, 18**
See also CA 104; 158

Mayhew, Henry 1812-1887 .... **NCLC 31**
See also DLB 18, 55

Mayle, Peter 1939(?)- .... **CLC 89**
See also CA 139; CANR 64

Maynard, Joyce 1953- .... **CLC 23**
See also CA 111; 129; CANR 64

Mayne, William (James Carter) 1928-**CLC 12**
See also AAYA 20; CA 9-12R; CANR 37; CLR 25; JRDA; MAICYA; SAAS 11; SATA 6, 68

Mayo, Jim
See L'Amour, Louis (Dearborn)

Maysles, Albert 1926- .... **CLC 16**
See also CA 29-32R

Maysles, David 1932- .... **CLC 16**

Mazer, Norma Fox 1931- .... **CLC 26**
See also AAYA 5; CA 69-72; CANR 12, 32; CLR 23; JRDA; MAICYA; SAAS 1; SATA 24, 67

Mazzini, Guiseppe 1805-1872 .... **NCLC 34**

McAuley, James Phillip 1917-1976 .. **CLC 45**
See also CA 97-100

McBain, Ed
See Hunter, Evan

McBrien, William Augustine 1930- .. **CLC 44**
See also CA 107

McCaffrey, Anne (Inez) 1926-**CLC 17; DAM NOV, POP**
See also AAYA 6; AITN 2; BEST 89:2; CA 25-28R; CANR 15, 35, 55; DLB 8; JRDA; MAICYA; MTCW; SAAS 11; SATA 8, 70

McCall, Nathan 1955(?)- .... **CLC 86**
See also CA 146

McCann, Arthur
See Campbell, John W(ood, Jr.)

McCann, Edson
See Pohl, Frederik

McCarthy, Charles, Jr. 1933-
See McCarthy, Cormac
See also CANR 42; DAM POP

McCarthy, Cormac 1933- **CLC 4, 57, 59, 101**
See also McCarthy, Charles, Jr.
See also DLB 6, 143

McCarthy, Mary (Therese) 1912-1989**CLC 1, 3, 5, 14, 24, 39, 59; SSC 24**
See also CA 5-8R; 129; CANR 16, 50, 64; DLB 2; DLBY 81; INT CANR-16; MTCW

McCartney, (James) Paul 1942-. **CLC 12, 35**
See also CA 146

McCauley, Stephen (D.) 1955- .... **CLC 50**
See also CA 141

McClure, Michael (Thomas) 1932-**CLC 6, 10**

See also CA 21-24R; CANR 17, 46; DLB 16

McCorkle, Jill (Collins) 1958-......... **CLC 51**
See also CA 121; DLBY 87

McCourt, James 1941-.......................**CLC 5**
See also CA 57-60

McCoy, Horace (Stanley) 1897-1955**TCLC 28**
See also CA 108; 155; DLB 9

McCrae, John 1872-1918................ **TCLC 12**
See also CA 109; DLB 92

McCreigh, James
See Pohl, Frederik

McCullers, (Lula) Carson (Smith) 1917-1967
   CLC 1, 4, 10, 12, 48, 100; DA; DAB; DAC;
   DAM MST, NOV; SSC 9, 24; WLC
See also AAYA 21; CA 5-8R; 25-28R; CABS
   1, 3; CANR 18; CDALB 1941-1968; DLB
   2, 7, 173; MTCW; SATA 27

McCulloch, John Tyler
See Burroughs, Edgar Rice

McCullough, Colleen 1938(?)- **CLC 27, 107;**
   DAM NOV, POP
See also CA 81-84; CANR 17, 46; MTCW

McDermott, Alice 1953-....................**CLC 90**
See also CA 109; CANR 40

McElroy, Joseph 1930- .... **CLC 5, 47**
See also CA 17-20R

McEwan, Ian (Russell) 1948- .... **CLC 13, 66;**
   DAM NOV
See also BEST 90:4; CA 61-64; CANR 14, 41;
   DLB 14; MTCW

McFadden, David 1940-.................... **CLC 48**
See also CA 104; DLB 60; INT 104

McFarland, Dennis 1950- .... **CLC 65**

McGahern, John 1934-**CLC 5, 9, 48; SSC 17**
See also CA 17-20R; CANR 29; DLB 14;
   MTCW

McGinley, Patrick (Anthony) 1937- **CLC 41**
See also CA 120; 127; CANR 56; INT 127

McGinley, Phyllis 1905-1978 .... **CLC 14**
See also CA 9-12R; 77-80; CANR 19; DLB 11,
   48; SATA 2, 44; SATA-Obit 24

McGinniss, Joe 1942- .... **CLC 32**
See also AITN 2; BEST 89:2; CA 25-28R;
   CANR 26; INT CANR-26

McGivern, Maureen Daly
See Daly, Maureen

McGrath, Patrick 1950-.................... **CLC 55**
See also CA 136

McGrath, Thomas (Matthew) 1916-1990**CLC**
   28, 59; DAM POET
See also CA 9-12R; 132; CANR 6, 33; MTCW;
   SATA 41; SATA-Obit 66

McGuane, Thomas (Francis III) 1939-**CLC 3,**
   7, 18, 45
See also AITN 2; CA 49-52; CANR 5, 24, 49;
   DLB 2; DLBY 80; INT CANR-24; MTCW

McGuckian, Medbh 1950- ..... **CLC 48; DAM**
   POET
See also CA 143; DLB 40

McHale, Tom 1942(?)-1982 .... **CLC 3, 5**
See also AITN 1; CA 77-80; 106

McIlvanney, William 1936- .... **CLC 42**
See also CA 25-28R; CANR 61; DLB 14

McIlwraith, Maureen Mollie Hunter
See Hunter, Mollie
See also SATA 2

McInerney, Jay 1955- ... **CLC 34; DAM POP**
See also AAYA 18; CA 116; 123; CANR 45;
   INT 123

McIntyre, Vonda N(eel) 1948- .... **CLC 18**
See also CA 81-84; CANR 17, 34; MTCW

McKay, Claude**TCLC 7, 41; BLC; DAB; PC 2**
See also McKay, Festus Claudius

See also DLB 4, 45, 51, 117

McKay, Festus Claudius 1889-1948
See McKay, Claude
See also BW 1; CA 104; 124; DA; DAC; DAM
   MST, MULT, NOV, POET; MTCW; WLC

McKuen, Rod 1933- .... **CLC 1, 3**
See also AITN 1; CA 41-44R; CANR 40

McLoughlin, R. B.
See Mencken, H(enry) L(ouis)

McLuhan, (Herbert) Marshall 1911-1980
   CLC 37, 83
See also CA 9-12R; 102; CANR 12, 34, 61;
   DLB 88; INT CANR-12; MTCW

McMillan, Terry (L.) 1951-**CLC 50, 61; DAM**
   MULT, NOV, POP
See also AAYA 21; BW 2; CA 140; CANR 60

McMurtry, Larry (Jeff) 1936-**CLC 2, 3, 7, 11,**
   27, 44; DAM NOV, POP
See also AAYA 15; AITN 2; BEST 89:2; CA 5-
   8R; CANR 19, 43, 64; CDALB 1968-1988;
   DLB 2, 143; DLBY 80, 87; MTCW

McNally, T. M. 1961- ....**CLC 82**

McNally, Terrence 1939- ...**CLC 4, 7, 41, 91;**
   DAM DRAM
See also CA 45-48; CANR 2, 56; DLB 7

McNamer, Deirdre 1950- ....**CLC 70**

McNeile, Herman Cyril 1888-1937
See Sapper
See also DLB 77

McNickle, (William) D'Arcy 1904-1977 **C L C**
   89; DAM MULT
See also CA 9-12R; 85-88; CANR 5, 45; DLB
   175; NNAL; SATA-Obit 22

McPhee, John (Angus) 1931- ....**CLC 36**
See also BEST 90:1; CA 65-68; CANR 20, 46,
   64; MTCW

McPherson, James Alan 1943-... **CLC 19, 77**
See also BW 1; CA 25-28R; CAAS 17; CANR
   24; DLB 38; MTCW

McPherson, William (Alexander) 1933- **C L C**
   34
See also CA 69-72; CANR 28; INT CANR-28

Mead, Margaret 1901-1978 .... **CLC 37**
See also AITN 1; CA 1-4R; 81-84; CANR 4;
   MTCW; SATA-Obit 20

Meaker, Marijane (Agnes) 1927-
See Kerr, M. E.
See also CA 107; CANR 37, 63; INT 107;
   JRDA; MAICYA; MTCW; SATA 20, 61

Medoff, Mark (Howard) 1940- ... **CLC 6, 23;**
   DAM DRAM
See also AITN 1; CA 53-56; CANR 5; DLB 7;
   INT CANR-5

Medvedev, P. N.
See Bakhtin, Mikhail Mikhailovich

Meged, Aharon
See Megged, Aharon

Meged, Aron
See Megged, Aharon

Megged, Aharon 1920-........................**CLC 9**
See also CA 49-52; CAAS 13; CANR 1

Mehta, Ved (Parkash) 1934- ....**CLC 37**
See also CA 1-4R; CANR 2, 23; MTCW

Melanter
See Blackmore, R(ichard) D(oddridge)

Melikow, Loris
See Hofmannsthal, Hugo von

Melmoth, Sebastian
See Wilde, Oscar (Fingal O'Flahertie Wills)

Meltzer, Milton 1915-........................**CLC 26**
See also AAYA 8; CA 13-16R; CANR 38; CLR
   13; DLB 61; JRDA; MAICYA; SAAS 1;
   SATA 1, 50, 80

Melville, Herman 1819-1891**NCLC 3, 12, 29,**
   45, 49; DA; DAB; DAC; DAM MST, NOV;
   SSC 1, 17; WLC
See also CDALB 1640-1865; DLB 3, 74; SATA
   59

Menander c. 342B.C.-c. 292B.C. ... **CMLC 9;**
   DAM DRAM; DC 3
See also DLB 176

Mencken, H(enry) L(ouis) 1880-1956 **T C L C**
   13
See also CA 105; 125; CDALB 1917-1929;
   DLB 11, 29, 63, 137; MTCW

Mendelsohn, Jane 1965(?)- .... **CLC 99**
See also CA 154

Mercer, David 1928-1980**CLC 5; DAM DRAM**
See also CA 9-12R; 102; CANR 23; DLB 13;
   MTCW

Merchant, Paul
See Ellison, Harlan (Jay)

Meredith, George 1828-1909 .. **TCLC 17, 43;**
   DAM POET
See also CA 117; 153; CDBLB 1832-1890;
   DLB 18, 35, 57, 159

Meredith, William (Morris) 1919-**CLC 4, 13,**
   22, 55; DAM POET
See also CA 9-12R; CAAS 14; CANR 6, 40;
   DLB 5

Merezhkovsky, Dmitry Sergeyevich 1865-1941
   TCLC 29

Merimee, Prosper 1803-1870**NCLC 6, 65; SSC**
   7
See also DLB 119

Merkin, Daphne 1954- .... **CLC 44**
See also CA 123

Merlin, Arthur
See Blish, James (Benjamin)

Merrill, James (Ingram) 1926-1995**CLC 2, 3,**
   6, 8, 13, 18, 34, 91; DAM POET
See also CA 13-16R; 147; CANR 10, 49, 63;
   DLB 5, 165; DLBY 85; INT CANR-10;
   MTCW

Merriman, Alex
See Silverberg, Robert

Merritt, E. B.
See Waddington, Miriam

Merton, Thomas 1915-1968**CLC 1, 3, 11, 34,**
   83; PC 10
See also CA 5-8R; 25-28R; CANR 22, 53; DLB
   48; DLBY 81; MTCW

Merwin, W(illiam) S(tanley) 1927- **CLC 1, 2,**
   3, 5, 8, 13, 18, 45, 88; DAM POET
See also CA 13-16R; CANR 15, 51; DLB 5,
   169; INT CANR-15; MTCW

Metcalf, John 1938-.......................... **CLC 37**
See also CA 113; DLB 60

Metcalf, Suzanne
See Baum, L(yman) Frank

Mew, Charlotte (Mary) 1870-1928 .. **TCLC 8**
See also CA 105; DLB 19, 135

Mewshaw, Michael 1943- ....**CLC 9**
See also CA 53-56; CANR 7, 47; DLBY 80

Meyer, June
See Jordan, June

Meyer, Lynn
See Slavitt, David R(ytman)

Meyer-Meyrink, Gustav 1868-1932
See Meyrink, Gustav
See also CA 117

Meyers, Jeffrey 1939- .... **CLC 39**
See also CA 73-76; CANR 54; DLB 111

Meynell, Alice (Christina Gertrude Thompson)
   1847-1922 .... **TCLC 6**
See also CA 104; DLB 19, 98

Meyrink, Gustav .... **TCLC 21**
See also Meyer-Meyrink, Gustav
See also DLB 81

Michaels, Leonard 1933- **CLC 6, 25; SSC 16**
See also CA 61-64; CANR 21, 62; DLB 130;
MTCW

Michaux, Henri 1899-1984 .... **CLC 8, 19**
See also CA 85-88; 114

Micheaux, Oscar 1884-1951 .... **TCLC 76**
See also DLB 50

Michelangelo 1475-1564 .... **LC 12**

Michelet, Jules 1798-1874 .... **NCLC 31**

Michener, James A(lbert) 1907(?)-1997 **C L C
1, 5, 11, 29, 60; DAM NOV, POP**
See also AITN 1; BEST 90:1; CA 5-8R; 161;
CANR 21, 45; DLB 6; MTCW

Mickiewicz, Adam 1798-1855 .... **NCLC 3**

Middleton, Christopher 1926- .... **CLC 13**
See also CA 13-16R; CANR 29, 54; DLB 40

Middleton, Richard (Barham) 1882-1911
TCLC 56
See also DLB 156

Middleton, Stanley 1919-.............. **CLC 7, 38**
See also CA 25-28R; CAAS 23; CANR 21, 46;
DLB 14

Middleton, Thomas 1580-1627 **LC 33; DAM
DRAM, MST; DC 5**
See also DLB 58

Migueis, Jose Rodrigues 1901- .... **CLC 10**

Mikszath, Kalman 1847-1910 .... **TCLC 31**

Miles, Jack .... **CLC 100**

Miles, Josephine (Louise) 1911-1985**CLC 1, 2,
14, 34, 39; DAM POET**
See also CA 1-4R; 116; CANR 2, 55; DLB 48

Militant
See Sandburg, Carl (August)

Mill, John Stuart 1806-1873 .... **NCLC 11, 58**
See also CDBLB 1832-1890; DLB 55

Millar, Kenneth 1915-1983 .... **CLC 14; DAM
POP**
See also Macdonald, Ross
See also CA 9-12R; 110; CANR 16, 63; DLB
2; DLBD 6; DLBY 83; MTCW

Millay, E. Vincent
See Millay, Edna St. Vincent

Millay, Edna St. Vincent 1892-1950 **TCLC 4,
49; DA; DAB; DAC; DAM MST, POET;
PC 6; WLCS**
See also CA 104; 130; CDALB 1917-1929;
DLB 45; MTCW

Miller, Arthur 1915-**CLC 1, 2, 6, 10, 15, 26, 47,
78; DA; DAB; DAC; DAM DRAM, MST;
DC 1; WLC**
See also AAYA 15; AITN 1; CA 1-4R; CABS
3; CANR 2, 30, 54; CDALB 1941-1968;
DLB 7; MTCW

Miller, Henry (Valentine) 1891-1980**CLC 1, 2,
4, 9, 14, 43, 84; DA; DAB; DAC; DAM
MST, NOV; WLC**
See also CA 9-12R; 97-100; CANR 33, 64;
CDALB 1929-1941; DLB 4, 9; DLBY 80;
MTCW

Miller, Jason 1939(?)-.......................... **CLC 2**
See also AITN 1; CA 73-76; DLB 7

Miller, Sue 1943- .... **CLC 44; DAM POP**
See also BEST 90:3; CA 139; CANR 59; DLB
143

Miller, Walter M(ichael, Jr.) 1923-**CLC 4, 30**
See also CA 85-88; DLB 8

Millett, Kate 1934- .... **CLC 67**
See also AITN 1; CA 73-76; CANR 32, 53;
MTCW

Millhauser, Steven (Lewis) 1943- **CLC 21, 54**

See also CA 110; 111; CANR 63; DLB 2; INT
111

Millin, Sarah Gertrude 1889-1968 ... **CLC 49**
See also CA 102; 93-96

Milne, A(lan) A(lexander) 1882-1956**TCLC 6;
DAB; DAC; DAM MST**
See also CA 104; 133; CLR 1, 26; DLB 10, 77,
100, 160; MAICYA; MTCW; YABC 1

Milner, Ron(ald) 1938- **CLC 56; BLC; DAM
MULT**
See also AITN 1; BW 1; CA 73-76; CANR 24;
DLB 38; MTCW

Milnes, Richard Monckton 1809-1885 **N C L C
61**
See also DLB 32, 184

Milosz, Czeslaw 1911- **CLC 5, 11, 22, 31, 56,
82; DAM MST, POET; PC 8; WLCS**
See also CA 81-84; CANR 23, 51; MTCW

Milton, John 1608-1674 ..... **LC 9; DA; DAB;
DAC; DAM MST, POET; PC 19; WLC**
See also CDBLB 1660-1789; DLB 131, 151

Min, Anchee 1957-.............................. **CLC 86**
See also CA 146

Minehaha, Cornelius
See Wedekind, (Benjamin) Frank(lin)

Miner, Valerie 1947-.......................... **CLC 40**
See also CA 97-100; CANR 59

Minimo, Duca
See D'Annunzio, Gabriele

Minot, Susan 1956-.............................. **CLC 44**
See also CA 134

Minus, Ed 1938-.................................. **CLC 39**

Miranda, Javier
See Bioy Casares, Adolfo

Mirbeau, Octave 1848-1917 .... **TCLC 55**
See also DLB 123

Miro (Ferrer), Gabriel (Francisco Victor) 1879-
1930 .... **TCLC 5**
See also CA 104

Mishima, Yukio 1925-1970**CLC 2, 4, 6, 9, 27;
DC 1; SSC 4**
See also Hiraoka, Kimitake
See also DLB 182

Mistral, Frederic 1830-1914 .... **TCLC 51**
See also CA 122

Mistral, Gabriela .... **TCLC 2; HLC**
See also Godoy Alcayaga, Lucila

Mistry, Rohinton 1952- .... **CLC 71; DAC**
See also CA 141

Mitchell, Clyde
See Ellison, Harlan (Jay); Silverberg, Robert

Mitchell, James Leslie 1901-1935
See Gibbon, Lewis Grassic
See also CA 104; DLB 15

Mitchell, Joni 1943- .... **CLC 12**
See also CA 112

Mitchell, Joseph (Quincy) 1908-1996**CLC 98**
See also CA 77-80; 152; DLBY 96

Mitchell, Margaret (Munnerlyn) 1900-1949
TCLC 11; DAM NOV, POP
See also CA 109; 125; CANR 55; DLB 9;
MTCW

Mitchell, Peggy
See Mitchell, Margaret (Munnerlyn)

Mitchell, S(ilas) Weir 1829-1914 ... **TCLC 36**

Mitchell, W(illiam) O(rmond) 1914-**CLC 25;
DAC; DAM MST**
See also CA 77-80; CANR 15, 43; DLB 88

Mitford, Mary Russell 1787-1855 ... **NCLC 4**
See also DLB 110, 116

Mitford, Nancy 1904-1973 .... **CLC 44**
See also CA 9-12R

Miyamoto, Yuriko 1899-1951 .... **TCLC 37**

See also DLB 180

Miyazawa Kenji 1896-1933 .... **TCLC 76**
See also CA 157

Mizoguchi, Kenji 1898-1956 .... **TCLC 72**

Mo, Timothy (Peter) 1950(?)-.......... **CLC 46**
See also CA 117; MTCW

Modarressi, Taghi (M.) 1931- .... **CLC 44**
See also CA 121; 134; INT 134

Modiano, Patrick (Jean) 1945- .... **CLC 18**
See also CA 85-88; CANR 17, 40; DLB 83

Moerck, Paal
See Roelvaag, O(le) E(dvart)

Mofolo, Thomas (Mokopu) 1875(?)-1948
TCLC 22; BLC; DAM MULT
See also CA 121; 153

Mohr, Nicholasa 1938-**CLC 12; DAM MULT;
HLC**
See also AAYA 8; CA 49-52; CANR 1, 32, 64;
CLR 22; DLB 145; HW; JRDA; SAAS 8;
SATA 8

Mojtabai, A(nn) G(race) 1938- **CLC 5, 9, 15,
29**
See also CA 85-88

Moliere 1622-1673 . **LC 28; DA; DAB; DAC;
DAM DRAM, MST; WLC**

Molin, Charles
See Mayne, William (James Carter)

Molnar, Ferenc 1878-1952 .. **TCLC 20; DAM
DRAM**
See also CA 109; 153

Momaday, N(avarre) Scott 1934- **CLC 2, 19,
85, 95; DA; DAB; DAC; DAM MST,
MULT, NOV, POP; WLCS**
See also AAYA 11; CA 25-28R; CANR 14, 34;
DLB 143, 175; INT CANR-14; MTCW;
NNAL; SATA 48; SATA-Brief 30

Monette, Paul 1945-1995 .... **CLC 82**
See also CA 139; 147

Monroe, Harriet 1860-1936............ **TCLC 12**
See also CA 109; DLB 54, 91

Monroe, Lyle
See Heinlein, Robert A(nson)

Montagu, Elizabeth 1917- .... **NCLC 7**
See also CA 9-12R

Montagu, Mary (Pierrepont) Wortley 1689-
1762 .... **LC 9; PC 16**
See also DLB 95, 101

Montagu, W. H.
See Coleridge, Samuel Taylor

Montague, John (Patrick) 1929- **CLC 13, 46**
See also CA 9-12R; CANR 9; DLB 40; MTCW

Montaigne, Michel (Eyquem) de 1533-1592
LC 8; DA; DAB; DAC; DAM MST; WLC

Montale, Eugenio 1896-1981**CLC 7, 9, 18; PC
13**
See also CA 17-20R; 104; CANR 30; DLB 114;
MTCW

Montesquieu, Charles-Louis de Secondat 1689-
1755 .... **LC 7**

Montgomery, (Robert) Bruce 1921-1978
See Crispin, Edmund
See also CA 104

Montgomery, L(ucy) M(aud) 1874-1942
TCLC 51; DAC; DAM MST
See also AAYA 12; CA 108; 137; CLR 8; DLB
92; DLBD 14; JRDA; MAICYA; YABC 1

Montgomery, Marion H., Jr. 1925- .... **CLC 7**
See also AITN 1; CA 1-4R; CANR 3, 48; DLB
6

Montgomery, Max
See Davenport, Guy (Mattison, Jr.)

Montherlant, Henry (Milon) de 1896-1972
CLC 8, 19; DAM DRAM

See also CA 85-88; 37-40R; DLB 72; MTCW

Monty Python
See Chapman, Graham; Cleese, John (Marwood); Gilliam, Terry (Vance); Idle, Eric; Jones, Terence Graham Parry; Palin, Michael (Edward)
See also AAYA 7

Moodie, Susanna (Strickland) 1803-1885 **NCLC 14**
See also DLB 99

Mooney, Edward 1951-
See Mooney, Ted
See also CA 130

Mooney, Ted .... **CLC 25**
See also Mooney, Edward

Moorcock, Michael (John) 1939-**CLC 5, 27, 58**
See also CA 45-48; CAAS 5; CANR 2, 17, 38, 64; DLB 14; MTCW; SATA 93

Moore, Brian 1921- **CLC 1, 3, 5, 7, 8, 19, 32, 90; DAB; DAC; DAM MST**
See also CA 1-4R; CANR 1, 25, 42, 63; MTCW

Moore, Edward
See Muir, Edwin

Moore, George Augustus 1852-1933**TCLC 7; SSC 19**
See also CA 104; DLB 10, 18, 57, 135

Moore, Lorrie .... **CLC 39, 45, 68**
See also Moore, Marie Lorena

Moore, Marianne (Craig) 1887-1972**CLC 1, 2, 4, 8, 10, 13, 19, 47; DA; DAB; DAC; DAM MST, POET; PC 4; WLCS**
See also CA 1-4R; 33-36R; CANR 3, 61; CDALB 1929-1941; DLB 45; DLBD 7; MTCW; SATA 20

Moore, Marie Lorena 1957-
See Moore, Lorrie
See also CA 116; CANR 39

Moore, Thomas 1779-1852 .... **NCLC 6**
See also DLB 96, 144

Morand, Paul 1888-1976 .... **CLC 41; SSC 22**
See also CA 69-72; DLB 65

Morante, Elsa 1918-1985 .... **CLC 8, 47**
See also CA 85-88; 117; CANR 35; DLB 177; MTCW

Moravia, Alberto 1907-1990**CLC 2, 7, 11, 27, 46; SSC 26**
See also Pincherle, Alberto
See also DLB 177

More, Hannah 1745-1833 .... **NCLC 27**
See also DLB 107, 109, 116, 158

More, Henry 1614-1687 .... **LC 9**
See also DLB 126

More, Sir Thomas 1478-1535 .... **LC 10, 32**

Moreas, Jean .... **TCLC 18**
See also Papadiamantopoulos, Johannes

Morgan, Berry 1919- .... **CLC 6**
See also CA 49-52; DLB 6

Morgan, Claire
See Highsmith, (Mary) Patricia

Morgan, Edwin (George) 1920- .... **CLC 31**
See also CA 5-8R; CANR 3, 43; DLB 27

Morgan, (George) Frederick 1922- . **CLC 23**
See also CA 17-20R; CANR 21

Morgan, Harriet
See Mencken, H(enry) L(ouis)

Morgan, Jane
See Cooper, James Fenimore

Morgan, Janet 1945- .... **CLC 39**
See also CA 65-68

Morgan, Lady 1776(?)-1859 .... **NCLC 29**
See also DLB 116, 158

Morgan, Robin 1941- .... **CLC 2**
See also CA 69-72; CANR 29; MTCW; SATA 80

Morgan, Scott
See Kuttner, Henry

Morgan, Seth 1949(?)-1990 .... **CLC 65**
See also CA 132

Morgenstern, Christian 1871-1914 . **TCLC 8**
See also CA 105

Morgenstern, S.
See Goldman, William (W.)

Moricz, Zsigmond 1879-1942 .... **TCLC 33**

Morike, Eduard (Friedrich) 1804-1875**NCLC 10**
See also DLB 133

Mori Ogai .... **TCLC 14**
See also Mori Rintaro

Mori Rintaro 1862-1922
See Mori Ogai
See also CA 110

Moritz, Karl Philipp 1756-1793 .... **LC 2**
See also DLB 94

Morland, Peter Henry
See Faust, Frederick (Schiller)

Morren, Theophil
See Hofmannsthal, Hugo von

Morris, Bill 1952- .... **CLC 76**

Morris, Julian
See West, Morris L(anglo)

Morris, Steveland Judkins 1950(?)-
See Wonder, Stevie
See also CA 111

Morris, William 1834-1896 .... **NCLC 4**
See also CDBLB 1832-1890; DLB 18, 35, 57, 156, 178, 184

Morris, Wright 1910- ...... **CLC 1, 3, 7, 18, 37**
See also CA 9-12R; CANR 21; DLB 2; DLBY 81; MTCW

Morrison, Arthur 1863-1945 .... **TCLC 72**
See also CA 120; 157; DLB 70, 135

Morrison, Chloe Anthony Wofford
See Morrison, Toni

Morrison, James Douglas 1943-1971
See Morrison, Jim
See also CA 73-76; CANR 40

Morrison, Jim .... **CLC 17**
See also Morrison, James Douglas

Morrison, Toni 1931-**CLC 4, 10, 22, 55, 81, 87; BLC; DA; DAB; DAC; DAM MST, MULT, NOV, POP**
See also AAYA 1, 22; BW 2; CA 29-32R; CANR 27, 42; CDALB 1968-1988; DLB 6, 33, 143; DLBY 81; MTCW; SATA 57

Morrison, Van 1945- .... **CLC 21**
See also CA 116

Morrissy, Mary 1958- .... **CLC 99**

Mortimer, John (Clifford) 1923-**CLC 28, 43; DAM DRAM, POP**
See also CA 13-16R; CANR 21; CDBLB 1960 to Present; DLB 13; INT CANR-21; MTCW

Mortimer, Penelope (Ruth) 1918- .... **CLC 5**
See also CA 57-60; CANR 45

Morton, Anthony
See Creasey, John

Mosca, Gaetano 1858-1941 .... **TCLC 75**

Mosher, Howard Frank 1943- .... **CLC 62**
See also CA 139

Mosley, Nicholas 1923- .... **CLC 43, 70**
See also CA 69-72; CANR 41, 60; DLB 14

Mosley, Walter 1952- **CLC 97; DAM MULT, POP**
See also AAYA 17; BW 2; CA 142; CANR 57

Moss, Howard 1922-1987 **CLC 7, 14, 45, 50; DAM POET**
See also CA 1-4R; 123; CANR 1, 44; DLB 5

Mossgiel, Rab
See Burns, Robert

Motion, Andrew (Peter) 1952- .... **CLC 47**
See also CA 146; DLB 40

Motley, Willard (Francis) 1909-1965**CLC 18**
See also BW 1; CA 117; 106; DLB 76, 143

Motoori, Norinaga 1730-1801 .... **NCLC 45**

Mott, Michael (Charles Alston) 1930-**CLC 15, 34**
See also CA 5-8R; CAAS 7; CANR 7, 29

Mountain Wolf Woman 1884-1960 .. **CLC 92**
See also CA 144; NNAL

Moure, Erin 1955- .... **CLC 88**
See also CA 113; DLB 60

Mowat, Farley (McGill) 1921-**CLC 26; DAC; DAM MST**
See also AAYA 1; CA 1-4R; CANR 4, 24, 42; CLR 20; DLB 68; INT CANAR-24; JRDA; MAICYA; MTCW; SATA 3, 55

Moyers, Bill 1934- .... **CLC 74**
See also AITN 2; CA 61-64; CANR 31, 52

Mphahlele, Es'kia
See Mphahlele, Ezekiel
See also DLB 125

Mphahlele, Ezekiel 1919-1983**CLC 25; BLC; DAM MULT**
See also Mphahlele, Es'kia
See also BW 2; CA 81-84; CANR 26

Mqhayi, S(amuel) E(dward) K(rune Loliwe) 1875-1945**TCLC 25; BLC; DAM MULT**
See also CA 153

Mrozek, Slawomir 1930- .... **CLC 3, 13**
See also CA 13-16R; CAAS 10; CANR 29; MTCW

Mrs. Belloc-Lowndes
See Lowndes, Marie Adelaide (Belloc)

Mtwa, Percy (?)- .... **CLC 47**

Mueller, Lisel 1924- .... **CLC 13, 51**
See also CA 93-96; DLB 105

Muir, Edwin 1887-1959 .... **TCLC 2**
See also CA 104; DLB 20, 100

Muir, John 1838-1914 .... **TCLC 28**
See also CA 165

Mujica Lainez, Manuel 1910-1984 .. **CLC 31**
See also Lainez, Manuel Mujica
See also CA 81-84; 112; CANR 32; HW

Mukherjee, Bharati 1940-**CLC 53; DAM NOV**
See also BEST 89:2; CA 107; CANR 45; DLB 60; MTCW

Muldoon, Paul 1951-**CLC 32, 72; DAM POET**
See also CA 113; 129; CANR 52; DLB 40; INT 129

Mulisch, Harry 1927- .... **CLC 42**
See also CA 9-12R; CANR 6, 26, 56

Mull, Martin 1943- .... **CLC 17**
See also CA 105

Mulock, Dinah Maria
See Craik, Dinah Maria (Mulock)

Munford, Robert 1737(?)-1783 .... **LC 5**
See also DLB 31

Mungo, Raymond 1946- .... **CLC 72**
See also CA 49-52; CANR 2

Munro, Alice 1931-.... **CLC 6, 10, 19, 50, 95; DAC; DAM MST, NOV; SSC 3; WLCS**
See also AITN 2; CA 33-36R; CANR 33, 53; DLB 53; MTCW; SATA 29

Munro, H(ector) H(ugh) 1870-1916
See Saki
See also CA 104; 130; CDBLB 1890-1914; DA; DAB; DAC; DAM MST, NOV; DLB 34, 162; MTCW; WLC

Murasaki, Lady .... **CMLC 1**

Murdoch, (Jean) Iris 1919-**CLC 1, 2, 3, 4, 6, 8, 11, 15, 22, 31, 51; DAB; DAC; DAM MST,**

NOV
See also CA 13-16R; CANR 8, 43; CDBLB
1960 to Present; DLB 14; INT CANR-8;
MTCW

Murfree, Mary Noailles 1850-1922 ...**SSC 22**
See also CA 122; DLB 12, 74

Murnau, Friedrich Wilhelm
See Plumpe, Friedrich Wilhelm

Murphy, Richard 1927- .... **CLC 41**
See also CA 29-32R; DLB 40

Murphy, Sylvia 1937- .... **CLC 34**
See also CA 121

Murphy, Thomas (Bernard) 1935- .. **CLC 51**
See also CA 101

Murray, Albert L. 1916- .... **CLC 73**
See also BW 2; CA 49-52; CANR 26, 52; DLB
38

Murray, Judith Sargent 1751-1820 **NCLC 63**
See also DLB 37

Murray, Les(lie) A(llan) 1938-**CLC 40; DAM**
POET
See also CA 21-24R; CANR 11, 27, 56

Murry, J. Middleton
See Murry, John Middleton

Murry, John Middleton 1889-1957 **TCLC 16**
See also CA 118; DLB 149

Musgrave, Susan 1951- .... **CLC 13, 54**
See also CA 69-72; CANR 45

Musil, Robert (Edler von) 1880-1942 . **T C L C**
12, 68; SSC 18
See also CA 109; CANR 55; DLB 81, 124

Muske, Carol 1945- .... **CLC 90**
See also Muske-Dukes, Carol (Anne)

Muske-Dukes, Carol (Anne) 1945-
See Muske, Carol
See also CA 65-68; CANR 32

Musset, (Louis Charles) Alfred de 1810-1857
NCLC 7

My Brother's Brother
See Chekhov, Anton (Pavlovich)

Myers, L(eopold) H(amilton) 1881-1944
TCLC 59
See also CA 157; DLB 15

Myers, Walter Dean 1937-.....**CLC 35; BLC;**
DAM MULT, NOV
See also AAYA 4; BW 2; CA 33-36R; CANR
20, 42; CLR 4, 16, 35; DLB 33; INT CANR-
20; JRDA; MAICYA; SAAS 2; SATA 41, 71;
SATA-Brief 27

Myers, Walter M.
See Myers, Walter Dean

Myles, Symon
See Follett, Ken(neth Martin)

Nabokov, Vladimir (Vladimirovich) 1899-1977
CLC 1, 2, 3, 6, 8, 11, 15, 23, 44, 46, 64;
DA; DAB; DAC; DAM MST, NOV; SSC
11; WLC
See also CA 5-8R; 69-72; CANR 20; CDALB
1941-1968; DLB 2; DLBD 3; DLBY 80, 91;
MTCW

Nagai Kafu 1879-1959 .... **TCLC 51**
See also Nagai Sokichi
See also DLB 180

Nagai Sokichi 1879-1959
See Nagai Kafu
See also CA 117

Nagy, Laszlo 1925-1978 .... **CLC 7**
See also CA 129; 112

Naipaul, Shiva(dhar Srinivasa) 1945-1985
CLC 32, 39; DAM NOV
See also CA 110; 112; 116; CANR 33; DLB
157; DLBY 85; MTCW

Naipaul, V(idiadhar) S(urajprasad) 1932-

CLC 4, 7, 9, 13, 18, 37, 105; DAB; DAC;
DAM MST, NOV
See also CA 1-4R; CANR 1, 33, 51; CDBLB
1960 to Present; DLB 125; DLBY 85;
MTCW

Nakos, Lilika 1899(?)- .... **CLC 29**

Narayan, R(asipuram) K(rishnaswami) 1906-
CLC 7, 28, 47; DAM NOV; SSC 25
See also CA 81-84; CANR 33, 61; MTCW;
SATA 62

Nash, (Frediric) Ogden 1902-1971 . **CLC 23;**
DAM POET; PC 21
See also CA 13-14; 29-32R; CANR 34, 61; CAP
1; DLB 11; MAICYA; MTCW; SATA 2, 46

Nashe, Thomas 1567-1601 .... **LC 41**

Nathan, Daniel
See Dannay, Frederic

Nathan, George Jean 1882-1958 .... **TCLC 18**
See also Hatteras, Owen
See also CA 114; DLB 137

Natsume, Kinnosuke 1867-1916
See Natsume, Soseki
See also CA 104

Natsume, Soseki 1867-1916 .... **TCLC 2, 10**
See also Natsume, Kinnosuke
See also DLB 180

Natti, (Mary) Lee 1919-
See Kingman, Lee
See also CA 5-8R; CANR 2

Naylor, Gloria 1950- **CLC 28, 52; BLC; DA;**
DAC; DAM MST, MULT, NOV, POP;
WLCS
See also AAYA 6; BW 2; CA 107; CANR 27,
51; DLB 173; MTCW

Neihardt, John Gneisenau 1881-1973 **CLC 32**
See also CA 13-14; CAP 1; DLB 9, 54

Nekrasov, Nikolai Alekseevich 1821-1878
NCLC 11

Nelligan, Emile 1879-1941 .... **TCLC 14**
See also CA 114; DLB 92

Nelson, Willie 1933- .... **CLC 17**
See also CA 107

Nemerov, Howard (Stanley) 1920-1991 **CLC 2,**
6, 9, 36; DAM POET
See also CA 1-4R; 134; CABS 2; CANR 1, 27,
53; DLB 5, 6; DLBY 83; INT CANR-27;
MTCW

Neruda, Pablo 1904-1973 **CLC 1, 2, 5, 7, 9, 28,**
62; DA; DAB; DAC; DAM MST, MULT,
POET; HLC; PC 4; WLC
See also CA 19-20; 45-48; CAP 2; HW; MTCW

Nerval, Gerard de 1808-1855 **NCLC 1, 67; PC**
13; SSC 18

Nervo, (Jose) Amado (Ruiz de) 1870-1919
TCLC 11
See also CA 109; 131; HW

Nessi, Pio Baroja y
See Baroja (y Nessi), Pio

Nestroy, Johann 1801-1862 .... **NCLC 42**
See also DLB 133

Netterville, Luke
See O'Grady, Standish (James)

Neufeld, John (Arthur) 1938- .... **CLC 17**
See also AAYA 11; CA 25-28R; CANR 11, 37,
56; MAICYA; SAAS 3; SATA 6, 81

Neville, Emily Cheney 1919- .... **CLC 12**
See also CA 5-8R; CANR 3, 37; JRDA;
MAICYA; SAAS 2; SATA 1

Newbound, Bernard Slade 1930-
See Slade, Bernard
See also CA 81-84; CANR 49; DAM DRAM

Newby, P(ercy) H(oward) 1918-1997 **CLC 2,**
13; DAM NOV

See also CA 5-8R; 161; CANR 32; DLB 15;
MTCW

Newlove, Donald 1928- .... **CLC 6**
See also CA 29-32R; CANR 25

Newlove, John (Herbert) 1938-.........**CLC 14**
See also CA 21-24R; CANR 9, 25

Newman, Charles 1938- .... **CLC 2, 8**
See also CA 21-24R

Newman, Edwin (Harold) 1919- ....**CLC 14**
See also AITN 1; CA 69-72; CANR 5

Newman, John Henry 1801-1890 ... **NCLC 38**
See also DLB 18, 32, 55

Newton, Suzanne 1936- .... **CLC 35**
See also CA 41-44R; CANR 14; JRDA; SATA
5, 77

Nexo, Martin Andersen 1869-1954 **TCLC 43**

Nezval, Vitezslav 1900-1958 .... **TCLC 44**
See also CA 123

Ng, Fae Myenne 1957(?)- .... **CLC 81**
See also CA 146

Ngema, Mbongeni 1955- .... **CLC 57**
See also BW 2; CA 143

Ngugi, James T(hiong'o) .... **CLC 3, 7, 13**
See also Ngugi wa Thiong'o

Ngugi wa Thiong'o 1938-**CLC 36; BLC; DAM**
MULT, NOV
See also Ngugi, James T(hiong'o)
See also BW 2; CA 81-84; CANR 27, 58; DLB
125; MTCW

Nichol, B(arrie) P(hillip) 1944-1988 . **CLC 18**
See also CA 53-56; DLB 53; SATA 66

Nichols, John (Treadwell) 1940- .... **CLC 38**
See also CA 9-12R; CAAS 2; CANR 6; DLBY
82

Nichols, Leigh
See Koontz, Dean R(ay)

Nichols, Peter (Richard) 1927-**CLC 5, 36, 65**
See also CA 104; CANR 33; DLB 13; MTCW

Nicolas, F. R. E.
See Freeling, Nicolas

Niedecker, Lorine 1903-1970 .... **CLC 10, 42;**
DAM POET
See also CA 25-28; CAP 2; DLB 48

Nietzsche, Friedrich (Wilhelm) 1844-1900
TCLC 10, 18, 55
See also CA 107; 121; DLB 129

Nievo, Ippolito 1831-1861 .... **NCLC 22**

Nightingale, Anne Redmon 1943-
See Redmon, Anne
See also CA 103

Nik. T. O.
See Annensky, Innokenty (Fyodorovich)

Nin, Anais 1903-1977 **CLC 1, 4, 8, 11, 14, 60;**
DAM NOV, POP; SSC 10
See also AITN 2; CA 13-16R; 69-72; CANR
22, 53; DLB 2, 4, 152; MTCW

Nishiwaki, Junzaburo 1894-1982 .... **PC 15**
See also CA 107

Nissenson, Hugh 1933- .... **CLC 4, 9**
See also CA 17-20R; CANR 27; DLB 28

Niven, Larry .... **CLC 8**
See also Niven, Laurence Van Cott
See also DLB 8

Niven, Laurence Van Cott 1938-
See Niven, Larry
See also CA 21-24R; CAAS 12; CANR 14, 44;
DAM POP; MTCW; SATA 95

Nixon, Agnes Eckhardt 1927- .... **CLC 21**
See also CA 110

Nizan, Paul 1905-1940 .... **TCLC 40**
See also CA 161; DLB 72

Nkosi, Lewis 1936- ...... **CLC 45; BLC; DAM**
MULT

See also BW 1; CA 65-68; CANR 27; DLB 157
Nodier, (Jean) Charles (Emmanuel) 1780-1844
    NCLC 19
    See also DLB 119
Nolan, Christopher 1965- .... **CLC 58**
    See also CA 111
Noon, Jeff 1957-............................... **CLC 91**
    See also CA 148
Norden, Charles
    See Durrell, Lawrence (George)
Nordhoff, Charles (Bernard) 1887-1947
    TCLC 23
    See also CA 108; DLB 9; SATA 23
Norfolk, Lawrence 1963- .... **CLC 76**
    See also CA 144
Norman, Marsha 1947-**CLC 28; DAM DRAM;**
    DC 8
    See also CA 105; CABS 3; CANR 41; DLBY
    84
Norris, Frank 1870-1902 .... **SSC 28**
    See also Norris, (Benjamin) Frank(lin, Jr.)
    See also CDALB 1865-1917; DLB 12, 71
Norris, (Benjamin) Frank(lin, Jr.) 1870-1902
    TCLC 24
    See also Norris, Frank
    See also CA 110; 160
Norris, Leslie 1921- .... **CLC 14**
    See also CA 11-12; CANR 14; CAP 1; DLB 27
North, Andrew
    See Norton, Andre
North, Anthony
    See Koontz, Dean R(ay)
North, Captain George
    See Stevenson, Robert Louis (Balfour)
North, Milou
    See Erdrich, Louise
Northrup, B. A.
    See Hubbard, L(afayette) Ron(ald)
North Staffs
    See Hulme, T(homas) E(rnest)
Norton, Alice Mary
    See Norton, Andre
    See also MAICYA; SATA 1, 43
Norton, Andre 1912- .... **CLC 12**
    See also Norton, Alice Mary
    See also AAYA 14; CA 1-4R; CANR 2, 31; DLB
    8, 52; JRDA; MTCW; SATA 91
Norton, Caroline 1808-1877 .... **NCLC 47**
    See also DLB 21, 159
Norway, Nevil Shute 1899-1960
    See Shute, Nevil
    See also CA 102; 93-96
Norwid, Cyprian Kamil 1821-1883 **NCLC 17**
Nosille, Nabrah
    See Ellison, Harlan (Jay)
Nossack, Hans Erich 1901-1978 .... **CLC 6**
    See also CA 93-96; 85-88; DLB 69
Nostradamus 1503-1566 .... **LC 27**
Nosu, Chuji
    See Ozu, Yasujiro
Notenburg, Eleanora (Genrikhovna) von
    See Guro, Elena
Nova, Craig 1945-.......................... **CLC 7, 31**
    See also CA 45-48; CANR 2, 53
Novak, Joseph
    See Kosinski, Jerzy (Nikodem)
Novalis 1772-1801 .... **NCLC 13**
    See also DLB 90
Novis, Emile
    See Weil, Simone (Adolphine)
Nowlan, Alden (Albert) 1933-1983 . **CLC 15;**
    DAC; DAM MST
    See also CA 9-12R; CANR 5; DLB 53

Noyes, Alfred 1880-1958 .... **TCLC 7**
    See also CA 104; DLB 20
Nunn, Kem ....**CLC 34**
    See also CA 159
Nye, Robert 1939-...**CLC 13, 42; DAM NOV**
    See also CA 33-36R; CANR 29; DLB 14;
    MTCW; SATA 6
Nyro, Laura 1947- ....**CLC 17**
Oates, Joyce Carol 1938-**CLC 1, 2, 3, 6, 9, 11,**
    15, 19, 33, 52, 108; DA; DAB; DAC; DAM
    MST, NOV, POP; SSC 6; WLC
    See also AAYA 15; AITN 1; BEST 89:2; CA 5-
    8R; CANR 25, 45; CDALB 1968-1988; DLB
    2, 5, 130; DLBY 81; INT CANR-25; MTCW
O'Brien, Darcy 1939- .... **CLC 11**
    See also CA 21-24R; CANR 8, 59
O'Brien, E. G.
    See Clarke, Arthur C(harles)
O'Brien, Edna 1936- **CLC 3, 5, 8, 13, 36, 65;**
    DAM NOV; SSC 10
    See also CA 1-4R; CANR 6, 41; CDBLB 1960
    to Present; DLB 14; MTCW
O'Brien, Fitz-James 1828-1862 ..... **NCLC 21**
    See also DLB 74
O'Brien, Flann .... **CLC 1, 4, 5, 7, 10, 47**
    See also O Nuallain, Brian
O'Brien, Richard 1942- ....**CLC 17**
    See also CA 124
O'Brien, (William) Tim(othy) 1946- .**CLC 7,**
    19, 40, 103; DAM POP
    See also AAYA 16; CA 85-88; CANR 40, 58;
    DLB 152; DLBD 9; DLBY 80
Obstfelder, Sigbjoern 1866-1900 ... **TCLC 23**
    See also CA 123
O'Casey, Sean 1880-1964**CLC 1, 5, 9, 11, 15,**
    88; DAB; DAC; DAM DRAM, MST;
    WLCS
    See also CA 89-92; CANR 62; CDBLB 1914-
    1945; DLB 10; MTCW
O'Cathasaigh, Sean
    See O'Casey, Sean
Ochs, Phil 1940-1976 ....**CLC 17**
    See also CA 65-68
O'Connor, Edwin (Greene) 1918-1968**CLC 14**
    See also CA 93-96; 25-28R
O'Connor, (Mary) Flannery 1925-1964 **C L C**
    1, 2, 3, 6, 10, 13, 15, 21, 66, 104; DA; DAB;
    DAC; DAM MST, NOV; SSC 1, 23; WLC
    See also AAYA 7; CA 1-4R; CANR 3, 41;
    CDALB 1941-1968; DLB 2, 152; DLBD 12;
    DLBY 80; MTCW
O'Connor, Frank .... **CLC 23; SSC 5**
    See also O'Donovan, Michael John
    See also DLB 162
O'Dell, Scott 1898-1989 .... **CLC 30**
    See also AAYA 3; CA 61-64; 129; CANR 12,
    30; CLR 1, 16; DLB 52; JRDA; MAICYA;
    SATA 12, 60
Odets, Clifford 1906-1963**CLC 2, 28, 98; DAM**
    DRAM; DC 6
    See also CA 85-88; CANR 62; DLB 7, 26;
    MTCW
O'Doherty, Brian 1934- ....**CLC 76**
    See also CA 105
O'Donnell, K. M.
    See Malzberg, Barry N(athaniel)
O'Donnell, Lawrence
    See Kuttner, Henry
O'Donovan, Michael John 1903-1966**CLC 14**
    See also O'Connor, Frank
    See also CA 93-96
Oe, Kenzaburo 1935- **CLC 10, 36, 86; DAM**
    NOV; SSC 20

See also CA 97-100; CANR 36, 50; DLB 182;
    DLBY 94; MTCW
O'Faolain, Julia 1932- .... **CLC 6, 19, 47, 108**
    See also CA 81-84; CAAS 2; CANR 12, 61;
    DLB 14; MTCW
O'Faolain, Sean 1900-1991 **CLC 1, 7, 14, 32,**
    70; SSC 13
    See also CA 61-64; 134; CANR 12; DLB 15,
    162; MTCW
O'Flaherty, Liam 1896-1984**CLC 5, 34; SSC 6**
    See also CA 101; 113; CANR 35; DLB 36, 162;
    DLBY 84; MTCW
Ogilvy, Gavin
    See Barrie, J(ames) M(atthew)
O'Grady, Standish (James) 1846-1928**T C L C**
    5
    See also CA 104; 157
O'Grady, Timothy 1951- .... **CLC 59**
    See also CA 138
O'Hara, Frank 1926-1966 . **CLC 2, 5, 13, 78;**
    DAM POET
    See also CA 9-12R; 25-28R; CANR 33; DLB
    5, 16; MTCW
O'Hara, John (Henry) 1905-1970**CLC 1, 2, 3,**
    6, 11, 42; DAM NOV; SSC 15
    See also CA 5-8R; 25-28R; CANR 31, 60;
    CDALB 1929-1941; DLB 9, 86; DLBD 2;
    MTCW
O Hehir, Diana 1922- .... **CLC 41**
    See also CA 93-96
Okigbo, Christopher (Ifenayichukwu) 1932-
    1967 ... **CLC 25, 84; BLC; DAM MULT,**
    POET; PC 7
    See also BW 1; CA 77-80; DLB 125; MTCW
Okri, Ben 1959-................................... **CLC 87**
    See also BW 2; CA 130; 138; DLB 157; INT
    138
Olds, Sharon 1942- .... **CLC 32, 39, 85; DAM**
    POET
    See also CA 101; CANR 18, 41; DLB 120
Oldstyle, Jonathan
    See Irving, Washington
Olesha, Yuri (Karlovich) 1899-1960 ... **CLC 8**
    See also CA 85-88
Oliphant, Laurence 1829(?)-1888 .. **NCLC 47**
    See also DLB 18, 166
Oliphant, Margaret (Oliphant Wilson) 1828-
    1897 .... **NCLC 11, 61; SSC 25**
    See also DLB 18, 159
Oliver, Mary 1935- .... **CLC 19, 34, 98**
    See also CA 21-24R; CANR 9, 43; DLB 5
Olivier, Laurence (Kerr) 1907-1989 **CLC 20**
    See also CA 111; 150; 129
Olsen, Tillie 1913-**CLC 4, 13; DA; DAB; DAC;**
    DAM MST; SSC 11
    See also CA 1-4R; CANR 1, 43; DLB 28; DLBY
    80; MTCW
Olson, Charles (John) 1910-1970**CLC 1, 2, 5,**
    6, 9, 11, 29; DAM POET; PC 19
    See also CA 13-16; 25-28R; CABS 2; CANR
    35, 61; CAP 1; DLB 5, 16; MTCW
Olson, Toby 1937-.............................. **CLC 28**
    See also CA 65-68; CANR 9, 31
Olyesha, Yuri
    See Olesha, Yuri (Karlovich)
Ondaatje, (Philip) Michael 1943-**CLC 14, 29,**
    51, 76; DAB; DAC; DAM MST
    See also CA 77-80; CANR 42; DLB 60
Oneal, Elizabeth 1934-
    See Oneal, Zibby
    See also CA 106; CANR 28; MAICYA; SATA
    30, 82
Oneal, Zibby .... **CLC 30**

See also Oneal, Elizabeth
See also AAYA 5; CLR 13; JRDA
O'Neill, Eugene (Gladstone) 1888-1953**TCLC 1, 6, 27, 49; DA; DAB; DAC; DAM DRAM, MST; WLC**
See also AITN 1; CA 110; 132; CDALB 1929-1941; DLB 7; MTCW
Onetti, Juan Carlos 1909-1994 ... **CLC 7, 10; DAM MULT, NOV; SSC 23**
See also CA 85-88; 145; CANR 32, 63; DLB 113; HW; MTCW
O Nuallain, Brian 1911-1966
See O'Brien, Flann
See also CA 21-22; 25-28R; CAP 2
Ophuls, Max 1902-1957 .... **TCLC 79**
See also CA 113
Opie, Amelia 1769-1853 .... **NCLC 65**
See also DLB 116, 159
Oppen, George 1908-1984 ...... **CLC 7, 13, 34**
See also CA 13-16R; 113; CANR 8; DLB 5, 165
Oppenheim, E(dward) Phillips 1866-1946 **TCLC 45**
See also CA 111; DLB 70
Opuls, Max
See Ophuls, Max
Origen c. 185-c. 254 .... **CMLC 19**
Orlovitz, Gil 1918-1973 .... **CLC 22**
See also CA 77-80; 45-48; DLB 2, 5
Orris
See Ingelow, Jean
Ortega y Gasset, Jose 1883-1955 .... **TCLC 9; DAM MULT; HLC**
See also CA 106; 130; HW; MTCW
Ortese, Anna Maria 1914- .... **CLC 89**
See also DLB 177
Ortiz, Simon J(oseph) 1941- .. **CLC 45; DAM MULT, POET; PC 17**
See also CA 134; DLB 120, 175; NNAL
Orton, Joe .... **CLC 4, 13, 43; DC 3**
See also Orton, John Kingsley
See also CDBLB 1960 to Present; DLB 13
Orton, John Kingsley 1933-1967
See Orton, Joe
See also CA 85-88; CANR 35; DAM DRAM; MTCW
Orwell, George **TCLC 2, 6, 15, 31, 51; DAB; WLC**
See also Blair, Eric (Arthur)
See also CDBLB 1945-1960; DLB 15, 98
Osborne, David
See Silverberg, Robert
Osborne, George
See Silverberg, Robert
Osborne, John (James) 1929-1994**CLC 1, 2, 5, 11, 45; DA; DAB; DAC; DAM DRAM, MST; WLC**
See also CA 13-16R; 147; CANR 21, 56; CDBLB 1945-1960; DLB 13; MTCW
Osborne, Lawrence 1958- .... **CLC 50**
Oshima, Nagisa 1932- .... **CLC 20**
See also CA 116; 121
Oskison, John Milton 1874-1947 . **TCLC 35; DAM MULT**
See also CA 144; DLB 175; NNAL
Ossoli, Sarah Margaret (Fuller marchesa d') 1810-1850
See Fuller, Margaret
See also SATA 25
Ostrovsky, Alexander 1823-1886**NCLC 30, 57**
Otero, Blas de 1916-1979 .... **CLC 11**
See also CA 89-92; DLB 134
Otto, Whitney 1955- .... **CLC 70**

See also CA 140
Ouida .... **TCLC 43**
See also De La Ramee, (Marie) Louise
See also DLB 18, 156
Ousmane, Sembene 1923- .... **CLC 66; BLC**
See also BW 1; CA 117; 125; MTCW
Ovid 43B.C.-18(?)**CMLC 7; DAM POET; PC 2**
Owen, Hugh
See Faust, Frederick (Schiller)
Owen, Wilfred (Edward Salter) 1893-1918 **TCLC 5, 27; DA; DAB; DAC; DAM MST, POET; PC 19; WLC**
See also CA 104; 141; CDBLB 1914-1945; DLB 20
Owens, Rochelle 1936- .... **CLC 8**
See also CA 17-20R; CAAS 2; CANR 39
Oz, Amos 1939-**CLC 5, 8, 11, 27, 33, 54; DAM NOV**
See also CA 53-56; CANR 27, 47; MTCW
Ozick, Cynthia 1928-**CLC 3, 7, 28, 62; DAM NOV, POP; SSC 15**
See also BEST 90:1; CA 17-20R; CANR 23, 58; DLB 28, 152; DLBY 82; INT CANR-23; MTCW
Ozu, Yasujiro 1903-1963 .... **CLC 16**
See also CA 112
Pacheco, C.
See Pessoa, Fernando (Antonio Nogueira)
Pa Chin .... **CLC 18**
See also Li Fei-kan
Pack, Robert 1929- .... **CLC 13**
See also CA 1-4R; CANR 3, 44; DLB 5
Padgett, Lewis
See Kuttner, Henry
Padilla (Lorenzo), Heberto 1932- ..... **CLC 38**
See also AITN 1; CA 123; 131; HW
Page, Jimmy 1944- .... **CLC 12**
Page, Louise 1955- .... **CLC 40**
See also CA 140
Page, P(atricia) K(athleen) 1916- **CLC 7, 18; DAC; DAM MST; PC 12**
See also CA 53-56; CANR 4, 22; DLB 68; MTCW
Page, Thomas Nelson 1853-1922 .... **SSC 23**
See also CA 118; DLB 12, 78; DLBD 13
Pagels, Elaine Hiesey 1943- .... **CLC 104**
See also CA 45-48; CANR 2, 24, 51
Paget, Violet 1856-1935
See Lee, Vernon
See also CA 104
Paget-Lowe, Henry
See Lovecraft, H(oward) P(hillips)
Paglia, Camille (Anna) 1947- .... **CLC 68**
See also CA 140
Paige, Richard
See Koontz, Dean R(ay)
Paine, Thomas 1737-1809 .... **NCLC 62**
See also CDALB 1640-1865; DLB 31, 43, 73, 158
Pakenham, Antonia
See Fraser, (Lady) Antonia (Pakenham)
Palamas, Kostes 1859-1943 .... **TCLC 5**
See also CA 105
Palazzeschi, Aldo 1885-1974 .... **CLC 11**
See also CA 89-92; 53-56; DLB 114
Paley, Grace 1922-**CLC 4, 6, 37; DAM POP; SSC 8**
See also CA 25-28R; CANR 13, 46; DLB 28; INT CANR-13; MTCW
Palin, Michael (Edward) 1943- .... **CLC 21**
See also Monty Python
See also CA 107; CANR 35; SATA 67

Palliser, Charles 1947- .... **CLC 65**
See also CA 136
Palma, Ricardo 1833-1919 .... **TCLC 29**
Pancake, Breece Dexter 1952-1979
See Pancake, Breece D'J
See also CA 123; 109
Pancake, Breece D'J .... **CLC 29**
See also Pancake, Breece Dexter
See also DLB 130
Panko, Rudy
See Gogol, Nikolai (Vasilyevich)
Papadiamantis, Alexandros 1851-1911**TCLC 29**
Papadiamantopoulos, Johannes 1856-1910
See Moreas, Jean
See also CA 117
Papini, Giovanni 1881-1956 .... **TCLC 22**
See also CA 121
Paracelsus 1493-1541 .... **LC 14**
See also DLB 179
Parasol, Peter
See Stevens, Wallace
Pareto, Vilfredo 1848-1923 .... **TCLC 69**
Parfenie, Maria
See Codrescu, Andrei
Parini, Jay (Lee) 1948- .... **CLC 54**
See also CA 97-100; CAAS 16; CANR 32
Park, Jordan
See Kornbluth, C(yril) M.; Pohl, Frederik
Park, Robert E(zra) 1864-1944 ...... **TCLC 73**
See also CA 122
Parker, Bert
See Ellison, Harlan (Jay)
Parker, Dorothy (Rothschild) 1893-1967**CLC 15, 68; DAM POET; SSC 2**
See also CA 19-20; 25-28R; CAP 2; DLB 11, 45, 86; MTCW
Parker, Robert B(rown) 1932-**CLC 27; DAM NOV, POP**
See also BEST 89:4; CA 49-52; CANR 1, 26, 52; INT CANR-26; MTCW
Parkin, Frank 1940- .... **CLC 43**
See also CA 147
Parkman, Francis, Jr. 1823-1893 ... **NCLC 12**
See also DLB 1, 30
Parks, Gordon (Alexander Buchanan) 1912-**CLC 1, 16; BLC; DAM MULT**
See also AITN 2; BW 2; CA 41-44R; CANR 26; DLB 33; SATA 8
Parmenides c. 515B.C.-c. 450B.C. **CMLC 22**
See also DLB 176
Parnell, Thomas 1679-1718 .... **LC 3**
See also DLB 94
Parra, Nicanor 1914- ...... **CLC 2, 102; DAM MULT; HLC**
See also CA 85-88; CANR 32; HW; MTCW
Parrish, Mary Frances
See Fisher, M(ary) F(rances) K(ennedy)
Parson
See Coleridge, Samuel Taylor
Parson Lot
See Kingsley, Charles
Partridge, Anthony
See Oppenheim, E(dward) Phillips
Pascal, Blaise 1623-1662 .... **LC 35**
Pascoli, Giovanni 1855-1912 .... **TCLC 45**
Pasolini, Pier Paolo 1922-1975 . **CLC 20, 37, 106; PC 17**
See also CA 93-96; 61-64; CANR 63; DLB 128, 177; MTCW
Pasquini
See Silone, Ignazio
Pastan, Linda (Olenik) 1932- **CLC 27; DAM**

POET
See also CA 61-64; CANR 18, 40, 61; DLB 5
Pasternak, Boris (Leonidovich) 1890-1960
**CLC 7, 10, 18, 63; DA; DAB; DAC; DAM
MST, NOV, POET; PC 6; WLC**
See also CA 127; 116; MTCW
Patchen, Kenneth 1911-1972 ... **CLC 1, 2, 18;
DAM POET**
See also CA 1-4R; 33-36R; CANR 3, 35; DLB
16, 48; MTCW
Pater, Walter (Horatio) 1839-1894 .. **NCLC 7**
See also CDBLB 1832-1890; DLB 57, 156
Paterson, A(ndrew) B(arton) 1864-1941
TCLC 32
See also CA 155
Paterson, Katherine (Womeldorf) 1932-**C L C
12, 30**
See also AAYA 1; CA 21-24R; CANR 28, 59;
CLR 7; DLB 52; JRDA; MAICYA; MTCW;
SATA 13, 53, 92
Patmore, Coventry Kersey Dighton 1823-1896
NCLC 9
See also DLB 35, 98
Paton, Alan (Stewart) 1903-1988 **CLC 4, 10,
25, 55, 106; DA; DAB; DAC; DAM MST,
NOV; WLC**
See also CA 13-16; 125; CANR 22; CAP 1;
MTCW; SATA 11; SATA-Obit 56
Paton Walsh, Gillian 1937-
See Walsh, Jill Paton
See also CANR 38; JRDA; MAICYA; SAAS 3;
SATA 4, 72
Patton, George S. 1885-1945 .... **TCLC 79**
Paulding, James Kirke 1778-1860 ... **NCLC 2**
See also DLB 3, 59, 74
Paulin, Thomas Neilson 1949-
See Paulin, Tom
See also CA 123; 128
Paulin, Tom .... **CLC 37**
See also Paulin, Thomas Neilson
See also DLB 40
Paustovsky, Konstantin (Georgievich) 1892-
1968 .... **CLC 40**
See also CA 93-96; 25-28R
Pavese, Cesare 1908-1950 ... **TCLC 3; PC 13;
SSC 19**
See also CA 104; DLB 128, 177
Pavic, Milorad 1929-.......................... **CLC 60**
See also CA 136; DLB 181
Payne, Alan
See Jakes, John (William)
Paz, Gil
See Lugones, Leopoldo
Paz, Octavio 1914-**CLC 3, 4, 6, 10, 19, 51, 65;
DA; DAB; DAC; DAM MST, MULT,
POET; HLC; PC 1; WLC**
See also CA 73-76; CANR 32; DLBY 90; HW;
MTCW
p'Bitek, Okot 1931-1982**CLC 96; BLC; DAM
MULT**
See also BW 2; CA 124; 107; DLB 125; MTCW
Peacock, Molly 1947- .... **CLC 60**
See also CA 103; CAAS 21; CANR 52; DLB
120
Peacock, Thomas Love 1785-1866 . **NCLC 22**
See also DLB 96, 116
Peake, Mervyn 1911-1968............. **CLC 7, 54**
See also CA 5-8R; 25-28R; CANR 3; DLB 15,
160; MTCW; SATA 23
Pearce, Philippa .... **CLC 21**
See also Christie, (Ann) Philippa
See also CLR 9; DLB 161; MAICYA; SATA 1,
67

Pearl, Eric
See Elman, Richard
Pearson, T(homas) R(eid) 1956- .... **CLC 39**
See also CA 120; 130; INT 130
Peck, Dale 1967- .... **CLC 81**
See also CA 146
Peck, John 1941- .... **CLC 3**
See also CA 49-52; CANR 3
Peck, Richard (Wayne) 1934-............ **CLC 21**
See also AAYA 1; CA 85-88; CANR 19, 38;
CLR 15; INT CANR-19; JRDA; MAICYA;
SAAS 2; SATA 18, 55
Peck, Robert Newton 1928- ..... **CLC 17; DA;
DAC; DAM MST**
See also AAYA 3; CA 81-84; CANR 31, 63;
CLR 45; JRDA; MAICYA; SAAS 1; SATA
21, 62
Peckinpah, (David) Sam(uel) 1925-1984**C L C
20**
See also CA 109; 114
Pedersen, Knut 1859-1952
See Hamsun, Knut
See also CA 104; 119; CANR 63; MTCW
Peeslake, Gaffer
See Durrell, Lawrence (George)
Peguy, Charles Pierre 1873-1914 ... **TCLC 10**
See also CA 107
Pena, Ramon del Valle y
See Valle-Inclan, Ramon (Maria) del
Pendennis, Arthur Esquir
See Thackeray, William Makepeace
Penn, William 1644-1718 .... **LC 25**
See also DLB 24
PEPECE
See Prado (Calvo), Pedro
Pepys, Samuel 1633-1703 **LC 11; DA; DAB;
DAC; DAM MST; WLC**
See also CDBLB 1660-1789; DLB 101
Percy, Walker 1916-1990**CLC 2, 3, 6, 8, 14, 18,
47, 65; DAM NOV, POP**
See also CA 1-4R; 131; CANR 1, 23, 64; DLB
2; DLBY 80, 90; MTCW
Perec, Georges 1936-1982 .... **CLC 56**
See also CA 141; DLB 83
Pereda (y Sanchez de Porrua), Jose Maria de
1833-1906 .... **TCLC 16**
See also CA 117
Pereda y Porrua, Jose Maria de
See Pereda (y Sanchez de Porrua), Jose Maria
de
Peregoy, George Weems
See Mencken, H(enry) L(ouis)
Perelman, S(idney) J(oseph) 1904-1979 **C L C
3, 5, 9, 15, 23, 44, 49; DAM DRAM**
See also AITN 1, 2; CA 73-76; 89-92; CANR
18; DLB 11, 44; MTCW
Peret, Benjamin 1899-1959 .... **TCLC 20**
See also CA 117
Peretz, Isaac Loeb 1851(?)-1915 .. **TCLC 16;
SSC 26**
See also CA 109
Peretz, Yitzhok Leibush
See Peretz, Isaac Loeb
Perez Galdos, Benito 1843-1920 .... **TCLC 27**
See also CA 125; 153; HW
Perrault, Charles 1628-1703 .... **LC 2**
See also MAICYA; SATA 25
Perry, Brighton
See Sherwood, Robert E(mmet)
Perse, St.-John .... **CLC 4, 11, 46**
See also Leger, (Marie-Rene Auguste) Alexis
Saint-Leger
Perutz, Leo 1882-1957 .... **TCLC 60**

See also DLB 81
Peseenz, Tulio F.
See Lopez y Fuentes, Gregorio
Pesetsky, Bette 1932- .... **CLC 28**
See also CA 133; DLB 130
Peshkov, Alexei Maximovich 1868-1936
See Gorky, Maxim
See also CA 105; 141; DA; DAC; DAM DRAM,
MST, NOV
Pessoa, Fernando (Antonio Nogueira) 1888-
1935 .... **TCLC 27; HLC; PC 20**
See also CA 125
Peterkin, Julia Mood 1880-1961 ...... **CLC 31**
See also CA 102; DLB 9
Peters, Joan K(aren) 1945-............... **CLC 39**
See also CA 158
Peters, Robert L(ouis) 1924- ....**CLC 7**
See also CA 13-16R; CAAS 8; DLB 105
Petofi, Sandor 1823-1849 .... **NCLC 21**
Petrakis, Harry Mark 1923-................**CLC 3**
See also CA 9-12R; CANR 4, 30
Petrarch 1304-1374 **CMLC 20; DAM POET;
PC 8**
Petrov, Evgeny .... **TCLC 21**
See also Kataev, Evgeny Petrovich
Petry, Ann (Lane) 1908-1997 ... **CLC 1, 7, 18**
See also BW 1; CA 5-8R; 157; CAAS 6; CANR
4, 46; CLR 12; DLB 76; JRDA; MAICYA;
MTCW; SATA 5; SATA-Obit 94
Petursson, Halligrimur 1614-1674 .... **LC 8**
Phaedrus 18(?)B.C.-55(?) .... **CMLC 25**
Philips, Katherine 1632-1664 .... **LC 30**
See also DLB 131
Philipson, Morris H. 1926- .... **CLC 53**
See also CA 1-4R; CANR 4
Phillips, Caryl 1958- . **CLC 96; DAM MULT**
See also BW 2; CA 141; CANR 63; DLB 157
Phillips, David Graham 1867-1911 **TCLC 44**
See also CA 108; DLB 9, 12
Phillips, Jack
See Sandburg, Carl (August)
Phillips, Jayne Anne 1952-**CLC 15, 33; SSC 16**
See also CA 101; CANR 24, 50; DLBY 80; INT
CANR-24; MTCW
Phillips, Richard
See Dick, Philip K(indred)
Phillips, Robert (Schaeffer) 1938- ... **CLC 28**
See also CA 17-20R; CAAS 13; CANR 8; DLB
105
Phillips, Ward
See Lovecraft, H(oward) P(hillips)
Piccolo, Lucio 1901-1969 .... **CLC 13**
See also CA 97-100; DLB 114
Pickthall, Marjorie L(owry) C(hristie) 1883-
1922 .... **TCLC 21**
See also CA 107; DLB 92
Pico della Mirandola, Giovanni 1463-1494**LC
15**
Piercy, Marge 1936- **CLC 3, 6, 14, 18, 27, 62**
See also CA 21-24R; CAAS 1; CANR 13, 43;
DLB 120; MTCW
Piers, Robert
See Anthony, Piers
Pieyre de Mandiargues, Andre 1909-1991
See Mandiargues, Andre Pieyre de
See also CA 103; 136; CANR 22
Pilnyak, Boris .... **TCLC 23**
See also Vogau, Boris Andreyevich
Pincherle, Alberto 1907-1990 .... **CLC 11, 18;
DAM NOV**
See also Moravia, Alberto
See also CA 25-28R; 132; CANR 33, 63;
MTCW

Pinckney, Darryl 1953- .... **CLC 76**
See also BW 2; CA 143
Pindar 518B.C.-446B.C. ..... **CMLC 12; PC 19**
See also DLB 176
Pineda, Cecile 1942- .... **CLC 39**
See also CA 118
Pinero, Arthur Wing 1855-1934 .. **TCLC 32;**
DAM DRAM
See also CA 110; 153; DLB 10
Pinero, Miguel (Antonio Gomez) 1946-1988
CLC 4, 55
See also CA 61-64; 125; CANR 29; HW
Pinget, Robert 1919-1997 .... **CLC 7, 13, 37**
See also CA 85-88; 160; DLB 83
Pink Floyd
See Barrett, (Roger) Syd; Gilmour, David; Mason, Nick; Waters, Roger; Wright, Rick
Pinkney, Edward 1802-1828 .... **NCLC 31**
Pinkwater, Daniel Manus 1941- .... **CLC 35**
See also Pinkwater, Manus
See also AAYA 1; CA 29-32R; CANR 12, 38;
CLR 4; JRDA; MAICYA; SAAS 3; SATA 46,
76
Pinkwater, Manus
See Pinkwater, Daniel Manus
See also SATA 8
Pinsky, Robert 1940-**CLC 9, 19, 38, 94; DAM**
POET
See also CA 29-32R; CAAS 4; CANR 58;
DLBY 82
Pinta, Harold
See Pinter, Harold
Pinter, Harold 1930-**CLC 1, 3, 6, 9, 11, 15, 27,**
58, 73; DA; DAB; DAC; DAM DRAM,
MST; WLC
See also CA 5-8R; CANR 33; CDBLB 1960 to
Present; DLB 13; MTCW
Piozzi, Hester Lynch (Thrale) 1741-1821
NCLC 57
See also DLB 104, 142
Pirandello, Luigi 1867-1936**TCLC 4, 29; DA;**
DAB; DAC; DAM DRAM, MST; DC 5;
SSC 22; WLC
See also CA 104; 153
Pirsig, Robert M(aynard) 1928-**CLC 4, 6, 73;**
DAM POP
See also CA 53-56; CANR 42; MTCW; SATA
39
Pisarev, Dmitry Ivanovich 1840-1868 **N C L C**
25
Pix, Mary (Griffith) 1666-1709 .... **LC 8**
See also DLB 80
Pixerecourt, Guilbert de 1773-1844**NCLC 39**
Plaatje, Sol(omon) T(shekisho) 1876-1932
TCLC 73
See also BW 2; CA 141
Plaidy, Jean
See Hibbert, Eleanor Alice Burford
Planche, James Robinson 1796-1880**NCLC 42**
Plant, Robert 1948- .... **CLC 12**
Plante, David (Robert) 1940- **CLC 7, 23, 38;**
DAM NOV
See also CA 37-40R; CANR 12, 36, 58; DLBY
83; INT CANR-12; MTCW
Plath, Sylvia 1932-1963 **CLC 1, 2, 3, 5, 9, 11,**
14, 17, 50, 51, 62; DA; DAB; DAC; DAM
MST, POET; PC 1; WLC
See also AAYA 13; CA 19-20; CANR 34; CAP
2; CDALB 1941-1968; DLB 5, 6, 152;
MTCW; SATA 96
Plato 428(?)B.C.-348(?)B.C. .... **CMLC 8; DA;**
DAB; DAC; DAM MST; WLCS
See also DLB 176

Platonov, Andrei .... **TCLC 14**
See also Klimentov, Andrei Platonovich
Platt, Kin 1911- .... **CLC 26**
See also AAYA 11; CA 17-20R; CANR 11;
JRDA; SAAS 17; SATA 21, 86
Plautus c. 251B.C.-184B.C. .... **DC 6**
Plick et Plock
See Simenon, Georges (Jacques Christian)
Plimpton, George (Ames) 1927- .... **CLC 36**
See also AITN 1; CA 21-24R; CANR 32;
MTCW; SATA 10
Pliny the Elder c. 23-79 .... **CMLC 23**
Plomer, William Charles Franklin 1903-1973
CLC 4, 8
See also CA 21-22; CANR 34; CAP 2; DLB
20, 162; MTCW; SATA 24
Plowman, Piers
See Kavanagh, Patrick (Joseph)
Plum, J.
See Wodehouse, P(elham) G(renville)
Plumly, Stanley (Ross) 1939- .... **CLC 33**
See also CA 108; 110; DLB 5; INT 110
Plumpe, Friedrich Wilhelm 1888-1931**T C L C**
53
See also CA 112
Po Chu-i 772-846 .... **CMLC 24**
Poe, Edgar Allan 1809-1849**NCLC 1, 16, 55;**
DA; DAB; DAC; DAM MST, POET; PC
1; SSC 1, 22; WLC
See also AAYA 14; CDALB 1640-1865; DLB
3, 59, 73, 74; SATA 23
Poet of Titchfield Street, The
See Pound, Ezra (Weston Loomis)
Pohl, Frederik 1919- .... **CLC 18; SSC 25**
See also CA 61-64; CAAS 1; CANR 11, 37;
DLB 8; INT CANR-11; MTCW; SATA 24
Poirier, Louis 1910-
See Gracq, Julien
See also CA 122; 126
Poitier, Sidney 1927- .... **CLC 26**
See also BW 1; CA 117
Polanski, Roman 1933- .... **CLC 16**
See also CA 77-80
Poliakoff, Stephen 1952- .... **CLC 38**
See also CA 106; DLB 13
Police, The
See Copeland, Stewart (Armstrong); Summers,
Andrew James; Sumner, Gordon Matthew
Polidori, John William 1795-1821 . **NCLC 51**
See also DLB 116
Pollitt, Katha 1949- .... **CLC 28**
See also CA 120; 122; MTCW
Pollock, (Mary) Sharon 1936-**CLC 50; DAC;**
DAM DRAM, MST
See also CA 141; DLB 60
Polo, Marco 1254-1324 .... **CMLC 15**
Polonsky, Abraham (Lincoln) 1910- **CLC 92**
See also CA 104; DLB 26; INT 104
Polybius c. 200B.C.-c. 118B.C. ...... **CMLC 17**
See also DLB 176
Pomerance, Bernard 1940- .... **CLC 13; DAM**
DRAM
See also CA 101; CANR 49
Ponge, Francis (Jean Gaston Alfred) 1899-1988
CLC 6, 18; DAM POET
See also CA 85-88; 126; CANR 40
Pontoppidan, Henrik 1857-1943 .... **TCLC 29**
Poole, Josephine .... **CLC 17**
See also Helyar, Jane Penelope Josephine
See also SAAS 2; SATA 5
Popa, Vasko 1922-1991 .... **CLC 19**
See also CA 112; 148; DLB 181
Pope, Alexander 1688-1744 **LC 3; DA; DAB;**

DAC; DAM MST, POET; WLC
See also CDBLB 1660-1789; DLB 95, 101
Porter, Connie (Rose) 1959(?)- .... **CLC 70**
See also BW 2; CA 142; SATA 81
Porter, Gene(va Grace) Stratton 1863(?)-1924
TCLC 21
See also CA 112
Porter, Katherine Anne 1890-1980**CLC 1, 3, 7,**
10, 13, 15, 27, 101; DA; DAB; DAC; DAM
MST, NOV; SSC 4
See also AITN 2; CA 1-4R; 101; CANR 1; DLB
4, 9, 102; DLBD 12; DLBY 80; MTCW;
SATA 39; SATA-Obit 23
Porter, Peter (Neville Frederick) 1929-**CLC 5,**
13, 33
See also CA 85-88; DLB 40
Porter, William Sydney 1862-1910
See Henry, O.
See also CA 104; 131; CDALB 1865-1917; DA;
DAB; DAC; DAM MST; DLB 12, 78, 79;
MTCW; YABC 2
Portillo (y Pacheco), Jose Lopez
See Lopez Portillo (y Pacheco), Jose
Post, Melville Davisson 1869-1930 **TCLC 39**
See also CA 110
Potok, Chaim 1929- . **CLC 2, 7, 14, 26; DAM**
NOV
See also AAYA 15; AITN 1, 2; CA 17-20R;
CANR 19, 35, 64; DLB 28, 152; INT CANR-
19; MTCW; SATA 33
Potter, (Helen) Beatrix 1866-1943
See Webb, (Martha) Beatrice (Potter)
See also MAICYA
Potter, Dennis (Christopher George) 1935-1994
CLC 58, 86
See also CA 107; 145; CANR 33, 61; MTCW
Pound, Ezra (Weston Loomis) 1885-1972
CLC 1, 2, 3, 4, 5, 7, 10, 13, 18, 34, 48, 50;
DA; DAB; DAC; DAM MST, POET; PC
4; WLC
See also CA 5-8R; 37-40R; CANR 40; CDALB
1917-1929; DLB 4, 45, 63; DLBD 15;
MTCW
Povod, Reinaldo 1959-1994 .... **CLC 44**
See also CA 136; 146
Powell, Adam Clayton, Jr. 1908-1972**CLC 89;**
BLC; DAM MULT
See also BW 1; CA 102; 33-36R
Powell, Anthony (Dymoke) 1905-**CLC 1, 3, 7,**
9, 10, 31
See also CA 1-4R; CANR 1, 32, 62; CDBLB
1945-1960; DLB 15; MTCW
Powell, Dawn 1897-1965 .... **CLC 66**
See also CA 5-8R
Powell, Padgett 1952- .... **CLC 34**
See also CA 126; CANR 63
Power, Susan 1961- .... **CLC 91**
Powers, J(ames) F(arl) 1917-**CLC 1, 4, 8, 57;**
SSC 4
See also CA 1-4R; CANR 2, 61; DLB 130;
MTCW
Powers, John J(ames) 1945-
See Powers, John R.
See also CA 69-72
Powers, John R. .... **CLC 66**
See also Powers, John J(ames)
Powers, Richard (S.) 1957- .... **CLC 93**
See also CA 148
Pownall, David 1938- .... **CLC 10**
See also CA 89-92; CAAS 18; CANR 49; DLB
14
Powys, John Cowper 1872-1963**CLC 7, 9, 15,**
46

See also CA 85-88; DLB 15; MTCW

Powys, T(heodore) F(rancis) 1875-1953
TCLC 9
See also CA 106; DLB 36, 162

Prado (Calvo), Pedro 1886-1952 .... **TCLC 75**
See also CA 131; HW

Prager, Emily 1952- .... **CLC 56**

Pratt, E(dwin) J(ohn) 1883(?)-1964 **CLC 19;**
DAC; DAM POET
See also CA 141; 93-96; DLB 92

Premchand .... **TCLC 21**
See also Srivastava, Dhanpat Rai

Preussler, Otfried 1923- .... **CLC 17**
See also CA 77-80; SATA 24

Prevert, Jacques (Henri Marie) 1900-1977
CLC 15
See also CA 77-80; 69-72; CANR 29, 61;
MTCW; SATA-Obit 30

Prevost, Abbe (Antoine Francois) 1697-1763
LC 1

Price, (Edward) Reynolds 1933-**CLC 3, 6, 13,**
43, 50, 63; DAM NOV; SSC 22
See also CA 1-4R; CANR 1, 37, 57; DLB 2;
INT CANR-37

Price, Richard 1949- .... **CLC 6, 12**
See also CA 49-52; CANR 3; DLBY 81

Prichard, Katharine Susannah 1883-1969
CLC 46
See also CA 11-12; CANR 33; CAP 1; MTCW;
SATA 66

Priestley, J(ohn) B(oynton) 1894-1984**CLC 2,**
5, 9, 34; DAM DRAM, NOV
See also CA 9-12R; 113; CANR 33; CDBLB
1914-1945; DLB 10, 34, 77, 100, 139; DLBY
84; MTCW

Prince 1958(?)- .... **CLC 35**

Prince, F(rank) T(empleton) 1912- .. **CLC 22**
See also CA 101; CANR 43; DLB 20

Prince Kropotkin
See Kropotkin, Peter (Aleksieevich)

Prior, Matthew 1664-1721 .... **LC 4**
See also DLB 95

Prishvin, Mikhail 1873-1954 .... **TCLC 75**

Pritchard, William H(arrison) 1932-**CLC 34**
See also CA 65-68; CANR 23; DLB 111

Pritchett, V(ictor) S(awdon) 1900-1997 **C L C**
5, 13, 15, 41; DAM NOV; SSC 14
See also CA 61-64; 157; CANR 31, 63; DLB
15, 139; MTCW

Private 19022
See Manning, Frederic

Probst, Mark 1925- .... **CLC 59**
See also CA 130

Prokosch, Frederic 1908-1989 ..... **CLC 4, 48**
See also CA 73-76; 128; DLB 48

Prophet, The
See Dreiser, Theodore (Herman Albert)

Prose, Francine 1947- .... **CLC 45**
See also CA 109; 112; CANR 46

Proudhon
See Cunha, Euclides (Rodrigues Pimenta) da

Proulx, E. Annie 1935- .... **CLC 81**

Proust, (Valentin-Louis-George-Eugene-)
Marcel 1871-1922 **TCLC 7, 13, 33; DA;**
DAB; DAC; DAM MST, NOV; WLC
See also CA 104; 120; DLB 65; MTCW

Prowler, Harley
See Masters, Edgar Lee

Prus, Boleslaw 1845-1912 .... **TCLC 48**

Pryor, Richard (Franklin Lenox Thomas) 1940-
CLC 26
See also CA 122

Przybyszewski, Stanislaw 1868-1927**TCLC 36**

See also CA 160; DLB 66

Pteleon
See Grieve, C(hristopher) M(urray)
See also DAM POET

Puckett, Lute
See Masters, Edgar Lee

Puig, Manuel 1932-1990**CLC 3, 5, 10, 28, 65;**
DAM MULT; HLC
See also CA 45-48; CANR 2, 32, 63; DLB 113;
HW; MTCW

Pulitzer, Joseph 1847-1911 .... **TCLC 76**
See also CA 114; DLB 23

Purdy, Al(fred Wellington) 1918-**CLC 3, 6, 14,**
50; DAC; DAM MST, POET
See also CA 81-84; CAAS 17; CANR 42; DLB
88

Purdy, James (Amos) 1923-**CLC 2, 4, 10, 28,**
52
See also CA 33-36R; CAAS 1; CANR 19, 51;
DLB 2; INT CANR-19; MTCW

Pure, Simon
See Swinnerton, Frank Arthur

Pushkin, Alexander (Sergeyevich) 1799-1837
NCLC 3, 27; DA; DAB; DAC; DAM
DRAM, MST, POET; PC 10; SSC 27;
WLC
See also SATA 61

P'u Sung-ling 1640-1715 .... **LC 3**

Putnam, Arthur Lee
See Alger, Horatio, Jr.

Puzo, Mario 1920-**CLC 1, 2, 6, 36, 107; DAM**
NOV, POP
See also CA 65-68; CANR 4, 42; DLB 6;
MTCW

Pygge, Edward
See Barnes, Julian (Patrick)

Pyle, Ernest Taylor 1900-1945
See Pyle, Ernie
See also CA 115; 160

Pyle, Ernie 1900-1945 .... **TCLC 75**
See also Pyle, Ernest Taylor
See also DLB 29

Pym, Barbara (Mary Crampton) 1913-1980
CLC 13, 19, 37
See also CA 13-14; 97-100; CANR 13, 34; CAP
1; DLB 14; DLBY 87; MTCW

Pynchon, Thomas (Ruggles, Jr.) 1937-**CLC 2,**
3, 6, 9, 11, 18, 33, 62, 72; DA; DAB; DAC;
DAM MST, NOV, POP; SSC 14; WLC
See also BEST 90:2; CA 17-20R; CANR 22,
46; DLB 2, 173; MTCW

Pythagoras c. 570B.C.-c. 500B.C. . **CMLC 22**
See also DLB 176

Qian Zhongshu
See Ch'ien Chung-shu

Qroll
See Dagerman, Stig (Halvard)

Quarrington, Paul (Lewis) 1953- ...... **CLC 65**
See also CA 129; CANR 62

Quasimodo, Salvatore 1901-1968 ..... **CLC 10**
See also CA 13-16; 25-28R; CAP 1; DLB 114;
MTCW

Quay, Stephen 1947- .... **CLC 95**

Quay, Timothy 1947- .... **CLC 95**

Queen, Ellery .... **CLC 3, 11**
See also Dannay, Frederic; Davidson, Avram;
Lee, Manfred B(ennington); Marlowe,
Stephen; Sturgeon, Theodore (Hamilton);
Vance, John Holbrook

Queen, Ellery, Jr.
See Dannay, Frederic; Lee, Manfred
B(ennington)

Queneau, Raymond 1903-1976 **CLC 2, 5, 10,**

42
See also CA 77-80; 69-72; CANR 32; DLB 72;
MTCW

Quevedo, Francisco de 1580-1645 ...... **LC 23**

Quiller-Couch, Arthur Thomas 1863-1944
TCLC 53
See also CA 118; DLB 135, 153

Quin, Ann (Marie) 1936-1973 .... **CLC 6**
See also CA 9-12R; 45-48; DLB 14

Quinn, Martin
See Smith, Martin Cruz

Quinn, Peter 1947- .... **CLC 91**

Quinn, Simon
See Smith, Martin Cruz

Quiroga, Horacio (Sylvestre) 1878-1937
TCLC 20; DAM MULT; HLC
See also CA 117; 131; HW; MTCW

Quoirez, Francoise 1935-..................... **CLC 9**
See also Sagan, Francoise
See also CA 49-52; CANR 6, 39; MTCW

Raabe, Wilhelm 1831-1910 .... **TCLC 45**
See also DLB 129

Rabe, David (William) 1940-... **CLC 4, 8, 33;**
DAM DRAM
See also CA 85-88; CABS 3; CANR 59; DLB 7

Rabelais, Francois 1483-1553**LC 5; DA; DAB;**
DAC; DAM MST; WLC

Rabinovitch, Sholem 1859-1916
See Aleichem, Sholom
See also CA 104

Rachilde 1860-1953 .... **TCLC 67**
See also DLB 123

Racine, Jean 1639-1699 . **LC 28; DAB; DAM**
MST

Radcliffe, Ann (Ward) 1764-1823**NCLC 6, 55**
See also DLB 39, 178

Radiguet, Raymond 1903-1923 ...... **TCLC 29**
See also DLB 65

Radnoti, Miklos 1909-1944 .... **TCLC 16**
See also CA 118

Rado, James 1939-............................. **CLC 17**
See also CA 105

Radvanyi, Netty 1900-1983
See Seghers, Anna
See also CA 85-88; 110

Rae, Ben
See Griffiths, Trevor

Raeburn, John (Hay) 1941- .... **CLC 34**
See also CA 57-60

Ragni, Gerome 1942-1991 .... **CLC 17**
See also CA 105; 134

Rahv, Philip 1908-1973 .... **CLC 24**
See also Greenberg, Ivan
See also DLB 137

Raine, Craig 1944- .... **CLC 32, 103**
See also CA 108; CANR 29, 51; DLB 40

Raine, Kathleen (Jessie) 1908- ..... **CLC 7, 45**
See also CA 85-88; CANR 46; DLB 20; MTCW

Rainis, Janis 1865-1929 .... **TCLC 29**

Rakosi, Carl .... **CLC 47**
See also Rawley, Callman
See also CAAS 5

Raleigh, Richard
See Lovecraft, H(oward) P(hillips)

Raleigh, Sir Walter 1554(?)-1618 . **LC 31, 39**
See also CDBLB Before 1660; DLB 172

Rallentando, H. P.
See Sayers, Dorothy L(eigh)

Ramal, Walter
See de la Mare, Walter (John)

Ramon, Juan
See Jimenez (Mantecon), Juan Ramon

Ramos, Graciliano 1892-1953 .... **TCLC 32**

Rampersad, Arnold 1941- .... **CLC 44**
    See also BW 2; CA 127; 133; DLB 111; INT
    133
Rampling, Anne
    See Rice, Anne
Ramsay, Allan 1684(?)-1758 .... **LC 29**
    See also DLB 95
Ramuz, Charles-Ferdinand 1878-1947**TCLC
33**
Rand, Ayn 1905-1982**CLC 3, 30, 44, 79; DA;
    DAC; DAM MST, NOV, POP; WLC**
    See also AAYA 10; CA 13-16R; 105; CANR
    27; MTCW
Randall, Dudley (Felker) 1914-**CLC 1; BLC;
    DAM MULT**
    See also BW 1; CA 25-28R; CANR 23; DLB
    41
Randall, Robert
    See Silverberg, Robert
Ranger, Ken
    See Creasey, John
Ransom, John Crowe 1888-1974**CLC 2, 4, 5,
    11, 24; DAM POET**
    See also CA 5-8R; 49-52; CANR 6, 34; DLB
    45, 63; MTCW
Rao, Raja 1909- ...... **CLC 25, 56; DAM NOV**
    See also CA 73-76; CANR 51; MTCW
Raphael, Frederic (Michael) 1931-**CLC 2, 14**
    See also CA 1-4R; CANR 1; DLB 14
Ratcliffe, James P.
    See Mencken, H(enry) L(ouis)
Rathbone, Julian 1935- .... **CLC 41**
    See also CA 101; CANR 34
Rattigan, Terence (Mervyn) 1911-1977**CLC 7;
    DAM DRAM**
    See also CA 85-88; 73-76; CDBLB 1945-1960;
    DLB 13; MTCW
Ratushinskaya, Irina 1954- .... **CLC 54**
    See also CA 129
Raven, Simon (Arthur Noel) 1927-.. **CLC 14**
    See also CA 81-84
Rawley, Callman 1903-
    See Rakosi, Carl
    See also CA 21-24R; CANR 12, 32
Rawlings, Marjorie Kinnan 1896-1953**TCLC
4**
    See also AAYA 20; CA 104; 137; DLB 9, 22,
    102; JRDA; MAICYA; YABC 1
Ray, Satyajit 1921-1992 .. **CLC 16, 76; DAM
    MULT**
    See also CA 114; 137
Read, Herbert Edward 1893-1968 ..... **CLC 4**
    See also CA 85-88; 25-28R; DLB 20, 149
Read, Piers Paul 1941- .... **CLC 4, 10, 25**
    See also CA 21-24R; CANR 38; DLB 14; SATA
    21
Reade, Charles 1814-1884 .... **NCLC 2**
    See also DLB 21
Reade, Hamish
    See Gray, Simon (James Holliday)
Reading, Peter 1946- .... **CLC 47**
    See also CA 103; CANR 46; DLB 40
Reaney, James 1926- ... **CLC 13; DAC; DAM
    MST**
    See also CA 41-44R; CAAS 15; CANR 42; DLB
    68; SATA 43
Rebreanu, Liviu 1885-1944 .... **TCLC 28**
Rechy, John (Francisco) 1934- **CLC 1, 7, 14,
    18, 107; DAM MULT; HLC**
    See also CA 5-8R; CAAS 4; CANR 6, 32, 64;
    DLB 122; DLBY 82; HW; INT CANR-6
Redcam, Tom 1870-1933 .... **TCLC 25**
Reddin, Keith .... **CLC 67**

Redgrove, Peter (William) 1932- . **CLC 6, 41**
    See also CA 1-4R; CANR 3, 39; DLB 40
Redmon, Anne .... **CLC 22**
    See also Nightingale, Anne Redmon
    See also DLBY 86
Reed, Eliot
    See Ambler, Eric
Reed, Ishmael 1938-**CLC 2, 3, 5, 6, 13, 32, 60;
    BLC; DAM MULT**
    See also BW 2; CA 21-24R; CANR 25, 48; DLB
    2, 5, 33, 169; DLBD 8; MTCW
Reed, John (Silas) 1887-1920 .... **TCLC 9**
    See also CA 106
Reed, Lou .... **CLC 21**
    See also Firbank, Louis
Reeve, Clara 1729-1807 .... **NCLC 19**
    See also DLB 39
Reich, Wilhelm 1897-1957 .... **TCLC 57**
Reid, Christopher (John) 1949- .... **CLC 33**
    See also CA 140; DLB 40
Reid, Desmond
    See Moorcock, Michael (John)
Reid Banks, Lynne 1929-
    See Banks, Lynne Reid
    See also CA 1-4R; CANR 6, 22, 38; CLR 24;
    JRDA; MAICYA; SATA 22, 75
Reilly, William K.
    See Creasey, John
Reiner, Max
    See Caldwell, (Janet Miriam) Taylor (Holland)
Reis, Ricardo
    See Pessoa, Fernando (Antonio Nogueira)
Remarque, Erich Maria 1898-1970 **CLC 21;
    DA; DAB; DAC; DAM MST, NOV**
    See also CA 77-80; 29-32R; DLB 56; MTCW
Remizov, A.
    See Remizov, Aleksei (Mikhailovich)
Remizov, A. M.
    See Remizov, Aleksei (Mikhailovich)
Remizov, Aleksei (Mikhailovich) 1877-1957
    TCLC 27
    See also CA 125; 133
Renan, Joseph Ernest 1823-1892 ... **NCLC 26**
Renard, Jules 1864-1910 .... **TCLC 17**
    See also CA 117
Renault, Mary .... **CLC 3, 11, 17**
    See also Challans, Mary
    See also DLBY 83
Rendell, Ruth (Barbara) 1930- . **CLC 28, 48;
    DAM POP**
    See also Vine, Barbara
    See also CA 109; CANR 32, 52; DLB 87; INT
    CANR-32; MTCW
Renoir, Jean 1894-1979 .... **CLC 20**
    See also CA 129; 85-88
Resnais, Alain 1922- .... **CLC 16**
Reverdy, Pierre 1889-1960 .... **CLC 53**
    See also CA 97-100; 89-92
Rexroth, Kenneth 1905-1982 **CLC 1, 2, 6, 11,
    22, 49; DAM POET; PC 20**
    See also CA 5-8R; 107; CANR 14, 34, 63;
    CDALB 1941-1968; DLB 16, 48, 165;
    DLBY 82; INT CANR-14; MTCW
Reyes, Alfonso 1889-1959 .... **TCLC 33**
    See also CA 131; HW
Reyes y Basoalto, Ricardo Eliecer Neftali
    See Neruda, Pablo
Reymont, Wladyslaw (Stanislaw) 1868(?)-1925
    TCLC 5
    See also CA 104
Reynolds, Jonathan 1942- .... **CLC 6, 38**
    See also CA 65-68; CANR 28
Reynolds, Joshua 1723-1792 .... **LC 15**

    See also DLB 104
Reynolds, Michael Shane 1937- ....**CLC 44**
    See also CA 65-68; CANR 9
Reznikoff, Charles 1894-1976 ....**CLC 9**
    See also CA 33-36; 61-64; CAP 2; DLB 28, 45
Rezzori (d'Arezzo), Gregor von 1914-**CLC 25**
    See also CA 122; 136
Rhine, Richard
    See Silverstein, Alvin
Rhodes, Eugene Manlove 1869-1934**TCLC 53**
R'hoone
    See Balzac, Honore de
Rhys, Jean 1890(?)-1979 **CLC 2, 4, 6, 14, 19,
    51; DAM NOV; SSC 21**
    See also CA 25-28R; 85-88; CANR 35, 62;
    CDBLB 1945-1960; DLB 36, 117, 162;
    MTCW
Ribeiro, Darcy 1922-1997 .... **CLC 34**
    See also CA 33-36R; 156
Ribeiro, Joao Ubaldo (Osorio Pimentel) 1941-
    CLC 10, 67
    See also CA 81-84
Ribman, Ronald (Burt) 1932- .... **CLC 7**
    See also CA 21-24R; CANR 46
Ricci, Nino 1959- .... **CLC 70**
    See also CA 137
Rice, Anne 1941- .... **CLC 41; DAM POP**
    See also AAYA 9; BEST 89:2; CA 65-68; CANR
    12, 36, 53
Rice, Elmer (Leopold) 1892-1967 **CLC 7, 49;
    DAM DRAM**
    See also CA 21-22; 25-28R; CAP 2; DLB 4, 7;
    MTCW
Rice, Tim(othy Miles Bindon) 1944- **CLC 21**
    See also CA 103; CANR 46
Rich, Adrienne (Cecile) 1929-**CLC 3, 6, 7, 11,
    18, 36, 73, 76; DAM POET; PC 5**
    See also CA 9-12R; CANR 20, 53; DLB 5, 67;
    MTCW
Rich, Barbara
    See Graves, Robert (von Ranke)
Rich, Robert
    See Trumbo, Dalton
Richard, Keith .... **CLC 17**
    See also Richards, Keith
Richards, David Adams 1950- **CLC 59; DAC**
    See also CA 93-96; CANR 60; DLB 53
Richards, I(vor) A(rmstrong) 1893-1979**C L C
    14, 24**
    See also CA 41-44R; 89-92; CANR 34; DLB
    27
Richards, Keith 1943-
    See Richard, Keith
    See also CA 107
Richardson, Anne
    See Roiphe, Anne (Richardson)
Richardson, Dorothy Miller 1873-1957**TCLC
3**
    See also CA 104; DLB 36
Richardson, Ethel Florence (Lindesay) 1870-
    1946
    See Richardson, Henry Handel
    See also CA 105
Richardson, Henry Handel .... **TCLC 4**
    See also Richardson, Ethel Florence (Lindesay)
Richardson, John 1796-1852**NCLC 55; DAC**
    See also DLB 99
Richardson, Samuel 1689-1761 .... **LC 1; DA;
    DAB; DAC; DAM MST, NOV; WLC**
    See also CDBLB 1660-1789; DLB 39
Richler, Mordecai 1931-**CLC 3, 5, 9, 13, 18, 46,
    70; DAC; DAM MST, NOV**
    See also AITN 1; CA 65-68; CANR 31, 62; CLR

17; DLB 53; MAICYA; MTCW; SATA 44;
SATA-Brief 27
Richter, Conrad (Michael) 1890-1968 **CLC 30**
See also AAYA 21; CA 5-8R; 25-28R; CANR
23; DLB 9; MTCW; SATA 3
Ricostranza, Tom
See Ellis, Trey
Riddell, J. H. 1832-1906 .... **TCLC 40**
Riding, Laura .... **CLC 3, 7**
See also Jackson, Laura (Riding)
Riefenstahl, Berta Helene Amalia 1902-
See Riefenstahl, Leni
See also CA 108
Riefenstahl, Leni .... **CLC 16**
See also Riefenstahl, Berta Helene Amalia
Riffe, Ernest
See Bergman, (Ernst) Ingmar
Riggs, (Rolla) Lynn 1899-1954 ..... **TCLC 56;
DAM MULT**
See also CA 144; DLB 175; NNAL
Riley, James Whitcomb 1849-1916 **TCLC 51;
DAM POET**
See also CA 118; 137; MAICYA; SATA 17
Riley, Tex
See Creasey, John
Rilke, Rainer Maria 1875-1926 **TCLC 1, 6, 19;
DAM POET; PC 2**
See also CA 104; 132; CANR 62; DLB 81;
MTCW
Rimbaud, (Jean Nicolas) Arthur 1854-1891
**NCLC 4, 35; DA; DAB; DAC; DAM MST,
POET; PC 3; WLC**
Rinehart, Mary Roberts 1876-1958 **TCLC 52**
See also CA 108
Ringmaster, The
See Mencken, H(enry) L(ouis)
Ringwood, Gwen(dolyn Margaret) Pharis
1910-1984 .... **CLC 48**
See also CA 148; 112; DLB 88
Rio, Michel 19(?)- .... **CLC 43**
Ritsos, Giannes
See Ritsos, Yannis
Ritsos, Yannis 1909-1990 .... **CLC 6, 13, 31**
See also CA 77-80; 133; CANR 39, 61; MTCW
Ritter, Erika 1948(?)- .... **CLC 52**
Rivera, Jose Eustasio 1889-1928 ... **TCLC 35**
See also HW
Rivers, Conrad Kent 1933-1968 .... **CLC 1**
See also BW 1; CA 85-88; DLB 41
Rivers, Elfrida
See Bradley, Marion Zimmer
Riverside, John
See Heinlein, Robert A(nson)
Rizal, Jose 1861-1896 .... **NCLC 27**
Roa Bastos, Augusto (Antonio) 1917- **CLC 45;
DAM MULT; HLC**
See also CA 131; DLB 113; HW
Robbe-Grillet, Alain 1922- **CLC 1, 2, 4, 6, 8,
10, 14, 43**
See also CA 9-12R; CANR 33; DLB 83; MTCW
Robbins, Harold 1916-1997 ..... **CLC 5; DAM
NOV**
See also CA 73-76; CANR 26, 54; MTCW
Robbins, Thomas Eugene 1936-
See Robbins, Tom
See also CA 81-84; CANR 29, 59; DAM NOV,
POP; MTCW
Robbins, Tom .... **CLC 9, 32, 64**
See also Robbins, Thomas Eugene
See also BEST 90:3; DLBY 80
Robbins, Trina 1938- .... **CLC 21**
See also CA 128
Roberts, Charles G(eorge) D(ouglas) 1860-1943

TCLC 8
See also CA 105; CLR 33; DLB 92; SATA 88;
SATA-Brief 29
Roberts, Elizabeth Madox 1886-1941 **TCLC
68**
See also CA 111; DLB 9, 54, 102; SATA 33;
SATA-Brief 27
Roberts, Kate 1891-1985 .... **CLC 15**
See also CA 107; 116
Roberts, Keith (John Kingston) 1935- **CLC 14**
See also CA 25-28R; CANR 46
Roberts, Kenneth (Lewis) 1885-1957 **TCLC 23**
See also CA 109; DLB 9
Roberts, Michele (B.) 1949- .... **CLC 48**
See also CA 115; CANR 58
Robertson, Ellis
See Ellison, Harlan (Jay); Silverberg, Robert
Robertson, Thomas William 1829-1871 **NCLC
35; DAM DRAM**
Robeson, Kenneth
See Dent, Lester
Robinson, Edwin Arlington 1869-1935 **T C L C
5; DA; DAC; DAM MST, POET; PC 1**
See also CA 104; 133; CDALB 1865-1917;
DLB 54; MTCW
Robinson, Henry Crabb 1775-1867 **NCLC 15**
See also DLB 107
Robinson, Jill 1936- .... **CLC 10**
See also CA 102; INT 102
Robinson, Kim Stanley 1952- .... **CLC 34**
See also CA 126
Robinson, Lloyd
See Silverberg, Robert
Robinson, Marilynne 1944- .... **CLC 25**
See also CA 116
Robinson, Smokey .... **CLC 21**
See also Robinson, William, Jr.
Robinson, William, Jr. 1940-
See Robinson, Smokey
See also CA 116
Robison, Mary 1949- .... **CLC 42, 98**
See also CA 113; 116; DLB 130; INT 116
Rod, Edouard 1857-1910 .... **TCLC 52**
Roddenberry, Eugene Wesley 1921-1991
See Roddenberry, Gene
See also CA 110; 135; CANR 37; SATA 45;
SATA-Obit 69
Roddenberry, Gene .... **CLC 17**
See also Roddenberry, Eugene Wesley
See also AAYA 5; SATA-Obit 69
Rodgers, Mary 1931- .... **CLC 12**
See also CA 49-52; CANR 8, 55; CLR 20; INT
CANR-8; JRDA; MAICYA; SATA 8
Rodgers, W(illiam) R(obert) 1909-1969 **CLC 7**
See also CA 85-88; DLB 20
Rodman, Eric
See Silverberg, Robert
Rodman, Howard 1920(?)-1985 .... **CLC 65**
See also CA 118
Rodman, Maia
See Wojciechowska, Maia (Teresa)
Rodriguez, Claudio 1934- .... **CLC 10**
See also DLB 134
Roelvaag, O(le) E(dvart) 1876-1931 **TCLC 17**
See also CA 117; DLB 9
Roethke, Theodore (Huebner) 1908-1963 **CLC
1, 3, 8, 11, 19, 46, 101; DAM POET; PC 15**
See also CA 81-84; CABS 2; CDALB 1941-
1968; DLB 5; MTCW
Rogers, Thomas Hunton 1927- .... **CLC 57**
See also CA 89-92; INT 89-92
Rogers, Will(iam Penn Adair) 1879-1935
TCLC 8, 71; DAM MULT

See also CA 105; 144; DLB 11; NNAL
Rogin, Gilbert 1929- .... **CLC 18**
See also CA 65-68; CANR 15
Rohan, Koda .... **TCLC 22**
See also Koda Shigeyuki
Rohlfs, Anna Katharine Green
See Green, Anna Katharine
Rohmer, Eric .... **CLC 16**
See also Scherer, Jean-Marie Maurice
Rohmer, Sax .... **TCLC 28**
See also Ward, Arthur Henry Sarsfield
See also DLB 70
Roiphe, Anne (Richardson) 1935- . **CLC 3, 9**
See also CA 89-92; CANR 45; DLBY 80; INT
89-92
Rojas, Fernando de 1465-1541 .... **LC 23**
**Rolfe, Frederick (William Serafino Austin
Lewis Mary)** 1860-1913 .... **TCLC 12**
See also CA 107; DLB 34, 156
Rolland, Romain 1866-1944 .... **TCLC 23**
See also CA 118; DLB 65
Rolle, Richard c. 1300-c. 1349 ...... **CMLC 21**
See also DLB 146
Rolvaag, O(le) E(dvart)
See Roelvaag, O(le) E(dvart)
Romain Arnaud, Saint
See Aragon, Louis
Romains, Jules 1885-1972 .... **CLC 7**
See also CA 85-88; CANR 34; DLB 65; MTCW
Romero, Jose Ruben 1890-1952 ..... **TCLC 14**
See also CA 114; 131; HW
Ronsard, Pierre de 1524-1585 ... **LC 6; PC 11**
Rooke, Leon 1934- .. **CLC 25, 34; DAM POP**
See also CA 25-28R; CANR 23, 53
Roosevelt, Theodore 1858-1919 ..... **TCLC 69**
See also CA 115; DLB 47
Roper, William 1498-1578 .... **LC 10**
Roquelaure, A. N.
See Rice, Anne
Rosa, Joao Guimaraes 1908-1967 ... **CLC 23**
See also CA 89-92; DLB 113
Rose, Wendy 1948- **CLC 85; DAM MULT; PC
13**
See also CA 53-56; CANR 5, 51; DLB 175;
NNAL; SATA 12
Rosen, R. D.
See Rosen, Richard (Dean)
Rosen, Richard (Dean) 1949- .... **CLC 39**
See also CA 77-80; CANR 62; INT CANR-30
Rosenberg, Isaac 1890-1918 .... **TCLC 12**
See also CA 107; DLB 20
Rosenblatt, Joe .... **CLC 15**
See also Rosenblatt, Joseph
Rosenblatt, Joseph 1933-
See Rosenblatt, Joe
See also CA 89-92; INT 89-92
Rosenfeld, Samuel
See Tzara, Tristan
Rosenstock, Sami
See Tzara, Tristan
Rosenstock, Samuel
See Tzara, Tristan
Rosenthal, M(acha) L(ouis) 1917-1996 . **C L C
28**
See also CA 1-4R; 152; CAAS 6; CANR 4, 51;
DLB 5; SATA 59
Ross, Barnaby
See Dannay, Frederic
Ross, Bernard L.
See Follett, Ken(neth Martin)
Ross, J. H.
See Lawrence, T(homas) E(dward)
Ross, Martin

See Martin, Violet Florence
See also DLB 135
Ross, (James) Sinclair 1908- **CLC 13; DAC;
DAM MST; SSC 24**
See also CA 73-76; DLB 88
Rossetti, Christina (Georgina) 1830-1894
**NCLC 2, 50, 66; DA; DAB; DAC; DAM
MST, POET; PC 7; WLC**
See also DLB 35, 163; MAICYA; SATA 20
Rossetti, Dante Gabriel 1828-1882 **NCLC 4;
DA; DAB; DAC; DAM MST, POET; WLC**
See also CDBLB 1832-1890; DLB 35
Rossner, Judith (Perelman) 1935-**CLC 6, 9, 29**
See also AITN 2; BEST 90:3; CA 17-20R;
CANR 18, 51; DLB 6; INT CANR-18;
MTCW
Rostand, Edmond (Eugene Alexis) 1868-1918
**TCLC 6, 37; DA; DAB; DAC; DAM
DRAM, MST**
See also CA 104; 126; MTCW
Roth, Henry 1906-1995 ..... **CLC 2, 6, 11, 104**
See also CA 11-12; 149; CANR 38, 63; CAP 1;
DLB 28; MTCW
Roth, Philip (Milton) 1933-**CLC 1, 2, 3, 4, 6, 9,
15, 22, 31, 47, 66, 86; DA; DAB; DAC;
DAM MST, NOV, POP; SSC 26; WLC**
See also BEST 90:3; CA 1-4R; CANR 1, 22,
36, 55; CDALB 1968-1988; DLB 2, 28, 173;
DLBY 82; MTCW
Rothenberg, Jerome 1931- .... **CLC 6, 57**
See also CA 45-48; CANR 1; DLB 5
Roumain, Jacques (Jean Baptiste) 1907-1944
TCLC 19; BLC; DAM MULT
See also BW 1; CA 117; 125
Rourke, Constance (Mayfield) 1885-1941
TCLC 12
See also CA 107; YABC 1
Rousseau, Jean-Baptiste 1671-1741 ..... **LC 9**
Rousseau, Jean-Jacques 1712-1778**LC 14, 36;
DA; DAB; DAC; DAM MST; WLC**
Roussel, Raymond 1877-1933 .... **TCLC 20**
See also CA 117
Rovit, Earl (Herbert) 1927- .... **CLC 7**
See also CA 5-8R; CANR 12
Rowe, Nicholas 1674-1718 .... **LC 8**
See also DLB 84
Rowley, Ames Dorrance
See Lovecraft, H(oward) P(hillips)
Rowson, Susanna Haswell 1762(?)-1824
NCLC 5
See also DLB 37
Roy, Gabrielle 1909-1983 **CLC 10, 14; DAB;
DAC; DAM MST**
See also CA 53-56; 110; CANR 5, 61; DLB 68;
MTCW
Rozewicz, Tadeusz 1921- ...**CLC 9, 23; DAM
POET**
See also CA 108; CANR 36; MTCW
Ruark, Gibbons 1941- ....**CLC 3**
See also CA 33-36R; CAAS 23; CANR 14, 31,
57; DLB 120
Rubens, Bernice (Ruth) 1923-.... **CLC 19, 31**
See also CA 25-28R; CANR 33; DLB 14;
MTCW
Rubin, Harold
See Robbins, Harold
Rudkin, (James) David 1936- .... **CLC 14**
See also CA 89-92; DLB 13
Rudnik, Raphael 1933- ....**CLC 7**
See also CA 29-32R
Ruffian, M.
See Hasek, Jaroslav (Matej Frantisek)
Ruiz, Jose Martinez...........................**CLC 11**

See also Martinez Ruiz, Jose
Rukeyser, Muriel 1913-1980**CLC 6, 10, 15, 27;
DAM POET; PC 12**
See also CA 5-8R; 93-96; CANR 26, 60; DLB
48; MTCW; SATA-Obit 22
Rule, Jane (Vance) 1931- ....**CLC 27**
See also CA 25-28R; CAAS 18; CANR 12; DLB
60
Rulfo, Juan 1918-1986 ....**CLC 8, 80; DAM
MULT; HLC; SSC 25**
See also CA 85-88; 118; CANR 26; DLB 113;
HW; MTCW
Rumi, Jalal al-Din 1297-1373 .... **CMLC 20**
Runeberg, Johan 1804-1877 .... **NCLC 41**
Runyon, (Alfred) Damon 1884(?)-1946**T C L C
10**
See also CA 107; DLB 11, 86, 171
Rush, Norman 1933- ....**CLC 44**
See also CA 121; 126; INT 126
Rushdie, (Ahmed) Salman 1947-**CLC 23, 31,
55, 100; DAB; DAC; DAM MST, NOV,
POP; WLCS**
See also BEST 89:3; CA 108; 111; CANR 33,
56; INT 111; MTCW
Rushforth, Peter (Scott) 1945- ....**CLC 19**
See also CA 101
Ruskin, John 1819-1900 .... **TCLC 63**
See also CA 114; 129; CDBLB 1832-1890;
DLB 55, 163; SATA 24
Russ, Joanna 1937-............................**CLC 15**
See also CA 25-28R; CANR 11, 31; DLB 8;
MTCW
Russell, George William 1867-1935
See Baker, Jean H.
See also CA 104; 153; CDBLB 1890-1914;
DAM POET
Russell, (Henry) Ken(neth Alfred) 1927-**C L C
16**
See also CA 105
Russell, Willy 1947-............................**CLC 60**
Rutherford, Mark ....**TCLC 25**
See also White, William Hale
See also DLB 18
Ruyslinck, Ward 1929- ....**CLC 14**
See also Belser, Reimond Karel Maria de
Ryan, Cornelius (John) 1920-1974 ..... **CLC 7**
See also CA 69-72; 53-56; CANR 38
Ryan, Michael 1946- ....**CLC 65**
See also CA 49-52; DLBY 82
Ryan, Tim
See Dent, Lester
Rybakov, Anatoli (Naumovich) 1911-**CLC 23,
53**
See also CA 126; 135; SATA 79
Ryder, Jonathan
See Ludlum, Robert
Ryga, George 1932-1987**CLC 14; DAC; DAM
MST**
See also CA 101; 124; CANR 43; DLB 60
S. H.
See Hartmann, Sadakichi
S. S.
See Sassoon, Siegfried (Lorraine)
Saba, Umberto 1883-1957 .... **TCLC 33**
See also CA 144; DLB 114
Sabatini, Rafael 1875-1950 .... **TCLC 47**
Sabato, Ernesto (R.) 1911-**CLC 10, 23; DAM
MULT; HLC**
See also CA 97-100; CANR 32; DLB 145; HW;
MTCW
Sacastru, Martin
See Bioy Casares, Adolfo
Sacher-Masoch, Leopold von 1836(?)-1895

NCLC 31
Sachs, Marilyn (Stickle) 1927- ....**CLC 35**
See also AAYA 2; CA 17-20R; CANR 13, 47;
CLR 2; JRDA; MAICYA; SAAS 2; SATA 3,
68
Sachs, Nelly 1891-1970 .... **CLC 14, 98**
See also CA 17-18; 25-28R; CAP 2
Sackler, Howard (Oliver) 1929-1982 **CLC 14**
See also CA 61-64; 108; CANR 30; DLB 7
Sacks, Oliver (Wolf) 1933-.................**CLC 67**
See also CA 53-56; CANR 28, 50; INT CANR-
28; MTCW
Sadakichi
See Hartmann, Sadakichi
Sade, Donatien Alphonse Francois Comte 1740-
1814 .... **NCLC 47**
Sadoff, Ira 1945-.................................**CLC 9**
See also CA 53-56; CANR 5, 21; DLB 120
Saetone
See Camus, Albert
Safire, William 1929-.........................**CLC 10**
See also CA 17-20R; CANR 31, 54
Sagan, Carl (Edward) 1934-1996 .....**CLC 30**
See also AAYA 2; CA 25-28R; 155; CANR 11,
36; MTCW; SATA 58; SATA-Obit 94
Sagan, Francoise .... **CLC 3, 6, 9, 17, 36**
See also Quoirez, Francoise
See also DLB 83
Sahgal, Nayantara (Pandit) 1927- ....**CLC 41**
See also CA 9-12R; CANR 11
Saint, H(arry) F. 1941- ....**CLC 50**
See also CA 127
St. Aubin de Teran, Lisa 1953-
See Teran, Lisa St. Aubin de
See also CA 118; 126; INT 126
Saint Birgitta of Sweden c. 1303-1373**C M L C
24**
Sainte-Beuve, Charles Augustin 1804-1869
NCLC 5
**Saint-Exupery, Antoine (Jean Baptiste Marie
Roger) de** 1900-1944**TCLC 2, 56; DAM
NOV; WLC**
See also CA 108; 132; CLR 10; DLB 72;
MAICYA; MTCW; SATA 20
St. John, David
See Hunt, E(verette) Howard, (Jr.)
Saint-John Perse
See Leger, (Marie-Rene Auguste) Alexis Saint-
Leger
Saintsbury, George (Edward Bateman) 1845-
1933 .... **TCLC 31**
See also CA 160; DLB 57, 149
Sait Faik .... **TCLC 23**
See also Abasiyanik, Sait Faik
Saki .... **TCLC 3; SSC 12**
See also Munro, H(ector) H(ugh)
Sala, George Augustus .... **NCLC 46**
Salama, Hannu 1936-.........................**CLC 18**
Salamanca, J(ack) R(ichard) 1922-**CLC 4, 15**
See also CA 25-28R
Sale, J. Kirkpatrick
See Sale, Kirkpatrick
Sale, Kirkpatrick 1937- ....**CLC 68**
See also CA 13-16R; CANR 10
Salinas, Luis Omar 1937- ......**CLC 90; DAM
MULT; HLC**
See also CA 131; DLB 82; HW
Salinas (y Serrano), Pedro 1891(?)-1951
TCLC 17
See also CA 117; DLB 134
Salinger, J(erome) D(avid) 1919-**CLC 1, 3, 8,
12, 55, 56; DA; DAB; DAC; DAM MST,
NOV, POP; SSC 2, 28; WLC**

See also AAYA 2; CA 5-8R; CANR 39; CDALB 1941-1968; CLR 18; DLB 2, 102, 173; MAICYA; MTCW; SATA 67

Salisbury, John
See Caute, (John) David

Salter, James 1925- .... **CLC 7, 52, 59**
See also CA 73-76; DLB 130

Saltus, Edgar (Everton) 1855-1921 . **TCLC 8**
See also CA 105

Saltykov, Mikhail Evgrafovich 1826-1889
    NCLC 16

Samarakis, Antonis 1919- .... **CLC 5**
See also CA 25-28R; CAAS 16; CANR 36

Sanchez, Florencio 1875-1910 .... **TCLC 37**
See also CA 153; HW

Sanchez, Luis Rafael 1936- .... **CLC 23**
See also CA 128; DLB 145; HW

Sanchez, Sonia 1934- ..... **CLC 5; BLC; DAM MULT; PC 9**
See also BW 2; CA 33-36R; CANR 24, 49; CLR 18; DLB 41; DLBD 8; MAICYA; MTCW; SATA 22

Sand, George 1804-1876 **NCLC 2, 42, 57; DA; DAB; DAC; DAM MST, NOV; WLC**
See also DLB 119

Sandburg, Carl (August) 1878-1967 **CLC 1, 4, 10, 15, 35; DA; DAB; DAC; DAM MST, POET; WLC**
See also CA 5-8R; 25-28R; CANR 35; CDALB 1865-1917; DLB 17, 54; MAICYA; MTCW; SATA 8

Sandburg, Charles
See Sandburg, Carl (August)

Sandburg, Charles A.
See Sandburg, Carl (August)

Sanders, (James) Ed(ward) 1939- .... **CLC 53**
See also CA 13-16R; CAAS 21; CANR 13, 44; DLB 16

Sanders, Lawrence 1920-1998 **CLC 41; DAM POP**
See also BEST 89:4; CA 81-84; CANR 33, 62; MTCW

Sanders, Noah
See Blount, Roy (Alton), Jr.

Sanders, Winston P.
See Anderson, Poul (William)

Sandoz, Mari(e Susette) 1896-1966 . **CLC 28**
See also CA 1-4R; 25-28R; CANR 17, 64; DLB 9; MTCW; SATA 5

Saner, Reg(inald Anthony) 1931- .... **CLC 9**
See also CA 65-68

Sannazaro, Jacopo 1456(?)-1530 .... **LC 8**

Sansom, William 1912-1976 **CLC 2, 6; DAM NOV; SSC 21**
See also CA 5-8R; 65-68; CANR 42; DLB 139; MTCW

Santayana, George 1863-1952 .... **TCLC 40**
See also CA 115; DLB 54, 71; DLBD 13

Santiago, Danny .... **CLC 33**
See also James, Daniel (Lewis)
See also DLB 122

Santmyer, Helen Hoover 1895-1986 **CLC 33**
See also CA 1-4R; 118; CANR 15, 33; DLBY 84; MTCW

Santoka, Taneda 1882-1940 .... **TCLC 72**

Santos, Bienvenido N(uqui) 1911-1996 . **C L C 22; DAM MULT**
See also CA 101; 151; CANR 19, 46

Sapper .... **TCLC 44**
See also McNeile, Herman Cyril

Sapphire 1950- .... **CLC 99**

Sappho fl. 6th cent. B.C.- ...... **CMLC 3; DAM POET; PC 5**

See also DLB 176

Sarduy, Severo 1937-1993 .... **CLC 6, 97**
See also CA 89-92; 142; CANR 58; DLB 113; HW

Sargeson, Frank 1903-1982 .... **CLC 31**
See also CA 25-28R; 106; CANR 38

Sarmiento, Felix Ruben Garcia
See Dario, Ruben

Saroyan, William 1908-1981 **CLC 1, 8, 10, 29, 34, 56; DA; DAB; DAC; DAM DRAM, MST, NOV; SSC 21; WLC**
See also CA 5-8R; 103; CANR 30; DLB 7, 9, 86; DLBY 81; MTCW; SATA 23; SATA-Obit 24

Sarraute, Nathalie 1900- **CLC 1, 2, 4, 8, 10, 31, 80**
See also CA 9-12R; CANR 23; DLB 83; MTCW

Sarton, (Eleanor) May 1912-1995 **CLC 4, 14, 49, 91; DAM POET**
See also CA 1-4R; 149; CANR 1, 34, 55; DLB 48; DLBY 81; INT CANR-34; MTCW; SATA 36; SATA-Obit 86

Sartre, Jean-Paul 1905-1980 **CLC 1, 4, 7, 9, 13, 18, 24, 44, 50, 52; DA; DAB; DAC; DAM DRAM, MST, NOV; DC 3; WLC**
See also CA 9-12R; 97-100; CANR 21; DLB 72; MTCW

Sassoon, Siegfried (Lorraine) 1886-1967 **C L C 36; DAB; DAM MST, NOV, POET; PC 12**
See also CA 104; 25-28R; CANR 36; DLB 20; MTCW

Satterfield, Charles
See Pohl, Frederik

Saul, John (W. III) 1942- **CLC 46; DAM NOV, POP**
See also AAYA 10; BEST 90:4; CA 81-84; CANR 16, 40

Saunders, Caleb
See Heinlein, Robert A(nson)

Saura (Atares), Carlos 1932- .... **CLC 20**
See also CA 114; 131; HW

Sauser-Hall, Frederic 1887-1961 ...... **CLC 18**
See also Cendrars, Blaise
See also CA 102; 93-96; CANR 36, 62; MTCW

Saussure, Ferdinand de 1857-1913 **TCLC 49**

Savage, Catharine
See Brosman, Catharine Savage

Savage, Thomas 1915- .... **CLC 40**
See also CA 126; 132; CAAS 15; INT 132

Savan, Glenn 19(?)- .... **CLC 50**

Sayers, Dorothy L(eigh) 1893-1957 **TCLC 2, 15; DAM POP**
See also CA 104; 119; CANR 60; CDBLB 1914-1945; DLB 10, 36, 77, 100; MTCW

Sayers, Valerie 1952- .... **CLC 50**
See also CA 134; CANR 61

Sayles, John (Thomas) 1950- . **CLC 7, 10, 14**
See also CA 57-60; CANR 41; DLB 44

Scammell, Michael 1935- .... **CLC 34**
See also CA 156

Scannell, Vernon 1922- .... **CLC 49**
See also CA 5-8R; CANR 8, 24, 57; DLB 27; SATA 59

Scarlett, Susan
See Streatfeild, (Mary) Noel

Schaeffer, Susan Fromberg 1941- **CLC 6, 11, 22**
See also CA 49-52; CANR 18; DLB 28; MTCW; SATA 22

Schary, Jill
See Robinson, Jill

Schell, Jonathan 1943- .... **CLC 35**
See also CA 73-76; CANR 12

Schelling, Friedrich Wilhelm Joseph von 1775-1854 .... **NCLC 30**
See also DLB 90

Schendel, Arthur van 1874-1946 ... **TCLC 56**

Scherer, Jean-Marie Maurice 1920-
See Rohmer, Eric
See also CA 110

Schevill, James (Erwin) 1920- .... **CLC 7**
See also CA 5-8R; CAAS 12

Schiller, Friedrich 1759-1805 **NCLC 39; DAM DRAM**
See also DLB 94

Schisgal, Murray (Joseph) 1926- .... **CLC 6**
See also CA 21-24R; CANR 48

Schlee, Ann 1934- .... **CLC 35**
See also CA 101; CANR 29; SATA 44; SATA-Brief 36

Schlegel, August Wilhelm von 1767-1845
    NCLC 15
See also DLB 94

Schlegel, Friedrich 1772-1829 .... **NCLC 45**
See also DLB 90

Schlegel, Johann Elias (von) 1719(?)-1749 **L C 5**

Schlesinger, Arthur M(eier), Jr. 1917- **CLC 84**
See also AITN 1; CA 1-4R; CANR 1, 28, 58; DLB 17; INT CANR-28; MTCW; SATA 61

Schmidt, Arno (Otto) 1914-1979 ...... **CLC 56**
See also CA 128; 109; DLB 69

Schmitz, Aron Hector 1861-1928
See Svevo, Italo
See also CA 104; 122; MTCW

Schnackenberg, Gjertrud 1953- ...... **CLC 40**
See also CA 116; DLB 120

Schneider, Leonard Alfred 1925-1966
See Bruce, Lenny
See also CA 89-92

Schnitzler, Arthur 1862-1931 **TCLC 4; SSC 15**
See also CA 104; DLB 81, 118

Schoenberg, Arnold 1874-1951 ...... **TCLC 75**
See also CA 109

Schonberg, Arnold
See Schoenberg, Arnold

Schopenhauer, Arthur 1788-1860 .. **NCLC 51**
See also DLB 90

Schor, Sandra (M.) 1932(?)-1990 ..... **CLC 65**
See also CA 132

Schorer, Mark 1908-1977 .... **CLC 9**
See also CA 5-8R; 73-76; CANR 7; DLB 103

Schrader, Paul (Joseph) 1946- .... **CLC 26**
See also CA 37-40R; CANR 41; DLB 44

Schreiner, Olive (Emilie Albertina) 1855-1920
    TCLC 9
See also CA 105; DLB 18, 156

Schulberg, Budd (Wilson) 1914- .. **CLC 7, 48**
See also CA 25-28R; CANR 19; DLB 6, 26, 28; DLBY 81

Schulz, Bruno 1892-1942 **TCLC 5, 51; SSC 13**
See also CA 115; 123

Schulz, Charles M(onroe) 1922- ...... **CLC 12**
See also CA 9-12R; CANR 6; INT CANR-6; SATA 10

Schumacher, E(rnst) F(riedrich) 1911-1977
    CLC 80
See also CA 81-84; 73-76; CANR 34

Schuyler, James Marcus 1923-1991 **CLC 5, 23; DAM POET**
See also CA 101; 134; DLB 5, 169; INT 101

Schwartz, Delmore (David) 1913-1966 **CLC 2, 4, 10, 45, 87; PC 8**
See also CA 17-18; 25-28R; CANR 35; CAP 2; DLB 28, 48; MTCW

Schwartz, Ernst

See Ozu, Yasujiro

Schwartz, John Burnham 1965- ...... **CLC 59**
See also CA 132

Schwartz, Lynne Sharon 1939- .... **CLC 31**
See also CA 103; CANR 44

Schwartz, Muriel A.
See Eliot, T(homas) S(tearns)

Schwarz-Bart, Andre 1928-........... **CLC 2, 4**
See also CA 89-92

Schwarz-Bart, Simone 1938-.............. **CLC 7**
See also BW 2; CA 97-100

Schwob, (Mayer Andre) Marcel 1867-1905
TCLC 20
See also CA 117; DLB 123

Sciascia, Leonardo 1921-1989 . **CLC 8, 9, 41**
See also CA 85-88; 130; CANR 35; DLB 177;
MTCW

Scoppettone, Sandra 1936- .... **CLC 26**
See also AAYA 11; CA 5-8R; CANR 41; SATA
9, 92

Scorsese, Martin 1942- .... **CLC 20, 89**
See also CA 110; 114; CANR 46

Scotland, Jay
See Jakes, John (William)

Scott, Duncan Campbell 1862-1947 **TCLC 6;
DAC**
See also CA 104; 153; DLB 92

Scott, Evelyn 1893-1963 .... **CLC 43**
See also CA 104; 112; CANR 64; DLB 9, 48

Scott, F(rancis) R(eginald) 1899-1985 **CLC 22**
See also CA 101; 114; DLB 88; INT 101

Scott, Frank
See Scott, F(rancis) R(eginald)

Scott, Joanna 1960- .... **CLC 50**
See also CA 126; CANR 53

Scott, Paul (Mark) 1920-1978 ...... **CLC 9, 60**
See also CA 81-84; 77-80; CANR 33; DLB 14;
MTCW

Scott, Walter 1771-1832 **NCLC 15; DA; DAB;
DAC; DAM MST, NOV, POET; PC 13;
WLC**
See also AAYA 22; CDBLB 1789-1832; DLB
93, 107, 116, 144, 159; YABC 2

Scribe, (Augustin) Eugene 1791-1861 **N C L C
16; DAM DRAM; DC 5**

Scrum, R.
See Crumb, R(obert)

Scudery, Madeleine de 1607-1701 .... **LC 2**

Scum
See Crumb, R(obert)

Scumbag, Little Bobby
See Crumb, R(obert)

Seabrook, John
See Hubbard, L(afayette) Ron(ald)

Sealy, I. Allan 1951- .... **CLC 55**

Search, Alexander
See Pessoa, Fernando (Antonio Nogueira)

Sebastian, Lee
See Silverberg, Robert

Sebastian Owl
See Thompson, Hunter S(tockton)

Sebestyen, Ouida 1924-..................... **CLC 30**
See also AAYA 8; CA 107; CANR 40; CLR 17;
JRDA; MAICYA; SAAS 10; SATA 39

Secundus, H. Scriblerus
See Fielding, Henry

Sedges, John
See Buck, Pearl S(ydenstricker)

Sedgwick, Catharine Maria 1789-1867 **N C L C
19**
See also DLB 1, 74

Seelye, John 1931- .... **CLC 7**

Seferiades, Giorgos Stylianou 1900-1971

See Seferis, George
See also CA 5-8R; 33-36R; CANR 5, 36;
MTCW

Seferis, George .... **CLC 5, 11**
See also Seferiades, Giorgos Stylianou

Segal, Erich (Wolf) 1937- ..**CLC 3, 10; DAM
POP**
See also BEST 89:1; CA 25-28R; CANR 20,
36; DLBY 86; INT CANR-20; MTCW

Seger, Bob 1945- ....**CLC 35**

Seghers, Anna ....**CLC 7**
See also Radvanyi, Netty
See also DLB 69

Seidel, Frederick (Lewis) 1936- ....**CLC 18**
See also CA 13-16R; CANR 8; DLBY 84

Seifert, Jaroslav 1901-1986 .. **CLC 34, 44, 93**
See also CA 127; MTCW

Sei Shonagon c. 966-1017(?) .... **CMLC 6**

Selby, Hubert, Jr. 1928- **CLC 1, 2, 4, 8; SSC 20**
See also CA 13-16R; CANR 33; DLB 2

Selzer, Richard 1928- .... **CLC 74**
See also CA 65-68; CANR 14

Sembene, Ousmane
See Ousmane, Sembene

Senancour, Etienne Pivert de 1770-1846
NCLC 16
See also DLB 119

Sender, Ramon (Jose) 1902-1982 **CLC 8; DAM
MULT; HLC**
See also CA 5-8R; 105; CANR 8; HW; MTCW

Seneca, Lucius Annaeus 4B.C.-65 **CMLC 6;
DAM DRAM; DC 5**

Senghor, Leopold Sedar 1906- **CLC 54; BLC;
DAM MULT, POET**
See also BW 2; CA 116; 125; CANR 47; MTCW

Serling, (Edward) Rod(man) 1924-1975 **C L C
30**
See also AAYA 14; AITN 1; CA 65-68; 57-60;
DLB 26

Serna, Ramon Gomez de la
See Gomez de la Serna, Ramon

Serpieres
See Guillevic, (Eugene)

Service, Robert
See Service, Robert W(illiam)
See also DAB; DLB 92

Service, Robert W(illiam) 1874(?)-1958 **TCLC
15; DA; DAC; DAM MST, POET; WLC**
See also Service, Robert
See also CA 115; 140; SATA 20

Seth, Vikram 1952- **CLC 43, 90; DAM MULT**
See also CA 121; 127; CANR 50; DLB 120;
INT 127

Seton, Cynthia Propper 1926-1982 ..**CLC 27**
See also CA 5-8R; 108; CANR 7

Seton, Ernest (Evan) Thompson 1860-1946
TCLC 31
See also CA 109; DLB 92; DLBD 13; JRDA;
SATA 18

Seton-Thompson, Ernest
See Seton, Ernest (Evan) Thompson

Settle, Mary Lee 1918- .... **CLC 19, 61**
See also CA 89-92; CAAS 1; CANR 44; DLB
6; INT 89-92

Seuphor, Michel
See Arp, Jean

**Sevigne, Marie (de Rabutin-Chantal) Marquise
de** 1626-1696 .... **LC 11**

Sewall, Samuel 1652-1730 .... **LC 38**
See also DLB 24

Sexton, Anne (Harvey) 1928-1974 **CLC 2, 4, 6,
8, 10, 15, 53; DA; DAB; DAC; DAM MST,
POET; PC 2; WLC**

See also CA 1-4R; 53-56; CABS 2; CANR 3,
36; CDALB 1941-1968; DLB 5, 169;
MTCW; SATA 10

Shaara, Michael (Joseph, Jr.) 1929-1988 **C L C
15; DAM POP**
See also AITN 1; CA 102; 125; CANR 52;
DLBY 83

Shackleton, C. C.
See Aldiss, Brian W(ilson)

Shacochis, Bob ....**CLC 39**
See also Shacochis, Robert G.

Shacochis, Robert G. 1951-
See Shacochis, Bob
See also CA 119; 124; INT 124

Shaffer, Anthony (Joshua) 1926- .... **CLC 19;
DAM DRAM**
See also CA 110; 116; DLB 13

Shaffer, Peter (Levin) 1926- **CLC 5, 14, 18, 37,
60; DAB; DAM DRAM, MST; DC 7**
See also CA 25-28R; CANR 25, 47; CDBLB
1960 to Present; DLB 13; MTCW

Shakey, Bernard
See Young, Neil

Shalamov, Varlam (Tikhonovich) 1907(?)-1982
CLC 18
See also CA 129; 105

Shamlu, Ahmad 1925- .... **CLC 10**

Shammas, Anton 1951- .... **CLC 55**

Shange, Ntozake 1948- **CLC 8, 25, 38, 74; BLC;
DAM DRAM, MULT; DC 3**
See also AAYA 9; BW 2; CA 85-88; CABS 3;
CANR 27, 48; DLB 38; MTCW

Shanley, John Patrick 1950- .... **CLC 75**
See also CA 128; 133

Shapcott, Thomas W(illiam) 1935- ... **CLC 38**
See also CA 69-72; CANR 49

Shapiro, Jane ....**CLC 76**

Shapiro, Karl (Jay) 1913- ... **CLC 4, 8, 15, 53**
See also CA 1-4R; CAAS 6; CANR 1, 36; DLB
48; MTCW

Sharp, William 1855-1905 .... **TCLC 39**
See also CA 160; DLB 156

Sharpe, Thomas Ridley 1928-
See Sharpe, Tom
See also CA 114; 122; INT 122

Sharpe, Tom ....**CLC 36**
See also Sharpe, Thomas Ridley
See also DLB 14

Shaw, Bernard .... **TCLC 45**
See also Shaw, George Bernard
See also BW 1

Shaw, G. Bernard
See Shaw, George Bernard

Shaw, George Bernard 1856-1950 **TCLC 3, 9,
21; DA; DAB; DAC; DAM DRAM, MST;
WLC**
See also Shaw, Bernard
See also CA 104; 128; CDBLB 1914-1945;
DLB 10, 57; MTCW

Shaw, Henry Wheeler 1818-1885 .. **NCLC 15**
See also DLB 11

Shaw, Irwin 1913-1984 **CLC 7, 23, 34; DAM
DRAM, POP**
See also AITN 1; CA 13-16R; 112; CANR 21;
CDALB 1941-1968; DLB 6, 102; DLBY 84;
MTCW

Shaw, Robert 1927-1978 .... **CLC 5**
See also AITN 1; CA 1-4R; 81-84; CANR 4;
DLB 13, 14

Shaw, T. E.
See Lawrence, T(homas) E(dward)

Shawn, Wallace 1943- .... **CLC 41**
See also CA 112

Shea, Lisa 1953-................................. **CLC 86**
See also CA 147

Sheed, Wilfrid (John Joseph) 1930-**CLC 2, 4, 10, 53**
See also CA 65-68; CANR 30; DLB 6; MTCW

Sheldon, Alice Hastings Bradley 1915(?)-1987
See Tiptree, James, Jr.
See also CA 108; 122; CANR 34; INT 108; MTCW

Sheldon, John
See Bloch, Robert (Albert)

Shelley, Mary Wollstonecraft (Godwin) 1797-1851**NCLC 14, 59; DA; DAB; DAC; DAM MST, NOV; WLC**
See also AAYA 20; CDBLB 1789-1832; DLB 110, 116, 159, 178; SATA 29

Shelley, Percy Bysshe 1792-1822 . **NCLC 18; DA; DAB; DAC; DAM MST, POET; PC 14; WLC**
See also CDBLB 1789-1832; DLB 96, 110, 158

Shepard, Jim 1956- .... **CLC 36**
See also CA 137; CANR 59; SATA 90

Shepard, Lucius 1947- .... **CLC 34**
See also CA 128; 141

Shepard, Sam 1943-**CLC 4, 6, 17, 34, 41, 44; DAM DRAM; DC 5**
See also AAYA 1; CA 69-72; CABS 3; CANR 22; DLB 7; MTCW

Shepherd, Michael
See Ludlum, Robert

Sherburne, Zoa (Morin) 1912- .... **CLC 30**
See also AAYA 13; CA 1-4R; CANR 3, 37; MAICYA; SAAS 18; SATA 3

Sheridan, Frances 1724-1766 .... **LC 7**
See also DLB 39, 84

Sheridan, Richard Brinsley 1751-1816**NCLC 5; DA; DAB; DAC; DAM DRAM, MST; DC 1; WLC**
See also CDBLB 1660-1789; DLB 89

Sherman, Jonathan Marc .... **CLC 55**

Sherman, Martin 1941(?)- .... **CLC 19**
See also CA 116; 123

Sherwin, Judith Johnson 1936- ... **CLC 7, 15**
See also CA 25-28R; CANR 34

Sherwood, Frances 1940- .... **CLC 81**
See also CA 146

Sherwood, Robert E(mmet) 1896-1955**TCLC 3; DAM DRAM**
See also CA 104; 153; DLB 7, 26

Shestov, Lev 1866-1938 .... **TCLC 56**

Shevchenko, Taras 1814-1861 .... **NCLC 54**

Shiel, M(atthew) P(hipps) 1865-1947**TCLC 8**
See Holmes, Gordon
See also CA 106; 160; DLB 153

Shields, Carol 1935- .... **CLC 91; DAC**
See also CA 81-84; CANR 51

Shields, David 1956- .... **CLC 97**
See also CA 124; CANR 48

Shiga, Naoya 1883-1971 ..... **CLC 33; SSC 23**
See also CA 101; 33-36R; DLB 180

Shilts, Randy 1951-1994 .... **CLC 85**
See also AAYA 19; CA 115; 127; 144; CANR 45; INT 127

Shimazaki, Haruki 1872-1943
See Shimazaki Toson
See also CA 105; 134

Shimazaki Toson 1872-1943 .... **TCLC 5**
See also Shimazaki, Haruki
See also DLB 180

Sholokhov, Mikhail (Aleksandrovich) 1905-1984 .... **CLC 7, 15**
See also CA 101; 112; MTCW; SATA-Obit 36

Shone, Patric

See Hanley, James

Shreve, Susan Richards 1939-........... **CLC 23**
See also CA 49-52; CAAS 5; CANR 5, 38; MAICYA; SATA 46, 95; SATA-Brief 41

Shue, Larry 1946-1985**CLC 52; DAM DRAM**
See also CA 145; 117

Shu-Jen, Chou 1881-1936
See Lu Hsun
See also CA 104

Shulman, Alix Kates 1932- .... **CLC 2, 10**
See also CA 29-32R; CANR 43; SATA 7

Shuster, Joe 1914- .... **CLC 21**

Shute, Nevil .... **CLC 30**
See also Norway, Nevil Shute

Shuttle, Penelope (Diane) 1947- .... **CLC 7**
See also CA 93-96; CANR 39; DLB 14, 40

Sidney, Mary 1561-1621 .... **LC 19, 39**

Sidney, Sir Philip 1554-1586 **LC 19, 39; DA; DAB; DAC; DAM MST, POET**
See also CDBLB Before 1660; DLB 167

Siegel, Jerome 1914-1996 .... **CLC 21**
See also CA 116; 151

Siegel, Jerry
See Siegel, Jerome

Sienkiewicz, Henryk (Adam Alexander Pius) 1846-1916 .... **TCLC 3**
See also CA 104; 134

Sierra, Gregorio Martinez
See Martinez Sierra, Gregorio

Sierra, Maria (de la O'LeJarraga) Martinez
See Martinez Sierra, Maria (de la O'LeJarraga)

Sigal, Clancy 1926-............................... **CLC 7**
See also CA 1-4R

Sigourney, Lydia Howard (Huntley) 1791-1865 **NCLC 21**
See also DLB 1, 42, 73

Siguenza y Gongora, Carlos de 1645-1700**LC 8**

Sigurjonsson, Johann 1880-1919 ... **TCLC 27**

Sikelianos, Angelos 1884-1951 .... **TCLC 39**

Silkin, Jon 1930- .... **CLC 2, 6, 43**
See also CA 5-8R; CAAS 5; DLB 27

Silko, Leslie (Marmon) 1948-**CLC 23, 74; DA; DAC; DAM MST, MULT, POP; WLCS**
See also AAYA 14; CA 115; 122; CANR 45; DLB 143, 175; NNAL

Sillanpaa, Frans Eemil 1888-1964 .... **CLC 19**
See also CA 129; 93-96; MTCW

Sillitoe, Alan 1928- .... **CLC 1, 3, 6, 10, 19, 57**
See also AITN 1; CA 9-12R; CAAS 2; CANR 8, 26, 55; CDBLB 1960 to Present; DLB 14, 139; MTCW; SATA 61

Silone, Ignazio 1900-1978 .... **CLC 4**
See also CA 25-28; 81-84; CANR 34; CAP 2; MTCW

Silver, Joan Micklin 1935- .... **CLC 20**
See also CA 114; 121; INT 121

Silver, Nicholas
See Faust, Frederick (Schiller)

Silverberg, Robert 1935- **CLC 7; DAM POP**
See also CA 1-4R; CAAS 3; CANR 1, 20, 36; DLB 8; INT CANR-20; MAICYA; MTCW; SATA 13, 91

Silverstein, Alvin 1933- .... **CLC 17**
See also CA 49-52; CANR 2; CLR 25; JRDA; MAICYA; SATA 8, 69

Silverstein, Virginia B(arbara Opshelor) 1937-**CLC 17**
See also CA 49-52; CANR 2; CLR 25; JRDA; MAICYA; SATA 8, 69

Sim, Georges
See Simenon, Georges (Jacques Christian)

Simak, Clifford D(onald) 1904-1988**CLC 1, 55**

See also CA 1-4R; 125; CANR 1, 35; DLB 8; MTCW; SATA-Obit 56

Simenon, Georges (Jacques Christian) 1903-1989 .. **CLC 1, 2, 3, 8, 18, 47; DAM POP**
See also CA 85-88; 129; CANR 35; DLB 72; DLBY 89; MTCW

Simic, Charles 1938- ....**CLC 6, 9, 22, 49, 68; DAM POET**
See also CA 29-32R; CAAS 4; CANR 12, 33, 52, 61; DLB 105

Simmel, Georg 1858-1918 .... **TCLC 64**
See also CA 157

Simmons, Charles (Paul) 1924-........ **CLC 57**
See also CA 89-92; INT 89-92

Simmons, Dan 1948-...... **CLC 44; DAM POP**
See also AAYA 16; CA 138; CANR 53

Simmons, James (Stewart Alexander) 1933-**CLC 43**
See also CA 105; CAAS 21; DLB 40

Simms, William Gilmore 1806-1870 **NCLC 3**
See also DLB 3, 30, 59, 73

Simon, Carly 1945-............................ **CLC 26**
See also CA 105

Simon, Claude 1913-1984 ..**CLC 4, 9, 15, 39; DAM NOV**
See also CA 89-92; CANR 33; DLB 83; MTCW

Simon, (Marvin) Neil 1927-**CLC 6, 11, 31, 39, 70; DAM DRAM**
See also AITN 1; CA 21-24R; CANR 26, 54; DLB 7; MTCW

Simon, Paul (Frederick) 1941(?)-..... **CLC 17**
See also CA 116; 153

Simonon, Paul 1956(?)- .... **CLC 30**

Simpson, Harriette
See Arnow, Harriette (Louisa) Simpson

Simpson, Louis (Aston Marantz) 1923-**CLC 4, 7, 9, 32; DAM POET**
See also CA 1-4R; CAAS 4; CANR 1, 61; DLB 5; MTCW

Simpson, Mona (Elizabeth) 1957- ... **CLC 44**
See also CA 122; 135

Simpson, N(orman) F(rederick) 1919-**CLC 29**
See also CA 13-16R; DLB 13

Sinclair, Andrew (Annandale) 1935-.**CLC 2, 14**
See also CA 9-12R; CAAS 5; CANR 14, 38; DLB 14; MTCW

Sinclair, Emil
See Hesse, Hermann

Sinclair, Iain 1943- .... **CLC 76**
See also CA 132

Sinclair, Iain MacGregor
See Sinclair, Iain

Sinclair, Irene
See Griffith, D(avid Lewelyn) W(ark)

Sinclair, Mary Amelia St. Clair 1865(?)-1946
See Sinclair, May
See also CA 104

Sinclair, May .... **TCLC 3, 11**
See also Sinclair, Mary Amelia St. Clair
See also DLB 36, 135

Sinclair, Roy
See Griffith, D(avid Lewelyn) W(ark)

Sinclair, Upton (Beall) 1878-1968 **CLC 1, 11, 15, 63; DA; DAB; DAC; DAM MST, NOV; WLC**
See also CA 5-8R; 25-28R; CANR 7; CDALB 1929-1941; DLB 9; INT CANR-7; MTCW; SATA 9

Singer, Isaac
See Singer, Isaac Bashevis

Singer, Isaac Bashevis 1904-1991**CLC 1, 3, 6, 9, 11, 15, 23, 38, 69; DA; DAB; DAC; DAM**

MST, NOV; SSC 3; WLC
See also AITN 1, 2; CA 1-4R; 134; CANR 1,
39; CDALB 1941-1968; CLR 1; DLB 6, 28,
52; DLBY 91; JRDA; MAICYA; MTCW;
SATA 3, 27; SATA-Obit 68
Singer, Israel Joshua 1893-1944 .... **TCLC 33**
Singh, Khushwant 1915- .... **CLC 11**
See also CA 9-12R; CAAS 9; CANR 6
Singleton, Ann
See Benedict, Ruth (Fulton)
Sinjohn, John
See Galsworthy, John
Sinyavsky, Andrei (Donatevich) 1925-1997
CLC 8
See also CA 85-88; 159
Sirin, V.
See Nabokov, Vladimir (Vladimirovich)
Sissman, L(ouis) E(dward) 1928-1976**CLC 9,
18**
See also CA 21-24R; 65-68; CANR 13; DLB 5
Sisson, C(harles) H(ubert) 1914- .... **CLC 8**
See also CA 1-4R; CAAS 3; CANR 3, 48; DLB
27
Sitwell, Dame Edith 1887-1964**CLC 2, 9, 67;
DAM POET; PC 3**
See also CA 9-12R; CANR 35; CDBLB 1945-
1960; DLB 20; MTCW
Siwaarmill, H. P.
See Sharp, William
Sjoewall, Maj 1935-............................. **CLC 7**
See also CA 65-68
Sjowall, Maj
See Sjoewall, Maj
Skelton, Robin 1925-1997 .... **CLC 13**
See also AITN 2; CA 5-8R; 160; CAAS 5;
CANR 28; DLB 27, 53
Skolimowski, Jerzy 1938- .... **CLC 20**
See also CA 128
Skram, Amalie (Bertha) 1847-1905 **TCLC 25**
Skvorecky, Josef (Vaclav) 1924- **CLC 15, 39,
69; DAC; DAM NOV**
See also CA 61-64; CAAS 1; CANR 10, 34,
63; MTCW
Slade, Bernard .... **CLC 11, 46**
See also Newbound, Bernard Slade
See also CAAS 9; DLB 53
Slaughter, Carolyn 1946- .... **CLC 56**
See also CA 85-88
Slaughter, Frank G(ill) 1908- .... **CLC 29**
See also AITN 2; CA 5-8R; CANR 5; INT
CANR-5
Slavitt, David R(ytman) 1935- ..... **CLC 5, 14**
See also CA 21-24R; CAAS 3; CANR 41; DLB
5, 6
Slesinger, Tess 1905-1945 .... **TCLC 10**
See also CA 107; DLB 102
Slessor, Kenneth 1901-1971 .... **CLC 14**
See also CA 102; 89-92
Slowacki, Juliusz 1809-1849........... **NCLC 15**
Smart, Christopher 1722-1771...**LC 3; DAM
POET; PC 13**
See also DLB 109
Smart, Elizabeth 1913-1986 .... **CLC 54**
See also CA 81-84; 118; DLB 88
Smiley, Jane (Graves) 1949-**CLC 53, 76; DAM
POP**
See also CA 104; CANR 30, 50; INT CANR-
30
Smith, A(rthur) J(ames) M(arshall) 1902-1980
CLC 15; DAC
See also CA 1-4R; 102; CANR 4; DLB 88
Smith, Adam 1723-1790 .... **LC 36**
See also DLB 104

Smith, Alexander 1829-1867 .... **NCLC 59**
See also DLB 32, 55
Smith, Anna Deavere 1950- .... **CLC 86**
See also CA 133
Smith, Betty (Wehner) 1896-1972 ..... **CLC 19**
See also CA 5-8R; 33-36R; DLBY 82; SATA 6
Smith, Charlotte (Turner) 1749-1806 **N C L C
23**
See also DLB 39, 109
Smith, Clark Ashton 1893-1961 .... **CLC 43**
See also CA 143
Smith, Dave .... **CLC 22, 42**
See also Smith, David (Jeddie)
See also CAAS 7; DLB 5
Smith, David (Jeddie) 1942-
See Smith, Dave
See also CA 49-52; CANR 1, 59; DAM POET
Smith, Florence Margaret 1902-1971
See Smith, Stevie
See also CA 17-18; 29-32R; CANR 35; CAP 2;
DAM POET; MTCW
Smith, Iain Crichton 1928- .... **CLC 64**
See also CA 21-24R; DLB 40, 139
Smith, John 1580(?)-1631 .... **LC 9**
Smith, Johnston
See Crane, Stephen (Townley)
Smith, Joseph, Jr. 1805-1844 .... **NCLC 53**
Smith, Lee 1944- .... **CLC 25, 73**
See also CA 114; 119; CANR 46; DLB 143;
DLBY 83; INT 119
Smith, Martin
See Smith, Martin Cruz
Smith, Martin Cruz 1942- ..... **CLC 25; DAM
MULT, POP**
See also BEST 89:4; CA 85-88; CANR 6, 23,
43; INT CANR-23; NNAL
Smith, Mary-Ann Tirone 1944- .... **CLC 39**
See also CA 118; 136
Smith, Patti 1946- .... **CLC 12**
See also CA 93-96; CANR 63
Smith, Pauline (Urmson) 1882-1959**TCLC 25**
Smith, Rosamond
See Oates, Joyce Carol
Smith, Sheila Kaye
See Kaye-Smith, Sheila
Smith, Stevie .... **CLC 3, 8, 25, 44; PC 12**
See also Smith, Florence Margaret
See also DLB 20
Smith, Wilbur (Addison) 1933- .... **CLC 33**
See also CA 13-16R; CANR 7, 46; MTCW
Smith, William Jay 1918- .... **CLC 6**
See also CA 5-8R; CANR 44; DLB 5; MAICYA;
SAAS 22; SATA 2, 68
Smith, Woodrow Wilson
See Kuttner, Henry
Smolenskin, Peretz 1842-1885 .... **NCLC 30**
Smollett, Tobias (George) 1721-1771 ... **LC 2**
See also CDBLB 1660-1789; DLB 39, 104
Snodgrass, W(illiam) D(e Witt) 1926-**CLC 2,
6, 10, 18, 68; DAM POET**
See also CA 1-4R; CANR 6, 36; DLB 5; MTCW
Snow, C(harles) P(ercy) 1905-1980**CLC 1, 4,
6, 9, 13, 19; DAM NOV**
See also CA 5-8R; 101; CANR 28; CDBLB
1945-1960; DLB 15, 77; MTCW
Snow, Frances Compton
See Adams, Henry (Brooks)
Snyder, Gary (Sherman) 1930-**CLC 1, 2, 5, 9,
32; DAM POET; PC 21**
See also CA 17-20R; CANR 30, 60; DLB 5,
16, 165
Snyder, Zilpha Keatley 1927-............ **CLC 17**
See also AAYA 15; CA 9-12R; CANR 38; CLR

31; JRDA; MAICYA; SAAS 2; SATA 1, 28,
75
Soares, Bernardo
See Pessoa, Fernando (Antonio Nogueira)
Sobh, A.
See Shamlu, Ahmad
Sobol, Joshua .... **CLC 60**
Soderberg, Hjalmar 1869-1941 ..... **TCLC 39**
Sodergran, Edith (Irene)
See Soedergran, Edith (Irene)
Soedergran, Edith (Irene) 1892-1923 . **T C L C
31**
Softly, Edgar
See Lovecraft, H(oward) P(hillips)
Softly, Edward
See Lovecraft, H(oward) P(hillips)
Sokolov, Raymond 1941- .... **CLC 7**
See also CA 85-88
Solo, Jay
See Ellison, Harlan (Jay)
Sologub, Fyodor .... **TCLC 9**
See also Teternikov, Fyodor Kuzmich
Solomons, Ikey Esquir
See Thackeray, William Makepeace
Solomos, Dionysios 1798-1857 .... **NCLC 15**
Solwoska, Mara
See French, Marilyn
Solzhenitsyn, Aleksandr I(sayevich) 1918-
**CLC 1, 2, 4, 7, 9, 10, 18, 26, 34, 78; DA;
DAB; DAC; DAM MST, NOV; WLC**
See also AITN 1; CA 69-72; CANR 40; MTCW
Somers, Jane
See Lessing, Doris (May)
Somerville, Edith 1858-1949 .... **TCLC 51**
See also DLB 135
Somerville & Ross
See Martin, Violet Florence; Somerville, Edith
Sommer, Scott 1951-........................... **CLC 25**
See also CA 106
Sondheim, Stephen (Joshua) 1930-. **CLC 30,
39; DAM DRAM**
See also AAYA 11; CA 103; CANR 47
Song, Cathy 1955- .... **PC 21**
See also CA 154; DLB 169
Sontag, Susan 1933-**CLC 1, 2, 10, 13, 31, 105;
DAM POP**
See also CA 17-20R; CANR 25, 51; DLB 2,
67; MTCW
Sophocles 496(?)B.C.-406(?)B.C.... **CMLC 2;
DA; DAB; DAC; DAM DRAM, MST; DC
1; WLCS**
See also DLB 176
Sordello 1189-1269 .... **CMLC 15**
Sorel, Julia
See Drexler, Rosalyn
Sorrentino, Gilbert 1929-**CLC 3, 7, 14, 22, 40**
See also CA 77-80; CANR 14, 33; DLB 5, 173;
DLBY 80; INT CANR-14
Soto, Gary 1952-. **CLC 32, 80; DAM MULT;
HLC**
See also AAYA 10; CA 119; 125; CANR 50;
CLR 38; DLB 82; HW; INT 125; JRDA;
SATA 80
Soupault, Philippe 1897-1990 .... **CLC 68**
See also CA 116; 147; 131
Souster, (Holmes) Raymond 1921-**CLC 5, 14;
DAC; DAM POET**
See also CA 13-16R; CAAS 14; CANR 13, 29,
53; DLB 88; SATA 63
Southern, Terry 1924(?)-1995 .... **CLC 7**
See also CA 1-4R; 150; CANR 1, 55; DLB 2
Southey, Robert 1774-1843 .... **NCLC 8**
See also DLB 93, 107, 142; SATA 54

Southworth, Emma Dorothy Eliza Nevitte
    1819-1899 .... NCLC 26
Souza, Ernest
    See Scott, Evelyn
Soyinka, Wole 1934-CLC 3, 5, 14, 36, 44; BLC;
    DA; DAB; DAC; DAM DRAM, MST,
    MULT; DC 2; WLC
    See also BW 2; CA 13-16R; CANR 27, 39; DLB
    125; MTCW
Spackman, W(illiam) M(ode) 1905-1990C L C
    46
    See also CA 81-84; 132
Spacks, Barry (Bernard) 1931- .... CLC 14
    See also CA 154; CANR 33; DLB 105
Spanidou, Irini 1946- .... CLC 44
Spark, Muriel (Sarah) 1918-CLC 2, 3, 5, 8, 13,
    18, 40, 94; DAB; DAC; DAM MST, NOV;
    SSC 10
    See also CA 5-8R; CANR 12, 36; CDBLB 1945-
    1960; DLB 15, 139; INT CANR-12; MTCW
Spaulding, Douglas
    See Bradbury, Ray (Douglas)
Spaulding, Leonard
    See Bradbury, Ray (Douglas)
Spence, J. A. D.
    See Eliot, T(homas) S(tearns)
Spencer, Elizabeth 1921- .... CLC 22
    See also CA 13-16R; CANR 32; DLB 6;
    MTCW; SATA 14
Spencer, Leonard G.
    See Silverberg, Robert
Spencer, Scott 1945- .... CLC 30
    See also CA 113; CANR 51; DLBY 86
Spender, Stephen (Harold) 1909-1995CLC 1,
    2, 5, 10, 41, 91; DAM POET
    See also CA 9-12R; 149; CANR 31, 54; CDBLB
    1945-1960; DLB 20; MTCW
Spengler, Oswald (Arnold Gottfried) 1880-1936
    TCLC 25
    See also CA 118
Spenser, Edmund 1552(?)-1599LC 5, 39; DA;
    DAB; DAC; DAM MST, POET; PC 8;
    WLC
    See also CDBLB Before 1660; DLB 167
Spicer, Jack 1925-1965 CLC 8, 18, 72; DAM
    POET
    See also CA 85-88; DLB 5, 16
Spiegelman, Art 1948- .... CLC 76
    See also AAYA 10; CA 125; CANR 41, 55
Spielberg, Peter 1929- .... CLC 6
    See also CA 5-8R; CANR 4, 48; DLBY 81
Spielberg, Steven 1947- .... CLC 20
    See also AAYA 8; CA 77-80; CANR 32; SATA
    32
Spillane, Frank Morrison 1918-
    See Spillane, Mickey
    See also CA 25-28R; CANR 28, 63; MTCW;
    SATA 66
Spillane, Mickey .... CLC 3, 13
    See also Spillane, Frank Morrison
Spinoza, Benedictus de 1632-1677 .... LC 9
Spinrad, Norman (Richard) 1940- .. CLC 46
    See also CA 37-40R; CAAS 19; CANR 20; DLB
    8; INT CANR-20
Spitteler, Carl (Friedrich Georg) 1845-1924
    TCLC 12
    See also CA 109; DLB 129
Spivack, Kathleen (Romola Drucker) 1938-
    CLC 6
    See also CA 49-52
Spoto, Donald 1941- .... CLC 39
    See also CA 65-68; CANR 11, 57
Springsteen, Bruce (F.) 1949- .... CLC 17

    See also CA 111
Spurling, Hilary 1940- .... CLC 34
    See also CA 104; CANR 25, 52
Spyker, John Howland
    See Elman, Richard
Squires, (James) Radcliffe 1917-1993CLC 51
    See also CA 1-4R; 140; CANR 6, 21
Srivastava, Dhanpat Rai 1880(?)-1936
    See Premchand
    See also CA 118
Stacy, Donald
    See Pohl, Frederik
Stael, Germaine de
    See Stael-Holstein, Anne Louise Germaine
        Necker Baronn
    See also DLB 119
Stael-Holstein, Anne Louise Germaine Necker
    Baronn 1766-1817 .... NCLC 3
    See also Stael, Germaine de
Stafford, Jean 1915-1979CLC 4, 7, 19, 68; SSC
    26
    See also CA 1-4R; 85-88; CANR 3; DLB 2, 173;
    MTCW; SATA-Obit 22
Stafford, William (Edgar) 1914-1993 CLC 4,
    7, 29; DAM POET
    See also CA 5-8R; 142; CAAS 3; CANR 5, 22;
    DLB 5; INT CANR-22
Stagnelius, Eric Johan 1793-1823 . NCLC 61
Staines, Trevor
    See Brunner, John (Kilian Houston)
Stairs, Gordon
    See Austin, Mary (Hunter)
Stannard, Martin 1947- .... CLC 44
    See also CA 142; DLB 155
Stanton, Elizabeth Cady 1815-1902TCLC 73
    See also DLB 79
Stanton, Maura 1946- .... CLC 9
    See also CA 89-92; CANR 15; DLB 120
Stanton, Schuyler
    See Baum, L(yman) Frank
Stapledon, (William) Olaf 1886-1950 . T C L C
    22
    See also CA 111; DLB 15
Starbuck, George (Edwin) 1931-1996CLC 53;
    DAM POET
    See also CA 21-24R; 153; CANR 23
Stark, Richard
    See Westlake, Donald E(dwin)
Staunton, Schuyler
    See Baum, L(yman) Frank
Stead, Christina (Ellen) 1902-1983 CLC 2, 5,
    8, 32, 80
    See also CA 13-16R; 109; CANR 33, 40;
    MTCW
Stead, William Thomas 1849-1912 TCLC 48
Steele, Richard 1672-1729 .... LC 18
    See also CDBLB 1660-1789; DLB 84, 101
Steele, Timothy (Reid) 1948- .... CLC 45
    See also CA 93-96; CANR 16, 50; DLB 120
Steffens, (Joseph) Lincoln 1866-1936 . T C L C
    20
    See also CA 117
Stegner, Wallace (Earle) 1909-1993CLC 9, 49,
    81; DAM NOV; SSC 27
    See also AITN 1; BEST 90:3; CA 1-4R; 141;
    CAAS 9; CANR 1, 21, 46; DLB 9; DLBY
    93; MTCW
Stein, Gertrude 1874-1946TCLC 1, 6, 28, 48;
    DA; DAB; DAC; DAM MST, NOV, POET;
    PC 18; WLC
    See also CA 104; 132; CDALB 1917-1929;
    DLB 4, 54, 86; DLBD 15; MTCW
Steinbeck, John (Ernst) 1902-1968CLC 1, 5, 9,

    13, 21, 34, 45, 75; DA; DAB; DAC; DAM
    DRAM, MST, NOV; SSC 11; WLC
    See also AAYA 12; CA 1-4R; 25-28R; CANR
    1, 35; CDALB 1929-1941; DLB 7, 9; DLBD
    2; MTCW; SATA 9
Steinem, Gloria 1934- .... CLC 63
    See also CA 53-56; CANR 28, 51; MTCW
Steiner, George 1929- ... CLC 24; DAM NOV
    See also CA 73-76; CANR 31; DLB 67; MTCW;
    SATA 62
Steiner, K. Leslie
    See Delany, Samuel R(ay, Jr.)
Steiner, Rudolf 1861-1925 .... TCLC 13
    See also CA 107
Stendhal 1783-1842NCLC 23, 46; DA; DAB;
    DAC; DAM MST, NOV; SSC 27; WLC
    See also DLB 119
Stephen, Adeline Virginia
    See Woolf, (Adeline) Virginia
Stephen, Leslie 1832-1904 .... TCLC 23
    See also CA 123; DLB 57, 144
Stephen, Sir Leslie
    See Stephen, Leslie
Stephen, Virginia
    See Woolf, (Adeline) Virginia
Stephens, James 1882(?)-1950 .... TCLC 4
    See also CA 104; DLB 19, 153, 162
Stephens, Reed
    See Donaldson, Stephen R.
Steptoe, Lydia
    See Barnes, Djuna
Sterchi, Beat 1949- .... CLC 65
Sterling, Brett
    See Bradbury, Ray (Douglas); Hamilton,
        Edmond
Sterling, Bruce 1954- .... CLC 72
    See also CA 119; CANR 44
Sterling, George 1869-1926 .... TCLC 20
    See also CA 117; DLB 54
Stern, Gerald 1925- .... CLC 40, 100
    See also CA 81-84; CANR 28; DLB 105
Stern, Richard (Gustave) 1928- ... CLC 4, 39
    See also CA 1-4R; CANR 1, 25, 52; DLBY 87;
    INT CANR-25
Sternberg, Josef von 1894-1969 .... CLC 20
    See also CA 81-84
Sterne, Laurence 1713-1768LC 2; DA; DAB;
    DAC; DAM MST, NOV; WLC
    See also CDBLB 1660-1789; DLB 39
Sternheim, (William Adolf) Carl 1878-1942
    TCLC 8
    See also CA 105; DLB 56, 118
Stevens, Mark 1951- .... CLC 34
    See also CA 122
Stevens, Wallace 1879-1955 TCLC 3, 12, 45;
    DA; DAB; DAC; DAM MST, POET; PC
    6; WLC
    See also CA 104; 124; CDALB 1929-1941;
    DLB 54; MTCW
Stevenson, Anne (Katharine) 1933-CLC 7, 33
    See also CA 17-20R; CAAS 9; CANR 9, 33;
    DLB 40; MTCW
Stevenson, Robert Louis (Balfour) 1850-1894
    NCLC 5, 14, 63; DA; DAB; DAC; DAM
    MST, NOV; SSC 11; WLC
    See also CDBLB 1890-1914; CLR 10, 11; DLB
    18, 57, 141, 156, 174; DLBD 13; JRDA;
    MAICYA; YABC 2
Stewart, J(ohn) I(nnes) M(ackintosh) 1906-
    1994 .... CLC 7, 14, 32
    See also CA 85-88; 147; CAAS 3; CANR 47;
    MTCW
Stewart, Mary (Florence Elinor) 1916-CLC 7,

35; DAB
 See also CA 1-4R; CANR 1, 59; SATA 12
Stewart, Mary Rainbow
 See Stewart, Mary (Florence Elinor)
Stifle, June
 See Campbell, Maria
Stifter, Adalbert 1805-1868NCLC **41**; SSC **28**
 See also DLB 133
Still, James 1906- .... **CLC 49**
  See also CA 65-68; CAAS 17; CANR 10, 26;
  DLB 9; SATA 29
Sting
 See Sumner, Gordon Matthew
Stirling, Arthur
 See Sinclair, Upton (Beall)
Stitt, Milan 1941- .... **CLC 29**
 See also CA 69-72
Stockton, Francis Richard 1834-1902
 See Stockton, Frank R.
 See also CA 108; 137; MAICYA; SATA 44
Stockton, Frank R. .... **TCLC 47**
 See also Stockton, Francis Richard
 See also DLB 42, 74; DLBD 13; SATA-Brief
  32
Stoddard, Charles
 See Kuttner, Henry
Stoker, Abraham 1847-1912
 See Stoker, Bram
 See also CA 105; DA; DAC; DAM MST, NOV;
  SATA 29
Stoker, Bram 1847-1912TCLC **8**; DAB; WLC
 See also Stoker, Abraham
 See also CA 150; CDBLB 1890-1914; DLB 36,
  70, 178
Stolz, Mary (Slattery) 1920- .... **CLC 12**
 See also AAYA 8; AITN 1; CA 5-8R; CANR
  13, 41; JRDA; MAICYA; SAAS 3; SATA 10,
  71
Stone, Irving 1903-1989 .. **CLC 7; DAM POP**
 See also AITN 1; CA 1-4R; 129; CAAS 3;
  CANR 1, 23; INT CANR-23; MTCW; SATA
  3; SATA-Obit 64
Stone, Oliver (William) 1946- .... **CLC 73**
 See also AAYA 15; CA 110; CANR 55
Stone, Robert (Anthony) 1937-CLC **5, 23, 42**
 See also CA 85-88; CANR 23; DLB 152; INT
  CANR-23; MTCW
Stone, Zachary
 See Follett, Ken(neth Martin)
Stoppard, Tom 1937-CLC **1, 3, 4, 5, 8, 15, 29,
  34, 63, 91; DA; DAB; DAC; DAM DRAM,
  MST; DC 6; WLC**
 See also CA 81-84; CANR 39; CDBLB 1960
  to Present; DLB 13; DLBY 85; MTCW
Storey, David (Malcolm) 1933-CLC **2, 4, 5, 8;
  DAM DRAM**
 See also CA 81-84; CANR 36; DLB 13, 14;
  MTCW
Storm, Hyemeyohsts 1935- ...... **CLC 3; DAM
  MULT**
 See also CA 81-84; CANR 45; NNAL
Storm, (Hans) Theodor (Woldsen) 1817-1888
  NCLC **1**; SSC **27**
Storni, Alfonsina 1892-1938 . TCLC **5; DAM
  MULT; HLC**
 See also CA 104; 131; HW
Stoughton, William 1631-1701 .... **LC 38**
 See also DLB 24
Stout, Rex (Todhunter) 1886-1975 ..... **CLC 3**
 See also AITN 2; CA 61-64
Stow, (Julian) Randolph 1935- .. **CLC 23, 48**
 See also CA 13-16R; CANR 33; MTCW
Stowe, Harriet (Elizabeth) Beecher 1811-1896

NCLC **3, 50; DA; DAB; DAC; DAM MST,
  NOV; WLC**
 See also CDALB 1865-1917; DLB 1, 12, 42,
  74; JRDA; MAICYA; YABC 1
Strachey, (Giles) Lytton 1880-1932 TCLC **12**
 See also CA 110; DLB 149; DLBD 10
Strand, Mark 1934- CLC **6, 18, 41, 71; DAM
  POET**
 See also CA 21-24R; CANR 40; DLB 5; SATA
  41
Straub, Peter (Francis) 1943-.. CLC **28, 107;
  DAM POP**
 See also BEST 89:1; CA 85-88; CANR 28;
  DLBY 84; MTCW
Strauss, Botho 1944- .... **CLC 22**
 See also CA 157; DLB 124
Streatfeild, (Mary) Noel 1895(?)-1986CLC **21**
 See also CA 81-84; 120; CANR 31; CLR 17;
  DLB 160; MAICYA; SATA 20; SATA-Obit
  48
Stribling, T(homas) S(igismund) 1881-1965
  CLC **23**
 See also CA 107; DLB 9
Strindberg, (Johan) August 1849-1912TCLC
  **1, 8, 21, 47; DA; DAB; DAC; DAM DRAM,
  MST; WLC**
 See also CA 104; 135
Stringer, Arthur 1874-1950 .... **TCLC 37**
 See also CA 161; DLB 92
Stringer, David
 See Roberts, Keith (John Kingston)
Stroheim, Erich von 1885-1957 ..... **TCLC 71**
Strugatskii, Arkadii (Natanovich) 1925-1991
  CLC **27**
 See also CA 106; 135
Strugatskii, Boris (Natanovich) 1933-CLC **27**
 See also CA 106
Strummer, Joe 1953(?)- .... **CLC 30**
Stuart, Don A.
 See Campbell, John W(ood, Jr.)
Stuart, Ian
 See MacLean, Alistair (Stuart)
Stuart, Jesse (Hilton) 1906-1984CLC **1, 8, 11,
  14, 34**
 See also CA 5-8R; 112; CANR 31; DLB 9, 48,
  102; DLBY 84; SATA 2; SATA-Obit 36
Sturgeon, Theodore (Hamilton) 1918-1985
  CLC **22, 39**
 See also Queen, Ellery
 See also CA 81-84; 116; CANR 32; DLB 8;
  DLBY 85; MTCW
Sturges, Preston 1898-1959 .... **TCLC 48**
 See also CA 114; 149; DLB 26
Styron, William 1925-CLC **1, 3, 5, 11, 15, 60;
  DAM NOV, POP; SSC 25**
 See also BEST 90:4; CA 5-8R; CANR 6, 33;
  CDALB 1968-1988; DLB 2, 143; DLBY 80;
  INT CANR-6; MTCW
Suarez Lynch, B.
 See Bioy Casares, Adolfo; Borges, Jorge Luis
Su Chien 1884-1918
 See Su Man-shu
 See also CA 123
Suckow, Ruth 1892-1960 .... **SSC 18**
 See also CA 113; DLB 9, 102
Sudermann, Hermann 1857-1928 .. **TCLC 15**
 See also CA 107; DLB 118
Sue, Eugene 1804-1857 .... **NCLC 1**
 See also DLB 119
Sueskind, Patrick 1949- .... **CLC 44**
 See also Suskind, Patrick
Sukenick, Ronald 1932- .... **CLC 3, 4, 6, 48**
 See also CA 25-28R; CAAS 8; CANR 32; DLB

  173; DLBY 81
Suknaski, Andrew 1942- .... **CLC 19**
 See also CA 101; DLB 53
Sullivan, Vernon
 See Vian, Boris
Sully Prudhomme 1839-1907 .... **TCLC 31**
Su Man-shu .... **TCLC 24**
 See also Su Chien
Summerforest, Ivy B.
 See Kirkup, James
Summers, Andrew James 1942- .... **CLC 26**
Summers, Andy
 See Summers, Andrew James
Summers, Hollis (Spurgeon, Jr.) 1916-CLC **10**
 See also CA 5-8R; CANR 3; DLB 6
Summers, (Alphonsus Joseph-Mary Augustus)
  Montague 1880-1948 .... **TCLC 16**
 See also CA 118
Sumner, Gordon Matthew 1951- ...... **CLC 26**
Surtees, Robert Smith 1803-1864 .. **NCLC 14**
 See also DLB 21
Susann, Jacqueline 1921-1974 .... **CLC 3**
 See also AITN 1; CA 65-68; 53-56; MTCW
Su Shih 1036-1101 .... **CMLC 15**
Suskind, Patrick
 See Sueskind, Patrick
 See also CA 145
Sutcliff, Rosemary 1920-1992CLC **26; DAB;
  DAC; DAM MST, POP**
 See also AAYA 10; CA 5-8R; 139; CANR 37;
  CLR 1, 37; JRDA; MAICYA; SATA 6, 44,
  78; SATA-Obit 73
Sutro, Alfred 1863-1933 .... **TCLC 6**
 See also CA 105; DLB 10
Sutton, Henry
 See Slavitt, David R(ytman)
Svevo, Italo 1861-1928 . TCLC **2, 35; SSC 25**
 See also Schmitz, Aron Hector
Swados, Elizabeth (A.) 1951- .... **CLC 12**
 See also CA 97-100; CANR 49; INT 97-100
Swados, Harvey 1920-1972 .... **CLC 5**
 See also CA 5-8R; 37-40R; CANR 6; DLB 2
Swan, Gladys 1934- .... **CLC 69**
 See also CA 101; CANR 17, 39
Swarthout, Glendon (Fred) 1918-1992CLC **35**
 See also CA 1-4R; 139; CANR 1, 47; SATA 26
Sweet, Sarah C.
 See Jewett, (Theodora) Sarah Orne
Swenson, May 1919-1989CLC **4, 14, 61, 106;
  DA; DAB; DAC; DAM MST, POET; PC
  14**
 See also CA 5-8R; 130; CANR 36, 61; DLB 5;
  MTCW; SATA 15
Swift, Augustus
 See Lovecraft, H(oward) P(hillips)
Swift, Graham (Colin) 1949- ...... **CLC 41, 88**
 See also CA 117; 122; CANR 46
Swift, Jonathan 1667-1745 LC **1; DA; DAB;
  DAC; DAM MST, NOV, POET; PC 9;
  WLC**
 See also CDBLB 1660-1789; DLB 39, 95, 101;
  SATA 19
Swinburne, Algernon Charles 1837-1909
  TCLC **8, 36; DA; DAB; DAC; DAM MST,
  POET; WLC**
 See also CA 105; 140; CDBLB 1832-1890;
  DLB 35, 57
Swinfen, Ann ....CLC **34**
Swinnerton, Frank Arthur 1884-1982CLC **31**
 See also CA 108; DLB 34
Swithen, John
 See King, Stephen (Edwin)
Sylvia

See Ashton-Warner, Sylvia (Constance)
Symmes, Robert Edward
See Duncan, Robert (Edward)
Symonds, John Addington 1840-1893 **N C L C 34**
See also DLB 57, 144
Symons, Arthur 1865-1945 .... **TCLC 11**
See also CA 107; DLB 19, 57, 149
Symons, Julian (Gustave) 1912-1994 **CLC 2, 14, 32**
See also CA 49-52; 147; CAAS 3; CANR 3, 33, 59; DLB 87, 155; DLBY 92; MTCW
Synge, (Edmund) J(ohn) M(illington) 1871-1909 .. **TCLC 6, 37; DAM DRAM; DC 2**
See also CA 104; 141; CDBLB 1890-1914; DLB 10, 19
Syruc, J.
See Milosz, Czeslaw
Szirtes, George 1948- .... **CLC 46**
See also CA 109; CANR 27, 61
Szymborska, Wislawa 1923- .... **CLC 99**
See also CA 154; DLBY 96
T. O., Nik
See Annensky, Innokenty (Fyodorovich)
Tabori, George 1914- .... **CLC 19**
See also CA 49-52; CANR 4
Tagore, Rabindranath 1861-1941 **TCLC 3, 53; DAM DRAM, POET; PC 8**
See also CA 104; 120; MTCW
Taine, Hippolyte Adolphe 1828-1893 . **N C L C 15**
Talese, Gay 1932- .... **CLC 37**
See also AITN 1; CA 1-4R; CANR 9, 58; INT CANR-9; MTCW
Tallent, Elizabeth (Ann) 1954- .... **CLC 45**
See also CA 117; DLB 130
Tally, Ted 1952- .... **CLC 42**
See also CA 120; 124; INT 124
Tamayo y Baus, Manuel 1829-1898 . **NCLC 1**
Tammsaare, A(nton) H(ansen) 1878-1940 **TCLC 27**
Tam'si, Tchicaya U
See Tchicaya, Gerald Felix
Tan, Amy (Ruth) 1952- **CLC 59; DAM MULT, NOV, POP**
See also AAYA 9; BEST 89:3; CA 136; CANR 54; DLB 173; SATA 75
Tandem, Felix
See Spitteler, Carl (Friedrich Georg)
Tanizaki, Jun'ichiro 1886-1965 **CLC 8, 14, 28; SSC 21**
See also CA 93-96; 25-28R; DLB 180
Tanner, William
See Amis, Kingsley (William)
Tao Lao
See Storni, Alfonsina
Tarassoff, Lev
See Troyat, Henri
Tarbell, Ida M(inerva) 1857-1944 . **TCLC 40**
See also CA 122; DLB 47
Tarkington, (Newton) Booth 1869-1946 **TCLC 9**
See also CA 110; 143; DLB 9, 102; SATA 17
Tarkovsky, Andrei (Arsenyevich) 1932-1986 **CLC 75**
See also CA 127
Tartt, Donna 1964(?)- .... **CLC 76**
See also CA 142
Tasso, Torquato 1544-1595 .... **LC 5**
Tate, (John Orley) Allen 1899-1979 **CLC 2, 4, 6, 9, 11, 14, 24**
See also CA 5-8R; 85-88; CANR 32; DLB 4, 45, 63; MTCW

Tate, Ellalice
See Hibbert, Eleanor Alice Burford
Tate, James (Vincent) 1943- ..... **CLC 2, 6, 25**
See also CA 21-24R; CANR 29, 57; DLB 5, 169
Tavel, Ronald 1940- .... **CLC 6**
See also CA 21-24R; CANR 33
Taylor, C(ecil) P(hilip) 1929-1981 ..... **CLC 27**
See also CA 25-28R; 105; CANR 47
Taylor, Edward 1642(?)-1729 ..... **LC 11; DA; DAB; DAC; DAM MST, POET**
See also DLB 24
Taylor, Eleanor Ross 1920- .... **CLC 5**
See also CA 81-84
Taylor, Elizabeth 1912-1975 ..... **CLC 2, 4, 29**
See also CA 13-16R; CANR 9; DLB 139; MTCW; SATA 13
Taylor, Frederick Winslow 1856-1915 **T C L C 76**
Taylor, Henry (Splawn) 1942- .... **CLC 44**
See also CA 33-36R; CAAS 7; CANR 31; DLB 5
Taylor, Kamala (Purnaiya) 1924-
See Markandaya, Kamala
See also CA 77-80
Taylor, Mildred D. .... **CLC 21**
See also AAYA 10; BW 1; CA 85-88; CANR 25; CLR 9; DLB 52; JRDA; MAICYA; SAAS 5; SATA 15, 70
Taylor, Peter (Hillsman) 1917-1994 **CLC 1, 4, 18, 37, 44, 50, 71; SSC 10**
See also CA 13-16R; 147; CANR 9, 50; DLBY 81, 94; INT CANR-9; MTCW
Taylor, Robert Lewis 1912- .... **CLC 14**
See also CA 1-4R; CANR 3, 64; SATA 10
Tchekhov, Anton
See Chekhov, Anton (Pavlovich)
Tchicaya, Gerald Felix 1931-1988 . **CLC 101**
See also CA 129; 125
Tchicaya U Tam'si
See Tchicaya, Gerald Felix
Teasdale, Sara 1884-1933 .... **TCLC 4**
See also CA 104; DLB 45; SATA 32
Tegner, Esaias 1782-1846 .... **NCLC 2**
Teilhard de Chardin, (Marie Joseph) Pierre 1881-1955 .... **TCLC 9**
See also CA 105
Temple, Ann
See Mortimer, Penelope (Ruth)
Tennant, Emma (Christina) 1937- **CLC 13, 52**
See also CA 65-68; CAAS 9; CANR 10, 38, 59; DLB 14
Tenneshaw, S. M.
See Silverberg, Robert
Tennyson, Alfred 1809-1892 ... **NCLC 30, 65; DA; DAB; DAC; DAM MST, POET; PC 6; WLC**
See also CDBLB 1832-1890; DLB 32
Teran, Lisa St. Aubin de .... **CLC 36**
See also St. Aubin de Teran, Lisa
Terence 195(?)B.C.-159B.C. **CMLC 14; DC 7**
Teresa de Jesus, St. 1515-1582 .... **LC 18**
Terkel, Louis 1912-
See Terkel, Studs
See also CA 57-60; CANR 18, 45; MTCW
Terkel, Studs .... **CLC 38**
See also Terkel, Louis
See also AITN 1
Terry, C. V.
See Slaughter, Frank G(ill)
Terry, Megan 1932- .... **CLC 19**
See also CA 77-80; CABS 3; CANR 43; DLB 7
Tertz, Abram

See Sinyavsky, Andrei (Donatevich)
Tesich, Steve 1943(?)-1996 .... **CLC 40, 69**
See also CA 105; 152; DLBY 83
Teternikov, Fyodor Kuzmich 1863-1927
See Sologub, Fyodor
See also CA 104
Tevis, Walter 1928-1984 .... **CLC 42**
See also CA 113
Tey, Josephine .... **TCLC 14**
See also Mackintosh, Elizabeth
See also DLB 77
Thackeray, William Makepeace 1811-1863 **NCLC 5, 14, 22, 43; DA; DAB; DAC; DAM MST, NOV; WLC**
See also CDBLB 1832-1890; DLB 21, 55, 159, 163; SATA 23
Thakura, Ravindranatha
See Tagore, Rabindranath
Tharoor, Shashi 1956- .... **CLC 70**
See also CA 141
Thelwell, Michael Miles 1939- .... **CLC 22**
See also BW 2; CA 101
Theobald, Lewis, Jr.
See Lovecraft, H(oward) P(hillips)
Theodorescu, Ion N. 1880-1967
See Arghezi, Tudor
See also CA 116
Theriault, Yves 1915-1983 .... **CLC 79; DAC; DAM MST**
See also CA 102; DLB 88
Theroux, Alexander (Louis) 1939- **CLC 2, 25**
See also CA 85-88; CANR 20, 63
Theroux, Paul (Edward) 1941- **CLC 5, 8, 11, 15, 28, 46; DAM POP**
See also BEST 89:4; CA 33-36R; CANR 20, 45; DLB 2; MTCW; SATA 44
Thesen, Sharon 1946- .... **CLC 56**
Thevenin, Denis
See Duhamel, Georges
Thibault, Jacques Anatole Francois 1844-1924
See France, Anatole
See also CA 106; 127; DAM NOV; MTCW
Thiele, Colin (Milton) 1920- .... **CLC 17**
See also CA 29-32R; CANR 12, 28, 53; CLR 27; MAICYA; SAAS 2; SATA 14, 72
Thomas, Audrey (Callahan) 1935- **CLC 7, 13, 37, 107; SSC 20**
See also AITN 2; CA 21-24R; CAAS 19; CANR 36, 58; DLB 60; MTCW
Thomas, D(onald) M(ichael) 1935-. **CLC 13, 22, 31**
See also CA 61-64; CAAS 11; CANR 17, 45; CDBLB 1960 to Present; DLB 40; INT CANR-17; MTCW
Thomas, Dylan (Marlais) 1914-1953 **TCLC 1, 8, 45; DA; DAB; DAC; DAM DRAM, MST, POET; PC 2; SSC 3; WLC**
See also CA 104; 120; CDBLB 1945-1960; DLB 13, 20, 139; MTCW; SATA 60
Thomas, (Philip) Edward 1878-1917 . **T C L C 10; DAM POET**
See also CA 106; 153; DLB 19
Thomas, Joyce Carol 1938- .... **CLC 35**
See also AAYA 12; BW 2; CA 113; 116; CANR 48; CLR 19; DLB 33; INT 116; JRDA; MAICYA; MTCW; SAAS 7; SATA 40, 78
Thomas, Lewis 1913-1993 .... **CLC 35**
See also CA 85-88; 143; CANR 38, 60; MTCW
Thomas, Paul
See Mann, (Paul) Thomas
Thomas, Piri 1928- .... **CLC 17**
See also CA 73-76; HW
Thomas, R(onald) S(tuart) 1913- **CLC 6, 13,**

48; DAB; DAM POET
See also CA 89-92; CAAS 4; CANR 30;
CDBLB 1960 to Present; DLB 27; MTCW

Thomas, Ross (Elmore) 1926-1995 .. **CLC 39**
See also CA 33-36R; 150; CANR 22, 63

Thompson, Francis Clegg
See Mencken, H(enry) L(ouis)

Thompson, Francis Joseph 1859-1907**TCLC 4**
See also CA 104; CDBLB 1890-1914; DLB 19

Thompson, Hunter S(tockton) 1939-..**CLC 9,
17, 40, 104; DAM POP**
See also BEST 89:1; CA 17-20R; CANR 23,
46; MTCW

Thompson, James Myers
See Thompson, Jim (Myers)

Thompson, Jim (Myers) 1906-1977(?)**CLC 69**
See also CA 140

Thompson, Judith .... **CLC 39**

Thomson, James 1700-1748 .... **LC 16, 29, 40;
DAM POET**
See also DLB 95

Thomson, James 1834-1882 **NCLC 18; DAM
POET**
See also DLB 35

Thoreau, Henry David 1817-1862**NCLC 7, 21,
61; DA; DAB; DAC; DAM MST; WLC**
See also CDALB 1640-1865; DLB 1

Thornton, Hall
See Silverberg, Robert

Thucydides c. 455B.C.-399B.C. ...... **CMLC 17**
See also DLB 176

Thurber, James (Grover) 1894-1961 .**CLC 5,
11, 25; DA; DAB; DAC; DAM DRAM,
MST, NOV; SSC 1**
See also CA 73-76; CANR 17, 39; CDALB
1929-1941; DLB 4, 11, 22, 102; MAICYA;
MTCW; SATA 13

Thurman, Wallace (Henry) 1902-1934**T C L C
6; BLC; DAM MULT**
See also BW 1; CA 104; 124; DLB 51

Ticheburn, Cheviot
See Ainsworth, William Harrison

Tieck, (Johann) Ludwig 1773-1853 **NCLC 5,
46**
See also DLB 90

Tiger, Derry
See Ellison, Harlan (Jay)

Tilghman, Christopher 1948(?)- ...... **CLC 65**
See also CA 159

Tillinghast, Richard (Williford) 1940-**CLC 29**
See also CA 29-32R; CAAS 23; CANR 26, 51

Timrod, Henry 1828-1867 .... **NCLC 25**
See also DLB 3

Tindall, Gillian (Elizabeth) 1938-.......**CLC 7**
See also CA 21-24R; CANR 11

Tiptree, James, Jr. .... **CLC 48, 50**
See also Sheldon, Alice Hastings Bradley
See also DLB 8

Titmarsh, Michael Angelo
See Thackeray, William Makepeace

Tocqueville, Alexis (Charles Henri Maurice
Clerel Comte) 1805-1859 ...**NCLC 7, 63**

Tolkien, J(ohn) R(onald) R(euel) 1892-1973
**CLC 1, 2, 3, 8, 12, 38; DA; DAB; DAC;
DAM MST, NOV, POP; WLC**
See also AAYA 10; AITN 1; CA 17-18; 45-48;
CANR 36; CAP 2; CDBLB 1914-1945; DLB
15, 160; JRDA; MAICYA; MTCW; SATA 2,
32; SATA-Obit 24

Toller, Ernst 1893-1939 .... **TCLC 10**
See also CA 107; DLB 124

Tolson, M. B.
See Tolson, Melvin B(eaunorus)

Tolson, Melvin B(eaunorus) 1898(?)-1966
CLC 36, 105; BLC; DAM MULT, POET
See also BW 1; CA 124; 89-92; DLB 48, 76

Tolstoi, Aleksei Nikolaevich
See Tolstoy, Alexey Nikolaevich

Tolstoy, Alexey Nikolaevich 1882-1945**T C L C
18**
See also CA 107; 158

Tolstoy, Count Leo
See Tolstoy, Leo (Nikolaevich)

Tolstoy, Leo (Nikolaevich) 1828-1910**TCLC 4,
11, 17, 28, 44, 79; DA; DAB; DAC; DAM
MST, NOV; SSC 9; WLC**
See also CA 104; 123; SATA 26

Tomasi di Lampedusa, Giuseppe 1896-1957
See Lampedusa, Giuseppe (Tomasi) di
See also CA 111

Tomlin, Lily ....**CLC 17**
See also Tomlin, Mary Jean

Tomlin, Mary Jean 1939(?)-
See Tomlin, Lily
See also CA 117

Tomlinson, (Alfred) Charles 1927-**CLC 2, 4, 6,
13, 45; DAM POET; PC 17**
See also CA 5-8R; CANR 33; DLB 40

Tomlinson, H(enry) M(ajor) 1873-1958**TCLC
71**
See also CA 118; 161; DLB 36, 100

Tonson, Jacob
See Bennett, (Enoch) Arnold

Toole, John Kennedy 1937-1969 **CLC 19, 64**
See also CA 104; DLBY 81

Toomer, Jean 1894-1967 .... **CLC 1, 4, 13, 22;
BLC; DAM MULT; PC 7; SSC 1; WLCS**
See also BW 1; CA 85-88; CDALB 1917-1929;
DLB 45, 51; MTCW

Torley, Luke
See Blish, James (Benjamin)

Tornimparte, Alessandra
See Ginzburg, Natalia

Torre, Raoul della
See Mencken, H(enry) L(ouis)

Torrey, E(dwin) Fuller 1937- .... **CLC 34**
See also CA 119

Torsvan, Ben Traven
See Traven, B.

Torsvan, Benno Traven
See Traven, B.

Torsvan, Berick Traven
See Traven, B.

Torsvan, Berwick Traven
See Traven, B.

Torsvan, Bruno Traven
See Traven, B.

Torsvan, Traven
See Traven, B.

Tournier, Michel (Edouard) 1924-**CLC 6, 23,
36, 95**
See also CA 49-52; CANR 3, 36: DLB 83;
MTCW; SATA 23

Tournimparte, Alessandra
See Ginzburg, Natalia

Towers, Ivar
See Kornbluth, C(yril) M.

Towne, Robert (Burton) 1936(?)- ......**CLC 87**
See also CA 108; DLB 44

Townsend, Sue ....**CLC 61**
See also Townsend, Susan Elaine
See also SATA 55, 93; SATA-Brief 48

Townsend, Susan Elaine 1946-
See Townsend, Sue
See also CA 119; 127; DAB; DAC; DAM MST

Townshend, Peter (Dennis Blandford) 1945-

CLC 17, 42
See also CA 107

Tozzi, Federigo 1883-1920 .... **TCLC 31**
See also CA 160

Traill, Catharine Parr 1802-1899 ..**NCLC 31**
See also DLB 99

Trakl, Georg 1887-1914 .... **TCLC 5; PC 20**
See also CA 104

Transtroemer, Tomas (Goesta) 1931-**CLC 52,
65; DAM POET**
See also CA 117; 129; CAAS 17

Transtromer, Tomas Gosta
See Transtroemer, Tomas (Goesta)

Traven, B. (?)-1969 ....**CLC 8, 11**
See also CA 19-20; 25-28R; CAP 2; DLB 9,
56; MTCW

Treitel, Jonathan 1959- ....**CLC 70**

Tremain, Rose 1943- ....**CLC 42**
See also CA 97-100; CANR 44; DLB 14

Tremblay, Michel 1942- **CLC 29, 102; DAC;
DAM MST**
See also CA 116; 128; DLB 60; MTCW

Trevanian ....**CLC 29**
See also Whitaker, Rod(ney)

Trevor, Glen
See Hilton, James

Trevor, William 1928- ..**CLC 7, 9, 14, 25, 71;
SSC 21**
See also Cox, William Trevor
See also DLB 14, 139

Trifonov, Yuri (Valentinovich) 1925-1981
CLC 45
See also CA 126; 103; MTCW

Trilling, Lionel 1905-1975 ...... **CLC 9, 11, 24**
See also CA 9-12R; 61-64; CANR 10; DLB 28,
63; INT CANR-10; MTCW

Trimball, W. H.
See Mencken, H(enry) L(ouis)

Tristan
See Gomez de la Serna, Ramon

Tristram
See Housman, A(lfred) E(dward)

Trogdon, William (Lewis) 1939-
See Heat-Moon, William Least
See also CA 115; 119; CANR 47; INT 119

Trollope, Anthony 1815-1882**NCLC 6, 33; DA;
DAB; DAC; DAM MST, NOV; SSC 28;
WLC**
See also CDBLB 1832-1890; DLB 21, 57, 159;
SATA 22

Trollope, Frances 1779-1863 ....**NCLC 30**
See also DLB 21, 166

Trotsky, Leon 1879-1940 ....**TCLC 22**
See also CA 118

Trotter (Cockburn), Catharine 1679-1749**L C
8**
See also DLB 84

Trout, Kilgore
See Farmer, Philip Jose

Trow, George W. S. 1943- ....**CLC 52**
See also CA 126

Troyat, Henri 1911- ....**CLC 23**
See also CA 45-48; CANR 2, 33; MTCW

Trudeau, G(arretson) B(eekman) 1948-
See Trudeau, Garry B.
See also CA 81-84; CANR 31; SATA 35

Trudeau, Garry B. ....**CLC 12**
See also Trudeau, G(arretson) B(eekman)
See also AAYA 10; AITN 2

Truffaut, Francois 1932-1984 .. **CLC 20, 101**
See also CA 81-84; 113; CANR 34

Trumbo, Dalton 1905-1976 ....**CLC 19**
See also CA 21-24R; 69-72; CANR 10; DLB

26

Trumbull, John 1750-1831 .... NCLC 30
See also DLB 31
Trundlett, Helen B.
See Eliot, T(homas) S(tearns)
Tryon, Thomas 1926-1991 . CLC 3, 11; DAM
POP
See also AITN 1; CA 29-32R; 135; CANR 32;
MTCW
Tryon, Tom
See Tryon, Thomas
Ts'ao Hsueh-ch'in 1715(?)-1763 .... LC 1
Tsushima, Shuji 1909-1948
See Dazai, Osamu
See also CA 107
Tsvetaeva (Efron), Marina (Ivanovna) 1892-
1941 .... TCLC 7, 35; PC 14
See also CA 104; 128; MTCW
Tuck, Lily 1938- .... CLC 70
See also CA 139
Tu Fu 712-770 .... PC 9
See also DAM MULT
Tunis, John R(oberts) 1889-1975 ..... CLC 12
See also CA 61-64; CANR 62; DLB 22, 171;
JRDA; MAICYA; SATA 37; SATA-Brief 30
Tuohy, Frank .... CLC 37
See also Tuohy, John Francis
See also DLB 14, 139
Tuohy, John Francis 1925-
See Tuohy, Frank
See also CA 5-8R; CANR 3, 47
Turco, Lewis (Putnam) 1934- ...... CLC 11, 63
See also CA 13-16R; CAAS 22; CANR 24, 51;
DLBY 84
Turgenev, Ivan 1818-1883 .... NCLC 21; DA;
DAB; DAC; DAM MST, NOV; DC 7; SSC
7; WLC
Turgot, Anne-Robert-Jacques 1727-1781 L C
26
Turner, Frederick 1943- .... CLC 48
See also CA 73-76; CAAS 10; CANR 12, 30,
56; DLB 40
Tutu, Desmond M(pilo) 1931- CLC 80; BLC;
DAM MULT
See also BW 1; CA 125
Tutuola, Amos 1920-1997CLC 5, 14, 29; BLC;
DAM MULT
See also BW 2; CA 9-12R; 159; CANR 27; DLB
125; MTCW
Twain, Mark TCLC 6, 12, 19, 36, 48, 59; SSC
26; WLC
See also Clemens, Samuel Langhorne
See also AAYA 20; DLB 11, 12, 23, 64, 74
Tyler, Anne 1941- . CLC 7, 11, 18, 28, 44, 59,
103; DAM NOV, POP
See also AAYA 18; BEST 89:1; CA 9-12R;
CANR 11, 33, 53; DLB 6, 143; DLBY 82;
MTCW; SATA 7, 90
Tyler, Royall 1757-1826 .... NCLC 3
See also DLB 37
Tynan, Katharine 1861-1931 .... TCLC 3
See also CA 104; DLB 153
Tyutchev, Fyodor 1803-1873 .... NCLC 34
Tzara, Tristan 1896-1963 ...... CLC 47; DAM
POET
See also CA 153; 89-92
Uhry, Alfred 1936-... CLC 55; DAM DRAM,
POP
See also CA 127; 133; INT 133
Ulf, Haerved
See Strindberg, (Johan) August
Ulf, Harved
See Strindberg, (Johan) August

Ulibarri, Sabine R(eyes) 1919-CLC 83; DAM
MULT
See also CA 131; DLB 82; HW
Unamuno (y Jugo), Miguel de 1864-1936
TCLC 2, 9; DAM MULT, NOV; HLC; SSC
11
See also CA 104; 131; DLB 108; HW; MTCW
Undercliffe, Errol
See Campbell, (John) Ramsey
Underwood, Miles
See Glassco, John
Undset, Sigrid 1882-1949TCLC 3; DA; DAB;
DAC; DAM MST, NOV; WLC
See also CA 104; 129; MTCW
Ungaretti, Giuseppe 1888-1970CLC 7, 11, 15
See also CA 19-20; 25-28R; CAP 2; DLB 114
Unger, Douglas 1952- .... CLC 34
See also CA 130
Unsworth, Barry (Forster) 1930- ..... CLC 76
See also CA 25-28R; CANR 30, 54
Updike, John (Hoyer) 1932-CLC 1, 2, 3, 5, 7,
9, 13, 15, 23, 34, 43, 70; DA; DAB; DAC;
DAM MST, NOV, POET, POP; SSC 13, 27;
WLC
See also CA 1-4R; CABS 1; CANR 4, 33, 51;
CDALB 1968-1988; DLB 2, 5, 143; DLBD
3; DLBY 80, 82; MTCW
Upshaw, Margaret Mitchell
See Mitchell, Margaret (Munnerlyn)
Upton, Mark
See Sanders, Lawrence
Urdang, Constance (Henriette) 1922-CLC 47
See also CA 21-24R; CANR 9, 24
Uriel, Henry
See Faust, Frederick (Schiller)
Uris, Leon (Marcus) 1924- CLC 7, 32; DAM
NOV, POP
See also AITN 1, 2; BEST 89:2; CA 1-4R;
CANR 1, 40; MTCW; SATA 49
Urmuz
See Codrescu, Andrei
Urquhart, Jane 1949- .... CLC 90; DAC
See also CA 113; CANR 32
Ustinov, Peter (Alexander) 1921-........CLC 1
See also AITN 1; CA 13-16R; CANR 25, 51;
DLB 13
U Tam'si, Gerald Felix Tchicaya
See Tchicaya, Gerald Felix
U Tam'si, Tchicaya
See Tchicaya, Gerald Felix
Vachss, Andrew (Henry) 1942- ...... CLC 106
See also CA 118; CANR 44
Vachss, Andrew H.
See Vachss, Andrew (Henry)
Vaculik, Ludvik 1926- .... CLC 7
See also CA 53-56
Vaihinger, Hans 1852-1933 .... TCLC 71
See also CA 116
Valdez, Luis (Miguel) 1940- .. CLC 84; DAM
MULT; HLC
See also CA 101; CANR 32; DLB 122; HW
Valenzuela, Luisa 1938- CLC 31, 104; DAM
MULT; SSC 14
See also CA 101; CANR 32; DLB 113; HW
Valera y Alcala-Galiano, Juan 1824-1905
TCLC 10
See also CA 106
Valery, (Ambroise) Paul (Toussaint Jules) 1871-
1945 .... TCLC 4, 15; DAM POET; PC 9
See also CA 104; 122; MTCW
Valle-Inclan, Ramon (Maria) del 1866-1936
TCLC 5; DAM MULT; HLC
See also CA 106; 153; DLB 134

Vallejo, Antonio Buero
See Buero Vallejo, Antonio
Vallejo, Cesar (Abraham) 1892-1938TCLC 3,
56; DAM MULT; HLC
See also CA 105; 153; HW
Vallette, Marguerite Eymery
See Rachilde
Valle Y Pena, Ramon del
See Valle-Inclan, Ramon (Maria) del
Van Ash, Cay 1918- .... CLC 34
Vanbrugh, Sir John 1664-1726 LC 21; DAM
DRAM
See also DLB 80
Van Campen, Karl
See Campbell, John W(ood, Jr.)
Vance, Gerald
See Silverberg, Robert
Vance, Jack .... CLC 35
See also Kuttner, Henry; Vance, John Holbrook
See also DLB 8
Vance, John Holbrook 1916-
See Queen, Ellery; Vance, Jack
See also CA 29-32R; CANR 17; MTCW
Van Den Bogarde, Derek Jules Gaspard Ulric
Niven 1921-
See Bogarde, Dirk
See also CA 77-80
Vandenburgh, Jane .... CLC 59
Vanderhaeghe, Guy 1951- .... CLC 41
See also CA 113
van der Post, Laurens (Jan) 1906-1996CLC 5
See also CA 5-8R; 155; CANR 35
van de Wetering, Janwillem 1931- .. CLC 47
See also CA 49-52; CANR 4, 62
Van Dine, S. S. .... TCLC 23
See also Wright, Willard Huntington
Van Doren, Carl (Clinton) 1885-1950 T C L C
18
See also CA 111
Van Doren, Mark 1894-1972 .... CLC 6, 10
See also CA 1-4R; 37-40R; CANR 3; DLB 45;
MTCW
Van Druten, John (William) 1901-1957T C L C
2
See also CA 104; 161; DLB 10
Van Duyn, Mona (Jane) 1921- CLC 3, 7, 63;
DAM POET
See also CA 9-12R; CANR 7, 38, 60; DLB 5
Van Dyne, Edith
See Baum, L(yman) Frank
van Itallie, Jean-Claude 1936- .... CLC 3
See also CA 45-48; CAAS 2; CANR 1, 48; DLB
7
van Ostaijen, Paul 1896-1928 .... TCLC 33
Van Peebles, Melvin 1932-. CLC 2, 20; DAM
MULT
See also BW 2; CA 85-88; CANR 27
Vansittart, Peter 1920- .... CLC 42
See also CA 1-4R; CANR 3, 49
Van Vechten, Carl 1880-1964 .... CLC 33
See also CA 89-92; DLB 4, 9, 51
Van Vogt, A(lfred) E(lton) 1912-........CLC 1
See also CA 21-24R; CANR 28; DLB 8; SATA
14
Varda, Agnes 1928- .... CLC 16
See also CA 116; 122
Vargas Llosa, (Jorge) Mario (Pedro) 1936-
CLC 3, 6, 9, 10, 15, 31, 42, 85; DA; DAB;
DAC; DAM MST, MULT, NOV; HLC
See also CA 73-76; CANR 18, 32, 42; DLB 145;
HW; MTCW
Vasiliu, Gheorghe 1881-1957
See Bacovia, George

See also CA 123
Vassa, Gustavus
  See Equiano, Olaudah
Vassilikos, Vassilis 1933- .... **CLC 4, 8**
  See also CA 81-84
Vaughan, Henry 1621-1695 .... **LC 27**
  See also DLB 131
Vaughn, Stephanie .... **CLC 62**
Vazov, Ivan (Minchov) 1850-1921 . **TCLC 25**
  See also CA 121; DLB 147
Veblen, Thorstein (Bunde) 1857-1929 **T C L C 31**
  See also CA 115
Vega, Lope de 1562-1635 .... **LC 23**
Venison, Alfred
  See Pound, Ezra (Weston Loomis)
Verdi, Marie de
  See Mencken, H(enry) L(ouis)
Verdu, Matilde
  See Cela, Camilo Jose
Verga, Giovanni (Carmelo) 1840-1922**T C L C 3; SSC 21**
  See also CA 104; 123
Vergil 70B.C.-19B.C. .... **CMLC 9; DA; DAB; DAC; DAM MST, POET; PC 12; WLCS**
Verhaeren, Emile (Adolphe Gustave) 1855-1916 **TCLC 12**
  See also CA 109
Verlaine, Paul (Marie) 1844-1896**NCLC 2, 51; DAM POET; PC 2**
Verne, Jules (Gabriel) 1828-1905**TCLC 6, 52**
  See also AAYA 16; CA 110; 131; DLB 123; JRDA; MAICYA; SATA 21
Very, Jones 1813-1880 .... **NCLC 9**
  See also DLB 1
Vesaas, Tarjei 1897-1970 .... **CLC 48**
  See also CA 29-32R
Vialis, Gaston
  See Simenon, Georges (Jacques Christian)
Vian, Boris 1920-1959 .... **TCLC 9**
  See also CA 106; DLB 72
Viaud, (Louis Marie) Julien 1850-1923
  See Loti, Pierre
  See also CA 107
Vicar, Henry
  See Felsen, Henry Gregor
Vicker, Angus
  See Felsen, Henry Gregor
Vidal, Gore 1925-**CLC 2, 4, 6, 8, 10, 22, 33, 72; DAM NOV, POP**
  See also AITN 1; BEST 90:2; CA 5-8R; CANR 13, 45; DLB 6, 152; INT CANR-13; MTCW
Viereck, Peter (Robert Edwin) 1916- . **CLC 4**
  See also CA 1-4R; CANR 1, 47; DLB 5
Vigny, Alfred (Victor) de 1797-1863**NCLC 7; DAM POET**
  See also DLB 119
Vilakazi, Benedict Wallet 1906-1947**TCLC 37**
Villiers de l'Isle Adam, Jean Marie Mathias Philippe Auguste Comte 1838-1889 **NCLC 3; SSC 14**
  See also DLB 123
Villon, Francois 1431-1463(?) .... **PC 13**
Vinci, Leonardo da 1452-1519 .... **LC 12**
Vine, Barbara .... **CLC 50**
  See also Rendell, Ruth (Barbara)
  See also BEST 90:4
Vinge, Joan D(ennison) 1948-**CLC 30; SSC 24**
  See also CA 93-96; SATA 36
Violis, G.
  See Simenon, Georges (Jacques Christian)
Visconti, Luchino 1906-1976 .... **CLC 16**
  See also CA 81-84; 65-68; CANR 39

Vittorini, Elio 1908-1966 .... **CLC 6, 9, 14**
  See also CA 133; 25-28R
Vizenor, Gerald Robert 1934-**CLC 103; DAM MULT**
  See also CA 13-16R; CAAS 22; CANR 5, 21, 44; DLB 175; NNAL
Vizinczey, Stephen 1933- .... **CLC 40**
  See also CA 128; INT 128
Vliet, R(ussell) G(ordon) 1929-1984 . **CLC 22**
  See also CA 37-40R; 112; CANR 18
Vogau, Boris Andreyevich 1894-1937(?)
  See Pilnyak, Boris
  See also CA 123
Vogel, Paula A(nne) 1951- .... **CLC 76**
  See also CA 108
Voight, Ellen Bryant 1943- .... **CLC 54**
  See also CA 69-72; CANR 11, 29, 55; DLB 120
Voigt, Cynthia 1942- .... **CLC 30**
  See also AAYA 3; CA 106; CANR 18, 37, 40; CLR 13,48; INT CANR-18; JRDA; MAICYA; SATA 48, 79; SATA-Brief 33
Voinovich, Vladimir (Nikolaevich) 1932-**C L C 10, 49**
  See also CA 81-84; CAAS 12; CANR 33; MTCW
Vollmann, William T. 1959-...**CLC 89; DAM NOV, POP**
  See also CA 134
Voloshinov, V. N.
  See Bakhtin, Mikhail Mikhailovich
Voltaire 1694-1778 **LC 14; DA; DAB; DAC; DAM DRAM, MST; SSC 12; WLC**
von Daeniken, Erich 1935- .... **CLC 30**
  See also AITN 1; CA 37-40R; CANR 17, 44
von Daniken, Erich
  See von Daeniken, Erich
von Heidenstam, (Carl Gustaf) Verner
  See Heidenstam, (Carl Gustaf) Verner von
von Heyse, Paul (Johann Ludwig)
  See Heyse, Paul (Johann Ludwig von)
von Hofmannsthal, Hugo
  See Hofmannsthal, Hugo von
von Horvath, Odon
  See Horvath, Oedoen von
von Horvath, Oedoen
  See Horvath, Oedoen von
von Liliencron, (Friedrich Adolf Axel) Detlev
  See Liliencron, (Friedrich Adolf Axel) Detlev von
Vonnegut, Kurt, Jr. 1922-**CLC 1, 2, 3, 4, 5, 8, 12, 22, 40, 60; DA; DAB; DAC; DAM MST, NOV, POP; SSC 8; WLC**
  See also AAYA 6; AITN 1; BEST 90:4; CA 1-4R; CANR 1, 25, 49; CDALB 1968-1988; DLB 2, 8, 152; DLBD 3; DLBY 80; MTCW
Von Rachen, Kurt
  See Hubbard, L(afayette) Ron(ald)
von Rezzori (d'Arezzo), Gregor
  See Rezzori (d'Arezzo), Gregor von
von Sternberg, Josef
  See Sternberg, Josef von
Vorster, Gordon 1924- .... **CLC 34**
  See also CA 133
Vosce, Trudie
  See Ozick, Cynthia
Voznesensky, Andrei (Andreievich) 1933- **CLC 1, 15, 57; DAM POET**
  See also CA 89-92; CANR 37; MTCW
Waddington, Miriam 1917- .... **CLC 28**
  See also CA 21-24R; CANR 12, 30; DLB 68
Wagman, Fredrica 1937- .... **CLC 7**
  See also CA 97-100; INT 97-100
Wagner, Linda W.

See Wagner-Martin, Linda (C.)
Wagner, Linda Welshimer
  See Wagner-Martin, Linda (C.)
Wagner, Richard 1813-1883 .... **NCLC 9**
  See also DLB 129
Wagner-Martin, Linda (C.) 1936- .... **CLC 50**
  See also CA 159
Wagoner, David (Russell) 1926-**CLC 3, 5, 15**
  See also CA 1-4R; CAAS 3; CANR 2; DLB 5; SATA 14
Wah, Fred(erick James) 1939- .... **CLC 44**
  See also CA 107; 141; DLB 60
Wahloo, Per 1926-1975 .... **CLC 7**
  See also CA 61-64
Wahloo, Peter
  See Wahloo, Per
Wain, John (Barrington) 1925-1994 .**CLC 2, 11, 15, 46**
  See also CA 5-8R; 145; CAAS 4; CANR 23, 54; CDBLB 1960 to Present; DLB 15, 27, 139, 155; MTCW
Wajda, Andrzej 1926- ....**CLC 16**
  See also CA 102
Wakefield, Dan 1932- .... **CLC 7**
  See also CA 21-24R; CAAS 7
Wakoski, Diane 1937-.**CLC 2, 4, 7, 9, 11, 40; DAM POET; PC 15**
  See also CA 13-16R; CAAS 1; CANR 9, 60; DLB 5; INT CANR-9
Wakoski-Sherbell, Diane
  See Wakoski, Diane
Walcott, Derek (Alton) 1930-**CLC 2, 4, 9, 14, 25, 42, 67, 76; BLC; DAB; DAC; DAM MST, MULT, POET; DC 7**
  See also BW 2; CA 89-92; CANR 26, 47; DLB 117; DLBY 81; MTCW
Waldman, Anne 1945- .... **CLC 7**
  See also CA 37-40R; CAAS 17; CANR 34; DLB 16
Waldo, E. Hunter
  See Sturgeon, Theodore (Hamilton)
Waldo, Edward Hamilton
  See Sturgeon, Theodore (Hamilton)
Walker, Alice (Malsenior) 1944- **CLC 5, 6, 9, 19, 27, 46, 58, 103; BLC; DA; DAB; DAC; DAM MST, MULT, NOV, POET, POP; SSC 5; WLCS**
  See also AAYA 3; BEST 89:4; BW 2; CA 37-40R; CANR 9, 27, 49; CDALB 1968-1988; DLB 6, 33, 143; INT CANR-27; MTCW; SATA 31
Walker, David Harry 1911-1992 .... **CLC 14**
  See also CA 1-4R; 137; CANR 1; SATA 8; SATA-Obit 71
Walker, Edward Joseph 1934-
  See Walker, Ted
  See also CA 21-24R; CANR 12, 28, 53
Walker, George F. 1947- . **CLC 44, 61; DAB; DAC; DAM MST**
  See also CA 103; CANR 21, 43, 59; DLB 60
Walker, Joseph A. 1935- .... **CLC 19; DAM DRAM, MST**
  See also BW 1; CA 89-92; CANR 26; DLB 38
Walker, Margaret (Abigail) 1915- **CLC 1, 6; BLC; DAM MULT; PC 20**
  See also BW 2; CA 73-76; CANR 26, 54; DLB 76, 152; MTCW
Walker, Ted ....**CLC 13**
  See also Walker, Edward Joseph
  See also DLB 40
Wallace, David Foster 1962- .... **CLC 50**
  See also CA 132; CANR 59
Wallace, Dexter

See Masters, Edgar Lee

Wallace, (Richard Horatio) Edgar 1875-1932 **TCLC 57**
See also CA 115; DLB 70

Wallace, Irving 1916-1990 . **CLC 7, 13; DAM NOV, POP**
See also AITN 1; CA 1-4R; 132; CAAS 1; CANR 1, 27; INT CANR-27; MTCW

Wallant, Edward Lewis 1926-1962 **CLC 5, 10**
See also CA 1-4R; CANR 22; DLB 2, 28, 143; MTCW

Walley, Byron
See Card, Orson Scott

Walpole, Horace 1717-1797 .... **LC 2**
See also DLB 39, 104

Walpole, Hugh (Seymour) 1884-1941 **TCLC 5**
See also CA 104; DLB 34

Walser, Martin 1927- .... **CLC 27**
See also CA 57-60; CANR 8, 46; DLB 75, 124

Walser, Robert 1878-1956 **TCLC 18; SSC 20**
See also CA 118; DLB 66

Walsh, Jill Paton .... **CLC 35**
See also Paton Walsh, Gillian
See also AAYA 11; CLR 2; DLB 161; SAAS 3

Walter, Villiam Christian
See Andersen, Hans Christian

Wambaugh, Joseph (Aloysius, Jr.) 1937- **CLC 3, 18; DAM NOV, POP**
See also AITN 1; BEST 89:3; CA 33-36R; CANR 42; DLB 6; DLBY 83; MTCW

Wang Wei 699(?)-761(?) .... **PC 18**

Ward, Arthur Henry Sarsfield 1883-1959
See Rohmer, Sax
See also CA 108

Ward, Douglas Turner 1930- .... **CLC 19**
See also BW 1; CA 81-84; CANR 27; DLB 7, 38

Ward, Mary Augusta
See Ward, Mrs. Humphry

Ward, Mrs. Humphry 1851-1920 .. **TCLC 55**
See also DLB 18

Ward, Peter
See Faust, Frederick (Schiller)

Warhol, Andy 1928(?)-1987 .... **CLC 20**
See also AAYA 12; BEST 89:4; CA 89-92; 121; CANR 34

Warner, Francis (Robert le Plastrier) 1937- **CLC 14**
See also CA 53-56; CANR 11

Warner, Marina 1946- .... **CLC 59**
See also CA 65-68; CANR 21, 55

Warner, Rex (Ernest) 1905-1986 ..... **CLC 45**
See also CA 89-92; 119; DLB 15

Warner, Susan (Bogert) 1819-1885 **NCLC 31**
See also DLB 3, 42

Warner, Sylvia (Constance) Ashton
See Ashton-Warner, Sylvia (Constance)

Warner, Sylvia Townsend 1893-1978 **CLC 7, 19; SSC 23**
See also CA 61-64; 77-80; CANR 16, 60; DLB 34, 139; MTCW

Warren, Mercy Otis 1728-1814 ...... **NCLC 13**
See also DLB 31

Warren, Robert Penn 1905-1989 **CLC 1, 4, 6, 8, 10, 13, 18, 39, 53, 59; DA; DAB; DAC; DAM MST, NOV, POET; SSC 4; WLC**
See also AITN 1; CA 13-16R; 129; CANR 10, 47; CDALB 1968-1988; DLB 2, 48, 152; DLBY 80, 89; INT CANR-10; MTCW; SATA 46; SATA-Obit 63

Warshofsky, Isaac
See Singer, Isaac Bashevis

Warton, Thomas 1728-1790 ..... **LC 15; DAM POET**
See also DLB 104, 109

Waruk, Kona
See Harris, (Theodore) Wilson

Warung, Price 1855-1911 .... **TCLC 45**

Warwick, Jarvis
See Garner, Hugh

Washington, Alex
See Harris, Mark

Washington, Booker T(aliaferro) 1856-1915 **TCLC 10; BLC; DAM MULT**
See also BW 1; CA 114; 125; SATA 28

Washington, George 1732-1799 .... **LC 25**
See also DLB 31

Wassermann, (Karl) Jakob 1873-1934 **TCLC 6**
See also CA 104; DLB 66

Wasserstein, Wendy 1950- ... **CLC 32, 59, 90; DAM DRAM; DC 4**
See also CA 121; 129; CABS 3; CANR 53; INT 129; SATA 94

Waterhouse, Keith (Spencer) 1929- . **CLC 47**
See also CA 5-8R; CANR 38; DLB 13, 15; MTCW

Waters, Frank (Joseph) 1902-1995 ... **CLC 88**
See also CA 5-8R; 149; CAAS 13; CANR 3, 18, 63; DLBY 86

Waters, Roger 1944- .... **CLC 35**

Watkins, Frances Ellen
See Harper, Frances Ellen Watkins

Watkins, Gerrold
See Malzberg, Barry N(athaniel)

Watkins, Gloria 1955(?)-
See hooks, bell
See also BW 2; CA 143

Watkins, Paul 1964- .... **CLC 55**
See also CA 132; CANR 62

Watkins, Vernon Phillips 1906-1967 **CLC 43**
See also CA 9-10; 25-28R; CAP 1; DLB 20

Watson, Irving S.
See Mencken, H(enry) L(ouis)

Watson, John H.
See Farmer, Philip Jose

Watson, Richard F.
See Silverberg, Robert

Waugh, Auberon (Alexander) 1939- .. **CLC 7**
See also CA 45-48; CANR 6, 22; DLB 14

Waugh, Evelyn (Arthur St. John) 1903-1966 **CLC 1, 3, 8, 13, 19, 27, 44, 107; DA; DAB; DAC; DAM MST, NOV, POP; WLC**
See also CA 85-88; 25-28R; CANR 22; CDBLB 1914-1945; DLB 15, 162; MTCW

Waugh, Harriet 1944- .... **CLC 6**
See also CA 85-88; CANR 22

Ways, C. R.
See Blount, Roy (Alton), Jr.

Waystaff, Simon
See Swift, Jonathan

Webb, (Martha) Beatrice (Potter) 1858-1943 **TCLC 22**
See also Potter, (Helen) Beatrix
See also CA 117

Webb, Charles (Richard) 1939- .... **CLC 7**
See also CA 25-28R

Webb, James H(enry), Jr. 1946- .... **CLC 22**
See also CA 81-84

Webb, Mary (Gladys Meredith) 1881-1927 **TCLC 24**
See also CA 123; DLB 34

Webb, Mrs. Sidney
See Webb, (Martha) Beatrice (Potter)

Webb, Phyllis 1927- .... **CLC 18**
See also CA 104; CANR 23; DLB 53

Webb, Sidney (James) 1859-1947 .. **TCLC 22**
See also CA 117

Webber, Andrew Lloyd .... **CLC 21**
See also Lloyd Webber, Andrew

Weber, Lenora Mattingly 1895-1971 **CLC 12**
See also CA 19-20; 29-32R; CAP 1; SATA 2; SATA-Obit 26

Weber, Max 1864-1920 .... **TCLC 69**
See also CA 109

Webster, John 1579(?)-1634(?) ... **LC 33; DA; DAB; DAC; DAM DRAM, MST; DC 2; WLC**
See also CDBLB Before 1660; DLB 58

Webster, Noah 1758-1843 .... **NCLC 30**

Wedekind, (Benjamin) Frank(lin) 1864-1918 **TCLC 7; DAM DRAM**
See also CA 104; 153; DLB 118

Weidman, Jerome 1913- .... **CLC 7**
See also AITN 2; CA 1-4R; CANR 1; DLB 28

Weil, Simone (Adolphine) 1909-1943 **TCLC 23**
See also CA 117; 159

Weinstein, Nathan
See West, Nathanael

Weinstein, Nathan von Wallenstein
See West, Nathanael

Weir, Peter (Lindsay) 1944- .... **CLC 20**
See also CA 113; 123

Weiss, Peter (Ulrich) 1916-1982 **CLC 3, 15, 51; DAM DRAM**
See also CA 45-48; 106; CANR 3; DLB 69, 124

Weiss, Theodore (Russell) 1916- **CLC 3, 8, 14**
See also CA 9-12R; CAAS 2; CANR 46; DLB 5

Welch, (Maurice) Denton 1915-1948 **TCLC 22**
See also CA 121; 148

Welch, James 1940- ..... **CLC 6, 14, 52; DAM MULT, POP**
See also CA 85-88; CANR 42; DLB 175; NNAL

Weldon, Fay 1931- .. **CLC 6, 9, 11, 19, 36, 59; DAM POP**
See also CA 21-24R; CANR 16, 46, 63; CDBLB 1960 to Present; DLB 14; INT CANR-16; MTCW

Wellek, Rene 1903-1995 .... **CLC 28**
See also CA 5-8R; 150; CAAS 7; CANR 8; DLB 63; INT CANR-8

Weller, Michael 1942- .... **CLC 10, 53**
See also CA 85-88

Weller, Paul 1958- .... **CLC 26**

Wellershoff, Dieter 1925- .... **CLC 46**
See also CA 89-92; CANR 16, 37

Welles, (George) Orson 1915-1985 **CLC 20, 80**
See also CA 93-96; 117

Wellman, Mac 1945- .... **CLC 65**

Wellman, Manly Wade 1903-1986 ... **CLC 49**
See also CA 1-4R; 118; CANR 6, 16, 44; SATA 6; SATA-Obit 47

Wells, Carolyn 1869(?)-1942 .... **TCLC 35**
See also CA 113; DLB 11

Wells, H(erbert) G(eorge) 1866-1946 **TCLC 6, 12, 19; DA; DAB; DAC; DAM MST, NOV; SSC 6; WLC**
See also AAYA 18; CA 110; 121; CDBLB 1914-1945; DLB 34, 70, 156, 178; MTCW; SATA 20

Wells, Rosemary 1943- .... **CLC 12**
See also AAYA 13; CA 85-88; CANR 48; CLR 16; MAICYA; SAAS 1; SATA 18, 69

Welty, Eudora 1909- . **CLC 1, 2, 5, 14, 22, 33, 105; DA; DAB; DAC; DAM MST, NOV; SSC 1, 27; WLC**
See also CA 9-12R; CABS 1; CANR 32; CDALB 1941-1968; DLB 2, 102, 143;

DLBD 12; DLBY 87; MTCW

Wen I-to 1899-1946 .... TCLC 28

Wentworth, Robert
See Hamilton, Edmond

Werfel, Franz (Viktor) 1890-1945 ... TCLC 8
See also CA 104; 161; DLB 81, 124

Wergeland, Henrik Arnold 1808-1845 N C L C
5

Wersba, Barbara 1932- .... CLC 30
See also AAYA 2; CA 29-32R; CANR 16, 38;
CLR 3; DLB 52; JRDA; MAICYA; SAAS 2;
SATA 1, 58

Wertmueller, Lina 1928- .... CLC 16
See also CA 97-100; CANR 39

Wescott, Glenway 1901-1987 .... CLC 13
See also CA 13-16R; 121; CANR 23; DLB 4,
9, 102

Wesker, Arnold 1932-.... CLC 3, 5, 42; DAB;
DAM DRAM
See also CA 1-4R; CAAS 7; CANR 1, 33;
CDBLB 1960 to Present; DLB 13; MTCW

Wesley, Richard (Errol) 1945- .... CLC 7
See also BW 1; CA 57-60; CANR 27; DLB 38

Wessel, Johan Herman 1742-1785 .... LC 7

West, Anthony (Panther) 1914-1987 CLC 50
See also CA 45-48; 124; CANR 3, 19; DLB 15

West, C. P.
See Wodehouse, P(elham) G(renville)

West, (Mary) Jessamyn 1902-1984 CLC 7, 17
See also CA 9-12R; 112; CANR 27; DLB 6;
DLBY 84; MTCW; SATA-Obit 37

West, Morris L(anglo) 1916- ...... CLC 6, 33
See also CA 5-8R; CANR 24, 49, 64; MTCW

West, Nathanael 1903-1940 TCLC 1, 14, 44;
SSC 16
See also CA 104; 125; CDALB 1929-1941;
DLB 4, 9, 28; MTCW

West, Owen
See Koontz, Dean R(ay)

West, Paul 1930- .... CLC 7, 14, 96
See also CA 13-16R; CAAS 7; CANR 22, 53;
DLB 14; INT CANR-22

West, Rebecca 1892-1983 ... CLC 7, 9, 31, 50
See also CA 5-8R; 109; CANR 19; DLB 36;
DLBY 83; MTCW

Westall, Robert (Atkinson) 1929-1993 CLC 17
See also AAYA 12; CA 69-72; 141; CANR 18;
CLR 13; JRDA; MAICYA; SAAS 2; SATA
23, 69; SATA-Obit 75

Westlake, Donald E(dwin) 1933- CLC 7, 33;
DAM POP
See also CA 17-20R; CAAS 13; CANR 16, 44;
INT CANR-16

Westmacott, Mary
See Christie, Agatha (Mary Clarissa)

Weston, Allen
See Norton, Andre

Wetcheek, J. L.
See Feuchtwanger, Lion

Wetering, Janwillem van de
See van de Wetering, Janwillem

Wetherell, Elizabeth
See Warner, Susan (Bogert)

Whale, James 1889-1957 .... TCLC 63

Whalen, Philip 1923- .... CLC 6, 29
See also CA 9-12R; CANR 5, 39; DLB 16

Wharton, Edith (Newbold Jones) 1862-1937
TCLC 3, 9, 27, 53; DA; DAB; DAC; DAM
MST, NOV; SSC 6; WLC
See also CA 104; 132; CDALB 1865-1917;
DLB 4, 9, 12, 78; DLBD 13; MTCW

Wharton, James
See Mencken, H(enry) L(ouis)

Wharton, William (a pseudonym) CLC 18, 37
See also CA 93-96; DLBY 80; INT 93-96

Wheatley (Peters), Phillis 1754(?)-1784 LC 3;
BLC; DA; DAC; DAM MST, MULT,
POET; PC 3; WLC
See also CDALB 1640-1865; DLB 31, 50

Wheelock, John Hall 1886-1978 .... CLC 14
See also CA 13-16R; 77-80; CANR 14; DLB
45

White, E(lwyn) B(rooks) 1899-1985 CLC 10,
34, 39; DAM POP
See also AITN 2; CA 13-16R; 116; CANR 16,
37; CLR 1, 21; DLB 11, 22; MAICYA;
MTCW; SATA 2, 29; SATA-Obit 44

White, Edmund (Valentine III) 1940- CLC 27;
DAM POP
See also AAYA 7; CA 45-48; CANR 3, 19, 36,
62; MTCW

White, Patrick (Victor Martindale) 1912-1990
CLC 3, 4, 5, 7, 9, 18, 65, 69
See also CA 81-84; 132; CANR 43; MTCW

White, Phyllis Dorothy James 1920-
See James, P. D.
See also CA 21-24R; CANR 17, 43; DAM POP;
MTCW

White, T(erence) H(anbury) 1906-1964 C L C
30
See also AAYA 22; CA 73-76; CANR 37; DLB
160; JRDA; MAICYA; SATA 12

White, Terence de Vere 1912-1994 ... CLC 49
See also CA 49-52; 145; CANR 3

White, Walter F(rancis) 1893-1955 TCLC 15
See also White, Walter
See also BW 1; CA 115; 124; DLB 51

White, William Hale 1831-1913
See Rutherford, Mark
See also CA 121

Whitehead, E(dward) A(nthony) 1933- CLC 5
See also CA 65-68; CANR 58

Whitemore, Hugh (John) 1936- .... CLC 37
See also CA 132; INT 132

Whitman, Sarah Helen (Power) 1803-1878
NCLC 19
See also DLB 1

Whitman, Walt(er) 1819-1892 .. NCLC 4, 31;
DA; DAB; DAC; DAM MST, POET; PC
3; WLC
See also CDALB 1640-1865; DLB 3, 64; SATA
20

Whitney, Phyllis A(yame) 1903- ..... CLC 42;
DAM POP
See also AITN 2; BEST 90:3; CA 1-4R; CANR
3, 25, 38, 60; JRDA; MAICYA; SATA 1, 30

Whittemore, (Edward) Reed (Jr.) 1919- CLC 4
See also CA 9-12R; CAAS 8; CANR 4; DLB 5

Whittier, John Greenleaf 1807-1892 NCLC 8,
59
See also DLB 1

Whittlebot, Hernia
See Coward, Noel (Peirce)

Wicker, Thomas Grey 1926-
See Wicker, Tom
See also CA 65-68; CANR 21, 46

Wicker, Tom .... CLC 7
See also Wicker, Thomas Grey

Wideman, John Edgar 1941- CLC 5, 34, 36,
67; BLC; DAM MULT
See also BW 2; CA 85-88; CANR 14, 42; DLB
33, 143

Wiebe, Rudy (Henry) 1934- .. CLC 6, 11, 14;
DAC; DAM MST
See also CA 37-40R; CANR 42; DLB 60

Wieland, Christoph Martin 1733-1813 N C L C
17
See also DLB 97

Wiene, Robert 1881-1938 .... TCLC 56

Wieners, John 1934- .... CLC 7
See also CA 13-16R; DLB 16

Wiesel, Elie(zer) 1928- CLC 3, 5, 11, 37; DA;
DAB; DAC; DAM MST, NOV; WLCS 2
See also AAYA 7; AITN 1; CA 5-8R; CAAS 4;
CANR 8, 40; DLB 83; DLBY 87; INT
CANR-8; MTCW; SATA 56

Wiggins, Marianne 1947- .... CLC 57
See also BEST 89:3; CA 130; CANR 60

Wight, James Alfred 1916-
See Herriot, James
See also CA 77-80; SATA 55; SATA-Brief 44

Wilbur, Richard (Purdy) 1921- CLC 3, 6, 9, 14,
53; DA; DAB; DAC; DAM MST, POET
See also CA 1-4R; CABS 2; CANR 2, 29; DLB
5, 169; INT CANR-29; MTCW; SATA 9

Wild, Peter 1940- .... CLC 14
See also CA 37-40R; DLB 5

Wilde, Oscar (Fingal O'Flahertie Wills)
1854(?)-1900 TCLC 1, 8, 23, 41; DA; DAB;
DAC; DAM DRAM, MST, NOV; SSC 11;
WLC
See also CA 104; 119; CDBLB 1890-1914;
DLB 10, 19, 34, 57, 141, 156; SATA 24

Wilder, Billy .... CLC 20
See also Wilder, Samuel
See also DLB 26

Wilder, Samuel 1906-
See Wilder, Billy
See also CA 89-92

Wilder, Thornton (Niven) 1897-1975 CLC 1, 5,
6, 10, 15, 35, 82; DA; DAB; DAC; DAM
DRAM, MST, NOV; DC 1; WLC
See also AITN 2; CA 13-16R; 61-64; CANR
40; DLB 4, 7, 9; MTCW

Wilding, Michael 1942- .... CLC 73
See also CA 104; CANR 24, 49

Wiley, Richard 1944- .... CLC 44
See also CA 121; 129

Wilhelm, Kate .... CLC 7
See also Wilhelm, Katie Gertrude
See also AAYA 20; CAAS 5; DLB 8; INT
CANR-17

Wilhelm, Katie Gertrude 1928-
See Wilhelm, Kate
See also CA 37-40R; CANR 17, 36, 60; MTCW

Wilkins, Mary
See Freeman, Mary Eleanor Wilkins

Willard, Nancy 1936- .... CLC 7, 37
See also CA 89-92; CANR 10, 39; CLR 5; DLB
5, 52; MAICYA; MTCW; SATA 37, 71;
SATA-Brief 30

Williams, C(harles) K(enneth) 1936- CLC 33,
56; DAM POET
See also CA 37-40R; CAAS 26; CANR 57; DLB
5

Williams, Charles
See Collier, James L(incoln)

Williams, Charles (Walter Stansby) 1886-1945
TCLC 1, 11
See also CA 104; DLB 100, 153

Williams, (George) Emlyn 1905-1987 CLC 15;
DAM DRAM
See also CA 104; 123; CANR 36; DLB 10, 77;
MTCW

Williams, Hugo 1942- .... CLC 42
See also CA 17-20R; CANR 45; DLB 40

Williams, J. Walker
See Wodehouse, P(elham) G(renville)

Williams, John A(lfred) 1925- ..... CLC 5, 13;

Author Index

BLC; DAM MULT
See also BW 2; CA 53-56; CAAS 3; CANR 6, 26, 51; DLB 2, 33; INT CANR-6

Williams, Jonathan (Chamberlain) 1929-
CLC 13
See also CA 9-12R; CAAS 12; CANR 8; DLB 5

Williams, Joy 1944- .... **CLC 31**
See also CA 41-44R; CANR 22, 48

Williams, Norman 1952- .... **CLC 39**
See also CA 118

Williams, Sherley Anne 1944-CLC 89; BLC;
DAM MULT, POET
See also BW 2; CA 73-76; CANR 25; DLB 41; INT CANR-25; SATA 78

Williams, Shirley
See Williams, Sherley Anne

Williams, Tennessee 1911-1983CLC 1, 2, 5, 7,
8, 11, 15, 19, 30, 39, 45, 71; DA; DAB;
DAC; DAM DRAM, MST; DC 4; WLC
See also AITN 1, 2; CA 5-8R; 108; CABS 3; CANR 31; CDALB 1941-1968; DLB 7; DLBD 4; DLBY 83; MTCW

Williams, Thomas (Alonzo) 1926-1990CLC 14
See also CA 1-4R; 132; CANR 2

Williams, William C.
See Williams, William Carlos

Williams, William Carlos 1883-1963CLC 1, 2,
5, 9, 13, 22, 42, 67; DA; DAB; DAC; DAM
MST, POET; PC 7
See also CA 89-92; CANR 34; CDALB 1917-1929; DLB 4, 16, 54, 86; MTCW

Williamson, David (Keith) 1942- ..... **CLC 56**
See also CA 103; CANR 41

Williamson, Ellen Douglas 1905-1984
See Douglas, Ellen
See also CA 17-20R; 114; CANR 39

Williamson, Jack .... **CLC 29**
See also Williamson, John Stewart
See also CAAS 8; DLB 8

Williamson, John Stewart 1908-
See Williamson, Jack
See also CA 17-20R; CANR 23

Willie, Frederick
See Lovecraft, H(oward) P(hillips)

Willingham, Calder (Baynard, Jr.) 1922-1995
CLC 5, 51
See also CA 5-8R; 147; CANR 3; DLB 2, 44; MTCW

Willis, Charles
See Clarke, Arthur C(harles)

Willy
See Colette, (Sidonie-Gabrielle)

Willy, Colette
See Colette, (Sidonie-Gabrielle)

Wilson, A(ndrew) N(orman) 1950- .. **CLC 33**
See also CA 112; 122; DLB 14, 155

Wilson, Angus (Frank Johnstone) 1913-1991
CLC 2, 3, 5, 25, 34; SSC 21
See also CA 5-8R; 134; CANR 21; DLB 15, 139, 155; MTCW

Wilson, August 1945- CLC 39, 50, 63; BLC;
DA; DAB; DAC; DAM DRAM, MST,
MULT; DC 2; WLCS
See also AAYA 16; BW 2; CA 115; 122; CANR 42, 54; MTCW

Wilson, Brian 1942- .... **CLC 12**

Wilson, Colin 1931- .... **CLC 3, 14**
See also CA 1-4R; CAAS 5; CANR 1, 22, 33; DLB 14; MTCW

Wilson, Dirk
See Pohl, Frederik

Wilson, Edmund 1895-1972CLC 1, 2, 3, 8, 24

See also CA 1-4R; 37-40R; CANR 1, 46; DLB 63; MTCW

Wilson, Ethel Davis (Bryant) 1888(?)-1980
CLC 13; DAC; DAM POET
See also CA 102; DLB 68; MTCW

Wilson, John 1785-1854 .... **NCLC 5**

Wilson, John (Anthony) Burgess 1917-1993
See Burgess, Anthony
See also CA 1-4R; 143; CANR 2, 46; DAC; DAM NOV; MTCW

Wilson, Lanford 1937- CLC 7, 14, 36; DAM
DRAM
See also CA 17-20R; CABS 3; CANR 45; DLB 7

Wilson, Robert M. 1944- .... **CLC 7, 9**
See also CA 49-52; CANR 2, 41; MTCW

Wilson, Robert McLiam 1964- .... **CLC 59**
See also CA 132

Wilson, Sloan 1920- .... **CLC 32**
See also CA 1-4R; CANR 1, 44

Wilson, Snoo 1948- .... **CLC 33**
See also CA 69-72

Wilson, William S(mith) 1932- .... **CLC 49**
See also CA 81-84

Wilson, Woodrow 1856-1924 .... **TCLC 73**
See also DLB 47

Winchilsea, Anne (Kingsmill) Finch Counte
1661-1720
See Finch, Anne

Windham, Basil
See Wodehouse, P(elham) G(renville)

Wingrove, David (John) 1954- .... **CLC 68**
See also CA 133

Wintergreen, Jane
See Duncan, Sara Jeannette

Winters, Janet Lewis .... **CLC 41**
See also Lewis, Janet
See also DLBY 87

Winters, (Arthur) Yvor 1900-1968 CLC 4, 8,
32
See also CA 11-12; 25-28R; CAP 1; DLB 48; MTCW

Winterson, Jeanette 1959-CLC 64; DAM POP
See also CA 136; CANR 58

Winthrop, John 1588-1649 .... **LC 31**
See also DLB 24, 30

Wiseman, Frederick 1930- .... **CLC 20**
See also CA 159

Wister, Owen 1860-1938 .... **TCLC 21**
See also CA 108; DLB 9, 78; SATA 62

Witkacy
See Witkiewicz, Stanislaw Ignacy

Witkiewicz, Stanislaw Ignacy 1885-1939
TCLC 8
See also CA 105

Wittgenstein, Ludwig (Josef Johann) 1889-1951
TCLC 59
See also CA 113

Wittig, Monique 1935(?)- .... **CLC 22**
See also CA 116; 135; DLB 83

Wittlin, Jozef 1896-1976 .... **CLC 25**
See also CA 49-52; 65-68; CANR 3

Wodehouse, P(elham) G(renville) 1881-1975
CLC 1, 2, 5, 10, 22; DAB; DAC; DAM
NOV; SSC 2
See also AITN 2; CA 45-48; 57-60; CANR 3, 33; CDBLB 1914-1945; DLB 34, 162; MTCW; SATA 22

Woiwode, L.
See Woiwode, Larry (Alfred)

Woiwode, Larry (Alfred) 1941- ... **CLC 6, 10**
See also CA 73-76; CANR 16; DLB 6; INT CANR-16

Wojciechowska, Maia (Teresa) 1927-CLC 26
See also AAYA 8; CA 9-12R; CANR 4, 41; CLR 1; JRDA; MAICYA; SAAS 1; SATA 1, 28, 83

Wolf, Christa 1929- .... **CLC 14, 29, 58**
See also CA 85-88; CANR 45; DLB 75; MTCW

Wolfe, Gene (Rodman) 1931- CLC 25; DAM
POP
See also CA 57-60; CAAS 9; CANR 6, 32, 60; DLB 8

Wolfe, George C. 1954- .... **CLC 49**
See also CA 149

Wolfe, Thomas (Clayton) 1900-1938TCLC 4,
13, 29, 61; DA; DAB; DAC; DAM MST,
NOV; WLC
See also CA 104; 132; CDALB 1929-1941; DLB 9, 102; DLBD 2, 16; DLBY 85; MTCW

Wolfe, Thomas Kennerly, Jr. 1931-
See Wolfe, Tom
See also CA 13-16R; CANR 9, 33; DAM POP; INT CANR-9; MTCW

Wolfe, Tom .... **CLC 1, 2, 9, 15, 35, 51**
See also Wolfe, Thomas Kennerly, Jr.
See also AAYA 8; AITN 2; BEST 89:1; DLB 152

Wolff, Geoffrey (Ansell) 1937- .... **CLC 41**
See also CA 29-32R; CANR 29, 43

Wolff, Sonia
See Levitin, Sonia (Wolff)

Wolff, Tobias (Jonathan Ansell) 1945- .. **C L C**
39, 64
See also AAYA 16; BEST 90:2; CA 114; 117; CAAS 22; CANR 54; DLB 130; INT 117

Wolfram von Eschenbach c. 1170-c. 1220
CMLC 5
See also DLB 138

Wolitzer, Hilma 1930- .... **CLC 17**
See also CA 65-68; CANR 18, 40; INT CANR-18; SATA 31

Wollstonecraft, Mary 1759-1797 .... **LC 5**
See also CDBLB 1789-1832; DLB 39, 104, 158

Wonder, Stevie .... **CLC 12**
See also Morris, Steveland Judkins

Wong, Jade Snow 1922- .... **CLC 17**
See also CA 109

Woodberry, George Edward 1855-1930
TCLC 73
See also DLB 71, 103

Woodcott, Keith
See Brunner, John (Kilian Houston)

Woodruff, Robert W.
See Mencken, H(enry) L(ouis)

Woolf, (Adeline) Virginia 1882-1941TCLC 1,
5, 20, 43, 56; DA; DAB; DAC; DAM MST,
NOV; SSC 7; WLC
See also CA 104; 130; CANR 64; CDBLB 1914-1945; DLB 36, 100, 162; DLBD 10; MTCW

Woolf, Virginia Adeline
See Woolf, (Adeline) Virginia

Woollcott, Alexander (Humphreys) 1887-1943
TCLC 5
See also CA 105; 161; DLB 29

Woolrich, Cornell 1903-1968 .... **CLC 77**
See also Hopley-Woolrich, Cornell George

Wordsworth, Dorothy 1771-1855 .. **NCLC 25**
See also DLB 107

Wordsworth, William 1770-1850 ..NCLC 12,
38; DA; DAB; DAC; DAM MST, POET;
PC 4; WLC
See also CDBLB 1789-1832; DLB 93, 107

Wouk, Herman 1915-CLC 1, 9, 38; DAM NOV,
POP

See also CA 5-8R; CANR 6, 33; DLBY 82; INT CANR-6; MTCW

Wright, Charles (Penzel, Jr.) 1935-**CLC 6, 13, 28**
See also CA 29-32R; CAAS 7; CANR 23, 36, 62; DLB 165; DLBY 82; MTCW

Wright, Charles Stevenson 1932- ... **CLC 49; BLC 3; DAM MULT, POET**
See also BW 1; CA 9-12R; CANR 26; DLB 33

Wright, Jack R.
See Harris, Mark

Wright, James (Arlington) 1927-1980**CLC 3, 5, 10, 28; DAM POET**
See also AITN 2; CA 49-52; 97-100; CANR 4, 34, 64; DLB 5, 169; MTCW

Wright, Judith (Arandell) 1915- **CLC 11, 53; PC 14**
See also CA 13-16R; CANR 31; MTCW; SATA 14

Wright, L(aurali) R. 1939- .... **CLC 44**
See also CA 138

Wright, Richard (Nathaniel) 1908-1960 **C L C 1, 3, 4, 9, 14, 21, 48, 74; BLC; DA; DAB; DAC; DAM MST, MULT, NOV; SSC 2; WLC**
See also AAYA 5; BW 1; CA 108; CANR 64; CDALB 1929-1941; DLB 76, 102; DLBD 2; MTCW

Wright, Richard B(ruce) 1937- ....**CLC 6**
See also CA 85-88; DLB 53

Wright, Rick 1945- .... **CLC 35**

Wright, Rowland
See Wells, Carolyn

Wright, Stephen 1946- .... **CLC 33**

Wright, Willard Huntington 1888-1939
See Van Dine, S. S.
See also CA 115; DLBD 16

Wright, William 1930- .... **CLC 44**
See also CA 53-56; CANR 7, 23

Wroth, LadyMary 1587-1653(?) .... **LC 30**
See also DLB 121

Wu Ch'eng-en 1500(?)-1582(?) .... **LC 7**

Wu Ching-tzu 1701-1754 .... **LC 2**

Wurlitzer, Rudolph 1938(?)- ... **CLC 2, 4, 15**
See also CA 85-88; DLB 173

Wycherley, William 1641-1715**LC 8, 21; DAM DRAM**
See also CDBLB 1660-1789; DLB 80

Wylie, Elinor (Morton Hoyt) 1885-1928 **TCLC 8**
See also CA 105; DLB 9, 45

Wylie, Philip (Gordon) 1902-1971 ... **CLC 43**
See also CA 21-22; 33-36R; CAP 2; DLB 9

Wyndham, John .... **CLC 19**
See also Harris, John (Wyndham Parkes Lucas) Beynon

Wyss, Johann David Von 1743-1818**NCLC 10**
See also JRDA; MAICYA; SATA 29; SATA-Brief 27

Xenophon c. 430B.C.-c. 354B.C. ... **CMLC 17**
See also DLB 176

Yakumo Koizumi
See Hearn, (Patricio) Lafcadio (Tessima Carlos)

Yanez, Jose Donoso
See Donoso (Yanez), Jose

Yanovsky, Basile S.
See Yanovsky, V(assily) S(emenovich)

Yanovsky, V(assily) S(emenovich) 1906-1989 **CLC 2, 18**
See also CA 97-100; 129

Yates, Richard 1926-1992 .... **CLC 7, 8, 23**
See also CA 5-8R; 139; CANR 10, 43; DLB 2; DLBY 81, 92; INT CANR-10

Yeats, W. B.
See Yeats, William Butler

Yeats, William Butler 1865-1939**TCLC 1, 11, 18, 31; DA; DAB; DAC; DAM DRAM, MST, POET; PC 20; WLC**
See also CA 104; 127; CANR 45; CDBLB 1890-1914; DLB 10, 19, 98, 156; MTCW

Yehoshua, A(braham) B. 1936- .. **CLC 13, 31**
See also CA 33-36R; CANR 43

Yep, Laurence Michael 1948-...........**CLC 35**
See also AAYA 5; CA 49-52; CANR 1, 46; CLR 3, 17; DLB 52; JRDA; MAICYA; SATA 7, 69

Yerby, Frank G(arvin) 1916-1991 **CLC 1, 7, 22; BLC; DAM MULT**
See also BW 1; CA 9-12R; 136; CANR 16, 52; DLB 76; INT CANR-16; MTCW

Yesenin, Sergei Alexandrovich
See Esenin, Sergei (Alexandrovich)

Yevtushenko, Yevgeny (Alexandrovich) 1933- **CLC 1, 3, 13, 26, 51; DAM POET**
See also CA 81-84; CANR 33, 54; MTCW

Yezierska, Anzia 1885(?)-1970 .... **CLC 46**
See also CA 126; 89-92; DLB 28; MTCW

Yglesias, Helen 1915- .... **CLC 7, 22**
See also CA 37-40R; CAAS 20; CANR 15; INT CANR-15; MTCW

Yokomitsu Riichi 1898-1947 .... **TCLC 47**

Yonge, Charlotte (Mary) 1823-1901**TCLC 48**
See also CA 109; DLB 18, 163; SATA 17

York, Jeremy
See Creasey, John

York, Simon
See Heinlein, Robert A(nson)

Yorke, Henry Vincent 1905-1974 ...... **CLC 13**
See also Green, Henry
See also CA 85-88; 49-52

Yosano Akiko 1878-1942 .... **TCLC 59; PC 11**
See also CA 161

Yoshimoto, Banana .... **CLC 84**
See also Yoshimoto, Mahoko

Yoshimoto, Mahoko 1964-
See Yoshimoto, Banana
See also CA 144

Young, Al(bert James) 1939- .**CLC 19; BLC; DAM MULT**
See also BW 2; CA 29-32R; CANR 26; DLB 33

Young, Andrew (John) 1885-1971 ...... **CLC 5**
See also CA 5-8R; CANR 7, 29

Young, Collier
See Bloch, Robert (Albert)

Young, Edward 1683-1765 .... **LC 3, 40**
See also DLB 95

Young, Marguerite (Vivian) 1909-1995 **C L C 82**
See also CA 13-16; 150; CAP 1

Young, Neil 1945- ....**CLC 17**
See also CA 110

Young Bear, Ray A. 1950- ..... **CLC 94; DAM MULT**
See also CA 146; DLB 175; NNAL

Yourcenar, Marguerite 1903-1987**CLC 19, 38, 50, 87; DAM NOV**
See also CA 69-72; CANR 23, 60; DLB 72; DLBY 88; MTCW

Yurick, Sol 1925- .... **CLC 6**

See also CA 13-16R; CANR 25

Zabolotskii, Nikolai Alekseevich 1903-1958 **TCLC 52**
See also CA 116

Zamiatin, Yevgenii
See Zamyatin, Evgeny Ivanovich

Zamora, Bernice (B. Ortiz) 1938-... **CLC 89; DAM MULT; HLC**
See also CA 151; DLB 82; HW

Zamyatin, Evgeny Ivanovich 1884-1937 **TCLC 8, 37**
See also CA 105

Zangwill, Israel 1864-1926 .... **TCLC 16**
See also CA 109; DLB 10, 135

Zappa, Francis Vincent, Jr. 1940-1993
See Zappa, Frank
See also CA 108; 143; CANR 57

Zappa, Frank ....**CLC 17**
See also Zappa, Francis Vincent, Jr.

Zaturenska, Marya 1902-1982 ......**CLC 6, 11**
See also CA 13-16R; 105; CANR 22

Zeami 1363-1443 .... **DC 7**

Zelazny, Roger (Joseph) 1937-1995 . **CLC 21**
See also AAYA 7; CA 21-24R; 148; CANR 26, 60; DLB 8; MTCW; SATA 57; SATA-Brief 39

Zhdanov, Andrei A(lexandrovich) 1896-1948 **TCLC 18**
See also CA 117

Zhukovsky, Vasily 1783-1852 .... **NCLC 35**

Ziegenhagen, Eric ....**CLC 55**

Zimmer, Jill Schary
See Robinson, Jill

Zimmerman, Robert
See Dylan, Bob

Zindel, Paul 1936-**CLC 6, 26; DA; DAB; DAC; DAM DRAM, MST, NOV; DC 5**
See also AAYA 2; CA 73-76; CANR 31; CLR 3, 45; DLB 7, 52; JRDA; MAICYA; MTCW; SATA 16, 58

Zinov'Ev, A. A.
See Zinoviev, Alexander (Aleksandrovich)

Zinoviev, Alexander (Aleksandrovich) 1922- **CLC 19**
See also CA 116; 133; CAAS 10

Zoilus
See Lovecraft, H(oward) P(hillips)

Zola, Emile (Edouard Charles Antoine) 1840-1902**TCLC 1, 6, 21, 41; DA; DAB; DAC; DAM MST, NOV; WLC**
See also CA 104; 138; DLB 123

Zoline, Pamela 1941- ....**CLC 62**
See also CA 161

Zorrilla y Moral, Jose 1817-1893 ....**NCLC 6**

Zoshchenko, Mikhail (Mikhailovich) 1895-1958 **TCLC 15; SSC 15**
See also CA 115; 160

Zuckmayer, Carl 1896-1977 .... **CLC 18**
See also CA 69-72; DLB 56, 124

Zuk, Georges
See Skelton, Robin

Zukofsky, Louis 1904-1978**CLC 1, 2, 4, 7, 11, 18; DAM POET; PC 11**
See also CA 9-12R; 77-80; CANR 39; DLB 5, 165; MTCW

Zweig, Paul 1935-1984 .... **CLC 34, 42**
See also CA 85-88; 113

Zweig, Stefan 1881-1942 .... **TCLC 17**
See also CA 112; DLB 81, 118

Zwingli, Huldreich 1484-1531 .... **LC 37**
See also DLB 179

Literary Criticism Series
Cumulative Topic Index

This index lists all topic entries in Gale's *Classical and Medieval Literature Criticism, Contemporary Literary Criticism, Literature Criticism from 1400 to 1800, Nineteenth-Century Literature Criticism,* and *Twentieth-Century Literary Criticism.*

Age of Johnson LC 15: 1-87
  Johnson's London, 3-15
  aesthetics of neoclassicism, 15-36
  "age of prose and reason," 36-45
  clubmen and bluestockings, 45-56
  printing technology, 56-62
  periodicals: "a map of busy life," 62-74
  transition, 74-86

Age of Spenser LC 39: 1-70
  Overviews, 2-21
  Literary Style, 22-34
  Poets and the Crown, 34-70

AIDS in Literature CLC 81: 365-416

Alcohol and Literature TCLC 70: 1-58
  overview, 2-8
  fiction, 8-48
  poetry and drama, 48-58

American Abolitionism NCLC 44: 1-73
  overviews, 2-26
  abolitionist ideals, 26-46
  the literature of abolitionism, 46-72

American Black Humor Fiction TCLC 54: 1-85
  characteristics of black humor, 2-13
  origins and development, 13-38
  black humor distinguished from related literary trends, 38-60
  black humor and society, 60-75
  black humor reconsidered, 75-83

American Civil War in Literature NCLC 32: 1-109
  overviews, 2-20
  regional perspectives, 20-54
  fiction popular during the war, 54-79
  the historical novel, 79-108

American Frontier in Literature NCLC

28: 1-103
  definitions, 2-12
  development, 12-17
  nonfiction writing about the frontier, 17-30
  frontier fiction, 30-45
  frontier protagonists, 45-66
  portrayals of Native Americans, 66-86
  feminist readings, 86-98
  twentieth-century reaction against frontier literature, 98-100

American Humor Writing NCLC 52: 1-59
  overviews, 2-12
  the Old Southwest, 12-42
  broader impacts, 42-5
  women humorists, 45-58

American Mercury, The TCLC 74: 1-80

American Popular Song, Golden Age of TCLC 42: 1-49
  background and major figures, 2-34
  the lyrics of popular songs, 34-47

American Proletarian Literature TCLC 54: 86-175
  overviews, 87-95
  American proletarian literature and the American Communist Party, 95-111
  ideology and literary merit, 111-7
  novels, 117-36
  Gastonia, 136-48
  drama, 148-54
  journalism, 154-9
  proletarian literature in the United States, 159-74

American Romanticism NCLC 44: 74-138
  overviews, 74-84
  sociopolitical influences, 84-104
  Romanticism and the American frontier, 104-15
  thematic concerns, 115-37

American Western Literature TCLC 46: 1-100
  definition and development of American Western literature, 2-7
  characteristics of the Western novel, 8-23
  Westerns as history and fiction, 23-34
  critical reception of American Western literature, 34-41
  the Western hero, 41-73
  women in Western fiction, 73-91
  later Western fiction, 91-9

Art and Literature TCLC 54: 176-248
  overviews, 176-93
  definitions, 193-219
  influence of visual arts on literature, 219-31
  spatial form in literature, 231-47

Arthurian Literature CMLC 10: 1-127
  historical context and literary beginnings, 2-27
  development of the legend through Malory, 27-64
  development of the legend from Malory to the Victorian Age, 65-81
  themes and motifs, 81-95
  principal characters, 95-125

Arthurian Revival NCLC 36: 1-77
  overviews, 2-12
  Tennyson and his influence, 12-43
  other leading figures, 43-73
  the Arthurian legend in the visual arts, 73-6

Australian Literature TCLC 50: 1-94
  origins and development, 2-21
  characteristics of Australian literature, 21-33
  historical and critical perspectives, 33-41
  poetry, 41-58
  fiction, 58-76

drama, 76-82
Aboriginal literature, 82-91

Beat Generation, Literature of the TCLC
42: 50-102
    overviews, 51-9
    the Beat generation as a social phenom-
        enon, 59-62
    development, 62-5
    Beat literature, 66-96
    influence, 97-100

The Bell Curve **Controversy** CLC 91: 281-
330

Bildungsroman **in Nineteenth-Century
Literature** NCLC 20: 92-168
    surveys, 93-113
    in Germany, 113-40
    in England, 140-56
    female *Bildungsroman,* 156-67

Bloomsbury Group TCLC 34: 1-73
    history and major figures, 2-13
    definitions, 13-7
    influences, 17-27
    thought, 27-40
    prose, 40-52
    and literary criticism, 52-4
    political ideals, 54-61
    response to, 61-71

Bly, Robert, *Iron John: A Book about Men
and Men's Work* CLC 70: 414-62

The Book of J CLC 65: 289-311

Buddhism and Literature TCLC 70: 59-
164
    eastern literature, 60-113
    western literature, 113-63

Businessman in American Literature
TCLC 26: 1-48
    portrayal of the businessman, 1-32
    themes and techniques in business
        fiction, 32-47

**Catholicism in Nineteenth-Century
American Literature** NCLC 64: 1-58
    overviews, 3-14

polemical literature, 14-46
Catholicism in literature, 47-57

Celtic Mythology CMLC 26: 1-111
    overviews, 2-22
    Celtic myth as literature and history, 22-
      48
    Celtic religion: Druids and divinities,
      48-80
    Fionn MacCuhaill and the Fenian cycle,
      80-111

Celtic Twilight
See **Irish Literary Renaissance**

Chartist Movement and Literature, The
NCLC 60: 1-84
    overview: nineteenth-century working-
      class fiction, 2-19
    Chartist fiction and poetry, 19-73
    the Chartist press, 73-84

Children's Literature, Nineteenth-Century
NCLC 52: 60-135
    overviews, 61-72
    moral tales, 72-89
    fairy tales and fantasy, 90-119
    making men/making women, 119-34

Civic Critics, Russian NCLC 20: 402-46
    principal figures and background, 402-9
    and Russian Nihilism, 410-6
    aesthetic and critical views, 416-45

**Colonial America: The Intellectual
Background** LC 25: 1-98
    overviews, 2-17
    philosophy and politics, 17-31
    early religious influences in Colonial
      America, 31-60
    consequences of the Revolution, 60-78
    religious influences in post-revolution-
      ary America, 78-87
    colonial literary genres, 87-97

**Colonialism in Victorian English Litera-
ture** NCLC 56: 1-77
    overviews, 2-34
    colonialism and gender, 34-51
    monsters and the occult, 51-76

Columbus, Christopher, Books on the

**Quincentennial of His Arrival in the New
World** CLC 70: 329-60

Comic Books TCLC 66: 1-139
    historical and critical perspectives, 2-48
    superheroes, 48-67
    underground comix, 67-88
    comic books and society, 88-122
    adult comics and graphic novels, 122-36

Connecticut Wits NCLC 48: 1-95
    general overviews, 2-40
    major works, 40-76
    intellectual context, 76-95

Crime in Literature TCLC 54: 249-307
    evolution of the criminal figure in
      literature, 250-61
    crime and society, 261-77
    literary perspectives on crime and
      punishment, 277-88
    writings by criminals, 288-306

**Czechoslovakian Literature of the
Twentieth Century** TCLC 42: 103-96
    through World War II, 104-35
    de-Stalinization, the Prague Spring, and
      contemporary literature, 135-72
    Slovak literature, 172-85
    Czech science fiction, 185-93

Dadaism TCLC 46: 101-71
    background and major figures, 102-16
    definitions, 116-26
    manifestos and commentary by
      Dadaists, 126-40
    theater and film, 140-58
    nature and characteristics of Dadaist
      writing, 158-70

Darwinism and Literature NCLC 32: 110-
206
    background, 110-31
    direct responses to Darwin, 131-71
    collateral effects of Darwinism, 171-205

de Man, Paul, Wartime Journalism of
CLC 55: 382-424

Detective Fiction, Nineteenth-Century
NCLC 36: 78-148
    origins of the genre, 79-100

history of nineteenth-century detective fiction, 101-33
significance of nineteenth-century detective fiction, 133-46

Detective Fiction, Twentieth-Century TCLC 38: 1-96
genesis and history of the detective story, 3-22
defining detective fiction, 22-32
evolution and varieties, 32-77
the appeal of detective fiction, 77-90

Disease and Literature TCLC 66: 140-283
overviews, 141-65
disease in nineteenth-century literature, 165-81
tuberculosis and literature, 181-94
women and disease in literature, 194-221
plague literature, 221-53
AIDS in literature, 253-82

The Double in Nineteenth-Century Literature NCLC 40: 1-95
genesis and development of the theme, 2-15
the double and Romanticism, 16-27
sociological views, 27-52
psychological interpretations, 52-87
philosophical considerations, 87-95

Dramatic Realism NCLC 44: 139-202
overviews, 140-50
origins and definitions, 150-66
impact and influence, 166-93
realist drama and tragedy, 193-201

Eastern Mythology CMLC 26: 112-92
heroes and kings, 113-51
cross-cultural perspective, 151-69
relations to history and society, 169-92

Electronic "Books": Hypertext and Hyperfiction CLC 86: 367-404
books vs. CD-ROMS, 367-76
hypertext and hyperfiction, 376-95
implications for publishing, libraries, and the public, 395-403

Eliot, T. S., Centenary of Birth CLC 55: 345-75

Elizabethan Drama LC 22: 140-240
origins and influences, 142-67
characteristics and conventions, 167-83
theatrical production, 184-200
histories, 200-12
comedy, 213-20
tragedy, 220-30

Elizabethan Prose Fiction LC 41: 1-70
overviews, 1-15
origins and influences, 15-43
style and structure, 43-69

The Encyclopedists LC 26: 172-253
overviews, 173-210
intellectual background, 210-32
views on esthetics, 232-41
views on women, 241-52

English Caroline Literature LC 13: 221-307
background, 222-41
evolution and varieties, 241-62
the Cavalier mode, 262-75
court and society, 275-91
politics and religion, 291-306

English Decadent Literature of the 1890s NCLC 28: 104-200
fin de siècle: the Decadent period, 105-19
definitions, 120-37
major figures: "the tragic generation," 137-50
French literature and English literary Decadence, 150-7
themes, 157-61
poetry, 161-82
periodicals, 182-96

English Essay, Rise of the LC 18: 238-308
definitions and origins, 236-54
influence on the essay, 254-69
historical background, 269-78
the essay in the seventeenth century, 279-93
the essay in the eighteenth century, 293-307

English Mystery Cycle Dramas LC 34: 1-88
overviews, 1-27
the nature of dramatic performances, 27-42
the medieval worldview and the mystery cycles, 43-67
the doctrine of repentance and the mystery cycles, 67-76
the fall from grace in the mystery cycles, 76-88

English Romantic Poetry NCLC 28: 201-327
overviews and reputation, 202-37
major subjects and themes, 237-67
forms of Romantic poetry, 267-78
politics, society, and Romantic poetry, 278-99
philosophy, religion, and Romantic poetry, 299-324

Espionage Literature TCLC 50: 95-159
overviews, 96-113
espionage fiction/formula fiction, 113-26
spies in fact and fiction, 126-38
the female spy, 138-44
social and psychological perspectives, 144-58

European Romanticism NCLC 36: 149-284
definitions, 149-77
origins of the movement, 177-82
Romantic theory, 182-200
themes and techniques, 200-23
Romanticism in Germany, 223-39
Romanticism in France, 240-61
Romanticism in Italy, 261-4
Romanticism in Spain, 264-8
impact and legacy, 268-82

Existentialism and Literature TCLC 42: 197-268
overviews and definitions, 198-209
history and influences, 209-19
Existentialism critiqued and defended, 220-35
philosophical and religious perspectives, 235-41
Existentialist fiction and drama, 241-67

Familiar Essay NCLC 48: 96-211
definitions and origins, 97-130
overview of the genre, 130-43
elements of form and style, 143-59
elements of content, 159-73
the Cockneys: Hazlitt, Lamb, and Hunt, 173-91
status of the genre, 191-210

Topic Index

Fear in Literature TCLC 74: 81-258
  overviews, 81
  pre-twentieth-century literature, 123
  twentieth-century literature, 182

Feminism in the 1990s: Commentary on Works by Naomi Wolf, Susan Faludi, and Camille Paglia CLC 76: 377-415

Feminist Criticism in 1990 CLC 65: 312-60

Fifteenth-Century English Literature LC 17: 248-334
  background, 249-72
  poetry, 272-315
  drama, 315-23
  prose, 323-33

Film and Literature TCLC 38: 97-226
  overviews, 97-119
  film and theater, 119-34
  film and the novel, 134-45
  the art of the screenplay, 145-66
  genre literature/genre film, 167-79
  the writer and the film industry, 179-90
  authors on film adaptations of their works, 190-200
  fiction into film: comparative essays, 200-23

French Drama in the Age of Louis XIV LC 28: 94-185
  overview, 95-127
  tragedy, 127-46
  comedy, 146-66
  tragicomedy, 166-84

French Enlightenment LC 14: 81-145
  the question of definition, 82-9
  Le siècle des lumières, 89-94
  women and the salons, 94-105
  censorship, 105-15
  the philosophy of reason, 115-31
  influence and legacy, 131-44

French Realism NCLC 52: 136-216
  origins and definitions, 137-70
  issues and influence, 170-98
  realism and representation, 198-215

French Revolution and English Literature

NCLC 40: 96-195
  history and theory, 96-123
  romantic poetry, 123-50
  the novel, 150-81
  drama, 181-92
  children's literature, 192-5

Futurism, Italian TCLC 42: 269-354
  principles and formative influences, 271-9
  manifestos, 279-88
  literature, 288-303
  theater, 303-19
  art, 320-30
  music, 330-6
  architecture, 336-9
  and politics, 339-46
  reputation and significance, 346-51

Gaelic Revival
See **Irish Literary Renaissance**

Gates, Henry Louis, Jr., and African-American Literary Criticism CLC 65: 361-405

Gay and Lesbian Literature CLC 76: 416-39

German Exile Literature TCLC 30: 1-58
  the writer and the Nazi state, 1-10
  definition of, 10-4
  life in exile, 14-32
  surveys, 32-50
  Austrian literature in exile, 50-2
  German publishing in the United States, 52-7

German Expressionism TCLC 34: 74-160
  history and major figures, 76-85
  aesthetic theories, 85-109
  drama, 109-26
  poetry, 126-38
  film, 138-42
  painting, 142-7
  music, 147-53
  and politics, 153-8

***Glasnost* and Contemporary Soviet Literature** CLC 59: 355-97

Gothic Novel NCLC 28: 328-402

development and major works, 328-34
  definitions, 334-50
  themes and techniques, 350-78
  in America, 378-85
  in Scotland, 385-91
  influence and legacy, 391-400

Graphic Narratives CLC 86: 405-32
  history and overviews, 406-21
  the "Classics Illustrated" series, 421-2
  reviews of recent works, 422-32

Greek Historiography CMLC 17: 1-49

Greek Mythology CMLC-26 193-320
  overviews, 194-209
  origins and development of Greek mythology, 209-29
  cosmogonies and divinities in Greek mythology, 229-54
  heroes and heroines in Greek mythology, 254-80
  women in Greek mythology, 280-320

Harlem Renaissance TCLC 26: 49-125
  principal issues and figures, 50-67
  the literature and its audience, 67-74
  theme and technique in poetry, fiction, and drama, 74-115
  and American society, 115-21
  achievement and influence, 121-2

Havel, Václav, Playwright and President CLC 65: 406-63

Historical Fiction, Nineteenth-Century NCLC 48: 212-307
  definitions and characteristics, 213-36
  Victorian historical fiction, 236-65
  American historical fiction, 265-88
  realism in historical fiction, 288-306

Holocaust and the Atomic Bomb: Fifty Years Later CLC 91: 331-82
  the Holocaust remembered, 333-52
  Anne Frank revisited, 352-62
  the atomic bomb and American memory, 362-81

Holocaust Denial Literature TCLC 58: 1-110
  overviews, 1-30

Robert Faurisson and Noam Chomsky,
 30-52
Holocaust denial literature in America,
 52-71
library access to Holocaust denial
 literature, 72-5
the authenticity of Anne Frank's diary,
 76-90
David Irving and the "normalization" of
 Hitler, 90-109

Holocaust, Literature of the TCLC 42:
355-450
 historical overview, 357-61
 critical overview, 361-70
 diaries and memoirs, 370-95
 novels and short stories, 395-425
 poetry, 425-41
 drama, 441-8

**Homosexuality in Nineteenth-Century
Literature** NCLC 56: 78-182
 defining homosexuality, 80-111
 Greek love, 111-44
 trial and danger, 144-81

**Hungarian Literature of the Twentieth
Century** TCLC 26: 126-88
 surveys of, 126-47
 Nyugat and early twentieth-century
  literature, 147-56
 mid-century literature, 156-68
 and politics, 168-78
 since the 1956 revolt, 178-87

Hysteria in Nineteenth-Century Literature
NCLC 64: 59-184
 the history of hysteria, 60-75
 the gender of hysteria, 75-103
 hysteria and women's narratives, 103-57
 hysteria in nineteenth-century poetry,
  157-83

Imagism TCLC 74: 259-454
 history and development, 260
 major figures, 288
 sources and influences, 352
 Imagism and other movements, 397
 influence and legacy, 431

Indian Literature in English TCLC 54:
308-406
 overview, 309-13
 origins and major figures, 313-25

the Indo-English novel, 325-55
Indo-English poetry, 355-67
Indo-English drama, 367-72
critical perspectives on Indo-English
 literature, 372-80
modern Indo-English literature, 380-9
Indo-English authors on their work,
 389-404

Industrial Revolution in Literature, The
NCLC 56: 183-273
 historical and cultural perspectives, 184-
  201
 contemporary reactions to the machine,
  201-21
 themes and symbols in literature, 221-73

**The Irish Famine as Represented in
Nineteenth-Century Literature** NCLC 64:
185-261
 overviews, 187-98
 historical background, 198-212
 famine novels, 212-34
 famine poetry, 234-44
 famine letters and eye-witness accounts,
  245-61

Irish Literary Renaissance TCLC 46: 172-
287
 overview, 173-83
 development and major figures, 184-202
 influence of Irish folklore and mythology, 202-22
 Irish poetry, 222-34
 Irish drama and the Abbey Theatre, 234-
  56
 Irish fiction, 256-86

Irish Nationalism and Literature NCLC
44: 203-73
 the Celtic element in literature, 203-19
 anti-Irish sentiment and the Celtic
  response, 219-34
 literary ideals in Ireland, 234-45
 literary expressions, 245-73

Italian Futurism
See **Futurism, Italian**

Italian Humanism LC 12: 205-77
 origins and early development, 206-18
 revival of classical letters, 218-23
 humanism and other philosophies, 224-
  39

humanisms and humanists, 239-46
the plastic arts, 246-57
achievement and significance, 258-76

Italian Romanticism NCLC 60: 85-145
 origins and overviews, 86-101
 Italian Romantic theory, 101-25
 the language of Romanticism, 125-45

Jacobean Drama LC 33: 1-37
 the Jacobean worldview: an era of
  transition, 2-14
 the moral vision of Jacobean drama, 14-
  22
 Jacobean tragedy, 22-3
 the Jacobean masque, 23-36

Jewish-American Fiction TCLC 62: 1-181
 overviews, 2-24
 major figures, 24-48
 Jewish writers and American life, 48-78
 Jewish characters in American fiction,
  78-108
 themes in Jewish-American fiction, 108-
  43
 Jewish-American women writers, 143-
  59
 the Holocaust and Jewish-American
  fiction, 159-81

Knickerbocker Group, The NCLC 56:
274-341
 overviews, 276-314
 Knickerbocker periodicals, 314-26
 writers and artists, 326-40

Lake Poets, The NCLC 52: 217-304
 characteristics of the Lake Poets and
  their works, 218-27
 literary influences and collaborations,
  227-66
 defining and developing Romantic
  ideals, 266-84
 embracing Conservatism, 284-303

Larkin, Philip, Controversy CLC 81: 417-
64

**Latin American Literature, Twentieth-
Century** TCLC 58: 111-98
 historical and critical perspectives, 112-
  36
 the novel, 136-45

the short story, 145-9
drama, 149-60
poetry, 160-7
the writer and society, 167-86
Native Americans in Latin American
  literature, 186-97

Madness in Twentieth-Century Literature
TCLC 50: 160-225
  overviews, 161-71
  madness and the creative process, 171-
  86
  suicide, 186-91
  madness in American literature, 191-207
  madness in German literature, 207-13
  madness and feminist artists, 213-24

Metaphysical Poets LC 24: 356-439
  early definitions, 358-67
  surveys and overviews, 367-92
  cultural and social influences, 392-406
  stylistic and thematic variations, 407-38

Modern Essay, The TCLC 58: 199-273
  overview, 200-7
  the essay in the early twentieth century,
  207-19
  characteristics of the modern essay, 219-
  32
  modern essayists, 232-45
  the essay as a literary genre, 245-73

Modern Japanese Literature TCLC 66:
284-389
  poetry, 285-305
  drama, 305-29
  fiction, 329-61
  western influences, 361-87

Modernism TCLC 70: 165-275
  definitions, 166-184
  Modernism and earlier influences, 184-
  200
  stylistic and thematic traits, 200-229
  poetry and drama, 229-242
  redefining Modernism, 242-275

**Muckraking Movement in American
Journalism** TCLC 34: 161-242
  development, principles, and major
  figures, 162-70
  publications, 170-9
  social and political ideas, 179-86
  targets, 186-208
  fiction, 208-19

decline, 219-29
impact and accomplishments, 229-40

**Multiculturalism in Literature and
Education** CLC 70: 361-413

Music and Modern Literature TCLC 62:
182-329
  overviews, 182-211
  musical form/literary form, 211-32
  music in literature, 232-50
  the influence of music on literature,
    250-73
  literature and popular music, 273-303
  jazz and poetry, 303-28

Native American Literature CLC 76: 440-
76

Natural School, Russian NCLC 24: 205-40
  history and characteristics, 205-25
  contemporary criticism, 225-40

Naturalism NCLC 36: 285-382
  definitions and theories, 286-305
  critical debates on Naturalism, 305-16
  Naturalism in theater, 316-32
  European Naturalism, 332-61
  American Naturalism, 361-72
  the legacy of Naturalism, 372-81

Negritude TCLC 50: 226-361
  origins and evolution, 227-56
  definitions, 256-91
  Negritude in literature, 291-343
  Negritude reconsidered, 343-58

New Criticism TCLC 34: 243-318
  development and ideas, 244-70
  debate and defense, 270-99
  influence and legacy, 299-315

The New World in Renaissance Literature
LC 31: 1-51
  overview, 1-18
  utopia vs. terror, 18-31
  explorers and Native Americans, 31-51

**New York Intellectuals and *Partisan
Review*** TCLC 30: 117-98
  development and major figures, 118-28

influence of Judaism, 128-39
Partisan Review, 139-57
literary philosophy and practice, 157-75
political philosophy, 175-87
achievement and significance, 187-97

The New Yorker TCLC 58: 274-357
  overviews, 274-95
  major figures, 295-304
  New Yorker style, 304-33
  fiction, journalism, and humor at *The
    New Yorker,* 333-48
  the new *New Yorker,* 348-56

Newgate Novel NCLC 24: 166-204
  development of Newgate literature, 166-
  73
  Newgate Calendar, 173-7
  Newgate fiction, 177-95
  Newgate drama, 195-204

**Nigerian Literature of the Twentieth
Century** TCLC 30: 199-265
  surveys of, 199-227
  English language and African life, 227-
  45
  politics and the Nigerian writer, 245-54
  Nigerian writers and society, 255-62

**Nineteenth-Century Native American
Autobiography** NCLC 64: 262-389
  overview, 263-8
  problems of authorship, 268-81
  the evolution of Native American
    autobiography, 281-304
  political issues, 304-15
  gender and autobiography, 316-62
  autobiographical works during the turn
    of the century, 362-88

Norse Mythology CMLC-26: 321-85
  history and mythological tradition, 322-
  44
  Eddic poetry, 344-74
  Norse mythology and other traditions,
  374-85

Northern Humanism LC 16: 281-356
  background, 282-305
  precursor of the Reformation, 305-14
  the Brethren of the Common Life, the
    Devotio Moderna, and education,
    314-40
  the impact of printing, 340-56

Novel of Manners, The NCLC 56: 342-96
    social and political order, 343-53
    domestic order, 353-73
    depictions of gender, 373-83
    the American novel of manners, 383-95

Nuclear Literature: Writings and Criticism in the Nuclear Age TCLC 46: 288-390
    overviews, 290-301
    fiction, 301-35
    poetry, 335-8
    nuclear war in Russo-Japanese literature, 338-55
    nuclear war and women writers, 355-67
    the nuclear referent and literary criticism, 367-88

Occultism in Modern Literature TCLC 50: 362-406
    influence of occultism on literature, 363-72
    occultism, literature, and society, 372-87
    fiction, 387-96
    drama, 396-405

Opium and the Nineteenth-Century Literary Imagination NCLC 20: 250-301
    original sources, 250-62
    historical background, 262-71
    and literary society, 271-9
    and literary creativity, 279-300

Periodicals, Nineteenth-Century British NCLC 24: 100-65
    overviews, 100-30
    in the Romantic Age, 130-41
    in the Victorian era, 142-54
    and the reviewer, 154-64

Plath, Sylvia, and the Nature of Biography CLC 86: 433-62
    the nature of biography, 433-52
    reviews of *The Silent Woman,* 452-61

Political Theory from the 15th to the 18th Century LC 36: 1-55
    Overview, 1-26
    Natural Law, 26-42
    Empiricism, 42-55

Polish Romanticism NCLC 52: 305-71
    overviews, 306-26
    major figures, 326-40

Polish Romantic drama, 340-62
influences, 362-71

Popular Literature TCLC 70: 279-382
    overviews, 280-324
    "formula" fiction, 324-336
    readers of popular literature, 336-351
    evolution of popular literature, 351-382

Pre-Raphaelite Movement NCLC 20: 302-401
    overview, 302-4
    genesis, 304-12
    Germ and *Oxford and Cambridge Magazine,* 312-20
    Robert Buchanan and the "Fleshly School of Poetry," 320-31
    satires and parodies, 331-4
    surveys, 334-51
    aesthetics, 351-75
    sister arts of poetry and painting, 375-94
    influence, 394-9

Preromanticism LC 40: 1-56
    overviews, 2-14
    defining the period, 14-23
    new directions in poetry and prose, 23-45
    the focus on the self, 45-56

Presocratic Philosophy CMLC 22: 1-56
    overviews, 3-24
    the Ionians and the Pythagoreans, 25-35
    Heraclitus, the Eleatics, and the Atomists, 36-47
    the Sophists, 47-55

Protestant Reformation, Literature of the LC 37: 1-83
    overviews, 1-49
    humanism and scholasticism, 49-69
    the reformation and literature, 69-82

Psychoanalysis and Literature TCLC 38: 227-338
    overviews, 227-46
    Freud on literature, 246-51
    psychoanalytic views of the literary process, 251-61
    psychoanalytic theories of response to literature, 261-88
    psychoanalysis and literary criticism, 288-312
    psychoanalysis as literature/literature as

psychoanalysis, 313-34

Rap Music CLC 76: 477-50

Renaissance Natural Philosophy LC 27: 201-87
    cosmology, 201-28
    astrology, 228-54
    magic, 254-86

Restoration Drama LC 21: 184-275
    general overviews, 185-230
    Jeremy Collier stage controversy, 230-9
    other critical interpretations, 240-75

Revising the Literary Canon CLC 81: 465-509

Robin Hood, Legend of LC 19: 205-58
    origins and development of the Robin Hood legend, 206-20
    representations of Robin Hood, 220-44
    Robin Hood as hero, 244-56

Rushdie, Salman, *Satanic Verses* Controversy CLC 55 214-63; 59: 404-56

Russian Nihilism NCLC 28: 403-47
    definitions and overviews, 404-17
    women and Nihilism, 417-27
    literature as reform: the Civic Critics, 427-33
    Nihilism and the Russian novel: Turgenev and Dostoevsky, 433-47

Russian Thaw TCLC 26: 189-247
    literary history of the period, 190-206
    theoretical debate of socialist realism, 206-11
    Novy Mir, 211-7
    Literary Moscow, 217-24
    Pasternak, *Zhivago,* and the Nobel Prize, 224-7
    poetry of liberation, 228-31
    Brodsky trial and the end of the Thaw, 231-6
    achievement and influence, 236-46

Salem Witch Trials LC-38: 1-145
    overviews, 2-30
    historical background, 30-65

Topic Index

judicial background, 65-78
the search for causes, 78-115
the role of women in the trials, 115-44

Salinger, J. D., Controversy Surrounding
In Search of J. D. Salinger CLC 55: 325-44

Science Fiction, Nineteenth-Century
NCLC 24: 241-306
background, 242-50
definitions of the genre, 251-6
representative works and writers, 256-75
themes and conventions, 276-305

Scottish Chaucerians LC 20: 363-412

Scottish Poetry, Eighteenth-Century LC 29: 95-167
overviews, 96-114
the Scottish Augustans, 114-28
the Scots Vernacular Revival, 132-63
Scottish poetry after Burns, 163-6

Sentimental Novel, The NCLC 60: 146-245
overviews, 147-58
the politics of domestic fiction, 158-79
a literature of resistance and repression, 179-212
the reception of sentimental fiction, 213-44

Sherlock Holmes Centenary TCLC 26: 248-310
Doyle's life and the composition of the Holmes stories, 248-59
life and character of Holmes, 259-78
method, 278-9
Holmes and the Victorian world, 279-92
Sherlockian scholarship, 292-301
Doyle and the development of the detective story, 301-7
Holmes's continuing popularity, 307-9

Slave Narratives, American NCLC 20: 1-91
background, 2-9
overviews, 9-24
contemporary responses, 24-7
language, theme, and technique, 27-70
historical authenticity, 70-5

antecedents, 75-83
role in development of Black American literature, 83-8

Spanish Civil War Literature TCLC 26: 311-85
topics in, 312-33
British and American literature, 333-59
French literature, 359-62
Spanish literature, 362-73
German literature, 373-5
political idealism and war literature, 375-83

Spanish Golden Age Literature LC 23: 262-332
overviews, 263-81
verse drama, 281-304
prose fiction, 304-19
lyric poetry, 319-31

Spasmodic School of Poetry NCLC 24: 307-52
history and major figures, 307-21
the Spasmodics on poetry, 321-7
Firmilian and critical disfavor, 327-39
theme and technique, 339-47
influence, 347-51

Steinbeck, John, Fiftieth Anniversary of
The Grapes of Wrath CLC 59: 311-54

Sturm und Drang NCLC 40: 196-276
definitions, 197-238
poetry and poetics, 238-58
drama, 258-75

Supernatural Fiction in the Nineteenth Century NCLC 32: 207-87
major figures and influences, 208-35
the Victorian ghost story, 236-54
the influence of science and occultism, 254-66
supernatural fiction and society, 266-86

Supernatural Fiction, Modern TCLC 30: 59-116
evolution and varieties, 60-74
"decline" of the ghost story, 74-86
as a literary genre, 86-92
technique, 92-101
nature and appeal, 101-15

Surrealism TCLC 30: 334-406
history and formative influences, 335-43
manifestos, 343-54
philosophic, aesthetic, and political principles, 354-75
poetry, 375-81
novel, 381-6
drama, 386-92
film, 392-8
painting and sculpture, 398-403
achievement, 403-5

Symbolism, Russian TCLC 30: 266-333
doctrines and major figures, 267-92
theories, 293-8
and French Symbolism, 298-310
themes in poetry, 310-4
theater, 314-20
and the fine arts, 320-32

Symbolist Movement, French NCLC 20: 169-249
background and characteristics, 170-86
principles, 186-91
attacked and defended, 191-7
influences and predecessors, 197-211
and Decadence, 211-6
theater, 216-26
prose, 226-33
decline and influence, 233-47

Theater of the Absurd TCLC 38: 339-415
"The Theater of the Absurd," 340-7
major plays and playwrights, 347-58
and the concept of the absurd, 358-86
theatrical techniques, 386-94
predecessors of, 394-402
influence of, 402-13

Tin Pan Alley
See **American Popular Song, Golden Age of**

Transcendentalism, American NCLC 24: 1-99
overviews, 3-23
contemporary documents, 23-41
theological aspects of, 42-52
and social issues, 52-74
literature of, 74-96

Travel Writing in the Nineteenth Century NCLC 44: 274-392

the European grand tour, 275-303
the Orient, 303-47
North America, 347-91

Travel Writing in the Twentieth Century
TCLC 30: 407-56
conventions and traditions, 407-27
and fiction writing, 427-43
comparative essays on travel writers,
443-54

True-Crime Literature CLC 99: 333-433
history and analysis, 334-407
reviews of true-crime publications, 407-
23
writing instruction, 424-29
author profiles, 429-33

***Ulysses* and the Process of Textual
Reconstruction** TCLC 26: 386-416
evaluations of the new *Ulysses,* 386-94
editorial principles and procedures, 394-
401
theoretical issues, 401-16

Utopian Literature, Nineteenth-Century
NCLC 24: 353-473
definitions, 354-74
overviews, 374-88
theory, 388-408
communities, 409-26
fiction, 426-53
women and fiction, 454-71

Utopian Literature, Renaissance LC-32:
1-63
overviews, 2-25
classical background, 25-33
utopia and the social contract, 33-9
origins in mythology, 39-48
utopia and the Renaissance country
house, 48-52
influence of millenarianism, 52-62

Vampire in Literature TCLC 46: 391-454
origins and evolution, 392-412
social and psychological perspectives,
413-44
vampire fiction and science fiction, 445-
53

Victorian Autobiography NCLC 40: 277-
363

development and major characteristics,
278-88
themes and techniques, 289-313
the autobiographical tendency in
Victorian prose and poetry, 313-47
Victorian women's autobiographies,
347-62

Victorian Fantasy Literature NCLC 60:
246-384
overviews, 247-91
major figures, 292-366
women in Victorian fantasy literature,
366-83

Victorian Novel NCLC 32: 288-454
development and major characteristics,
290-310
themes and techniques, 310-58
social criticism in the Victorian novel,
359-97
urban and rural life in the Victorian
novel, 397-406
women in the Victorian novel, 406-25
Mudie's Circulating Library, 425-34
the late-Victorian novel, 434-51

Vietnam War in Literature and Film CLC
91: 383-437
overview, 384-8
prose, 388-412
film and drama, 412-24
poetry, 424-35

Vorticism TCLC 62: 330-426
Wyndham Lewis and Vorticism, 330-8
characteristics and principles of
Vorticism, 338-65
Lewis and Pound, 365-82
Vorticist writing, 382-416
Vorticist painting, 416-26

Women's Diaries, Nineteenth-Century
NCLC 48: 308-54
overview, 308-13
diary as history, 314-25
sociology of diaries, 325-34
diaries as psychological scholarship,
334-43
diary as autobiography, 343-8
diary as literature, 348-53

Women Writers, Seventeenth-Century LC
30: 2-58

overview, 2-15
women and education, 15-9
women and autobiography, 19-31
women's diaries, 31-9
early feminists, 39-58

World War I Literature TCLC 34: 392-486
overview, 393-403
English, 403-27
German, 427-50
American, 450-66
French, 466-74
and modern history, 474-82

Yellow Journalism NCLC 36: 383-456
overviews, 384-96
major figures, 396-413

Young Playwrights Festival
1988—CLC 55: 376-81
1989—CLC 59: 398-403
1990—CLC 65: 444-8

Contemporary Literary Criticism
Cumulative Nationality Index

ALBANIAN
Kadare, Ismail 52

ALGERIAN
Althusser, Louis 106
Camus, Albert 1, 2, 4, 9, 11, 14, 32, 63, 69
Cixous, Helene 92
Cohen-Solal, Annie 50

AMERICAN
Abbey, Edward 36, 59
Abbott, Lee K(ittredge) 48
Abish, Walter 22
Abrams, M(eyer) H(oward) 24
Acker, Kathy 45
Adams, Alice (Boyd) 6, 13, 46
Addams, Charles (Samuel) 30
Adler, C(arole) S(chwerdtfeger) 35
Adler, Renata 8, 31
Ai 4, 14, 69
Aiken, Conrad (Potter) 1, 3, 5, 10, 52
Albee, Edward (Franklin III) 1, 2, 3, 5, 9, 11, 13, 25, 53, 86
Alexander, Lloyd (Chudley) 35
Alexie, Sherman (Joseph Jr.) 96
Algren, Nelson 4, 10, 33
Allen, Edward 59
Allen, Paula Gunn 84
Allen, Woody 16, 52
Allison, Dorothy E. 78
Alta 19
Alter, Robert B(ernard) 34
Alther, Lisa 7, 41
Altman, Robert 16
Alvarez, Julia 93
Ammons, A(rchie) R(andolph) 2, 3, 5, 8, 9, 25, 57, 108
Anaya, Rudolfo A(lfonso) 23
Anderson, Jon (Victor) 9
Anderson, Poul (William) 15
Anderson, Robert (Woodruff) 23
Angell, Roger 26
Angelou, Maya 12, 35, 64, 77
Anthony, Piers 35
Apple, Max (Isaac) 9, 33
Appleman, Philip (Dean) 51
Archer, Jules 12
Arendt, Hannah 66, 98
Arnow, Harriette (Louisa) Simpson 2, 7, 18
Arrick, Fran 30
Arzner, Dorothy 98
Ashbery, John (Lawrence) 2, 3, 4, 6, 9, 13, 15, 25, 41, 77
Asimov, Isaac 1, 3, 9, 19, 26, 76, 92
Attaway, William (Alexander) 92
Auchincloss, Louis (Stanton) 4, 6, 9, 18, 45
Auden, W(ystan) H(ugh) 1, 2, 3, 4, 6, 9, 11, 14, 43

Auel, Jean M(arie) 31, 107
Auster, Paul 47
Bach, Richard (David) 14
Badanes, Jerome 59
Baker, Elliott 8
Baker, Nicholson 61
Baker, Russell (Wayne) 31
Bakshi, Ralph 26
Baldwin, James (Arthur) 1, 2, 3, 4, 5, 8, 13, 15, 17, 42, 50, 67, 90
Bambara, Toni Cade 19, 88
Banks, Russell 37, 72
Baraka, Amiri 1, 2, 3, 5, 10, 14, 33
Barbera, Jack (Vincent) 44
Barnard, Mary (Ethel) 48
Barnes, Djuna 3, 4, 8, 11, 29
Barondess, Sue K(aufman) 8
Barrett, William (Christopher) 27
Barth, John (Simmons) 1, 2, 3, 5, 7, 9, 10, 14, 27, 51, 89
Barthelme, Donald 1, 2, 3, 5, 6, 8, 13, 23, 46, 59
Barthelme, Frederick 36
Barzun, Jacques (Martin) 51
Bass, Rick 79
Baumbach, Jonathan 6, 23
Bausch, Richard (Carl) 51
Baxter, Charles (Morley) 45, 78
Beagle, Peter S(oyer) 7, 104
Beattie, Ann 8, 13, 18, 40, 63
Becker, Walter 26
Beecher, John 6
Begiebing, Robert J(ohn) 70
Behrman, S(amuel) N(athaniel) 40
Belitt, Ben 22
Bell, Madison Smartt 41, 102
Bell, Marvin (Hartley) 8, 31
Bellow, Saul 1, 2, 3, 6, 8, 10, 13, 15, 25, 33, 34, 63, 79
Benary-Isbert, Margot 12
Benchley, Peter (Bradford) 4, 8
Benedikt, Michael 4, 14
Benford, Gregory (Albert) 52
Bennett, Hal 5
Bennett, Jay 35
Benson, Jackson J. 34
Benson, Sally 17
Bentley, Eric (Russell) 24
Berendt, John (Lawrence) 86
Berger, Melvin H. 12
Berger, Thomas (Louis) 3, 5, 8, 11, 18, 38
Bergstein, Eleanor 4
Bernard, April 59
Berriault, Gina 54
Berrigan, Daniel 4
Berrigan, Ted 37
Berry, Chuck 17
Berry, Wendell (Erdman) 4, 6, 8, 27, 46

Berryman, John 1, 2, 3, 4, 6, 8, 10, 13, 25, 62
Bessie, Alvah 23
Bettelheim, Bruno 79
Betts, Doris (Waugh) 3, 6, 28
Bidart, Frank 33
Bishop, Elizabeth 1, 4, 9, 13, 15, 32
Bishop, John 10
Blackburn, Paul 9, 43
Blackmur, R(ichard) P(almer) 2, 24
Blaise, Clark 29
Blatty, William Peter 2
Blessing, Lee 54
Blish, James (Benjamin) 14
Bloch, Robert (Albert) 33
Bloom, Harold 24, 103
Blount, Roy (Alton) Jr. 38
Blume, Judy (Sussman) 12, 30
Bly, Robert (Elwood) 1, 2, 5, 10, 15, 38
Bochco, Steven 35
Bogan, Louise 4, 39, 46, 93
Bogosian, Eric 45
Bograd, Larry 35
Bonham, Frank 12
Bontemps, Arna(ud Wendell) 1, 18
Booth, Philip 23
Booth, Wayne C(layson) 24
Bottoms, David 53
Bourjaily, Vance (Nye) 8, 62
Bova, Ben(jamin William) 45
Bowers, Edgar 9
Bowles, Jane (Sydney) 3, 68
Bowles, Paul (Frederick) 1, 2, 19, 53
Boyle, Kay 1, 5, 19, 58
Boyle, T(homas) Coraghessan 36, 55, 90
Bradbury, Ray (Douglas) 1, 3, 10, 15, 42, 98
Bradley, David (Henry Jr.) 23
Bradley, John Ed(mund Jr.) 55
Bradley, Marion Zimmer 30
Brady, Joan 86
Brammer, William 31
Brancato, Robin F(idler) 35
Brand, Millen 7
Branden, Barbara 44
Branley, Franklyn M(ansfield) 21
Brautigan, Richard (Gary) 1, 3, 5, 9, 12, 34, 42
Braverman, Kate 67
Brennan, Maeve 5
Breslin, Jimmy 4, 43
Bridgers, Sue Ellen 26
Brin, David 34
Brodkey, Harold (Roy) 56
Brodsky, Joseph 4, 6, 13, 36, 100
Brodsky, Michael (Mark) 19
Bromell, Henry 5
Broner, E(sther) M(asserman) 19
Bronk, William 10
Brooks, Cleanth 24, 86

Brooks, Gwendolyn **1, 2, 4, 5, 15, 49**
Brooks, Mel **12**
Brooks, Peter **34**
Brooks, Van Wyck **29**
Brosman, Catharine Savage **9**
Broughton, T(homas) Alan **19**
Broumas, Olga **10, 73**
Brown, Alan **99**
Brown, Claude **30**
Brown, Dee (Alexander) **18, 47**
Brown, Rita Mae **18, 43, 79**
Brown, Rosellen **32**
Brown, Sterling Allen **1, 23, 59**
Brown, (William) Larry **73**
Browne, (Clyde) Jackson **21**
Browning, Tod **16**
Bruccoli, Matthew J(oseph) **34**
Bruce, Lenny **21**
Bryan, C(ourtlandt) D(ixon) B(arnes) **29**
Buchwald, Art(hur) **33**
Buck, Pearl S(ydenstricker) **7, 11, 18**
Buckley, William F(rank) Jr. **7, 18, 37**
Buechner, (Carl) Frederick **2, 4, 6, 9**
Bukowski, Charles **2, 5, 9, 41, 82, 108**
Bullins, Ed **1, 5, 7**
Burke, Kenneth (Duva) **2, 24**
Burnshaw, Stanley **3, 13, 44**
Burr, Anne **6**
Burroughs, William S(eward) **1, 2, 5, 15, 22, 42, 75**
Busch, Frederick **7, 10, 18, 47**
Bush, Ronald **34**
Butler, Octavia E(stelle) **38**
Butler, Robert Olen (Jr.) **81**
Byars, Betsy (Cromer) **35**
Byrne, David **26**
Cage, John (Milton Jr.) **41**
Cain, James M(allahan) **3, 11, 28**
Caldwell, Erskine (Preston) **1, 8, 14, 50, 60**
Caldwell, (Janet Miriam) Taylor (Holland) **2, 28, 39**
Calisher, Hortense **2, 4, 8, 38**
Cameron, Carey **59**
Cameron, Peter **44**
Campbell, John W(ood Jr.) **32**
Campbell, Joseph **69**
Campion, Jane **95**
Canby, Vincent **13**
Canin, Ethan **55**
Capote, Truman **1, 3, 8, 13, 19, 34, 38, 58**
Capra, Frank **16**
Caputo, Philip **32**
Card, Orson Scott **44, 47, 50**
Carey, Ernestine Gilbreth **17**
Carlisle, Henry (Coffin) **33**
Carlson, Ron(ald F.) **54**
Carpenter, Don(ald Richard) **41**
Carr, Caleb **86**
Carr, John Dickson **3**
Carr, Virginia Spencer **34**
Carroll, James P. **38**
Carroll, Jim **35**
Carruth, Hayden **4, 7, 10, 18, 84**
Carson, Rachel Louise **71**
Carver, Raymond **22, 36, 53, 55**
Casey, John (Dudley) **59**
Casey, Michael **2**
Casey, Warren (Peter) **12**
Cassavetes, John **20**
Cassill, R(onald) V(erlin) **4, 23**
Cassity, (Allen) Turner **6, 42**
Castaneda, Carlos **12**
Castedo, Elena **65**

Catton, (Charles) Bruce **35**
Caunitz, William J. **34**
Cavanna, Betty **12**
Chabon, Michael **55**
Chappell, Fred (Davis) **40, 78**
Charyn, Jerome **5, 8, 18**
Chase, Mary Ellen **2**
Chayefsky, Paddy **23**
Cheever, John **3, 7, 8, 11, 15, 25, 64**
Cheever, Susan **18, 48**
Cherryh, C. J. **35**
Chester, Alfred **49**
Childress, Alice **12, 15, 86, 96**
Chute, Carolyn **39**
Ciardi, John (Anthony) **10, 40, 44**
Cimino, Michael **16**
Cisneros, Sandra **69**
Clampitt, Amy **32**
Clancy, Tom **45**
Clark, Eleanor **5, 19**
Clark, Walter Van Tilburg **28**
Clarke, Shirley **16**
Clavell, James (duMaresq) **6, 25, 87**
Cleaver, (Leroy) Eldridge **30**
Clifton, (Thelma) Lucille **19, 66**
Coburn, D(onald) L(ee) **10**
Codrescu, Andrei **46**
Coen, Ethan **108**
Coen, Joel **108**
Cohen, Arthur A(llen) **7, 31**
Coles, Robert (Martin) **108**
Collier, Christopher **30**
Collier, James L(incoln) **30**
Collins, Linda **44**
Colter, Cyrus **58**
Colum, Padraic **28**
Colwin, Laurie (E.) **5, 13, 23, 84**
Condon, Richard (Thomas) **4, 6, 8, 10, 45, 100**
Connell, Evan S(helby) Jr. **4, 6, 45**
Connelly, Marc(us Cook) **7**
Conroy, Donald Pat(rick) **30, 74**
Cook, Robin **14**
Cooke, Elizabeth **55**
Cook-Lynn, Elizabeth **93**
Cooper, J(oan) California **56**
Coover, Robert (Lowell) **3, 7, 15, 32, 46, 87**
Coppola, Francis Ford **16**
Corcoran, Barbara **17**
Corman, Cid **9**
Cormier, Robert (Edmund) **12, 30**
Corn, Alfred (DeWitt III) **33**
Corso, (Nunzio) Gregory **1, 11**
Costain, Thomas B(ertram) **30**
Cowley, Malcolm **39**
Cozzens, James Gould **1, 4, 11, 92**
Crane, R(onald) S(almon) **27**
Crase, Douglas **58**
Creeley, Robert (White) **1, 2, 4, 8, 11, 15, 36, 78**
Crews, Harry (Eugene) **6, 23, 49**
Crichton, (John) Michael **2, 6, 54, 90**
Cristofer, Michael **28**
Crow Dog, Mary (Ellen) **93**
Crowley, John **57**
Crumb, R(obert) **17**
Cryer, Gretchen (Kiger) **21**
Cudlip, David **34**
Cummings, E(dward) E(stlin) **1, 3, 8, 12, 15, 68**
Cunningham, J(ames) V(incent) **3, 31**
Cunningham, Julia (Woolfolk) **12**
Cunningham, Michael **34**

Currie, Ellen **44**
Dacey, Philip **51**
Dahlberg, Edward **1, 7, 14**
Daitch, Susan **103**
Daly, Elizabeth **52**
Daly, Maureen **17**
Dannay, Frederic **11**
Danticat, Edwidge **94**
Danvers, Dennis **70**
Danziger, Paula **21**
Davenport, Guy (Mattison Jr.) **6, 14, 38**
Davidson, Donald (Grady) **2, 13, 19**
Davidson, Sara **9**
Davis, Angela (Yvonne) **77**
Davis, Harold Lenoir **49**
Davison, Peter (Hubert) **28**
Dawson, Fielding **6**
Deer, Sandra **45**
Delany, Samuel R(ay Jr.) **8, 14, 38**
Delbanco, Nicholas (Franklin) **6, 13**
DeLillo, Don **8, 10, 13, 27, 39, 54, 76**
Deloria, Vine (Victor) Jr. **21**
Del Vecchio, John M(ichael) **29**
de Man, Paul (Adolph Michel) **55**
De Marinis, Rick **54**
Demby, William **53**
Denby, Edwin (Orr) **48**
De Palma, Brian (Russell) **20**
Deren, Maya **16, 102**
Derleth, August (William) **31**
Deutsch, Babette **18**
De Vries, Peter **1, 2, 3, 7, 10, 28, 46**
Dexter, Pete **34, 55**
Diamond, Neil **30**
Dick, Philip K(indred) **10, 30, 72**
Dickey, James (Lafayette) **1, 2, 4, 7, 10, 15, 47**
Dickey, William **3, 28**
Dickinson, Charles **49**
Didion, Joan **1, 3, 8, 14, 32**
Dillard, Annie **9, 60**
Dillard, R(ichard) H(enry) W(ilde) **5**
Disch, Thomas M(ichael) **7, 36**
Dixon, Stephen **52**
Dobyns, Stephen **37**
Doctorow, E(dgar) L(aurence) **6, 11, 15, 18, 37, 44, 65**
Dodson, Owen (Vincent) **79**
Doerr, Harriet **34**
Donaldson, Stephen R. **46**
Donleavy, J(ames) P(atrick) **1, 4, 6, 10, 45**
Donovan, John **35**
Doolittle, Hilda **3, 8, 14, 31, 34, 73**
Dorn, Edward (Merton) **10, 18**
Dos Passos, John (Roderigo) **1, 4, 8, 11, 15, 25, 34, 82**
Douglas, Ellen **73**
Dove, Rita (Frances) **50, 81**
Dowell, Coleman **60**
Drexler, Rosalyn **2, 6**
Drury, Allen (Stuart) **37**
Duberman, Martin (Bauml) **8**
Dubie, Norman (Evans) **36**
Du Bois, W(illiam) E(dward) B(urghardt) **1, 2, 13, 64, 96**
Dubus, Andre **13, 36, 97**
Duffy, Bruce **50**
Dugan, Alan **2, 6**
Dumas, Henry L. **6, 62**
Duncan, Lois **26**
Duncan, Robert (Edward) **1, 2, 4, 7, 15, 41, 55**
Dunn, Katherine (Karen) **71**
Dunn, Stephen **36**
Dunne, John Gregory **28**

Durang, Christopher (Ferdinand) 27, 38
Durban, (Rosa) Pam 39
Dworkin, Andrea 43
Dylan, Bob 3, 4, 6, 12, 77
Eastlake, William (Derry) 8
Eberhart, Richard (Ghormley) 3, 11, 19, 56
Eberstadt, Fernanda 39
Eckert, Allan W. 17
Edel, (Joseph) Leon 29, 34
Edgerton, Clyde (Carlyle) 39
Edmonds, Walter D(umaux) 35
Edson, Russell 13
Edwards, Gus 43
Ehle, John (Marsden Jr.) 27
Eigner, Larry 9
Eiseley, Loren Corey 7
Eisenstadt, Jill 50
Eliade, Mircea 19
Eliot, T(homas) S(tearns) 1, 2, 3, 6, 9, 10, 13, 15, 24, 34, 41, 55, 57
Elkin, Stanley L(awrence) 4, 6, 9, 14, 27, 51, 91
Elledge, Scott 34
Elliott, George P(aul) 2
Ellis, Bret Easton 39, 71
Ellison, Harlan (Jay) 1, 13, 42
Ellison, Ralph (Waldo) 1, 3, 11, 54, 86
Ellmann, Lucy (Elizabeth) 61
Ellmann, Richard (David) 50
Elman, Richard 19
Ephron, Nora 17, 31
Epstein, Daniel Mark 7
Epstein, Jacob 19
Epstein, Joseph 39
Epstein, Leslie 27
Erdman, Paul E(mil) 25
Erdrich, Louise 39, 54
Erickson, Steve 64
Eshleman, Clayton 7
Estleman, Loren D. 48
Eugenides, Jeffrey 81
Everett, Percival L. 57
Everson, William (Oliver) 1, 5, 14
Exley, Frederick (Earl) 6, 11
Ezekiel, Tish O'Dowd 34
Fagen, Donald 26
Fair, Ronald L. 18
Fante, John (Thomas) 60
Farina, Richard 9
Farley, Walter (Lorimer) 17
Farmer, Philip Jose 1, 19
Farrell, James T(homas) 1, 4, 8, 11, 66
Fast, Howard (Melvin) 23
Faulkner, William (Cuthbert) 1, 3, 6, 8, 9, 11, 14, 18, 28, 52, 68
Fauset, Jessie Redmon 19, 54
Faust, Irvin 8
Fearing, Kenneth (Flexner) 51
Federman, Raymond 6, 47
Feiffer, Jules (Ralph) 2, 8, 64
Feinberg, David B. 59
Feldman, Irving (Mordecai) 7
Felsen, Henry Gregor 17
Ferber, Edna 18, 93
Ferlinghetti, Lawrence (Monsanto) 2, 6, 10, 27
Ferrigno, Robert 65
Fiedler, Leslie A(aron) 4, 13, 24
Field, Andrew 44
Fierstein, Harvey (Forbes) 33
Fisher, M(ary) F(rances) K(ennedy) 76, 87
Fisher, Vardis (Alvero) 7
Fitzgerald, Robert (Stuart) 39

Flanagan, Thomas (James Bonner) 25, 52
Fleming, Thomas (James) 37
Foote, Horton 51, 91
Foote, Shelby 75
Forbes, Esther 12
Forche, Carolyn (Louise) 25, 83, 86
Ford, John 16
Ford, Richard 46
Ford, Richard 99
Foreman, Richard 50
Forman, James Douglas 21
Fornes, Maria Irene 39, 61
Forrest, Leon 4
Fosse, Bob 20
Fox, Paula 2, 8
Fox, William Price (Jr.) 22
Francis, Robert (Churchill) 15
Frank, Elizabeth 39
Fraze, Candida (Merrill) 50
Frazier, Ian 46
Freeman, Judith 55
French, Albert 86
French, Marilyn 10, 18, 60
Friedan, Betty (Naomi) 74
Friedman, B(ernard) H(arper) 7
Friedman, Bruce Jay 3, 5, 56
Frost, Robert (Lee) 1, 3, 4, 9, 10, 13, 15, 26, 34, 44
Fuchs, Daniel 34
Fuchs, Daniel 8, 22
Fuller, Charles (H. Jr.) 25
Fulton, Alice 52
Fussell, Paul 74
Gaddis, William 1, 3, 6, 8, 10, 19, 43, 86
Gaines, Ernest J(ames) 3, 11, 18, 86
Gaitskill, Mary 69
Gallagher, Tess 18, 63
Gallant, Roy A(rthur) 17
Gallico, Paul (William) 2
Galvin, James 38
Gann, Ernest Kellogg 23
Garcia, Cristina 76
Gardner, Herb(ert) 44
Gardner, John (Champlin) Jr. 2, 3, 5, 7, 8, 10, 18, 28, 34
Garrett, George (Palmer) 3, 11, 51
Garrigue, Jean 2, 8
Gass, William H(oward) 1, 2, 8, 11, 15, 39
Gates, Henry Louis Jr. 65
Gaye, Marvin (Penze) 26
Gelbart, Larry (Simon) 21, 61
Gelber, Jack 1, 6, 14, 79
Gellhorn, Martha (Ellis) 14, 60
Gent, Peter 29
George, Jean Craighead 35
Gertler, T. 34
Ghiselin, Brewster 23
Gibbons, Kaye 50, 88
Gibson, William 23
Gibson, William (Ford) 39, 63
Gifford, Barry (Colby) 34
Gilbreth, Frank B. Jr. 17
Gilchrist, Ellen 34, 48
Giles, Molly 39
Gilliam, Terry (Vance) 21
Gilroy, Frank D(aniel) 2
Gilstrap, John 99
Ginsberg, Allen 1, 2, 3, 4, 6, 13, 36, 69
Giovanni, Nikki 2, 4, 19, 64
Glasser, Ronald J. 37
Gluck, Louise (Elisabeth) 7, 22, 44, 81
Godwin, Gail (Kathleen) 5, 8, 22, 31, 69
Goines, Donald 80

Gold, Herbert 4, 7, 14, 42
Goldbarth, Albert 5, 38
Goldman, Francisco 76
Goldman, William (W.) 1, 48
Goldsberry, Steven 34
Goodman, Paul 1, 2, 4, 7
Gordon, Caroline 6, 13, 29, 83
Gordon, Mary (Catherine) 13, 22
Gordon, Sol 26
Gordone, Charles 1, 4
Gould, Lois 4, 10
Goyen, (Charles) William 5, 8, 14, 40
Graham, Jorie 48
Grau, Shirley Ann 4, 9
Graver, Elizabeth 70
Gray, Amlin 29
Gray, Francine du Plessix 22
Gray, Spalding 49
Grayson, Richard (A.) 38
Greeley, Andrew M(oran) 28
Green, Hannah 3
Green, Julien 3, 11, 77
Green, Paul (Eliot) 25
Greenberg, Joanne (Goldenberg) 7, 30
Greenberg, Richard 57
Greene, Bette 30
Greene, Gael 8
Gregor, Arthur 9
Griffin, John Howard 68
Griffin, Peter 39
Grisham, John 84
Grumbach, Doris (Isaac) 13, 22, 64
Grunwald, Lisa 44
Guare, John 8, 14, 29, 67
Guest, Barbara 34
Guest, Judith (Ann) 8, 30
Guild, Nicholas M. 33
Gunn, Bill 5
Gurganus, Allan 70
Gurney, A(lbert) R(amsdell) Jr. 32, 50, 54
Gustafson, James M(oody) 100
Guterson, David 91
Guthrie, A(lfred) B(ertram) Jr. 23
Guthrie, Woody 35
Guy, Rosa (Cuthbert) 26
Hacker, Marilyn 5, 9, 23, 72, 91
Hailey, Elizabeth Forsythe 40
Haines, John (Meade) 58
Haldeman, Joe (William) 61
Haley, Alex(ander Murray Palmer) 8, 12, 76
Hall, Donald (Andrew Jr.) 1, 13, 37, 59
Halpern, Daniel 14
Hamill, Pete 10
Hamilton, Edmond 1
Hamilton, Virginia 26
Hammett, (Samuel) Dashiell 3, 5, 10, 19, 47
Hamner, Earl (Henry) Jr. 12
Hannah, Barry 23, 38, 90
Hansberry, Lorraine (Vivian) 17, 62
Hansen, Joseph 38
Hanson, Kenneth O(stlin) 13
Hardwick, Elizabeth 13
Harjo, Joy 83
Harlan, Louis R(udolph) 34
Harling, Robert 53
Harmon, William (Ruth) 38
Harper, Michael S(teven) 7, 22
Harris, MacDonald 9
Harris, Mark 19
Harrison, Harry (Max) 42
Harrison, James (Thomas) 6, 14, 33, 66
Harrison, Kathryn 70
Harriss, Will(ard Irvin) 34

Hart, Moss 66
Hartman, Geoffrey H. 27
Haruf, Kent 34
Hass, Robert 18, 39, 99
Haviaras, Stratis 33
Hawkes, John (Clendennin Burne Jr.) 1, 2, 3, 4, 7, 9, 14, 15, 27, 49
Hayden, Robert E(arl) 5, 9, 14, 37
Hayman, Ronald 44
H. D. 3, 8, 14, 31, 34, 73
Hearne, Vicki 56
Hearon, Shelby 63
Heat-Moon, William Least 29
Hecht, Anthony (Evan) 8, 13, 19
Hecht, Ben 8
Heifner, Jack 11
Heilbrun, Carolyn G(old) 25
Heinemann, Larry (Curtiss) 50
Heinlein, Robert A(nson) 1, 3, 8, 14, 26, 55
Heller, Joseph 1, 3, 5, 8, 11, 36, 63
Hellman, Lillian (Florence) 2, 4, 8, 14, 18, 34, 44, 52
Helprin, Mark 7, 10, 22, 32
Hemingway, Ernest (Miller) 1, 3, 6, 8, 10, 13, 19, 30, 34, 39, 41, 44, 50, 61, 80
Hempel, Amy 39
Henley, Beth 23
Hentoff, Nat(han Irving) 26
Herbert, Frank (Patrick) 12, 23, 35, 44, 85
Herbst, Josephine (Frey) 34
Herlihy, James Leo 6
Herrmann, Dorothy 44
Hersey, John (Richard) 1, 2, 7, 9, 40, 81, 97
Heyen, William 13, 18
Higgins, George V(incent) 4, 7, 10, 18
Highsmith, (Mary) Patricia 2, 4, 14, 42, 102
Highwater, Jamake (Mamake) 12
Hijuelos, Oscar 65
Hill, George Roy 26
Hillerman, Tony 62
Himes, Chester (Bomar) 2, 4, 7, 18, 58, 108
Hinton, S(usan) E(loise) 30
Hirsch, Edward 31, 50
Hirsch, E(ric) D(onald) Jr. 79
Hoagland, Edward 28
Hoban, Russell (Conwell) 7, 25
Hobson, Laura Z(ametkin) 7, 25
Hochman, Sandra 3, 8
Hoffman, Alice 51
Hoffman, Daniel (Gerard) 6, 13, 23
Hoffman, Stanley 5
Hoffman, William M(oses) 40
Hogan, Linda 73
Holland, Isabelle 21
Hollander, John 2, 5, 8, 14
Holleran, Andrew 38
Holmes, John Clellon 56
Honig, Edwin 33
hooks, bell 94
Horgan, Paul (George Vincent O'Shaughnessy) 9, 53
Horovitz, Israel (Arthur) 56
Horwitz, Julius 14
Hougan, Carolyn 34
Howard, Maureen 5, 14, 46
Howard, Richard 7, 10, 47
Howe, Fanny 47
Howe, Irving 85
Howe, Susan 72
Howe, Tina 48
Howes, Barbara 15
Hubbard, L(afayette) Ron(ald) 43
Huddle, David 49

Hughart, Barry 39
Hughes, (James) Langston 1, 5, 10, 15, 35, 44, 108
Hugo, Richard F(ranklin) 6, 18, 32
Humphrey, William 45
Humphreys, Josephine 34, 57
Hunt, E(verette) Howard (Jr.) 3
Hunt, Marsha 70
Hunter, Evan 11, 31
Hunter, Kristin (Eggleston) 35
Hurston, Zora Neale 7, 30, 61
Huston, John (Marcellus) 20
Hustvedt, Siri 76
Hwang, David Henry 55
Hyde, Margaret O(ldroyd) 21
Hynes, James 65
Ian, Janis 21
Ignatow, David 4, 7, 14, 40
Ingalls, Rachel (Holmes) 42
Inge, William (Motter) 1, 8, 19
Innaurato, Albert (F.) 21, 60
Irving, John (Winslow) 13, 23, 38
Isaacs, Susan 32
Isler, Alan (David) 91
Ivask, Ivar Vidrik 14
Jackson, Jesse 12
Jackson, Shirley 11, 60, 87
Jacobs, Jim 12
Jacobsen, Josephine 48, 102
Jakes, John (William) 29
Janowitz, Tama 43
Jarrell, Randall 1, 2, 6, 9, 13, 49
Jeffers, (John) Robinson 2, 3, 11, 15, 54
Jen, Gish 70
Jennings, Waylon 21
Jensen, Laura (Linnea) 37
Joel, Billy 26
Johnson, Charles (Richard) 7, 51, 65
Johnson, Denis 52
Johnson, Diane 5, 13, 48
Johnson, Joyce 58
Jones, Edward P. 76
Jones, Gayl 6, 9
Jones, James 1, 3, 10, 39
Jones, LeRoi 1, 2, 3, 5, 10, 14
Jones, Louis B. 65
Jones, Madison (Percy Jr.) 4
Jones, Nettie (Pearl) 34
Jones, Preston 10
Jones, Robert F(rancis) 7
Jones, Thom 81
Jong, Erica 4, 6, 8, 18, 83
Jordan, June 5, 11, 23
Jordan, Pat(rick M.) 37
Just, Ward (Swift) 4, 27
Justice, Donald (Rodney) 6, 19, 102
Kadohata, Cynthia 59
Kahn, Roger 30
Kaletski, Alexander 39
Kallman, Chester (Simon) 2
Kaminsky, Stuart M(elvin) 59
Kanin, Garson 22
Kantor, MacKinlay 7
Kaplan, David Michael 50
Kaplan, James 59
Karl, Frederick R(obert) 34
Katz, Steve 47
Kauffman, Janet 42
Kaufman, Bob (Garnell) 49
Kaufman, George S. 38
Kaufman, Sue 3, 8
Kazan, Elia 6, 16, 63
Kazin, Alfred 34, 38

Keaton, Buster 20
Keene, Donald 34
Keillor, Garrison 40
Kellerman, Jonathan 44
Kelley, William Melvin 22
Kellogg, Marjorie 2
Kemelman, Harry 2
Kennedy, Adrienne (Lita) 66
Kennedy, William 6, 28, 34, 53
Kennedy, X. J. 8, 42
Kenny, Maurice (Francis) 87
Kerouac, Jack 1, 2, 3, 5, 14, 29, 61
Kerr, Jean 22
Kerr, M. E. 12, 35
Kerr, Robert 55
Kerrigan, (Thomas) Anthony 4, 6
Kesey, Ken (Elton) 1, 3, 6, 11, 46, 64
Kesselring, Joseph (Otto) 45
Kessler, Jascha (Frederick) 4
Kettelkamp, Larry (Dale) 12
Keyes, Daniel 80
Kherdian, David 6, 9
Kienzle, William X(avier) 25
Killens, John Oliver 10
Kincaid, Jamaica 43, 68
King, Martin Luther Jr. 83
King, Stephen (Edwin) 12, 26, 37, 61
King, Thomas 89
Kingman, Lee 17
Kingsley, Sidney 44
Kingsolver, Barbara 55, 81
Kingston, Maxine (Ting Ting) Hong 12, 19, 58
Kinnell, Galway 1, 2, 3, 5, 13, 29
Kirkwood, James 9
Kizer, Carolyn (Ashley) 15, 39, 80
Klappert, Peter 57
Klein, Norma 30
Klein, T(heodore) E(ibon) D(onald) 34
Knapp, Caroline 99
Knebel, Fletcher 14
Knight, Etheridge 40
Knowles, John 1, 4, 10, 26
Koch, Kenneth 5, 8, 44
Komunyakaa, Yusef 86, 94
Koontz, Dean R(ay) 78
Kopit, Arthur (Lee) 1, 18, 33
Kosinski, Jerzy (Nikodem) 1, 2, 3, 6, 10, 15, 53, 70
Kostelanetz, Richard (Cory) 28
Kotlowitz, Robert 4
Kotzwinkle, William 5, 14, 35
Kozol, Jonathan 17
Kozoll, Michael 35
Kramer, Kathryn 34
Kramer, Larry 42
Kristofferson, Kris 26
Krumgold, Joseph (Quincy) 12
Krutch, Joseph Wood 24
Kubrick, Stanley 16
Kumin, Maxine (Winokur) 5, 13, 28
Kunitz, Stanley (Jasspon) 6, 11, 14
Kushner, Tony 81
Kuzma, Greg 7
L'Amour, Louis (Dearborn) 25, 55
Lancaster, Bruce 36
Landis, John 26
Langer, Elinor 34
Lapine, James (Elliot) 39
Larsen, Eric 55
Larsen, Nella 37
Larson, Charles R(aymond) 31
Lasch, Christopher 102

Latham, Jean Lee 12
Lattimore, Richmond (Alexander) 3
Laughlin, James 49
Lear, Norman (Milton) 12
Leavitt, David 34
Lebowitz, Fran(ces Ann) 11, 36
Lee, Andrea 36
Lee, Chang-rae 91
Lee, Don L. 2
Lee, George W(ashington) 52
Lee, Helen Elaine 86
Lee, Lawrence 34
Lee, Manfred B(ennington) 11
Lee, (Nelle) Harper 12, 60
Lee, Shelton Jackson 105
Lee, Stan 17
Leet, Judith 11
Leffland, Ella 19
Le Guin, Ursula K(roeber) 8, 13, 22, 45, 71
Leiber, Fritz (Reuter Jr.) 25
Leimbach, Marti 65
Leithauser, Brad 27
Lelchuk, Alan 5
Lemann, Nancy 39
L'Engle, Madeleine (Camp Franklin) 12
Lentricchia, Frank (Jr.) 34
Leonard, Elmore (John Jr.) 28, 34, 71
Lerman, Eleanor 9
Lerman, Rhoda 56
Lester, Richard 20
Levertov, Denise 1, 2, 3, 5, 8, 15, 28, 66
Levi, Jonathan 76
Levin, Ira 3, 6
Levin, Meyer 7
Levine, Philip 2, 4, 5, 9, 14, 33
Levinson, Deirdre 49
Levitin, Sonia (Wolff) 17
Lewis, Janet 41
Leyner, Mark 92
L'Heureux, John (Clarke) 52
Lieber, Joel 6
Lieberman, Laurence (James) 4, 36
Lifton, Robert Jay 67
Lightman, Alan P(aige) 81
Ligotti, Thomas (Robert) 44
Lindbergh, Anne (Spencer) Morrow 82
Linney, Romulus 51
Lipsyte, Robert (Michael) 21
Lish, Gordon (Jay) 45
Littell, Robert 42
Loewinsohn, Ron(ald William) 52
Logan, John (Burton) 5
Lopate, Phillip 29
Lord, Bette Bao 23
Lorde, Audre (Geraldine) 18, 71
Louie, David Wong 70
Lowell, Robert (Traill Spence Jr.) 1, 2, 3, 4, 5,
　8, 9, 11, 15, 37
Loy, Mina 28
Lucas, Craig 64
Lucas, George 16
Ludlam, Charles 46, 50
Ludlum, Robert 22, 43
Ludwig, Ken 60
Lurie, Alison 4, 5, 18, 39
Lynch, David (K.) 66
Lynn, Kenneth S(chuyler) 50
Lytle, Andrew (Nelson) 22
Maas, Peter 29
Macdonald, Cynthia 13, 19
MacDonald, John D(ann) 3, 27, 44
Macdonald, Ross 1, 2, 3, 14, 34, 41
MacInnes, Helen (Clark) 27, 39

Maclean, Norman (Fitzroy) 78
MacLeish, Archibald 3, 8, 14, 68
MacShane, Frank 39
Madden, (Jerry) David 5, 15
Madhubuti, Haki R. 6, 73
Mailer, Norman 1, 2, 3, 4, 5, 8, 11, 14, 28, 39,
　74
Major, Clarence 3, 19, 48
Malamud, Bernard 1, 2, 3, 5, 8, 9, 11, 18, 27,
　44, 78, 85
Malcolm X 82
Maloff, Saul 5
Malone, Michael (Christopher) 43
Malzberg, Barry N(athaniel) 7
Mamet, David (Alan) 9, 15, 34, 46, 91
Mamoulian, Rouben (Zachary) 16
Mano, D. Keith 2, 10
Manso, Peter 39
Margulies, Donald 76
Markfield, Wallace 8
Markson, David M(errill) 67
Marquand, John P(hillips) 2, 10
Marques, Rene 96
Marshall, Garry 17
Marshall, Paule 27, 72
Martin, Steve 30
Martin, Valerie 89
Maso, Carole 44
Mason, Bobbie Ann 28, 43, 82
Masters, Hilary 48
Mastrosimone, William 36
Matheson, Richard Burton 37
Mathews, Harry 6, 52
Mathews, John Joseph 84
Matthews, William 40
Matthias, John (Edward) 9
Matthiessen, Peter 5, 7, 11, 32, 64
Maupin, Armistead 95
Maxwell, William (Keepers Jr.) 19
May, Elaine 16
Maynard, Joyce 23
Maysles, Albert 16
Maysles, David 16
Mazer, Norma Fox 26
McBrien, William Augustine 44
McCaffrey, Anne (Inez) 17
McCall, Nathan 86
McCarthy, Cormac 4, 57, 59, 101
McCarthy, Mary (Therese) 1, 3, 5, 14, 24, 39,
　59
McCauley, Stephen (D.) 50
McClure, Michael (Thomas) 6, 10
McCorkle, Jill (Collins) 51
McCourt, James 5
McCullers, (Lula) Carson (Smith) 1, 4, 10, 12,
　48, 100
McDermott, Alice 90
McElroy, Joseph 5, 47
McFarland, Dennis 65
McGinley, Phyllis 14
McGinniss, Joe 32
McGrath, Thomas (Matthew) 28, 59
McGuane, Thomas (Francis III) 3, 7, 18, 45
McHale, Tom 3, 5
McInerney, Jay 34
McIntyre, Vonda N(eel) 18
McKuen, Rod 1, 3
McMillan, Terry (L.) 50, 61
McMurtry, Larry (Jeff) 2, 3, 7, 11, 27, 44
McNally, Terrence 4, 7, 41, 91
McNally, T. M. 82
McNamer, Deirdre 70
McNickle, (William) D'Arcy 89

McPhee, John (Angus) 36
McPherson, James Alan 19, 77
McPherson, William (Alexander) 34
Mead, Margaret 37
Medoff, Mark (Howard) 6, 23
Mehta, Ved (Parkash) 37
Meltzer, Milton 26
Mendelsohn, Jane 99
Meredith, William (Morris) 4, 13, 22, 55
Merkin, Daphne 44
Merrill, James (Ingram) 2, 3, 6, 8, 13, 18, 34,
　91
Merton, Thomas 1, 3, 11, 34, 83
Merwin, W(illiam) S(tanley) 1, 2, 3, 5, 8, 13,
　18, 45, 88
Mewshaw, Michael 9
Meyers, Jeffrey 39
Michaels, Leonard 6, 25
Michener, James A(lbert) 1, 5, 11, 29, 60
Miles, Jack 100
Miles, Josephine (Louise) 1, 2, 14, 34, 39
Millar, Kenneth 14
Miller, Arthur 1, 2, 6, 10, 15, 26, 47, 78
Miller, Henry (Valentine) 1, 2, 4, 9, 14, 43, 84
Miller, Jason 2
Miller, Sue 44
Miller, Walter M(ichael Jr.) 4, 30
Millett, Kate 67
Millhauser, Steven (Lewis) 21, 54
Milner, Ron(ald) 56
Miner, Valerie 40
Minot, Susan 44
Minus, Ed 39
Mitchell, Joseph (Quincy) 98
Modarressi, Taghi (M.) 44
Mohr, Nicholasa 12
Mojtabai, A(nn) G(race) 5, 9, 15, 29
Momaday, N(avarre) Scott 2, 19, 85, 95
Monette, Paul 82
Montague, John (Patrick) 13, 46
Montgomery, Marion H. Jr. 7
Mooney, Ted 25
Moore, Lorrie 39, 45, 68
Moore, Marianne (Craig) 1, 2, 4, 8, 10, 13, 19,
　47
Morgan, Berry 6
Morgan, (George) Frederick 23
Morgan, Robin 2
Morgan, Seth 65
Morris, Bill 76
Morris, Wright 1, 3, 7, 18, 37
Morrison, Jim 17
Morrison, Toni 4, 10, 22, 55, 81, 87
Mosher, Howard Frank 62
Mosley, Walter 97
Moss, Howard 7, 14, 45, 50
Motley, Willard (Francis) 18
Mountain Wolf Woman 92
Moyers, Bill 74
Mueller, Lisel 13, 51
Mukherjee, Bharati 53
Mull, Martin 17
Mungo, Raymond 72
Murphy, Sylvia 34
Murray, Albert L. 73
Muske, Carol 90
Myers, Walter Dean 35
Nabokov, Vladimir (Vladimirovich) 1, 2, 3, 6,
　8, 11, 15, 23, 44, 46, 64
Nash, (Fredric) Ogden 23
Naylor, Gloria 28, 52
Neihardt, John Gneisenau 32
Nelson, Willie 17

Nationality Index

Nemerov, Howard (Stanley) 2, 6, 9, 36
Neufeld, John (Arthur) 17
Neville, Emily Cheney 12
Newlove, Donald 6
Newman, Charles 2, 8
Newman, Edwin (Harold) 14
Newton, Suzanne 35
Nichols, John (Treadwell) 38
Niedecker, Lorine 10, 42
Nin, Anais 1, 4, 8, 11, 14, 60
Nissenson, Hugh 4, 9
Niven, Larry 8
Nixon, Agnes Eckhardt 21
Norman, Marsha 28
Norton, Andre 12
Nova, Craig 7, 31
Nunn, Kem 34
Nyro, Laura 17
Oates, Joyce Carol 1, 2, 3, 6, 9, 11, 15, 19, 33, 52, 108
O'Brien, Darcy 11
O'Brien, (William) Tim(othy) 7, 19, 40, 103
Ochs, Phil 17
O'Connor, Edwin (Greene) 14
O'Connor, (Mary) Flannery 1, 2, 3, 6, 10, 13, 15, 21, 66, 104
O'Dell, Scott 30
Odets, Clifford 2, 28, 98
O'Donovan, Michael John 14
O'Grady, Timothy 59
O'Hara, Frank 2, 5, 13, 78
O'Hara, John (Henry) 1, 2, 3, 6, 11, 42
O Hehir, Diana 41
Olds, Sharon 32, 39, 85
Oliver, Mary 19, 34, 98
Olsen, Tillie 4, 13
Olson, Charles (John) 1, 2, 5, 6, 9, 11, 29
Olson, Toby 28
Oneal, Zibby 30
Oppen, George 7, 13, 34
Orlovitz, Gil 22
Ortiz, Simon J(oseph) 45
Otto, Whitney 70
Owens, Rochelle 8
Ozick, Cynthia 3, 7, 28, 62
Pack, Robert 13
Pagels, Elaine Hiesey 104
Paglia, Camille (Anna) 68
Paley, Grace 4, 6, 37
Palliser, Charles 65
Pancake, Breece D'J 29
Parini, Jay (Lee) 54
Parker, Dorothy (Rothschild) 15, 68
Parker, Robert B(rown) 27
Parks, Gordon (Alexander Buchanan) 1, 16
Pastan, Linda (Olenik) 27
Patchen, Kenneth 1, 2, 18
Paterson, Katherine (Womeldorf) 12, 30
Peacock, Molly 60
Pearson, T(homas) R(eid) 39
Peck, John 3
Peck, Richard (Wayne) 21
Peck, Robert Newton 17
Peckinpah, (David) Sam(uel) 20
Percy, Walker 2, 3, 6, 8, 14, 18, 47, 65
Perelman, S(idney) J(oseph) 3, 5, 9, 15, 23, 44, 49
Pesetsky, Bette 28
Peterkin, Julia Mood 31
Peters, Joan K(aren) 39
Peters, Robert L(ouis) 7
Petrakis, Harry Mark 3
Petry, Ann (Lane) 1, 7, 18

Philipson, Morris H. 53
Phillips, Jayne Anne 15, 33
Phillips, Robert (Schaeffer) 28
Piercy, Marge 3, 6, 14, 18, 27, 62
Pinckney, Darryl 76
Pineda, Cecile 39
Pinkwater, Daniel Manus 35
Pinsky, Robert 9, 19, 38, 94
Pirsig, Robert M(aynard) 4, 6, 73
Plante, David (Robert) 7, 23, 38
Plath, Sylvia 1, 2, 3, 5, 9, 11, 14, 17, 50, 51, 62
Platt, Kin 26
Plimpton, George (Ames) 36
Plumly, Stanley (Ross) 33
Pohl, Frederik 18
Poitier, Sidney 26
Pollitt, Katha 28
Polonsky, Abraham (Lincoln) 92
Pomerance, Bernard 13
Porter, Connie (Rose) 70
Porter, Katherine Anne 1, 3, 7, 10, 13, 15, 27, 101
Potok, Chaim 2, 7, 14, 26
Pound, Ezra (Weston Loomis) 1, 2, 3, 4, 5, 7, 10, 13, 18, 34, 48, 50
Povod, Reinaldo 44
Powell, Adam Clayton Jr. 89
Powell, Dawn 66
Powell, Padgett 34
Power, Susan 91
Powers, J(ames) F(arl) 1, 4, 8, 57
Powers, John R. 66
Powers, Richard (S.) 93
Prager, Emily 56
Price, (Edward) Reynolds 3, 6, 13, 43, 50, 63
Price, Richard 6, 12
Prince 35
Pritchard, William H(arrison) 34
Probst, Mark 59
Prokosch, Frederic 4, 48
Prose, Francine 45
Proulx, E. Annie 81
Pryor, Richard (Franklin Lenox Thomas) 26
Purdy, James (Amos) 2, 4, 10, 28, 52
Puzo, Mario 1, 2, 6, 36, 107
Pynchon, Thomas (Ruggles Jr.) 2, 3, 6, 9, 11, 18, 33, 62, 72
Quay, Stephen 95
Quay, Timothy 95
Queen, Ellery 3, 11
Quinn, Peter 91
Rabe, David (William) 4, 8, 33
Rado, James 17
Raeburn, John (Hay) 34
Ragni, Gerome 17
Rahv, Philip 24
Rakosi, Carl 47
Rampersad, Arnold 44
Rand, Ayn 3, 30, 44, 79
Randall, Dudley (Felker) 1
Ransom, John Crowe 2, 4, 5, 11, 24
Raphael, Frederic (Michael) 2, 14
Rechy, John (Francisco) 1, 7, 14, 18, 107
Reddin, Keith 67
Redmon, Anne 22
Reed, Ishmael 2, 3, 5, 6, 13, 32, 60
Reed, Lou 21
Remarque, Erich Maria 21
Rexroth, Kenneth 1, 2, 6, 11, 22, 49
Reynolds, Jonathan 6, 38
Reynolds, Michael Shane 44
Reznikoff, Charles 9

Ribman, Ronald (Burt) 7
Rice, Anne 41
Rice, Elmer (Leopold) 7, 49
Rich, Adrienne (Cecile) 3, 6, 7, 11, 18, 36, 73, 76
Richter, Conrad (Michael) 30
Riding, Laura 3, 7
Ringwood, Gwen(dolyn Margaret) Pharis 48
Rivers, Conrad Kent 1
Robbins, Harold 5
Robbins, Tom 9, 32, 64
Robbins, Trina 21
Robinson, Jill 10
Robinson, Kim Stanley 34
Robinson, Marilynne 25
Robinson, Smokey 21
Robison, Mary 42, 98
Roddenberry, Gene 17
Rodgers, Mary 12
Rodman, Howard 65
Roethke, Theodore (Huebner) 1, 3, 8, 11, 19, 46, 101
Rogers, Thomas Hunton 57
Rogin, Gilbert 18
Roiphe, Anne (Richardson) 3, 9
Rooke, Leon 25, 34
Rose, Wendy 85
Rosen, Richard (Dean) 39
Rosenthal, M(acha) L(ouis) 28
Rossner, Judith (Perelman) 6, 9, 29
Roth, Henry 2, 6, 11, 104
Roth, Philip (Milton) 1, 2, 3, 4, 6, 9, 15, 22, 31, 47, 66, 86
Rothenberg, Jerome 6, 57
Rovit, Earl (Herbert) 7
Ruark, Gibbons 3
Rudnik, Raphael 7
Rukeyser, Muriel 6, 10, 15, 27
Rule, Jane (Vance) 27
Rush, Norman 44
Russ, Joanna 15
Ryan, Cornelius (John) 7
Ryan, Michael 65
Sachs, Marilyn (Stickle) 35
Sackler, Howard (Oliver) 14
Sadoff, Ira 9
Safire, William 10
Sagan, Carl (Edward) 30
Saint, H(arry) F. 50
Salamanca, J(ack) R(ichard) 4, 15
Sale, Kirkpatrick 68
Salinas, Luis Omar 90
Salinger, J(erome) D(avid) 1, 3, 8, 12, 55, 56
Salter, James 7, 52, 59
Sanchez, Sonia 5
Sandburg, Carl (August) 1, 4, 10, 15, 35
Sanders, (James) Ed(ward) 53
Sanders, Lawrence 41
Sandoz, Mari(e Susette) 28
Saner, Reg(inald Anthony) 9
Santiago, Danny 33
Santmyer, Helen Hoover 33
Santos, Bienvenido N(uqui) 22
Sapphire 99
Saroyan, William 1, 8, 10, 29, 34, 56
Sarton, (Eleanor) May 4, 14, 49, 91
Saul, John (W. III) 46
Savage, Thomas 40
Savan, Glenn 50
Sayers, Valerie 50
Sayles, John (Thomas) 7, 10, 14
Schaeffer, Susan Fromberg 6, 11, 22
Schell, Jonathan 35

Schevill, James (Erwin) 7
Schisgal, Murray (Joseph) 6
Schlesinger, Arthur M(eier) Jr. 84
Schnackenberg, Gjertrud 40
Schor, Sandra (M.) 65
Schorer, Mark 9
Schrader, Paul (Joseph) 26
Schulberg, Budd (Wilson) 7, 48
Schulz, Charles M(onroe) 12
Schuyler, James Marcus 5, 23
Schwartz, Delmore (David) 2, 4, 10, 45, 87
Schwartz, John Burnham 59
Schwartz, Lynne Sharon 31
Scoppettone, Sandra 26
Scorsese, Martin 20, 89
Scott, Evelyn 43
Scott, Joanna 50
Sebestyen, Ouida 30
Seelye, John 7
Segal, Erich (Wolf) 3, 10
Seger, Bob 35
Seidel, Frederick (Lewis) 18
Selby, Hubert Jr. 1, 2, 4, 8
Selzer, Richard 74
Serling, (Edward) Rod(man) 30
Seton, Cynthia Propper 27
Settle, Mary Lee 19, 61
Sexton, Anne (Harvey) 2, 4, 6, 8, 10, 15, 53
Shaara, Michael (Joseph Jr.) 15
Shacochis, Bob 39
Shange, Ntozake 8, 25, 38, 74
Shanley, John Patrick 75
Shapiro, Jane 76
Shapiro, Karl (Jay) 4, 8, 15, 53
Shaw, Irwin 7, 23, 34
Shawn, Wallace 41
Shea, Lisa 86
Sheed, Wilfrid (John Joseph) 2, 4, 10, 53
Shepard, Jim 36
Shepard, Lucius 34
Shepard, Sam 4, 6, 17, 34, 41, 44
Sherburne, Zoa (Morin) 30
Sherman, Jonathan Marc 55
Sherman, Martin 19
Sherwin, Judith Johnson 7, 15
Shields, Carol 91
Shields, David 97
Shilts, Randy 85
Shreve, Susan Richards 23
Shue, Larry 52
Shulman, Alix Kates 2, 10
Shuster, Joe 21
Siegel, Jerome 21
Sigal, Clancy 7
Silko, Leslie (Marmon) 23, 74
Silver, Joan Micklin 20
Silverberg, Robert 7
Silverstein, Alvin 17
Silverstein, Virginia B(arbara Opshelor) 17
Simak, Clifford D(onald) 1, 55
Simic, Charles 6, 9, 22, 49, 68
Simmons, Charles (Paul) 57
Simmons, Dan 44
Simon, Carly 26
Simon, (Marvin) Neil 6, 11, 31, 39, 70
Simon, Paul (Frederick) 17
Simpson, Louis (Aston Marantz) 4, 7, 9, 32
Simpson, Mona (Elizabeth) 44
Sinclair, Upton (Beall) 1, 11, 15, 63
Singer, Isaac Bashevis 1, 3, 6, 9, 11, 15, 23, 38, 69
Sissman, L(ouis) E(dward) 9, 18
Slaughter, Frank G(ill) 29

Slavitt, David R(ytman) 5, 14
Smiley, Jane (Graves) 53, 76
Smith, Anna Deavere 86
Smith, Betty (Wehner) 19
Smith, Clark Ashton 43
Smith, Dave 22, 42
Smith, Lee 25, 73
Smith, Martin Cruz 25
Smith, Mary-Ann Tirone 39
Smith, Patti 12
Smith, William Jay 6
Snodgrass, W(illiam) D(e Witt) 2, 6, 10, 18, 68
Snyder, Gary (Sherman) 1, 2, 5, 9, 32
Snyder, Zilpha Keatley 17
Sokolov, Raymond 7
Sommer, Scott 25
Sondheim, Stephen (Joshua) 30, 39
Sontag, Susan 1, 2, 10, 13, 31, 105
Sorrentino, Gilbert 3, 7, 14, 22, 40
Soto, Gary 32, 80
Southern, Terry 7
Spackman, W(illiam) M(ode) 46
Spacks, Barry (Bernard) 14
Spanidou, Irini 44
Spencer, Elizabeth 22
Spencer, Scott 30
Spicer, Jack 8, 18, 72
Spiegelman, Art 76
Spielberg, Peter 6
Spielberg, Steven 20
Spillane, Mickey 3, 13
Spinrad, Norman (Richard) 46
Spivack, Kathleen (Romola Drucker) 6
Spoto, Donald 39
Springsteen, Bruce (F.) 17
Squires, (James) Radcliffe 51
Stafford, Jean 4, 7, 19, 68
Stafford, William (Edgar) 4, 7, 29
Stanton, Maura 9
Starbuck, George (Edwin) 53
Steele, Timothy (Reid) 45
Stegner, Wallace (Earle) 9, 49, 81
Steinbeck, John (Ernst) 1, 5, 9, 13, 21, 34, 45, 75
Steinem, Gloria 63
Steiner, George 24
Sterling, Bruce 72
Stern, Gerald 40, 100
Stern, Richard (Gustave) 4, 39
Sternberg, Josef von 20
Stevens, Mark 34
Stevenson, Anne (Katharine) 7, 33
Still, James 49
Stitt, Milan 29
Stolz, Mary (Slattery) 12
Stone, Irving 7
Stone, Oliver (William) 73
Stone, Robert (Anthony) 5, 23, 42
Storm, Hyemeyohsts 3
Stout, Rex (Todhunter) 3
Strand, Mark 6, 18, 41, 71
Straub, Peter (Francis) 28, 107
Stribling, T(homas) S(igismund) 23
Stuart, Jesse (Hilton) 1, 8, 11, 14, 34
Sturgeon, Theodore (Hamilton) 22, 39
Styron, William 1, 3, 5, 11, 15, 60
Sukenick, Ronald 3, 4, 6, 48
Summers, Hollis (Spurgeon Jr.) 10
Susann, Jacqueline 3
Swados, Elizabeth (A.) 12
Swados, Harvey 5
Swan, Gladys 69

Swarthout, Glendon (Fred) 35
Swenson, May 4, 14, 61, 106
Talese, Gay 37
Tallent, Elizabeth (Ann) 45
Tally, Ted 42
Tan, Amy (Ruth) 59
Tartt, Donna 76
Tate, James (Vincent) 2, 6, 25
Tate, (John Orley) Allen 2, 4, 6, 9, 11, 14, 24
Tavel, Ronald 6
Taylor, Eleanor Ross 5
Taylor, Henry (Splawn) 44
Taylor, Mildred D. 21
Taylor, Peter (Hillsman) 1, 4, 18, 37, 44, 50, 71
Taylor, Robert Lewis 14
Terkel, Studs 38
Terry, Megan 19
Tesich, Steve 40, 69
Tevis, Walter 42
Theroux, Alexander (Louis) 2, 25
Theroux, Paul (Edward) 5, 8, 11, 15, 28, 46
Thomas, Audrey (Callahan) 7, 13, 37, 107
Thomas, Joyce Carol 35
Thomas, Lewis 35
Thomas, Piri 17
Thomas, Ross (Elmore) 39
Thompson, Hunter S(tockton) 9, 17, 40, 104
Thompson, Jim (Myers) 69
Thurber, James (Grover) 5, 11, 25
Tilghman, Christopher 65
Tillinghast, Richard (Williford) 29
Tiptree, James Jr. 48, 50
Tolson, Melvin B(eaunorus) 36, 105
Tomlin, Lily 17
Toole, John Kennedy 19, 64
Toomer, Jean 1, 4, 13, 22
Torrey, E(dwin) Fuller 34
Towne, Robert (Burton) 87
Traven, B. 8, 11
Trevanian 29
Trilling, Lionel 9, 11, 24
Trow, George W. S. 52
Trudeau, Garry B. 12
Trumbo, Dalton 19
Tryon, Thomas 3, 11
Tuck, Lily 70
Tunis, John R(oberts) 12
Turco, Lewis (Putnam) 11, 63
Turner, Frederick 48
Tyler, Anne 7, 11, 18, 28, 44, 59, 103
Uhry, Alfred 55
Ulibarri, Sabine R(eyes) 83
Unger, Douglas 34
Updike, John (Hoyer) 1, 2, 3, 5, 7, 9, 13, 15, 23, 34, 43, 70
Urdang, Constance (Henriette) 47
Uris, Leon (Marcus) 7, 32
Vachss, Andrew (Henry) 106
Valdez, Luis (Miguel) 84
Van Ash, Cay 34
Vance, Jack 35
Vandenburgh, Jane 59
Van Doren, Mark 6, 10
Van Duyn, Mona (Jane) 3, 7, 63
Van Peebles, Melvin 2, 20
Van Vechten, Carl 33
Vaughn, Stephanie 62
Vidal, Gore 2, 4, 6, 8, 10, 22, 33, 72
Viereck, Peter (Robert Edwin) 4
Vinge, Joan D(ennison) 30
Vizenor, Gerald Robert 103
Vliet, R(ussell) G(ordon) 22

Nationality Index

Vogel, Paula A(nne) 76
Voight, Ellen Bryant 54
Voigt, Cynthia 30
Vollmann, William T. 89
Vonnegut, Kurt Jr. 1, 2, 3, 4, 5, 8, 12, 22, 40, 60
Wagman, Fredrica 7
Wagner-Martin, Linda (C.) 50
Wagoner, David (Russell) 3, 5, 15
Wakefield, Dan 7
Wakoski, Diane 2, 4, 7, 9, 11, 40
Waldman, Anne 7
Walker, Alice (Malsenior) 5, 6, 9, 19, 27, 46, 58, 103
Walker, Joseph A. 19
Walker, Margaret (Abigail) 1, 6
Wallace, David Foster 50
Wallace, Irving 7, 13
Wallant, Edward Lewis 5, 10
Wambaugh, Joseph (Aloysius Jr.) 3, 18
Ward, Douglas Turner 19
Warhol, Andy 20
Warren, Robert Penn 1, 4, 6, 8, 10, 13, 18, 39, 53, 59
Wasserstein, Wendy 32, 59, 90
Waters, Frank (Joseph) 88
Watkins, Paul 55
Webb, Charles (Richard) 7
Webb, James H(enry) Jr. 22
Weber, Lenora Mattingly 12
Weidman, Jerome 7
Weiss, Theodore (Russell) 3, 8, 14
Welch, James 6, 14, 52
Wellek, Rene 28
Weller, Michael 10, 53
Welles, (George) Orson 20, 80
Wellman, Mac 65
Wellman, Manly Wade 49
Wells, Rosemary 12
Welty, Eudora 1, 2, 5, 14, 22, 33, 105
Wersba, Barbara 30
Wescott, Glenway 13
Wesley, Richard (Errol) 7
West, (Mary) Jessamyn 7, 17
West, Paul 7, 14, 96
Westlake, Donald E(dwin) 7, 33
Whalen, Philip 6, 29
Wharton, William (a pseudonym) 18, 37
Wheelock, John Hall 14
White, Edmund (Valentine III) 27
White, E(lwyn) B(rooks) 10, 34, 39
Whitney, Phyllis A(yame) 42
Whittemore, (Edward) Reed (Jr.) 4
Wicker, Tom 7
Wideman, John Edgar 5, 34, 36, 67
Wieners, John 7
Wiesel, Elie(zer) 3, 5, 11, 37
Wiggins, Marianne 57
Wilbur, Richard (Purdy) 3, 6, 9, 14, 53
Wild, Peter 14
Wilder, Billy 20
Wilder, Thornton (Niven) 1, 5, 6, 10, 15, 35, 82
Wiley, Richard 44
Wilhelm, Kate 7
Willard, Nancy 7, 37
Williams, C(harles) K(enneth) 33, 56
Williams, John A(lfred) 5, 13
Williams, Jonathan (Chamberlain) 13
Williams, Joy 31
Williams, Norman 39
Williams, Sherley Anne 89
Williams, Tennessee 1, 2, 5, 7, 8, 11, 15, 19, 30, 39, 45, 71
Williams, Thomas (Alonzo) 14
Williams, William Carlos 1, 2, 5, 9, 13, 22, 42, 67
Williamson, Jack 29
Willingham, Calder (Baynard Jr.) 5, 51
Wilson, August 39, 50, 63
Wilson, Brian 12
Wilson, Edmund 1, 2, 3, 8, 24
Wilson, Lanford 7, 14, 36
Wilson, Robert M. 7, 9
Wilson, Sloan 32
Wilson, William S(mith) 49
Winters, (Arthur) Yvor 4, 8, 32
Winters, Janet Lewis 41
Wiseman, Frederick 20
Wodehouse, P(elham) G(renville) 1, 2, 5, 10, 22
Woiwode, Larry (Alfred) 6, 10
Wojciechowska, Maia (Teresa) 26
Wolfe, Gene (Rodman) 25
Wolfe, George C. 49
Wolfe, Tom 1, 2, 9, 15, 35, 51
Wolff, Geoffrey (Ansell) 41
Wolff, Tobias (Jonathan Ansell) 39, 64
Wolitzer, Hilma 17
Wonder, Stevie 12
Wong, Jade Snow 17
Woolrich, Cornell 77
Wouk, Herman 1, 9, 38
Wright, Charles (Penzel Jr.) 6, 13, 28
Wright, Charles Stevenson 49
Wright, James (Arlington) 3, 5, 10, 28
Wright, Richard (Nathaniel) 1, 3, 4, 9, 14, 21, 48, 74
Wright, Stephen 33
Wright, William 44
Wurlitzer, Rudolph 2, 4, 15
Wylie, Philip (Gordon) 43
Yates, Richard 7, 8, 23
Yep, Laurence Michael 35
Yerby, Frank G(arvin) 1, 7, 22
Yglesias, Helen 7, 22
Young, Al(bert James) 19
Young, Marguerite (Vivian) 82
Young Bear, Ray A. 94
Yurick, Sol 6
Zamora, Bernice (B. Ortiz) 89
Zappa, Frank 17
Zaturenska, Marya 6, 11
Zelazny, Roger (Joseph) 21
Ziegenhagen, Eric 55
Zindel, Paul 6, 26
Zoline, Pamela 62
Zukofsky, Louis 1, 2, 4, 7, 11, 18
Zweig, Paul 34, 42

ANTIGUAN
Edwards, Gus 43
Kincaid, Jamaica 43, 68

ARGENTINIAN
Bioy Casares, Adolfo 4, 8, 13, 88
Borges, Jorge Luis 1, 2, 3, 4, 6, 8, 9, 10, 13, 19, 44, 48, 83
Cortazar, Julio 2, 3, 5, 10, 13, 15, 33, 34, 92
Costantini, Humberto 49
Dorfman, Ariel 48, 77
Guevara, Che 87
Mujica Lainez, Manuel 31
Puig, Manuel 3, 5, 10, 28, 65
Sabato, Ernesto (R.) 10, 23
Valenzuela, Luisa 31, 104

ARMENIAN
Mamoulian, Rouben (Zachary) 16

AUSTRALIAN
Anderson, Jessica (Margaret) Queale 37
Astley, Thea (Beatrice May) 41
Brinsmead, H(esba) F(ay) 21
Buckley, Vincent (Thomas) 57
Buzo, Alexander (John) 61
Carey, Peter 40, 55, 96
Clark, Mavis Thorpe 12
Clavell, James (duMaresq) 6, 25, 87
Courtenay, Bryce 59
Davison, Frank Dalby 15
Elliott, Sumner Locke 38
FitzGerald, Robert D(avid) 19
Grenville, Kate 61
Hall, Rodney 51
Hazzard, Shirley 18
Hope, A(lec) D(erwent) 3, 51
Hospital, Janette Turner 42
Jolley, (Monica) Elizabeth 46
Jones, Rod 50
Keneally, Thomas (Michael) 5, 8, 10, 14, 19, 27, 43
Koch, C(hristopher) J(ohn) 42
Lawler, Raymond Evenor 58
Malouf, (George Joseph) David 28, 86
Matthews, Greg 45
McAuley, James Phillip 45
McCullough, Colleen 27, 107
Murray, Les(lie) A(llan) 40
Porter, Peter (Neville Frederick) 5, 13, 33
Prichard, Katharine Susannah 46
Shapcott, Thomas W(illiam) 38
Slessor, Kenneth 14
Stead, Christina (Ellen) 2, 5, 8, 32, 80
Stow, (Julian) Randolph 23, 48
Thiele, Colin (Milton) 17
Weir, Peter (Lindsay) 20
West, Morris L(anglo) 6, 33
White, Patrick (Victor Martindale) 3, 4, 5, 7, 9, 18, 65, 69
Wilding, Michael 73
Williamson, David (Keith) 56
Wright, Judith (Arandell) 11, 53

AUSTRIAN
Adamson, Joy(-Friederike Victoria) 17
Bachmann, Ingeborg 69
Bernhard, Thomas 3, 32, 61
Bettelheim, Bruno 79
Frankl, Viktor E(mil) 93
Gregor, Arthur 9
Handke, Peter 5, 8, 10, 15, 38
Hochwaelder, Fritz 36
Jandl, Ernst 34
Lang, Fritz 20, 103
Lind, Jakov 1, 2, 4, 27, 82
Sternberg, Josef von 20
Wellek, Rene 28
Wilder, Billy 20

BARBADIAN
Brathwaite, Edward Kamau 11
Clarke, Austin C(hesterfield) 8, 53
Kennedy, Adrienne (Lita) 66
Lamming, George (William) 2, 4, 66

BELGIAN
Crommelynck, Fernand 75
Ghelderode, Michel de 6, 11

Levi-Strauss, Claude **38**
Mallet-Joris, Francoise **11**
Michaux, Henri **8, 19**
Sarton, (Eleanor) May **4, 14, 49, 91**
Simenon, Georges (Jacques Christian) **1, 2, 3,
    8, 18, 47**
van Itallie, Jean-Claude **3**
Yourcenar, Marguerite **19, 38, 50, 87**

BOTSWANAN
Head, Bessie **25, 67**

BRAZILIAN
Amado, Jorge **13, 40, 106**
Andrade, Carlos Drummond de **18**
Cabral de Melo Neto, Joao **76**
Dourado, (Waldomiro Freitas) Autran **23, 60**
Drummond de Andrade, Carlos **18**
Lispector, Clarice **43**
Ribeiro, Darcy **34**
Ribeiro, Joao Ubaldo (Osorio Pimentel) **10,
    67**
Rosa, Joao Guimaraes **23**

BULGARIAN
Bagryana, Elisaveta **10**
Belcheva, Elisaveta **10**
Canetti, Elias **3, 14, 25, 75, 86**
Kristeva, Julia **77**

CAMEROONIAN
Beti, Mongo **27**

CANADIAN
Acorn, Milton **15**
Aquin, Hubert **15**
Atwood, Margaret (Eleanor) **2, 3, 4, 8, 13, 15,
    25, 44, 84**
Avison, Margaret **2, 4, 97**
Barfoot, Joan **18**
Bellow, Saul **1, 2, 3, 6, 8, 10, 13, 15, 25, 33,
    34, 63, 79**
Berton, Pierre (Francis De Marigny) **104**
Birney, (Alfred) Earle **1, 4, 6, 11**
Bissett, Bill **18**
Blais, Marie-Claire **2, 4, 6, 13, 22**
Blaise, Clark **29**
Bowering, George **15, 47**
Bowering, Marilyn R(uthe) **32**
Buckler, Ernest **13**
Buell, John (Edward) **10**
Callaghan, Morley Edward **3, 14, 41, 65**
Campbell, Maria **85**
Carrier, Roch **13, 78**
Child, Philip **19, 68**
Chislett, (Margaret) Anne **34**
Clarke, Austin C(hesterfield) **8, 53**
Cohen, Leonard (Norman) **3, 38**
Cohen, Matt **19**
Coles, Don **46**
Cook, Michael **58**
Cooper, Douglas **86**
Coupland, Douglas **85**
Craven, Margaret **17**
Davies, (William) Robertson **2, 7, 13, 25, 42,
    75, 91**
de la Roche, Mazo **14**
Donnell, David **34**
Ducharme, Rejean **74**
Dudek, Louis **11, 19**
Engel, Marian **36**
Everson, R(onald) G(ilmour) **27**
Faludy, George **42**

Ferron, Jacques **94**
Finch, Robert (Duer Claydon) **18**
Findley, Timothy **27, 102**
Fraser, Sylvia **64**
Frye, (Herman) Northrop **24, 70**
Gallant, Mavis **7, 18, 38**
Garner, Hugh **13**
Gilmour, David **35**
Glassco, John **9**
Gotlieb, Phyllis Fay (Bloom) **18**
Govier, Katherine **51**
Gunnars, Kristjana **69**
Gustafson, Ralph (Barker) **36**
Haig-Brown, Roderick (Langmere) **21**
Hailey, Arthur **5**
Harris, Christie (Lucy) Irwin **12**
Hebert, Anne **4, 13, 29**
Highway, Tomson **92**
Hillis, Rick **66**
Hine, (William) Daryl **15**
Hodgins, Jack **23**
Hood, Hugh (John Blagdon) **15, 28**
Hospital, Janette Turner **42**
Hyde, Anthony **42**
Jacobsen, Josephine **48, 102**
Jiles, Paulette **13, 58**
Johnston, George (Benson) **51**
Jones, D(ouglas) G(ordon) **10**
Kelly, M(ilton) T(erry) **55**
King, Thomas **89**
Kinsella, W(illiam) P(atrick) **27, 43**
Klein, A(braham) M(oses) **19**
Kogawa, Joy Nozomi **78**
Krizanc, John **57**
Kroetsch, Robert **5, 23, 57**
Kroker, Arthur (W.) **77**
Lane, Patrick **25**
Laurence, (Jean) Margaret (Wemyss) **3, 6, 13,
    50, 62**
Layton, Irving (Peter) **2, 15**
Levine, Norman **54**
Lightfoot, Gordon **26**
Livesay, Dorothy (Kathleen) **4, 15, 79**
MacEwen, Gwendolyn (Margaret) **13, 55**
MacLennan, (John) Hugh **2, 14, 92**
MacLeod, Alistair **56**
Macpherson, (Jean) Jay **14**
Maillet, Antonine **54**
Major, Kevin (Gerald) **26**
McFadden, David **48**
McLuhan, (Herbert) Marshall **37, 83**
Metcalf, John **37**
Mitchell, Joni **12**
Mitchell, W(illiam) O(rmond) **25**
Moore, Brian **1, 3, 5, 7, 8, 19, 32, 90**
Morgan, Janet **39**
Moure, Erin **88**
Mowat, Farley (McGill) **26**
Munro, Alice **6, 10, 19, 50, 95**
Musgrave, Susan **13, 54**
Newlove, John (Herbert) **14**
Nichol, B(arrie) P(hillip) **18**
Nowlan, Alden (Albert) **15**
Ondaatje, (Philip) Michael **14, 29, 51, 76**
Page, P(atricia) K(athleen) **7, 18**
Pollock, (Mary) Sharon **50**
Pratt, E(dwin) J(ohn) **19**
Purdy, Al(fred Wellington) **3, 6, 14, 50**
Quarrington, Paul (Lewis) **65**
Reaney, James **13**
Ricci, Nino **70**
Richards, David Adams **59**
Richler, Mordecai **3, 5, 9, 13, 18, 46, 70**

Ringwood, Gwen(dolyn Margaret) Pharis **48**
Ritter, Erika **52**
Rooke, Leon **25, 34**
Rosenblatt, Joe **15**
Ross, (James) Sinclair **13**
Roy, Gabrielle **10, 14**
Rule, Jane (Vance) **27**
Ryga, George **14**
Scott, F(rancis) R(eginald) **22**
Shields, Carol **91**
Skelton, Robin **13**
Skvorecky, Josef (Vaclav) **15, 39, 69**
Slade, Bernard **11, 46**
Smart, Elizabeth **54**
Smith, A(rthur) J(ames) M(arshall) **15**
Souster, (Holmes) Raymond **5, 14**
Suknaski, Andrew **19**
Theriault, Yves **79**
Thesen, Sharon **56**
Thomas, Audrey (Callahan) **7, 13, 37, 107**
Thompson, Judith **39**
Tremblay, Michel **29, 102**
Urquhart, Jane **90**
Vanderhaeghe, Guy **41**
Van Vogt, A(lfred) E(lton) **1**
Vizinczey, Stephen **40**
Waddington, Miriam **28**
Wah, Fred(erick James) **44** ·
Walker, David Harry **14**
Walker, George F. **44, 61**
Webb, Phyllis **18**
Wiebe, Rudy (Henry) **6, 11, 14**
Wilson, Ethel Davis (Bryant) **13**
Wright, L(aurali) R. **44**
Wright, Richard B(ruce) **6**
Young, Neil **17**

CHILEAN
Alegria, Fernando **57**
Allende, Isabel **39, 57, 97**
Donoso (Yanez), Jose **4, 8, 11, 32, 99**
Dorfman, Ariel **48, 77**
Neruda, Pablo **1, 2, 5, 7, 9, 28, 62**
Parra, Nicanor **2, 102**

CHINESE
Chang, Jung **71**
Ch'ien Chung-shu **22**
Ding Ling **68**
Lord, Bette Bao **23**
Mo, Timothy (Peter) **46**
Pa Chin **18**
Peake, Mervyn **7, 54**
Wong, Jade Snow **17**

COLOMBIAN
Garcia Marquez, Gabriel (Jose) **2, 3, 8, 10, 15,
    27, 47, 55, 68**

CONGOLESE
Tchicaya, Gerald Felix **101**

CUBAN
Arenas, Reinaldo **41**
Cabrera Infante, G(uillermo) **5, 25, 45**
Calvino, Italo **5, 8, 11, 22, 33, 39, 73**
Carpentier (y Valmont), Alejo **8, 11, 38**
Fornes, Maria Irene **39, 61**
Garcia, Cristina **76**
Guevara, Che **87**
Guillen, Nicolas (Cristobal) **48, 79**
Lezama Lima, Jose **4, 10, 101**
Padilla (Lorenzo), Heberto **38**

Nationality Index

Sarduy, Severo **6, 97**

CZECH
Friedlander, Saul **90**
Havel, Vaclav **25, 58, 65**
Holub, Miroslav **4**
Hrabal, Bohumil **13, 67**
Klima, Ivan **56**
Kohout, Pavel **13**
Kundera, Milan **4, 9, 19, 32, 68**
Lustig, Arnost **56**
Seifert, Jaroslav **34, 44, 93**
Skvorecky, Josef (Vaclav) **15, 39, 69**
Vaculik, Ludvik **7**

DANISH
Abell, Kjeld **15**
Bodker, Cecil **21**
Dinesen, Isak **10, 29, 95**
Dreyer, Carl Theodor **16**
Hoeg, Peter **95**

DUTCH
de Hartog, Jan **19**
Mulisch, Harry **42**
Ruyslinck, Ward **14**
van de Wetering, Janwillem **47**

EGYPTIAN
Chedid, Andree **47**
Mahfuz, Najib **52, 55**

ENGLISH
Ackroyd, Peter **34, 52**
Adams, Douglas (Noel) **27, 60**
Adams, Richard (George) **4, 5, 18**
Adcock, Fleur **41**
Aickman, Robert (Fordyce) **57**
Aiken, Joan (Delano) **35**
Aldington, Richard **49**
Aldiss, Brian W(ilson) **5, 14, 40**
Allingham, Margery (Louise) **19**
Almedingen, E. M. **12**
Alvarez, A(lfred) **5, 13**
Ambler, Eric **4, 6, 9**
Amis, Kingsley (William) **1, 2, 3, 5, 8, 13, 40, 44**
Amis, Martin (Louis) **4, 9, 38, 62, 101**
Anderson, Lindsay (Gordon) **20**
Anthony, Piers **35**
Archer, Jeffrey (Howard) **28**
Arden, John **6, 13, 15**
Armatrading, Joan **17**
Arthur, Ruth M(abel) **12**
Arundel, Honor (Morfydd) **17**
Atkinson, Kate **99**
Auden, W(ystan) H(ugh) **1, 2, 3, 4, 6, 9, 11, 14, 43**
Ayckbourn, Alan **5, 8, 18, 33, 74**
Ayrton, Michael **7**
Bagnold, Enid **25**
Bailey, Paul **45**
Bainbridge, Beryl (Margaret) **4, 5, 8, 10, 14, 18, 22, 62**
Ballard, J(ames) G(raham) **3, 6, 14, 36**
Banks, Lynne Reid **23**
Barker, Clive **52**
Barker, George Granville **8, 48**
Barker, Howard **37**
Barker, Pat(ricia) **32, 94**
Barnes, Julian (Patrick) **42**
Barnes, Peter **5, 56**
Barrett, (Roger) Syd **35**

Bates, H(erbert) E(rnest) **46**
Beer, Patricia **58**
Bennett, Alan **45, 77**
Berger, John (Peter) **2, 19**
Berkoff, Steven **56**
Bermant, Chaim (Icyk) **40**
Betjeman, John **2, 6, 10, 34, 43**
Billington, (Lady) Rachel (Mary) **43**
Binyon, T(imothy) J(ohn) **34**
Blunden, Edmund (Charles) **2, 56**
Bogarde, Dirk **19**
Bolt, Robert (Oxton) **14**
Bond, Edward **4, 6, 13, 23**
Booth, Martin **13**
Bowen, Elizabeth (Dorothea Cole) **1, 3, 6, 11, 15, 22**
Bowie, David **17**
Boyd, William **28, 53, 70**
Bradbury, Malcolm (Stanley) **32, 61**
Bragg, Melvyn **10**
Braine, John (Gerard) **1, 3, 41**
Brenton, Howard **31**
Brittain, Vera (Mary) **23**
Brooke-Rose, Christine **40**
Brookner, Anita **32, 34, 51**
Brophy, Brigid (Antonia) **6, 11, 29, 105**
Brunner, John (Kilian Houston) **8, 10**
Bunting, Basil **10, 39, 47**
Burgess, Anthony **1, 2, 4, 5, 8, 10, 13, 15, 22, 40, 62, 81, 94**
Byatt, A(ntonia) S(usan Drabble) **19, 65**
Caldwell, (Janet Miriam) Taylor (Holland) **2, 28, 39**
Campbell, (John) Ramsey **42**
Carter, Angela (Olive) **5, 41, 76**
Causley, Charles (Stanley) **7**
Caute, (John) David **29**
Chambers, Aidan **35**
Chaplin, Charles Spencer **16**
Chapman, Graham **21**
Chatwin, (Charles) Bruce **28, 57, 59**
Chitty, Thomas Willes **11**
Christie, Agatha (Mary Clarissa) **1, 6, 8, 12, 39, 48**
Churchill, Caryl **31, 55**
Clark, (Robert) Brian **29**
Clarke, Arthur C(harles) **1, 4, 13, 18, 35**
Cleese, John (Marwood) **21**
Colegate, Isabel **36**
Comfort, Alex(ander) **7**
Compton-Burnett, I(vy) **1, 3, 10, 15, 34**
Cooney, Ray **62**
Copeland, Stewart (Armstrong) **26**
Cornwell, David (John Moore) **9, 15**
Costello, Elvis **21**
Coward, Noel (Peirce) **1, 9, 29, 51**
Creasey, John **11**
Crispin, Edmund **22**
Dabydeen, David **34**
Dahl, Roald **1, 6, 18, 79**
Daryush, Elizabeth **6, 19**
Davie, Donald (Alfred) **5, 8, 10, 31**
Davies, Rhys **23**
Day Lewis, C(ecil) **1, 6, 10**
Deighton, Len **4, 7, 22, 46**
Delaney, Shelagh **29**
Dennis, Nigel (Forbes) **8**
Dickinson, Peter (Malcolm) **12, 35**
Drabble, Margaret **2, 3, 5, 8, 10, 22, 53**
Duffy, Maureen **37**
du Maurier, Daphne **6, 11, 59**
Durrell, Lawrence (George) **1, 4, 6, 8, 13, 27, 41**

Eagleton, Terry **63**
Edgar, David **42**
Edwards, G(erald) B(asil) **25**
Eliot, T(homas) S(tearns) **1, 2, 3, 6, 9, 10, 13, 15, 24, 34, 41, 55, 57**
Elliott, Janice **47**
Ellis, A. E. **7**
Ellis, Alice Thomas **40**
Empson, William **3, 8, 19, 33, 34**
Enright, D(ennis) J(oseph) **4, 8, 31**
Ewart, Gavin (Buchanan) **13, 46**
Fairbairns, Zoe (Ann) **32**
Farrell, J(ames) G(ordon) **6**
Feinstein, Elaine **36**
Fenton, James Martin **32**
Figes, Eva **31**
Fisher, Roy **25**
Fitzgerald, Penelope **19, 51, 61**
Fleming, Ian (Lancaster) **3, 30**
Follett, Ken(neth Martin) **18**
Forester, C(ecil) S(cott) **35**
Forster, E(dward) M(organ) **1, 2, 3, 4, 9, 10, 13, 15, 22, 45, 77**
Forsyth, Frederick **2, 5, 36**
Fowles, John **1, 2, 3, 4, 6, 9, 10, 15, 33, 87**
Francis, Dick **2, 22, 42, 102**
Fraser, George MacDonald **7**
Fraser, (Lady) Antonia (Pakenham) **32, 107**
Frayn, Michael **3, 7, 31, 47**
Freeling, Nicolas **38**
Fry, Christopher **2, 10, 14**
Fugard, Sheila **48**
Fuller, John (Leopold) **62**
Fuller, Roy (Broadbent) **4, 28**
Gardam, Jane **43**
Gardner, John (Edmund) **30**
Garfield, Leon **12**
Garner, Alan **17**
Garnett, David **3**
Gascoyne, David (Emery) **45**
Gee, Maggie (Mary) **57**
Gerhardie, William Alexander **5**
Gilliatt, Penelope (Ann Douglass) **2, 10, 13, 53**
Glanville, Brian (Lester) **6**
Glendinning, Victoria **50**
Gloag, Julian **40**
Godden, (Margaret) Rumer **53**
Golding, William (Gerald) **1, 2, 3, 8, 10, 17, 27, 58, 81**
Graham, Winston (Mawdsley) **23**
Graves, Richard Perceval **44**
Graves, Robert (von Ranke) **1, 2, 6, 11, 39, 44, 45**
Gray, Simon (James Holliday) **9, 14, 36**
Green, Henry **2, 13, 97**
Greene, Graham (Henry) **1, 3, 6, 9, 14, 18, 27, 37, 70, 72**
Griffiths, Trevor **13, 52**
Grigson, Geoffrey (Edward Harvey) **7, 39**
Gunn, Thom(son William) **3, 6, 18, 32, 81**
Haig-Brown, Roderick (Langmere) **21**
Hailey, Arthur **5**
Hall, Rodney **51**
Hamburger, Michael (Peter Leopold) **5, 14**
Hamilton, (Anthony Walter) Patrick **51**
Hampton, Christopher (James) **4**
Hare, David **29, 58**
Harrison, Tony **43**
Hartley, L(eslie) P(oles) **2, 22**
Harwood, Ronald **32**
Hastings, Selina **44**
Hawking, Stephen W(illiam) **63, 105**

Headon, (Nicky) Topper **30**
Heppenstall, (John) Rayner **10**
Herriot, James **12**
Hibbert, Eleanor Alice Burford **7**
Hill, Geoffrey (William) **5, 8, 18, 45**
Hill, Susan (Elizabeth) **4**
Hinde, Thomas **6, 11**
Hitchcock, Alfred (Joseph) **16**
Hocking, Mary (Eunice) **13**
Holden, Ursula **18**
Holdstock, Robert P. **39**
Hollinghurst, Alan **55, 91**
Hooker, (Peter) Jeremy **43**
Hopkins, John (Richard) **4**
Household, Geoffrey (Edward West) **11**
Howard, Elizabeth Jane **7, 29**
Hughes, David (John) **48**
Hughes, Richard (Arthur Warren) **1, 11**
Hughes, Ted **2, 4, 9, 14, 37**
Huxley, Aldous (Leonard) **1, 3, 4, 5, 8, 11, 18, 35, 79**
Idle, Eric **21**
Ingalls, Rachel (Holmes) **42**
Isherwood, Christopher (William Bradshaw) **1, 9, 11, 14, 44**
Ishiguro, Kazuo **27, 56, 59**
Jacobson, Dan **4, 14**
Jagger, Mick **17**
James, C(yril) L(ionel) R(obert) **33**
James, P. D. **18, 46**
Jellicoe, (Patricia) Ann **27**
Jennings, Elizabeth (Joan) **5, 14**
Jhabvala, Ruth Prawer **4, 8, 29, 94**
Johnson, B(ryan) S(tanley William) **6, 9**
Johnson, Pamela Hansford **1, 7, 27**
Jolley, (Monica) Elizabeth **46**
Jones, David (Michael) **2, 4, 7, 13, 42**
Jones, Diana Wynne **26**
Jones, Mervyn **10, 52**
Jones, Mick **30**
Josipovici, Gabriel **6, 43**
Kavan, Anna **5, 13, 82**
Kaye, M(ary) M(argaret) **28**
Keates, Jonathan **34**
King, Francis (Henry) **8, 53**
Kirkup, James **1**
Koestler, Arthur **1, 3, 6, 8, 15, 33**
Kops, Bernard **4**
Kureishi, Hanif **64**
Lanchester, John **99**
Larkin, Philip (Arthur) **3, 5, 8, 9, 13, 18, 33, 39, 64**
Leavis, F(rank) R(aymond) **24**
le Carre, John **3, 5, 9, 15, 28**
Lee, Laurie **90**
Lee, Tanith **46**
Lehmann, Rosamond (Nina) **5**
Lennon, John (Ono) **12, 35**
Lessing, Doris (May) **1, 2, 3, 6, 10, 15, 22, 40, 94**
Levertov, Denise **1, 2, 3, 5, 8, 15, 28, 66**
Levi, Peter (Chad Tigar) **41**
Lewis, C(live) S(taples) **1, 3, 6, 14, 27**
Lively, Penelope (Margaret) **32, 50**
Lodge, David (John) **36**
Loy, Mina **28**
Luke, Peter (Ambrose Cyprian) **38**
MacInnes, Colin **4, 23**
Mackenzie, Compton (Edward Montague) **18**
Macpherson, (Jean) Jay **14**
Maitland, Sara (Louise) **49**
Manning, Olivia **5, 19**
Markandaya, Kamala **8, 38**

Masefield, John (Edward) **11, 47**
Mason, Nick **35**
Maugham, W(illiam) Somerset **1, 11, 15, 67, 93**
Mayle, Peter **89**
Mayne, William (James Carter) **12**
McEwan, Ian (Russell) **13, 66**
McGrath, Patrick **55**
Mercer, David **5**
Metcalf, John **37**
Middleton, Christopher **13**
Middleton, Stanley **7, 38**
Mitford, Nancy **44**
Mo, Timothy (Peter) **46**
Moorcock, Michael (John) **5, 27, 58**
Mortimer, John (Clifford) **28, 43**
Mortimer, Penelope (Ruth) **5**
Mosley, Nicholas **43, 70**
Mott, Michael (Charles Alston) **15, 34**
Murdoch, (Jean) Iris **1, 2, 3, 4, 6, 8, 11, 15, 22, 31, 51**
Naipaul, V(idiadhar) S(urajprasad) **4, 7, 9, 13, 18, 37, 105**
Newby, P(ercy) H(oward) **2, 13**
Nichols, Peter (Richard) **5, 36, 65**
Noon, Jeff **91**
Norfolk, Lawrence **76**
Nye, Robert **13, 42**
O'Brien, Richard **17**
O'Faolain, Julia **6, 19, 47, 108**
Olivier, Laurence (Kerr) **20**
Orton, Joe **4, 13, 43**
Osborne, John (James) **1, 2, 5, 11, 45**
Osborne, Lawrence **50**
Page, Jimmy **12**
Page, Louise **40**
Page, P(atricia) K(athleen) **7, 18**
Palin, Michael (Edward) **21**
Parkin, Frank **43**
Paulin, Tom **37**
Peake, Mervyn **7, 54**
Pearce, Philippa **21**
Phillips, Caryl **96**
Pinter, Harold **1, 3, 6, 9, 11, 15, 27, 58, 73**
Plant, Robert **12**
Poliakoff, Stephen **38**
Poole, Josephine **17**
Potter, Dennis (Christopher George) **58, 86**
Powell, Anthony (Dymoke) **1, 3, 7, 9, 10, 31**
Pownall, David **10**
Powys, John Cowper **7, 9, 15, 46**
Priestley, J(ohn) B(oynton) **2, 5, 9, 34**
Prince, F(rank) T(empleton) **22**
Pritchett, V(ictor) S(awdon) **5, 13, 15, 41**
Pym, Barbara (Mary Crampton) **13, 19, 37**
Quin, Ann (Marie) **6**
Raine, Craig **32, 103**
Raine, Kathleen (Jessie) **7, 45**
Rathbone, Julian **41**
Rattigan, Terence (Mervyn) **7**
Raven, Simon (Arthur Noel) **14**
Read, Herbert Edward **4**
Read, Piers Paul **4, 10, 25**
Reading, Peter **47**
Redgrove, Peter (William) **6, 41**
Reid, Christopher (John) **33**
Renault, Mary **3, 11, 17**
Rendell, Ruth (Barbara) **28, 48**
Rhys, Jean **2, 4, 6, 14, 19, 51**
Rice, Tim(othy Miles Bindon) **21**
Richard, Keith **17**
Richards, I(vor) A(rmstrong) **14, 24**
Roberts, Keith (John Kingston) **14**

Roberts, Michele (B.) **48**
Rudkin, (James) David **14**
Rushdie, (Ahmed) Salman **23, 31, 55, 100**
Rushforth, Peter (Scott) **19**
Russell, (Henry) Ken(neth Alfred) **16**
Russell, Willy **60**
Sacks, Oliver (Wolf) **67**
Sansom, William **2, 6**
Sassoon, Siegfried (Lorraine) **36**
Scammell, Michael **34**
Scannell, Vernon **49**
Schlee, Ann **35**
Schumacher, E(rnst) F(riedrich) **80**
Scott, Paul (Mark) **9, 60**
Shaffer, Anthony (Joshua) **19**
Shaffer, Peter (Levin) **5, 14, 18, 37, 60**
Sharpe, Tom **36**
Shaw, Robert **5**
Sheed, Wilfrid (John Joseph) **2, 4, 10, 53**
Shute, Nevil **30**
Shuttle, Penelope (Diane) **7**
Silkin, Jon **2, 6, 43**
Sillitoe, Alan **1, 3, 6, 10, 19, 57**
Simonon, Paul **30**
Simpson, N(orman) F(rederick) **29**
Sinclair, Andrew (Annandale) **2, 14**
Sinclair, Iain **76**
Sisson, C(harles) H(ubert) **8**
Sitwell, Dame Edith **2, 9, 67**
Slaughter, Carolyn **56**
Smith, Stevie **3, 8, 25, 44**
Snow, C(harles) P(ercy) **1, 4, 6, 9, 13, 19**
Spender, Stephen (Harold) **1, 2, 5, 10, 41, 91**
Spurling, Hilary **34**
Stannard, Martin **44**
Stewart, J(ohn) I(nnes) M(ackintosh) **7, 14, 32**
Stewart, Mary (Florence Elinor) **7, 35**
Stoppard, Tom **1, 3, 4, 5, 8, 15, 29, 34, 63, 91**
Storey, David (Malcolm) **2, 4, 5, 8**
Streatfeild, (Mary) Noel **21**
Strummer, Joe **30**
Summers, Andrew James **26**
Sumner, Gordon Matthew **26**
Sutcliff, Rosemary **26**
Swift, Graham (Colin) **41, 88**
Swinfen, Ann **34**
Swinnerton, Frank Arthur **31**
Symons, Julian (Gustave) **2, 14, 32**
Szirtes, George **46**
Taylor, Elizabeth **2, 4, 29**
Tennant, Emma (Christina) **13, 52**
Teran, Lisa St. Aubin de **36**
Thomas, D(onald) M(ichael) **13, 22, 31**
Tindall, Gillian (Elizabeth) **7**
Tolkien, J(ohn) R(onald) R(euel) **1, 2, 3, 8, 12, 38**
Tomlinson, (Alfred) Charles **2, 4, 6, 13, 45**
Townshend, Peter (Dennis Blandford) **17, 42**
Treitel, Jonathan **70**
Tremain, Rose **42**
Tuohy, Frank **37**
Turner, Frederick **48**
Unsworth, Barry (Forster) **76**
Ustinov, Peter (Alexander) **1**
Vansittart, Peter **42**
Vine, Barbara **50**
Wain, John (Barrington) **2, 11, 15, 46**
Walker, Ted **13**
Walsh, Jill Paton **35**
Warner, Francis (Robert le Plastrier) **14**
Warner, Marina **59**
Warner, Rex (Ernest) **45**
Warner, Sylvia Townsend **7, 19**

Waterhouse, Keith (Spencer) 47
Waters, Roger 35
Waugh, Auberon (Alexander) 7
Waugh, Evelyn (Arthur St. John) 1, 3, 8, 13, 19, 27, 44, 107
Waugh, Harriet 6
Webber, Andrew Lloyd 21
Weldon, Fay 6, 9, 11, 19, 36, 59
Weller, Paul 26
Wesker, Arnold 3, 5, 42
West, Anthony (Panther) 50
West, Paul 7, 14, 96
West, Rebecca 7, 9, 31, 50
Westall, Robert (Atkinson) 17
White, Patrick (Victor Martindale) 3, 4, 5, 7, 9, 18, 65, 69
White, T(erence) H(anbury) 30
Whitehead, E(dward) A(nthony) 5
Whitemore, Hugh (John) 37
Wilding, Michael 73
Williams, Hugo 42
Wilson, A(ndrew) N(orman) 33
Wilson, Angus (Frank Johnstone) 2, 3, 5, 25, 34
Wilson, Colin 3, 14
Wilson, Snoo 33
Wingrove, David (John) 68
Winterson, Jeanette 64
Wodehouse, P(elham) G(renville) 1, 2, 5, 10, 22
Wright, Rick 35
Wyndham, John 19
Yorke, Henry Vincent 13
Young, Andrew (John) 5

ESTONIAN
Ivask, Ivar Vidrik 14

FIJI ISLANDER
Prichard, Katharine Susannah 46

FILIPINO
Santos, Bienvenido N(uqui) 22

FINNISH
Haavikko, Paavo Juhani 18, 34
Salama, Hannu 18
Sillanpaa, Frans Eemil 19

FRENCH
Adamov, Arthur 4, 25
Anouilh, Jean (Marie Lucien Pierre) 1, 3, 8, 13, 40, 50
Aragon, Louis 3, 22
Audiberti, Jacques 38
Ayme, Marcel (Andre) 11
Barthes, Roland (Gerard) 24, 83
Bataille, Georges 29
Baudrillard, Jean 60
Beauvoir, Simone (Lucie Ernestine Marie Bertrand) de 1, 2, 4, 8, 14, 31, 44, 50, 71
Beckett, Samuel (Barclay) 1, 2, 3, 4, 6, 9, 10, 11, 14, 18, 29, 57, 59, 83
Bonnefoy, Yves 9, 15, 58
Bresson, Robert 16
Breton, Andre 2, 9, 15, 54
Butor, Michel (Marie Francois) 1, 3, 8, 11, 15
Camus, Albert 1, 2, 4, 9, 11, 14, 32, 63, 69
Carrere, Emmanuel 89
Cayrol, Jean 11
Celine, Louis-Ferdinand 1, 3, 4, 7, 9, 15, 47
Cendrars, Blaise 18, 106
Chabrol, Claude 16

Char, Rene(-Emile) 9, 11, 14, 55
Chedid, Andree 47
Cixous, Helene 92
Clair, Rene 20
Cocteau, Jean (Maurice Eugene Clement) 1, 8, 15, 16, 43
Cousteau, Jacques-Yves 30
del Castillo, Michel 38
Derrida, Jacques 24, 87
Destouches, Louis-Ferdinand 9, 15
Duhamel, Georges 8
Duras, Marguerite 3, 6, 11, 20, 34, 40, 68, 100
Ernaux, Annie 88
Federman, Raymond 6, 47
Foucault, Michel 31, 34, 69
Fournier, Pierre 11
Francis, Claude 50
Gallo, Max Louis 95
Gary, Romain 25
Gascar, Pierre 11
Genet, Jean 1, 2, 5, 10, 14, 44, 46
Giono, Jean 4, 11
Godard, Jean-Luc 20
Goldmann, Lucien 24
Gontier, Fernande 50
Gracq, Julien 11, 48
Gray, Francine du Plessix 22
Green, Julien 3, 11, 77
Guillevic, (Eugene) 33
Ionesco, Eugene 1, 4, 6, 9, 11, 15, 41, 86
Japrisot, Sebastien 90
Jouve, Pierre Jean 47
Kristeva, Julia 77
Lacan, Jacques (Marie Emile) 75
Laurent, Antoine 50
Le Clezio, J(ean) M(arie) G(ustave) 31
Leduc, Violette 22
Leger, (Marie-Rene Auguste) Alexis Saint-Leger 11
Leiris, Michel (Julien) 61
Levi-Strauss, Claude 38
Mallet-Joris, Francoise 11
Malraux, (Georges-)Andre 1, 4, 9, 13, 15, 57
Mandiargues, Andre Pieyre de 41
Marcel, Gabriel Honore 15
Mauriac, Claude 9
Mauriac, Francois (Charles) 4, 9, 56
Merton, Thomas 1, 3, 11, 34, 83
Modiano, Patrick (Jean) 18
Montherlant, Henry (Milon) de 8, 19
Morand, Paul 41
Nin, Anais 1, 4, 8, 11, 14, 60
Perec, Georges 56
Perse, St.-John 4, 11, 46
Pinget, Robert 7, 13, 37
Ponge, Francis (Jean Gaston Alfred) 6, 18
Prevert, Jacques (Henri Marie) 15
Queneau, Raymond 2, 5, 10, 42
Quoirez, Francoise 9
Renoir, Jean 20
Resnais, Alain 16
Reverdy, Pierre 53
Rio, Michel 43
Robbe-Grillet, Alain 1, 2, 4, 6, 8, 10, 14, 43
Rohmer, Eric 16
Romains, Jules 7
Sachs, Nelly 14, 98
Sagan, Francoise 3, 6, 9, 17, 36
Sarduy, Severo 6, 97
Sarraute, Nathalie 1, 2, 4, 8, 10, 31, 80
Sartre, Jean-Paul 1, 4, 7, 9, 13, 18, 24, 44, 50, 52
Sauser-Hall, Frederic 18

Schwarz-Bart, Andre 2, 4
Schwarz-Bart, Simone 7
Simenon, Georges (Jacques Christian) 1, 2, 3, 8, 18, 47
Simon, Claude 4, 9, 15, 39
Soupault, Philippe 68
Steiner, George 24
Tournier, Michel (Edouard) 6, 23, 36, 95
Troyat, Henri 23
Truffaut, Francois 20, 101
Tuck, Lily 70
Tzara, Tristan 47
Varda, Agnes 16
Wittig, Monique 22
Yourcenar, Marguerite 19, 38, 50, 87

FRENCH GUINEAN
Damas, Leon-Gontran 84

GERMAN
Amichai, Yehuda 9, 22, 57
Arendt, Hannah 66, 98
Arp, Jean 5
Becker, Jurek 7, 19
Benary-Isbert, Margot 12
Bienek, Horst 7, 11
Boell, Heinrich (Theodor) 2, 3, 6, 9, 11, 15, 27, 32, 72
Buchheim, Lothar-Guenther 6
Bukowski, Charles 2, 5, 9, 41, 82, 108
Eich, Guenter 15
Ende, Michael (Andreas Helmuth) 31
Enzensberger, Hans Magnus 43
Fassbinder, Rainer Werner 20
Figes, Eva 31
Grass, Guenter (Wilhelm) 1, 2, 4, 6, 11, 15, 22, 32, 49, 88
Habermas, Juergen 104
Hamburger, Michael (Peter Leopold) 5, 14
Heidegger, Martin 24
Herzog, Werner 16
Hesse, Hermann 1, 2, 3, 6, 11, 17, 25, 69
Heym, Stefan 41
Hildesheimer, Wolfgang 49
Hochhuth, Rolf 4, 11, 18
Hofmann, Gert 54
Johnson, Uwe 5, 10, 15, 40
Kroetz, Franz Xaver 41
Kunze, Reiner 10
Lenz, Siegfried 27
Levitin, Sonia (Wolff) 17
Mueller, Lisel 13, 51
Nossack, Hans Erich 6
Preussler, Otfried 17
Remarque, Erich Maria 21
Riefenstahl, Leni 16
Sachs, Nelly 14, 98
Schmidt, Arno (Otto) 56
Schumacher, E(rnst) F(riedrich) 80
Seghers, Anna 7
Strauss, Botho 22
Sueskind, Patrick 44
Walser, Martin 27
Weiss, Peter (Ulrich) 3, 15, 51
Wellershoff, Dieter 46
Wolf, Christa 14, 29, 58
Zuckmayer, Carl 18

GHANIAN
Armah, Ayi Kwei 5, 33

GREEK
Broumas, Olga 10, 73

Elytis, Odysseus **15, 49, 100**
Haviaras, Stratis **33**
Karapanou, Margarita **13**
Nakos, Lilika **29**
Ritsos, Yannis **6, 13, 31**
Samarakis, Antonis **5**
Seferis, George **5, 11**
Spanidou, Irini **44**
Vassilikos, Vassilis **4, 8**

GUADELOUPEAN
Conde, Maryse **52, 92**
Schwarz-Bart, Simone **7**

GUATEMALAN
Asturias, Miguel Angel **3, 8, 13**

GUINEAN
Laye, Camara **4, 38**

GUYANESE
Dabydeen, David **34**
Harris, (Theodore) Wilson **25**

HUNGARIAN
Faludy, George **42**
Koestler, Arthur **1, 3, 6, 8, 15, 33**
Konrad, Gyoergy **4, 10, 73**
Lengyel, Jozsef **7**
Lukacs, George **24**
Nagy, Laszlo **7**
Szirtes, George **46**
Tabori, George **19**
Vizinczey, Stephen **40**

ICELANDIC
Gunnars, Kristjana **69**
Laxness, Halldor **25**

INDIAN
Ali, Ahmed **69**
Anand, Mulk Raj **23, 93**
Desai, Anita **19, 37, 97**
Ezekiel, Nissim **61**
Ghosh, Amitav **44**
Mahapatra, Jayanta **33**
Markandaya, Kamala **8, 38**
Mehta, Ved (Parkash) **37**
Mistry, Rohinton **71**
Mukherjee, Bharati **53**
Narayan, R(asipuram) K(rishnaswami) **7, 28, 47**
Rao, Raja **25, 56**
Ray, Satyajit **16, 76**
Rushdie, (Ahmed) Salman **23, 31, 55, 100**
Sahgal, Nayantara (Pandit) **41**
Sealy, I. Allan **55**
Seth, Vikram **43, 90**
Singh, Khushwant **11**
Tharoor, Shashi **70**
White, T(erence) H(anbury) **30**

IRANIAN
Modarressi, Taghi (M.) **44**
Shamlu, Ahmad **10**

IRISH
Banville, John **46**
Beckett, Samuel (Barclay) **1, 2, 3, 4, 6, 9, 10, 11, 14, 18, 29, 57, 59, 83**
Behan, Brendan **1, 8, 11, 15, 79**
Blackwood, Caroline **6, 9, 100**
Boland, Eavan (Aisling) **40, 67**

Bowen, Elizabeth (Dorothea Cole) **1, 3, 6, 11, 15, 22**
Boyle, Patrick **19**
Brennan, Maeve **5**
Brown, Christy **63**
Carroll, Paul Vincent **10**
Clarke, Austin **6, 9**
Colum, Padraic **28**
Cox, William Trevor **9, 14, 71**
Day Lewis, C(ecil) **1, 6, 10**
Dillon, Eilis **17**
Donleavy, J(ames) P(atrick) **1, 4, 6, 10, 45**
Doyle, Roddy **81**
Durcan, Paul **43, 70**
Friel, Brian **5, 42, 59**
Gebler, Carlo (Ernest) **39**
Hanley, James **3, 5, 8, 13**
Hart, Josephine **70**
Heaney, Seamus (Justin) **5, 7, 14, 25, 37, 74, 91**
Johnston, Jennifer **7**
Kavanagh, Patrick (Joseph) **22**
Keane, Molly **31**
Kiely, Benedict **23, 43**
Kinsella, Thomas **4, 19**
Lavin, Mary **4, 18, 99**
Leonard, Hugh **19**
Longley, Michael **29**
Mac Laverty, Bernard **31**
MacNeice, (Frederick) Louis **1, 4, 10, 53**
Mahon, Derek **27**
McGahern, John **5, 9, 48**
McGinley, Patrick (Anthony) **41**
McGuckian, Medbh **48**
Montague, John (Patrick) **13, 46**
Moore, Brian **1, 3, 5, 7, 8, 19, 32, 90**
Morrison, Van **21**
Morrissy, Mary **99**
Muldoon, Paul **32, 72**
Murphy, Richard **41**
Murphy, Thomas (Bernard) **51**
Nolan, Christopher **58**
O'Brien, Edna **3, 5, 8, 13, 36, 65**
O'Brien, Flann **1, 4, 5, 7, 10, 47**
O'Casey, Sean **1, 5, 9, 11, 15, 88**
O'Connor, Frank **23**
O'Doherty, Brian **76**
O'Faolain, Julia **6, 19, 47, 108**
O'Faolain, Sean **1, 7, 14, 32, 70**
O'Flaherty, Liam **5, 34**
Paulin, Tom **37**
Rodgers, W(illiam) R(obert) **7**
Simmons, James (Stewart Alexander) **43**
Trevor, William **7, 9, 14, 25, 71**
White, Terence de Vere **49**
Wilson, Robert McLiam **59**

ISRAELI
Agnon, S(hmuel) Y(osef Halevi) **4, 8, 14**
Amichai, Yehuda **9, 22, 57**
Appelfeld, Aharon **23, 47**
Bakshi, Ralph **26**
Friedlander, Saul **90**
Grossman, David **67**
Kaniuk, Yoram **19**
Levin, Meyer **7**
Megged, Aharon **9**
Oz, Amos **5, 8, 11, 27, 33, 54**
Shammas, Anton **55**
Sobol, Joshua **60**
Yehoshua, A(braham) B. **13, 31**

ITALIAN

Antonioni, Michelangelo **20**
Bacchelli, Riccardo **19**
Bassani, Giorgio **9**
Bertolucci, Bernardo **16**
Bufalino, Gesualdo **74**
Buzzati, Dino **36**
Calasso, Roberto **81**
Calvino, Italo **5, 8, 11, 22, 33, 39, 73**
De Sica, Vittorio **20**
Eco, Umberto **28, 60**
Fallaci, Oriana **11**
Fellini, Federico **16, 85**
Fo, Dario **32**
Gadda, Carlo Emilio **11**
Ginzburg, Natalia **5, 11, 54, 70**
Giovene, Andrea **7**
Landolfi, Tommaso **11, 49**
Levi, Primo **37, 50**
Luzi, Mario **13**
Montale, Eugenio **7, 9, 18**
Morante, Elsa **8, 47**
Moravia, Alberto **2, 7, 11, 27, 46**
Ortese, Anna Maria **89**
Palazzeschi, Aldo **11**
Pasolini, Pier Paolo **20, 37, 106**
Piccolo, Lucio **13**
Pincherle, Alberto **11, 18**
Quasimodo, Salvatore **10**
Ricci, Nino **70**
Sciascia, Leonardo **8, 9, 41**
Silone, Ignazio **4**
Ungaretti, Giuseppe **7, 11, 15**
Visconti, Luchino **16**
Vittorini, Elio **6, 9, 14**
Wertmueller, Lina **16**

JAMAICAN
Bennett, Louise (Simone) **28**
Cliff, Jimmy **21**
Marley, Bob **17**
Thelwell, Michael Miles **22**

JAPANESE
Abe, Kobo **8, 22, 53, 81**
Enchi Fumiko (Ueda) **31**
Endo, Shusaku **7, 14, 19, 54, 99**
Ibuse Masuji **22**
Ichikawa, Kon **20**
Ishiguro, Kazuo **27, 56, 59**
Kawabata, Yasunari **2, 5, 9, 18, 107**
Kurosawa, Akira **16**
Mishima, Yukio **2, 4, 6, 9, 27**
Oe, Kenzaburo **10, 36, 86**
Oshima, Nagisa **20**
Ozu, Yasujiro **16**
Shiga, Naoya **33**
Tanizaki, Jun'ichiro **8, 14, 28**
Yoshimoto, Banana **84**

KENYAN
Ngugi, James T(hiong'o) **3, 7, 13**
Ngugi wa Thiong'o **36**

MARTINICAN
Cesaire, Aime (Fernand) **19, 32**
Fanon, Frantz **74**
Glissant, Edouard **10, 68**

MEXICAN
Castellanos, Rosario **66**
Fuentes, Carlos **3, 8, 10, 13, 22, 41, 60**
Ibarguengoitia, Jorge **37**
Lopez Portillo (y Pacheco), Jose **46**

Nationality Index

Lopez y Fuentes, Gregorio **32**
Paz, Octavio **3, 4, 6, 10, 19, 51, 65**
Rulfo, Juan **8, 80**

MOROCCAN
Arrabal, Fernando **2, 9, 18, 58**

NEW ZEALANDER
Adcock, Fleur **41**
Ashton-Warner, Sylvia (Constance) **19**
Baxter, James K(eir) **14**
Campion, Jane **95**
Frame, Janet **2, 3, 6, 22, 66, 96**
Gee, Maurice (Gough) **29**
Grace, Patricia **56**
Hilliard, Noel (Harvey) **15**
Hulme, Keri **39**
Ihimaera, Witi **46**
Marsh, (Edith) Ngaio **7, 53**
Sargeson, Frank **31**

NICARAGUAN
Alegria, Claribel **75**
Cardenal, Ernesto **31**

NIGERIAN
Achebe, (Albert) Chinua(lumogu) **1, 3, 5, 7, 11, 26, 51, 75**
Clark, John Pepper **38**
Ekwensi, Cyprian (Odiatu Duaka) **4**
Emecheta, (Florence Onye) Buchi **14, 48**
Okigbo, Christopher (Ifenayichukwu) **25, 84**
Okri, Ben **87**
Soyinka, Wole **3, 5, 14, 36, 44**
Tutuola, Amos **5, 14, 29**

NORTHERN IRISH
Simmons, James (Stewart Alexander) **43**
Wilson, Robert McLiam **59**

NORWEGIAN
Friis-Baastad, Babbis Ellinor **12**
Heyerdahl, Thor **26**
Vesaas, Tarjei **48**

PAKISTANI
Ali, Ahmed **69**
Ghose, Zulfikar **42**

PARAGUAYAN
Roa Bastos, Augusto (Antonio) **45**

PERUVIAN
Allende, Isabel **39, 57, 97**
Arguedas, Jose Maria **10, 18**
Goldemberg, Isaac **52**
Vargas Llosa, (Jorge) Mario (Pedro) **3, 6, 9, 10, 15, 31, 42, 85**

POLISH
Agnon, S(hmuel) Y(osef Halevi) **4, 8, 14**
Becker, Jurek **7, 19**
Bermant, Chaim (Icyk) **40**
Bienek, Horst **7, 11**
Brandys, Kazimierz **62**
Dabrowska, Maria (Szumska) **15**
Gombrowicz, Witold **4, 7, 11, 49**
Herbert, Zbigniew **9, 43**
Konwicki, Tadeusz **8, 28, 54**
Kosinski, Jerzy (Nikodem) **1, 2, 3, 6, 10, 15, 53, 70**
Lem, Stanislaw **8, 15, 40**
Milosz, Czeslaw **5, 11, 22, 31, 56, 82**

Mrozek, Slawomir **3, 13**
Polanski, Roman **16**
Rozewicz, Tadeusz **9, 23**
Singer, Isaac Bashevis **1, 3, 6, 9, 11, 15, 23, 38, 69**
Skolimowski, Jerzy **20**
Szymborska, Wislawa **99**
Wajda, Andrzej **16**
Wittlin, Jozef **25**
Wojciechowska, Maia (Teresa) **26**

PORTUGUESE
Migueis, Jose Rodrigues **10**

PUERTO RICAN
Marques, Rene **96**
Pinero, Miguel (Antonio Gomez) **4, 55**
Sanchez, Luis Rafael **23**

ROMANIAN
Appelfeld, Aharon **23, 47**
Arghezi, Tudor **80**
Blaga, Lucian **75**
Celan, Paul **10, 19, 53, 82**
Cioran, E(mil) M. **64**
Codrescu, Andrei **46**
Ionesco, Eugene **1, 4, 6, 9, 11, 15, 41, 86**
Rezzori (d'Arezzo), Gregor von **25**
Tzara, Tristan **47**
Wiesel, Elie(zer) **3, 5, 11, 37**

RUSSIAN
Aitmatov, Chingiz (Torekulovich) **71**
Akhmadulina, Bella Akhatovna **53**
Akhmatova, Anna **11, 25, 64**
Aksyonov, Vassily (Pavlovich) **22, 37, 101**
Aleshkovsky, Yuz **44**
Almedingen, E. M. **12**
Asimov, Isaac **1, 3, 9, 19, 26, 76, 92**
Bakhtin, Mikhail Mikhailovich **83**
Bitov, Andrei (Georgievich) **57**
Brodsky, Joseph **4, 6, 13, 36, 100**
Deren, Maya **16, 102**
Ehrenburg, Ilya (Grigoryevich) **18, 34, 62**
Eliade, Mircea **19**
Gary, Romain **25**
Goldberg, Anatol **34**
Grade, Chaim **10**
Grossman, Vasily (Semenovich) **41**
Iskander, Fazil **47**
Kaletski, Alexander **39**
Krotkov, Yuri **19**
Leonov, Leonid (Maximovich) **92**
Limonov, Edward **67**
Nabokov, Vladimir (Vladimirovich) **1, 2, 3, 6, 8, 11, 15, 23, 44, 46, 64**
Olesha, Yuri (Karlovich) **8**
Pasternak, Boris (Leonidovich) **7, 10, 18, 63**
Paustovsky, Konstantin (Georgievich) **40**
Rahv, Philip **24**
Rand, Ayn **3, 30, 44, 79**
Ratushinskaya, Irina **54**
Rybakov, Anatoli (Naumovich) **23, 53**
Sarraute, Nathalie **1, 2, 4, 8, 10, 31, 80**
Shalamov, Varlam (Tikhonovich) **18**
Sholokhov, Mikhail (Aleksandrovich) **7, 15**
Sinyavsky, Andrei (Donatevich) **8**
Solzhenitsyn, Aleksandr I(sayevich) **1, 2, 4, 7, 9, 10, 18, 26, 34, 78**
Strugatskii, Arkadii (Natanovich) **27**
Strugatskii, Boris (Natanovich) **27**
Tarkovsky, Andrei (Arsenyevich) **75**
Trifonov, Yuri (Valentinovich) **45**

Troyat, Henri **23**
Voinovich, Vladimir (Nikolaevich) **10, 49**
Voznesensky, Andrei (Andreievich) **1, 15, 57**
Yanovsky, V(assily) S(emenovich) **2, 18**
Yevtushenko, Yevgeny (Alexandrovich) **1, 3, 13, 26, 51**
Yezierska, Anzia **46**
Zaturenska, Marya **6, 11**
Zinoviev, Alexander (Aleksandrovich) **19**

SALVADORAN
Alegria, Claribel **75**
Argueta, Manlio **31**

SCOTTISH
Banks, Iain M(enzies) **34**
Brown, George Mackay **5, 48, 100**
Cronin, A(rchibald) J(oseph) **32**
Dunn, Douglas (Eaglesham) **6, 40**
Graham, W(illiam) S(ydney) **29**
Gray, Alasdair (James) **41**
Grieve, C(hristopher) M(urray) **11, 19**
Hunter, Mollie **21**
Jenkins, (John) Robin **52**
Kelman, James **58, 86**
Laing, R(onald) D(avid) **95**
MacBeth, George (Mann) **2, 5, 9**
MacCaig, Norman (Alexander) **36**
MacDiarmid, Hugh **2, 4, 11, 19, 63**
MacInnes, Helen (Clark) **27, 39**
MacLean, Alistair (Stuart) **3, 13, 50, 63**
McIlvanney, William **42**
Morgan, Edwin (George) **31**
Smith, Iain Crichton **64**
Spark, Muriel (Sarah) **2, 3, 5, 8, 13, 18, 40, 94**
Taylor, C(ecil) P(hilip) **27**
Walker, David Harry **14**
Young, Andrew (John) **5**

SENEGALESE
Ousmane, Sembene **66**
Senghor, Leopold Sedar **54**

SOMALIAN
Farah, Nuruddin **53**

SOUTH AFRICAN
Abrahams, Peter (Henry) **4**
Breytenbach, Breyten **23, 37**
Brink, Andre (Philippus) **18, 36, 106**
Brutus, Dennis **43**
Coetzee, J(ohn) M(ichael) **23, 33, 66**
Courtenay, Bryce **59**
Fugard, (Harold) Athol **5, 9, 14, 25, 40, 80**
Fugard, Sheila **48**
Gordimer, Nadine **3, 5, 7, 10, 18, 33, 51, 70**
Harwood, Ronald **32**
Head, Bessie **25, 67**
Hope, Christopher (David Tully) **52**
Kunene, Mazisi (Raymond) **85**
La Guma, (Justin) Alex(ander) **19**
Millin, Sarah Gertrude **49**
Mphahlele, Ezekiel **25**
Mtwa, Percy **47**
Ngema, Mbongeni **57**
Nkosi, Lewis **45**
Paton, Alan (Stewart) **4, 10, 25, 55, 106**
Plomer, William Charles Franklin **4, 8**
Prince, F(rank) T(empleton) **22**
Smith, Wilbur (Addison) **33**
Tolkien, J(ohn) R(onald) R(euel) **1, 2, 3, 8, 12, 38**
Tutu, Desmond M(pilo) **80**

van der Post, Laurens (Jan) **5**
Vorster, Gordon **34**

SPANISH
Alberti, Rafael **7**
Aleixandre, Vicente **9, 36**
Alfau, Felipe **66**
Alonso, Damaso **14**
Arrabal, Fernando **2, 9, 18, 58**
Azorin **11**
Benet, Juan **28**
Buero Vallejo, Antonio **15, 46**
Bunuel, Luis **16, 80**
Casona, Alejandro **49**
Castedo, Elena **65**
Cela, Camilo Jose **4, 13, 59**
Cernuda (y Bidon), Luis **54**
del Castillo, Michel **38**
Delibes, Miguel **8, 18**
Espriu, Salvador **9**
Gironella, Jose Maria **11**
Gomez de la Serna, Ramon **9**
Goytisolo, Juan **5, 10, 23**
Guillen, Jorge **11**
Matute (Ausejo), Ana Maria **11**
Otero, Blas de **11**
Rodriguez, Claudio **10**
Ruiz, Jose Martinez **11**
Saura (Atares), Carlos **20**
Sender, Ramon (Jose) **8**

SRI LANKAN
Gunesekera, Romesh **91**

ST. LUCIAN
Walcott, Derek (Alton) **2, 4, 9, 14, 25, 42, 67, 76**

SWEDISH
Beckman, Gunnel **26**
Bergman, (Ernst) Ingmar **16, 72**
Ekeloef, (Bengt) Gunnar **27**
Johnson, Eyvind (Olof Verner) **14**
Lagerkvist, Paer (Fabian) **7, 10, 13, 54**
Martinson, Harry (Edmund) **14**
Sjoewall, Maj **7**
Spiegelman, Art **76**
Transtroemer, Tomas (Goesta) **52, 65**
Wahloo, Per **7**
Weiss, Peter (Ulrich) **3, 15, 51**

SWISS
Canetti, Elias **3, 14, 25, 75, 86**
Cendrars, Blaise **18, 106**
Duerrenmatt, Friedrich **1, 4, 8, 11, 15, 43, 102**
Frisch, Max (Rudolf) **3, 9, 14, 18, 32, 44**
Hesse, Hermann **1, 2, 3, 6, 11, 17, 25, 69**
Pinget, Robert **7, 13, 37**
Sauser-Hall, Frederic **18**
Sterchi, Beat **65**
von Daeniken, Erich **30**

TRINIDADIAN
Guy, Rosa (Cuthbert) **26**
James, C(yril) L(ionel) R(obert) **33**
Lovelace, Earl **51**
Naipaul, Shiva(dhar Srinivasa) **32, 39**
Naipaul, V(idiadhar) S(urajprasad) **4, 7, 9, 13, 18, 37, 105**

TURKISH
Hikmet, Nazim **40**
Kemal, Yashar **14, 29**

Seferis, George **5, 11**

UGANDAN
p'Bitek, Okot **96**

URUGUAYAN
Galeano, Eduardo (Hughes) **72**
Onetti, Juan Carlos **7, 10**

WELSH
Abse, Dannie **7, 29**
Arundel, Honor (Morfydd) **17**
Clarke, Gillian **61**
Dahl, Roald **1, 6, 18, 79**
Davies, Rhys **23**
Francis, Dick **2, 22, 42, 102**
Hughes, Richard (Arthur Warren) **1, 11**
Humphreys, Emyr Owen **47**
Jones, David (Michael) **2, 4, 7, 13, 42**
Jones, Terence Graham Parry **21**
Levinson, Deirdre **49**
Llewellyn Lloyd, Richard Dafydd Vivian **7, 80**
Mathias, Roland (Glyn) **45**
Norris, Leslie **14**
Roberts, Kate **15**
Rubens, Bernice (Ruth) **19, 31**
Thomas, R(onald) S(tuart) **6, 13, 48**
Watkins, Vernon Phillips **43**
Williams, (George) Emlyn **15**

YUGOSLAVIAN
Andric, Ivo **8**
Cosic, Dobrica **14**
Kis, Danilo **57**
Krleza, Miroslav **8**
Pavic, Milorad **60**
Popa, Vasko **19**
Simic, Charles **6, 9, 22, 49, 68**
Tesich, Steve **40, 69**

Nationality Index

CLC-108 Title Index

"Acceptance" (Hughes) **108**:297

Une affaire de viol (Himes) **108**:229

"All He Needs Is Feet" (Himes) **108**:227, 235

American Appetites (Oates) **108**:374, 381, 386, 388

Angel of Light (Oates) **108**:352

"The Arc Inside and Out" (Ammons) **108**:16-7, 54

"As I Grow Older" (Hughes) **108**:283

Ask Your Mama: 12 Moods for Jazz (Hughes) **108**:283-84, 335

The Assassins: A Book of Hours (Oates) **108**:386, 391

The Assignation (Oates) **108**:374-76

"At Least I Have Made a Woman of Her" (Oates) **108**:348

At Terror Street and Agony Way (Bukowski) **108**:113

At Terror Street and Agony Way (Bukowski) **108**:112

"Ballad" (Ammons) **108**:12

"Ballad of Mary's Son" (Hughes) **108**:299

"Ballad of the Girl Whose Name Is Mud" (Hughes) **108**:330

Barfly (Bukowski) **108**:88, 91, 94

Barton Fink (The Coen Brothers) **108**:147, 149, 151-64, 166-67, 169-71

"Beans with Garlic" (Bukowski) **108**:112

Because It Is Bitter and Because It Is My Heart (Oates) **108**:374-75, 378, 386, 388, 390

Bellefleur (Oates) **108**:348, 371, 374-75, 378, 385, 391

Beneath the Fortinaria (Bukowski) **108**:110

"Big Meeting" (Hughes) **108**:298

The Big Sea: An Autobiography (Hughes) **108**:284, 290, 292, 295-96, 311-12, 314, 317, 323

"The Bitter River" (Hughes) **108**:283

Black Misery (Hughes) **108**:336

Black on Black: Baby Sister and Selected Writings (Himes) **108**:227

Black Water (Oates) **108**:374, 395-96

"Blessed Assurance" (Hughes) **108**:329

Blind Man with a Pistol (Himes) **108**:234, 237-40, 242, 247, 249-52, 265, 268-72, 277, 278-79

Blood Simple (The Coen Brothers) **108**:120-30, 133, 135-40, 142, 145-47, 149, 151-52, 157-62, 165-70

A Bloodsmoor Romance (Oates) **108**:348, 375, 385, 391

"The Bloodstained Bridal Gown; or, Xavier Kilgarvan's Last Case" (Oates) **108**:349-51, 353

"Blues I'm Playing" (Hughes) **108**:313, 315

"Blues Montage" (Hughes) **108**:335

"Boogie 1 a.m." (Hughes) **108**:299-304

"Bop Bop against That Curtain" (Bukowski) **108**:87

"Bourn" (Ammons) **108**:21

"The Boyfriend" (Oates) **108**:382

"Breaking Out" (Ammons) **108**:56

"Bridge" (Ammons) **108**:28

"Brown America in Jail: Kilby" (Hughes) **108**:318

"The Buck" (Oates) **108**:383

The Bukowski/Purdy Letters: A Decade of Dialogue, 1964-1974 (Bukowski) **108**:81, 114-15

"Burn and burn and burn" (Bukowski) **108**:113

Burning in Water Drowning in Flame: Selected Poems 1955-1973 (Bukowski) **108**:110

By the North Gate (Oates) **108**:341, 368

"Café: 3 A.M." (Hughes) **108**:329-30

The Call of Service: A Witness to Idealism (Coles) **108**:207, 209

The Call of Stories (Coles) **108**:193, 201

A Case of Rape (Himes)
    See *Une affaire de viol*

Cast the First Stone (Himes) **108**:228-29, 231, 259

"Catalyst" (Ammons) **108**:6

"the catch" (Bukowski) **108**:114

Chicanos (Coles) **108**:194

Children of Crisis (Coles) **108**:186-88, 193-94, 203-05, 210, 214

Childwold (Oates) **108**:386, 391

"Christ in Alabama" (Hughes) **108**:298, 328

"Christmas Eve" (Ammons) **108**:51, 53, 58

"Christmas Gift" (Himes) **108**:235

"The City Limits" (Ammons) **108**:11

"Class" (Bukowski) **108**:85-6

"Close-Up" (Ammons) **108**:21

"Coast of Trees" (Ammons) **108**:56

A Coast of Trees (Ammons) **108**:24, 55

"Cold Rheum" (Ammons) **108**:61

The Collected Poems (Ammons) **108**:24, 28, 55

Collected Poems, 1951-1971 (Ammons) **108**:5-6, 8-9, 24, 27

The Collected Poems of Langston Hughes (Hughes) **108**:334-35

The Collected Stories of Chester Himes (Himes) **108**:227-28, 234-35, 241

"Coming to Summer" (Ammons) **108**:19

"Configurations" (Ammons) **108**:11, 23

"Conserving the Magnitude of Uselessness" (Ammons) **108**:28

"Coon Song" (Ammons) **108**:5, 8, 30

"Corson's Inlet" (Ammons) **108**:10, 14-17, 28, 45

Corson's Inlet (Ammons) **108**:5, 24, 46, 60

Cotton Comes to Harlem (Himes) **108**:233, 239, 256, 269, 276-77

"Cowards from the Colleges" (Hughes) **108**:319

"Craps" (Oates) **108**:384

"Crazy in the Stir" (Himes) **108**:227

"Cross" (Hughes) **108**:314, 334-35

Crucifix in a Deathhand: New Poems, 1963-1965 (Bukowski) **108**:81, 110

"The Cruel Suitor" (Oates) **108**:350-51

"Dark Song" (Ammons) **108**:8

"a day at the oak tree meet" (Bukowski) **108**:75

"Daybreak in Alabama" (Hughes) **108**:332-33

The Days Run Away Like Wild Horses over the Hills (Bukowski) **108**:81

"The Dead" (Oates) **108**:354, 368, 370-71

"Death Valley" (Oates) **108**:384

"Desire" (Hughes) **108**:332

"Devil's Half-Acre; or, The Mystery of the 'Cruel Suitor'" (Oates) **108**:349

Diversifications (Ammons) **108**:12, 24, 55

Do with Me What You Will (Oates) **108**:344, 391

Don't You Want to Be Free? (Hughes) **108**:295

"Doxology" (Ammons) **108**:19

"Dream Boogie" (Hughes) **108**:299-300, 302-04

"Dream Boogie: Variation" (Hughes) **108**:299, 301, 303-04

The Dream Keeper and Other Poems (Hughes) **108**:283

"Dream Variations" (Hughes) **108**:296, 300

"Driving Through" (Ammons) **108**:19

"Dunes" (Ammons) **108**:23

"Easter Morning" (Ammons) **108**:56-7

"Easy Boogie" (Hughes) **108**:299-304

The Eclipse (Oates) **108**:376

The End of a Primitive (Himes) **108**:230, 232

Erections, Ejaculations, Exhibitions, and General Tales of Ordinary Madness (Bukowski)
    See *Life and Death in the Charity Ward*

"Essay on Poetics" (Ammons) **108**:11, 32-3, 35-6, 40, 43, 46

"The Expense of Spint" (Oates) **108**:368, 370-71

Expensive People (Oates) **108**:343, 385, 391

Expressions of Sea Level (Ammons) **108**:2, 5, 7, 26, 46

"Extremes and Moderations" (Ammons) **108**:9, 11, 38, 44

Factotum (Bukowski) **108**:72, 97-8, 103-04, 106, 108

"Family" (Oates) **108**:384-85

Famous American Negroes (Hughes) **108**:286

Famous Negro Heroes of America (Hughes) **108**:286

Famous Negro Music Makers (Hughes) **108**:283

Fargo (The Coen Brothers) **108**:165-71

"Father and Son" (Hughes) **108**:315, 317, 327

Fight for Freedom (Hughes) **108**:284, 286

Fine Clothes to the Jew (Hughes) **108**:293-94, 310, 319, 323

"Fire" (Hughes) **108**:297

The First Book of Jazz (Hughes) **108**:300

The First Book of Negroes (Hughes) **108**:291-92

Flannery O'Connor's South (Coles) **108**:179, 180, 183

Flower, Fist, and Bestial Wail (Bukowski) **108**:81

"The Foot-Washing" (Ammons) **108**:51

"For Harold Bloom" (Ammons) **108**:17

For Love of Imabelle (Himes) **108**:232, 236-39, 241, 264, 267-70, 275

"For marilyn m" (Bukowski) **108**:111

Foxfire: Confessions of a Girl Gang (Oates) **108**:393

"Freedom's Plow" (Hughes) **108**:283

"The Fuck Machine" (Bukowski) **108**:85

"Fulfillment" (Hughes) **108**:332

Garbage (Ammons) **108**:46-9, 59, 60-1

A Garden of Earthly Delights (Oates) **108**:341-42, 391

"Getting to Know All about You" (Oates) **108**:384

"Give Us Our Peace" (Hughes) **108**:334

"Givings" (Ammons) **108**:56

Godded and Codded (O'Faolain) **108**:399, 425

The Goddess and Other Women (Oates) **108**:372

Title Index

"The Golden Mean" (Ammons) **108**:22
"Good Morning Revolution" (Hughes) **108**:294, 296
Good Morning, Revolution: Uncollected Social Protest Writings (Hughes) **108**:318-21
"Goodbye Christ" (Hughes) **108**:294, 297, 320
"Grace Abounding" (Ammons) **108**:57
"Grandparents: Can They Love Too Much?" (Coles) **108**:194
"Gravelly Run" (Ammons) **108**:20
"Great Poets Die in Steaming Pots of Shit" (Bukowski) **108**:85
"Guide" (Ammons) **108**:21, 50
"The Gut-Wrenching Machine" (Bukowski) **108**:85
"Halfway" (Ammons) **108**:24
Ham on Rye (Bukowski) **108**:88, 102
"Hard Daddy" (Hughes) **108**:329
"Hardweed Path Going" (Ammons) **108**:4
"Harlem" (Hughes) **108**:333
Harvard Diaries (Coles) **108**:194
"Havana Dreams" (Hughes) **108**:324
"have you ever kissed a panther" (Bukowski) **108**:74
"He Beats His Women" (Bukowski) **108**:84
"he wrote in lovely blood" (Bukowski) **108**:75
"Headwaiter" (Himes) **108**:235, 241
Heat and Other Stories (Oates) **108**:374, 379, 383, 385
The Heat's On (Himes) **108**:233, 236, 238-39, 268
"Heavy Breathing" (Hughes) **108**:331
"Her Whole Existence" (Himes) **108**:227
"Here to Yonder" (Hughes) **108**:321
"Hibernaculum" (Ammons) **108**:33-4, 36, 42, 45, 53
Hibernaculum (Ammons) **108**:60
"His Last Day" (Himes) **108**:227, 258
Hollywood (Bukowski) **108**:88-9, 91
"Home" (Hughes) **108**:315
"Hope" (Hughes) **108**:336
"Hostage" (Oates) **108**:384
"Hot" (Bukowski) **108**:113
Hot Day, Hot Night (Himes)
  See *Blind Man with a Pistol*
"House Hunting" (Oates) **108**:381
"House in Toas" (Hughes) **108**:310
"How I Contemplated the World from the Detroit House of Correction and Began My Life Over Again" (Oates) **108**:367-68
Hudsucker Proxy (The Coen Brothers) **108**:155-61, 166, 169
"Hymn" (Ammons) **108**:50-1, 54, 57-8
"I didn't want to" (Bukowski) **108**:106
"I Don't Want to Die" (Himes) **108**:227
I Lock My Door upon Myself (Oates) **108**:379-81, 385
"I Love My Friend" (Hughes) **108**:331
"I Set It My Task" (Ammons) **108**:19
"I, Too, Sing America" (Hughes) **108**:283, 314, 324
"I Went Out in the Sun" (Ammons) **108**:18
I Wonder As I Wander: An Autobiographical Journey (Hughes) **108**:284, 290-91, 298, 318, 324
"If Anything Will Level with You Water Will" (Ammons) **108**:28
If He Hollers Let Him Go (Himes) **108**:228, 231, 236, 253-55, 267, 271, 274
"An Improvisation for the Stately Dwelling" (Ammons) **108**:56
"In a Mexican City" (Hughes) **108**:323
In Darkest America (Oates) **108**:376

"In Memoriam Mae Noblitt" (Ammons) **108**:56
Indians (Coles) **108**:194
"Interference" (Ammons) **108**:21
Invisible Woman: New and Selected Poems, 1970-1982 (Oates) **108**:348
The Irish Signorina (O'Faolain) **108**:407
It Catches My Heart in Its Hands: New and Selected Poems, 1955-1963 (Bukowski) **108**:110, 114
"It's Half an Hour Later Before" (Ammons) **108**:12
"Jazzonia" (Hughes) **108**:296
"Jim Crow's Funeral" (Hughes) **108**:284
Jim Crow's Last Stand (Hughes) **108**:283
"Joshua Tree" (Ammons) **108**:21
"Joy" (Hughes) **108**:332
The Judas Cloth (O'Faolain) **108**:423-24
"Judgment Day" (Hughes) **108**:297
"The Killers" (Bukowski) **108**:85
"Kind" (Ammons) **108**:24
"Knife" (Oates) **108**:382
"Ladies and Gentleman" (Oates) **108**:385
"The Lady with the Pet Dog" (Oates) **108**:354, 368, 371
"Lady's Boogie" (Hughes) **108**:299-304
Lake Effect Country (Ammons) **108**:16, 57
The Langston Hughes Reader (Hughes) **108**:285
Laughing to Keep from Crying (Hughes) **108**:285
"left with the day" (Bukowski) **108**:75
"Leila Lee" (Oates) **108**:384
"Lenin" (Hughes) **108**:321
"Let America Be America Again" (Hughes) **108**:283
"Letter" (Hughes) **108**:291
"Letter to the Academy" (Hughes) **108**:294
Life and Death in the Charity Ward (Bukowski) **108**:83
"The life of Borodin" (Bukowski) **108**:111
"Little Old Spy" (Hughes) **108**:324
"Loneliness" (Bukowski) **108**:86
Lonely Crusade (Himes) **108**:220-21, 224, 228, 231-32, 236, 253-61, 271, 274
"Long Trip" (Hughes) **108**:333
"Lost" (Bukowski) **108**:113
"Ma Lord" (Hughes) **108**:298
"Madam" (Hughes) **108**:326
"Madam and Her Madam" (Hughes) **108**:326
"Madam and the Number Writer" (Hughes) **108**:297
"A Man" (Bukowski) **108**:86
"Man in the Cellar" (O'Faolain) **108**:407, 413
"Mansion" (Ammons) **108**:21
"March Moon" (Hughes) **108**:330
"March Song" **108**:20
Marriages and Infidelities (Oates) **108**:354, 369, 370
"Mary Winosky" (Hughes) **108**:292
Marya: A Life (Oates) **108**:386, 390, 393
"Mechanism" (Ammons) **108**:3, 4
"The Metamorphosis" (Oates) **108**:354
"Mexican Games" (Hughes) **108**:323
Migrants (Coles) **108**:194, 210-12
Miller's Crossing (The Coen Brothers) **108**:145-47, 149-51, 153, 156-58, 161-63, 166-67, 169
Montage of a Dream Deferred (Hughes) **108**:283, 291, 299, 328, 334-35
The Moral Intelligence of Children (Coles) **108**:216
The Moral Life of Children (Coles) **108**:184, 186-88, 208, 211-12, 216
"Mother to Son" (Hughes) **108**:296, 309
"Motion for Motion" (Ammons) **108**:23

"Mountain Liar" (Ammons) **108**:20
Mountaineers and Eskimos (Coles) **108**:194, 210
"Mulatto" (Hughes) **108**:327
Mulatto (Hughes) **108**:284, 291
My Life of Absurdity (Himes) **108**:228-29, 234, 241, 256
Mysteries of Winterthurn (Oates) **108**:348-49, 351, 354, 385, 391
"The Myth" (Oates) **108**:355, 357
"Naked" (Oates) **108**:382
"Negro" (Hughes) **108**:309
"The Negro Artist and the Racial Mountain" (Hughes) **108**:290, 294, 307, 320, 323, 325, 333
"The Negro Mother" (Hughes) **108**:297
"A Negro Speaks of Rivers" (Hughes) **108**:296, 309, 311-12, 323, 334
"Nelly Meyers" (Ammons) **108**:4
"New Heaven and Earth" (Oates) **108**:356
A New Song (Hughes) **108**:295, 297
"A nice day" (Bukowski) **108**:112
"A Nigger" (Himes) **108**:235
"Nightmare Boogie" (Hughes) **108**:299, 301, 303-04
No Country for Young Men (O'Faolain) **108**:406, 409-10, 414-15, 417-18, 422
"No Neck and Bad as Hell" (Bukowski) **108**:86
Northfield Poems (Ammons) **108**:5
Not in God's Image (O'Faolain) **108**:414
Not without Laughter (Hughes) **108**:285, 293-94, 326
Notes of a Dirty Old Man (Bukowski) **108**:80, 83
The Obedient Wife (O'Faolain) **108**:413
"Old poet" (Bukowski) **108**:111
"Old Walt" (Hughes) **108**:333
Ommateum with Doxology (Ammons) **108**:5, 12, 14, 26, 46, 60
On Boxing (Oates) **108**:362-63, 365-67, 374
"On Medicine and Literature" (Coles) **108**:192
"One Friday Morning" (Hughes) **108**:285
One Way Ticket (Hughes) **108**:291
"An Open Letter to the South" (Hughes) **108**:294
The Panther and the Lash: Poems of Our Times (Hughes) **108**:286, 290, 334
"Parting" (Ammons) **108**:56
"Passion" (Oates) **108**:382
Pinktoes (Himes) **108**:228, 234
"Plan B" (Himes) **108**:234, 241-42, 251-53
The Political Life of Children (Coles) **108**:184, 186-88, 210, 214
"Politics" (Bukowski) **108**:87
Popo and Fifina (Hughes) **108**:294
"Portrait" (Ammons) **108**:24
Post Office (Bukowski) **108**:66, 70, 72, 81-3, 90, 96-7, 100, 106
"A Pot of Soothing Herbs" (O'Faolain) **108**:408-09
"Powder-White Faces" (Hughes) **108**:324
"Prayer Meeting" (Hughes) **108**:297
"Prediction" (Himes) **108**:234, 251, 278
"The Prescriptive Stalls As" (Ammons) **108**:13
The Primitive (Himes) **108**:229, 232, 254, 259
"Prison Mass" (Himes) **108**:235
Privileged Ones (Coles) **108**:194
"Prospecting" (Ammons) **108**:20
Pulp (Bukowski) **108**:93-95, 115, 116
The Quality of Hurt (Himes) **108**:223, 228-29, 234, 241, 259-60
"Radioactive Red Caps" (Hughes) **108**:284
A Rage in Harlem (Himes)
  See *For Love of Imabelle*
Raising Arizona (The Coen Brothers) **108**:129-

33, 135-44, 146-47, 149, 151, 156-57, 159-62, 165-66, 168-72, 175
"Rapids" (Ammons) **108**:56
"the rat" (Bukowski) **108**:75
The Real Cool Killers (Himes) **108**:237-38, 242, 244, 246-47, 250, 267, 275
The Really Short Poems of A.R. Ammons (Ammons) **108**:47, 61
"Refusal to Mourn the Death by Fire of a Child in London (Ammons) **108**:21
La Reine des Pommes (Himes) **108**:232, 241
The Rise of Life on Earth (Oates) **108**:379, 381, 385
"Ritual for Eating the World" (Ammons) **108**:20
"River" (Ammons) **108**:22
"Roland Hayes Beaten" (Hughes) **108**:319
"Ruby Brown" (Hughes) **108**:326
Run Man Run (Himes) **108**:234
Run with the Hunted (Bukowski) **108**:94-5
"The Sacred Marriage" (Oates) **108**:354-58, 368-69
"Saliences" (Ammons) **108**:11, 23
"Salute to the Passing" (Himes) **108**:235
"Same in Blues" (Hughes) **108**:328
"Saturday Night" (Hughes) **108**:297
Scenes from American Life (Oates) **108**:389
"Scottsboro" (Hughes) **108**:330
"Selahl" (Hughes) **108**:308
Selected Poems (Ammons) **108**:5, 17, 21-2, 24
The Selected Poems: Expanded Editions (Ammons) **108**:24
The Selected Poems of Langston Hughes (Hughes) **108**:292, 295, 315, 319, 334-35
"Seventy-five Dollars" (Hughes) **108**:292
Sharecroppers (Coles) **108**:194, 210
"the shoelace" (Bukowski) **108**:75
"Shopping" (Oates) **108**:381-82
"Silhouette" (Hughes) **108**:328
"Silver" (Ammons) **108**:4
Simple Stakes a Claim (Hughes) **108**:284
Simple's Uncle Sam (Hughes) **108**:286
"Singling & Doubling Together" (Ammons) **108**:16, 38, 57, 58
"Sinner" (Hughes) **108**:297
"Sister" (Hughes) **108**:328
"Six Inches" (Bukowski) **108**:85
"Slaves on the Block" (Hughes) **108**:328
The Snow Poems (Ammons) **108**:10-3, 24, 27-8, 35, 37, 55, 58
"So I Said I Am Ezra" (Ammons) **108**:14
Solstice (Oates) **108**:386, 389-90
"Something about a Viet Cong Flag" (Bukowski) **108**:87
"Song for a Dark Girl" (Hughes) **108**:299
"A Song of the Soul of Central" (Hughes) **108**:309
Soul/Mate (Oates) **108**:386-88
The South Goes North (Coles) **108**:210-11, 214
South of No North (Bukowski) **108**:77, 86-87
"Southern Gentlemen, White Prostitutes, Mill-Owners, and Negroes" (Hughes) **108**:318
"Southern Mammy Sings" (Hughes) **108**:325-26
"Sphere" (Ammons) **108**:27
Sphere: The Form of a Motion (Ammons) **108**:11, 13, 15, 24, 27-8, 35-8, 54-5, 60
The Spiritual Life of Children (Coles) **108**:203, 206-07, 209, 216
"S-sss-ss-sh!" (Hughes) **108**:330
"Stalkings" (Oates) **108**:371, 374
"Still" (Ammons) **108**:23
"Stop Staring at My Tits, Mister" (Bukowski) **108**:85
"Strange Hurt" (Hughes) **108**:330
"Strictly Business" (Himes) **108**:235

A Study of Courage and Fear (Coles) **108**:193
Sumerian Vistas (Ammons) **108**:24
"Sunday before Noon" (Bukowski) **108**:113
"Sunday by the Combination" (Hughes) **108**:297
"Sundays before noon" (Bukowski) **108**:112
"Sundays in Summer" (Oates) **108**:384
"Swamps" (Oates) **108**:371
Sweet and Sour Animal Book (Hughes) **108**:335-36
The Sweet Flypaper of Life (Hughes) **108**:289-90
"Sweetened Change" (Ammons) **108**:56
"Swells" (Ammons) **108**:56
"Sylvester's Dying Bed" (Hughes) **108**:297
"Tambourines" (Hughes) **108**:297
"Tang" (Himes) **108**:234-35
Tape for the Turn of the Year (Ammons) **108**:5, 11-2, 48, 52-5, 58-9, 61
"Terrain" (Ammons) **108**:22
That Red Wheelbarrow (Coles) **108**:195
them (Oates) **108**:374, 377-78, 391-92
The Third Generation (Himes) **108**:224, 228-31, 259
"This Is" (Ammons) **108**:28
"This Is What Killed Dylan Thomas" (Bukowski) **108**:86
"Those Who Have No Turkey" (Hughes) **108**:292
Three Lovers (O'Faolain) **108**:399, 424-25, 428
"Tiger" (Hughes) **108**:307
Times of Surrender (Coles) **108**:192, 196
"Tired" (Hughes) **108**:320
"To Artina" (Hughes) **108**:333
"To Certain Negro Leaders" (Hughes) **108**:319
"To the Little Fort, San Lázaro, on the Ocean Front Havana" (Hughes) **108**:324
"To What Red Hell" (Himes) **108**:227
"Tom Mooney" (Hughes) **108**:294
Tone Clusters (Oates) **108**:376
"Too Sensitive" (Bukowski) **108**:85
"The Tragedy of the Leaves" (Bukowski) **108**:110
"Transformations" (Oates) **108**:354
"A Treeful of Cleavage Flared Branching" (Ammons) **108**:19
The Triumph of the Spider Monkey (Oates) **108**:386
"Turkish Delight" (O'Faolain) **108**:415
"The Turn of the Screw" (Oates) **108**:354
"Twelve Flying Monkeys Who Won't Copulate Properly" (Bukowski) **108**:85
"The Twins" (Bukowski) **108**:111
"Twins" (Oates) **108**:384
Unholy Loves (Oates) **108**:386, 390
"The Unique/Universal" (Oates) **108**:356
"Unmailed, Unwritten Letters" (Oates) **108**:369
"Unsaid" (Ammons) **108**:9
"Up to the Crater of an Old Volcano" (Hughes) **108**:323
Uplands (Ammons) **108**:55
Upon the Sweeping Flood, and Other Stories (Oates) **108**:341
"The Vanity of Human Wishes" (Ammons) **108**:22
"View from the screen" (Bukowski) **108**:111
"The Virgin in the Rose-Bower; or, The Tragedy of Glen Mawr Manor" (Oates) **108**:349, 351, 353
"The Virgin of Guadalupe" (Hughes) **108**:323
"Visit" (Ammons) **108**:28
Walker Percy: An American Search (Coles) **108**:179
The Ways of White Folks (Hughes) **108**:313, 315
The Weary Blues (Hughes) **108**:282, 290, 293-94, 296, 310, 312, 319, 323
"The Whaleboat Struck" (Ammons) **108**:19

What I Lived For (Oates) **108**:394-95
"When I Set Fire to the Reed Patch" (Ammons) **108**:19
"When She Wears Red" (Hughes) **108**:293, 309
"Where Are You Going, Where Have You Been?" (Oates) **108**:375, 386
"The White House" (Hughes) **108**:307
"White Trash" (Oates) **108**:383
"Whose Timeless Reach" (Ammons) **108**:19
"Why Don't You Come Live with Me It's Time" (Oates) **108**:384
"The Wide Land" (Ammons) **108**:20
"The Wind Coming Down From" (Ammons) **108**:21
"Winter Scene" (Ammons) **108**:24
"With Hopes of Hemp" (Ammons) **108**:19
With Shuddering Fall (Oates) **108**:341, 362, 386
Women (Bukowski) **108**:96, 100-03, 105-09
Women in the Wall (O'Faolain) **108**:400-01
Women of Crisis (Coles) **108**:188
Wonderland (Oates) **108**:374-75, 378, 385, 386, 391
"The Word Crys Out" (Ammons) **108**:12
"Words of Comfort" (Ammons) **108**:12
"Would You Suggest Writing as a Career?" (Bukowski) **108**:85
"Yarrow" (Oates) **108**:384
You Must Remember This (Oates) **108**:374, 378, 390
"Zombie" (Oates) **108**:395-96

Title Index

ISBN 0-7876-2031-9

90000